Guide to First Edition Prices 2000/1

Also Edited by R.B. Russell

Aklo: A Volume of the Fantastic
(with Mark Valentine and Roger Dobson)

Tartarus Press Guide to First Edition Prices, 1998/9

Tartarus Press Guide to First Edition Prices, 1997

The Secret of the Sangraal and Other Writings by Arthur Machen

Tales From Tartarus: Collected Stories
(with Rosalie Parker)

Ritual and Other Stories by Arthur Machen

Translation

Le Grand Meaulnes by Alain-Fournier

Bibliography

Sylvia Townsend Warner: A Bibliography
(forthcoming, with J. Lawrence Mitchell)

Guide to
First Edition Prices 2000/1

Edited by
R.B. Russell

Tartarus Press

Guide to First Edition Prices, 2000/1, edited by R.B. Russell
Published by The Tartarus Press, November 1999, at:
5 Birch Terrace, Hangingbirch Lane, Horam, East Sussex, TN21 OPA

Book printed and bound by the Atheneum Press Ltd., Tyne and Wear

ISBN 1 872621 45 7

A CIP catalogue record for this book is available from the British Library.

ACKNOWLEDGEMENTS

Many thanks to the various bookdealers and collectors who have made suggestions, corrections, and have given us the encouragement to continue! Many thanks also to those dealers whose catalogues have been invaluable reference material. We would also like to specifically thank the following: The Margery Allingham Society, Dr Gail-Nina Anderson, Eric Arthur, Mike Ashley, Ted Ball, Chris Barker, Mike Berro, Peter Carter, Shelley Cox, Clarissa Cridland & the Friends of the Chalet School (4 Rock Terrace, Coleford, Bath, BA3 5NF), Richard Dalby, David Downes, David Jarman, Norman Gates, Edward Mendelson, Gary Morris & the Compton-Burnett Cabal, A. Reynolds Morse, Cynthia Reavell of the Tilling Society, Ryan Roberts, Barry and Susan Russell, Colin Scott-Sutherland, Ed Seiler, David Tibbetts, David Tibet, Mark Valentine, and the staff of Heathfield and Hastings Libraries.

INTRODUCTION

In *For the Love of Books* (1934), Paul Jordan Smith suggests that a collector should aim to acquire only those volumes which he or she enjoys. He says that he has no interest "... in those who gather books as small boys accumulate their marbles or fat dowagers their diamonds." A shelf full of books that have been acquired for love will always provide enjoyment, whereas those acquired for the sake of fashion or investment can be the cause of embarrassment or grief.

However, in the real world the laws of supply and demand can make the most ephemeral title (especially the most ephemeral) worth thousands of pounds. No matter how we view our books they will also have a monetary value. This is the point of the Tartarus Press *Guide to First Edition Prices*. This edition of the *Guide* contains entries for over 20,000 collectable books and we hope that we might just help you spot a rarity nobody else has seen, or save you from paying more than you need to for a book you are uncertain about.

Bookdealers will often charge widely varying prices for apparently identical books. One of the most important reasons for this is the condition of the volume involved. The importance of dust wrappers cannot be over-emphasised, as the most extreme variations in price are usually between books offered with and without their original dust wrappers. It should also be remembered that inscriptions by previous owners (unless famous), notes in margins etc, will further decrease the value of a book.

The majority of values in the *Guide* are assumed to be the prices asked by the average provincial bookdealer selling a title to a collector. However, it has been rightly pointed out that the more rare and expensive titles will rarely be seen in such bookshops. Specialist dealers are more expensive, and have often had to pay a high price to obtain their stock.

Another important point that must be made is that the *Guide* represents the prices that a dealer might charge a collector, not the price at which they would buy books for their own stock. My own personal experience is that a dealer will often offer the vendor a quarter of the re-sale value of an ordinary book. For a large number of very indifferent titles the proportion will be considerably less. However, a very desirable and expensive book will often be bought for much nearer its eventual re-sale value. In *For the Love of Books* Paul Jordan Smith comments that "... the book business—with notably slight exceptions—is characterized by honesty, courtesy, amiability and (though I despise the word) service." This is still true today, and anyone offering a book for sale should remember that there is nothing wrong with a dealer attempting to make an honest profit. Most dealers choose their profession out of a "love of books", but they would not be there to sell you the books if they could not make a living!

Wherever possible each value in this *Guide* has been checked against copies of the book offered for sale in the last two years. In many cases two values are given. The first value is for a book with a dust wrapper which is good for its age (very good for recent books, only fair for older titles), and the second value is for a very good copy without a dust wrapper. Where there is only one value suggested, then it is usually the case that the publication was either issued without a dust wrapper, or is a paperback or booklet. (We have also imposed a cut-off date of 1920, before which books are given a single value, without dust wrappers. The survival of dust wrappers from before this time is so rare that it is very difficult to value these volumes accurately.)

The rate of appreciation in the value of collectable first editions is impossible to predict, but it should be remembered that copies in poor condition, acquired for little, will have little re-sale value. If you can afford it, it is always a better investment to buy a fine copy. Advertisements for investment opportunities always carry the caveat (usually in very small print) that prices may go down as well as up. A recent example is the collectors who a few years ago remembered with affection, from their childhood, the exploits of Billy Bunter. These avid collectors were retired and often well-to-do, but many of them have now passed on, and prices must be revised downwards as the demand decreases.

Once again, please remember that this is only a guide. Limitations of space make it impossible to comment on the complexities of different "states", variant bindings etc. If in any doubt, especially if you are about to make an expensive purchase, please do consult any other available author-specific bibliography which will give much more detailed information. Ask a bookdealer!

This edition of our *Guide* is rather different to those which have gone before. In the past we were heavily reliant on contributions from various dealers and collectors, but this time I have personally reviewed each and every title. We hope that this approach makes for a little more consistency. One major advantage of this new approach is that I have been able to research values for books both with and without dust wrapper, a distinction previously lacking.

Of course, this *Guide* represents the opinion of one person, and it is inevitable that some errors may have crept in. One frequent criticism of our previous *Guides* has been the omission of certain authors. We will never be able to do justice to every collectable author, but a number of new entries suggested by dealers and collectors are included in this edition. As ever, suggestions for future editions of the *Guide* are welcomed.

No one can learn the tricks of the book trade overnight. This *Guide* does not explain how to become a bookdealer, or how to get one step ahead of the trade. It is unlikely that it will help anyone make their fortune, and nobody can be an expert on all of the titles listed here. I have only been able to compile the *Guide* thanks to the experience of the countless bookdealers who have advertised books for sale over the last few years.

NOTES

Entries are listed alphabetically by author, then chronologically by publication. Limited editions are noted simply as ***x** copies*. If it is a 'signed' edition then it is assumed that it was the author who did the signing, unless noted otherwise. Trade editions are described first, followed by other limited editions, large paper copies etc, unless these issues preceded the trade edition. If a book was re-issued under a new title then it is listed under the original title but noted thus:

ditto, as ***Starship***, Criterion (U.S.), 1959 . . £15

If a book was issued pseudonomously then a note follows the date, ie. *(pseud. "Fred Smith")*

REFERENCES

Ahern, Allen and Patricia, ***Collected Books, A Guide to their Values, 1998 Edition***, Putnam's, 1997.

Browning, D.C. (editor), ***Everyman's Dictionary of Literary Biography***, Everyman, 1970.

Cole, Michael (editor), ***Annual Register of Book Values, Modern First Editions***, The Clique. (various editions)

Connolly, Joseph, ***Modern First Editions***, Orbis, 1993.

Jackson, Crispin (editor), ***Collecting Children's Books***, Book and Magazine Collector, 1995.

Ousby, Ian (editor), ***The Cambridge Guide to Literature in English***, Guild Publishing, 1989.

Ward, K. Anthony, ***First Editions, A Field Guide***, Scolar Press, 1994.

Woodcock, George, ***20th-Century Fiction***, Macmillan, 1983.

The Book and Magazine Collector, various issues.

INDEX OF AUTHORS

J.R. ACKERLEY

(b.1896 d.1967)

For many years Ackerley was literary editor of *The Listener*. *My Father and Myself* is considered by many to be his masterpiece.

Novel

We Think the World of You, The Bodley Head, 1960 . . . . £20/£5

Poetry

Cambridge Poets 1914-1920, Heffers, 1920 (ed. E. Davison) . . . . £100/£25

Poems by Four Authors, Bowes & Bowes, 1923 £45

Micheldever and Other Poems, McKelvie, 1972 (350 numbered copies, wraps) £25

Other Titles

The Prisoners of War: A Play in Three Acts, Chatto & Windus, 1925 . . . . £75/£35

ditto, Chatto & Windus, 1925 (wraps) £45

Hindoo Holiday: An Indian Journey, Chatto & Windus, 1932. . . . . £75/£10

My Dog Tulip: Life with an Alsatian, Secker & Warburg, 1956 . . . . £20/£5

My Father and Myself, The Bodley Head, 1968 . . . . £15/£5

E.M. Forster: A Portrait, McKelvie, 1972 (wraps) £10

The Letters of J.R. Ackerley, Duckworth, 1975 . . . . £10/£5

My Sister and Myself, Hutchinson, 1982 . £10/£5

Edited by Ackerley

Escapers All, The Bodley Head, 1932 . . £20/£5

PETER ACKROYD

(b.1949)

A wide-ranging and versatile writer, Ackroyd is best known as a novelist and biographer. His life of T.S. Eliot won the Whitbread and Heinemann Awards for 1984, and his monumental biography of Dickens is much acclaimed.

Novels

The Great Fire of London, Hamish Hamilton, 1982 . . . . £100/£30

The Last Testament of Oscar Wilde, Hamish Hamilton, 1983 . . . . £50/£15

ditto, Harper & Row (U.S.), 1983 . . . . £20/£5

Hawksmoor, Hamish Hamilton, 1985 . . £50/£10

ditto, Harper & Row (U.S.), 1985 . . . . . £15/£5

Chatterton, Hamish Hamilton, 1987 . . . . £20/£5

ditto, Hamish Hamilton, 1987 (150 signed copies, glassine d/w) . . . . £50/£45

ditto, Grove Press (U.S.), 1988 . . . . . £10/£5

First Light, Hamish Hamilton, 1989 . . . . £15/£5

ditto, Grove Weidenfeld (U.S.), 1989 . . . £10/£5

English Music, Hamish Hamilton, 1992. . . £15/£5

ditto, London Limited Editions, 1992, (150 signed, numbered copies, glassine d/w) £40

ditto, Knopf (U.S.), 1992 . . . . £10/£5

ditto, The Franklin Library, 1992 (full leather, signed, limited edition) £40

The House of Doctor Dee, Hamish Hamilton, 1993 . . . . £10/£5

Dan Leno and the Limehouse Golem, Sinclair-Stevenson, 1994 . . . . £10/£5

ditto, as ***The Trial of Elizabeth Cree***, Doubleday (U.S.) 1995 . . . . £10/£5

Milton in America, Sinclair-Stevenson, 1996 . £10/£5

ditto, Doubleday (U.S.), 1997 . . . . . £10/£5

Verse

Ouch, Curiously Strong Press, 1971, (approx 500 xeroxed copies, sheets, usually in stapled wraps) £150

London Lickpenny, Ferry Press, 1973, (274 signed copies of edition of 500, illustrated card wraps) £50

ditto, Ferry Press, 1973, (200 unsigned copies of edition of 500, illustrated card wraps) . . . £35

ditto, Ferry Press, 1973, (26 signed copies of edition of 500, with additional holograph poem, illustrated card wraps). £125

Country Life, Ferry Press, 1978, (324 signed copies of edition of 350, card wraps) £50

ditto, Ferry Press, 1978, (26 signed copies of edition of 350, with additional holograph poem, card wraps) £100

The Diversions of Purley, Hamish Hamilton, 1987 . . . . £15/£5

Biography

Ezra Pound and His World, Thames & Hudson, 1980 . . . . £15/£5

ditto, Scribner's, 1980 . . . . £10/£5

T.S. Eliot, Hamish Hamilton, 1984 . . . £15/£5

ditto, Simon & Schuster, 1984 . . . . . £10/£5

Dickens, Sinclair-Stevenson, 1990 . . . £20/£5

ditto, London Limited Editions, 1990, (150 signed copies, glassine d/w) . . . . £50/£40

ditto, HarperCollins (U.S.), 1990. . . . . £10/£5

Blake, Sinclair-Stevenson, 1995 . . . . . £10/£5

ditto, Knopf (U.S.), 1996 . . . . £10/£5

The Life of Thomas More, Chatto & Windus 1998 . . . . £10/£5

ditto, Doubleday (U.S.), 1998 . . . . . £10/£5

Miscellaneous

Notes for a New Culture: An Essay on Modernism, Vision Press, 1976 . . . . £75/£30
Dressing Up, Transvestism and Drag: The History of an Obsession, Thames & Hudson, 1979 . £60/£20
ditto, Simon and Schuster, 1979 . . . . . £25/£10
Dickens' London: An Imaginative Vision, Headline, 1987 (introduced by Peter Ackroyd) . . . £10/£5
Introduction to Dickens, Sinclair-Stevenson, 1991 . . . . £10/£5

DOUGLAS ADAMS

(b.1952)

Author of *The Hitch-Hiker's Guide To The Galaxy* and related science fiction silliness, the *Hitchhikers* adventures were first heard on the radio, became books, and were then televised.

Novels

The Hitch-Hiker's Guide To The Galaxy, Pan, 1979 (wraps) £10
ditto, Arthur Barker, n.d. [1980] (first hardback edition) . . . . £45/£15
ditto, Harmony (U.S.), 1980 . . . . . . £15/£5
The Restaurant At The End Of The Universe, Pan, 1980 (wraps) £5
ditto, Arthur Barker, 1980 (first hardback edition) . . . . £25/£10
ditto, Harmony (U.S.), 1980 . . . . £10/£5
Life, The Universe and Everything, Pan, 1982 £5
ditto, Arthur Barker, 1982 (first hardback edition) . . . . £15/£5
ditto, Harmony (U.S.), 1982 . . . . £10/£5
So Long, And Thanks For All The Fish, Pan, 1984 . . . . £10/£5
ditto, Harmony (U.S.), 1985 . . . . £10/£5
Dirk Gently's Holistic Detective Agency, Heinemann, 1987 . . . . £10/£5
ditto, Simon & Schuster (U.S.), 1987 . . . . £10/£5
The Long Dark Tea-Time Of The Soul, Heinemann, 1988 . . . . £10/£5
ditto, Simon & Schuster (U.S.), 1988 . . . . £10/£5
Mostly Harmless, Heinemann, 1992 . . . . £10/£5
ditto, Harmony (U.S.), 1992 . . . . £10/£5
Starship Titanic, Harmony Books (U.S.), 1997 (with Terry Jones) . . . . £10/£5

Omnibus Editions

The Hitch-Hiker's Guide To The Galaxy: A Trilogy in Four Parts, Heinemann, 1986 . . . . . £20/£5
ditto: ***A Trilogy in Five Parts***, Heinemann, 1995 . . . . £10/£5

Others

The Meaning of Liff, Pan, 1983 (with John Lloyd, wraps). £5
The Hitch-Hiker's Guide To The Galaxy: The Original Radio Scripts, Pan, 1985 (wraps) . £5
Last Chance To See ..., Heinemann, 1990 (with Mark Carwardine) . . . . £5/£5
The Deeper Meaning of Liff, Pan, 1990, (with John Lloyd). . . . . £5/£5
Doctor Who - Pirate Planet, Titan Books, 1994 (wraps) £5

RICHARD ADAMS

(b.1920)

The classic *Watership Down* won the Guardian Award and Carnegie Medal. Much of Adams' best work is concerned with man's cruelty to animals. The first issue of *The Girl in a Swing* was withdrawn through fear of libel, and among the changes made was the name of the heroine.

Watership Down, Rex Collings, 1972 . . . £450/£75
ditto, Macmillan (U.S.), 1972. . . . . . . £35/£10
ditto, Penguin, 1976 (first illustrated edition, in slipcase) . . . . £50/£15
ditto, deluxe illustrated edition (limited to 250 signed, numbered copies, slipcase) . . . . . £600/£500
Shardik, Allen Lane, 1974 . . . . . . £15/£5
ditto, Simon and Schuster (U.S.), [1974] . . . £10/£5
Plague Dogs, Allen Lane, 1977 . . . . . £10/£5
The Girl in a Swing, Allen Lane, 1980 (withdrawn first issue) . . . . £45/£15
ditto, Knopf (U.S.), 1980 (withdrawn issue). £40/£15
ditto, Allen Lane, 1980 (second issue, revised edition,) . . . . £10/£5
ditto, Knopf (U.S.), 1980 (revised edition) . . £10/£5
The Iron Wolf and Other Stories, Allen Lane, 1980 . . . . £10/£5
ditto, as ***The Unbroken Web: Stories & Fables***, Crown (U.S.), 1980 . . . . £10/£5
The Legend of Te Tuna, Sylvester & Orphanos, 1982 . . . . £15/£5
ditto, Sidgwick & Jackson, 1986 . . . . . £10/£5
Maia, Viking, 1984 . . . . £10/£5
ditto, Knopf (U.S.), 1985 . . . . £10/£5
The Bureaucrats, Viking Kestrel, 1985 . . . £10/£5
Traveller, Knopf (U.S.), 1988 . . . . . £10/£5
ditto, Hutchinson, 1988 . . . . £10/£5
Tales from Watership Down, Hutchinson, 1996 £10/£5
ditto, Knopf (U.S.), 1996 . . . . £10/£5

Verse

The Tyger Voyage, Cape, 1976 . . . . . . £15/£5
ditto, Knopf (U.S.), 1976 . . . . £10/£5
The Ship's Cat, Cape, 1977 . . . . . . £10/£5
ditto, Knopf (U.S.), 1977 . . . . £10/£5

Non Fiction

Nature Through the Seasons, Kestrel, 1975 (with Max Hooper) . . . . £10/£5
ditto, Simon & Schuster (U.S.), 1975 . . . £10/£5
Nature Day and Night, Kestrel, 1978 (with Max Hooper) . . . . £10/£5
ditto, Viking (U.S.), 1978 . . . . £10/£5
Voyage Through the Antarctic, Allen Lane, 1982 (with Ronald Lockley). . . . . £10/£5
ditto, Knopf (U.S.), 1983 . . . . £10/£5
The Nature Diary, Viking, 1985 . . . . £10/£5
Day Gone By, Hutchinson, 1988 . . . . . . £10/£5
ditto, Knopf (U.S.), 1991 . . . . £10/£5

ROBERT AICKMAN
(b.1914 d.1981)

British short story writer, critic, lecturer and novelist. He edited *The Fontana Book of Great Ghost Stories* between 1964 and 1972.

Short Stories

We Are For the Dark - Six Ghost Stories, Cape, 1951 (with Elizabeth Jane Howard) . . . . £200/£75
Dark Entries, Collins, 1964 . . . . . £300/£100
Powers of Darkness, Collins, 1966 . . . £250/£100
Sub Rosa, Gollancz, 1968 . . . . . £125/£75
ditto, Gollancz, 1968 (40 signed copies). . £300/£200
Cold Hand in Mine, Gollancz, 1975. . . . £75/45
ditto, Scribners (U.S.), 1975 . . . . . £50/£10
Tales of Love and Death, Gollancz, 1977 . £100/£45
Painted Devils: Strange Stories, Scribner (U.S.), 1979 . . . . £40/£10
Intrusions: Strange Tales, Gollancz, 1980 . £75/£45
Night Voices: Strange Stories, Gollancz, 1985 . . . . £35/£10
The Wine-dark Sea, Arbor House (U.S.), 1988. . . . . £20/£10
ditto, Mandarin, 1990 . . . . £5
The Unsettled Dust, Mandarin, 1990 (wraps) . . £10

Novels

The Late Breakfasters, Gollancz, 1964 . . £100/£45
ditto, Portway, 1978 . . . . £20/£10
The Model, Arbor House (U.S.), 1987 . . . . £25
ditto, Robinson, 1988 . . . . £15

Others

The Attempted Rescue, Gollancz, 1966 . . £200/£75

ALAIN-FOURNIER
(b.1886 d.1914)

Alain-Fournier was the pen name of Henri Fournier, author of one novel, *Le Grand Meaulnes*, published in France in 1913. Often translated into English as *The Wanderer* or *The Lost Domain*, it is a classic novel of a lost childhood love.

The Wanderer, Houghton Mifflin (U.S.), 1928 (translated by Françoise Delisle) . . . £50/£15
ditto, Constable, 1929 . . . . £50/£15
Towards the Lost Domain: Letters from London, 1905, Carcanet, 1986 (edited and translated by W.J. Strachan) . . . . £15/£5
Le Grand Meaulnes and Miracles, Tartarus Press, 1999 . . . . £25/£10

CECIL ALDIN
(b.1870 d.1925)

A British comic illustrator in the 1890s, Aldin later became a successful sporting artist.

Children's

Spot, An Autobiography, Houlston, 1894 (14 illustrations) £100
Wonderland Wonders, by Rev. John Isabell, Home Words, 1895 (frontispiece and 19 illustrations, also contributions by Louis Wain) £65
Two Little Runaways, by James Buckland, Longman, 1898 . . . . £75
A Cockney in Arcadia, by Harry Spurr, George Allen, 1899 (28 illustrations by Aldin and John Hassall) £75
Two Well-Worn Shoe Stories, Sands, 1899 . . £200
Ten Little Puppy Dogs, Sands, [1902] . . . £175
Faithful Friends, Blackie, 1902 . . . . . £75
Bubble and Squeak, by P. Robinson, Isbister, 1902 . . . . £300
A Dog Day, or The Angel in the House, by Walter Emanuel, Heinemann, 1902 (28 illustrations) £100
The House Annual, Gale & Palden, 1902 . . £75
The Young Folks Birthday Book, Hills, 1902 £50
The Snob: Some Episodes In a Mis-spent Youth, by Walter Emanuel, Lawrence & Bullen, 1904 (19 colour plates). £100
A Gay Dog: The Story of a Foolish Year, by Walter Emanuel, Heinemann, 1905 (24 colour plates) £150

The Dogs of War, by Walter Emanuel, Bradbury Agnew, [1906] £100
The Happy Annual, Heinemann, 1907 (with John Hassall) £65
Old Christmas, by Washington Irving, Hodder & Stoughton, 1908 (27 colour plates, 6 b/w plates) £125
Farm Friends for Little Folk, Blackie, 1908 £75
The Playtime Picture Books, Lawrence & Jellicoe, 1909 (series) . . . . £150 each
Pussy and Her Ways, Henry Frowde/Hodder & Stoughton, [1909] £200
Doggie and His Ways, Henry Frowde/Hodder & Stoughton, [1909] £200
The Black Puppy Book, Henry Frowde/Hodder & Stoughton, [1909] £200
The White Puppy Book, Henry Frowde/Hodder & Stoughton, [1909] £200
The White Kitten Book, Henry Frowde/Hodder & Stoughton, [1909] (11 colour plates) . . . £200
Pickles, A Puppy Dog's Tale, Henry Frowde/Hodder & Stoughton, [1909] (24 colour illustrations). . £300
Rough and Tumble, Henry Frowde/Hodder & Stoughton, [1909] £300
Field Babies, Henry Frowde/Hodder & Stoughton, [1910] (24 colour plates) £175
The Twins, Henry Frowde/Hodder & Stoughton, [1910] (24 full-page colour plates) £300
The Red Puppy Book, Henry Frowde/Hodder & Stoughton, [1910] (12 colour plates) . . . £175
My Pets, Henry Frowde/Hodder & Stoughton, [1910] £75
An Old-Fashioned Christmas Eve, by Washington Irving, Hodder & Stoughton, 1910 . . . . £45
An Old-Fashioned Christmas Day, by Washington Irving, Hodder & Stoughton, 1910 . . . . £45
The Posthumous Papers of the Pickwick Club, by Charles Dickens, Chapman & Hall/Lawrence & Jellicoe, 1910 (2 vols, vol. I with 13 colour plates, vol. II with 11 colour plates) £200
My Book of Doggies: Stories and Pictures for Little Folk, Blackie, [1910] £100
Puppy Tails, by Richard Waylett, Lawrence & Jellicoe, [1910]. £125
Farm Babies, by May Byron, Henry Frowde/Hodder & Stoughton, [1911] (24 full-page colour illustrations) £300
Farmyard Puppies, Henry Frowde/Hodder & Stoughton, [1911] (12 colour illustrations). . £150
Merry and Bright, Henry Frowde/Hodder & Stoughton, [1911] (24 full-page colour illustrations) £300
Mac: A Story of a Dog, Henry Frowde/Hodder & Stoughton, [1912] £325
The Mongrel Puppy Book, Henry Frowde/Hodder & Stoughton, [1912] (12 colour plates) . . . £175
Black Beauty, by Anna Sewell, Jarrold, [1912] (18 colour plates) £100
White-Ear and Peter: The Story of a Fox and a Fox-Terrier, by Neils Heiberg, Macmillan, 1912 (16 colour plates) £175
Cecil Aldin's Happy Family, by May Byron, Henry Frowde/Hodder & Stoughton, [1912] (6 parts, illustrated in colour) . . . . . . £75 each
ditto, Henry Frowde/Hodder & Stoughton, [1912] (single volume edition) £75
Cecil Aldin's Merry Party, by May Byron, Henry Frowde/Hodder & Stoughton, [1913] (6 parts, illustrated in colour) . . . . . . £75 each
ditto, Henry Frowde/Hodder & Stoughton, [1913] (single volume edition) £75
My Dog, by Maurice Maeterlinck, Allen, 1913 (6 colour plates) £75
Zoo Babies, by G.E. Farrow, Henry Frowde/Hodder & Stoughton, 1913 . . . . £125
The Merry Puppy Book, Milford, 1913 (36 colour plates) £275
The Underdog, by Sidney Trist, Animals' Guardian, 1913 (4 illustrations). £75
Cecil Aldin's Rag Book, The Animals' School Treat, by Clifton Bingham, Dean: 'Rag Book' series No. 70, [1913] (24 colour illustrations) £150
The Bobtail Puppy Book, Henry Frowde/Hodder & Stoughton, [1914] £200
Jack and Jill, by May Byron, Henry Frowde/Hodder & Stoughton, [1914] £300
The Dog Who Wasn't What He Thought He Was, by Walter Emanuel, Raphael Tuck, [1914] (24 colour plates). £300
Animal Revels, by May Byron, Henry Frowde/Hodder & Stoughton, [c.1914] £75
Animal Frolics, by May Byron, Henry Frowde/Hodder & Stoughton, [1914] £75
Mouflou, by Ouida, T.C. & E.C. Jack, 1915 . £100
The Cecil Aldin Painting Books, Lawrence & Jellicoe, [1915] £100
Jock and Some Others, by Richard Waylett, Gale & Polden, [1916] (16 full-page colour illustrations, 15 b/w) £250
The Merry Party, Humphrey Milford, [1918] . £150
Bunnyborough, Humphrey Milford, [1919] . £275
ditto, Eyre & Spottiswoode, 1946 (15 colour plates, issued in dustjacket) £50
Gyp's Hour of Bliss, by Gladys Davidson, Collins, 1919 . . . . £200
The Great Adventure, Humphrey Milford, [1920] (17 colour plates) £200
Cecil Aldin Letter Books, Humphrey Milford, [1920] £100
Us, Humphrey Milford, [1922] £150
Dogs of Character, Eyre & Spottiswoode, 1927 £75

A Dozen Dogs Or So, by P.R. Chalmers, Eyre & Spottiswoode, 1927 (13 colour plates) £100
Sleeping Partners: A Series of Episodes, Eyre & Spottiswoode, [1929] (20 colour plates) . . . £250
Jerry: The Story of an Exmoor Pony, by Eleanor E. Helme and Nance Paul, Eyre & Spottiswoode, [1930] (11 full-page b/w illustrations) £45
An Artist's Model, Witherby, 1930 (20 colour plates) £200
Mrs Tickler's Caravan, Eyre & Spottiswoode, 1931 . . . . £50
Lost, Stolen or Strayed, by Marion Ashmore, Eyre & Spottiswoode, 1931 (30 b/w illustrations and colour frontispiece) £45
Flax, Police Dog, by Svend Fleuron, Eyre & Spottiswoode, [1931] (10 b/w illustrations) . £35
The Bunch Book, by James Douglas, Eyre & Spottiswoode, 1932 (51 b/w illustrations and coloured frontispiece) £35
The Joker, and Jerry Again, by Eleanor E. Helme and Nance Paul, Eyre & Spottiswoode, 1932 . . . £45
The Cecil Aldin Book, Eyre & Spottiswoode, 1932 (8 colour plates and 95 b/w illustrations) £45
Scarlet, Blue and Green, by Duncan Fife, Macmillan, 1932 (5 colour plates, 7 half-tone and 25 b/w illustrations) £75
His Apologies, by Rudyard Kipling, Doubleday Doran (U.S.), 1932 . . . . £45
Dogs of Every Day, by Patrick Chalmers, Eyre & Spottiswoode, 1933 (12 full-page mono plates) £75
Who's Who in the Zoo, Eyre & Spottiswoode, 1933 (4 colour plates and 35 full-page b/w illustrations) £50
Hotspur the Beagle, by John Vickerman, Constable, 1934 . . . . £50
Just Among Friends, Eyre & Spottiswoode, 1935 £175
How to Draw Dogs, John Lane: The Bodley Head, 1935 . . . . £150
Smuggler's Gallows, by William E.S. Hope, Eyre & Spottiswoode, 1936 . . . . £30

Others

Old Inns, Heinemann, 1921 (16 plates) . . . £75
Old Manor Houses, Heinemann, 1923 (12 plates) £45

RICHARD ALDINGTON

(b.1892 d.1962)

Richard Aldington, poet, novelist and literary scholar, is probably best known for being one of the first three Imagist poets, along with Ezra Pound and H.D.

Novels

Death of a Hero, Chatto & Windus, 1929 . £150/£40
ditto, Covici, Friede (U.S.), 1929. . . . . £75/£20
ditto, Babou & Kahane (Paris), 1930 (first unexpurgated edition, 300 copies, 2 vols, tissue d/w) . . . . £200/£165
The Colonel's Daughter. A Novel, Chatto & Windus, 1931 . . . . £20/£5
ditto, Chatto & Windus, 1931 (210 signed, numbered copies) £125
ditto, Doubleday (U.S.), 1931 . . . . . £20/£5
Stepping Heavenward, - A Record, Orioli (Florence), 1931 (808 signed, numbered copies) . . £64/£45
ditto, Chatto & Windus, 1931 . . . . £25/£5
All Men are Enemies: A Romance, Chatto & Windus, 1932 . . . . £20/£5
ditto, Chatto & Windus, 1933 (110 signed copies) £100
ditto, Doubleday (U.S.), 1933 . . . . £20/£5
Women Must Work, Chatto & Windus, 1934 . £20/£5
ditto, Doubleday (U.S.), 1934 . . . . . £20/£5
Very Heaven, Heinemann, 1937 . . . . £15/£5
ditto, Doubleday (U.S.), 1937 . . . . . £15/£5
Seven Against Reeves: A Comedy-Farce, Heinemann, 1938 . . . . £15/£5
ditto, Doubleday (U.S.), 1938 . . . . £15/£5
Rejected Guest, Viking (U.S.), 1939. . . . £20/£5
ditto, Heinemann, 1939 . . . . £15/£5
The Romance of Casanova: a Novel, Duell, Sloan, and Pearce (U.S.), 1946 . . . . £15/£5
ditto, Heinemann, 1946 . . . . £15/£5

Short Stories

Roads to Glory, Chatto & Windus, 1930 . £65/£15
ditto, Chatto & Windus, 1930 (360 numbered copies) £90
ditto, Doubleday (U.S.), 1931 . . . . £30/£10
Two Stories, Elkin Mathews & Marrot, 1930 (530 signed, numbered copies) . . . . . . £100/£75
At All Costs, Heinemann, 1930 . . . . £15/£5
ditto, Heinemann, 1930 (275 signed, numbered copies) £75
Last Straws, Hours Press (Paris), 1930 (500 numbered copies out of 700) £100
ditto, Hours Press (Paris), 1930 (200 signed, numbered copies out of 700) £2000
Soft Answers, Chatto & Windus, 1932 . . . . £20/£5
ditto, Chatto & Windus, 1932 (110 signed copies) £90
ditto, Doubleday (U.S.), 1932 . . . . £20/£5

Verse

Images (1910-1915), The Poetry Bookshop, 1915 (wraps) £200
ditto, as ***Images Old and New***, Four Seas Company (U.S.), 1916 (wraps) £75
The Love of Myrrhine and Konallis And Other Prose Poems, The Clerk's Press (U.S.), 1917 (40 copies, wraps) £250

ditto, Pascal Covici (U.S.), 1926 (150 signed copies) . . . . £75/£45
ditto, Pascal Covici (U.S.), 1926 (unsigned copies). . . . . £25/£5
Reverie, A Little Book of Poems for H.D., The Clerk's Press (U.S.), 1917 (50 copies, wraps) . . . £150
Images of War, Beaumont Press, 1919 (30 numbered, signed copies, in box) £400
ditto, (50 copies on cartridge paper numbered 31 to 80) £200
ditto, (120 unsigned copies on hand-made paper, numbered 81 to 200). £75
ditto, Allen & Unwin, 1919 . . . . £20
ditto, Four Seas Company (U.S.), 1921 (wraps). £65
Images of Desire, Elkin Mathews/Riverside Press, 1919 (signed, numbered, wraps) £95
Images, The Egoist Ltd, 1919 (wraps) . . . £45
War and Love (1915-1918), Four Seas Company (U.S.), 1919 . . . . £45
The Berkshire Kennet, Curwen Press, 1923 (50 copies, wraps). £150
Collected Poems 1915-1923, Allen & Unwin, 1933 . . . . £35/£15
Exile and Other Poems, Allen & Unwin, 1923 (750 copies) £50
A Fool i' the Forest: a Phantasmagoria, Allen & Unwin, 1924 . . . . £15/£5
Hark the Herald, Hours Press (Paris), 1928 (100 numbered, signed copies) £300
The Eaten Heart, Hours Press (Paris), 1929 (200 numbered, signed copies) £300
ditto, Chatto & Windus, 1933 . . . . £20/£10
Movietones: Invented and Set Down by Richard Aldington, 1928-1929, privately printed, 1932 (10 copies) £7,500
Love and the Luxembourg, Covici, Friede (U.S.), 1930 (475 signed copies, slipcase) . . . . £45/£25
ditto, as ***A Dream in the Luxembourg***, Chatto & Windus, 1930 (308 signed copies) . . . £45/£25
The Poems of Richard Aldington, Doubleday (U.S.), 1934 . . . . £15/£5
Life Quest, Chatto & Windus, 1935 . . . . £15/£5
ditto, Doubleday (U.S.), 1935 . . . . . £10/£5
The Crystal World, Heinemann, 1937 . . . £10/£5

Others

Literary Studies and Reviews, Allen & Unwin 1924 . . . . £10/£5
Voltaire, Routledge, 1925. . . . . . . £10/£5
ditto, Dutton (U.S.), 1924. . . . . £10/£5
French Studies and Reviews, Allen & Unwin, 1926 . . . . £10/£5
ditto, Dial Press (U.S.), 1926 . . . . £10/£5
D.H. Lawrence: An Indiscretion, University of Washington Book Store (U.S.), 1927 (wraps) . £25
ditto, as ***D.H. Lawrence***, Chatto & Windus, 1930 (250 signed copies) . . . . £45/£25
Remy de Gourment. A Modern Man of Letters, University of Washington Book Store (U.S.), 1928 (wraps) £25
Balls and Another Book for Suppression, Lahr, 1930 (100 copies, wraps) £45
Balls, privately printed, 1932 (99 + copies, single folded sheet) £200
The Squire Heinemann, 1934 . . . . . . £2,750
D.H. Lawrence: a Complete List of His Works, Together with a Critical Appreciation, Heinemann, [1935?] . . . . £35/£10
Artifex: Sketches and Ideas, Chatto and Windus, 1935 . . . . £20/£5
ditto, Doubleday, 1935 . . . . £15/£5
W. Somerset Maugham, An Appreciation, Doubleday (U.S.), 1939 (wraps) £25
Life for Life's Sake, A Book of Reminiscences, Viking (U.S.), 1941 . . . . £40/£20
The Duke, Being an Account of the Life and Achievments of the 1st Duke of Wellington, Viking (U.S.), 1943 . . . . £10/£5
ditto, as ***Wellington***, Heinemann, 1946 . . . £10/£5
Jane Austen, Ampersand Press (U.S.), 1948 £45/£20
Four English Portraits 1801-1851, Evans, 1948 . . . . £15/£5
The Strange Life of Charles Waterton, Evans, 1949 . . . . £20/£5
ditto, Duell, Sloan, and Pearce (U.S.), 1949. . £15/£5
D.H. Lawrence: An Appreciation, Penguin, 1950 (wraps) £5
ditto, as ***D.H. Lawrence, Portrait of a Genius, But ...***, Heinemann, 1950 . . . . £25/£10
Pinorman: Personal Recollections of Norman Douglas, Pino Orioli, and Charles Prentice, Heinemann, 1954 . . . . £15/£5
Ezra Pound & T.S. Eliot - A Lecture, The Peacocks Press, 1954 (350 signed, numbered copies, glassine d/w) . . . . £75/£65
ditto, The Peacocks Press, 1954 (10 trial copies, azure paper, signed) £250
A.E. Housman & W.B. Yeats: Two Lectures, The Peacocks Press, 1955 (350 copies of 360, glassine d/w) . . . . £75/£65
Lawrence L'Imposteur: T.E. Lawrence, the Legend and the Man, Amiot-Dumont (Paris), 1954 £35/£10
ditto, as ***Lawrence of Arabia: A Biographical Enquiry***, Collins, 1955 . . . . . . £50/£20
Introduction to Mistral, Heinemann, 1956 . £15/£5
ditto, Southern Illinois Univ. Press (U.S.), 1960 £10/£5
Frauds, Heinemann, 1957 . . . . . . £10/£5
A Tourist's Rome, Melissa Press (France), [1960 or 1961] (wraps). £75
Portrait of a Rebel, The Life and Works of Robert

Louis Stevenson, Evans, 1957 . . . . . £15/£5

A Letter from Richard Aldington and a Summary Bibliography of Count Potocki's Published Works, Melissa Press (France), 1962 . . . . . £100

D.H. Lawrence in Selbstzeugnissen und Bilddokumenten, Rowohlt Taschenbuch (Hamburg), 1961 . . . . £10/£5

Selected Critical Writings 1928-60, Southern Illinois Univ. Press (U.S.), 1970. . . . . . . £10/£5

A Passionate Prodigality: Letters to Alan Bird from Richard Aldington 1949-1962, New York Public Library and Readers Books (U.S.), 1975 . £10/£5

Literary Lifelines: The Richard Aldington - Lawrence Durrell Correspondence, Faber, 1981 . . £10/£5

ditto, Viking (U.S.), 1981 . . . . £10/£5

BRIAN ALDISS
(b.1925)

First published during the 1950s, Aldiss is best known for science fiction novels. He is able to push the genre to the limits of convention, however. *Barefoot in the Head* owes much to Joyce, and *A Report on Probability* is in essence an 'anti-novel'.

Novels

The Brightfount Diaries, Faber, 1955 . . £100/£40

Non-Stop, Faber, 1958 . . . . £75/£30

ditto, as ***Starship***, Criterion (U.S.), 1959 . £60/£20

Vanguard from Alpha, Ace (U.S.), 1959 (paperback double with Kenneth Bulmer's *The Changeling Worlds*) £5

ditto, as ***Equator***, Digit, 1961 (wraps) . . £5

Bow Down to Nul, Ace (U.S.), 1960 (paperback double with Manly Wade Wellman's *The Dark Destroyers*) £5

ditto, as ***The Interpreter***, Digit, 1961 (wraps) . £5

The Male Response, Beacon Press (U.S.), 1961 (wraps) £10

ditto, Dobson, 1963 . . . . £20/£5

The Primal Urge, Ballantine (U.S.), 1961 (wraps) £5

ditto, Sphere, 1967 (wraps) £5

Hothouse, Faber, 1962 . . . . . . £50/£20

ditto, as ***The Long Aftermath of Earth***, NAL (U.S.), 1962 (abridged, wraps) £5

The Dark Light Years, Faber, 1964 . . . £25/£10

ditto, NAL (U.S.), 1964 (wraps) £5

Greybeard, Harcourt Brace (U.S.), 1964 . £50/£10

ditto, Faber, 1964 . . . . £30/£10

Earthworks, Faber, 1965 . . . . . . £30/£10

ditto, Doubleday (U.S.), 1966 . . . . £15/£5

An Age, Faber, 1967 . . . . £25/£10

ditto, as ***Cryptozoic***, Doubleday, 1968 . . £15/£5

Report on Probability A, Faber, 1968 . . £15/£5

ditto, Doubleday (U.S.), 1968 . . . . £15/£5

Barefoot in the Head, Faber, 1969 . . . £15/£5

ditto, Doubleday (U.S.), 1970 . . . . £15/£5

The Hand-Reared Boy, Weidenfeld, 1970 . £15/£5

ditto, McCann (U.S.), 1970 . . . . . £15/£5

A Soldier Erect, Weidenfeld, 1971 . . . £15/£5

ditto, McCann (U.S.), 1971 . . . . . £15/£5

Frankenstein Unbound, Cape, 1973 . . £25/£10

ditto, Random House (U.S.), [1974] . . . £15/£5

The Eighty-Minute Hour, Doubleday (U.S.), 1974 . . . . £15/£5

ditto, Cape, 1974 . . . . £15/£5

The Malacia Tapestry, Cape, 1976 . . £10/£5

ditto, Harper & Row (U.S.), [1977] . . . £10/£5

Brothers of the Head, Pierrot (UK & US), 1977 . . . . £10/£5

ditto, as ***Brothers of the Head***, and ***Where the Lines Converge***, Panther, 1979 (wraps) £5

Enemies of the System, Cape, 1978 . . . £10/£5

ditto, Harper & Row (U.S.), 1978 . . . £10/£5

A Rude Awakening, Weidenfeld, 1978 . . £10/£5

ditto, Random House (U.S.), 1979 . . . £10/£5

Life in the West, Weidenfeld, 1980 . . . £10/£5

ditto, Carroll & Graf (U.S.), 1990 . . . £10/£5

Moreau's Other Island, Cape, 1980 . . . £10/£5

ditto, as ***An Island Called Moreau***, Simon & Schuster (U.S.), 1981 . . . . £10/£5

Helliconia Spring, Cape, 1982 . . . . £10/£5

ditto, Atheneum (U.S.), 1982 . . . . . £10/£5

Helliconia Summer, Cape, 1983 . . . . £10/£5

ditto, Atheneum (U.S.), 1983 . . . . . £10/£5

Helliconia Winter, Cape, 1985 . . . . £10/£5

ditto, Atheneum (U.S.), 1985 . . . . . £10/£5

The Year Before Yesterday, Watts (U.S.) 1987. . . . . £10/£5

ditto, as ***Cracken at Critical***, Kerosina, 1987 £15/£5

ditto, Kerosina, 1987 (250 signed, numbered copies, with dustjacket and in slipcase with *The Magic of the Past*) . . . . £45 the set

ditto, Kerosina, 1987 (26 lettered, ¼ leather copies) £75

The Magic of the Past, Kerosina, 1987 (350 copies, wraps) £25

ditto, Kerosina, 1987 (250 cloth copies without jacket, in slipcase with *Cracken at Critical*) . . £45 the set

Forgotten Life, Gollancz, 1988 . . . . £10/£5

ditto, Atheneum (U.S.), 1989 . . . . . £10/£5

Sex and the Black Machine, Avernus: Titan Books, 1988 (wraps) £20

Dracula Unbound, HarperCollins (U.S.), 1991 £10/£5

ditto, Gollancz, 1991 . . . . £10/£5

Remembrance Day, HarperCollins (U.S.), 1992 . . . . £10/£5

ditto, St. Martin's Press (U.S.), 1993 . . £10/£5

Short Stories

Space, Time and Nathaniel, Faber, 1957 . £150/£45

ditto, as ***No Time Like Tomorrow***, NAL (U.S.), 1959 (wraps) £5

The Canopy of Time, Faber, 1959 . . . . £50/£15

ditto, as ***Galaxies Like Grains of Sand***, NAL (U.S.), 1960 (wraps) £5

The Airs of Earth, Faber, 1963 . . . . £45/£20

ditto, as ***Starswarm***, NAL (U.S.), 1964 (wraps) £5

Best SF Stories of Brian W. Aldiss, Faber, 1965 . . . . £15/£5

ditto, as ***Who Can Replace a Man?***, Harcourt Brace (U.S.), 1966 . . . . £10/£5

ditto, Faber, 1971 (revised edition) . . . . £10/£5

The Saliva Tree and Other Strange Growths, Faber, 1966 . . . . £50/£20

Intangibles Inc. and Other Stories, Faber, 1969 . . . . £20/£5

ditto, as ***Neanderthal Planet***, Avon, Science Fiction Book Club (U.S.), 1970 . . . . £10/£5

The Moment of Eclipse, Faber, 1970 . . . £10/£5

ditto, as ***Moment of Eclipse***, Doubleday (U.S.), 1972 . . . . £10/£5

The Comic Inferno, Daw Books (U.S.), 1972 . £10/£5

ditto, as ***The Book of Brian Aldiss***, N.E.L., 1973 . . . . £10/£5

Last Orders, Cape, 1977 . . . . £10/£5

ditto, Carroll & Graf (U.S.) 1989. . . . . . £10/£5

New Arrivals, Old Encounters, Cape, 1979. . £10/£5

ditto, Harper & Row (U.S.), 1979 . . . . . £10/£5

A Romance of the Equator, Birmingham Science Fiction Group, 1980 (wraps) £15

ditto, as ***A Romance of the Equator: Best Fantasy Stories***, Gollancz, 1989 . . . . £10/£5

ditto, Atheneum (U.S.), 1990 . . . . £10/£5

The Life of Samuel Johnson, as edited (ie. written) by Aldiss, Oxford Polytechnic Press, 1980 (60 signed, numbered copies) £35

Foreign Bodies, Chapman (Singapore), 1981 . £15/£5

Seasons in Flight, Cape, 1984 . . . . . £10/£5

ditto, Atheneum (U.S.), 1986 . . . . £10/£5

My Country 'Tis Not Only of Thee, Aldiss Appreciation Society, 1986 (100 signed copies) £25

Best SF Stories of Brian W. Aldiss, Gollancz, 1988 (new collection) . . . . £10/£5

ditto, as ***Man in His Time***, Atheneum (U.S.), 1989 . . . . £10/£5

Bodily Functions, Avernus, 1991 (100 signed copies) . . . . £60/£40

The Secret of This Book, HarperCollins, 1995 £10/£5

ditto, as ***Common Clay: 20 Odd Stories***, St Martin's (U.S.), 1996 . . . . £10/£5

Verse

Pile: A Poem, Cape, 1979 (illustrated by Mike Wilks) £15

ditto, Holt Rineheart (U.S.), 1980 . . . . . £10

Farewell to a Child, Priapus, 1982 (315 of 350 unsigned copies) £15

ditto, Priapus, 1982 (35 signed, numbered copies of 350) £25

At the Caligula Hotel, Sinclair Stevenson, 1995 (wraps) £10

Non Fiction

Cities and Stones: A Traveller's Yugoslavia, Faber, 1966 . . . . £10/£5

The Shape of Further Things, Faber, 1970. . £10/£5

ditto, Doubleday (U.S.), 1971 . . . . . . £10/£5

Billion Year Spree: The History of Science Fiction, Weidenfeld, 1973 . . . . £10/£5

ditto, Doubleday (U.S.), 1973 . . . . . . £10/£5

Science Fiction Art, N.E.L., 1977 (oversized soft cover) £35

Science Fiction as Science Fiction, Bran's Head Books, 1979 (wraps) £5

This World and Nearer Ones: Essays Exploring the Familiar, Weidenfeld, 1979 . . . . . £10/£5

ditto, Kent State (U.S.), 1981 (wraps) . . . £5

The Pale Shadow of Science, Serconia Press (U.S.), 1985 . . . . £10/£5

Trillion Year Spree: The History of Science Fiction, Gollancz, 1986 (with David Wingrove) . £25/£10

ditto, Gollancz, 1986 (100 signed copies of 126, slipcase) £75

ditto, Gollancz, 1986 (26 signed, lettered copies of 126) £150

ditto, Atheneum (U.S.), 1986 . . . . £10/£5

...And the Lurid Glare of the Comet, Serconia Press (U.S.), 1986 . . . . £10/£5

Ruins, Century Hutchinson, 1987 . . . . £10/£5

Detached Retina, Liverpool Science Fiction Texts and Studies, No.4, 1994 . . . . £15

ditto, Liverpool Science Fiction Texts and Studies, No.4, 1994 (wraps) £10

Omnibus Editions

A Brian Aldiss Omnibus, Sidgwick & Jackson, 1969 . . . . £15/£5

Brian Aldiss Omnibus 2, Sidgwick & Jackson, 1971 . . . . £15/£5

Miscellaneous

Science Fiction Blues, co-written with Ken Campbell, Avernus, 1988 (wraps, stage sketches) . . . £5

Bury my Heart at W.H. Smith's, Hodder & Stoughton, 1990 . . . . £10/£5

ditto, Avernus, 1990 (250 signed, numbered copies, with six extra chapters) . . . . . £40/£20

MARGERY ALLINGHAM

(b.1904 d.1966)

An author of detective fiction from its "Golden Age", whose hero is an aristocratic adventurer known as Albert Campion.

Albert Campion Titles

The Crime at Black Dudley, Jarrolds, 1929 £250/£100
ditto as the *Black Dudley Murder*, Doubleday (U.S.), 1930 . . . . £75/£45
Mystery Mile, Jarrolds, 1930 . . . . . . £150/£75
ditto, Doubleday (U.S.), 1930 . . . . . £40/£20
Look to the Lady, Jarrolds, 1931. . . . . £125/£75
ditto as ***The Gyrth Chalice Mystery***, Doubleday (U.S.), 1931 . . . . £40/£15
Police at the Funeral, Heinemann, 1931 . £100/£50
ditto, Doubleday (U.S.), 1932 . . . . £40/£15
Sweet Danger, Heinemann, 1933 . . . £100/£50
ditto, as ***Kingdom of Death,*** Doubleday (U.S.), 1933 . . . . £50/£20
Death of a Ghost, Heinemann, 1934. . . £100/£50
ditto, Doubleday (U.S.), 1934 . . . . £40/£15
Flowers for the Judge, Heinemann, 1936 . £75/£35
ditto, Doubleday (U.S.), 1936 . . . . £20/£10
Dancers in Mourning, Heinemann, 1937 . £75/£35
ditto, Doubleday (U.S.), 1937 . . . . £20/£10
The Case of the Late Pig, Hodder & Stoughton, 1937 (wraps) £75
Mr. Campion Criminologist, Doubleday (U.S.), 1937 . . . . £50/£25
The Fashion in Shrouds, Heinemann, 1938 £75/£35
ditto, Doubleday (U.S.), 1938 . . . . £25/£10
Mr Campion and Others, Heinemann, 1939 £250/£150
Traitor's Purse, Heinemann, 1941 . . . £50/£20
ditto, Doubleday (U.S.), 1941 . . . . £25/£10
Coroner's Pidgin, Heinemann, 1945. . . £50/£20
ditto, as ***Pearls Before Swine***, Doubleday (U.S.), 1945 . . . . £40/£10
The Case Book of Mr Campion, Spivak (U.S.), 1947 . . . . £20
More Work for the Undertaker, Heinemann, 1948 . . . . £25/£10
ditto, Doubleday (U.S.), 1949 . . . . £20/£5
The Tiger in the Smoke, Chatto and Windus, 1952 . . . . £25/£10
ditto, Doubleday (U.S.), 1952 . . . . £20/£5
The Beckoning Lady, Chatto and Windus, 1955 . . . . £20/£5
ditto, as ***The Estate of the Beckoning Lady***, Doubleday (U.S.), 1955 . . . . £20/£5
Hide My Eyes, Chatto and Windus, 1958 . £20/£5
ditto, as ***Tether's End***, Doubleday (U.S.), 1958 . . . . £20/£5
The China Governess, Doubleday (U.S.), 1962 . . . . £20/£5
ditto, Chatto and Windus, 1963 . . . . £20/£5
The Mysterious Mr Campion, An Allingham Omnibus, Chatto and Windus, 1963 . . £20/£5
The Mind Readers, Morrow (U.S.), 1965 . £20/£5
ditto, Chatto and Windus, 1965 . . . . . £20/£5
Mr Campion's Lady, An Allingham Omnibus, Chatto and Windus, 1965 . . . . £20/£5
Mr Campion's Clowns, An Allingham Omnibus, Chatto and Windus, 1967 . . . . . £10/£5
Cargo of Eagles, Chatto and Windus, 1968. £15/£5
ditto, Morrow (U.S.), 1968 . . . . . . £20/£5
The Allingham Casebook, Chatto and Windus, 1969 . . . . £10/£5
ditto, Morrow (U.S.), 1969 . . . . . . £10/£5
The Allingham Minibus, Chatto and Windus, 1973 . . . . £10/£5
ditto, Morrow (U.S.), 1973 . . . . . . £5
ditto, as ***Mr. Campion's Lucky Day and other Stories***, Penguin, 1992 . . . . £5
ditto, Carroll & Graf (U.S.), 1992 . . . . £5
The Return of Mr Campion, Hodder & Stoughton, 1989 . . . . £10/£5
ditto, St Martin's (U.S.), 1990 . . . . £10/£5

Books written as "Maxwell March"

Other Man's Danger, Collins, 1933 . . . £40/£15
ditto, as ***The Man of Dangerous Secrets***, Doubleday (U.S.), 1933 . . . . £35/£15
The Rogues' Holiday, Collins, 1935. . . £35/£15
ditto, Doubleday (U.S.), 1935 . . . . £35/£15
The Shadow in the House, Collins (Crime Club) 1936 . . . . £30/£10
ditto, Doubleday (U.S.), 1936 . . . . . £30/£10

Other crime Titles

The White Cottage Mystery, Jarrolds, 1928 £40/£20
ditto, Carroll & Graf (U.S.), 1990 . . . . . £20
Black Plumes, Doubleday (U.S.), 1940 . . £20/£10
ditto, Heinemann, 1940 . . . . . . £25/£10
Wanted: Someone Innocent, Stamford House (U.S.), 1946 . . . . £20
Deadly Duo, Doubleday (U.S.), 1949. . . £20/£10
ditto, as ***Take Two at Bedtime***, World's Work, 1950 . . . . £20/£10
No Love Lost, World's Work, 1954 . . . £20/£10
ditto, Doubleday (U.S.), 1954 . . . . . £20/£10
The Darings of the Red Rose, Crippen & Landru (U.S.), 1995 . . . . £5

Other Titles

Blackkerchief Dick, Hodder and Stoughton, 1923 . . . . £450/£65
ditto, as ***Black'erchief Dick***, Doubleday (U.S.), 1923 . . . . £250/£35

Dance of the Years, Michael Joseph, 1943 . £15/£5

Play
Water in a Sieve, French, 1925 (wraps) . . . £20

Non Fiction
The Oaken Heart, Michael Joseph, 1941 . £25/£10
ditto, Doubleday (U.S.), 1941 . . . . £20/£5

ERIC AMBLER
(b.1909 d.1998)

A popular and influential thriller writer who deftly directs his heroes through fast-moving plots.

The Dark Frontier, Hodder & Stoughton, 1936 . . . . £1,500/£200
Uncommon Danger, Hodder & Stoughton, 1937 . . . . £1,500/£200
Epitaph for a Spy, Hodder & Stoughton, 1938 . . . . £1,250/£100
ditto, Knopf (U.S.), 1952 . . . . . . £150/£25
Cause for Alarm, Hodder & Stoughton, 1938 . . . . £1,250/£100
ditto, Knopf (U.S.), 1939 . . . . . . £150/£25
The Mask of Dimitrios, Hodder & Stoughton, 1939 . . . . £2,000/£300
Journey into Fear, Hodder & Stoughton, 1940 . . . . £500/£50
ditto, Knopf (U.S.), 1940 . . . . . . £50/£15
Skytip, Doubleday (U.S.), 1950 (pseud. 'Eliot Reed', written with Charles Rhoda). . . . . £75/£15
ditto, Hodder & Stoughton, 1951 . . . £75/£15
Judgement on Deltchev, Hodder & Stoughton, 1951 . . . . £50/£25
ditto, Knopf (U.S.), 1951 . . . . . . £15/£10
Tender to Danger, Doubleday (U.S.), 1951 (pseud. 'Eliot Reed', written with Charles Rhoda) . £75/£15
ditto, as ***Tender to Moonlight***, Hodder & Stoughton, 1951 . . . . £75/£15
The Malas Affair, Collins, 1953 (pseud. 'Eliot Reed', written with Charles Rhoda). . . . . £75/£15
The Schirmer Inheritance, Heinemann, 1953 £40/£15
ditto, Knopf (U.S.), 1953 . . . . . . £20/£5
Charter to Danger, Collins, 1954 (pseud. 'Eliot Reed', written with Charles Rhoda). . . . . £75/£15
The Night Comers, Heinemann, 1956 . . £15/£5
ditto as ***State of Siege***, Knopf (U.S.), 1956 . £15/£5
Passage of Arms, Heinemann, 1959 . . . £15/£5
ditto, Knopf (U.S.), 1959 . . . . . . £10/£5
The Light of Day, Heinemann, 1962. . . £15/£5
ditto, Knopf (U.S.), 1963 . . . . £10/£5
A Kind of Anger, Bodley Head, 1964 . . . £15/£5
ditto, Atheneum (U.S.), 1964 . . . . . . £10/£5
The Jealous God Stellar Press, 1964 (200 copies, wraps). £50
Dirty Story, Bodley Head, 1967 . . . . £15/£5
ditto, Atheneum (U.S.), 1967 . . . . . . £10/£5
The Intercom Conspiracy, Atheneum (U.S.), 1969 . . . . £15/£5
ditto, Weidenfeld & Nicolson, 1970 . . . . £15/£5
The Levanter, Weidenfeld & Nicolson, 1972 . £15/£5
ditto, Atheneum (U.S.), 1972 . . . . . . £10/£5
Doctor Frigo, Weidenfeld & Nicolson, 1974 . £15/£5
ditto, Atheneum (U.S.), 1974 . . . . . . £10/£5
Send No More Roses, Weidenfeld & Nicolson, 1977 . . . . £10/£5
ditto as ***The Siege of the Villa Lipp***, Random House (U.S.) 1977 . . . . £20/£5
The Care of Time, Farrar Straus Giroux (U.S.), 1981 . . . . £10/£5
ditto, Farrar Straus Giroux (U.S.), 1981 (300 signed copies, slipcase) . . . . £35/£15
ditto, Weidenfeld & Nicolson, 1981 . . . £10/£5

Short Stories
The Army of the Shadows and Other Stories, Eurographica (Helsinki), 1986 (350 signed copies) . . . . £75/£45
Waiting for Orders, Mysterious Press (U.S.), 1991 . . . . £10/£5
ditto, Mysterious Press (U.S.), 1991 (26 signed copies, slipcase) . . . . £150/£100
The Story So Far, Weidenfeld & Nicholson, 1993 . . . . £10/£5

Essays
The Ability to Kill and Other Pieces, Bodley Head, 1962 (first issue with essay) . . . . £125/£65
ditto, Bodley Head, 1963 (2nd issue) £45/£10
ditto, The Mysterious Press (U.S.), [1987] (250 signed copies in slipcase) . . . . £25/£15
ditto, The Mysterious Press (U.S.), [1987] (unlimited edition in dustjacket). . . . . . . £10/£5

Autobiography
Here Lies Eric Ambler, Weidenfeld & Nicolson, 1985 . . . . £10/£5
ditto, Farrar Straus Giroux (U.S.) 1986 . . £10/£5
ditto, Farrar Straus Giroux (U.S.) 1986 (100 signed copies, slipcase) . . . . £50/£30

Edited by Ambler
To Catch a Spy, Bodley Head, 1964 . . . £15/£5
ditto, Atheneum (U.S.), 1965 . . . . . £10/£5

KINGSLEY AMIS
(b.1922 d.1995)

A poet and novelist who has the ability to be satirical and inventive whilst being thoroughly readable.

Novels

Lucky Jim, Gollancz, 1953 [1954] . . . £500/£75
ditto, Doubleday (U.S.), 1954 . . . . £50/£20
That Uncertain Feeling, Gollancz, 1955 . £50/£10
ditto, Harcourt Brace (U.S.), 1956 . . . £25/£10
I Like it Here, Gollancz, 1958 . . . . £35/£10
ditto, Harcourt Brace (U.S.), 1958 . . . £25/£10
Take a Girl Like You, Gollancz, 1960 . . £45/£15
ditto, Harcourt Brace (U.S.), 1961 . . . £15/£5
One Fat Englishman, Gollancz, 1963 . . £15/£5
ditto, Harcourt Brace (U.S.), 1964 . . . £10/£5
The Egyptologists (with Robert Conquest), Jonathan Cape, 1965 . . . . £25/£10
ditto, Random House (U.S.), 1966 . . . £15/£5
The Anti-Death League, Gollancz, 1966 . £15/£5
ditto, Harcourt Brace (U.S.), 1966 . . . £10/£5
Colonel Sun, Jonathan Cape, 1968 (pseud. 'Robert Markham') . . . . £25/£5
ditto, Harper (U.S.), 1968 . . . . . . £20/£5
I Want it Now, Jonathan Cape, 1968 . . . £15/£5
ditto, Harcourt Brace (U.S.), 1969 . . . £10/£5
The Green Man, Jonathan Cape, 1969 . . £15/£5
ditto, Harcourt Brace (U.S.), 1970 . . . £10/£5
Girl, 20, Jonathan Cape, 1971 . . . . £10/£5
ditto, Harcourt Brace (U.S.), 1972 . . . £10/£5
The Riverside Villas Murder, Jonathan Cape, 1973 . . . . £12/£5
ditto, Harcourt Brace (U.S.), 1973 . . . £10/£5
Ending Up, Jonathan Cape, 1974 . . . £12/£5
ditto, Harcourt Brace (U.S.), 1974 . . . £10/£5
The Alteration, Jonathan Cape, 1976 . . £15/£5
ditto, Viking Press (U.S.), 1977 . . . . £10/£5
Jake's Thing, Hutchinson, 1978 . . . . £10/£5
ditto, Viking Press (U.S.), 1979 . . . . £10/£5
Russian Hide-and-Seek, Hutchinson, 1980 . £10/£5
Stanley and the Women, Hutchinson, 1984 . £10/£5
ditto, Summit (U.S.), 1985 . . . . . . £10/£5
The Old Devils, Hutchinson, 1986 . . . £15/£5
ditto, Hutchinson/London Limited Editions, 1986 (250 signed copies, tissue jacket) . . . . . £50/£45
ditto, Summit (U.S.), 1986 . . . . £10/£5
Difficulties With Girls, Hutchinson, 1988 . . £10/£5
ditto, Hutchinson, 1988 (500 numbered proof copies, wraps) £15
ditto, Summit (U.S.), 1989 . . . . . . £10/£5
The Folks That Live on the Hill, Hutchinson, 1990 . . . . £10/£5
ditto, Hutchinson, 1990 (500 numbered proof copies) £40
ditto, Summit (U.S.), 1990 . . . . . . £10/£5
The Russian Girl, Hutchinson, 1992. . . £10/£5
ditto, Viking (U.S.), 1992. . . . . . . £10/£5
We Are All Guilty, Reinhardt Books/Viking, 1991 . . . . £10/£5
You Can't Do Both, London Limited Editions, 1994 (150 copies in glassine d/w). . . . . . £45/£35
ditto, Hutchinson, 1994 . . . . £10/£5
The Biographer's Moustache, Flamingo/Harper Collins, 1995 . . . . £10/£5

Omnibus Editions

The Kingsley Amis Omnibus, Hutchinson, 1992 . . . . £10/£5

Short Stories

My Enemy's Enemy, Gollancz, 1962 . . £35/£10
ditto, Harcourt Brace (U.S.), 1963 . . . £10/£5
Dear Illusion, Covent Garden Press, 1972 (500 copies, wraps). £15
ditto, Covent Garden Press, 1972 (100 signed copies, wraps) £30
The Darkwater Hall Mystery, Tragara Press (Edinburgh), 1978 (165 copies, wraps). . . . £50
Collected Short Stories, Hutchinson, 1980 . £10/£5
The Crime of the Century, Hutchinson, 1989 £10/£5
ditto, Mysterious Press (U.S.), 1989 . . . £10/£5
ditto, Mysterious Press (U.S.), 1989 (100 signed copies in slipcase) £40
Mrs Barrett's Secret and Other Stories, Hutchinson, 1993 . . . . £5/£2

Verse

Bright November, Fortune Press, [1947] . £150/£75
A Frame of Mind, Reading School of Art, 1953 (250 numbered copies, wraps) £175
Fantasy Poets No.22, Fantasy Press, 1954 (wraps) £175
A Case of Samples: Poems, 1946-1956, Gollancz, 1956. . . . . £75/£25
ditto, Harcourt Brace (U.S.), 1957 . . . £45/£15
Penguin Modern Poets No.2, Penguin, 1962, (with Dom Moraes and Peter Porter, wraps) £5
The Evans Country, Fantasy Press, 1962 (wraps) £40
A Look Round the Estate: Poems, 1957-1967, Jonathan Cape, 1967 . . . . £25/£10
ditto, Harcourt Brace (U.S.), 1968 . . . £10/£5
Wasted and ***Kipling at Batemans***, Poem of the Month Club, 1973 (broadsheet) £10
Collected Poems 1944-1979, Hutchinson, 1979 . . . . £10/£5
ditto, Viking (U.S.), 1980 . . . . £10/£5

Non Fiction

Socialism and the Intellectuals, Fabian Press, 1957

(wraps) £35
New Maps of Hell: A Survey of Science Fiction, Harcourt Brace (U.S.), 1960 . . . . £25/£10
ditto, Gollancz, 1961 . . . . £25/£10
The James Bond Dossier, Jonathan Cape, 1965 . . . . £35/£5
ditto, NAL (U.S.), 1965 . . . . £15/£5
Lucky Jim's Politics, Conservative Policy Centre, 1968 (wraps) £25
What Became of Jane Austen? and Other Questions, Jonathan Cape, 1970 . . . . . . £25/£5
ditto, Harcourt Brace (U.S.), 1971 . . . . £10/£5
On Drink, Jonathan Cape, 1972 . . . . . £15/£5
ditto, Harcourt Brace (U.S.), 1973 . . . £15/£5
Rudyard Kipling and his World, Thames & Hudson, 1975 . . . . £10/£5
ditto, Scribner (U.S.), 1975 . . . . . . £10/£5
An Arts Policy?, Centre for Policy Studies, 1979 (wraps) £5
Every Day Drinking, Hutchinson, 1983 . . . . £10/£5
How's Your Glass? A Quizzical Look at Drinks and Drinking, Weidenfeld & Nicolson, 1984 . £10/£5
Selected Non-Fiction, Hutchinson, 1990 . £10/£5
Memoirs, Hutchinson, 1991 . . . . . £10/£5
ditto, Summit (U.S.), 1991 . . . . . . £10/£5

MARTIN AMIS
(b.1949)

The son of Kingsley Amis, Martin wrote his first novel at the age of 21.

Novels
The Rachel Papers, Cape, 1973 . . . . £200/£30
ditto, Knopf (U.S.), 1974 . . . . £75/£15
Dead Babies, Cape, 1975 . . . . £173/£30
ditto, Knopf (U.S.), 1976 . . . . £45/£10
ditto, as ***Dark Secrets***, Triad, 1977 (wraps) . . £10
Success, Cape, 1978 . . . . £50/£10
ditto, Harmony (U.S.), 1987 . . . . . . £10/£5
Other People: A Mystery Story, Cape, 1981 £50/£10
ditto, Viking Press (U.S.), 1981 . . . . . £10/£5
Money: A Suicide Note, Cape, 1984. . . . £50/£10
ditto, Viking Press (U.S.), 1985 . . . . . £10/£5
London Fields, Cape, 1989 . . . . . . £15/£5
ditto, London Limited Editions, 1989 (150 signed copies, glassine d/w) . . . . £75/£50
ditto, Harmony (U.S.), 1990 . . . . . . £10/£5
Time's Arrow, or the Nature of the Offence, Cape, 1991 . . . . £15/£5
ditto, London Limited Editions, 1991 (200 signed copies, glassine d/w) . . . . £75/£50
ditto, Harmony (U.S.), 1991 . . . . . . £10/£5
The Information, Flamingo, 1995 . . . . £10/£5
ditto, Flamingo, 1995 (350 signed, numbered copies of 376, slipcase) . . . . £60/£45
ditto, Harmony (U.S.), 1995 . . . . . . £10/£5

Short Stories
Einstein's Monsters, Cape, 1987. . . . . £25/£10
ditto, Harmony (U.S.), 1987 . . . . . . £15/£5
Two Stories, Moorhouse & Sorensen, 1994 (26 signed copies, bound in aluminium, of 326) . . . £200
ditto, Moorhouse & Sorensen, 1994 (100 signed copies bound in clothof 326) £75
ditto, Moorhouse & Sorensen, 1994 (200 signed copies in card coversof 326) £25

Non Fiction
Invasion of the Space Invaders, Hutchinson, 1982 (wraps) £50
The Moronic Inferno and Other Visits to America, Cape, 1986 . . . . £25/£10
ditto, Viking Press (U.S.), 1987 . . . . . £10/£5
Visiting Mrs Nabokov and Other Excursions, Cape, 1993 . . . . £10/£5
ditto, Harmony (U.S.), 1993 . . . . . . £10/£5

MAYA ANGELOU
(b. 1928)

Maya Angelou is a poet, historian, author, actress, playwright, civil-rights activist, producer and director. Her books of autobiography have become international bestsellers.

Autobiography
I Know Why the Caged Bird Sings, Random House (U.S.), 1969 . . . . £125/£45
Gather Together in My Name, Random House (U.S.), 1974 . . . . £45/£20
Singin' and Swingin' and Gettin' Merry Like Christmas, Random House (U.S.), 1976 . £25/£10
The Heart of a Woman, Random House (U.S.), 1981 . . . . £25/£10
All God's Children Need Traveling Shoes, Random House (U.S.), 1986 . . . . £30/£10
ditto, Franklin Library (U.S.), 1986 (signed copies) £50

Essays
Wouldn't Take Nothing for my Journey Now, Random House (U.S.), 1993 . . . . £15/£5
Even the Stars Look Lonesome, Random House (U.S.), 1997 . . . . £15/£5

Poetry

Just Give Me a Cool Drink of Water 'fore I Diiie, Random House (U.S.), 1971 . . . . . £50/£20

Oh Pray My Wings are Gonna Fit Me Well, Random House (U.S.), 1975 . . . . £30/£10

And Still I Rise, Random House (U.S.), 1978 £40/£15

Shaker, Why Don't You Sing?, Random House (U.S.), 1983 . . . . £30/£10

Now Sheba Sings the Song, Dutton/Dial (U.S.), 1987 . . . . £25/£10

I Shall Not Be Moved, Random House (U.S.), 1990 . . . . £20/£5

On the Pulse of the Morning, Random House (U.S.), 1993 (wraps) £15

The Complete Collected Poems of Maya Angelou, Random House (U.S.), 1994 . . . . £10/£5

EDWARD ARDIZZONE

(b.1900 d.1979)

Ardizzone studied at the Westminster School of Art and in 1927 became a full-time artist. He is best known for his illustrations of children's books, some of which he wrote himself.

Children's Books written and illustrated by Ardizzone

Little Tim and the Brave Sea Captain, O.U.P., [1936] . . . . £350/£200

ditto, O.U.P., 1955 (revised edition) . . . £25/£10

Lucy Brown and Mr Grimes, O.U.P., [1937] . . . . £275/£150

ditto, O.U.P., 1970 (revised edition) . . . £30/£10

Tim and Lucy go to Sea, O.U.P., [1938] £275/£150

ditto, O.U.P., 1958 (revised edition) . . . £25/£10

Nicholas the Fast-Moving Diesel, Eyre & Spottiswoode [1947]. . . . . £250/£150

Paul, The Hero of the Fire, Puffin, 1948 (wraps) £35

ditto, Constable, 1962 (revised edition) . . £20/£5

Tim to the Rescue, O.U.P., 1949. . . . £200/£100

Tim and Charlotte, O.U.P., 1951 . . . £175/£75

Tim in Danger, O.U.P., 1953 . . . . £125/£50

Tim all Alone, O.U.P., 1956 . . . . . £50/£25

Johnny the Clockmaker, O.U.P., 1960 . . £50/£25

Tim's Friend Towser, O.U.P., 1962 . . . £50/£25

Peter the Wanderer, O.U.P., 1963 . . . . £40/£20

Diana and her Rhinoceros, The Bodley Head, 1964 . . . . £40/£20

Sarah and Simon and No Red Paint, Constable [1965] . . . . £40/£20

Tim and Ginger, O.U.P., 1965 . . . . £35/£20

The Little Girl and the Tiny Doll, Constable, 1966 (with Aingelda Ardizzone) . . . . . £35/£20

Tim to the Lighthouse, O.U.P., 1968 . . £30/£15

Johnny's Bad Day, The Bodley Head, 1970 £25/£15

Tim's Last Voyage, The Bodley Head, 1972 £25/£15

Ship's Cook Ginger: Another Time Story, The Bodley Head, 1977 . . . . £20/£5

The Adventures of Tim, The Bodley Head, 1977 . . . . £20/£5

Children's Books illustrated by Ardizzone

Tom, Dick and Harriet, by Albert N. Lyons, Cresset Press, 1937 . . . . £250/£100

Great Expectations, by Charles Dickens, Heritage Press, 1939 . . . . £55/£25

ditto, Limited Editions Club (U.S.) [1939] £350/£200

MIMFF, by H.J. Kaeser, O.U.P., 1939 . . £55/£25

Peacock Pie, by Walter de la Mare, Faber, 1946 . . . . £50/£25

The Pilgrim's Progress, by John Bunyan, Faber, 1947. . . . . £60/£30

Three Brothers and a Lady, by Margaret Black, Acorn Press, 1947 . . . . £45/£20

A True and Pathetic History of Desbarollda, The Waltzing Mouse, by Noel Langley, Lindsay Drummond, 1947 . . . . £45/£20

Hey Nonny Yes: Passions and Conceits from Shakespeare, edited by Hallam Fordham, John Lehmann, 1947 . . . . £35/£15

The Life and Adventures of Nicholas Nickleby, Ealing Studios, 1947 (promotional booklet) £75

Charles Dickens' Birthday Book, edited by Enid Dickens Hawksley, Faber, 1948 . . . . £40/£15

The Otterbury Incident, by Cecil Day Lewis, Putnam, 1948 . . . . £45/£20

The Rose and the Ring, by William Makepeace Thackeray, Guilford Press/Wilfrid David, 1948 . . . . £30/£15

MIMFF in Charge, by H.J. Kaeser, (translated by David Ascoli), O.U.P., 1949 . . . . £35/£20

The Tale of Ali Baba, (translated by J.C. Mardrus and E. Powys Mathers), Limited Editions Club (U.S.), 1949 (2,500 signed copies) £75

Somebody's Rocking My Dreamboat, by Noel Langley and Hazel Pynegar, Barker, 1949 . . . £30/£15

The Humour of Dickens, News Chronicle, 1952 £20

The Blackbird in the Lilac, by James Reeves, O.U.P., 1952 . . . . £35/£15

MIMFF Takes Over, by H.J. Kaeser, O.U.P., 1954 . . . . £30/£15

The Fantastic Tale of the Plucky Sailor and the Postage Stamp, by Stephen Corrin, Faber, 1954 . . . . £25/£10

The Little Bookroom, by Eleanor Farjeon, O.U.P., 1955 . . . . £30/£15

The Suburban Child, by James Kenward, O.U.P., 1955 . . . . £40/£15

Minnow on the Say, by Phillippa Pearce, O.U.P., 1955 . . . . £40/£20

David Copperfield, by Charles Dickens, (abridged by S. Wood), O.U.P., 1955 . . . . £30/£15

Bleak House, Charles Dickens, (abridged by S. Wood), O.U.P., 1955 . . . . £30/£15

Sun Slower, Sun Faster, by Meriol Trevor, Collins, 1955 . . . . £35/£15

Pigeons and Princesses, by James Reeves, Heinemann, 1956 . . . . £35/£15

Marshmallow, by Claire Newberry, Studio, 1956 £20

St Luke's Life of Christ (translated by J.B. Phillips), Collins, 1956 . . . . £25/£10

Wandering Moon, by James Reeves, Heinemann, 1957 . . . . £35/£15

A Stickful of Nonpareil, by George Scurfield, (500 copies) CUP, 1956 . . . . £50

Hunting with Mr Jorrocks, by Robert Surtees (edited by Lionel Gough) O.U.P., 1956. . . . £45/£20

Prefabulous Animiles, by James Reeves, Heinemann, 1957 . . . . £30/£15

The School in Our Village, by Joan M. Goldman, Batsford, 1957 . . . . £30/£15

The Boy Down Kitchiner Street, by Leslie Paul, Faber, 1957 . . . . £30/£15

Lottie, by John Symonds, The Bodley Head, 1957 . . . . £30/£15

MIMFF-Robinson, by H.J. Kaeser, (translated by Ruth Michaelis and Jena & Arthur Ratcliff), O.U.P., 1958 . . . . £30/£15

The Story of Joseph, by Walter de la Mare, Faber, 1958 . . . . £30/£15

Jim at the Corner, by Eleanor Farjeon, O.U.P., 1958 £40/£20

Pinky Pye, by Eleanor Estes, Constable, 1959 £30/£15

The Nine Lives of Island Mackenzie, by Ursula Moray Williams, Chatto & Windus, 1959 . . . £25/£10

Titus in Trouble, by James Reeves, The Bodley Head, 1959 . . . . £30/£15

Exploits of Don Quixote, by Cervantes, (abridged by James Reeves), Blackie [1959] . . . . £30/£15

Story of Moses, by Walter de la Mare, Faber, 1959 . . . . £30/£15

Elfrida and the Pig, by John Symonds, Harrap, 1959 . . . . £35/£15

Holiday Trench, by Joan Ballantyne, Nelson, 1959 . . . . £20/£10

The Godstone and the Blackymor, by T.H. White, Cape, 1959 . . . . £35/£15

The Story of Samuel and Saul, by Walter de la Mare, Faber, 1960 . . . . £30/£15

Kidnappers at Coombe, by Joan Ballantyne, Nelson, 1960 . . . . £25/£10

The Rib of the Green Umbrella, by Naomi Mitchison, Collins, 1960 . . . . £30/£15

Eleanor Farjeon's Book, edited by Eleanor Graham, Puffin, 1960 (wraps) £15

Merry England, by Cyril Ray, Vista Books, 1960 . . . . £35/£15

Italian Peepshow, by Eleanor Farjeon, O.U.P., 1960 . . . . £35/£15

The Penny Fiddle: Poems for Children, by Robert Graves, Cassell, 1960 . . . . . . £65/£35

ditto, Doubleday (U.S.), 1960 . . . . . . £45/£10

Boyhoods of the Great Composers, O.U.P., 1960 &, 1963 (2 vols) . . . . £40/£20

Hurdy Gurdy, by James Reeves, Heinemann, 1961 . . . . £40/£20

No Mystery for the Maitlands, by Joan Ballantyne, Nelson, 1961 . . . . £35/£15

Down in the Cellar, by Nicholas Gray, Dobson, 1961 . . . . £30/£15

The Adventures of Huckleberry Finn, by Mark Twain, Heinemann, 1961 . . . . £35/£15

The Adventures of Tom Sawyer, by Mark Twain, Heinemann, 1961 . . . . £35/£15

Stories from the Bible, by Walter de la Mare, Faber, 1961 . . . . £30/£15

The Witch Family, by Eleanor Estes, Constable, 1962 . . . . £35/£15

Naughty Children, by Christianna Brand, Gollancz, 1962 . . . . £45/£20

Sailor Rumbelow and Britannia, by James Reeves, Heinemann, 1962 . . . . £40/£20

Peter Pan, by J.M. Barrie, Brockhampton Press, 1962. . . . . £45/£20

A Ring of Bells, by John Betjeman, John Murray, 1962 . . . . £35/£15

The Story of Let's Make an Opera, by Eric Crosier, O.U.P., 1962 . . . . £30/£15

The Singing Cupboard, by Dan Farralla, Blackie, 1962 . . . . £35/£15

Mrs Malone, by Eleanor Farjeon, O.U.P., 1962 . . . . £35/£15

Stig of the Dump, by Clive King, Puffin Original, 1963 (wraps) £20

Kaleidoscope, by Eleanor Farjeon, O.U.P., 1963 . . . . £40/£20

Swanhilda-of-the-Swans, by Dana Farralla, Blackie [1964] . . . . £30/£15

Ann at Highwood Hall, by Robert Graves, Cassell, 1964 . . . . £30/£15

ditto, Doubleday (U.S.), 1964 . . . . . £20/£10

Three Tall Tales, by James Reeves, Abelard-Schumann, 1964 . . . . £30/£15

The Alley, by Eleanor Estes, Harcourt Brace (U.S.), 1964 . . . . £25/£15

Nurse Matilda, by Christianna Brand, Brockhampton Press, 1965 . . . . £35/£15

Island of Fish in the Trees, by Eva-Lis Wuorio,

Dobson, 1964. . . . . £35/£15

The Land of Right Up and Down, by Eva-Lis Wuorio, Dobson, 1965 . . . . £35/£15

Open the Door, edited by Margery Fisher, Brockhampton Press, 1965 . . . . . . £30/£15

The Story of Jackie Thimble, by James Reeves, Chatto & Windus, 1965 . . . . £30/£15

Old Perisher, by Diana Ross, Faber, 1965 . £30/£15

The Old Nurse's Stocking Basket, by Eleanor Farjeon, O.U.P., 1965 . . . . £30/£15

The Truants and Other Poems for Children, by John Walsh, Heinemann, 1965 . . . . . £30/£15

The Growing Summer, by Noel Streatfield, Collins, 1966 . . . . £40/£15

Long Ago When I Was Young, by E. Nesbit, Whiting & Wheaton, 1966 . . . . £30/£15

Daddy Longlegs, by Jean Webster, Brockhampton Press, 1966 . . . . £30/£15

The Land of Green Ginger, by Noel Langley, Puffin, 1966, (wraps). £15

The Dragon, by Archibald Marshall, Warne, 1966. . . . . £25/£10

The Secret Shoemaker and Other Stories, by James Reeves, Abelard-Schumann, 1966 . . . £45/£15

Timothy's Song, by W.J. Lederer, Lutterworth Press, 1966 . . . . £25/£10

The Year Round, by Leonard Clark, Hart-Davis, 1966 . . . . £25/£10

Rhyming Will, by James Reeves, Hamish Hamilton, 1967 . . . . £40/£20

Travels with a Donkey, by Robert Louis Stevenson, Folio Society, 1967 . . . . £20/£10

Miranda The Great, by Eleanor Estes, Harcourt Brace (U.S.), 1967 . . . . £20/£10

A Likely Place, by Paula Fox, Macmillan [1967] . . . . £20/£10

Kali and the Golden Mirror, by Eva-Lis Wuorio, World Publishing, 1967 . . . . . . £30/£15

The Stuffed Dog, by John Symonds, Barker, 1967 . . . . £25/£10

Nurse Matilda Goes to Town, by Christianna Brand, Brockhampton Press, 1967 . . . . . £25/£10

Robinson Crusoe, by Daniel Defoe, Nonesuch Press, 1968 . . . . £25/£10

Upside-Down Willie, by Dorothy Clewes, Hamish Hamilton, 1968 . . . . £20/£10

Special Branch Willie, by Dorothy Clewes, Hamish Hamilton, 1969 . . . . £20/£10

The Angel and the Donkey, by James Reeves, Hamish Hamilton, 1969 . . . . £20/£10

Dick Wittington, retold by Kathleen Lines, The Bodley Head, 1970 . . . . £15/£5

Fire Brigade Willie, by Dorothy Clewes, Hamish Hamilton, 1970 . . . . £25/£10

Home From the Sea, by Robert Louis Stevenson, (verse, selected and introduced by Ivor Brown), The Bodley Head, 1970 . . . . £15/£5

How the Moon Began, by James Reeves, Abelard-Schumann, 1971 . . . . £20/£10

The Old Ballad of the Babes in the Wood, The Bodley Head, 1972 . . . . £15/£5

The Second Best Children in the World, by Mary Lavin, Longmans, 1972 . . . . £15/£5

The Tunnel of Hugsy Goode, by Eleanor Estes, Harcourt Brace (U.S.), 1972 . . . . . £15/£5

The Little Fire Engine, by Graham Greene, The Bodley Head, 1973 . . . . £20/£10

The Little Train, by Graham Greene, The Bodley Head, 1973 . . . . £20/£10

Complete Poems for Children, by James Reeves, Heinemann, 1973 . . . . £15/£5

The Night Ride, by Aingelda Ardizzone, The Bodley Head, 1973 . . . . £15/£5

The Little Horse Bus, by Graham Greene, The Bodley Head, 1974 . . . . £25/£10

The Little Steam Roller, by Graham Greene, The Bodley Head, 1974 . . . . £25/£10

The Lion That Flew, by James Reeves, Chatto & Windus, 1974 (issued without d/w). . . . £20/£10

Nurse Matilda goes to Hospital, by Christianna Brand, Brockhampton Press, 1974 . . . . . . £25/£10

More Prefabulous Animiles, by James Reeves, Heinemann, 1975 . . . . £15/£5

Ardizzone's Kilvert, Cape, 1976 . . . . . £15/£5

Arcadian Ballads, by James Reeves, Heinemann, 1978 . . . . £15/£5

Ardizzone's Hans Andersen, Deutsch, 1978 £20/£10

A Child's Christmas in Wales, by Dylan Thomas, Dent, 1978 . . . . £25/£10

The James Reeves Story Book, Heinemann, 1978 . . . . £15/£5

Ardizzone's English Fairy Tales, Deutsch, 1980 . . . . £15/£5

Adult Books written and illustrated by Ardizzone

Baggage to the Enemy, John Murray, 1941 £45/£20

The Young Ardizzone: An Autobiographical Fragment, Studio Vista, 1970 . . . . . £25/£10

Diary of a War Artist, The Bodley Head, 1974 £25/£10

From Edward Ardizzone's Indian Diary, Stellar Press/The Bodley Head, 1983 (225 copies, wraps) £50

Indian Diary, The Bodley Head, 1984 . . £20/£10

Adult Books illustrated by Ardizzone

In a Glass Darkly, by Sheridan Le Fanu, Peter Davis, 1929 . . . . £200/£75

ditto, Peter Davis, 1929 (second impression) £75/£35

The Library, by George Crabbe, De la More Press, 1930 . . . . £60/£30

The Mediterranean, edited by Paul Bloomfield, Cassell, 1935 . . . . £50/£20
The Local, by Maurice Gorham, Cassell, 1939 £25/£10
My Uncle Silas, by H.E. Bates, Cape, 1939 £150/£75
The Road to Bordeaux, by C.D. Freeman and D. Cooper, Cresset Press, 1940. . . . . . £25/£10
The Battle of France, by A. Maurois, The Bodley Head, 1940 . . . . £25/£10
Women, O.U.P., 1943 (wraps) £10
The Poems of Francois Villon, Cresset Press, 1946 . . . . £40/£15
Back to the Local, by Maurice Gorham, Percival Marshall, 1949 . . . . £30/£15
The Londoners, by Maurice Gorham, Percival Marshall, 1951 . . . . £30/£15
Showmen and Suckers, by Maurice Gorham, Percival Marshall, 1951 . . . . £30/£15
The Modern Prometheus, by Zara Nuber, Forge Press, 1952 . . . . £15/£5
The Warden, by Anthony Trollope, O.U.P., 1952 . . . . £35/£15
Barchester Towers, by Anthony Trollope, O.U.P., 1953 . . . . £35/£15
Christmas Eve, by Cecil Day Lewis, Faber, 1954 . . . . £15/£5
The Newcomes, by William Makepeace Thackeray, Limited Edition Club, 1954, (1,500 signed copies, slipcase, 2 vols) £45
The Tale of an Old Tweed Jacket, by Eric Keown, Moss Bros, [1955] . . . . £50/£20
The History of Henry Esmond, by William Makepeace Thackeray, The Limited Editions Club (U.S.), 1956 (1,500 signed, numbered copies, slipcase) . . £100
Sugar for the Horse, by H.E. Bates, Joseph, 1957 . . . . £25/£10
Not Such An Ass, by Henry Cecil, Hutchinson, 1961 . . . . £20/£5
Folk Songs of England, Ireland, Scotland and Wales, by W. Cole, Doubleday (U.S.), 1961 . . £20/£5
London Since, 1912, by John T. Hayes, Museum of London, 1962 . . . . £20/£5
The Thirty-Nine Steps, by John Buchan, Dent, 1964 . . . . £20/£5
The Milldale Riot, by Freda P. Nichols, Ginn, 1965 . . . . £20/£5
Know About English Law, by Henry Cecil, Blackie, 1965 . . . . £20/£5
The Short Stories, by Charles Dickens, Limited Edition Club (U.S.), 1971, (1,500 signed copies, slipcase) £75
Learn More About English Law, by Henry Cecil, William Luscombe, 1974 . . . . . . £10/£5
Fragment, Macmillan, 1984 . . . . . £10/£5

MICHAEL ARLEN
(b.1895 d.1956)

Born Dikran Kouyoumdjian in Bulgaria of Armenian ancestry, Arlen became a naturalised British subject in 1922 and was a popular writer during the 1920s and 30s.

Short Stories
The Romantic Lady and Other Stories, Collins, [1921] . . . . £50/£20
ditto, Doran (U.S.), 1921 . . . . . . £45/£15
These Charming People, Collins, [1923] . £35/£10
ditto, Doran (U.S.), 1924 . . . . . . £25/£10
May Fair, In Which Are Told the Last Adventures of These Charming People, Collins, [1925] . £40/£10
ditto, Doran (U.S.), [1925] . . . . . £15/£5
ditto, Doran (U.S.), [1925] (550 signed copies in slipcase) . . . . £50/£40
Ghost Stories, Collins, [1927] . . . . £40/£15
Babes in the Wood, Hutchinson, [1929]. . £25/£10
ditto, Doran (U.S.), 1929 . . . . . . £15/£5
The Ancient Sin and Other Stories, Collins, 1930 . . . . £15/£5
The Short Stories of Michael Arlen, Collins, 1933 . . . . £15/£5
The Crooked Coronet and Other Misrepresentations of the Real Facts of Life, Heinemann, 1937 . £15/£5
ditto, Doran (U.S.), 1937 . . . . . . £15/£5

Novels
The London Venture, Heinemann, 1920 . £45/£15
ditto, Doran (U.S.), 1920 . . . . . . £40/£15
'Piracy': A Romantic Chronicle of These Days, Collins, [1922] . . . . £40/£10
ditto, Doran, 1923 . . . . £25/£10
The Green Hat: A Romance for a Few People, Collins, 1924 . . . . £75/£20
ditto, Doran, 1924 . . . . £25/£10
Young Men in Love, Hutchinson, [1927] . £25/£10
ditto, Doran, 1927 . . . . £20/£5
Lily Christine, Hutchinson, [1928] . . . £25/£15
ditto, Doran, 1928 . . . . £15/£5
Men Dislike Women, Heinemann, 1931. . £15/£5
ditto, Doran, 1931 . . . . £15/£5
A Young man Comes to London, Keliher & Co., 1931 (brochure to promote Dorchester Hotel) . . £30
Man's Mortality, Heinemann, 1933 . . £15/£5
ditto, Doran, 1933 . . . . £15/£5
Hell! Said the Duchess: A Bed-Time Story, Heinemann, [1934] . . . . £25/£10
ditto, Doran, 1934 . . . . £15/£5
The Flying Dutchman, Heinemann, 1939 . £15/£5
ditto, Doran, 1939 . . . . £15/£5

Plays

The Zoo, Samuel French, 1927 (wraps, with Winchell Smith) £10
Good Losers, Samuel French, 1933 (wraps, with Walter Hackett) £10

ISAAC ASIMOV

(b.1920 d.1992)

Born in Russia, Asimov was taken to the U.S. in infancy. A hugely successful science fiction writer, his many non-fiction writings have also served to make scientific ideas popular and easily understandable.

Novels

Pebble in the Sky, Doubleday (U.S.), 1950 . £200/£50
ditto, Sidgwick & Jackson, 1968 . . . . £60/£20
The Stars, Like Dust, Doubleday (U.S.), 1951 £75/£35
Foundation, Gnome Press (U.S.), 1951 . . £125/£50
ditto, Weidenfeld, 1953 . . . . £75/£40
Foundation and Empire, Gnome Press (U.S.), 1952 . . . . £100/£50
The Currents of Space, Doubleday (U.S.), 1952 . . . . £75/£35
ditto, Boardman, 1955. . . . . £30/£10
Second Foundation, Gnome Press (U.S.), 1953 . . . . £100/£50
The Caves of Steel, Doubleday (U.S.), 1954 £50/£20
ditto, Boardman, 1954. . . . . £30/£10
The End of Eternity, Doubleday (U.S.), 1955 £40/£15
The Naked Sun, Doubleday (U.S.), 1957 . £50/£20
ditto, Joseph, 1958. . . . . £25/£10
The Death Dealers, Avon (U.S.), 1958 (wraps) £10
ditto, as ***A Whiff of Death***, Walker (U.S.), 1968 . . . . £25/£10
ditto, Gollancz, 1968 . . . . £25/£10
Fantastic Voyage, Houghton Miffin (U.S.), 1966 . . . . £25/£10
ditto, Dobson, 1966 . . . . £25/£10
The Gods Themselves, Doubleday (U.S.), 1972 . . . . £25/£10
ditto, Gollancz, 1972 . . . . £25/£5
Authorised Murder, Doubleday (U.S.), 1976 . £15/£5
ditto, Gollancz, 1976 . . . . £15/£5
Murder at the Aba, Doubleday (U.S.), 1976 . £10/£5
Foundation's Edge, Doubleday (U.S.), 1982 . £15/£5
ditto, Whispers Press (U.S.), 1982 (1,000 signed, numbered copies, no d/w) £75
ditto, Whispers Press (U.S.), 1982 (26 signed, lettered copies, all edges gilt, slipcase, no d/w) £300
ditto, Granada, 1982 . . . . £10/£5
Robots of Dawn, Doubleday (U.S.), 1983 . . £15/£5
ditto, Granada, 1984 . . . . £10/£5
Foundation and Earth, Doubleday (U.S.), 1986 . . . . £10/£5
ditto, Grafton, 1986 . . . . £10/£5
Fantastic Voyage II: Destination Britain, Doubleday (U.S.), 1987 . . . . £10/£5
ditto, Grafton, 1987 . . . . £10/£5
Prelude to Foundation, Doubleday (U.S.), 1988 . . . . £10/£5
ditto, Grafton, 1988 . . . . £10/£5
Azazel, Doubleday (U.S.), 1988 . . . . £10/£5
ditto, Doubleday (U.K.), 1989 . . . . . £10/£5
Nemesis, Doubleday (U.S.), 1989 . . . . £10/£5
ditto, Doubleday (U.K.), 1989 . . . . . £10/£5
Nightfall, Doubleday (U.S.), 1990 (with Robert Silverberg) . . . . £10/£5
ditto, Gollancz, 1990 . . . . £10/£5
Child of Time, Gollancz, 1991 . . . . . £10/£5
The Positronic Man, Doubleday (U.S.), 1992 (with Robert Silverberg) . . . . £10/£5
ditto, Gollancz, 1992 . . . . £10/£5
Forward the Foundation, Doubleday (U.S.), 1993 . . . . £10/£5
Magic: The Final Fantasy Collection, Harper (U.S.) 1996 . . . . £10/£5
ditto, Voyager, 1996 . . . . £10/£5

Short Stories

I, Robot, Gnome Press (U.S.), 1950 . . . £500/£100
ditto, Grayson, 1952 . . . . £75/£35
The Martian Way and Other Stories, Doubleday (U.S.), 1955 . . . . £50/£15
ditto, Dobson, 1964 . . . . £50/£20
Earth Is Room Enough, Doubleday (U.S.), 1957 . . . . £35/£20
Nine Tomorrows: Tales of the Near Future, Doubleday (U.S.), 1959 . . . . £20/£5
ditto, Dobson, 1963 . . . . £20/£5
The Rest of the Robots, Doubleday (U.S.), 1964 . . . . £20/£5
ditto, Dobson, 1967 . . . . £15/£5
Through a Glass, Clearly, New English Library, 1967 . . . . £10/£5
Asimov's Mysteries, Doubleday (U.S.), 1968 . £10/£5
ditto, Rapp & Whiting, 1968 . . . . . . £10/£5
Nightfall and Other Stories, Doubleday (U.S.), 1969 . . . . £10/£5
ditto, Rapp & Whiting, 1969 . . . . . . £10/£5
The Early Asimov, Doubleday (U.S.), 1972. £10/£5
The Best of Isaac Asimov, Sidgwick & Jackson, 1973 . . . . £10/£5
ditto, Doubleday (U.S.), 1974 . . . . . £10/£5
Tales of the Black Widowers, Doubleday (U.S.), 1974 . . . . £10/£5
ditto, Gollancz, 1975 . . . . £10/£5
Buy Jupiter and Other Stories, Doubleday (U.S.),

1975 . . . . £10/£5
ditto, Gollancz, 1976 . . . . £10/£5
The Bicentennial Man and Other Stories, Doubleday (U.S.), 1976 . . . . £10/£5
ditto, Gollancz, 1977 . . . . £10/£5
More Tales of the Black Widowers, Doubleday (U.S.), 1976 . . . . £10/£5
ditto, Gollancz, 1977 . . . . £10/£5
The Key Word and Other Mysteries, Walker (U.S.), 1977 . . . . £10/£5
The Casebook of the Black Widowers, Doubleday (U.S.), 1980 . . . . £10/£5
ditto, Gollancz, 1980 . . . . £10/£5
Three Science Fiction Tales, Targ Editions (U.S.), 1981 (250 signed copies in plain d/w) . . £35/£25
Banquets of the Black Widowers, Doubleday (U.S.), 1985 . . . . £10/£5
ditto, Granada, 1985 . . . . £10/£5
Alternative Asimovs, Doubleday (U.S.), 1986 . £10/£5
Robot Dreams, Berkley (U.S.), 1986 . . . . £10/£5
ditto, Gollancz, 1987 . . . . £10/£5
The Best Science Fiction of Isaac Asimov, Doubleday (U.S.), 1986 . . . . £10/£5
ditto, Grafton, 1987 . . . . £10/£5
The Best Mysteries of Isaac Asimov, Doubleday (U.S.), 1986 . . . . £10/£5
ditto, Grafton, 1987 . . . . £10/£5
The Asimov Chronicles: Fifty Years of Isaac Asimov, Dark Harvest (U.S.), 1989 . . . . . . £10/£5
ditto, Century, 1991 . . . . £10/£5
Robot Visions, NAL, 1990 . . . . £10/£5
ditto, Gollancz, 1990 . . . . £10/£5
Puzzles of the Black Widowers, Doubleday (U.S.), 1990 . . . . £10/£5
ditto, Doubleday (U.K.), 1990 . . . . . . £10/£5
The Complete Stories I, Doubleday (U.S.), 1990 . . . . £10/£5
The Complete Stories, Harper/Collins, 1992 . £10/£5
Gold: The Final Science Fiction Collection, Harper Collins, 1995 . . . . £10/£5

Children's Titles written as 'Paul French'
David Starr: Space Ranger, Doubleday (U.S.), 1953 . . . . £65/£35
Lucky Starr and the Pirates of the Asteroids, Doubleday (U.S.), 1954 . . . . £40/£15
Lucky Starr and the Oceans of Venus, Doubleday (U.S.), 1954 . . . . £25/£10
Lucky Starr and the Big Sun of Mercury, Doubleday (U.S.), 1956 . . . . £20/£10
Lucky Starr and the Moons of Jupiter, Doubleday (U.S.), 1957 . . . . £15/£5
Lucky Starr and the Rings of Saturn, Doubleday (U.S.), 1958 . . . . £15/£10

MABEL LUCIE ATTWELL
(b.1879 d.1964)

Attwell illustrated not only classic children's books such as *Alice in Wonderland*, but drew comic strips and produced her own books, postcards and annuals.

'Bunty and the Boo Boos' Titles
Bunty and the Boo Boos, Valentine, [1921] . £125
The Boo Boos and Bunty's Baby, Valentine, [1921] £125
The Boo Boos at School, Valentine, [1921]. . £125
The Boo Boos at the Seaside, Valentine, [1921] £125
The Boo Boos at Honeysweet Farm, Valentine, [1921] £125
The Boo Boos and Santa Claus, Valentine, [1921] £125

Annuals
The Lucie Attwell Annual No. 1, Partridge, 1922 £175
The Lucie Attwell Annual No. 2, Partridge, 1923 £150
The Lucie Attwell Annual No. 3, Partridge, 1924 £150
Lucie Attwell's Children's Book, Partridge, 1925-32 . . . . £150 each
Lucie Attwell's Annual, Dean, 1934-35, 1937-41 . . . . £100 each
Lucie Attwell's Annual, Dean, 1942 . . . . £75
Lucie Attwell's Annual, Dean, 1945-68 . . . £50
Lucie Attwell's Annual, Dean, 1969-74 . . . £40

Others written and illustrated by Attwell
Peggy: The Lucie Attwell Cut-Out Dressing Doll, Valentine, [1921]. £100
Stitch Stitch, Valentine, [1922] £100
Comforting Thoughts, Valentine, [1922] . . £45
Baby's Book, Raphael Tuck, [1922] £75
All About Bad Babies, John Swain, [c1925] . £50
All About the Seaside, John Swain, [c1925] . £45
All About Fairies, Swain, [c1925] £50
All About the Country, John Swain, [c1925] . £45
All About School, John Swain, [c1925] . . . £45
All About Fido, John Swain, [c1925] . . . £50
Lucie Attwell's Rainy-Day Tales, Partridge [1931] (with other authors) £100
Lucie Attwell's Rock-Away Tales, London, 1931 (with other authors) £80
Lucie Attwell's Fairy Book, Partridge, 1932 £150
Lucie Attwell's Happy-Day Tales, Partridge, [1932] £80
Lucie Attwell's Quiet Time Tales, Partridge, [1932] £80
Lucie Attwell's Painting Book, Dean, [1934] . £50
Lucie Attwell's Great Big Midget Book, Dean, [1934] £80
Lucie Attwell's Great Big Midget Book, Dean, [1935]

(different from above) £80
Lucie Attwell's Playtime Pictures, Carlton Publishing Co, 1935 . . . . £60
Lucie Attwell's Story Book, Dean, [1943] . . . £50
Lucie Attwell's Story Book, Dean, [1945] (different from above) £50
Lucie Attwell's Jolly Book, Dean, [1953] . . £40
Lucie Attwell's Nursery Rhymes Pop-Up Book, Dean, 1958 . . . . £35
Lucie Attwell's Storytime Tales, Dean, [1959] . £20
Lucie Attwell's Book of Verse, Dean, 1960 . . £20
Lucie Attwell's Book of Rhymes, Dean, 1962 . £20
Stories for Everyday, Dean, 1964 . . . . . £15
A Little Bird Told Me, Dean, 1964 . . . . . £15
A Little Bird Told Me Another Story, Dean, 1966 £15
Tinie's Book of Prayers, Dean, 1967 . . . . £15
Lucie Attwell's Tiny Rhymes Pop-Up Book, Dean, 1967 . . . . £25
Lucie Attwell's Tell Me A Story Pop-Up Book, Dean, 1968 . . . . £25
Lucie Attwell's Book of Rhymes, Dean, 1969 . £15

Books illustrated by Attwell

That Little Limb, by May Baldwin, Chambers, 1905 . . . . £50
The Amateur Cook, by K Burrill, Chambers, 1905 £40
Troublesome Ursula, by Mabel Quiller-Couch, Chambers, 1905. . . . . £50
Dora: A High School Girl, by May Baldwin, Chambers, 1906. . . . . £50
A Boy and a Secret, by Raymond Jacberns, Chambers, 1908 . . . . £30
The Little Tin Soldier, by Graham Mar, Chambers, 1909 . . . . £40
The February Boys, by Mrs Molesworth, Chambers, 1909 . . . . £50
Old Rhymes, Raphael Tuck, 1909 . . . . . £35
The Old Pincushion, by Mrs Molesworth, Chambers, 1910 . . . . £45
Mother Goose, Raphael Tuck, 1910 . . . . . £125
Alice in Wonderland, by Lewis Carroll, Raphael Tuck [1910] (twelve colour plates by Attwell) . . £150
My Dolly's House ABC, Raphael Tuck, [c.1910] £125
Grimm's Fairy Tales, Cassell [1910] (four full-page illustrations by Attwell) £100
Tabitha Smallways, by Raymond Jacberns, Chambers, 1911 . . . . £50
Grimm's Fairy Stories, Raphael Tuck, 1912 (twelve colour plates by Attwell) £125
Troublesome Topsy and Her Friends, by May Baldwin, Chambers, 1913 . . . . . . £40
Hans Andersen's Fairy Tales, Raphael Tuck [1914] (twelve colour plates by Attwell) £125
A Band of Mirth, by L.T. Meade, Chambers, 1914 £40
The Water Babies, by Charles Kingsley, Raphael Tuck [1915] (twelve colour plates by Attwell) . . . £150
Children's Stories from French Fairy Tales, by Doris Ashley, Raphael Tuck, 1917 . . . . . . £140
Peeping Pansy, by Marie, Queen of Roumania, Hodder & Stoughton [1919] (issued with d/w) . . . £300
Wooden, by Archibald Marshall, Collins, [1920] £60
Peter Pan and Wendy, by J.M. Barrie, Hodder & Stoughton [1921]. £200
The Lost Princess: A Fairy Tale, by Marie, Queen of Roumania, Partridge, 1924 . . . . . £95
Children's Stories, Whitman Publishing Co. [c.1930] £200

MARGARET ATWOOD

(b.1939)

Atwood is a Canadian writer, most popularly known for her prose following the success of *Cat's Eye*. A versatile writer, she works successfully in various genres.

Verse

Double Persephone, Hawkshead Press (Canada), 1961 (wraps) £1,000
The Circle Game, Cranbrook Academy, 1964 (15 copies) £2,500
ditto, Contact Press (Canada), 1966 (wraps). . £150
ditto, House of Anansi (Canada), 1967 (100 signed copies) £200
ditto, House of Anansi (Canada), 1967 (wraps) £25
Talismans for Children, Cranbrook Academy, 1965 . (10 copies). £250
Kaleidoscopes: Baroque, Cranbrook Academy, 1965 (20 copies) £350
Speeches for Doctor Frankenstein, Cranbrook Academy, 1966 (10 copies). £450
Expeditions, Cranbrook Academy, 1966 (15 handwritten copies) £1,000
The Animals in that Country, O.U.P. (Canada), 1968 . . . . £100/£25
ditto, O.U.P. (Canada), 1968 (wraps). . . . £25
ditto, Little, Brown (U.S.), [1969] . . . £35/£10
What Was in the Garden?, Unicorn (U.S.), 1969 £30
The Journals of Susanna Moodie, O.U.P. (Canada), 1970 . . . . £25
ditto, Manuel and Abel Bello-Sanchez (Canada), 1980 (20 deluxe signed copies, numbered I-XX) . £450
ditto, Manuel and Abel Bello-Sanchez (Canada), 1980 (100 signed copies) £45
Oratorio for Sasquatch, Man and Two Androids: Poems for Voices, C.B.C. (Canada), 1970 . £20
Procedures for Underground, O.U.P. (Canada), 1970. . . . . £15

ditto, Little, Brown (U.S.), 1970 . . . . . . £10
Power Politics, Anansi (Canada), 1971 . . £75/£20
ditto, Anansi (Canada), 1971 (wraps) . . £25
ditto, Harper (U.S.), 1973 . . . . £20/£5
You Are Happy, O.U.P. (Canada), 1974 . . £20
ditto, Harper (U.S.), 1974 . . . . . . £10/£5
Selected Poems, O.U.P. (Canada), 1976 . . . £20
ditto, Simon & Schuster (U.S.), 1978 . . . £10/£5
Marsh, Hawk, Dreadnought, 1977 . . . . £20
Two-headed Poems, O.U.P. (Canada), 1978 . £20
ditto, Simon & Schuster (U.S.), 1980 . . . £10/£5
A Poem for Grandmothers, Square Zero Editions (U.S.), 1978 . . . . £40
True Stories, O.U.P. (Canada), 1981 . . . £20
ditto, Simon & Schuster (U.S.), 1982 . . £20/£10
ditto, Cape, 1982 . . . . £20/£10
Notes Towards a Poem that can Never be Written, Salamander Press (Canada), 1981 (200 numbered, signed copies) £100
Snake Poems, Salamander Press (Canada), 1983 (100 numbered, signed copies) £175
Interlunar, O.U.P. (Canada), 1984 . . . . £15
ditto, Cape, 1988 . . . . £15/£5
Selected Poems 2, O.U.P. (Canada), 1986 . £15
ditto, Houghton Mifflin (U.S.), 1987 . . £10/£5
ditto, as ***Poems, 1976-1986***, Virago, 1992 . £10
Selected Poems, 1966-1984, O.U.P. (Canada), 1990 . . . . £15
Poems, 1965-1975, Virago, 1991 . . . £10
ditto, Houghton Mifflin (U.S.), 1987 . . . £10/£5
Good Bones, Harbour Front Reading Series (Canada), 1992 (150 signed copies) £15
Murder in the Dark, Virago, 1995 (wraps) . . £5
Morning in the Burned House, McClelland & Stewart (Canada), [1995] . . . . £10/£5
ditto, Virago, 1995 (wraps) £5
ditto, Houghton Mifflin (U.S.), 1995 . . . . £10/£5
Bones and Murder, Virago, 1995 (wraps) . . £5

Novels
The Edible Woman, McClelland & Stewart (Canada), 1969 . . . . £200/£35
ditto, Deutsch, 1969 . . . . £150/£30
ditto, Little, Brown (U.S.), 1970 . . . . £75/£15
Surfacing, McClelland & Stewart (Canada), 1972 . . . . £40/£15
ditto, Deutsch, 1973 . . . . £40/£15
ditto, Simon & Schuster (U.S.), 1973 . . . £15/£5
Lady Oracle, McClelland & Stewart (Canada), 1976 . . . . £20/£5
ditto, Simon & Schuster (U.S.), 1976 . . £15/£5
ditto, Deutsch, 1977 . . . . £15/£5
Life Before Man, McClelland & Stewart (Canada), 1979 . . . . £20/£5
ditto, Simon & Schuster (U.S.), 1979 . . . £15/£5
ditto, Cape, 1980 . . . . £15/£5
Bodily Harm, McClelland & Stewart (Canada), 1981 . . . . £20/£5
ditto, Simon & Schuster (U.S.), 1982 . . £10/£5
ditto, Cape, 1982 . . . . £10/£5
The Handmaid's Tale, McClelland & Stewart (Canada), 1985 . . . . £35/£10
ditto, Houghton Mifflin (U.S.), 1986 . . . £25/£5
ditto, Cape, 1986 . . . . £25/£5
Cat's Eye, McClelland & Stewart (Canada), 1988 . . . . £30/£10
ditto, Doubleday (U.S.), 1989 . . . . . £15/£5
ditto, Bloomsbury, 1989 . . . . £15/£5
Robber Bride, McClelland & Stewart (Canada), 1993 . . . . £30/£10
ditto, Doubleday (U.S.), 1993 . . . . . £15/£5
ditto, Bloomsbury, 1993 . . . . £10/£5
Alias Grace, McClelland & Stewart (Canada), 1996 . . . . £30/£10
ditto, Doubleday (U.S.), 1996 . . . . . £15/£5
ditto, Bloomsbury, 1996 . . . . £10/£5
The Margaret Atwood Omnibus, Deutsch, 1987 . . . . £10/£5

Short Stories
Dancing Girls and Other Stories, McClelland & Stewart (Canada), 1977 . . . . . . £35/£10
ditto, Simon & Schuster (U.S.), 1982 . . £25/£5
ditto, Cape, 1982 . . . . £25/£5
Encounters with the Element Man, Ewert (U.S.), 1982 . . . . £60
ditto, Ewert (U.S.), 1982 (100 copies, wraps) . £25
Murder in the Dark: Short Fictions and Prose Poems, Coach House Press (Canada), 1983 . . . . £20
ditto, Cape, 1984 . . . . £10/£5
Bluebeard's Egg and Other Stories, McClelland & Stewart (Canada), 1983 . . . . . . £25/£10
ditto, Houghton Mifflin (U.S.), 1986 . . . £10/£5
ditto, Cape, 1987 . . . . £10/£5
Unearthing Suite, Grand Union Press, 1983 (175 copies) £75
Hurricane Hazel and Other Stories, Eurographica, (Helsinki), 1987 (350 signed copies) . . £75/£50
Wilderness Tips, McClelland & Stewart (Canada), 1991 . . . . £15/£5
ditto, Doubleday (U.S.), 1991 . . . . . £10/£5
ditto, Bloomsbury, 1991 . . . . £10/£5
Good Bones, Coach House (Canada), 1992 . . £20/£5
ditto, Bloomsbury, 1992 . . . . £10/£5
Good Bones and Simple Murders, Doubleday (U.S.), 1994 . . . . £10/£5

Children's
Up in the Tree, McClelland & Stewart (Canada), 1978 . . . . £15/£5

Anna's Pet, Lorimer (Canada), 1980 (with Joyce Barkhouse) £20
For the Birds, Douglas & McIntyre (Canada), 1990 . . . . £10
Princess Prunella and the Purple Peanut, Key Porter Kids, 1995 . . . . £5

Criticism
Survival: A Thematic Guide to Canadian Literature, Anansi (Canada), 1972 . . . . £20/£10
Second Words: Selected Critical Prose, Anansi, (Canada), 1982 . . . . £20/£10
ditto, Beacon Press (U.S.), 1984 . . . . . £10
New Critical Essays, Macmillan, 1994 . . £10/£5
Strange Things: The Malevolent North in Canadian Literature, O.U.P., 1995 . . . . . . £10/£5

Other
Margaret Atwood: Conversations, Ontario Review Press (Canada), 1990 . . . . . . £15/£5
ditto, Virago, 1991 . . . . £10
Winner of the Welsh Arts Council International Writer's Prize, Welsh Arts Council, 1982 (wraps) £5

W.H. AUDEN
(b.1907 d.1973)

Auden's early poetry was markedly left-wing, but Christianity was the dominant influence in his later life and art. He is considered to be one of the most influential poets of the twentieth century.

Verse
Poems, privately printed by Stephen Spender, 1928 (30 copies, orange wraps) £10,000
Poems, Faber, 1930 (wraps) £300
The Orators: an English Study, Faber, [1932] . . . . £75/£25
ditto, Random House (U.S.), 1967 . . . £10/£5
The Dance of Death, Faber, 1933 . . . £100/£25
The Witnesses, privately printed, 1933 (broadside, 20 copies, illustrated by Gwen Raverat) . . . £3,000
Poem, privately printed, 1933 (22 copies, wraps) £5,000
Two Poems, privately printed, 1934 (22 copies, wraps) £5,000
Poems, Random House (U.S.), 1934. . . . £45/£20
Our Hunting Fathers, privately printed, 1935 (22 copies, wraps) £5,000
Sonnet, privately printed, 1935 (22 copies, wraps) £5,000
Look Stranger!, Faber, 1936 . . . . . £100/£35
ditto, as ***On This Island***, Random House (U.S.), [1937]. . . . . £35/£15
Spain, Faber, [1937] (wraps) £75
Deux Poemes, Hours Press (Paris), 1937 (100 copies). £275
Night Mail, G.P.O., 1938 (broadside). . . . £40
Selected Poems, Faber, 1938 . . . . . £75/£25
Journey to a War, Faber, 1939 (with Christopher Isherwood) . . . . £100/£35
ditto, Random House (U.S.), 1939 . . . £75/£25
Another Time, Faber, 1940 . . . . . £50/£25
ditto, Random House (U.S.), 1940 . . . £25/£10
Some Poems, Faber, 1940 . . . . . £25/£10
New Year Letter, Faber, 1941 . . . . £30/£15
ditto, as ***The Double Man***, Random House (U.S.), 1941 . . . . £75/£45
Three Songs for St Cecilia's Day, privately printed, 1941 (250 copies, wraps) £125
For the Time Being, Random House (U.S.), 1944 . . . . £75/£20
ditto, Faber, 1945 . . . . £25/£10
The Collected Poetry, Random House, 1945 £40/£15
Litany and Anthem for St Matthew's Day, privately printed, 1946 (single sheet) £50
The Age of Anxiety, Random House (U.S.), [1947] . . . . £30/£10
ditto, Faber, 1948 . . . . £15/£10
Collected Shorter Poems 1930-1944, Faber, 1950 . . . . £30/£10
Nones, Random House (U.S.), 1951 . . . £35/£10
ditto, Faber, 1952 . . . . £25/£5
Mountains, Faber Ariel Poem, 1954 (wraps) . £15
The Shield of Achilles, Faber, 1955 . . . £20/£10
ditto, Random House (U.S.), 1955 . . . £15/£5
The Old Man's Road, Voyages Press (U.S.), 1956 (50 signed copies, wraps) £300
ditto, Voyages Press (U.S.), 1956 (750 copies, wraps). £20
W.H. Auden: A Selection by the Author, Penguin, 1958 (wraps) £5
ditto, as ***Selected Poetry of W.H. Auden***, Modern Library (U.S.), 1959 . . . . £10/£5
Goodbye to the Mezzogiorno, All'Insegna del Pesce d'Oro (Spain), 1958 (1,000 numbered copies, wraps). £30
Homage to Clio, Random House (U.S.), 1960 £25/£10
ditto, Faber, 1960 . . . . £25/£10
About the House, Random House (U.S.), 1965 £20/£10
ditto, Faber, 1966 . . . . £20/£10
Collected Shorter Poems, 1927-1957, Faber, 1966 . . . . £25/£10
ditto, Random House (U.S.), 1967 . . . £20/£10
Marginalia, Ibex Press (U.S.), 1966 (150 signed copies, wraps) £150
Selected Poems, Faber, 1968 (wraps) . . . £5
Collected Longer Poems, Faber, 1968 . . £20/£5

ditto, Random House (U.S.), 1969 . . . £15/£5
City Without Walls, Faber, 1969 . . . . £10/£5
ditto, Random House (U.S.), 1970 . . . . £10/£5
Natural Linguistics, Poem-of-the-month-Club, 1970 (1,000 signed copies, broadsheet) £50
Academic Graffiti, Faber, 1971 . . . . . . £10/£5
ditto, Random House (U.S.), 1972 . . . . . £10/£5
Epistle to a Godson, Faber, 1972 . . . . £15/£5
ditto, Random House (U.S.), 1972 . . . . . £15/£5
The Ballad of Barnaby, no place, 1973 (broadside) £25
Thank You Fog: Last Poems, Faber, 1974 £15/£5
ditto, Random House (U.S.), 1974 . . . £15/£5
Collected Poems, Faber, 1976 . . . £15/£5
ditto, Random House (U.S.), 1976 . . . £15/£5
ditto, Franklin Centre (U.S.), 1976 (full leather edition) £40
The English Auden, Faber, 1977 . . . . £15/£5
ditto, Random House (U.S.), 1978 . . . £15/£5
Norse Poems, Athlone Press, 1981 . . . £15/£5

Plays
The Dog Beneath the Skin (with Christopher Isherwood), Faber, 1935. . . . . . . £100/£25
ditto, Random House (U.S.), 1935 . . . £35/£20
The Ascent of F6, Faber, 1936 (with Christopher Isherwood) . . . . £50/£10
ditto, Random House (U.S.), 1937 . . . £25/£10
On the Frontier, Faber, [1938] (with Christopher Isherwood) . . . . £75/£25
ditto, Random House (U.S.), 1939 . . . £50/£10

Prose
Letters from Iceland, Faber, 1937 (with Louis MacNeice) . . . . £75/£25
ditto, Harcourt Brace (U.S.), 1937 . . . . £50/£15
Education Today and Tomorrow, Hogarth Press, 1939 (with T. S. Worsley, wraps) £30
The Enchafèd Flood or The Romantic Iconography of the Sea, Random House (U.S.), 1950 . £25/£10
ditto, Faber, 1951 . . . . £15/£5
Making, Knowing and Judging, O.U.P., 1956 (wraps) £20
The Dyer's Hand, Random House (U.S.), 1962 . . . . £20/£10
ditto, Faber and Faber 1963 . . . . . . £10/£10
Louis MacNeice - A Memorial Address, privately printed Faber, 1963 (1,500 copies, wraps) . . £25
Selected Essays, Faber, 1964 (wraps) . . . £15
Secondary Worlds, Random House (U.S.), 1968 . . . . £15/£5
ditto, Faber, 1969 . . . . £15/£5
Forewords and Afterwords, Faber, 1973 . £15/£5
ditto, Viking (U.S.), 1973 . . . . £10/£5

Others
The Rake's Progress, Boosey and Hawkes Ltd, 1951 (libretto, with Chester Kallman, wraps) . . £50
The Magic Flute, Random House, 1956 (libretto, with Chester Kallman). . . . . £15/£5
ditto, Faber, 1957 . . . . £15/£5
Elegy for Young Lovers, Schott, 1961 (libretto, with Chester Kallman, wraps) £25
The Bassarids, Schott, 1966 (libretto with Chester Kallman, wraps) £25
A Certain World, Viking (U.S.), [1970] . . £25/£10
ditto, Faber, 1971 . . . . £15/£5

JANE AUSTEN
(b.1775 d.1817)

Generally regarded as the greatest of English women novelists, Austen's novels are particularly noted for their sparkling social comedy and accurate portrayal of human relationships.

Novels
Sense and Sensibility, T. Egerton, 1811, (3 vols in original boards) £8,000
ditto, T. Egerton, 1811, (other bindings). . £3,000
Pride and Prejudice, T. Egerton, 1813, (3 vols in original boards) £8,000
ditto, T. Egerton, 1813, (other bindings). . £3,000
Mansfield Park, T. Egerton, 1814, (3 vols in original boards) £6,500
ditto, T. Egerton, 1814, (other bindings). . £3,000
Emma, J. Murray, 1816, (3 vols in original boards) £9,000
ditto, J. Murray, 1816, (other bindings) . . £2,500
Northanger Abbey and Persuasion, J. Murray, 1818, (4 vols in original boards) £5,000
ditto J. Murray, 1818, (other bindings) . . . £2,000

Miscellaneous
The Watsons, Mathews and Marrot, 1871 . . £750
Letters, R. Bentley, 1884, (2 vols) £300
Charades, Spottiswoode & Co., 1895 . . . £200
Love and Freindship (sic) ***and Other Early Works*** *(Volume the second)*, Chatto and Windus, 1922 £50
ditto, Chatto and Windus, 1922 (260 copies, special edition) £100
ditto, Stokes (U.S.), 1922 . . . . £40
ditto, (*Volume the First)*, Clarendon Press, 1933 £40
ditto, (*Volume the Second)*, Clarendon Press, 1951 £40
Five Letters from Jane Austen to her Niece, Fanny Knight, Clarendon Press, 1924 (250 copies) . £75
Fragment of a Novel, O.U.P., 1925 ('Sanditon') £35
ditto, O.U.P., 1925 (250 copies on handmade paper) .

. . . . £100
Lady Susan, O.U.P., 1925 . . . . £35
ditto, O.U.P., 1925 (250 copies on handmade paper) £100
Two Chapters from Persuasion, O.U.P., 1926 . £25
Plan of a Novel, Clarendon Press, 1926 (350 copies) £75
Letters, O.U.P., 1932, (2 vols) £75
Three Evening Prayers, Colt Press (U.S.), 1940 £40
Sanditon: A Facsimile of the Manuscript, O.U.P., 1975 . . . . £25
ditto, Houghton Mifflin (U.S.), 1975. . . . £10/£5
Jane Austen's Sir Charles Grandison, O.U.P., 1980 . . . . £20

REV. W. AWDRY CHRISTOPHER AWDRY

(b. 1911 d.1998, b.1940)

Thomas the Tank Engine is the most famous of all of the Rev. Awdry's railway characters, in a series of books which have been continued by his son, Christopher.

"Railway Series" Titles by Rev. W. Awdry
The Three Railway Engines, Edmund Ward, 1945 (illustrated by Middleton) . . . . . £40/£10
Thomas the Tank Engine, Edmund Ward, 1946 (illustrated by Payne) . . . . . . £50/£15
James the Red Engine, Edmund Ward, 1948 (illustrated by Dalby) . . . . . . £30/£10
Tank Engine Thomas Again, Edmund Ward, 1949 (illustrated by Dalby) . . . . . . £30/£10
Troublesome Engines, Edmund Ward, 1950 (illustrated by Dalby) . . . . . . £25/£5
Henry the Green Engine, Edmund Ward, 1951 (illustrated by Dalby) . . . . . . £25/£5
Toby the Tram Engine, Edmund Ward, 1952 (illustrated by Dalby) . . . . . . £25/£5
Gordon the Big Engine, Edmund Ward, 1953 (illustrated by Dalby) . . . . . . £25/£5
Edward the Blue Engine, Edmund Ward, 1954 (illustrated by Dalby) . . . . . . £25/£5
Four Little Engines, Edmund Ward, 1955 (illustrated by Dalby) . . . . £25/£5
Percy the Small Engine, Edmund Ward, 1956 (illustrated by Dalby) . . . . . . £20/£5
The Eight Famous Engines, Edmund Ward, 1957 (illustrated by Kenney) . . . . . . £20/£5
Duck and the Diesel Engine, Edmund Ward, 1958 (illustrated by Kenney) . . . . . . £15/£5
The Little Old Engine, Edmund Ward, 1959 (illustrated by Kenney) . . . . . . £15/£5
The Twin Engines, Edmund Ward, 1960 (illustrated by Kenney) . . . . £15/£5
Branch Line Engines, Edmund Ward, 1961 (illustrated by Kenney) . . . . £15/£5
Gallant Old Engine, Edmund Ward, 1962 (illustrated by Kenney) . . . . £15/£5
Stepney the "Bluebell" Engine, Edmund Ward, 1963 (illustrated by G. & P. Edwards) . . . . £15/£5
Mountain Engines, Edmund Ward, 1964 (illustrated by G. & P. Edwards). . . . . £15/£5
Very Old Engines, Edmund Ward, 1965 (illustrated by G. & P. Edwards) . . . . £15/£5
Main Line Engines, Edmund Ward, 1966 (illustrated by G. & P. Edwards). . . . . £15/£5
Small Railway Engines, Kaye & Ward, 1967 (illustrated by G. & P. Edwards) . . . £15/£5
Enterprising Engines, Kaye & Ward, 1968 (illustrated by G. & P. Edwards). . . . . . . £15/£5
Oliver the Western Engine, Kaye & Ward, 1969 (illustrated by G. & P. Edwards) . . . . £15/£5
Duke the Lost Engine, Kaye & Ward, 1970 (illustrated by G. & P. Edwards). . . . . . . £15/£5
Tramway Engines, Kaye & Ward, 1972 (illustrated by G. & P. Edwards) . . . . £15/£5

"Railway Series" Titles by Christopher Awdry
Really Useful Engines, Kaye & Ward, 1983 (illustrated by Spong). . . . . £10/£5
James and the Diesel Engines, Kaye & Ward, 1984 (illustrated by Spong) . . . . . . £10/£5
Great Little Engines, Kaye & Ward, 1985 (illustrated by Spong). . . . . £10/£5
More about Thomas the Tank Engine, Kaye & Ward, 1986 (illustrated by Spong) . . . . . £10/£5
Gordon the High-Speed Engine, Kaye & Ward, 1987 (illustrated by Spong) . . . . . . £10/£5

ALAN AYCKBOURN

(b.1939)

A popular playwright, Ayckbourn excels at highlighting the neuroses and anxieties of the English middle-class.

Relatively Speaking, Evans, 1968 (wraps) . . £45
ditto, French (U.S.), 1968 (wraps) £15
Playbill One, edited by Alan Durband, Hutchinson Educational, 1969 (contains "Ernie's Incredible Illucinations" wraps). £10
We Who Are About To ..., Methuen, 1970 (contains "Countdown") (wraps) £10
How the Other Half Loves, French (U.S.), 1972

(wraps) £15
ditto, Evans, 1972 (wraps) £15
Time and Time Again, French, 1973 (wraps) . £15
ditto, French (U.S.), 1973 (wraps) £15
Absurd Person Singular, French, 1974 (wraps) £15
ditto, French (U.S.), 1974 (wraps) £15
The Norman Conquests, French, 1975 (wraps). £30
ditto, French (U.S.), 1975 (wraps) £25
ditto, Chatto & Windus, 1975 . . . . £25/£10
Absent Friends, French, 1975 (wraps) . . . £15
ditto, French (U.S.), 1975 (wraps) £15
Bedroom Farce, French, 1977 (wraps) . . . £15
ditto, French (U.S.), 1977 (wraps) £15
Three Plays, Chatto & Windus, 1977 . . £20/£10
ditto, Grove Press, 1979 . . . . £20/£10
Just Between Ourselves, French, 1978 (wraps). £10
ditto, French (U.S.), 1978 (wraps) £10
Ten Times Table, French, 1978 (wraps). . . £10
ditto, French (U.S.), 1978 (wraps) £10
Joking Apart, French, 1979 (wraps) . . . £15
ditto, French (U.S.), 1979 (wraps) £15
ditto, Chatto & Windus, 1979 . . . . £15/£5
Confusions, French, 1979 (wraps) £10
ditto, French (U.S.), 1979 (wraps) £10
Sisterly Feelings, French, 1981 (wraps) . . . £10
ditto, French (U.S.), 1981 (wraps) £10
Taking Steps, French, 1981 (wraps) £10
ditto, French (U.S.), 1981 (wraps) £10
Suburban Strains, French, 1982 (wraps) . . £5
ditto, French (U.S.), 1982 (wraps) £5
Season's Greetings, French, 1982 (wraps) . . £5
ditto, French (U.S.), 1982 (wraps) £5
Way Upstream, French, 1983 (wraps) . . . £5
ditto, French (U.S.), 1983 (wraps) £5
Intimate Exchanges, French, 1985 (2 vols, wraps) £15
ditto, French (U.S.), 1985 (2 vols, wraps) . . £15
Chorus of Disapproval, French, 1985 (wraps) . £5
ditto, French (U.S.), 1985 (wraps) £5
Woman in Mind, Faber, 1986 . . . . . £5
A Small Family Business, Faber, 1987 . . . £5
Henceforward, Faber, 1988 . . . . . . £5
Mr A's Amazing Maze Plays, Faber, 1989 . . £5
A Man of the Moment, Faber, 1990 . . . . £5
Invisible Friends, Faber, 1991 . . . . . £5
Callisto 5, Faber, 1992 . . . . £5
My Very Own Story, Faber, 1992 . . . . . £5

'BB'

(b.1905 d.1990)

'BB' was the pseudonym used by Denys James Watkins-Pitchford, an author and illustrator of countryside books for both adults and children.

Adult Books written and illustrated by 'BB'
The Sportsman's Bedside Book, Eyre & Spottiswoode, 1937 . . . . £50/£20
The Countryman's Bedside Book, Eyre & Spottiswoode, 1941 . . . . £50/£20
The Idle Countryman, Eyre & Spottiswoode, 1943 . . . . £50/£20
The Fisherman's Bedside Book, Eyre & Spottiswoode, 1945 . . . . £75/£25
The Wayfaring Tree, Hollis & Carter, 1945 £50/£15
The Shooting Man's Bedside Book, Eyre & Spottiswoode, 1948 . . . . £40/£15
A Stream in Your Garden, Eyre & Spottiswoode, 1948 . . . . £35/£15
Be Quiet and Go A-Angling, Lutterworth, 1949 (pseud. Michael Traherne) . . . . . £125/£75
Confessions of a Carp Fisher, Eyre & Spottiswoode, 1950 . . . . £100/£45
Letters from Compton Deverell, Eyre & Spottiswoode, 1950 . . . . £25/£10
Tides Ending, Hollis & Carter, 1950 . . £75/£35
Dark Estuary, Hollis & Carter, 1953 . . £75/£35
A Carp Water (Wood Pool), Putnam, 1958 . £125/£65
Autumn Road to the Isles, Kaye, 1959 . . £40/£15
The White Road Westward, Kaye, 1961 . £35/£15
The September Road to Caithness, Kaye, 1962 . . . . £35/£15
Pegasus Book of the Countryside, Hamish Hamilton, 1964 . . . . £35/£15
The Summer Road to Wales, Kaye, 1964 . £35/£15
A Summer of the Nene, Kaye, 1967 . . . . £60/£25
Recollections of a Longshore Gunner, Boydell, 1976. . . . . £30/£10
A Child Alone: The Memoirs of 'BB', Michael Joseph, 1978 . . . . £50/£25
Ramblings of a Sportsman-Naturalist, Michael Joseph, 1979 . . . . £35/£15
The Naturalist's Bedside Book, Michael Joseph, 1980 . . . . £25/£10
The Quiet Fields, Michael Joseph. 1981 . £30/£15
Indian Summer, Michael Joseph, 1984 . . £25/£10
The Best of 'BB', Michael Joseph, 1985. . £25/£10
Fisherman's Folly, Boydell, 1987 (wraps) . . £5

Children's Books written and illustrated by 'BB'
Wild Lone: The Story of a Pytchley Fox, Eyre & Spottiswoode, 1938 . . . . £100/£35
Manka, The Sky Gipsy, Eyre & Spottiswoode, 1939 . . . . £75/£30
The Little Grey Men: A Story for the Young in Heart, Eyre & Spottiswoode, 1942 . . . . . £50/£20
ditto, Eyre & Spottiswoode, 1946 (8 colour plates). . . . . £150/£75
Brendon Chase, Hollis & Carter, 1944 . . £50/£20
Down the Bright Stream, Eyre & Spottiswoode, [1948]

. . . . £50/£20
Meeting Hill: BB's Fairy Book, Hollis & Carter, 1948 . . . . £75/£30
The Wind in the Wood, Hollis & Carter, 1952 £40/£15
Fairy Tales of Long Ago, Dent, 1952 . . £25/£10
The Forest of Boland Light Railway, Eyre & Spottiswoode, 1955 . . . . £40/£15
Monty Woodpig's Caravan, Ward, 1957 . £75/£30
Ben the Bullfinch, Hamish Hamilton, 1957. £35/£15
Wandering Wind, Hamish Hamilton, 1957 . £35/£15
Bill Badger and the Wandering Wind, Methuen, 1981 . . . . £50/£20
Alexander, Blackwell, 1957 [1958] . . . £65/£25
Monty Woodpig and his Bubblebuzz Car, Ward, 1958 . . . . £100/£35
Mr Bumstead, Eyre & Spottiswoode, 1958 . £60/£25
The Wizard of Boland, Ward, 1959 . . . £35/£15
Bill Badger's Winter Cruise, Hamish Hamilton, 1959 . . . . £50/£20
Bill Badger and the Pirates, Hamish Hamilton, 1960 . . . . £50/£20
Bill Badger's Finest Hour, Hamish Hamilton, 1961 . . . . £50/£20
Bill Badger's Whispering Reeds Adventure, Hamish Hamilton, 1962 . . . . £50/£20
Lepus the Brown Hare, Benn, 1962 . . . . £40/£15
Bill Badger's Big Mistake, Hamish Hamilton, 1963 . . . . £45/£20
Granny's Wonderful Chair, by Frances Browne, Dent, 1963 . . . . £30/£10
Bill Badger and the Big Store Robbery, Hamish Hamilton, 1967 . . . . £40/£15
The Whopper, Benn, 1967 . . . . . £200/£75
At the Back O'Ben Dee, Benn, 1968 . . . £50/£20
Bill Badger's Voyage to the World's End, Kaye & Ward, 1969 . . . . £50/£20
The Tyger Tray, Methuen, 1971 . . . . £45/£20
The Pool of the Black Witch, Methuen, 1974 £30/£10
Lord of the Forest, Methuen, 1975 . . . £25/£10
Stories of the Wild, Benn, 1975 (with A.L.E. Fenton and A. Windsor Richards) . . . . . . £25/£10
More Stories of the Wild, Benn, 1977 (with A. Windsor Richards) . . . . £25/£10
A Child Alone, Joseph, 1978 . . . . . . £25/£10

Other Books illustrated by 'BB'

Sport in Wildest Britain, by H.V. Prichard, Philip Allan, 1936 . . . . £30/£10
Winged Company, by R.G. Walmsley, Eyre & Spottiswoode, 1940 . . . . £25/£10
England is a Village, by C.H. Warren, Eyre & Spottiswoode, 1940 . . . . £15/£5
Southern English, by E. Benfield, Eyre & Spottiswoode, 1942 . . . . £15/£5
Narrow Boat, by L.T.C. Rolt, Eyre & Spottiswoode, 1944 . . . . £25/£10
It's My Delight, by B. Vesey-Fitzgerald, Eyre & Spottiswoode, 1947 . . . . £15/£5
Philandering Angler, by A. Applin, Hurst & Blackett, [1948]. . . . . £25/£10
A Sportsman Looks at Eire, by J.B. Drought, Hutchinson, 1949 . . . . £30/£10
Landmarks, by A.G. Street, Eyre & Spottiswoode, 1949 . . . . £25/£10
Red Vagabond, by G.D. Adams, Batchworth Press, 1951 . . . . £10/£5
The White Foxes of Gorfenletch, by H. Tegner, Hollis & Carter, 1954 . . . . £25/£10
The Secret of Orra, by E. Vipont, Blackwell, 1957 . . . . £30/£10
The Long Night, by William Mayne, Blackwell, 1957 [1958]. . . . . £40/£15
The Long-Bow, by Ronald Welch, Blackwell, 1958 . . . . £20/£10
Sailors All by Peter Dawlish, Blackwell, 1958 £15/£5
A Snowdon Stream, by W.H. Canaway, Putnam: Fisherman's Choice Series, 1958 . . . £25/£10
Trout Fisherman's Saga, by I.D. Owen, Putnam: Fisherman's Choice Series, 1959 . . . £25/£10
Thirteen O'Clock by William Mayne, Blackwell, 1960. . . . . £25/£10
Vix: The Story of a Fox Cub, by A. Windsor-Richards, E. Benn, 1960 . . . . £25/£5
Beasts of the North Country, by H. Tegner, Galley Press, 1961 . . . . £10/£5
Birds of the Lonely Lake, by A. Windsor-Richards, Benn, 1961 . . . . £20/£5
Prince Prigio and Prince Ricardo, by Andrew Lang, Dent, 1961 . . . . £20/£5
The Rogue Elephant, by Arthur Catherall, Dobson, 1962 . . . . £40/£15
Guns This Way, by H.W. Pearson-Rogers, Witherby, 1962 . . . . £25/£10
King Todd, by N. Burke, Putnam, 1963 . . £20/£5
A Cabin in the Woods, by A. Windsor-Richards, Friday Press, 1963 . . . . £25/£10
Red Ivory, by A.R. Channel, Dobson, 1964 (pseud. Arthur Catherall) . . . . £20/£5
The Lost Princess, by George Macdonald, Dent, 1965. . . . . £25/£10
To Do With Birds, by H. Tegner, H. Jenkins, 1965 . . . . £15/£5
The Wild White Swan, by A. Windsor-Richards, Friday Press, 1965 . . . . £30/£10
Jungle Rescue, by A.R. Channel, Dobson, 1967 . . . . £25/£10
Great Nature Stories, by A. Windsor-Richards, E. Benn, 1967 . . . . £15/£5
The Shadow on the Moor, by I. Alan, 8th Duke of Northumberland, privately printed, 1967 (200 copies).

. . . . £450
Where Vultures Fly, by G. Summers, Collins, 1974 . . . . £15/£5
Stories of the Wild, by A.L.E. Fenton and A.W. Richards, Benn, 1975 . . . . £25/£10
More Stories of the Wild, by A. Windsor-Richards, Benn, 1977 . . . . £25/£10

BERYL BAINBRIDGE

(b.1934)

Bainbridge's books, usually controversial, often involve several deaths.

Novels

A Weekend with Claud, New Authors Limited, Hutchinson, 1967 . . . . £30/£10
ditto, as ***A Weekend with Claude***, Duckworth, 1981 . . . . £10/£5
ditto, Braziller (U.S.), 1981 . . . . . £15/£5
Another Part of the Wood, Hutchinson, 1968 £35/£15
ditto, Duckworth, 1979 . . . . . . £10/£5
ditto, Braziller (U.S.), 1980 . . . . . £10/£5
Harriet Said ..., Duckworth, 1972 . . . £20/£5
ditto, Braziller (U.S.), 1972 . . . . . £15/£5
The Dressmaker, Duckworth, 1973 . . £15/£5
ditto, as ***The Secret Glass***, Braziller (U.S.), 1973 . . . . £15/£5
The Bottle Factory Outing, Duckworth, 1974 £15/£5
ditto, Braziller (U.S.), 1974 . . . . . £10/£5
Sweet William, Duckworth, 1975 . . . £12/£5
ditto, Braziller (U.S.), 1975 . . . . . £10/£5
A Quiet Life, Duckworth, 1976 . . . . £12/£5
ditto, Braziller (U.S.), 1977 . . . . . £10/£5
Injury Time, Duckworth, 1977 . . . . £12/£5
ditto, Braziller (U.S.), 1977 . . . . . £10/£5
Young Adolf, Duckworth, 1978 . . . . £12/£5
ditto, Braziller (U.S.), 1979 . . . . . £10/£5
Winter Garden, Duckworth, 1980 . . . £10/£5
ditto, Braziller (U.S.), 1981 . . . . . £10/£5
Watson's Apology, Duckworth, 1984 . . £10/£5
ditto, McGraw Hill (U.S.), 1985 . . . . £10/£5
Filthy Lucre, Duckworth, 1986 . . . . £10/£5
An Awfully Big Adventure, Duckworth, 1989 £10/£5
ditto, HarperCollins (U.S.), 1991. . . . £10/£5
The Birthday Boys, Duckworth, 1991 . . £10/£5
ditto, Carroll & Graf, 1991 . . . . . £10/£5
Every Man for Himself, Duckworth, 1996 . £10/£5
ditto, Carroll & Graf, 1996 . . . . . £10/£5
Master Georgie, Duckworth, 1998 . . . £10/£5

Omnibus Editions

A Bainbridge Omnibus, Duckworth, 1989 . £10/£5

Short Stories

Mum and Mr Armitage: Selected Stories, Duckworth, 1985 . . . . £10/£5
ditto, McGraw Hill (U.S.), 1987 . . . . £10/£5
Collected Stories, Penguin, 1994 (wraps) . . £5

Travel

English Journey: or, The Road to Milton Keynes, Duckworth, 1984 . . . . £10/£5
ditto, Braziller (U.S.), 1984 . . . . . . £10/£5
Forever England: North and South, Duckworth, 1987 . . . . £10/£5

Essays

Something Happened Yesterday, Duckworth, 1993 (wraps) £5

R.M. BALLANTYNE

(b.1825 d.1894)

A Scottish author, Ballantyne's first published work was an account of his time as a fur trader in Canada, followed by a series of popular adventure stories. By the time of his death he had written over 80 books in 40 years.

Snowflakes and Sunbeams, or The Young Fur-Traders, Nelson, 1856 . . . . £100
Three Little Kittens, Nelson, [1856] (pseud. 'Comus') £50
My Mother, Nelson, 1857 (pseud. 'Comus'). . £50
The Butterfly's Ball, Nelson, 1857 (pseud. 'Comus') £75
Mister Fox, Nelson, 1857 (pseud. 'Comus') . . £50
Ungava, A Tale of Esquimaux Land, Nelson, 1858 [1857]. £50
The Coral Island, A Tale of the Pacific Ocean, Nelson, 1858 [1857] £300
The Robber Kitten, Nelson, 1858 (pseud. 'Comus') £75
Martin Rattler, or A Boy's Adventures in the Forests of Brazil, Nelson, 1858 . . . . £75
Mee-a-ow! or Good Advice to Cats and Kittens, Nelson, 1859 . . . . £75
The World of Ice, or Adventures in the Polar Regions, Nelson, 1860 [1859] £75
The Dog Crusoe, A Tale of the Western Prairies, Nelson, 1861 [1860] £100
The Golden Dream, or Adventures in the Far West, Shaw, 1861 [1860] £100
The Gorilla Hunters, A Tale of the Wilds Of Africa, Nelson, 1861 . . . . £100
The Red Eric, or The Whaler's Last Cruise: A Tale, Routledge, 1861 . . . . £75

Man on the Ocean, A Book for Boys, Nelson, 1863 [1862]. £75
The Wild Man of the West, A Tale of the Rocky Mountains, Routledge, 1863 [1862] £100
Ballantyne's Miscellany, Nisbet, 1863-1886 (15 vols). £500
Gascoyne, The Sandal-Wood Trader, A Tale of the Pacific, Nisbet. 1864 [1863] £75
The Lifeboat, A Tale of Our Coast Heroes, Nisbet, 1864 . . . . £50
Freaks on the Fells, or Three Months' Rustication: And Why I did not Become a Sailor, Routledge, 1865 [1864]. £75
The Lighthouse, Being the Story of a Great Fight Between Man and the Sea, Nisbet, 1865 . . £50
Shifting Winds, A Tough Yarn, Nisbet, 1866 . £50
Silver Lake, or Lost in the Snow, Jackson, 1867 £50
Fighting the Flames, A Tale of the London Fire Brigade, Nisbet, 1868 . . . . £75
Away in the Wilderness, or Life Among the Red-Indians and Fur-Traders of North America, Porter S. Coates (U.S.), 1869 . . . . £100
Deep Down, A Tale of the Cornish Mines, Nisbet, 1869 . . . . £50
Erling the Bold, A Tale of the Norse Sea-Kings, Nisbet, 1869 . . . . £50
The Floating Lights of the Godwin Sands, A Tale, Nisbet, 1870 . . . . £50
The Iron Horse, or Life on the Line: A Tale of the Grand National Trunk Railway, Nisbet, 1871 £100
The Norsemen in the West, or America Before Columbus, Nisbet, 1872. . . . . £75
The Pioneers, A Tale of the Western Wilderness, Nisbet, 1872 . . . . £75
Black Ivory, A Tale of Adventure among the Slavers of East Africa, Nisbet, 1873 . . . . . £75
Life in the Red Brigade, A Story for Boys, Routledge [1873]. £50
The Ocean and Its Wonders, Nelson, 1874 . . £25
The Pirate City, An Algerine Tale, Nisbet, 1875 £75
Rivers of Ice, A Tale Illustrative of Alpine Adventure and Glacier Action, Nisbet, 1875 . . . . £50
Under the Waves, or Diving In Deep Waters, A Tale, Nisbet, 1876 . . . . £50
The Settler and the Savage, A Tale of Peace and War in South Africa, Nisbet, 1877 . . . . . £75
In the Track of the Troops, A Tale of Modern War, Nisbet, 1878 . . . . £50
Jarwin and Cuffy, A Tale, Warne, [1878] . . £50
Six Months at the Cape, or Letters to Periwinkle from South Africa, Nisbet, 1879 [1878] £75
Post Haste, A Tale of Her Majesty's Mails, Nisbet, 1880 [1879] £75
Philosopher Jack, A Tale of the Southern Seas, Nisbet, 1880 . . . . £50
The Lonely Island, or the refuge of the Mutineers, Nisbet, 1880 . . . . £50
The Redman's Revenge, A Tale of the Red River Flood, Nisbet, 1880 . . . . £75
The Collected Works of Ensign Sopht, Late of the Volunteers, Nisbet, 1881 . . . . . . £150
My Doggy and I, Nisbet, [1881] £50
The Giant of the North, or Pokings Round the Pole, Nisbet, 1882 [1881] £75
The Kitten Pilgrims, or Great Battles and Grand Victories, Nisbet, [1882] £75
The Battery and the Boiler, or Adventures in the Laying of Submarine Cable, Nisbet, 1883 [1882] £75
The Madman and the Pirate, Nisbet, 1883 . . £50
Battles with the Sea, or Heroes of the Lifeboat and Rocket, Nisbet, 1883. . . . . £50
The Young Trawlers, A Story of Life and ***Death and Rescue on the North Sea***, Nisbet, 1884 . . . £50
Dusty Diamonds Cut and Polished, A Tale of City-Arab Life and Adventure, Nisbet, 1884 [1883] £50
Twice Bought, A Tale of the Oregon Gold Fields, Nisbet, 1885 [1884] £50
The Rover of the Andes, A Tale of Adventure in South America, Nisbet, 1885 . . . . £50
The Island Queen, A Tale of the Southern Hemisphere, Nisbet, 1885 . . . . £50
Red Rooney, or Last of the Crew, Nisbet, 1886 £50
The Big Otter, A Tale of the Great Nor'West, Routledge, 1887 [1886] £50
Blue Lights, or Hot Work in the Soudan: A Tale of Soldier Life, Nisbet, 1888 . . . . £50
The Middy and the Moors, An Algerine Story, Nisbet, 1888 . . . . £50
The Crew of the Water Wagtail, A Story of Newfoundland, Nisbet, [1889] £50
The Garrett and the Garden, or Low Life High Up, and ***Jeff Benson, or The Young Coastguardsman***, Nisbet, [1890] £50
Charlie to the Rescue, A Tale of the Sea and the Rockies, Nisbet, 1890 . . . . £50
The Coxswain's Bride, or The Rising Tide and Other Tales, Nisbet, 1891 . . . . £50
The Hot Swamp, A Romance of Old Albion, Nisbet, 1892 . . . . £50
Hunted and Harried, A Tale of the Scottish Covenanters, Nisbet, [1892] £50
The Walrus Hunters, A Romance of the Realms of Ice, Nisbet, 1893 . . . . £50
Fighting the Whales, Blackie, [1915] . . . £20
The Jolly Kitten Book, Blackie, [1925] . . £20/£10
Ballantyne Omnibus for Boys, Collins, [1932] £10/£5

J. G. BALLARD
(b.1930)

Despite shifting from avant-garde science fiction to surreal contemporary writing, Ballard is best known as the author of the *Empire of the Sun*, based on his own experiences of internment by the Japanese in World War two.

Novels

The Wind from Nowhere, Berkley (U.S.), 1962 (wraps) £10
ditto, Penguin, 1967 (wraps) £5
The Drowned World, Berkley (U.S.), 1962 (wraps) £10
ditto, Gollancz, 1963 . . . . £250/£75
The Drought, Cape, 1965. . . . . . . £125/£45
The Crystal World, Cape, 1966 . . . . . £100/£45
ditto, Farrar Straus (U.S.), 1966 . . . . . £45/£10
Crash!, Cape, 1973 . . . . £100/£45
ditto, Farrar Straus (U.S.), 1973 . . . . £40/£15
Concrete Island, Cape, 1974 . . . . . £65/£25
ditto, Farrar Straus (U.S.), 1974 . . . . £25/£10
High Rise, Cape, 1975 . . . . £55/£15
ditto, Holt Rinehart (U.S.), 1977 . . . . £15/£5
The Unlimited Dream Company, Cape, 1979 £20/£5
ditto, Holt Rinehart (U.S.), 1979 . . . . £15/£5
Hello America, Cape, 1981 . . . . . £20/£5
ditto, Carroll & Graf (U.S.), 1988 . . . . £15/£5
Empire of the Sun, Gollancz, 1984 . . . £20/£5
ditto, Gollancz, 1984 (100 signed copies, slipcase) . . . . £200/£150
ditto, Simon & Schuster (U.S.), 1985 . . £10/£5
The Day of Creation, Gollancz, 1987 . . £15/£5
ditto, Gollancz, 1987 (100 signed copies in slipcase) . . . . £75/£65
ditto, Farrar Straus (U.S.), 1988 . . . . . £10/£5
Running Wild, Hutchinson, 1988 (novella) . £10/£5
ditto, Farrar Straus (U.S.), 1989 . . . . £10/£5
The Kindness of Women, Harper Collins, 1991 £10/£5
ditto, Farrar Straus (U.S.), 1991 . . . . . £10/£5
Rushing to Paradise, Harper Collins, 1994 . £10/£5
ditto, Picador (U.S.), 1995 . . . . . £10/£5
Cocaine Nights, Harper Collins, 1996 . . £10/£5

Short Stories

The Voices of Time and Other Stories, Berkley (U.S.), 1962 (wraps) £15
ditto, Gollancz, 1985 . . . . £20/£10
Billenium and Other Stories, Berkley (U.S.), 1962 (wraps). £15
The Four-Dimensional Nightmare, Gollancz, 1963 . . . . £300/£125
Passport to Eternity and Other Stories, Berkley (U.S.), 1963 (wraps) £15
The Terminal Beach, Berkley (U.S.), 1964 (wraps) £10
ditto, Gollancz, 1964 . . . . £125/£45
The Impossible Man and Other Stories, Berkley (U.S.), 1966 (wraps) £20
The Day of Forever, Panther, 1967 (wraps). . £10
ditto, Gollancz, 1986 (hardback) . . . . . £15/£5
The Disaster Area, Cape, 1967 . . . . £100/£45
The Overloaded Man, Panther, 1967 (wraps) . £10
The Atrocity Exhibition, Cape, 1970 . . £150/£45
Vermilion Sands, Berkley (U.S.), 1971 (wraps) £15
ditto, Cape, 1973 . . . . £100/£35
Chronopolis 1972, Putnam (U.S.), 1971. . £20/£10
Low Flying Aircraft, Cape, 1976 . . . . £20/£10
The Best of J.G. Ballard, Sidgwick & Jackson, 1977 . . . . £25/£10
The Best Sort Stories of J.G. Ballard, Holt, Rinehart and Winston, 1978 . . . . £25/£10
The Venus Hunters, Granada, 1980 (wraps) . £10
ditto, Gollancz, 1986 . . . . £20/£10
Myths of the Near Future, Cape, 1982 . . £20/£10
Memories of the Space Age, Arkham House (Sauk City, U.S.), 1988 . . . . £25/£10
War Fever, Collins, 1990 . . . . . . £10/£5
ditto, Farrar Straus (U.S.), 1991 . . . . £10/£5

Others

Why I Want to Fuck Ronald Reagan, Unicorn Bookshop, 1968 (50 signed copies of 250) . £200
ditto, Unicorn Bookshop, 1968 (200 unsigned copies of 250) £100
Users Guide to the Millennium, HarperCollins, 1996 . . . . £10/£5
ditto, Picador (U.S.), 1996 . . . . . . £10/£5

IAIN BANKS
(b.1954)

The Wasp Factory was a controversial success, and Banks has become more than a cult writer. His subsequent works of fiction and science fiction often stray into the realm of the bizarre and the sinister.

Novels

The Wasp Factory, Macmillan, 1984 . . £100/£35
ditto, Houghton Mifflin (U.S.), 1984. . . £20/£5
Walking on Glass, Macmillan, 1985. . . £25/£10
ditto, Houghton Mifflin (U.S.), 1986. . . £10/£5
The Bridge, Macmillan, 1986 . . . . £20/£10
ditto, St Martin's (U.S.), 1989 . . . . £10/£5
Consider Phlebas, Macmillan, 1987. . . £35/£10
ditto, Macmillan, 1987 (176 signed copies, slipcase) . . . . £75/£60

ditto, St Martin's (U.S.), 1988 . . . . £10/£5
Espedair Street, Macmillan, 1987 . . . £20/£10
The Player of Games, Macmillan, 1988. . £35/£10
ditto, Macmillan, 1988 (201 signed copies, slipcase) . . . . £75/£60
ditto, St Martin's (U.S.), 1989 . . . . £10/£5
Canal Dreams, Macmillan, 1989 . . . £15/£5
ditto, Doubleday (U.S.), 1991 . . . . £10/£5
Use of Weapons, Orbit, 1990. . . . . £20/£5
ditto, Bantam (U.S.), 1992 . . . . . . £10/£5
The Crow Road, Scribners, 1992. . . . £10/£5
Complicity, Little, Brown, 1993 . . . . £10/£5
ditto, Doubleday (U.S.), 1992 . . . . £10/£5
Against a Dark Background, Orbit, 1993 . £20/£5
Feersum Endjinn, Orbit, 1994 . . . . £20/£5
ditto, Bantam (U.S.), 1995 (wraps) £5
Whit, Little, Brown, 1995. . . . . . . £10/£5
Excession, Orbit, 1996 . . . . . . £10/£5
ditto, Bantam (U.S.), 1997 (wraps) £5
A Song of Stone, Abacus, 1997 . . . . £10/£5
ditto, Simon & Schuster (U.S.), 1998 . . £10/£5
Inversions, Orbit, 1998 . . . . £10/£5

Others

Cleaning Up, Birmingham Science Fiction Group, 1987 (500 signed copies, wraps) £35
The State of the Art, Ziesing (U.S.), 1989 . . £10/£5
ditto, Ziesing (U.S.), 1989 (400 signed copies) £35/£20
ditto, Orbit, 1991 (contains further uncollected stories) . . . . £10/£5

HELEN BANNERMAN

(b.1863 d.1946)

Born in Scotland, Helen Bannerman married an army doctor and settled in India where she wrote *Little Black Sambo* for her own children. She returned in later life to her native land.

The Story of Little Black Sambo, Grant Richards' 'Dumpy Books for Children', No. 4, 1899 (anonymous) £6,000
The Story of Little Black Mingo, Nisbet, 1901 (anonymous) £250
The Story of Little Black Quibba, Nisbet, 1902 (anonymous) £250
Little Degchie-Head: An Awful Warning to Bad Babas, Nisbet, 1903 (anonymous) £200
Pat and the Spider: The Biter Bit, Nisbet, 1904 (anonymous) £150
The Story of the Teasing Monkey, Nisbet, 1906 (anonymous) £150
The Story of Little Black Quasha, Stokes, 1908 (anonymous) £100
The Story of Little Black Bobtail, Nisbet, 1909 (anonymous) £75
The Story of Sambo and the Twins, Nisbet [1937]. . . . . £150/£50
The Story of Little White Squibba, Chatto & Windus, 1966 . . . . £25/£10

JOHN BANVILLE

(b.1945)

Banville is a well respected Irish author, whose novel *The Book of Evidence* was shortlisted for the Booker prize.

Novels

Nightspawn, Secker & Warburg, 1970 . . £250/£50
ditto, Norton (U.S.), 1971. . . . . . £50/£35
Birchwood, Secker & Warburg, 1971 . . £50/£20
ditto, Norton (U.S.), 1973. . . . . . £25/£10
Doctor Copernicus, Secker & Warburg, 1976 £45/£15
ditto, Norton (U.S.), 1976. . . . . . £25/£10
Kepler, Secker & Warburg, 1981 . . . £35/£10
ditto, Godline (U.S.), 1983 . . . . . . £10/£5
The Newton Letter: an Interlude, Secker & Warburg, 1982 . . . . £20/£5
ditto, Godline (U.S.), 1987 . . . . . £10/£5
Mefisto, Secker & Warburg, 1986 . . . £20/£5
ditto, Godline (U.S.), 1989 . . . . . £10/£5
The Book of Evidence, Secker & Warburg, 1989 . . . . £25/£10
ditto, Scribner (U.S.), 1990 . . . . . £10/£5
Ghosts, Secker & Warburg, 1993 . . . £15/£5
ditto, Knopf (U.S.), 1993 . . . . . . £10/£5
Athena, Secker & Warburg, 1995 . . . £10/£5
ditto, Knopf (U.S.), 1995 . . . . . . £10/£5
The Untouchable, Picador, 1997. . . . £10/£5
ditto, Knopf (U.S.), 1997 . . . . . . £10/£5

Short Stories

Long Lankin, Secker & Warburg, 1970 . . £150/£75
ditto, Galley Press (Dublin), 1984 (revised edition) . . . . £20/£5

CLIVE BARKER

(b.1952)

A novelist and short story writer in the horror genre, Barker was born in Liverpool but now lives in Los Angeles. He also illustrates his own work, and writes, directs and produces for the stage and screen.

'Books of Blood' Titles

Books of Blood, Vols. 1-6, Sphere, 1984-85 (first issue with original covers, wraps) £45
Books of Blood, Vols. 1-6, Sphere, 1984-85 (second issue with Barker designed covers, wraps) . . £20
ditto, Vols. 1 and 2, Sphere, 1984 (hardback) . £40
ditto, Vol. 1, Weidenfeld & Nicolson, 1985 . . £15
ditto, Vol. 2, Weidenfeld & Nicolson, 1985 . . £15
ditto, Vol. 3, Weidenfeld & Nicolson, 1985 . . £15
ditto, Vols. 1-3, Weidenfeld & Nicholson, 1985 (200 signed, numbered sets, slipcase) £100
ditto, Vols. 4 & 5, Leisure circle, 1985 . . . £20
ditto, Vol. 4, Weidenfeld and Nicholson, 1986 . £15
ditto, Vol. 5, Weidenfeld and Nicholson, 1986 . £15
ditto, Vol. 6, Weidenfeld and Nicholson, 1986 . £15
ditto, Vols. 4-6, Weidenfeld and Nicholson, 1986 (200 signed, numbered sets, slipcase) £100

Other Titles

The Damnation Game, Weidenfeld & Nicolson, 1985 . . . . £30
ditto, Weidenfeld & Nicolson, 1985 (250 signed, numbered copies, slipcase) £100
ditto, Putnam (U.S.), 1987 . . . . £20
The Inhuman Condition, Poseidon Press (U.S.), 1986 . . . . £10
The Hellbound Heart, Dark Harvest (U.S.), 1986 £15
Weaveworld, Poseidon (U.S.), 1987 . . . . . £15
ditto, Poseidon (U.S.), 1987 (500 signed, numbered copies) £75
ditto, Collins, 1987 . . . . £10
ditto, Collins, 1987 (500 signed, numbered copies, slipcase) £75
Cabal, Poseidon (U.S.), 1988. . . . . . . £10
ditto, Poseidon (U.S.), 1988 (750 signed, numbered copies) £50
ditto, Fontana, 1988 (wraps) £5
The Great and Secret Show, Collins, 1989 . . £10
ditto, Collins, 1989 (500 signed copies, slipcase) £45
ditto, Harper & Row (U.S.), 1990 . . . . £10
Imajica, HarperCollins (U.S.), 1991 . . . . £10
ditto, HarperCollins (U.S.), 1991 (500 signed copies, slipcase) £50
ditto, HarperCollins, 1991 . . . . . . £10
Pandemonium, Eclipse (U.S.), 1991 (wraps) . £10
The Thief of Always, HarperCollins (U.S.), 1992 £10
ditto, HarperCollins, 1992 . . . . . . £10
The Yattering and Jack, Eclipse (U.S.), 1992 (with Steve Niles, wraps) £10
Clive Barker's Revelations, Eclipse (U.S.), 1992 (with Steve Niles, wraps) £10
The Age of Desire, Eclipse (U.S.), 1992 (wraps) £10
ditto, Eclipse, 1993 (wraps) £10
The Life of Death, Eclipse (U.S.), 1993 (wraps) £10
Everville, HarperCollins, 1994 . . . . . £10
ditto, HarperCollins (U.S.), 1994. . . . . . £10
Sacrament, HarperCollins, 1996 . . . . . . £10
Imajica, Volume 2, Reconciliations, HarperCollins, 1996 . . . . £10

PAT BARKER

(b.1943)

Pat Barker is a novelist and short story writer whose *The Ghost Road*, the last of her "Regeneration trilogy", won the Booker Prize in 1995.

Union Street, Virago, 1982 . . . . . . £150/£35
ditto, Virago, 1982 (wraps) £10
ditto, Putnam (U.S.), 1983 . . . . . . £50/£15
Blow Your House Down, Virago, 1984 . . £100/£25
ditto, Virago, 1984 (wraps) £10
ditto, Putnam (U.S.), 1984 . . . . . . £20/£5
The Century's Daughter, Virago, 1986 . . £25/£10
ditto, Virago, 1986 (wraps) £5
ditto, Putnam (U.S.), 1986 . . . . . £15/£5
The Man Who Wasn't There, Virago, 1989 £25/£5
ditto, Ballantine (U.S.), 1988 (wraps) . . . £5
Regeneration, Viking, 1991. . . . . . £75/£25
ditto, Dutton (U.S.), 1992 . . . . . . £35/£15
The Eye in the Door, Viking, 1993 . . . £50/£15
ditto, Dutton (U.S.), 1994 . . . . . . £20/£5
The Ghost Road, Viking, 1995 . . . . . £50/£15
ditto, Dutton (U.S.), 1995 . . . . . . £10/£5
The Regeneration Trilogy, Viking, 1996 . £10/£5
Another World, Viking, 1998 . . . . . £10/£5
ditto, Farrar, Straus & Giroux(U.S.), 1999 . £10/£5

JULIAN BARNES

(b.1946)

A clever and inventive post-modernist writer, Barnes moves between genres, probing the boundaries of convention.

Novels

Metroland, Cape, 1980 . . . . £150/£40
ditto, St Martin's Press (U.S.), 1980 . . . £75/£25

Before She Met Me, Cape, 1982 . . . . £40/£10
ditto, McGraw-Hill (U.S.), 1986 (wraps) . . £5
Flaubert's Parrot, Cape, 1984 . . . . £100/£20
ditto, Knopf (U.S.), 1985 . . . . . . £20/£5
Staring at the Sun, Cape, 1986 . . . . £20/£5
ditto, London Limited Editions, 1986 (150 signed copies, glassine dustjacket) . . . . . £50/£40
ditto, Knopf (U.S.), 1987 . . . . £10/£5
A History of the World in 10½ Chapters, Cape, 1989 . . . . £25/£10
ditto, Knopf (U.S.), 1989 . . . . . . £15/£5
Talking it Over, Cape, 1991 . . . . . £15/£5
ditto, London Limited Editions, 1991 (200 signed copies, glassine dustjacket) . . . . . £50/£40
ditto, Knopf (U.S.), 1991 . . . . . . £10/£5
Bodlivo Svinche, Obsidian (Bulgaria), 1992 (wraps) £10
ditto, as ***The Porcupine***, Cape, 1992 (novella) £10/£5
ditto, Knopf (U.S.), 1992 . . . . . . £10/£5
England, England, Cape, 1998 . . . . . £10/£5

Novels as 'Dan Kavanagh'
Duffy, Cape, 1980 . . . . £40/£10
ditto, Pantheon (U.S.), 1986 (wraps) . . . £5
Fiddle City, Cape, 1981 . . . . £45/£10
ditto, Pantheon (U.S.), 1986 (wraps) £5
Putting the Boot In, Cape, 1985 . . . . . £25/£10
Going to the Dogs, Viking UK, 1987 . . £25/£10
ditto, Viking (U.S.), 1987 . . . . . . £10/£5
The Duffy Omnibus, Penguin, 1991 . . . . £5

Short Stories
Cross Channel, Cape, 1996 . . . . . . £10/£5
ditto, Cape, 1996 (50 special copies, signed and numbered) £225
ditto, Knopf (U.S.), 1996 . . . . . . £10/£5

Other
Letters from London, 1990-1995, Picador, 1995 . . . . £10/£5
ditto, Vintage (U.S.) 1995. . . . . . . £10/£5

H.E. BATES
(b.1906 d.1974)

A British author of popular novels, novellas and short stories, many of which have been adapted for television. He is perhaps best known for the Larkin family novels, including *The Darling Buds of May*.

Novels
The Two Sisters, Cape, 1926 . . . . . £175/£45
Catherine Foster, Cape, 1929 . . . . £95/£35
Charlotte's Row, Cape, 1931 . . . . £75/£25
The Fallow Land, Cape, 1932 . . . . £75/£25
The Poacher, Cape, 1935 . . . . . . £65/£25
ditto, Macmillan (U.S.), 1935. . . . . £25/£10
A House of Women, Cape, 1936 . . . . £65/£25
"Spella Ho", Cape, 1938 . . . . . . £35/£10
Fair Stood the Wind for France, Joseph, 1944 . . . . £20/£10
ditto, Little, Brown (U.S.), 1944 . . . . £10/£5
The Cruise of the 'Breadwinner', Joseph, 1946 £15/£5
The Purple Plain, Joseph, 1947 . . . . £15/£5
ditto, Little, Brown (U.S.), 1947 . . . . £10/£5
The Jacaranda Tree, Joseph [1949] . . . £15/£5
ditto, Little, Brown (U.S.), 1949 . . . . £10/£5
Dear Life, Joseph, 1949 . . . . . . £10/£5
The Scarlet Sword, Joseph, 1950 . . . £10/£5
ditto, Little, Brown (U.S.), 1951 . . . . £10/£5
Love for Lydia, Joseph, 1952. . . . . £10/£5
ditto, Little, Brown (U.S.), 1952 . . . . £10/£5
The Feast of July, Joseph, 1954 . . . . £10/£5
ditto, Little, Brown (U.S.), 1954 . . . . £10/£5
The Sleepless Moon, Joseph, 1956 . . . £10/£5
ditto, Little, Brown (U.S.), 1956 . . . . £10/£5
Death of a Huntsman, Joseph, 1957 . . £10/£5
ditto, as ***Summer in Salandar***, Little, Brown and Co. (U.S.), 1957 . . . . £10/£5
The Darling Buds of May, Joseph, 1958 . £20/£10
ditto, Little, Brown (U.S.), 1958 . . . . £10/£5
A Breath of French Air, Joseph, 1959 . . £10/£5
ditto, Little, Brown (U.S.), 1959 . . . . £10/£5
When the Green Woods Laugh, Joseph, 1960 £10/£5
The Day of the Tortoise, Joseph, 1961 . . £10/£5
The Crown of Wild Myrtle, Joseph, 1962 . £10/£5
ditto, Farrar, Straus (U.S.), 1963 . . . . £10/£5
Oh! to be in England, Joseph, 1963 . . . £10/£5
ditto, Farrar, Straus (U.S.), 1964 . . . . £10/£5
A Moment in Time, Joseph, 1964 . . . £10/£5
ditto, Farrar, Straus (U.S.), 1964 . . . . £10/£5
The Distant Horns of Summer, Joseph, 1967 £10/£5
A Little of What You Fancy, Joseph, 1970 . £10/£5
The Triple Echo, Joseph, 1970 . . . . £10/£5

Short Stories
The Spring Song, and In View of the Fact That ... Two Stories, Archer, 1927 (100 numbered, signed copies, wraps) £175
ditto, Lantern Press (U.S.), 1927 (50 signed copies) £175
Day's End, Cape, 1928 . . . . £150/£45
Seven Tales and Alexander, Scholartis Press, 1929 (50 signed copies of an edition of 1,000) . . £200
ditto, Scholartis Press, 1929 (950 unsigned copies of an edition of 1,000) . . . . £25/£15
The Tree, A Story, Blue Moon Booklets, 1930 (wraps) £35

The Hessian Prisoner, Furnival Books, 1930 (550 signed copies) £75
Mrs. Esmond's Life, privately printed, 1931 (300 signed copies) £75
ditto, privately printed, 1931 (50 signed copies, leaf of manuscript bound in) £275
A Threshing Day, Foyle, 1931 (300 signed copies) £100
A German Idyll, Golden Cockerel Press, 1932 (307 signed copies) £250
The Black Boxer, Pharos Editions (Cape), 1932, (100 signed copies) . . . . £175/£125
The Story Without an End and The Country Doctor, White Owl Press, 1932 . . . . . . £15/£5
ditto, White Owl Press, 1932 (125 signed copies) . . . . £50/£25
Sally Go Round the Moon, White Owl Press, 1932 . . . . £30/£10
ditto, White Owl Press, 1932 (129 signed copies) . . . . £50/£35
ditto, White Owl Press, 1932 (21 signed copies with lea of manuscript bound in) £250
The House with the Apricot and Two Other Tales, Golden Cockerel Press, 1933 (300 signed copies). £175
The Woman Who Had Imagination, Cape, 1934 . . . . £35/£15
ditto, Macmillan (U.S.), 1934. . . . . . £30/£10
Thirty Tales, Cape, Traveller's Library, 1934 £15/£5
Cut and Come Again: Fourteen Stories, Cape, 1935 . . . . £35/£15
The Duet, A Story, Grayson Books, 1935 (285 signed copies) . . . . £125/£40
Something Short and Sweet, Cape, 1937 . £25/£5
Country Tales, Readers Union, 1938 (tissue jacket) . . . . £35/£25
ditto, Cape, 1940 . . . . £10/£5
My Uncle Silas, Cape, 1939 . . . . . . £150/£75
The Flying Goat, Cape, 1939 . . . . £50/£25
The Beauty of the Dead and Other Stories, Cape, 1940, ... £20/£10
The Greatest People in the World. 1942 Cape (pseud. Flying Officer 'X') . . . . £45/£15
How Sleep the Brave and other Stories by Flying Officer 'X', Cape, 1943 . . . . . . £35/£15
The Daffodil Sky, Cape, 1943 . . . . £20/£10
The Bride Comes to Evensford, Cape, 1943 £20/£5
Thirty-One Selected Tales, Cape, 1947 . £10/£5
Dear Life, Joseph, 1950 . . . . £15/£5
Colonel Julian and Other Stories, Joseph, 1951 . . . . £35/£10
ditto, Little, Brown (U.S.), 1952 . . . . . £10/£5
Twenty Tales, Cape, 1951 . . . . . . £15/£5
The Nature of Love, Joseph, 1953 . . . £15/£5
Sugar for the Horse, Joseph, 1957 . . . £25/£10
The Watercress Girl and other Stories, Joseph. 1959 . . . . £20/£10
ditto, Little, Brown, 1959 . . . . £20/£5
An Aspidistra in Babylon: Four Novellas, Joseph, 1960 . . . . £15/£5
Now Sleeps the Crimson Petal and Other Stories, Joseph, 1961 . . . . £15/£5
The Golden Oriole: Five Novellas, Joseph, 1962 . . . . £15/£5
ditto, Little, Brown (U.S.), 1962 . . . . £10/£5
Seven by Five: Stories 1926-1961, Joseph, 1963 . . . . £20/£10
ditto, as ***The Best of H. E. Bates***, Little, Brown and Co. (U.S.), 1963 . . . . £15/£5
The Fabulous Mrs V., Joseph, 1964. . . . £15/£5
The Wedding Party, Joseph, 1965 . . . £15/£5
The Wild Cherry Tree, Joseph, 1968 . . £15/£5
The Four Beauties, Joseph, 1968 . . . £15/£5
The Song of the Wren, Joseph, 1972 . . £10/£5
The Yellow Meads of Asphodel, Joseph, 1976 £10/£5
A Month by the Lake & Other Stories, New Directions (U.S.), 1987 . . . . £15/£5
Elephants Nest in a Rhubarb Tree & Other Stories, New Directions (U.S.), 1989 . . . . £15/£5

Plays

The Last Bread, Labour Publishing Co., 1926 (wraps) £125
The Day of Glory, Joseph, 1945 . . . . £20/£5

Children's

The Seekers, Bumpus, 1926 (tissue jacket) . £60/£50
The Seasons and the Gardener, C.U.P., 1940 £25/£10
Achilles the Donkey, Dobson Books, 1962 . £45/£20
Achilles and Diana, Dobson Books, 1964 . £45/£20
Achilles and the Twins, Dobson Books, 1964 £45/£20
The White Admiral, Dobson. 1968 . . . £45/£20

Verse

Song for December, privately printed, 1928 (wraps) £100
Christmas 1930, privately printed, 1930 (wraps) £100
Holly and Sallow, Blue Moon, 1931 (100 signed copies, broadside) £45

Autobiography

The Vanished World, Joseph, 1969 . . . . £15/£5
ditto, Univ. of Missouri Press (U.S.), 1969 . £10/£5
The Blossoming World, Joseph 1971 . . . £10/£5
ditto, Univ. of Missouri Press (U.S.), 1971 . £10/£5
A Love of Flowers, Joseph, 1971 . . . £10/£5
The World in Ripeness, Joseph,1972 . . £10/£5

Others

Flowers and Faces, Golden Cockerel Press, 1935 (325

signed copies) £175
Through the Woods: The English Woodland - April to April, Gollancz, 1936 . . . . £35/£10
Down the River, Gollancz, 1937 . . . . . £35/£10
ditto, Henry Holt & Co. (U.S.), 1937 . . £100/£70
In the Heart of the Country, Country Life, 1943 (illustrated by Tunnicliffe) . . . . . . £35/£15
O More Than Happy Countryman, Country Life, 1943 (illustrated by Tunnicliffe) . . . . . . £35/£15
Country Life, Penguin Books, 1943 (wraps) . £5
There's Freedom in the Air: The Official Story of the Allied Air Forces from the Occupied Countries, H.M.S.O., 1944 (anonymous, wraps) £20
The Tinkers of Elstow, [no place] 1946 . . . . £35
Edward Garnett, Parrish, 1950 . . . . . £25/£10
The Country of White Clover, Joseph, 1952 £25/£5
ditto, Joseph, 1952 (100 signed copies) . . . £75
The Face of England, Batsford Ltd, 1952 . £10/£5

L. FRANK BAUM

(b.1856 d.1919)

An American author who had a varied career until he started to write for children with *Mother Goose in Prose*. Three years later he brought out the classic *The Wonderful Wizard of Oz*. In this and its 13 sequels, Baum was attempting to write fantasies with distinctly American origins.

Mother Goose in Prose, Chicago (U.S.), [1897] £2,500
Father Goose, His Book, Chicago (U.S.), 1899 £2,500
A New Wonderland, Russell (U.S.), 1900 . £2,000
ditto, as ***The Surprising Adventures of the Magical Monarch of Mo and His People***, Bobbs-Merrill (U.S.). [1903] £750
The Wonderful Wizard of Oz, Hill (U.S.), 1900 £4,500
ditto, as ***The New Wizard of Oz***, Bobbs-Merrill (U.S.) [1903] £500
ditto, Hodder & Stoughton, 1906 . . . . . . £500
American Fairy Tales, Chicago (U.S.), 1901 . £1,000
Dot and Tot of Merryland, Hill (U.S.), 1901 . £1,000
The Master Key: An Electrical Fairy Tale, Bobbs-Merrill (U.S.), 1901 . . . . £600
ditto, Stevens & Brown, [1902] £500
The Life and Adventures of Santa Claus, Bobbs-Merrill (U.S.), 1902 . . . . £2,500
ditto, Stevens & Brown, 1902 . . . . . £2,000
The Enchanted Island of Yew, Bobbs-Merrill (U.S.), [1903] £500
The Marvellous Land of Oz, Reilly & Britton (U.S.), 1904 . . . . £7,500
Queen Zixi of Ix, Century (U.S.), 1905 . . . . £250
ditto, Hodder & Stoughton, 1905 . . . . . . £200
The Woggle-Bug Book, Reilly & Britton (U.S.), 1905 . . . . £1,000
John Dough and The Cherub, Reilly & Britton (U.S.), 1906 . . . . £250
ditto, Constable, 1906 . . . . £200
Ozma of Oz, Reilly & Britton (U.S.), 1907 . . £500
The Last Egyptian: A Romance of the Nile; Reilly & Britton (U.S.), 1908 . . . . £225
Dorothy and the Wizard of Oz, Reilly & Britton (U.S.), 1908 . . . . £500
The Road to Oz, Reilly & Britton (U.S.), 1909 . £500
The Emerald City of Oz, Reilly & Britton (U.S.), 1910 . . . . £500
The Sea Fairies, Reilly & Britton (U.S.), 1911 . £250
Sky Island, Reilly & Britton (U.S.), 1912 . . £200
The Patchwork Girls of Oz, Reilly & Britton (U.S.), 1913 . . . . £500
Tik-Tok of Oz, Reilly & Britton (U.S.), 1914 . £500
The Scarecrow of Oz, Reilly & Britton (U.S.), 1915 . . . . £400
Rinkitink in Oz, Reilly & Britton (U.S.), 1916 . £500
The Lost Princess of Oz, Reilly & Britton (U.S.), 1917 . . . . £400
The Tin Woodman of Oz, Reilly & Britton (U.S.), 1918 . . . . £400
The Magic of Oz, Reilly & Lee (U.S.), 1919 . £400
Glinda of Oz, Reilly & Lee (U.S.), 1920 . . £250

BEANO ANNUALS

The Beano is arguably the most famous of all children's comics, first appearing on 30th July 1938. The first Beano Annual was issued in 1940

The Beano Book 1940, D.C. Thomson, 1940 . £850
The Beano Book 1941, D.C. Thomson, 1941 . £750
The Beano Book 1942, D.C. Thomson, 1942 . £650
The Magic Beano Book 1943, D.C. Thomson, 1943 . . . . £500
The Magic Beano Book 1944, D.C. Thomson, 1944 . . . . £450
The Magic Beano Book 1945, D.C. Thomson, 1945 . . . . £400
The Magic Beano Book 1946, D.C. Thomson, 1946 . . . . £300
The Magic Beano Book 1947, D.C. Thomson, 1947 . . . . £250
The Magic Beano Book 1948, D.C. Thomson, 1948 . . . . £200
The Magic Beano Book 1949, D.C. Thomson, 1949 . . . . £175
The Magic Beano Book 1950, D.C. Thomson, 1950 . . . . £125

The Beano Book 1951, D.C. Thomson, 1951 . £75
The Beano Book 1952, D.C. Thomson, 1952 . £50
The Beano Book 1953, D.C. Thomson, 1953 . £50
The Beano Book 1954, D.C. Thomson, 1954 . £40
The Beano Book 1955, D.C. Thomson, 1955 . £35
The Beano Book 1956, D.C. Thomson, 1956 . £35
The Beano Book 1957, D.C. Thomson, 1957 . £35
The Beano Book 1958, D.C. Thomson, 1958 . £35
The Beano Book 1959, D.C. Thomson, 1959 . £35
The Beano Book 1960, D.C. Thomson, 1960 . £30
The Beano Book 1961, D.C. Thomson, 1961 . £30
The Beano Book 1962, D.C. Thomson, 1962 . £30
The Beano Book 1963, D.C. Thomson, 1963 . £30
The Beano Book 1964, D.C. Thomson, 1964 . £30
The Beano Book 1965, D.C. Thomson, 1965 . £25
The Beano Book 1966, D.C. Thomson, 1966 . £20
The Beano Book 1967-69, D.C. Thomson, 1967-69 . . . . £15 each
The Beano Book 1970-75, D.C. Thomson, 1970-75 . . . . £10 each
The Beano Book 1976-80, D.C. Thomson, 1976-80 . . . . £5 each

---

AUBREY BEARDSLEY

(b.1872 d.1898)

British illustrator and writer who came to prominence in the 1890s. His sinuous black and white illustrations became as synonymous with the 'decadence' of the period as did the name of Oscar Wilde.

Major Works

Le Morte d'Arthur, by Thomas Malory, Dent, 1893-4, (12 parts, green wraps) . . . . . the set £2,500
ditto, Dent, 1893-4, (12 parts, handmade paper, grey wraps). . . . . the set £3,250
ditto, Dent, 1893, (2 vols). £800
ditto, Dent, 1893, (3 vols, 300 copies, handmade paper) £2,000
Bon Mots, Dent, 1893-94, (3 vols) . . . . £75 each
ditto, Dent, 1893-94, (100 numbered copies, large paper issue, 3 vols) . . . . £350 each
Salome, by Oscar Wilde, Lane and Mathews, 1894 (755 copies) £1,500
ditto, Lane and Mathews, 1894 (125 copies, on Japan vellum, large paper issue) £2,500
The Rape of the Lock, by Alexander Pope, [Smithers], privately printed, 1896 (1,000 copies) £350
ditto, [Smithers], privately printed, 1896 (25 copies on Japan vellum). £5,000
Lysistrata of Aristophanes, [Smithers], privately printed, 1896 (100 copies) £4,500
A Book of Fifty Drawings, Smithers, 1897 (500 copies) £200
ditto, Smithers, 1897 (50 copies on Japan vellum) £3,000
The Pierrot of the Minute, Leonard Smithers, 1897 (300 copies printed on handmade paper) . . £500
ditto, Leonard Smithers, 1897 (30 copies printed on Japanese vellum) £2,000
ditto, Grolier Club (U.S.), 1923 (300 copies printed on Dutch antique paper) £200
A Second Book of Fifty Drawings, Smithers, 1898 . . . . £200
Mademoiselle de Maupin, by Theophile Gautier, Smithers, 1898 (portfolio, 50 numbered copies) £2,500
Volpone, by Ben Jonson, Smithers, 1898 (1,000 copies) £250
ditto, Smithers, 1898 (100 numbered copies on Japan vellum) £1,750
The Early Work of Aubrey Beardsley, Bodley Head, 1899 . . . . £250
ditto, Bodley Head, 1912 . . . . £75
The Later Work of Aubrey Beardsley, Bodley Head, 1901 . . . . £250
ditto, Bodley Head, 1912 . . . . £75
Under the Hill, John Lane, 1904 . . . . . . £175
ditto, John Lane, 1904 (50 copies on Japan vellum) £1,500
ditto, Olympia Press (Paris), 1959 . . . . £100
The Uncollected Works of Aubrey Beardsley, Bodley Head, 1925 . . . . £150

Other Titles illustrated by Beardsley

Plays, by John Davidson, Mathews & Lane, 1894 £50
A London Garland, Macmillan, 1895 . . . £75
Tales of Mystery and Wonder, by Edgar Allen Poe, Stone & Kimball (U.S.), 1895 . . . . . . £150
Earl Lavender, by John Davidson, Ward & Downey, 1895 . . . . £50
An Evil Motherhood, by Walt Ruding, Elkin Mathews, 1895 . . . . £30
Sappho, by H.T. Wharton, Lane, 1896 . . . . £35
A Book of Bargains, by V. O'Sullivan, Smithers, 1896 . . . . £125
Verses, Leonard Smithers, 1896 (300 copies. Cover design by Aubrey Beardsley) £300
ditto, Leonard Smithers, 1896 (30 copies on Japanese Vellum) £2,000
The Life and Times of Madame du Barry, by Douglas, Smithers, 1897 . . . . £75
The House of Sin, by V. O'Sullivan, Smithers, 1897 . . . . £125
Decorations, in Verse & Prose, Leonard Smithers, 1899 . . . . £250
The Poems of Ernest Dowson, John Lane, 1905 (edited and with a memoir by Arthur Symons) £150

Other Titles containing illustrations by Beardsley

Aubrey Beardsley, by Arthur Symons, Unicorn Press, 1898 . . . . £60

ditto, Dent, 1905 . . . . £25

The Last Letters of Aubrey Beardsley, ed. by John Gray, Longmans, 1904 . . . . £75

Aubrey Beardsley, by Robert Ross, Lane, 1909 £45

The Beardsley Period, by O. Burdett, Bodley Head, 1925 . . . . £15

The Best of Beardsley, by R.A. Walker, Bodley Head, 1948 . . . . £20

A Beardsley Miscellany, ed. by R.A. Walker, London, 1949 . . . . £20

Beardsley: A Catalogue of an Exhibition, V&A Museum, 1966 . . . . £10

Beardsley, by B. Reade, London, 1967 . . . . £10

Aubrey Beardsley's Erotic Universe, by D. Stanford, NEL, 1967 . . . . £10

Aubrey Beardsley, by Stanley Weintraub, W.H. Allen, 1967 . . . . £15/£5

Beardsley and His World, by Brigid Brophy, Thames & Hudson, 1976 . . . . £15/£5

Others

The Story of Venus and Tanhauser, A Romantic Novel, Smithers, 1907 ('Under the Hill', 250 numbered copies on handmade paper, no illustrations) £150

ditto, Smithers, 1907 ('Under the Hill', 50 numbered copies on Japan vellum, no illustrations) . . . £350

Letters to Leonard Smithers, First Editions Club, 1937 . . . . £50

SAMUEL BECKETT

(b.1906 d.1989)

An individual and experimental Irish playwright, novelist and poet who received the Nobel Prize for Literature in 1969.

Our Exagmination Round His Factification for Incamination of 'Work in Progress', Shakespeare & Co (Paris), 1929 (300 copies, wraps) £300

ditto, Shakespeare & Co (Paris), 1929 (96 large paper copies) £600

ditto, Faber, 1936 . . . . £150/£65

ditto, New Directions (U.S.), 1939 . . . . . £50

Whoroscope, Hours Press, 1930 (200 numbered copies of 300, wraps) £1,000

ditto, Hours Press, 1930 (100 signed, numbered copies of 300, wraps) £4,000

ditto, Grove Press (U.S.), 1957 . . . . £25/£10

Proust, Chatto & Windus, 1931 . . . £150/£65

ditto, Grove Press (U.S.), 1957 (250 signed copies) £200

ditto, Grove Press (U.S.), 1957 (wraps) . . . £20

More Pricks than Kicks, Chatto & Windus, 1934 . . . . £400/£150

ditto, Grove Press (U.S.), 1970 . . . . . £25/£10

Echo's Bones, Europa Press (Paris), 1935 (327 copies) £250

Murphy, Routledge, 1938. . . . . . . £500/£200

ditto, Grove Press (U.S.), [c. 1957] . . . . £65/£35

ditto, Grove Press (U.S.), [c. 1957] (100 signed copies, acetate d/w) . . . . £250/£245

Molloy, Éditions de Minuit (Paris), 1951 (550 numbered copies, wraps) £100

ditto, Grove Press (U.S.), 1955 . . . . . £65/£35

ditto, Olympia Press (Paris), 1955 (wraps) . £100

ditto, Calder, 1959. . . . . £100/£45

Malone Meurt, Éditions de Minuit (Paris), [1951] (wraps) £50

ditto, as ***Malone Dies***, Grove Press (U.S.), 1956 . . . . £65/£35

ditto, Grove Press (U.S.), 1956 (100 signed copies, acetate d/w) . . . . £100/£90

ditto, as ***Malone Dies***, Calder, 1958 . . . . £100/£45

En Attendant Godot, Éditions de Minuit (Paris), 1952 (wraps) £200

ditto, as ***Waiting for Godot***, Grove Press (U.S.), 1954 (wraps) £75

ditto, Faber, 1956 . . . . £75/£40

L'Innommable, Éditions de Minuit (Paris), 1953 (wraps) £50

The Unnamable, Calder, 1959 . . . . . £25/£10

ditto, Grove Press (U.S.), 1959 (100 numbered copies) £100

Watt, Olympia Press (Paris), 1953 (1,100 numbered copies, wraps) £125

ditto, Grove Press (U.S.), 1953 (100 copies) £125/£45

ditto, Calder, 1963. . . . . £20/£10

Nouvelles et Textes pour Rien, Éditions de Minuit (Paris), 1955 (1,185 numbered copies, wraps). £40

Fin de Partie, Éditions de Minuit (Paris), 1957 (wraps) £75

Tous Ceux Qui Tombent, Éditions de Minuit (Paris), 1957 (wraps) £50

ditto, as ***All That Fall***, Faber, 1958 . . . . . £20

ditto, Grove Press (U.S.), 1958 . . . . . £25/£10

Endgame, Faber, 1958 . . . . £75/£35

ditto, Grove Press (U.S.), 1958 . . . . . £50/£20

From an Abandoned Work, Faber, 1958 . . £20

Krapp's Last Tape and Embers, Faber, 1959 . £25

ditto, Grove Press (U.S.), 1960 . . . . . £20/£10

Three Novels, Grove Press (U.S.), 1959. . £20/£10

La dernière bande, Éditions de Minuit (Paris), 1959 [1960] (wraps) £45

ditto, Éditions de Minuit (Paris), 1959 [1960] (40 numbered copies, wraps) £250
Molloy, Malone Dies, The Unnamable: A Trilogy, Olympia Press (Paris), 1959 (wraps) . . . £40
ditto, as ***The Trilogy***, Calder, 1960 . . . . £20/£10
Poems in English, Calder, 1961 . . . . £40/£15
ditto, Calder, 1961 (100 signed copies, slipcase) £250
ditto, Grove Press (U.S.), 1963 . . . . . £20/£5
Comment c'est, Éditions de Minuit (Paris), 1961 (wraps) £40
ditto, as ***How It Is***, Calder, 1964 . . . . £25/£10
ditto, as ***How It Is***, Calder, 1964 (100 signed copies, slipcase) £250
Happy Days, Grove Press (U.S.), 1961 . . £20/£10
ditto, Faber, 1962 . . . . £20/£10
ditto, as ***Oh Les Beaux Jours***, Éditions de Minuit (Paris), 1963 (412 copies, wraps) £75
Play and Two Short Pieces for Radio, Faber, 1964 . . . . £20/£10
ditto, Faber, 1964 (signed, limited edition) . . £150
Proust and Three Dialogues with Georges Duthuit, Calder, 1965 . . . . £15/£5
Imagination Morte Immaginez, Éditions de Minuit (Paris), 1965 (612 signed copies) £175
ditto, as ***Imagination Dead Imagine***, Calder, 1966 . . . . £15/£5
Comedie et actes diversz, Éditions de Minuit (Paris), 1966 (112 copies, wraps) £150
Come and Go, Calder, 1967 . . . . £15/£5
ditto, Calder, 1967 (100 signed copies, slipcase) £250
Eh Joe and Other Writings, Faber, 1967 . £35/£10
Stories & Texts for Nothing, Grove Press (U.S.), 1967 . . . . £35/£10
Têtes Mortes, Éditions de Minuit (Paris), 1967 (wraps) £45
No's Knife, Calder, 1967 . . . . £10/£5
ditto, Calder, 1967 (100 signed copies, slipcase) £250
Poèms, Éditions de Minuit (Paris), 1968 (limited edition, wraps) £125
ditto, Éditions de Minuit (Paris), 1978 . . . £45
Sans, Éditions de Minuit (Paris), 1969 (742 copies, wraps) £45
ditto as ***Lessness***, Calder, 1970 . . . . . £15/£5
ditto, Calder, 1970 (100 signed copies, slipcase) £250
The Lost Ones, Éditions de Minuit (Paris), 1970 (92 of 399 copies) £150
ditto, Éditions de Minuit (Paris), 1970 (201 of 399 copies) £75
ditto, Calder, 1972 . . . . £15/£5
ditto, Calder, 1972 (100 signed copies, slipcase) £250
Premier Amour, Éditions de Minuit (Paris), 1970 (92 of 399 copies) £150
ditto, Éditions de Minuit (Paris), 1970 (201 of 399 copies) £75

ditto, as ***First Love***, Calder, 1973 . . . . £15/£5
ditto, Grove Press (U.S.), 1974 . . . . £15/£5
Mercier et Camier, Éditions de Minuit (Paris), 1970 . . . . £45
ditto, as ***Mercier and Camier***, Calder, 1974. £15/£5
Six Residua, Calder, 1972 (wraps) £5
Film, Faber, 1972 . . . . £10
Breath and Other Short Plays, Faber, 1972 (hardback) . . . . £60/£25
ditto, Faber, 1972 (wraps). £10
ditto, Faber, 1972 (signed, limited edition) . . £125
Not I, Faber, 1973 . . . . £10
The North, Enitharmon Press, 1973 (137 signed, numbered copies, wraps) £125
ditto Enitharmon Press, 1973 (15 copies with three extra etchings, heavyweight paper, wraps) . £1,000
Still, M'Arte Edizioni (Milan), 1974 (30 signed copies of 160 with extra portfolio of plates, slipcase) £1,750
ditto, M'Arte Edizioni (Milan), 1974 (72 signed copies of 160, slipcase) £1,000
All Strange Away, Gotham Book Mart (U.S.), 1976 . . . . £50/£15
ditto, Calder, 1979 . . . . £10/£5
Footfalls, Faber, 1976. . . . . £10
Pour finir encore et autres foirades, Éditions de Minuit (Paris), 1976 (wraps) £15
That Time, Calder, 1976 . . . . £10/£5
For to End Yet Again and Other Fizzles, Calder, 1976 . . . . £10/£5
ditto as ***Fizzles***, Grove Press (U.S.), 1977 . £10/£5
Ends and Odds, Calder, 1977 . . . . . £10/£5
ditto, Grove Press (U.S.), 1977 . . . . . £10/£5
Collected Poems in French and English, Calder, 1977 . . . . £15/£5
Four Novellas, Calder, 1978 . . . . . £10/£5
Six Residua, Calder, 1978 . . . . £5
Three Occasional Pieces, Faber, 1982 (wraps) . £5
Worstward Ho, Calder, 1983 . . . . . . £15/£5
ditto, as ***Cap au pire***, Éditions de Minuit (Paris), 1991 (wraps) £15
Company, Éditions de Minuit (Paris), 1979 (wraps) £10
ditto, Calder, 1980 . . . . £15/£5
ditto, Calder, 1980 (100 signed copies, slipcase) £250
ditto, Grove Press (U.S.), 1980 . . . . £10/£5
Mirlitonnades, Éditions de Minuit (Paris), 1979 (wraps) £10
Rockaby and Other Short Pieces, Grove Press (U.S.), 1981 . . . . £15/£5
Ill Seen Ill Said, Grove Press (U.S.), 1981 . £15/£5
ditto, Calder, 1982 . . . . £15/£5
ditto, Lord John Press (U.S.), 1982 (299 signed copies of 325) £100
ditto, Lord John Press (U.S.), 1982 (26 signed, lettered copies of 325) £250

ditto, as ***Mal vu mal dit***, Éditions de Minuit (Paris), 1987 (wraps) £20
ditto, Éditions de Minuit (Paris), 1987 (99 numbered copies, wraps) £75
Disjecta, Calder, 1983. . . . . £30/£10
ditto, Grove Press (U.S.), 1983 . . . . . £15/£5
Quoi Ou, Éditions de Minuit (Paris), 1983 (99 copies, wraps) £75
Catastrophe, Lord John Press (U.S.), 1983 (100 signed copies, broadside) £150
Collected Shorter Plays, Calder, 1984 . . . . £5
ditto, Grove Press, 1984 . . . . £5
Collected Poems, 1930-1978, Calder, 1984 . £10
Collected Shorter Prose, 1945-1980, Calder, 1984 £10
The Collected Works, Grove Press (U.S.), (16 vols 200 signed, numbered sets) £300
As the Story Was Told, Rampant Lions Press, 1987 (325 numbered copies) £60
ditto, Calder, 1990. . . . . £10/£5
Stirrings Still, Calder/Blue Moon Books, [1988] (200 of 226 signed, numbered copies, slipcase) . . £1,000
ditto, Calder/Blue Moon Books, [1988] (26 lettered, signed copies of 226, slipcase) £1,750
ditto, Calder/Blue Moon Books, [1988] (15 roman-numeraled "hors de commerce" copies, slipcase) £2,000
Le Monde et le Pantalon, Éditions de Minuit (Paris), 1989 (99 copies, wraps) £45
Nohow On, Calder, 1989 . . . . £10/£5
ditto, Limited Editions Club (U.S.), [1989] (550 copies in box) £450
Comment dire, Éditions de Minuit (Paris), 1989 (wraps) £5
Dream of Fair to Middling Women, Black Cat Press (Dublin), 1992 . . . . £15/£5
Eleutheria, Éditions de Minuit (Paris), 1995 (wraps) £10

MAX BEERBOHM

(b.1872 d.1956)

Humorist, caricaturist, essayist and novelist, and survivor of the 1890s decadent scene.

Novels

The Happy Hypocrite, Wayside Press (U.S.), 1896 (wraps) £125
ditto, John Lane, 1897. . . . . £50
Zuleika Dobson, Heinemann, 1911 . . . . £100
ditto, John Lane (U.S.), 1912 . . . . £50
A Christmas Garland, Heinemann, 1912 . . £50
ditto, Dutton & Co. (U.S.), 1912 . . . . . . £25
Seven Men, Heinemann, 1919 . . . . £75/£15
ditto, Knopf (U.S.) 1920 (2,000 copies) . . £35/£15
ditto, as ***Seven Men and Two Others***, Heinemann, 1946 . . . . £10/£5
The Dreadful Dragon of Hay Hill, Heinemann, 1928 . . . . £35/£10

Prose

The Works of Max Beerbohm, Scribners (U.S.), 1896 (1,000 copies, of which 401 were pulped) . . £200
ditto, John Lane, 1896. . . . . £100
More, John Lane, 1899 . . . . £50
Yet Again, Chapman and Hall, 1909. . . . . £50
And Even Now, Heinemann, 1920 . . . . £50/£10
Around Theatres, Heinemann, 1924 (2 vols) £35/£10
ditto, Knopf (U.S.) 1930 . . . . £15/£5
A Variety of Things, Heinemann, 1928 . . £25/£10
ditto, Knopf (U.S.) 1928 (2,000 copies) . . £25/£10
Lytton Strachey, CUP, 1943 (wraps). . . . £10
ditto, Knopf (U.S.) 1943 . . . . £15/£5
Mainly on the Air, Heinemann, 1946 . . . £20/£5
ditto, Knopf (U.S.) 1947 . . . . £10/£5
Sherlockiana: A Reminiscence of Sherlock Holmes, Hill (U.S.), 1948 (36 copies) £250
Letters Of Max Beerbohm, 1892-1956, John Murray, 1988 . . . . £10/£5
ditto, Norton (U.S.), 1989. . . . . . . £10/£5

Drawings and Caricatures

Caricatures of Twenty-Five Gentleman, Leonard Smithers, 1896 (500 copies). £400
Poets' Corner, Heinemann, 1904. . . . £150
ditto, Penguin, 1943 . . . . £15
A Book of Caricatures, Methuen, 1907 . . £150
Cartoons: The Second Childhood of John Bull, Stephen Swift, [1911] £125
Fifty Caricatures, Heinemann, 1913. . . . . £75
ditto, Dutton (U.S.), 1913. . . . . £45
A Survey, Heinemann, 1921 . . . . . £125/£50
ditto, Heinemann, 1921 (275 signed, numbered copies) . . . . £250/£175
ditto, Doubleday, 1921 . . . . . . £100/£50
Rossetti and His Circle, Heinemann, 1922 . £125/£50
ditto, Heinemann, 1922 (380 signed, numbered copies) . . . . £250/£175
Things New and Old, Heinemann, 1923. . £100/£45
ditto, Heinemann, 1923 (350 signed, numbered copies, with additional signed coloured plate) . . £250/£175
Observations, Heinemann, 1925 . . . . . £75/£45
The Heroes and Heroines of Bitter Sweet, [Leadley, 1931] (900 numbered copies, portfolio) . . £200

Edited by Beerbohm

Herbert Beerbohm Tree, Hutchinson, 1920. £20/£10

BRENDAN BEHAN
(b.1923 d.1964)

An Irish playwright, Behan spent many years in prison as a result of his IRA activities. Although released in 1947, it was in prison that he started to write, and his first success came with the publication of *The Quare Fellow* in 1956.

Plays
The Quare Fellow, Methuen, 1956 . . . £75/£25
The Hostage, Methuen, 1958. . . . . £50/£25
ditto, Grove Press (U.S.), 1958 . . . . £40/£20
Borstal Boy, Random House (U.S.), 1971 . £15/£5
Richard's Cork Leg, Methuen, 1973. . . . £10/£5
ditto, Grove Press (U.S.), 1974 . . . . £10/£5
An Giall and The Hostage, C. Smythe, 1988 . £5

Novels
Borstal Boy, Knopf (U.S.), 1957. . . . £40/£15
ditto, Hutchinson, 1958 . . . . . . £50/£20
Hold Your Hour and Have Another, Hutchinson, 1963 . . . . £20/£5
ditto, Little, Brown (U.S.), 1964 . . . . £10/£5
The Scarperer, Hutchinson, 1964 . . . £15/£5
ditto, Doubleday (U.S.), 1964 . . . . £10/£5
Confessions of an Irish Rebel, Hutchinson, 1965 . . . . £20/£5
ditto, Geis (U.S.), 1966 . . . . . . £15/£5

Verse
Poems and A Play in Irish, Gallery Press (Dublin), 1981 . . . . £10

Non Fiction
Brendan Behan's Island, Hutchinson, 1962 £20/£5
ditto, Geis (U.S.), 1962 . . . . . . £15/£5
Brendan Behan's New York, Hutchinson, 1964 £15/£5
ditto, Geis (U.S.), 1964 . . . . . . £15/£5

Miscellaneous
After the Wake: Uncollected Prose, O'Brien Press (Ireland), 1983 . . . . £10

HILAIRE BELLOC
(b.1870 d.1953)

Belloc was a poet, novelist, essayist, and travel writer, but is best known and most often collected for his humorous verse for children.

Verse
Verses and Sonnets, Ward & Downey, 1896 . £150
The Bad Child's Book of Beasts, Alden Press, 1896 . . . . £95
More Beasts (For Worse Children), Arnold, 1897 £75
The Modern Traveller, Arnold, 1898 . . . £75
A Moral Alphabet, Arnold, 1899. . . . . £75
Cautionary Tales for Children, Eveleigh Nash, 1907 . . . . £50
Verses, Duckworth, 1910 . . . . . . £50
More Peers, Stephen Swift, 1911 . . . . £45
Sonnets and Verse, Duckworth, 1923 . . £45/£10
ditto, Duckworth, 1923 (525 signed copies). . £75
The Chanty of the Nowa, Faber, Arial Poem, 1928 £15
ditto, Faber, Arial Poem, 1928 (500 signed, large paper copies) £50
New Cautionary Tales, Duckworth, 1930 . £75/£20
ditto, Duckworth, 1930 (110 signed copies). . £125
In Praise of Wine: A Heroic Poem, Peter Davies, 1931 . . . . £25/£10
Ladies and Gentlemen, Duckworth, 1932 . £25/£10
The Verse of Hilaire Belloc, The Nonesuch Press, 1954 (1,250 numbered copies) £35

Novels
Emmanuel Burden, Methuen, 1904 . . . . £45
Mr Clutterbuck's Election, Eveleigh Nash, 1908 £25
A Change in the Cabinet, Methuen, 1909 . . £25
Pongo and the Bull, Constable, 1910 . . . £50
Mr Girondin, Nelson, 1911 . . . . . . £20
The Green Overcoat, Arrowsmith, 1912 . . £35
The Mercy of Allah, Chatto & Windus, 1922 £75/£20
Mr Petre, Arrowsmith, 1925 . . . . . £45/£15
ditto, McBride (U.S.), 1925 . . . . . £45/£15
The Emerald, Arrowsmith, 1926. . . . £45/£15
ditto, Harpers (U.S.), 1926 . . . . . £45/£15
The Haunted House, Arrowsmith, 1927 . £200/£95
ditto, Harper (U.S.), 1928. . . . . . £90/£25
But Soft, We Are Observed, Arrowsmith, 1928. . . . . £35/£10
Belinda, Constable, 1928 . . . . . . £45/£15
The Missing Masterpiece, Arrowsmith, 1929 £75/£20
The Man Who Made Gold, Arrowsmith, 1930 £45/£15
ditto, Harper (U.S.), 1931. . . . . . £25/£10
The Post-Master General, Arrowsmith, 1932 £100/£25
ditto, Lippincott (U.S.), 1932. . . . . £25/£10
The Hedge and the Horse, Cassell, 1936 . £25/£10

History
Danton, John Nisbet & Co., 1899 . . . . . £50
ditto, Putnams (U.S.), 1928 . . . . . . £20/£10
Robespierre, John Nisbet & Co., 1901 . . . £40
The Eye Witness, Eveleigh Nash, 1908 . . . £40
Marie Antoinette, Methuen, 1909 . . . . . £40
The French Revolution, Williams and Norgate, 1911 . . . . £30
The Battle of Blenheim, Stephen Swift, 1911 . £20

Malplaquet, Stephen Swift, 1911 . . . . £20
Crecy, Stephen Swift, 1911 . . . . . . £20
Poitiers, Stephen Swift, 1911 . . . . £20
Waterloo, Stephen Swift, 1912 . . . . . £20
Turcoing, Stephen Swift, 1912 . . . . . £20
Warfare in England, Williams & Norgate, 1912 £20
The Book of the Bayeaux Tapestry, Chatto and Windus, 1914. . . . . £30
History of England, (Vol. 11), Catholic Publications Society of America, 1915 . . . . . . £15
Land and Water Map of the War, Land and Water, 1915 . . . . £25
A General Sketch of the European War: The First Phase, Nelson, 1915. . . . . £40
The Two Maps of Europe, Arthur Pearson, 1915 £30
The Last Days of the French Monarchy, Chapman and Hall, 1916 . . . . £10
A General Sketch of the European War: The Second Phase, Nelson, 1916. . . . . £40
The Second Year of the War, Land and Water, 1916 . . . . £30
The Principles of War, by Foch, Chapman & Hall, 1919 (translation) £25
Precepts and Judgements, by Foch, Chapman & Hall, 1919 (translation) £25
The Jews, Constable, 1922 . . . . £20/£5
The Campaign of 1812, Nelson, 1924 . . £30/£10
History of England Vol. 1, Methuen, 1925 . £25/£10
Miniatures of French History, Nelson, 1925 £25/£10
Mrs Markham's New History of England, Cayme Press, 1926 . . . . £25/£10
History of England Vol. 2, Methuen, 1927 . £25/£10
Oliver Cromwell, Benn, 1927 . . . . . £20/£5
History of England Vol. 3, Methuen, 1928 . £25/£10
James II, Faber & Gwyer, 1928 . . . . £25/£10
ditto, as ***James the Second***, Lippincott (U.S.), 1928 . . . . £25/£10
How the Reformation Happened, Cape, 1928 £15/£5
ditto, McBride & Co (U.S.), 1928 . . . . £15/£5
Joan of Arc, Cassell, 1929 . . . . . . £25/£10
Richelieu, Benn, 1930 . . . . £15/£5
Wolsey, Cassell, 1930 . . . . £15/£5
ditto, Lippincott (U.S.), 1930 . . . . . . £15/£5
History of England Vol. 4, Methuen, 1931 . £25/£5
Cranmer, Cassell, 1931 . . . . £15/£5
ditto, Lippincott (U.S.), 1931 . . . . . . £15/£5
The Tactics and Strategy of the Great Duke of Marlborough, Arrowsmith, 1931 . . . . £40/£10
Six British Battles, Arrowsmith, 1931 . . . £20/£5
Napoleon, Cassell, 1932 . . . . £15/£5
ditto, Lippincott (U.S.), 1932 . . . . . . £15/£5
William the Conqueror, Peter Davies, 1933 £15/£10
Beckett, Catholic Truth Society, 1933 . . £15/£5
Charles I, Cassell, 1933 . . . . £15/£5
ditto, Lippincott (U.S.), 1933 . . . . . . £15/£5
Cromwell, Cassell, 1934 . . . . £15/£5
A Shorter History of England, Harrap, 1934 £25/£10
Milton, Cassell, 1935 . . . . £25/£5
The Battleground, Cassell, 1936 . . . . . £15/£5
ditto, Lippincott (U.S.), 1936 . . . . . . £15/£5
Characters of the Reformation, Sheed & Ward (U.S.), 1936 . . . . £15/£5
The Crusade, Cassell, 1937 . . . . £25/£5
The Crisis of Our Civilization, Cassell, 1937 (wraps) £10
ditto, Fordham University Press (U.S.), 1937 . £10
The Great Heresies, Sheed & Ward (U.S.), 1938 . . . . £15/£5
Monarchy: A Study of Louis XIV, Cassell, 1938 . . . . £15/£5
ditto, as ***Louis XIV***, Harper (U.S.), 1938 . £15/£15
The Last Rally, Cassell, 1940 . . . . £15/£5
Elizabethan Commentary, Cassell, 1942 . £15/£5

Travel

Paris, Arnold, 1900 . . . . £25
The Path to Rome, Allen, 1902 . . . . . £25
The Old Road, Constable, 1904 . . . . . £25
Esto Perpetua, Duckworth, 1906. . . . . £45
Sussex, A.C. Black, 1906 . . . . £25
The Historic Thames, Dent, 1907 . . . . £20
The Pyrenees, Methuen, 1909 . . . . . £25
The River of London, Foulis, 1912 . . . . £20
The Four Men, Foulis, 1912 . . . . . . £20
The Stane Street, Constable, 1913 . . . £20/£5
The Road, Charles Hobson, 1923 . . . £25/£10
The Contrast, Arrowsmith, 1923. . . . £15/£5
ditto, McBride (U.S.), 1924 . . . . . £10/£5
The Cruise of the Nona, Constable, 1925 . £40/£15
ditto, Houghton Mifflin, 1925 . . . . . £25/£10
The Highway and its Vehicles, The Studio, 1926 £15
Many Cities, Constable, 1928 . . . . . £20/£5
Return to the Baltic, Constable, 1938 . . . £20/£5
On Sailing the Sea, Methuen, 1939 . . . . £10/£5
Places, Sheed and Ward (U.S.), 1941 . . £10/£5
ditto, Cassell, 1942 . . . . £10/£5

Politics

Socialism and the Servile State, ILP, 1910 . £10
The Party System and Cecil Chesterton, Stephen Swift, 1911 . . . . £15
The Servile State, Foulis, 1912 . . . . . £20
ditto, Henry Holt (U.S.), 1946 . . . . £10/£5
The Free Press, Allen & Unwin, 1918 . . £25/£10
The House of Commons and the Monarchy, Allen & Unwin, 1920 . . . . £25/£5
Economics for Helen, Arrowsmith, 1924 . £20/£10
The Political Effort, True Temperance Association, 1924 . . . . £15

Literature

Caliban's Guide to Letters, Duckworth, 1903 . £35

The Romance of Tristan and Iseult, Allen, 1903 (translation) £20

Avril, Being Essays on the Poetry of the French Renaissance, Duckworth, 1904 . . . . . . £20

On the Place of Gilbert Chesterton in English Letters, Sheed and Ward, 1940 . . . . . . £15/£5

Religion

An Open Letter on the Decay of Faith, Burns & Oates, 1906 . . . . £20

The Catholic Church and Historical Truth, W. Watson, 1908. . . . . £10

An Examination of Socialism, Catholic Truth Society, 1908 . . . . £10

The Church and Socialism, Catholic Truth Society, 1908 . . . . £10

The Ferrer Case, Catholic Truth Society, 1909 £10

Anti-Catholic History, Catholic Truth Society, 1914 . . . . £10

Religion and Liberty, Catholic Truth Society, 1918 £10

The Catholic Church and the Purchase of Private Property, Catholic Truth Society, 1920 . . £10

A Companion to Mr Wells' Outline of History, Sheed & Ward, 1926 . . . . £25/£10

Mr Belloc Still Objects, Sheed and Ward, 1927 £15/£5

The Catholic Church and History, Burns, Oates & Washbourne, 1927 . . . . . . £10/£5

Survivals and New Arrivals, Sheed & Ward, 1929 . . . . £10/£5

ditto, Macmillan (U.S.), 1929. . . . . £10/£5

The Case of Dr Coulton, Sheed & Ward, 1931 £10/£5

The Catholic and the War, Burns & Oates, 1940 . . . . £10/£5

Essays

At the Sign of the Lion, Mosher (U.S.), 1896 (950 copies) £20

ditto, Mosher (U.S.), 1916 . . . . . . £15

Hills and Seas, Methuen, 1906 . . . . . £25

On Nothing, Methuen, 1908 . . . . . . £15

On Everything, Methuen, 1909 . . . . . £15

On Anything, Methuen, 1910 . . . . . £15

On Something, Methuen, 1910 . . . . . £15

First and Last, Methuen, 1911 . . . . . £10

This and That, Methuen, 1912 . . . . . £10

On, Methuen, 1923 . . . . £15/£5

Hilaire Belloc: Essays, Harrap, 1926 . . . £15/£5

Short Talks with the Dead, Cayme Press, 1926 £20/£5

A Conversation with an Angel, Jonathan Cape, 1928 . . . . £20/£5

Conversations with a Cat, Cassell, 1930 . £25/£10

ditto, Harper & Brothers (U.S.), 1931 . . £20/£5

Essays of a Catholic, Sheed & Ward, 1931 £15/£5

Nine Nines, Blackwell, 1931 . . . . . £15/£5

An Essay on the Restoration of Property, Distributist League, 1936 . . . . £10

An Essay on the Nature of Contemporary England, Constable, 1937 . . . . £15/£5

The Silence of the Sea, Sheed & Ward (U.S.), 1940 . . . . £15/£5

ditto, Cassell, 1941 . . . . . . £15/£5

Others

Lambkin's Remains, by 'H.B.', J.C.R. 1900. . £100

The Great Inquiry, Duckworth, 1903 . . . £30

A Pamphlet, 1930, privately printed (for Belloc's 60th birthday) £65

On Translation, Clarendon Press, 1931 . . £30/£15

The Issue, Sheed & Ward, 1937 . . . . £15/£5

The Question and the Answer, Longman's Green, 1938 . . . . £15/£5

The Test in Poland, Weekly Review, 1939 . . £10

SAUL BELLOW

(b.1915)

American novelist, and recipient of the Nobel Prize for Literature in 1976, Bellow's writings frequently address the problems of those living in urban areas, and their place in the modern world.

Novels

Dangling Man, Vanguard Press (U.S.), 1944 £200/£75

ditto, Lehmann, 1946 . . . . £125/£35

The Victim, Vanguard Press (U.S.), 1945 . £75/£25

ditto, Lehmann, 1948 . . . . £75/£25

The Adventures of Augie March, Viking (U.S.), 1953. . . . . £50/£20

ditto, Weidenfeld, 1954 . . . . . . £40/£15

Seize the Day, with Three Short Stories and a One Act Play, Viking (U.S.), 1956 . . . . . £50/£15

ditto, Weidenfeld, 1957 . . . . . . £40/£15

Henderson the Rain King, Viking (U.S.), 1959 . . . . £30/£10

ditto, Weidenfeld, 1959 . . . . . . £30/£10

Herzog, Viking (U.S.), 1964 . . . . . £45/£15

ditto, Weidenfeld, 1965 . . . . . . £20/£5

Mr Sammler's Planet, Viking (U.S.), 1970 . £20/£5

ditto, Weidenfeld, 1970 . . . . . . £15/£5

Humboldt's Gift, Viking (U.S.), 1975 . . £20/£5

ditto, Alison Press/Secker & Warburg, 1975 £20/£5

The Dean's December, Harper (U.S.), 1982 £10/£5

ditto, Harper, 1982 (500 signed copies, glassine wrapper, slipcase) .. . . £75/£65

ditto, Secker & Warburg, 1982 . . . . . £10/£5

More Die of Heartbreak, Morrow (U.S.), 1987 £10/£5

ditto, Alison Press, 1987 . . . . £10/£5

Short Stories

Mosby's Memoirs and Other Stories, Viking (U.S.), 1968 . . . . £44/£15
ditto, Weidenfeld, 1969 . . . . £10/£5
Him with His Foot in His Mouth and Other Stories, Harper (U.S.), 1984 . . . . £10/£5
ditto, Secker & Warburg, 1984 . . . . . £10/£5
A Theft, Penguin, 1989 (wraps) £10
The Bellarosa Connection, Penguin (U.S.), 1989 (wraps) £10
ditto, Penguin , 1989 (wraps) £10
Something to Remember Me By, Secker & Warburg, 1992 . . . . £10/£5

Plays

The Last Analysis, Viking (U.S.), 1965 . . £60/£25
ditto, Weidenfeld, 1966 . . . . £15/£5

Others

To Jerusalem and Back, Viking (U.S.), 1976 £10/£5
ditto, Secker & Warburg, 1976 . . . . . £10/£5
The Nobel Lecture, U.S. Information Service (Stockholm), 1977 . . . . £35
ditto, Targ editions (U.S.), 1979 (350 signed copies, tissue wraps) . . . . £75/£65
It All Adds Up, Penguin (U.S.), 1994 . . £10/£5
ditto, Secker & Warburg, 1994 . . . . £10/£5

ALAN BENNETT

(b.1934)

An actor and playwright, Alan Bennett's quiet, self-effacing style has been as popular with television audiences as it has with the readers of his books.

Plays

Beyond the Fringe, Souvenir Press, 1963 . £40/£10
ditto, French (U.S.), 1964 (wraps) £10
Forty Years On, Faber, 1969 . . . . . . £45/£15
Getting On, Faber, 1971 . . . . . . £20/£5
ditto, Faber, 1971 (wraps). £5
Habeas Corpus, Faber, 1973 . . . . . . £20/£5
ditto, Faber, 1973 (wraps). £5
The Old Country, Faber, 1978 (wraps) £10
Enjoy, Faber, 1980 (wraps) £10
Office Suite: Two One-Act Plays, Faber, 1981 (wraps) £15
Objects of Affection, BBC, 1983 (wraps) . . £10
The Writer in Disguise, Faber, 1985. . . £5/£10
Two Kafka Plays, Faber, 1987 (wraps) . . . £5
Talking Heads, BBC, 1987 (wraps) £5
ditto, as ***Single Spies and Talking Heads***, Summit (U.S.), 1989 . . . . £15/£5

Screenplays

A Private Function, Faber, 1985 (wraps) £5
Prick Up Your Ears, Faber, 1987 (wraps) . . . £5
The Madness of King George, Faber, 1992 (wraps) £5
ditto, Random House (U.S.), 1995 . . . . £10/£5

Others

Writing Home, Faber, 1994 . . . . . . £10/£5
ditto, Random House (U.S.), 1995 . . . . £10/£5

ARNOLD BENNETT

(b.1867 d.1931)

Born in the Staffordshire Potteries, this novelist, short story writer, playwright and journalist's reputation today rests principally on his novels about the lives of ordinary people.

A Man from the North, John Lane, 1898 . . £100
Polite Farces for the Drawing Room, Lamley, 1900 . . . . £40
Anna of the Five Towns, Chatto & Windus, 1902 £100
The Grand Babylon Hotel, Chatto & Windus, 1902 . . . . £25
The Gates of Wrath, Chatto & Windus, 1903 . £40
Leonora, Chatto & Windus, 1903 . . . . £35
A Great Man, Chatto & Windus, 1904 . . . £25
Teresa of Watling Street, Chatto & Windus, 1904 £20
Sacred and Profane Love, Chatto & Windus, 1905 £25
Hugo, Chatto & Winds, 1906 . . . . . £25
The Sinews of War (with Eden Philpotts), T. Werner Laurie, 1906 . . . . £35
Whom God Hath Joined, David Nutt, 1906 . £10
The City of Pleasure, Chatto & Windus, 1907 . £10
The Ghost: A Fantasia on Modern Times, Chatto & Windus, 1907. . . . . £25
The Grim Smile of the Five Towns, Chatto & Windus, 1908 . . . . £25
Buried Alive, Chapman & Hall, 1908 . . . £20
The Old Wives' Tale, Chapman & Hall, 1908 . £50
ditto, Ernest Benn, 1927 (500 signed copies, 2 vols, slipcase) £100
The Statue (with Eden Philpotts), Cassell, 1908 £20
The Glimpse: An Adventure of the Soul, Chapman & Hall, 1909 . . . . £15
Cupid and Commonsense, New Age Press, 1909 £10
What the Public Wants, Duckworth, 1909 . . £10
Clayhanger, Methuen, 1910 . . . . . . £30
Helen with the High Hand, Chapman & Hall, 1910 . . . . £10

The Card, Methuen, 1911 . . . . £15
Hilda Lessways, Methuen, 1911 . . . . . £30
The Honeymoon, Methuen, 1911 . . . . £10
The Matador of the Five Towns, Methuen, 1912 £10
Milestones (with Edward Knoblauch), Methuen, 1912 . . . . £10
The Regent, Methuen, 1913 . . . . £20
The Great Adventure, Methuen, 1913 . . . £10
The Price of Love, Methuen, 1914 . . . . £20
These Twain, Methuen, 1916. . . . . £95/£15
The Lion's Share, Cassell, 1916 . . . . £95/£15
The Pretty Lady, Cassell, 1918 . . . . £95/£15
The Roll Call, Hutchinson, 1918. . . . £85/£10
The Title, Chatto & Windus, 1918 . . . £85/£10
Judith, Chatto & Windus, 1919 . . . . £85/£10
Lilian, Cassell, 1922 . . . . £75/£10
Mr Prohack, Methuen, 1922 . . . . . £65/£10
The Love Match, Chatto & Windus, 1922 . £45/£10
Body and Soul, Chatto & Windus, 1922. . £45/£10
Riceyman Steps, Cassell, 1923 . . . . . £75/£15
ditto, Doran (U.S.), 1923 . . . . £30/£10
Don Juan de Marana, T. Werner Laurie, 1923 (1,000 signed copies) . . . . £50/£35
The Bright Island, Golden Cockerel Press, 1924 (200 signed copies) £60
London Life (with Edward Knoblauch), Chatto & Windus, 1924. . . . . £45/£10
The Clayhanger Family, Methuen, 1925 . £45/£10
ditto, Methuen, 1925 (200 signed copies) . . £60
Lord Riango, Cassell, 1926 . . . . . . £30/£10
The Strange Vanguard, Cassell, 1929 . . £30/£10
Piccadilly, Readers Library Publishing Co., 1929 . . . £30/£10
Imperial Palace, Cassell, 1930 . . . . £30/£10
ditto, Cassell, 1930 (100 signed copies, 2 vols) . £150
Venus Rising from the Sea, Cassell, 1931 (350 numbered copies, in slipcase) £60
ditto, Cassell, 1932 . . . . £25/£10
Dream of Destiny, Cassell, 1932. . . . . £25/£10
Flora, Rich & Cowan, 1933 . . . . . . £25/£10
The Snake Charmer, Rich & Cowan, 1933 . £25/£10

E.F. BENSON
(b.1867 d.1940)

Benson's first book, *Dodo* was a huge success. Known for his light society novels, especially the 'Mapp and Lucia' series and also his supernatural fiction, of which *The Room in the Tower* is perhaps the most highly regarded.

Novels
Dodo: A Detail of Today, Methuen, 1893 (2 vols) £100
The Rubicon, Methuen, 1894 (2 vols) £40
The Judgement Books, Osgood McIlvaine, 1895 £30
Limitations, Innes, 1896 . . . . £30
ditto, Harpers (U.S.), 1896 . . . . £25
The Babe, B.A., Putnams (U.S.), 1896 . . . . £30
ditto, Putnams, 1897 . . . . £20
The Vintage, Methuen, 1898 . . . . £30
The Money Market, Arrowsmith, 1898 . . . . £30
The Capsina, Methuen, 1899. . . . . £30
Mammon and Co., Heinemann, 1899 . . . £30
The Princess Sophia, Heinemann, 1900. . . £25
The Luck of the Vails, Heinemann, 1901 . . £35
Scarlet and Hyssop, Heinemann, 1902 . . . £20
The Book of Months, Heinemann, 1903. . . £20
ditto, Harper & Bros (U.S.) 1903. . . . . £15
An Act in a Backwater, Heinemann, 1903 . . £20
The Valkyries, Dean, 1903 . . . . £20
The Relentless City, Heinemann. 1903 . . . £20
ditto, Harper & Bros (U.S.) 1903. . . . . £20
The Challoners, Heinemann, 1904 . . . . £20
ditto, A.L. Burt Co (U.S.), 1904 . . . . . £15
The Image in the Sand, Heinemann, 1905 . . £25
The Angel of Pain, Lippincott (Philadelphia), 1905 . . . . £25
ditto, Heinemann, 1906 . . . . £20
Paul, Heinemann, 1906 . . . . £40
The House of Defense, Macleod & Allen, 1906 £20
ditto, Authors and Newspapers Association (U.S.), 1906 . . . . £15
Sheaves, Stanley Paul, 1907 . . . . £20
The Blotting Book, Heinemann, 1908 . . . £20
ditto, Doubleday (U.S.), 1908 . . . . . . £20
The Climber, Heinemann, 1908 . . . . . . £20
A Reaping, Heinemann, 1909 . . . . . . £20
Daisy's Aunt, Nelson, 1910 . . . . £40
The Osbornes, Smith Elder, 1910 . . . . . £20
Margery, Doubleday (U.S.), 1910 . . . . . £20
ditto, as ***Juggernaut***, Heinemann, 1911 . . . £20
Account Rendered, Heinemann, 1911 . . . . £20
Mrs Ames, Hodder & Stoughton, 1912 . . . . £20
The Weaker Vessel, Heinemann, 1913 . . . . £20
Thorley Weir, Heinemann, 1913 . . . . . . £20
Dodo's Daughter: A Sequel to Dodo, Century Co. (U.S.), 1913 . . . . £20
ditto, as ***Dodo the Second***, Hodder & Stoughton, 1914 . . . . £20
Arundel, Unwin, 1914 . . . . £20
The Oakleyites, Hodder & Stoughton, 1915 . £20
David Blaize, Hodder & Stoughton, 1916 . . £20
Mike, Cassell, 1916 . . . . £20
The Freaks of Mayfair, Foulis, 1916 . . . . £45
ditto, Doran (U.S.), [1918] £30
Mr Teddy, Unwin, 1917 . . . . £15
An Autumn Sowing, Collins, 1917 . . . . . £15
David Blaize and the Blue Door, Hodder & Stoughton,

1918 . . . . £15
Up and Down, Hutchinson, 1918 . . . . £15
Across the Stream, John Murray, 1919 . . £45/£15
ditto, Doran (U.S.), 1919 . . . . £35/£15
Robin Linnet, Hutchinson, 1919 . . . . £35/£15
Queen Lucia, Hutchinson, 1920 . . . . £45/£15
Dodo Wonders, Hutchinson, 1921 . . . £35/£15
Lovers and Friends, Unwin, 1921 . . . £35/£15
Miss Mapp, Hutchinson, 1922 . . . . £35/£15
Peter, Cassell, 1922 . . . . £30/£10
Colin: A Novel, Hutchinson, [1923] . . . £30/£10
David of King's, Hodder & Stoughton, 1924 £30/£10
Alan, Unwin, 1924 . . . . £30/£10
Colin II, Hutchinson, [1925] . . . . . £30/£10
Rex, Hodder & Stoughton. 1925 . . . . £30/£10
Mezzanine, Cassell, 1926 . . . . . . £30/£10
Pharisees and Publicans, Hutchinson, 1926 £30/£10
Lucia in London, Hutchinson, 1927 . . . £30/£10
Paying Guests, Hutchinson, 1929 . . . £30/£10
The Inheritor, Hutchinson, [1930] . . . £45/£15
ditto, Doran (U.S.), 1930 . . . . £45/£15
Mapp & Lucia, Hodder & Stoughton, 1931 . £45/£15
Secret Lives, Hodder & Stoughton, 1932 . £30/£10
Travail of Gold, Hodder & Stoughton, 1933 £25/£10
Raven's Brood, Arthur Barker, 1934 . . £35/£10
ditto, Doran (U.S.), 1934 . . . . . . £25/£10
Lucia's Progress, Hodder & Stoughton, 1935 £250/£75
All About Lucia, Doubleday (U.S.), 1936 (the first four Lucia novels in one vol.) . . . . . £25/£10
Old London, Appleton-Century, 1937, (4 vols. in dust wrappers slipcase) . . . . £50/£20
Trouble for Lucia, Hodder & Stoughton, 1939 . . . . £200/£45
ditto, Doran (U.S.), 1939 . . . . £100/£35

Short Stories
Six Common Things, Osgood McIlvaine, 1893 £25
A Double Overture, C.H. Sergel (U.S.), 1894 £20
The Countess of Lowndes Square and Other Stories, Cassell, 1920 . . . . £300/£100
The Male Impersonator, Elkin Mathews & Marrot, 1929 (530 signed copies) . . . . . £45/£25
Desirable Residences, O.U.P., 1991 . . . £10/£5
Fine Feathers, O.U.P., 1994 . . . . . £10/£5

Ghost Stories
The Room in the Tower, Mills & Boon, [1912] £100
Visible and Invisible, Hutchinson, 1923 . . £250/£75
ditto, Doran (U.S.), 1924 . . . . . . £200/£75
'And the Dead Spake' & The Horror Horn, Doran (U.S.), 1923 . . . . £75/£25
Expiation & Naboth's Vineyard, Doran (U.S.), 1924 . . . . £75/£25
The Face, Doran (U.S.), 1924 . . . . £100/£35
The Temple, Doran (U.S.), 1925 . . . . £75/£25
A Tale of an Empty House & Bagnell Terrace, Doran (U.S.), 1925 . . . . £75/£25
ditto, as ***The Tale of an Empty House***, Black Swan/Corgi, 1985 (wraps) £5
ditto, Black Swan/Corgi, 1986 (limited edition hardback) . . . . £25/£10
Spook Stories, Hutchinson, [1928] . . . . £225/£75
The Step, H.V. Marrot, 1930 . . . . £100/£35
More Spook Stories, Hutchinson, [1934] . £225/£75
The Horror Horn, Panther, 1974 (wraps) . . £5
The Flint Knife, Equation, 1988 (wraps) . . £15

Collaborations with Eustace Miles
Daily Training, Hurst & Blackett, 1902 . . . . £30
Cricket of Abel, Hirst and Shrewsbury, Hurst & Blackett, 1903 . . . . £65
The Mad Annual, Grant Richards, 1903 . . . £30
A Book of Golf, Hurst Blackett, 1903 . . . . £30
Diversions Day by Day, Hurst & Blackett, 1905 £30

Non Fiction
Sketches from Marlborough, 1888 (anonymous) £100
English Figure-Skating, Bell, 1908 . . . . £25
Winter Sports in Switzerland, George Allen, 1913 £45
Skating Calls, Bell, 1909 . . . . £20
Deutschland Uber Allah, Hodder & Stoughton, 1917 . . . . £15
Crescent and Iron Cross, Hodder & Stoughton, 1918 . . . . £25
The White Eagle of Poland, Hodder & Stoughton, 1918 . . . . £25
ditto, Doran (U.S.), 1919 . . . . £45/£25
Poland and Mittel-Europa, Hodder & Stoughton, 1918 . . . . £25/£10
The Social Value of Temperance, True Temperance Association, 1919 . . . . £15
Our Family Affairs, 1867-1896, Cassell, 1920 £25£10
Mother, Hodder & Stoughton, 1925 . . . £25/£10
Sir Frances Drake, John Lane the Bodley Head, 1927. . . . . £25/£10
ditto, Harper (U.S.), 1927 . . . . . . £20/£10
The Life of Alcibiades, Ernest Benn, 1928 . £35/£10
Ferdinand Magellan, John Lane the Bodley Head, 1929 . . . . £25/£10
ditto, Harper (U.S.), 1930 . . . . . £20/£10
Henry James: Letters to A.C. Benson/Auguste Monod, Elkin Mathews & Marrot, 1930 (1,050 numbered copies) £20
As We Were: A Victorian Peepshow, Longmans, 1930 . . . . £25/£10
As We Are: A Modern Revue, Longmans, 1932 . . . . £25/£10
Charlotte Brontë, Longmans, 1932 . . . £25/£10
King Edward VII, Longmans, 1933 . . . £25/£10
The Outbreak of War, Peter Davies, 1933 . £50/£20

Queen Victoria, Longmans (U.S.), 1935 . £25/£10
ditto, Longmans, 1935. . . . . . . £20/£10
The Kaiser and English Relations, Longmans, 1934 . . . . £20/£10
Queen Victoria's Daughters, Appleton-Century (U.S.), 1938 . . . . £20/£10
ditto, as ***Daughters of Queen Victoria***, Cassell, 1939 . . . . £20/£10
Final Edition: An Informal Autobiography, Longmans, 1940 . . . . £20/£10
ditto, Appleton-Century (U.S.), 1940 . . £20/£10

Others
Bensoniana: Maxims by E.F. Benson, Siegle Hill Watteau, 1912 . . . . £40
ditto, A.L. Humphreys, 1912 . . . . £40
Thoughts from E.F. Benson, Harrap, 1913 . £30
Thoughts from E.F. Benson, Holden & Hardingham, 1916 (leather bound). £75
ditto, Holden & Hardingham, 1916 (cloth bound) £25

LORD BERNERS
(b.1883 d.1950)

Millionaire, composer, author and eccentric.

Fiction
The Camel, Constable, 1936 . . . . . . £75/£35
The Girls of Radcliff Hall, privately published, 1937 (wraps) £80
Far from the Madding War, Constable, 1941 £65/£25
Count Omega, Constable 1941 . . . . £75/£35
Percy Wallingford and Mr Pidger, Blackwell, 1941 (wraps) £45
The Romance of a Nose, Constable, 1941 . £65/£25

Autobiography
First Childhood, Constable, 1934 . . . £75/£45
A Distant Prospect, Constable, 1945 . . £35/£10

Music
Intermezzo from "The Triumph of Neptune", J. & W. Chester, Ltd, 1927 (quarto, wraps) . . £75
Three Songs in the German Manner, J. & W. Chester, Ltd, [n.d.] (quarto, wraps) £95
Luna Park - Fantastic Ballet in One Act, J. & W. Chester, Ltd, [n.d., c.1930] (quarto, wraps) . £150
Trois Chansons, J. & W. Chester, Ltd, 1920 (quarto, wraps). £85
Suite from The Triumph of Neptune, J. & W. Chester, Ltd, [n.d.] (quarto, wraps) £50

JOHN BETJEMAN
(b.1906 d.1984)

As a broadcasting personality, commenting on the superficial and the middle class, Betjeman somehow missed serious recognition for his verse during his lifetime, despite becoming Poet Laureate in 1972.

Verse
Mount Zion or In Touch with the Infinite, James Press, [1931] £600
Continual Dew, John Murray, 1937 . . . £150/£45
Sir John Piers by 'Epsilon', Mullingar (Ireland), 1938, (150 copies) £250
Old Lights for New Chancels, John Murray, 1940 . . . . £60/£25
New Bats in Old Belfries, John Murray, 1945 £40/£20
Slick, But not Streamlined, Doubleday (U.S.), 1947 (ed W.H. Auden) . . . . £65/£15
Selected Poems, John Murray, 1948 . . . £45/£15
ditto, John Murray, 1948 (18 copies). . . . £250
A Few Late Chrysanthemums, John Murray, 1954 . . . . £25/£10
Poems in the Porch, SPCK, 1954 (wraps) . . £15
John Betjeman: A Selection, Edward Hulton Pocket Poets, 1958, (wraps) £5
Collected Poems, John Murray, 1958 . . £40/£15
ditto, John Murray, 1958 (100 signed copies) . £175
ditto, Houghton Mifflin (U.S.), 1959. . . £15/£5
Summoned by Bells, John Murray, 1960 . £20/£10
ditto, John Murray, 1960 (125 signed, numbered copies) £250
ditto, Houghton Mifflin (U.S.), 1960. . . £15/£5
A Ring of Bells, John Murray, 1962 . . £15/£5
ditto, Houghton Mifflin (U.S.), 1963. . . £15/£5
High and Low, John Murray, 1966 . . £15/£5
ditto, John Murray, 1966 (100 signed copies) £200
ditto, Houghton Mifflin (U.S.), 1967. . . £10/£5
Six Betjeman Songs, Duckworth, 1967 (wraps) £20
A Wembley Lad and The Crem, Poem of the Month Club, 1971 (signed broadsheet) £75
A Nip in the Air, John Murray, 1974 . . £15/£5
ditto, John Murray, 1974 (175 copies, signed by the author) £175
ditto, Norton (U.S.), [1974] . . . . . £10/£5
Betjeman in Miniature, Selected Poems, 1976 . £10
The Best of Betjeman, John Murray, 1978 £10/£5
Church Poems, John Murray, 1981 (first issue, withdrawn) . . . . £85/£40
ditto, John Murray, 1981 (second issue) . . £20/£5
ditto, John Murray, 1981 (100 copies, signed by the author and John Piper) £175
Uncollected Poems, John Murray, 1982. . £10/£5
Betjeman's Cornwall, John Murray, 1984 . £10/£5
Ah Middlesex, Warren, 1984 (250 copies) . . £30

Prose

Ghastly Good Taste, Chapman & Hall, 1933 . £150

ditto, Chapman & Hall, 1933 (200 signed copies in a slipcase) £250

Cornwall Illustrated in a series of views, Architectural Press, 1934 . . . . £45

Devon, Architectural Press, 1936 . . . . £45

An Oxford University Chest, John Miles, 1938 . . . . £125/£35

A Handbook on Paint, with Hugh Casson, Silicate Paint Co., 1939 (wraps) £50

Antiquarian Prejudice, Hogarth Sixpenny Pamphlets No. 3, 1939 (card wraps) £30

Vintage London, Collins, 1942 . . . . . £25

English Cities and Small Towns, Britain in Pictures/ Collins, 1943 . . . . £20/£5

John Piper, Penguin Modern Painters, 1944, (wraps) £15

Murray's Buckinghamshire Architectural Guide, John Murray, 1949 (edited with John Piper) . . £30/£5

Murray's Berkshire Architectural Guide, John Murray, 1949 (edited with John Piper) . . £30/£5

Shropshire, Faber Shell Guide, 1951 . . £25/£10

The English Scene, CUP/NBL, 1951 (wraps) . £5

First and Last Loves, John Murray, 1952 . £30/£5

The English Town in the Last Hundred Years, CUP, 1956 (Rede Lecture, wraps) £5

Collins Guide to English Parish Churches, Collins, 1958 . . . . £25/£5

Ground Plan to Skyline (pseud. 'Richard M. Farran'), Newman Neame, 1960 . . . . £25

English Churches, with Basil Clarke, Studio Vista, 1964 . . . . £15/£5

The City of London Churches, Pitkin Pictorial, 1965 (wraps) £5

Victorian and Edwardian London from Old Photographs, Batsford, 1969 . . . . £15/£5

ditto, Viking (U.S.), 1969 . . . . £10

Ten Wren Churches, Editions Elector, 1970 (100 copies, folder) £150

Victorian and Edwardian Oxford from Old Photographs, with David Vaisey, Batsford, 1971 . . . . £15/£5

Victorian and Edwardian Brighton from Old Photographs, with J. S. Gray, Batsford, 1972 £15/£5

London's Historic Railway Stations, John Murray, 1972 . . . . £25/£5

A Pictorial History of English Architecture, John Murray, 1972 . . . . £20/£5

ditto, John Murray, 1972 (100 signed copies, slipcase). . . . . £200/£190

ditto, Macmillan (U.S.), 1972. . . . . . £10/£5

West Country Churches, Society of Saints Peter & Paul, 1973 (wraps) £20

Victorian and Edwardian Cornwall from Old Photographs, with A. L. Rowse, Batsford, 1974 . . . . £15/£5

Archie and the Strict Baptists, John Murray, 1977 . . . . £20/£5

ditto, Lippincott (U.S.), 1978 . . . . . £15/£5

Metroland, BBC Publications, 1977 . . . . . £10

Ode on the Marriage of H.R.H. Prince Charles to Lady Diana Spencer, Warren Editions, 1981 (125 signed copies, broadsheet) £75

ALGERNON BLACKWOOD

(b.1869 d.1951)

Important British writer of supernatural fiction, Blackwood mined all aspects of the genre, and towards the end of his life became something of a radio and television personality.

Novels

Jimbo: A Fantasy, Macmillan, 1909 . . . £50

The Education of Uncle Paul, Macmillan, 1909 £45

ditto, Holt (U.S.), 1914 . . . . £20

The Human Chord, Macmillan, 1910 . . . £45

The Centaur, Macmillan, 1911 . . . . . . £50

A Prisoner in Fairyland, Macmillan, 1913 . . £30

The Extra Day, Macmillan, 1915 . . . . £30

Julius Levallon, Cassell, 1916 . . . . . £30

ditto, Dutton (U.S.), 1916 . . . . £25

The Wave: An Egyptian Aftermath, Macmillan, 1916. . . . . £30

ditto, Dutton (U.S.), 1916 . . . . £20

The Promise of Air, Macmillan, 1918 . . £75/£30

ditto, Dutton (U.S.), 1918 . . . . . . £50/£15

The Garden of Survival, Macmillan, 1918 . £75/£30

ditto, Dutton (U.S.), 1918 . . . . . . £45/£15

The Bright Messenger, Cassell, 1921 . . £65/£30

Short Story Collections

The Empty House and Other Ghost Stories, Nash, 1906 . . . . £250

The Listener and Other Stories, Nash, 1907 . £125

ditto, Vaughan & Gomme (U.S.), 1914 (limited to 500 copies) £100

John Silence, Physician Extraordinary, Nash, 1908 . . . . £250

ditto, John W. Luce (U.S.), 1909 . . . . £150

The Lost Valley and Other Stories, Nash, 1910 £150

Pan's Garden, A Volume of Nature Stories, Macmillan, 1912 . . . . £75

Incredible Adventures, Macmillan, 1914 . . £75

Ten Minute Stories, Murray, 1914 . . . . £75

Day and Night Stories, Cassell, 1917 . . . £75

ditto, Dutton, 1917. . . . . £75/£35

The Wolves of God, Cassell, 1921 (with Wilfrid Wilson) . . . . £250/£50
Tongues of Fire and Other Sketches, Jenkins, 1924 . . . . £250/£50
ditto, Dutton, 1925. . . . . £75/£35
The Willows and Other Queer Tales, Collins, [1925] . . . . £200/£45
Ancient Sorceries and Other Tales, Collins, [1927] . . . . £100/£30
The Dance of Death and Other Tales, Jenkins, 1927 . . . . £75/£25
ditto, Dial Press (U.S.), 1928 . . . . £20
Strange Stories, Heinemann, 1929 . . . . £35/£10
ditto, as ***The Best Supernatural Tales of Algernon Blackwood***, Causeway Books (U.S.), 1973 (abridged facsimile of above edition) . . . . . . £10/£5
Full Circle, Mathews & Marrot, 1929 (530 signed, numbered copies) . . . . £45/£25
Short Stories of Today and Yesterday, Harrap & Co, 1930 . . . . £20/£10
Shocks, Grayson, 1935 . . . . £30/£10
The Tales of Algernon Blackwood, Secker, 1938 . . . . £25/£10
Selected Tales of Algernon Blackwood, Penguin, 1942 . . . . £10
Selected Short Stories of Algernon Blackwood, Armed Services Editions (U.S.), [1942], ... £20
The Doll and One Other, Arkham House (Sauk City, U.S.), 1946 . . . . £45/£20
Tales of the Uncanny and Supernatural, Nevill, 1949 . . . . £15/£5
In the Realm of Terror, Pantheon Books (U.S.), 1957 . . . . £5
Selected Tales of Algernon Blackwood, John Baker, 1964 . . . . £10/£5
Tales of the Mysterious and Macabre, Spring Books, 1967 . . . . £10/£5

Children's Books
Sambo and Snitch, Blackwell, 1927. . . . . £60
Mr Cupboard, Blackwell, 1928 . . . . . . £50
Dudley and Gilderoy: A Nonsense, Benn, 1929 . . . . £25/£10
ditto, Dutton (U.S.), 1929. . . . . £20/£10
By Underground, Blackwell, 1930 . . . . £45
The Parrot and the Cat, Blackwell, 1931 . . . £45
The Italian Conjuror, Blackwell, 1932 . . . £45
Maria (Of England) In the Rain, Blackwell, 1933 £45
Sergeant Poppett and Policeman James, Blackwell, 1934 . . . . £45
The Fruit Stoners, Grayson, [1934] . . . £35/£20
ditto, Dutton (U.S.), 1935. . . . . . . £20/£10
ditto, Blackwell, 1935 (extract) £30
How the Circus Came to Tea, Blackwell, 1936 £45
The Adventures of Dudley and Gilderoy, Dutton, 1941 (adapted by Marion B. Cottren) . . . £20/£10

Plays
Karma: A Reincarnation Play, Macmillan, 1918 (with Violet Pearn) £15
ditto, Dutton (U.S.), 1918 . . . . £15
Through the Crack, Samuel French, 1925 (with Violet Pearn) £15

Other Works
Episodes Before Thirty, Cassell, 1923 . . . £25
ditto, Dutton (U.S.), 1924 . . . . £20
Adventures Before Thirty, Cape, 1934 . . . £15

CHRISTOPHER BLAYRE

(b.1861 d.1943)

Pseudonym used by Edward Herron-Allen, a scientist and polymath whose scholarly writings range from hard sciences to the occult. He wrote several entertaining works of weird fiction which are highly sought after by collectors.

The Purple Sapphire and other Posthumous Papers, Allan, [1921] . . . . £100/£45
ditto, as ***The Strange Papers of Dr. Blayre***, Allan, 1932 . . . . £75/£35
The Cheetah-Girl, privately printed, 1923 (20 copies). £1,500
ditto, Tartarus Press, 1998 (99 copies) . . £75/£45
Some Women of the University, Sorelle Nessuno, Nubiana [Stockwell], 1934 (100 copies) . . £450
The Collected Strange Papers of Christopher Blayre, Tartarus Press, 1998 . . . . £25/£15

ROBERT BLOCH

(b.1917 d.1994)

Author of horror and crime stories, often underlain by a black humour. *Psycho* became the best known of his novels following Hitchcock's classic film.

Novels
The Scarf, Dial Press (U.S.), 1947 . . . £100/£35
ditto, New English Library, 1972 (wraps) . . £5
The Will to Kill, Ace (U.S.), 1954 (wraps) . . £10
The Kidnapper, Lion (U.S.), 1954 (wraps) . . £10
Spiderweb, Ace (U.S.), 1954 (wraps) . . . £10
Shooting Star, Ace (U.S.), 1958 (wraps) . . £10
Psycho, Simon & Schuster (U.S.), 1959 . . £125/£35
ditto, Robert Hale, 1960 . . . . . . £25/£10

The Dead Beat, Simon & Schuster (U.S.), 1960 . . . £10/£5
ditto, Robert Hale, 1971 . . . . £10/£5
Firebug, Regency (U.S.), 1961 (wraps) . . . £10
ditto, Corgi, 1977 (wraps). £5
The Couch, Fawcett (U.S.), 1962 (wraps) . . £5
ditto, Frederick Muller, 1962 . . . . . £10/£5
Terror, Belmont (U.S.), 1962 (wraps) . . . £5
ditto, Corgi, 1964 (wraps). £5
Ladies' Day/This Crowded Earth, Belmont (U.S.), 1968 (wraps) £5
The Star Stalker, Pyramid (U.S.), 1968 (wraps) £5
The Todd Dossier, Delacorte (U.S.), 1969 (pseud. 'Collier Young') . . . . £35/£10
ditto, Macmillan, 1969 (pseud. 'Collier Young') . . £30/£10
It's All In Your Mind, Curtis (U.S.), 1971 (wraps) £5
Sneak Preview, Paperback Library (U.S.), 1971 (wraps) £5
Night World, Simon & Schuster (U.S.), 1972 £25/£10
ditto, Robert Hale, 1974 . . . . £20/£5
American Gothic, Simon & Schuster (U.S.), 1974 . £20/£5
ditto, W. H. Allen, 1975 . . . . £10/£5
Strange Eons, Whispers Press (U.S.), 1978 [1979] . £20/£5
ditto, Whispers Press (U.S.), 1978 [1979] (300 signed copies, slipcase) . . . . £75/£50
There is a Serpent in Eden, Zebra Books, 1979 (wraps) £5
Psycho II, Warner Books (U.S.), 1982 (wraps) £5
ditto, Whispers Press (U.S.), 1982 . . . £20/£10
ditto, Whispers Press (U.S.), 1982 (750 signed, numbered copies, slipcase) . . . . . £75/£65
ditto, Whispers Press (U.S.), 1982 (26 signed, lettered copies, slipcase) . . . . £250/£240
ditto, Corgi, 1983 (wraps). £5
Twilight Zone - The Movie, Warner Books (U.S.), 1983 (wraps) £5
ditto, Transworld, 1983 (wraps) £5
Night of the Ripper, Robert Hale, 1986 . . £10/£5
ditto, Doubleday (U.S.), 1984 . . . . £10/£5
Unholy Trinity, Scream Press, 1986 . . . £25/£10
ditto, Scream Press (U.S.), 1986 (500 signed, numbered copies, slipcase) £75
Lori, Tor (U.S.), 1989. . . . . £10/£5
Screams, Underwood/Miller, 1989 . . . £25/£10
ditto, Underwood/Miller, 1989, (300 signed copies, slipcase) . . . . £50/£40
Psycho III: The Psycho House, Tor (U.S.), 1990 £10

Short Stories

Sea Kissed, Utopian Publications, [1945], (wraps) £50
The Opener of the Way, Arkham House (U.S.), 1945 . . . . £200/£65
ditto, Neville Spearman, 1974 . . . . . £10/£5
Terror in the Night, Ace (U.S.), 1958 (wraps) £10
Pleasant Dreams, Arkham House (U.S.), 1960 . . £75/£25
ditto, Whiting & Wheaton, 1967 . . . . . £20/£5
Blood Runs Cold, Simon and Schuster (U.S.), 1961 . £45/£10
ditto, Robert Hale, 1963 . . . . £10/£5
Nightmares, Belmont Books (U.S.), 1961 (wraps) £5
Atoms and Evil, Fawcett (U.S.), 1962 (wraps) £5
ditto, Frederick Muller, 1963 (wraps) . . . £5
ditto, Hale, 1976 (hardback) . . . . . £15/£5
More Nightmares, Belmont Books (U.S.), [1962] (wraps) £5
Yours Truly, Jack the Ripper, Belmont Books (U.S.), [1962] (wraps) £5
ditto, as ***The House of the Hatchet***, Tandem, 1965 (wraps) £5
Horror-7, Belmont (U.S.), 1963 (wraps) . . £5
ditto, Four Square, 1965 (wraps) £5
Bogey Men: Ten Tales, Pyramid Books (U.S.), 1963 (wraps) £5
Tales in a Jugular Vein, Pyramid Books (U.S.), 1965 (wraps) £5
ditto, Sphere, 1970 (wraps) £5
The Skull of the Marquis de Sade, Pyramid Books (U.S.), 1965 (wraps) £5
ditto, Robert Hale, 1975 . . . . £10/£5
Chamber of Horrors, Award (U.S.), 1966 (wraps) £5
ditto, Corgi, 1977 (wraps). £5
The Living Demons, Belmont Books, 1967 (wraps) £5
ditto, Sphere, 1970 (wraps) £5
Dragons and Nightmares, Mirage Press (U.S.), 1968 (1,000 copies) . . . . £40/£15
Bloch and Bradbury, Tower (U.S.), 1969 (wraps) £5
ditto, Sphere, 1970 (wraps) £5
Fear Today, Gone Tomorrow, Award (U.S.), 1971 (wraps) £5
The King of Terrors, Mysterious Press (U.S.), 1977 (250 signed copies, slipcase) . . . . £50/£40
ditto, Robert Hale, 1978 . . . . . . £10/£5
Cold Chills, Doubleday (U.S.), 1977 . . £20/£10
ditto, Robert Hale, 1978 . . . . £10/£5
The Best of Robert Bloch, Ballantine (U.S.), 1977 (wraps) £5
Out of the Mouths of Graves, Mysterious Press (U.S.), 1978 . . . . £10/£5
ditto, Mysterious Press (U.S.), 1978 (250 signed copies, slipcase) . . . . £50/£45
Such Stuff As Screams Are Made Of, Ballantine (U.S.), 1978 (wraps) £5
The Selected Stories of Robert Bloch, Underwood/ Muller (U.S.), 1987 (3 vols, 500 copies, slipcase, no dust jackets) . . . . . £35 each, £100 the set
Midnight Pleasures, Doubleday (U.S.), 1987 £10/£5

Lost in Space and Time With Lefty Feep, Creatures at Large Press (U.S.), 1987 (wraps) £10
ditto, Creatures at Large Press (U.S.), 1987 (250 signed copies in d/w and slipcase) . . . . . . £45/£35
Fear and Trembling, Tor (U.S.), 1989 (wraps) £5

Others
The Eighth Stage of Fandom, Advent (U.S.), 1962 . . . . £75/£45
ditto, Advent (U.S.), 1962 (100 numbered, signed copies) £200

EDMUND BLUNDEN
(b.1896 d.1974)

Remembered primarily as a war poet, Blunden was later inspired by his adopted county of Kent.

Poetry
Poems, privately printed, 1914 (100 copies, wraps) £1,000
Poems Translated from the French, privately printed, 1914 (100 copies, wraps) £500
The Barn, privately printed, 1916 (50 copies, wraps). £500
Three Poems, privately printed, 1916 (50 copies, wraps). £500
The Harbingers, privately printed, 1916 (200 copies, 'The Barn' and 'Three Poems' bound together, wraps) £250
Pastorals, Erskine Macdonald, 1916 (wraps) . £100
ditto, Erskine Macdonald, 1916 (fifty cloth copies) £250
The Waggoner and Other Poems, Sidgwick & Jackson, 1920 . . . . £100/£35
The Shepherd and Other Poems of Peace and War, Cobden-Sanderson, 1922 . . . . . £75/£25
To Nature, The Beaumont Press, 1923 (310 numbered copies) £50
ditto, The Beaumont Press, 1923 (80 signed, numbered copies) £150
Masks of Time: A New Collection of Poems, The Beaumont Press, 1925 (310 numbered copies) £50
ditto, The Beaumont Press, 1925 (80 signed, numbered copies) £150
The Augustan Books of Modern Poetry, Benn, 1925 (wraps) £5
English Poems, Cobden-Sanderson, 1926 . £25/£10
Retreat, Cobden-Sanderson, 1928 . . . . £25/£10
ditto, Cobden-Sanderson, 1928 (112 signed, numbered copies). £100
Japanese Garland, The Beaumont Press, 1928 (310 numbered copies) £45
ditto, The Beaumont Press, 1928 (eighty signed, numbered copies) £100
Winter Nights: A Reminiscence, Faber, 1928 (wraps) £5
ditto, Faber, 1928 (500 signed, numbered, large paper copies) £45
Near and Far, Cobden-Sanderson, 1929 . £25/£10
ditto, Cobden-Sanderson, 1929 (160 signed, numbered copies). . . . . £75/£45
Poems 1914-1930, Cobden-Sanderson, 1930 £25/£10
ditto, Cobden-Sanderson, 1930 (200 signed, numbered copies). . . . . £65/£35
Halfway House: A Miscellany of New Poems, Cobden-Sanderson, 1932 . . . . . £25/£10
Choice or Chance: New Poems, Cobden-Sanderson, 1934 . . . . £20/£10
ditto, Cobden-Sanderson, 1934 (45 signed, numbered copies) £65
An Elegy and Other Poems, Cobden-Sanderson, 1937 . . . . £20/£10
Poems 1930-1940, Macmillan, 1940 [1941] £20/£10
Shells by a Stream: New Poems, Macmillan, 1944 . . . . £20/£10
After the Bombing and Other Short Poems, Macmillan, 1949 . . . . £15/£5
Eastward: A Selection of Verses, privately printed, 1950 (250 copies) £40
Poems of Many Years, Collins, 1957 . £15/£5
A Hong Kong House: Poems 1951-1981, Collins, 1982 . . . . £10/£5
Eleven Poems, The Golden Head Press, 1965 [1966] (wraps) £15
ditto, The Golden Head Press, 1965 [1966] (21 signed copies) £100
A Selection of the Shorter Poems, privately printed, 1966 (wraps) £5
The Midnight Skaters: Poems for Young Readers, The Bodley Head, 1968 . . . . £10/£5
A Selection from the Poems, privately printed, 1969 (wraps) £5
Selected Poems, Carcanet, 1982 . . . . . £5
Overtones of War: Poems of the First World War, Duckworth, 1996. . . . . £10/£5

Prose
The Bonadventure: A Random Journal of an Atlantic Holiday, Cobden-Sanderson, 1922 £75/£25
Christ's Hospital: A Retrospect, Christophers, 1923 . . . . £50/£20
On the Poems of Henry Vaughan, Cobden-Sanderson, 1927 . . . . £20/£10
Undertones of War, Cobden-Sanderson, 1928 . . . . £75/£25
ditto, The Folio Society, 1989 . . . . £10
Nature in English Literature, The Hogarth Press,

1929 . . . . £20/£5

Leigh Hunt, Cobden-Sanderson, 1930 . . £40/£10

De Bello Germanico: A Fragment of Trench History, G.A. Blunden, 1930 (250 copies) . . £100

ditto, G.A. Blunden, 1930 (25 signed copies) . £200

Votive Tablets: Studies Chiefly Appreciative of English Authors and Books, Cobden-Sanderson, 1931 . . . . £20/£10

ditto, Cobden-Sanderson, 1931 (60 signed, numbered copies) £100

The Face of England, Longmans Green, 1932 . . . . £25/£10

We'll Shift our Ground, or Two On a Tour, Cobden-Sanderson, 1933 (with Sylvia Norman) . £30/£15

Charles Lamb and His Contemporaries, CUP, 1933 . . . . £15/£5

The Mind's Eye, Cape, 1934 . . . . £15/£5

Keat's Publisher: A Memoir of John Taylor (1781-1864), Cape, 1938 . . . . . . £15/£5

English Villages, Collins, 1941 . . . . £15/£5

Thomas Hardy, Macmillan, 1941 [1942] . £20/£10

Cricket Country, Collins, 1944 . . . . £25/£10

Shelley: A Life Story, Collins, 1946 . . £15/£10

John Keats, British Council, Longmans, 1950 (wraps) £5

Charles Lamb, British Council, Longmans, 1954 (wraps) £5

War Poets 1914-1918, British Council, Longmans, 1958 (wraps) £5

ENID BLYTON

(b.1897 d.1968)

Prolific children's author, best known for the 'Famous Five', 'Secret Seven' and 'Noddy' books. There are too many titles to list here, so only the most collectable have been included.

'Famous Five' Titles

Five on a Treasure Island: An Adventure Story, Hodder & Stoughton, 1942 . . . . . £150/£50

Five Go Adventuring Again, Hodder & Stoughton, 1943 . . . . £125/£35

Five Run Away Together, Hodder & Stoughton, 1944 . . . . £125/£35

Five Go To Smuggler's Top, Hodder & Stoughton, 1945 . . . . £100/£35

Five Go off in a Caravan, Hodder & Stoughton, 1946. . . . . £75/£25

Five on Kirrin Island Again, Hodder & Stoughton, 1947 . . . . £75/£25

Five Go Off to Camp, Hodder & Stoughton, 1948 . . . . £75/£25

Five Get Into Trouble, Hodder & Stoughton, 1949 . . . . £40/£15

Five Fall into an Adventure, Hodder & Stoughton, 1950 . . . . £40/£15

Five on a Hike Together, Hodder & Stoughton, 1951 . . . . £40/£15

Five Have a Wonderful Time, Hodder & Stoughton [1952]. . . . . £30/£10

Five Go Down to the Sea, Hodder & Stoughton, 1953 . . . . £30/£10

Five Go to Mystery Moor, Hodder & Stoughton, 1954. . . . . £30/£10

Five Have Plenty of Fun, Hodder & Stoughton, 1955 . . . . £30/£10

Five on a Secret Trail, Hodder & Stoughton, 1956 . . . . £30/£10

Five Go To Billycock Hill, Hodder & Stoughton, 1957 . . . . £30/£10

Five get into a Fix, Hodder & Stoughton [1958] . . . . £30/£10

The Famous Five Special, Hodder & Stoughton, 1959 (contains ***Five Go Off to Camp***, ***Five Go Off in a Caravan*** and ***Five Have a Wonderful Time***) . . . . £15/£5

Five on Finniston Farm, Hodder & Stoughton [1960] . . . . £30/£10

Five Go To Demon's Rocks, Hodder & Stoughton, 1961 . . . . £30/£10

Five Have a Mystery to Solve, Hodder & Stoughton, 1962 . . . . £30/£10

Five are Together Again, Hodder & Stoughton, 1963 . . . . £30/£10

The Famous Five Big Book, Hodder & Stoughton, 1964 (contains ***Five on a Treasure Island***, ***Five Go Adventuring Again*** and ***Five Run Away Together***) . . . . £15/£5

'Adventure' Titles

The Island of Adventure, Macmillan, 1944 . £75/£15

The Castle of Adventure, Macmillan, 1946 . £50/£15

The Valley of Adventure, Macmillan, 1947 . £35/£10

The Sea of Adventure, Macmillan, 1948 . £35/£10

The Mountain of Adventure, Macmillan, 1949. . . . . £35/£10

The Ship of Adventure, Macmillan, 1950 . £30/£10

The Circus of Adventure, Macmillan, 1952. £30/£10

The River of Adventure, Macmillan, 1955 . £30/£10

'Secret Seven' Titles

The Secret Seven, Brockhampton Press, 1949 £50/£10

Secret Seven Adventure, Brockhampton Press, 1950 . . . . £35/£10

Well Done, Secret Seven, Brockhampton Press, 1951 . . . . £30/£10

Secret Seven on the Trail, Brockhampton Press, 1952

. . . . £30/£10

Go Ahead Secret Seven, Brockhampton Press, 1953 . . . . £30/£10

Good Work, Secret Seven, Brockhampton Press, 1954 . . . . £30/£10

Secret Seven Win Through, Brockhampton Press, 1955 . . . . £30/£10

Three Cheers Secret Seven, Brockhampton Press, 1956 . . . . £30/£10

Secret Seven Mystery, Brockhampton Press, 1957 . . . . £25/£10

Puzzle for the Secret Seven, Brockhampton Press, 1958 . . . . £25/£10

Secret Seven Fireworks, Brockhampton Press, 1959 . . . . £25/£10

Good Old Secret Seven, Brockhampton Press, 1960 . . . . £25/£10

Shock for the Secret Seven, Brockhampton Press, 1961 . . . . £20/£10

Look out Secret Seven, Brockhampton Press, 1962 . . . . £15/£10

Fun for the Secret Seven, Brockhampton Press, 1963 . . . . £15/£10

'Mystery' Titles

The Mystery of the Burnt Cottage, Methuen, 1943 . . . . £95/£45

The Mystery of the Disappearing Cat, Methuen, 1944 . . . . £95/£45

The Mystery of the Secret Room, Methuen, 1945 . . . . £95/£45

The Mystery of the Spiteful Letters, Methuen, 1946 . . . . £65/£20

The Mystery of the Missing Necklace, Methuen, 1947 . . . . £65/£20

The Mystery of the Hidden House, Methuen, 1948 . . . . £50/£15

The Mystery of the Pantomime Cat, Methuen, 1949 . . . . £50/£15

The Mystery of the Invisible Thief, Methuen, 1950 . . . . £30/£10

The Mystery of the Vanished Prince: Being the Ninth Adventure of the Five Find-Outers and Dog, Methuen, 1951 . . . . £30/£10

The Mystery of the Strange Bundle, Methuen, 1952 . . . . £30/£10

The Mystery of Holly Lane, Methuen, 1953 £25/£10

The Mystery of Tally-Ho Cottage, Methuen, 1954 . . . . £25/£10

The Mystery of the Missing Man, Methuen, 1956 . . . . £25/£10

The Mystery of the Strange Messages, Methuen, 1957 . . . . £25/£10

The Mystery of Banshee Towers, Methuen, 1961 . . . . £25/£10

'St Clare's School' Titles

Methuen, 1941-45 . . . . £30/£10 each

'Malory Towers' Titles

Methuen, 1946-51 . . . . £25/£10 each

'Noddy' Titles

Sampson Low, 1949-64, numbered Noddy books, 1-25, ... £30/£10 each

Noddy's House of Books, Sampson Low [1951] ('The Tiny Noddy Book Nos. 1-6, in card case, no d/w) . . . . £65 the set

The Big Noddy Book, Sampson Low, 1952 (no d/w) £35

Enid Blyton's Noddy's Ark of Books, Sampson Low, [1952] (5 books, cardboard case, no d/w) £65 the set

Noddy Cut-Out Model Book, Sampson Low, 1953 . . . . £50

Noddy's Garage of Books, Sampson Low [1953] (5 books, in cardboard case, no d/w) . . £65 the set

Noddy's Castle of Books, Sampson Low [1954] (5 books, in cardboard case, no d/w) . . £65 the set

The Noddy Toy Station Book Nos. 1-5, Sampson Low [1956]. . . . . £65 the set

Noddy's Shop of Books Nos. 1-5, Sampson Low [1958]. . . . . £65 the set

Noddy's Tall Blue (Green-Orange-Pink-Red-Yellow) Book, Sampson Low [1960]. . . . £65 the set

Others

Sports and Games, [Birn, 1920] £75

Responsive Singing Games, J. Saville, 1923 . £75

Songs of Gladness, J. Saville, 1924 . . . . £75

The Enid Blyton Book of Fairies, Newnes [1924] . . . . £75/£45

The Enid Blyton Book of Bunnies, Newnes [1925] . . . . £75/£45

The Enid Blyton Book of Brownies, Newnes [1926] . . . . £75/£45

Tales Half Told, Nelson, 1926 . . . . . £75/£45

The Play's the Thing: Musical Plays for Children, Home Library Book Co. [1927]. . . £125/£45

Let's Pretend, Nelson [1928] . . . . . £40/£15

The Red Pixie Book, Newnes [1934] . . £75/£45

The Green Goblin Book, Newnes [1935] . . £40/£15

The Yellow Fairy Book, Newnes [1936] . £40/£15

The Secret Island, Blackwell, 1948 . . . . £40/£15

The Enchanted Wood, Newnes, 1939 . . £40/£15

The Secret of Spiggy Holes, Blackwood [1940] . . . . £40/£15

The Babar Story Book, Methuen, 1941 . . £50/£15

The Three Golliwogs, Newnes, 1944 . . £40/£15

Rubbalong Tale Showbook, Werner Laurie, 1950 (complete with cut-outs) £75

Mary Mouse Showbook, Werner Laurie, 1950 (complete with cut-outs) £75

Verse

Child Whispers, J. Saville, [1922] (booklet) . £100
ditto, J. Saville, 1923 . . . . £45/£25
Real Fairies, J. Saville, 1923 . . . . . £125/£50
Silver and Gold, Nelson [1925] . . . . £75/£45

LUCY M. BOSTON

(b.1892 d.1990)

A British author who was inspired to write The Children of Green Knowe after buying the 800 year-old Grey Manor in Cambridgeshire in 1935

Green Knowe Titles

The Children of Green Knowe, Faber, 1954 £45/£20
The Chimneys of Green Knowe, Faber, 1958 £25/£10
The River at Green Knowe, Faber, 1959 . £25/£10
A Stranger at Green Knowe, Faber, 1961 . £25/£10
An Enemy at Green Knowe, Faber, 1964 . £25/£10
The Stones of Green Knowe, Faber, 1954 . £20/£5

Other Titles

Yew Hall, Faber, 1954 . . . . £30/£10
The Castle of Yew, Bodley Head, 1965 . . £15/£5
The Sea Egg, Faber, 1967 . . . . . £15/£5
The House that Grew, Faber, 1969 . . . £15/£5
Persephone, Faber, 1969 . . . . . . £15/£5
The Horned Man, Faber, 1970 . . . . £15/£5
Nothing Said, Faber, 1971 . . . . . £15/£5
The Guardians of the House, Bodley Head, 1974 . . . . £15/£5
The Fosil Snake, Bodley Head, 1975 . . £15/£5
Time is Undone, privately printed, 1954 (750 copies, wraps) £15

ELIZABETH BOWEN

(b.1899 d.1973)

Anglo-Irish novelist and short story writer noted for her attention to detail and subtlety of style.

Short Stories

Encounters: Stories, Sidgwick & Jackson, 1923 . . . . £125/£45
ditto, Boni & Liveright, 1926 . . . . . £65/£20
Ann Lee's and Other Stories, Sidgwick & Jackson, 1926 . . . . £75/£30
ditto, Boni & Liveright, 1926 . . . . . £45/£20
Joining Charles and Other Stories, Constable, 1929 . . . . £75/£25
ditto, Dial Press, 1929 . . . . £45/£20
The Cat Jumps and Other Stories, Gollancz, 1934 . . . . £45/£20
Look at All Those Roses, Gollancz, 1941 . £35/£15
ditto, Knopf (U.S.), 1941 . . . . £20/£10
The Demon Lover and Other Stories, Cape, [1945] . . . . £20£10
ditto, as ***Ivy Gripped the Steps and Other Stories***, Knopf (U.S.), 1946 . . . . £20/£10
Selected Stories, Fridberg (Dublin), 1946 . . £15
Stories, Knopf (U.S.), 1959 . . . . £10/£5
A Day in the Dark and Other Stories, Cape, 1965 . . . . £10/£5
The Collected Stories, Cape, 1981 . . . . £10/£5
ditto, Random House (U.S.), 1982 . . . . £10/£5

Novels

The Hotel, Constable, 1927 . . . . . £75/£15
ditto, Dial Press, 1928 . . . . £50/£15
The Last September, Constable, 1929 . . £65/£20
ditto, Dial Press, 1929 . . . . £45/£15
Friends and Relations, Constable, 1931 . £50/£15
ditto, Dial Press, 1931 . . . . £30/£15
To the North, Gollancz, 1931 . . . . £50/£15
ditto, Knopf (U.S.), 1933 . . . . . . £30/£15
The House in Paris, Gollancz, 1935 . . . £50/£15
ditto, Knopf (U.S.), 1936 . . . . £20/£5
The Death of the Heart, Gollancz, 1938 . £35/£10
ditto, Knopf (U.S.), 1939 . . . . £20/£5
The Heat of the Day, Cape, 1949 . . . . £20/£5
ditto, Knopf (U.S.), 1949 . . . . £10/£5
A World of Love, Cape, 1955 . . . . . £15/£5
ditto, Knopf (U.S.), 1955 . . . . £10/£5
The Little Girls, Cape, 1964 . . . . . £10/£5
ditto, Knopf (U.S.), 1964 . . . . £10/£5
Eva Trout, Knopf (U.S.), 1968 . . . . £10/£5
ditto, Cape, 1969 . . . . £10/£5

Non Fiction

Bowen's Court, Longman, 1942 . . . . . £35/£10
ditto, Knopf (U.S.), 1942 . . . . £30/£10
English Novelists, Collins, 1942 . . . . £10/£5
ditto, Hastings House (U.S.), 1942 . . . . £10/£5
Seven Winters, Cuala Press (Dublin), 1942 (450 numbered copies) £60
ditto, Longman, 1943 . . . . £10/£5
ditto, Knopf (U.S.), 1943 . . . . £10/£5
Anthony Trollope: A New Judgement, O.U.P., 1946 . . . . £15/£5
Why Do I Write?: An Exchange of Views Between Elizabeth Bowen, Graham Greene, and V.S. Pritchett, Marshall, 1948 . . . . . £20/£5
Collected Impressions, Longman, 1950 . . £10/£5

ditto, Knopf (U.S.), 1950 . . . . £10/£5
The Shelbourne, Harrap, 1951 . . . . £25/£10
*ditto, as **The Shelbourne Hotel***, Knopf (U.S.), 1951 . . . . £20/£5
A Time in Rome, Longman, 1960 . . . £10/£5
ditto, Knopf (U.S.), 1960 . . . . £10/£5
Afterthought: Pieces About Writing, Longman, 1962. . . . . £10/£5
ditto, Knopf (U.S.), 1962 . . . . £10/£5
Pictures and Conversations, Knopf (U.S.), 1975 . . . . £10/£5

Children's
The Good Tiger, Knopf (U.S.), 1965 . . . £10/£5
ditto, Cape, 1970 . . . . £10/£5

WILLIAM BOYD
(b.1952)

Born in Ghana, Boyd's first two books remain highly collectable, although he is currently slightly out of vogue.

A Good Man in Africa, Hamish Hamilton, 1981 . . . . £225/£45
ditto, Morrow (U.S.), 1982 . . . . . . £35/£10
On the Yankee Station and Other Stories, Hamish Hamilton, 1982 . . . . £150/£35
ditto, Morrow (U.S.), 1984 . . . . . . £15/£5
An Ice Cream War, Hamish Hamilton, 1982 £35/£10
ditto, Morrow (U.S.), 1983 . . . . . . £15/£5
Stars and Bars, Hamish Hamilton, 1984 . £20/£5
ditto, Morrow (U.S.), 1985 . . . . . . £10/£5
School Ties, Hamish Hamilton, 1985 . £20/£5
ditto, Penguin, 1985 (wraps) £5
ditto, Morrow (U.S.), 1986 . . . . . . £10/£5
The New Confessions, Hamish Hamilton, 1987 £20/£5
ditto, Morrow (U.S.), 1988 . . . . . £10/£5
Brazzaville Beach, Sinclair Stevenson, 1990 £20/£5
ditto, London Limited Editions, 1990 (150 signed copies, cellophane d/w) . . . . . . £50/£45
ditto, Morrow (U.S.), 1991 . . . . . . £10/£5
The Blue Afternoon, Sinclair Stevenson, 1993 £10/£5
ditto, London Limited Editions, 1993 (150 signed copies, cellophane d/w) £50
ditto, Knopf (U.S.), 1995 . . . . £10/£5
The Destiny of Nathalie 'X' and Other Short Stories, Sinclair Stevenson, 1990 . . . . . . £10/£5
ditto, Knopf (U.S.), 1997 . . . . £10/£5
Cork, Ulysses, 1994 (236 copies) £50

MALCOLM BRADBURY
(b.1932)

A novelist and critic, *The History Man* is his best regarded novel, satirising the university culture of the 1960s and 70s.

Novels
Eating People is Wrong, Secker & Warburg, 1959 . . . . £125/£45
ditto, Knopf (U.S.), 1960 . . . . £35/£10
Stepping Westward, Secker & Warburg, 1965 £75/£25
ditto, Houghton & Mifflin (U.S.), 1966 . . £15/£5
The History Man, Secker & Warburg, 1975 £50/£15
ditto, Houghton & Mifflin (U.S.), 1976 . . £15/£5
Rates of Exchange, Secker & Warburg, 1983 £15/£5
ditto, Knopf (U.S.), 1983 . . . . . . £10/£5
Doctor Criminale, Secker & Warburg, 1992 £10/£5
ditto, Viking (U.S.), 1992 . . . . . . £10/£5

Novella
Cuts, Hutchinson, 1987 . . . . . . £10/£5
ditto, Harper (U.S.), 1987 . . . . . . £10/£5

Short Stories
Who Do You Think You Are?, Secker & Warburg, 1976 . . . . £15/£5

Criticism etc.
Phogey! How to Have Class in a Classless Society, Parrish, 1960 . . . . £25/£10
All Dressed Up and Nowhere to Go, Parrish, 1962 . . . . £25/£10
Evelyn Waugh, Oliver & Boyd, 1964 (wraps) . £25
What is a Novel?, Arnold, 1969 . . . . . . £15
The Social Context of Modern English Literature, Blackwell, 1971 . . . . £15/£5
Possibilities: Essays on the State of the Novel, O.U.P., 1973 . . . . £10
Saul Bellow, Methuen, 1982 (wraps) £10
The Modern American Novel, O.U.P., 1983 £10/£5
ditto, Viking (U.S.), 1993 . . . . . . £10/£5
Why Come to Slaka?, Secker & Warburg, 1986 £10
ditto, Penguin (U.S.), 1988 . . . . . . £10
My Strange Quest for Mensonge: Structuralism's Hidden Hero, Deutsch, 1987 . . . . £10/£5
ditto, Penguin (U.S.), 1988 . . . . £10
No, Not Bloomsbury, Deutsch, 1987 . . £10/£5
ditto, Columbia Univ. Press (U.S.), 1988 . £10/£5
The Modern World: Ten Great Writers, Secker & Warburg, 1988 . . . . £10/£5
ditto, Viking (U.S.), 1989 . . . . . . £10/£5
Unsent Letters: Irreverent Notes From a Literary Life, Secker & Warburg, 1988 . . . . £10/£5
ditto, Viking (U.S.), 1988 . . . . . . £10/£5

From Puritanism to Post-modernism: The Story of American Literature, Routledge, 1991 (with Richard Ruland) . . . . £10/£5
ditto, Viking (U.S.), 1991 . . . . . . £10/£5
The Modern British Novel, Secker & Warburg, 1993 . . . . £10/£5
Dangerous Pilgrimages, Secker & Warburg, 1995 . . . . £10/£5
ditto, Viking (U.S.), 1996 . . . . . . £10/£5

RAY BRADBURY

(b.1920)

American author of fiction in various genres, Bradbury originally emerged from the science fiction pulp magazines and is considered a leading writer in the field.

Novels

Fahrenheit 451, Ballantine (U.S.), 1953 (wraps) £25
ditto, Ballantine (U.S.), 1953 (200 signed, numbered copies) £1,000
ditto, Hart-Davis, 1954 . . . . . . £75/£20
ditto, Limited Editions Club (U.S.), 1982 (2,000 signed, numbered copies) . . . . . £75/£45
Dandelion Wine, Doubleday (U.S.), 1957 . £50/£20
ditto, Hart-Davis, 1957 . . . . . . £45/£15
Something Wicked This Way Comes, Simon & Schuster (U.S.), 1962 . . . . . £125/£50
ditto, Hart-Davis, 1963 . . . . . . £50/£15
Death is a Lonely Business, Knopf (U.S.), 1985 . . . . £10/£5
ditto, Grafton, 1986 . . . . £10/£5
ditto, Franklin Press (U.S.), 1985 (signed, limited edition, full leather) £40
A Graveyard for Lunatics, Knopf (U.S.), 1990 £10/£5
ditto, Grafton, 1990 . . . . £10/£5

Omnibus Editions

The Novels of Ray Bradbury, Granada, 1984 £10/£5

Short Stories

Dark Carnival, Arkham House (Sauk City, U.S.), 1947 . . . . £250/£75
ditto, Hamish Hamilton, 1948 . . . . £50/£20
The Martian Chronicles, Doubleday (U.S.), 1950 £300/£100
ditto, as ***The Silver Locusts***, Hart-Davis, 1951 . . . . £100/£45
The Pedestrian, Roy Squires (U.S.), [1951] (card wraps) £50
The Illustrated Man, Doubleday (U.S.), 1951 £75/£25
ditto, Hart-Davis, 1952 . . . . . . £35/£10
The Golden Apples of the Sun, Doubleday (U.S.), 1953 . . . . £100/£35
ditto, Hart-Davis, 1953 . . . . . . £40/£15
The October Country, Ballantine (U.S.), 1955 £75/£30
ditto, Hart-Davis, 1956 . . . . . . £60/£25
A Medicine for Melancholy, Doubleday (U.S.), 1959 . . . . £40/£15
ditto, as ***The Day it Rained Forever***, Hart-Davis, 1959 . . . . £25/£10
The Machineries of Joy, Simon & Schuster (U.S.), 1964 . . . . £40/£15
ditto, Hart-Davis, 1964 . . . . . . £20/£5
The Vintage Bradbury, Random House (U.S.), 1965 . . . . £15/£5
The Autumn People, Ballantine (U.S.), 1965 (cartoons, wraps) £10
Tomorrow Midnight, Ballantine (U.S.), 1966 (cartoons, wraps) £15
Twice Twenty Two, Doubleday (U.S.), 1966 £20/£10
I Sing the Body Electric!, Knopf (U.S.), 1969 £45/£10
ditto, Hart-Davis, 1970 . . . . . . £20/£10
Bloch and Bradbury (with Robert Bloch), Tower (U.S.), 1969 (wraps) £5
Fever Dreams and Other Stories (with Robert Bloch), Sphere, 1970 (wraps) £5
The Small Assassin, New English Library, 1962 . . . . £10/£5
Selected Stories, Harrap, 1975 (ed Anthony Adams) . . . . £10/£5
Long After Midnight, Knopf (U.S.), 1976 . £15/£5
ditto, Hart-Davis MacGibbon, 1977 . . . £10/£5
The Best of Bradbury, Bantam (U.S.), 1976 (wraps) £10
To Sing Strange Songs, Wheaton, 1979. . . £10
The Stories of Ray Bradbury, Knopf (U.S.), 1980 . . . . £20/£10
ditto, Granada, 1980, (two vols, wraps) . . . £5
The Last Circus, and The Electrocution, Lord John Press (U.S.), 1980 (300 signed copies, slipcase) £50
Dinosaur Tales, Bantam (U.S.), 1983 (wraps) £5
A Memory for Murder, Dell (U.S.), 1984, (wraps) £5
The Toynbee Convector, Knopf (U.S.), 1988 £20/£10
ditto, Knopf (U.S.), 1988 (350 signed copies) £100/£85
ditto, Grafton, 1989 . . . . £5

Verse

Old Ahab's Friend, Squires (U.S.), 1971 (445 unsigned copies of 485, wraps) £20
ditto, Squires (U.S.), 1971 (40 signed copies of 485) £75
That Son of Richard III, Squires (U.S.), 1974 (400 unsigned copies of 485, wraps) £20
ditto, Squires (U.S.), 1974 (85 signed copies of 485) £50
Twin Hieroglyphs that Swim the River Dust, Lord

John Press (U.S.), 1978 (300 signed copies of edition of 326) £25
The Bike Repairman, Lord John Press (U.S.), 1978 (limited edition) £25
The Poet Considers His Resources, Lord John Press (U.S.), 1979 (200 signed copies, broadside) . . £25
The Aqueduct, Squires (U.S.), 1979 (230 copies, wraps) £25
The Attic Where The Meadow Greens, Lord John Press (U.S.), 1980 (300 copies, signed) . . . £40
ditto, Lord John Press (U.S.), 1980 (75 deluxe copies, signed) £75
The Love Affair, Lord John Press (U.S.), 1983 (300 signed copies) . . . . £35/£30
ditto, Lord John Press (U.S.), 1983 (100 signed deluxe copies) £45
Forever and the Earth, Croissant (U.S.), 1984 (300 signed copies, tissue d/w) £35
The Complete Poems of Ray Bradbury, Ballantine (U.S.), 1982 . . . . £5

Plays
The Meadow, (in ***Best One-Act Plays of, 1947-48***) Dodd Mead (U.S.), 1948 . . . . £15
The Anthem Sprinters and Other Antics, Dial Press (U.S.), 1963 . . . . £15/£5
The Day it Rained Forever, French (U.S.), 1966 £5
The Pedestrian, French (U.S.), 1966 . . . . £5
The Wonderful Ice Cream Suit and Other Plays, Bantam (U.S.), 1972 . . . . £10
ditto, Hart-Davis, 1973 . . . . £15/£5
Pillar of Fire and Other Plays of Today, Tomorrow and beyond Tomorrow, Bantam (U.S.), 1975 £10

Children's Books
Switch on the Night, Pantheon (U.S.), 1955 . £40
ditto, Hart-Davis, 1955 . . . . £20/£10
R is for Rocket, Doubleday (U.S.), 1962 . £45/£15
ditto, Hart-Davis, 1968 . . . . £15/£5
S is for Space, Doubleday (U.S.), 1966 . . £40/£15
ditto, Hart-Davis, 1968 . . . . £15/£5
The Hallowe'en Tree, Knopf (U.S.), 1972 . £15/£5
ditto, Hart-Davis MacGibbon, 1973 . . . . . £10
When Elephants Last in the Dooryard Boomed: Celebrations for Almost any Day of the Year, Knopf (U.S.), 1973 . . . . £15/£5
ditto, Hart-Davis, 1975 . . . . £10/£5
Where Robot Mice and Robot Men Run Round in Robot Towns: New Poems both Light and Dark, Knopf (U.S.), 1977 . . . . £15/£5
ditto, Granada, 1979 . . . . £10/£5
The Haunted Computer and the Android Pope, Knopf (U.S.), 1981 . . . . £10/£5
ditto, Granada, 1981 . . . . £10/£5

Miscellaneous
The Circus of Dr Lao and Other Improbable Stories (ed by Ray Bradbury), Bantam, 1956 (wraps) £5
Teacher's Guide: Science Fiction with Lewy Olfson, Bantam (U.S.), 1969 . . . . £5
Mars and the Mind of Man, Harper (U.S.), 1973 £5
Zen and the Art of Writing, and The Joy of Writing, Capra Press (U.S.), 1973 (250 signed copies) £60
The Mummies of Guanajuato. Photographs by Archie Lieberman, Abrams (U.S.), 1978 . . . £50/£20
Beyond, 1984: Remembrance of Things Future, Targ (U.S.), 1979 (350 signed copies, acetate dust wrapper) £50
Flatland: A Romance of Many Dimensions, by Edwin Abbott, (with an introduction by Bradbury, limited edition), Arion Press, 1980 . . . . . . £100
Fantasmas Para Siempre, Ediciones Libreria (Buenos Aires), 1980 . . . . £75/£45
ditto, as ***The Ghosts of Forever***, Rizzoli (U.S.), 1981 . . . . £50/£30
Los Angeles. Photographs by West Light, Skyline Press (U.S.), 1984 . . . . £5
Orange County. Photographs by Bill Ross and others, Skyline Press (U.S.), 1985 . . . . . . £5
The Art of 'Playboy', Playboy Press, 1985 . £25/£15

JOHN BRAINE
(b.1922 d.1986)

A novelist best known for *Room at the Top*, a classic novel of the 'Angry Young Men' School.

Room at the Top, Eyre & Spottiswoode, 1957 £75/£20
ditto, Houghton Mifflin (U.S.), 1957 . . . £25/£10
The Void, Eyre & Spottiswoode, 1959 . . £10/£5
Life at the Top, Eyre & Spottiswoode, 1962 £20/£5
ditto, Houghton Mifflin (U.S.), 1962 . . . £15/£5
The Jealous God, Eyre & Spottiswoode, 1964 £10/£5
The Crying Game, Eyre & Spottiswoode, 1968 . . . . £15/£5
Stay with Me till Morning, Eyre & Spottiswoode, 1970 . . . . £10/£5
The Queen of a Distant Country, Methuen, 1972 . . . . £10/£5
Writing a Novel, Eyre Methuen, 1974 . . £10/£5
The Pious Agent, Eyre Methuen, 1975 . . £10/£5
Waiting for Sheila, Eyre Methuen, 1976 . £10/£5
Finger of Fire, Eyre Methuen, 1977 . . . £10/£5
J.B. Priestley, Weidenfeld & Nicolson, 1979 £10/£5
One and Last Love, Eyre Methuen, 1981 . £10/£5
The Two of Us, Methuen, 1984 . . . . £10/£5
These Golden Days, Methuen, 1985 . . . £10/£5

ERNEST BRAMAH

(b. 1868 d.1942)

Ernest Bramah Smith is read for his Kai Lung and Max Carrados stories, the former featuring a Chinese philosopher, the latter a blind detective.

Kai Lung Titles

The Wallet of Kai Lung, Grant Richards, 1900 £200
ditto, L.C. Page and Company (U.S.), 1900 . £100
ditto, Grant Richards's Colonial Library, 1900 . £150
ditto, Grant Richards, 1923 (200 signed copies) . . . £300/£150
ditto, Doran (U.S.), [1923] . . . . . . £150/£30
The Transmutation of Ling, Grant Richards, 1911 (500 copies?) £100
ditto, Brentano's (U.S.), 1912 (500 copies?) . £100
Kai Lung's Golden Hours, Grant Richards, 1922 . . . . . £150/£50
ditto, Doran (U.S.), 1923 . . . . . . £95/£40
ditto, Grant Richards, 1924 (200 signed copies) . . . £350/£200
The Story of Wan and the Remarkable Shrub ..., Doubleday Doran (U.S.), 1927 (wraps) . . £150
ditto, as ***Kai Lung Unrolls His Mat***, Richards Press, 1928 (the above title comprises two chapters from this book) . . . . £75/£45
ditto, Doran (U.S.), 1928 . . . . . . £65/£25
The Moon of Much Gladness, Cassell, 1932 £100/£50
ditto, as ***The Return of Kai Lung***, Sheridan House (U.S.), 1937 . . . . £75/£45
The Kai Lung Omnibus, Philip Allan, 1936 £75/£25
Kai Lung Beneath the Mulberry-Tree, Richards Press, 1940 . . . . £150/£45
ditto, Arno Press (U.S.), 1978 . . . . . £15
Kin Weng and the Miraculous Tusk, City of Birmingham School of Printing, 1941 . . . £50
The Celestial Omnibus, Richards Press, 1963 £35/£10
Kai Lung: Six, Non-Profit Press (U.S.), 1974 (250 copies) . . . . £50/£15

Max Carrados Titles

Max Carrados, Methuen, 1914 . . . . £400/£150
ditto, Hyperion Press (U.S.), 1975 . . . . £20
The Eyes of Max Carrados, Grant Richards, 1923 . . . . . £250/£125
ditto, Doran (U.S.), 1924 . . . . £75/£40
Max Carrados Mysteries, Hodder & Stoughton, 1927 . . . . . £175/£100
ditto, Penguin (U.S.), 1964 . . . . £10
The Bravo of London, Cassell, 1934 . . £600/£175

Kai Lung & Max Carrados Titles

The Specimen Case, Hodder & Stoughton, 1924 . . . . . £200/£50
ditto, Doran (U.S.), 1925 . . . . £100/£45
Short Stories of Today and Yesterday, Harrap, 1929 . . . . . £65/£20

Other Fiction

The Mirror of Kong Ho, Chapman & Hall, 1905 . . . . . £100/£45
ditto, Doubleday (U.S.), 1930 . . . . . £45/£20
What Might Have Been, John Murray, 1907 (anonymous) £200
ditto, as ***The Secret of the League: The Story of a Social War***, Nelson, [1909] £75
ditto, as ***The Secret of the League: The Story of a Social War***, Specular Press (U.S.), 1995 (wraps) £10
A Little Flutter, Cassell, 1930 . . . . . . £100

Non Fiction

English Farming and Why I Turned It Up, Leadenhall Press, 1894 . . . . £150
A Handbook for Writers and Artists, Deacon, 1898 . . . . . £100
A Guide to the Varieties and Rarity of English Regal Copper Coins, Methuen, 1929 . . . . . . £50

ANGELA BRAZIL

(b.1868 d.1947)

A British born author who found success with school stories for girls.

A Terrible Tomboy, Gay & Bird, 1904 . . . . £100
The Fortunes of Philippa, Blackie, 1907 [1906] £75
The Third Class at Miss Kaye's, Blackie, 1909 [1908] £75
The Nicest Girl in the School, Blackie, 1910 . £65
Bosom Friends: A Seaside Story, Nelson, [1910] £50
The Manor House School, Blackie, 1911 . . £45
A Fourth Form Friendship, Blackie, 1912 . . £45
The New Girl at St. Chad's, Blackie, 1912 . . £45
A Pair of Schoolgirls, Blackie, [1912] £45
The Leader of the Lower School, Blackie, [1914] £45
The Youngest Girl in the Fifth, Blackie, [1914] £45
The Girls of St. Cyprian's, Blackie, [1914] . . £45
The School by the Sea, Blackie, [1914] . . . £45
The Jolliest Term on Record, Blackie, [1915] . £40
For the Sake of the School, Blackie, [1915] . £40
The Luckiest Girl in the School, Blackie. [1916] £35
The Slap-Bang Boys, T. C. & E. G, Jack, [1917] £35
The Madcap of the School, Blackie, [1918] . £35
A Patriotic Schoolgirl, Blackie, [1918] . . . £30

For the School Colours, Blackie, [1918] . . £25
A Harum-Scarum Schoolgirl, Blackie, [1919] . £25
The Head Girl at The Gables, Blackie, [1919] . £20
Two Little Scamps and a Puppy, Nelson, [1919] £25
A Gift from the Sea, Nelson, [1920] . . . £75/£20
A Popular Schoolgirl, Blackie, [1920] . . £75/£20
The Princess of the School, Blackie, [1920] £75/£20
A Fortunate Term, Blackie, [1921] . . . £75/£20
Loyal to the School, Blackie, [1921] . . £75/£20
Moniteress Merle, Blackie, [1922] . . . £75/£20
The School in the South, Blackie. [1922] . £75/£20
The Khaki Boys and Other Stories, Nelson, [1923] . . . . £75/£20
Schoolgirl Kitty, Blackie, [1923]. . . . £75/£20
Captain Peggie, Blackie, [1924] . . . . £50/£15
Joan's Best Chum, Blackie, [1926] . . . £50/£15
Queen of the Dormitory and Other Stories, Cassell, [1926]. . . . . £50/£15
Ruth of St. Ronans, Blackie, [1927]. . . . £45/£15
At School with Rachel, Blackie, [1928] . . £45/£15
St. Catherine's College, Blackie, [1929] . £40/£10
The Little Green School, Blackie, [1931] . £40/£10
Nesta's New School, Blackie, [1932] . . £40/£10
Jean's Golden Term, Blackie, [1934] . . £40/£10
The School at the Turrets, Blackie, [1935] . £40/£10
An Exciting Term, Blackie, [1936] . . . £35/£10
Jill's Jolliest School, Blackie, 1937 . . . £35/£10
The School on the Cliff, Blackie, [1938] . £35/£10
The School on the Moor, Blackie, [1939] . £35/£10
The New School at Scawdale, Blackie, [1940] £35/£10
Five Jolly Schoolgirls, Blackie, [1941] . . £25/£10
The Mystery of the Moated Grange, Blackie [1942] . . . . £25/£10
The Secret of the Border Castle, Blackie, [1943] . . . . £25/£10
The School in the Forest, Blackie, [1944] . £25/£10
Three Terms at Uplands, Blackie, [1945] . £25/£10
The School on the Loch, Blackie, [1946] . £25/£10

Plays
The Mischievous Brownie, Paterson, 'Children's Plays' series No. 1, [1913] £40
The Fairy Gifts, Paterson, 'Children's Plays' series No. 2, [1913] £40
The Enchanted Fiddle, Paterson, 'Children's Plays' series No. 3, [1913] £40
The Wishing Princess, Paterson, 'Children's Plays' series No. 4, [1913] £40

Autobiography
My Own Schooldays, Blackie, [1925] £45

ELINOR BRENT-DYER
(b.1894 d.1969)

Born Gladys Eleanor May Dyer, this British author of stories for girls worked for many years as a teacher.

'Chalet School' Titles
The School at the Chalet, Chambers, 1925 . £300/£75
Jo of the Chalet School, Chambers, 1926 . £250/£50
The Princess of the Chalet School, Chambers, 1927 . . . . £250/£50
The Head Girl of the Chalet School, Chambers, 1928. . . . . £250/£50
The Rivals of the Chalet School, Chambers, 1929 . . . . £250/£50
Eustacia Goes to the Chalet School, Chambers, 1930 . . . . £250/£50
The Chalet School and Jo, Chambers, 1931 £250/£50
The Chalet School in Camp, Chambers, 1932 . . . . £250/£50
The Exploits of the Chalet School Girls, Chambers, 1933 . . . . £250/£50
The Chalet School and the Lintons, Chambers, 1934 . . . . £250/£50
The New House at the Chalet School, Chambers, 1935 . . . . £250/£50
Jo Returns to the Chalet School, Chambers, 1936 . . . . £250/£50
The New Chalet School, Chambers, 1938 . £180/£40
The Chalet School in Exile, Chambers, 1940 (Nazi d/w) . . . . £350/£30
The Chalet School Goes To It, Chambers, 1941 . . . . £65/£30
The Highland Twins at the Chalet School, Chambers, 1942 . . . . £65/£30
Lavender Laughs in the Chalet School, Chambers, 1943 . . . . £65/£30
Gay from China at the Chalet School, Chambers, 1944 . . . . £65/£30
Jo to the Rescue, Chambers, 1945 . . . £65/£30
The Chalet School Book for Girls, Chambers, 1947 . . . . £45
The Second Chalet School Book for Girls, Chambers, 1948 . . . . £45
The Third Chalet School Book for Girls, Chambers, 1949 . . . . £75/£40
Three Go to the Chalet School, Chambers, 1949 . . . . £50/£25
The Chalet School and the Island, Chambers, 1950 . . . . £50/£25
Peggy of the Chalet School, Chambers, 1950 £40/£25
Carola Storms the Chalet School, Chambers, 1951 . . . . £50/£25
The Chalet School and Rosalie, Chambers, 1951 (wraps) £75

Guide to First Edition Prices, 2000/1

The Wrong Chalet School, Chambers, 1952 £40/£25
Shocks for the Chalet School, Chambers, 1952 . . . . £50/£25
The Chalet School in the Oberland, Chambers, 1952 . . . . £60/£30
Bride Leads the Chalet School, Chambers, 1953 . . . . £75/£35
Changes for the Chalet School, Chambers, 1953 . . . . £60/£30
The Chalet Girls' Cook Book, Chambers, 1953 . . . . £100/£75
Joey Goes to the Oberland, Chambers, 1954 £60/£35
The Chalet School and Barbara, Chambers, 1954. . . . . £60/£25
Tom Tackles the Chalet School, Chambers, 1955 . . . . £60/£35
The Chalet School Does it Again, Chambers, 1955 . . . . £75/£40
A Chalet Girl from Kenya, Chambers, 1955 £50/£30
Mary-Lou of the Chalet School, Chambers, 1956 . . . . £50/£25
A Genius at the Chalet School, Chambers, 1956 . . . . £50/£25
A Problem for the Chalet School, Chambers, 1956 . . . . £50/£25
The New Mistress at the Chalet School, Chambers, 1957 . . . . £50/£25
Excitements at the Chalet School, Chambers, 1957 . . . . £45/£25
The Coming of Age at the Chalet School, Chambers, 1958 . . . . £45/£25
The Chalet School and Richenda, Chambers, 1958 . . . . £45/£25
Trials for the Chalet School, Chambers, 1959 £45/£25
Theodora and the Chalet School, Chambers, 1959 . . . . £45/£25
Joey and Co. in Tirol, Chambers, 1960 . . £50/£25
Ruey Richardson, Chaletian, Chambers, 1960 £65/£30
A Leader in the Chalet School, Chambers, 1961 . . . . £50/£25
The Chalet School Wins the Trick, Chambers, 1961 . . . . £50/£25
A Future Chalet School Girl, Chambers, 1962 £55/£30
The Feud in the Chalet School, Chambers, 1962 . . . . £55/£25
The Chalet School Triplets, Chambers, 1963 £45/£25
The Chalet School Reunion, Chambers, 1963 (with d/w, chart and yellow band). . . . . . £100/£30
Jane and the Chalet School, Chambers, 1964 £45/£25
Redheads at the Chalet School, Chambers, 1964 . . . . £45/£25
Adrienne and the Chalet School, Chambers, 1965 . . . . £45/£25
Summer Term at the Chalet School, Chambers, 1965. . . . . £45/£25
Challenge for the Chalet School, Chambers, 1966 . . . . £45/£25
Two Sams at the Chalet School, Chambers, 1967 . . . . £45/£25
Althea Joins the Chalet School, Chambers, 1969 . . . . £45/£25
Prefects of the Chalet School, Chambers, 1970 . . . . £60/£25

'La Rochelle' Titles

Gerry Goes to School, Chambers, 1922 . . £150/£50
ditto, Lippincott (Philadelphia), 1923 . . . £150/£50
A Head Girl's Difficulties, Chambers, 1923 £150/£50
The Maids of La Rochelle, Chambers, 1924 £150/£50
Seven Scamps, Chambers, 1927 . . . . . £150/£50
Heather Leaves School, Chambers, 1929 . £150/£50
Janie of La Rochelle, Chambers, 1932 . . £125/£45
Janie Steps in, Chambers, 1953 . . . . . £45/£10

'Chudleigh Hold' Titles

Chudleigh Hold, Chambers 1954 . . . . £45/£10
The Condor Crags Adventure, Chambers 1954 . . . . £45/£10
Top Secret, Chambers 1955 . . . . . . £45/£10

Other Titles

A Thrilling Term at Janeways, Nelson, 1927 . . . . £150/£50
The New Housemistress, Nelson, 1928 . . £45/£10
Judy the Guide, Nelson, 1928 . . . . . £100/£45
The School by the River, Burns, Oates & Washbourne, 1930 . . . . £300/£75
The Feud in the Fifth Remove, Girl's Own Paper, 1931 . . . . £75/£25
The Little Marie-Jose, Burns, Oates & Washbourne, 1932 . . . . £300/£75
Carnation of the Upper Fourth, Girl's Own Paper, 1934 . . . . £75/£25
Elizabeth the Gallant, Butterworth, 1935 . £250/£100
Monica Turns Up Trumps, Girl's Own Paper, 1936 . . . . £65/£25
Caroline the Second, Girl's Own Paper, 1937 £75/£25
They Both Liked Dogs, Girl's Own Paper, 1938 . . . . £75/£25
The Little Missus, Chambers, 1942 . . . £75/£25
The Lost Staircase, Chambers, 1946. . . £75/£25
Lorna at Wynyards, Lutterworth, 1947 . . £75/£25
Stepsisters for Lorna, Temple, 1948. . . £75/£25
Fardingales, Latimer House, 1950 . . . £75/£25
Verena Visits New Zealand, Chambers, 1951 £150/£50
Bess on Her Own in Canada, Chambers, 1951. . . . . £150/£50
Quintette in Queensland, Chambers, 1951 £150/£50
Sharlie's Kenya Diary, Chambers, 1951 £150/£50
The 'Susannah' Adventure, Chambers, 1953 £50/£20

Nesta Steps Out, Oliphants, 1954 . . . £50/£20
Kennelmaid Nan, Lutterworth, 1954 . . £50/£20
Beechy of the Harbour School, Oliphants, 1955 . . . . £50/£20
Leader in Spite of Herself, Oliphants, 1956 £50/£20
The School at Skelton Hall, Max Parrish, 1962 . . . . £50/£20
Trouble at Skelton Hall, Max Parrish, 1963 £50/£20

Short Stories

Sunday and Everyday Reading for the Young (contains 'Jack's Revenge'), Wells, Gardner, Darton, 1914 . . . . £15
The Big Book for Girls (contains 'The Lady in the Yellow Gown'), Humphrey Milford/O.U.P., 1925 £10
The Golden Story Book for Girls (contains 'The Lady in the Yellow Gown'), Humphrey Milford/O.U.P., 1931 . . . . £10
Stories of the Circus, Book 4 (magazine, contains 'Carlotta to the Rescue'), c.1931. . . . . . £10
The Children's Circus Book (contains 'Carlotta to the Rescue'), Associated Newspapers c.1934 . . £10
Come to the Circus (contains 'Carlotta to the Rescue'), P.R. Gawthorn c.1938 . . . . £10
The Second Coronet Book for Girls (contains 'Cavalier Maid'), Sampson Low [n.d.]. £10
My Favourite Story (contains 'Rescue in the Snows'), Thames [n.d.] £10
Sceptre Girls' Story Annual (contains 'House of Secrets'), Purnell [n.d.] £10
Girl's Own Annual, Vol 57 (contains 'The Robins Make Good'), Girl's Own [n.d.] £15
My Treasure Hour Bumper Annual (contains 'The Chalet School Mystery'), Murrays Sales and Service Co., 1970 . . . . £10

ANNE BRONTË

(b.1820 d.1849)

Not held in as much esteem as her sisters, *Agnes Grey* was originally published alongside *Wuthering Heights*.

Poems by Currer, Ellis and Acton Bell, Aylott & Jones, 1846, first issue (with Charlotte and Emily Brontë) £20,000
ditto, second issue £2,500
ditto, Smith, Elder & Co, 1846 [1848], second edition £1,500
ditto, Lea and Blanchard (U.S.), 1848 . . . £500
Wuthering Heights with ***Agnes Grey***, Newby, 1847, (pseud. Ellis and Acton Bell, 3 vols) . . £25,000
The Tenant of Wildfell Hall, Newby, 1848, (pseud. Acton Bell, 3 vols) £20,000
ditto, Harper (U.S.), 1848 . . . . £1,500

CHARLOTTE BRONTË

(b.1816 d.1855)

Sister to Emily and Anne, Charlotte was the only Brontë to achieve literary fame in her own lifetime. Charlotte was a champion of the female spirit, her *Jane Eyre* an enduring classic.

Poems by Currer, Ellis and Acton Bell, Aylott & Jones, 1846, first issue (with Anne and Emily Brontë) £20,000
ditto, second issue £2,500
ditto, Smith, Elder & Co, 1846 [1848], second edition £1,500
ditto, Lea and Blanchard (U.S.), 1848 . . £500
Jane Eyre, Smith, Elder & Co., 1847, (3 vols, first issue, with advertisements dated June, 1847) £20,000
ditto, (second issue, ads dated October, 1847) . £5,000
ditto, Harper (U.S.), 1848 (wraps) £750
Shirley, Smith, Elder & Co., 1849, (3 vols) . £2,500
ditto, Harper (U.S.), 1850 (1 vol.) £200
Villette, Smith, Elder & Co., 1853, (3 vols) . . £2,500
ditto, Harper (U.S.), 1853 (1 vol.) £200
The Professor, Smith, Elder & Co., 1857, (2 vols) £750
ditto, Smith, Elder & Co., 1857, second state, (2 vols rebound together) £250
ditto, Harper (U.S.), 1857 (1 vol.) £150

Minor Works

The Last Sketch - Emma: A Fragment, The Cornhill Magazine Vol I, 1860 . . . . £100
The Twelve Adventurers and Other Stories, Hodder & Stoughton, 1925 . . . . £30
The Spell, O.U.P., 1931 . . . . £30/£10
Legends of Angria, edited by Fannie E. Ratchford, Yale University Press (U.S.), 1933 . . . . . £25
The Poems of Charlotte Brontë and Patrick Branwell Brontë, edited by T.J. Wise and J.A. Symington, O.U.P., 1934 . . . . £50
The Miscellaneous and Unpublished Writings of Charlotte and Patrick Branwell Brontë, edited by T.J. Wise and J.A. Symington, O.U.P., 1934 (2 vols). £75
Tales from Angria, edited by Phyllis Bentley, Collins, 1954 . . . . £10
The Search After Happiness, Harvill Press, 1969 £10
Five Novelettes, edited by Winifred Gerin, The Folio Society, 1971 . . . . £10
A Leaf from an Unopened Volume, The Brontë Society, 1986 . . . . £5

EMILY BRONTË
(b.1818 d.1848)

Wuthering Heights, now regarded as a classic novel, was published shortly after Charlotte's *Jane Eyre*, and the pseudonyms used by the sisters were originally thought to conceal the identity of a single male author. Emily's poems are often seen as some of the finest lyric verse in the English language.

Poems by Currer, Ellis and Acton Bell, Aylott & Jones, 1846, first issue (with Anne and Charlotte Brontë) £20,000
ditto, second issue £2,500
ditto, Smith, Elder & Co, 1846 [1848], second edition £1,500
Wuthering Heights with Agnes Grey, Newby, 1847, (pseud. Ellis and Acton Bell, 3 vols) . . . £25,000

JOCELYN BROOKE
(b.1908 d.1966)

A novelist and poet, Brooke is considered a fine stylist.

The Orchid Series
The Military Orchid, Bodley Head, 1948 . £60/£20
A Mine of Serpents, Bodley Head, 1949 . £60/£20
The Goose Cathederal, Bodley Head, 1950. £40/£15

Other Fiction
The Scapegoat, Bodley Head, 1948 . . . . £40/£15
ditto, Harper & Brothers (U.S.), 1949 . . £20/£10
The Image of a Drawn Sword, Bodley Head, 1950 . . . . £60/£20
ditto, Knopf (U.S.), 1951 . . . . . £15/£5
The Passing of a Hero, Bodley Head, 1953 £40/£15
Private View: Four Portraits, Barrie, 1954 . £30/£15
The Dog at Clambercrown, Bodley Head, 1955 . . . . £45/£15
ditto, Vanguard Press (U.S.), 1955 . . . £20/£10
The Crisis in Bulgaria, or Ibsen to the Rescue!, Chatto & Windus, 1956 . . . . £35/£15
Conventional Weapons, Faber, 1961 . . £25/£10
ditto, as ***The Name of Greene***, Vanguard Press (U.S.), 1961 . . . . £20/£10

Poetry
Six Poems, privately printed, 1928 (50 signed, numbered copies) £150
December Spring, Bodley Head, 1946 . . £30/£15
The Elements of Death and other poems, Hand and Flower Press, 1952 (card wraps) £20

Children's
The Wonderful Summer, Lehmann, 1949 . £50/£20

Non Fiction
The Wild Orchids of Britain, Bodley Head, 1950 (40 specially bound, signed copies of 1,140) . . £250
ditto, Bodley Head, 1950 (1,100 copies of 1,140) . . . . £175/£145
The Flower in Season, Bodley Head, 1952 . £35/£15
Ronald Firbank: A Critical Study, Barker, 1951 . . . . £25/£15
ditto, Roy (U.S.), 1951 . . . . £15/£5
Elizabeth Bowen, British Council/Longmans Green, 1952 (wraps) £5
Aldous Huxley, British Council/Longmans Green, 1953 (wraps) £5
ditto, revised edition, British Council/Longmans Green, 1958 (wraps) £5
Ronald Firbank and John Betjeman, British Council/Longmans Green, 1962 (wraps) . . £5
The Birth of a Legend, Bertram Rota, 1964 (65 signed, numbered copies, wraps) £90

RUPERT BROOKE
(b.1887 d.1915)

Born and educated at Rugby, the future war poet subsequently went up to Cambridge University. Although already a published poet, Brooke achieved his greatest fame posthumously. He died of blood-poisoning aboard ship on his way to the great engagement of the Dardanelles at the age of 28.

The Pyramids, Rugby Press, 1904 (wraps) . . £4,500
The Bastille, Rugby Press, 1905 (wraps) . . £2,500
Prize Compositions, Rugby Press, 1905 (wraps) £1,500
Poems, Sidgwick & Jackson, 1911 . . . . £1,000
1914 and Other Poems, Sidgwick & Jackson, 1915 . . . . £500
ditto, Doubleday, Page (U.S.), 1915 (87 copyright copies) £750
1914, Five Sonnets, Sidgwick & Jackson, 1915 (wraps) £100
War Poems, privately printed, 1915 . . . . . £500
The Collected Poems of Rupert Brooke, Lane (U.S.), 1916 (with a Memoir by Edward Marsh) . . £50
ditto, Sidgwick & Jackson, 1918 . . . . . . £50
ditto, Riccardi Press, 1919 (1,000 numbered copies) £50

Lithuania, A Drama in One Act, Chicago Little Theatre (U.S.), 1915 (wraps) £175
ditto, Sidgwick & Jackson, 1935 (wraps) . . £25
The Old Vicarage, Grantchester, Sidgwick & Jackson, 1916 (with woodcut by Noel Rooke) . . . £75
Letters from America, Scribner (U.S.), 1916 . £25
ditto, Sidgwick & Jackson, 1916 . . . . . . £20
John Webster and the Elizabethan Drama, John Lane (U.S.), 1916 . . . . £50
ditto, Sidgwick & Jackson, 1916 . . . . . . £40
Selected Poems, Sidgwick & Jackson, 1917 . £20
The Poetical Works of Rupert Brooke, Faber & Faber, 1946 . . . . £12
Democracy and the Arts, Hart-Davis, 1946 (preface by Geoffrey Keynes) . . . . £25/£10
ditto, Hart-Davis, 1946 (240 numbered copies) £100
The Prose of Rupert Brooke, Sidgwick & Jackson, 1956 (edited and with an introduction by Christopher Hassall) . . . . £20/£5
The Letters of Rupert Brooke, Faber & Faber, 1968 . . . . £250/£10
ditto, Harcourt Brace (U.S.), 1968 . . . . £20/£10

ANITA BROOKNER
(b.1928)

Brookner's very literary novels are haunted by solitary, sad women and the failures of their relationships.

A Start in Life, Cape, 1981 . . . . . . £45/£15
ditto, as ***The Debut***, Linden Press (U.S.), 1981 £15/£5
Providence, Cape, 1982 . . . . £25/£5
ditto, Pantheon (U.S.), 1984 . . . . . . £20/£5
Look at Me, Cape, 1983 . . . . £25/£5
ditto, Pantheon (U.S.), 1983 . . . . . . £15/£5
Hotel Du Lac, Cape, 1984 . . . . . . £40/£10
ditto, Pantheon (U.S.), 1985 . . . . . . £15/£5
Family and Friends, Cape, 1985 . . . . £15/£5
ditto, London Limited Editions, 1985 (250 signed copies) . . . . £60/£55
ditto, Pantheon (U.S.), 1985 . . . . . . £15/£5
A Misalliance, Cape, 1986 . . . . . . £15/£5
ditto, as ***The Misalliance***, Pantheon (U.S.), 1987 . . . . £15/£5
A Friend From England, Cape, 1987 . . £15/£5
ditto, Pantheon (U.S.), 1988 . . . . . . £15/£5
Latecomers, Cape, 1988 . . . . £10/£5
ditto, Pantheon (U.S.), 1989 . . . . . . £10/£5
Lewis Percy, Cape, 1989 . . . . £10/£5
ditto, Pantheon (U.S.), 1990 . . . . . . £10/£5
Brief Lives, Cape, 1990 . . . . £10/£5
ditto, Random House (U.S.), 1991 . . . £10/£5
A Closed Eye, Cape, 1991 . . . . . . £10/£5
ditto, Random House (U.S.), 1992 . . . £10/£5
Fraud, Cape, 1992 . . . . £10/£5
ditto, Random House (U.S.), 1992 . . . £10/£5
A Family Romance, Cape, 1993 . . . . £10/£5
A Private View, Cape, 1994 . . . . . . £10/£5
ditto, Random House (U.S.), 1994 . . . £10/£5
Incidents in the Rue Laugier, Cape, 1995 . £10/£5
ditto, Random House (U.S.), 1994 . . . £10/£5
Altered States, Cape, 1996 . . . . . £10/£5
ditto, Random House (U.S.), 1996 . . . £10/£5
Visitors, Cape, 1997 . . . . £10/£5

FREDRIC BROWN
(b.1906 d.1972)

One of the most collectable authors of the pulp era, Brown's work is usually very original, well-plotted and fast-moving.

Novels

The Fabulous Clipjoint, Dutton (U.S.), 1947 £300/£50
ditto, Boardman, 1949 (wraps) £35
The Dead Ringer, Dutton (U.S.), 1948 . . £200/£35
ditto, Boardman, 1949 (wraps) £30
Murder Can be Fun, Dutton (U.S.), 1948 . £175/£35
ditto, Boardman, 1951. . . . . £75/£20
The Bloody Moonlight, Dutton (U.S.), 1949 £175/£35
ditto, as ***Murder in Moonlight***, Boardman, 1949 . . . . £50/£15
The Screaming Mimi, Dutton (U.S.), 1949 £250/£50
ditto, Boardman, 1950. . . . . £75/£20
What Mad Universe, Dutton (U.S.), 1949 . £175/£35
ditto, Boardman, 1951. . . . . £75/£20
Compliments of a Fiend, Dutton (U.S.), 1950 . . . . £175/£35
ditto, Boardman, 1951. . . . . £75/£20
Here Comes a Candle, Dutton (U.S.), 1950 £175/£35
ditto, Boardman, 1951. . . . . £75/£20
Night of the Jabberwock, Dutton (U.S.), 1950 . . . . £175/£35
ditto, Boardman, 1951. . . . . £75/£20
The Case of the Dancing Sandwiches, Dell (U.S.), 1951 (wraps) £200
Death has Many Doors, Dutton (U.S.), 1951 £150/£25
ditto, Boardman, 1952. . . . . £75/£20
The Far Cry, Dutton (U.S.), 1951 . . . . £150/£25
ditto, Boardman, 1952. . . . . £75/£20
We All Killed Grandma, Dutton (U.S.), 1951 £125/£25
ditto, Boardman, 1952. . . . . £50/£15
The Deep End, Dutton (U.S.), 1952 . . . £150/£25
ditto, Boardman, 1953. . . . . £50/£15
Madball, Dell (U.S.), 1953 (wraps) £50

ditto, Muller Gold Medal, 1962 (wraps) . . . £10
The Lights in the Sky are Stars, Dutton (U.S.), 1953 . . . . £125/£25
ditto, as ***Project Jupiter***, Boardman, 1954 . £50/£15
His Name Was Death, Dutton (U.S.), 1954 £125/£25
ditto, Boardman, 1955. . . . . £50/£15
The Wench is Dead, Dutton (U.S.), 1955 . £125/£25
Martians Go Home, Dutton (U.S.), 1955 . £150/£35
ditto, Grafton, 1987 (wraps) £10
The Lenient Beast, Dutton (U.S.), 1956. . £125/£25
ditto, Boardman, 1957. . . . . £50/£15
Rogue in Space, Dutton (U.S.), 1957 . . £125/£25
One For the Road, Dutton (U.S.), 1958 . . £125/£25
ditto, Boardman, 1959. . . . . £50/£15
The Office, Dutton (U.S.), 1958 . . . . £200/£35
ditto, Dennis McMillan (U.S.), 1987 (425 copies) . . . . £40/£10
The Late Lamented, Dutton (U.S.), 1959 . £100/£20
ditto, Boardman, 1959. . . . . £50/£15
Knock Three-One-Two, Dutton (U.S.), 1959 £150/£35
ditto, Boardman, 1960. . . . . £50/£15
The Murderers, Dutton (U.S.), 1961 . . £100/£20
ditto, Boardman, 1962. . . . . £45/£15
The Mind Thing, Bantam (U.S.), 1961 (wraps) £15
ditto, Hamlyn, 1979 (wraps) £10
The Five-Day Nightmare, Dutton (U.S.), 1963. . . . . £100/£20
ditto, as ***Five Day Nightmare***, Boardman, 1963 . . . . £45/£15
Mrs Murphy's Underpants, Dutton (U.S.), 1963 . . . . £100/£20
ditto, Boardman, 1965. . . . . £45/£15
4 Novels by Fredric Brown, Zomba, 1983 (*Night of the Jabberwock, The Screaming Mimi, Knock Three-One-Two* and *The Fabulous Clipjoint*) . . . £30/£10

Short Stories

Space on My Hands, Shasta (U.S.), 1951 . £250/£35
ditto, Corgi, 1953 (wraps). £15
Mostly Murder: Eighteen Short Stories, Dutton (U.S.), 1953 . . . . £150/£35
ditto, Boardman, 1954. . . . . £100/£25
Angels and Spaceships, Dutton (U.S.), 1954 £125/£25
ditto, Gollancz, 1955 . . . . £50/£15
Honeymoon in Hell, Bantam (U.S.), 1958 (wraps) £15
The Shaggy Dog and Other Murders, Dutton (U.S.), 1963 . . . . £125/£25
ditto, Boardman, 1954. . . . . £45/£15
Carnival of Crime, Southern Illinois University Press (U.S.), 1985 . . . . £35/£10
Nightmares and Geezenstacks, Bantam (U.S.), 1961 (wraps) £20
ditto, Corgi, 1962 (wraps). £10
Daymares, Lancer (U.S.), 1968 (wraps) . . . £10
Paradox Lost, Random House (U.S.), 1973 £25/£5
ditto, Hale, 1975 . . . . £20/£5
The Best of Fredric Brown, Doubleday (U.S.), 1976 . . . . £35/£10
The Best Short Stories of Fredric Brown, NEL, 1982 (wraps) £5
And the Gods Laughed, Phantasia Press (U.S.), 1987 (1,525 copies) . . . . £25/£10
ditto, Phantasia Press (U.S.), 1987 (475 numbered copies) . . . . £50/£15

Fredric Brown in the Pulp Detectives

Homicide Sanatarium, Dennis McMillan (U.S.), 1984 (300 numbered copies) . . . . . . £100/£25
Before She Kills, Dennis McMillan (U.S.), 1984 (350 numbered copies) . . . . £75/£20
Madman's Holiday, Dennis McMillan (U.S.), 1985 (350 numbered copies) . . . . £75/£20
The Case of the Dancing Sandwiches, Dennis McMillan (U.S.), 1985 (400 numbered copies) . . . . £75/£20
The Freak Show Murders, Dennis McMillan (U.S.), 1985 (350 numbered copies) . . . . . £50/£15
30 Corpses Every Thursday, Dennis McMillan (U.S.), 1985 (375 numbered copies) . . . . . £50/£15
Pardon My Ghoulish Laughter, Dennis McMillan (U.S.), 1986 (400 numbered copies) . . £50/£15
Red is the Hue of Hell, Dennis McMillan (U.S.), 1986 (400 numbered copies) . . . . £50/£15
Sex Life on the Planet Mars, Dennis McMillan (U.S.), 1986 (400 numbered copies) . . . . £100/£25
Brother Monster, Dennis McMillan (U.S.), 1987 (400 numbered copies) . . . . £50/£15
Nightmare in the Darkness, Dennis McMillan (U.S.), 1987 (425 numbered copies) . . . . £50/£15
Who Was That Blonde I saw You Kill Last Night?, Dennis McMillan (U.S.), 1988 (450 numbered copies) . . . . £40/£10
Three Corpse Parlay, Dennis McMillan (U.S.), 1988 (450 numbered copies) . . . . . . £40/£10
Selling Death Short, Dennis McMillan (U.S.), 1988 (450 numbered copies) . . . . . . £30/£10
Whispering Death, Dennis McMillan (U.S.), 1989 (450 numbered copies) . . . . £30/£10
Happy Ending, Dennis McMillan (U.S.), 1990 (450 numbered copies) . . . . £30/£10
The Water Walker, Dennis McMillan (U.S.), 1990 (425 numbered copies) . . . . . . £30/£10
The Gibbering Night, Dennis McMillan (U.S.), 1991 (425 numbered copies) . . . . . . £25/£10
The Pickled Punks, Dennis McMillan (U.S.), 1991 (450 numbered copies) . . . . . . £25/£10

Poetry

Fermented Ink, privately published (U.S.), 1932 (wraps) £750

Shadow Suite, privately published (U.S.), 1932 (wraps) £750

Children's

Mitkey Astromouse, Quist (U.S. & U.K.), 1971 . . . . £75/£25

JEAN de BRUNHOFF

(b.1899 d.1937)

The creator of Barbar the Elephant, after his death de Brunhoff's series of books were continued by his son, Laurent.

The Story of Barbar, the Little Elephant, Methuen, 1934 . . . . £160
Barbar's Travels, Methuen, 1937 . . . . £150
Barbar the King, Methuen, 1936. . . . . £145
Barbar's ABC, Methuen, 1937 . . . . . £150
Barbar's Friend Zephir, Methuen, 1937 . . £75
Barbar at Home, Methuen, 1938 . . . . £125
Barbar and Father Christmas, Methuen, 1940. £100

'Babar' Books by Laurent de Brunhoff

Barbar and that Rascal Arthur, Methuen, 1948 £60
Picnic at Barbar's, Methuen, 1950 . . . . £60
Barbar's Visit to Bird Island, Methuen, 1952 . £45
Barbar's Castle, Methuen, 1962 . . . . . £25
Serafina the Giraffe, Methuen, 1964 [1965] . £20
Barbar's French Lessons, Cape, 1965 . . . £20
Serafina's Lucky Find, Methuen, 1967 . . . £20
Barbar and the Professor, Methuen, 1972 . £10
Barbar's Book of Colour, Methuen, 1985 . . £10

JOHN BUCHAN

(b.1875 d.1940)

Prolific Scottish writer whose talents ranged across novels, biographies, essays and poetry. Buchan's Richard Hannay mystery novels are still popular, and his historical romances have attracted much praise.

Historical Romances

Sir Quixote of the Moors, Fisher Unwin, 1895 . £200
John Burnet of Barns, John Lane, 1898 . . . £75
Grey Weather, Moorland Tales, John Lane, 1899 £75
A Lost Lady of Old Years, John Lane, 1899 . £50
Salute to Adventurers, Nelson [1915] . . . £50
ditto, Doran (U.S.), 1915 . . . . £25
The Path of the King, Hodder & Stoughton [1921] . . . . £50/£15
Midwinter, Hodder & Stoughton [1923]. . £65/£15
ditto, Doran (U.S.), 1923 . . . . £45/£10
Witch Wood, Hodder & Stoughton, 1927 . £150/£35
ditto, Houghton Mifflin (U.S.), 1927. . . . £45/£10
The Blanket of the Dark, Hodder & Stoughton, 1931 . . . . £100/£20
The Free Fishers, Hodder & Stoughton, 1934 £75/£20
ditto, Houghton Mifflin (U.S.), 1934. . . £45/£10

The Richard Hannay Books

The Thirty-Nine Steps, Blackwood, 1915 . . £175
Greenmantle, Hodder & Stoughton, 1916 . . £75
Mr Standfast, Hodder & Stoughton, 1918 . . £45
ditto, Doran (U.S.), 1919 . . . . £25
The Three Hostages, Hodder & Stoughton [1924] . . . . £75/£15
ditto, Houghton Mifflin (U.S.), 1924. . . . £45/£10
The Courts of the Morning, Hodder & Stoughton, 1929 . . . . £75/£10
The Island of Sheep, Hodder & Stoughton, 1936 . . . . £75/£10

The Edward Leithen Books

The Power House, Blackwood, 1916 . . . . £50
John MacNab, Hodder & Stoughton [1925] £200/£50
ditto, Houghton Mifflin (U.S.), 1925. . . . £45/£10
The Dancing Floor, Hodder & Stoughton [1926] . . . . £150/£45
The Runagates Club and Other Stories, Hodder & Stoughton, 1928 . . . . £200/£45
ditto, Houghton Mifflin (U.S.), 1928. . . . £45/£20
The Gap in the Curtain, Hodder & Stoughton, 1932 . . . . £150/£45
ditto, Houghton Mifflin (U.S.), 1932. . . . £45/£20
Sick Heart River, Hodder & Stoughton, 1941 £75/£15
ditto, as ***Mountain Meadow***, Houghton Mifflin (U.S.),1941 . . . . £45/£10

The Dickson McCunn Books

Huntingtower, Hodder & Stoughton, 1922 . £75/£15
Castle Gay, Hodder & Stoughton, 1930 . . £100/£15
ditto, Houghton Mifflin (U.S.), 1930. . . . £45/£10
The House of the Four Winds, Hodder & Stoughton, 1935 . . . . £75/£15
ditto, Houghton Mifflin (U.S.), 1935. . . . £45/£10

Contemporary Adventures

The Half-Hearted, Isbister, 1900 . . . . . £125
The Watcher by the Threshold and Other Tales, Blackwood, 1902. . . . . £100
Prester John, Nelson, 1910 . . . . £50
ditto, Doran (U.S.), 1910 . . . . £25
A Prince of the Captivity, Hodder & Stoughton, 1933 . . . . £100/£15

Miscellaneous

A Lodge in the Wilderness, Blackwood, 1906 . £150

The Moon Endureth, Tales and Fancies, Blackwood, 1912 . . . . £100

ditto, Sturgis & Walton (U.S.), 1912. . . . . £25

The Island of Sheep (by 'Cadmus & Harmonia'), Hodder & Stoughton, 1919 . . . . £45

Omnibus Editions

The Four Adventures of Richard Hannay, Hodder & Stoughton, 1930 . . . . £30/£10

The Adventures of Sir Edward Leithen, Hodder & Stoughton, 1933 . . . . £30/£10

Four Tales, Hodder & Stoughton, 1936. . . £30/£10

The Adventures of Dickson McCunn, Hodder & Stoughton, 1937 . . . . £30/£10

A Five-Fold Salute to Adventure, Hodder & Stoughton, 1939 . . . . £30/£10

Adventures of Richard Hannay, Houghton Mifflin & Co., 1939 . . . . £20/£5

Adventurers All, Houghton Mifflin (U.S.), 1942 . . . . £40/£10

Verse

Sir Walter Raleigh, Blackwell, 1897 (wraps) . £150

The Pilgrim Fathers, Blackwell, 1898 (wraps) . £150

Poems, Scots and English, Jack, 1917 . . . . £50

Children's

Sir Walter Raleigh, T. Nelson & Sons, [1911] . £70

The Magic Walking Stick, Hodder & Stoughton, 1932 . . . . £40/£10

The Long Traverse, Hodder & Stoughton, 1941 . . . . £40/£10

Non Fiction

Scholar Gipsies, John Lane, 1896 . . . . . £150

Brasenose College, F.E. Robinson, 1898 . . £125

The African Colony, Blackwood, 1903 . . . £125

The Law Relating to Taxation of Foreign Income ..., Stevens and Sons, 1905 . . . . £200

Some Eighteenth Century Byways and other essays, Blackwood, 1908. . . . . £75

The Marquis of Montrose, T. Nelson & Sons, 1913 . . . . £35

Andrew Jameson, Lord Ardwall, Blackwood, 1913 . . . . £45

Nelson's History of the War, T. Nelson & Sons, [1915-1919] (24 vols) £250

ditto, as ***A History of the Great War***, Nelson, 1921-22 (4 vols, condensed version of the above) . . £100

ditto, Nelson, 1921-22 (500 numbered, signed copies, 4 vols) £275

ditto, Houghton Mifflin (U.S.), 1923 (4 vols) . £75

These for Remembrance, privately printed, 1919 £450

The History of the South African Forces in France, T. Nelson & Sons, [1920] . . . . . . £100/£25

Francis and Riversdale Grenfell: A Memoir, T. Nelson & Sons, [1920] . . . . £75/£15

A Book of Escapes and Hurried Journeys, T. Nelson & Sons, [1922] . . . . £150/£45

The Last Secrets: the final mysteries of exploration, T. Nelson & Sons, [1923]. . . . . . £150/£35

ditto, Houghton Mifflin (U.S.), 1924. . . . £45/£10

Days to Remember: the British Empire in the Great War, T. Nelson & Sons, 1923 (with Henry Newbolt) . . . . £75/£20

Lord Minto: A Memoir, T. Nelson & Sons, [1924] . . . . £75/£20

The History of the Royal Scots Fusiliers, 1678-1918, T. Nelson & Sons, [1925] . . . . . £150/£65

Homilies and Recreations, T. Nelson & Sons, [1926] . . . . £50/£10

ditto, T. Nelson & Sons, [1926] (large paper edition, 200 signed and numbered copies) £150

Montrose, T. Nelson & Sons, [1928] . . . £35/£10

ditto, Houghton Mifflin (U.S.), 1928. . . £45/£10

The Kirk in Scotland, 1560-1929, Hodder and Stoughton, [1930] (with George Adam Smith) . . . . £100/£25

Sir Walter Scott, Cassell, [1932] . . . . . £30/£5

Julius Caesar, P. Davies, 1932 . . . . . £30/£5

The Massacre of Glencoe, P. Davies, 1933 . £50/£20

ditto, Putnam (U.S.), 1933 . . . . . . £35/£10

Gordon at Khartoum, P. Davies, 1934 . . £50/£20

Oliver Cromwell, Hodder and Stoughton, [1934] . . . . £50/£20

ditto, Houghton Mifflin (U.S.), 1934. . . . £35/£10

The King's Grace:, 1910-35, Hodder and Stoughton, [1935]. . . . . £30/£10

ditto, Hodder and Stoughton, 1935 (large paper edition, 500 numbered, signed copies) £100

Augustus, Hodder and Stoughton, 1937 . . £50/£20

ditto, Houghton Mifflin (U.S.), 1937. . . . £35/£10

Memory Hold-the-Door, Hodder and Stoughton, 1940 . . . . £15/£5

Comments and Characters, T. Nelson & Sons, [1940] . . . . £75/£25

Canadian Occasions, Hodder and Stoughton, [1940] . . . . £25/£10

The Clearing House: a John Buchan Anthology, Hodder and Stoughton, 1946 . . . . . £10/£5

Life's Adventure: a John Buchan Anthology, Hodder and Stoughton, 1947 . . . . £15/£5

ANTHONY BUCKERIDGE
(b.1912)

Buckeridge was a teacher whose first successes were radio plays for adults. The immortal Jennings appeared later on, first on the radio and then in a series of children's novels.

Children's Novels
Jennings Goes to School, Collins, 1950. . £50/£10
Jennings Follows a Clue, Collins, 1951. . £40/£10
Jennings' Little Hut, Collins, 1951 . . . £30/£10
Jennings and Darbishire, Collins, 1952 . £25/£10
Jennings' Diary, Collins, 1953 . . . . £20/£10
A Funny Thing Happened!, Lutterworth Press [1953] . . . . £20/£10
Rex Milligan's Busy Term, Lutterworth Press, 1953 . . . . £20/£10
According to Jennings, Collins, 1954 . . £20/£10
Our Friend Jennings, Collins, 1955. . . £20/£10
Rex Milligan Raises the Roof, Lutterworth Press, 1955 . . . . £20/£10
Rex Milligan Holds Forth, Lutterworth Press, 1955 . . . . £20/£10
Thanks to Jennings, Collins, 1957 . . . £20/£10
Take Jennings, for Instance, Collins, 1958. £20/£10
Jennings, as Usual, Collins, 1959 . . . £20/£10
The Trouble with Jennings, Collins, 1960 . £20/£10
Just Like Jennings, Collins, 1961 . . . £20/£10
Rex Milligan Reporting, Lutterworth Press, 1961 . . . . £20/£10
Leave It to Jennings, Collins, 1963 . . . £20/£10
Jennings, of Course!, Collins, 1964. . . £20/£10
Especially Jennings!, Collins, 1965 . . . £20/£10
A Bookful of Jennings!, Collins, 1966 (anthology) . . . . £20/£10
ditto, as ***The Best of Jennings***, Collins, 1972 £10/£5
Jennings Abounding, Collins, 1967. . . £20/£5
Jennings in Particular, Collins, 1968 . . £20/£5
Trust Jennings!, Collins, 1969 . . . . £20/£5
The Jennings Report, Collins, 1970. . . £50/£10
Typically Jennings!, Collins, 1971 . . . £20/£5
Speaking of Jennings, Collins, 1973 . . £20/£5
Jennings at Large, Armada, 1977 (wraps) . . £5
ditto, Severn House, 1980. . . . . . £20/£5
Jennings Again!, Macmillan, 1991 . . . £10/£5
Jennings Unlimited, Macmillan, 1993. . . £10/£5
That's Jennings, Macmillan, 1994 . . . £10/£5

Plays
Jennings Abounding, A Comedy with Music, Samuel French , 1980 (wraps) £5

ANTHONY BURGESS
(b.1917 d.1993)

Born John Burgess Wilson, this inventive, satirical author often presents a bleak outlook on life. He has produced very distinctive, well received novels, his best known work being the classic *The Clockwork Orange.*

Novels
Time for a Tiger, Heinemann, 1956 . . . £350/£75
The Enemy in the Blanket, Heinemann, 1958 . . . . £100/£45
Beds in the East, Heinemann, 1959 . . . £50/£20
The Right to an Answer, Heinemann, 1960. £50/£20
ditto, Norton (U.S.), 1961. . . . . . £25/£10
The Doctor is Sick, Heinemann, 1960 . . £75/£25
ditto, Norton (U.S.), 1966. . . . . . £25/£10
The Worm and the Ring, Heinemann, 1961 £300/£125
Devil of a State, Heinemann, 1961 . . . £25/£10
ditto, Norton (U.S.), 1962. . . . . . £15/£5
One Hand Clapping, Peter Davies, 1961 (pseud. 'Joseph Kell') . . . . £125/£45
ditto, Knopf (U.S.), 1961 . . . . . . £20/£5
A Clockwork Orange, Heinemann, 1962 (black boards) . . . . £400/£100
ditto, Norton (U.S.), 1963. . . . . . £200/£75
The Wanting Seed, Heinemann, 1962 . . £75/£35
ditto, Norton (U.S.), 1963. . . . . . £10/£5
Honey for the Bears, Heinemann, 1963 . . £25/£10
ditto, Norton (U.S.), 1964. . . . . . £10/£5
Inside Mr Enderby, Heinemann, 1963 (pseud. 'Joseph Kell') . . . . £100/£45
Nothing Like the Sun, Heinemann, 1964 . £25/£10
ditto, Norton (U.S.), 1964. . . . . . £10/£5
The Eve of Saint Venus, Sidgwick & Jackson, 1964 . . . . £25/£10
A Vision of Battlements, Sidgwick & Jackson, 1964 . . . . £25/£10
ditto, Norton (U.S.), 1966. . . . . . £10/£5
Tremor of Intent, Heinemann, 1966 . . . £25/£10
ditto, Norton (U.S.), 1966. . . . . . £10/£5
Enderby Outside, Heinemann, 1968 . . . £35/£10
Enderby, Norton (U.S.), 1968 . . . . £10/£5
MF, Cape, 1971 . . . . £15/£5
ditto, Knopf (U.S.), 1971 . . . . . . £10/£5
Napoleon Symphony, Cape, 1974 . . . £10/£5
ditto, Knopf (U.S.), 1974 . . . . . . £10/£5
The Clockwork Testament; or Enderby's End, Hart-Davis MacGibbon, 1974. . . . . . £10/£5
ditto, Knopf (U.S.), 1974 . . . . . . £10/£5
Moses: A Narrative, Dempsey & Squires, 1976 . . . . £10/£5
ditto, Stonehill (U.S.), 1976 . . . . . £10/£5
Beard's Roman Women, McGraw Hill (U.S.), 1976 .

. . . . £10/£5
ditto, Hutchinson, 1977 . . . . £10/£5
Abba Abba, Faber, 1977 . . . . £10/£5
ditto, Little, Brown, (U.S.), 1977. . . . £10/£5
1985, Hutchinson, 1978 . . . . £10/£5
ditto, Little, Brown, (U.S.), 1978. . . . £10/£5
Man of Nazareth, McGraw Hill (U.S.), 1979 £10/£5
ditto, Magnum, 1980 . . . . £10/£5
Earthly Powers, Hutchinson, 1980 . . . £10/£5
ditto, Simon and Schuster (U.S.), 1980 . . £10/£5
The End of the World News, Hutchinson, 1982 £10/£5
ditto, McGraw Hill (U.S.), 1983 . . . . £10/£5
Enderby's Dark Lady, Hutchinson, 1984 . £10/£5
ditto, McGraw Hill (U.S.), 1984 . . . . £10/£5
The Kingdom of the Wicked, Hutchinson, 1985 £10/£5
ditto, Franklin Library (U.S.), 1985 (signed edition) £30
ditto, Arbor House (U.S.), 1985 . . . . £10/£5
The Pianoplayers, Hutchinson, 1986 . . £10/£5
ditto, Arbor House (U.S.), 1986 . . . . £10/£5
The Old Iron, Hutchinson, 1989 . . . . £10/£5
ditto, Random House (U.S.), 1989 . . . £10/£5
Mozart and the Wolf Gang, Hutchinson, 1991 £10/£5
Byrne, Hutchinson, 1995 . . . . £10/£5

Autobiography
Little Wilson and Big God, Weidenfeld & Nicholson (U.S.), 1986 . . . . £10/£5
ditto, Heinemann, 1987 . . . . £10/£5
You've Had Your Time, Heinemann, 1990 . £10/£5
ditto, Grove Weidenfeld (U.S.), 1991 . . £10/£5

Literary Criticism & Biography
English Literature: A Survey for Students, Longmans, Green, 1958 (written as 'John Burgess Wilson') £50
The Novel Today, Longmans, Green, 1963 (wraps) £10
Language Made Plain, English University Press, 1964 . . . . £35/£10
ditto, Crowell (U.S.), 1965 . . . . . £10/£5
Here Comes Everybody, Faber, 1965 . . £20/£10
The Novel Now, Faber, 1967 . . . . . £15/£5
ditto, Norton (U.S.), 1967. . . . . . £10/£5
Urgent Copy, Literary Studies, Cape, 1968 . £30/£10
ditto, Norton (U.S.), 1969. . . . . . £15/£5
Shakespeare, Cape, 1970 . . . . . . £20/£10
ditto, Knopf (U.S.), 1970 . . . . . . £15/£5
Joysprick, Deutsch, 1973 . . . . . . £30/£10
Ernest Hemingway and his World, Thames & Hudson, 1978 . . . . £15/£5
ditto, Scribner (U.S.), 1978 . . . . . £10/£5
Ninety-Nine Novels, Allison & Busby, 1984 £10/£5
ditto, Simon & Schuster (U.S.), 1984 . . £10/£5
Flame into Being: The Life and Works of D.H. Lawrence, Heinemann, 1985 . . . . £10/£5
ditto, Arbor House (U.S.), 1985 . . . . £10/£5

Mouthful of Air, Hutchinson, 1992 . . . £10/£5
ditto, Morrow (U.S.), 1992 . . . . . . £10/£5

Miscellaneous Works
A Long Trip to Teatime, Dempsey & Squires, 1976 . . . . £15/£5
ditto, Stonehill (U.S.), 1976 . . . . . £10/£5
New York, Time-Life Books, 1977 . . . £10/£5
The Land Where Ice-Cream Grows, Benn, 1979 . . . . £10/£5
ditto, Doubleday (U.S.), 1979 . . . . £10/£5
This Man and Music, Hutchinson, 1982 . £10/£5
ditto, McGraw Hill (U.S.), 1983 . . . . £10/£5
Homage to Qwert Yuiop, Hutchinson, 1985 £10/£5
ditto, McGraw Hill (U.S.), 1986 . . . . £10/£5
Oberon Old and New, Hutchinson, 1985 . £10/£5
Carmen, Hutchinson, 1986 . . . . . £10/£5
Blooms of Dublin, Hutchinson, 1986 . . £10/£5

W.J. BURLEY
(b.1914)

Burley worked as an engineer until he won a mature state scholarship to Oxford where he read Zoology. Later working as a teacher, he is famous for his 'Wycliffe' detective novels set in Cornwall.

'Wycliffe' Novels
Three Toed Pussy, Gollancz, 1968 . . . £75/£25
To Kill A Cat, Gollancz, 1970 . . . . £75/£25
ditto, Walker (U.S.), c.1970 . . . . . £35/£15
Guilt-Edged, Gollancz, 1971 . . . . . £45/£20
ditto, as ***Wycliffe and the Guilt Edged Alibi***, Corgi, 1994 (wraps) £5
Death in a Salubrious Place, Gollancz, 1973 £45/£15
ditto, Walker (U.S.), 1973 . . . . . £15/£5
ditto, as ***Wycliffe and Death in a Salubrious Place***, Corgi, 1995 (wraps) £5
Death in Stanley Street, Gollancz, 1975 . £45/£15
ditto, as ***Wycliffe and Death in Stanley Street***, Corgi, 1990 (wraps) £5
Wycliffe and the Pea-Green Boat, Gollancz, 1975 . . . . £45/£15
ditto, Walker (U.S.), 1975 . . . . . £15/£5
Wycliffe and the Schoolgirls, Gollancz, 1976 £45/£15
ditto, Walker (U.S.), 1976 . . . . . £15/£5
Wycliffe and the Scapegoat, Gollancz, 1978 £40/£10
ditto, Doubleday (U.S.), 1979 . . . . £15/£5
Wycliffe in Paul's Court, Gollancz, 1980 . £30/£10
ditto, Doubleday (U.S.), 1980 . . . . £15/£5
Wycliffe's Wild Goose Chase, Gollancz, 1982 £30/£10
ditto, Doubleday (U.S.), 1982 . . . . £10/£5
Wycliffe and the Beales, Gollancz, 1983 . £30/£10

ditto, Doubleday (U.S.), 1984 . . . . £10/£5
Wycliffe and the Four Jacks, Gollancz, 1985 £25/£10
ditto, Doubleday (U.S.), 1986 . . . . £10/£5
Wycliffe and the Quiet Virgin, Gollancz, 1986 £25/£10
ditto, Doubleday (U.S.), 1986 . . . . £10/£5
Wycliffe and the Winsor Blue, Gollancz, 1987 £20/£10
ditto, Doubleday (U.S.), 1987 . . . . £10/£5
Wycliffe and the Tangled Web, Gollancz, 1988 £15/£5
ditto, Doubleday (U.S.), 1989 . . . . £10/£5
Wycliffe and the Cycle of Death, Gollancz, 1990 . . . . £10/£5
ditto, Doubleday (U.S.), 1991 . . . . £10/£5
Wycliffe and the Dead Flautist, Gollancz, 1991 £10/£5
ditto, St Martin's Press (U.S.), 1992 . . . £10/£5
Wycliffe and the Last Rites, Gollancz, 1992 £10/£5
ditto, St Martin's Press (U.S.), 1993 . . . £10/£5
Wycliffe and the Dunes Mystery, Gollancz, 1994 . . . . £10/£5
ditto, St Martin's Press (U.S.), 1994 . . . £10/£5
Wycliffe and the House of Fear, Gollancz, 1995 . . . . £10/£5
ditto, St Martin's Press (U.S.), 1996 . . . £10/£5
Wycliffe Omnibus, Gollancz, 1996 . . . £10/£5
Wycliffe and the The Redhead, Gollancz, 1997 £10/£5
ditto, St. Martin's Press (U.S.) 1998 . . . £10/£5

Other Novels
A Taste of Power: A Novel, Gollancz, 1966 £65/£30
Death in Willow Pattern, Gollancz, 1969 . £45/£20
The Schoolmaster, Gollancz, 1977 . . . £25/£10
ditto, Walker (U.S.), 1977 . . . . . . £10/£5
The Sixth Day: A Novel, Gollancz, 1978 . £25/£10
Charles and Elizabeth: A Gothic Novel, Gollancz, 1979 . . . . £20/£10
ditto, Walker (U.S.), 1981 . . . . . £10/£5
The House of Care: A Novel, Gollancz, 1981 £20/£10

Non Fiction
City of Truro, 1877-1977, O. Blackford, Truro, 1977 (wraps) £5

FRANCES HODGSON BURNETT
(b.1849 d.1924)

Novelist and children's writer, Burnett was born in Manchester but spent many years in America, where she died. Her sentimental children's stories have often been filmed, with varying degrees of success.

Children's Books
Little Lord Fauntleroy, Scribners (U.S.), 1886 . £300
ditto, Warne, 1886. . . . . £100
Sara Crewe; or What Happened at Miss Minchin's, Unwin, 1887 . . . . £45
Sara Crewe, and Editha's Burglar, Warne, 1888 £30
Little Saint Elizabeth and Other Child Stories, Warne, 1890 . . . . £15
Children I Have Known, Osgood McIlvaine, 1892 [1891]. £30
The One I Knew the Best of All, Warne, 1893 . £15
The Captain's Youngest and Other Stories, Warne, 1894 . . . . £15
Two Little Pilgrims' Progress, Warne, 1895 . £25
A Little Princess, Warne, 1905 . . . . . £40
Racketty Packetty House, Warne, 1907. . . £30
The Troubles of Queen Silver-Bell, Warne, 1907 £30
The Secret Garden, Stokes (U.S.), 1911 . . £500
ditto, Heinemann, 1911 . . . . £350
My Robin, Putnam, 1913 . . . . £25
The Land of the Blue Flower, Putnam, 1912 . £30
The Lost Prince, Hodder & Stoughton, 1915 . £30
The Little Hunchback Zia, Heinemann, 1916 . £50
The Cozy Lion, Tom Stacey, 1972 . . . £10/£5
The Spring Cleaning, Tom Stacey, 1973 . £10/£5

Adult Books
Novels and Novellas
That Lass O'Lowrie's: A Lancashire Story, Scribners (U.S.), 1887 . . . . £75
ditto, Warne [1877] £30
Dolly: A Love Story, Routledge [1877] . . . £20
ditto, Warne, 1893 (new edition) £10
Theo: A Love Story, Ward Lock [1877]. . . £20
ditto, Warne, 1877 (new edition) £20
Pretty Polly Pemberton: A Love Story, Routledge, 1878 . . . . £20
Kathleen: A Love Story, Routledge, 1878 . . £20
ditto, as ***Kathleen Mavourneen***, Chatto & Windus, 1879. . . . . £20
Miss Crespigny: A Love Story, Routledge [1878] £20
Haworth's, Macmillan, 1879 (2 vols) . . . £50
Louisiana, and That Lass O'Lowrie's, Macmillan, 1880 . . . . £30
A Fair Barbarian, Warne [1881] £20
Through One Administration, Warne, 1883 (3 vols) £75
A Woman's Will; or, Miss Defarge, Warne, 1887 £20
The Fortunes of Philippa Fairfax, Warne, 1888 £30
The Pretty Sister of Jose, Spencer Blackett, 1889 (wraps) £20
A Lady of Quality, Warne, 1896 . . . . . £10
His Grace of Ormonde, Warne, 1897 . . . £10
In Connection with the De Willoughby Claim, Warne, 1899 . . . . £10
The Making of a Marchioness, Smith Elder, 1901 £15
The Methods of Lady Walderhurst, Smith Elder, 1902 . . . . £10
In the Closed Room, Hodder & Stoughton, 1904 £50

The Dawn of Tomorrow, Warne, 1907 . . . £10
The Shuttle, Heinemann, 1907 . . . . . £10
T. Tembarom, Hodder & Stoughton [1913]. . £10
The White People, Heinemann, 1920 . . . £15/£5
The Head of the House of Coombe, Heinemann, 1922 . . . . £15/£5
Robin, Heinemann, 1922 . . . . £15/£5

Short Stories
Surly Tim and Other Stories, Ward Lock [1877] £20
Our Neighbour Opposite, Routledge [1878] . £20
Natalie and Other Stories, Warne [1879] . . £20
Lindsay's Luck, Routledge, 1879 . . . . £20
The Tide on the Moaning Bar and A Quiet Life, Routledge [1879]. £20

EDGAR RICE BURROUGHS
(b.1875 d.1950)

The 'Tarzan' titles are Burroughs' best known, but his many 'Martian' and other science fiction stories are of seminal importance in the development of the genre.

'Tarzan' Titles
Tarzan of the Apes, McClurg (U.S.), 1914 . . £1,000
The Return of Tarzan, McClurg (U.S.), 1915 . £150
The Beasts of Tarzan, McClurg (U.S.), 1916 . £150
The Son of Tarzan, McClurg (U.S.), 1917 . . £150
Tarzan and the Jewels of Opar, McClurg (U.S.), 1918 . . . . £150
Jungle Tales of Tarzan, McClurg (U.S.), 1919 . . . . £50
Tarzan the Untamed, McClurg (U.S.), 1920 £450/£50
Tarzan the Terrible, McClurg (U.S.), 1921 . £400/£50
Tarzan and the Golden Lion, McClurg (U.S.), 1923 . . . . £400/£50
Tarzan and the Ant Men, McClurg (U.S.), 1924 . . . . £350/£50
Tarzan, Lord of the Jungle, McClurg (U.S.), 1928 . . . . £350/£50
Tarzan and the Lost Empire, Metropolitan (U.S.), 1929 . . . . £300/£50
Tarzan at the Earth's Core, Metropolitan (U.S.), 1930 . . . . £250/£50
Tarzan the Invincible, ERB Inc. (U.S.), 1931 . . . . £250/£50
Tarzan Triumphant, ERB Inc. (U.S.), 1932 . . . . £250/£50
Tarzan and the City of Gold, ERB Inc. (U.S.), 1933 . . . . £250/£50
Tarzan and the Lion Man, ERB Inc. (U.S.), 1934 . . . . £250/£50
Tarzan and the Leopard Man, ERB Inc. (U.S.), 1935 . . . . £250/£50
Tarzan's Quest, ERB Inc. (U.S.), 1936 . . £200/£50
Tarzan and the Forbidden City, ERB Inc. (U.S.), 1938 . . . . £150/£50
Tarzan and the Tarzan Twins with Jad-Bal-Ja the Golden Lion, Whitman (U.S.), 1936 . . . £175
Tarzan the Magnificent, ERB Inc. (U.S.), 1939 . . . . £100/£35
Tarzan and the Foreign Legion, ERB Inc. (U.S.), 1947 . . . . £75/£25
Tarzan the Madman, Canaveral (U.S.), 1964 £75/£25
Tarzan and the Castaways, Canaveral (U.S.), 1965 . . . . £75/£25

'Mars' Titles
A Princess of Mars, McClurg (U.S.), 1917 . . £200
The Gods of Mars, McClurg (U.S.), 1918 . . £75
The Warlord of Mars, McClurg (U.S.), 1919 . £60
Thuvia, Maid of Mars, McClurg (U.S.), 1920 . . . . £150/£40
Chessmen of Mars, McClurg (U.S.), 1922 . £125/£35
Master Mind of Mars, McClurg (U.S.), 1928 £125/£25
Fighting Man of Mars, Metropolitan (U.S.), 1931 . . . . £125/£25
Sword of Mars, ERB Inc. (U.S.), 1936 . . £175/£25
Synthetic Man of Mars, ERB Inc. (U.S.), 1940 . . . . £100/£25
Llana of Gathol, ERB Inc. (U.S.), 1948 . £100/£25
John Carter of Mars, Canaveral (U.S.), 1964 £50/£25

'Venus' Titles
Pirates of Venus, ERB Inc. (U.S.), 1934 . £125/£35
Lost on Venus, ERB Inc. (U.S.), 1935 . . £100/£25
Carson on Venus, ERB Inc. (U.S.), 1939 . £100/£25
Escape on Venus, ERB Inc. (U.S.), 1946 . £100/£25

'Pellucidar' Titles
At the Earth's Core, McClurg (U.S.), 1922 . £250/£75
Pellucidar, McClurg (U.S.), 1923 . . . £250/£50
Tanar of Pellucidar, Metropolitan (U.S.), 1930 . . . . £175/£50
Back to the Stone Age, ERB Inc. (U.S.), 1937 . . . . £150/£50
Land of Terror, ERB Inc. (U.S.), 1944 . . £175/£50
Savage Pellucidar, Canaveral (U.S.), 1963 . £45/£20

'Old West' Titles
The Bandit of Hell's Bend, McClurg (U.S.), 1925 . . . . £400/£75
The War Chief, McClurg (U.S.), 1927 . . £250/£75
Apache Devil, ERB Inc. (U.S.), 1933 . . £200/£50
The Oakdale Affair/The Rider, ERB Inc. (U.S.), 1937 . . . . £200/£50
The Deputy Sheriff of Comanche Country, ERB Inc. (U.S.), 1940 . . . . £200/£50

Others

The Girl from Hollywood, McCauley (U.S.), 1923 . . . . £200/£50

The Land That Time Forgot, McClurg (U.S.), 1924 . . . . £200/£50

The Cave Girl, McClurg (U.S.), 1925 . . . £150/£50

The Eternal Lover, McClurg (U.S.), 1925 . £175/£50

The Moon Maid, McClurg (U.S.), 1926 . £175/£50

Jungle Girl, ERB Inc. (U.S.), 1932 . . £175/£50

The Lad and the Lion, ERB Inc. (U.S.), 1938 . . . . £175/£50

The Girl from Farris, Wilma Co. (U.S.), 1959 . . . . £150/£50

WILLIAM S. BURROUGHS

(b.1914 d.1997)

A controversial American 'beat' novelist who wrote of his experience as a heroin addict in *Junkie* and *The Naked Lunch.* The latter became a cult classic, banned on the grounds of obscenity.

Novels

Junkie: Confessions of an Unredeemed Drug Addict, Ace (U.S.), 1953 (pseud. 'William Lee', bound back to back with *Narcotic Agent,* wraps) £150

ditto, Digit, 1957 . . . . £75

ditto, as ***Junky***, Penguin, 1977 . . . . . . £5

The Naked Lunch, Olympia Press (Paris), 1959 (wrappers, with d/w) . . . . £275/£150

ditto, as ***Naked Lunch***, Grove Press (U.S.), 1959 [1962] . . . . £100/£25

ditto, Calder, 1964 . . . . £45/£15

ditto, Grove Press (U.S.), 1984 (500 signed copies in box) £100

The Soft Machine, Olympia Press (Paris), 1961 (wrappers, with d/w) . . . . £150/£75

ditto, Grove Press (U.S.), 1966 . . . . . £45/£20

ditto, Calder & Boyars, 1968 . . . . . . £45/£15

The Ticket That Exploded, Olympia Press (Paris), 1962 (wrappers, with d/w) . . . . . £125/£75

ditto, Grove Press (U.S.), 1967 . . . . £30/325

ditto, Calder & Boyars 1968 . . . . . . £45/£15

Dead Fingers Talk, Olympia Press (Paris), 1963 (wrappers) £75

ditto, Calder 1963 . . . . £50/£25

Nova Express, Grove Press (U.S.), 1964 . £45/£15

ditto, Cape 1966 . . . . £35/£15

The Wild Boys: A Book of the Dead, Grove Press (U.S.), 1971 . . . . £15

ditto, Calder & Boyars, 1972 . . . . . . £25/£10

Port of Saints, Covent Garden Press, 1973 [1975] (100 signed copies of 200) . . . . £250/£200

ditto, Covent Garden Press, 1973 [1975] (100 unsigned copies of 200) . . . . £125/£75

ditto, Blue Wind Press (U.S.), 1980 . . . £20/£5

ditto, Blue Wind Press (U.S.), 1980 (200 signed copies, slipcase) . . . . £125/£100

ditto, Calder 1983 . . . . £20/£5

Short Novels, Calder, 1978 . . . . . . £20/£10

Blade Runner: A Movie, Blue Wind Press (U.S.), 1979 . . . . £25/£10

Cities of the Red Night: A Boy's Book, Calder, 1981 . . . . £25/£10

ditto, Holt Rinehart (U.S.), 1981 . . . . £20/£5

ditto, Holt Rinehart (U.S.), 1981 (500 signed, numbered copies, slipcase, no d/w) £175

The Place of Dead Roads, Holt Rinehart (U.S.), 1983 . . . . £20/£5

ditto, Holt Rinehart (U.S.), 1983 (300 signed, numbered copies, slipcase, no d/w) £175

ditto, Calder 1984 . . . . £20/£5

Queer, Viking (U.S.), 1985 . . . . . . £15/£5

ditto, Picador, 1985 . . . . £15/£5

The Western Lands, Viking (U.S.), 1987 . £10/£5

ditto, Picador 1988 . . . . £10/£5

Stories

Exterminator!, Viking (U.S.), 1974 . . . £30/£10

ditto, Calder & Boyars, 1974 . . . . . . £30/£10

Early Routines, Cadmus (U.S.), 1981 (26 of 151 signed copies) £150

ditto, Cadmus (U.S.), 1981 (125 of 151 signed copies, glassine d/w) . . . . £100/£90

ditto, Cadmus (U.S.), 1981 . . . . . . £25/£10

Verse

The Exterminator, Auerhahn Press (U.S.), 1960 (with Brion Gysin, wraps) £50

Minutes to Go, Two Cities (Paris), 1960 (with Gysin, Corso and Beiles, wraps) £50

Others

Letter from a Master Addict to Dangerous Drugs, privately published, 1957 (stapled sheets) . . £200

Yage Letters, City Lights Books (U.S.), 1963 (with Allen Ginsburg, wraps) £50

Takis, Gall Schwarz, 1962 (wraps) £25

Roosevelt After Inauguration, Fuck You Press (U.S.), 1964 (pseud. 'Willy Lee', wraps) £45

Time, 'C' Press (U.S.), 1965 (with Brion Gysin, 886 copies of 986, wraps) £100

ditto, 'C' Press (U.S.), 1965 (100 signed copies of 986, wraps) £500

ditto, 'C' Press (U.S.), 1965 (14 copies with page of manuscript and an original drawing by Gysin) £1,500

ditto, Urgency Press Rip-Off, 1972 (495 copies) £100
Valentine's Day Reading, American Theatre for Poets (U.S.), 1965 (wraps) £20
Health Bulletin: Apo-33, Fuck You Press (U.S.), 1965 . . . . £25
White Subway, Aloes Books, (1965) (975 copies of 1,000, wraps). £60
ditto, Aloes Books, (1965) (25 signed copies of 1,000) £500
Apo-33 Bulletin: A Metabolic Regulator, City Lights Books (U.S.), 1966 (wraps) £75
So Who Owns Death TV?, Beach Books (U.S.), 1967 (with Claude Pelieu and Carl Weissner, wraps) £100
The Dead Star, Nova Broadcast Press (U.S.), 1969 (wraps) £30
Fernseh-Tuberkulose, Nova Press (Frankfurt), 1969 (with Claude Pelieu and Carl Weissner) . . . £30
Academy Series, Urgency Press Rip Off, [1969] (650 copies, wraps) £50
The Job, Interviews with William S. Burroughs, Grove Press (U.S.), 1970 . . . . . . £60/£25
The Third Mind, Viking (U.S.), 1978 . . . £15/£5
Alf's Smile, Unicorn Books, 1971 (189 copies). £200
Electronic Revolution, 1970-71, Blackmoor Head Press, 1971 (100 signed copies of 500, wraps) £200
ditto, Blackmoor Head Press, 1971 (400 copies of 500, wraps). £75
A Book of Breething, Chopin, 1974 (wraps) . £15
ditto, Chopin, 1974 (350 numbered copies, wraps) £45
ditto, Chopin, 1974 (50 bound, signed copies) £245
ditto, Blue Wind Press (U.S.), 1975 (wraps) . £10
ditto, Blue Wind Press (U.S.), 1975 (175 signed copies) £75
Ah Pook is Here and Other Texts, Calder, 1979 . . . . £50/£20
A William Burroughs Reader, Picador, 1982 . £10
The Adding Machine, Selected Essays, Calder, 1985 . . . . £20/£5
ditto, Seaver Books (U.S.), 1986 . . . . £15/£5
Interzone, Picador, 1989 . . . . . . £15/£5
ditto, Viking, 1989. . . . . £15/£5
The Letters of William S. Burroughs, 1945-59, Picador, 1993. . . . . £15/£5
My Education, A Book of Dreams, Picador, 1995 . . . . £10/£5
ditto, Viking, 1995. . . . . £10/£5

A.S. BYATT

(b.1936)

A novelist and critic, and sister of Margaret Drabble, Byatt won the Booker prize for *Possession*, her best known work.

Novels

Shadow of a Sun, Chatto & Windus, 1964 . £100/£35
ditto, as ***Shadow of the Sun***, Harcourt Brace (U.S.), 1964 . . . . £100/£35
The Game, Chatto & Windus, 1967 . . . £75/£25
ditto, Scribner (U.S.), 1968 . . . . . £50/£15
The Virgin in the Garden, Chatto & Windus, 1978 . . . . £25/£10
ditto, Knopf (U.S.), 1979 . . . . . . £15/£5
Still Life, Chatto & Windus and The Hogarth Press, 1985 . . . . £20/£5
ditto, Scribner (U.S.), 1985 . . . . . £15/£5
Possession, Chatto & Windus, 1990 . . . £20/£5
ditto, Random House (U.S.), 1990 . . . £15/£5
Babel Tower, Chatto & Windus, 1996 . . £10/£5
ditto, Random House (U.S.), 1996 . . . £10/£5

Short Stories and Novellas

Sugar and Other Stories, Chatto & Windus, 1987 . . . . £25/£10
ditto, Scribner (U.S.), 1987 . . . . . £20/£5
Angels and Insects, Chatto & Windus, 1992 £20/£5
ditto, London Limited Editions, 1992 (150 signed copies, acetate d/w) . . . . £65/£50
ditto, Random House (U.S.), 1992 . . . £10/£5
Matisse Stories, Chatto & Windus, 1993 . £15/£5
ditto, Random House (U.S.), 1993 . . . £10/£5

Djinn in the Nightingale's Eye, Five Fairy Stories, Chatto and Windus, 1994 . . . . . £10/£5
ditto, Random House (U.S.), 1994 . . . £10/£5

Non Fiction

Degrees of Freedom: The Novels of Iris Murdoch, Chatto & Windus, 1965 . . . . . . £50/£25
ditto, Barnes & Noble (U.S.), 1965 . . . £45/£20
Wordsworth and Coleridge in their Time, Nelson, 1970 . . . . £45/£20
ditto, Crane, Russak (U.S.), 1973 . . . £25/£10
ditto, as *Unruly Times: Wordsworth and Coleridge in Their Times*, Hogarth Press, 1989 . . . £10/£5
Iris Murdoch, Longman, 1970 . . . . . £10
ditto, Crane-Russak (U.S.), 1973 . . . . . £10
Ford Madox Ford and the Prose Tradition, Chatto & Windus, 1982. . . . . £25/£10
ditto, Knopf (U.S.), 1982 . . . . . . £20/£10
Passions of the Mind, Chatto & Windus, 1991 £10/£5
ditto, Turtle Bay (U.S.), 1992. . . . . £10/£5
Imagining Characters, Six Conversations with Women Writers, Chatto & Windus, 1995 (with Ignes Sodre) . . . . £20/£10
ditto, as ***Imagining Characters: Conversations about Women Writers***, Vintage Books (U.S.), 1997 . £5

RANDOLPH CALDECOTT
(b.1846 d.1886)

A British illustrator, Caldecott produced a series of popular picture books which are said to have had an influence on Beatrix Potter.

'Picture Books'

The House that Jack Built, Routledge, [1878-84] £30
The Diverting History of John Gilpin, Routledge, [1878-84] £30
The Mad Dog, Routledge, [1878-84] . . . £75
The Babes in the Wood, Routledge, [1878-84] . £30
The Milkmaid, Routledge, [1878-84] . . . £30
Sing a Song for Sixpence, Routledge, [1878-84] £25
The Queen of Hearts, Routledge, [1878-84] . £25
The Farmer's Boy, Routledge, [1878-84] . . £25
Hey Diddle Diddle and Baby Bunting, Routledge, [1878-84] £25
The Three Jovial Huntsmen, Routledge, [1878-84] £25
A Frog He Would A-Wooing Go, Routledge, [1878-84] £25
The Fox Jumps Over the Parson's Gate, Routledge, [1878-84] £25
Come Lasses and Lads, Routledge, [1878-84] . £25
Ride a Cock Horse to Banbury Cross and A Farmer Went Trotting upon his Grey Mare, Routledge, [1878-84] £25
An Elegy on the Glory of her Sex, Mrs Mary Blaize, by Dr Oliver Goldsmith, Routledge, [1878-84]. £25
The Great Panjandrum Himself, Routledge, [1878-84] £25
R. Caldecott's Picture Book, Vol. One, Routledge, [1879] (containing the first four 'Picture Books') £50
R. Caldecott's Picture Book, Vol. Two, Routledge, [1881] (containing the second four 'Picture Books') £50
R. Caldecott's Collection of Pictures and Songs, Routledge, [1881] (reissue of Caldecott's 'Picture Book' Vols One and Two) £50
The Hey Diddle Diddle Picture Book, Routledge, [1883] (contains 4 'Picture Books') £50
The Panjandrum Picture Book, Routledge, [1885] (contains 4 'Picture Books') £50
The Complete Collection of Randolph Caldecott's Pictures and Songs, Routledge, [1887] (contains all sixteen 'Picture Books', 800 copies) . . . £250
R. Caldicott's Picture Books, Routledge, [1889-1892] (contains the first four 'Picture Books') . . . £50
Randolph Caldecott's Second Collection of Pictures and Songs, Warne, [1895] (reissue of *The Hey Diddle Diddle Picture Book* and *The Panjandrum Picture Book*) £50

Other Titles illustrated by Randolph Caldecott

Frank Mildmay, or The Naval Officer, by Captain Marryat, Routledge [1873] £35
Baron Bruno, or The Unbelieving Philosopher and Other Fairy Stories, by Louisa Morgan, Macmillan, 1875 . . . . £45
Old Christmas, From the Sketchbook of Washington Irving, Macmillan, 1876. . . . . . . £35
Bracebridge Hall, or The Humorists, by Washington Irving, Macmillan. 1877 [1876]. £35
What the Blackbird Said, A Story in Four Chirps, by Mrs Frederick Locker, Routledge, 1881 . . £45
Jackanapes, by Juliana Horatia Ewing, S.P.C.K., 1884 [1883]. £25
Some of Aesop's Fables with Modern Instances, Macmillan 1883 . . . . £30
Daddy Darwin's Dovecote, A Country Tale, by Juliana Horatia Ewing, S.P.C.K., [1884] £25
Lob Lie-By-The-Fire, by Juliana Horatia Ewing, S.P.C.K. [1885] £25
Fables de la Fontaine, Macmillan, 1885 . . £30
Jack and the Beanstalk, by Hallam Tennyson, Macmillan, 1886 . . . . £30
The Owls of Olynn Belfry, by A.Y.D., Field & Tuer, [1886]. £30
Jackanapes, by Juliana Horatia Ewing, S.P.C.K., [1892] (contains *Daddy Darwin's Dovecote* and *Lob Lie-By-The-Fire*) £25
Randolph Caldecott's Painting Book, S.P.C.K. [1895] £45

TRUMAN CAPOTE
(b.1924 d.1984)

American short story writer and novelist whose career developed after he won the O. Henry prize in 1946.

Novels

Other Voices, Other Rooms, Random House (U.S.), 1948 . . . . £100/£35
ditto, Heinemann, 1948 . . . . £50/£20
The Grass Harp, Random House (U.S.), 1951 £75/£25
ditto, Heinemann, 1952 . . . . £45/£15
Answered Prayers: The Unfinished Novel, Random House (U.S.), 1987 . . . . £10/£5
ditto, Hamish Hamilton, 1986 . . . . . £10/£55

Short Stories

A Tree of Night and Other Stories, Random House (U.S.), 1949 . . . . £65/£25
ditto, Heinemann, 1950 . . . . £20/£10
Breakfast at Tiffany's, Random House (U.S.), 1958 . . . . £100/£35

ditto, Heinemann, 1959 . . . . £35/£10
A Christmas Memory, Random House (U.S.), 1966 (no d/w) £125
One Christmas, Random House (U.S.), 1983 (no d/w, slipcase) £20
ditto, Random House (U.S.), 1983 (500 numbered copies signed by the author) £125
ditto, Hamish Hamilton, 1983 . . . . £10/£5
Three by Truman Capote, Random House (U.S.), 1985 . . . . £20/£5

Plays
The Grass Harp, Random House (U.S.), [1952] . . . . £60/£25
The Thanksgiving Visitor, Random House (U.S.), 1967 (300 signed, numbered copies, slipcase) . £125
ditto, Random House (U.S.), 1968 (slipcase) . . £25
ditto, Hamish Hamilton, 1969 . . . . . £15/£5
House of Flowers, Random House (U.S.), 1968 . . . . £200/£100
Trilogy: An Experiment in Multimedia. with Elinor Perry, Macmillan (U.S.), 1969 . . . . £15/£5

Non Fiction
Local Color, Random House (U.S.), 1950 . £100/£60
ditto, Random House (U.S.), 1950 (200 numbered copies) £200
The Muses are Heard: An Account, Random House (U.S.), 1956 . . . . £50/£25
ditto, Heinemann, 1957 . . . . £25/£10
Observations, Simon & Schuster (U.S.), 1959 (glassine d/w, slipcase) . . . . £175/£150
ditto, Weidenfeld and Nicolson, 1959 (glassine d/w, slipcase) . . . . £175/£150
In Cold Blood: A True Account of a Multiple Murder and its Consequences, Random House (U.S.), 1965 . . . . £25/£10
ditto, Hamish Hamilton, 1966 . . . . . £20/£5
The Dogs Bark: Public People and Private Places, Random House (U.S.), 1973 . . . . . £15/£5
ditto, Weidenfeld and Nicolson, 1974 . . £10/£5
Then it All Came Down: Criminal Justice Today Discussed by Police, Criminals and Correcting Officers with Comments by Truman Capote, Random House (U.S.), 1976 . . . . . £35/£10
Music for Chameleons, Random House (U.S.), 1980 . . . . £15/£5
ditto, Random House (U.S.), 1980 (350 signed copies, slipcase) £125
ditto, Hamish Hamilton, 1980 . . . . £10/£5

Collections
Selected Writings of Truman Capote, Random House (U.S.), 1963 . . . . £20/£5
ditto, Hamish Hamilton, 1963 . . . . . £10/£5
A Capote Reader, Random House (U.S.), 1987 £10/£5
ditto, Hamish Hamilton, 1987 . . . . £10/£5

PETER CAREY

(b.1943)

An Australian author of novels and stories which have been described as post-modern fables.

Novels
Bliss, Univ. of Queensland Press (Australia), 1981 . . . . £45/£15
ditto, Faber, 1981 . . . . £35/£10
ditto, Harper (U.S.), 1981 . . . . . . £25/£10
Illywhacker, Univ. of Queensland Press (Australia), 1985 . . . . £20/£10
ditto, Faber, 1985 . . . . £20/£5
ditto, Harper (U.S.), 1985 . . . . . . £15/£5
Oscar and Lucinda, Univ. of Queensland Press (Australia), 1988 . . . . £20/£10
ditto, Faber, 1988 . . . . £10/£5
ditto, Harper (U.S.), 1988 . . . . . . £10/£5
The Tax Inspector, Univ. of Queensland Press (Australia), 1991 . . . . £10/£5
ditto, Faber, 1991 . . . . £10/£5
ditto, Knopf (U.S.), 1991 . . . . . . £10/£5
ditto, Franklin Library (U.S.), 1991 (signed edition) £30
The Unusual Life of Tristan Smith, Univ. of Queensland Press (Australia), 1994. . . £10/£5
ditto, Faber, 1994 . . . . £10/£5
ditto, Knopf (U.S.), 1995 . . . . . . £10/£5
Jack Maggs, Univ. of Queensland Press (Australia), 1997 . . . . £10/£5
ditto, Faber, 1997 . . . . £10/£5
ditto, Knopf (U.S.), 1998 . . . . . . £10/£5

Short Stories
The Fat Man in History, Univ. of Queensland Press (Australia), 1974 . . . . £45/£20
ditto, Faber, 1980 . . . . £30/£10
ditto, Random House (U.S.), 1980 . . . £25/£10
War Crimes, Univ. of Queensland Press (Australia), 1979 . . . . £45/£25
Collected Stories, Faber, 1995 . . . . £15/£5

Others
Bliss: The Screenplay, Univ. of Queensland Press (Australia), 1986 . . . . £10/£5
ditto, as ***Bliss: The Film***, Faber, 1986 . . . £10/£5
A Letter to Our Son, Univ. of Queensland Press (Australia), 1994 . . . . £10/£5
Big Bazoohley, Faber, 1995 . . . . . £10/£5

LEWIS CARROLL

(b.1832 d.1898)

Born Charles Lutwidge Dodgson, Carroll was a humorist and children's writer. *Alice's Adventures in Wonderland* was an immediate success.

Alice's Adventures in Wonderland, Macmillan, 1865 (withdrawn, illustrated by Sir John Tenniel) £200,000
ditto, Appleton (U.S.), 1866 (illustrated by Sir John Tenniel) £3,500
ditto, Macmillan, 1866 (illustrated by Sir John Tenniel) £3,000
ditto, as ***Alice's Adventures Under Ground***, Macmillan, 1886 . . . . £150
ditto, Macmillan, 1889 (illustrated by Gertrude Thomson). £125
ditto, Harper (U.S.), 1901 (illustrated by Peter Newell) £100
ditto, Mansfield (U.S.), 1896 (illustrated by Blanche McManus) £75
ditto, Ward Lock, 1907 (illustrated by Blanche McManus) £75
ditto, Cassell, 1907 (illustrated by Charles Robinson) £100
ditto, Heinemann, [1907] (illustrated by Arthur Rackham). £150
ditto, Heinemann, [1907] (illustrated by Arthur Rackham, deluxe limited edition) £1,250
ditto, Routledge, 1907 (illustrated by Thomas Maybank). £100
ditto, Chatto & Windus, 1907 (illustrated by Millicent Sowerby) £100
ditto, Nelson, 1908 (illustrated by Harry Rountree) £75
ditto, Raphael Tuck [1910] (12 colour plates by Mabel Lucie Attwell) £150
ditto, Dutton (U.S.), 1929 (illustrated by Willy Pogany) . . . . £35/£10
ditto, Dutton (U.S.), 1929 (signed, limited edition, illustrated by Willy Pogany). £250
ditto, Black Sun Press, Paris, 1930 (illustrated by Marie Lurencin) £1,500
ditto, with extra plates £4,500
ditto, Random House (U.S.), 1969 (illustrated by Salvador Dali) £3,000
Phantasmagoria and Other Poems, Macmillan, 1869 . . . . £250
ditto, Macmillan, 1911 (miniature edition) . . . £25
The Songs from Alice's Adventures in Wonderland, Weekes, [1870] (wraps) £75
Through the Looking Glass, Macmillan, 1872 (illustrated by Sir John Tenniel) £250
ditto, Mansfield (U.S.), 1899 (illustrated by Blanche McManus) £50
ditto, Harper (U.S.), 1902 (illustrated by Peter Newell) £100
The Hunting of the Snark, An Agony in Eight Fits, Macmillan, 1876 . . . . £450
Rhyme? and Reason?, Macmillan, 1883 . . . £150
A Tangled Tale, Macmillan, 1885 . . . . . £100
The Game of Logic, Macmillan, 1886 (with envelope, card and 9 counters) £100
Symbolic Logic, Macmillan, 1896 . . . . £500
Sylvie and Bruno, Macmillan, 1889 . . . . £50
Sylvie and Bruno Concluded, Macmillan, 1893 £45
Three Sunsets and Other Poems, Macmillan, 1898 £30
The Lewis Carroll Picture Book, T. Fisher Unwin, 1899 . . . . £50
Feeding the Mind, Chatto & Windus, 1907 (boards) £25
ditto, Chatto & Windus, 1907 (wraps) £20
ditto, Chatto & Windus, 1907 (leather binding). £45
Bruno's Revenge, Collins [1924] £15
Further Nonsense, Verse and Prose, T. Fisher Unwin, 1926 . . . . £35/£15
The Collected Verse of Lewis Carroll, Macmillan, 1932 . . . . £50/£20
For the Train, Denis Archer, 1932 . . . . £40/£15
The Rectory Umbrella and Mischmasch, Cassell & Co., 1932 . . . . £40/£15
Useful and Instructive Poetry, Butler and Tanner, 1954 . . . . £25/£10
ditto, Macmillan (U.S.), 1954. . . . . . £25/£10
The Diaries of Lewis Carroll, Cassell, 1953 [1954] (2 vols) . . . . £75/£45
The Rectory Magazine, University of Texas (U.S.), 1975 . . . . £20/£10
The Letters of Lewis Carroll, Macmillan, 1979 (2 vols) . . . . £25/£20
ditto, as ***The Selected Letters of Lewis Carroll***, Macmillan, 1982 (1 vol.) . . . . . £10/£5
Alice in Wonderland and Through the Looking Glass, Stockholm, 1946 (illustrated by Mervyn Peake) £200
ditto, Wingate, 1954 . . . . £100

ANGELA CARTER

(b.1940 d.1992)

Carter was a novelist and short story writer whose work explores the territory of magic realism.

Novels

Shadow Dance, Heinemann, 1966 . . . £125/£45
ditto, as ***Honeybuzzard***, Simon and Schuster (U.S.), 1966 . . . . £100/£45
The Magic Toyshop, Heinemann, 1967 . . £100/£45

ditto, Simon and Schuster (U.S.), 1968 . . £40/£15
Several Perceptions, Heinemann, 1968 . . £50/£15
ditto, Simon and Schuster (U.S.), 1968 . . £30/£10
Heroes and Villains, Heinemann, 1969 . . £50/£15
ditto, Simon and Schuster (U.S.), 1969 . . £30/£15
Love, Hart-Davis, 1971 . . . . . . £40/£15
The Infernal Desire Machines of Doctor Hoffman, Hart-Davis, 1972. . . . . £45/£15
ditto, as ***The War of Dreams***, Harcourt Brace (U.S.), 1974 . . . . £35/£15
The Passion of New Eve, Gollancz, 1977 . £20/£5
ditto, Harcourt Brace (U.S.), 1977 . . . . £20/£5
Nights at the Circus, Chatto & Windus, 1984 £20/£5
ditto, Viking (U.S.), 1986. . . . . . . £20/£5
Wise Children, Chatto & Windus, 1991 . . £20/£5
ditto, Farrar Straus (U.S.), 1992 . . . . £10/£5

Short Stories
Fireworks: Nine Profane Pieces, Quartet, 1974 . . . . £35/£10
ditto as ***Fireworks: Nine Stories in Various Disguises***, Harper & Row (U.S.), 1981 . . . . . . £15/£5
The Bloody Chamber and Other Stories, Gollancz, 1979 . . . . £20/£5
ditto, Harper (U.S.), 1979. . . . . . . £20/£5
Black Venus, Chatto & Windus, 1985 . . £20/£5
ditto, as ***Saints and Strangers*** Viking (U.S.), 1986 . . . . £20/£5
Wayward Girls and Wicked Women, Virago, 1986 (wraps) £5
American Ghosts and Old World Wonders, Chatto & Windus, 1993. . . . . £20/£5
Burning Your Boats, The Complete Short Stories, Chatto & Windus, 1995 . . . . . . £20/£10
ditto, Holt (U.S.), 1996 . . . . . . £15/£5

Children's Fiction
Miss Z, The Dark Young Lady, Heinemann, 1970 . . . . £35/£15
ditto, Simon & Schuster (U.S.), 1970 . . £25/£10
The Donkey Prince, Simon & Schuster (U.S.), 1970 . . . . £20/£10
The Fairy Tales of Charles Perrault, Gollancz, 1977 . . . . £40/£20
Martin Leman's Comic and Curious Cats, Gollancz, 1979 . . . . £15
ditto, Crown (U.S.), 1979. . . . . . . £10
The Music People, Hamish Hamilton, 1980 (with Leslie Carter). £10
Moonshadow, Gollancz, 1982 (with Justin Todd) £35
Sleeping Beauty and Other Favourite Fairy Tales, Gollancz, 1983 . . . . £10
ditto, Schocken, 1984 . . . . £10/£5

Verse
The Unicorn, The Location Press, 1966 (150 copies, wraps). £50

Others
The Sadeian Woman, Virago, 1979 . . . . £35
ditto, Pantheon (U.S.), 1979 . . . . . . £15/£5
Nothing Sacred, Selected Writings, Virago, 1982 (wraps) £5
Come Unto These Yellow Sands, Bloodaxe Books, 1984 . . . . £15
Expletives Deleted, Chatto & Windus, 1992 . £10
The Curious Room, Collected Dramatic Works, Chatto & Windus, 1996 . . . . £10/£5
ditto, Secker & Warburg (U.S.), 1997 . . £10/£5

RAYMOND CARVER
(b.1938 d.1988)

American short story writer and poet, Carver's work has been translated into more than twenty languages.

Fiction
Put Yourself in My Shoes, Capra (U.S.), 1974 (wraps) £50
Will you Please Be Quiet, Please?, McGraw-Hill (U.S.), 1976 . . . . £250/£100
Furious Seasons and Other Stories, Capra (U.S.), 1977 (100 signed copies) £500
ditto, Capra (U.S.), 1977 (wraps). £50
What We Talk About When We Talk About Love, Knopf (U.S.), 1981 . . . . £50/£25
The Pheasant, Metacom (U.S.), 1982 (150 signed copies, wraps) £100
ditto, Metacom (U.S.), 1982 (26 lettered signed copies) £300
Cathedral, Knopf (U.S.), 1983 . . . . £50/£45
The Stories of Raymond Carver, Picador, 1985 (wraps) £10
My Father's Life, Babcock & Koontz (U.S.), 1986 (200 signed copies, wraps) £75
Those Days: Early Writings by Raymond Carver, Raven (U.S.), 1987 (100 signed, numbered copies, wraps). £125
ditto, Raven (U.S.), 1987 (26 signed, lettered copies) £250
ditto, Raven (U.S.), 1987 (14 presentation copies) £500
Where I'm Calling From: New and Selected Stories, Atlantic Monthly (U.S.), 1988 . . . . £25/£10
ditto, Franklin Library (U.S.), 1988 (signed) . £75
ditto, Harvill, 1993 . . . . £20/£10
Elephant and Other Stories, Collins Harvill, 1988 . . . . £20/£10

Three Stories, Engdahl Typography, 1990 (400 copies) . . . . £50/£25

Poetry

Near Klamath, English Club of Sacramento State College (U.S.), 1968 (wraps) £1,250
Winter Insomnia, Kayak (U.S.), 1970 (wraps) . £45
At Night the Salmon Move, Capra (U.S.), 1976 (100 signed copies) £250
Distress Sale, Lord John Press, 1981 (150 signed copies) £75
Two Poems, Scarab (U.S.), 1982 ("The Baker" and "Louise", 100 signed copies, wraps) £125
This Water, Ewart (U.S.), 1985 (100 signed copies, wraps). £100
ditto, Ewart (U.S.), 1985 (26 signed, lettered copies) £200
Where Water Comes Together with Other Water, Random House, 1985 . . . . £40/£15
Ultramarine, Random House (U.S.), 1986 . £30/£10
In a Marine Light: Selected Poems, Collins Harvill, 1987 . . . . £25/£10
The Painter and the Fish, Ewart (U.S.), 1988 (26 signed copies, hardcover) £200
ditto, Ewart (U.S.), 1988 (74 signed, copies, wraps) £100
A New Path to the Waterfall, Atlantic Monthly (U.S.), 1989 . . . . £25/£10
ditto, Atlantic Monthly (U.S.), 1989 (200 signed copies, slipcase). . . . . £75/£65
ditto, Collins Harvill, 1989 . . . . . . £25/£10
All of Us, Collins Harvill, 1996 . . . . . £25/£10
ditto, Knopf (U.S.), 1998 . . . . £20/£10

Essays, Poems, and Stories

Fires, Capra (U.S.), 1983 (250 signed, hardback copies) . . . . £75/£65
ditto, Capra (U.S.), 1983 (wraps). £25
ditto, Collins Harvill, 1985 . . . . . . £25/£10
Music, Ewart (U.S.), 1985 (26 signed, lettered copies, wraps). £150
ditto, Ewart (U.S.), 1985 (100 signed, numbered copies, wraps) £45
No Heroics, Please: Uncollected Writings, Collins Harvill, 1991 . . . . £25/£10
diito, Vintage Contemporaries (U.S.), 1992 . . £10

Screenplay

Dostoevsky: A Screenplay, Capra (U.S.), 1985 (with Tess Gallagher, bound in with ***King Dog*** by Le Guin, wraps). £25
ditto, Capra (U.S.), 1985 (200 copies signed by all authors, wraps) £100

JOYCE CARY

(b.1888 d.1957)

A novelist, perhaps best known for his *The Horse's Mouth*, made into a film with Alec Guinness.

Aissa Saved, Benn, 1932 . . . . . . £75/£20
ditto, Harper & Row (U.S.), 1962 . . . £20/£10
The African Witch, Gollancz, 1936 . . . £75/£20
ditto, Morrow (U.S.), 1936 . . . . . £15/£5
Castle Corner, Gollancz, 1938, ... £75/£20
ditto, Harper & Row (U.S.) 1963. . . . £20/£10
Mister Johnson, Gollancz, 1939 . . . . £75/£20
ditto, Harper & Row (U.S.), 1948 . . . £10/£5
Charley Is My Darling, Joseph, 1940 . . £50/£10
ditto, Harper & Row (U.S.), 1959 . . . £10/£5
A House of Children, Joseph, 1941 . . . £35/£10
ditto, Harper & Row (U.S.), 1955 . . . £10/£5
Herself Surprised, Joseph, 1941 . . . . £35/£10
ditto, Harper & Row (U.S.), 1941 . . . £10/£5
To Be a Pilgrim, Joseph, 1942 . . . . £35/£10
ditto, Harper & Row (U.S.), 1942 . . . £10/£5
The Horse's Mouth, Joseph, 1944 . . . £45/£15
ditto, Harper & Row (U.S.), 1944. . . . £10/£5
The Moonlight, Joseph, 1946 . . . . £35/£10
ditto, Harper & Row (U.S.), 1946. . . . £10/£5
A Fearful Joy, Joseph, 1949 . . . . . £25/£10
ditto, Harper & Row (U.S.), 1949. . . . . £10/£5
Prisoner of Grace, Joseph, 1952 . . . . £25/£10
ditto, Harper & Row (U.S.), 1952. . . . £10/£5
Except the Lord, Joseph, 1953 . . . . £20/£5
ditto, Harper & Row (U.S.), 1953. . . . £10/£5
Not Honour More, Joseph, 1955. . . . £20/£5
ditto, Harper & Row (U.S.), 1955. . . . £10/£5
The Horse's Mouth and The Old Strife at Plant's, George Rainbird/Joseph, 1957 . . . . £20/£10
The Captive and the Free, Joseph, 1959 . £20/£10
ditto, Harper & Row (U.S.), 1959. . . . £10/£5
Spring Song and Other Stories, Joseph, 1960 £15/£10
ditto, Harper & Row (U.S.), 1960. . . . £10/£5
Cock Jarvis, Joseph, 1974 . . . . . £10/£5
ditto, St. Martin's (U.S.), 1975 . . . . £10/£5

Verse

Marching Soldier, Joseph, 1945 . . . . £25/£10
The Drunken Sailor: A Ballad-Epic, Joseph, 1947 . . . . £20/£10

Others

Power in Men, Liberal Book Club/Nicholson & Watson, 1939. . . . . £20/£10
ditto, Nicholson & Watson, 1939. . . . £100/£50
ditto, Univ. of Washington Pr. (U.S.), 1963 . £10/£5
The Case for African Freedom, Secker & Warburg, 1941 . . . . £20/£10

ditto, Secker & Warburg, 1941 (revised edition) . . . £20/£10

ditto, as ***The Case for African Freedom and Other Writings on Africa***, Univ. of Texas (U.S.), 1962 . . . £10/£5

Process of Real Freedom, Joseph, 1943. . £35/£10

Britain and West Africa, Longman's Green and Co., 1946 (wraps) £20

Art and Reality, Ways of the Creative Process, Cambridge University Press, 1958 . . . £10/£5

ditto, Harper & Row (U.S.), 1958. . . . £10/£5

Memoir of the Bobotes, University of Texas (U.S.), 1960 . . . . £15/£5

ditto, Joseph, 1964. . . . . £10/£5

Selected Essays, Joseph, 1976 . . . . £15/£5

ditto, St. Martin's (U.S.), 1976 . . . . £10/£5

WILLA CATHER

(b.1873 d.1947)

O Pioneers was Cather's first popular success, and serious critical recognition was to come with the award of the Pulitzer Prize for *One of Ours*, and the Prix Femina Americaine in 1933.

Novels

Alexander's Bridge, Houghton Mifflin/Riverside Press (U.S.), 1912 (blue cloth). £50

ditto, Heinemann, 1912 . . . . £35

O Pioneers!, Houghton Mifflin/Riverside Press (U.S.), 1913 (tan or cream cloth) £75

ditto, Heinemann, 1913 . . . . £35

The Song of the Lark, Houghton Mifflin/Riverside Press (U.S.), 1915 . . . . £45

ditto, Murray, 1916 . . . . £25

My Ántonia, Houghton Mifflin/Riverside Press (U.S.), 1918 . . . . £45

ditto, Heinemann, 1919 . . . . £25

One of Ours, Knopf (U.S.), 1922 (35 signed, on Japanese vellum of 345 copies, glassine d/w) . . . £1,500/£1,250

ditto, Knopf (U.S.), 1922 (310 signed of 345 copies, slipcase) . . . . £500/£400

ditto, Knopf (U.S.), 1922 . . . . . . £100/£25

ditto, Knopf (U.S.), 1922 (250 special copies) £75/£25

ditto, Heinemann, 1923 . . . . £75/£25

A Lost Lady, Knopf (U.S.), 1923. . . . £150/£45

ditto, Knopf (U.S.), 1923 (220 signed copies, slipcase) . . . . £650/£550

ditto, Heinemann, 1924 . . . . £75/£25

The Professor's House, Knopf (U.S.), 1925 (40 signed, on Japanese vellum of 225 copies, glassine d/w) . . . . £600/£500

ditto, Knopf (U.S.), 1925 (185 signed of 225 copies, slipcase) . . . . £350/£300

ditto, Knopf (U.S.), 1925 . . . . £65/£20

ditto, Heinemann, 1925 . . . . £35/£10

My Mortal Enemy, Knopf (U.S.), 1926 (220 signed copies, slipcase) . . . . £450/£350

ditto, Knopf (U.S.), 1926 . . . . £65/£20

ditto, Heinemann, 1928 . . . . £35/£10

Death Comes for the Archbishop, Knopf (U.S.), 1927 (50 signed copies on Japanese vellum) . . £2,000

ditto, Knopf (U.S.), 1927 (175 signed copies) . £750

ditto, Knopf (U.S.), 1927 . . . . £75/£20

ditto, Heinemann, 1927 . . . . £35/£10

ditto, Knopf (U.S.), 1929 (170 signed copies) . . . . £350/£250

Shadows on the Rock, Knopf (U.S.), 1931 £75/£15

ditto, Knopf (U.S.), 1931 (619 signed, numbered copies) . . . . £250/£200

ditto, Cassell, 1932 . . . . £30/£10

Lucy Gayheart, Knopf (U.S.), 1935 . . . . £50/£10

ditto, Knopf (U.S.), 1935 (749 signed, numbered copies, d/w and slipcase) . . . . . £250/£175

ditto, Cassell, 1935 . . . . £25/£10

Sapphira and the Slave Girl, Knopf (U.S.), 1940 . . . . £45/£10

ditto, Knopf (U.S.), 1940 (525 signed, numbered copies) . . . . £200/£150

ditto, Cassell, 1941 . . . . £15/£5

Short Stories

The Troll Garden, McClure, Phillips & Co. (U.S.), 1905 . . . . £100

Youth and the Bright Medusa, Knopf (U.S.), 1920 . . . . £100/£35

ditto, Knopf (U.S.), 1920 (35 signed copies) £400/£500

ditto, Heinemann, 1921 . . . . £75/£25

The Fear that Walks by Noonday, Phoenix Bookshop, 1931 (30 numbered copies) £500

Obscure Destinies, Knopf (U.S.), 1932 (260 signed, numbered copies, d/w and slipcase) . £200/£150

ditto, Knopf (U.S.), 1932 . . . . £35/£10

ditto, Cassell, 1932 . . . . £25/£10

The Old Beauty and Others, Knopf (U.S.), 1948 . . . . £30/£10

ditto, Cassell, 1956 . . . . £10/£5

Five Stories, Vintage Books (U.S.), 1956 (wraps) £100

Early Stories of Willa Cather, Dodd, Mead & Co. (U.S.), 1957 . . . . £20/£10

Willa Cather's Collected Short Fiction, University of Nebraska Press (U.S.), 1965 . . . . . £20/£5

Uncle Valentine and Other Stories, University of Nebraska Press (U.S.), 1973 . . . . . £15/£5

Verse

April Twilights, Gorham Press (U.S.), 1903. . £200

April Twilights and other poems, Knopf (U.S.), 1923 (450 signed, numbered copies, slipcase) £150/£125
ditto, Knopf (U.S.), 1923 . . . . . . £50/£20

Essays
Not Under Forty, Knopf (U.S.), 1936 . . £20/£10
ditto, Knopf (U.S.), 1936 (313 signed, numbered copies on Japanese vellum, d/w and slipcase) . £250/£200
ditto, Cassell, 1936 . . . . £20/£5

Others
My Autobiography, by S.S. McClure, Stokes (U.S.), 1914 (written by Cather). £15
ditto, Murray, 1914 . . . . £10
December Night, Knopf (U.S.), 1933 . . £75/£35
Willa Cather on Writing, Knopf (U.S.), 1949 £30/£10
Writing from Willa Cather's Campus Years, Univ. of Nebraska Press (U.S.), 1950 . . . . £25/£10
Father Junipero's Holy Family, Robbins (U.S.), 1955 (200 copies) . . . . £250/£200
Willa Cather in Europe, Knopf (U.S.), 1956 £20/£5
The Kingdom of Art, Univ. of Nebraska Press (U.S.), 1966 . . . . £25/£10
The World and the Parish, Univ. of Nebraska Press (U.S.), 1970 (2 vols) . . . . £30/£10

RAYMOND CHANDLER
(b.1888 d.1959)

An American novelist and short story writer, Chandler was 45 before he started writing, and in *The Big Sleep* introduced one of the most famous fictional detectives of all time, Philip Marlowe.

Novels
The Big Sleep, Knopf (U.S.), 1939 . . £4,500/£250
ditto, Hamish Hamilton, 1939 . . . £750/£100
Farewell My Lovely, Knopf (U.S.), 1940 £2,000/£250
ditto, Hamish Hamilton, 1940 . . . £750/£100
The High Window, Knopf (U.S.), 1942 . £2,000/£250
ditto, Hamish Hamilton, 1943 . . . £650/£100
The Lady in the Lake, Knopf (U.S.), 1943 . . . . £2,500/£250
ditto, Hamish Hamilton, 1944 . . . £650/£100
The Little Sister, Hamish Hamilton, 1949 . £250/£75
ditto, Houghton Mifflin (U.S.), 1949. . . £175/£65
The Long Goodbye, Hamish Hamilton, 1953 £75/£20
ditto, Houghton Mifflin (U.S.), 1954. . . £45/£20
Playback, Hamish Hamilton, 1958 . . . £75/£20
ditto, Houghton Mifflin (U.S.), 1958 . . £45/£20

Short Stories
Five Murderers, Avon (U.S.), 1944 (wraps) . £150
Five Sinister Characters, Avon (U.S.), 1945 (wraps) £75
Finger Man and Other Stories, Avon (U.S.), [1946] (wraps) £60
Red Wind, World (U.S.), 1946 . . . . £35/£10
Spanish Blood, World (U.S.), 1946 . . . £25/£10
Trouble is My Business, Penguin, 1950 (wraps) £10
ditto, Pocket Books (U.S.), 1951 . . . . . £10
The Simple Art of Murder, Houghton Mifflin (U.S.), 1950 . . . . £200/£30
ditto, Hamish Hamilton, 1950 . . . . £150/£30
Smart Aleck Kill, Hamish Hamilton, 1953 . £100/£25
Pearls are a Nuisance, Houghton Mifflin (U.S.), 1953 . . . . £125/£35
ditto, Hamish Hamilton, 1953 . . . . £100/£25
Killer in the Rain, Hamish Hamilton, 1964 . £45/£15
ditto, Houghton Mifflin (U.S.), 1964. . . £30/£10
The Smell of Fear, Hamish Hamilton, 1965 £30/£10

Omnibus Editions
The Raymond Chandler Omnibus, Hamish Hamilton, 1953 . . . . £65/£15
The Second Raymond Chandler Omnibus, Hamish Hamilton, 1962 . . . . £50/£10
The Raymond Chandler Omnibus, Knopf (U.S.), 1964 . . . . £50/£10

Others
Raymond Chandler Speaking, Houghton Mifflin (U.S.), 1962 . . . . £45/£10
The Notebooks of Raymond Chandler and English Summer - A Gothic Romance, The Ecco Press (U.S.), 1976 . . . . £45/£20
Letters, Raymond Chandler and James M. Fox, Nevile & Yellin (U.S.), 1978 (350 numbered copies) £45
Backfire: Story for the Screen, Santa Barbara Press (U.S.), 1984 . . . . £30
ditto, Santa Barbara Press (U.S.), 1984 (26 lettered copies, signed by Robert Parker, splicase) . . £200
ditto, Santa Barbara Press (U.S.), 1984 (100 signed, numbered copies, splicase) £65
Raymond Chandler's Unknown Thriller: The Screenplay of 'Playback', Mysterious Press (U.S.), 1985 . . . . £30/£15
ditto, Mysterious Press (U.S.), 1985 (250 copies, signed by Robert Parker, slipcase) . . . . £100/£75
ditto, Mysterious Press (U.S.), 1985 (26 signed, lettered copies, splicase) . . . . £200/£175
ditto, Harrap, 1985 . . . . £20/£10
Poodle Springs, Putnam (U.S.), 1989 . . £10/£5
ditto, Macdonald, 1990 (250 copies signed by Parker) . . . . £35/£30
ditto, Macdonald, 1990 . . . . . . £10/£5

LESLIE CHARTERIS

(b.1907 d.1993)

Leslie Charteris was born in Singapore to a Chinese father and English mother. Educated and living in England for several years he wrote a number of crime novels before he hit upon the character of Simon Templar, a gentleman burglar nicknamed 'The Saint'. He later moved to America, and in 1941 became an American citizen.

'Saint' Novels

Meet-the Tiger!, Ward Lock, 1928 . . . £500/£100
ditto, Doubleday (U.S.), 1929 . . . . £300/£65
ditto, as ***The Saint Meets The Tiger***, Hodder & Stoughton, 1963 . . . . £15/£5
The Last Hero, Hodder & Stoughton, [1930] £250/£45
ditto, Doubleday (U.S.), 1931 . . . . £250/£45
ditto, as ***The Saint Closes The Case***, Hodder & Stoughton, 1951 . . . . £25/£10
Knight Templar, Hodder & Stoughton, [1930] . . . . £250/£35
ditto, as ***The Avenging Saint***, Doubleday (U.S.), 1931 . . . . £200/£35
She was a Lady, Hodder & Stoughton, 1931 £200/£35
ditto, as ***Angels of Doom***, Doubleday (U.S.), 1932 . . . . £150/£25
ditto, as ***The Saint Meets His Match***, Hodder & Stoughton, 1950 . . . . £25/£10
Getaway, Hodder & Stoughton, 1932 . . . £125/£20
ditto, as ***Getaway: The New Saint Mystery***, Doubleday (U.S.), 1933 . . . . £125/£20
ditto, as ***The Saint's Getaway***, Hodder & Stoughton, 1950 . . . . £25/£10
The Saint in New York, Hodder & Stoughton, 1935 . . . . £125/£20
ditto, Doubleday (U.S.), 1935 . . . . £125/£15
The Saint Overboard, Hodder & Stoughton, 1936 . . . . £125/£15
ditto, Doubleday (U.S.), 1936 . . . . £125/£15
Thieves' Picnic, Hodder & Stoughton, 1937 £100/£15
ditto, Doubleday (U.S.), 1937 . . . . £75/£15
ditto, as ***The Saint Bids Diamonds***, Hodder & Stoughton, 1950 . . . . £20/£10
Prelude for War, Hodder & Stoughton, 1938 £75/£15
ditto, Doubleday (U.S.), 1938 . . . . £75/£10
ditto, as ***The Saint Plays With Fire***, Hodder & Stoughton, 1951 . . . . £20/£10
The Saint in Miami, Doubleday (U.S.), 1940 £50/£10
ditto, Hodder & Stoughton, 1941. . . . £35/£10
The Saint Steps In, Doubleday (U.S.), 1943 £45/£10
ditto, Hodder & Stoughton, 1944. . . . £35/£10
The Saint Sees it Through, Doubleday (U.S.), 1946 . . . . £40/£10
ditto, Hodder & Stoughton, 1947. . . . . £30/£10
The Saint and the Fiction Makers, Doubleday (U.S.), 1968 . . . . £20/£10
ditto, Hodder & Stoughton, 1969. . . . . £20/£10
The Saint in Pursuit, Doubleday (U.S.), 1970 £20/£5
ditto, Hodder & Stoughton, 1971. . . . . £20/£5
The Saint and the People Importers, Hodder & Stoughton, 1971 (wraps). £10
ditto, Doubleday (U.S.), 1972 . . . . £15/£5
ditto, Hodder & Stoughton, 1973. . . . . £15/£5
The Saint and the Hapsburg Necklace, Doubleday (U.S.), 1976 . . . . £15/£5
ditto, Hodder & Stoughton, 1976. . . . . £15/£5
Send for The Saint, Hodder & Stoughton, 1977 £15/£5
ditto, Doubleday (U.S.), 1978 . . . . £15/£5
The Saint and the Templar Treasure, Doubleday (U.S.), 1979 . . . . £15/£5
ditto, Hodder & Stoughton, 1979. . . . . £15/£5
Count on The Saint, Doubleday (U.S.), 1980 £10/£5
ditto, Hodder & Stoughton, 1980. . . . . £10/£5
Salvage for The Saint, Doubleday (U.S.), 1983 £10/£5
ditto, Hodder & Stoughton, 1983 . . . . £10/£5

'Saint' Novellas and Short Stories

Enter The Saint, Hodder & Stoughton, [1930] . . . . £200/£45
ditto, Doubleday (U.S.), 1931 . . . . £150/£45
Featuring The Saint, Hodder & Stoughton, 1931 . . . . £75/£25
Alias The Saint, Hodder & Stoughton, 1931 £75/£25
The Holy Terror, Hodder & Stoughton, 1932 £65/£25
ditto, as ***The Saint Versus Scotland Yard***, Doubleday (U.S.), 1932 . . . . £65/£25
Once More The Saint, Hodder & Stoughton, 1933. . . . . £65/£25
ditto, as ***The Saint and Mr Teal***, Doubleday (U.S.), 1933 . . . . £65/£25
The Brighter Buccaneer, Hodder & Stoughton, 1933 . . . . £65/£25
ditto, Doubleday (U.S.), 1933 . . . . £50/£25
The Misfortunes of Mr Teal, Hodder & Stoughton, 1934 . . . . £50/£25
ditto, Doubleday (U.S.), 1934 . . . . £50/£25
ditto, as ***The Saint In London***, Hodder & Stoughton, 1952 . . . . £50/£25
Boodle, Hodder & Stoughton, 1934 . . . . £50/£25
ditto, ***The Saint Intervenes***, Doubleday (U.S.), 1934 . . . . £50/£25
The Saint Goes On, Hodder & Stoughton, 1934 . . . . £50/£25
ditto, Doubleday (U.S.), 1935 . . . . £50/£25
The Ace of Knaves, Hodder & Stoughton, 1937 . . . . £50/£25
ditto, Doubleday (U.S.), 1937 . . . . £50/£25

Follow The Saint, Doubleday (U.S.), 1938 . £50/£25
ditto, Hodder & Stoughton, 1939. . . . £50/£25
The Happy Highwayman, Doubleday (U.S.), 1939 . . . . £50/£25
ditto, Hodder & Stoughton, 1939. . . . £50/£25
The Saint Goes West, Doubleday (U.S.), 1942 £45/£15
ditto, Hodder & Stoughton, 1942 . . . £45/£15
The Saint on Guard, Doubleday (U.S.), 1944 £45/£15
ditto, Hodder & Stoughton, 1945. . . . £35/£10
Call For The Saint, Doubleday (U.S.), 1948 £45/£15
ditto, Hodder & Stoughton, 1948. . . . £30/£10
Saint Errant, Doubleday (U.S.), 1948 . . £35/£10
ditto, Hodder & Stoughton, 1949. . . . £25/£10
The Saint in Europe, Doubleday (U.S.), 1953 £35/£10
ditto, Hodder & Stoughton, 1954. . . . £25/£10
The Saint on the Spanish Main, Doubleday (U.S.), 1955 . . . . £30/£10
ditto, Hodder & Stoughton, 1956. . . . £25/£10
The Saint Around the World, Doubleday (U.S.), 1956 . . . . £25/£10
ditto, Hodder & Stoughton, 1957. . . . £25/£10
Thanks to The Saint, Doubleday (U.S.), 1957 £25/£10
ditto, Hodder & Stoughton, 1958. . . . £25/£10
Señor Saint, Doubleday (U.S.), 1958 . . £25/£10
ditto, Hodder & Stoughton, 1959. . . . £25/£10
The Saint to the Rescue, Doubleday (U.S.), 1959 . . . . £25/£10
ditto, Hodder & Stoughton, 1961 . . . £25/£10
Trust The Saint, Doubleday (U.S.), 1962 . £25/£10
ditto, Hodder & Stoughton, 1962. . . . £25/£10
The Saint in the Sun, Doubleday (U.S.), 1963 £25/£10
ditto, Hodder & Stoughton, 1964. . . . £25/£10
Vendetta for The Saint, Doubleday (U.S.), 1964 . . . . £25/£10
ditto, Hodder & Stoughton, 1965 . . . £25/£10
The Saint on TV, Doubleday (U.S.), 1968 . £25/£10
ditto, Hodder & Stoughton, 1968. . . . £25/£10
The Saint Returns, Doubleday (U.S.), 1968 £25/£10
ditto, Hodder & Stoughton, 1969. . . . £25/£10
The Saint Abroad, Doubleday (U.S.), 1969. . £20/£5
ditto, Hodder & Stoughton, 1970. . . . . £15/£5
Catch The Saint, Hodder & Stoughton, 1975 . £15/£5
ditto, Doubleday (U.S.), 1975 . . . . . £15/£5
The Saint in Trouble, Doubleday (U.S.), 1978 . £15/£5
ditto, Hodder & Stoughton, 1979 . . . £15/£5

Collected Editions

Wanted for Murder, Doubleday (U.S.), 1931 £75/£25
The First Saint Omnibus, Hodder & Stoughton, 1939 . . . . £35/£10
ditto, Doubleday (U.S.), 1939 . . . . £35/£10
ditto, as ***Arrest the Saint***, PermaBooks (U.S.), 1951 . . . . £20/£10
The Saint Two in One, Sun Dial Press (U.S.), 1942 . . . . £15/£5
The Saint at Large, Sun Dial Press (U.S.), 1943 . . . . £15/£5
Paging the Saint, Jacobs (U.S.), 1945 (wraps) £25
The Second Saint Omnibus, Doubleday (U.S.), 1951 . . . . £25/£10
ditto, Hodder & Stoughton, 1952. . . . £25/£10
Concerning The Saint, Avon (U.S.), 1958 (wraps) £25
The Saint Cleans Up, Avon (U.S.), 1959 (wraps) £25
The Saint Magazine Reader, Doubleday (U.S.), 1966 . . . . £15/£5
ditto, as ***The Saint's Choice***, Hodder & Stoughton, 1976 . . . . £15/£5
Saints Alive, Hodder & Stoughton, 1974 . . £15/£5
The Saint: Good as Gold, The Ellery Queen Mystery Club (U.S.), 1979 . . . . £10
The Fantastic Saint, Doubleday (U.S.), 1982 . £10/£5
ditto, Hodder & Stoughton, 1982. . . . . £10/£5
The Saint: Five Complete Novels, Avenel Books (U.S.), 1983 . . . . £10/£5

Other Titles

X Esquire, Ward Lock, 1927 . . . . . £125/£65
The White Rider, Ward Lock, 1928 . . . £150/£50
ditto, Doubleday (U.S.), 1930 . . . . £75/£25
Daredevil, Ward Lock, 1929 . . . . . £150/£50
ditto, Doubleday (U.S.), 1929 . . . . £75/£10
The Bandit, Ward Lock, 1929 . . . . £150/£50
ditto, Doubleday (U.S.), 1930 . . . . . £75/£10
Killer of Bulls, Heinemann, 1937 (with Juan Belmonte) . . . . £75/£25
ditto, Doubleday (U.S.), 1937 . . . . . £75/£25
Lady on a Train, Shaw Press (U.S.), 1945 (wraps) £50
Spanish for Fun, Hodder & Stoughton, 1964 (wraps) £10
***Paleneo**: A Universal Sign Language*, Hodder & Stoughton, 1972 (wraps). £10

BRUCE CHATWIN

(b.1940 d.1989)

A travel writer and novelist, Chatwin's first book, *In Patagonia*, won both the Hawthornden Prize and the E.M. Forster Award of the American Academy of Arts and Letters.

Novels

The Viceroy of Ouidah, Jonathan Cape, 1980 £35/£10
ditto, Summit (U.S.), 1980 . . . . . £10/£5
On the Black Hill, Jonathan Cape, 1982 . £25/£10
ditto, Viking, 1982. . . . . £10/£5
The Songlines, Jonathan Cape, 1987 . . £35/£10
ditto, London Limited Editions, 1987 (150 signed copies, glassine wrapper) . . . . £350/£235

ditto, Viking (U.S.), 1987 . . . . £20/£5
ditto, Franklin Library (U.S.), 1987 (200 signed copies) £150
Utz, Jonathan Cape, 1988 . . . . . . £15/£5
ditto, Viking (U.S.), 1989 . . . . . . £10/£5

Travel
In Patagonia, Jonathan Cape, 1977 . . . . £250/£100
ditto, Summit (U.S.) . . . . £75/£35
Patagonia Revisited, Russell, 1985 (with Paul Theroux) . . . . £20/£10
ditto, Russell, 1985 (250 copies, cellophane d/w) . . . . £175/£150
ditto, Houghton Mifflin (U.S.), 1986 . . . . £20/£10
ditto, as ***Nowhere Is a Place***, Sierra Club (U.S.), 1991 . . . . £20/£10

Short Stories
The Attractions of France, Colophon Press, 1993 (26 lettered copies of 211 bound in cloth) £200
ditto, Colophon Press, 1993 (175 numbered copies of 211, wraps) £35

Biography
What am I Doing Here?, Jonathan Cape, 1989 £20/£5
ditto, Viking (U.S.), 1989 . . . . £10/£5
Photographs and Notebooks, Cape, 1993 . £20/£5
ditto, Viking (U.S.), 1993 . . . . £15/£5

Others
Lady Lisa Lyon, Viking (U.S.), 1983 (Robert Mapplethorpe, text by Chatwin, wraps) . . £20
ditto, St. Martin's Press (U.S.), 1983 . . . . £75/£50
The Morality of Things, Typographeum (U.S.), 1993 (175 copies, no d/w) £100
The Anatomy of Restlessness, Selected Writings, 1969-89, Cape, 1996 . . . . £15/£5
ditto, Viking (U.S.), 1996 . . . . £15/£5

G.K. CHESTERTON
(b.1874 d.1936)

Poet, novelist, journalist and essayist, Chesterton is best remembered for his detective stories featuring Father Brown, an unassuming Catholic priest.

'Father Brown' Stories
The Innocence of Father Brown, Cassell, 1911 £250
ditto, John Lane (U.S.), 1911 . . . . . . £100
The Wisdom of Father Brown, Cassell, 1914 . £35
ditto, John Lane (U.S.), 1915 . . . . £20
The Incredulity of Father Brown, Cassell, 1926 . . . . £750/£35
ditto, Dodd Mead (U.S.), 1927 . . . . . £300/£25
The Secret of Father Brown, Cassell, 1927 . £500/£20
ditto, Harper & Bros (U.S.), 1928 . . . £200/£20
The Scandal of Father Brown, Cassell, 1935 . . . . £400/£20
ditto, Dodd Mead (U.S.), 1935 . . . . . £200/£20

Omnibus Editions of 'Father Brown' Stories
The Father Brown Stories, Cassell, 1929 . £45/£20
ditto, as ***The Father Brown Omnibus***, Dodd Mead (U.S.), 1933 . . . . £35/£15

Novels
The Napoleon of Notting Hill, John Lane, 1904 £20
ditto, John Lane (U.S.), 1906 . . . . £20
The Man who was Thursday, Arrowsmith, [1908] £65
ditto, Dodd Mead (U.S.), 1908 . . . . . . £50
The Ball and the Cross, John Lane (U.S.),1909 £25
ditto, Wells Gardner, 1910 . . . . £20
Manalive, Nelson, 1912 . . . . £25
ditto, John Lane (U.S.), 1912 . . . . £15
The Flying Inn, Methuen, 1914 . . . . . £45
The Return of Don Quixote, Chatto & Windus, 1927 . . . . £75/£20
ditto, Dodd Mead (U.S.), 1927 . . . . . £65/£15

Short Stories
The Club of Queer Trades, Harper & Bros, 1905 £250
ditto, Harper & Bros (U.S.), 1905 . . . . £250
The Man who Knew too Much, Cassell, 1922 . . . . £250/£25
ditto, Harper & Bros (U.S.), 1922 . . . £200/£20
Tales of the Long Bow, Cassell, 1925 . . £500/£40
The Sword of Wood, Elkin Mathews & Marrott, 1928 (530 signed copies) . . . . £55/£45
The Poet and the Lunatics, Cassell, 1929 . £250/£25
Four Faultless Felons, Cassell, 1930 . . £250/£25
ditto, Dodd Mead (U.S.), 1930 . . . . . £65/£15
The Paradoxes of Mr Pond, Cassell, 1937 . £100/£25

Plays
Magic, A Fantastic Comedy, Martin Secker, 1913 £25
ditto, Martin Secker, 1913 (150 signed copies) . £75
The Judgement of Dr. Johnson, Sheed & Ward, 1927 . . . . £75/£20
ditto, Putnam's (U.S.), 1928 . . . . . £50/£10
The Surprise, Sheed & Ward, 1953 . . . £20/£10

Verse
Greybeards at Play, Brimley Johnson, 1900 . £125
The Wild Knight and Other Poems, Grant Richards, 1900 . . . . £75
The Ballad of the White Horse, Methuen, 1911 £15
ditto, Methuen, 1911 (100 signed copies, handmade paper) £75

The Nativity, Albany (U.S.), 1911 (wraps) . . . £20
Poems, Burns & Oats Ltd, 1915 . . . . . £10
Wine, Water and Song, Methuen, 1915 . . . . £10
The Ballad of St. Barbara and Other Verses, Cecil Palmer, 1922 . . . . £35/£10
The Queen of Seven Swords, Sheed & Ward, 1926 . . . . £35/£10
Collected Poems, Cecil Palmer, 1927 . . . £35/£10
ditto, Cecil Palmer, 1927 (350 signed copies, slipcase). £125

Others
The Defendant, Brimley Johnson, 1901 . . . . £25
Twelve Types, Humphreys, 1902 . . . . . . £20
Robert Browning, Macmillan, 1903 . . . . . £20
G.F. Watts, Duckworth, 1904 . . . . . . £15
Charles Dickens, Methuen, 1906 . . . . . £25
ditto, as ***Charles Dickens, a critical study***, Dodd Mead (U.S.), 1906 . . . . £25
ditto, as ***Varied Types***, Dodd Mead & Co. (U.S.), 1908 . . . . £20
All Things Considered, Methuen, 1908 . . . . £20
George Bernard Shaw, John Lane and the Bodley Head, 1909 . . . . £25
ditto, John Lane (U.S.), 1909 . . . . £15
Tremendous Trifles, Methuen, 1909. . . . £20
Five Types, Humphries, 1910 (wraps) . . . £20
Alarms and Discursions, Methuen, 1910 . . £15
ditto, Dodd Mead & Co (U.S.), 1911. . . . . £15
William Blake, Duckworth, 1910 . . . . . £15
Appreciations and Criticisms of the Works of Dickens, Dent & Sons, 1911 . . . . £15
ditto, Dutton (U.S.), 1911. . . . . £15
The Future of Religion. Mr. G.K. Chesterton's Reply to Mr. Bernard Shaw, The Heritics Club (U.S.), 1911 (wraps) £50
A Miscellany of Men, Methuen, 1912 . . . . £15
ditto, Dodd Mead & Co (U.S.), 1912. . . . . £15
Victorian Age in Literature, Williams & Norgate, 1913 . . . . £10
The Barbarism of Berlin, Cassell, 1914 (wraps) £15
ditto, as ***The Appetite of Tyranny***, Dodd Mead & Co (U.S.), 1915 . . . . £15
The Crimes of England, Cecil, Palmer & Hayward, 1915 (wraps) £20
Lord Kitchener, privately published, 1917 (wraps) £75
A Short History Of England, John Lane, 1917 . £20
ditto, John Lane (U.S.), 1917 . . . . £20
Utopia of Usurers and Other Essays, Boni & Liveright (U.S.), 1917 . . . . £75
Eugenics and Other Evils, Cassell, 1922 . £150/£15
ditto, Dodd Mead & Co. (U.S.) 1922 . . . £150/£15
What I Saw In America, Hodder & Stoughton, 1922 . . . . £150/£10
Fancies Versus Fads, Dodd, Mead and Co. (U.S.) 1923 . . . . £150/£10
St Francis of Assisi, Hodder & Stoughton, 1923 . . . . £100/£10
The Superstitions of the Sceptic, Heffers, 1925 (wraps) £35
The Everlasting Man, Dodd, Mead and Co. (U.S.) 1925 . . . . £150/£20
William Cobbett, Hodder & Stoughton, 1925 £100/£15
The Outline of Sanity, Methuen, 1926 . . £100/£15
ditto, Dodd, Mead and Co. (U.S.) 1927 . . £75/£20
The Catholic Church and Conversion, Burns, Oates & Washbourne, 1926 . . . . £75/£15
Robert Louis Stevenson, Hodder and Stoughton, [1927]. . . . . £75/£15
The Resurrection of Rome, Hodder & Stoughton, [1930]. . . . . £75/£15
ditto, Dodd, Mead and Co. (U.S.), 1927 . . £75/£15
Come to Think of It, Methuen, 1930 . . £50/£15
Chaucer, Faber & Faber, 1932 . . . . . £50/£15
ditto, Farrar & Rinehart (U.S.), 1932. . . £45/£15
Christendom in Dublin, Sheed & Ward (U.S.), 1933 . . . . £35/£15
All I Survey, Methuen, 1933 . . . . . £35/£15
ditto, Dodd, Mead and Co. (U.S.), 1933 . . £35/£15
St. Thomas Aquinas, Hodder & Stoughton, 1933 . . . . £35/£15
ditto, Sheed & Ward (U.S.), 1933 . . . . £35/£15
Avowals and Denials, Methuen, 1934 . . £35/£15
The Well and the Shallows, Sheed & Ward (U.S.), 1935 . . . . £35/£15
Autobiography of G.K. Chesterton, Sheed & Ward (U.S.), 1936 . . . . £35/£15
The Coloured Lands, Sheed & Ward, 1938. £35/£15
ditto, Sheed & Ward (U.S.), 1938 . . . . £35/£15
The Common Man, Sheed & Ward, 1950 . £25/£10
A Handful Of Authors, Sheed And Ward, 1953 . . . . £15/£5
The Glass Walking-Stick and Other Essays from the Illustrated London News, Metheun, 1955 . £15/£5
Lunacy and Letters, Sheed & Ward, 1958 . £15/£5

AGATHA CHRISTIE
(b.1890 d.1976)

The Queen of detective fiction, and creator of the immortal Hercule Poirot and Miss Marple.

Novels
The Mysterious Affair at Styles, John Lane (U.S.), 1920 . . . . £6,000/£600
ditto, John Lane, 1921 . . . . £5,000/£600
The Secret Adversary, John Lane, 1922 £4,000/£500
ditto, Dodd Mead (U.S.), 1922 . . . £4,000/£300

Murder on the Links, John Lane, 1923 £3,000/£300
ditto, Dodd Mead (U.S.), 1923 . . . £2,500/£200
The Man in the Brown Suit, John Lane, 1924 . . . . £3,000/£300
ditto, Dodd Mead (U.S.), 1924 . . . £2,000/£300
The Secret of Chimneys, John Lane, 1925 £2,000/£250
ditto, Dodd Mead (U.S.), 1925 . . . £2,000/£250
The Murder of Roger Ackroyd, Collins, 1926 . . . . £4,000/£400
ditto, Dodd Mead (U.S.), 1926 . . . £3,500/£350
The Big Four, Collins, 1927 . . . . £1,500/£100
ditto, Dodd Mead (U.S.), 1927 . . . £1,000/£100
The Mystery of the Blue Train, Collins, 1928 . . . . £1,000/£75
ditto, Dodd Mead (U.S.), 1928 . . . . £500/£75
The Seven Dials Mystery, Collins, 1929. £1,500/£100
ditto, Dodd Mead (U.S.), 1929 . . . . £500/£75
The Murder at the Vicarage, Collins, 1930 . . . . £1,500/£100
ditto, Dodd Mead (U.S.), 1930 . . . . £750/£75
Giant's Bread, Collins, 1930 (pseud. 'Mary Westmacott') . . . . £1,000/£100
ditto, Doubleday (U.S.), 1930 . . . . £500/£75
The Sittaford Mystery, Collins, 1931 . £1,000/£100
ditto, as ***The Murder at Hazelmoor***, Dodd Mead (U.S.), 1931 . . . . £400/£75
Peril at End House, Collins, 1931 . . £1,000/£75
ditto, Dodd Mead (U.S.), 1932 . . . . £450/£75
Lord Edgware Dies, Collins, 1933 . . £1,000/£75
ditto, as ***Thirteen at Dinner***, Dodd Mead (U.S.), 1933 . . . . £750/£75
Why Didn't They Ask Evans?, Collins, 1934 . . . . £1,500/£100
ditto, as ***Boomerang Clue***, Dodd Mead (U.S.), 1935 . . . . £750/£75
Murder on the Orient Express, Collins, 1934 . . . . £2,000/£200
ditto, as ***Murder on the Calais Coach***, Dodd Mead (U.S.), 1942 . . . . £1,500/£100
Murder in Three Acts, Dodd Mead (U.S.), 1934 . . . . £750/£75
ditto, as ***Three Act Tragedy***, Collins, 1935 £500/£75
Unfinished Portrait, Collins, 1934, (pseud. 'Mary Westmacott') . . . . £750/£75
ditto, Doubleday (U.S.), 1934 . . . . £200/£35
Death in the Clouds, Collins, 1935 . . . £500/£75
ditto, as ***Death in the Air***, Dodd Mead (U.S.), 1935 . . . . £250/£35
The A.B.C. Murders: A New Poirot Mystery, Collins, 1936 . . . . £500/£75
ditto, Dodd Mead (U.S.), 1936 . . . . £250/£35
Cards on the Table, Collins, 1936 . . . £500/£75
ditto, Dodd Mead (U.S.), 1936 . . . . £250/£25
Murder in Mesopotamia, Collins, 1936. . £500/£150
ditto, Dodd Mead (U.S.), 1936 . . . . £250/£25

Death on the Nile, Collins, 1937. . . . £1,000/£125
ditto, Dodd Mead (U.S.), 1938 . . . . £250/£75
Dumb Witness, Collins, 1937 . . . . £500/£75
ditto, as ***Poirot Loses a Client***, Dodd Mead (U.S.), 1937 . . . . £350/£75
Appointment With Death: A Poirot Mystery, Collins, 1938 . . . . £450/£75
ditto, Dodd Mead (U.S.), 1938 . . . . £200/£25
Hercule Poirot's Christmas, Collins, 1939 . £500/£75
ditto, as ***Murder for Christmas, A Poirot Story***, Dodd Mead, 1939 . . . . £300/£75
Murder Is Easy, Collins, 1939 . . . . £300/£75
ditto, as ***Easy to Kill***, Dodd Mead, 1939. . £200/£50
Ten Little Niggers, Collins, 1939 . . £1,500/£200
ditto, as ***And Then There Were None***, Dodd Mead, 1940 . . . . £250/£50
One, Two, Buckle My Shoe, Collins, 1940 £500/£75
ditto, as ***The Patriotic Murders***, Dodd Mead, 1941 . . . . £300/£75
Sad Cypress, Collins, [1940] . . . . . £300/£75
ditto, Dodd Mead (U.S.), 1940 . . . . £125/£50
Evil Under the Sun, Collins, 1941 . . . £250/£75
ditto, Dodd Mead (U.S.), 1941 . . . . £250/£75
N or M?, Collins, 1941 . . . . . . £250/£75
ditto, Dodd Mead (U.S.), 1941 . . . . £250/£75
The Body in the Library, Collins, 1942 . . . £200/£75
ditto, Dodd Mead (U.S.), 1942 . . . . £200/£75
The Moving Finger, Dodd Mead (U.S.), 1942 . . . . £150/£40
ditto, Collins, 1943 . . . . £150/£40
Five Little Pigs, Collins, 1942 . . . . £200/£75
ditto, as ***Murder in Retrospect***, Dodd Mead (U.S.), 1942 . . . . £150/£40
Death Comes as the End, Dodd Mead (U.S.), 1942 . . . . £200/£50
ditto, Collins, 1945 . . . . £125/£40
Towards Zero, Collins, 1944 . . . . . £125/£40
ditto, Dodd Mead (U.S.), 1944 . . . . £125/£40
Absent in the Spring, Collins, 1944 (pseud. 'Mary Westmacott') . . . . £125/£40
ditto, Farrar & Rinehart (U.S.), 1944. . . £125/£40
Sparkling Cyanide, Collins, 1945 . . . £125/£40
ditto, as ***Remembered Death***, Dodd Mead (U.S.), 1945 . . . . £125/£40
The Hollow, Collins, 1946 . . . . £125/£50
ditto, Dodd Mead (U.S.), 1946 . . . . £125/£40
Taken at the Flood, Collins, 1948 . . . . £125/£40
ditto, as ***There is a Tide***, Dodd Mead (U.S.), 1948 . . . . £125/£40
The Rose and the Yew Tree, Heinemann, 1948 (pseud. 'Mary Westmacott') . . . . £125/£40
ditto, Rinehart (U.S.), 1948 . . . . . £125/£40
Crooked House, Collins, 1949 . . . . £125/£40
ditto, Dodd Mead (U.S.), 1949 . . . . £100/£25
A Murder is Announced, Collins, 1950 . . £60/£15

ditto, Dodd Mead (U.S.), 1950 . . . . £50/£15
They Came to Baghdad, Collins, 1951 . . £45/£15
ditto, Dodd Mead (U.S.), 1951 . . . . £45/£15
They Do It with Mirrors, Collins, 1951 . . £45/£15
ditto, as ***Murder with Mirrors***, Dodd Mead (U.S.), 1951 . . . . £45/£15
Mrs McGinty's Dead, Collins, 1952 . . . £45/£15
ditto, Dodd Mead (U.S.), 1952 . . . . £45/£15
A Daughter's a Daughter, Heinemann, 1951 (pseud. 'Mary Westmacott') . . . . £45/£10
After the Funeral, Collins, 1953 . . . . £45/£10
ditto, as ***Funerals are Fatal***, Dodd Mead (U.S.), 1953 . . . . £40/£10
A Pocket Full of Rye, Collins, 1953 . . . £40/£10
ditto, Dodd Mead (U.S.), 1954 . . . . £40/£10
Destination Unknown, Collins, 1954 . . £40/£10
ditto, as ***So Many Steps to Death***, Dodd Mead (U.S.), 1955 . . . . £40/£10
Hickory, Dickory, Dock, Collins, 1955 . . £40/£10
ditto, as ***Hickory, Dickory, Death***, Dodd Mead (U.S.), 1955 . . . . £25/£10
Dead Man's Folly, Collins, 1956 . . . £40/£10
ditto, Dodd Mead (U.S.), 1956 . . . . £40/£10
The Burden, Heinemann, 1956 (pseud. 'Mary Westmacott') . . . . £40/£10
4.50 from Paddington, Collins, 1957 . . . £40/£10
ditto, as ***What Mrs McGillicuddy Saw!***, Dodd Mead (U.S.), 1957 . . . . £35/£10
Ordeal by Innocence, Collins, 1958 . . . £35/£10
ditto, Dodd Mead (U.S.), 1958 . . . . £35/£10
Cat Among the Pigeons, Collins, 1959 . . £35/£10
ditto, Dodd Mead (U.S.), 1959 . . . . £25/£10
The Pale Horse, Collins, 1961 . . . . £20/£10
ditto, Dodd Mead (U.S.), 1962 . . . . £20/£10
The Mirror Crack'd from Side to Side, Collins, 1962 . . . . £20/£10
ditto, as ***The Mirror Crack'd***, Dodd Mead (U.S.), 1963 . . . . £20/£10
The Clocks, Collins, 1963 . . . . . £15/£5
ditto, Dodd Mead (U.S.), 1964 . . . . £15/£5
A Caribbean Mystery, Collins, 1964. . . £15/£5
ditto, Dodd Mead (U.S.), 1965 . . . . £15/£5
At Bertram's Hotel, Collins, 1965 . . . £15/£5
ditto, Dodd Mead (U.S.), 1965 . . . . £15/£5
Third Girl, Collins, 1966 . . . . . £15/£5
ditto, Dodd Mead (U.S.), 1967 . . . . £15/£5
Endless Night, Collins, 1967 . . . . . £15/£5
ditto, Dodd Mead (U.S.), 1968 . . . . £15/£5
By the Pricking of My Thumbs, Collins, 1968 £15/£5
ditto, Dodd Mead (U.S.), 1968 . . . . £15/£5
Passenger to Frankfurt, Collins, 1970 . . £15/£5
ditto, Dodd Mead (U.S.), 1970 . . . . £15/£5
Nemesis, Collins, 1971 . . . . . £15/£5
ditto, Dodd Mead (U.S.), 1971 . . . . £15/£5
Elephants Can Remember, Collins, 1972 . £15/£5
ditto, Dodd Mead (U.S.), 1972 . . . . £15/£5
Postern of Fate, Collins, 1973 . . . . £15/£5
ditto, Dodd Mead (U.S.), 1973 . . . . £15/£5
Murder on Board; Three Complete Mystery Novels, Dodd Mead (U.S.), 1974 . . . . . £15/£5
Curtain: Hercule Poirot's Last Case, Collins, 1975 . . . . £15/£5
ditto, Dodd Mead (U.S.), 1975 . . . . £15/£5
Sleeping Murder, Collins, 1976 . . . . £15/£5
ditto, Dodd Mead (U.S.), 1976 . . . . £10/£5

Short Stories

Poirot Investigates, John Lane, 1924 £3,000/£300
ditto, Dodd Mead (U.S.), 1924 . . . £2,000/£200
Partners in Crime, Collins, 1929 . . . £750/£75
ditto, Dodd Mead (U.S.), 1929 . . . . £300/£75
The Underdog, Reader's Library, 1929 (with story by Oppenheim) . . . . £400/£150
The Mysterious Mr Quinn, Collins, 1930 . £500/£150
ditto, Dodd Mead (U.S.), 1930 . . . . £500/£100
The Thirteen Problems, Collins, 1932 . . £200/£50
ditto, as ***The Tuesday Club Murders***, Dodd Mead (U.S.), 1933 . . . . £200/£50
The Hound of Death and Other Stories, Odhams, 1933 . . . . £250/£75
Parker Pyne Investigates, Collins, 1934 £250/£75
ditto, as ***Mr Parker Pyne, Detective***, Dodd Mead (U.S.), 1934 . . . . £200/£65
The Listerdale Mystery and Other Stories, Collins, 1934 . . . . £200/£50
Murder in the Mews and Other Stories, Collins, 1937 . . . . £200/£50
ditto, as ***Dead Man's Mirror and Other Stories***, Dodd Mead (U.S.), 1937 . . . . £300/£75
The Regatta Mystery and Other Stories, Dodd Mead (U.S.), 1939 . . . . £200/£50
The Labours of Hercules: Short Stories, Collins, 1947 . . . . £65/£20
ditto, as ***Labours of Hercules***, Dodd Mead (U.S.), 1947 . . . . £65/£20
Witness for the Prosecution, Dodd Mead (U.S.), 1948 . . . . £50/£15
Three Blind Mice and Other Stories, Dodd Mead (U.S.), 1950 . . . . £40/£10
Under Dog and Other Stories, Dodd Mead (U.S.), 1951 . . . . £40/£10
The Adventure of the Christmas Pudding, Collins, 1960 . . . . £75/£25
Double Sin and Other Stories, Dodd Mead (U.S.), 1961 . . . . £30/£10
13 for Luck, Dodd Mead (U.S.), 1961 . . £20/£10
ditto, Collins, 1966 . . . . £20/£10
Star over Bethlehem and Other Stories, Collins, 1965 (pseud. 'A. C. Mallowan') . . . . . £15/£5
ditto, Dodd Mead (U.S.), 1965 . . . . . £10/£5

Surprise! Surprise!, Dodd Mead (U.S.), 1965 £15/£5
13 Clues for Miss Marple, Dodd Mead, 1965 £15/£5
The Golden Ball and Other Stories, Dodd Mead (U.S.), 1971 . . . . £10/£5
Hercule Poirot's Early Cases, Collins, 1974 £15/£5
ditto, Dodd Mead (U.S.), 1974 . . . . . £10/£5
Miss Marple's Final Cases and Others, Collins, 1979 . . . . £15/£5
ditto, Dodd Mead (U.S.), 1979 . . . . . £10/£5
Remembrance, Souvenir Press, 1988 . . £10/£5

Verse
The Road of Dreams, Bles, 1925 . . . . £500/£100
ditto, as ***Poems***, Collins, 1973 (glassine d/w) £45/£40
ditto, Dodd Mead (U.S.), 1973 (glassine d/w) £25/£20

Plays
Black Coffee, Ashley, 1934 (wraps) £125
ditto, French, 1952 (wraps) £35
Ten Little Niggers, French, 1944 (wraps) . . . £50
ditto, as ***Ten Little Indians***, French (U.S.), 1946 (wraps) £10
Appointment with Death, French, 1945 (wraps) £50
Murder on the Nile, French, 1946 (wraps) . . £40
ditto, French (U.S.), 1946 (wraps) £20
The Hollow, French, 1952 (wraps) £35
ditto, French (U.S.), 1952 (wraps) £20
The Mousetrap, French, 1954 (wraps) £100
ditto, French (U.S.), 1954 (wraps) . . . £75
Witness for the Prosecution, French (U.S.), 1954 (wraps) £40
ditto, French, 1956 (wraps) £40
The Spider's Web, French, 1957 (wraps) . . £30
ditto, French (U.S.), 1957 (wraps) £10
Towards Zero, Dramatist's Play Service (U.S.), 1957 (wraps) £50
ditto, French, 1958 (wraps) £35
Verdict, French, 1958 (wraps) £35
The Unexpected Guest, French, 1958 (wraps) . £35
Go Back for Murder, French, 1960 (wraps) . £35
Rule of Three, French, 1963 (3 vols, wraps) . £50
Akhmaton, Collins, 1973 . . . . . . £15/£5
ditto, Dodd Mead (U.S.), 1973 . . . . . £15/£5

Travel
Come Tell Me How You Live, Collins, 1946 £65/£10
ditto, Dodd Mead (U.S.), 1946 . . . . . £50/£10

Autobiography
Autobiography, Collins, 1977 . . . . . £15/£5
ditto, Dodd Mead (U.S.), 1977 . . . . . £10/£5

JOHN CLARE
(b.1793 d.1864)

A poet who excels in his descriptions of rural life, and the thoughts and feelings of humble country folk.

Verse
Poems Descriptive of Rural Life and Scenery, Taylor & Hessey, 1820 . . . . £750
The Village Minstrel and Other Poems, Taylor & Hessey (and) Stamford: E. Drury, 1821 . . £300
The Shephers Calendar, Taylor, 1827 . . . . £300
The Rural Muse, Whittaker & Co., 1835 . . . £200
Poems Chiefly From Manuscript, Cobden-Sanderson, 1920 . . . . £75/£45

Others
Sketches in the Life of John Clare, Cobden-Sanderson, 1931 . . . . £60/£30
The Letters of John Clare, Routledge & Kegan Paul, 1951 . . . . £30/£10

ARTHUR C. CLARKE
(b.1917)

Clarke's much admired science fiction has successfully popularised and experimented with speculative science.

Novels
Prelude to Space, World Editions (U.S.), 1951 (wraps) £15
ditto, Sidgwick & Jackson, 1953 . . . . . £125/£35
The Sands of Mars, Sidgwick & Jackson, 1951 . . . . £125/£35
ditto, Gnome Press (U.S.), 1952 . . . . . £75/£35
Islands in the Sky, Winston (U.S.), 1952 . £125/£35
ditto, Sidgwick & Jackson, 1952 . . . . £100/£35
Against the Fall of Night, Gnome Press (U.S.), 1953 . . . . £125/£35
Childhood's End, Ballantine (U.S.), 1953 . £250/£75
ditto, Sidgwick & Jackson, 1954 . . . . . £95/£35
Earthlight, Ballantine (U.S.), 1955 . . . . £200/£75
ditto, Muller, 1955. . . . . £125/£45
The City and the Stars, Harcourt Brace (U.S.), 1956 . . . . £100/£35
ditto, Muller, 1956. . . . . £75/£35
The Deep Range, Harcourt Brace (U.S.), 1957 . . . . £75/£25
ditto, Muller, 1957. . . . . £75/£25
A Fall of Moondust, Harcourt Brace (U.S.), 1961 . . . . £75/£25
ditto, Gollancz, 1961 . . . . £75/£25

Dolphin Island, Holt Rinehart (U.S.), 1963 . £50/£20
ditto, Gollancz, 1963 . . . . £50/£20
Glide Path, Harcourt Brace (U.S.), 1963 . £50/£20
ditto, Sidgwick & Jackson, 1969 . . . . . £50/£20
2001: A Space Odyssey, NAL (U.S.), 1968 £175/£45
ditto, Hutchinson, 1968 . . . . £100/£45
The Lion of Comarre, Harcourt Brace (U.S.), 1968 . . . . £45/£15
ditto, Gollancz, 1970 . . . . £45/£15
Rendezvous with Rama, Harcourt Brace (U.S.), 1973 . . . . £45/£15
ditto, Gollancz, 1973 . . . . £45/£15
Imperial Earth, Gollancz, 1975 . . . . £25/£10
ditto, Harcourt Brace (U.S.), 1976 . . . . £25/£10
The Fountains of Paradise, Gollancz, 1979 £25/£10
ditto, Harcourt Brace (U.S.), 1979 . . . £25/£10
2010: Odyssey Two, Granada, 1982 . . £20/£5
ditto, Granada, 1982 (author's name misspelt "Clark" on title page) . . . . £75/£45
ditto, Phantasia (U.S.), 1982 (650 signed copies, slipcase) . . . . £75/£65
ditto, Phantasia (U.S.), 1982 (26 signed, lettered copies, leather box) . . . . £450/£425
ditto, Ballantine (U.S.), 1982 . . . . . £15/£5
The Songs of Distant Earth, Grafton, 1986. £15/£5
ditto, Ballantine (U.S.), 1986 . . . . . £15/£5
Odyssey Three, Ballantine (U.S.), 1988 . . £15/£5
ditto, Grafton, 1988 . . . . £15/£5
Cradle, Gollancz, 1988 (with Gentry Lee) . £15/£5
ditto, Warner (U.S.), 1988 . . . . . . £15/£5
Rama II, Gollancz, 1989 (with Gentry Lee). £20/£10
ditto, Ballantine (U.S.), 1989 . . . . . £10/£5
Beyond the Fall of Night, Putnam (U.S.), 1990 (with Gregory Benford) . . . . £10/£5
ditto, as ***Against the Fall of Night***, Gollancz, 1991 . . . . £10/£5
The Ghost from the Grand Banks, Bantam (U.S.), 1990 . . . . £10/£5
ditto, Gollancz, 1990 . . . . £10/£5
The Garden of Rama, Gollancz, 1991 (with Gentry Lee) . . . . £10/£5
ditto, Bantam (U.S.), 1991 . . . . . £10/£5
Rama Revealed, Gollancz, 1993 (with Gentry Lee) . . . . £10/£5
ditto, Bantam (U.S.), 1994 . . . . . £10/£5
The Hammer of God, Gollancz, 1993 . . £10/£5
ditto, Bantam (U.S.), 1993 . . . . . . £10/£5

Stories
Expedition to Earth, Ballantine (U.S.), 1953 £175/£45
ditto, Sidgwick & Jackson, 1954 . . . . £90/£25
Reach for Tomorrow, Ballantine (U.S.), 1956 . . . . £125/£35
ditto, Gollancz, 1962 . . . . £75/£25
Tales from the White Hart, Ballantine (U.S.), 1957 . . . . £100/£25
ditto, Sidgwick & Jackson, 1972 . . . . £30/£10
The Other Side of the Sky, Harcourt Brace (U.S.), 1958 . . . . £100/£35
ditto, Gollancz, 1961 . . . . £35/£10
Tales of Ten Worlds, Harcourt Brace (U.S.), 1962 . . . . £25/£10
ditto, Gollancz, 1963 . . . . £25/£10
The Nine Billion Names of God, Harcourt Brace (U.S.), 1967 . . . . £15/£5
A Meeting with Medusa, Harcourt Brace (U.S.), 1971 . . . . £15/£5
The Wind from the Sun, Harcourt Brace (U.S.), 1971 . . . . £15/£5
Of Time and Stars, Gollancz, 1972 . . . £15/£5
Report on Planet Three and Other Speculations, Gollancz, 1972 . . . . £15/£5
The Sentinel, Berkley (U.S.), 1983 . . . £10/£5
ditto, Panther, 1985 . . . . £10/£5
Tales from Planet Earth, Century, 1989 . £10/£5

Miscellaneous collections
Across the Sea of Stars, Harcourt Brace (U.S.), 1959 . . . . £45/£10
From the Oceans, From the Stars, Harcourt Brace (U.S.), 1962 . . . . £50/£25
Prelude to Mars, Harcourt Brace (U.S.), 1965 £35/£10
An Arthur C. Clarke Omnibus, Sidgwick & Jackson, 1965 . . . . £25/£10
An Arthur C. Clarke Second Omnibus, Sidgwick & Jackson, 1968 . . . . £25/£10
The Lost Worlds of 2001, NAL (U.S.), 1972 £25/£10
ditto, Sidgwick & Jackson, 1972 . . . . £25/£10
Best of Arthur C. Clarke: 1937-1971, Sidgwick & Jackson, 1973 . . . . £25/£10

HARRY CLARKE
(b.1889 d.1931)

An Irish artist in the tradition of Beardsley, but whose detail and decoration are distinctively his own.

Illustrated by Clarke
Hans Andersen's Fairy Tales, Harrap, [1916] (125 signed copies) £1,000
ditto, Harrap, [1916] (full leather edition) . . £450
ditto, Harrap, [1916] (cloth edition) £200
ditto, Bretano's (U.S.), 1916 . . . . . . £175
Tales of Mystery and Imagination, by Edgar Allan Poe, Harrap, 1919 (170 signed copies). . . £2,000
ditto, Harrap, [1919] (morocco leather edition) . £400
ditto, Harrap, [1919] (cloth edition) £200
ditto, Harrap, [1923] (new edition with colour plates,

antique leather) £250
ditto, Harrap, [1923] (new edition with colour plates, cloth edition) . . . . £250/£125
The Year's at the Spring, Harrap, 1920 (250 signed copies) £450
ditto, Harrap, 1920 (cloth edition) . . . £200/£100
ditto, Bretano's (U.S.), 1920 . . . . . £150/£75
The Fairy Tales of Perrault, Harrap, [1922] (Persian levant leather edition) £350
ditto, Harrap, [1922] (Buckram edition) . . £250/£150
ditto, Harrap, [1922] (cloth edition) . . . £200/£125
ditto, Dodge (U.S.), [1922] . . . . . . £200/£125
Faust, by Goethe, Harrap, 1925 (1,000 signed copies) . . . . £600/£450
Elixir of Life Being a slight account of the romantic rise to fame of a great house, John Jameson & Son Limited (Dublin), 1925 . . . . . . £750/£450
Selected Poems of Algernon Charles Swinburne, John Lane, 1928 . . . . £400/£125
ditto, Dodd, Mead (U.S.), 1928 . . . . . £350/£125

WILKIE COLLINS
(b.1824 d.1889)

A friend of Charles Dickens, Collins was a popular and skilful author of sensation fiction.

Memoirs of the Life of William Collins, R.A. Longmans, 1848 (2 vols) £1,250
Antonina, or the Fall of Rome, Bentley, 1850 (3 vols) £300
Rambles Beyond Railways: Notes in Cornwall Taken A-Foot, Bentley, 1851 . . . . £250
Mr Wray's Cash-Box, Bentley, 1852 . . . £250
Basil: A Story of Modern Life, Bentley, 1852 (3 vols) £250
Hide and Seek, Bentley, 1854 (3 vols) . . . £600
After Dark, Smith & Elder, 1855 (3 vols) . . £200
The Dead Secret, Bradbury and Evans, 1857 (2 vols) £750
The Queen of Hearts, Hurst & Blackett, 1859 (3 vols) £750
The Woman in White, Sampson Low, 1860 (3 vols) £4,500
No Name, Sampson Low, 1862 (3 vols) . . . £500
My Miscellanies, Sampson Low, 1863 (3 vols) . £350
Armadale, Smith, Elder & Co., 1866 (2 vols) . £250
The Moonstone, William Tinsley, 1868 (3 vols) £2,500
Man and Wife, F. S. Ellis, 1870 (3 vols) . . £500
Poor Miss Finch, Bentley, 1872 (3 vols) . . £250
The New Magdalen, Bentley, 1873 (2 vols) . £250
Miss or Mrs? and Other Stories, Bentley, 1873 £250
The Frozen Deep and Other Tales, Bentley, 1874 (2 vols) £500
The Law and the Lady, Chatto & Windus, 1875 (3 vols) £450
The Two Destinies, Chatto & Windus, 1876 (2 vols) £250
The Haunted Hotel and My Lady's Money, Chatto & Windus, 1879 (2 vols) £350
A Rogue's Life, Bentley, 1879 . . . . . £250
The Fallen Leaves, Chatto & Windus, 1879 (3 vols) £125
Jezebel's Daughter, Chatto & Windus, 1880 (3 vols) £125
The Black Robe, Chatto & Windus, 1881 (3 vols) £125
Heart and Science, Chatto & Windus, 1883 (3 vols) £125
I Say No, Chatto & Windus, 1884 (3 vols) . . £125
The Evil Genius, Chatto & Windus, 1886 (3 vols) £125
The Guilty River, Arrowsmith, 1886. . . . £125
Little Novels, Chatto & Windus, 1887 (3 vols) . £250
The Legacy of Cain, Chatto & Windus, 1889 (3 vols) £125
Blind Love, Chatto & Windus, 1890 (3 vols, completed by Walter Besant) £50
The Lazy Tour of Two Idle Apprentices, Chapman & Hall, 1890 (in collaboration with Charles Dickens) £100

IVY COMPTON-BURNETT
(b.1892 d.1969)

The author of incisive, if claustrophobic domestic novels, told principally through the dialogue of her characters.

Dolores, Blackwood, 1911 . . . . . . £325
Pastors and Masters, A Study, Heath Cranton, 1925 . . . . £165/£100
Brothers and Sisters, Heath Cranton, 1929 £150/£75
ditto, Zero Press (U.S.), 1956 (includes introductory pamphlet) . . . . £25/£10
Men and Wives, Heinemann, 1931 . . . £90/£40
More Women than Men, Heinemann, 1933. £90/£40
A House and its Head, Heinemann, 1935 . £65/£25
Daughters and Sons, Gollancz, 1937 . . £65/£25
A Family and its Fortune, Gollancz, 1939 . £60/£25
Parents and Children, Gollancz, 1941 . £60/£25
Elders and Betters, Gollancz, 1944 . . £50/£15
Manservant and Maidservant, Gollancz, 1947 . . . . £30/£10
ditto, as ***Bullivant and the Lamb***, Knopf (U.S.), 1948 .

. . . . £30/£10
Two Worlds and their Ways, Gollancz, 1949 £30/£10
ditto, Knopf (U.S.), 1949 . . . . £30/£10
Darkness and Day, Gollancz, 1951 . . £30/£10
ditto, Knopf (U.S.), 1951 . . . . £30/£10
The Present and the Past, Gollancz, 1953 . £20/£5
ditto, Messner (U.S.), 1953 . . . . . . £20/£5
Mother and Son, Gollancz, 1955 . . . . £20/£5
ditto, Messner (U.S.), 1955 . . . . . . £20/£5
A Father and his Fate, Gollancz, 1957 . £20/£5
ditto, Messner (U.S.), 1958 . . . . . £20/£5
A Heritage and its History, Gollancz, 1959. £20/£5
ditto, Simon & Schuster (U.S.), 1960 . . £20/£5
The Mighty and their Fall, Gollancz, 1961 £20/£5
ditto, Simon & Schuster (U.S.), 1962 . . £20/£5
A God and His Gifts, Gollancz, 1963 . . £20/£5
ditto, Simon & Schuster (U.S.), 1964 . . £20/£5
The Last and the First, Gollancz, 1971 . £15/£5
ditto, Knopf (U.S.), 1971 . . . . . . £10/£5
Collected Works, Gollancz, 1972 (deluxe edition of 500 sets in 19 vols) £350

CYRIL CONNOLLY
(b.1903 d.1974)

Principally a critic and literary editor, Connolly founded the influential literary magazine *Horizon*.

The Rock Pool, Obelisk Press (Paris), 1936 (wraps) £200
ditto, Scriber (U.S.), 1936. . . . . . . £75/£40
ditto, Hamish Hamilton, 1947 . . . . £25/£10
Enemies of Promise, Routledge, 1938 . . £200/£50
ditto, Little, Brown (U.S.), 1939 . . . . £75/£25
The Unquiet Grave, Horizon, 1944 (500 numbered hardback copies of 1,000, pseud. "Palinurus"). £75
ditto, Horizon, 1944 (500 numbered copies of 1,000, wraps) £75
ditto, Hamish Hamilton, [1945] (new edition) £15/£5
ditto, Harper (U.S.), 1945 (new edition) . . £15/£5
The Condemned Playground, Routledge, [1945] . . . . £25/£10
ditto, Macmillan, 1946 . . . . . . £15/£5
The Missing Diplomats, Queen Anne Press, 1952 (wraps) £25
Ideas and Places, Weidenfeld, 1953 . . £25/£10
ditto, Harper (U.S.), 1953. . . . . . £25/£10
The Golden Horizon, Weidenfeld, 1953 . £15/£5
ditto, University Books (U.S.), 1955 . . . £10/£5
Les Pavillons, Macmillan (U.S.), 1962 (with Jerome Zerbe) . . . . £25/£10
ditto, Hamish Hamilton, 1962 . . . . £25/£10
Previous Convictions, Hamish Hamilton, 1963 £20/£10
ditto, Harper (U.S.), 1964 . . . . £15/£5
The Modern Movement: 100 Key Books from England, France and America, 1880-1950, Deutsch/Hamilton, 1965 . . . . £45/£15
ditto, Atheneum (U.S.), 1966 . . . . . £45/£15
ditto, H.R.C. (U.S.), 1971 (wraps) £20
ditto, H.R.C. (U.S.), 1971 (520 copies, cloth) . £50
The Evening Colonnade, Bruce & Watson, 1973 . . . . £10/£5
ditto, Harcourt Brace (U.S.), 1975 . . . . £10/£5
A Romantic Friendship: The Letters of Cyril Connolly to Noel Blakiston, Constable, 1975 . . £15/£5
Journal and Memoir, Collins, 1983 . . . £10/£5
ditto, Ticknor & Fields (U.S.), 1984 . . . £10/£5
Shade Those Laurels, Bellew, 1990 . . . £10/£5
ditto, Panthen (U.S.), 1990 . . . . . . £10/£5

JOSEPH CONRAD
(b.1857 d.1924)

Conrad served for twenty years at sea, becoming a naturalised British subject in 1886. The sea provided the background for a number of powerful, novels. His classic 'Heart of Darkness' was first published in *Youth: A Narrative, and Other Stories* in 1902.

Novels
Almayer's Folly, T. Fisher Unwin, 1895 . . £750
ditto, Macmillan (U.S.), 1895. . . . . . £250
An Outcast of the Islands, T. Fisher Unwin, 1896 £400
ditto, Appleton (U.S.), 1896 . . . . £200
The Children of the Sea, Dodd Mead (U.S.), 1897. . . . . £400
ditto, as ***The Nigger of the Narcissus***, Heinemann, August 1898 (copyright edition, 7 copies, wraps) £4,000
ditto, as ***The Nigger of the Narcissus***, Heinemann, 1898 (first issue: 16 pages of advertisements) . £200
ditto, as ***The Nigger of the Narcissus***, Heinemann, 1898 (second issue: 32 pages of advertisements) £200
Lord Jim, William Blackwood, 1900 . . . £200
ditto, Doubleday (U.S.), 1900 . . . . . £150
The Secret Agent, Methuen, 1907 . . . . £200
Nostromo, Harper (U.K. and U.S.), 1909 . . £150
Under Western Eyes, Methuen, 1911 . . . £200
ditto, Harper (U.S.), 1911 . . . . £75
Chance, Methuen, 1913 (postponed first issue, 50 copies) £1,250
ditto, Methuen, 1914 (authorised issue) . . . £200
ditto, Doubleday (U.S.), 1914 . . . . . . £75
Victory, An Island Tale, Doubleday (U.S.), 1915 £65
ditto, Methuen, 1915 . . . . £50
The Shadow Line, Dent, 1917 . . . . . . £45

ditto, Doubleday (U.S.), 1917 . . . . . . £20
The Arrow of Gold, Doubleday (U.S.), 1919 . £20
ditto, T. Fisher Unwin, 1919 . . . . £20
The Rescue, Doubleday (U.S.), 1920 . . £150/£20
ditto, Dent, 1920 (40 copies for private distribution) £950
ditto, Dent, 1920 (trade edition, green cloth) £150/£20
The Rover, T. Fisher Unwin, 1923 . . . . £100/£15
ditto, Doubleday (U.S.), 1923 . . . . £75/£15
Suspense, Dent, 1925 . . . . £100/£15
ditto, Doubleday (U.S.), 1923 (limited edition of 377 copies) . . . . £100/£45
ditto, Doubleday (U.S.), 1923 . . . . . £75/£15
The Sisters, Crosby Gaige (U.S.), 1928 (926 copies) £45

Titles written with Ford Maddox Hueffer/Ford
The Inheritors, McClure, Phillips & Co. (U.S.), 1901 . . . . £100
ditto, Heinemann, 1901 . . . . £100
Romance, Smith Elder, 1903 . . . . £100
ditto, McClure (U.S.), 1904 . . . . £40
The Nature of a Crime, Duckworth, 1924 . £60/£20
ditto, Doubleday (U.S.), 1924 . . . . . £60/£20

Short Stories
Tales of Unrest, Scribners (U.S.), 1898 . . £250
ditto, T. Fisher Unwin, 1898 . . . . £225
Youth: A Narrative, and Other Stories, William Blackwood, 1902. . . . . £250
ditto, McClure, Phillips & Co. (U.S.), 1903 . . £100
Typhoon, Putnam/Knickerbocker Press, 1902 . £200
ditto, as ***Typhoon and Other Stories***, Heinemann, 1903 . . . . £150
A Set of Six, Methuen, 1908 . . . . £150
'Twixt Land and Sea, Dent, 1912 . . . . . £75
ditto, Hodder & Stoughton/Doran (U.S.), 1912 . £75
Within the Tides, Dent, 1915. . . . . . . £150
Tales of Hearsay, T. Fisher Unwin, 1925 . £50/£10
ditto, Doubleday (U.S.), 1925 . . . . £45/£10

Plays
One Day More: A Play in One Act, privately printed, Clement Shorter, 1917 (25 copies) £1,000
ditto, Beaumont Press, 1919 (250 copies) . . £200
ditto, Beaumont Press, 1919 (24 copies on Japanese vellum) £500
The Secret Agent: A Drama, privately printed, Canterbury, 1921. . . . . £100
ditto, T. Werner Laurie, 1923 (printed for subscribers only, 1,000 signed copies) . . . . . . £400/£300
Laughing Anne, Moorland Press, 1923 (200 signed, numbered copies) £450
Laughing Anne and One More Day, John Castle, 1924 . . . . £40/£10
Three Plays, Methuen, 1934 (contains 'One Day More', 'The Secret Agent' and 'Laughing Anne') . £30/£10

Miscellaneous
The Nigger of the Narcissus: A Preface, privately printed, 1902 (100 copies, wraps) £300
The Mirror of the Sea, Methuen, [1906] . . £100
ditto, Harper (U.S.), 1906. . . . . £45
Some Reminiscences, Eveleigh Nash, 1912. . £75
Notes on Life and Letters, Dent, 1921 (33 copies, privately printed). £750
ditto, Dent, 1921 (trade edition) . . . . £100/£20
Notes On My Books, Heinemann, 1921 (250 signed copies) £250
The Dover Patrol: A Tribute, privately printed, Canterbury, 1922, (75 copies, wraps) . . . £400
Five Letters by Joseph Conrad, privately printed, 1925 (100 numbered copies, wraps) £350
Notes by Joseph Conrad, privately printed, 1925 (100 numbered copies, wraps) £350
Last Essays, Dent, 1926 . . . . £75/£20
ditto, Doubleday (U.S.), 1926 . . . . . £60/£20
Joseph Conrad's Letters to His Wife, privately printed, 1927 (220 copies, signed by his widow) . . £200
Letters ... 1895 to 1924, Nonesuch Press, 1928 (925 numbered copies) £45
A Sketch of Joseph Conrad's Life Written by Himself, privately printed, 1939 (75 copies) £150
Letters to William Blackwood, Duke University Press (U.S.), 1958 . . . . £25/£10
Congo Diary and other Uncollected Pieces, Doubleday (U.S.), 1979 . . . . £20/£10

HUBERT CRACKANTHORPE
(b.1870 d.1896)

In 1892 Crackanthorpe founded *The Albermarle*, a short-lived magazine of high reputation. His own writings gained notoriety, dealing with taboo subjects such as adultery, prostitution and social degradation.

Wreckage: Seven Studies, Heinemann, 1893 . £75
Sentimental Studies & A Set of Village Tales, Heinemann, 1895 . . . . £50
Vignettes, A Miniature Journal of Whim and Sentiment, John Lane/The Bodley Head, 1896 £45
Last Studies, Heinemann, 1897 . . . . . . £45
The Light Sovereign: A Farcical Comedy in Three Acts, privately printed, Lady Henry Harland, 1917 (with Henry Harland) £120
Collected Stories (1893-1897) of Hubert Crackanthorpe, Scholar's facsimiles and Reprints (U.S.), 1969 . . . . £25

WALTER CRANE

(b.1845 d.1915)

A successful British artist, Crane was a colleague of William Morris, sharing many of Morris's political and artistic beliefs.

'Aunt Mavor' and Walter Crane Sixpenny Toy Books

The House that Jack Built, Ward, Lock & Tyler, 1865 . . . . £100
The Comical Cat, Ward, Lock & Tyler, 1865 . . £75
The Affecting Story of Jenny Wren, Ward, Lock & Tyler, 1865 . . . . £75
The Railroad Alphabet, Routledge, 1865 . . £75
The Farmyard Alphabet, Routledge, 1865 . . £75
Cock Robin, Frederick Warne, 1866. . . . £75
Sing A Song of Sixpence, Frederick Warne, 1866 £75
A Gaping-Wide-Mouth Waddling Frog, Frederick Warne, [1866] £75
The Old Courtier, Frederick Warne, 1867 . . £75
Multiplication Rule in Verse, Routledge, [1867] £75
Chattering Jack's Picture Book, Routledge, [1867] £75
How Jessie Was Lost, Routledge, [1868] . . £75
Grammar in Rhyme, Routledge, [1868]. . . £75
Annie and Jack in London, Routledge, [1869]. £75
One, Two, Buckle My Shoe, Routledge, [1869] £75
The Fairy Ship, Routledge, 1870 . . . £75
The Adventures of Puffy, Routledge, 1870 . . £75
This Little Pig Went To Market, Routledge, [1870] £75
King Luckieboy's Party, Routledge, 1870 . . £125
King Luckieboy's Picture Book, Routledge, 1871 £125
Routledge's Book of Alphabets, Routledge, 1871 £75
Noah's Ark Alphabet, Routledge, 1872 . . . £75
My Mother, Routledge, 1873. . . . . . . £75
Ali Baba and the Forty Thieves, Routledge, 1873 £75
The Three Bears, Routledge, 1873 . . . . £75
Cinderella, Routledge, 1873 . . . . . . £75
Walter Crane's New Toy Book, Routledge, 1873 £250
Walter Crane's Picture Book, Routledge, 1874 £250
Valentine and Orson, Routledge, 1874 . . . £75
Puss in Boots, Routledge, 1874 . . . . . £75
Old Mother Hubbard, Routledge, 1874 . . . £75
The Marquis of Caraba's Picture Book, Routledge, [1874]. £75
The Absurd ABC, Routledge, 1874 . . . . £65
The Frog Prince, Routledge: 'Walter Crane Shilling Series', 1874 . . . . £75
Goody Two Shoes, Routledge: 'Walter Crane Shilling Series', 1874 . . . . £75
Beauty and the Beast, Routledge: 'Walter Crane Shilling Series', 1874 . . . . £75
The Alphabet of Old Friends, Routledge: 'Walter Crane Shilling Series', 1874 . . . . . . £75
Little Red Riding Hood, Routledge, 1875 . . . £75
Jack and the Beanstalk, Routledge, 1875 . . £75
The Bluebeard Picture Book, Routledge, 1875. £75
Baby's Own Alphabet, Routledge, 1875. . . £75
The Yellow Dwarf, Routledge: 'Walter Crane Shilling Series', 1875 . . . . £75
The Hind in the Wood, Routledge: 'Walter Crane Shilling Series', 1875 . . . . £75
Princess Belle Etoile, Routledge: 'Walter Crane Shilling Series', 1875 . . . . £75
Aladdin's Picture Book, Routledge: 'Walter Crane Shilling Series', 1875 [1876] £75
Song of Sixpence Toy Book, Warner, [1876] . £75
The Three Bears Picture Book, Routledge, [1876] £75
The Sleeping Beauty in the Wood, Routledge, 1876 . . . . £45
Walter Crane's Picture Books Vol. 1: The Little Pig: His Picture Book, John Lane, 1895 . . . £50
Walter Crane's Picture Books Vol. 2: Mother Hubbard: Her Picture Book, John Lane, 1897 £50
Walter Crane's Picture Books Vol. 3: Cinderella's Picture Book, John Lane, 1897 . . . . £50
Walter Crane's Picture Books Vol. 4: Red Riding Hood's Picture Book, John Lane, 1898 . . £50
Beauty and the Beast Picture Book, John Lane: Large Series Vol. l, 1901 . . . . £40
Goody Two Shoes Picture Book, John Lane: Large Series Vol. 2, 1901 . . . . £40
The Song of Sixpence Picture Book, John Lane: Large Series Vol. 3, 1909 . . . . £40
The Buckle My Shoe Picture Book, John Lane: Large Series Vol. 4, 1910 . . . . £40
Puss in Boots and ***The Forty Thieves***, John Lane, 1914 . . . . £40
The Sleeping Beauty and ***Bluebeard***, John Lane, 1914 . . . . £40
The Three Bears and ***Mother Hubbard***, John Lane, 1914 . . . . £40

Books written by Mary Molesworth, illustrated by Crane

Tell Me A Story, Macmillan, 1875 . . . . £50
Carrots, Macmillan, 1876. . . . . . . £45
The Cuckoo Clock, Macmillan, 1877 . . . £45
Grandmother Dear, Macmillan, 1878 . . . £40
The Tapestry Room, Macmillan, 1879 . . . £35
A Christmas Child, Macmillan, 1880 . . . £35
The Adventures of Herr Baby, Macmillan, 1881 £30
Rosy, Macmillan, 1882 . . . . £30
Two Little Waifs, Macmillan, 1883 . . . . £30
Christmas-Tree Land, Macmillan, 1884 . . £30
Us, An Old fashioned Story, Macmillan, 1885 . £30

Four Winds Farm, Macmillan, 1886 . . . . £25
Little Miss Piggy, Macmillan, 1887 . . . . £25
A Christmas Posy, Macmillan, 1888. . . . £25
The Rectory Children, Macmillan, 1889 . . £25
The Children of the Castle, Macmillan, 1890 . £25
Studies and Stories, A. D. Innes, 1893 . . . £25

Other Titles illustrated by Crane

The New Forest: Its History and Scenery, by John de Capel Wise, Smith & Elder, 1863 . . . . £75
A Merrie Heart, by Cassell, 1871 . . . . £100
Mrs Mundi at Home, by Walter Crane, Marcus Ward, 1875 . . . . £75
The Quiver of Love: A Collection of Valentines, Marcus Ward, 1876 . . . . £75
The Baby's Opera: Old Rhymes with New Dresses, by Walter Crane, Routledge, 1877 . . . . . . £75
The Baby's Bouquet, by Walter Crane, Routledge, 1878 . . . . £75
The Necklace of Princess Fiorimonde, by Mary de Morgan, Macmillan, 1880 . . . . £50
The First of May: A Fairy Masque, by John R Wise, Henry Southeran, 1881, (300 copies, signed by Crane) £300
ditto, Henry Southeran, 1881, (folio edition, 200 copies, signed by Crane). £750
Household Stories, by the Brothers Grimm, Macmillan, 1882 . . . . £75
Art and the Formation of Taste, by Lucy Crane, Macmillan, 1882 . . . . £65
Pan Pipes: A Book of Old Songs, by Theodore Marzials, Routledge, 1883 . . . . £145
The Golden Primer, Parts 1 & 2, by Professor J.M.D. Meiklejohn, William Blackwood, 1884-5 (2 vols) £50
Folk and Fairy Tales, by Mrs Burton Harrison, Ward & Downey, 1885 . . . . £50
Slateandpencilvania: Being the Adventures of Dick on a Desert Island, by Walter Crane, Marcus Ward, 1885 . . . . £150
Little Queen Annie, by Walter Crane, Marcus Ward, 1886 . . . . £150
Pothooks and Perseverance, by Walter Crane, Marcus Ward, 1886 . . . . £175
A Romance of the Three Rs, by Walter Crane, Marcus Ward, 1886 . . . . £125
The Sirens Three: A Poem, by Walter Crane, Macmillan, 1886 . . . . £125
Legends for Lionel in Pen and Pencil, by Walter Crane, Cassell, 1887 . . . . £125
The Baby's Own Aesop, by Walter Crane, Routledge, 1887 . . . . £125
Echoes of Hellas, Parts 1 & 2, by Professor George C. Warr, Marcus Ward, 1887-88 (2 vols) . . . £125
The Happy Prince and Other Tales, by Oscar Wilde, David Nutt, 1888. . . . . £750
The Book of Wedding Days, Compiled by K.E.J. Reid, Longmans, 1889 . . . . £65
Flora's Feast: A Masque of Flowers, by Walter Crane, Cassell, 1889 . . . . £100
Society for the Encouragement of Arts, Manufacture and Commerce: Lectures by Walter Crane, W. Trounce, 1891 . . . . £50
Queen Summer: or the Tourney of the Lily and the Rose, by Walter Crane, Cassell, 1891 . . . £125
Renascence: A Book of Verse, by Walter Crane, Elkin Mathews, 1891 . . . . £75
The Claims of Decorative Art, by Walter Crane, Lawrence & Bullen, 1892 . . . . £75
A Wonder Book for Boys and Girls, by Nathaniel Hawthorne, Osgood, McIlvaine, 1892 . . . £150
Columbia's Courtship, by Walter Crane, Prang & Co. (U.S.), 1893 . . . . £75
The Old Garden and Other Verses, by Margaret Delane, Osgood, McIlvaine, 1893 . . . . £50
The Tempest, by William Shakespeare, Dent, 1893 £50
The History of Reynard the Fox, by F.S. Ellis, David Nutt, 1894 . . . . £50
The Story of the Glittering Plain, by William Morris, Kelmscott Press, 1894 (257 copies) £2,000
The Merry Wives of Windsor, by William Shakespeare, George Allen, 1894 . . . . £50
Two Gentlemen of Verona, by William Shakespeare, Dent, 1894 . . . . £50
The Faerie Queen, by Edmund Spenser, George Allen, 1894-97 (issued in 19 parts). . . . . £500 the set
ditto, George Allen, 1897 (6 vols, 1,000 sets) . . . . £750 the set
A Book of Christmas Verse, Methuen, 1895 . £50
Cartoons for the Cause, Twentieth Century Press, 1896 . . . . £500
Of the Decorative Illustration of Books Old and New, by Walter Crane, Bell, 1896. . . . . . . £75
The Work of Walter Crane, Virtue & Co., 1898 £100
A Floral Fantasy in an Old English Garden, by Walter Crane, Harper, 1898. . . . . . £125
The Shepherd's Calendar, by Edmund Spenser, Harper, 1898 . . . . £75
The Bases of Design, by Walter Crane, Bell, 1898 £75
Triplets, by Walter Crane, Routledge, 1899 (500 numbered copies) £250
Don Quixote, translated by Judge Parry, Blackie, 1900 . . . . £50
Line and Form, by Walter Crane, Bell, 1900 . £45
Walter Crane's Picture Book, Frederick Warne, 1900 (750 copies, bound in vellum) £300
A Masque of Days, Cassell, 1901 . . . . £125
The Art of Walter Crane, by Paul George Konody, Bell, 1902. . . . . £200
A Flower Wedding, by Walter Crane, Cassell, 1905 . . . . £75

Flowers from Shakespeare's Garden, by Walter Crane, Cassell, 1906 . . . . £125
India Impressions, by Walter Crane, Methuen, 1907 . . . . £75
An Artists Reminiscences, by Walter Crane, Methuen, 1907 . . . . £65
A Child's Socialist Reader, by A.A. Watts, Methuen, 1907 . . . . £50
The Rosebud and Other Tales, by Arthur Kelly, Fisher & Unwin, 1909 . . . . £50
King Arthur's Knights, by H. Gilbert, Jack, 1911 £50
William Morris to Whistler, by Walter Morris, Bell, 1911 (350 copies) £200
Rumbo Rhymes, by A. Calmour, Harper, 1911 . £100
Robin Hood, by H. Gilbert, Jack, 1912 . . . . £50
The Story of Greece, by M. MacGregor, Jack, 1913 . . . . £50
Michael Mouse Unfolds His Tale, by Walter Crane, Yale University Press (U.S.), 1956 . . . . £50

JOHN CREASEY

(b.1908 d.1973)

An author whose output was prodigious, Creasey is best known for his detective fiction.

Department Z Novels

The Death Miser, Melrose, 1932. . . . £40/£10
Redhead, Hurst & Blackett, 1934 . . . £35/£10
First came a Murder, Melrose, 1934 . . £30/£10
Death Round the Corner, Melrose, 1935 . £30/£10
The Mark of the Crescent, Melrose, 1935 . £30/£10
Thunder in Europe, Melrose, 1936 . . . £25/£5
The Terror Trap, Melrose, 1936 . . . . £25/£5
Carriers of Death, Melrose, 1937 . . . £25/£5
Days of Danger, Melrose, 1937 . . . . £25/£5
Death Stands By, Long, 1938 . . . . £25/£5
Menace, Long, 1938 . . . . £25/£5
Murder Must Wait, Melrose, 1939 . . . £20/£5
Panic, Long, 1939 . . . . £20/£5
Death By Night, Long, 1940 . . . . . £20/£5
The Island of Peril, Long, 1940 . . . . £20/£5
Sabotage, Long, 1941 . . . . £20/£5
Go Away Death, 1941 . . . . £20/£5
The Day of Disaster, Long, 1942 . . . £20/£5
Prepare for Action, Stanley Paul, 1942 . . £20/£5
No Darker Crime, Stanley Paul, 1943 . . £20/£5
Dark Peril, Stanley Paul, 1944 . . . . £20/£5
The Peril Ahead, Stanley Paul, 1946 . . £20/£5
The League of Dark Men, Stanley Paul, 1947 £20/£5
Department of Death, Evans, 1949 . . . £20/£5
The Enemy Within, Evans, 1950. . . . £15/£5
Dead or Alive, Evans, 1951 . . . . . £15/£5
A Kind of Prisoner, Hodder & Stoughton, 1954 £15/£5
The Black Spiders, Hodder & Stoughton, 1957 £15/£5

Sexton Blake Paperbacks

The Case of the Murdered Financier, Amalgamated Press, 1937 . . . . £10
The Great Air Swindle, Amalgamated Press, 1939 £10
The Man from Fleet Street, Amalgamated Press, 1940 . . . . £10
The Case of the Mad Inventor, Amalgamated Press, 1942 . . . . £10
Private Carter's Crime, Amalgamated Press, 1943 £10

The Toff Novels

Introducing The Toff, Long, 1938 . . . . £35/£10
The Toff Goes On, Long, 1939 . . . . £35/£10
The Toff Steps Out, Long, 1939 . . . . £35/£10
Here Comes The Toff, Long, 1940 . . . £30/£10
The Toff Breaks In, Long, 1940 . . . . £30/£10
Salute the Toff, Long, 1941 . . . . . £30/£10
The Toff Proceeds, Long, 1941 . . . . £30/£10
The Toff Goes to Market, Long, 1942 . . £20/£5
The Toff is Back, Long, 1942 . . . . . £20/£5
The Toff Among the Millions, Long, 1943 . £20/£5
Accuse the Toff, Long, 1943 . . . . . £20/£5
The Toff and the Curate, Long, 1944 . . £20/£5
The Toff and the Great Illusion, Long, 1944 £20/£5
Feathers for the Toff, Long, 1945 . . . £20/£5
The Toff and the Lady, Long, 1946 . . . £20/£5
The Toff on Ice, Long, 1946 . . . . . £20/£5
Hammer the Toff, Long, 1947 . . . . £20/£5
The Toff in Town, Long, 1948 . . . . £20/£5
The Toff Takes Shares, Long, 1948 . . . £20/£5
The Toff and Old Harry, Long, 1949 . . £20/£5
The Toff on Board, Long, 1949 . . . . £20/£5
Fool The Toff, Evans, 1950 . . . . . £15/£5
Kill The Toff, Evans, 1950 . . . . . £15/£5
A Knife for The Toff, Evans, 1951 . . . £15/£5
The Toff Goes Gay, Evans, 1951 . . . £15/£5
Hunt The Toff, Evans, 1952 . . . . . £15/£5
Call The Toff, Hodder & Stoughton, 1953 . £15/£5
The Toff Down Under, Hodder & Stoughton, 1953 . . . . £15/£5
The Toff at Butlins, Hodder & Stoughton, 1954 £15/£5
The Toff at the Fair, Hodder & Stoughton, 1954 . . . . £15/£5
A Six for The Toff, Hodder & Stoughton, 1955 £15/£5
The Toff and the Deep Blue Sea, Hodder & Stoughton, 1955 . . . . £15/£5
Make-Up for The Toff, Hodder & Stoughton, 1956 . . . . £15/£5
The Toff in New York, Hodder & Stoughton, 1956 . . . . £15/£5
Model for The Toff, Hodder & Stoughton, 1957 . . . . £15/£5

The Toff on Fire, Hodder & Stoughton, 1957 £15/£5
The Toff and the Stolen Tresses, Hodder & Stoughton, 1958 . . . . £15/£5
The Toff on the Farm, Hodder & Stoughton, 1958 . . . . £15/£5
Double for The Toff, Hodder & Stoughton, 1959 . . . . £15/£5
The Toff and the Runaway Bride, Hodder & Stoughton, 1959 . . . . £15/£5
A Rocket for The Toff, Hodder & Stoughton, 1960 . . . . £10/£5
The Toff and the Kidnapped Child, Hodder & Stoughton, 1960 . . . . £10/£5
Follow The Toff, Hodder & Stoughton, 1961 £10/£5
The Toff and the Teds, Hodder & Stoughton, 1961 . . . . £10/£5
A Doll for The Toff, Hodder & Stoughton, 1963 . . . . £10/£5
Leave it to The Toff, Hodder & Stoughton, 1963 . . . . £10/£5
The Toff and the Spider, Hodder & Stoughton, 1965 . . . . £10/£5
The Toff in Wax, Hodder & Stoughton, 1966 £10/£5
A Bundle for The Toff, Hodder & Stoughton, 1967 . . . . £10/£5
Stars for The Toff, Hodder & Stoughton, 1968 £10/£5
The Toff and the Golden Boy, Hodder & Stoughton, 1969 . . . . £10/£5
The Toff and the Fallen Angels, Hodder & Stoughton, 1970 . . . . £10/£5
Vote for The Toff, Hodder & Stoughton, 1971 £10/£5
The Toff and the Trip-Trip-Triplets, Hodder & Stoughton, 1972 . . . . £10/£5
The Toff and the Terrified Taxman, Hodder & Stoughton, 1973 . . . . £10/£5
The Toff and the Sleepy Cowboy, Hodder & Stoughton, 1975 . . . . £10/£5

The Toff Short Stories
The Toff on the Trail, Everybody's Books, [n.d.] £10
Murder out of the Past, Barrington Gray, 1953 £10

Dr Palfrey Novels
Traitor's Doom, Long, 1942 . . . . . £30/£10
The Legions of the Lost, Long 1943. . . . £30/£10
The Valley of Fear, Long, 1943 . . . . . £30/£10
Dangerous Quest, Long, 1944 . . . . £20/£5
Death in the Rising Sun, Long, 1945 . . £20/£5
The Hounds of Vengeance, Long, 1945 . £20/£5
Shadow of Doom, Long, 1946 . . . . £20/£5
The House of the Bears, Long, 1946 . . £20/£5
Dark Harvest, Long, 1947 . . . . £20/£5
The Wings of Peace, Long, 1948 . . . £20/£5
Sons of Satan, Long, 1948 . . . . . £20/£5
The Dawn of Darkness, Long, 1949. . . £20/£5
The League of Light, Evans, 1949 . . . £20/£5
The Man Who Shook the World, Evans, 1950 £15/£5
The Prophet of Fire, Evans, 1951 . . . £15/£5
The Children of Hate, Evans, 1952 . . . £15/£5
The Touch of Death, Hodder & Stoughton, 1954 . . . . £15/£5
The Mists of Fear, Hodder & Stoughton, 1955 £15/£5
The Flood, Hodder & Stoughton, 1956 . . £15/£5
The Plague of Silence, Hodder & Stoughton, 1958 . . . . £15/£5
The Drought, Hodder & Stoughton, 1959 . £15/£5
The Terror, Hodder & Stoughton, 1962. . £10/£5
The Depths, Hodder & Stoughton, 1963 . £10/£5
The Sleep, Hodder & Stoughton, 1964 . . £10/£5
The Inferno, Hodder & Stoughton, 1965 . £10/£5
The Flame, Hodder & Stoughton, 1967. . £10/£5
The Blight, Hodder & Stoughton, 1968 . . £10/£5
The Oasis, Hodder & Stoughton, 1970 . . £10/£5
The Smog, Hodder & Stoughton, 1970 . . £10/£5
The Unbegotten, Hodder & Stoughton, 1971 £10/£5
The Insulators, Hodder & Stoughton, 1972 £10/£5
The Voiceless One, Hodder & Stoughton, 1973 £10/£5
The Thunder-Maker, Hodder & Stoughton, 1976 . . . . £10/£5
The Whirlwind, Hodder & Stoughton, 1979 £10/£5

Inspector West Novels
Inspector West Takes Charge, Stanley Paul, 1942 . . . . £25/£10
Inspector West at Home, Stanley Paul, 1944 £25/£10
Inspector West Regrets, Stanley Paul, 1945 £25/£10
Holiday for Inspector West, Stanley Paul, 1946 £15/£5
Battle for Inspector West, Stanley Paul, 1948 £15/£5
Triumph for Inspector West, Stanley Paul, 1948 . . . . £15/£5
Inspector West Kicks Off, Stanley Paul, 1949 £15/£5
Inspector West Alone, Evans, 1950 . . . £10/£5
Inspector West Cries Wolf, Evans, 1950 . £10/£5
A Case for Inspector West, Evans, 1951 . £10/£5
Puzzle for Inspector West, Evans, 1951. . £10/£5
Inspector West at Bay, Evans, 1952 . . . £10/£5
A Gun for Inspector West, Hodder & Stoughton, 1953 . . . . £10/£5
Send for Inspector West, Hodder & Stoughton, 1953 . . . . £10/£5
A Beauty for Inspector West, Hodder & Stoughton, 1954 . . . . £10/£5
Inspector West Makes Haste, Hodder & Stoughton, 1955 . . . . £10/£5
Two for Inspector West, Hodder & Stoughton, 1955 . . . . £10/£5
Parcels for Inspector West, Hodder & Stoughton, 1956 . . . . £10/£5
A Prince for Inspector West, Hodder & Stoughton, 1956 . . . . £10/£5

Accident for Inspector West, Hodder & Stoughton, 1957 . . . . £10/£5
Find Inspector West, Hodder & Stoughton, 1957 . . . . £10/£5
Murder, London - New York, Hodder & Stoughton, 1958 . . . . £10/£5
Strike for Death, Hodder & Stoughton, 1958 £10/£5
Death of a Racehorse, Hodder & Stoughton, 1959 . . . . £10/£5
The Case of the Innocent Victims, Hodder & Stoughton, 1959 . . . . £10/£5
Murder on the Line, Hodder & Stoughton, 1960 . . . . £10/£5
Death in Cold Print, Hodder & Stoughton, 1961 . . . . £10/£5
The Scene of the Crime, Hodder & Stoughton, 1961 . . . . £10/£5
Policeman's Dread, Hodder & Stoughton, 1962 £10/£5
Hang the Little Man, Hodder & Stoughton, 1963 . . . . £10/£5
Look Three Ways at Murder, Hodder & Stoughton, 1964 . . . . £10/£5
Murder, London - Australia, Hodder & Stoughton, 1965 . . . . £10/£5
Murder, London - South Africa, Hodder & Stoughton, 1966 . . . . £10/£5
The Executioners, Hodder & Stoughton, 1967 £10/£5
So Young to Burn, Hodder & Stoughton, 1968 £10/£5
Murder, London - Miami, Hodder & Stoughton, 1969 . . . . £10/£5
A Part for a Policeman, Hodder & Stoughton, 1970 . . . . £10/£5
Alibi, Hodder & Stoughton, 1971 . . . £10/£5
A Splinter of Glass, Hodder & Stoughton, 1972 £10/£5
The Theft of Magna Carter, Hodder & Stoughton, 1973 . . . . £10/£5
The Extortioners, Hodder & Stoughton, 1974 £10/£5
A Sharp Rise in Crime, Hodder & Stoughton, 1978 . . . . £10/£5

Other Titles

Seven Times Seven, Melrose, 1932 . . . . £75/£25
Men, Maids and Murder, Melrose, 1933 . £75/£25
Four of the Best, Hodder & Stoughton, 1955 £20/£5
The Mountain of the Blind, Hodder & Stoughton, 1960 . . . . £10/£5
The Foothills of Fear, Hodder & Stoughton, 1961 . . . . £10/£5
The Masters of Bow Street, Hodder & Stoughton, 1972 . . . . £10/£5

Children's

The Men Who Died Laughing, D.C. Thomson, 1935 (wraps) £10
The Killer Squad, Newnes, 1936 (wraps) . . £10
Our Glorious Term, Sampson Low, [n.d.] . £10/£5
The Captain of the Fifth, Sampson Low, [n.d.] £10/£5
Blazing the Air Trail, Sampson Low, 1936 . £10/£5
The Jungle Flight Mystery, Sampson Low, 1936 . . . . £10/£5
The Mystery 'Plane, Sampson Low, 1936 . £10/£5
Murder by Magic, Amalgamated Press, 1937 (wraps) £10
The Mysterious Mr Rocco, Mellifont, 1937 (wraps) £10
The S.O.S. Flight, Sampson Low, 1937 . . £10/£5
The Secret Aeroplane, Sampson Low, 1937 £10/£5
The Treasure Flight, Sampson Low, 1937 . £10/£5
The Air Marauders, Sampson Low, 1937 . £10/£5
The Black Biplane, Sampson Low, 1937 . £10/£5
The Mystery Flight, Sampson Low, 1937 . £10/£5
The Double Motive, Mellifont, 1938 . . £10/£5
The Double-Cross of Death, Mellifont, 1938 (wraps) £5
The Missing Hoard, Mellifont, 1938 (wraps) . £5
Mystery at Manby House, North News Syndicate, 1938 (wraps) £5
The Fighting Flyers, Sampson Low, 1938 . £10/£5
The Flying Stowaways, Sampson Low, 1938 £10/£5
The Miracle 'Plane, Sampson Low, 1938 . £10/£5
Dixon Hawke, Secret Agent, D.C. Thomson, 1939 (wraps) £5
Documents of Death, Mellifont, 1939 (wraps) . £5
The Hidden Hoard, Mellifont, 1939 (wraps) . £5
Mottled Death, D.C. Thomson, 1939 (wraps) . £5
The Blue Flyer, Mellifont, 1939 (wraps) . . £5
The Jumper, Northern News Syndicate, 1939 (wraps) £5
The Mystery of Blackmoor Prison, Mellifont, 1939 (wraps) £5
The Sacred Eye, D.C. Thomson, 1939 . . £10/£5
The Ship of Death, D.C. Thomson, 1939 (wraps) £5
Peril By Air, Newnes, 1939 (wraps) . . . £5
The Flying Turk, Sampson Low, 1939 . . £10/£5
The Monarch of the Skies, Sampson Low, 1939 . . . . £10/£5
The Fear of Felix Corder, Fleetway, [n.d.] (wraps) £5
John Brand, Fugitive, Fleetway, [n.d.] (wraps) £5
The Night of Dread, Fleetway, [n.d.] (wraps) . £5
Dazzle - Air Ace No. 1, Newnes, 1940 (wraps) . £5
Dazzle and the Red Bomber, Newnes, n.d. (wraps) £5
Five Missing Men, Newnes, 1940 (wraps) . . £5
The Poison Gas Robberies, Mellifont, 1940 (wraps) £5
The Cinema Crimes, Pemberton, 1945 (wraps) £5
The Missing Monoplane, Sampson Low, 1947 £10/£5

EDMUND CRISPIN

(b.1921 d.1978)

Successful author of detective fiction. He was also a prolific editor of detective and science fiction anthologies.

Novels

The Case of the Gilded Fly, Gollancz, 1944 £200/£75
ditto, as ***Obsequies at Oxford***, Lippincott (U.S.), 1945. . . . . £100/£45
Holy Disorders, Gollancz, 1946 . . . . . £100/£25
ditto, Lippincott (U.S.), 1946. . . . . . £50/£20
The Moving Toyshop, Gollancz, 1946 . . £100/£25
ditto, Lippincott (U.S.), 1946. . . . . . £50/£20
Swan Song, Gollancz, 1947 . . . . . . £100/£25
ditto, as ***Dead and Dumb***, Lippincott (U.S.), 1947 . . . . £75/£20
Love Lies Bleeding, Gollancz, 1948 . . . . £75/£20
ditto, Lippincott (U.S.), 1948. . . . . . £45/£15
Buried for Pleasure, Gollancz, 1948 . £75/£20
ditto, Lippincott (U.S.), 1948. . . . . . £45/£15
Frequent Hearses, Gollancz, 1950 . . . . £35/£15
ditto, as ***Sudden Vengeance***, Dodd Mead (U.S.), 1950 . . . . £20/£10
The Long Divorce, Gollancz, 1951 . . . . £35/£15
ditto, Dodd Mead (U.S.), 1951 . . . . . £20/£10
ditto, as ***A Noose for Her***, Spivak, 1952. . £20/£10
The Glimpses of the Moon, Gollancz, 1977 £25/£10
ditto, Walker (U.S.), 1978 . . . . . . £10/£5

Stories

Beware of the Trains: 16 Stories, Gollancz, 1953 . . . . £35/£15
ditto, Walker (U.S.), 1962 . . . . . . £25/£10
Fen Country: 26 stories, Gollancz, 1979 . £25/£10
ditto, Walker (U.S.), 1979 . . . . . . £10/£5

RICHMAL CROMPTON

(b.1890 d.1969)

Born Richmal Crompton Lamburn, she began writing short stories for magazines while working as a teacher. When these stories were first collected together the resultant *Just William* was an immediate success.

'William' Titles

Just William, Newnes [1922] . . . . £1,500/£100
More William, Newnes, 1922 . . . . . £500/£75
William Again, Newnes, 1923 . . . . . £250/£30
William the Fourth, Newnes, 1924 . . . . £200/£25
Still William, Newnes, 1925 . . . . . . £200/£25
William the Conqueror, Newnes, 1926 . . £200/£25
William the Outlaw, Newnes, 1927 . . . . £200/£25
William in Trouble, Newnes, 1927 . . . . £200/£25
William the Good, Newnes, 1928 . . . . £200/£25
William, Newnes, 1929 . . . . £350/£45
William the Bad, Newnes, 1930 . . . . . £350/£45
William's Happy Days, Newnes, 1930 . . £350/£45
William's Crowded Hours, Newnes, 1931 . £350/£45
William the Pirate, Newnes, 1932 . . . . £350/£45
William the Rebel, Newnes, 1933 . . . . £350/£45
William the Gangster, Newnes, 1934 . . £350/£45
William the Detective, Newnes, 1935 . . £350/£45
Sweet William, Newnes, 1936 . . . . . £350/£45
William the Showman, Newnes, 1937 . . £350/£45
William the Dictator, Newnes, 1938. . . £350/£45
William and A.R.P., Newnes, 1939 (title later changed to ***William's Bad Resolution***) . . . . . £300/£45
William and the Evacuees, Newnes, 1940 (title later changed to ***William the Film Star***). . . . £500/£75
William Does His Bit, Newnes, 1941 . . . £300/£45
William Carries On, Newnes, 1941 . . . . £200/£45
William and the Brains Trust, Newnes, 1945 . . . . £100/£35
Just William's Luck, Newnes, 1948 . . . . £60/£20
William the Bold, Newnes, 1950. . . . . £60/£20
William and the Tramp, Newnes, 1952 . . . £50/£15
William and the Moon Rocket, Newnes, 1954 £50/£15
William and the Space Animal, Newnes, 1956 . . . . £50/£15
William's Television Show, Newnes, 1958 . £50/£15
William the Explorer, Newnes, 1960 . . . £60/£20
William's Treasure Trove, Newnes, 1962 . £50/£20
William and the Witch, Newnes, 1964 . . . £75/£25
William and the Ancient Briton, Mayfair, 1965 . . . . £15/£5
William and the Monster, Mayfair, 1965 . £15/£5
William the Globetrotter, Mayfair, 1965 . £15/£5
William the Cannibal, Mayfair, 1965 . . £15/£5
William and the Pop Singers, Newnes, 1965 £65/£25
William and the Masked Ranger, Newnes, 1966 . . . . £65/£25
William the Superman, Newnes, 1968 . . . £75/£25
William the Lawless, Newnes, 1970 . . . . £300/£75

Adult Novels

The Innermost Room, Melrose, 1923 . . . £200/£50
The Hidden Light, Hodder & Stoughton, [1924] . . . . £150/£35
Anne Morrison, Jarrolds, 1925 . . . . . £150/£35
The Wildings, Hodder & Stoughton, [1925] £125/£30
David Wilding, Hodder & Stoughton, [1926] £125/£30
The House, Hodder & Stoughton, [1926] . £175/£35
Millicent Dorrington, Hodder & Stoughton, [1927] . . . . £100/£25
Leadon Hill, Hodder & Stoughton, [1927] . £100/£25
The Thorn Bush, Hodder & Stoughton, [1928]. . .

. . . . £100/£25
Roofs Off!, Hodder & Stoughton, [1928] . £75/£20
The Four Graces, Hodder & Stoughton, [1929] . . . . £150/£35
Abbot's End, Hodder & Stoughton, [1929] £150/£35
Blue Flames, Hodder & Stoughton, [1930] £75/£20
Naomi Godstone, Hodder & Stoughton, [1930] . . . . £75/£20
Portrait of a Family, Macmillan, 1931 . . £75/£20
The Odyssey of Euphemia Tracy, Macmillan, 1932 . . . . £75/£20
Marriage of Hermione, Macmillan, 1932 . £50/£20
The Holiday, Macmillan, 1933 . . . . £50/£20
Chedsy Place, Macmillan, 1934 . . . . £50/£20
The Old Man's Birthday, Macmillan, 1934 £50/£20
Quartet, Macmillan, 1935 . . . . . £50/£20
Caroline, Macmillan, 1936 . . . . . £50/£20
There are Four Seasons, Macmillan, 1937 £45/£15
Journeying Wave, Macmillan, 1938. . . £50/£20
Merlin Bay, Macmillan, 1939 . . . . £50/£20
Steffan Green, Macmillan, 1940 . . . . £50/£20
Narcissa, Macmillan, 1941 . . . . . £50/£20
Mrs Frensham Describes a Circle, Macmillan, 1942 . . . . £35/£15
Weatherley Parade, Macmillan, 1943 . . £20/£5
Westover, Hutchinson, [1946] . . . . £20/£5
The Ridleys, Hutchinson, [1947]. . . . £20/£5
Family Roundabout, Hutchinson, [1948] . £20/£5
Frost at Morning, Hutchinson, 1950 . . £20/£5
Linden Rise, Hutchinson, 1952 . . . . £20/£5
The Gypsy's Baby, Hutchinson, 1954 . . £40/£15
Four in Exile, Hutchinson, 1955. . . . £25/£5
Matty and the Dearingroydes, Hutchinson, 1956 . . . . £20/£5
Blind Man's Buff, Hutchlnson, 1957 . . £20/£5
Wiseman's Folly, Hutchinson, 1959 . . . £20/£5
The Inheritor, Hutchinson, 1960. . . . £10/£5

Adult Short Stories

Kathleen and I, and, Of Course, Veronica, Hodder & Stoughton, [1926] . . . . £100/£25
Enter—Patricia, Newnes, [1927] . . . £50/£15
A Monstrous Regiment, Hutchinson, [1927] £125/£40
Mist, Hutchinson, [1928] . . . . . . £175/£45
The Middle Things, Hutchinson, [1928] . £150/£45
Felicity Stands By, Newnes, [1928] . . £75/£25
Sugar and Spice, Ward Lock, 1929 . . £75/£25
Ladies First, Hutchinson, [1929]. . . . £150/£45
The Silver Birch, Hutchinson, [1931] . . £150/£45
The First Morning, Hutchinson, [1936]. . £150/£45

E.E. CUMMINGS

(b.1894 d., 1962)

An innovative American poet, much influenced by slang and jazz, whose work is characterised by unconventional punctuation and typography. He usually signed his work 'e.e.cummings'.

Verse

Tulips and Chimneys, Seltzer (U.S.), 1923 . . £300
XLI Poems, Dial Press (U.S.), 1925 . . . £250/£50
Is 5, Boni & Liveright (U.S.), 1926 (77 signed copies, slipcase) £500
W [ViVa], Liveright Inc. (U.S.), 1931 . . . £175
ditto, Liveright Inc. (U.S.), 1931 (95 signed copies, glassine d/w) £500
No Thanks, Golden Eagle Press (U.S.), 1935 (900 copies) . . . . £120/£50
Tom, Arrow Editions (U.S.), 1935 (1500 copies) . . . . £200/£60
1/20, Roger Roughton, 1936 (tissue d/w) . £250/£235
Collected Poems, Harcourt Brace (U.S.), 1938 . . . . £75/£25
1 x 1, Holt (U.S.), 1944 . . . . £100/£35
ditto, Horizon, 1947 . . . . £40/£15
XAIPE: Seventy-One Poems, O.U.P. (U.S.), 1950 . . . . £60/£25
Poems, 1923-1954, Harcourt Brace (U.S.), 1954 . . . . £40/£10
95 Poems, Harcourt Brace (U.S.), 1958 (300 signed copies, slipcase) £250
ditto, Harcourt Brace (U.S.), 1958 (5,000 signed copies) . . . . £20/£10
100 Selected Poems, Grove Press (U.S.), 1959 . . . . £35/£10
Selected Poems, Faber, 1960 . . . . . . £25/£10
73 Poems, Harcourt (U.S.), 1963. . . . £25/£5
Collected Poems, MacGibbon & Kee (U.S.), 1968 (2 vols) . . . . £50/£20
Complete Poems 1913--1962, Harcourt Brace (U.S.), 1972 . . . . £25/£10
Poems 1905-1962, Marchim Press, 1973 (225 numbered copies) £75
Complete Poems 1910--1962, Granada, 1981 (2 vols in slipcase) . . . . £65/£45
Etcetera: The Unpublished Poems, Liveright (U.S.), 1983 . . . . £45/£15
Hist Whist and Other Poems for Children, Norton (U.S.), 1984 . . . . £25/£10

Fiction

The Enormous Room, Boni & Liveright (U.S.), 1911 . . . . £1,000/£350
ditto, Cape, 1928 . . . . £250/£100

Eimi, William Sloane (U.S.), [1933]. . . . £75/£35
ditto, Covivi, Friede (U.S.), 1933 (1,381 signed, numbered copies) . . . . £150/£125

Others
Him, Boni & Liveright (U.S.), 1927 . . . £100/£20
ditto, Boni & Liveright (U.S.), 1927 (160 signed, numbered copies, slipcase) £200
Santa Claus, Holt (U.S.), 1946 (250 signed copies) £200
ditto, Holt (U.S.), 1946 . . . . . . £75/£25
i: Six Nonlectures, Harvard University Press (U.S.), 1953 . . . . £40/£10
Fairy Tales, Harcourt Brace (U.S.), 1965 . £25/£10
Selected Letters, Harcourt Brace (U.S.), 1969 £25/£10
ditto, Deutsch, 1972 . . . . £20/£5

ROALD DAHL
(b.1916 d.1990)

Principally a children's writer, although his short stories for adults are also well known. In the past Dahl's books for children often met with disapproval due to the unpleasant ends met by some of his characters - but it is precisely this that children seem to enjoy.

Children's Titles
The Gremlins, Random House (U.S.), [1943] . . . . £750/£150
ditto, Collins, [1944] (boards, no d/w) . . . £400
James and the Giant Peach, Knopf (U.S.), 1961 . . . . £150/£40
ditto, Allen & Unwin, 1967 (boards, no d/w) . £75
Charlie and the Chocolate Factory, Knopf (U.S.), 1964 . . . . £150/£40
ditto, Allen & Unwin, 1967 (boards, no d/w) . £75
The Magic Finger, Harper (U.S.), 1966. . £125/£50
ditto, Allen & Unwin, 1968 (boards, no d/w) . £50
Fantastic Mr Fox, Knopf (U.S.), 1970 . . £30/£10
ditto, Allen & Unwin, 1970 (boards, no d/w) . £15
Charlie and the Great Glass Elevator, Knopf (U.S.), 1972 . . . . £50/£15
ditto, Allen & Unwin, 1973 (boards, no d/w) . £40
Danny, The Champion of the World, Cape, 1975 . . . . £25/£10
ditto, Knopf (U.S.), 1975 . . . . £20/£5
The Wonderful Story of Henry Sugar and Six More, Cape, 1977 . . . . £25/£10
ditto, Knopf (U.S.), 1977 . . . . £20/£5
The Enormous Crocodile, Cape, 1978 . . £20/£10
ditto, Knopf (U.S.), 1978 . . . . . . £20/£5
The Twits, Cape, 1980 . . . . . . £25/£10
ditto, Knopf (U.S.), 1981 . . . . £20/£10
George's Marvellous Medicine, Cape, 1981 £25/£20
ditto, Knopf (U.S.), 1982 . . . . £20/£5
Roald Dahl's Revolting Rhymes, Cape, 1983 (no d/w) £25
ditto, Knopf (U.S.), 1983 . . . . £20/£5
The BFG, Cape, 1982. . . . . £25/£10
ditto, Farrar Straus (U.S.), 1982 . . . . £20/£5
Dirty Beasts, Cape 1983 (no d/w) £25
ditto, Farrar Straus (U.S.), 1983 . . . . £20/£5
The Witches, Cape, 1983 . . . . £25/£10
ditto, Farrar Straus (U.S.), 1983 . . . . £20/£5
The Giraffe, the Pelly and Me, Cape, 1985. £15/£5
ditto, Farrar Straus (U.S.), 1985 . . . . £15/£5
Matilda, Cape, 1988 . . . . £15/£5
ditto, Viking Kestrel (U.S.), 1988 . . . . £15/£5
Rhyme Stew, Cape, 1989 . . . . . . £15/£5
ditto, Viking Penguin (U.S.), 1990 . . . £15/£5
Esio Trot, Cape, 1990. . . . . £15/£5
ditto, Viking Penguin (U.S.), 1990 . . . . £15/£5
Roald Dahl's Guide to Railway Safety, British Rail, 1991 (wraps) £5
The Vicar of Nibbleswicke, Random Century, 1991 . . . . £10/£5
ditto, Viking Penguin (U.S.), 1991 . . . £10/£5
The Min Pins, Cape, 1991 . . . . . . £10/£5

Adult Novels
Sometime Never, Scribner (U.S.), 1948 . . £100/£35
ditto, Collins, 1949 . . . . £125/£35
My Uncle Oswald, Michael Joseph, 1979 . £10/£5
ditto, Knopf (U.S.), 1980 . . . . £10/£5

Short Stories
Over to You, Reynal & Hitchcock (U.S.), 1946. . . . . £150/£50
ditto, Hamish Hamilton, 1946 . . . . . £125/£50
Someone Like You, Knopf (U.S.), 1953. . £75/£20
ditto, Secker & Warburg, 1954 . . . . £50/£20
Kiss Kiss, Knopf (U.S.), 1960 . . . . £35/£10
ditto, Michael Joseph, 1960 . . . . . £35/£10
Switch Bitch, Knopf (U.S.), 1974 . . . £20/£5
ditto, Michael Joseph, 1974 . . . . . . £20/£5
Two Fables, Viking (U.S.), 1986. . . . £10/£5
ditto, Viking (U.S.), 1986 (300 signed copies) . £50

Autobiography
Boy: Tales of Childhood, Cape, 1984 . . £20/£5
ditto, Farrar Straus, 1984 (signed, limited edition) £50
ditto, Farrar Straus, 1984 . . . . £10/£5
Going Solo, Cape, 1986 . . . . £10/£5

DANIEL DEFOE

(b.1660 d.1730)

Daniel Defoe can be regarded as the father of the English novel, of modern journalism and the art of political propaganda. A prolific writer, he was at one time employed by the government as a policy adviser and in undercover espionage work.

Robinson Crusoe

The Life and Strange Surprizing Adventures of Robinson Crusoe; W. Taylor, London 1719 (first edition, first issue, anonymous) £12,000

ditto, later impressions, W. Taylor, London 1719 (anonymous) £1,250

ditto, McKnight Kauffer Edition, Etchells & MacDonald, 1929 (illustrated by E. McKnight Kauffer, limited edition, 525 copies) . . . £400

ditto, Edward Gordon Craig Edition, Basilisk Press, 1979 (illustrated by Edward Gordon Craig, limited edition, 500 copies, slipcase) £400

Robinson Crusoe Sequels and Omnibuses

The Farther Adventures of Robinson Crusoe, W. Taylor, London, 1719 (anonymous) . . £1,000

Serious Reflections During the Life and Surprising Adventures of Robinson Crusoe, W. Taylor, London 1720 (anonymous) £1,000

ditto, First Joint Edition of Parts I and II, W. Mears/ T. Woodward, London 1726 (2 vols made up of the abridged seventh edition of ***The Life and Strange Adventures of Robinson Crusoe*** and the fifth edition of ***The Farther Adventures of Robinson Crusoe***) £500

The Life and Strange Surprising Adventures of Robinson Crusoe, John Stockdale, London 1790 (first Stockdale Edition, together with 'The Life of Daniel De Foe' and a bibliography of his writings by George Chalmers. 2 vols). £500

The Life and Adventures of Robinson Crusoe, sold by J. Walter, London 1790 (first joint edition of Parts I, II and III, printed at the Logographic Press, includes 'The True-Born Englishman, A Satire' and 'The Original Power of the People of England examined and asserted', 3 vols). £500

ditto, Constable Press, 1925 (reissued with facsimiles of Stothard's plates, as ***The Life and Strange Surprising Adventures of Robinson Crusoe***, with an introduction by Charles Whibley. 3 vols, limited edition, 775 copies) £300

ditto, Cruikshank Edition, John Major, 1831 (illustrated by George Cruikshank and Thomas Stothard, with introductory verses by Bernard Barton. 2 vols) £500

ditto, Ayton Symington Edition, Dent, 1903 (illustrated by J. Ayton Symington) £30

Fiction Titles

The Life . . . of Captain Singleton, J. Brotherton, London 1720 (anonymous) £500

Moll Flanders, W. Chetwood/T. Edling, London [1722] (anonymous) £10,000

A Journal of the Plague Year, E. Nutt, London 1722 (anonymous) £500

The History . . . of Col. Jacque, Commonly Call'd Col. Jack, J. Brotherton, London 1722 (anonymous) £500

The Fortunate Mistress, or . . . Roxana, T. Werner, London 1724 (anonymous) £500

Memoirs of a Cavalier, A. Bell, London 1720 . £500

Non Fiction

The Shortest-Way With Dissenters published annonymously, MDCCII [1702] £3,000

The History of the Union of Great Britain, Heirs and Successors of Andrew Anderson, Edinburgh 1709 (in 6 parts) £300

The Family Instructor [Vol I], Emanuel Matthews, London/J. Button, Newcastle-upon-Tyne 1715 (anonymous) £200

The Family Instructor [Vol II], Emanuel Matthews, London 1718 (2 parts) (anonymous) . . . £200

ditto, Thos. Longman, London 1741 (first combined edition, 2 vols) £200

The Compleat English Tradesman [Vol I], Charles Rivington, London 1726 [1725] (anonymous). £200

The Compleat English Tradesman [Vol II], Charles Rivington, London 1732 (2 parts, anonymous) £200

ditto, C. Rivington, London 1732 (first combined edition, 2 vols) £200

A Tour Thro' the Whole Island of Great Britain, G. Strahan, London 1724-27 [1726] (3 vols, anonymous) £1,000

ditto, Peter Davis, 1927 (abridged version, 2 vols, limited edition, 1,000 copies) £300

A System of Magick, Roberts, 1727 . . . . £750

LEN DEIGHTON

(b.1929)

Len Deighton worked as an illustrator until his first novel was published in 1962. He is best known for his popular thrillers and spy novels.

Novels

The Ipcress File, Hodder & Stoughton, 1962 £300/£35

ditto, Simon & Schuster (U.S.), 1963 . . £100/£20

ditto, Franklin Library (U.S.), 1988 (signed edition) £65

Horse Under Water, Cape, 1963, (with loose crossword competition) . . . . £50/£20

ditto, Cape, 1963, (without loose crossword competition) . . . . £25/£10
ditto, Putnam (U.S.), 1968 . . . . . £25/£10
Funeral in Berlin, Cape, 1964 . . . . £25/£10
ditto, Putnam (U.S.), 1965 . . . . . £15/£5
Billion Dollar Brain, Putnam (U.S.), 1966 . £25/£5
ditto, Cape, 1966 . . . . £20/£5
An Expensive Place to Die, Putnam (U.S.), 1967 . . . . £20/£5
ditto, Cape, 1967 (with wallet of documents) £25/£10
ditto, Cape, 1967 (without wallet of documents) £10/£5
Only When I Larf, privately printed, (limited edition, 150 copies in plastic binding) £125
ditto, Joseph, 1968 (boards) . . . . . £50/£10
ditto, Joseph, 1968 (wraps) £20
ditto, as ***Only When I Laugh***, The Mysterious Press (U.S.), 1987 . . . . £20/£5
Bomber, Cape, 1970 . . . . £20/£5
ditto, Harper & Row, 1970 . . . . . . £15/£5
Declarations of War, Cape, 1971 (short stories) £25/£5
ditto, as ***Eleven Declarations of War***, Harcourt Brace (U.S.),1975 . . . . £15/£5
Close-Up, Cape, 1972. . . . . £15/£5
ditto, Atheneum (U.S.), 1972 . . . . . £10/£5
Spy Story, Cape, 1974. . . . . £20/£5
ditto, Harcourt Brace (U.S.), 1974 . . . £10/£5
Yesterday's Spy, Cape, 1975 . . . . . . £15/£5
ditto, Harcourt Brace (U.S.), 1975 . . . £10/£5
Twinkle, Twinkle, Little Spy, Cape, 1976 . £15/£5
ditto, as ***Catch a Falling Spy***, Harcourt Brace (U.S.), 1976 . . . . £10/£5
SS-GB, Cape, 1978 . . . . £10/£5
ditto, Knopf (U.S.), 1979 . . . . . . £10/£5
XPD, Hutchinson, 1981 . . . . £10/£5
ditto, Knopf (U.S.), 1981 . . . . £10/£5
Goodbye, Mickey Mouse, Hutchinson, 1982 £10/£5
ditto, Knopf (U.S.), 1982 . . . . £10/£5
Berlin Game, Hutchinson, 1983 . . . . £10/£5
ditto, Knopf (U.S.), 1984 . . . . £10/£5
Mexico Set, Hutchinson, 1984 . . . . £10/£5
ditto, Knopf (U.S.), 1985 . . . . £10/£5
London Match, Hutchinson, 1985 . . . £10/£5
ditto, Knopf (U.S.), 1986 . . . . £10/£5
Winter, Hutchinson, 1987. . . . . . . £10/£5
ditto, Knopf (U.S.), 1987 . . . . £10/£5
Spy Hook, Hutchinson, 1988 . . . . . £10/£5
ditto, Knopf (U.S.), 1988 . . . . £10/£5
Spy Line, Hutchinson, 1989 . . . . . £10/£5
ditto, Knopf (U.S.), 1989 . . . . £10/£5
Spy Sinker, Hutchinson, 1989 . . . . £15/£5
ditto, HarperCollins (U.S.), 1990. . . . . £15/£5
MAMista, Hutchinson, 1991 . . . . . £10/£5
ditto, HarperCollins (U.S.), 1991. . . . . £10/£5
City of Gold, Century, 1992 . . . . . £10/£5
ditto, HarperCollins (U.S.), 1992. . . . £10/£5
Violent Ward, Scorpion Press, 1993 (130 signed copies) £50
ditto, Harper Collins, 1993 . . . . . £10/£5
ditto, Harper Collins (U.S.), 1993 . . . £10/£5
Faith, Harper Collins, 1994 . . . . . £10/£5
ditto, Harper Collins (U.S.), 1994 . . . £10/£5
Hope, Scorpion Press, 1995 (15 copies of edition of 114) £75
ditto, Scorpion Press, 1995 (99 copies of edition of 114, glassine d/w) £45
ditto, HarperCollins, 1995 . . . . £10/£5
ditto, HarperCollins (U.S.), 1995. . . . £10/£5
Charity, HarperCollins, 1996. . . . . £10/£5
ditto, HarperCollins (U.S.), 1996. . . . £10/£5

Omnibus Editions

Game, Set and Match, Hutchinson, 1986 . £10/£5
ditto, Knopf (U.S.), 1989 . . . . £10/£5
Hook Line and Sinker, Hutchinson, 1991 . £10/£5

Cookery Titles

Ou Est le Garlic, Penguin, 1965 (wraps) . . £30
ditto, Harper & Row (U.S.), 1977 . . . . £10/£5
ditto, as ***Basic French Cooking***, Cape, 1979 £10/£5
ditto, as ***Basic French Cookery Course***, Century Hutchinson, 1990 . . . . £10/£5
Action Cookbook, Len Deighton's Guide to Eating, Cape, 1965 (printed boards, clear d/w). . £40/£35
ditto, as ***Cookstrip Cookbook***, Bernard Geiss (U.S.), 1966 . . . . £10/£5

Others

The Assassination of President Kennedy, Cape/ Jackdaw, 1967 (Portfolio containing 12 reproductions, 1 cut-out model and 5 broadsides, with Rand and Loxton) £150
Len Deighton's London Dossier, Cape, 1967 £40/£20
Len Deighton's Continental Dossier, Joseph, 1968 . . . . £40/£20
Fighter: The True Story of the Battle of Britain, Cape, 1977 . . . . £15/£5
ditto, Knopf (U.S.), 1978 . . . . . . £10/£5
Airshipwreck, Cape, 1978 (postcard laid in) £15/£5
ditto, Hart Rinehart (U.S.), 1979 . . . . £10/£5
Blitzkrieg, Cape, 1979 . . . . . . £10/£5
ditto, Knopf (U.S.), 1980 . . . . £10/£5
Battle of Britain, Cape, 1980. . . . . . £10/£5
ditto, Coward McCann & Geoghegan (U.S.), 1980 . . . . £10/£5
Blood, Tears and Folly: *An Objective Look at World War II*, Cape, 1993 . . . . £10/£5
ditto, Harper Collins (U.S.), 1993 . . . £10/£5
Pests, A Play in Three Acts, Martin, 1994 (50 signed, numbered copies of 226, slipcase) . . . £75/£65
ditto, Martin, 1994 (150 signed, numbered copies of

226) . . . . £50/£40
ditto, Martin, 1994 (26 signed, lettered copies of 226) . . . . £100/£90

WALTER DE LA MARE
(b.1873 d.1956)

British author, poet and critic, whose delicate and lyrical poems of fantasy and childhood are still admired today.

Verse

Songs of Childhood, Longmans, 1902 (pseud. 'Walter Ramal') £350
ditto, Longmans, 1923 (enlarged and revised) £25/£10
ditto, Longmans, 1923 (310 signed copies) £150/£100
Poems, Murray, 1906 . . . . £50
The Listeners and Other Poems, Constable, 1912 £30
A Child's Day, A Book of Rhymes, Constable, 1912 . . . . £30
Peacock Pie, A Book of Rhymes, Constable, 1913 £25
The Old Men, Flying Fame, 1913 . . . . . £25
The Sunken Garden and Other Poems, Beaumont Press, 1917 (270 copies). £75
Motley and Other Poems, Constable, 1918 . . £25
Flora: A Book of Drawings, by Pamela Bianco, Heinemann, 1919 (with 27 poems by de la Mare) £30
Poems, 1901 to 1918, Constable, 1920, (2 vols) . . £65/£25
ditto, Constable, 1920, (210 signed, numbered sets) £150
The Veil and Other Poems, Constable, 1921 £50/£15
Down-Adown-Derry, A Book of Fairy Poems, Constable, 1922 . . . . £100/£50
Thus Her Tale, A Poem, Porpoise Press, 1923 (50 copies, wraps) £35
A Ballad of Christmas, Selwyn & Blount, 1924 (100 copies) £30
Before Dawn, Selwyn & Blount, 1924 (100 copies) £30
The Hostage, Selwyn & Blount, 1925 (100 copies) £30
St Andrews, A & C Black, 1926 (with Rudyard Kipling) . . . . £45/£15
Alone, Faber, 1927 (Ariel Poem No.4, wraps) . £10
Selected Poems, Holt (U.S.), 1927 . . . . £25/£10
Stuff and Nonsense and So On, Constable, 1927 . . . . £45/£15
ditto, as ***Stuff and Nonsense***, Faber, 1946 (enlarged and revised edition of above) . . . . £15/£5
The Captive and Other Poems, Bowling Green Press (U.S.), 1928 (600 signed copies, glassine wraps) . . . . £45/£40
Self to Self, Faber, 1928 (Ariel Poem No. 11, wraps) £10
A Snowdrop, Faber, 1929 (Ariel Poem No. 20, wraps). £10
News, Faber, 1930 (Ariel Poem No. 31, wraps) £10
To Lucy, Faber, 1931 (Ariel Poem No. 33, wraps) £10
Poems for Children, Constable, 1930 . . . £30/£10
The Sunken Garden and Other Verses, Birmingham School of Printing, 1931 (different selection to 1917 edition) £20
Two Poems, privately printed, 1931 (100 copies, wraps) £25
Old Rhymes and New, Constable, 1932 (2 vols) . . . . £50/£20
The Fleeting and Other Poems, Constable, 1933 . . . . £25/£10
ditto, Constable, 1933 (150 signed copies) . £65/£30
Poems, 1919 to 1934, Constable, 1935 . . £30/£15
This Year, Next Year, Faber, 1937 . . . £75/£25
Poems, Corvinus Press, 1937 (40 copies) . . £125
Memory and Other Poems, Constable, 1938 £15/£5
Two Poems by Walter de la Mare and - but! - Arthur Rogers, privately printed, 1938 (200 copies) . £45
Haunted: A Poem, Linden Broadsheet No. 4, 1939 £20
Bells and Grass, a book of rhymes, Faber, 1941 . . . . £15/£5
Collected Poems, Faber, 1942 . . . . £20/£10
Time Passes and Other Poems, Faber, 1942 £15/£5
Collected Rhymes and Verses, Faber, 1944. £15/£5
The Burning-Glass and Other Poems, Faber, 1945 . . . . £15/£5
The Traveller, Faber, 1946 . . . . . £35/£10
Two Poems, Dropmore Press, 1946 . . . . £15
Rhymes and Verses, Collected Poems for Children, Holt (U.S.), 1947. . . . . . . £15/£5
Inward Companion, Faber, 1950 . . . £15/£5
Winged Chariot, Faber, 1951 . . . . £10/£5
O Lovely England and Other Poems, Faber, 1953 . . . . £10/£5
The Winnowing Dream, Faber, 1954 (Ariel Poem, wraps) £5
Selected Poems, Faber, 1954 . . . . . £10/£5
The Morrow, privately printed, 1955 (50 copies, wraps) £20
Poems, Puffin, 1962 (wraps) £5

Children's Stories

The Three Mulla-Mulgars, Duckworth, 1910 (later re-titled ***The Three Royal Monkeys***) £35
ditto, Duckworth, 1910 (250 signed copies). . £125
Broomsticks and Other Tales, Constable, 1925 (278 signed copies, slipcase) . . . . £200/£165
ditto, Constable, 1925 . . . . £45/£15
Miss Jemima, Blackwell, 1925 . . . . . £25
Lucy, Blackwell, 1925 . . . . £25
Old Joe, Blackwell, 1925 . . . . £25

Readings: Traditional Tales, told by de la Mare, Blackwell, 1925-28 (set of 6 vols) £125
Told Again: Traditional Tales, Blackwell, 1927 . . . . £35/£15
Stories from the Bible, Faber, 1929 . . . £25/£10
The Dutch Cheese and The Lovely Myfanwy, Knopf (U.S.), 1931 . . . . £25/£10
The Lord Fish and Other Tales, Faber, 1933 £25/£10
ditto, Faber, 1933 (60 signed copies, d/w, slipcase)£250
Mr Bumps and His Monkey, J.C. Winston (U.S.), 1942 . . . . £20/£5
The Old Lion and Other Stories, Faber, 1942 £10/£5
The Magic Jacket and Other Stories, Faber, 1943 . . . . £10/£5
The Scarecrow and Other Stories, Faber, 1945 £10/£5
The Dutch Cheese and Other Stories, Faber, 1946 . . . . £10/£5
Collected Stories for Children, Faber, 1947 £10/£5
Selected Stories and Verses, Puffin, 1952 (wraps) £5
Jack and the Beanstalk, Hulton Press, 1951 (from ***Told Again***) . . . . £10/£5
Dick Whittington, Hulton Press, 1951 . . £10/£5
Snow White, Hulton Press, 1952 . . . . £10/£5
Cinderella, Hulton Press, 1952 . . . . £10/£5
A Penny a Day and Other Stories, Knopf (U.S.), 1960 . . . . £15/£5

Novels
Henry Brocken, Murray, 1904 . . . . . £45
The Return, Arnold, 1910 . . . . . . £30
Memoirs of a Midget, Collins, 1921 . . . £65/£10
ditto, Collins, 1921 (210 signed, numbered copies) £75
The Walter de la Mare Omnibus, Collins, 1933 . . . . £25/£10

Short Stories
Lispet, Lispet and Vaine, Bookman's Journal, 1923 (Vine Books No.3, 200 signed copies) . . . £100
The Riddle and Other Stories, Selwyn & Blount, 1923 . . . . £45/£15
Ding Dong Bell, Selwyn & Blount, 1924 . £25/£10
Two Tales: 'The Green Room' and 'The Connoisseur', Bookman's Journal, 1925 (200 signed copies) . £50
The Connoisseur and Other Stories, Collins, 1926 . . . . £40/£15
Seaton's Aunt, Faber, 1927 (wraps) £20
At First Sight, Crosby Gaige (U.S.), 1928 (650 signed copies) £30
On the Edge, Faber, 1930 . . . . . £65/£25
A Forward Child, Faber, 1934 . . . . £20/£5
The Wind Blows Over, Faber, 1936 . . . £30/£10
The Almond Tree, Todd, 1943 (from ***The Riddle***) £15
The Orgy, Todd, 1943 (from ***On the Edge***) . £15
A Beginning and Other Stories, Faber, 1955 £25/£5
Eight Tales, Arkham House (U.S.), 1971 . £10/£5
Story and Rhyme, Dent, 1921 . . . . £10/£5
Seven Short Stories, Faber, 1931 . . . £50/£15
ditto, Faber, 1931 (100 signed copies) £300
The Nap and Other Stories, Nelson Classics, 1938 . . . . £10/£5
Stories, Essays and Poems, Dent, Everyman's Library, 1938 . . . . £10/£5
The Picnic and Other Stories, Faber, 1941 . £10/£5
Best Stories of Walter de la Mare, Faber, 1942 £10/£5
The Collected Tales of Walter de la Mare, Knopf (U.S.), 1950 . . . . £15/£5
Ghost Stories, Folio Society, 1956 (slipcase) £10/£5
Walter de la Mare: A Selection from his Writings, Faber, 1956 . . . . £10/£5
Some Stories, Faber, 1962 . . . . . £10/£5

Miscellaneous
M.E. Coleridge: An Appreciation, The Guardian, 1907 (limited edition) £25
Rupert Brooke and the Intellectual Imagination, Sidgwick & Jackson, 1919 . . . . £20
Some Thoughts on Reading, Yellowsands Press, 1923 (340 copies) £20
The Printing of Poetry, Cambridge University Press, 1931 (limited to 90 copies) £25
Lewis Carroll, Faber, 1932 . . . . . £30/£10
Poetry in Prose, Humphrey Milford, 1936 . . £15
Arthur Thompson: A Memoir, privately printed, 1938 . . . . £10
An Introduction to Everyman, Dent, 1938 (400 copies) £25
Pleasures and Speculations, Faber, 1940 . £15/£5
Private View, Faber, 1953 . . . . . £15/£5

MAURICE AND EDWARD DETMOLD

(b.1883 d.1908, b.1883 d.1957)

Brothers who collaborated in illustrating until the suicide of the former. Edward continued illustrating books until the late 1920s.

Books illustrated by Maurice and Edward Detmold
Pictures from Birdland, Dent, 1899 . . . £300
Sixteen Illustrations of Subjects from Kipling's 'Jungle Book', Macmillan, 1903 (portfolio) . £750
The Jungle Book, Macmillan, 1908 . . . . £75

Books illustrated by Edward Detmold
The Fables of Aesop, Hodder & Stoughton, 1909 £100
ditto, Hodder & Stoughton, 1909 (750 signed copies) £500
Birds and Beasts, by Camille Lemonnier, Allen, 1911 .

. . . . £50
The Book of Baby Beasts, by Florence E. Dugdale, Frowde/Hodder & Stoughton, [1911] . . . £75
The Life of the Bee, by Maurice Maeterlinck, Allen, 1911 . . . . £150
Hours of Gladness, by Maurice Maeterlinck, Allen, 1912 . . . . £125
The Book of Baby Birds, by Florence E. Dugdale, Frowde/Hodder & Stoughton, [1912] . . . £75
The Book of Baby Pets, by Florence E. Dugdale, Frowde/Hodder & Stoughton, [1915] . . . £75
The Book of Baby Dogs, by Charles J. Kaberry, Frowde/Hodder & Stoughton, [1915] . . . £50
Twenty-Four Nature Pictures, Dent, [1919] (portfolio) £450
Birds in Town and Village, by W.H. Hudson, Dent, 1919 . . . . £45
Our Little Neighbours, by Charles J. Kaberry, Frowde/Hodder & Stoughton, [1921] . . £125/£50
Fabre's Book of Insects, by J.H.C. Fabre, Hodder & Stoughton, [1921] . . . . £150/£50
Rainbow House for Boys and Girls, by Arthur Vine Hall, Cape, 1923 . . . . £75/£25
The Arabian Nights - Tales from the Thousand and One Nights, Hodder & Stoughton, [1924] . . £200
ditto, Hodder & Stoughton, [1924] (100 signed copies) £750
The Fantastic Creatures of Edward Julius Detmold, Pan, 1976 (wraps) £10

COLIN DEXTER
(b.1930)

A crime writer whose Inspector Morse is pre-eminent among the contemporary television detectives.

Novels
Last Bus to Woodstock, Macmillan, 1975 . £500/£50
ditto, St Martin's Press (U.S.), 1975 . . . £350/£40
Last Seen Wearing, Macmillan, 1976 . . £400/£50
ditto, St Martin's Press (U.S.), 1976 . . . . £300/£30
The Silent World of Nicholas Quinn, Macmillan, 1977 . . . . £250/£45
ditto, St Martin's Press (U.S.), 1977 . . . £150/£20
Service of All the Dead, Macmillan, 1979 . £150/£15
ditto, St Martin's Press (U.S.), 1980 . . . £75/£10
The Dead of Jericho, Macmillan, 1980 . . £100/£15
ditto, St Martin's Press (U.S.), 1980 . . . £50/£10
Riddle of the Third Mile, Macmillan, 1983 . £100/£15
ditto, St Martin's Press (U.S.), 1983 . . . £50/£10
The Secret of Annexe 3, Macmillan, 1986 . £50/£10
ditto, St Martin's Press (U.S.), 1987 . . . £25/£10
The Wench is Dead, Macmillan, 1989 . . £25/£5
ditto, St Martin's Press (U.S.), 1990 . . . £15/£5
The Jewel That Was Ours, Scorpion Press, 1991 (150 signed copies, quarter leather) £100
ditto, Scorpion Press, 1991 (20 signed deluxe copies) £200
ditto, Macmillan, 1991 . . . . £25/£5
ditto, Crown (U.S.), 1992 . . . . £10/£5
The Way Through the Woods, Macmillan, 1992 . . . . £15/£5
ditto, Scorpion Press, 1992 (150 signed copies, quarter leather) £75
ditto, Scorpion Press, 1992 (20 signed deluxe copies) £200
ditto, Crown (U.S.), 1993 . . . . . . £10/£5
Daughters of Cain, Macmillan, 1992 . . £10/£5
ditto, Crown (U.S.), 1994 . . . . . . £10/£5
Death is Now My Neighbour, Macmillan, 1996 £10/£5
ditto, as ***Death is Now My Neighbor***, Crown (U.S.), 1997 . . . . £10/£5

Short Stories
Morse's Greatest Mystery and Other Stories, Macmillan, 1993 . . . . £10/£5
ditto, Scorpion Press, 1993 (99 signed copies, quarter leather) £100
ditto, Scorpion Press, 1993 (20 signed deluxe copies) £200
ditto, Crown (U.S.), 1993 . . . . . . £10/£5
Inside Story, Macmillan, 1993 (for American Express, wraps). £15
Neighbourhood Watch, Macmillan, 1993 (150 numbered copies) £65
ditto, Macmillan, 1993 (50 signed, numbered copies) £145
A Good as Gold, Macmillan, 1994 . . . . . £5

Omnibus Editions
An Inspector Morse Omnibus, Macmillan, 1991 £10
The Second Inspector Morse Omnibus, Macmillan, 1992 . . . . £10
The Third Inspector Morse Omnibus, Macmillan, 1993 . . . . £10

MICHAEL DIBDIN
(b.1947)

A popular crime writer, Dibdin is considered by some to be the next P.D. James.

The Last Sherlock Holmes Story, Jonathan Cape, 1978 . . . . £200/£50
ditto, Pantheon (U.S.), 1978 . . . . . £20/£5
A Rich Full Death, Jonathan Cape, 1986 . £50/£15

Ratking, Faber, 1988 . . . . £50/£15
ditto, Bantam (U.S.), 1989 . . . . . £15/£5
The Tryst, Faber, 1989 . . . . . . £20/£5
ditto, Summit (U.S.), 1990 . . . . . £15/£5
Vendetta, Faber, 1990. . . . . . . £15/£5
ditto, Doubleday (U.S.), 1991 . . . . £15/£5
Dirty Tricks, Faber, 1991 . . . . . . £15/£5
ditto, Summit (U.S.), 1991 . . . . . £15/£5
Cabal, Faber, 1992 . . . . £15/£5
ditto, Doubleday (U.S.), 1993 . . . . £15/£5
The Dying of the Light, Faber, 1993 . . £10/£5
ditto, Pantheon (U.S.), 1993 . . . . . . £10/£5
Dead Lagoon, Faber, 1994 . . . . . £10/£5
ditto, Pantheon (U.S.), 1994 . . . . . £10/£5
Dark Spectre, Faber, 1995 . . . . . £10/£5
ditto, Pantheon (U.S.), 1995 . . . . . £10/£5
Cosi Fan Tuti, Faber, 1996 . . . . . £10/£5
ditto, Pantheon (U.S.), 1996 . . . . . £10/£5
A Long Finish, Faber, 1998 . . . . . £10/£5
ditto, Pantheon (U.S.), 1998. . . . . . £10/£5

PHILIP K. DICK

(b.1928 d.1982)

Dick was an American writer of science fiction, often dealing in his work with the effects of mechanisation, hallucinogenic drugs and schizophrenic delusions.

Solar Lottery, Ace Books (U.S.), 1955 (wraps) £25
ditto, as ***World of Chance***, Rich & Cowan, 1956 . . . . £350/£150
ditto, Gregg Press (U.S.), 1979 . . . . . £40
A Handful of Darkness, Rich & Cowan, 1955 . . . . £450/£150
ditto, Gregg Press (U.S.), 1978 . . . . . £50
The World Jones Made, Ace Books (U.S.), 1956 (wraps) £15
ditto, Sidgwick & Jackson, 1968 . . . . . . £100
The Man Who Japed, Ace Books (U.S.), 1956 (wraps) £15
ditto, Eyre Methuen, 1978 . . . . . £50/£15
Eye in the Sky, Ace Books (U.S.), 1957 (wraps) £10
ditto, Gregg Press (U.S.), 1979 . . . . . £50
The Cosmic Puppets, Ace Books (U.S.), 1957 (wraps) £10
ditto, Severn House, 1986. . . . . . £25/£5
The Variable Man, Ace Books (U.S.), 1957 (wraps) £15
Time Out Of Joint, Lippincott (U.S.), 1959 £300/£75
ditto, Science Fiction Book Club, 1961 . . £25/£10
Dr Futurity, Ace Books (U.S.), 1960 (wraps) £10
Vulcan's Hammer, Ace Books (U.S.), 1960 (wraps) £10
The Man in the High Castle, Putnam (U.S.), 1962 . . . . £200/£45
ditto, Penguin, 1965 (wraps) £10
ditto, Gollancz, 1975 . . . . £25/£10
The Game Players of Titan, Ace Books (U.S.), 1963 (wraps) £10
ditto, White Lion, 1974 . . . . . . £25/£10
Martian Time-Slip, Ballantine Books (U.S.), 1964 (wraps) £10
ditto, New English Library, 1976. . . . . £50/£10
The Simulacra, Ace Books (U.S.), 1964 (wraps) £15
ditto, Eyre Methuen, 1977 . . . . . . £50/£10
The Penultimate Truth, Belmont (U.S.), 1964 (wraps) £10
ditto, Jonathan Cape, 1967 . . . . . . £125/£45
Clans of the Alphane Moon, Ace Books (U.S.), 1964 (wraps) £10
The Three Stigmata of Palmer Eldritch, Doubleday (U.S.), 1965 . . . . £125/£45
ditto, Jonathan Cape, 1966 . . . . . . £50/£10
Dr Bloodmoney, Ace Books (U.S.), 1965 (wraps) £10
Now Wait for Last Year, Doubleday (U.S.), 1966 . . . . £125/£45
The Crack in Space, Ace Books (U.S.), 1966 (wraps) £10
ditto, Severn House, 1989. . . . . . £20/£5
The Unteleported Man, Ace Books (U.S.), 1966 (wraps) £10
ditto, Berkley (U.S.), 1983 (wraps, revised version) £10
ditto, as ***Lies Inc.***, Gollancz, 1984 (further revisions) . . . . £15/£5
The Zap Gun, Pyramid (U.S.), 1967 (wraps) . £10
ditto, Gregg Press (U.S.), 1979 . . . . . . £50
Counter-Clock World, Berkley (U.S.), 1967 (wraps) £10
ditto, White Lion, 1977 . . . . . . £75/£20
The Ganymede Takeover, Ace Books (U.S.), 1967 (with Ray Nelson, wraps) £10
ditto, Severn House, 1988. . . . . . £15/£5
Do Androids Dream of Electric Sheep?, Doubleday (U.S.), 1969 . . . . £250/£100
ditto, Rapp & Whiting, 1969 . . . . . £45/£20
Ubik, Doubleday (U.S.), 1969 . . . . £200/£45
ditto, Rapp & Whiting, 1970 . . . . . £45/£15
Galactic Pot-Healer, Berkeley (U.S.), 1969 (wraps) £10
ditto, Gollancz, 1971 . . . . £45/£10
The Preserving Machine, Ace Books (U.S.), 1969 (wraps) £10
ditto, Gollancz, 1971 . . . . £45/£10
A Maze of Death, Doubleday (U.S.), 1970 . £150/£45
ditto, Gollancz, 1972 . . . . £35/£10
Our Friends from Frolix 8, Ace Books (U.S.), 1970 (wraps) £10
ditto, Kinnell, 1989 . . . . £15/£5

A Philip K. Dick Omnibus, Sidgwick & Jackson, 1970 . . . . £50/£15
We Can Build You, Daw Books (U.S.), 1972 (wraps) £10
ditto, Severn House, 1988. . . . . . £15/£5
The Book of Philip K. Dick, Daw Books (U.S.), 1973 (wraps) £10
ditto, as ***The Turning Wheel***, Coronet, 1977 (wraps) £10
Flow My Tears, The Policeman Said, Doubleday (U.S.), 1974 . . . . £25/£10
ditto, Gollancz, 1974 . . . . £25/£10
Confessions of a Crap Artist, Entwhistle Books (U.S.), 1975 (500 copies) £125
ditto, Entwhistle Books (U.S.), 1975 (90 signed copies) £250
ditto, Entwhistle Books (U.S.), 1975 (500 copies, wraps). £25
ditto, Magnum, 1979 (wraps) £10
Deus Irae, Doubleday (U.S.), 1976 (with Roger Zelazny) . . . . £35/£10
ditto, Gollancz, 1977 . . . . £25/£10
A Scanner Darkly, Doubleday (U.S.), 1977. £35/£10
ditto, Gollancz, 1977 . . . . £25/£10
The Best of Philip K. Dick, Ballantine (U.S.), 1977 (wraps) £10
The Golden Man, Berkeley (U.S.), 1980 (wraps) £10
Valis, Bantam (U.S.), 1981 (wraps) £10
ditto, Kerosina, 1987 . . . . £25/£10
ditto, Kerosina, 1987 (limited edition) . . £60/£50
ditto, Kerosina, 1987 (signed edition) . . . £150
ditto, Kerosina, 1987 (leather bound edition) . £250
The Divine Invasion, Simon Schuster/Timescape (U.S.), 1981 . . . . £15/£5
The Transmigration of Timothy Archer, Simon & Schuster, 1982 . . . . £15/£5
ditto, Gollancz, 1982 . . . . £10/£5
The Man Whose Teeth Were Exactly Alike, Ziesling (U.S.), 1984 . . . . £15
In Milton Lumky Territory, Dragon Press, 1985 . . . . £15/£5
ditto, Gollancz, 1986 . . . . £10/£5
I Hope I Shall Arrive Soon, Doubleday (U.S.), 1985 . . . . £15/£5
ditto, Gollancz, 1986 . . . . £10/£5
Ubik: The Screenplay, Corroboree Press (U.S.), 1985 . . . . £100/£45
ditto, Corroboree Press (U.S.), 1985 (deluxe edition) £250
Puttering About in a Small Land, Chicago Academy (U.S.), 1985 . . . . £15/£5
Radio Free Albemuth, Arbor House (U.S.), 1985 . . . . £15/£5
ditto, Severn House, 1987. . . . . . £15/£5
Humpty Dumpty in Oakland, Gollancz, 1986 £15/£5
Mary and the Giant, Arbor House (U.S.), 1987 £15/£5
ditto, Arbor House (U.S.), 1987 (50 copies bound in quarter leather) £100
ditto, Gollancz, 1988 . . . . £15/£5
Collected Stories, Underwood Miller, 1987 (5 vols) £125
ditto, Underwood Miller, 1987 (cased limited edition) £150
ditto, Underwood Miller, 1987 (signed edition). £300
ditto, Gollancz, 1988/89 (vols 1 and 2) £25
ditto, Gollancz, 1990 (vols 3 and 4) £25
Cosmogony and Cosmology, Kerosina, 1987 £25/£10
Nick and the Glimmung, Gollancz, 1988 . £15/£5
The Broken Bubble, Morrow/Arbor House (U.S.), 1988 . . . . £15/£5
ditto, Gollancz, 1989 . . . . £15/£5
ditto, Ultramarine Press, 1989 (150 copies, quarter leather) £125
ditto, Ultramarine Press, 1989 (26 copies, full leather) £200

CHARLES DICKENS

(b.1812 d.1870)

An acclaimed and prolific author, Dickens' position as one of the 'greats' of English literature is beyond dispute.

Sketches by 'Boz', first series, John Macrone MDCCCXXXVI 1836 (2 vols, illustrated by George Cruikshank, dark green cloth) £2,500
ditto, second series, John Macrone, MDCCCXXXVII 1837 (1 vol., illustrated by George Cruikshank, pink cloth) £750
ditto, monthly parts (20 parts, 13 extra plates by George Cruikshank, pink wrapper) Chapman & Hall, November 1837-June 1839 . . . . . . £10,000
ditto, first 1 vol. (octavo) edition dated '1837' (monthly parts, bound with wrapper in glossy brown or purple cloth, with 40 plates by George Cruikshank) Chapman & Hall, 1839 . . . . £250
The Posthumous Papers of the Pickwick Club edited by 'Boz', (20 monthly parts in, 19. Parts I & II Illustrated by Robert Seymour, part III by R. W. Buss and parts IV-XIX/XX by Phiz. Green wrappers) Chapman & Hall, April 1836-Nov 1837 . . £5,000
ditto, later issue £750
ditto, first book edition (1 vol., monthly parts bound with or without wrappers. 43 illustrations by R. Seymour and Phiz. Cloth or red morocco binding), Chapman & Hall, 1837 . . . . . . £750
Oliver Twist, (by 'Boz', 3 vols, illustrated by George Cruikshank, brown cloth), Richard Bentley 1838 . .

. . . . £6,000
ditto, (10 monthly parts with illustrations by George Cruikshank, green wrappers), Bradbury & Evans, January-October 1846 . . . . £6,000
ditto, first, 1 vol. edition, (as above, with slate-coloured cloth), Bradbury & Evans, MDCCCXLVI 1846 £200
Nicholas Nickleby, (20 monthly parts in 19, illustrated by Phiz, green wrappers), Chapman & Hall, April 1838-October 1839 . . . . £3,000
ditto, first book edition (monthly parts in 1 vol., illustrated by Phiz, cloth or half and full morocco binding), Chapman & Hall, 1839 . . . . . £300
Master Humphrey's Clock, (contains first publication of 'The Old Curiosity Shop' and 'Barnaby Rudge'. 88 weekly parts, illustrated by G. Cattermole, Phiz & Daniel Maclise, white wrappers), Chapman & Hall, April 1840-Nov 1841 . . . . £1,000
ditto (20 monthly parts, illustrated as above, green wrappers), Chapman & Hall April 1840-Nov 1841 . . . . £1,250
ditto, first book edition (3 vols, weekly or monthly parts, illustrated as above, bound with or without wrappers. brown or purple cloth binding), Chapman & Hall, MDCCCXL/MDCCCXLI 1841 . . . . £250
The Old Curiosity Shop, (original monthly parts from 'Master Humphrey's Clock', cloth binding), Chapman & Hall, 1841 . . . . £750
Barnaby Rudge, (original monthly parts from 'Master Humphrey's Clock', cloth binding), Chapman & Hall, 1841 . . . . £750
Martin Chuzzlewit, (20 monthly parts in 19, illustrated by Phiz, green wrappers), Chapman & Hall, Jan 1843-July 1844 . . . . £1,250
ditto, first book edition (made up of unsold monthly parts, Prussian blue cloth binding) Chapman & Hall, MDCCCXXLIV 1844 . . . . £250
Dombey and Son, (20 monthly parts in 19, illustrated by Phiz), Bradbury & Evans, 1848 . . . . £1,000
ditto, first book edition (monthly parts bound in dark green cloth.) Bradbury & Evans, 1848 . . . . £450
David Copperfield, (20 monthly parts in 19, illustrated by Phiz, green wrappers), Bradbury & Evans, May 1849-Nov, 1850 . . . . £5,000
ditto, first book edition (monthly parts bound in dark green cloth.) Bradbury & Evans, 1850 . . . . £450
Bleak House, (20 monthly parts in 19, illustrated by Phiz, blue wrappers, Bradbury & Evans, March 1852-Sept 1853 . . . . £1,000
ditto, first book edition (monthly parts bound in cloth), Bradbury & Evans, 1853 . . . . £250
Hard Times, Bradbury & Evans, 1854 (1 vol., green cloth) £500
Little Dorrit, (20 monthly parts in 19, illustrated by Phiz, blue wrappers), Bradbury & Evans, Dec 1855-June 1857 . . . . £1,000
ditto, first book edition (monthly parts bound in green cloth and morocco), Bradbury & Evans, 1857 £250
A Tale of Two Cities, (8 parts in 7, illustrated by Phiz, blue wrappers), Chapman & Hall June-Dec MDCCCLIX 1859 . . . . £7,500
ditto, first book edition (monthly parts bound in red cloth), Chapman & Hall, 1859 . . . . . £500
Great Expectations, (3 vols, purple or plum cloth), Chapman & Hall, MDCCCLXI 1861 . . . £7,500
Our Mutual Friend, (20 monthly parts in 19, illustrated by Marcus Stone, green wrappers) Chapman & Hall, May 1864-May 1865 . . . . £1,000
ditto, first book edition (2 vols of monthly parts bound in brown cloth) Chapman & Hall, 1865 . . . £450
The Mystery of Edwin Drood, (unfinished, six monthly parts, illustrated by Luke Fildes with cover design by Charles Alston Collins, green wrappers), Chapman & Hall, April-Sept 1870 . . . . £500
ditto, first book edition (monthly parts bound in green cloth), Chapman & Hall, 1870 . . . . . . £75

BENJAMIN DISRAELI
(b.1804 d.1881)

Perhaps beter-known as a politician, Disraeli was also a successful and popular novelist of the nineteenth century.

Vivian Grey, Colburn, 1826-27 (5 vols; anonymous) £1,000
The Voyage of Captain Popanilla, Colburn, 1828 £300
The Young Duke, Colburn, 1831 (3 vols) . . £750
Contarini Fleming: A Pyschologlcal Auto-biography, John Murray, 1832 (4 vols) £500
ditto, as ***The Young Venetian***, John Murray, 1834 £250
The Wondrous Tale of Alroy, and ***The rise of Iskander***, Saunders & Otley, 1833 (3 vols) . £250
A Year at Hartlebury, or The Election, Saunders & Otley, 1834 (as 'Cherry' and 'Fair Star', with Sarah Disraeli, 2 vols) £300
Henrietta Temple, Colburn, 1836 (3 vols) . . £500
Venetia, or The Poet's Daughter, Colburn, 1837 (3 vols) £500
Coningsby, or The New Generation, Colburn, 1844 (3 vols) £500
Sybil, or The Two Nations, Colburn, 1845 (3 vols) £500
Tancred, or The New Crusade, Colburn, 1847 (3 vols) £400
Lothair, Longman, 1870 (3 vols). £250
Endymion, Longman, 1880 (3 vols) £250
Ixion in Heaven, Cape, 1925. . . . . £25/£10

LORD ALFRED DOUGLAS
(b.1870 d.1945)

Notorious for his tempestuous affair with Oscar Wilde, Douglas was also a serious poet of some merit.

Verse

Poemes, Mercur de France, (Paris), 1896 . . £150
ditto, Mercur de France, (Paris), 1896 (50 deluxe copies) £250
ditto, Mercur de France, (Paris), 1896 (25 grande deluxe copies) £500
Perkin Warbeck and Some Other Poems, Chiswick Press, 1897 (50 copies) £300
The City of the Soul, Grant Richards, 1899 . . £75
Sonnets, W.H. Smith & Son/Academy Publishing Company, 1909 . . . . £75
ditto, Arden Press, 1909 (large paper edition) . £150
Collected Poems, Martin Secker, 1919 . . . . £25
ditto, Martin Secker, 1919 (200 copies, signed by the author) £200
In Excelsis, Martin Secker, 1924. . . . . £40/£15
ditto, Martin Secker, 1924 (100 signed copies) . £200
Nine Poems, privately printed for A.J.A. Symons, 1926 (50 copies) £500
Selected Poems, Martin Secker, 1924 . . £10/£5
Lord Alfred Douglas [***'Selected Poems'***], Ernest Benn, 'Augustan Books of Modern Poetry', [1926] (wraps) £5
Collected Satires, The Fortune Press, 1926 (550 copies) £50
ditto, The Fortune Press, 1926 (250 numbered copies signed by the author). £200
Complete Poems and Light Verse, Martin Secker, 1928 . . . . £35/£15
Lyrics, Rich & Cowan, 1935 . . . . . . £35/£15
ditto, Rich & Cowan, 1935 (50 copies signed by the author, cloth slipcase) £250
Sonnets, Rich & Cowan, 1935 . . . . . £35/£15
ditto, Rich & Cowan, 1935 (edition limited to 50 copies signed by the author, cloth slipcase) £250
Sonnets, Richards Press, 1943 (pocket edition) £15/£5

Prose

New Preface to "The Life and Confessions of Oscar Wilde", The Fortune Press, 1925 . . . . . £50
The Autobiography of Lord Alfred Douglas, Martin Secker, 1929 . . . . £35/£10
The Principles of Poetry, Richards Press, 1943 (1,000 copies, wraps) £15

NORMAN DOUGLAS
(b.1868 d.1952)

A travel writer and novelist, Douglas's *South Wind* is perhaps his best known novel.

Pamphlets

Zur Fauna Santorins, Leipzig, 1892 (c.50 copies, no wraps). £500
Contributions to an Avifauna of Baden, London, 1894 (no wraps, pseud. G. Norman Douglass) . . £500
On the Herpetology of the Grand Duchy of Baden, London, 1894 (50 copies, pseud. G. Norman Douglass) £500
Report on the Pumice Stone Industry of the Lipari Islands, H.M.S.O., 1895 . . . . . . £350
ditto, Hours Press, 1928 (80 copies) £250
On the Darwinian Hypothesis of Sexual Selection, London, 1895 (25 copies, pseud. G. Norman Douglass) £300

Capri Monographs

The Blue Grotto and its Literature, privately printed, 1904 (100 copies) £250
The Forestal Conditions of Capri, privately printed, 1904 (100 copies) £250
Fabio Giordano's Relation of Capri, privately printed, 1906 (250 copies) £200
Three Monographs, privately printed, 1906 (250 copies) £200
The Life of the Venerable Suor Serafina Di Dio, privately printed, 1907 (100 copies) . . . £250
Some Antiquarian Notes, privately printed, 1907 (250 copies) £200
Dislecta Membra, privately printed, 1915 (100 copies) £250
Index, privately printed, 1915 (100 copies) . . £250

Novels

South Wind, Martin Secker, 1917 . . . . £150
ditto, Martin Secker, 1922 (150 signed copies) . £150
ditto, Dodd Mead (U.S.), 1918 . . . . . . £150
ditto, Limited Editions Club (U.S.), 1932 . . £50
They Went, Chapman & Hall, 1920 . . . . £65
In the Beginning, privately printed (Florence), 1927 (700 signed, numbered copies) . . . . £150/£75
ditto, Chatto & Windus, 1928 . . . . £40/£15
ditto, John Day (U.S.), 1928 . . . . . £50/£20
Nerinda, G. Orioli (Florence), 1929 (475 signed, numbered copies) . . . . £150/£75

Short Stories

Unprofessional Tales, T. Fisher Unwin, 1901 (pseud. 'Normyx') £300

Travel/Belles Lettres
Siren Land, J.M. Dent, 1911 . . . . . . £200
Fountains in the Sand, Martin Secker, 1912 . £100
ditto, James Pott (U.S.), 1912. . . . . . . £25
Old Calabria, Martin Secker, 1915 . . . . £100
Alone, Chapman & Hall, 1921 . . . . £75/£25
Together, Chapman & Hall, 1923 . . . £75/£25
ditto, Chapman & Hall, 1923 (275 signed copies) £125
One Day, Hours Press (Paris), 1929 (300 copies) £200
ditto, Hours Press (Paris) (200 signed copies) . £350
Summer Islands, Desmond Harmsworth, 1931 £35/£15
ditto, Desmond Harmsworth, 1931 (500 numbered copies) . . . . £100/£35
ditto, Corvinus Press, 1942 [1944] (45 copies, various papers and bindings) £350
ditto, Colophon (U.S.), 1931 . . . . . . £25
ditto, Colophon (U.S.), 1931 (550 signed copies) £100
Footnote on Capri, Sidgwick & Jackson, 1952 £20/£5
ditto, McBride (U.S.), 1952 . . . . . £20/£5

Others
London Street Games, St Catherine's Press, 1916 £150
ditto, Chatto & Windus, 1931 . . . . £25/£10
ditto, Chatto & Windus, 1931 (110 signed copies) £75
D.H. Lawrence and Maurice Magnus: A Plea for Better Manners, privately printed (Florence), 1924 (wraps) £65
Experiments, privately printed (Florence), 1925 (300 signed, numbered copies) . . . . . £200/£100
ditto, Chapman & Hall, 1925 . . . . . £25/£10
ditto, McBride (U.S.), 1925 . . . . . . £25/£10
Birds and Beasts of the Greek Anthology, privately printed (Florence), 1927 (500 signed, numbered copies . . . . £200/£100
ditto, Chapman & Hall, 1928 . . . . . £40/£20
ditto, Cape & Smith (U.S.), 1929. . . . . £25/£10
Some Limericks, privately printed (Florence), 1928 (110 signed numbered copies) £250
ditto, privately printed (Florence), 1928 (750 unnumbered copies) £100
ditto, privately printed (by Guy d'Isere for David Moss, U.S.), 1928 (750 numbered copies). . . . £75
ditto, privately printed (Florence), 1929 (1,000 numbered copies for subscribers) £100
How About Europe?, privately printed (Florence), 1929 (550 signed, numbered copies) . . £150/£100
ditto, Chatto & Windus, 1930 . . . . £25/£10
The Angel of Manfredonia, The Windsor Press, 1929 (225 numbered copies) £50
Three of Them, Chatto & Windus, 1930 . £25/£10
Capri: Materials for a Description of the Island, G. Orioli (Florence), 1930 (525 signed, numbered copies) £200
ditto, G. Orioli (Florence), 1930 (100 signed copies) £500
Paneros, G. Orioli (Florence), 1930 (250 copies) £200
ditto, Chatto & Windus, 1931 (650 numbered copies) £75
ditto, McBride (U.S.), 1932 (750 copies, box) £65/£50
Looking Back, Chatto & Windus, 1933 (2 vols, 535 signed, numbered sets) £150
ditto, Chatto & Windus, 1934 (1 vol.) . . £35/£15
ditto, Harcourt, Brace (U.S.), 1933 (1 vol.) . £100/£25
An Almanac, privately printed (Lisbon), 1941 (25 [c.50] signed, numbered copies) £400
ditto, Secker & Warburg, 1945 . . . . £25/£10
Late Harvest, Lindsay Drummond, 1946 . £20/£5
Venus in the Kitchen, Heinemann, 1952 . £25/£5
ditto, Viking (U.S.), 1953 . . . . . . £25/£5

ERNEST DOWSON
(b.1867 d.1900)

Dowson was one of the best of the decadent poets of the 1890s. He also prepared translations and wrote short stories before dying of tuberculosis at the age of thirty-two.

Verse
Verses, Leonard Smithers, 1896 (300 copies. Cover design by Aubrey Beardsley) £300
ditto, Leonard Smithers, 1896 (30 copies on Japanese Vellum) £2,000
The Pierrot of the Minute, Leonard Smithers, 1897 (illustrated by Aubrey Beardsley, 300 copies printed on handmade paper) £400
ditto, Leonard Smithers, 1897 (30 copies printed on Japanese vellum) £2,500
ditto, Grolier Club (U.S.), 1923 (300 copies printed on Dutch antique paper) £200
Decorations, in Verse & Prose, Leonard Smithers, 1899 . . . . £400
The Poems of Ernest Dowson, John Lane, 1905 (edited and with a memoir by Arthur Symons. Illustrated by Aubrey Beardsley) £125
Cynara: A Little Book of Verse, Thomas Mosher (U.S.), 1907 (950 copies, slipcase) £45
Poetical Works of Ernest Dowson, Cassell/John Lane, 1934 (edited by Desmond Flower) . . . £25/£10
ditto, Cassell's Pocket Library, 1950 . . . £10/£5
The Poems of Ernest Dowson, The Unicorn Press, 1946 . . . . £15/£5
The Poems of Ernest Dowson, University of Pennsylvania Press (U.S.), 1962 (edited by Mark Longaker). . . . . £20/£5

Prose
A Comedy of Masks, Heinemann, 1893 (with Arthur

Moore. Novel in 3 vols) £200
Dilemmas, Elkin Matthews, 1895 (short stories) £100
Adrian Rome, Methuen, 1899 (with Arthur Moore) £75
The Stories of Ernest Dowson, University of Pennsylvania (U.S.), 1947 . . . . . £20/£10
ditto, W.H. Allen [1949] (edited by Mark Longaker) . . . . £15/£5
The Letters of Ernest Dowson, Fairleigh Dickinson (U.S.), 1967 (collected and edited by Desmond Flower & Henry Maas) . . . . £30/£20
ditto, Cassell, 1967 . . . . £30/£20
Bouquet, Whittington Press, 1991 . . . . £90
New Letters from Ernest Dowson, Whittington Press, 1984 (220 copies, signed by Desmond Flower) £50

Important Translations
La Terre, by Emile Zola, Lutetian Society, 1894 £100
Majesty, by Couperus, T. Fisher Unwin, 1894 (translated with A. Teixera de Mattos) £35
La Fille Aux Yeux D'Or, by Honore de Balzac, Leonard Smithers, 1896 (illustrated by Charles Conder) £75
Memoirs of Cardinal Dubois, Leonard Smithers, 1899 (2 vols) , ... £75
La Pucelle D'Orleans, by Voltaire, Lutetian Society, 1899 (500 sets, 2 vols) £125
The Conficantes of a King, by Edmond & Jules de Goncourt, T.N. Foulis, 1907 . . . . . £25
The Story of the Beauty and the Beast, John Lane, 1908 [1907] (illustrated by Charles Conder) . £40
Dangerous Acquaintances, by Pierre Choderlos de Lacios, Nonesuch Press, 1940 (illustrated by Charles Laborde) £40

SIR ARTHUR CONAN DOYLE

(b.1859 d.1930)

Best known, of course, for his creation of the ever-popular detective, Sherlock Holmes. Conan Doyle also wrote historical fiction, the genre of which he was most fond.

Sherlock Holmes Titles
A Study in Scarlet, Ward Lock, 1888 (wraps) £45,000
The Sign of Four, Spencer Blackett, 1890 . . £3,500
The Adventures of Sherlock Holmes, George Newnes, 1892 . . . . £2,000
ditto, Harper (U.S.), 1892. . . . . £750
The Memoirs of Sherlock Holmes, George Newnes, 1894 [1893] £1,000
ditto, Harper (U.S.), 1894. . . . . £600
The Hound of the Baskervilles, George Newnes, 1902 . . . . £2,000
ditto, McClure, Phillips (U.S.), 1902. . . . . £500
The Return of Sherlock Holmes, McClure, Phillips (U.S.), 1905 . . . . £500
ditto, George Newnes, 1905 . . . . £1,500
The Valley of Fear, Doran (U.S.), 1914. . . . £300
ditto, Smith Elder, 1915 . . . . £300
His Last Bow, John Murray, 1917 . . . . £300
ditto, Doran (U.S.), 1917 . . . . £100
The Case-Book of Sherlock Holmes, John Murray, 1927 . . . . £2,500/£300
ditto, Doran (U.S.), 1927 . . . . £750/£100

Novels
The Mystery of Cloomber, Ward and Downey 1889 [1888] (wraps) £150
ditto, Fenno (U.S.), 1895 . . . . £75
Micah Clarke, Longmans Green, 1889 . . . . £250
The Firm of Girdlestone, Chatto & Windus, 1890 £250
The White Company, Smith Elder, 1891 (3 vols) £3,000
ditto, Smith Elder, 1892 (1 vol.) £75
The Doings of Raffles Haw, Lovell (U.S.), 1891 £200
ditto, Cassell, 1892 . . . . £250
The Great Shadow, Arrowsmith's Christmas Annual, 1892 (wraps) £400
Beyond the City, Rand McNally (U.S.), [1892] £100
The Great Shadow, and Beyond the City, Arrowsmith [1893] £50
ditto, Harper (U.S.), 1893. . . . . £50
The Refugees, Longmans Green, 1893 (3 vols) £3,000
ditto, Longmans Green [August], 1893 (1 vol.) . £100
ditto, Harper (U.S.), 1893. . . . . £100
The Parasite, Constable, 1894 . . . . . . £150
ditto, Constable, 1894 (wraps) £150
Rodney Stone, Smith Elder, 1896 . . . . . £100
ditto, Appleton (U.S.) 1896 . . . . £75
Uncle Bernac, Horace Cox, 1896 [Jan 1897] (wraps, copyright edition: Chapters 1-10 only) . . . £1,500
ditto, Smith Elder, 1897 . . . . £150
ditto, Appleton (U.S.) 1897 . . . . £150
A Desert Drama, being the tragedy of the Korosko, Lippincott (U.S.), 1898 . . . . £100
ditto, as ***The Tragedy of Korosko***, Smith Elder, 1898 . . . . £100
Sir Nigel, Smith Elder, 1906 . . . . . £65
ditto, McClure, Phillips (U.S.), 1906. . . . . £50
The Lost World, Hodder & Stoughton, [1912] . £250
ditto, Hodder & Stoughton, [1912] (large paper edition, 190 of 1,000 copies comprise the first issue) £1,000
ditto, Henry Frowde/Hodder & Stoughton, [1912] (large paper edition, 810 of 1,000 copies comprise the second issue) £150
ditto, Doran (U.S.), 1912 . . . . £100
The Land Of Mist, Hutchinson, [1926] . £2,000/£200
ditto, Doran (U.S.),1926 . . . . . . £500/£50

The Maracot Deep, John Murray, 1929 (novel and 3 short stories) . . . . £750/£75

Short Stories

Mysteries and Adventures, Walter Scott, [1890] £1,500
ditto, Walter Scott, [1890], (wraps) £1,000
The Captain of the Polestar, Longmans, 1890 . £50
Round the Red Lamp, Methuen, 1894 . . . £45
ditto, Appleton (U.S.), 1894 . . . . £45
The Exploits of Brigadier Gerard, Newnes, 1896 (advertisements dated 10/2/96) £75
ditto, Newnes, 1896 (later advertisements) . . £60
ditto, Appleton (U.S.), 1896 . . . . £45
The Green Flag, Smith Elder, 1900 . . . . £50
Adventures of Gerard, Newnes, 1903 . . . £50
ditto, McClure, Phillips (U.S.), 1903. . . . £30
The Croxley Master, A Great Tale of the Prize Ring, McClure, Phillips (U.S.), 1907 . . . . . £50
Round the Fire Stories, Smith Elder, 1908 . . £30
ditto, McClure, Phillips (U.S.), 1908. . . . £30
The Last Galley, Smith Elder, 1911 . . . . . £50
ditto, Doubleday (U.S.), 1911 . . . . . . £30
Danger, John Murray, 1918 . . . . £30

Plays

Waterloo, Samuel French, 1907 . . . . . . £150

MARGARET DRABBLE
(b.1939)

Drabble's novels often explore the struggle of the individual against convention or repression. She was awarded a C.B.E. in 1980 for her services to English literature.

Novels

A Summer Bird-Cage, Weidenfeld, 1963 . £75/£25
ditto, Morrow (U.S.), 1964 . . . . . £25/£10
The Garrick Year, Weidenfeld, 1964 . . £50/£20
ditto, Morrow (U.S.), 1965 . . . . . £25/£10
The Millstone, Weidenfeld, 1965 . . . £40/£15
ditto, Morrow (U.S.), 1966 . . . . . £10/£5
Jerusalem the Golden, Weidenfeld, 1967 . £25/£10
ditto, Morrow (U.S.), 1967 . . . . . £10/£5
The Waterfall, Weidenfeld, 1969 . . . £15/£5
ditto, Knopf (U.S.), 1969 . . . . . . £10/£5
The Needle's Eye, Weidenfeld, 1972 . . £15/£5
ditto, Knopf (U.S.), 1972 . . . . . . £10/£5
The Realms of Gold, Weidenfeld, 1975 . . £10/£5
ditto, Knopf (U.S.), 1975 . . . . . . £10/£5
The Ice Age, Wieidenfeld, 1977 . . . . £10/£5
ditto, Knopf (U.S.), 1977 . . . . . . £10/£5
The Middle Ground, Weidenfeld, 1980 . . £10/£5
ditto, Knopf (U.S.), 1980 . . . . £10/£5
The Radiant Way, Weidenfeld & Nicolson, 1987 . . . . £10/£5
ditto, Knopf (U.S.), 1987 . . . . £10/£5
A Natural Curiosity, Viking, 1989 . . . £10/£5
ditto, London Limited Editions, 1989 (150 signed copies) . . . . £65/£45
ditto, Viking (U.S.), 1989. . . . . . . £10/£5
The Gates of Ivory, Viking, 1991 . . . . £10/£5
ditto, Viking (U.S.), 1992. . . . . . . £10/£5

Non Fiction

Wordsworth, Evans, 1966 . . . . . . £20/£5
Virginia Woolf: A Personal Debt, Aloe Editions (U.S.), 1973 (110 signed copies, wraps) . . . £100
Arnold Bennett: A Biography, Weidenfeld, 1974 . . . . £10/£5
ditto, Knopf (U.S.), 1974 . . . . £10/£5
A Writer's Britain: Landscape in Literature, Thames & Hudson, 1979 . . . . £20/£10
ditto, Knopf (U.S.), 1979 . . . . £20/£10
The Tradition of Women's Fiction: Lectures in Japan, O.U.P., (Tokyo), 1985 . . . . . . £15/£5
Case for Equality, Fabian Society, 1988 . . . £10
Stratford Revisited: A Legacy of the Sixties, Celandine Press, 1989 (150 signed copies, wraps) . . . £15
Safe As Houses: An Examination of Home Ownership and Mortgage Tax Relief, Chatto & Windus, 1990 . . . . £5
Angus Wilson: A Biography, Secker & Warburg, 1995 . . . . £10/£5
ditto, St. Martin's Press (U.S.), 1996 . . . . £10/£5

Children's

For Queen and Country: Britain in the Victorian Age, Deutsch, 1978 . . . . £15
ditto, Seabury Press (U.S.), 1979. . . . . . £10

DAPHNE DU MAURIER
(b.1907 d.1989)

Du Maurier is the author of tense romances set against the background of Cornwall, her home for most of her life.

Novels

The Loving Spirit, Heinemann, 1931 . . . £150/£25
ditto, Doubleday (U.S.), 1931 . . . . . £65/£15
I'll Never Be Young Again, Heinemann, 1932 £75/£15
ditto, Doubleday (U.S.), 1932 . . . . . £45/£15
The Progress of Julius, Heinemann, 1933 . £25/£10
Jamaica Inn, Gollancz, 1936 . . . . . £40/£10
ditto, Doubleday (U.S.), 1936 . . . . . £35/£10

Rebecca, Gollancz, 1938 . . . . . . £250/£50
ditto, Doubleday (U.S.), 1938 . . . . £100/£20
Frenchman's Creek, Gollancz, 1941 . . £35/£10
ditto, Doubleday (U.S.), 1942 . . . . £25/£5
Hungry Hill, Gollancz, 1943 . . . . . £10/£5
ditto, Doubleday (U.S.), 1943 . . . . £10/£5
The King's General, Gollancz, 1946 . . £10/£5
ditto, Doubleday (U.S.), 1946 . . . . £10/£5
The Parasites, Gollancz, 1949 . . . . £15/£5
ditto, Doubleday (U.S.), 1950 . . . . £10/£5
My Cousin Rachel, Gollancz, 1951 . . . £10/£5
ditto, Doubleday (U.S.), 1952 . . . . £10/£5
Mary Anne, Gollancz, 1954 . . . . . £10/£5
ditto, Doubleday (U.S.), 1954 . . . . £10/£5
The Daphne du Maurier Omnibus, Gollancz, 1956 (contains ***Rebecca***, ***Jamaica Inn*** and ***Frenchman's Creek***). . . . . £10/£5
The Scapegoat, Gollancz, 1957 . . . . £10/£5
ditto, Doubleday (U.S.), 1957 . . . . £10/£5
Castle Dor, Gollancz, 1962 (with Sir Arthur Quiller-Couch) . . . . £15/£5
ditto, Doubleday (U.S.), 1962 . . . . £10/£5
The Glassblowers, Gollancz, 1963 . . . £10/£5
ditto, Doubleday (U.S.), 1963 . . . . £10/£5
The Daphne du Maurier Tandem, Gollancz, 1964 (contains ***Mary Anne*** and ***My Cousin Rachel***) £10/£5
The Flight of the Falcon, Gollancz, 1965 . £10/£5
ditto, Doubleday (U.S.), 1965 . . . . £10/£5
The House on the Strand, Gollancz, 1969 . £10/£5
ditto, Doubleday (U.S.), 1969 . . . . £10/£5
Rule Britannia, Gollancz, 1972 . . . . £10/£5
ditto, Doubleday (U.S.), 1972 . . . . £10/£5
Three Famous Daphne du Maurier Novels, Gollancz, 1982 (contains *The Flight of the Falcon, The House on the Strand* and *The King's General*) £10/£5
Four Great Cornish Novels, Gollancz, 1982 (contains *Jamaica Inn, Rebecca, Frenchman's Creek* and *My Cousin Rachel*) . . . . £10/£5

Short Stories

Happy Christmas, Doubleday (U.S.), 1940 . £25/£10
ditto, Todd Publishing Co., 1943 . . . . . £20
Consider the Lilies, Polybooks/Todd Publishing Co., 1943 (wraps) £20
Escort, Polybooks/Todd Publishing Co., 1943 (wraps). £20
Nothing Hurts for Long; and Escort, Polybooks/Todd Publishing Co., 1943 (wraps) £20
Spring Picture, Todd Publishing Co., 1944 (wraps) £20
Leading Lady, Polybooks/Vallancey Press, 1945 (wraps) £20
London and Paris, Polybooks/Vallancey Press, 1945 (wraps) £20
The Apple Tree, Gollancz, 1952 (later published as ***The Birds***) . . . . £35/£10
Early Stories, Bantam Books, 1954 . . . . £15
The Breaking Point, Gollancz, 1959 (later published as ***The Blue Lenses***) . . . . . . £10/£5
ditto, Doubleday (U.S.), 1959 . . . . £10/£5
The Treasury of du Maurier Short Stories, Gollancz, 1960 (contains ***The Apple Tree*** and ***The Breaking Point***) . . . . £10/£5
The Lover, Ace Wraps (U.S.), 1961 . . . . £5
Not After Midnight, Gollancz, 1971 (later published as ***Don't Look Now***) . . . . £15/£5
Echoes from the Macabre, Gollancz, 1976 . £10/£5
ditto, Doubleday (U.S.), 1976 . . . . £10/£5
The Rendezvous, Gollancz, 1980 . . . £10/£5
Classics of the Macabre, Gollancz, 1987 . £15/£5
ditto, Gollancz, 1987 (250 signed copies in slipcase) £40

Plays

Rebecca, Gollancz, 1940 . . . . . . £20/£5
The Years Between, Gollancz, 1945 . . . £20/£5
ditto, Doubleday (U.S.), 1946 . . . . £20/£5
September Tide, Gollancz, 1946 . . . . £20/£5
ditto, Doubleday (U.S.), 1950 . . . . £20/£5
The Little Photographer, Samuel French, 1979 (wraps, adapted by Derek Hoddinott) £5
My Cousin Rachel, Samuel French, 1979, (wraps, adapted by Diana Morgan) £5

Biographies

Gerald: A Portrait, Gollancz, 1934 . . . £20/£10
The du Mauriers, Gollancz, 1937 . . . £20/£10
The Infernal World of Branwell Brontë, Gollancz, 1960 . . . . £10/£5
ditto, Doubleday (U.S.), 1960 . . . . . £10/£5
The Golden Lads, Gollancz, 1975 . . . £10/£5
The Winding Stair: Francis Bacon, His Rise And Fall, Gollancz, 1976. . . . . . . £10/£5
ditto, Doubleday (U.S.), 1977 . . . . . £10/£5
Growing Pains: The Shaping of a Writer, Gollancz, 1977 . . . . £10/£5
The Rebecca Notebook & Other Memories, Doubleday (U.S.), 1980 . . . . . . £10/£5
ditto, Gollancz, 1981 . . . . £10/£5

Miscellaneous

Come Wind, Come Weather, Heinemann, 1940 (wraps) £10
Vanishing Cornwall, Gollancz, 1967 . . . £15/£5
ditto, Doubleday (U.S.), 1967 . . . . . £10/£5
ditto, Gollancz, 1981 (colour edition) . . £15/£5

GEORGE DU MAURIER

(b.1834 d.1896)

Principally a novelist and critic, du Maurier's *Trilby* brought the author fame. He also wrote humorous verse.

Novels

Peter Ibbetson, Osgood, McIlvaine, 1892 (s vols) £90
ditto, Harper (U.S.), 1892. . . . . £20
Trilby, Osgood, McIlvaine, 1894, (3 vols) . . £250
ditto, Harper (U.S.), 1894. . . . . £20
The Martian, Harper (U.S.), 1897 . . . . £25
ditto, Harper (U.K.), 1898 . . . . . . £25
Svengali, W.H. Allen, 1982 (first unexpurgated edition of ***Trilby***) . . . . £10/£5

Others

English Society at Home, Bradbury, Agnew & Co., 1880 . . . . £35
Society Pictures, Bradbury, Agnew & Co., 1890-91 (2 vols) £25
English Society, Osgood, McIlvaine, 1897 . . £20
Social Pictorial Satire, Harper & Bros., 1898 . £20
ditto, Harper (U.S.), 1898. . . . . . . £20
A Legend of Camelot, Bradbury, Agnew & Co., 1898 . . . . £20
The Young du Marier: A Selection of his Letters, Peter Davies, 1951 . . . . £10/£5

EDMUND DULAC

(b.1882 d.1953)

A French illustrator, and rival to Arthur Rackham, Dulac illustrated many 'gift book' editions of popular fairy tales.

Written and illustrated by Dulac

Lyrics Pathetic and Humorous From A to Z, Warne, 1908 . . . . £350
ditto, Warne, 1908 [1909], (portfolio of 24 plates, cloth-covered box) £2,500
A Fairy Garland: Being Fairy Tales from the Old French, Cassell, 1928 . . . . . £350/£75
ditto, Cassell, 1928 (deluxe edition, 1,000 signed copies, slipcase and glassine d/w) . . £400/£300
ditto, Scribner's (U.S.), 1929 . . . . . £200/£75

Illustrated by Dulac

The Novels of the Brontë Sisters, by The Brontës, Dent, 1905 (10 vols) . . . . £25 each
Fairies I Have Met, by Mrs R. Stawell, John Lane [1901]. £60
ditto, Hodder & Stoughton, [1910] £50
ditto, as ***My Days With the Fairies***, Hodder & Stoughton, [1913] £125
Stories from The Arabian Nights, retold by Laurence Housman, Hodder & Stoughton, 1907 . . . £150
ditto, Hodder & Stoughton, 1907 (deluxe edition, 350 signed copies) £1,000
ditto, Scribner's (U.S.), 1907 . . . . . . £150
The Tempest, by William Shakespeare, Hodder & Stoughton, [1908] £150
ditto, Hodder & Stoughton, [1908] (deluxe edition, 500 signed copies) £750
The Rubaiyat of Omar Khyyam, by Edward Fitzgerald, Hodder & Stoughton, [1909] £100
ditto, Hodder & Stoughton, [1909] (deluxe edition, 750 signed copies) £500
The Sleeping Beauty, retold by Sir Arthur Quiller-Couch, Hodder & Stoughton, [1910] £250
ditto, Hodder & Stoughton, [1910] (deluxe edition, 1,000 signed copies) £750
Stories from Hans Anderson, Hodder & Stoughton, 1911 . . . . £250
ditto, Hodder & Stoughton, 1911 (deluxe edition, 750 signed copies) £1,000
ditto, Hodder & Stoughton, 1911 (deluxe edition, 100 signed copies, morocco binding) £2,500
The Bells and Other Poems, by Edgar Allan Poe, Hodder & Stoughton, [1912] £150
ditto, Hodder & Stoughton, [1912] (deluxe edition, 750 signed copies) £600
Princess Badoura: A Tale from The Arabian Nights, retold by Laurence Housman, Hodder & Stoughton, [1913]. £150
ditto, Hodder & Stoughton, [1913] (deluxe edition, 750 signed copies) £750
Sinbad the Sailor and Other Stories from the Arabian Nights, Hodder & Stoughton, [1914] . . . £350
ditto, Hodder & Stoughton, [1914] (deluxe edition, 500 signed copies) £1,750
Edmund Dulac's Picture-Book for the French Red Cross, Hodder & Stoughton, [1915] . . . £40
The Dreamer of Dreams, by Queen Marie of Roumania, Hodder & Stoughton, [1915] . . £45
The Stealers of Light, by Queen Marie of Roumania, Hodder & Stoughton, 1916 . . . . . . £35
Edmund Dulac's Fairy-Book, Hodder & Stoughton, [1916]. £125
ditto, Hodder & Stoughton, [1916] (deluxe edition, 350 signed copies) £600
ditto, Hodder & Stoughton, 1919 (extra plate) . £100
Tanglewood Tales, by Nathaniel Hawthorne, Hodder & Stoughton, [1918] £100
ditto, Hodder & Stoughton, [1918] (deluxe edition, 500 signed copies) £500
The Kingdom of the Pearl, by Leonard Rosenthal,

Nisbet, [1920], (675 copies). . . . . . £350/£200
ditto, Nisbet, [1920] (100 signed copies) . . £1,250
ditto, Brentano's (U.S.) 1920 (675 numbered copies) . . . . £350/£200
Four Plays for Dancers, by W.B. Yeats, Macmillan, 1921 . . . . £100
The Green Lacquer Pavilion, by Helen Beauclerk, Collins, 1926 . . . . £25/£10
ditto, Doran (U.S.) 1926 . . . . £60/£20
Treasure Island, by Robert Louis Stevenson, Benn, 1927 . . . . £300/£150
ditto, Benn, 1927 (deluxe edition, 50 signed copies) £3,000
ditto, Doran (U.S.) [1927] . . . . . . £125/£65
Gods and Mortals in Love, by Hugh Ross Williamson, Country Life, [1936]. . . . . £250/£50
The Daughters of the Stars, by Mary C. Crary, Hatchard, 1939 . . . . £25/£15
ditto, Hatchard, 1939 (deluxe edition, 500 copies signed by author and artist) £125
The Golden Cockerel, by Alexander Pushkin, Limited Editions Club (U.S.), [1950], (1,500 signed, numbered copies, slipcase) . . . . £100/£85
ditto, Heritage Press, (U.S.), 1950 (slipcase) £50/£45
The Marriage of Cupid and Psyche, by Walter Pater, Limited Editions Club (U.S.), [1951], (1,500 signed, numbered copies) . . . . £100/£85
ditto, Heritage Press, (U.S.), 1951 (slipcase) £35/£30
The Masque of Comus, by John Milton, Limited Editions Club (U.S.), 1954, (1,500 numbered copies, slipcase) . . . . £100/£85
ditto, Heritage Press, (U.S.), 1955 (slipcase) £35/£30

DOUGLAS DUNN

(b.1942)

A Scottish poet whose early work shows the influence of Philip Larkin.

Verse

Terry Street, Faber, 1969 . . . . £25/£10
Backwaters, The Review, 1971 (wraps) £20
Night, Poem of the Month Club, 1971 (broadsheet) £15
The Happier Life, Faber, 1972 . . . . . £25/£10
ditto, Chilmark (U.S.), [no date] . . . . £15/£5
Love or Nothing, Faber, 1974 (wraps) . . . £15
Barbarians, Faber, 1979 (wraps). £25
St Kilda's Parliament, Faber, 1981 (wraps). . £10
Europa's Lover, Bloodaxe, 1982 (wraps) . . £10
Northlight, Faber, 1988 . . . . . . £15/£5
Elegies, Faber, 1985 . . . . £15/£5
Selected Poems 1964-1983, Faber, 1986 . . £10
New and Selected Poems 1966-1988, Ecco Press (U.S.), 1989 . . . . £10/£5
Dante's Drum-Kit, Faber, 1993 . . . . . £10/£5
Boyfriends and Girlfriends, Faber, 1995 . £10/£5

Stories

Secret Villages, Faber, 1985 . . . . . . £20/£5
ditto, Dodd Mead, 1985 . . . . £15/£5

Others

Under the Influence: Douglas Dunn on Philip Larkin, Edinburgh University Press Library, 1987 £10
Poll Tax, the Fiscal Fake: Why We Should Fight the Community Charge, Chatto & Windus, 1990 . £5

LORD DUNSANY

(b.1878 d.1957)

A versatile Irish writer, Dunsany is read and appreciated today for his contributions to the genre of heroic fantasy.

Short Stories

The Gods of Pegana, Elkin Mathews, 1905. . £125
Time and the Gods, W. Heinemann, 1906 . . £90
ditto, Luce (U.S.), 1913 . . . . £75
ditto, Putnam's, 1922 [1923] (250 copies signed by Dunsany and Sime) £275
The Sword of Welleran, George Allen, 1908 (the first issue has 'George Allen & Sons' at base of spine) £100
ditto, George Allen, 1908 (second issue with 'George Allen' at base of spine) £80
A Dreamer's Tales, George Allen, 1910 . . £90
ditto, Luce (U.S.), 1911 . . . . £60
The Fortress Unvanquishable, Save for Sacnoth, School of Arts Press, 1910 (30 copies). . . . £450
Selections from the Writings of Lord Dunsany, Cuala Press, 1912 (250 copies) £200
The Book of Wonder, W. Heinemann, 1912 . £35
ditto, Luce (U.S.), 1912 . . . . £25
Fifty-One Tales, Elkin Mathews, 1915 . . . £45
ditto, Kennerly (U.S.), 1915 . . . . . . £20
Tales of Wonder, Elkin Mathews, 1916 . . . . £40
ditto, as ***The Last Book of Wonder***, Luce (U.S.), 1916 . . . . £60
Tales of War, Talbot Press/T. Fisher Unwin, 1918 £75
ditto, Little, Brown (U.S.), 1918 . . . . . £15
Unhappy Far Off Things, Elkin Mathews, 1919 £20
ditto, Little, Brown (U.S.), 1919 . . . . . £15
Tales of Three Hemispheres, Luce (U.S.), 1919 . . . . £75/£20
ditto, T. Fisher Unwin, 1920 . . . . £75/£20
The Travel Tales of Mr. Joseph Jorkens, Putnam's, 1931 . . . . £75/£35

ditto, Putnam's (U.S.), 1931 . . . . . . £75/£35
Mr Jorkens Remembers Africa, W. Heinemann, 1934 . . . . £75/£40
Jorkens Has A Large Whiskey, Putnam, 1940 . . . . £75/£35
The Fourth Book of Jorkens, Jarrolds [1947] £65/£20
ditto, Arkham House (U.S.), 1948 . . . . £45/£20
The Man Who Ate the Phoenix, Jarrolds [1949] . . . . £45/£15
The Little Tales of Smethers, Jarrolds, 1952 £45/£20
Jorkens Borrows Another Whiskey, Michael Joseph, 1954 . . . . £40/£15
The Edge of the World, Ballantine Adult Fantasy, 1970 (wraps) £5
Beyond the Fields We Know, Ballantine Adult Fantasy, 1972 (wraps) £5
Gods, Men and Ghosts: The Best Supernatural Fiction of Lord Dunsany, Dover, 1972 (wraps) £5
Over the Hills and Far Away, Ballantine Adult Fantasy, 1974 (wraps) £5

Novels

The Chronicles of Rodriguez, Putnam's, 1922 (500 copies numbered and signed by Dunsany and Sime) . . . . £250/£200
ditto, Putnam's, 1924 . . . . £75/£25
ditto, as ***Don Rodriguez, Chronicles of Shadow Valley***, Putnam's (U.S.), 1924 . . . . . . £75/£25
The King of Elfland's Daughter, Putnam's, 1924 (250 copies numbered and signed by Dunsany and Sime) . . . . £225/£200
ditto, Putnam's, 1924 . . . . £90/£35
ditto, Putnam's (U.S.), 1924 . . . . . £75/£25
The Charwoman's Shadow, Putnam's, 1926 £75/£20
ditto, Putnam's (U.S.), 1926 . . . . . £75/£20
The Blessing of Pan, Putnam's, 1927 . . £75/£20
ditto, Putnam's (U.S.), 1928 . . . . . . £75/£20
The Curse of the Wise Woman, W. Heinemann, 1933 . . . . £50/£15
ditto, Longman's (U.S.), 1933 . . . . . £20
Up in the Hills, W. Heinemann, 1935 . . £45/£15
ditto, Putnam's (U.S.), 1935 . . . . . £45/£15
Rory and Bran, W. Heinemann, 1936 . . £45/£10
ditto, Putnam's (U.S.), 1937 . . . . . £25/£10
My Talks with Dean Spanley, W. Heinemann, 1936 . . . . £30/£10
ditto, Putnam's (U.S.), 1936 . . . . . £25/£10
The Story of Mona Sheehy, W. Heinemann, 1939 . . . . £75/£25
Guerrilla, W. Heinemann, 1944 . . . . £25/£10
ditto, Bobbs-Merrill (U.S.), 1944. . . . . £20/£5
The Strange Journeys of Colonel Polders, Jarrolds, 1950 . . . . £40/£20
ditto, Jarrolds (U.S.), 1950 . . . . . £40/£20
The Last Revolution, Jarrolds, 1951 . . . £40/£20
His Fellow Men, Jarrolds, 1952 . . . . . £40/£20

Plays

Five Plays, Grant Richards, 1914 . . . . £30
ditto, Little, Brown (U.S.), 1914 . . . . . £20
Plays of Gods and Men, Talbot Press, 1917 . £30
ditto, Luce (U.S.), 1917 . . . . £20
If, Putnam's, 1921 . . . . £25/£10
ditto, Putnam's, 1921 (large paper issue) . . £35
ditto, Putnam's (U.S.), 1921 . . . . . £25/£10
The Laughter of the Gods, Putnam's, 1922 (from ***Plays of Gods and Men***, wraps) £15
The Tents of the Arabs, Putnam's, [1922] (from ***Plays of Gods and Men***, wraps) £15
The Queen's Enemies, Putnam's, 1922 (from ***Plays of Gods and Men***, wraps) £15
A Night at an Inn, Putnam's, 1922 (from ***Plays of Gods and Men***, wraps) £15
Plays of Near and Far, Putnam's, 1922 (500 copies) £50
ditto, Putnam's, 1923 . . . . £25/£10
ditto, Putnam's (U.S.), 1923 . . . . . £25/£10
The Gods of the Mountain, Putnam's, 1923 (from ***Five Plays***, wraps) £10
The Golden Dome, Putnam's, 1923 (from ***Five Plays***, wraps). £10
King Argimenes and the Unknown Warrior, Putnam's, 1923 (from ***Five Plays***, wraps) £10
The Glittering Gate, Putnam's, 1923 (from ***Five Plays***, wraps). £10
The Lost Silk Hat, Putnam's, 1923 (from ***Five Plays***, wraps). £10
The Compromise of the King of the Golden Isles, Putnam's [1923] (from ***Plays of Near and Far***, wraps) £10
The Flight of the Queen, Putnam's [1923] (from ***Plays of Near and Far***, wraps) £10
Cheezo, Putnam's [1923] (from ***Plays of Near and Far***, wraps). £10
A Good Bargain, Putnam's [1923] (from ***Plays of Near and Far***, wraps) £10
If Shakespeare Lived To-day, Putnam's [1923] (from ***Plays of Near and Far***, wraps) £10
Fame and the Poet, Putnam's [1923] (from ***Plays of Near and Far***, wraps) £10
Alexander, and Three Small Plays, Putnam's, 1925 . . . . £25/£10
ditto, Putnam's, 1925 (250 copies) £60
ditto, Putnam's (U.S.), 1923 . . . . . £25/£10
Alexander, Putnam's, 1925 (from ***Alexander, and Three Small Plays***, wraps) £10
The Old King's Tale, Putnam's, 1925 (from ***Alexander, and Three Small Plays***, wraps) £10
The Evil Kettle, Putnam's, 1925 (from ***Alexander, and Three Small Plays***, wraps) £10
The Amusements of Khan Kharuda, Putnam's, 1925

(from ***Alexander, and Three Small Plays***, wraps) £10
Seven Modern Comedies, Putnam's, 1928 . £25/£10
ditto, Putnam's, 1928 (250 copies) £60
ditto, Putnam's (U.S.), 1929 . . . . . £25/£10
Atlanta in Wimbledon, Putnam's, 1928 (from ***Seven Modern Comedies***, wraps) £10
The Raffle, Putnam's, 1928 (from ***Seven Modern Comedies***, wraps) £10
The Journey of the Soul, Putnam's, 1928 (from ***Seven Modern Comedies***, wraps) £10
In Holy Russia, Putnam's, 1928 (from ***Seven Modern Comedies***, wraps) £10
His Sainted Grandmother, Putnam's, 1928 (from ***Seven Modern Comedies***, wraps) £10
The Hopeless Passion of Mr Bunyon, Putnam's, 1928 (from ***Seven Modern Comedies***, wraps) . . £10
The Jest of Hahalaba, Putnam's, 1928 (from ***Seven Modern Comedies***, wraps) £10
The Old Folk of the Centuries, Elkin Mathews & Marrot, 1930 (100 signed copies of 900) . £75/£65
ditto, Elkin Mathews & Marrot, 1930 (800 unsigned copies of 900) . . . . £45/£20
Lord Adrian, Golden Cockerel Press, 1933 (325 copies, glassine d/w) £125
Mr Faithful, Samuel French [1935] (wraps) . £15
Plays for Earth and Air, W. Heinemann, 1937 £25/£10

Verse

Fifty Poems, Putnam's, 1929 (250 copies) . £125/£20
ditto, Putnam's, 1929 . . . . £50/£20
Mirage Water, Putnam's, 1938 . . . . . £20
War Poems, Hutchinson [1941] £15
Wandering Songs, Hutchinson [1943] £15
A Journey, Macdonald [1944] (250 copies, initialed 'D', leather bound in slipcase) £45
ditto, Macdonald [1944] (trade edition) . . £15/£5
The Year, Jarrolds, 1946 . . . . £15/£5
To Awaken Pegasus, George Ronald, 1949. £25/£10

Autobiography

Patches of Sunlight, W. Heinemann, 1938 . £35/£15
ditto, Reynal Hitchcock (U.S.), 1938. . . £20/£10
While the Sirens Slept, Jarrolds [1944] . . £30/£10
The Sirens Wake, Jarrolds, 1945. . . . . £25/£10

Miscellaneous

If I Were Dictator, Methuen, 1934 . . . . £35/£10
My Ireland, Jarrolds, 1937 . . . . . . £30/£10
ditto, Jarrolds, 1950 (revised edition) . . £20/£5
The Donnellan Lectures, 1943, W. Heinemann, 1945 . . . . £10/£5
A Glimpse from the Watch Tower, Jarrolds, 1946 . . . . £25/£10
The Ghosts of the Heaviside Layer and other Phantasms, Owlswick Press (U.S.), 1980 £20/£10

GERALD DURRELL

(b.1925 d.1995)

Brother of Lawrence, Gerald Durrell wrote popular travel and natural history books, and was appointed an OBE in 1983.

Non Fiction

The Overloaded Ark, Faber & Faber, 1953 £15/£5
ditto, Viking (U.S.), 1953 . . . . £10/£5
Three Singles to Adventure, Hart-Davis, 1954 £15/£5
The Bafut Beagles, Hart-Davis, 1954 . . £10/£5
ditto, Viking (U.S.), 1954 . . . . £10/£5
The Drunken Forest, Hart-Davis, 1956 . . £10/£5
ditto, Viking (U.S.), 1956 . . . . £10/£5
My Family and Other Animals, Hart-Davis, 1956 . . . . £20/£10
ditto, Viking (U.S.), 1957 . . . . £20/£5
Encounters With Animals, Hart-Davis, 1958 £15/£5
A Zoo in My Luggage, Hart-Davis, 1960 . £10/£5
ditto, Viking (U.S.), 1956 . . . . £10/£5
The Whispering Land, Hart-Davis, 1961 . £10/£5
ditto, Viking (U.S.), 1962 . . . . £10/£5
Menagerie Manor, Hart-Davis, 1964 . . £10/£5
ditto, Viking (U.S.), 1964 . . . . £10/£5
Two In The Bush, Collins, 1966 . . . . £10/£5
ditto, Viking (U.S.), 1966 . . . . £10/£5
Birds, Beasts & Relatives, Collins, 1969 . £10/£5
ditto, Viking (U.S.), 1969 . . . . £10/£5
Fillets of Plaice, Collins, 1971 . . . . £10/£5
ditto, Viking (U.S.), 1971 . . . . £10/£5
Catch Me a Colobus, Collins, 1972 . . . £10/£5
ditto, Viking (U.S.), 1972 . . . . £10/£5
Beasts in My Belfry, Collins, 1973 . . . £10/£5
The Stationary Ark, Collins, 1976 . . . £10/£5
ditto, Simon & Schuster (U.S.), 1976 . . £10/£5
Golden Bats and Pink Pigeons, Collins, 1977 £10/£5
ditto, Simon & Schuster (U.S.), 1977 . . £10/£5
The Garden of the Gods, Collins, 1978 . . £10/£5
The Amateur Naturalist, Hamish Hamilton, 1982 . . . . £10/£5
ditto, as ***A Practical Guide for the Amateur Naturalist***, Knopf (U.S.), 1983 . . . . £10/£5
How To Shoot An Amateur Naturalist, Collins, 1982 . . . . £10/£5
ditto, Little, Brown (U.S.), 1984 . . . . . £10/£5
Durrell in Russia, McDonald, 1986 (with Lee Durrell) . . . . £10/£5
ditto, Simon & Schuster (U.S.), 1986 . . £10/£5
Ark's Anniversary, Collins, 1990 . . . £10/£5
ditto, Arcade (U.S.), 1991. . . . . . . £10/£5
Gerald Durrell's Army, J. Murray, 1992 . £10/£5
Best of Durrell, HarperCollins, 1996 . . £10/£5

Novel
Rosy is My Relative, Collins, 1968 . . . £15/£5
ditto, Viking (U.S.), 1968 . . . . £10/£5
The Mockery Bird, Collins, 1981 . . . £10/£5
ditto, Simon & Schuster (U.S.), 1981 . . £10/£5

Short Stories
The Picnic & Suchlike Pandemonium, Collins, 1979 . . . . £10/£5
ditto, as ***The Picnic & Other Inimitable Stories***, Simon & Schuster (U.S.), 1980 . . . . . . £10/£5

Children's
The New Noah, Collins, 1955 . . . . £10/£5
Island Zoo, Collins, 1961 . . . . . . £10/£5
Look at Zoos, Collins, 1961 . . . . . £10/£5
My Favourite Animal Stories, Collins, 1962 £10/£5
The Donkey Rustlers, Collins, 1968 . . . £10/£5
ditto, Viking (U.S.), 1968 . . . . . . £10/£5
The Talking Parcel, Collins, 1974 . . . £10/£5
Fantastic Flying Journey, Conran Octopus, 1987 . . . . £10/£5
ditto, Simon & Schuster (U.S.), 1987 . . £10/£5
Animal Family Adventures with Gerald Durrell, Price Stern Sloan, 1988 . . . . £10/£5
Fantastic Dinosaur Adventure, Conran Octopus, 1989 . . . . £10/£5
ditto, Simon & Schuster (U.S.), 1989 . . £10/£5
Toby the Tortoise, M. O'Mara Books, 1991. £10/£5
ditto, Little, Brown (U.S.), 1991 . . . . £10/£5

LAWRENCE DURRELL
(b.1912 d.1990)

Novelist, poet and travel writer, much of Lawrence Durrell's work owes a debt to the Mediterranean where he spent most of his life.

Verse
Quaint Fragment, Cecil Press, 1931 . . £15,000
ditto, Cecil Press, 1931 (wraps) £15,000
Ten Poems, Caduceus Press, 1932 (wraps) . . £2,500
Ballade of Slow Decay, privately printed, 1932 (single sheet, folded) £2,000
Transition, Caduceus Press, 1934 . . . . £2,500
A Private Country, Faber, 1943 . . . . £500/£35
Cities, Plains and People, Faber, 1946 . . £50/£20
On Seeming to Presume, Faber, 1948 . . £25/£10
Deus Loci, Ischia, 1950 (200 signed copies, wraps) £200
The Tree of Idleness, Faber, 1955 . . . £25/£10
Selected Poems, Faber, 1956 (wraps) . . . £10
ditto, Grove Press (U.S.), 1956 . . . . £10/£5
Collected Poems, Faber, 1960 . . . . . £15/£5
ditto, Dutton (U.S.), 1960. . . . . . . £10/£5
Beccafico Le Becfigue, La Licorne (France), 1963 (150 signed copies, wraps) £125
La Descente du Styx, La Murène (France), 1964 (250 signed copies, wraps) £100
ditto, as ***Down the Styx***, Capricorn Press (U.S.), 1971 (200 of 1,000 copies) £50
ditto, as ***Down the Styx***, Capricorn Press (U.S.), 1971 (800 of 1,000 copies, wraps) £25
Selected Poems, 1935-1963, Faber, 1964 (wraps) £10
The Ikons, Faber, 1966 . . . . £15/£5
ditto, Dutton (U.S.), 1967. . . . . . . £10/£5
Nothing Is Lost, Sweet Self, Turret, 1967 (100 signed copies, wraps with d/w) £100
In Arcadia, Turret, 1968 (100 signed copies, wraps with d/w) £100
The Red Limbo Lingo, Faber, 1971 (1,200 copies, glassine d/w, slipcase) £45
ditto, Faber, 1971 (100 signed copies) . . . £200
On the Suchness of the Old Boy, Turret, 1972 (226 signed copies, wraps) £75
Vega and Other Poems, Faber, 1973 . . £10/£5
Lifelines - Four Poems, Tragara Press, 1974 (15 signed copies of 115, wraps) £250
ditto, Tragara Press, 1974 (100 copies of 115, wraps) £75
Collected Poems: 1931-1974, Faber, 1980 . £25/£10
ditto, Faber, 1980 (26 signed copies, with signed etching by Henry Moore, slipcase) £300
ditto, Viking (U.S.), 1980. . . . . . . £20/£10

Parody
Bromo Bombasts, Caduceus Press, 1933 (100 copies) £2,500

Novels
Pied Piper of Lovers, Cassell, 1935 . £2,000/£1,250
Panic Spring, Faber, 1937 (pseud. Charles Norden) . . . . £1,250/£750
ditto, Covici Friede (U.S.), 1937 . . . £500/£150
The Black Book, Obelisk Press (Paris), 1938 (wraps) £400
ditto, Dutton (U.S.), 1960. . . . . . . £10/£5
ditto, Faber, 1973 . . . . £10/£5
Cefalû, Editions Poetry, 1947 . . . . £50/£20
ditto, as ***The Dark Labyrinth***, Ace (U.S.), 1958 (wrappers) £10
ditto, Faber, 1961 . . . . £10/£5
Justine, Faber, 1957 . . . . £200/£65
ditto, Dutton (U.S.), 1957. . . . . . . £75/£25
White Eagles over Serbia, Faber, 1957 . . £50/£25
ditto, Criterion (U.S.), 1957 . . . . . £50/£25
Balthazar, Faber, 1958 . . . . . . £50/£25

ditto, Dutton (U.S.), 1958 . . . . £25/£10
Mountolive, Faber, 1958 . . . . £50/£25
ditto, Dutton (U.S.), 1959 . . . . £20/£5
Clea, Faber, 1960 . . . . £35/£10
ditto, Dutton (U.S.), 1960 . . . . £15/£5
The Alexandria Quartet, Faber, 1962 . . £60/£25
ditto, Faber, 1962 (500 signed copies, slipcase) . . . . £300/£250
ditto, Dutton (U.S.), 1962 . . . . £50/£20
ditto, Dutton (U.S.), 1962 (199 signed, numbered copies) . . . . £300/£250
Tunc, Faber, 1968 . . . . £15/£5
ditto, Dutton (U.S.), 1968 . . . . £10/£5
Nunquam, Faber, 1970 . . . . £15/£5
ditto, Dutton (U.S.), 1970 . . . . £10/£5
The Revolt of Aphrodite, Faber, 1973 . . £25/£10
Monsieur, or, The Prince of Darkness, Faber, 1974 . . . . £15/£5
ditto, Viking (U.S.), 1974 . . . . £10/£5
Livia or Buried Alive, Faber, 1978 . . . £10/£5
ditto, Viking (U.S.), 1979 . . . . £10/£5
Constance or Solitary Practices, Faber, 1982 £10/£5
ditto, Viking (U.S.), 1982 . . . . £10/£5
Sebastian or Ruling Passions, Faber, 1983 . £10/£5
ditto, Viking (U.S.), 1984 . . . . £10/£5
Quinx or The Ripper's Tale, Faber, 1985 . £10/£5
ditto, Viking (U.S.), 1985 . . . . £10/£5
The Avignon Quintet, Faber, 1992 . . . £10/£5

Plays
Sappho, Faber, 1950 . . . . £35/£15
ditto, Dutton (U.S.), 1958 . . . . £10/£5
An Irish Faustus, Faber, 1963 . . . . £20/£5
ditto, Dutton (U.S.), 1964 . . . . £10/£5
Acte, Faber, 1965 . . . . £10/£5
ditto, Dutton (U.S.), 1965 . . . . £10/£5

Short Stories
Zero and Asylum in the Snow, privately printed (Rhodes), 1946 (50 copies, wraps) £250
ditto, as ***Two Excursions into Reality***, Circle Editions (U.S.), 1947 . . . . £50/£20
Esprit de Corps, Faber, 1957 . . . . . . £20/£5
ditto, Dutton (U.S.), 1958 . . . . £10/£5
Stiff Upper Lip, Faber, 1958 . . . . . . £10/£5
ditto, Dutton (U.S.), 1959 . . . . £10/£5
Sauve Qui Peut, Faber, 1966 . . . . . . £10/£5
ditto, Dutton (U.S.), 1967 . . . . £10/£5
The Best of Antrobus, Faber, 1974 . . . £15/£5

Non Fiction
Prospero's Cell, Faber, 1945 . . . . . £75/£15
ditto, Dutton (U.S.), 1960 . . . . £15/£5
Key to Modern Poetry, Nevill, 1952 . . . £30/£10
Reflections on a Marine Venus, Faber, 1953 £50/£15
ditto, Dutton (U.S.), 1960 . . . . £15/£5
Bitter Lemons, Faber, 1957 . . . . . . £25/£10
ditto, Dutton (U.S.), 1958 . . . . £20/£5
Art and Outrage, Putnam, 1959 . . . . £20/£5
ditto, Dutton (U.S.), 1960 . . . . £15/£5
Lawrence Durrell and Henry Miller: A Private Correspondence, Dutton (U.S.), 1963 . . £25/£10
ditto, Faber, 1963 . . . . £25/£10
Spirit of Place, Faber, 1969 . . . . . . £20/£5
ditto, Dutton (U.S.), 1969 . . . . £15/£5
Le Grand Suppositoire, Editions Pierre Belfond (Paris), 1972 . . . . £10/£5
ditto, as ***The Big Supposer***, Abelard-Schuman, 1973 (English translation) . . . . £10/£5
ditto, as ***The Big Supposer***, Grove Press (U.S.), 1974 . . . . £10/£5
Blue Thirst, Capra Press (U.S.), 1975 (250 signed copies, glassine d/w) . . . . £50/£45
Sicilian Carousel, Faber, 1977 . . . . . £15/£5
ditto, Viking (U.S.), 1977 . . . . £10/£5
The Greek Islands, Faber, 1978 . . . . £15/£5
ditto, Viking (U.S.), 1978 . . . . £10/£5
A Smile in the Mind's Eye, Wildwood House, 1980 . . . . £15/£5
Literary Lifelines: The Richard Aldington - Lawrence Durrell Correspondence, Faber, 1981 . . £10/£5
ditto, Viking (U.S.), 1981 . . . . £10/£5
The Durrell/Miller Letters, Faber, 1988 . . £10/£5
Letters to Jean Fanchette, 1958-1963, Editions Two Cities, 1988 (1,800 of 2,000 copies, wraps) . £10
ditto, Editions Two Cities, 1988 (200 signed copies of 2,000, wraps) £150
Caesar's Vast Ghost: Aspects of Provence, Faber, 1990 . . . . £10/£5

BERESFORD EGAN

(b.1905 d.1984)

As an artist Egan's wickedly satirical black and white line drawings were at their most effective in *The Sink of Solitude*, a lampoon of the reactions to Radclyffe Hall's *The Well of Loneliness*.

Written and illustrated by Egan
Pollen, Denis Archer, 1933 (patterned boards) . £40
ditto, Denis Archer, 1933 (orange boards) . . £30
No Sense in Form: A Tragedy of Manners, Denis Archer, 1933 . . . . £40
But The Sinners Triumph, Fortune Press, 1934 . . . . £45/£20
Epitaph, A Double Bedside Book for Singular People, Fortune Press, [1943] £20

Epilogue, A Potpourri of Prose, Verse and Drawings, Fortune Press, [1946] £20
Bun-Ho!, Floris Bakeries Ltd, 1959 (edited and decorated by Egan) £50
Storicards, Barrigan Press, 1960 (5 cards) the set £50

Illustrated by Egan
The Sink of Solitude: A Broadside, preface by P.R. Stevensen, lampoons by various hands, Hermes Press, 1928 (250 numbered, signed copies) £150
ditto, Hermes Press, 1928 (wraps) £50
Policeman of The Lord: A Political Satire, Sophistocles Press, 1929 (500 numbered copies) . . £125
ditto, Sophistocles Press 1929 (wraps) £50
Les Fleurs du Mal, In Pattern and Prose, by Baudelaire, translated by C. Bower Adcock, Sophistocles Press and T. Werner Laurie, 1929 (500 signed copies) £150
ditto, Godwin (U.S.), 1933 (pirated edition). . £20
ditto, Sylvan Press (U.S.), 1947 (1,499 numbered copies) £40
ditto, Sylvan Press (U.S.), 1947 (un-numbered copies). £20
Aphrodite, by Pierre Loüys, The Fortune Press, 1929 (1,075 copies) £50
Cyprian Masques, by Pierre Loüys, The Fortune Press, 1929 . . . . £50
De Sade, by Beresford Egan and Brian de Shane, The Fortune Press, 1929 (1,600 copies). £50
The Adventures of King Pausole, by Pierre Loüys, Fortune Press, 1930 (1,200 copies). £50
Income and Outcome: A Study in Personal Finance, by Nigel Balchin, Hamish Hamilton, 1936. . £35
Pobottle, by Heavy Duty Alloys Ltd 1935-39, (advertising, 7 vols) . . . . £125 the set

Others
Beresford Egan: An Introduction to His Work, by Paul Allen, Scorpion Press, 1966 (limited edition) . . . . £35/£20
ditto, Scorpion Press, 1966 (25 signed copies, with extra plate) . . . . £125/£100

GEORGE ELIOT
(b.1819 d.1880)

George Eliot was the pseudonym of Mary Anne Evans, novelist, critic and poet. Her great power is her detailed depiction of character and motivation chiefly among middle class provincial society.

Novels
Adam Bede, Blackwood, 1859 (3 vols) . . . £1,500
The Mill on the Floss, Blackwood, 1860 (3 vols) £500
Silas Marner, The Weaver of Raveloe, Blackwood, 1861 . . . . £600
Romola, Smith, Elder & Co., 1863 (3 vols) . . £750
Felix Holt, The Radical, Blackwood, 1866 (3 vols) £450
Middlemarch, A Study of Provincial Life, Blackwood, 1871-1872 (8 parts bound together as vols) . £2,000
ditto, Blackwood, 1874 (4 vols in book form) . £2,000
Daniel Deronda, Blackwood, 1874-1876 (8 parts, blue/grey wraps) £2,000
ditto, Blackwood, 1874-1876 (8 parts bound together as 1 vol.). £1,250
ditto, Blackwood, 1876 (4 vols in book form) . £1,250

Short Stories
Scenes of Clerical Life, Blackwood, 1858 (2 vols). £7,500

Essays
Impressions of Theophrastus Such, Blackwood, 1879 . . . . £175
Essays and Leaves from a Note-Book, Blackwood, 1884 . . . . £175

Verse
The Spanish Gypsy, Blackwood, 1868 . . . . £600
The Legend of Jubal and Other Poems, Blackwood, 1874 . . . . £500

Translations
The Life of Jesus, Critically Examined by D. F. Strauss, Chapman, 1846 (3 vols) £2,000
Feuerbach's Essence of Christianity, Chapman, 1854 (3 vols) £1,000

T.S. ELIOT
(b.1888 d.1965)

The American-born poet, critic and dramatist lived most of his adult life in England. Eliot received both the Nobel Prize for Literature and the Order of Merit in 1948.

Verse
Prufrock and Other Observations, Egoist Ltd, 1917 (wraps) £3,500
Poems, Hogarth Press, 1919 (wraps). . . . £3,500
Ara Vus Prec (sic), Ovid Press, 1920 (30 numbered, signed copies) £4,000
ditto, Ovid Press, 1920 (220 numbered copies) £2,000
ditto, as ***Poems***, Knopf (U.S.), 1920 . . £1,000/£450
The Waste Land, Boni & Liveright, 1922 (approx 500

of 1,000 copies with flexible black cloth) . . £4,000
ditto, Boni & Liveright, 1922 (later copies, approx 500 of 1,000, with stiff black cloth and "a" dropped from "mountain" on p. 41, line 339) £2,000
ditto, Hogarth Press, 1923 . . . . £1,750
Homage to John Dryden, Hogarth Press, 1924 (wraps) £200
Poems, 1909-1925, Faber & Gwyer, 1925 £450/£100
ditto, Faber & Gwyer, 1925 (85 numbered and signed copies) £2,500
ditto, Harcourt Brace (U.S.), 1932 . . . £75/£45
Journey of the Magi, Faber & Gwyer, 1927 (wraps) £35
ditto, Faber & Gwyer, 1927 (350 copies) . . £75
ditto, Rudge (U.S.), (27 copies, copyright edition) £750
A Song for Simeon, Faber & Gwyer, 1928 . . £30
ditto, Faber & Gwyer, 1928 (500 numbered, signed large paper copies) £300
Animula, Faber, [1929] £25
ditto, Faber, [1929] (400 numbered, signed copies, slipcase) £350
Ash-Wednesday, Faber, 1930 . . . . . £75
ditto, Faber/Fountain Press, 1930 (600 signed copies, glassine d/w, slipcase) £750
ditto, Putnam (U.S.), 1930 . . . . . . £35
Marina, Faber, [1930] (wraps) £30
ditto, Faber, [1930] (400 numbered, signed copies) £200
Triumphal March, Faber, 1931 (wraps). . . £25
ditto, Faber, 1931 (300 numbered, signed copies) £200
Collected Poems, 1909-1935, Faber, 1936 . £45/£15
ditto, Harcourt Brace (U.S.), 1936 . . . . £25/£10
Old Possum's Book of Practical Cats, Faber, 1939 . . . . £450/£75
ditto, Harcourt Brace (U.S.), 1939 . . . £400/£75
The Waste Land and Other Poems, Faber, 1940 . . . . £25/£10
ditto, Harcourt Brace (U.S.), 1955 . . . £10/£5
East Coker, New English Weekly, 1940 (stapled, unbound supplement) £50
ditto, Faber, 1940 . . . . £45
Burnt Norton, Faber, 1941 (wraps) £35
The Dry Salvages, Faber, 1941 (wraps) . . . £25
Little Gidding, Faber, 1942 (wraps) £25
Four Quartets, Harcourt Brace (U.S.), 1943 £500/£150
ditto, Faber, 1944 . . . . £125/£45
ditto, Faber, 1960 (290 signed copies) . . . £2,000
A Sermon, CUP, 1948 (300 copies, not for sale, wraps) £75
Selected Poems, Penguin, 1948 . . . . . . £5
ditto, Harcourt Brace (U.S.), 1967 . . . . £5
The Undergraduate Poems, Harvard Advocate, 1949, (unauthorised publication, 1,000 copies, wraps) £75
Poems Written in Early Youth, privately printed (Stockholm), 1950 (12 copies only) . . . £2,000
ditto, Faber, 1967 . . . . £15
ditto, Farrar Straus (U.S.), 1967 . . . . . £10
The Complete Poems and Plays, 1909-1950, Harcourt Brace (U.S.), 1952 . . . . £30/£15
The Cultivation of Christmas Trees, Faber, 1954 (wraps & envelope) £45
ditto, Farrar Straus (U.S.), 1956 . . . . . . £10
Collected Poems, 1909-1962, Faber, 1963 . . £25
ditto, Farrar Straus (U.S.), 1963 . . . . . . £20
The Complete Poems and Plays, Faber, 1968 . £15
The Waste Land: A Facsimile and Transcript, Faber, 1971 . . . . £30
ditto, Faber, 1971 (500 copies, in slipcase) . . £100
ditto, Harcourt Brace (U.S.), 1971 . . . . . £25

Prose

Ezra Pound: His Metric and Poetry, Knopf (U.S.), 1917 . . . . £300/£150
The Sacred Wood, Methuen, 1920 . . . . £300/£40
ditto, Knopf (U.S.), 1921 . . . . £250/£25
Shakespeare and the Stoicism of Seneca, O.U.P., 1927 (wraps) £125
For Lancelot Andrewes, Faber & Gwyer, 1928 . . . . £200/£25
ditto, Doubleday (U.S.), 1929 . . . . £150/£15
Dante, Faber, 1929 . . . . £100/£35
ditto, Faber, 1929 (125 numbered, signed copies, glassine d/w) . . . . £750/£700
Thoughts After Lambeth, Faber, 1931 (wraps). £20
ditto, Faber, 1931 (boards) . . . . . . £50/£15
Charles Whibley: A Memoir, O.U.P., 1931 (wraps) £25
Selected Essays, 1917-1931, Faber, 1932 . £65/£20
ditto, Faber, 1932 (115 numbered, signed copies, cellophane d/w) . . . . £1,500/£1,400
ditto, Harcourt Brace (U.S.), 1932 . . . £65/£20
John Dryden: The Poet, the Dramatist, the Critic, Holliday, 1931 . . . . £100/£40
ditto, Holliday, 1931 (110 signed copies) . . £600
The Use of Poetry and the Use of Criticism, Faber, 1933 . . . . £150/£20
ditto, Harvard University Press (U.S.), 1933 £125/£15
After Strange Gods, Faber, 1934. . . . £200/£25
ditto, Harcourt Brace (U.S.), 1934 . . . £125/£20
Elizabethan Essays, Faber, 1934. . . . £150/£25
Essays Ancient and Modern, Faber, 1936 . £35/£10
ditto, Harcourt Brace (U.S.), 1936 . . . . £20/£5
The Idea of a Christian Society, Faber, 1939 £25/£10
ditto, Harcourt Brace (U.S.), 1940 . . . £15/£5
Points of View, Faber, 1941 . . . . . £15/£5
The Classics and the Man of Letters, O.U.P., 1942 (wraps) £15
The Music of Poetry, Jackson and Co., 1942 (wraps) £40
Reunion by Destruction, Vacher & Sons, 1943 £45

What is a Classic?, Faber, 1945 (Virgil Society issue, wraps) £95
ditto, Faber, 1945 . . . . £45/£20
On Poetry, Concord, 1947, (750 copies, not for sale, wraps) £100
Milton, Cumberlege, 1947, (500 copies, wraps) £50
Notes Towards the Definition of Culture, Faber, 1948 . . . . £40/£15
ditto, Harcourt Brace (U.S.), 1949 . . . £20/£10
From Poe to Valéry, Harcourt Brace (U.S.), 1948 (1,500 copies, not for sale, boards and envelope) . . . . £75/£65
The Aims of Poetic Drama, Poets' Theatre Guild, 1949 (wraps) £25
Poetry and Drama, Harvard University Press (U.S.), 1951 . . . . £40/£15
ditto, Faber, 1951 . . . . £25/£10
The Value and Use of Cathedrals in England Today, Chichester Cathedral, 1952 (wraps) £35
An Address to the Members of the London Library, Queen Anne Press, 1952 (500 copies, wraps) . £40
Selected Prose, Penguin, 1953 . . . . . £5
American Literature and the American Language, Washington University, 1953 (500 copies, wraps) £75
The Three Voices of Poetry, National Book League, 1953 (wraps) £25
ditto, CUP (U.S.), 1954 . . . . £10
Religious Drama: Mediaeval and Modern, House of Books (NY), 1954 (300 numbered copies, glassine d/w) . . . . £350/£300
ditto, House of Books (NY), 1954 (26 lettered and signed copies) £1,500
The Literature of Politics, Conservative Political Centre, 1955 (wraps). £20
The Frontiers of Criticism, Univ of Minnesota, 1956 (10,050 copies, not for sale, wraps). £35
On Poetry and Poets, Faber, 1957 . . . . £35/£10
ditto, Farrar Straus (U.S.), 1957 . . . . . £20/£10
Geoffrey Faber, 1889-1961, Faber, 1961 (100 copies, not for sale) . . . . £200/£125
George Herbert, Longmans, 1962 (wraps) . . £15
Knowledge and Experience in the Philosophy of F.H. Bradley, Faber, 1964 . . . . £30/£10
ditto, Farrar Straus (U.S.), 1964 . . . . £20/£10
To Criticize the Critic and Other Writings, Faber, 1965 . . . . £25/£10
ditto, Farrar Straus (U.S.), 1965 . . . . . £15/£5
The Letters of T.S. Eliot, Vol. 1, 1898-1922, Faber, 1988 . . . . £15/£5

Drama

Sweeney Agonistes, Faber, 1932 . . . . . £50/£20
The Rock, Faber, 1934 (wraps) £20
ditto, Faber, 1934 (hardback) . . . . . £35/£10
ditto, Harcourt Brace (U.S.), 1934 . . . . £20/£10
Murder in the Cathedral, Goulden, 1935 (750 copies, wraps) £250
ditto, Faber, 1935 (first complete edition) . £75/£15
ditto, Harcourt Brace (U.S.), 1935 . . . . £60/£14
The Family Reunion, Faber, 1939 . . . £30/£10
ditto, Harcourt Brace (U.S.), 1939 . . . £25/£10
The Cocktail Party, Faber, 1950 . . . . £40/£10
ditto, Harcourt Brace (U.S.), 1950 . . . £30/£10
The Confidential Clerk, Faber, 1954 . . £25/£10
ditto, Harcourt Brace (U.S.), 1954 . . . £15/£10
The Elder Statesman, Faber, 1959 . . £25/£10
ditto, Farrar Straus (U.S.), 1959 . . . . £15/£5
Collected Plays, Faber, 1962 . . . . . £20/£10

ALICE THOMAS ELLIS

(b.1932)

An author whose novels are fashionable as well as respected, Ellis has also written a number of non-fiction books.

Novels

The Sin Eater, Duckworth, 1977. . . . £35/£15
The Birds of the Air, Duckworth, 1980 . . £20/£5
ditto, Viking Press (U.S.),1981 . . . . £15/£5
The 27th Kingdom, Duckworth, 1982 . . £10/£5
The Other Side of the Fire, Duckworth, 1983 £10/£5
ditto, Elisabeth Sifton (U.S.),1984 . . . £10/£5
Unexplained Laughter, Duckworth, 1985 . £10/£5
ditto, Harper (U.S.), 1987. . . . . . . £10/£5
The Clothes in the Wardrobe, Duckworth, 1987 . . . . £10/£5
The Skeleton in the Cupboard, Duckworth, 1988 . . . . £10/£5
The Fly in the Ointment, Duckworth, 1989. £10/£5
The Inn at the Edge of the World, Viking , 1990 . . . . £10/£5
Pillars of Gold, Viking, 1992. . . . . £10/£5
Fairy Tale, Viking, 1996 . . . . . . £10/£5
ditto, Moyer Bell (U.S.), 1998 . . . . £10/£5

Cookery

Natural Baby Food: A Cookery Book, Duckworth, 1977 (pseud. Brenda O'Casey) . . . . £10/£5
Darling, You Shouldn't Have Gone to So Much Trouble, Cape, 1980 (pseud. Anna Haycraft, with Caroline Blackwood) . . . . £10/£5

Others

Home Life, Duckworth, 1986 . . . . £10/£5
ditto, Akadine Press (U.S.), 1997. . . . £10/£5
Secrets of Strangers, Duckworth, 1986 (with Tom Pitt-Aikens) . . . . £10/£5

More Home Life, Duckworth, 1987 . . . . £10/£5
Home Life 3, Duckworth 1988 . . . . £10/£5
Loss of the Good Authority: The Cause of Delinquency, Viking (U.S.), 1989 (with Tom Pitt-Aikens) . . . . £10/£5
Home Life 4, Duckworth, 1989 . . . . . £10/£5
A Welsh Childhood, Joseph, 1990 . . . . £10/£5

JOHN MEADE FALKNER
(b.1858 d.1932)

A British industrialist and antiquarian, Falkner turned his hand to novel writing and local history. In *The Lost Stradivarius* he created an enduring classic.

Novels
The Lost Stradivarius, Blackwood, 1895 . . £250
Moonfleet, Arnold, 1898 . . . . £300
ditto, Little, Brown & Co. (U.S.) 1951 . . £10/£25
The Nebuly Coat, Arnold, 1903 . . . . £100

Verse
Poems, Westminster Press, [c. 1935] (wraps) . £20

Others
Handbook for Travellers in Oxfordshire, John Murray, 1894 (anonymous) £30
A History of Oxfordshire, John Murray, 1899 . £30
Handbook for Berkshire, Edward Stanford, 1902 £30
Bath in History and Social Tradition, John Murray, 1918 (anonymous) £20
A History of Durham Cathedral Library, Durham Country Advertiser, 1925 . . . . £75

ELEANOR FARJEON
(b.1881 d.1965)

Eleanor Farjeon was born in Buckingham Street, London, where Samuel Pepys once lived. Part of a literary circle which included Edward Thomas and Rupert Brooke, she is best known for her often beautifully illustrated children's poems and stories.

Children's Books, Prose
Martin Pippin in the Apple-Orchard, Collins, 1921 . . . . £20/£10
ditto, Collins, 1925 (illustrated by C. E. Brock)£40/£20
ditto, O.U.P., 1952 (illustrated by Richard Kennedy) . . . . £30/£15
Basil Blackwell 'Continuous Stories' Series:
7 Tom Cobble, 1925 . . . . £20
11 The Wonderful Knight, 1927 . . . . . . £20
17 A Bad Day for Martha, 1928 . . . . . . £20
21 The King's Daughter Cries for the Moon, 1929 . . . . £20
27 Westwoods, 1930 . . . . £20
51 The Clumber Pup, 1934 . . . . £10
63 And I Dance Mine Own Child, 1935 . . . £10
68 Jim and the Pirates, 1936. . . . . . . £10
Mighty Men: Achilles to Julius Caesar, Blackwell, 1924 (illustrated by Hugh Chesterman) . £15/£5
Mighty Men: Beowulf to Harold, Blackwell, 1925 (illustrated by Hugh Chesterman) . . . £15/£5
Mighty Men (contains both above books), Blackwell, 1928 . . . . £20/£10
Nuts and May: A Medley for Children, Collins, 1926 (illustrated by Rosalind Thornycroft) . . £100/£50
The King's Barn, or, Joan's Tale, Collins, 1927 . . . . £20/£10
The Mill of Dreams, or, Jennifer's Tale, Collins, 1927 . . . . £20/£10
Young Gerard; or, Joyce's Tale, Collins, 1927 . . . . £20/£10
Kaleidoscope, Collins, 1928 . . . . . £15/£5
ditto, O.U.P., 1963 (illustrated by Edward Ardizzone) . . . . £40/£20
The Tale of Tom Tiddler, Collins, 1929. . £20/£10
The Perfect Zoo, Harrap, 1929 . . . . £20/£10
Tales from Chaucer: The Canterbury Tales Done into Prose, Medici Society, 1930 (illustrated by W. Russell Flint) . . . . £60/£30
The Old Nurse's Stocking Basket, University of London Press, 1931 (illustrated by E. H. Whydale) . . . . £25/£10
ditto, O.U.P., 1965 (illustrated by Edward Ardizzone) . . . . £30/£15
Perkin the Pedlar, Faber, 1932 (illustrated by Clare Leighton) . . . . £20/£10
ditto, O.U.P., 1956 (illustrated by Dodie Masterman) . . . . £15/£5
Katy Kruse at the Seaside, Harrap, 1932 . £20/£10
Pannychis, High House Press, 1933 (200 copies, illustrated by Clare Leighton) £75
ditto, High House Press, Shaftesbury, 1933 (deluxe 25 copies) £250
Ameliaranne's Prize Packet, Harrap, 1933 (illustrated by S.B. Pearse) . . . . £50/£25
Italian Peepshow and Other Stories, Blackwell, 1934 . . . . £10/£5
ditto, O.U.P., 1960 (illustrated by Edward Ardizzone) . . . . £30/£15
Ameliaranne's Washing Day, Harrap, 1934 (illustrated by S.B. Pearse) . . . . £45/£20
Jim at the Corner and Other Stories, Blackwell, 1934 (illustrated by Irene Mountfort) . . . . £15/£5
ditto, O.U.P., 1958 (illustrated by Edward Ardizzone)

. . . . £40/£20
Ten Saints, O.U.P., 1936 (illustrated by Helen Sewell) . . . . £20/£10
Lector Readings, Nelson, 1937 . . . . £10/£5
The Wonders of Herodotus, Nelson, 1937 . £10/£5
Paladins in Spain, Nelson, 1937 (illustrated by Katherine Tozer) . . . . £10/£5
Martin Pippin in the Daisy Field, Michael Joseph, 1937 (illustrated by Isobel and John Morton Sale) . . . . £30/£10
One Foot in Fairyland: Sixteen Tales, Michael Joseph, 1938 . . . . £10/£5
The New Book of Days, O.U.P., 1941 (illustrated by P. Gough and M.M. Hawes) . . . . . . £15/£5
The Silver Curlew, O.U.P., 1953 (illustrated by E.H. Shepard) . . . . £30/£15
ditto, Goodchild, 1983 . . . . £10/£5
The Glass Slipper, O.U.P., 1955 (illustrated by E.H. Shepard) . . . . £30/£15
ditto, Goodchild, 1983 . . . . £10/£5
The Little Bookroom, O.U.P., 1955 (illustrated by Edward Ardizzone) . . . . £30/£15
ditto, O.U.P., 1972 (wraps) £5
ditto, Puffin, 1977 (wraps) £5
Mr Garden, Hamish Hamilton, 1966 . . £10/£5

Verse

Nursery Rhymes of London Town, Duckworth, 1916 . . . . £75
More Nursery Rhymes of London Town, Duckworth, 1917 . . . . £75
All the Way to Alfriston, Greenleaf Press, 1918 (illustrated by Robin Guthrie) £75
Singing Games for Children, Dent, 1919 . . £50
A First Chap-Book of Rounds/A Second Chap-Book of Rounds, Dent, 1919 (2 vols, music by Harry Farjeon) £40
Tunes of a Penny Piper, Selwyn & Blount, 1922 (illustrated by John Aveten) . . . . . £15/£5
Songs for Music and Lyrical Poems, Selwyn & Blount, 1922 (illustrated by John Aveten) £15/£5
All the Year Round, Collins, 1923 . . . £15/£5
ditto, as ***Around the Seasons***, Hamish Hamilton, 1969 . . . . £10/£5
The Country Child's Alphabet, Poetry Bookshop, 1924 (illustrated by W.M. Rothenstein, boards) £150/£75
ditto, Poetry Bookshop, 1924 (illustrated by W.M. Rothenstein, wraps) £100
The Town's Child's Alphabet, Poetry Bookshop, 1924 (illustrated by David Jones, boards) . . £150/£75
ditto, Poetry Bookshop, 1924 (illustrated by David Jones, wraps) £100
Young Folk and Old, High House Press, 1925 £15/£5
Songs from 'Punch' for Children, Saville, 1925 £15/£5
Singing Games from Arcady, Blackwell, 1926 £15/£5
Joan's Door, Collins, 1926 (illustrated by Will Townsend) . . . . £15/£5
Come Christmas, Collins, 1927 (illustrated by Molly McArthur) . . . . £15/£5
An Alphabet of Magic, The Medici Society, 1928 (illustrated by Margaret Tarrant) . . £30/£15
Kings and Queens, Gollancz, 1932 (with Herbert Farjeon, illustrated by R. Thorncroft) . . £50/£25
ditto, Dent, 1940 & 1953 (revised/enlarged edition) . . . . £30/£15
ditto, Dent, 1983 (illustrated by Robin Jacques) £15/£5
ditto, Puffin, 1987 (wraps) £5
Heroes and Heroines, Gollancz, 1933 (with Herbert Farjeon, illustrated by Rosalind Thornycroft) £30/£15
Over the Garden Wall, Faber, 1933 (illustrated by Gwen Raverat) . . . . £35/£15
Songs of Kings and Queens, Arnold, 1938 (with Herbert Farjeon) . . . . £10/£5
Sing for Your Supper, Michael Joseph, 1938 (illustrated by Isobel and John Morton-Sale) £10/£5
A Sussex Alphabet, Pear Tree Press, 1939 (illustrated by Sheila M. Thompson) . . . . . . £100/£45
Cherrystones, Michael Joseph, 1945 (illustrated by Isobel and John Morton-Sale) . . . . £10/£5
The Mulberry Bush, Michael Joseph, 1945 (illustrated by Isobel and John Morton-Sale) . . . . £10/£5
The Starry Floor, Michael Joseph, 1949 (illustrated by Isobel and John Morton-Sale) . . . . . £10/£5
Mrs Malone, Michael Joseph, 1950 (illustrated by David Knight) . . . . £10/£5
ditto, O.U.P., 1962 (illustrated by Edward Ardizzone) . . . . £35/£15
Silver Sand and Snow, Michael Joseph, 1951 £10/£5
The Children's Bells: A Selection of Poems, O.U.P., 1957 (illustrated by Peggy Fortnum) . . £15/£5
A Puffin Quartet of Poets (includes other poets), Puffin, 1958 (wraps) £5
Then There Were Three, Michael Joseph, 1958 (contains 'Cherrystones', 'The Mulberry Bush' and 'The Starry Floor') . . . . £15/£5
Morning Has Broken, Mowbray, Oxford, 1981 £10/£5
Invitation to a Mouse and Other Poems, Pelham, 1981 (illustrated by Anthony Maitland) . . . £10/£5
Something I Remember, Blackie, 1987 (selected poems edited by Anne Harvey) . . . . £10/£5
ditto, Puffin, 1989 (wraps) £5

Plays

Granny Gray: Children's Plays and Games With Music and Without, Dent, 1939 (illustrated by Joan Jefferson Farjeon) . . . . £20/£10
ditto, O.U.P., 1956 (illustrated by Peggy Fortnum) . . . . £15/£5
The Glass Slipper (with Herbert Farjeon), Samuel French, 1945 (wraps) £5

ditto, Allen Wingate, 1946 (illustrated by Hugh Stevenson) . . . . £10/£5
The Silver Curlew: A Fairy Tale, Samuel French, 1953 (wraps) £5

Children's Omnibuses
Eleanor Farjeon's Book: Stories, Verses, Plays, Puffin, 1960 (edited by Eleanor Graham, illustrated by Edward Ardizzone, wraps) £15

Adult Books, Fiction: Novels
The Soul of Kol Nikon, Collins, [1923] . . £20/£5
Ladybrook, Collins, 1931 . . . . £10/£5
The Fair of St James: A Fantasia, Faber, 1932 . . . . £10/£5
The Humming Bird, Michael Joseph, 1936 £10/£5
Miss Granby's Secret, Michael Joseph, 1940 £10/£5
Brave Old Woman, Michael Joseph, 1941 £10/£5
The Fair Venetian, Michael Joseph, 1943 £10/£5
Golden Coney: The Story of a Cat, Michael Joseph, 1943 . . . . £10/£5
Ariadne and the Bull, Michael Joseph, [1945] £10/£5
The Two Bouquets, Michael Joseph, 1948 . £10/£5
Love Affair, Michael Joseph, 1949 . . . £10/£5

Fiction: Short Stories
Gypsy and Ginger, Dent, 1920 . . . . £15/£5
Faithful Jenny Dove and Other Tales, Collins, 1925 . . . . £10/£5
ditto, as ***Faithful Jenny Dove and Other Illusions***, Michael Joseph, 1963 . . . . . . £10/£5

Verse
Pan Worship and Other Poems, Elkin Matthews, 1908 . . . . £15
Dream-Songs for the Beloved, Orpheus Press, 1911 . . . . £10
Sonnets and Poems, Blackwell, 1918 . . . £10
Tomfooleries, as ***Tomfool***, Daily Herald, 1920 £15/£5
Moonshine, as ***Tomfool***, Labour Publishing Co./Allen & Unwin, 1921 . . . . £15/£5
The ABC of the BBC, Collins, 1928 (illustrated by T.C. Derrick) . . . . £25/£15
Snowfall, Favil Press, 1928 . . . . . £15/£5
A Collection of Poems, Collins, 1929 . . £10/£5
First and Second Love: Sonnets, Michael Joseph, 1947 . . . . £15/£5
ditto, O.U.P., 1959. . . . . £10/£5

Plays (with Herbert Farjeon)
The Two Bouquets: A Victorian Comedy with Music, Gollancz, 1936 . . . . £15/£5
Aucassin and Nicolette, Chappell, 1952. . £10/£5
A Room at the Inn: A Christmas Masque, privately printed, 1956 . . . . £15/£5

Operas and Operettas (with Herbert Farjeon)
Floretta, Henderson & Spalding, 1899 . . . £10
The Registry Office, Henderson & Spalding, 1900 £10
A Gentleman of the Road, Boosey & Hawkes, 1903 . . . . £10

Miscellaneous
Trees, Batsford, 1914 (essay). £15
A Nursery in the Nineties, Gollancz, 1935 (memoirs) . . . . £20/£10
ditto, O.U.P., 1980 (wraps) £5
Magic Casements, Allen & Unwin, 1941 (essays) . . . . £15/£5
Dark World of Animals, Sylvan Press, 1945 £10/£5
Elizabeth Myers, St Albert's Press, Aylesford, 1957 (memoir) £10
Edward Thomas: The Last Four Years ('The Memoirs of Eleanor Farjeon, Book One'), O.U.P., 1958£20/£10
ditto, O.U.P, 1979 (wraps) £5
You Come Too, Bodley Head, 1964 (a selection of poems by Robert Frost, introduced by Eleanor Farjeon) . . . . £10/£5
The Green Roads, Bodley Head, 1965 (a selection of poems edited and introduced by Eleanor Farjeon) . . . . £20/£10

G.E. FARROW
(b.1862)

An author of children's stories, somewhat in the tradition of Lewis Carroll, Farrow is perhaps collected as much for the artists who illustrated his books as on his own account.

The Wallypug of Why, Hutchinson, [1895] (illustrated by Harry Furniss, vignettes by Dorothy Furniss) £100
ditto, Dodd, Mead and Co. (U.S.), 1896 . . . . £25
The King's Gardens: An Allegory, Hutchinson, 1896 (illustrated by A.L. Bowley). £45
The Missing Prince, Hutchinson, 1896 (illustrated by Harry Furniss, vignettes by Dorothy Furniss) £45
The Wallypug in London, Methuen, 1898 [1897] (illustrated by Alan Wright) £65
Adventures in Wallypug-land, Methuen, 1898 (illustrated by Alan Wright) £65
The Little Panjandrum's Dodo, Skeffington, 1899 (illustrated by Alan Wright) £45
The Mandarin's Kite, or Little Tsu-Foo and Another Boy, Skeffington, 1900 (illustrated by Alan Wright) £20
Baker Minor and the Dragon, Pearson, 1902 [1901] (illustrated by Alan Wright) £45
The New Panjandrum, Pearson, 1902 [1901]

(illustrated by Alan Wright) £45
An A.B.C. of Every-day People, Dean, [1902] (illustrated by John Hassall) £65
In Search of the Wallypug, Pearson, 1903 [1902] (illustrated by Alan Wright) £65
Absurd Ditties, Routledge, 1903 (illustrated by John Hassall) £45
Professor Philanerpan, Pearson, 1904 [1903] . £35
All About the Wallypug, Raphael Tuck, [1904]. £45
The Cinematograph Train and Other Stories, Johnson, 1904 (illustrated by Alan Wright) . £65
Pixie Pickles: The Adventures of Pixene and Pixette in their Woodland Haunts, Skeffington, [1904] (illustrated by H.B. Neilson) £65
Wallypug Tales, Raphael Tuck, [1904] £45
Round the World A.B.C., Nister, [1904] (illustrated by John Hassall) £55
The Wallypug Birthday Book, Routledge, 1904 (illustrated by Alan Wright) £45
The Wallypug in Fogland, Pearson, 1904 (illustrated by Alan Wright) £65
Ruff and Ready, The Fairy Guide by May Byron and G.E. Farrow, Cooke, [1905] (illustrated by John Hassall) £40
The Mysterious 'Mr Punch', A School Story, Christian Knowledge Society, [1905] £30
The Wallypug Book, Traherne, [1905] £50
The Wallypug in the Moon, or His Badjesty, Pearson, 1905 (illustrated by Alan Wright) £50
The Adventures of Ji, Partridge, [1906] (illustrated by G.C. Tresidder) £40
Essays in Bacon, An Autograph Book, Treherne, [1906] £40
The Escape of the Mullingong, A Zoological Nightmare, Blackie, 1907 [1906] (illustrated by Gordon Browne) £35
The Adventures of a Dodo, Unwin, [1907] (illustrated by Willy Pogany). £65
ditto, as ***A Mysterious Voyage, or The Adventures of a Dodo***, Partridge, [1910] (illustrated by K.M. Roberts) £35
The Dwindleberry Zoo, Blackie, 1909 [1908] (illustrated by Gordon Browne). £35
The Mysterious Shin Shira, Hodder & Stoughton, [1915]. £25
Zoo Babies, Frowde/Hodder & Stoughton, 1913 (illustrated by Cecil Aldin) £125
Don't Tell, Cooke, [no date] (illustrated by John Hassall) £40
Ten Little Jappy Chaps, Treherne, [no date] (illustrated by John Hassall) £30

Parodies

Lovely Man, Being the Views ol Mistress A. Grosapatch, Skeffington, 1904 . . . . . . £40

WILLIAM FAULKNER

(b.1897 d.1962)

A Nobel Prize winning American novelist, Faulkner often pushed the boundaries of narrative convention.

Novels

Soldier's Pay, Boni & Liveright (U.S.), 1926 . . . . £3,500/£250
ditto, Chatto and Windus, 1930 . . . . £750/£250
Mosquitoes, Privately printed, 1927 . £2,500/£1,000
ditto, Boni & Liveright, 1927. . . . £2,000/£450
ditto, Garden City (U.S.), 1937 . . . . £125/£50
ditto, Chatto and Windus, 1964 . . . . £45/£20
Sartoris, Harcourt Brace (U.S.), 1929 £1,250/£150
ditto, Chatto and Windus, 1933 . . . . £200/£75
The Sound and the Fury, Cape & Smith (U.S.), 1929 . . . . £2,500/£200
ditto, Chatto and Windus, 1931 . . . £750/£150
As I Lay Dying, Jonathan Cape & Harrison Smith (U.S.), 1930 . . . . £2,500/£1,000
ditto, Chatto and Windus, 1935 . . . £700/£125
Sanctuary, Cape & Smith (U.S.), 1931 £2,000/£250
ditto, Chatto and Windus, 1931 . . . £1,000/£100
Idyll in the Desert, Random House (U.S.), 1931 (400 signed, numbered copies, glassine d/w) £1,250/£1,000
Miss Zilphia Gant, Book Club of Texas (U.S.), 1932 (300 copies) . . . . £1,000/£200
Light in August, Smith & Haas (U.S.), 1932 (glassine d/w over paper d/w) . . . . . . £750/£100
ditto, Chatto and Windus, 1933 . . . £200/£75
Pylon, Smith & Haas (U.S.), 1935 . . £250/£35
ditto, Smith & Haas, 1935 (310 signed copies, slipcase) . . . . £1,000/£800
ditto, Chatto and Windus, 1936 . . . £250/£40
Absalom, Absalom!, Random House (U.S.), 1936 . . . . £750/£125
ditto, Random House, 1936 (300 signed copies) £1,500
ditto, Chatto and Windus, 1937. . . . £350/£45
The Unvanquished, Random House (U.S.), 1938 . . . . £500/£100
ditto, Random House, 1938 (250 signed copies) £1,500
ditto, Chatto and Windus, 1938 . . . £350/£45
The Hamlet, Random House (U.S.), 1940 £750/£100
ditto, Random House, 1940 (250 signed copies) £1,500
ditto, Chatto and Windus, 1940 . . . . £150/£35
Intruder in the Dust, Random House (U.S.), 1948 . . . . £175/£35
ditto, Chatto and Windus, 1949 . . . . £100/£30
Notes on a Horsethief, Levee Press (U.S.), 1950 [1951] (975 signed, numbered copies, tissue d/w). . . . . £700/£650
Requiem for a Nun, Random House (U.S.), 1951 .

. . . . £75/£30
ditto, Random House, 1951 (750 signed, numbered copies) £650
ditto, Chatto and Windus, 1953 . . . . £45/£20
A Fable, Random House (U.S.), 1954 . £125/£20
ditto, Random House, 1954 (1,000 signed copies, glassine d/w, slipcase) . . . . £800/£650
ditto, Chatto and Windus, 1954 . . . . £60/£25
The Town, Random House (U.S.), 1957. . £50/£20
ditto, Chatto and Windus, 1958 . . . . £45/£15
The Mansion, Random House (U.S.), 1959. £50/£20
ditto, Chatto and Windus, 1960 . . . . £40/£15
The Reivers, Random House (U.S.), 1962 . £50/£20
ditto, Chatto and Windus, 1962 . . . . £40/£15

Short Stories
These Thirteen, Cape & Smith (U.S.), 1931 £750/£200
ditto, Cape & Smith (U.S.), 1931 (299 signed copies, plain tissue d/w). . . . . . . £2,250/£2,000
ditto, Chatto and Windus, 1933 . . . . £500/£50
Doctor Martino and Other Stories, Smith & Haas (U.S.), 1934 . . . . £900/£250
ditto, Smith & Haas (U.S.), 1934 (360 signed, numbered copies) £1,000
ditto, Chatto and Windus, 1934 . . . . £300/£50
The Wild Palms, Random House (U.S.), 1939 . . . . £750/£50
ditto, Random House (U.S.), 1939 (250 signed copies) £1,500
ditto, Chatto and Windus, 1939 . . . . £250/£40
Go Down, Moses and Other Stories, Random House (U.S.), 1942 . . . . £650/£125
ditto, Random House (U.S.), 1942 (100 signed copies) £7,500
ditto, Chatto and Windus, 1942. . . . £300/£60
Knight's Gambit, Random House (U.S.), 1948 £75/£25
ditto, Chatto and Windus, 1951 . . . . £50/£15
Collected Stories, Random House (U.S.), 1950 £50/£15
ditto, Chatto and Windus, 1951 . . . . £35/£10
Big Woods, Random House (U.S.), 1955 . £75/£30
The Collected Stories, Chatto and Windus, 1958 (3 vols) . . . . £75/£45
Selected Short Stories, Random House (U.S.), 1962 . . . . £35/£10
Uncollected Stories, Chatto, 1980 . . . . £20/£5

Verse
Vision in Spring, privately printed (U.S.), 1921 . . . . £20,000
The Marble Faun, Four Seas (U.S.), 1924 . . . . £15,000/£7,500
This Earth: A Poem, Equinox (U.S.), 1932. . £2,500
A Green Bough, Smith & Haas, 1933 . £400/£150
ditto, Smith & Haas, 1933(360 signed copies) . . . . £1,500/£600

Others
An Address by William Faulkner, Delta State Teachers College (U.S.), 1952 (wraps) £1,500
Faulkner's Country, Chatto and Windus, 1955. . . . . £35/£15
New Orleans Sketches, Rutgers University Press (U.S.), 1958 . . . . £45/£15
ditto, Sidgwick and Jackson, 1959 . . . £35/£10
Early Prose and Poetry, Little, Brown (U.S.), 1962 . . . . £30/£10
ditto, Cape, 1962 . . . . £25/£10
Essays, Speeches, and Public Letters, Random House (U.S.), 1966 . . . . £25/£10
ditto, Chatto and Windus, 1966 . . . . £25/£10
Selected Letters, Franklin Library (U.S.), 1976. £45

RONALD FIRBANK
(b.1886 d.1926)

An eccentric, Roman Catholic author of witty and artificial novels.

Novels
Vainglory, Grant Richards, 1915. . . . . £50
ditto, Brentano's (U.S.), 1925. . . . . £75/£25
Inclinations, Grant Richards, 1916 . . . . £75
Caprice, Grant Richards, 1917 . . . . . £75
Valmouth, Grant Richards, 1919. . . . . £75
Prancing Nigger, Brentano's (U.S.), 1924 . £150/£25
ditto, as ***Sorrow in Sunlight***, Brentano's, 1924 (1,000 numbered copies) . . . . . £150/£30
Concerning the Eccentricities of Cardinal Pirelli, Grant Richards, 1926, ... £150/£30
The Artificial Princess, Duckworth, 1934 . £100/£25
ditto, Centaur Press 1934, (60 copies) . . . £200

Short Stories
Odette d'Antrevernes and A Study in Temperament, Elkin Mathews, 1905, (wraps) . . . £250
ditto, Elkin Mathews, 1905, (10 copies on Japanese vellum) £1,000
ditto, as ***Odette: A Fairy Tale for Weary People***, Grant Richards, 1916 (wraps) £75
Santal, Grant Richards, 1921 (wraps) . . . £75
ditto, Bonacio & Saul with Grove Press (U.S.),1955 . . . . £30/£15
Two Early Stories, Albondocani Press (U.S.), 1971 (226 copies) £40

Biography
The Flower Beneath the Foot, Grant Richards, 1923 . . . . £150/£65
ditto, Brentano (U.S.),1924 . . . . . £45/£15

Others

The Princess Zoubaroff - A Play, Grant Richards, 1920 . . . . £125/£50

A Letter from Arthur Ronald Firbank to Madame Albani, Centaur Press, 1934 (50 facsimile copies of letter, issued in envelope) . . . . . . £100/£75

The New Rythum and Other Pieces, Duckworth, 1962 . . . . £20/£10

ditto, New Directions (U.S.),1963 . . . £20/£10

The Wind and the Roses, Alan Clodd, 1966 (poem limited to 50 copies) £125

Far Away, Typographical Lab University of Iowa, 1966 (100 copies) £75

An Early Flemish Painter, The Enitharmon Press/Miriam L. Benkowitz, 1969 (300 copies) £35

When Widows Love and A Tragedy in Green, The Enitharmon Press, 1980 (300 copies) . . . £40

Collected Editions

The Works of Ronald Firbank, Duckworth, 1929, (235 numbered sets, 5 vols) £1,000

Rainbow Edition, Duckworth, 1929-1930, (8 vols). £250

The Complete Ronald Firbank, Duckworth, 1961, (1 vol.) . . . . £15/£5

F. SCOTT FITZGERALD

(b.1896 d.1940)

An American novelist and short story writer synonymous with the jazz age, *The Great Gatsby* is his enduring classic.

Novels

This Side of Paradise, Scribners (U.S.), 1920 . . . . £6,000/£250

ditto, Collins, 1921 . . . . £2,000/£200

The Beautiful and Damned, Scribner (U.S.), 1922 . . . . £4,000/£200

ditto, Collins, 1922 . . . . £1,500/£100

The Great Gatsby, Scribner (U.S.), 1925 £10,000/£700

ditto, Chatto & Windus, 1926 (original binding) . . . . £1,000/£100

ditto, Chatto & Windus, 1926 [1927] (cheap edition) . . . . £800/£75

Tender is the Night, Scribner (U.S.), 1934 (first issue jacket, no reviews) . . . . . . £2,500/£100

ditto, Scribner (U.S.), 1934 (second issue jacket with reviews) . . . . £1,000/£100

ditto, Chatto & Windus, 1934 (original binding) . . . . £200/£75

ditto, Chatto & Windus, 1934 [1936] (cheap edition) . . . . £150/£65

ditto, Grey Walls Press, 1953 . . . . . £75/£20

Last Tycoon, Scribner (U.S.), 1941 (unfinished) . . . . £250/£50

ditto, Grey Walls Press, 1949. . . . . . £60/£15

Short Stories

Flappers and Philosophers, Scribner (U.S.), 1920 . . . . £3,500/£500

ditto, Collins, 1922 . . . . £1,500/£250

Tales of the Jazz Age, Scribner (U.S.), 1922 . . . . £3,000/£350

ditto, Collins, 1923 . . . . £1,500/£100

All the Sad Young Men, Scribner (U.S.), 1926 . . . . £1,500/£200

John Jackson's Arcady, Baker (U.S.), 1928 (wraps) £1,000

Taps at Reveille, Scribner (U.S.), 1935 £1,250/£200

The Stories, Scribners (U.S.), 1951 . . . £50/£15

Borrowed Time, Grey Walls Press, 1951 . £45/£25

Afternoon of an Author, privately printed Princeton University Press (U.S.), 1957 . . . . £35/£10

ditto, Scribners (U.S.), 1958 . . . . . £25/£10

ditto, Bodley Head, 1958 . . . . . . £25/£10

The Mystery of Raymond Mortgage, Random House (U.S.), [1960] (750 copies, wraps) £150

The Pat Hobby Stories, Scribners (U.S.), 1962 . . . . £25/£10

ditto, Penguin, 1967 . . . . £5

Dearly Beloved, Windhover Press/University of Iowa (U.S.), 1969 (no d/w) £25

The Basil and Josephine Stories, Scribners (U.S.), 1973 . . . . £20/£5

Bits of Paradise, Scribners (U.S.), 1974. . £25/£10

ditto, Bodley Head, 1973 . . . . . . £25/£10

The Price Was High, Harcourt Brace (U.S.), 1979 . . . . £20/£5

ditto, Quartet, 1979 . . . . £15/£5

Others

The Vegetable: From President to Postman, Scribners, 1923 . . . . £750/£100

The Crack-Up, New Directions (U.S.), 1945 £350/£45

ditto, New Directions ("British Empire" issue), 1945 . . . . £250/£35

ditto, Grey Walls Press, 1947. . . . . £40/£15

The Letters, Scribners (U.S.), 1963 . . . £75/£20

ditto, Bodley Head, 1964 . . . . . . £20/£10

The Apprentice Fiction, Rutgers U.P., 1965 £25/£10

Thoughtbook of Francis Scott Key Fitzgerald, Princeton University Library (U.S.), 1965 (glassine d/w) . . . . £30/£20

In His Own Time, Kent State U.P., 1971 . £25/£10

Dear Scott / Dear Max, Scribners (U.S.), 1971 . . . . £25/£10

ditto, Cassell, 1973 . . . . £20/£10

As Ever, Scott Fitz, Lippincott (U.S.), 1972 . . . £25/£10
ditto, Woburn, 1973 . . . . £20/£10
Preface to This Side of Paradise, Windhover Press (U.S.), 1975 (150 copies) £75
The Notebooks, Harcourt Brace, 1978 . . . £20/£10
The Correspondence, Random House (U.S.), 1980 . . . . £20/£10

PENELOPE FITZGERALD

(b.1916)

A Booker Prize winning novelist, Fitzgerald's novels are humorous and understated while often painfully revealing.

Novels

The Golden Child, Duckworth, 1977 . . . £50/£20
ditto, Scribner (U.S.), 1978 . . . . . £30/£10
The Bookshop, Duckworth, 1978 . . . £40/£15
ditto, as ***The Book Shop***, Houghton Mifflin (U.S.), 1997 (wraps) £5
Offshore, Collins, 1979 . . . . . . £20/£5
ditto, Henry Holt (U.S.), 1979 . . . . £20/£5
Human Voices, Collins, 1980 . . . . £20/£5
At Freddies, Collins, 1985 . . . . . £15/£5
ditto, Godine (U.S.), 1983 . . . . . £15/£5
Innocence, Collins, 1986 . . . . . . £10/£5
ditto, Holt (U.S.), 1987 . . . . . . £10/£5
The Beginning of Spring, Collins, 1988 . £10/£5
ditto, Holt (U.S.), 1989 . . . . . . £10/£5
The Gate of Angels, Collins, 1990 . . . £10/£5
ditto, Doubleday (U.S.), 1992 . . . . £10/£5
The Blue Flower, Flamingo, 1995 . . . £10/£5
ditto, Houghton Mifflin (U.S.), 1997. . . £10/£5

Others

Edward Burne-Jones: A Biography, Joseph, 1975 . . . . £45/£15
The Knox Brothers, Macmillan, 1977 . . £10/£5
ditto, Coward McCann (U.S.), 1977 . . . £10/£5
Charlotte Mew and Her Friends: With a Selection of Her Poems, Collins, 1984 . . . . . £10/£5
ditto, Addison Wesley (U.S.), 1988 . . . £10/£5

IAN FLEMING

(b.1908 d.1964)

Famous for the legendary James Bond stories. The condition of the early books is of paramount importance in determining their value.

Bond Titles

Casino Royale, Cape, 1953 . . . . £2,500/£500
ditto, Macmillan (U.S.), 1954. . . . . £500/£75
Live and Let Die, Cape, 1954 . . . £1,500/£300
ditto, Macmillan (U.S.), 1955. . . . . £300/£35
Moonraker, Cape, 1955 . . . . . £1,500/£250
ditto, Macmillan (U.S.), 1955. . . . . £300/£35
Diamonds are Forever, Cape, 1956 . . . £750/£50
ditto, Macmillan (U.S.), 1956. . . . . £100/£50
From Russia, with Love, Cape, 1957 . . £450/£45
ditto, Macmillan (U.S.), 1957. . . . . £50/£20
Dr No, Cape, 1958 . . . . £250/£40
ditto, Macmillan (U.S.), 1958. . . . . £35/£15
Goldfinger, Cape, 1959 . . . . . . £150/£35
ditto, Macmillan (U.S.), 1959. . . . . £35/£15
For Your Eyes Only, Cape, 1960 (short stories) . . . . £125/£35
ditto, Viking (U.S.), 1960. . . . . . £35/£15
Thunderball, Cape, 1961 . . . . . . £75/£20
ditto, Viking (U.S.), 1961. . . . . . . £25/£15
The Spy Who Loved Me, Cape, 1962 . . £75/£20
ditto, Viking (U.S.), 1962. . . . . . . £25/£15
On Her Majesty's Secret Service, Cape, 1963 £50/£20
ditto, Cape, 1963 (250 signed copies, glassine d/w) . . . . £3,000/£2,500
ditto, NAL (U.S.), 1963 . . . . £35/£15
You Only Live Twice, Cape, 1964 . . . £40/£15
ditto, NAL (U.S.), 1964 . . . . £20/£10
The Man with the Golden Gun, Cape, 1965 £35/£15
ditto, NAL (U.S.), 1965 . . . . £20/£10
Octopussy and The Living Daylights, Cape, 1966 (short stories) . . . . £25/£10
ditto, NAL (U.S.), 1966 . . . . £20/£10
see also ***The Ivory Hammer: The Year at Sotherby's***, Longman, 1963 (Contains Bond story 'The Property of a Lady') . . . . £45/£20
ditto, Holt, Rinehart & Winston (U.S.), 1964 £40/£15

Non Fiction

The Diamond Smugglers, Cape, 1957 . . £100/£35
ditto, Macmillan (U.S.), 1958. . . . . £40/£20
Thrilling Cities, Cape, 1963 . . . . . £30/£15
ditto, NAL (U.S.), 1964 . . . . £15/£10
Ian Fleming Introduces Jamaica, Deutsch, 1965 . . . . £20/£10
ditto, Hawthorne (U.S.), 1965 . . . . . £15/£10

Children's

Chitty Chitty Bang Bang, Cape, 1964-64 (3 books) . . . . £30 each, £175 the set
ditto, Random House (U.S.), 1964. . . . £10/£5

FORD MADDOX FORD

(b.1873 d.1939)

A novelist and editor, he was actually born Ford Hermann Hueffer, although, unless noted otherwise, titles listed below were published as either Ford Maddox Ford, Ford Maddox Hueffer or F. Maddox Hueffer.

Novels

The Shifting of the Fire, T. Fisher Unwin, 1892 (pseud. 'H. Ford Hueffer') £250
The Benefactor, Brown, Langham & Co., 1905 £100
The Fifth Queen, Alston Rivers, 1906 . . . £75
ditto, Vanguard Press (U.S.), [c.1963] . . £15/£5
Privy Seal, Alston Rivers, 1907 . . . . . £50
An English Girl, Methuen & Co., 1907 . . . £50
The Fifth Queen Crowned, Eveleigh Nash, 1908 £50
Mr Apollo, Methuen & Co., 1908 . . . . £50
The Half Moon, Eveleigh Nash, 1909 . . . £50
A Call, Chatto & Windus, 1910 . . . . . £50
The Portrait, Methuen & Co., 1910 . . . . £50
The Simple Life Limited, John Lane, 1911 (pseud. 'Daniel Chaucer') £50
Ladies Whose Bright Eyes, Constable & Co., 1911 . . . . £50
ditto, Lippincott (U.S.), 1935 . . . . . £65/£20
The Panel, Constable & Co., 1912 . . . . £50
The New Humpty-Dumpty, John Lane, 1912 (pseud. 'Daniel Chaucer') £50
Mr Fleight, Howard Latimer, 1913 . . . . £50
The Young Lovell, Chatto & Windus, 1913 . . £50
The Good Soldier, John Lane, 1915 . . . . . £1,000
Zeppelin Nights: A London Entertainment, John Lane/Bodley Head, 1915 (with Violet Hunt) £100
The Marsden Case, Duckworth, 1923 . . £75/£25
Some Do Not, Duckworth, 1924 . . . . £100/£25
ditto, Seltzer (U.S.), 1925 . . . . . . £65/£20
No More Parades, Duckworth, 1925 . . £125/£25
A Man Could Stand Up, Duckworth, 1926 £100/£25
ditto, Boni (U.S.), 1926 . . . . . . £75/£15
The Last Post, The Literary Guild of America (U.S.), 1928 . . . . £75/£15
ditto, as ***Last Post***, Duckworth, 1928. . . £75/£15
A Little Less Than Gods, Duckworth, [1928] £75/£20
ditto, Viking (U.S.), 1928 . . . . . . £75/£20
No Enemy, Macaulay (U.S.), 1929 . . . £150/£35
When the Wicked Man, Horace Liveright (U.S.), 1931 . . . . £75/£20
ditto, Jonathan Cape, 1932 . . . . . £50/£20
The Rash Act, Long & Smith (U.S.), 1933 . £50/£20
ditto, Jonathan Cape, 1933 . . . . . £50/£20
Henry for Hugh, Lippincott (U.S.), 1934 . £50/£20
Vive le Roy, Lippincott (U.S.), 1936 . . . £50/£20
ditto, George Allen and Unwin, 1937 . . £50/£20

With Joseph Conrad

The Inheritors, McClure, Phillips & Co. (U.S.), 1901 . . . . £100
ditto, Heinemann, 1901 . . . . £100
Romance, Smith Elder, 1903 . . . . £100
ditto, McClure (U.S.), 1904 . . . . £40
The Nature of a Crime, Duckworth, 1924 . £60/£20
ditto, Doubleday (U.S.), 1924 . . . . . £60/£20

Verse

New Poems, Rudge (U.S.), 1927 (325 signed copies, glassine d/w) £150
Selected Poems, Pym Randall, 1971 (1,000 copies) . . . . £25/£15
ditto, Pym Randall, 1971 (50 copies) . . £175/£125

Others

The Brown Owl: A Fairy Story, Unwin, 1892 (as Ford H. Hueffer) £300
ditto, Putnam, 1892 . . . . £250
The Cinque Ports: A Historical and Descriptive Record, Blackwood, 1900 . . . . . . £400
Rossetti: A Critical Essay on His Art, Duckworth, [1902] £15
The Soul of London: A Survey of a Modern City, Rivers, 1905 . . . . £50
The Heart of the Country: A Survey of a Modern Land, Duckworth, 1906 . . . . £50
The Critical Attitude, Duckworth, 1911 (as Ford Maddox Hueffer) £35
Henry James: A Critical Study, Secker, 1913 . £50
Between St. Dennis and St. George: A Sketch of Three Civilizations, Hodder and Stoughton, 1915 £45
Women and Men, Three Mountains Press (Paris), 1923 (300 numbered copies, wraps) £350
Mister Bosphorus and the Muses; or, A Short History of Poetry in Britain, Duckworth, 1923 . . £125/£20
ditto, Duckworth, 1923 (70 copies signed by artist) . . . . £400/£200
New York is Not America, Duckworth, 1927 £125/£20
ditto, Boni (U.S.), 1927 . . . . . . £75/£20
New York Essays, Rudge (U.S.), 1927 (750 signed copies) £200
The English Novel, Lippincott (U.S.), 1929 £50/£15
ditto, Constable, 1930 . . . . £45/£15
Provence, from Minstrels to the Machine, Allen and Unwin, 1935 . . . . £40/£15
ditto, Lippincott (U.S.), 1935 . . . . . . £40/£15
Great Trade Route, Oxford UP (U.S.), 1937 £25/£15
The March of Literature from Confucius to Modern Times, Dial Press (U.S.), 1938 . . . . . £50/£20
Your Mirror to My Times, Holt Rinehart and Winston (U.S.), 1971 . . . . £10/£5

C.S. FORESTER
(b.1899 d.1966)

Best remembered for the Hornblower series, and for *The African Queen.*

'Hornblower' Novels
Beat to Quarters, Little, Brown (U.S.), 1937 £300/£35
ditto, as ***The Happy Return***, Joseph, 1937 £300/£35
A Ship of the Line, Little, Brown (U.S.), 1938 . . . . £200/£35
ditto, Joseph, 1938. . . . . £200/£35
Flying Colours, Little, Brown (U.S.), 1939 . £175/£50
ditto, The Book Society/Joseph, 1939 . . £175/£50
ditto, Joseph, 1939. . . . . £100/£35
Commodore Hornblower, Little, Brown (U.S.), 1945 . . £25/£10
ditto, as ***The Commodore***, Joseph, 1945. . £25/£10
Lord Hornblower, Little, Brown (U.S.), 1946 £25/£10
ditto, Joseph, 1946. . . . . £25/£10
Mr Midshipman Hornblower, Little, Brown (U.S.), 1950 . . . . £20/£10
ditto, Joseph, 1950. . . . . £20/£10
Lieutenant Hornblower, Little, Brown (U.S.), 1952 . £20/£10
ditto, Joseph, 1952. . . . . £20/£10
Hornblower and the Atropos, Little, Brown (U.S.), 1953 . . . . £20/£10
ditto, Joseph, 1953. . . . . £20/£10
Admiral Hornblower in the West Indies, Little, Brown (U.S.), 1958 . . . . £20/£10
ditto, as ***Hornblower in the West Indies***, Joseph, 1958 . £20/£10
Hornblower and the Hotspur, Little, Brown (U.S.), 1962 . . . . £15/£5
ditto, Joseph, 1962. . . . . £10/£5
The Hornblower Companion, Joseph, 1964 £50/£20
ditto, Little, Brown (U.S.), 1964 . . . . £50/£10
Hornblower and the Crisis: An Unfinished Novel, Joseph, 1967 . . . . £20/£10
ditto, Little, Brown (U.S.), 1967 . . . . £20/£10

'Hornblower' Omnibus Editions
Young Hornblower, Joseph, 1964 . . . £20/£5
Captain Hornblower R.N., Joseph, 1965 . £20/£5
Admiral Hornblower, Joseph, 1968 . . . £20/£5

Other Novels
A Pawn Among Kings, Methuen, 1924 . . £750/£100
Napoleon and His Court, Methuen, 1924 £450/£75
The Paid Piper, Methuen, 1924 . . . . £750/£100
Josephine, Napoleon 's Empress, Methuen, 1925 . . . £300/£65
Payment Deferred, Bodley Head, 1926 £250/£45
ditto, Little, Brown (U.S.), 1942 . . . . £25/£10
Love Lies Dreaming, Bodley Head, 1927 £250/£100
ditto, Bobbs-Merrill (U.S.), 1927. . . . £250/£100
The Wonderful Week, Bodley Head, 1927 £250/£100
Victor Emmanuel II and the Union of Italy, Methuen, 1927 . . . . £250/£100
Louis XIV, King of France and Navarre, Dodd, Mead (U.S.), 1928 . . . . £100/£45
Brown on Resolution, Bodley Head, 1929 £100/£35
ditto, as ***Single-Handed***, Putnam (U.S.), 1929 . . . . £100/£30
Lord Nelson, Bobbs-Merrill (U.S.), 1929 £100/£35
Two and Twenty, Bodley Head, 1931 . £200/£100
ditto, Appleton-Century Co. (U.S.), 1931 £200/£100
Death to the French, Bodley Head, 1932 £200/£100
The Gun, John Lane, 1933 . . . . . £150/£60
ditto, as ***Rifleman Dodd and the Gun***, 1933 £100/£45
The Peacemaker, Heinemann, 1934 . . . £200/£75
The African Queen, Little, Brown (U.S.), 1935 . . . £750/£200
ditto, Heinemann, 1935 . . . . . . £350/£75
The General, Joseph, 1936 . . . . . £200/£35
ditto, Little, Brown (U.S.), 1936 . . . . £200/£35
The Captain from Connecticut, Joseph, 1941 £35/£15
ditto, Little, Brown (U.S.), 1941 . . . . £25/£10
The Ship, Joseph, 1943 . . . . . . £35/£15
ditto, Little, Brown (U.S.), 1943 . . . . £25/£10
The Bedchamber Mystery, S.J. Reginald Saunders (Canada), 1944 . . . . £100/£40
The Sky and the Forest, Joseph, 1948 . . £20/£10
ditto, Little, Brown (U.S.), 1948 . . . . £20/£10
Randall and the River of Time, Little, Brown (U.S.), 1950 . . . . £20/£10
ditto, Joseph, 1951. . . . . £20/£10
The Nightmare, Joseph, 1954 . . . . £25/£15
The Good Shepherd, Joseph, 1955 . . . £20/£10
ditto, Little, Brown (U.S.), 1955 . . . . £20/£10
Hunting the Bismarck, Joseph, 1959 . . £20/£10
ditto, as ***The Last Nine Days of the Bismarck***, Little, Brown (U.S.), 1959 . . . . £20/£10

Short Stories
The Man in the Yellow Raft, Joseph, 1969 £20/£10
Gold From Crete, Little, Brown, 1970 . . £20/£10
ditto, Joseph (U.S.), 1971 . . . . £20/£10

Others
The Voyage of the Annie Marble, John Lane, 1929 . . £150/£35
The Annie Marble in Germany, John Lane, 1930 . . . £150/£35
The Earthly Paradise, Joseph, 1940 . . £50/£20
ditto, as ***To the Indies***, Little, Brown (U.S.), 1940 . . . £40/£20
The Age of Fighting Sail: The Story of the Naval War of 1812, Doubleday (U.S.), 1956 . . . £25/£10

Long Before Forty, Little, Brown (U.S.), 1967 £25/£10

Editor
The Adventures of John Wetherell, Joseph, 1954 . . . £20/£10
ditto, Doubleday (U.S.), 1954 . . . . £20/£10

Children's
Marionettes At Home, Joseph, 1936. . . . £75/£40
Poo-Poo and the Dragons, Little, Brown (U.S.), 1942 . . . £75/£40
The Barbary Pirates, Random House (U.S.), 1953 . . . £45/£20
Hornblower Goes to Sea, Joseph, 1954 . . £45/£20
Hornblower's Triumph, Joseph, 1955 . . £45/£20

E.M. FORSTER
(b.1879 d.1970)

A novelist and essayist, Forster's writings often reflect his loathing of public schools, imperialism, and the repression of civil liberties. His books have been popularised recently by the successful film makers Merchant and Ivory.

Novels
Where Angels Fear to Tread, Blackwood, 1905 £500
ditto, Knopf (U.S.), 1920 . . . . . £1,000/£400
The Longest Journey, Blackwood, 1907 . . £250
ditto, Knopf (U.S.), 1922 . . . . . . £250/£75
A Room with a View, Arnold, 1908 . . . . £500
ditto, Putnam (U.S.), 1911 . . . . . . £100
Howard's End, Arnold, 1910. . . . . . £350
ditto, Putnam (U.S.), 1910 . . . . . . £100
The Story of the Siren, Hogarth Press, 1920 (wraps) £150
A Passage to India, Arnold, 1924 . . . £500/£200
ditto, Arnold, 1924 (200 numbered signed copies, fawn paper boards, grey slipcase) £3,500
ditto, Harcourt Brace (U.S.), 1924 . . . £250/£50
ditto, as ***The Manuscripts of A Passage to India***, Arnold, 1978 (1,500 copies) . . . . £35/£15
Maurice, Arnold, 1971 . . . . . . £25/£10
ditto, Norton (U.S.), 1971. . . . . . £20/£5

Short Stories
The Celestial Omnibus and Other Stories, Sidgwick & Jackson, 1911 . . . . £100
ditto, Knopf (U.S.), 1923 . . . . £35
The Eternal Moment, Sidgwick & Jackson, 1928 . . . . £45/£15
ditto, Harcourt Brace (U.S.), 1928 . . . £40/£10
The Collected Tales, Knopf (U.S.), 1947 . £20/£10
ditto, as ***The Collected Short Stories***, Sidgwick & Jackson, 1948 . . . . £20/£10
The Life to Come, Arnold, 1972 . . . . £25/£10
ditto, Norton (U.S.), 1973. . . . . . £15/£5

Essays
Pharos and Pharillon, Hogarth Press, 1923 (900 copies) £75
ditto, Knopf (U.S.), 1923 . . . . . . £500/£200
Anonymity: An Enquiry, Hogarth Press, 1925 (boards) £40
ditto, Hogarth Press, 1925 (wraps) £25
A Letter to Madam Blanchard, Hogarth Press, 1931 (wraps) £25
ditto, Harcourt Brace (U.S.), 1932 (wraps) . . £20
Abinger Harvest, Arnold, 1936 (unauthorised version, cream d/w decorated orange) . . . . £125/£75
ditto, Arnold, 1936 (authorised version) . . £45/£20
ditto, Harcourt Brace (U.S.), 1936 . . . £75/£25
What I Believe, Hogarth Press, 1939 (wraps) . . £25
Nordic Twilight, Macmillan, 1940 (wraps) . . . £15
The Challenge of Our Time, Marshall, 1948 . . £25
Two Cheers for Democracy, Arnold, 1951 . £25/£10
ditto, Harcourt Brace (U.S.), 1951 . . . £25/£5

Others
The Government of Egypt, Labour Research Dept., [1920] (wraps) £100
Alexandria, A History and a Guide, Whitehead Morris, 1922 . . . . £200
ditto, Whitehead Morris, 1922 (revised edition with maps and plans) £45
ditto, Whitehead Morris, 1922 (250 signed copies) £250
ditto, Doubleday (U.S.), 1961 . . . . . £20/£10
Aspects of the Novel, Arnold, 1927 . . . £100/£25
ditto, Harcourt Brace (U.S.), 1927 . . . . £75/£20
Goldsworthy Lowes Dickinson, Arnold, 1934 £45/£20
ditto, Harcourt Brace (U.S.), 1934 . . . £45/£20
Reading as Usual, Tottenham Public Libraries, 1939 (wraps) £100
England's Pleasant Land, Hogarth Press, 1940 . . . . £40/£20
Virginia Woolf, CUP, 1942 (wraps) £25
ditto, Harcourt Brace (U.S.), 1942 . . . £50/£20
The Development of English Prose Between 1918 and 1930, Jackson, 1945 (wraps) £20
Desmond McCarthy, Mill House Press, 1952 (64 copies) £250
ditto, Mill House Press, 1952 (8 copies). . . £1,000
The Hill of Devi, Arnold, 1953 . . . . £40/£15
ditto, Harcourt Brace (U.S.), 1953 . . . £40/£15
I Assert There is an Alternative to Humanism, The Ethical Union, 1955 . . . . £45
Battersea Rise, privately printed (Harcourt Brace U.S.), 1955 . . . . £45

Marianne Thornton, Arnold, 1956 . . . £25/£10
ditto, Arnold, 1956 (200 signed copies, slipcase) £250
ditto, Harcourt Brace (U.S.), 1956 . . . £15/£5
E.K. Bennett, privately printed, 1958 . . . . £15
A View Without a Room, Albondocani Press (U.S.), 1973 (200 numbered copies, wraps) . . . £50
Letters to Donald Windham, Campbell (Verona), 1975 (300 copies) £75
Commonplace Book, Scolar Press, 1978 (facsimile, 350 numbered copies, boxed) £45
Selected Letters, Vol. 1, Collins, 1983 . . . £15/£5
ditto, Harvard University Press (U.S.), 1983 £15/£5
Selected Letters, Vol. 2, Collins, 1984 . . . £15/£5
ditto, Harvard University Press (U.S.), 1984 £15/£5

FREDERICK FORSYTH

(b.1938)

The author of the phenomenally successful *The Day of the Jackal*, Forsyth's forte is the tense thriller.

Novels

The Biafra Story, Penguin Special, 1969 (wraps) £50
The Day of the Jackal, Hutchinson, 1971 . £35/£10
ditto, Viking (U.S.), 1971 . . . . . . £25/£10
The Odessa File, Hutchinson, 1972 . . . £15/£5
ditto, Viking (U.S.), 1972 . . . . . . £10/£5
The Dogs of War, Hutchinson, 1974. . . £15/£5
ditto, Viking (U.S.), 1974 . . . . . . £10/£5
The Shepherd, Hutchinson, 1975 . . . £10/£5
ditto, Viking (U.S.), 1976 . . . . . . £10/£5
The Devil's Alternative, Hutchinson, 1979 . £10/£5
ditto, Viking (U.S.), 1980 . . . . . . £10/£5
The Fourth Protocol, Hutchinson, 1984 . £10/£5
ditto, Viking (U.S.), 1984 . . . . . . £10/£5
The Negotiator, Bantam, 1989 . . . . £10/£5
ditto, London Limited editions, 1989 (150 signed copies, glasssine d/w) . . . . . £65/£50
ditto, Bantam (U.S.), 1989 . . . . . £10/£5
The Deceiver, Bantam, 1991 . . . . . £10/£5
ditto, Bantam (U.S.), 1991 . . . . . £10/£5
Fist of God, Bantam, 1994 . . . . . £10/£5
ditto, Bantam (U.S.), 1994 . . . . . £10/£5
Icon, Bantam, 1996 . . . . . . £10/£5
ditto, Bantam (U.S.), 1996 . . . . . £10/£5

Short Stories

No Comebacks, Hutchinson, 1982 . . . £10/£5
ditto, Viking (U.S.), 1982 . . . . . . £10/£5
ditto, Eurographica (Helsinki), 1986 (350 signed copies) . . . . £40/£25

DION FORTUNE

(b.1890 d.1946)

British occultist and writer of occult fiction, Fortune's books were published under her own name as well as the pseudonyms V.M. Steele and Violet M. Firth.

Dion Fortune Novels

The Demon Lover, Noel Douglas, [1927] . £65/£25
The Winged Bull, Williams & Norgate, 1935 £65/£25
The Goat-Foot God, Williams & Norgate, 1936 . . . £65/£25
The Sea Priestess, Inner Light, 1938 . . £65/£25
Moon Magic, Aquarian Press, 1956 (wraps) £20

Dion Fortune Short Stories

The Secrets of Dr Taverner, Noel Douglas, 1926 . . . . £65/£25

Dion Fortune Non Fiction

The Esoteric Philosophy of Love and Marriage, Rider, 1923 . . . . £45/£20
Esoteric Orders and Their Work, Rider, 1928 £45/£20
Sane Occultism, Rider, 1929 . . . . . £35/£15
The Training and Work of an Initiate, Rider, 1930 . . . . £35/£15
Mystical Meditations Upon the Collects, Rider, 1930 . . . . £35/£15
Spiritualism in the Light of Occult Science, Rider, 1931 . . . . £35/£15
Psychic Self-Defence, Rider, 1931 . . . £45/£20
Through the Gates of Death, Inner Light, 1932 . . . . £35/£15
The Mystical Cabalah, Williams & Norgate, 1935 . . . . £45/£20
Practical Occultism in Daily Life, Williams & Norgate, 1935 . . . . £35/£15
The Cosmic Doctrine, Inner Light, 1949 . £20/£10
Applied Magic, Aquarian Press, 1962 . . £20/£10
Aspects of Occultism, Aquarian Press, 1962 £20/£10
The Magical Battle of Britain, Golden Gates Press, 1994 . . . . £15/£5

V.M. Steele Novels

The Scarred Wrists, Stanley Paul, [1935] . £25/£10
Hunters of Humans, Stanley Paul, [1936] . £25/£10
Beloved of Ishmael, Stanley Paul, [1937] . £25/£10

Violet M. Firth, Non Fiction

Machinery of the Mind, Allen & Unwin, 1922 £50/£20
The Psychology of the Servant Problem, C.W. Daniel, 1925 . . . . £20/£10
The Soya Bean, C.W. Daniel, 1925 . . . £20/£10
The Problem of Purity, Rider, [1928] . . £20/£10
Avalon of the Heart, Muller, 1934 . . . £20/£10

Violet M. Firth verse
Violets, Mendip Press, [1904] £25
More Violets, Jarrold, [1906] £25

JOHN FOWLES
(b.1926)

Fowles has become both popularly and critically acclaimed as a modern literary figure due to his experimental style and the broad humanist content of his novels.

Novels
The Collector, Jonathan Cape, 1963 (first issue d/w without reviews quoted). . . . . . £300/£75
ditto, Jonathan Cape, 1963 (later issue d/w with reviews). . . . . £250/£75
ditto, Little, Brown (U.S.), 1963 . . . . . £200/£45
The Magus, Little, Brown (U.S.), 1965 . . £125/£25
ditto, Jonathan Cape, 1966 . . . . . . £125/£25
ditto, Jonathan Cape, 1977 (revised edition) £20/£10
ditto, Little, Brown (U.S.), 1978 (revised edition) . . . . £20/£10
The French Lieutenant's Woman, Jonathan Cape, 1969 . . . . £80/£20
ditto, Little, Brown (U.S.), 1969 . . . . . £30/£10
The Ebony Tower, Jonathan Cape, 1974 (novellas) . . . . £20/£5
ditto, Little, Brown (U.S.), 1974 . . . . . £15/£5
ditto, Little, Brown (U.S.), 1974 (signed issue, with a special tipped-in leaf signed by John Fowles) . . . . £175/£150
Daniel Martin, Little, Brown (U.S.), 1977 . £15/£5
ditto, Jonathan Cape, 1977 . . . . . £15/£5
Mantissa, Jonathan Cape, 1982 . . . . £10/£5
ditto, Little, Brown (U.S.), 1982 . . . . £10/£5
ditto, Little, Brown (U.S.), 1982 (500 signed copies, slipcase) . . . . £65/£50
A Maggot, Jonathan Cape, 1985 . . . . £15/£5
ditto, Cape/London Limited Editions, 1985 (500 signed copies, glassine d/w) . . . . £50/£45
ditto, Little, Brown (U.S.), 1985 . . . . £10/£5
ditto, Little, Brown (U.S.), 1985 (260 signed copies) £75

Other Titles
The Aristos, Little, Brown (U.S.), 1964 . . £300/£65
ditto, Jonathan Cape, 1965 . . . . . £300/£65
My Recollections of Kafka, University of Manitoba Press, 1970 (25 copies, wraps) £750
Poems, Ecco Press (U.S.), 1973 . . . . . £40/£15
Cinderella, by Perrault, translated by John Fowles, Jonathan Cape, 1974 . . . . . . £45/£20
Shipwreck, Jonathan Cape, 1974 (photographs with text by John Fowles) . . . . . . £25/£10
ditto, Little, Brown (U.S.), 1975 . . . . £15/£5
Ourika, Tom Taylor (U.S.), 1977 (500 signed copies) £200
Islands, Jonathan Cape, 1978 (photographs with text by John Fowles) . . . . £15/£5
ditto, Little, Brown (U.S.), 1979 . . . . £10/£5
ditto, Little, Brown (U.S.), 1979 (160 signed, numbered copies, slipcase) . . . . £200/£175
Conditional, Lord John Press (U.S.), 1979 (broadside, 150 numbered, signed copies) £200
The Tree, Aurum Press, 1979 (photographs with text by John Fowles) . . . . £25/£10
ditto, Little, Brown (U.S.), 1980 . . . . £10/£5
A Letter from Charles I Concerning Lyme, Lyme Regis Museum, 1980 (100 signed sets of 2 printed sheets). £100
The Enigma of Stonehenge, Jonathan Cape, 1980 (photographs with text by John Fowles) . £15/£5
ditto, Summit (U.S.), 1980 . . . . . . £10/£5
A Brief History of Lyme, Friends of the Lyme Regis Museum, 1981 (wraps). £15
The French Lieutenant's Woman, A Screenplay, Cape, 1981 . . . . £20/£5
ditto, Little, Brown (U.S.), 1981 . . . . £15/£5
ditto, Little, Brown (U.S.), 1981 (360 signed copies, slipcase) . . . . £125/£100
Photographs of Lyme Regis, Skelton Press, 1982 (25 signed copies) £1,000
A Short History of Lyme Regis, Dovecote Press, 1982 . . . . £25/£10
ditto, Little, Brown (U.S.), 1983 . . . . £10/£5
Of Memories and Magpies, Tom Taylor (U.S.), 1983 (200 copies, wraps) £300
Land, Heinemann, 1985 . . . . . . £45/£10
ditto, Little, Brown (U.S.), 1985 . . . . £45/£10
Poor Koko, Eurographica (Helsinki), 1987 (350 signed, numbered copies, wraps) £75
The Enigma, Eurographica (Helsinki), 1987 (350 signed, numbered copies, wraps) £75
Behind the Magus, Colophon Press, 1994 (26 signed, lettered copies bound in goatskin) £200
ditto, Colophon Press, 1994 (signed copies, wraps) £75
The Nature of Nature and The Tree, Yolla Bolly Press (U.S.), 1995 (140 signed copies, boards, slipcase) . . . . £525/£500
ditto, Yolla Bolly Press (U.S.), 1995 (275 signed copies, wraps) £175
Wormholes, Colophon Press, 1998 (signed copies, slipcase) £175
ditto, Cape, 1998 . . . . £15/£5
ditto, Holt (U.S.), 1998 . . . . . . £15/£5
ditto, Holt (U.S.), 1998 (150 signed copies, slipcase) . . . . £175/£150

DICK FRANCIS
(b.1920)

A former steeplechase jockey, Francis has become a highly popular and collectable thriller writer, setting his novels in the world of horse racing.

Novels

Dead Cert, Michael Joseph, 1962 . £1,250/£400
ditto, Holt Rinehart (U.S.), 1962 . . . . £450/£100
Nerve, Michael Joseph, 1964 . . . . . £400/£75
ditto, Harper (U.S.), 1964 . . . . . . £300/£65
For Kicks, Michael Joseph, 1965 . . . £200/£25
ditto, Harper (U.S.), 1965 . . . . . . £50/£10
Odds Against, Michael Joseph, 1965 . . £75/£15
ditto, Harper (U.S.), 1966 . . . . . . £35/£10
Flying Finish, Michael Joseph, 1966 . . £100/£25
ditto, Harper (U.S.), 1967 . . . . . . £25/£10
Blood Sport, Michael Joseph, 1967 . . . £60/£15
ditto, Harper (U.S.), 1968 . . . . . . £15/£5
Forfeit, Michael Joseph, 1968 . . . . £50/£15
ditto, Harper (U.S.), 1969 . . . . . . £15/£5
Enquiry, Michael Joseph, 1969 . . . . £40/£10
ditto, Harper (U.S.), 1969 . . . . . . £15/£5
Rat Race, Michael Joseph, 1970 . . . . £30/£10
ditto, Harper (U.S.), 1971 . . . . . . £15/£5
Bonecrack, Michael Joseph, 1971 . . . £25/£5
ditto, Harper (U.S.), 1972 . . . . . . £15/£5
Smokescreen, Michael Joseph, 1972 . . £25/£5
ditto, Harper (U.S.), 1972 . . . . . . £15/£5
Slay-Ride, Michael Joseph, 1973 . . . . £25/£5
ditto, Harper (U.S.), 1974 . . . . . . £15/£5
Knock Down, Michael Joseph, 1974 . . . £25/£5
ditto, Harper (U.S.), 1975 . . . . . . £15/£5
Across the Board, Harper (U.S.), 1975 (contains *Flying Finish, Blood Sport* and *Enquiry*) . . . £15/£5
High Stakes, Michael Joseph, 1975 . . . £25/£5
ditto, Harper (U.S.), 1976 . . . . . . £15/£5
In The Frame, Michael Joseph, 1976 . . £25/£5
ditto, Harper (U.S.), 1977 . . . . . . £15/£5
Risk, Michael Joseph, 1977 . . . . £15/£5
ditto, Harper (U.S.), 1978 . . . . . . £15/£5
Three Winners, Michael Joseph, 1977, (contains *Dead Cert, Nerve* and *For Kicks*) . . . . . £10/£5
Trial Run, Michael Joseph, 1978 . . . £15/£5
ditto, Harper (U.S.), 1979 . . . . . . £15/£5
Three Favourites, Michael Joseph, 1978, (contains *Odds Against, Flying Finish* and *Blood Sport*) £10/£5
Whip Hand, Michael Joseph, 1979 . . . £10/£5
ditto, Harper (U.S.), 1980 . . . . . . £10/£5
Three To Follow, Michael Joseph, 1979, (contains *Forfeit, Enquiry* and *Rat Race*) . . . . £10/£5
Reflex, Michael Joseph, 1980 . . . . £10/£5
ditto, Putnam (U.S.), 1981 . . . . . . £10/£5
Twice Shy, Michael Joseph, 1981 . . . . £10/£5
ditto, Putnam (U.S.), 1982 . . . . . . £10/£5
Banker, Michael Joseph, 1982 . . . . £10/£5
ditto, Putnam (U.S.), 1983 . . . . . . £10/£5
The Danger, Michael Joseph, 1983 . . . £10/£5
ditto, Putnam (U.S.), 1984 . . . . . . £10/£5
Proof, Michael Joseph, 1984 . . . . . £10/£5
ditto, Putnam (U.S.), 1985 . . . . . . £10/£5
Break In, Michael Joseph, 1985 . . . . £10/£5
ditto, Putnam (U.S.), 1986 . . . . . . £10/£5
Bolt, Michael Joseph, 1986 . . . . . £10/£5
ditto, Putnam (U.S.), 1987 . . . . . . £10/£5
Hot Money, Michael Joseph, 1987 . . . £10/£5
ditto, Putnam (U.S.), 1988 (250 signed copies, slipcase) . . . . £60/£50
ditto, Putnam (U.S.), 1988 . . . . . . £10/£5
The Edge, Michael Joseph, 1988 . . . . £10/£5
ditto, Putnam (U.S.), 1989 . . . . . . £10/£5
Straight, Michael Joseph, 1989 . . . . £10/£5
ditto, Michael Joseph, 1989, (500 signed copies, bound in quarter leather, in slipcase) . . . . . £75/£65
ditto, Putnam (U.S.), 1989 . . . . . . £10/£5
Longshot, Michael Joseph, 1990 . . . . £10/£5
ditto, Putnam (U.S.), 1990 . . . . . . £10/£5
Comeback, Michael Joseph, 1991 . . . £10/£5
ditto, Putnam (U.S.), 1991 . . . . . . £10/£5
Driving Force, Michael Joseph, 1992 . . £10/£5
ditto, Putnam (U.S.), 1992 . . . . . . £10/£5
Decider, Michael Joseph, 1993 . . . . £10/£5
ditto, Putnam (U.S.), 1993 . . . . . . £10/£5
Wild Horses, Michael Joseph, 1994 . . . £10/£5
ditto, Scorpion Press, 1994, (99 signed, numbered copies, bound in quarter leather) £65
ditto, Scorpion Press, 1994, (20 signed, lettered copies, deluxe binding) £125
ditto, Putnam (U.S.), 1994 . . . . . . £10/£5
Come to Grief, Michael Joseph, 1995 . . £10/£5
To the Hilt, Michael Joseph, 1996 . . . £10/£5
ditto, Scorpion Press, 1996, (99 signed, numbered copies, bound in quarter leather) £65
ditto, Scorpion Press, 1996, (15 signed, lettered copies, deluxe binding) £125
ditto, Putnam (U.S.), 1996 . . . . . . £10/£5

Miscellaneous

The Sport of Queens, Michael Joseph, 1957, (autobiography) . . . . £250/£50
ditto, second edition (revised), Michael Joseph, 1968 . . . . £10/£5
ditto, Harper (U.S.), 1969 . . . . . . £40/£10
Best Racing and Chasing Stories, Faber, 1966, (edited, with an introduction by, Dick Francis and John Welcome) . . . . £15/£5
The Racing Man's Bedside Book, Faber, 1969, (edited

by Dick Francis and John Welcome) . . . £15/£5
Best Racing and Chasing Stories Two, Faber, 1972, edited, with an introduction by Dick Francis and John Welcome . . . . £15/£5
Lester: The Official Biography, Michael Joseph, 1986 . . . . £10/£5
ditto, Michael Joseph, 1986, (500 signed copies, in slipcase) . . . . £50/£45
Great Racing Stories, Bellew, 1989, edited by Dick Francis . . . . £10/£5
ditto, Bellew, 1989, (deluxe 75 numbered copies, signed by Dick Francis and John Welcome; bound in full leather) £225
ditto, Bellew, 1989, (standard limited 175 numbered copies, signed by Dick Francis and John Wellcome; bound in quarter leather) £200

GEORGE MACDONALD FRASER
(b.1925)

A novelist and historian, Fraser's successful Flashman books have made an unlikely hero out of the bully who originally appeared in *Tom Brown's Schooldays.*

Novels
Flashman, Barrie & Jenkins, 1969 . . . £75/£25
ditto, World Publishing Co./New American Library (U.S.), 1969 . . . . £60/£20
Royal Flash, Barrie & Jenkins, 1970 . . £65/£20
ditto, Knopf (U.S.), 1970 . . . . £50/£20
Flash for Freedom, Barrie & Jenkins, 1971 £65/£20
ditto, Knopf (U.S.), 1972 . . . . £45/£20
Flashman at the Charge, Barrie & Jenkins, 1973 . . . . £65/£20
ditto, Knopf (U.S.), 1973 . . . . £35/£20
Flashman in the Great Game, Barrie & Jenkins, 1975 . . . . £45/£15
ditto, Knopf (U.S.), 1975 . . . . £30/£10
Flashman's Lady, Barrie & Jenkins, 1977 . £50/£15
ditto, Knopf (U.S.), 1978 . . . . £30/£10
Flashman and the Redskins, Collins, 1982. £35/£10
ditto, Knopf (U.S.), 1982 . . . . £25/£10
Flashman and the Dragon, Collins, 1985 . £25/£5
ditto, Knopf (U.S.), 1986 . . . . £20/£5
Flashman and the Mountain of Light, Collins, 1990 . . . . £25/£5
ditto, Knopf (U.S.), 1991 . . . . £20/£5
Flashman and the Angel of the Lord, Collins, 1994 . . . . £25/£5
ditto, Scorpion Press, 1994 (119 signed copies, glassine d/w) . . . . £150/£125
ditto, Knopf (U.S.), 1995 . . . . £10/£5

Short Stories
The General Danced at Dawn, Collins, 1970 £65/£20
ditto, Knopf (U.S.), 1973 . . . . £45/£10
McAuslan in the Rough, Barrie & Jenkins, 1974 . . . . £45/£15
ditto, Knopf (U.S.), 1974 . . . . £35/£10
The Sheik and the Dustbin, Collins, 1988 £25/£10

Others
The Steel Bonnets, Barrie & Jenkins, 1971 £75/£25
ditto, Knopf (U.S.), 1972 . . . . £65/£20
Mr American, Collins, 1980 . . . . . . £45/£10
ditto, Simon & Schuster (U.S.), 1980 . . £15/£5
The Pyrates, Collins, 1983 . . . . . . £35/£10
ditto, Knopf (U.S.), 1984 . . . . £25/£10
The Hollywood History of the World, Joseph, 1988 . . . . £40/£10
ditto, Beech Tree/Morrow (U.S.), 1988 . . £25/£10
Quartered Safe Out Here, Collins, 1992 . £10/£5
The Candlemass Road, Collins, 1993 . . £10/£5
Black Ajax, Collins, 1997 . . . . . . £10/£5
ditto, Carroll & Graf (U.S.), 1998 . . . £10/£5

MICHAEL FRAYN
(b.1933)

A journalist, novelist and dramatist, Frayn established his reputation as a sixties satirist. His best known work is the drama *Noises Off,* describing an appalling touring company of actors.

Novels
The Tin Men, Collins, 1965 . . . . . £20/£5
ditto, Little, Brown (U.S.), 1966 . . . . £15/£5
The Russian Interpreter, Collins, 1966 . . £20/£5
ditto, Viking (U.S.), 1966 . . . . £10/£5
Towards the End of Morning, Collins, 1967 £10/£5
ditto, as ***Against Entropy***, Viking (U.S.), 1967 £10/£5
A Very Private Life, Collins, 1968 . . . £10/£5
ditto, Viking (U.S.), 1968 . . . . £10/£5
Sweet Dreams, Collins, 1973 . . . . . £10/£5
ditto, Viking (U.S.), 1973 . . . . £10/£5
The Trick of It, Viking (U.K.), 1989 . . £10/£5
ditto, Viking (U.S.), 1989 . . . . £10/£5
A Landing on the Sun, Viking (U.K.), 1991 £10/£5
ditto, Viking (U.S.), 1992 . . . . £10/£5
Now You Know, Viking (U.K.), 1992 . . £10/£5
ditto, Viking (U.S.), 1993 . . . . £10/£5

Plays
The Two of Us, French, 1970 (wraps) . . . £5
ditto, Fontana, 1970 (wraps) £5
Alphabetical Order, French, 1976 (wraps) . . £5

Donkey's Years, French, 1977 (wraps) . . . £5
ditto, Eyre Methuen, 1977 (wraps) £10
Clouds, French, 1977 (wraps) £5
ditto, Eyre Methuen, 1977 (wraps) £10
Make and Break, French, 1980 (wraps) . . £5
ditto, Methuen, 1980 (wraps) £5
Noises Off, Methuen, 1982 (wraps) £5
ditto, French (U.S.), 1985 (wraps) £5
Benefactors, Methuen, 1984 (wraps) . . . £5
Plays I, Methuen, 1986 (wraps) £5
Balmoral, Methuen, 1987 (wraps) £5
First and Last, Methuen, 1989 (wraps) . . . £5
Look Look, Methuen, 1990 (wraps) £5
Listen to this: 21 Short Plays and Sketches, Methuen, 1991 (wraps) £5

Screenplay
Clockwise, Methuen, 1986 (wraps) £5

Others
The Day of the Dog, Collins, 1962 . . . £25/£10
ditto, Doubleday (U.S.), 1963 . . . . £10/£5
The Book of Fub, Collins, 1963 . . . . £10/£5
ditto, as ***Never Put off to Gomorrah***, Pantheon (U.S.), 1964 . . . . £10/£5
On the Outskirts, Collins, 1964 . . . . £10/£5
At Bay in Gear Street, Fontana, 1967 (wraps) £5
Constructions, Wildwood House, 1974 . . £10/£5
The Original Frayn, Salamander Press, 1983 £10/£5

ROBERT FROST

(b.1874 d.1963)

An American poet with the distinctive voice of his own country, whose poetry often addresses the problems of a solitary character attempting to make sense of the world.

[Twilight] Five Poems, (1894) £10,000
A Boy's Will, David Nutt, 1913 (1st issue, bronze cloth) £2,500
ditto, David Nutt, 1913 (2nd issue, 135 signed, numbered copies, cream wraps) £1,750
ditto, David Nutt, 1913 (2nd issue, cream wraps) £500
ditto, Holt (U.S.), 1915 . . . . £300
North of Boston, David Nutt, 1914 . . . £1,500
ditto, Holt (U.S.), 1914 [1915] £1,500
Mountain Interval, Holt (U.S.), 1916 . . . £150
Selected Poems, Holt (U.S.), 1923 . . . £500/£100
diitto, Heinemann, 1923 . . . . £50
New Hampshire, Holt (U.S.), 1923 . . . £400/£125
ditto, Holt (U.S.), 1923 (350 signed copies, slipcase) . . . . £600/£500
ditto, Grant Richards, 1924 . . . . . . £350/£75
ditto, The New Dresden Press (Hanover), 1955 (750 signed, numbered copies, semi-transparent d/w) . . . . £300/£200
West-Running Brook, Holt (U.S.), 1928 . £150/£50
ditto, Holt (U.S.), 1928 (1,000 signed copies, slipcase, glasine d/w) . . . . £300/£250
A Way Out, Harbor Press (U.S.), 1929 (485 signed copies, glassine d/w) . . . . £225/£200
The Lovely Shall Be Choosers, Random House (U.S.), 1929 (475 copies, wraps) £100
The Cows in the Corn, Slide Mountain Press (U.S.), 1929 (91 signed copies) . . . . . . £600/£400
Collected Poems, Random House (U.S.), 1930 . . . . £100/£20
ditto, Random House (U.S.), 1930 (1,000 signed copies) £300
ditto, Longman, 1930 . . . . £100/£20
The Lone Striker, Holt (U.S.), 1933 (wraps in envelope) . . . . £45/£25
A Further Range, Holt (U.S.), 1936 . . . £45/£15
ditto, Spiral Press (U.S.), 1936 (800 signed copies) £250
ditto, Cape, 1937 . . . . £25/£10
Selected Poems, Cape, 1936 . . . . . . £20/£5
From Snow to Snow, Holt (U.S.), 1936 . . £250/£100
A Witness Tree, Holt (U.S.), 1942 . . . £25/£10
ditto, Spiral Press (U.S.), 1942 (735 signed copies, slipcase) . . . . £250/£225
ditto, Cape, 1943 . . . . £20/£10
A Masque of Reason, Holt (U.S.), 1945 . £25/£10
ditto, Holt (U.S.), 1945 (800 signed copies, slipcase) . . . . £150/£125
ditto, Cape, 1948 . . . . £20/£5
Steeple Bush, Holt (U.S.), 1947 . . . . £25/£10
ditto, Holt (U.S.), 1947 (750 signed copies, slipcase) . . . . £150/£125
A Masque of Mercy, Holt (U.S.), 1947 . . £25/£10
ditto, Holt (U.S.), 1947 (751 signed copies, slipcase) . . . . £150/£125
Hard Not to be a King, House of Books (U.S.), 1951 (300 signed copies) £300
The Complete Poems, Holt (U.S.), 1949 (500 signed copies) £350
ditto, Limited Editions Club (U.S.), 1950 (signed, 2 vols in slipcase) . . . . £350/£300
ditto, Cape, 1951 . . . . £45/£10
A Cabin in the Clearing, Blumenthal (U.S.), 1951 (wraps) £45
My Objection to Being Stepped On, Blumenthal (U.S.), 1957 (wraps) £25
A Wishing Well, Blumenthal (U.S.), 1959 (wraps) £25
In the Clearing, Holt (U.S.), 1961 . . . £20/£5
ditto, Spiral Press (U.S.), 1961 (1500 signed copies) . . . . £150/£125

The Prophets Really Prophecy as Mystics, Blumenthal (U.S.), 1962 . . . . £25
The Poetry of Robert Frost, Holt (U.S.), 1969 £15/£5
ditto, Cape, 1971 . . . . £15/£5

ALAN GARNER
(b.1934)

A writer of children's literature, the majority of Garner's books are set in his native Cheshire. His books are an evocative mix of myth, fantasy and reality.

The Weirdstone of Brisingamen: A Tale of Alderley, Collins, 1960 . . . . £125/£25
ditto, Philomel (U.S.), 1960 . . . . . . £35/£10
The Moon of Gomrath, Collins, 1963 . . £100/£25
ditto, Philomel (U.S.), 1963 . . . . . . £25/£10
Elidor, Collins, 1965 (Illustrated by Charles Keeping) . . . . £50/£15
ditto, Walck (U.S.), [1965] . . . . . . £25/£10
Holly from the Bongs: A Nativity Play, Collins, 1966 . . . . £45/£15
The Old Man of Mow, Collins, 1967 (Photographs by Roger Hill) . . . . £40/£15
ditto, Doubleday (U.S.), 1967 . . . . £15/£5
The Owl Service, Collins, 1967 . . . . £50/£10
ditto, Philomel (U.S.), 1967 . . . . . £25/£10
Red Shift, Collins, 1973 . . . . £20/£10
ditto, Macmillan (U.S.), 1973. . . . . £20/£10
The Guizer: A Book of Fools, Hamish Hamilton, 1975 . . . . £15/£5
ditto, Greenwillow(U.S.), 1976 . . . . £15/£5
The Stone Book, Collins, 1976 (illustrated by Michael Foreman) . . . . £15/£5
ditto, Collins (U.S.), 1976. . . . . . . £15/£5
Tom Fobble's Day, Collins, 1977 (illustrated by Michael Foreman) . . . . £15/£5
ditto, Collins (U.S.), 1979. . . . . . . £15/£5
Granny Reardun, Collins, 1977 (illustrated by Michael Foreman) . . . . £15/£5
ditto, Collins (U.S.), 1978. . . . . . . £15/£5
The Aimer Gate, Collins, 1978 (illustrated by Michael Foreman) . . . . £15/£5
ditto, Collins (U.S.), 1979. . . . . . . £15/£5
Fairy Tales of Gold, Collins, 1979 (4 vols) . £35/£10
ditto, Philomel (U.S.), 1980 (1 vol.) . . . £15/£5
The Lad of the Gad, Collins, 1980 . . . £15/£5
ditto, Philomel (U.S.), 1981 . . . . . . £15/£5
The Stone Book Quartet, Collins, 1983 . . £20/£5
A Bag of Moonshine, Collins, 1986 (illustrated by Patrick Lynch) . . . . £15/£5
ditto, Delacorte Press(U.S.), 1986 . . . £15/£5
Jack and the Beanstalk, HarperCollins, 1992 £10/£5
Strandloper, Harvill Press, 1996 . . . £10/£5

Verse
The Breadhorse, Collins, 1975 (illustrated by Albin Trowski) . . . . £35/£15

Plays
Potter Thompson, O.U.P., 1975 . . . . £15/£5

DAVID GARNETT
(b.1892 d.1981)

Principally a novelist, whose early works have a light, fantastic touch, Garnett was associated with the Bloomsbury Group. His *Aspects of Love* was recently turned into a successful stage musical.

Novels
Dope-Darling: A Story of Cocaine, Werner Laurie, [1919] (pseud. 'Leda Burke') £75
Lady Into Fox, Chatto & Windus, 1922. . £25/£10
ditto, Knopf (U.S.), 1923 . . . . £15/£5
A Man in the Zoo, Chatto & Windus, 1924 £20/£10
ditto, Chatto & Windus, 1924 (110 signed, numbered copies) £50
ditto, Knopf (U.S.), 1924 . . . . . . £15/£5
The Sailor's Return, Chatto & Windus, 1925 £20/£10
ditto, Chatto & Windus, 1925 (160 signed, numbered copies) £50
ditto, Knopf (U.S.), 1925 . . . . £15/£5
Go She Must!, Chatto & Windus, 1927 . . £20/£10
ditto, Chatto & Windus, 1927 (160 signed, numbered copies) £50
ditto, Knopf (U.S.), 1927 . . . . £15/£5
No Love, Chatto & Windus, 1929 . . . £15/£5
ditto, Chatto & Windus, 1929 (160 signed, numbered copies) £50
The Grasshoppers Come, Chatto & Windus, 1931 . . . . £15/£5
ditto, Chatto & Windus, 1931 (210 signed, numbered copies) £45
A Rabbit in the Air, Chatto & Windus, 1932 £15/£5
ditto, Chatto & Windus, 1932 (110 signed, numbered copies) £50
ditto, Brewer, Warren & Putnam (U.S.), 1932 £15/£5
Pocahontas, or the Nonpareil of Virginia, Chatto & Windus, 1933. . . . . £15/£5
ditto, Chatto & Windus, 1933 (550 signed, numbered copies) £40
Beany-Eye, Chatto & Windus, 1935 . . . £10/£5
ditto, Chatto & Windus, 1935 (110 signed, numbered copies) £50

ditto, Harcourt, Brace (U.S.), 1935 . . . £15/£5
Aspects of Love, Chatto & Windus, 1955 . £25/£10
ditto, Harcourt, Brace (U.S.), 1955 . . . £15/£5
A Shot in the Dark, Longmans, 1958 . . £10/£5
ditto, Little, Brown (U.S.), 1958 . . . . £10/£5
A Net for Venus, Longmans, 1959 . . . £10/£5
Two By Two: A Story of Survival, Longmans, 1963 . . . . £10/£5
Ulterior Motives, Longmans, 1966 . . . £10/£5
A Clean Slate, Hamish Hamilton, 1971 . . £10/£5
The Sons of the Falcon, Macmillan, 1972 £10/£5
Plough Over the Bones, Macmillan, 1973 £10/£5
Up She Rises, Macmillan, 1977 . . . . £10/£5

Short Stories
The Old Dovecote and Other Stories, Elkin Mathews & Marrot: No.8 in the Woburn Books series, 1928 (530 signed copies) . . . . £50/£35
A Terrible Day, William Jackson: No.9 in the Furnival Books series, 1932 (550 signed copies) . £50/£35
First 'Hippy' Revolution, San Marcos Press, (New Mexico), 1970 . . . . £10
Purl and Plain, Macmillan, 1973 . . . £10/£5

Autobiography
The Golden Echo, Chatto & Windus, 1953 . £10/£5
ditto, Harcourt, Brace (U.S.), 1954 . . . £10/£5
The Flowers of the Forest, Chatto & Windus, 1955 . . . . £10/£5
Familiar Faces, Chatto & Windus, 1962 . £10/£5
ditto, Harcourt, Brace (U.S.), 1962 . . . £10/£5

Miscellaneous
Never Be a Bookseller, Knopf (U.S.), 1929 (2,000 copies, none for sale) £75
ditto, The Fleece Press, 1995 (400 copies) . . £20
War in the Air: September 1939 to May 1941, Chatto & Windus, 1941 . . . . £30/£10
The Battle of Britain, Puffin Picture Book No.21, 1941 (wraps) £10
The Campaign in Greece and Crete, Chatto & Windus, 1942. . . . . £10
A Historical Pageant of Huntingdonshire in Celebration of the Coronation of Her Majesty Elizabeth II, privately printed, (Huntingdon), 1953 (souvenir programme) £15
The White/Garnett Letters, Cape, 1968 . . £15/£5
ditto, Viking (U.S.), 1968 . . . . £10/£5
The Master Cat: The True and Unexpurgated Story of Puss in Boots, Macmillan, 1974 . . . £10/£5
Sir Geoffrey Keynes: A Tribute, privately printed, 1978 . . . . £10
Great Friends: Portraits of Seventeen Writers, Macmillan, 1979 . . . . £30/£10
ditto, Atheneum (U.S.), 1980 . . . . £25/£10

ELIZABETH GASKELL
(b.1810 d.1865)

A novelist whose work earned the respect of Dickens, Mrs Gaskell is principally remembered for her friendship with Charlotte Brontë, and her biography The Life of Charlotte Brontë

Novels
Mary Barton, A Tale of Manchester Life, Chapman & Hall, 1848 (anonnymous, 2 vols) £750
Libbie Marsh's Three Eras, A Lancashire Tale, Hamilton, Adams & Co., 1850 . . . . . £500
The Sexton's Hero, Johnson, Rawson & Co., Manchester, 1850 . . . . £500
The Moorland Cottage, Chapman & Hall, 1850 £500
Ruth, A Novel, Chapman & Hall, 1853 (3 vols) £750
Cranford, Chapman & Hall, 1853 (anon) . . £1,000
North and South, Chapman & Hall, 1855 (2 vols) £500
The Sexton's Hero and Christmas Storms and Sunshine, Chapman & Hall, 1855 . . . . £100
A Dark Night's Work, Smith Elder, 1863 . . £350
Sylvia's Lovers, Smith Elder, 1863 (3 vols) . . £400
Wives and Daughters, An Everyday Story, Smith Elder, 1866 (illustrated by George du Maurier, 2 vols) £400

Short Stories
Lizzie Leigh and Other Tales, Smith Elder, 1855 [1854]) £250
Round the Sofa, Sampson Low, 1858 (2 vols) £400
ditto, as ***My Lady Ludlow and Other Tales***, Sampson Low, 1861 (1 vol.) £250
Right at Last and Other Tales, Sampson Low, 1860 . . . . £250
Lois the Witch and Other Tales, Tauchnitz, 1861 £35
Cousin Phyllis and Other Tales, Smith Elder, 1865 (illustrated by George du Maurier) £250
The Grey Woman and Other Tales, Smith Elder, 1865 (illustrated by George du Maurier) £250
The Half-Brothers, Gulliver Book Co., [1943] £25
The Squire's Story, Todd Publishing Co., 1943 £10/£5
The Cage at Cranford and Other Stories, Nelson Classics, [1937] . . . . £10/£5
Mrs Gaskell's Tales of Mystery and Horror, Gollancz, 1978 . . . . £10/£5

Miscellaneous
The Life of Charlotte Brontë, Smith Elder, 1857 (2 vols) £500
Letters of Charlotte Brontë, privately printed, 1915 (25 copies) £100
My Diary, The Early Years of My Daughter

Marianne, privately printed by Clement Shorter, 1923 (50 copies, wraps) £75
Letters of Mrs Gaskell and Charles Eliot Norton, 1855-1865, O.U.P., 1932 . . . . . £20/£10
The Letters of Elizabeth Gaskell, Manchester University Press, [1966] . . . . . . £20/£10

Collected Editions
The Novels and Tales of Elizabeth Gaskell, Smith Elder, 1878-82 (7 vols) £150
The Works of Elizabeth Gaskell, Smith Elder, 1906 (8 vols) £100

STELLA GIBBONS
(b.1902 d.1989)

Author of many novels, but collected mainly for her first, the classic *Cold Comfort Farm.*

Novels
Cold Comfort Farm, Longmans, 1932 . . £500/£75
Bassett, Longmans, 1934 . . . . . . £25/£10
Enbury Heath, Longmans, 1935 . . . . £25/£10
Miss Linsey and Pa, Longmans, 1936 . . £25/£10
Nightingale Wood, Longmans, 1938 . . £25/£10
My American: A Romance, Longmans, 1939 £25/£10
The Rich House, Longmans, 1941 . . . £20/£5
Ticky, Longmans, 1943 . . . . . . £20/£5
The Bachelor, Longmans, 1944 . . . . £20/£5
Westwood, or, The Gentle Powers, Longmans, 1946 . . . . £20/£5
Conference at Cold Comfort Farm, Longmans, 1949 . . . . £35/£10
The Matchmaker, Longmans, 1949 . . . £10/£5
The Swiss Summer, Longmans, 1951 . . £10/£5
Fort of the Bear, Longmans, 1953 . . . £10/£5
The Shadow of a Sorcerer, Hodder & Stoughton, 1955 . . . . £10/£5
Here Be Dragons, Hodder & Stoughton, 1956 £10/£5
White Sand and Grey Sand, Hodder & Stoughton, [1958] . . . . £10/£5
A Pink Front Door, Hodder & Stoughton, [1959] . . . . £10/£5
The Weather at Tregulla, Hodder & Stoughton, [1962] . . . . £10/£5
The Wolves Were in the Sledge, Hodder & Stoughton, 1964 . . . . £10/£5
The Charmers, Hodder & Stoughton, 1965 . £10/£5
Starlight, Hodder & Stoughton, 1967 . . £10/£5
The Snow-Woman, Hodder & Stoughton, 1969 £10/£5
The Woods in Winter, Hodder & Stoughton, 1970 . . . . £10/£5

Short Stories
Roaring Tower and Other Short Stories, Longmans, 1937 . . . . £25/£10
Christmas at Cold Comfort Farm and Other Stories, Longmans, 1940 . . . . £35/£10
Beside the Pearly Water and Other Stories, Peter Nevill, 1954 . . . . £20/£5

Verse
The Mountain Beast and Other Poems, Longmans, 1930 (wraps) £40
The Priestess and Other Poems, Longmans, 1934 (wraps) £25
The Lowland Venus and Other Poems, Longmans, 1938 (wraps) £25
Collected Poems, Longmans, 1950 . . . . £10/£5
ditto, Theodore Brun, 1950 (150 copies) . £40/£20

Children's
The Untidy Gnome, Longmans, 1935 . . £35/£10

GILES' ANNUALS

The distinctive cartoons drawn by Carl Giles, published in the Daily Express, have been collected together annually.

No. 1, 1946 . . . . £200
No. 2, 1947 . . . . £225
No. 3, 1949 . . . . £100
No. 4, 1950 . . . . £90
No. 5, 1951 . . . . £125
No. 6, 1952 . . . . £45
No. 7, 1953 . . . . £45
No. 8, 1954 . . . . £25
No. 9, 1955 . . . . £25
No. 10, 1956 . . . . £15
No. 11, 1957 . . . . £15
No. 12, 1958 . . . . £15
No. 13, 1959 . . . . £15
No. 14, 1960 . . . . £5
No. 15, 1961 . . . . £5
No. 16, 1962 . . . . £10
No. 17, 1963 . . . . £10
No. 18, 1964 . . . . £5
No. 19, 1965 . . . . £5
No. 20, 1966 . . . . £5
No. 21, 1967 . . . . £10
No. 22, 1968 . . . . £5
No. 23, 1969 . . . . £5
No. 24, 1970 . . . . £5
No. 25, 1971 . . . . £5
No. 26, 1972 . . . . £5

WARWICK GOBLE
(b.1862 d.1943)

A British illustrator, Goble's work owes a great debt to Chinese and Japanese art.

Children's Books

The Grim House, by Mrs Molesworth, Nisbet, 1899 . . . . £25

The Water Babies, by Charles Kingsley, Macmillan, 1909 (32 colour plates) £300

ditto, Macmillan, 1909 (260 copies) £1,250

ditto, Macmillan, 1910 (16 colour plates) . . £50

Green Willow and Other Japanese Fairy Tales, by Grace James, Macmillan, 1910 (40 colour plates) £250

ditto, Macmillan, 1910 (500 copies) £1,500

ditto, Macmillan, 1912 (16 colour plates) . . £50

Folk Tales of Bengal, by Lal Behari Day, Macmillan, 1912 . . . . £100

ditto, Macmillan, 1912 (150 copies) £1,000

Peeps at Many Lands - Turkey, by Julius Van Millingen, A. & C. Black, 1911 (12 colour plates) £15

Stories from the Pentamerone, by Giovanni Battista Basile, Macmillan, 1911. . . . . . . £100

ditto, Macmillan, 1911 (150 copies) £750

The Fairy Book, by D.M. Craik, Macmillan, 1913 (32 colour plates). £200

The Book of Fairy Poetry, Dora Owen, ed., Longmans, 1920 (16 colour plates) £250

Kidnapped, Macmillan (U.S.), 1925 (3 colour plates) . . . . £100/£45

Others

The Oracle of Baal, by J. Provand Webster, Lippincott (U.S.), 1896 . . . . £50

Constantinople, A.&C. Black, 1906 (63 colour plates) £150

The Greater Abbeys of England, Chatto & Windus, 1908 (60 watercolours) £40

Indian Myth and Legend, by Donald A. Mackenzie, Gresham , 1913 (8 colour plates) £40

SIR WILLIAM GOLDING
(b.1911 d.1993)

Golding's novels often place his characters in extreme situations, facing moral dilemmas. *Lord of the Flies* is his disturbing classic.

Novels

Lord of the Flies, Faber, 1954 . . . £1,000/£200

ditto, Coward McCann (U.S.), 1955 . . . £350/£150

The Inheritors, Faber, 1955 . . . . . £350/£100

ditto, Harcourt Brace (U.S.), 1962 . . . . £35/£15

Pincher Martin, Faber, 1956. . . . . . £125/£35

ditto as ***The Two Deaths of Christopher Martin***, Harcourt Brace (U.S.), 1956 . . . . . £40/£10

Free Fall, Faber, 1959 . . . . . . £75/£20

ditto, Harcourt Brace (U.S.), 1960 . . . £25/£10

The Spire, Faber, 1964 . . . . £40/£10

ditto, Harcourt Brace (U.S.), 1964 . . . £15/£5

The Pyramid, Faber, 1967 . . . . . . £40/£10

ditto, Harcourt Brace (U.S.), 1967 . . . £15/£5

Darkness Visible, Faber, 1979 . . . . £25/£10

ditto, Farrar Straus (U.S.), 1979 . . . . £15/£5

Rites of Passage, Faber, 1980 . . . . £25/£10

ditto, Farrar Straus (U.S.), 1980 . . . . £15/£5

The Paper Men, Faber, 1984. . . . . £15/£5

ditto, Farrar Straus (U.S.), 1984 . . . . £15/£5

Close Quarters, Faber, 1987 . . . . . £15/£5

ditto, Farrar Straus (U.S.), 1987 . . . . £10/£5

Fire Down Below, Faber, 1989 . . . . £10/£5

ditto, Farrar Straus (U.S.), 1989 . . . . £10/£5

Double Tongue, Faber, 1995. . . . . . £10/£5

ditto, Farrar Straus (U.S.), 1995 . . . . . £10/£5

Short Stories

Sometime, Never: Three Tales of Imagination, Eyre & Spottiswoode, 1956 . . . . £75/£35

ditto, Ballantine (U.S.), 1956 . . . . . . £50/£20

The Ladder and the Tree, Marlborough College Press, 1961 (wraps) £1,500

The Scorpion God, Faber, 1971 . . . . £45/£15

ditto, Harcourt Brace (U.S.), 1972 . . . . £15/£5

Collected Editions

To the Ends of the Earth: A Sea Trilogy ("*Rites of Passage*", "*Close Quarters*" & "*Fire Down Below*"), Faber, 1991 .. . . £15/£5

ditto, Faber, 1991 (400 signed copies, glassine d/w) . . . . £150/£135

Others

Poems, Macmillan, 1934 (wraps) £3,000

ditto, Macmillan (U.S.), 1935. . . . . . . £500

The Brass Butterfly, A Play in Three Acts, Faber, 1958 . . . . £100/£45

The Hot Gates and Other Occasional Pieces, Faber, 1965 . . . . £35/£10

ditto, Harcourt Brace (U.S.), 1965 . . . £15/£5

A Moving Target, Faber, 1982 . . . . . £10/£5

ditto, Farrar Straus (U.S.), 1982 . . . . £10/£5

Nobel Lecture, Sixth Chamber Press, 1983 (500 copies, wraps). £25

Nobel Lecture, Sixth Chamber Press, 1983 (signed copies, wraps) £65

ditto, Sixth Chamber Press, 1983 (deluxe edition, 50 signed copies, slipcase) . . . . . . £250/£225
An Egyptian Journal, Faber, 1985 . . . £10/£5
ditto, Farrar Straus (U.S.), 1985 . . . . £10/£5

ROBERT GRAVES

(b.1895 d.1985)

Known particularly for his poetry, fiction and his early autobiography, *Goodbye to All That*, Graves lived on Majorca for most of his life.

Verse

Over the Brazier, The Poetry Bookshop, 1916 (wraps) £600
ditto, The Poetry Bookshop, 1920 . . . . £150/£45
Goliath and David, Chiswick Press, 1916 (200 copies, wraps). £1,000
Fairies and Fusiliers, Heinemann, 1917 . £450/£75
ditto, Knopf (U.S.), 1918 . . . . £300/£35
Treasure Box, [Chiswick Press, 1919] (200 copies, wraps). £750
ditto, [Chiswick Press, 1919] (200 copies, boards and d/w) £1,250
Country Sentiment, Secker, 1920 . . . £200/£75
ditto, Knopf (U.S.), 1920 . . . . . . £125/£65
The Pier-Glass, Secker, 1921 . . . . £300/£75
ditto, Knopf (U.S.), 1921 . . . . £200/£45
Whipperginny, Heinemann, 1923 . . . £200/£50
ditto, Knopf (U.S.), 1923 . . . . £125/£35
The Feather Bed, Hogarth Press, 1923 (250 copies, signed by the author). £250
Mock Beggar Hall, Hogarth Press, 1923 . . £250
Welchman's Hose, The Fleuron, 1925 (525 copies, glassine d/w) . . . . £250/£235
Poems, Benn, 1925 (wraps) £100
The Marmosite's Miscellany, Hogarth Press, 1925 (pseud. 'John Doyle') £400
Poems, 1914-1926, Heinemann, 1927 . . £300/£100
ditto, Doubleday, Doran (U.S.), 1929 . . £200/£65
Poems, 1914-1927, Heinemann, 1927 (115 signed, numbered copies, slipcase and d/w) . £600/£450
Poems, 1929, Seizin Press, 1929 (225 signed, numbered copies) £300
Ten Poems More, Hours Press (Paris), 1930 (200 signed copies) £350
Poems, 1926-1930, Heinemann, 1931 (first issue with misbound title-page) . . . . £75/£25
To Whom Else?, Seizen Press (Majorca), 1931 (200 signed copies) £250
Poems, 1930-1933, Barker, 1933 . . . . . £75
Collected Poems, Cassell, 1938 . . . . £50/£20
ditto, Random House (U.S.), 1939 . . . £25/£10
No More Ghosts: Selected Poems, Faber, 1940 . . . . £45/£15
Poems, Eyre & Spottiswoode, 1943 (wraps) . £30
Poems, 1938-1945, Cassell, 1946 . . . £30/£10
ditto, Creative Age Press (U.S.), 1946 . . £30/£10
Collected Poems, 1914-1947, Cassell, 1948 £45/£15
Poems and Satires, Cassell, 1951 . . . £30/£10
Poems, 1953, Cassell, 1953 . . . . . £25/£10
ditto, Cassell, 1953 (250 signed, numbered copies, tissue d/w) . . . . £200/£175
Collected Poems, 1955, Doubleday (U.S.), 1955 . . . . £25/£10
Poems Selected by Himself, Penguin, 1957 (wraps) £5
The Poems of Robert Graves, Doubleday (U.S.), 1958 . . . . £15/£5
Collected Poems, 1959, Cassell, 1959 . . £75/£35
More Poems, 1961, Cassell, 1961 . . . £15/£5
Collected Poems, Doubleday (U.S.), 1961 . £30/£10
New Poems, 1962, Cassell, 1962. . . . £20/£5
The More Deserving Cases: Eighteen Old Poems for Reconsideration, Marlborough College Press, 1962 (350 signed copies) £75
ditto, Marlborough College Press, 1962 (400 signed copies, bound in morocco) £125
Man Does, Woman Is, Cassell, 1964 . . £25/£10
ditto, Cassell, 1964 (175 copies, signed by the author) . . . . £150/£100
ditto, Doubleday (U.S.), 1964 . . . . £25/£10
Love Respelt, Cassell, 1965 (250 signed copies) . . . . £200/£150
ditto, Doubleday (U.S.), 1966 . . . . £25/£10
Collected Poems, 1965, Cassell, 1965 . . £15/£5
Seventeen Poems Missing From 'Love Respelt', privately printed, 1966 (330 copies, signed by the author) . . . . £150/£100
Colophon to 'Love Respelt', privately printed, 1967 (386 copies, signed by the author) . . . £100/£75
Poems, 1965-1968, Cassell, 1968 . . . £15/£5
Poems About Love, Cassell, 1969 . . . £25/£10
Love Respelt Again, Doubleday (U.S.), 1969 (1,000 numbered copies, signed by the author) . £75/£50
Beyond Giving, privately printed, 1969 (536 copies, signed by the author, card covers, d/w). . £75/£60
Poems, 1968-1970, Cassell, 1970 . . . £20/£10
Advice from a Mother, Poem of the Month Club, 1970 (broadsheet) £25
The Green-Sailed Vessel, privately printed, 1971 (536 copies) . . . . £65/£45
Poems: Abridged for Dolls and Princes, Cassell, 1971 . . . . £25/£10
Poems, 1970-1972, Cassell, 1972 . . . £25/£10
Deya: A Portfolio, Motif Editions, 1972 (75 signed copies) £225
Timeless Meeting: Poems, privately printed, 1973 (536

signed, numbered copies) . . . . . . £75/£50
At the Gate, Stellar Press (U.S.), 1974 (536 copies) . . . . £75/£50
Collected Poems, 1975, Cassell, 1975 . . £25/£10
New Collected Poems, Doubleday (U.S.), 1977 . . . . £25/£10
Across the Gulf, Late Poems, The New Seizin Press, 1992 (175 copies) £75

Fiction
My Head! My Head!, Secker, 1925 (500 copies) . . . . £350/£200
ditto, Knopf (U.S.), 1925 . . . . £125/£50
The Shout, Mathews & Marrot, 1929 (530 signed, numbered copies) . . . . £175/£125
No Decency Left, Cape, 1932 (pseud. Barbara Rich, with Laura Riding) . . . . £250/£100
The Real David Copperfield, Barker, 1933 £75/£35
ditto, as ***David Copperfield***, Harcourt Brace (U.S.), 1934 (abridged version condensed by Robert Graves) . . . . £45/£15
I, Claudius, Barker, 1934 (black cloth) £600/£250
ditto, Barker, 1934 (remainder copies, orange cloth) . . . . £500/£200
ditto, Smith & Haas (U.S.), 1934 . . . . £250/£25
Claudius the God and his Wife Messalina, Barker, 1934 . . . . £250/£75
ditto, Smith & Haas (U.S.), 1935 . . . . £75/£15
Antigua, Penny, Puce, Constable/Selzin Press, 1936 . . . . £250/£75
ditto, as ***The Antigua Stamp***, Random House (U.S.), 1937 . . . . £60/£15
Count Belisarius, Cassell, 1938 . . . . £75/£15
ditto, Random House (U.S.), 1938 . . . £50/£10
Sergeant Lamb of the Ninth, Methuen, 1940 £75/£10
ditto, Random House (U.S.), 1941 . . . £25/£10
Proceed, Sergeant Lamb, Methuen, 1941 . £75/£25
ditto, Random House (U.S.), 1941 . . . £65/£20
Wife to Mr Milton: The Story of Mary Powell, Cassell, 1943 . . . . £40/£15
ditto, Creative Age Press (U.S.), 1944 . . £25/£10
The Golden Fleece, Cassell, 1944 . . . £45/£15
ditto, as ***Hercules, My Shipmate***, Creative Age Press (U.S.), 1945 . . . . £35/£15
King Jesus, Creative Age Press (U.S.), 1946 £25/£10
ditto, Cassell, 1946 . . . . £25/£10
Watch the North Wind Rise, Creative Age Press (U.S.), 1949 . . . . £40/£15
ditto, as ***Seven Days in New Crete***, Cassell, 1949 . . . . £35/£10
The Islands of Unwisdom, Doubleday (U.S.), 1949 . . . . £25/£10
ditto, as ***The Isles of Unwisdom***, Cassell, 1950 £25/£10
Homer's Daughter, Cassell, 1955 . . . £35/£10
ditto, Doubleday (U.S.), 1955 . . . . . £25/£10
Catacrok! Mostly Stories, Mostly Funny, Cassell, 1956 . . . . £30/£10
They Hanged My Saintly Billy, Cassell, 1957 £25/£10
ditto, Doubleday (U.S.), 1957 . . . . . £25/£10
Collected Short Stories, Doubleday (U.S.), 1964 . . . . £30/£10
ditto, Cassell, 1965 . . . . £25/£10

Plays
John Kemp's Wager: A Ballad Opera, Blackwell, 1925 (100 signed, numbered copies) £450
ditto, Blackwell, 1925 (750 unsigned copies) . £75
ditto, French (U.S.), 1925 (250 copies) . . . £175

Children's Books
The Penny Fiddle: Poems for Children, Cassell, 1960 (illustrated by Edward Ardizzone) . . . £65/£35
ditto, Doubleday (U.S.), 1960 . . . . . £45/£10
The Big Green Book, Crowell-Collier (U.S.), 1962 (illustrated by Maurice Sendak). . . . £25/£10
ditto, Puffin, 1978 (wraps) £5
Ann at Highwood Hall: Poems for Children, Cassell, 1964 (illustrated by Edward Ardizzone) . £20/£10
ditto, Doubleday (U.S.), 1964 . . . . £20/£10
Two Wise Children, Quist (U.S.), 1967 . . £25/£10
The Poor Boy Who Followed His Star, Cassell, 1968 . . . . £25/£10
ditto, Doubleday (U.S.), 1969 . . . . . £25/£10
An Ancient Castle, Peter Owen, 1980 . . £15/£5
ditto, Kesend (U.S.), 1981 . . . . . £10/£5

As Editor
Oxford Poetry, 1921, Blackwell, 1921 (with Alan Porter and Richard Hughes). £100
ditto, Appleton (U.S.), 1922 . . . . £25
John Skelton (Laureate), Benn, 1927 . . £35/£15
The Less Familiar Nursery Rhymes, Benn, 1927 . . . . £35/£10
T.E. Lawrence To His Biographers, Faber, 1938 (2 vols, 500 signed copies, with d/ws, in slipcase) . . . . £450/£400
ditto, Doubleday Doran, 1938 (2 vols, 500 signed copies, with d/ws, in slipcase) . . . £450/£400
The Comedies of Terence, Doubleday (U.S.), 1962 £25
ditto, Cassell, 1963 . . . . £10

Translations
Almost Forgotten Germany, by George Schwarz, (with Laura Riding), Constable/Seizin Press, 1936 £250/£60
The Transformation of Lucius, Otherwise Known as the Golden Ass, by Lucius Apuleius, Penguin, 1950 (2,000 signed, numbered copies, slipcase) £50/£40
ditto, Penguin, 1950 (wraps) £5
ditto, Farrar, Straus, Giroux (U.S.), 1951 . £20/£5
The Cross and the Sword from 'Enriquillio', by

Manuel de Jesus Galvan, University Press: Bloomington (U.S.), 1954 . . . . . £45/£15
ditto, Gollancz, 1956 . . . . £45/£10
The Infant with the Globe from 'El Nino do la Bola', by Pedro de Alarcon, Trianon Press, 1955 £25/£10
ditto, Yoseleff (U.S.), 1959 . . . . . £20/£10
Winter in Majorca, by George Sand, Cassell, 1956 . . . . £15/£5
ditto, Valldemosa Edition(Mallorca), 1959 (wraps) £10
Pharsalia, by Lucan, Penguin, 1956 (wraps) . . £5
ditto, Penguin (U.S.), 1957 . . . . . . £10/£5
The Twelve Caesars, by Suetonius, Penguin, 1957 (wraps) £5
The Anger of Achilles: Homer's Iliad, Homer, Doubleday (U.S.)., 1959. . . . . . . £35/£10
ditto, Cassell, 1960 . . . . £20/£10
The Rubaiyat of Omar Khayyam, by Omar Khayyam, (with Omar Ali-Shah), Cassell, 1967 . . £20/£5
ditto, Doubleday (U.S.), 1968 . . . . £20/£5
The Song of Songs, Clarkson Potter (U.S.), 1973 . . . . £15/£5
ditto, Collins, 1973 . . . . £15/£5

Others

On English Poetry, Knopf (U.S.), 1922 . . £200/£30
ditto, Heinemann, 1922 . . . . £150/£25
The Meaning of Dreams, Cecil Palmer, 1924 £100/£35
ditto, Greenberg (U.S.), 1925. . . . . £50/£20
Poetic Unreason and Other Studies, Cecil Palmer, 1925 . . . . £150/£60
Contemporary Techniques of Poetry: A Political Analogy, Hogarth Press, 1925 (wraps) . . . £45
Another Future of Poetry, Hogarth Press, 1926 £100
Impenetrability, or the Proper Habit of English, Hogarth Press, 1927 . . . . £200
The English Ballad: A Short Critical Survey, Benn, 1927 . . . . £75/£25
ditto, as ***English and Scottish Ballads***, Heinemann, 1957 (revised edition) . . . . . . £25/£10
Lars Porsena, or 'The Future of Swearing and Improper Language', Kegan Paul, Trench, Trubner, 1927 . . . . £100/£25
ditto, Dutton (U.S.), 1927 . . . . . £75/£20
ditto, as ***The Future of Swearing and Improper Language***, Kegan Paul, Trench, Trubner, 1936 (revised edition) . . . . £25/£10
ditto, as ***The Future of Swearing and Improper Language***, Martin Brian & O'Keefe, 1972 (100 signed copies) £125
A Survey of Modernist Poetry, Heinemann, 1927 (with Laura Riding) . . . . £75/£20
ditto, Doubleday (U.S.), 1928 . . . . £50/£15
Lawrence and the Arabs, Cape, 1927 . . £150/£30
ditto, as ***Lawrence and the Arabian Adventure***, Doubleday (U.S.), 1928 . . . . . . £100/£20

A Pamphlet Against Anthologies, Cape, 1928 (with Laura Riding). £75
ditto, Doubleday (U.S.), 1928 . . . . £75/£25
Mrs Fisher, or The Future of Humour, Kegan Paul, Trench, Trubner, 1928 . . . . £75/£25
ditto, Dutton (U.S.), 1928. . . . . . . £75/£25
Goodbye to All That: An Autobiography, Cape, 1929 (first issue). . . . . £1,000/£750
ditto, Cape, 1929 (second issue). . . . . . £200/£20
ditto, Cape & Smith (U.S.), 1930. . . . £45/£15
But it Still Goes On: An Accumulation, Cape, 1930 (1st impression) . . . . £150/£100
ditto, Cape, 1930 (2nd impression) . . £45/£15
ditto, Cape & Smith (U.S.), 1931. . . . £35/£10
The Long Weekend (with Alan Hodge), Faber, 1940 . . . . £40/£10
ditto, Macmillan (U.S.), 1941. . . . . £25/£10
The Reader Over Your Shoulder (with Alan Hodge), Cape, 1943 . . . . £40/£10
ditto, Macmillan (U.S.), 1943. . . . . £25/£10
The White Goddess, Faber, 1948 . . . £75/£20
ditto, Creative Age Press (U.S.), 1948 . . £65/£15
The Common Asphodel: Collected Essays on Poetry, 1922-1949, Hamish Hamilton, 1949 . . £75/£20
Occupation: Writer, Creative Age Press (U.S.), 1950 . . . . £35/£10
ditto, Cassell, 1951 . . . . £25/£10
The Nazarene Gospel Restored (with Joshua Podro), Cassell, 1953 . . . . £100/£25
ditto, Doubleday (U.S.), 1954 . . . . £65/£15
The Greek Myths, Penguin, 1955 (2 vols, wraps) £10
ditto, Cassell , 1958 . . . . £20/£10
The Crowning Privilege: The Clark Lectures, 1954-5, Cassell, 1955 . . . . £25/£10
ditto, Doubleday (U.S.), 1956 . . . . £20/£5
Adam's Rib, Trianon Press, 1955 (illustrated by James Metcalf) . . . . £50/£15
ditto, Trianon Press, 1955 (250 signed, numbered copies, slipcase) . . . . £175/£150
ditto, Yoseloff (U.S.), 1955 . . . . . £45/£15
Jesus in Rome (with Joshua Podro), Cassell, 1957 . . . . £45/£20
Steps, Cassell, 1958 . . . . £25/£10
5 Pens in Hand, Doubleday (U.S.), 1958 . £30/£10
Food for Centaurs, Doubleday (U.S.), 1960 £45/£15
Greek Gods and Heroes, Doubleday (U.S.), 1960 . . . . £25/£10
ditto as ***Myths of Ancient Greece***, Cassell, 1961 . . . . £25/£10
Selected Poetry and Prose, Hutchinson, 1961, (edited James Reeves) . . . . £10/£5
Oxford Addresses on Poetry, Cassell, 1962. £20/£5
ditto, Doubleday (U.S.), 1962 . . . . . £20/£5
The Siege and Fall of Troy, Cassell, 1962 (illustrated by Walter Hodges) . . . . £15/£5

ditto, Doubleday (U.S.), 1962 . . . . . £15/£5
Hebrew Myths: The Book of Genesis, Doubleday (U.S.), 1964 (with Raphael Patai) . . . £35/£10
ditto, Cassell, 1964 . . . . £35/£10
Majorca Observed, Cassell, 1965 . . . . £15/£5
ditto, Doubleday (U.S.), 1965 . . . . . £15/£5
Mammon and the Black Goddess, Cassell, 1965 . . . . £20/£5
ditto, Doubleday (U.S.), 1965 . . . . . £20/£5
Poetic Craft and Principle, Cassell, 1967 . £15/£5
Greek Myths and Legends, Cassell, 1968 . £10/£5
The Crane Bag, Cassell, 1969 . . . . £10/£5
On Poetry: Collected Talks and Essays, Doubleday (U.S.), 1969 . . . . £20/£5
Difficult Questions, Easy Answers, Cassell, 1972 . . . . £15/£5
ditto, Doubleday (U.S.), 1973 . . . . £15/£5
Collected Letters, Moyer Bell, (U.K./U.S.), 1984 & 1988 (2 vols) . . . . £50/£25

ALASDAIR GRAY
(b.1934)

An inventive writer of bizarre tales, strangely written.

Novels
Lanark, Canongate, 1981 . . . . . . £125/£20
ditto, Harper Colophon (U.S.), 1981 (wraps) . £10
ditto, Braziller (U.S.), 1985 . . . . . £50/£20
1982 Janine, Cape, 1984 . . . . . . £10/£5
ditto, Viking (U.S.), 1984 . . . . . . £10/£5
The Fall of Kelvin Walker, Canongate, 1985 £10/£5
ditto, Braziller (U.S.), 1986 . . . . . £10/£5
Something Leather, Cape, 1990 . . . . £10/£5
ditto, Random House (U.S.), 1990 . . . £10/£5
McGrotty and Ludmilla, Dog and Bone, 1990 (wraps) £10
Poor Things, Bloomsbury, 1991 . . . . £10/£5
ditto, Harcourt (U.S.), 1992 . . . . . £10/£5
History Maker, Canongate, 1994 . . . . £10/£5
ditto, Harcourt (U.S.), 1994 . . . . . £10/£5

Short Stories
The Comedy of the White Dog, Print Studio Press, 1979 (600 numbered copies, wraps) . . . £75
Unlikely Stories, Mostly, Canongate, 1983 . £20/£5
ditto, Penguin (U.S.), 1984 . . . . . £10/£5
Lean Tales, Cape, 1985 (with James Kelman and Agnes Owens) . . . . £20/£5
Ten Tales Tall and True, Bloomsbury, 1993 £10/£5
ditto, Harcourt (U.S.), 1993 . . . . . £10/£5
Mavis Belfrage, Bloomsbury, 1996 . . . £10/£5

Others
Dialogue, Scottish Theatre Magazine, 1971 . . £25
Self-portrait, Saltaire Society, 1988 (wraps) . £20
The Anthology of Prefaces, Canongate, 1989 . £10
Old Negatives: Four Verse Sequences, Cape, 1989 (500 signed copies) . . . . £25/£15

HENRY GREEN
(b.1905 d.1973)

Henry Green was the pseudonym of the novelist Henry Vincent Yorke.

Novels
Blindness, Dutton (U.S.), 1926 . . . . £600/£100
ditto, Dent, 1926 . . . . £600/£100
Living, Dutton (U.S.), 1929 . . . . . £250/£60
ditto, Dent, 1929 . . . . £250/£75
Party Going, Hogarth Press, 1939 . . . £500/£100
ditto, Longman (Toronto), 1939 . . . . £250/£75
ditto, Viking (U.S.), 1951 . . . . . . £20/£5
Caught, Hogarth Press, 1943 . . . . . £250/£50
ditto, Macmillan (Toronto), 1943 . . . £100/£45
ditto, Viking (U.S.), 1950 . . . . . . £20/£5
Loving, Hogarth Press, 1945 . . . . . £225/£50
ditto, Macmillan (Toronto), 1945 . . . £100/£45
ditto, Viking (U.S.), 1949 . . . . . . £25/£5
Back, Hogarth Press, 1946 . . . . . £100/£40
ditto, Oxford (Toronto), 1946 . . . . £60/£20
ditto, Viking (U.S.), 1950 . . . . . . £20/£5
Concluding, Hogarth Press, 1948 . . . £40/£15
ditto, Viking (U.S.), 1950 . . . . . . £20/£5
Nothing, Hogarth Press, 1950 . . . . £40/£15
ditto, Viking (U.S.), 1950 . . . . . . £15/£5
Doting, Hogarth Press, 1951 . . . . . £40/£15
ditto, Viking (U.S.), 1952 . . . . . . £15/£5

Others
Pack My Bag, Hogarth Press, 1940 . . . £250/£75
ditto, Macmillan (Toronto), 1940 . . . £100/£40
ditto, New Directions (U.S.), 1993 . . . . £10/£5
Surviving, The Uncollected Writings of Henry Green, Chatto & Windus [1992] . . . . . £20/£5
ditto, Viking (U.S.), 1993 . . . . . . £15/£5

KATE GREENAWAY

(b.1846 d.1901)

British author and illustrator whose first success, *Under the Window*, had a major influence on children's fashion of the time.

Aunt Louisa's Nursery Favourite, Warne, 1870 £250
Diamonds and Toads, Warne, [1871] £750
Puck and Blossom, by Rosa Mulholland, Marcus Ward, 1875 . . . . £200
Fairy Gifts, by K. Knox, 1875 . . . . . . £150
Seven Birthdays, 1876 . . . . £150
A Quiver of Love: A Collection of Valentines, Marcus Ward, 1876 . . . . £75
Under the Window, by Kate Greenaway, Routledge, [1879]. £100
The 'Little Folks' Painting Book, Cassell/Peter Galpin, [1879]. £250
Kate Greenaway's Birthday Book for Children, Routledge, [1880] £100
Topo, Marcus Ward, 1880 . . . . £50
Mother Goose, or The Old Nursery Rhymes, Routledge, [1881] £100
A Day in a Child's Life, Routledge, 1881 . . £100
Little Ann and Other Poems, by J. and A. Taylor, Routledge, [1883] £100
Language of Flowers, Routledge, [1884] . . £100
A Painting Book, Routledge, [1884] (wraps.) . £200
Songs for the Nursery, Routledge, 1884 . . £100
Marigold Garden, Routledge, [1885] . . . £100
Kate Greenaway's Album, Routledge, 1885 (8 copies) £6,000
Kate Greenaway's Alphabet, Routledge, [1885] (miniature book, card covers) £100
English Spelling Book, Routledge, 1885 . . £200
Dame Wiggins of Lee and Her Seven Wonderful Cats, George Allen, 1885 . . . . £50
A Apple Pie, Routledge, [1886] £100
Rhymes for the Young Folk, Cassell, 1886 . . £100
Queen Victoria's Jubilee Garland, Routledge, 1887 . . . . £150
Baby's Birthday Book, Marcus Ward, [1887] . £100
Pied Piper of Hamelin, by R. Browning, Routledge, [1888]. £100
The Royal progress of King Pepito, by Beatrice Cresswell, SPCK, [1889] £75
Kate Greenaway's Book of Games, Routledge, [1889] £175
The April Baby's Book of Tunes, by the author of 'Elizabeth and her German Garden', Routledge, 1900. . . . . £150
Littledom Castle and Other Tales, by Mabel H, Spielmann, Routledge, 1903 . . . . . £75

Almanacks
(assuming original envelope no longer present)
1883, Routledge, [1882] £125
1884, Routledge, [1883] £125
1885, Routledge, [1884] £125
1886, Routledge, [1885] £125
1887, Routledge, [1886] £100
1888, Routledge, [1887] £100
1889, Routledge, [1888] £150
1890, Routledge, [1889] £100
1891, Routledge, [1890] £100
1892, Routledge, [1891] £100
1893, Routledge, [1892] £100
1894, Routledge, [1893] £125
1895, Routledge, [1894] £125
1897, Routledge, [1896] (leather binding) . . £500

Calendars
Calendar of the Seasons, 1876/1877/1881/1882, Marcus Ward . . . . £75 each
A Calendar of the Months, Marcus Ward, 1884 £50
Kate Greenaway's Calendar, 1884/1897/1899, Routledge . . . . £100 each

---

GRAHAM GREENE

(b.1904 d.1991)

Popularly known for his novels, Greene is equally acclaimed as a short story writer, playwright, critic and essayist. From his first real success, *Stamboul Train*, to *Brighton Rock* and a host of well-known books, he appears preoccupied with the themes of guilt, pursuit and failure, much of which can be seen to stem from his conversion to Catholicism.

Novels
The Man Within, Heinemann, 1929 . . £1,500/£250
ditto, Doubleday (U.S.), 1929 . . . . . £350/£75
The Name of Action, Heinemann, 1930 . £1,250/£250
ditto, Doubleday (U.S.), 1931 . . . . . £350/£75
Rumour at Nightfall, Heinemann, 1931 . £3,000/£250
ditto, Doubleday (U.S.), 1932 . . . . . £350/£75
Stamboul Train, Heinemann, 1932 . . £1,750/£300
ditto, Doubleday (U.S.), 1933 . . . . . £400/£75
It's A Battlefield, Heinemann, 1934 . . £1,500/£100
ditto, Doubleday (U.S.), 1934 . . . . . £150/£45
England Made Me, Heinemann, 1935 . £1,500/£500
ditto, Doubleday (U.S.), 1935 . . . . £150/£35
This Gun For Hire, Doubleday (U.S.), 1936 £250/£75
ditto, as ***A Gun for Sale***, Heinemann, 1936 . . . . £2,000/£300
Brighton Rock, Viking (U.S.), 1938 . . . £450/£75
ditto, Heinemann, 1938 . . . . . . £5,000/£350

The Confidential Agent, Heinemann, 1939 . . . . £1,500/£200
ditto, Viking (U.S.), 1939 . . . . £300/£45
The Power and the Glory, Heinemann, 1940 . . . . £2,000/£750
ditto as ***The Labyrinthine Ways***, Viking (U.S.), 1940 (first state) . . . . £750/£450
ditto as ***The Labyrinthine Ways***, Viking (U.S.), 1940 (second state with pp. 165 and 256 in correct order) . . . . £150/£35
The Ministry of Fear, Heinemann, 1943 . £400/£45
ditto, Viking (U.S.), 1943 . . . . £150/£30
The Heart of the Matter, Heinemann, 1948 £100/£15
ditto, Viking (U.S.), 1948 . . . . . . £50/£10
The Third Man, Viking (U.S.), 1950 . . £175/£15
The Third Man and The Fallen Idol, Heinemann, 1950 . . . . £100/£15
ditto, Eurographica (Helsinki), 1988 (500 signed copies) . . . . £200/£150
The End of the Affair, Heinemann, 1951 . £75/£15
ditto, Viking (U.S.), 1951 . . . . . . £35/£10
Loser Takes All, Heinemann, 1955 . . . . £75/£15
ditto, Viking (U.S.), 1957 . . . . £35/£10
The Quiet American, Heinemann, 1955 . . £40/£10
ditto, Viking (U.S.), 1956 . . . . £30/£10
Our Man in Havana, Heinemann, 1958 . . £40/£10
ditto, Viking (U.S.), 1958 . . . . £30/£10
A Burnt Out Case, Heinemann, 1961 . . £25/£5
ditto, Viking (U.S.), 1961 . . . . . . £15/£5
The Comedians, Viking (U.S.), 1966 (500 advance copies, acetate d/w) . . . . . . £75/£50
ditto, Bodley Head, 1966 . . . . £20/£5
ditto, Viking (U.S.), 1966 . . . . £15/£5
Travels wlth My Aunt, Bodley Head, 1969 £15/£5
ditto, Viking (U.S.), 1970 . . . . £15/£5
The Honorary Consul, Bodley Head, 1973 £15/£5
ditto, Viking (U.S.), 1973 . . . . £15/£5
The Human Factor, Bodley Head, 1978 . £15/£5
ditto, Simon & Schuster (U.S.), 1978 . . . £15/£5
Dr Fischer of Geneva or The Bomb Party, Bodley Head, 1980 . . . . £15/£5
ditto, Simon & Schuster (U.S.), 1980 . . . £15/£5
ditto, Simon & Schuster (U.S.), 1980, (500 signed copies, slipcase) . . . . £150/£125
How Father Quixote Became a Monsignor, Sylvester & Orphanos (U.S.), 1980 (330 numbered copies, acetate d/w) . . . . £150/£125
Monsignor Quixote, Lester & Orpen Dennys (Canada), 1982 . . . . £15/£5
ditto, Bodley Head, 1982 . . . . £15/£5
ditto, Simon & Schuster (U.S.), 1982 . . . £10/£5
ditto, Simon & Schuster (U.S.), 1982, (250 signed copies in slipcase) . . . . £150/£125
The Tenth Man, Bodley Head, 1985 . . . £15/£5
ditto, Simon & Schuster (U.S.), 1985 . . £10/£5
The Captain and the Enemy, Reinhardt, 1988 £15/£5
ditto, Viking (U.S.), 1988 . . . . £10/£5

Short stories
The Bear Fell Free, Grayson, 1935 (285 signed copies) . . . . £750/£300
The Basement Room, Cresset Press, 1935 . £500/£150
Twenty Four Stories, Cresset Press, 1939 (with James Laver and Sylvia Townsend Warner) . . £75/£30
Nineteen Stories, Heinemann, 1947 . . . £150/£45
ditto, Viking (U.S.), 1949 . . . . . . £50/£10
ditto, as ***Twenty-One Stories***, Heinemann, 1954 (extra stories added) . . . . £35/£10
A Visit to Morin, Heinemann, [1959] (250 copies) . . . . £200/£100
A Sense of Reality, Bodley Head, 1963 . . £50/£15
ditto, Viking (U.S.), 1963 . . . . £35/£10
May We Borrow Your Husband?, Bodley Head, 1967 . . . . £20/£5
ditto, Bodley Head, 1967 (500 signed copies, glassine d/w) . . . . £150/£125
ditto, Viking (U.S.), 1967 . . . . £15/£5
The Collected Stories, Bodley Head/Heinemann, 1972 . . . . £20/£5
ditto, Viking (U.S.), 1973 . . . . £15/£5
Shades of Greene, Bodley Head/Heinemann, 1975 £15
The Last Word and Other Stories, Reinhardt, 1990 . . . . £10/£5

Plays
The Living Room, Heinemann, 1953 . . £45/£10
ditto, Viking (U.S.), 1954 . . . . £20/£5
The Potting Shed, Viking (U.S.), 1957 . . £50/£15
ditto, Heinemann, 1958 £25/£10
The Complaisant Lover, Heinemann, 1959 £50/£15
ditto, Viking (U.S.), 1961 . . . . £15/£5
Carving a Statue, Bodley Head, 1964 £45/£15
The Return of A.J. Raffles, Bodley Head, 1975 (wraps) £10
ditto, Bodley Head, 1975 (250 signed copies) . . . . £250/£100
ditto, Simon & Schuster (U.S.), 1978 . . £15/£5
The Great Jowett, Bodley Head, 1981 (525 signed copies, glassine d/w) . . . . £150/£125
Yes & No and For Whom the Bell Chimes, Bodley Head, 1983 (775 signed copies, glassine d/w) . . . . £100/£80
Yes & No - A Play in One Act, Eurographica (Helsinki), 1984 (350 signed copies, wraps) . £100

Travel
Journey Without Maps, Heinemann, 1936 . . . . £4,000/£1,000
ditto, Doubleday (U.S.), 1936 . . . . . £175/£45
The Lawless Roads, Longman, 1939 . £1,000/£250

ditto, as ***Another Mexico***, Viking (U.S.), 1939 . . . . £250/£50

Children's

The Little Train, Eyre & Spottiswoode, 1946 (anonymous) . . . . £450/£100
ditto, Lothrop (U.S.), 1958 . . . . . £250/£50
The Little Fire Engine, Parrish, 1950 . . £250/£45
ditto, as ***The Little Red Fire Engine***, Lothrop (U.S.), 1952. . . . . £100/£35
The Little Horse Bus, Parrish, 1952 . . . £200/£45
ditto, Lothrop (U.S.), 1954 . . . . . £75/£25
The Little Steam Roller, Parrish, 1953 . . £200/£45
ditto, Lothrop (U.S.), 1955 . . . . . £75/£25

Others

Babbling April, Blackwell, 1925. . . . £1,500/£750
To Beg I am Ashamed, Vanguard Press (U.S.), 1938 (pseud. 'Sheila Cousins', with Ronald Matthews) . . . . £200/£25
Men At Work, Penguin New Writing, 1941 . . £20
British Dramatists, Collins, 1942 . . . . £40/£10
Why Do I Write?: An Exchange of Views Between Elizabeth Bowen, Graham Greene, and V.S. Pritchett, Marshall, 1948 . . . . . £25/£10
The Lost Childhood, Eyre & Spottiswoode, 1951 . . . . £40/£15
ditto, Viking (U.S.), 1952. . . . . . £20/£5
In Search of a Character: Two African Journals, Bodley Head, 1961 . . . . £20/£5
ditto, Viking (U.S.), 1961. . . . . . . £20/£5
Introductions to Three Novels, Norstedt (Stockholm), 1962 (wraps) £40
The Revenge, An Autobiographical Fragment, The Stellar Press, 1963 (300 copies, wraps) . . . £150
Victorian Detective Fiction, A Catalogue of the Collection made by Dorothy Glover and Graham Greene, Bodley Head, 1966 (500 signed copies) . . . . £250/£150
Collected Essays, Bodley Head, 1969 . . £20/£5
ditto, Viking (U.S.), 1969. . . . . . . £15/£5
Mr Visconti, Bodley Head, 1969 (300 copies, wraps) £200
The Virtue of Disloyalty, Bodley Head, 1969 (300 copies, wraps) £200
A Sort of Life, Bodley Head, 1971 . . . £10/£5
ditto, Simon & Schuster (U.S.), 1971 . . £10/£5
The Pleasure Dome: The Collected Film Criticism, 1935-1940, Secker & Warburg, 1972 . . £15/£5
ditto, Simon & Schuster (U.S.), 1972 . . £10/£5
Lord Rochester's Monkey, Bodley Head, 1974 £15/£5
ditto, Viking (U.S.), 1974. . . . . . . £10/£5
An Impossible Woman, The Memories of Dottoressa Moor of Capri, Bodley Head, 1975 . . £20/£5
Ways of Escape, Lester & Orpen Dennys (Canada), 1980 . . . . £25/£5
ditto, Lester & Orpen Dennys (Canada), 1980 (150 signed copies, slipcase) . . . . £250/£225
ditto, Bodley Head, 1980 . . . . £10/£5
ditto, Simon & Schuster (U.S.), 1980 . . . £10/£5
J'Accuse: The Darker Side of Nice, *ditto*, Lester & Orpen Dennys (Toronto), 1982 (wraps and d/w) . . . . £25/£15
ditto, Bodley Head, 1982 (wraps and d/w) . £25/£15
The Other Man: Conversations with Graham Greene, Bodley Head, 1983 . . . . £20/£5
ditto, Simon & Schuster (U.S.), 1983 . . . £20/£5
A Quick Look Behind, Sylvester & Orphanos, 1983 (330 copies, slipcase) . . . . . . £75/£50
Getting to Know The General, Bodley Head, 1984 . . . . £15/£5
ditto, Simon & Schuster (U.S.), 1984 . . . £10/£5
The Monster of Capri, Eurographica (Helsinki), 1985 (500 signed copies) . . . . . . £175/£125
Why the Epigraph?, Nonesuch, 1989 (950 signed copies, glassine dw) . . . . . . £150/£125
Dear David, Dear Graham, A Bibliophilic Correspondence, The Alembic Press, 1989 (50 of 250 copies, slipcase) . . . . £125/£100
ditto, The Alembic Press, 1989 (200 of 250 copies) £75
Yours, etc: Letters to the Press, Reinhardt, 1989 . . . . £10/£5
ditto, Viking (U.S.), 1990. . . . . . . £10/£5
Reflections on Travels with My Aunt, Firsts & Co., 1989 (250 signed copies, wraps) £150
Reflections 1923-1988, Reinhardt, 1990 . £10/£5
ditto, Viking (U.S.), 1990. . . . . . . £10/£5
A World of My Own, Reinhardt, 1992 . . £10/£5
ditto, Viking (U.S.), 1994. . . . . . . £10/£5

THOM GUNN

(b.1929)

While not commanding the respect he once did, Gunn remains a well-regarded post-war poet.

Verse

Poetry from Cambridge, 1951-1952, Fortune Press, 1952 . . . . £45
The Fantasy Poets No. 16, Fantasy Press, 1953 (approx 300 copies, wraps) £250
Fighting Terms, Fantasy Press, 1954 (approx 300 copies) £300
ditto, Hawks Well Press (U.S.), 1958 (1,500 copies, wraps). £35
ditto, Faber, 1966 . . . . £20/£5
Poetry from Cambridge, 1952-1954, Fantasy Press, 1955 (wraps) £125

The Sense of Movement, Faber, 1957 . . £35/£10
ditto, University of Chicago Press (U.S.), 1959 £35/£10
My Sad Captains, Faber, 1961 . . . . £40/£10
ditto, University of Chicago Press (U.S.), 1961 £15
Selected Poems, Faber 1962 (with Ted Hughes) £15/£5
A Geography, Stone Wall Press (U.S.), 1966 (220 copies, wraps) £35
Positives, Faber 1966 . . . . £20/£5
ditto, University of Chicago Press (U.S.), 1967 £20/£5
Touch, Faber, [1967] . . . . . . £20/£5
ditto, University of Chicago Press (U.S.), 1968 £15/£5
The Garden of the Gods, Pym-Randall Press (U.S.), [1968] (200 of 226, signed copies, wraps) . . £35
ditto, Pym-Randall Press (U.S.), [1968] (26 lettered copies of 226, wraps) £150
The Explorers, Gilbertson (U.S.), 1969 (6 copies) £300
ditto, Gilbertson (U.S.), 1969 (deluxe issue of 10 copies) £200
ditto, Gilbertson (U.S.), 1969 (special issue of 20 copies) £150
ditto, Gilbertson (U.S.), 1969 (ordinary issue of 64 copies) £75
The Fair in the Woods, Sycamore Press, 1969 (broadsheet, 500 copies). £10
Poems 1950-1966: A Selection, Faber 1969 (wraps) £10
Sunlight, Albondocani Press (U.S.), 1969 (150 numbered copies) £35
Moly, Faber, 1971 . . . . £25/£10
ditto, Farrar Straus (U.S.), 1973 . . . . £10/£5
Last Days at Teddington, John Roberts Press, 1971 (broadsheet, 1,000 copies) £10
Poem After Chaucer, Albondocani Press (U.S.), 1971 (320 copies) £35
The Spell, Steane, 1973 (broadsheet, 500 copies) £10
Songbook, Albondocani Press (U.S.), 1973 (230 copies, wraps) £35
To the Air, Godine, 1974 . . . . £20
Mandrakes, The Rainbow Press, [1974] (150 signed copies, slipcase) . . . . £200/£175
Jack Straw's Castle, Hallman, 1975 (300 copies, wraps). £15
ditto, Hallman, 1976 (100 signed hardback copies) £45
ditto, as ***Jack Straw's Castle and Other Poems***, Faber 1976 (750 hardback copies). . . . . £20/£5
ditto, Faber 1976 (100 numbered, signed hardback copies) . . . . £45/£25
ditto, Faber 1976 (4,000 wraps copies) £5
ditto, Farrar Straus (U.S.), 1976 . . . . . £15/£5
The Missed Beat, Janus Press (U.S.), 1976 (50 copies, slipcase) . . . . £150/£125
ditto, Gruffyground Press, 1976 (approx 70 copies, wraps) £25
A Crab, The Pirates, 1978 . . . . £20
Games of Chance, Abattoir, 1979 (220 copies) £25
Selected Poems 1950-1975, Faber, 1979 . £10/£5
ditto, Farrar Straus (U.S.), 1979 . . . . £10/£5
Talbot Road, Helikon Press, 1981 (150 signed, numbered copies, wraps) £25
The Passages of Joy, Faber, 1982 . . . £10/£5
ditto, Farrar Straus Giroux (U.S.), 1982 . . £10/£5
Sidewalks, Albondocani Press (U.S.), 1985 (200 signed copies, wraps) £45
Lament, Doe Press (U.S.), 1985 (150 signed copies, wraps). £25
The Hurtless Trees, privately printed, 1986 (signed, wraps and d/w) £50
Night Sweats, Barth (U.S.), 1987 (200 signed, numbered copies, wraps) £50
ditto, Barth (U.S.), 1987 (wraps) £20
ditto, as ***The Man with Night Sweats***, Faber, 1992 . . . . £15/£5
ditto, Farrar Straus Giroux (U.S.), 1992 . . £15/£5
Undesirables, Pig Press, 1988 . . . . . £10
At the Barriers, NADJA, 1989 . . . . . £10
Death's Door, Red Hydra Press, 1989 (20 signed, quarter morocco copies) £200
ditto, Red Hydra Press, 1989 (60 signed copies) £100

H. RIDER HAGGARD

(b.1856 d.1925)

A successful British writer of heroic adventure novels, Haggard's strengths are his story-telling abilities and the authentic background to his books.

Novels

Dawn, Hurst & Blackett, 1884 (3 vols) . . . £3,000
ditto, Lovell (U.S.), 1887 . . . . £150
The Witch's Head, Hurst & Blackett, 1885 [1884] (3 vols) £5,000
ditto, Appleton (U.S.), 1885 . . . . . . £150
King Solomon's Mines, Cassell, 1885 . . . £1,000
ditto, Cassell (U.S.), 1885. . . . . . £1,5000
She, Harper (U.S.), 1886 (wraps) £200
ditto, Longmans, 1887. . . . . £175
Jess, Smith, Elder, & Co., 1887 . . . . . £200
ditto, Harper (U.S.), 1887. . . . . . . £95
Allan Quartermain, Longmans, 1887 . . . £450
ditto, Longmans, 1887 (112 large paper copies) £1,500
Maiwa's Revenge, Longmans, 1888 . . . . £45
ditto, Harper (U.S.), 1888. . . . . . . £45
Mr Meeson's Will, Spencer Blackett, 1888 . . £45
ditto, Harper (U.S.), 1888. . . . . . . £45
Colonel Quaritch V.C., Longmans, 1888 (3 vols) £400
Cleopatra, Longmans, 1889 . . . . . . £35
ditto, Longmans, 1889 (50 large paper copies) £2,000
ditto, Harper (U.S.), 1889 (wraps) £175

Allan's Wife, Spencer Blackett, 1889 . . . £200
ditto, Longmans, 1889 (100 large paper copies) £2,000
Beatrice, Longman's, 1890 . . . . £30
The World's Desire, Longmans, 1890 (with Andrew Lang) £30
ditto, Harper (U.S.), 1890. . . . . £30
Eric Brighteyes, Longmans, 1891 . . . . £35
ditto, Harper (U.S.), 1891. . . . . £30
Nada the Lily, Longmans, 1892 . . . . . £35
ditto, Longmans(U.S.), 1892 . . . . £30
Montezuma's Daughter, Longmans (U.S.), 1893 £35
ditto, Longmans, 1893. . . . . £30
The People of the Mist, Longmans, 1894 . . £65
ditto, Longmans (U.S.), 1894. . . . . . . £35
Joan Haste, Longmans, 1895 . . . . . . £65
ditto, Longmans (U.S.), 1895. . . . . . . £35
Heart of the World, Longmans (U.S.), 1895 . £65
ditto, Longmans, 1896. . . . . £35
The Wizard, Arrowsmith, 1896 (wraps) . . . £55
ditto, Longmans (U.S.), 1896 . . . . . . £45
Doctor Therne, Longmans, 1898. . . . . . £45
ditto, Longmans (U.S.), 1898 . . . . . . £75
Allan the Hunter, Lothrop (U.S.), 1898. . . £100
Swallow, Longmans, 1899 . . . . £45
Black Heart and White Heart, Longmans, 1900 £100
ditto, as ***Elissa***, Longmans (U.S.), 1900. . . £75
Lysbeth, Longmans, 1901. . . . . £45
ditto, Longmans (U.S.), 1901 . . . . . . £45
Pearl-Maiden, Longmans, 1903 . . . . . £35
ditto, Longmans (U.S.), 1903 . . . . . . £35
Stella Fregelius, Longmans (U.S.), 1903 . . £35
ditto, Longmans, 1904. . . . . £35
The Brethren, Cassell, 1904 . . . . . . £35
ditto, McClure, Phillips (U.S.), 1904 . . . £35
Ayesha, Ward Lock, 1905 . . . . £55
ditto, Doubleday. (U.S.), 1905 . . . . . . £35
The Way of the Spirit, Hutchinson, 1906 . . £35
Benita, Cassell, 1906 . . . . £35
ditto, as ***The Spirit of Bambatse***, Longmans (U.S.), 1906 . . . . £35
Fair Margaret, Hutchinson, 1907 . . . . £35
ditto, as ***Margaret***, Longmans (U.S.), 1907 . . £35
The Ghost Kings, Cassell, 1908 . . . . . £35
ditto, as ***The Lady of the Heavens***, Lovell (U.S.), 1908 . . . . £35
The Yellow God, Cupples and Leon (U.S.), 1908 £35
ditto, Cassell, 1909 . . . . £35
The Lady of Blossholme, Hodder & Stoughton, 1909 . . . . £45
Morning Star, Cassell, 1910 . . . . £35
ditto, Longmans (U.S.), 1910. . . . . . . £25
Queen Sheba's Ring, Eveleigh Nash, 1910 . . £35
Red Eve, Hodder & Stoughton, 1911 . . . £35
The Mahatma and The Hare, Longmans, 1911 £55
Marie, Cassell, 1912 . . . . £25
Child of Storm, Cassell, 1913 . . . . . . £25
ditto, Longmans (U.S.), 1913. . . . . . . £25
The Wanderer's Necklace, Cassell, 1914 . . £45
ditto, Longmans (U.S.), 1914. . . . . . . £25
The Holy Flower, Ward Lock, 1915. . . . . £25
ditto, as Allan and ***The Holy Flower***, Longmans (U.S.), 1915 . . . . £25
The Ivory Child, Cassell, 1916 . . . . . . £35
ditto, Longmans (U.S.), 1916. . . . . . . £25
Finished, Ward Lock, 1917 . . . . £35
Love Eternal, Cassell, 1918 . . . . £25
Moon of Israel, Murray, 1918 . . . . . . £45
When the World Shook, Cassell, 1919 . . . £35
ditto, Longmans (U.S.), 1919. . . . . . . £25
The Ancient Allan, Cassell, 1920 . . . £250/£35
ditto, Longmans (U.S.), 1920. . . . . £250/£35
Smith and the Pharaohs, Arrowsmith, 1920 £300/£75
ditto, Longmans (U.S.), 1920. . . . . £250/£35
She and Allan, Longmans (U.S.), 1921 . . £125/£45
ditto, Hutchinson, 1921 . . . . £275/£65
The Virgin of the Sun, Cassell, 1922 . . £100/£35
ditto, Doubleday (U.S.), 1922 . . . . £100/£25
Wisdom's Daughter, Hutchinson, 1923 . . £200/£35
ditto, Doubleday (U.S.), 1923 . . . . £200/£35
Heu-Heu, Hutchinson, 1924 . . . . . £100/£45
Queen of the Dawn, Doubleday Page (U.S.) 1925 . . . . £125/£25
ditto, Hutchinson, 1925 . . . . £125/£35
The Treasure of the Lake, Hutchinson, 1926 £150/£45
ditto, Doubleday (U.S.), 1926 . . . . £125/£25
Allan and the Ice Gods, Doubleday Page (U.S.) 1927 . . . . £125/£25
ditto, Hutchinson, 1927 . . . . £150/£45
Mary of Marion Isle, Hutchinson, 1929. . £150/£45
ditto, as ***Marion Isle***, Doubleday (U.S.), 1929 £100/£25
Belshazzar, Stanley Paul, 1930 . . . . £175/£55
ditto, Doubleday (U.S.), 1930 . . . . £100/£25

Non Fiction

Cetywayo and His White Neighbours, Trubner, 1882 . . . . £450
A Farmer's Year, Longmans, 1899 . . . . £100
The Last Boer War, Kegan Paul, 1899 . . . £50
ditto, as ***A History of The Transvaal***, New Amsterdam Book Co. (U.S.), 1899 . . . . £75
A Winter Pilgrimage, Longmans, 1901 . . . £50
Rural England, Longmans, 1902 (2 vols) . . £60
A Gardener's Year, Longmans, 1905 . . . £60
The Poor and the Land, Longmans, 1905 . . £60
Regeneration, Longmans, 1910 . . . . . . £20
Rural Denmark, Longmans, 1911 . . . . . £50
The Days of My Life, Longmans, 1926 (2 vols) £150
The Private Diaries of Sir H. Rider Haggard 1914-1925, Stein & Day (U.S.), 1980. . . . £10/£5

Miscellaneous

An Heroic Effort, 1893 . . . . £35
Church and State, 1895 . . . . £30
East Norfolk Representation, 1895 . . . . . £30
Lord Kimberly in Norfolk, 1895 . . . . . . £30
Speeches of the Earl of Iddesleigh, NSPCC, 1895 £30
A Visit to Victoria Hospital, 1897 . . . . £30
Rural England, Royal Institution of Great Britain, 1903 . . . . £30
The Real Wealth of England, Dr Barnados, 1908 £25
The Royal Commission on Coast Erosion, HMSO, 1907-1911 (3 vols) £45
Letters to the Right Honorable Lewis Harcourt, HMSO, 1913-1914 (2 vols) £45
A Call to Arms, 1914 . . . . £25
The After-War Settlement and Employment of Ex-Servicemen, Saint Catherine Press, 1916 . . . £30
The Salvation Army, 1920 . . . . £25
A Note on Religion, Longmans, 1927 (wraps) . . £25

RADCLYFFE HALL

(b.1880 d.1943)

Hall's notoriety stems from the publication in 1928, and subsequent suppression in Britain for obscenity, of *The Well of Loneliness*. The book, a sympathetic study of lesbian love, was not republished in Britain until 1949.

Novels

The Forge, Arrowsmith, 1924 . . . . . £175/£50
The Unlit Lamp, Cassell, 1924 . . . . . £175/£50
ditto, Cape And Smith (U.S.), [1929] . . . £100/£25
A Saturday Life, Arrowsmith, 1925 . . . £100/£30
ditto, Cape And Smith (U.S.), [1930] . . . £75/£20
Adam's Breed, Cassell, 1926 . . . . . £100/£30
ditto, Cape And Smith (U.S.), [1929] . . . £45/£10
The Well of Loneliness, Cape, 1928 . . . £125/£25
ditto, Pegasus Press (Paris), 1928 . . . £125/£40
ditto, Covici-Friede, 1928 (glassine d/w, slipcase) . . . . £125/£100
ditto, Covici-Friede, 1929 (225 signed copies, 2 vols, slipcase) £250
The Master of the House, Cape, 1932 . . . £50/£15
ditto, Cape, 1932 (172 signed, numbered copies, slipcase) . . . . £200/£145
ditto, Cape And Ballou (U.S.), 1932 . . . . £45/£10
The Sixth Beatitude, Heinemann, 1936 . . . £45/£10
ditto, Heinemann, 1936 (125 signed, numbered copies, slipcase) . . . . £175/£135

Short Stories

Mrs Ogilvy Finds Herself, Heinemann, 1934 £75/£20

Verse

Twixt Earth and Stars, Bumpus, 1906 . . . . £150
A Sheaf of Verses, Bumpus, 1908 . . . . . £125
Poems of Past and Present, Chapman & Hall, 1910 . . . . £75
Songs of Three Counties, Chapman & Hall, 1913 £60
The Forgotten Island, Chapman & Hall, 1915 £60

Others

Your John: Letters of Radclyffe Hall, New York University (U.S.), 1997 . . . . £10/£5

PATRICK HAMILTON

(b.1904 d.1962)

Born in Sussex, Hamilton was a typically English writer, relishing the art of understatement.

Novels

Monday Morning, Constable, 1925 . . . £200/£45
ditto, Houghton Mifflin (U.S.), 1925. . . £75/£20
Craven House, Constable, 1926 . . . . £150/£35
ditto, Houghton Mifflin (U.S.), 1927. . . £75/£20
ditto, Constable, 1943 (revised edition) . . £75/£20
Twopence Coloured, Constable, 1928 . . £125/£35
ditto, Houghton Mifflin (U.S.), 1928. . . £75/£20
The Midnight Bell: A Love Story, Constable, 1929 . . . . £100/£25
ditto, Little, Brown (U.S.), 1930 . . . . £75/£20
The Siege of Pleasure, Constable, 1932 . £100/£25
ditto, Little, Brown (U.S.), 1932 . . . . £75/£20
The Plains of Cement, Constable, 1934 . . £100/£25
ditto, Little, Brown (U.S.), 1935 . . . . £75/£20
Twenty Thousand Streets Under The Sky: A London Trilogy, Constable, 1935 . . . . . £50/£20
Impromptu in Moribundia, Constable, 1939 £200/£65
Hangover Square, or The Man with Two Minds: A Story of Darkest Earls Court, Constable, 1941 . . . . £75/£15
ditto, Random House (U.S.), 1942 . . . £65/£15
The Slaves of Solitude, Constable, 1947 . £45/£15
ditto, as ***Riverside***, Random House (U.S.), 1947 . . . . £45/£15
The West Pier, Constable, 1951 . . . . £45/£15
ditto, Doubleday (U.S.), 1952 . . . . £45/£15
Mr Stimpson and Mr Gorse, Constable, 1953 £45/£15
Unknown Assailant, Constable, 1955 . . £45/£15

Plays

Rope: A Play, with a Preface on Thrillers, Constable, 1929 . . . . £50/£20
Gaslight: A Victorian Thriller, Constable, 1939 (wraps) £10

Money With Menaces and To The Public Danger: Two Radio Plays, Constable, 1939 . . . £30/£10
This Is Impossible, French, 1942 (wraps) . . £10
The Duke in Darkness, Constable, 1943 . £30/£10
The Man Upstairs, Constable, 1954 . . . £25/£10

DASHIELL HAMMETT

(b.1894 d.1961)

American creator of tough detective fiction, his best known centring around the 'private eye' Sam Spade.

Novels

Red Harvest, Knopf (U.S.), 1929 . . £5,000/£750
ditto, Knopf /Cassell, 1929 . . . . . £2,000/£350
The Dain Curse, Knopf (U.S.), 1929 £1,250/£250
ditto, Knopf /Cassell, 1929 . . . . . £500/£100
The Maltese Falcon, Knopf (U.S.), 1930 £7,000/£750
ditto, Knopf /Cassell 1930 . . . . £1,250/£250
The Glass Key, Knopf /Cassell, 1931 £1,500/£250
ditto, Knopf (U.S.), 1931 . . . . . £1,500/£250
The Thin Man, Knopf (U.S.), 1934 . . £1,500/£175
ditto, Barker 1934 . . . . £500/£100
$106,000 Blood Money, Spivak (U.S.), 1943 (wraps) £150
ditto, as ***Blood Money***, World (U.S.), 1943 . £30/£10
ditto, as ***The Big Knock-over***, Spivak (U.S.), 1948 (wraps) £35

Short Stories

The Adventures of Sam Spade, Spivak (U.S.), 1944 (wraps) £200
ditto, as ***They Can Only Hang You Once***, Spivak (U.S.), 1949 (wraps) £75
The Continental OP, Spivak (U.S.), 1945 (wraps) £75
The Return of the Continental Op, Spivak (U.S.), 1945 (wraps) £50
Hammett Homicides, Spivak (U.S.), 1946 (wraps) £50
Dead Yellow Women, Spivak (U.S.), 1947 (wraps) £50
Nightmare Town, Spivak (U.S.), 1948 (wraps) £50
The Creeping Siamese, Spivak (U.S.), 1950 (wraps) £35
Women in the Dark, Spivak (U.S.), 1951 (wraps) £35
A Man Named Thin and Other Stories, Ferman (U.S.), 1952 . . . . £35
The Big Knockover: Selected Stories and Short Novels, Random House (U.S.), 1966 . . £10/£5
ditto, as ***The Hammett Story Omnibus***, Cassell, 1966 . . . . £10/£5

THOMAS HARDY

(b.1840 d.1928)

Acknowledged as one of the great novelists, Hardy was also a prolific poet. Much of his writing is set in his native Dorset, fictionalised as Wessex.

Novels

Desperate Remedies, Tinsley Bros., 1871, (3 vols, anon.) £5,000
ditto, Holt (U.S.), 1874, (1 vol.) £200
ditto, Ward & Downey, 1889, (1 vol.) . . . £100
Under the Greenwood Tree, Tinsley Bros., 1872, (2 vols) £5,000
ditto, Tinsley Bros., 1873, (1 vol.) . . £1,000
ditto, Holt (U.S.), 1874, (1 vol.) £200
A Pair of Blue Eyes, Tinsley Bros., 1873 (3 vols) £2,000
ditto, Holt (U.S.), 1873, (1 vol.) £200
ditto, Henry S. King, 1877 (1 vol.) £200
Far from the Madding Crowd, Smith, Elder, 1874 (2 vols) £2,000
ditto, Holt (U.S.), 1874, (1 vol.) £150
ditto, Smith, Elder, 1875 (2 vols) . . . £1,000
ditto, Smith, Elder, 1877 (1 vol.) £200
The Hand of Ethelberta, Smith, Elder, 1876, (2 vols, 11 illustrations by George du Marier) . . £2,000
ditto, Holt (U.S.), 1876, (1 vol.) £150
ditto, Smith, Elder, 1877, (1 vol., 6 illustrations by George du Maurier) £200
The Return of the Native, Smith, Elder, 1878, (3 vols) £2,000
ditto, Holt (U.S.), 1878, (1 vol.) £150
ditto, Kegan Paul, 1880 [1879], (1 vol.) . . . £200
The Trumpet-Major, Smith, Elder, 1880 (3 vols) £2,000
ditto, Holt (U.S.), 1880, (1 vol.) £150
ditto, Samson Low, 1881 (1 vol.) £200
Fellow-Townsmen, Harper (U.S.), 1880 (cloth) £750
ditto, Harper (U.S.), 1880 (wraps) £450
A Laodicean, Holt (U.S.), 1881, (1 vol.) . . £250
ditto, Samson Low, 1881 (3 vols) . . £1,500
ditto, Samson Low, 1882 (1 vol.). £150
Two on a Tower, Samson Low, 1882 (3 vols) £2,000
ditto, Holt (U.S.), 1882, (1 vol.) £150
ditto, Samson Low, 1883, (3 vols) . . . £1,000
ditto, Samson Low, 1883, (1 vol.) £150
The Romantic Adventures of a Milkmaid, Munro's (U.S.), 1883 (wraps) £600
The Mayor of Casterbridge, Smith Elder, 1886, (2 vols) £3,000
ditto, Holt (U.S.), 1886, (1 vol.) £200
ditto, Samson Low, 1887, (1 vol.) £200
The Woodlanders, Macmillan, 1887, (3 vols) £1,000
ditto, Harper (U.S.), 1887, (1 vol.) £150

ditto, Macmillan, 1887, (1 vol.) £75
Tess of the D'Urbervilles, Osgood McIlvaine, 1891, (3 vols) £3,000
ditto, Harper (U.S.), 1892, (1 vol.) £200
ditto, Osgood McIlvaine, 1892, (3 vols) . . . £750
ditto, Osgood McIlvaine, 1892, ('fifth' [third] edition, 1 vol.) £100
Jude the Obscure, Osgood McIlvaine, 1896 [1895], (1 vol.) £200
ditto, Harper (U.S.), 1896, (1 vol.) £100
The Well-Beloved, Osgood McIlvaine, 1897, (1 vol.) £100
ditto, Harper (U.S.), 1897, (1 vol.) £100
Our Exploits at West Poley, O.U.P., 1952 £150/£60

Short Stories
Wessex Tales, Macmillan, 1888, (2 vols) . £1,250
ditto, Macmillan, 1889, (1 vol.) £75
ditto, Osgood McIlvaine, 1896, (1 vol.) £45
A Group of Noble Dames, Osgood McIlvaine, 1891 . . . . £150
ditto, Harper (U.S.), 1891. . . . . £75
Life's Little Ironies, Osgood McIlvaine, 1894 £125
ditto, Macmillan (U.S.), 1894. . . . . £75
A Changed Man and Other Tales, Macmillan, 1913 . . . . £50
ditto, Harper (U.S.), 1913. . . . . £75
Old Mrs Chundle, Crosby Gaige (U.S.), 1929 (755 numbered copies) £75

Collection Editions
Wessex Novels Edition, Osgood McIlvaine, 1895-97, (17 vols) . . . . £2,000 the set, £50-£75 each
The Writings, Autograph Edition, Harper & Bros, [1911] (153 signed copies, 20 vols) £2,500 the set
Wessex Edition, Macmillan, 1912-31, (24 vols; maroon cloth) . . . . £1,500 the set, £30 each
Melstock Edition, Macmillan, 1919-20, (37 vols, limited to 500 sets, signed by the author) £4,000 set

Magazine Serialisations
A Pair of Blue Eyes, Tinsley's Magazine, Sept 1872-July 1873 . . . . £200 (for set)
Far From the Madding Crowd, Cornhill Magazine, Jan-Sept 1874 . . . . £200 (for set)
The Hand of Ethelberta, Cornhill Magazine, July 1875-May, 1876 . . . . £200 (for set)
The Return of the Native, Belgravia, Jan-December 1878 . . . . £200 (for set)
The Trumpet Major, Good Words, Jan-December 1880 . . . . £200 (for set)
A Laodicean, Harper's, December 1880-December 1881 . . . . £200 (for set)
Two on a Tower, Atlantic Monthly, May-December 1882 . . . . £200 (for set)
The Mayor of Casterbridge, Graphic, June 1885-May 1886 . . . . £250 (for set)
The Woodlanders, Macmillan's Magazine, May 1886-April 1887 . . . . £200 (for set)
Tess of the D'Urbervilles, Graphic, July-December 1891 . . . . £250 (for set)
Jude the Obscure, Harper's, December 1894-November 1895 (first instalment as 'The Simpleton', the 'Hearts Insurgent') . . . . . . £200 (for set)
The Well-Beloved, as ***The Pursuit of the Well-Beloved,*** Illustrated London News, October-December 1892 . . . . £200 (for set)

Verse
Wessex Poems and Other Verses, Harper (U.S. & U.K.), 1898 . . . . £500
ditto, Harper (U.S. & U.K.), 18982 (presentation binding) £1,250
Poems Of The Past And The Present, Harper (U.S. & U.K.), 1902 . . . . £500
ditto, Harper (U.S. & U.K.), 1902 (presentation binding) £1,250
The Dynasts, Macmillan, 1904, 1906 [1905], 1908 . . . . £500
ditto, Macmillan, 1910 (1 vol.) £100
ditto, Macmillan, 1927 (525 signed large paper copies, 3 vols, tissue d/w, slipcase) . . . . £500/£400
Time's Laughingstocks and Other Verses, Macmillan, 1909 . . . . £150
Song of the Soldiers, privately printed by Clement Shorter, 1914 (single sheet, 12 copies) . . . £750
ditto, privately printed at Hove by E. Williams, 1914 (single sheet) £100
The Oxen, privately printed at Hove by E. Williams, 1915 (wraps) £150
Selected Poems, Macmillan, 1916 . . . . . £150
ditto, Warner, 1921 . . . . £100
Moments of Vision and Miscellaneous Verses, Macmillan, 1917. . . . . £100
Collected Poems, Macmillan, 1919 . . . . . £125
Late Lyrics and Earlier with Many Other Verses, Macmillan, 1922 . . . . £125/£50
The Famous Tragedy of the Queen of Cornwall, Macmillan, 1923 . . . . £200/£75
ditto, Macmillan, 1923 (1,000 numberd copies, no d/w) £75
Human Shows. Far Phantasies. Songs, and Trifles, Macmillan, 1925 . . . . £150/£65
ditto, Macmillan (U.S.), 1925 (100 numbered copies, no d/w) £150
ditto, Macmillan (U.S.), 1925. . . . . . £100/£45
Yuletide in a Younger World, Faber, 1927 (wraps) £250
ditto, Rudge (U.S.), 1927 (27 copyright copies, wraps) £400

Winter Words In Various Moods and Metres, Macmillan, 1928 . . . . £75/£35
ditto, Macmillan (U.S.), 1928 (500 copies, slipcase) . . . . £150/£125

THOMAS HARRIS

(b.1940)

Famous since the release of the film of *The Silence of the Lambs*, aficionados also recommend that *Red Dragon* should not be overlooked.

Novels

Black Sunday, Putnam (U.S.), 1975 . . . . £25/£5
ditto, Hodder & Stoughton, 1975. . . . . £20/£5
Red Dragon, Putnam (U.S.), 1981 . . . . £20/£5
ditto, Bodley Head, 1982 . . . . £15/£5
The Silence of the Lambs, St Martin's Press (U.S.), 1988 . . . . £30/£5
ditto, Heinemann, 1988 . . . . £25/£5

L.P. HARTLEY

(b.1895 d.1972)

Novelist and short story writer, Leslie Poles Hartley's work won a number of awards, but he is best known for *The Go-Between*, an evocative portrayal of a small boy's view of Edwardian England, which won the Heinemann Foundation Award.

Short Stories

Night Fears and Other Stories, Putnam, 1924 . . . . £200/£50
The Killing Bottle, Putnam, 1931 . . . . £100/£35
The Travelling Grave, Arkham House (U.S.), 1948 . . . . £65/£20
ditto, Barrie, 1951 . . . . £75/£25
A White Wand and Other Stories, Hamilton, 1954. . . . . £25/£5
Two for the River, Hamilton, 1961 . . . . £20/£5
The Collected Stories, Hamilton, 1968 . . £10/£5
ditto, Horizon Press (U.S.), 1969. . . . . £10/£5
Mrs Carteret Receives, Hamilton, 1971 . . £10/£5

Novels

Simonetta Perkins, Putnam, 1925 . . . . £125/£40
ditto, Putnam (U.S.), 1925 . . . . . . £75/£20
The Shrimp and the Anemone, Putnam, 1944 £75/£20
ditto, as ***The West Window***, Putnam (U.S.), 1945 . . . . £40/£10
The Sixth Heaven, Putnam, 1946 . . . . £25/£5
ditto, Doubleday (U.S.), 1947 . . . . . £15/£5
Eustace and Hilda, Putnam, 1947 . . . . £20/£5
ditto, British Book Centre (U.S.), 1958 . . £15/£5
The Boat, Putnam, 1950 . . . . £20/£5
ditto, Doubleday (U.S.), 1950 . . . . . £10/£5
My Fellow Devils, Barrie, 1951 . . . . . £15/£5
ditto, British Book Centre (U.S.), 1959 . . £15/£5
The Go-Between, Hamilton, 1953 . . . . £30/£10
ditto, Knopf (U.S.), 1954 . . . . £20/£5
A Perfect Woman, Hamilton, 1955 . . . . £10/£5
ditto, Knopf (U.S.), 1956 . . . . £10/£5
The Hireling, Hamilton, 1957 . . . . . £10/£5
ditto, Rinehart (U.S.), 1958 . . . . . . £10/£5
Facial Justice, Hamilton, 1960 . . . . . £10/£5
ditto, Doubleday (U.S.), 1961 . . . . . £10/£5
The Brickfield, Hamilton, 1964 . . . . . £10/£5
The Betrayal, Hamilton, 1966 . . . . . £10/£5
Poor Clare, Hamilton, 1968 . . . . . . £10/£5
The Love-Adept, Hamilton, 1969 . . . . £10/£5
My Sister's Keeper, Hamilton, 1970 . . . £10/£5
The Harness Room, Hamilton, 1971 . . . £10/£5
The Will and the Way, Hamilton, 1973 . . £10/£5

Others

The Novelist's Responsibility, Hamilton, 1967 £20/£5

SEAMUS HEANEY

(b.1939)

The acclaimed Irish poet who moved away from powerful nature poetry to deal with political and cultural issues. Heaney was awarded the Nobel Prize for Literature in 1995.

Verse

Eleven Poems, Festival (Belfast), 1965 (wraps) £400
Death of a Naturalist, Faber, 1966 . . . . £250/£50
ditto, O.U.P. (U.S.), 1966. . . . . . . £150/£35
ditto, Faber, 1969 (wraps). £20
A Lough Neagh Sequence, Phoenix Pamphlet, Poets Press, 1969 (950 copies, wraps) £75
ditto, Phoenix Pamphlet, Poets Press, 1969 (50 signed copies, wraps) £400
Door into the Dark, Faber, 1969. . . . . £200/£45
ditto, OUP (U.S.), 1969 . . . . £150/£35
ditto, Faber, 1972 (wraps). £20
Night Drive: Poems, Gilbertson, 1970, (100 signed copies) £150
ditto, Gilbertson, 1970, (25 of the above containing poem in author's hand) £450
ditto, Crediton, 1970 (100 signed copies, wraps) £450
A Boy Driving His Father to Confession, Sceptre Press, 1970 (150 numbered copies, wraps) £100

ditto, Sceptre Press, 1970 (50 signed copies, wraps) £250
Land, Poem of the month Club, 1979 (signed broadside) £75
Wintering Out, Faber, 1972 (wraps) £75
ditto, Faber, 1973 . . . . £45/£10
ditto, O.U.P. (U.S.), 1973 . . . . £30/£10
Stations, Ulsterman Publications, 1975 (wraps) £50
North, Faber, 1975 . . . . £250/£75
ditto, Faber, 1975 (wraps) £35
ditto, O.U.P. (U.S.), 1976 . . . . £125/£35
Bog Poems, Rainbow Press, 1975 (150 signed copies, slipcase) . . . . £600/£550
In Their Element, Arts Council of Northern Ireland, 1977 . . . . £25
Ugolino, Carpenter, 1978 (125 signed copies, hardback, no d/w) £450
After Summer, Gallery Press (Dublin), 1979 (250 signed copies) . . . . £200/£125
Field Work, Faber, 1979 . . . . £45/£10
ditto, Faber, 1979 (wraps) £25
ditto, Farrar Straus (U.S.), 1979 . . . . . £30/£5
Gravities, Charlotte Press, 1979 (wraps) . . . £20
Selected Poems 1965-1975, Faber, 1980 £35/£10
ditto, Faber, 1980 (wraps) £15
ditto, Farrar Straus (U.S.), 1980 . . . . . £30/£5
Holly, Loughcrew, 1981 (121 signed copies, wraps) £150
Sweeney Praises the Trees, Kelly/Winterton Press (U.S.), 1981 (110 copies, wraps) £250
Poems and a Memoir, The Limited Editions Club (U.S.), 1982 (1,500 signed copies, slipcase) . . . . £175/£150
An Open Letter, Field Day, (Derry), 1983 (wraps) £40
Sweeney Astray, Field Day, (Derry), 1983 £60/£20
ditto, Field Day, (Derry), 1983 (wraps) . . . £25
ditto, Faber, 1984 . . . . £30/£10
ditto, Faber, 1984 (wraps) £15
ditto, Farrar Straus (U.S.), 1984 . . . . . £15/£5
ditto, Farrar Straus (U.S.), 1984 (350 signed copies, slipcase . . . . £100/£75
Station Island, Faber, 1984 . . . . . . £30/£10
ditto, Faber, 1984 (wraps) £15
ditto, Farrar Straus (U.S.), 1984 . . . . . £20/£5
Verses for a Fordham Commencement, Nadja (U.S.), 1984 (200 signed, numbered copies, wraps) £100
ditto, Nadja (U.S.), 1984 (26 signed, lettered copies on hand-made paper, boards) £300
Hailstones, Gallery Press (Dublin), 1984 (250 signed copies) £75
ditto, Gallery Press (Dublin), 1984 (500 unsigned copies, wraps) £50
From the Republic of Conscience, Amnesty International, 1985 (2,000 copies, wraps) . . £20
Towards a Collaboration, Arts Council of Northern Ireland, 1986 (wraps) £15
The Haw Lantern, Faber, 1987 . . . . . £25/£5
ditto, Faber, 1987 (wraps) £10
ditto, Farrar Straus (U.S.), 1987 . . . . . £10/£5
ditto, Farrar Straus (U.S.), 1987 (250 signed copies, slipcase) £100
An Upstairs Outlook, Linen Hall, 1989 (wraps) £15
Railway Children, Poems on the Underground, 1989 (200 copies, broadside) £35
The Fire Gaze, Cheltenham Festival of Literature, 1989 (broadside) £15
New Selected Poems 1966-87, Faber, 1990 £20/£5
ditto, Faber, 1990 (25 signed copies of 125, slipcase) £500
ditto, Faber, 1990 (100 signed copies of 125, slipcase). £150
ditto, Faber, 1990 (wraps) £5
ditto, Farrar Straus (U.S.), 1990 . . . . . £15/£5
ditto, Farrar Straus (U.S.), 1990 (200 signed copies, slipcase) . . . . £125/£100
The Place of Waiting, Scholars Press (U.S.), 1990 £10
The Tree Clock, Linen Hall, 1990 (750 copies) £75
ditto, Linen Hall, 1990 (100 signed copies, slipcase) £300
ditto, Faber, 1990 . . . . £10
The Earth House, Cheltenham Festival of Literature, 1990 (broadside) £15
Seeing Things, Faber 1991 . . . . . . £15/£5
ditto, Faber 1991 (250 signed copies, slipcase) £150
ditto, Faber, 1991 (wraps) £5
Squarings, Hieroglyph Editions (Dublin), 1991 (100 signed copies in slipcase) £750
The Water Pause, Cheltenham Festival of Literature, 1991 (broadside) £15
Sweeney's Flight, Faber, 1992 . . . . . £10/£5
ditto, Farrar Straus (U.S.), 1992 . . . . . £10/£5
Iron Spike, Ewart (U.S.), 1992 (100 signed copies, broadside) £75
The Air Station, Cheltenham Festival of Literature, 1992 (broadside) £15
The Gravel Walks, Lenoir Rhyne College, 1992 (wraps) £100
The Midnight Verdict, Gallery Press (Dublin), 1993 (925 copies) . . . . £45/£15
ditto, Gallery Press (Dublin), 1993 (75 signed copies) £200
Poet's Chair, Ewart (U.S.), 1993 (100 signed copies, broadside) £100
Keeping Going, Ewart (U.S.), 1993 (50 signed copies, boards, no d/w) £150
ditto, Ewart (U.S.), 1993 (150 signed copies, wraps) £125
Laments: Jan Kochanowski (1530-1584), Faber 1995 (translation, with Stanislaw Baranczak) . . £10
ditto, Farrar Straus (U.S.), 1995 . . . . . £10/£5

The Spirit Level, Faber, 1996 . . . . £15/£5
ditto, Farrar Straus (U.S.), 1996 (200 signed, numbered copies with audio cassette in slipcase) . . . £150
ditto, Farrar Straus (U.S.), 1996 (with audio cassette in slipcase) . . . . £25/£10
Opened Ground: Poems 1966-1996, Faber, 1998 . . . . £15/£5
ditto, Faber, 1998 (300 signed, numbered copies in slipcase) £150
ditto, Farrar Straus (U.S.), 1998 . . . . £10/£5

Others

The Fire i' the Flint: Reflections on the Poetry of Gerard Manley Hopkins, British Academy/O.U.P., 1975 (wraps) £20
Robert Lowell: A Memorial Lecture and an Eulogy, privately printed, 1978 (wraps) £100
The Makings of Music: Reflections on the Poetry of Wordsworth and Yeats, University of Liverpool, 1978 (wraps) £15
Preoccupations: Selected Prose 1968-1978, Faber, 1980 . . . . £45/£15
ditto, Farrar Straus (U.S.), 1980 . . . . £15/£5
Among the Schoolchildren, Queen's University, (Belfast), 1983 (green wraps) £45
ditto, Queen's University, (Belfast), 1983 (blue wraps) £10
Place and Displacement, Dove Cottage, 1984 (wraps) £15
The Government of the Tongue, Faber, 1988 £10/£5
ditto, Farrar Straus (U.S.), 1988 . . . . £15/£5
The Cure at Troy, Field Day, 1989 (500 signed copies) . . . . £125/£100
ditto, Faber, 1989 (wraps). £5
ditto, Farrar Straus (U.S.), 1991 . . . . £25/£5
The Redress of Poetry, Clarendon Press, 1990 £10
ditto, Faber, 1995 . . . . £20/£5
ditto, Farrar Straus (U.S.), 1995 . . . . £10/£5
Dylan the Durable? On Dylan Thomas, Bennington College, 1992 (1,000 numbered copies, wraps) £25
Joy or Night, Univ. College of Swansea, 1993 (wraps) £20
Crediting Poetry, Gallery Books, 1995 (wraps) £25
Commencement Address, Univ. of North Carolina (U.S.), 1998 (100 signed copies, wraps) . . £125

ROBERT A. HEINLEIN

(b.1907 d.1988)

An influential American science fiction writer, Heinlein was first published in *Astounding SF* magazine in 1939.

Novels

The Discovery of the Future, Novacious Press (U.S.), 1941 (wraps) £1,000
Rocket Ship Galileo, Scribners (U.S.), 1947 £300/£75
ditto, New English Library, 1971 (wraps) . . £10
Beyond This Horizon, Fantasy Press (U.S.), 1948 . . . . £150/£45
ditto, Fantasy Press (U.S.), 1948 (500 signed, numbered copies) . . . . £750/£500
Space Cadet, Scribners (U.S.), 1948. . . £150/£45
ditto, Gollancz, 1966 . . . . £125/£35
Red Planet, Scribners (U.S.), 1949 . . . £125/£35
ditto, Gollancz, 1963 . . . . £150/£35
Sixth Column, Gnome Press (U.S.), 1949 £125/£35
ditto, Mayflower, 1962 (wraps) £10
Farmer in the Sky, Scribners (U.S.), 1950 £125/£35
ditto, Gollancz, 1962 . . . . £125/£25
The Man who Sold the Moon, Shasta (U.S.), 1950 . . . . £125/£45
ditto, Sidgwick & Jackson, 1953 . . . . £100/£25
Waldo and Magic Inc., Doubleday (U.S.), 1950 . . . . £125/£35
Between Planets, Scribners (U.S.), 1951 £175/£45
ditto, Gollancz, 1968 . . . . £150/£35
The Green Hills of Earth, Shasta (U.S.), 1951 . . . . £175/£45
ditto, Sidgwick & Jackson, 1954 . . . . £150/£35
The Puppet Masters, Doubleday (U.S.), 1951 £250/£75
ditto, Museum Press, 1953 . . . . . £200/£50
Universe, Dell Books (U.S.), 1951 (wraps) . . £45
The Rolling Stones, Scribners (U.S.), 1952 £150/£45
ditto, as ***Space Family Stone***, Gollancz, 1969 £125/£45
Assignment in Eternity, Fantasy Press (U.S.), 1953 (500 numbered, signed copies) . . . £400/£250
ditto, Fantasy Press (U.S.), 1953 . . . £200/£75
ditto, Museum Press, 1955 . . . . . £175/£50
Revolt in 2100, Shasta (U.S.), 1953 . . . £250/£75
Starman Jones, Scribners (U.S.), 1953 . . £150/£45
ditto, Sidgwick & Jackson, 1954 . . . . £100/£35
The Star Beast, Scribners (U.S.), 1954 . . £150/£45
ditto, New English Library, 1971 (wraps) . . £10
Tunnel in the Sky, Scribners (U.S.), 1955 £150/£50
ditto, Gollancz, 1965 . . . . £100/£35
Double Star, Doubleday (U.S.), 1956 . . £500/£150
ditto, Michael Joseph, 1958 . . . . . £250/£100
Time for the Stars, Scribners (U.S.), 1956 £125/£35
ditto, Gollancz, 1963 . . . . £70/£20
Citizen of the Galaxy, Scribners (U.S.), 1957 £200/£50
ditto, Gollancz, 1969 . . . . £75/£25
The Door into Summer, Doubleday (U.S.), 1957 . . . . £200/£75
ditto, Panther, 1960 (wraps) £5
ditto, Gollancz, 1967 . . . . £125/£45
Have Space Suit - Will Travel, Scribners (U.S.), 1958 . . . . £175/£50

ditto, Gollancz, 1970 . . . . £125/£25
Methuselah's Children, Gnome Press (U.S.), 1958 . . . . £150/£35
ditto, Gollancz, 1963 (abridged version). . £125/£35
The Robert Heinlein Omnibus, Science Fiction Book Club, 1958 . . . . £25/£10
The Menace from Earth, Gnome Press (U.S.), 1959 . . . . £200/£65
ditto, Dobson, 1966 . . . . £75/£25
Starship Troopers, Putnam (U.S.), 1959 £1,000/£250
ditto, New English Library, 1961 (wraps) . . £10
The Unpleasant Profession of Jonathan Hoag, Gnome Press (U.S.), 1959 . . . . . £175/£45
ditto, Dobson, 1964 . . . . £100/£35
Stranger in a Strange Land, Putnam (U.S.), 1961 . . . . £450/£75
ditto, New English Library, 1965 (wraps) . . £10
Orphans of the Sky, Gollancz, 1963. . . . £250/£75
ditto, Putnam (U.S.), 1964 . . . . . £200/£45
Glory Road, Putnam (U.S.), 1963 . . . £250/£65
ditto, New English Library, 1965 (wraps) . . £10
Podkayne of Mars, Putnam (U.S.), 1963 £500/£125
ditto, New English Library, 1969 (wraps) . . £15
Farnham's Freehold, Putnam (U.S.), 1964 £175/£45
ditto, Dobson, 1965 . . . . £75/£25
Three by Heinlein, Doubleday (U.S.), 1965 £75/£25
ditto, as ***A Heinlein Triad***, Gollancz, 1966 £35/£10
The Moon is a Harsh Mistress, Putnam (U.S.), 1966 . . . . £150/£45
ditto, Dobson, 1967 . . . . £75/£25
The Worlds of Robert Heinlein, Ace Books (U.S.), 1966 (wraps) £10
ditto, New English Library, 1970 (wraps) . . . £10
A Robert Heinlein Omnibus, Sidgwick & Jackson, 1966 . . . . £25/£10
The Past Through Tomorrow, Putnam (U.S.), 1967 . . . . £150/£50
ditto, New English Library, 1977 (2 vols) . £35/£10
I Will Fear No Evil, Putnam (U.S.), 1970 . £50/£15
ditto, New English Library, 1971. . . . £45/£15
Time Enough For Love, Putnam (U.S.), 1973 . . . . £125/£45
ditto, New English Library, 1974. . . . £100/£35
Best of Robert Heinlein, Sidgwick & Jackson, 1973 . . . . £25/£10
The Notebooks of Lazarus Long, Putnam (U.S.), 1978 (wraps) £10
Destination Moon, Gregg Press (U.S.), 1979 £45
Expanded Universe, Grosset & Dunlap (U.S.), 1980 . . . . £50/£15
The Number of the Beast, New English Library, 1980 . . . . £35/£10
ditto, Fawcett (U.S.), 1980 . . . . . £50/£15
ditto, Fawcett (U.S.), 1980 (wraps) £10
Friday, Holt Rinehart (U.S.), 1982 . . . £15/£5
ditto, Ballantine/Del Ray (U.S.), 1984 (500 signed, numbered copies, slipcase) . . . . £125/£100
ditto, New English Library, 1982. . . . £20/£5
Job, Ballantine/Del Ray (U.S.), 1984 . . . £15/£5
ditto, Ballantine/Del Ray (U.S.), 1984 (750 signed, numbered copies, slipcase) . . . . . £100/£75
ditto, New English Library, 1984. . . . £20/£5
The Cat Who Walks Through Walls, Putnam (U.S.), 1985 . . . . £15/£5
ditto, Putnam (U.S.), 1984 (350 signed, numbered copies, slipcase) . . . . £125/£100
ditto, New English Library, 1986. . . . £20/£5
To Sail Beyond the Sunset, Ace/Putnam (U.S.), 1987 . . . . £15/£5
ditto, Michael Joseph, 1987 . . . . . £15/£5

JOSEPH HELLER
(b.1923)

Heller, an American author, is chiefly known for *Catch-22*, an anti-war satire which drew on his own experience of military service.

Novels
Catch-22, Simon & Schuster (U.S.), 1961 £650/£200
ditto, Cape, 1962 . . . . £150/£45
ditto, Franklin Library (U.S.), 1978 (signed) . £75
ditto, Simon & Schuster (U.S.), 1994 (750 signed, numbered copies, slipcase) . . . . . £150/£125
Something Happened, Knopf (U.S.), 1974 £20/£5
ditto, Knopf (U.S.), 1974 (350 signed, numbered copies, d/w and slipcase) . . . . . £100/£75
ditto, Cape, 1974 . . . . £20/£5
Good as Gold, Franklin Library (U.S.), 1979 (limited edition) £20
ditto, Franklin Library (U.S.), 1979 (signed copies from unspecified limited edition) £100
ditto, Simon & Schuster (U.S.), 1979 . . £20/£5
ditto, Simon & Schuster (U.S.), 1979 (500 signed copies, acetate d/w, slipcase) . . . . £100/£75
ditto, Cape, 1979 . . . . £20/£5
God Knows, Knopf (U.S.), 1984 . . . . £20/£5
ditto, Knopf (U.S.), 1984 (350 signed copies, d/w and slipcase) . . . . £75/£50
ditto, Cape, 1984 . . . . £10/£5
ditto, Franklin Library (U.S.), 1984 (signed limited edition) £35
Picture This, Putnam (U.S.), 1988 . . . £15/£5
ditto, Macmillan, 1988 . . . . . . £15/£5
ditto, Macmillan, 1988 (50 proof copies) . . £50
Closing Time, Simon & Schuster (U.S.), 1994 £15/£5
ditto, Simon & Schuster (U.S.), 1994 (750 signed, numbered copies, slipcase, no d/w) . . . £65/£50

Plays

We Bombed in New Haven, Knopf (U.S.), 1968 . . . . £35/£10

ditto, Cape, 1969 . . . . £25/£5

Catch-22, French (U.S.), 1971 . . . . . £20

Clevinger's Trial, French (U.S.), 1973 . . . £20

Non Fiction

No Laughing Matter, Knopf (U.S.), 1986 (with Speed Vogel). . . . . £15/£5

ditto, Cape, 1986 . . . . £15/£5

ERNEST HEMINGWAY

(b.1899 d.1961)

One of the most famous American novelists of the twentieth century, Hemingway's great successes were *A Farewell to Arms*, set during the First World War, and *For Whom the Bell Tolls* with the Spanish Civil War as its background.

Novels

The Torrents of Spring, Scribner (U.S.), 1926 . . . . £2,000/£350

ditto, Jonathan Cape, 1933 . . . . . . £300/£50

The Sun Also Rises, Scribner (U.S.), 1926 £1,000/£100

ditto, as ***Fiesta***, Jonathan Cape, 1927 . . . £750/£200

A Farewell to Arms, Scribner (U.S.), 1929 £500/£75

ditto, Scribner (U.S.), 1929 (510 signed copies, glassine d/w, slipcase). . . . . . . £2,500/£2,000

ditto, Jonathan Cape, 1929 . . . . . . £300/£65

To Have and to Have Not, Scribner (U.S.), 1937 . . . . £250/£75

ditto, Jonathan Cape, 1937 . . . . . £75/£20

For Whom the Bell Tolls, Scribner (U.S.), 1940 . . . . £200/£45

ditto, Jonathan Cape, 1941 . . . . . £150/£15

Across the River and into the Trees, Jonathan Cape, 1950 . . . . £75/£25

ditto, Scribner (U.S.), 1950 (24 advance copies containing errors) £10,000

ditto, Scribner (U.S.), 1950 . . . . . . £75/£20

The Old Man and the Sea, Scribner (U.S.), 1952 . . . . £250/£75

ditto, Jonathan Cape, 1952 . . . . . £25/£5

Islands in the Stream, Scribner (U.S.), 1970 £25/£5

ditto, Collins, 1970 . . . . £15/£5

The Garden of Eden, Scribner (U.S.), 1986 £20/£5

ditto, Hamish Hamilton, 1987 . . . . £15/£5

Short Stories

Three Stories and Ten Poems, privately printed, Contact Publishing Co., 1923 (300 copies, wraps) £1,500

In Our Time, Three Mountains Press (Paris), 1924 (170 copies) £6,000

ditto, Boni & Liveright (U.S.), 1925 . . £2,000/£300

ditto, Jonathan Cape, 1926 . . . . . £250/£50

Men Without Women, Scribner (U.S.), 1927 (first state weighing 15.5 ounces) . . . . . . £2,000/£150

ditto, Scribner (U.S.), 1927 (second state weighing 13.8 ounces) . . . . £750/£100

ditto, Jonathan Cape, 1928 . . . . . £150/£25

Winner Take Nothing, Scribner (U.S.), 1933 . . . . £450/£100

ditto, Jonathan Cape, 1934 . . . . . £200/£45

The Fifth Column and The First Forty-Nine Stories, Scribner (U.S.), 1938 . . . . £400/£50

ditto, Jonathan Cape, 1939 . . . . . £200/£35

The Nick Adams Stories, Scribner (U.S.), 1972 . . . . £75/£20

A Divine Gesture, A Fable, Aloe Editions (U.S.), 1974 (200 copies, wraps) £75

Others

Death in the Afternoon, Scribner (U.S.), 1932 . . . . £500/£150

ditto, Jonathan Cape, 1932 . . . . . £200/£65

Green Hills of Africa, Scribner (U.S.), 1935 £450/£100

ditto, Jonathan Cape, 1936 . . . . . . £75/£25

The Spanish War, Fact, 1938 (card wraps) . . £75

The Essential Hemingway, Jonathan Cape, 1947 . . . . £25/£5

The Collected Poems, [no place], [c.1955] (pirated, wraps). £150

A Moveable Feast, Scribner (U.S.), 1964 . £65/£20

ditto, Jonathan Cape, 1964 . . . . . £75/£20

By-Line, Scribner, 1967 . . . . £65/£15

ditto, Collins, 1968 . . . . £45/£15

Bastard Sheet Note for A Farewell to Arms, Cohn (U.S.), 1971 (93 copies, single sheet) . . . £250

Eighty-Eight Poems, Harcourt Brace (U.S.), 1980 . . . . £25/£10

Selected Letters, 1917-1961, Scribners (U.S.), 1981 . . . . £25/£10

ditto, Scribners (U.S.), 1981 (500 copies signed by editor, glassine d/w, slipcase) . . . £75/£50

ditto, Granada, 1981 . . . . £25/£10

The Dangerous Summer, Scribner (U.S.), 1985 £20/£5

ditto, Hamish Hamilton, 1985 . . . . £20/£5

On Writing, Granada, 1985 . . . . . . £10

G.A. HENTY

(b.1832 d.1902)

Henty was a popular nineteenth century author of patriotic stories for boys.

A Search for a Secret, Tinsley Brothers, 1867 (3 vols, blue or green cloth) £2,000
The March to Magdala, Tinsley Brothers, 1868 . . . . £2,000
All But Lost, Tinsley Brothers, 1869 (3 vols, blue boards) £2,000
Out on the Pampas, or The Young Settlers, Griffith & Farran, 1871 [1870] (blue or brown boards) £1,000
The Young Franc-Tireurs, Griffith & Farran, 1872 [1871] (blue, red or green boards). £650
The March to Coomassie, Tinsley Brothers, 1874 £500
Seaside Maidens, Tinsley Brothers, 1880 (orange boards) £625
The Young Buglars, Griffith & Farran, 1880 [1879] (red or green boards) £500
The Cornet of Horse, Sampson Low & Marston, 1881 (red boards). £500
In Times of Peril, Griffith & Farran, 1881 (red or blue boards) £700
Facing Death, Blackie, [1882] (blue or brown boards) £500
Winning His Spurs, Sampson Low & Marston, 1882 . . . . £300
Friends Though Divided, Griffith & Farran, 1883 £400
Jack Archer, Sampson Low & Marston, 1883 £400
Under Drake's Flag, Blackie, 1883 [1882] (green or brown boards) £200
ditto, as ***Cast Ashore***, Blackie, 1906 . . . . £45
By Sheer Pluck, Blackie, 1884 [1883] (red boards) £300
With Clive in India, Blackie, 1884 [1883] (red, brown or blue boards) £200
ditto, as ***The Young Captain***, Blackie, 1906 £50
ditto, as ***Charlie Marryat***, Blackie, 1906 . . £50
The Young Colonists, Routledge, 1885 [1884] (blue and gold boards) £200
True to the Old Flag, Blackie, 1885 [1884]. . £200
In Freedom's Cause, Blackie, 1885 [1884]. . £100
ditto, as ***A Highland Chief***, Blackie, 1906 . . £50
St. George For England, Blackie, 1885 [1884] £100
The Lion of the North, Blackie, 1886 [1885] (brown or green boards). £150
The Dragon and the Raven, Blackie, 1886 [1885] (brown or green boards) £200
For Name and Fame, Blackie, 1886 [1885] (brown or grey boards) £200
Through the Fray, Blackie, 1886 [1885] (brown or red boards) £150
Yarns on the Beach, Blackie, 1886 [1885] (brown or red boards) £350
The Young Carthaginian, Blackie, 1887 [1886] (blue or green boards) £200
The Bravest of the Brave, Blackie, 1887 [1886] (red or blue boards) £150
A Final Reckoning, Blackie, 1887 [1886] (blue or green boards). £100
ditto, as ***Among the Bushrangers***, Blackie, 1906 £50
With Wolfe in Canada, Blackie 1887 [1886] £200
The Sovereign Reader: Scenes from the Life and Reign of Queen Victoria, Blackie, [1887] (red or purple boards) £175
In the Reign of Terror, Blackie, 1888 . . . £150
Sturdy and Strong, Blackie, 1888 [1887] (red, blue or orange boards) £150
Orange and Green, Blackie 1888 [1887] (red, blue or orange boards) £100
ditto, as ***Cornet Walter***, Blackie, 1906 . . . £50
Bonnie Prince Charlie, Blackie, 1888 [1887] (brown or red boards). £100
For the Temple, Blackie, 1888 [1887] (brown, red or blue boards) £200
Gabriel Allen MP, Spencer & Blackett, [1888] (red boards) £250
Captain Bayley's Heir, Blackie, 1889 (red, brown or blue boards) £100
The Cat of Bubastes, Blackie, 1889 [1888] . . £200
The Lion of St Mark, Blackie, 1889 [1888] (red, blue or grey boards) £75
The Curse of Carne's Hold, Spencer & Blackett, 1889 (2 vols, blue boards) £500
The Plague Ship, S.P.C.K. 'Penny Library of Fiction' series, 1889 (wraps) £600
By Pike and Dyke, Blackie, 1890 [1889] (brown or green boards). £125
One of the 28th, Blackie, 1890 [1889] . . . £200
Tales of Daring and Danger, Blackie, 1889 [1890] (blue or green boards) £300
With Lee in Virginia, Blackie, 1890 [1889] (brown or blue boards) £150
Those Other Animals, Henry & Co., [1891] (green boards) £250
By England's Aid, Blackie, 1891 [1890] (blue or brown boards) £150
By Right of Conquest, Blackie, 1891 [1890] (green or brown boards) £100
Maori and Settler, Blackie, 1891 . . . . . £100
A Chapter of Adventures, Blackie, 1891 [1890] £1,000
A Hidden Foe, Sampson Low & Marston, [1891] (2 vols, grey boards) £2,000
The Dash for Khartoum, Blackie, 1892 [1891] £100
Held Fast for England, Blackie, 1892 [1891] (red, grey or brown boards) £100
Redskin and Cowboy, Blackie, 1892 [1891] (red, green or brown boards) £100

ditto, as ***An Indian Raid***, Blackie, 1906. . . . £50
The Ranch in the Valley, S.P.C.K. 'Penny Library of Fiction' series, 1892 (wraps) £500
Beric the Briton, Blackie, 1893 [1892] (blue or brown boards) £150
Condemned as Nihilist, Blackie, 1893 [1892] (brown or blue boards) £150
In Greek Waters, Blackie, 1893 [1892] (grey, brown or green boards). £100
Tales from the Works of G. A. Henty, Blackie, 1893 (red boards) £100
Rujub the Juggler, Chatto & Windus, 1893 (3 vols, blue boards) £750
A Jacobite Exile, Blackie, 1894 [1893] . . . £200
Through the Sikh War, Blackie, 1894 [1893] (green boards) £100
St Bartholomew's Eve, Blackie, 1894 [1893] (green, blue or red boards) £100
Dorothy's Double, Chatto & Windus, 1894 (3 vols) £750
When London Burned, Blackie, 1895 [1894] (blue boards) £200
Cuthbert Hartington and A Woman of the Commune, F.V. White, 1895. . . . . £200
Wulf the Saxon, Blackie, 1895 [1894] (green boards) £75
In the Heart of the Rockies, Blackie, 1895 [1894] (grey boards) £100
A Knight of the White Cross, Blackie, 1896 [1895] (green boards) £150
Bears and Dacoits, Blackie, [1896] (wraps) £300
Surly Joe, Blackie, [1896] (wraps) £200
White-Faced Dick, Blackie, [1896] (limp cloth cover) £200
Through Russian Snows, Blackie, 1896 [1895] (grey boards) £100
The Tiger of Mysore, Blackie, 1896 [1895] (blue boards) £100
On the Irrawaddy, Blackie, 1897 [1896] (blue boards) £150
At Agincourt, Blackie, 1897 (grey boards) . . £150
With Cochrane the Dauntless, Blackie, 1897 (blue boards) £100
The Queen's Cup, Chatto & Windus, 1897 (three vols, green or blue boards) £600
With Moore at Corunna, Blackie, 1898 [1897] (green or blue boards) £100
Colonel Thorndyke's Secret, Chatto & Windus, 1898 (pink boards). £150
With Frederick the Great, Blackie, 1898 [1897] (red boards) £100
Under Wellington's Command, Blackie, 1899 [1898] (blue boards). £100
At Aboukir and Acre, Blackie, 1899 [1898] (red boards) £100
Both Sides the Border, Blackie, 1899 [1898] (blue boards) £75
The Lost Heir, James Bowden, 1899 (green boards) £150
On the Spanish Main, Chambers, [1899] (red wraps) £100
At Duty's Call, Chambers, [1899] £75
A Roving Commission, Blackie, 1900 [1899] (red boards) £100
Won by the Sword, Blackie, 1900 [1899] (blue boards) £75
No Surrender!, Blackie, 1900 [1899] (red boards). £100
Do Your Duty, Blackie, [1900] (blue or green boards) £150
The Soul Survivors, Chambers, [1901] (red wraps) £100
In the Irish Brigade, Blackie, 1901 [1900] (green boards) £100
Out With Garibaldi, Blackie, 1901 [1900] (blue boards) £65
John Hawke's Fortune, Chapman & Hall:, Young People's Library' series, 1901 (paper cover) £65
With Buller in Natal, Blackie, 1901 (blue boards) £65
Queen Victoria, Blackie, 1901 (purple boards) £50
To Herat and Cabul, Blackie, 1902 [1901] (blue boards) £65
With Roberts in Pretoria, Blackie, 1902 [1901] (red boards) £150
At the Point of the Bayonet, Blackie, 1902 [1901] (green boards) £65
In the Hands of the Cave Dwellers, Blackie, 1903 [1902]. £150
The Treasure of the Incas, Blackie, 1903 [1902] (green boards) £75
With the British Legion, Blackie, 1903 [1902] (blue or green boards). £75
With Kitchener in the Soudan, Blackie, 1903 [1902] (red boards) £65
Through Three Campaigns, Blackie, 1904 [1903] (red boards) £65
With the Allies to Pekin, Blackie, 1904 [1903] (green boards) £65
By Conduct and Courage, Blackie, 1905 [1904] (red boards) £100
Gallant Deeds, Chambers, 1905 (white or grey boards) £65
In the Hands of the Malays, Blackie, 1905 (red boards) £65
A Soldier's Daughter, Blackie, 1906 [1905] (red, blue or green boards) £65
ditto, as ***The Two Prisoners***, Blackie, 1906 [1905] £45

JAMES HERBERT

(b.1943)

Often thought of as the British version of Stephen King, Herbert may not have King's world-wide sales, but he is just as successful in the United Kingdom.

Novels

The Rats, New English Library, 1974 . . £200/£50
ditto, as ***Deadly Eyes***, Signet (U.S.), 1975 (wraps) £5
ditto, (***The Rats***) New English Library, 1985, (limited edition, limitation unknown) . . . £30/£10
The Fog, New English Library, 1975 . . £150/£45
ditto, Signet (U.S.), 1975 (wraps) £5
ditto, New English Library, 1988, (3,000 copies) . . . . £30/£10
The Survivor, New English Library, 1976 £75/£25
ditto, Signet (U.S.), 1977 (wraps) £5
ditto, New English Library, 1988, (2,000 copies) . . . . £30/£10
Fluke, New English Library, 1977 . . . £50/£15
ditto, Signet (U.S.), 1978 (wraps) £5
The Spear, New English Library, 1978 . . £20/£5
Lair, New English Library, 1979 . . . . £200/£50
ditto, Signet (U.S.), 1979 (wraps) £5
ditto, New English Library, 1985, (limited edition, limitation unknown) . . . . £100/£25
The Dark, New English Library, 1980 . . £30/£10
ditto, New English Library, 1988, (2,000 copies) . . . . £30/£10
The Jonah, New English Library, 1981 . . £25/£5
ditto, Signet (U.S.), 1981 (wraps) £5
ditto, New English Library, 1985, (limited edition, limitation unknown) . . . . £25/£5
Shrine, New English Library, 1983 . . . £25/£5
ditto, Signet (U.S.), 1985 (wraps) £5
Domain, New English Library, 1984 . . £20/£5
ditto, Signet (U.S.), 1985 (wraps) £5
Moon, New English Library, 1985 . . . £15/£5
ditto, Crown (U.S.), 1985 . . . . £10/£5
The Magic Cottage, Hodder & Stoughton, 1986 £10/£5
ditto, New American Library (U.S.), 1987 £10/£5
Sepulchre, Hodder & Stoughton, 1987 . . £10/£5
ditto, Putnam's (U.S.), 1988 . . . . . . £10/£5
Haunted, Hodder & Stoughton, 1988 . . £10/£5
ditto, Hodder & Stoughton, 1988 (250 signed copies, slipcase, no d/w) . . . . £75/£50
ditto, Putnam's (U.S.), 1989 . . . . . . £10/£5
Creed, Hodder & Stoughton, 1990 . . . £10/£5
Portent, Hodder & Stoughton, 1992 . . . £10/£5
ditto, Hodder & Stoughton, 1992 (pre-publication issue, with d/w) . . . . £35/£10
The City, Pan Macmillan, 1994 (wraps) £5
ditto, Pan Macmillan, 1994 (1,000 copies, signed by author and artist in silver, some with flyer) £25
The Ghosts of Sleath, Harper Collins, 1994 £10/£5
ditto, Harper Collins, 1994, (over-sized edition, 500 signed copies) . . . . £40/£20
'48, Harper Collins, 1994 . . . . £10/£5

Others

James Herbert's Dark Places, Harper Collins, 1983 . . . . £15/£5

From 1990 Hodder & Stoughton have published Uniform Editions of the above titles, each edition limited to 3,000 copies . . . . £25/£5 each

---

JAMES HERRIOT

(b.1916 d.1995)

Born James Alfred Wight in Sunderland, he studied at Glasgow Veterinary College and joined a practice in the Yorkshire Dales in 1937. The television series, *All Creatures Great and Small,* has helped make his books enormously successful.

Novels

If Only They Could Talk, Joseph, 1970 . . £45/£10
It Shouldn't Happen to a Vet, Joseph, 1972 £20/£5
Let Sleeping Vets Lie, Joseph, 1973 . . . £15/£5
Vet In Harness, Joseph, 1974 . . . . £10/£5
All Creatures Great and Small, Joseph, 1975 £20/£5
Vets Might Fly, Joseph, 1976 . . . . £10/£5
All Things Bright and Beautiful, Joseph, 1976 £10/£5
Vet in a Spin, Joseph, 1977 . . . . . £10/£5
All Things Wise and Wonderful, Joseph, 1978 £10/£5
James Herriot's Yorkshire, Joseph, 1979 £10/£5
The Lord God Made Them All, Joseph, 1981 £10/£5
The Best of James Herriot, Joseph, 1982 £10/£5
Moses the Kitten, Joseph, 1984 . . . . £15/£5
Only One Woof, Joseph, 1985 . . . . . £15/£5
James Herriot's Dog Stories, Joseph, 1986 £10/£5
The Christmas Day Kitten, Joseph, 1986 £15/£5
Bonny's Big Day, Joseph, 1987 . . . . £15/£5
The Market Square Dog, Joseph, 1989 . . £15/£5
Oscar Cat-About-Town, Joseph, 1990 . . £15/£5
Smudge's Day Out, Joseph, 1991 . . . £15/£5
Blossom Comes Home, Joseph, 1991 . . £15/£5
Every Living Thing, Joseph, 1992 . . . . £10/£5
James Herriot's Cat Stories, Joseph, 1994 £10/£5
James Herriot's Favourite Dog Stories, Joseph, 1992. . . . . £10/£5

PATRICIA HIGHSMITH

(b.1921 d.1995)

A cult crime writer born in Fort Worth, Texas, Highsmith began writing at the age of fifteen. She started out writing speech bubbles for comic strips such as *Superman*. Her first novel, *Strangers on a Train*, was filmed by Hitchcock in 1951. She lived in Europe during her later years and died in Switzerland.

Novels

Strangers on a Train, Harper (U.S.), 1950 £650/£125
ditto, Cresset Press, 1951 . . . . £250/£65
The Price of Salt, Coward McCann (U.S.), 1952 (pseud. 'Claire Morgan') . . . . . . £200/£50
ditto, as ***Carol*** , Bloomsbury, 1990 . . . . £10/£5
The Blunderer, Coward McCann (U.S.), 1954 . . . . £200/£50
ditto, Cressett Press, 1956 . . . . . . £175/£50
The Talented Mr Ripley, Coward McCann (U.S.), 1955 . . . . £200/£50
ditto, Cressett Press, 1957. . . . . . . £150/£40
Deep Water, Harper (U.S.), 1957 . . . £75/£25
ditto, Heinemann, 1958 . . . . £50/£20
A Game for the Living, Harper (U.S.), 1958 £50/£20
ditto, Heinemann, 1959 . . . . £35/£15
This Sweet Sickness, Harper (U.S.), 1960 . £35/£15
ditto, Heinemann, 1961 . . . . £25/£5
The Cry of the Owl, Harper (U.S.), 1962 £30/£10
ditto, Heinemann, 1963 . . . . £25/£5
The Two Faces of January, Doubleday (U.S.), 1964 . . . . £30/£10
ditto, Heinemann, 1964 . . . . £25/£5
The Glass Cell, Doubleday (U.S.), 1964 . £35/£10
ditto, Heinemann, 1965 . . . . £35/£10
The Story-Teller, Doubleday (U.S.), 1965 £25/£10
ditto, as ***A Suspension of Mercy***, Heinemann, 1965 . . . . £20/£5
Those Who Walk Away, Doubleday (U.S.), 1967 . . . . £20/£5
ditto, Heinemann, 1967 . . . . £15/£5
The Tremor of Forgery, Doubleday (U.S.), 1969 . . . . £20/£5
ditto, Heinemann, 1969 . . . . £15/£5
Ripley Under Ground, Doubleday (U.S.), 1970 £25/£5
ditto, Heinemann, 1971 . . . . £15/£5
A Dog's Ransom, Knopf (U.S.), 1972 . . £20/£5
ditto, Heinemann, 1972 . . . . £15/£5
Ripley's Game, Knopf (U.S.), 1974 . . . £20/£5
ditto, Heinemann, 1974 . . . . £15/£5
Edith's Diary, Simon & Schuster (U.S.), 1977 £15/£5
ditto, Heinemann, 1977 . . . . £15/£5
The Boy Who Followed Ripley, Heinemann, 1980 . . . . £15/£5
ditto, Lippincott (U.S.), 1980 . . . . . £10/£5
The People Who Knock on the Door, Heinemann, 1983 . . . . £10/£5
ditto, Mysterious Press (U.S.), [1985] (250 signed copies, slipcase, no d/w) . . . . £25/£15
ditto, Mysterious Press (U.S.), [1985] . . £10/£5
Found in the Street, Heinemann, 1986 . . £10/£5
ditto, Atlantic Monthly Press (U.S.), 1986 £10/£5
Ripley Under Water, Bloomsbury, 1991 £10/£5
ditto, London Limited Editions, 1991 (150 signed copies, glassine d/w) £40
ditto, Knopf (U.S.), 1992 . . . . £10/£5
Small G: A Summer Idyll, Bloomsbury, 1995 £10/£5

Short Stories

The Snail-Watcher, Doubleday (U.S.), 1970 £20/£5
ditto, as ***Eleven***, Heinemann, 1970 . . . . £20/£5
Kleine Geschichten Fur Weiberfeinde, Diogenes (Germany), 1974 . . . . £25/£10
ditto, as ***Little Tales of Misogyny***, Heinemann, 1977 . . . . £20/£5
ditto, as ***Little Tales of Misogyny***, Mysterious Press (U.S.), [1986] (250 signed copies, slipcase, no d/w) . . . . £25/£15
ditto, as ***Little Tales of Misogyny***, Mysterious Press (U.S.), [1986]. . . . . £10/£5
The Animal-Lover's Book of Beastly Murder, Heinemann, 1975 . . . . £20/£5
ditto, Mysterious Press (U.S.), [1986] (250 signed copies, slipcase, no d/w) . . . . . . £25/£15
ditto, Mysterious Press (U.S.), [1986] . . £10/£5
Slowly, Slowly in the Wind, Heinemann, 1979 £20/£5
ditto, Mysterious Press, [1984] (250 signed copies, slipcase and d/w) . . . . £25/£15
ditto, Mysterious Press, [1984] . . . . £10/£5
The Black House, Heinemann, 1981 . . £15/£5
ditto, Mysterious Press (U.S.), [1988] (250 signed copies, slipcase, no d/w) . . . . . . £25/£15
ditto, Mysterious Press (U.S.), [1988] . . £10/£5
Mermaids on the Golf Course and Other Stories, Heinemann, 1985 . . . . £15/£5
ditto, Mysterious Press (U.S.), 1988 . . . £10/£5
The Man Who Wrote Books in His Head and Other Stories, Eurographica (Helsinki), 1986 (350 signed copies, wraps and d/w) £50
Tales of Natural and Unnatural Catastrophes, Bloomsbury, 1987 . . . . £15/£5
ditto, Atlantic Monthly Press (U.S.), 1989 £10/£5
Where the Action Is and Other Stories, Eurographica (Helsinki), 1989 (350 signed copies, wraps and d/w) £50
Tales of Obsession, Severn House, 1994 £10/£5

Children's

Miranda the Panda is on the Verandah, Coward McCann (U.S.), 1958 (with Doris Sanders) £50/£15

Miscellaneous

Plotting and Writing Suspense Fiction, Writer (U.S.), 1966 . . . . £25/£10
ditto, Poplar Press, 1983 . . . . £10/£5

SUSAN HILL

(b.1942)

A novelist whose work frequently explores states of loneliness.

Novels

The Enclosure, Hutchinson, 1961 . . . £50/£20
Do Me a Favour, Hutchinson 1963 . . . £45/£20
Gentlemen and Ladies, Hamilton, 1968. . £25/£10
ditto, Walker (U.S.), 1969 . . . . . £15/£5
A Change for the Better, Hamilton 1969 . £25/£10
I'm the King of the Castle, Hamilton, 1970. £20/£5
ditto, Viking (U.S.), 1970. . . . . . £10/£5
Strange Meeting, Hamilton, 1971 . . . £15/£5
ditto, Saturday Review Press (U.S.), 1972 . £10/£5
The Bird of Night, Hamilton, 1972 . . . £15/£5
ditto, Saturday Review Press (U.S.), 1972 . £10/£5
In the Springtime of the Year, Hamilton, 1974 £10/£5
ditto, Saturday Review Press (U.S.), 1974 . £10/£5
The Woman in Black, Hamilton 1983 . . £25/£10
ditto, Godine (U.S.), 1986 . . . . . £15/£5
Can It Be True?, Hamilton 1988. . . . £10/£5
ditto, Viking Kestrel (U.S.), 1998 . . . £15/£5
Air and Angels, Sinclair-Stevenson, 1991 . £10/£5
The Mist in the Mirror, Sinclair-Stevenson, 1992 . . . . £10/£5
Mrs. de Winter, Sinclair Stevenson 1993 . £10/£5
ditto, Morrow (U.S.), 1993 . . . . . £10/£5

Short Stories

The Albatross and Other Stories, Hamilton, 1971 . . . . £15/£5
ditto, Saturday Review/Dutton (U.S.), 1971. £10/£5
The Custodian, Covent Garden Press, 1972 (100 of 600 signed copies, wraps) £30
ditto, Covent Garden Press, 1972 (500 of 600 copies) £15
A Bit of Singing and Dancing, Hamilton, 1973 £15/£5
Lanterns Across the Snow, Joseph 1987 . £10/£5
ditto, Potter (U.S.), 1988 . . . . . . £10/£5
The Glass Angels, Walker Books 1991 . . £10/£5
ditto, Candlewick Press (U.S.), 1991. . . £10/£5
Beware Beware, Walker Books 1993 . . £10/£5
ditto, Candlewick Press (U.S.), 1993. . . £10/£5
Christmas Collection, Candlewick Press (U.S.), 1994 . . . . £10/£5

Others

The Magic Apple Tree, Hamilton 1982 . . £10/£5
ditto, Holt, Rinehart & Winston (U.S.), 1992 £15/£5
Through the Kitchen Window, Hamilton 1984 £10/£5
ditto, Stemmer House (U.S.), 1984 . . . £10/£5
Through the Garden Gate, Hamilton 1986 . £10/£5
The Lighting Of The Lamps, Hamilton 1987 £10/£5
The Spirit of Britain, An Illustrated guide to Literary Britain, Headline, 1994 . . . . £10/£5

WILLIAM HOPE HODGSON

(b.1877 d.1918)

Hodgson was born in Essex and spent many of his earlier years at sea with the Merchant Marine. He is known for his ghost and horror stories, many of which have a maritime theme. Hodgson was killed in an artillery bombardment near Ypres in April, 1918.

The Boats of 'Glen Carrig', Chapman & Hall, 1907 . . . . £1,000
The House on the Borderland, Chapman & Hall, 1908 . . . . £1,500
The Ghost Pirates, Stanley Paul, 1909 . . . £750
The Night Land, Eveleigh Nash, 1912 . . . . £1,000
Poems and The Dream of X, R. Harold Paget (U.S.), 1912 (wraps) £150
Carnacki the Ghost-Finder, Eveleigh Nash, 1913 . . . . £550
ditto, Mycroft & Moran (U.S.), 1947 . . £100/£30
Men of the Deep Waters, Eveleigh Nash, 1914 £350
The Luck of the Strong, Eveleigh Nash, 1916 . £200
Captain Gault, Eveleigh Nash, 1917. . . . £175
ditto, Mcbride & Co. (U.S.), 1918 . . . . £100
The Calling of the Sea, Selwyn & Blount, 1920 . . . . £175
The Voice of the Ocean, Selwyn & Blount, 1921 . . . . £150
The House on the Borderland and Other Novels, Arkham House (U.S.), 1946. . . . . £250/£75
Deep Waters, Arkham House (U.S.), 1967 . £75/£30
Out of the Storm, Donald Grant (U.S.), 1975 £35/£10
The Dream of X, Donald Grant (U.S.), 1977 £30/£10
Poems of the Sea, Ferret, 1977, (illustrated, 500 copies) . . . . £40/£15
The Haunted "Pampero": Uncollected Fantasies and Mysteries, Donald Grant (U.S.), 1996 (500 copies signed by editor) . . . . £30/£10
Terrors of the Sea: Unpublished and Uncollected Fantasies, Donald M. Grant (U.S.), 1996 . £30/£10

E. T. A. HOFFMANN
(b.1776 d.1822)

A German writer and musician, Hoffman's opera *Undine* is his only musical work revived today, but his fantasies and romances are very highly regarded.

The Devil's Elixir, Blackwood and Cadell, 1824 (2 vols) £250
Hoffmann's Strange Stories from the German, Burnham Brothers (U.S.), 1855 . . . . . . £250
Hoffmann's Fairy Tales, Burnham Brothers (U.S.), 1857 . . . . £250
Weird Tales, Nimmo, 1885 (2 vols) £200
The Serapion Brethren, Bohn's Standard Library, George Bell, Vol. 1, 1886, Vol. 2 1892 . . £250
Tales of Hoffmann, Harrap, [1932] . . . £200/£45
The Tales of Hoffmann, Heritage Press (U.S.), 1943 . . . . £150/£35
Tales of Hoffmann, A. A. Wyn (U.S.), 1946 £75/£25
The Best Tales of Hoffmann, Dover Publications (U.S.), 1967 (wraps) £10
Selected Writings of E. T. A. Hoffmann, University of Chicago Press, (U.S. & U.K., 1969 (2 vols) £75/£35

HEINRICH HOFFMANN
(b.1809 d.1894)

German author and illustrator whose 'Struwwelpeter' stories were hugely popular.

The English Struwwelpeter, or Pretty Stories and Funny Pictures for Little Children, Leipzig, 1848, (first English edition) £4,000
Dean's Sixpenny 'English Struwwelpeters', Dean, 1859 (numbered 1-9 and 11-14) . . . . £100 each
Slovenly Peter, Limited Editions Club (U.S.), 1935 (translated by Mark Twain, 1,500 copies) . . £250
King Nut-Cracker, or The Dream of Poor Reinhold: A Fairy Tale, London [printed Leipzig], [1853] £250
Kindergarten Toys and How to Use Them: A Practical Explanation of The First Six Gifts of Froebel's Kindergarten, London, [1874] £100

GEOFFREY HOUSEHOLD
(b.1900 d.1988)

Household is a pseudonym for Edward West. He is best known for his second novel, *Rogue Male*, although he wrote twenty thrillers and adventure stories. His work is characterised by an interest in the psychology of the chase.

Novels
The Third Hour, Chatto & Windus, 1937 . £50/£15
ditto, Little, Brown (U.S.), 1938 . . . . £35/£10
Rogue Male, Chatto & Windus, 1939 . . £200/£40
ditto, Little, Brown (U.S.), 1939 . . . . £125/£20
Arabesque, Chatto & Windus, 1948 . . . £35/£10
ditto, Little, Brown (U.S.), 1948 . . . . £20/£5
The High Place, Joseph, 1950 . . . . £20/£5
ditto, Little, Brown (U.S.), 1950 . . . . £10/£5
A Rough Shoot, Joseph, 1951 . . . £20/£5
ditto, Little, Brown (U.S.), 1951 . . . . £10/£5
A Time to Kill, Little, Brown (U.S.), 1951 . £20/£5
ditto, Joseph, 1952. . . . . £10/£5
Fellow Passenger, Joseph, 1955 . . . . £10/£5
ditto, Little, Brown (U.S.), 1955 . . . . £10/£5
Watcher in the Shadows, Joseph, 1960 . . £10/£5
ditto, Little, Brown (U.S.), 1960 . . . . £10/£5
Thing to Love, Joseph, 1963 . . . . . £10/£5
ditto, Little, Brown (U.S.), 1963 . . . . £10/£5
Olura, Joseph, 1965 . . . . £10/£5
ditto, Little, Brown (U.S.), 1965 . . . . £10/£5
The Courtesy of Death, Joseph, 1967 . . £10/£5
ditto, Little, Brown (U.S.), 1967 . . . . £10/£5
Dance of the Dwarfs, Joseph, 1968 . . . £10/£5
ditto, Little, Brown (U.S.), 1968 . . . . £10/£5
Doom's Caravan, Joseph , 1971 . . . . £10/£5
ditto, Little, Brown (U.S.), 1971 . . . . £10/£5
The Three Sentinels, Joseph, 1972 . . . £10/£5
ditto, Little, Brown (U.S.), 1972 . . . . £10/£5
The Lives and Times of Bernardo Brown, Joseph, 1973 . . . . £10/£5
ditto, Little, Brown (U.S.), 1974 . . . . £10/£5
Red Anger, Joseph, 1975 . . . . . . £10/£5
ditto, Little, Brown (U.S.), 1976 . . . . £10/£5
Hostage: London, Joseph, 1977 . . . . £10/£5
ditto, Little, Brown (U.S.), 1977 . . . . £10/£5
The Last Two Weeks of George Rivac, Joseph, 1978 . . . . £10/£5
ditto, Little, Brown (U.S.), 1978 . . . . £10/£5
The Sending, Joseph, 1980 . . . . . £10/£5
ditto, Little, Brown (U.S.), 1980 . . . . £10/£5
Summon the Bright Water, Joseph, 1981 . £10/£5
ditto, Little, Brown (U.S.), 1981 . . . . £10/£5
Rogue Justice, Joseph, 1982 . . . . . £10/£5
ditto, Little, Brown (U.S.), 1983 . . . . £10/£5
Face to the Sun, Joseph, 1988 . . . . £10/£5

Short Stories

The Salvation of Pisco Gabar, Chatto & Windus, 1938 . . . . £50/£15
ditto, Little, Brown (U.S.), 1940 . . . . £20/£5
Tales of Adventurers, Joseph, 1952 . . . £15/£5
ditto, Little, Brown (U.S.), 1952 . . . . £10/£5
The Brides of Solomon, Joseph, 1958 . . £15/£5
ditto, Little, Brown (U.S.), 1958 . . . . £10/£5
Sabres on the Sand, Joseph, 1966 . . . £10/£5
ditto, Little, Brown (U.S.), 1966 . . . . £10/£5
The Europe That Was, David & Charles, 1979 £10/£5
ditto, St Martin's (U.S.), 1979 . . . . £10/£5
Capricorn and Cancer, Joseph, 1981 . . £10/£5
Arrows of Desire, Joseph, 1985 . . . . £10/£5
ditto, Little, Brown (U.S.), 1986 . . . . £10/£5
The Days of Your Fathers, Joseph, 1987 . £10/£5
ditto, Little, Brown (U.S.), 1987 . . . . £10/£5

Children's

The Terror of Villadonga, Hutchinson, 1936 £75/£25
ditto, as ***The Spanish Cave***, Little, Brown (U.S.), 1936 (revised edition) . . . . £50/£20
The Exploits of Xenophon, Random House (U.S.), 1955 . . . . £10/£5
ditto, as ***Xenophon's Adventure***, Bodley Head, 1961 . . . . £10/£5
Prisoner of the Indies, Bodley Head, 1967 . £10/£5
ditto, Little, Brown (U.S.), 1967 . . . . £10/£5
Escape Into Daylight, Bodley Head, 1976 . £10/£5

A. E. HOUSMAN

(b.1859 d.1936)

Housman was both a scholar and a poet. Although his output of verse was relatively small it is very highly regarded.

Verse

A Shropshire Lad, Kegan Paul, Trench, Trubner & Co., 1896 . . . . £1,500
ditto, John Lane (U.S.), 1897 . . . . . £1,500
Last Poems, Grant Richards, [1922] . . . £40/£15
ditto, Henry Holt (U.S.), 1922 . . . . £35/£15
A Fragment, privately printed, 1930 (37 copies, two folded leaves). £100
Three Poems, privately printed, Dept of English, University College, London, 1935 . . . . £45
[***For my Funeral***], C.U.P., 1936 (300 copies, two folded leaves). £40
More Poems, Cape, 1936 . . . . . . £25/£10
ditto, Cape, 1936 (379 deluxe copies) . . £125/£65
ditto, Knopf (U.S.), 1936 . . . . . . £20/£10
Collected Poems, Cape, 1939 . . . . . £25/£10
ditto, Henry Holt (U.S.), 1940 . . . . . £25/£10
Stars, Venice, 1939 (10 copies signed by the artist, F. Prokosch, wraps) £125
The Manuscript Poems of A.E. Housman, University of Minnesota Press (U.S.), 1955 . . . . £30/£15

Prose

Introductory Lecture, C.U.P., 1892 (wraps) . £350
ditto, privately printed, C.U.P., 1933 (100 copies, wraps) £100
ditto, C.U.P., 1937. . . . . £35/£10
ditto, Macmillan & C.U.P. (U.S.), 1937 . . £30/£10
The Name and Nature of Poetry, C.U.P., 1933 . . . . £45/£15
ditto, Macmillan (U.S.), 1933. . . . . . £45/£15
Jubilee Address to King George V, C.U.P., 1935 (2 copies of 26 on vellum) £1,250
ditto, C.U.P., 1935 (24 copies of 26). £600
Letters to E. H. Blakeney, privately printed (18 copies) £175
A. E. H., W. W., privately printed, 1944 (12 copies) £175
Thirty Letters to Witter Bynner, Knopf (U.S.), 1957 (700 copies) . . . . £45/£20
To Joseph Ishill, Oriole Press (U.S.), 1959 . . £25
Selected Prose, C.U.P., 1961 . . . . . . £20
The Confines of Criticism, C.U.P., 1969 . . £20
Letters, Hart-Davis, 1971 . . . . £20
Classical Papers, C.U.P., 1962 (3 vols) . . . £40
Fifteen Letters to Walter Ashburner, Tragara Press, 1976 (125 copies) £35

ELIZABETH JANE HOWARD

(b.1923)

Howard took up writing novels and short stories after spending the war years as an Air Raid Warden in London.

Novels

The Beautiful Visit, Jonathan Cape, 1950 . £40/£15
ditto, Random House (U.S.), 1950 . . . £20/£5
The Long View, Jonathan Cape, 1956 . . £15/£5
ditto, Reynal (U.S.), 1956. . . . . . £10/£5
The Sea Change, Jonathan Cape, 1959 . . £10/£5
ditto, Harper (U.S.), 1960 . . . . . £10/£5
After Julius, Jonathan Cape, 1965 . . . £10/£5
ditto, Viking (U.S.), 1965 . . . . . £10/£5
Something in Disguise, Jonathan Cape, 1969 £10/£5
ditto, Viking (U.S.), 1970 . . . . . £10/£5
Odd Girl Out, Jonathan Cape, 1972 . . . £10/£5
ditto, Viking (U.S.), 1972 . . . . . £10/£5
Mr Wrong, Jonathan Cape, 1975. . . . £10/£5
ditto, Viking (U.S.), 1975 . . . . . £10/£5

Getting it Right, Hamish Hamilton, 1982 . £10/£5
ditto, Viking (U.S.), 1982 . . . . . £10/£5
The Light Years, Macmillan, 1990 . . . £10/£5
ditto, Pocket Books (U.S.), 1990. . . . £10/£5
Making Time, Macmillan, 1991 . . . . £10/£5
ditto, Pocket Books (U.S.), 1992. . . . £10/£5
Casting Off, Macmillan, 1995 . . . . £10/£5
ditto, Pocket Books (U.S.), 1996. . . . £10/£5

Short Stories
We Are For the Dark, Jonathan Cape, 1951 (with Robert Aickman). . . . . £250/£75

As Editor
The Lover's Companion, David & Charles, 1978 . . . . £10/£5

Miscellaneous
Howard and Maschler on Food, Michael Joseph, 1987 (with Fay Maschler) . . . . £10/£5

ROBERT E. HOWARD
(b.1906 d.1936)

A Texan writer of pulp fiction, his range extended beyond his 'Conan' tales through westerns and sports stories.

'Conan' Novels
Conan the Conqueror: The Hyperborean Age, Gnome Press (U.S.), 1950 . . . . £200/£100
ditto, Boardman, 1954. . . . . £125/£50
The Return of Conan, Gnome Press (U.S.), 1957 (by L. Sprague de Camp & Bjorn Nyberg) . . £125/£50
People of the Black Circle, Grant (U.S.), 1974 . . . . £35/£15
Red Nails, Grant (U.S.), 1975 . . . . £25/£10
A Witch Shall Be Born, Grant (U.S.), 1975 £25/£10
The Hour of the Dragon, Grant (U.S.), 1989 £20/£10

'Conan' Stories
The Sword of Conan: The Hyperborean Age, Gnome Press (U.S.), 1952 . . . . £200/£75
King Conan: The Hyperborean Age, Gnome Press (U.S.), 1953 . . . . £200/£75
The Coming of Conan, Gnome Press (U.S.), 1953 . . . . £150/£65
Conan the Barbarian, Gnome Press (U.S.), 1954 . . . . £150/£65
Tales of Conan, Gnome Press (U.S.), 1955 (with L. Sprague de Camp) . . . . £125/£50
Conan the Adventurer, Lancer (U.S.), 1966 (wraps) £10
Conan the Usurper, Lancer (U.S.), 1967 (wraps) £10
The Tower of the Elephant, Grant (U.S.), 1975 . . . . £25/£10
The Devil in Iron, Grant (U.S.), 1976 . . £25/£10
Rogues in the House, Grant (U.S.), 1976 . £25/£10
Queen of the Black Coast, Grant (U.S.), 1978 £25/£10
Black Colossus, Grant (U.S.), 1979 . . . £25/£10
Jewels of Gwahlur, Grant (U.S.), 1979 . . £25/£10
The Pool of the Black One, Grant (U.S.), 1986 . . . . £25/£10
The Conan Chronicles, Orbit, 1990 (two vols, wraps). £10

Other Novels
Almuric, Ace (U.S.), 1964 (wraps) £10
ditto, N.E.L., 1971 (wraps) £5

Other Short Stories
A Gent from Bear Creek, Herbert Jenkins, 1937 . . . . £1,750/£1,000
ditto, Grant (U.S.), 1966 . . . . £25/£5
Skull-Face and Others, Arkham House (U.S.), 1946 . . . . £500/£200
ditto, as ***Skull-Face Omnibus***, Spearman, 1974 . . . . £35/£20
The Dark Man and Others, Arkham House (U.S.), 1963 . . . . £145/£45
ditto, as ***The Dark Man Omnibus***, Panther 1978 (two vols, wraps) £10
The Pride of Bear Creek, Grant (U.S.), 1966 £45/£15
King Kull, Lancer (U.S.), 1967 (wraps, with Lin Carter) £5
Bran Mak Morn, Dell (U.S.), 1969 (wraps) . £5
ditto, Sphere, 1976 (wraps) £5
ditto, as ***Kull***, Grant (U.S.), 1985 (revised text) £20/£10
Wolfshead, Lancer (U.S.), 1968 (wraps) . . £5
Red Shadows, Grant (U.S.), 1968 . . . £125/£30
Red Blades of Black Cathay, Grant (U.S.), 1971 (with Tevis Clyde Smith) . . . . £75/£25
Marchers of Valhalla, Grant (U.S.), 1972 . £20/£5
ditto, Sphere, 1977 (wraps) £5
The Vultures, Fictioneer (U.S.), 1973 . . £20/£10
The Sowers of the Thunder, Grant (U.S.), 1973 . . . . £35/£10
ditto, Sphere, 1977 (wraps) £5
Worms of the Earth, Grant (U.S.), 1974 . £25/£10
ditto, Orbit/Futura, 1976 (wraps) £5
The Incredible Adventures of Dennis Dorgan, Fax (U.S.), 1974 . . . . £15/£5
The Lost Valley of Iskander, Fax (U.S.), 1974 £15/£5
ditto, Orbit/Futura, 1976 (wraps). £5
Tigers of the Sea, Grant (U.S.), 1974 . . £20/£5
ditto, Sphere, 1977 (wraps) £5
Black Vulmea's Vengeance and Other Tales of Pirates, Grant (U.S.), 1976 . . . . . £15/£5

The Iron Man and Other Tales of the Ring, Grant (U.S.), 1976 . . . . £10/£5
The Swords of Shahrazar, Fax (U.S.), 1976 £10/£5
ditto, Orbit/Futura, 1976 (wraps) £5
Son of the White Wolf, Fax (U.S.), 1977 . £10/£5
ditto, Futura, 1977 (wraps) £5
Three-Bladed Doom, Futura, 1977 (wraps) . . £5
Mayhem on Bear Creek, Fax (U.S.), 1979 . £15/£5
The Road to Azrael, Grant (U.S.), 1979 . £15/£5
Lord of the Dead, Grant (U.S.), 1981 . . £15/£5
Cthulhu: The Mythos and Kindred Horrors, Baen (U.S.), 1987 . . . . £20/£5
Post Oaks and Sand Roughs, Grant (U.S.), 1991 . . . . £15/£5

Verse
Always Comes Evening, Arkham House (U.S.), 1957 . . . . £300/£100
Etchings in Ivory: Poems in Prose, Glenn Lord (U.S.), 1968 . . . . £150/£50
Singers in the Shadows, Grant (U.S.), 1970 (500 copies) . . . . £75/£25
Echoes from an Iron Harp, Grant (U.S.), 1972 . . . . £45/£15
Rhymes of Death, McHaney (U.S.), 1975 (600 numbered copies) £40
Shadows of Dreams, Grant (U.S.), 1991 . £20/£10

L. RON HUBBARD
(b.1911 d.1986)

Although he has written a number of very collectable science fiction titles, L. Ron Hubbard is best-known as the founder of Scientology.

Novels
Buckskin Brigades, Macauley (U.S.), 1937 . . . . £1,250/£200
ditto, Wright & Brown, [1938] . . . . £450/£75
Final Blackout, Hadley Publishing (U.S.), 1948 . . . . £200/£65
ditto, New Era, 1989 . . . . £15/£5
Death's Deputy, Fantasy Publishing (U.S.), 1948 . . . . £125/£35
ditto, Fantasy Publishing/Gnome Press, 1959 £75/£25
Slaves of Sleep, Shasta (U.S.), 1938 . . . £200/£75
ditto, Shasta (U.S.), 1938 (250 signed copies) . . . . £1,250/£1000
Triton, Fantasy Publishing (U.S.), 1949 . . £100/£25
The Kingslayer, Fantasy Publishing (U.S.), 1949 . . . . £100/£25
Typewriter in the Sky and Fear, Gnome Press (U.S.), 1951 . . . . £100/£25
ditto, Fantasy Publishing/Gnome (U.S.), 1959 £45/£20
From Death to the Stars, Fantasy Publishing (U.S.), 1953) . . . . £350/£65
Return to Tomorrow, Ace (U.S.), 1954 (wraps) £10
ditto, Panther, 1957 (wraps) £5
Fear and the Ultimate Adventure, Berkley Medallion (U.S.), 1970 (wraps) £10
Seven Steps to the Arbiter, Major Books (U.S.) 1975 (wraps) £10
Battlefield Earth, St. Martin's Press (U.S.), 1982 . . . . £20/£5
ditto, Quadrant, 1984 . . . . £15/£5
Mission Earth, Bridge Publications (U.S.), 1985-87 (ten vols: 'The Invader's Plan', 'Death Quest', 'Black Genesis', 'The Enemy Within', 'An Alien Affair', 'Fortune of Fear', 'Voyage of Vengeance', 'Disaster', 'Villainy Victorious' and 'The Doomed Planet') . . . . £10/£5 each
ditto, New Era, 1986-88 (10 vols) . . £10/£5 each
ditto, Bridge Publications (U.S.), 1987 (set) £200

Short Stories
Ole Doc Methuselah, Theta Press (U.S.), 1970 £75/£25
ditto, New Era, 1993 . . . . . £10/£5
Lives You Wished to Lead but Never Dared, Theta Books (U.S.), 1978 . . . . £150/£45

Dianetics
Dianetics: The Modern Science of Mental Health, Hermitage House, 1950 . . . . . £300/£150

TED HUGHES
(b.1930 d.1998)

Hughes is chiefly known for his poetry which often depicts the cruelties of the animal world, and the malevolence of creatures of his own invention. In 1984 he was made Poet Laureate.

Verse
The Hawk in the Rain, Faber, 1957 . . . £200/£50
ditto, Harper (U.S.), 1957. . . . . . . £100/£35
Pike, Gehenna Press, 1959 (broadsheet, 150 signed copies) £225
Lupercal, Faber, 1960. . . . . . . £125/£45
ditto, Harper (U.S.), 1960. . . . . . £75/£25
Selected Poems, Faber, 1962 (with Thom Gunn) . . . . £15/£5
The Burning of the Brothel, Turret Books, 1966 (75 numbered and signed copies) £200
ditto, Turret Books, 1966 (225 unsigned copies) £75
Recklings, Turret Books, 1966 (150 numbered and signed copies) £200

Scapegoats and Rabies, Poet & Printer, 1967 (approx. 400 copies) £50
Wodwo, Faber, 1967 . . . . £40/£15
ditto, Harper (U.S.), 1967. . . . . . . £15/£5
Animal Poems, Gilbertson, 1967 (6 signed copies with poems handwritten by Hughes) £750
ditto, Gilbertson, 1967 (10 signed copies with three manuscript poems) £450
ditto, Gilbertson, 1967 (20 signed copies with 1 manuscript poem) £250
ditto, Gilbertson, 1967 (64 signed copies) . . £100
Gravestones, Bartholomew, 1967 (set of 6 broadsheets, 40 sets printed) £150
I Said Goodbye to Earth, Turret Books, 1969 (broadsheet, 75 signed copies) £150
A Crow Hymn, Sceptre Press, 1970 (21 signed copies for sale) £150
ditto, Sceptre Press, 1970 (64 unsigned copies). £45
The Martyrdom of Bishop Farrar, Gilbertson, 1970 (100 signed copies) £100
A Few Crows, Rougemont Press, 1970 (75 signed copies) £125
ditto, Rougemont Press, 1970 (75 unsigned copies) £45
Crow, Faber, 1970. . . . . £40/£10
ditto, Harper (U.S.), 1971. . . . . . . £25/£10
Fighting for Jerusalem, Northumberland Arts, 1970 (poster) £25
Crow Wakes, Poet & Printer, 1971 (100 copies) £75
Eat Crow, Rainbow Press, 1971 (150 signed, numbered copies) £150
Poems, Rainbow Press, 1971 (with Ruth Fainlight and Alan Sillitoe, 300 copies, numbered and signed by all three poets) £150
Selected Poems, 1957-1967, Faber, 1972 (wraps) £10
ditto, Harper (U.S.), 1973. . . . . £10
Prometheus on His Crag, Rainbow Press, 1973 (160 copies signed by Hughes and Leonard Baskin) £175
Cave Birds, Scolar Press, 1975 (10 sheets issued in box, 125 sets printed) £200
ditto, Faber, 1978 (trade edition) . . . . . £25/£5
The Interrogator: A Titled Vultress, Scolar Press, 1975 . . . . £15/£5
The New World, O.U.P., 1975 . . . . . £15/£5
Eclipse, Sceptre Press, 1976 (50 signed copies) £75
ditto, Sceptre Press, 1976 (200 unsigned copies) £25
Gaudete, Faber, 1977 . . . . £20/£5
ditto, Harper (U.S.), 1977. . . . . . . £10/£5
Chiasmadon, Janus Press (U.S.), 1977 (175 signed copies) £100
Sunstruck, Sceptre Press, 1977 (50 signed copies) £100
ditto, Sceptre Press, 1977 (200 numbered copies) £30
A Solstice, Sceptre Press, 1978 (500 signed copies) £100
ditto, Sceptre Press, 1978 (250 numbered copies) £25
Orts, Rainbow Press, 1978 (200 numbered and signed copies) £100
Moortown Elegies, Rainbow Press, 1978 (6 author's copies) £750
ditto, Rainbow Press, 1978 (26 lettered A-Z) . £250
ditto, Rainbow Press, 1978 (143 numbered copies) £125
Adam and the Sacred Nine, Rainbow Press, 1979 (200 numbered and signed copies) £125
Remains of Elmet, Rainbow Press, 1979 (numbered 1-70, signed by Hughes and the artist, leather bound) £250
ditto, Rainbow Press, 1979 (numbered 71-180 signed by Hughes, ordinary binding) £75
ditto, Faber, 1979 . . . . £25/£10
The Threshold, Steam Press, 1979 (100 copies of 12 leaves, illustrated by Ralph Steadman, and signed by Hughes and Steadman) £225
Night Arrival of Sea-Trout, The Iron Wolf, Puma, Morrigu Press, 1979 (three broadsheets, 30 sets) £100
Brooktrout, Morrigu Press, 1979 (broadsheet, 60 copies) £40
Pan, Morrigu Press, 1979 (broadsheet, 60 copies) £50
Woodpecker, Morrigu Press, 1979 (broadsheet, 60 copies) £50
Moortown, Faber, 1979 . . . . . . £20/£5
ditto, Harper (U.S.), 1980. . . . . . . £10/£5
Wolverine, Morrigu Press, 1979, (broadsheet, 75 copies) £40
Four Tales Told by an Idiot, Sceptre Press, 1979 (450 numbered copies) £25
ditto, Sceptre Press, 1979 (100 signed copies) . £100
In the Black Chapel, Victoria and Albert Museum, 1979 (poster) £25
Eagle, Morrigu Press, 1980, (broadsheet, 75 copies) £35
Mosquito, Morrigu Press, 1980, (broadsheet, 60 copies) £35
Catadrome, Morrigu Press, 1980, (broadsheet, 75 copies) £35
Caddis, Morrigu Press, 1980, (broadsheet, 75 copies) £35
Visitation, Morrigu Press, 1980, (broadsheet, 75 copies) £35
A Primer of Birds, Gehenna Press, 1981 (signed by Hughes and artist, Leonard Baskin). £75
Selected Poems, 1957-1981, Faber, 1982 . £15/£5
ditto, as ***New Selected Poems***, Harper (U.S.), 1982 . . . . £10/£5
River, Faber, 1983. . . . . £25/£5
ditto, Harper (U.S.), 1984. . . . . £15/£5
Weasels at Work, Morrigu Press, 1983 (75 copies) £35
Fly Inspects, Morrigu Press, 1983 (75 copies) . £35
Mice are Funny Little Creatures, Morrigu Press, 1983 (75 copies) £35

Flowers and Insects: Some Birds and a Pair of Spiders, Faber, 1986 . . . . £15/£5
ditto, Knopf (U.S.), 1986 . . . . £10/£5
Moortown Diary, Faber, 1989 . . . . £15/£5
ditto, Faber, 1989 (wraps). £5
Wolf-Watching, Faber, 1989 . . . . . . £15/£5
Rain-Charm for the Duchy, Faber, 1992 . £15/£5
ditto, Faber, 1992 (signed, limited edition) . . £100
ditto, Faber, 1992 (wraps). £5
Three Books: Remains of Elmet, Cave Birds, River, Faber, 1993 . . . . £5
Elmet, Faber, 1984 . . . . £30/£10
Earth Dances, Old Stile Press, 1994. . . . £75
New Selected Poems, 1957-94, Faber, 1995 £15/£5
Ted Hughes Poetry, Collins Educational, 1997 £10/£5
Birthday Letters, Faber, 1998 . . . . £20/£5

Children's Verse
Meet My Folks!, Faber, 1961 . . . . . £75/£20
ditto, Bobbs-Merrill (U.S.), 1973. . . . £15/£5
The Earth-Owl and Other Moon-People, Faber, 1963 . . . . £40/£15
ditto, as ***Moon Whales and Other Moon People***, Viking (U.S.), 1976 . . . . £15/£5
ditto, as ***Moonwhales***, Faber, 1988 . . . £10/£5
Nessie the Mannerless Monster, Faber, 1964 £50/£15
ditto, as ***Nessie the Monster***, Bobbs-Merrill (U.S.), 1974 . . . . £15/£5
Five Autumn Songs for Children's Voices, Gilbertson, 1968 (9 copies for sale with a verse in manuscript & a watercolour) £250
ditto, Gilbertson, 1968 (27 copies with a verse in manuscript) £200
ditto, Gilbertson, 1968 (150 signed copies) . . £75
ditto, Gilbertson, 1968 (312 numbered copies) . £25
Spring Summer Autumn Winter, Rainbow Press, 1974 (140 numbered and signed copies) £175
ditto, as ***Season Songs***, Doubleday (U.S.), 1975 £10/£5
ditto, Faber, 1976 . . . . £10/£5
Earth-Moon, Rainbow Press, 1976 (226 signed and numbered copies) £150
Moon Bells and Other Poems, Chatto & Windus, 1978 . . . . £15/£5
Under the North Star, Faber, 1981 . . . . £20/£5
ditto, Viking (U.S.), 1981 . . . . £15/£5
The Cat and the Cuckoo, Sunstone Press, [1987] . . . . £20/£5
ditto, Sunstone Press, [1987] (250 signed copies in d/w and slipcase) . . . . £75/£50
ditto, Faber, 1991 . . . . £10/£5
Under the North Star and Others, Faber, 1990 £20/£5
The Mermaids Purse, Faber, 1991 . . . . £15/£5
Collected Animal Poems, Faber, 1995 (4 vols) £30/£10
ditto, Faber, 1996 (1 vol.). . . . . . . £10/£5

Children's Prose
How the Whale Became, Faber, 1963 . . £50/£15
ditto, Atheneum (U.S.), 1964 . . . . . . £25/£10
The Iron Man, Faber, 1968 . . . . . . £50/£15
ditto, as ***The Iron Giant***, Harper (U.S.), 1968 £15/£5
What is the Truth?, Faber, 1984 . . . . . £15/£5
ditto, Harper (U.S.), 1984 . . . . £10/£5
Ffangs the Vampire Bat and the Kiss of Truth, Faber, 1986 . . . . £10/£5
Tales of the Early World, Faber, 1988 . . £10/£5
The Iron Woman, Faber, 1993 . . . . . £10/£5
Dreamfighter and Other Creation Tales, Faber, 1995 . . . . £10/£5
Shaggy and Spotty, Faber, 1997 . . . £10/£5

Others
Poetry in the Making, Faber, 1967 . . . £50/£15
ditto, as ***Poetry Is***, Doubleday (U.S.), 1970 . £25/£10
Seneca's Oedipus, Faber, 1969 . . . . £25/£5
ditto, Doubleday (U.S.), 1972 . . . . £20/£5
The Coming of the Kings and Other Plays, Faber, 1970 . . . . £25/£5
ditto, as ***Tiger's Bones and Other Plays for Children***, Viking (U.S.), 1974 . . . . £15/£5
Shakespeare's Poem, Lexham Press, 1971 (75 signed copies) £100
Orpheus, Dramatic Publishing Company (U.S.), 1973 (1,023 copies) £30
Henry Williamson, Rainbow Press, 1979 (200 signed copies, wraps) £50
T.S. Eliot: A Tribute, Faber, 1987 (privately printed, 250 copies) £75
Shakespeare and the Goddess of Complete Being, Faber, 1992 . . . . £10/£5
Winter Pollen: Occasional Prose, Faber, 1994 £10/£5
Difficulties of a Bridegroom, Faber, 1995 £10/£5

ALDOUS HUXLEY

(b.1894 d.1963)

A novelist and short story writer, much of Huxley's work is marked by a certain despair and disgust, none more so than his great novel of the future, *Brave New World*.

Verse
The Burning Wheel, Blackwell, 1916 (wraps) . £450
Jonah, Holywell, 1917 (approx. 50 signed copies, wraps) £750
The Defeat of Youth and Other Poems, Blackwell, 1918 (500 copies, wraps) £100
Leda, Chatto & Windus, 1920 . . . . . . £75
ditto, Chatto & Windus, 1920 (160 numbered and

signed copies) £250
ditto, Doran (U.S.), 1920 . . . . £45
ditto, Doran (U.S.), 1920 (361 numbered and signed copies) £100
Selected Poems, Blackwell, 1925 . . . . £50/£15
ditto, Blackwell, 1925 (100 signed copies) . . £250
ditto, Appleton (U.S.), 1925 . . . . . . £30/£10
Arabia Infelix, Fountain Press (U.S.), Chatto & Windus, 1929 (692 signed, numbered copies, glassine d/w) . . . . £100/£75
Apennine, Slide Mountain Press (U.S.), 1930 (91 signed, numbered copies, glasine d/w) . . £200/£175
The Cicadas and Other Poems, Chatto & Windus, 1931 . . . . £35/£10
ditto, Chatto & Windus, 1931 (160 signed, numbered copies) £175
ditto, Doubleday Doran (U.S.), 1931. . . £25/£10
Verses and a Comedy, Chatto & Windus, 1946 £20

Short Stories

Limbo, Chatto & Windus, 1920 (6 stories and a play) . . . . £75/£25
ditto, Doran (U.S.), 1920 . . . . £45/£15
Mortal Coils, Chatto & Windus, 1922 . . . £75/£25
ditto, Doran (U.S.), 1922 . . . . £45/£15
Little Mexican and Other Stories, Chatto & Windus, 1924 . . . . £100/£35
ditto, Doran (U.S.), 1924 . . . . £75/£25
Two or Three Graces and Other Stories, Chatto & Windus, 1926. . . . . £75/£25
ditto, Doran (U.S.), 1926 . . . . £50/£15
Brief Candles, Chatto & Windus, 1930 . . £75/£15
ditto, Doubleday Doran (U.S.), 1930. . . . £50/£10
ditto, Fountain Press (U.S.), 1930 (800 signed copies) £150
Collected Short Stories, Chatto & Windus, 1957 . . . . £15/£5
ditto, Harper (U.S.), 1957. . . . . . . £15/£5

Novels

Crome Yellow, Chatto & Windus, 1921 . . £250/£75
ditto, Doran (U.S.), 1922 . . . . £175/£45
Antic Hay, Chatto & Windus, 1923 . . . £175/£40
ditto, Doran (U.S.), 1923 . . . . £100/£25
Those Barren Leaves, Chatto & Windus, 1925 £75/£15
ditto, Doran (U.S.), 1925 . . . . £65/£15
ditto, Doran, 1925 (250 signed, numbered copies) £200
Point Counter Point, Chatto & Windus, 1928 £125/£25
ditto, Chatto & Windus, 1928 (256 signed and numbered copies) £200
ditto, Doubleday Doran (U.S.), 1928. . . . £75/£15
Brave New World, Chatto & Windus, 1932 £500/£150
ditto, Chatto & Windus, 1932 (324 signed numbered copies) £1,250
ditto, Doubleday Doran (U.S.), 1932. . . £250/£75
ditto, Doubleday Doran (U.S.), 1932 (250 signed numbered copies) £750
Eyeless in Gaza, Chatto & Windus, 1936 . £65/£15
ditto, Chatto & Windus, 1936 (200 signed, numbered copies) £175
ditto, Harper (U.S.), 1936. . . . . . £40/£10
After Many a Summer, Chatto & Windus, 1939 . . . . £65/£15
ditto, Harper (U.S.), 1939. . . . . . £40/£10
Time Must Have a Stop, Chatto & Windus, 1944 . . . . £25/£10
ditto, Harper (U.S.), 1944. . . . . . £25/£10
Ape and Essence, Chatto & Windus, 1948 . £20/£5
ditto, Harper (U.S.), 1948. . . . . . . £10/£5
The Genius and the Goddess, Chatto & Windus, 1955 . . . . £15/£5
ditto, Harper (U.S.), 1955. . . . . . £10/£5
Island, Chatto & Windus, 1961 . . . . £10/£5
ditto, Harper (U.S.), 1961. . . . . . . £10/£5

Drama

The World of Light, Chatto & Windus, 1931 £35/£10
ditto, Chatto & Windus, 1931 (160 signed, numbered copies) £150
ditto, Doubleday Doran (U.S.), 1931. . . £25/£5
The Gioconda Smile, Chatto & Windus, 1948 £25/£5
ditto, Harper (U.S.), 1948. . . . . . . £20/£5

Others

On the Margin, Chatto & Windus, 1923 . £75/£20
ditto, Doran (U.S.), 1923 . . . . £20/£5
Along the Road, Chatto & Windus, 1925 . £75/£20
ditto, Doran (U.S.), 1925 . . . . £20/£5
ditto, Doran, 1925 (250 signed, numbered copies) . . . . £175/£45
Essays New and Old, Chatto & Windus, 1926 (650 signed, numbered copies) £75
ditto, Doran (U.S.), 1927 . . . . £25/£5
Jesting Pilate, Chatto & Windus, 1926 . . £100/£20
ditto, Doran (U.S.), 1926 . . . . £75/£20
Proper Studies, Chatto & Windus, 1927. . £35/£10
ditto, Chatto & Windus, 1927 (260 signed copies) £125
ditto, Doubleday Doran (U.S.), 1928. . . £25/£15
Do What You Will, Chatto & Windus, 1929 £50/£15
ditto, Doubleday Doran (U.S.), 1929. . . £35/£10
Holy Face and Other Essays, The Fleuron Press, 1929 (300 numbered copies) £175
Vulgarity in Literature, Chatto & Windus, 1930, No. 1 of the 'Dolphin's Books' . . . . £20/£10
ditto, Chatto & Windus, 1930 (260 signed, numbered copies) £125
Music at Night and Other Essays, Chatto & Windus, 1931 . . . . £25/£10
ditto, Chatto & Windus/Fountain Press 1931 (842 signed, numbered copies) £100

ditto, Doubleday Doran (U.S.), 1931 . . . £15/£5
Rotunda, Chatto & Windus, 1932 . . . . £25/£10
T.H. Huxley as a Man of Letters, Macmillan, 1932 . . . . £25
Texts and Pretexts, Chatto & Windus, 1932 (214 signed copies) £175
ditto, Chatto & Windus, 1932 . . . . . £25/£5
ditto, Harper (U.S.), 1933 . . . . £20/£5
Beyond the Mexique Bay, Chatto & Windus, 1934 . . . . £125/£25
ditto, Chatto & Windus, 1934 (210 signed, numbered copies) £200
ditto, Harper (U.S.), 1934 . . . . £45/£10
The Olive Tree and Other Essays, Chatto & Windus, 1936 . . . . £45/£10
ditto, Chatto & Windus, 1936 (160 signed, numbered copies) £200
ditto, Harper (U.S.), 1937 . . . . £35/£10
What Are You Going to do About It? The Case for Constructive Peace, Chatto & Windus, 1936 (wraps) £35
ditto, Harper (U.S.), 1937 . . . . £15
Ends and Means, Chatto & Windus, 1937 . £15/£5
ditto, Chatto & Windus, 1937 (160 signed, numbered copies) £150
ditto, Harper (U.S.), 1937 . . . . £15/£5
The Most Agreeable Vice, Ward Ritchie Press (U.S.), 1938 (500 copies, wraps) £250
Beyond the Swarm, Ward Ritchie Press (U.S.), 1939 (300 copies, wraps) £250
Grey Eminence, Chatto & Windus, 1941 . £15/£5
ditto, Harper (U.S.), 1941 . . . . £15/£5
The Art of Seeing, Chatto & Windus, 1942 . £25/£5
ditto, Harper (U.S.), 1942 . . . . £25/£5
The Perennial Philosophy, Chatto & Windus, 1945 . . . . £30/£5
ditto, Harper (U.S.), 1945 . . . . £25/£5
Science, Liberty and Peace, Chatto & Windus, 1946 . . . . £15/£5
ditto, Harper (U.S.), 1946 . . . . £15/£5
The Prisons, Trianon Press, 1949 (212 signed and numbered copies, slipcase) £250
ditto, Trianon Press, 1949 (1,000 unsigned copies) £45
ditto, Zeitlin & Ver Brugge (U.S.), 1949 (212 signed and numbered copies, slipcase) £250
Themes and Variations, Chatto & Windus, 1950 . . . . £15/£5
ditto, Harper (U.S.), 1950 . . . . £15/£5
The Devils of Loudun, Chatto & Windus, 1952 £25/£5
ditto, Harper (U.S.), 1952 . . . . £20/£5
The Doors of Perception, Chatto & Windus, 1954 . . . . £45/£10
ditto, Harper (U.S.), 1954 . . . . £40/£10
Adonis and the Alphabet, Chatto & Windus, 1956 . . . . £15/£5
ditto, as ***Tomorrow and Tomorrow and Tomorrow***, Harper (U.S.), 1956 . . . . £15/£5
Heaven and Hell, Chatto & Windus, 1956 . £25/£5
ditto, Harper (U.S.), 1956 . . . . £10/£5
Brave New World Revisited, Chatto & Windus, 1958 . . . . £30/£5
ditto, Harper (U.S.), 1958 . . . . £25/£5

HAMMOND INNES

(b.1913 d.1998)

Ralph Hammond Innes' thrillers have been translated into many languages, and appear in book club and wraps editions throughout the world.

Novels

The Doppelganger, Jenkins, 1936 . . . £450/£60
Air Disaster, Jenkins, 1937 . . . . . £350/£50
Sabotage Broadcast, Jenkins, 1938 . . . £350/£50
All Roads Lead to Friday, Jenkins, 1939 . £350/£50
Wreckers Must Breathe, Collins, 1940 . . £250/£45
The Trojan Horse, Collins, 1940 . . . £200/£30
Attack Alarm, Collins, 1941 . . . . . £100/£20
Dead and Alive, Collins, 1946 . . . . £60/£15
The Lonely Skier, Collins, 1947 . . . . £60/£15
The Killer Mine, Collins, 1947 . . . . £40/£5
Maddon's Rock, Collins, 1948 . . . . £40/£5
The Blue Ice, Collins, 1948 . . . . . £40/£5
The White South, Collins, 1949 . . . . £35/£5
The Angry Mountain, Collins, 1950 . . . £35/£5
Air Bridge, Collins, 1951 . . . . . . £35/£5
Campbell's Kingdom, Collins, 1952 . . . £35/£5
The Strange Land, Collins, 1954 . . . £25/£5
The Mary Deare, Collins, 1956 . . . . £25/£5
The Land God Gave to Cain, Collins, 1958 £25/£5
The Doomed Oasis, Collins, 1960 . . . £30/£5
Atlantic Fury, Collins, 1962 . . . . . £20/£5
The Strode Venturer, Collins, 1965 . . . £15/£5
Levkas Man, Collins, 1971 . . . . . £15/£5
Golden Soak, Collins, 1973 . . . . . £10/£5
North Star, Collins, 1974 . . . . . . £10/£5
The Big Footprints, Collins, 1977 . . . £10/£5
Solomon's Seal, Collins, 1980 . . . . £10/£5
The Black Tide, Collins, 1982 . . . . £10/£5
High Stand, Collins, 1985 . . . . . £10/£5
Medusa, Collins, 1988 . . . . £10/£5
Isvik, Chapmans, 1991 . . . . £10/£5
The Delta Connection, Macmillan, 1996 . £10/£5

Children's (pseud. 'Ralph Hammond')

Cocos Island, Collins, 1950 . . . . . £35/£10
Isle of Strangers, Collins, 1951 . . . . £35/£10

Saracen's Tower, Collins, 1952 . . . . £35/£10
Black Gold on the Double Diamond, Collins, 1953 . . . . £35/£10

Non Fiction
Harvest of Journeys, Collins, 1960 . . . £15/£5
Scandinavia, Time-Life (U.S.), 1963 . . . £10
Sea and Islands, Collins, 1967 . . . . £10/£5
The Conquistadores, Collins, 1969 . . . £10/£5
ditto, Collins, 1969 (deluxe leather-bound edition) £200
Hammond Innes Introduces Australia, Andre Deutsch, 1971 . . . . £10/£5
The Last Voyage: Captain Cook's Lost Diary, Collins, 1979 . . . . £15/£5
Hammond Innes' East Anglia, Hodder and Stoughton, 1986 . . . . £15/£5

MICHAEL INNES
(b.1906 d.1994)

Innes is the pseudonym used by J.I.M. Stewart when writing his many detective novels. These range from the ingenious and urbane through to straightforward chase novels.

Death at the President's Lodging, Gollancz, 1936 . . . . £200/£45
ditto, as ***Seven Suspects***, Dodd Mead (U.S.), 1936 . . . . £200/£55
Hamlet, Revenge!, Gollancz, 1937 . . . £150/£35
ditto, Dodd Mead (U.S.), 1938 . . . . £150/£35
Lament for a Maker, Gollancz, 1938 . . £250/£45
ditto, Dodd Mead (U.S.), 1938 . . . . £250/£45
Stop Press, Gollancz, 1939 . . . . . . £125/£25
There Came Both Mist and Snow, Gollancz, 1940 . . . . £100/£25
ditto, as ***A Comedy of Terrors***, Dodd Mead (U.S.), 1940 . . . . £250/£45
The Secret Vanguard, Gollancz, 1940 . . £100/£25
ditto, Dodd Mead (U.S.), 1941 . . . . £75/£25
Appleby on Ararat, Gollancz, 1941 . . . £200/£45
ditto, Dodd Mead (U.S.), 1941 . . . . £75/£25
The Daffodil Affair, Gollancz, 1942. . . £50/£15
ditto, Dodd Mead (U.S.), 1942 . . . . £50/£15
The Weight of the Evidence, Gollancz, 1944 £45/£15
ditto, Dodd Mead (U.S.), 1943 . . . . £45/£15
Appleby's End, Gollancz, 1945 . . . . £40/£15
From London Far, Gollancz, 1946 . . . £40/£15
What Happened at Hazelwood, Gollancz, 1946 . . . . £40/£15
A Night of Errors, Gollancz, 1948 . . . £35/£10
The Journeying Boy, Gollancz, 1949 . . £30/£10
Operation Pax, Gollancz, 1951 . . . . £30/£10
ditto, as ***The Paper Thunderbolt***, Dodd Mead (U.S.), 1951 . . . . £20/£5
A Private View, Gollancz, 1952 . . . . £25/£5
ditto, as ***One-Man Show***, Dodd Mead (U.S.), 1952 . . . . £20/£5
Christmas at Candleshoe, Gollancz, 1953 . £20/£5
The Man from the Sea, Gollancz, 1955 . . £20/£5
ditto, Dodd Mead (U.S.), 1951? . . . . £15/£5
Old Hall, New Hall, Gollancz, 1956. . . £20/£5
Appleby Plays Chicken, Gollancz, 1956. . £20/£5
The Long Farewell, Gollancz, 1958 . . . £20/£5
ditto, Dodd Mead (U.S.), 1958 . . . . £15/£5
Hare Sitting Up, Gollancz, 1959. . . . £20/£5
ditto, Dodd Mead (U.S.), 1959 . . . . £15/£5
The New Sonia Wayward, Gollancz, 1960 . £15/£5
ditto, as ***The Case of Sonia Wayward***, Dodd Mead (U.S.), 1960 . . . . £15/£5
Silence Observed, Gollancz, 1961 . . . £15/£5
A Connoisseur's Case, Gollancz, 1962 . . £15/£5
ditto, as ***The Crabtree Affair***, Dodd Mead (U.S.), 1962 . . . . £15/£5
Money from Holme, Gollancz, 1964 . . £15/£5
Appleby Intervenes, Dodd Mead (U.S.), 1965 £15/£5
The Bloody Wood, Gollancz, 1964 . . . . £15/£5
ditto, Dodd Mead (U.S.), 1966 . . . . £15/£5
A Change of Heir, Gollancz, 1966 . . . £15/£5
ditto, Dodd Mead (U.S.), 1966 . . . . £15/£5
Appleby at Allington, Gollancz, 1968 . . £15/£5
A Family Affair, Gollancz, 1969. . . . £15/£5
Death at the Chase, Gollancz, 1970 . . . £15/£5
ditto, Dodd Mead (U.S.), 1970 . . . . £15/£5
An Awkward Lie, Gollancz, 1971 . . . £15/£5
ditto, Dodd Mead (U.S.), 1971 . . . . £15/£5
The Open House, Gollancz, 1972 . . . £15/£5
ditto, Dodd Mead (U.S.), 1972 . . . . £15/£5
Appleby's Answer, Gollancz, 1973 . . . £15/£5
ditto, Dodd Mead (U.S.), 1973 . . . . £15/£5
Appleby's Other Story, Gollancz, 1974 . . £15/£5
ditto, Dodd Mead (U.S.), 1974 . . . . £15/£5
The Mysterious Commission, Gollancz, 1974 £15/£5
ditto, Dodd Mead (U.S.), 1974 . . . . £15/£5
The Gay Phoenix, Gollancz, 1976 . . . £15/£5
ditto, Dodd Mead (U.S.), 1976 . . . . £15/£5
Honeybath's Haven, Gollancz, 1977 . . £10/£5
ditto, Dodd Mead (U.S.), 1977 . . . . £10/£5
The Ampersand Papers, Gollancz, 1978 . £10/£5
ditto, Dodd Mead (U.S.), 1978 . . . . £10/£5
Going It Alone, Gollancz, 1980 . . . . £10/£5
ditto, Dodd Mead (U.S.), 1980 . . . . £10/£5
Lord Mullion's Secret, Gollancz, 1981 . . £10/£5
ditto, Dodd Mead (U.S.), 1981 . . . . £10/£5
Sheikhs and Adders, Gollancz, 1982 . . £10/£5
ditto, Dodd Mead (U.S.), 1984 . . . . £10/£5
Appleby and Honeybath, Gollancz, 1983 . £10/£5

ditto, Dodd Mead (U.S.), 1983 . . . . . £10/£5
Carson's Conspiracy, Gollancz, 1984 . . £10/£5
ditto, Dodd Mead (U.S.), 1984 . . . . £10/£5
Appleby and the Ospreys, Gollancz, 1986 .. £10/£5
ditto, Dodd Mead (U.S.), 1986 . . . . £10/£5

Short Stories
Appleby Talking, Gollancz, 1954 . . . . £15/£5
Appleby Talks Again, Gollancz, 1956 . . £15/£5
The Appleby File, Gollancz, 1975 . . . £15/£5
ditto, Dodd Mead (U.S.), 1975 . . . . £10/£5

CHRISTOPHER ISHERWOOD
(b.1904 d.1986)

Isherwood is usually remembered for the novels *Mr Norris Changes Trains* and *Goodbye to Berlin*. The latter included the sketch 'Sally Bowles', which was dramatised and turned into the popular musical *Cabaret*.

Novels
All the Conspirators, Cape, 1928 . . £1,000/£100
ditto, New Directions (U.S.), 1958 . . . £25/£10
The Memorial, Hogarth Press, 1931 . . . £200/£100
ditto, New Directions (U.S.), 1946 . . . £25/£10
Mr Norris Changes Trains, Hogarth Press, 1935 . . . . £1,000/£100
ditto, as ***The Last of Mr Norris***, Morrow (U.S.), 1935 . . . . £250/£40
Sally Bowles, Hogarth Press, 1937 . . . £350/£50
Goodbye to Berlin, Hogarth Press, 1939 £600/£100
ditto, Random House (U.S.), 1939 . . . £250/£75
Prater Violet, Random House (U.S.), 1945 . £100/£15
ditto, Methuen, 1946 . . . . £75/£15
The World in the Evening, Random House (U.S.), 1954 . . . . £25/£5
ditto, Methuen, 1954 . . . . £20/£5
Down There on a Visit, Simon & Schuster (U.S.), 1962 . . . . £20/£5
ditto, Methuen, 1962 . . . . £15/£5
A Single Man, Simon & Schuster (U.S.), 1964 £20/£5
ditto, Methuen, 1964 . . . . £15/£5
A Meeting by the River, Simon & Schuster (U.S.), 1967 . . . . £15/£5
ditto, Methuen, 1967 . . . . £15/£5

Omnibus Editions
The Berlin Stories, New Directions (U.S.), 1946 . . . . £25/£10
ditto, as ***The Berlin of Sally Bowles***, Hogarth Press, 1975 . . . . £15/£5

Plays
The Dog Beneath the Skin, Faber, 1935 (with W.H. Auden) . . . . £100/£25
ditto, Random House (U.S.), 1935 . . . £35/£20
The Ascent of F6, Faber, 1936 (with W.H. Auden) . . . . £50/£10
ditto, Random House (U.S.), 1937 . . . £25/£10
On The Frontier, Faber, 1938 (with W.H. Auden) . . . . £75/£25
ditto, Random House (U.S.), 1939 . . . £50/£10

Verse
People One Ought to Know, Doubleday, 1982 £10/£5
ditto, Macmillan, 1982 . . . . . . £10/£5

Others
Lions and Shadows, Hogarth Press, 1938 . £200/£50
ditto, New Directions (U.S.), 1948 . . . £65/£25
Journey to a War, Faber, 1939 (with W.H. Auden) . . . . £100/£35
ditto, Random House (U.S.), 1939 . . . £75/£25
The Condor and the Cows, Random House (U.S.), 1949 . . . . £45/£15
ditto, Methuen, 1949 . . . . £40/£10
Ramakrishna and His Disciples, Simon & Schuster (U.S.), 1965 . . . . £20/£5
ditto, Methuen, 1965 . . . . £20/£5
Exhumations, Simon & Schuster (U.S.), 1966 £15/£5
ditto, Methuen, 1966 . . . . £15/£5
Kathleen and Frank, Simon & Schuster (U.S.), 1971 . . . . £10/£5
ditto, Methuen, 1971 . . . . £10/£5
Frankenstein: The True Story, Avon (U.S.), 1973 (wraps) £5
Christopher and His Kind, Farrar, Strauss and Giroux (U.S.), 1976 . . . . £10/£5
ditto, Farrar, Strauss/Sylvester & Orphanos (U.S.), 1976 (130 signed copies, slipcase) . . . . £250/£245
ditto, Eyre Methuen, 1977 . . . . . . £10/£5
My Guru and His Disciple, Farrar Straus (U.S.), 1980. . . . . £10/£5
ditto, Eyre Methuen, 1980 . . . . . . £10/£5
October, Twelvetrees Press (U.S.), 1980 (150 numbered, signed copies, slipcase) £250
ditto, Twelvetrees Press (U.S.), 1980 (26 signed, lettered copies) £400
ditto, Twelvetrees Press (U.S.), 1980 (wraps) . £20
ditto, Methuen, 1982 (1,000 copies, wraps) . . £20
Diaries, Volume One: 1939-1960, Methuen, 1996 . . . . £15/£5
ditto, HarperCollins (U.S.), 1997 . . . . £15/£5

KAZUO ISHIGURO

(b.1954)

A product of Malcolm Bradbury's creative writing course at the University of East Anglia, Ishiguro's slim, studied novels have become very fashionable following the successful film adaptation of *The Remains of the Day*.

A Pale View of Hills, Faber, 1982 . . . £300/£40
ditto, Putnam (U.S.), 1982 . . . . . . £75/£20
An Artist of the Floating World, Faber, 1986 £45/£10
ditto, Putnam (U.S.), 1986 . . . . . £25/£5
The Remains of the Day, Faber 1989 . . £95/£25
ditto, Knopf (U.S.), 1989 . . . . . . £75/£20
The Unconsoled, Faber 1995. . . . . £15/£5
ditto, Knopf (U.S.), 1995 . . . . . . £15/£5

HENRY JAMES

(b.1843 d.1916)

Highly regarded American (later British) author of early modernist fiction, often producing comedies of manners featuring the American abroad.

Roderick Hudson, Osgood (U.S.) 1876 [1875] £450
ditto, Macmillan, 1879 (3 vols) £2,500
The American, Osgood (U.S.), 1877 . . . £450
ditto, Ward Lock, 1877 (pirated U.K. first edition) £450
ditto, Macmillan, 1879 (authorised U.K. first edition) £400
Watch and Ward, Houghton Osgood (U.S.), 1878 . . . . £400
ditto, Houghton Osgood (U.K.), 1878 . . £400
The Europeans, Macmillan, 1878, (2 vols) . . £500
ditto, Houghton Osgood (U.S.), 1879 . . . £100
Confidence, Chatto & Windus, 1880 [1879] (2 vols) £1,000
ditto, Houghton Osgood (U.S.), 1880 . . . £100
Washington Square; The Pension Beaurepas; A Bundle of Letters, Harper (U.S.), 1881 [1882] £400
ditto, Macmillan, 1881 (2 vols) £1,000
The Portrait of a Lady, Macmillan, 1881, (3 vols) £4,000
ditto, Houghton Mifflin (U.S.), 1882. . . . £250
The Bostonians, Macmillan, 1886, (3 vols) . . £2,500
ditto, Macmillan (U.S.), 1886. . . . . . £200
The Princess Casamassima, Macmillan, 1886, (3 vols) £2,500
ditto, Macmillan (U.S.), 1886. . . . . . £100
The Reverberator, Macmillan, 1888, (2 vols) £1,000
ditto, Macmillan (U.S.), 1888. . . . . . £100
The Tragic Muse, Houghton Mifflin (U.S.), 1890 (2 vols) £500
ditto, Macmillan, 1890, (2 vols) £500
The Other House, Heinemann, 1896, (2 vols) . £500
ditto, Macmillan (U.S.), 1896. . . . . . £65
The Spoils of Poynton, Heinemann, 1897 . . £125
ditto, Houghton Mifflin (U.S.), 1897. . . . £65
What Maisie Knew, Stone (U.S.), 1897 . . . £100
ditto, Heinemann, 1897 (tulips on front cover) . £400
ditto, Heinemann, 1897 (irises on front cover) . £100
In the Cage, Duckworth, 1898 . . . . . £50
ditto, Herbert S. Stone & Co. (U.S.), 1898 . . £50
The Awkward Age, Heinemann, 1899 . . . £75
ditto, Harper (U.S.), 1899. . . . . . . £75
The Sacred Fount, Scribners (U.S.), 1901 (2 vols) £75
ditto, Methuen, 1901 . . . . £50
The Wings of the Dove, Scribners (U.S.), 1902 (2 vols) £200
ditto, Archibald Constable, 1902 . . . . . £200
The Ambassadors, Macmillan, 1903. . . . £75
ditto, Harper (U.S.), 1903 . . . . £50
The Golden Bowl, Scribners (U.S.), 1905 (2 vols). £150
ditto, Methuen, 1905 . . . . £100
The Ivory Tower, Collins, 1917 . . . . . £50
ditto, Scribner (U.S.), 1917 . . . . . . £45
The Sense of the Past, Collins, 1917 (unfinished) £25
ditto, Scribner (U.S.), 1917 . . . . . . £25

Collected Editions

The Collective Edition, Macmillan, 1883, (14 vols) £1,000
ditto, Macmillan, 1883, (14 vols, wraps). . . £600
The New York Edition, Scribners (U.S.), 1907-9, 1918 (26 vols) £2,500
ditto, Scribners (U.S.), 1907-9 (156 copies on handmade paper) £5,000

Short Stories

A Passionate Pilgrim, Osgood (U.S.), 1875 £500
ditto, Macmillan, 1879 (3 vols) £500
Daisy Miller; An International Episode, Four Meetings, Macmillan, 1879 (2 vols) . . . £450
The Madonna of the Future and Other Tales, Macmillan, 1879 (2 vols) £450
Tales of Three Cities, Macmillan, 1884 . . . £75
Stories Revived, Macmillan, 1885 (3 vols) . . £400
The Aspern Papers; Louis Pallant, The Modern Warning, Macmillan, 1888 (2 vols) . . . £350
A London Life; The Patagonia; The Liar; Mrs Temperley, Macmillan, 1889 (2 vols) . . . £250
ditto, Macmillan (U.S.), 1889. . . . . . £75
The Lesson of the Master; The Marriages; The Pupil; Brooksmith; The Solution; Sir Edmund Orme, Macmillan (U.S.), 1892 . . . . £75

ditto, Macmillan, 1892 . . . . £75
The Real Thing and Other Tales, Macmillan (U.S.), 1893 . . . . £75
ditto, Macmillan, 1893 . . . . £75
The Private Life; The Wheel of Time; Lord Beaupre; The Visits; Collaboration; Owen Wingrave, Osgood McIlvane, 1893 . . . . £100
ditto, Harpers (U.S.), 1893 . . . . . . £75
Terminations; The Death of the Lion; The Coxon Fund; The Middle Years; The Altar of the Dead, Heinemann, 1895 . . . . £75
ditto, Harpers (U.S.), 1895 . . . . £75
Embarrassments; The Figure in the Carpet; Glasses; The Next Time; The Way it Came, Heinemann, 1896 . . . . £75
The Two Magics: The Turn of the Screw; Covering End, Heinemann, 1898 . . . . £150
ditto, Macmillan (U.S.), 1898. . . . . . £150
The Soft Side, Methuen, 1900 . . . . . £75
ditto, Macmillan (U.S.), 1900. . . . . . . £75
The Better Sort, Methuen, 1903 . . . . . £50
ditto, Scribners (U.S.), 1900 . . . . . . £35
The Finer Grain, Scribners (U.S.), 1910 . . £35
ditto, Methuen, 1910 . . . . £35
The Outcry, Methuen, 1911 . . . . £25
ditto, Scribners (U.S.), 1911 . . . . . . £25
A Small Boy and Others, Macmillan, 1913 . . £25
ditto, Scribners (U.S.), 1913 . . . . . . £25
Notes of a Son and a Brother, Macmillan, 1914 £25
ditto, Scribners (U.S.), 1914. . . . . . . £25
The Ghostly Tales of Henry James, Rutgers University Press (U.S.), 1948 [1949] . . . . . £25/£5
ditto, as ***Stories of the Supernatural***, Barrie & Jenkins, 1971 . . . . £15/£5

Plays
Theatricals: Two Comedies - Tenants [and] ***Disengaged***, Osgood McIlvaine, 1894 . . . £100
ditto, Harpers (U.S.), 1894 . . . . . . £100
Theatricals: Second Series - The Album; The Reprobate, Osgood McIlvaine, 1895 . . . £75
ditto, Harpers (U.S.), 1895 [1894] £70
The Complete Plays of Henry James, Lippincott (U.S.), 1949 . . . . £45/£15
ditto, Hart-Davis, 1949 . . . . £45/£15

Non Fiction
French Poets and Novelists, Macmillan, 1878 . £300
Hawthorne, Macmillan, 1879 . . . . . . £125
ditto, Harpers (U.S.), 1880 . . . . £45
Portraits of Places, Macmillan, 1883 . . . £100
ditto, Osgood (U.S.), 1884 . . . . £100
Partial Portraits, Macmillan, 1888 . . . . £75
Essays in London and Elsewhere, Osgood McIlvaine, 1893 . . . . £75
A Little Tour in France, Heinemann, 1900 . . £50
ditto, Heinemann, 1900 (150 copies on Japanese vellum) £350
ditto, Houghton, Mifflin (U.S.), 1900 . . . £75
ditto, Cambridge Riverside Press (U.S.), 1900 (250 numbered large paper copies) £150
William Whetmore Story and His Friends, Blackwood, 1903 (2 vols) £150
ditto, Houghton, Mifflin (U.S.), 1903 (2 vols) . £150
English Hours, Heinemann, 1905 . . . . £50
ditto, Houghton, Mifflin (U.S.), 1905 . . . £50
ditto, Cambridge Riverside Press (U.S.), 1905 (400 large paper copies) £125
The American Scene, Chapman & Hall, 1907 . £50
ditto, Scribner's (U.S.), 1946 . . . . . £30/£10
Italian Hours, Heinemann, 1909. . . . . £75
Notes on Novelists, Dent, 1914 . . . . . £40
ditto, Scribner's (U.S.), 1914 . . . . . . £40
The Middle Years, Collins, [1917] £40
ditto, Scribner's (U.S.), 1917 . . . . . . £40
Within the Rim and Other Essays, Collins, [1919] £40
The Letters of Henry James, Macmillan, 1920 (2 vols) . . . . £200/£45
ditto, Scribner's (U.S.), 1920 (2 vols) . . £200/£45
The Painter's Eye, Hart-Davis, 1956 . . £35/£10
The House of Fiction, Hart-Davis, 1957 . £30/£10

M.R. JAMES
(b.1862 d.1936)

A distinguished scholar and academic, James was awarded the Order of Merit in 1930. He had a penchant for the macabre and supernatural, and is famous for his ghost stories.

Ghost Stories
Ghost Stories of an Antiquary, Edward Arnold, 1904 . . . . £500
More Ghost Stories, Edward Arnold, 1911 . . £250
A Thin Ghost, Edward Arnold, 1919 . . . £40
A Warning to the Curious, Edward Arnold, 1925 . . . . £100/£35
Wailing Well, Mill House Press, 1928 (157 numbered copies) £200
Collected Ghost Stories, Edward Arnold, 1931 £75/£15
Two Ghost Stories: A Centenary, Ghost Story Press, 1993 (200 numbered copies) £85

Other Titles
Old Testament Legends, Longmans, 1913 . . £35
The Five Jars, Edward Arnold, 1922 . . £250/£75
ditto, Ash-Tree Press, 1995 . . . . . £75/£25
Abbeys, Great Western Railway, 1925 . . . £20

ditto, Doubleday (U.S.), 1926 . . . . . . £20
Eton and Kings, William and Norgate, 1926 . £15
Suffolk and Norfolk, Dent, 1930 . . . £30/£10
Letters to a Friend, Edward Arnold, 1956 . £25/£10

Edited/Translated by M. R. James
The Apocryphal New Testament, Clarendon Press, 1924 . . . . £25
Judith, Medici, 1928 (illustrated by W.R. Flint) £35
The Book of Tobit & The History of Susanna, Medici, 1929 . . . . £35
Hans Anderson, Forty Stories, Faber and Faber, 1930 . . . . £30/£15
The New Testament, Dent, 1934-6 (4 vols) . . £40

P.D. JAMES
(b.1920)

Born in Oxford but educated at Cambridge Girl's High School, P.D. James worked in the Civil Service and did not begin writing until her forties. She is famous for her detective fiction, much of which has been successfully televised.

Novels
Cover Her Face, Faber, 1962 . . . £1,000/£250
ditto, Scribner (U.S.), 1966 . . . . . £150/£35
A Mind to Murder, Faber, 1963 . . . . £750/£200
ditto, Scribner (U.S.), 1967 . . . . . £125/£25
Unnatural Causes, Faber, 1967 . . . . £400/£100
ditto, Scribner (U.S.), 1967 . . . . . £75/£20
Shroud for a Nightingale, Faber, 1971 . £125/£25
ditto, Scribner (U.S.), 1971 . . . . . £50/£15
An Unsuitable Job for a Woman, Faber, 1972 £75/£25
ditto, Scribner (U.S.), 1972 . . . . . £35/£10
The Black Tower, Faber, 1975 . . . £50/£15
ditto, Scribner (U.S.), 1974 . . . . . £20/£5
Death of an Expert Witness, Faber, 1977 . £35/£10
ditto, Scribner (U.S.), 1977 . . . . . £15/£5
Innocent Blood, Faber, 1980 . . . . . £35/£10
ditto, Scribner (U.S.), 1980 . . . . . £15/£5
P.D. James Omnibus, Faber, 1982 . . . £15/£5
The Skull Beneath the Skin, Faber, 1982 . £25/£5
ditto, Scribner (U.S.), 1982 . . . . . £15/£5
A Taste for Death, Faber, 1986 . . . . £20/£5
ditto, Knopf (U.S.), 1986 . . . . £10/£5
Devices and Desires, Faber, 1989 . . . £15/£5
ditto, Franklin Press (U.S.), 1990 (signed) . . £45
ditto, Knopf (U.S.), 1990 . . . . £10/£5
The Second P. D. James Omnibus, Faber, 1990 . . . . £10/£5
The Children of Men, Faber, 1992 . . . £20/£5
ditto, Knopf (U.S.), 1993 . . . . £10/£5
Original Sin, Faber, 1994. . . . . . . £20/£5
ditto, London Limited Editions, 1994 (150 signed copies, acetate d/w) . . . . £45/£40
ditto, Knopf (U.S.), 1995 . . . . £10/£5
A Certain Justice, Faber, 1997 . . . . £10/£5
ditto, Knopf (U.S.), 1997 . . . . £10/£5

Non Fiction
The Maul and the Pear Tree, Constable, 1971, (with T.A. Critchley) . . . . £25/£10
ditto, Mysterious Press (U.S.), 1986 . . . £15/£5
Bad Language in Church, Prayer Book Society, 1988 (wraps) £10

RICHARD JEFFERIES
(b.1848 d.1887)

British essayist, novelist, and chronicler of rural life.

Novels
The Scarlet Shawl, Tinsley Bros., 1874 . . . £250
Restless Human Hearts, Tinsley Bros., 1875 (3 vols) £300
World's End, Tinsley Bros., 1877 (3 vols) . . £275
Greene Ferne Farm, Smith, Elder & Co., 1880 £75
The Dewy Morn, Bentley, 1884, (2 vols) . . £125
After London, or Wild England, Cassell & Co., 1885 . . . . £75
Amaryllis at the Fair, Sampson, Low & Co., 1887 . . . . £100
The Early Fiction of Richard Jefferies, Simpkin, Marshall & Co., 1896 . . . . £25
ditto, 1896 (large paper, 50 numbered copies) . £100

Short Story
T.T.T., Arthur Young, 1896 (100 copies) . . £150

Children's
Wood Magic, A Fable, Cassell, Petter & Galpin, 1881, (2 vols) £200
Bevis, The Story of a Boy, Sampson, Low & Co., 1882, (3 vols) £750

Non Fiction
Reporting, Editing and Authorship: Practical Hints for Beginners in Literature, John Snow & Co., [1873]. £600
Jack Brass, Emperor of England, Pettit and Co., 1873 . . . . £400
A Memoir of the Goddards of North Wilts Compiled from Ancient Records, Registers and Family Papers, Simmons & Botten, [1873] £600
Suez-cide!! or How Miss Britannia Bought a Dirty

Puddle and Lost her Sugar Plums, John Snow, 1876 . . . . £300
The Gamekeeper at Home, or Sketches of Natural History & Rural Life, Smith, Elder & Co., 1878 (anonymous) £100
Wild Life in a Southern County, Elder & Co., 1879 (anonymous) £100
The Amateur Poacher, Elder & Co., 1879 (anonymous) £150
Hodge and His Masters, Elder & Co., 1880, (2 vols) £125
Round About a Great Estate, Elder & Co., 1880 £90
Nature Near London, Chatto & Windus, 1883 . £100
The Story of My Heart, My Autobiography, Longmans, 1883 . . . . £150
Red Deer, Longmans, 1884 . . . . . . £125
The Life of the Fields, Chatto & Windus, 1884 £75
The Open Air, Chatto & Windus, 1885 . . . . £75
Field and Hedgerow, Being the Last Essays of Richard Jefferies Collected by His Widow, Longmans, Green & Co., 1889 . . . . £75
ditto, Longmans, Green & Co., 1889 (large paper, 200 numbered copies) £125
The Toilers of the Field, Longmans, Green & Co., 1892 . . . . £25
ditto, Longmans, Green & Co., 1892 (large paper, 105 numbered copies) £75
Jefferies Land, A History of Swindon and Its Environs, Simpkin, Marshall & Co., 1896. . . £75
ditto, Simpkin, Marshall & Co., 1896 (large paper, 50 numbered copies) £100
The Hills and the Vale, Duckworth, 1909 . . £25
The Nature Diaries and Notebooks of Richard Jefferies, With an Essay 'A Tangle of Autumn' Now Printed for the First Time, Grey Walls Press, 1941 . . . . £35/£15
ditto, Grey Walls Press, 1941 (large paper, 105 numbered copies) £75
Chronicles of the Hedges And Other Essays, Phoenix House, 1948 . . . . £15/£5
The Old House at Coate, Lutterworth Press, 1948 . . . . £25/£10
ditto, Harvard University Press, 1948 . . . £20/£10
Beauty Is Immortal (Felise of the Dewy Morn), With Some Hitherto Uncollected Essays and Manuscripts, Worthing Cavalcade, 1948 . . . . £20
Field and Farm, Essays Now Collected With Some From Manuscripts, Phoenix House, 1957 . £25/£10
Landscape and Labour, Moonraker Press, 1979 . . . . £10/£5
By the Brook, Eric & Joan Stevens, 1981 (170 numbered copies) £25
ditto, Eric & Joan Stevens, 1981 (20 leather bound copies in slipcase) £75
The Birth of a Naturalist, Tern Press, 1985 (300 numbered copies) £50
ditto, Tern Press, 1985 (20 leather-bound copies in slipcase) . . . . £125/£100

JEROME K. JEROME

(b.1859 d.1927)

First employed as a railway clerk at Euston Station, then as an actor, Jerome was best known as a novelist, but was also a successful dramatist and popular journalist.

Novels

Three Men in a Boat, Arrowsmith, 1889, (first issue, address: "Quay Street") £125
ditto, Arrowsmith, 1889, (second issue, address: "11 Quay Street") £60
ditto, Holt (U.S.), 1890 . . . . £50
Diary of a Pilgrimage, Arrowsmith, 1891 . . £30
ditto, Holt (U.S.), 1891 . . . . £20
Three Men on the Bummel, Arrowsmith, 1900 £30
Paul Kelver, Hutchinson, 1902 . . . . . £30
ditto, Dodd, Mead (U.S.), 1902 . . . . . . £20
Tommy & Co, Hutchinson, 1904. . . . . £20
ditto, Dodd, Mead (U.S.), 1904 . . . . . £15
They and I, Hutchinson, 1909 . . . . . £20
ditto, Dodd, Mead (U.S.), 1909 . . . . . £15
All Roads Lead to Calvary, Hutchinson, 1919 . £15
ditto, Dodd, Mead (U.S.), 1919 . . . . . £15
Anthony John, Cassell, 1923. . . . . . . £15

Short Stories

John Ingerfield and Other Stories, McClure, 1894 . . . . £30
ditto, Holt (U.S.), 1894 . . . . £25
The Observations of Henry, Arrowsmith, 1901 £25
ditto, Dodd, Mead (U.S.), 1901 . . . . . . £15
Tea Table Talk, Hutchinson, 1903 . . . . . £15
The Passing of the Third Floor Back, Hurst & Blackett, 1907 . . . . £15
Malvina of Brittany, Cassell, 1916 . . . . . £15

Plays

Barbara, Lacy, 1886 . . . . £20
Sunset, Fitzgerald (U.S.), [1888]. £20
Fennel, French, [1888] £15
Woodbarrow Farm, French, [1888] £15
The Prude's Progress, French, 1895. . . . . £15
Miss Hobbs, French, 1902 . . . . £15
Fanny and the Servant Problem, Lacy, 1909 . £15
The Passing of the Third Floor Back, Hurst & Blackett, 1910 . . . . £15
The Master of Mrs Chilvers, Fisher Unwin, 1911 £10

Robina in Search of a Husband, Lacy, 1914 . £10
The Celebrity, Hodder & Stoughton, 1926 . . £10
The Soul of Nicholas Snyders, Hodder & Stoughton, 1927 . . . . £10

Other Works
On Stage-and Off, Field & Tuer, 1885 . . . £75
ditto, Leadenhall Press, 1891, (illustrated by Kenneth M. Skeaping) £35
The Idle Thoughts of an Idle Fellow, Field & Tuer, 1886 . . . . £25
ditto, Holt (U.S.), 1890 . . . . £50
Stage-Land, Chatto & Windus, 1889 . . . £25
ditto, Holt (U.S.), 1906 . . . . £50
Told After Supper, Leadenhall Press, 1893 . . £45
Novel Notes, Leadenhall Press, 1893 . . . . £35
Sketches in Lavender, Blue and Green, Longman, 1897 . . . . £25
ditto, Holt (U.S.), 1907 . . . . £50
The Second Thoughts of an Idle Fellow, Hurst & Blackett, 1898 . . . . £20
ditto, Dodd, Mead (U.S.), 1898 . . . . . £15
American Wives and Others, Stokes (U.S.), 1904 £20
Idle Ideas in 1905, Hurst & Blackett, 1905 . £15
The Angel and the Author - and Others, Hurst & Blackett, 1908 . . . . £15
Thoughts from Jerome K. Jerome, Sesame Booklets, 1913 . . . . £10
A Miscellany of Sense and Nonsense, Arrowsmith, 1923 . . . . £15
My Life and Times, Hodder & Stoughton, 1926 . . . . £35/£15
ditto, Harper (U.S.), 1926. . . . . . . £35/£15

RUTH PRAWER JHABVALA
(b.1927)

Born in Cologne, Ruth Prawer Jhabvala fled with her Polish/Jewish family to England in 1939. She married an Indian architect in 1951 and moved to Delhi. Her first novel was published in 1955. She is also known for her short stories and film scripts written for the Merchant/Ivory partnership.

Novels
To Whom She Will, George Allen & Unwin, 1955 £75
ditto as ***Amrita***, Norton (U.S.), 1956 . . £25/£10
The Nature of Passion, George Allen & Unwin, 1956 . . . . £50/£20
ditto, Norton (U.S.), 1957. . . . . . . £20/£5
Esmond in India, George Allen & Unwin, 1958 . . . . £50/£20
ditto, Norton (U.S.), 1958. . . . . . . £20/£5
The Householder, John Murray, 1960 . . £50/£20
ditto, Norton (U.S.), 1960. . . . . . . £10/£5
Get Ready for Battle, John Murray, 1962 . £40/£15
ditto, Norton (U.S.), 1963. . . . . . . £10/£5
A Backward Place, John Murray, 1965 . . £25/£10
ditto, Norton (U.S.), 1965. . . . . . . £10/£5
A New Dominion, John Murray, 1972 . . £25/£10
ditto, as ***Travellers***, Harper & Row (U.S.), 1973 £10/£5
Heat and Dust, John Murray, 1975 . . . £25/£10
ditto, Harper (U.S.), 1976 . . . . . . £20/£5
In Search of Love and Beauty, John Murray, 1983 . . . . £10/£5
ditto, Morrow (U.S.), 1983 . . . . . . £10/£5
Three Continents, John Murray, 1987 . . £10/£5
ditto, Morrow (U.S.), 1987 . . . . . . £10/£5
Poet and Dancer, John Murray, 1993 . . £10/£5
ditto, Doubleday (U.S.), 1993 . . . . . £10/£5
Shards of Memory, John Murray, 1995 . . £10/£5
ditto, Doubleday (U.S.), 1995 . . . . . £10/£5

Short Stories
Like Birds Like Fishes, John Murray, 1963. £30/£10
ditto, Norton (U.S.), 1964. . . . . . . £10/£5
A Stronger Climate, John Murray, 1968 . £25/£10
ditto, Norton (U.S.), 1969. . . . . . . £10/£5
An Experience of India, John Murray, 1971 £25/£10
ditto, Norton (U.S.), 1972. . . . . . . £10/£5
How I Became a Holy Mother, John Murray, 1976 . . . . £10/£5
ditto, Harper (U.S.), 1976. . . . . . . £10/£5
Out of India: Selected Stories, Morrow (U.S.), 1986 . . . . £10/£5
ditto, John Murray, 1987 . . . . £10/£5
East Into Upper East: Plain Tales From New York and New Delhi, Counterpoint (U.S.), 1998 £10/£5

CAPTAIN W.E. JOHNS
(b.1893 d.1968)

In 1916 Johns joined the newly formed Royal Flying Corps, and remained in the Air Force until 1930. He founded the monthly *Popular Flying* magazine in which Captain James Bigglesworth made his first appearance.

'Biggles' Titles
The Camels Are Coming, Hamilton [1932] (pseud. 'William Earle') . . . . £750/£200
The Cruise of the Condor: A Biggles Story, Hamilton [1933]. . . . . £500/£150
'Biggles' of the Camel Squadron, Hamilton [1934] . . . . £450/£125
Biggles Flies Again, Hamilton [1934] . . £450/£125

ditto, Penguin, 1941 (wraps) £75
Biggles Learns to Fly, Boys' Friend Library, 1935 (wraps) £150
ditto, Brockhampton Press, 1955 (first hardback edition) . . . . £30/£10
Biggles Flies East, O.U.P., 1935. . . . . £450/£100
Biggles Hits the Trail, O.U.P., 1935. . . . £400/£100
Biggles in France, Boys' Friend Library, 1935 (wraps) £150
The Black Peril: A 'Biggles' Story, Hamilton [1935] . . . . £700/£175
Biggles in Africa, O.U.P., 1936 . . . . £450/£100
Biggles & Co, O.U.P., 1936 . . . . £400/£100
Biggles - Air Commodore, O.U.P., 1937 . £350/£75
Biggles Flies West, O.U.P., 1937 . . . £350/£75
Biggles Flies South, O.U.P., 1938 . . . £300/£50
Biggles Goes to War, O.U.P., 1938 . . . £300/£50
Biggles Flies North, O.U.P., 1939 . . . £200/£35
Biggles in Spain, O.U.P., 1939 . . . . £200/£35
The Rescue Flight: A 'Biggles' Story, O.U.P., 1939 . . . . £250/£45
Biggles in the Baltic: A Tale of the Second Great War, O.U.P., 1940 . . . . £350/£75
Biggles in the South Seas, O.U.P., 1940 . £300/£50
Biggles - Secret Agent, O.U.P., 1940 . . £200/£35
Spitfire Parade: Stories of Biggles in War-Time, O.U.P., 1941 . . . . £300/£50
Biggles Sees it Through, O.U.P., 1941 . . £300/£50
Biggles Defies the Swastika, O.U.P., 1941 . £350/£75
Biggles in the Jungle, O.U.P., 1942 . . . £200/£35
Biggles Sweeps the Desert, Hodder & Stoughton, 1942 . . . . £25/£10
Biggles - Charter Pilot, O.U.P., 1943 . . £150/£30
Biggles 'Fails to Return', Hodder & Stoughton, 1943 . . . . £25/£10
Biggles in Borneo, O.U.P., 1943. . . . £150/£30
Biggles in the Orient, Hodder & Stoughton, 1945 . . . . £25/£10
Biggles Delivers the Goods, Hodder & Stoughton, 1946 . . . . £15/£5
Sergeant Bigglesworth CID, Hodder & Stoughton, 1947 . . . . £20/£5
Biggles Hunts Big Game, Hodder & Stoughton, 1948 . . . . £15/£5
Biggles' Second Case, Hodder & Stoughton, 1948 . . . . £25/£5
Biggles Breaks the Silence, Hodder & Stoughton, 1949 £15/£5
Biggles Takes a Holiday, Hodder & Stoughton, 1949 . . . . £15/£5
Biggles Gets His Men, Hodder & Stoughton, 1950 . . . . £15/£5
Another Job for Biggles, Hodder & Stoughton, 1951 . . . . £15/£5
Biggles Goes to School, Hodder & Stoughton, 1951 . . . . £20/£5
Biggles Works It Out, Hodder & Stoughton, 1951 . . . . £15/£5
Biggles - Air Detective, Marks & Spencer, 1951 . . . . £10/£5
Biggles Follows On, Hodder & Stoughton, 1952 . . . . £20/£5
Biggles Takes the Case, Hodder & Stoughton, 1952 . . . . £15/£5
Biggles and the Black Raider, Hodder & Stoughton, 1953 . . . . £15/£5
Biggles in the Blue, Brockhampton Press, 1953 £25/£5
Biggles of the Special Air Police, Thames [1953] . . . . £15/£5
Biggles in the Gobi, Hodder & Stoughton, 1953 £25/£5
Biggles and the Pirate Treasure and Other Biggles Adventures, Brockhampton Press, 1954 . £25/£5
Biggles Cuts it Fine, Hodder & Stoughton, 1954 . . . . £20/£5
Biggles, Foreign Legionnaire, Hodder & Stoughton, 1954 . . . . £20/£5
Biggles, Pioneer Airfighter, Thames [1954] £15/£5
Biggles' Chinese Puzzle and Other Biggles Adventures, Brockhampton Press, 1955 . £20/£5
Biggles in Australia, Hodder & Stoughton, 1955 . . . . £25/£5
Biggles of 266, Thames [1956] . . . . £10/£5
Biggles Takes Charge, Brockhampton Press, 1956 . . . . £20/£5
No Rest For Biggles, Hodder & Stoughton, 1956 . . . . £20/£5
Biggles Makes Ends Meet, Hodder & Stoughton, 1957 . . . . £20/£5
Biggles of the Interpol, Brockhampton Press, 1957 . . . . £25/£5
Biggles on the Home Front, Hodder & Stoughton, 1957 . . . . £25/£5
Biggles Buries a Hatchet, Brockhampton Press, 1958 . . . . £25/£5
Biggles on Mystery Island, Hodder & Stoughton [1958]. . . . . £25/£5
Biggles Presses On, Brockhampton Press, 1958 £25/£5
Biggles at World's End, Brockhampton Press, 1959 . . . . £25/£5
Biggles' Combined Operation, Hodder & Stoughton [1959]. . . . . £25/£5
Biggles in Mexico, Brockhampton Press, 1959 £25/£5
Biggles and the Leopards of Zinn, Brockhampton Press, 1960 . . . . £25/£5
Biggles Goes Home, Hodder & Stoughton [1960] . . . . £25/£5
Biggles and the Missing Millionaire, Brockhampton Press, 1961 . . . . £25/£5
Biggles and the Poor Rich Boy, Brockhampton Press, 1961 . . . . £20/£5

Biggles Forms a Syndicate, Hodder & Stoughton, 1961 . . . . £25/£5
Biggles Goes Alone, Hodder & Stoughton [1962] . . . . £25/£5
Biggles Sets a Trap, Hodder & Stoughton, 1962 . . . . £25/£5
Orchids for Biggles, Hodder & Stoughton, 1962 . . . . £25/£5
Biggles and the Planet That Disappeared: A Story of the Air Police, Hodder & Stoughton, 1963 £30/£10
Biggles Flies to Work, Dean [1963] . . . . £10/£5
Biggles' Special Case, Brockhampton Press, 1963 . . . . £25/£5
Biggles Takes A Hand, Hodder & Stoughton [1963] . . . . £40/£15
Biggles Takes it Rough, Brockhampton Press, 1963 . . . . £40/£15
Biggles and the Black Mask, Hodder & Stoughton, 1964 . . . . £40/£15
Biggles and the Lost Sovereigns, Brockhampton Press, 1964 . . . . £30/£10
Biggles Investigates and Other Stories of the Air Police, Brockhampton Press, 1965 . . . . £30/£10
Biggles and the Blue Moon, Brockhampton Press, 1965 . . . . £75/£20
Biggles and the Plot That Failed, Brockhampton Press, 1965 . . . . £75/£20
Biggles Looks Back: A Story of Biggles and the Air Police, Hodder & Stoughton, 1965 . . . . £50/£15
Biggles Scores a Bull, Hodder & Stoughton, 1965 . . . . £50/£15
Biggles in the Terai, Brockhampton Press, 1966 . . . . £75/£20
Biggles and the Gun Runners, Brockhampton Press, 1966 . . . . £75/£20
Biggles and the Penitent Thief, Brockhampton Press, 1967 . . . . £75/£20
Biggles Sorts It Out, Brockhampton Press, 1967 . . . . £75/£20
Biggles and the Dark Intruder, Knight, 1967 (wraps) £20
ditto, Brockhampton Press, 1970 . . . . . £50/£15
Biggles in the Underworld, Brockhampton Press, 1968 . . . . £80/£25
The Boy Biggles, Dean, 1968 . . . . . £10/£5
Biggles and the Deep Blue Sea, Brockhampton Press, 1968 . . . . £75/£20
Biggles and the Little Green God, Brockhampton Press, 1969 . . . . £100/£30
Biggles and the Noble Lord, Brockhampton Press, 1969 . . . . £75/£20
Biggles Sees Too Much, Brockhampton Press, 1970 . . . . £100/£30
Biggles of the Royal Flying Corps, Purnell, 1978 . . . . £15/£5

Biggles Omnibuses
The Biggles Omnibus, O.U.P., 1938 . . . £200/£65
The Biggles Flying Omnibus, O.U.P., 1940 £200/£65
The Third Biggles Omnibus, O.U.P., 1941 . £200/£65
The First Biggles Omnibus, Hodder and Stoughton, 1953 . . . . £20/£5
The Biggles Air Detective Omnibus, Hodder and Stoughton, 1956 . . . . £20/£5
The Biggles Adventure Omnibus, Hodder and Stoughton, 1965 . . . . £25/£5
The Bumper Biggles Book, Chancellor, 1983 £10/£5
The Best of Biggles, Chancellor, 1985 . . £10/£5

'Worrals' Books
Worrals of the W.A.A.F., Lutterworth Press, 1941 . . . . £50/£15
Worrals Carries On, Lutterworth Press, 1942 £25/£10
Worrals Flies Again, Hodder & Stoughton, 1942 . . . . £20/£5
Worrals On the War-Path, Hodder & Stoughton, 1943 . . . . £20/£5
Worrals Goes East, Hodder & Stoughton, 1944 £20/£5
Worrals of the Islands: A Story of the War in the Pacific, Hodder & Stoughton, 1945 . . £15/£5
Worrals in the Wilds, Hodder & Stoughton, 1947 . . . . £10/£5
Worrals Down Under, Lutterworth Press, 1948 £10/£5
Worrals Goes Afoot, Lutterworth Press, 1949 £10/£5
Worrals In the Wastelands, Lutterworth Press, 1949 . . . . £10/£5
Worrals Investigates, Lutterworth Press, 1950 £10/£5

'Gimlet' Books
King of the Commandos, University of London Press, 1943 . . . . £25/£5
Gimlet Goes Again, University of London Press, 1944 . . . . £25/£5
Gimlet Comes Home, University of London Press, 1946 . . . . £10/£5
Gimlet Mops Up, Brockhampton Press, 1947 £10/£5
Gimlet's Oriental Quest, Brockhampton Press, 1948 . . . . £10/£5
Gimlet Lends a Hand, Brockhampton Press, 1949 . . . . £10/£5
Gimlet Bores In, Brockhampton Press, 1950 £10/£5
Gimlet Off the Map, Brockhampton Press, 1951 . . . . £10/£5
Gimlet Gets the Answer, Brockhampton Press, 1952 . . . . £10/£5
Gimlet Takes a Job, Brockhampton Press, 1954 . . . . £10/£5

Science Fiction Titles
Kings of Space: A Story of Interplanetary Explorations, Hodder & Stoughton, 1954 . £10/£5

Return to Mars, Hodder & Stoughton, 1955 £10/£5
Now to the Stars, Hodder & Stoughton, 1956 £10/£5
To Outer Space, Hodder & Stoughton, 1957 £10/£5
The Edge of Beyond, Hodder & Stoughton [1958] . . . . £20/£5
The Death Rays of Ardilla, Hodder & Stoughton [1959] . . . . £10/£5
To Worlds Unknown: A Story of Interplanetary Explorations, Hodder & Stoughton [1960] £20/£5
The Quest for the Perfect Planet, Hodder & Stoughton, 1961 . . . . £10/£5
Worlds of Wonder: More Adventures in Space, Hodder & Stoughton, 1962 . . . . . £10/£5
The Man Who Vanished into Space, Hodder & Stoughton [1963] . . . . £10/£5

Others

Mossyface, 'The Weekly Telegraph Novel', 1922 (pseud. 'William Earle', wraps) £600
ditto, Mellifont, 1932 (wraps) £200
Modern Boys Book of Aircraft, Amalgamated Press, 1931 . . . . £50/£15
The Pictorial Flying Course, John Hamilton [1932] (by Johns and H.M. Schofield) . . . . £250/£75
Fighting Planes and Aces, John Hamilton [1932] . . . . £250/£75
The Spy Flyers, John Hamilton, 1933 . . . £500/£125
The Raid, John Hamilton [1935] . . . . . £250/£75
The Air VC's, John Hamilton [1935] . . . £250/£75
Some Milestones in Aviation, John Hamilton [1935] . . . . £200/£45
Blue Blood Runs Red, Newnes [1936] (pseud. 'Jon Early') . . . . £500/£125
Modern Boy's Book of Adventure Stories, Amalgamated Press, 1936 . . . . £50/£15
Ace High, Ace, 1936 . . . . £100/£30
Air Adventures, Ace, 1936 . . . . . . £100/£30
Sky High: A 'Steeley' Adventure, Newnes [1936] . . . . £250/£75
Steeley Flies Again, Newnes [1936] . . . . £250/£75
Flying Stories, John Hamilton, 1937. . . . £100/£25
Murder By Air: A 'Steeley' Adventure, Newnes [1937] . . . . £250/£75
The Passing Show, My Garden/Newnes, , 1937 . . . . £75/£20
Desert Night: A Romance, John Hamilton [1938] . . . . £200/£45
The Murder at Castle Deeping: A 'Steeley' Adventure, John Hamilton [1938] . . . . . £400/£100
Champion of the Main, O.U.P., 1938 . . . £250/£75
Wings of Romance: A 'Steeley' Adventure, Newnes, 1939 . . . . £250/£75
Modern Boy's Book of Pirates, Amalgamated Press, [1939] . . . . £200/£50
The Unknown Quantity, John Hamilton, [1940] . . . . £200/£50
Sinister Service: A Tale, O.U.P., 1942 . . . £100/£25
The Rustlers of Rattlesnake Valley, Nelson, 1948 . . . . £25/£5
Dr Vane Answers the Call, Latimer House, 1950 . . . . £100/£25
Short Sorties, Latimer House, 1950 . . . . £100/£25
Sky Fever and Other Stories, Latimer House, [1953] . . . . £100/£25
Adventure Bound, Nelson, 1955 . . . . . . £10/£5
Adventure Unlimited, Nelson, 1957 . . . . £10/£5
No Motive for Murder, Hodder & Stoughton [1958] . . . . £100/£25
The Man Who Lost His Way, Macdonald, 1959 . . . . £100/£25
The Biggles Book of Heroes, Parrish, 1959 £50/£15
Adventures of the Junior Detection Club, Parrish [1960] . . . . £50/£15
Where the Golden Eagle Soars, Hodder & Stoughton [1960] . . . . £25/£5
The Biggles Book of Treasure Hunting, Parrish, 1962 . . . . £50/£15
Out of the Blue, John Hamilton [no date] . £100/£25

Illustrated by Johns

Desert Wings, by Clark Venable, John Hamilton [1931] (real name Covington Clarke') . . . . . £25/£10
Aces Up, by Clark Venable, John Hamilton [1931] (real name Covington Clarke') . . . . . . £25/£10
For Valour, by Clark Venable, John Hamilton [1931] (real name Covington Clarke') . . . . . £25/£10

B.S. JOHNSON

(b.1933 d.1973)

A controversial and experimental novelist, Johnson's books have been purposefully issued with pages which are black, blank, and containing holes. *The Unfortunates* was published in the form of loose sections to be shuffled and read in no particular order.

Novels

Travelling People, Constable, 1963 . . . . £125/£45
ditto, Transworld, 1964 (wraps) £10
Albert Angelo, Constable, 1964 . . . . . £100/£35
ditto, Panther, 1967 (wraps) £10
ditto, New Directions (U.S.), 1987 . . . . . £10/£5
Trawl, Secker & Warburg, 1966 . . . . . £75/£35
ditto, Panther, 1968 (wraps) £10
The Unfortunates, Panther [with Secker & Warburg], 1969 (27 loose sections in box) £150
House Mother Normal, Trigram Press, 1971 (26 signed, lettered copies) £200

ditto, Trigram Press, 1971 (100 signed, numbered copies) £100
ditto, Collins, 1971 . . . . £45/£20
ditto, Quartet, 1973 (wraps) £10
ditto, Bloodaxe, 1984 (wraps) £10
ditto, New Directions (U.S.), 1987 . . . £10/£5
Christie Malry's Own Double Entry, Collins, 1973 . . . . £25/£5
ditto, Viking (U.S.), 1973 . . . . £20/£5
See The Old Lady Decently, Collins, 1973 . £25/£5
ditto, Viking (U.S.), 1975 . . . . £15/£5

Short Stories
Statement Against Corpses, Constable, 1964 (with Zulfikar Ghose) . . . . £75/£25
Aren't You Rather Young to be Writing Your Memoirs?, Hutchinson, 1973 . . . . . . £20
Everybody Knows Somebody Who's Dead, Covent Garden Press, 1973 (100 signed, numbered copies) . . . . £100/£65

Poetry
Poems, Constable, 1964 . . . . £25
Poems Two, Trigram Press, 1972 (100 signed copies) £75
ditto, Trigram Press, 1972 (hardback) . . £25/£5
ditto, Trigram Press, 1972 (wraps) £10
A Dublin Unicorn, Byron Press, 1975 (250 copies) £45

Others
Street Children, Hodder & Stoughton, 1964 (with photographs by Julia Trevelyan) . . . £15/£5
The Evacuees, Gollancz, 1968 . . . . . £10/£5
You're Human Like the Rest of Them, Penguin New English Dramatists, 1970 (wraps) £5
London Consequences, Greater London Arts Association, 1972 (edited with Margaret Drabble) . . . . £15/£5
All Bull: The National Serviceman, Allison & Busby, 1973 . . . . £10/£5

JAMES JOYCE

(b.1882 d.1941)

Novelist, short story writer, poet and father of modernism, Joyce's *Ulysses* and *Finnegan's Wake* revolutionised narrative form and paved the way for the modern novel.

Verse
Chamber Music, Elkin Mathews, 1907 . . . £1,500
ditto, Cornhill Co. (U.S.), 1918 (unauthorised edition) £225
ditto, Huebsch (U.S.), 1918 (authorised edition) £225
Pomes Penyeach, Shakespeare and Co. (Paris), 1927 . . . . £250
ditto, Shakespeare and Co. (Paris), 1927 (100 signed copies) £2,000
ditto, Sylvia Beach (U.S.), 1931 . . . . . . £250
ditto, Obelisk Press, 1932 . . . . £200
ditto, Faber, 1933 (wraps) £35
Collected Poems, Black Sun Press (U.S.), 1936 (800 copies, glassine d/w) . . . . £400/£350
ditto, Black Sun Press (U.S.), 1936 (50 signed copies, tissue d/w, slipcase) . . . . . £4,000/£3,500
ditto, Viking (U.S.), 1937 . . . . £250/£65

Short Stories
Dubliners, Grant Richards, 1914 . . . . . £1,500
ditto, Huebsch (U.S.), 1916 . . . . £650

Novels
A Portrait of the Artist as a Young Man, Huebsch (U.S.), 1916 . . . . £500
ditto, Egoist Ltd, 1916 [1917] £250
Ulysses, Shakespeare Press (Paris), 1922, (900 numbered copies) £10,000
ditto, Shakespeare Press (Paris), 1922 (100 signed, numbered copies) £40,000
ditto, Egoist Press, 1922 (2,000 numbered copies, wraps) £1,750
ditto, Shakespeare Press (Paris), 1924 . . . £200
ditto, Random House (U.S.), 1934 (first copyright printing, 100 copies) £750
ditto, Random House (U.S.), 1934 (second printing) . . . . £250/£50
ditto, Bodley Head, 1936 (900 copy edition) . . . . £1,250/£500
ditto, Bodley Head, 1936 (100 signed copies, slipcase) . . . . £7,500/£6,500
ditto, Bodley Head, 1937 . . . . £250/£100
Finnegan's Wake, Faber, 1939 . . . £1,000/£250
ditto, Faber/Viking, 1939 (425 signed copies, glassine d/w) £4,000
ditto, Viking (U.S.), 1939 . . . . £250/£25
Stephen Hero, Cape, 1944 . . . . . £250/£100
ditto, New Directions (U.S.), 1944 . . . £100/£30

Fragments
Anna Livia Plurabelle, Crosby Gaige (U.S.), 1928 (800 signed copies) £650
ditto, Crosby Gaige (U.S.), 1928 (500 unsigned copies) £400
ditto, Faber, 1930 (wraps) £50
Tales Told of Shem and Shaun, Black Sun Press (Paris), 1929 (500 copies, wraps, slipcase) £700/£600
ditto, Black Sun Press (Paris), 1929 (100 signed copies)

. . . . £3,500

Haveth Childers Everywhere, Fountain Press (U.S.), 1930 (685 copies) £1,000

ditto, Fountain Press (U.S.), 1930 (100 signed copies, glassine d/w, slipcase) £4,000

ditto, Faber, 1931 (wraps). £75

Two Tales of Shem and Shaun, Faber, 1932 £125/£45

The Mime of Mick Nick and the Maggies, Servire Press, 1934 (wraps, slipcase) . . . . £300/£250

ditto, Servire Press, 1934 (29 signed copies, wraps, slipcase) £5,000

Storiella As She is Syung, Corvinus Press, 1937 (150 numbered copies, slipcase) £2,000

ditto, Corvinus Press, 1937 (25 signed copies, slipcase) . . . . £7,500/£7,000

Letters

The Letters Vol. I, Faber, 1957 . . . . £50/£20

The Letters Vol. II, Faber, 1966 . . . . £25/£10

The Letters Vol. III, Faber, 1966 . . . £25/£10

Others

Exiles, Grant Richards, 1918 . . . . . . £200

ditto, Huebsch (U.S.), 1918 . . . . £200

The Critical Writings, Faber, 1959 . . . £40/£15

ditto, Viking (U.S.), 1959. . . . . £40/£15

The Cat and the Devil, Dodd Mead (U.S.), [1964] . . . . £50/£20

ditto, Faber, 1965 . . . . £50/£20

ERICH KÄSTNER

(b.1899 d.1974)

A German writer in a wide range of genres, he is collected principally for his children's works, notably *Emil and the Detectives.*

Emil and the Detectives, Cape, 1931 (illustrated by Walter Trier) . . . . £150/£40

Annaluise and Anton, Cape, 1932 (illustrated by Walter Trier) . . . . £95/£25

The 35th of May, Cape, 1933 (illustrated by Walter Trier) . . . . £45/£15

The Flying Classroom, Cape, 1934 (illustrated by Walter Trier) . . . . £60/£20

Emil and the Three Twins, Cape, 1935 (illustrated by Walter Trier) . . . . £60/£20

Lottie and Lisa, Cape, 1950 (illustrated by Walter Trier) . . . . £55/£20

The Animals Conference, Collins, 1955 . £60/£20

The Little Man, Cape, 1966 (illustrated by Horst Lemke) . . . . £25/£10

Till Eulenspiegel the Clown, Cape, 1967 (illustrated by Walter Trier) . . . . £75/£20

Puss in Boots, Cape, 1967 (illustrated by Walter Trier) . . . . £45/£15

The Little Man and the Little Miss, Cape, 1969 (illustrated by Horst Lemke) . . . . . £20/£5

Collected Edition

Emil, Cape, 1949 . . . . £10/£5

Others

When I was a Little Boy, Cape, 1959 . . . £10/£5

Let's Face It, Cape, 1963 . . . . £10/£5

JOHN KEATS

(b.1795 d.1821)

Along with Wordsworth, Keats is one of the best known and most widely read of the English Romantic poets.

Poetry

Poems, Ollier, 1817 . . . . £12,500

Endymion, Taylor & Hessey, 1818 . . . . . £7,500

Lamia, Isabella, The Eve of St Agnes, and Other Poems, Taylor & Hessey, 1820 . . . . . £7,500

Miscellaneous

Life, Letters and Literary Remains of John Keats, Moxon, 1848 (2 vols) £250

The Letters of John Keats, Reeves & Turner, 1895 . . . . £75

Letters ... to Fanny Brawne, privately printed, 1878-79 (50 copies) £450

Anatomical and Physiological Notebook, O.U.P., 1934 (350 copies) £50

JACK KEROUAC

(b.1922 d.1969)

The semi-autobiographical novelist of the Beat Generation in 1950s San Francisco.

Fiction

The Town and the City, Harcourt Brace (U.S.), 1950 (pseud. 'John Kerouac') . . . . . £500/£125

ditto, Eyre & Spottiswoode, 1951 . . . £175/£50

On the Road, Viking (U.S.), 1957 . . £1,500/£300

ditto, Andre Deutsch, 1958 . . . . . . £400/£75

The Subterraneans, Grove Press (U.S.), 1958 . . . . £650/£50

ditto, Grove Press (U.S.), 1958 (100 numbered copies) £400
ditto, Grove Press (U.S.), 1958 (wraps) £20
ditto, Andre Deutsch, 1962 . . . . . . £200/£50
The Dharma Bums, Viking (U.S.), 1958 . £200/£50
ditto, Andre Deutsch, 1959 . . . . . . £75/£25
Doctor Sax: Faust Part Three, Grove Press (U.S.), 1959 . . . . £500/£75
ditto, Grove Press (U.S.), 1959 (26 signed, lettered copies) £2,000
ditto, Grove Press (U.S.), 1959 (4 signed, numbered copies) £4,000
ditto, Evergreen, 1961 (wraps) £10
ditto, Deutsch, 1977 . . . . £50/£15
Maggie Cassidy, Avon (U.S.), 1959 (wraps) . £30
ditto, Panther, 1960 (wraps) £10
ditto, Deutsch, 1974 . . . . £50/£15
Excerpts from Visions of Cody, New Directions (U.S.), 1959 (750 signed, numbered copies) . . . £500
ditto, Andre Deutsch, 1973 . . . . . £50/£15
Tristessa, Avon (U.S.), 1960 (wraps) . . . £15
ditto, World Distributors, 1963 (wraps) . . . £10
Book of Dreams, City Light Books (U.S.), 1961 £50
Big Sur, Farrar Straus (U.S.), 1962 . . . £125/£25
ditto, Andre Deutsch, 1963 . . . . . . £75/£20
Visions of Gerard, Farrar Straus (U.S.), 1963 £100/£25
ditto, Andre Deutsch, 1964 (with ***Tristessa***) £50/£15
Desolation Angels, Coward McCann (U.S.), 1965 . . . . £125/£25
ditto, Andre Deutsch, 1966 . . . . . . £75/£25
Satori in Paris, Grove Press (U.S.), 1966 . £100/£20
ditto, Andre Deutsch, 1967 . . . . . . £25/£10
Vanity of Dulouz: An Adventurous Education, 1935-46, Coward McCann (U.S.), 1968 . . . £75/£20
ditto, Andre Deutsch, 1969 . . . . . . £50/£20
Pic and the Subterraneans, Grove Press (U.S.), 1971 . . . . £45/£10
ditto, Andre Deutsch, 1973 . . . . . . £40/£10
Old Angel Midnight, Unicorn Press, 1976 (wraps) £25
ditto, Midnight Press (U.S.), 1985 (wraps) . . £25
Take Care of My Ghost, Ghost Press (U.S.), 1977 (with Ginsberg, wraps) £20
ditto, Ghost Press (U.S.), 1977 (200 copies signed by Ginsberg, wraps) £100
Baby Driver: A Story About Myself, St. Martin's (U.S.), 1981 . . . . £20/£5
ditto, Andre Deutsch, 1981 . . . . . . £20/£5
San Francisco Blues, Beat Books (U.S.), 1983 £25
Two Stories, Pacific Red Car (U.S.), 1984 (100 copies, wraps). £30
The Great Western Bus Ride, Pacific Red Car (U.S.), 1984 (100 copies) £30
Celine and Other Tales, Pacific Red Car (U.S.), 1985 (100 copies) £30
The Vision of the Hooded White Angels, Pacific Red Car (U.S.), 1985 (100 copies) £30
Home at Christmas, Pacific Red Car (U.S.), [no date] £25

Verse

Mexico City Blues, Grove Press (U.S.), 1959 . . . . £750/£150
ditto, Grove Press (U.S.), 1959 (26 signed, lettered copies) £1,500
ditto, Grove Press (U.S.), 1959 (4 signed, numbered copies) £2,500
Hymn - God Pray For Me, Jubilee Magazine (U.S.), [1959], (broadsheet) £45
The Scripture of the Golden Eternity, Totem Press/Corinth Books (U.S.), 1960 (wraps) . . £125
Rimbaud, City Light Books (U.S.), 1960 (broadsheet) £50
'I demand that the human race ceases multiplying its kind...', Pax #17 (U.S.), 1962 (broadsheet) £50
Poem, Jubilee Magazine (U.S.), [1962] (broadsheet) £45
A Pun for Al Gepi, privately printed (U.S.) (100 copies, broadsheet) £50
Hugo Weber, Portents (U.S.), 1967 (200 copies, broadsheet) £45
Someday You'll be Lying, privately printed (U.S.), 1968 (broadsheet) £45
A Last Haiku, privately printed (U.S.), 1969 (broadsheet) £35
Scattered Poems, City Lights (U.S.), 1971 (wraps) £30
Trip, Trap, Grey Fox Press (U.S.), 1973 (wraps) £40
Heaven and Other Poems, Grey Fox Press (U.S.), 1977 . . . . £40

Others

Lonesome Traveller, McGraw Hill (U.S.), 1960 . . . . £100/£20
ditto, Andre Deutsch, 1962 . . . . . . £50/£15
Pull My Daisy, Grove Press (U.S.), 1961 (wraps) £75
ditto, Evergreen, 1961 (wraps) £35

KEN KESEY

(b.1935)

An American novelist, Kesey volunteered, in the 1960s, for Government drug experiments. His *One flew over the Cuckoo's Nest* draws on his experience of working as an aide on a psychiatric ward in a veteran's hospital.

Novels

One Flew over the Cuckoo's Nest, Viking (U.S.), 1962 . . . . £500/£75
ditto, Methuen, 1963 . . . . £125/£25

Sometimes a Great Notion, Viking (U.S.), 1964 . . . . £100/£25
ditto, Methuen, 1966 . . . . £75/£20
Demon Box, Viking (U.S.), 1986 . . . £15/£5
ditto, Methuen, 1986 . . . . £10/£5
The Further Inquiry, Viking (U.S.), 1990 . £10/£5
Sailor Song, Viking (U.S.), 1992 . . . £10/£5

Children's
Little Tricker the Squirrel Meets Big Double the Bear, Viking (U.S.), 1990 . . . . £25/£10
Sea Lion, Viking (U.S.), 1991 . . . . £25/£10

Others
Kesey's Garage Sale, Viking (U.S.), 1973 . £25/£10
Kesey, Northwest Review Books (U.S.), 1977 (hardback, no d/w) £50
ditto, Northwest Review Books (U.S.), 1977 (wraps) £15
The Day After Superman Died, Lord John Press (U.S.), 1980 (350 signed copies) £65

STEPHEN KING
(b.1947)

One of the most successful of living writers, King's breakthrough was *Carrie*, a book which has now sold over 12 million copies.

Novels
Carrie, Doubleday (U.S.), 1974 . . . £250/£100
ditto, New English Library, 1974. . . . £250/£100
Salem's Lot, Doubleday (U.S.), 1975 ('Doctor Cody' on d/w) . . . . £200/£125
ditto, Doubleday (U.S.), 1975 ('Father Cody' on d/w) . . . . £600/£125
ditto, New English Library, 1976. . . . £150/£50
The Shining, Doubleday (U.S.), 1977 . . £225/£75
ditto, New English Library, 1977. . . . £150/£50
Rage, Signet/New American Library (U.S.), 1977 (pseud. 'Richard Bachman', wraps) £25
ditto, New English Library, 1983 (wraps) . . £15
The Stand, Doubleday (U.S.), 1978 . . . £200/£50
ditto, New English Library, 1979. . . . £150/£50
The Dead Zone, Viking (U.S.), 1979 . . £50/£20
ditto, Macdonald & Jane, 1979 . . . . £75/£25
The Long Walk, Signet/New American Library (U.S.), 1979 (pseud. 'Richard Bachman', wraps) . . £25
Firestarter, Phantasia Press (U.S.), 1980 (725 copies in d/w and slipcase). . . . . £500/£200
ditto, Phantasia Press (U.S.), 1980 (26 lettered copies, bound in asbestos) £4,000
ditto, Viking (U.S.), 1980. . . . . . . £25/£10
ditto, Macdonald & Jane, 1980 . . . . . £25/£10
Roadwork, Signet/New American Library (U.S.), 1981 (pseud. "Richard Bachman", wraps) . . . £15
ditto, New English Library, 1983 (wraps) . . £10
Cujo, Viking (U.S.), 1981 . . . . . . £25/£10
ditto, Mysterious Press (U.S.), 1981 (750 numbered, signed copies) . . . . £300/£150
ditto, Mysterious Press (U.S.), 1981 (lettered, signed copies) £500
ditto, Macdonald, 1982 . . . . £25/£10
The Running Man, Signet /New American Library (U.S.), 1982 (pseud. 'Richard Bachman', wraps) £20
ditto, New English Library, 1983 (wraps) . . £10
Creepshow, NAL/Plume (U.S.), 1982 (wraps) . £25
The Dark Tower: The Gunslinger, Grant (U.S.), 1982 . . . . £200/£65
ditto, Grant (U.S.), 1982 (lettered, signed edition, d/w and slipcase) . . . . £1,500/£1,000
ditto, Grant (U.S.), 1982 (500 numbered, signed copies, d/w and slipcase) . . . . £600/£400
ditto, Sphere, 1988, (wraps) £10
Christine, Grant (U.S.), 1983 (lettered, signed edition) £2,000
ditto, Grant (U.S.), 1983 (1,000 signed copies, slipcase) . . . . £350/£200
ditto, Viking (U.S.), 1983. . . . . . . £25/£5
ditto, Hodder & Stoughton, 1983. . . . . £25/£5
Cycle of the Werewolf, Land of Enchantment (U.S.), 1983 . . . . £200/£75
ditto, Land of Enchantment (U.S.), 1983 (8 presentation copies) £2,500
ditto, Land of Enchantment (U.S.), 1983 (250 copies) . . . . £500/£250
ditto, Land of Enchantment (U.S.), 1983 (100 copies with original drawing) . . . . . £1,000/£500
ditto, New English Library, 1985 (wraps) . . £10
Selected Works, Heinemann/Octopus, 1983. £15/£5
Pet Sematary, Doubleday (U.S.), 1983 . . £20/£5
ditto, Hodder & Stoughton, 1984. . . . £20/£5
The Eyes of the Dragon, Philtrum (U.S.), 1984 (1,000 signed copies numbered in black ink, slipcase, no d/w) £450
ditto, Philtrum (U.S.), 1984 (250 signed copies numbered in red ink, slipcase, no d/w) £750
ditto, Viking (U.S.), 1987. . . . . . . £15/£5
ditto, Macdonald, 1987 . . . . £15/£5
The Talisman, Viking, 1984 (with Peter Straub) £20/£5
ditto, Grant (U.S.), 1984 (70 numbered copies signed by authors and artists, slipcase, 2 vols). . £500/£400
ditto, Grant (U.S.), 1984 (1,200 signed, numbered copies, no d/w, slipcase, 2 vols). . . . £225/£150
ditto, Viking (U.K.), 1984 . . . . . . £15/£5
Thinner, New American Library (U.S.), 1984 (pseud. 'Richard Bachman') . . . . £40/£10
ditto, New English Library, 1985 (pseud. 'Richard

Bachman') . . . . £25/£10
The Bachman Books, New American Library, 1985 (pseud. "Richard Bachman") . . . . £20/£5
ditto, New English Library, 1986. . . . . £20/£5
Silver Bullet, New American Library/Signet (U.S.), 1985 (wraps) £10
It, Hodder & Stoughton, 1986 . . . . £20/£5
ditto, Viking (U.S.), 1986 . . . . . . £15/£5
Misery, Viking (U.S.), 1987 . . . . . £20/£5
ditto, Hodder & Stoughton, 1987. . . . £15/£5
The Dark Tower II: The Drawing of the Three, Grant (U.S.), 1987 . . . . £30/£10
ditto, Grant (U.S.), 1987 (800 signed copies, d/w and slipcase) . . . . £300/£250
ditto, Grant (U.S.), 1987 (52? lettered copies, d/w and slipcase) . . . . £650/£500
ditto, Sphere, 1989 (wraps) £10
The Tommyknockers, Putnum (U.S.), 1987. £15/£5
ditto, Hodder & Stoughton, 1988. . . . £15/£5
The Dark Half, Hodder & Stoughton, 1989. £10/£5
ditto, Viking (U.S.), 1989 . . . . . . £10/£5
The Stand, Doubleday (U.S.), 1990 (complete and uncut edition). . . . . £10/£5
ditto, Doubleday (U.S.), 1990 (52 signed, lettered copies) £1,000
ditto, Doubleday (U.S.), 1990 (1,250 signed copies, bound in full leather, in wooden box) . . . £500
ditto, Hodder & Stoughton, 1990. . . . £10/£5
The Dark Tower III: The Wastelands, Grant (U.S.), 1991 . . . . £25/£10
ditto, Grant (U.S.), 1991 (1,250 signed copies, d/w and slipcase). . . . . £275/£200
ditto, Sphere, 1991, (wraps) £10
Needful Things, Hodder & Stoughton, [1991] £10/£5
ditto, Viking (U.S.), 1991 . . . . . . £10/£5
Gerald's Game, Viking (U.S.), 1992. . . £10/£5
ditto, Hodder & Stoughton, 1992. . . . £10/£5
Dolores Claiborne, Book Club Associates, 1992 . . . . £10/£5
ditto, Viking (U.S.), 1992 . . . . . . £10/£5
ditto, Hodder & Stoughton, 1992. . . . £10/£5
ditto, Hodder & Stoughton, 1992 ('Special Limited Christmas Gift Edition', slipcase) . . . £75/£45
Insomnia, Ziesing (U.S.), 1994 (1,250 signed copies, d/w and case) . . . . £200/£150
ditto, Ziesing (U.S.), 1994 ("Gift edition", d/w and slipcase) . . . . £75/£45
ditto, Viking (U.S.), 1994 . . . . . . £10/£5
ditto, Hodder & Stoughton, 1994. . . . £10/£5
ditto, Hodder & Stoughton, 1994 (200 signed, numbered copies, slipcase, no d/w) £200
Rose Madder, Hodder & Stoughton, 1994 . £10/£5
ditto, Hodder & Stoughton, 1994 (250 signed copies, slipcase, no d/w) . . . . £150/£100
ditto, Viking (U.S.), 1995 . . . . . . £10/£5
The Green Mile, Penguin/Signet (U.S.), 1996 (six paperbacks) . . . . £15 the set
ditto, Penguin, 1996 (six paperbacks) . . £15 the set
ditto, Penguin/Plume (U.S.), 1997 (1 vol.) . . . £5
Desperation, Viking (U.S.), 1996 . . . £10/£5
ditto, Hodder & Stoughton, 1996. . . . £10/£5
Desperation and ***The Regulator***, Hodder Headline, 1996 (250 sets in single slipcase, the former signed, the latter pseud. 'Richard Bachman') . . £250/£200
The Dark Tower IV: Wizard and Glass, Grant (U.S.), 1997 . . . . £25/£10
ditto, Grant (U.S.), 1991 (1,200 signed copies, d/w and slipcase). . . . . £250/£150
ditto, Hodder & Stoughton, 1988, (wraps) . . £10
ditto, Hodder & Stoughton, 1988, (500 copies, no d/w) £200
Bag of Bones, Simon & Schuster/Scribner (U.S.), 1998 . . . . £10/£5
ditto, Hodder & Stoughton, 1998. . . . £10/£5
ditto, Hodder & Stoughton, 1998 (2,000 signed copies) . . . . £45/£15

Short Stories

Night Shift, Doubleday (U.S.), 1978. . . £250/£60
ditto, New English Library, 1978. . . . £225/£45
Different Seasons, Viking (U.S.), 1982 . . £25/£10
ditto, Macdonald, 1982 . . . . . . £20/£15
The Plant, Philtrum (U.S.), 1982 (200 signed copies, wraps). £1,000
ditto, Philtrum (U.S.), 1982 (26 signed, lettered copies, wraps). £1,500
The Plant - Part Two, Philtrum (U.S.), 1983 (200 copies, wraps) £1,000
ditto, Philtrum (U.S.), 1983 (26 signed, lettered copies, wraps). £1,500
Skeleton Crew, Putnam (U.S.), 1985. . . . £45
ditto, as ***Stephen King's Skeleton Crew***, Scream Press (U.S.), 1985 (1,000 copies numbered in silver ink and signed by author and artist, slipcase) . . £300/£200
ditto, Scream Press (U.S.), 1985, (69 leather-bound, zippered copies) £1,500
ditto, Scream Press (U.S.), 1985 (17 presentation copies) £2,000
ditto, Scream Press (U.S.), 1985 (52 lettered copies) £750
ditto, Putnam), 1985 . . . . £20/£5
ditto, Macdonald, 1985 . . . . £20/£5
The Plant - Part Three, Philtrum (U.S.), 1985 (200 copies, wraps) £1,000
ditto, Philtrum (U.S.), 1985 (26 signed, lettered copies, wraps). £1,500
My Pretty Pony, Whitney Museum of American Art (U.S.), 1989 (250 copies) £1,750
ditto, Knopf (U.S.), 1989 . . . . £30/£10
Dolan's Cadillac, Lord John Press (U.S.), 1989 (26

lettered, signed copies) £1,500
ditto, Lord John Press (U.S.), 1989 (100 presentation copies, quarter-bound in leather) £300
ditto, Lord John Press (U.S.), 1989 (250 numbered, signed copies, quarter-bound in leather) . . £250
ditto, Lord John Press (U.S.), 1989 (1,000 numbered, signed copies, no d/w) £100
Four Past Midnight, Viking (U.S.), 1990 . £10/£5
ditto, Hodder & Stoughton, 1990. . . . £10/£5
Nightmares and Dreamscapes, Viking (U.S.), 1993 . . . . £10/£5
ditto, Hodder & Stoughton, 1993. . . . £10/£5

Others
Danse Macabre, Everest House (U.S.), 1981 £50/£20
ditto, Everest House (U.S.), 1981 (250 signed, numbered copies, slipcase, tissue d/w) . . £450/£150
ditto, Everest House (U.S.), 1981 (signed, lettered copies, slipcase, tissue d/w) . . . . . £750/£450
ditto, Everest House (U.S.), 1981 (35 publishers copies, no slipcase or d/w) £750
ditto, Macdonald Futura, 1981 . . . . £25/£10
Letters from Hell, Lord John Press (U.S.), 1988 (500 signed copies, broadside in wraps) £100

RUDYARD KIPLING

(b.1865 d.1936)

Often considered a poet of British imperialism, Kipling's work has caused much controversy, though poems such as *If* and his 'Jungle Book' stories remain firmly entrenched in our colonial mythology.

Verse
Schoolboy Lyrics, privately printed (Lahore), 1881 (wraps) £5,000
Echoes, privately printed (Lahore), 1884 (published anonymously, with Alice Kipling, wraps) . . £5,000
Departmental Ditties, Civil and Military Gazette (Lahore), 1886 (wraps) £1,000
ditto, Thacker, Spink & Co. (Calcutta), 1886 . £250
ditto, Thackar & Co. (London), 1890 . . . £40
Barrack-Room Ballads and Other Verses, Methuen, 1892 . . . . £50
ditto, Methuen, 1892 (large paper edition, 225 copies) £200
ditto, Methuen, 1892 (deluxe edition, 30 copies on half-vellum) £300
The Seven Seas, Methuen, 1896 . . . . . £25
ditto, Methuen, 1896 (large paper edition, 150 copies) £100
ditto, Methuen, 1896 (deluxe edition, 30 copies on half-vellum) £250
An Almanac of Twelve Sports, Heinemann, 1898 [1897]. £100
Early Verse, Macmillan, 1900 . . . . . £50
The Five Nations, Methuen, 1903 . . . . £20
ditto, Methuen, 1903 (large paper edition, 200 copies) £200
ditto, Methuen, 1903 (deluxe edition, 30 copies on full vellum. £300
A Song of the English, Hodder & Stoughton, [c.1909] (30 colour plates illustrated by W. Heath Robinson) £100
ditto, Hodder & Stoughton, [c.1909] (deluxe edition, 500 copies signed by the artist, 30 colour plates, full vellum) £200
ditto, Hodder & Stoughton, [1912], (12 colour plates) £20
ditto, Hodder & Stoughton/Daily Telegraph, [1915] (16 colour plates). £40
ditto, Hodder & Stoughton, [1919] (16 colour plates) £20
The Dead King, Hodder & Stoughton, 1910 (illustrated by W. Heath Robinson) £25
ditto, Hodder & Stoughton, 1910 (illustrated by W. Heath Robinson, wraps) £25
Collected Verse, Doubleday Page (U.S.), 1910 (9 colour plates by W. Heath Robinson) . . . £100
Collected Verse, Hodder & Stoughton, 1912 . £15
ditto, Hodder & Stoughton, 1912 (deluxe edition, 100 copies on full vellum) £125
A History of England, O.U.P./Hodder & Stoughton, 1911 (quarto, with C.R.L. Fletcher) . . . £20
ditto, O.U.P./Hodder & Stoughton, 1911 (octavo edition for schools) £15
Songs from Books, Macmillan, 1913 . . . £20
Twenty Poems, Methuen, 1918 (wraps) . . . £15
The Years Between, Methuen, 1919 . . . . £20
ditto, Methuen, 1919 (Large Paper edition, 100 copies) £100
ditto, Methuen, 1919 (deluxe edition, 30 copies on vellum) £150
Verse: Inclusive Edition 1885-1918, Hodder & Stoughton, 1919 (3 vols) £50
ditto, Hodder & Stoughton, 1919 (deluxe edition, 100 signed sets on vellum) £500
A Kipling Anthology: Verse, Methuen, 1922 £15/£5
Songs for Youth, Hodder & Stoughton, [1924] £25/£10
A Choice of Songs, Methuen, 1925 . . . £15/£5
Sea and Sussex, Macmillan, 1926 (illustrated by Donald Maxwell). . . . . £30/£15
ditto, Macmillan, 1926 (500 copies on half-vellum) £175
Songs of the Sea, Macmillan, 1927 (illustrated by Donald Maxwell). . . . . £30/£10
ditto, Macmillan, 1927 (500 copies on half-vellum) £175

Poems 1886-1929, Macmillan, 1929 (3 vols, illustrated by Francis Dodd). . . . . £50/£20
ditto, Macmillan, 1929 (deluxe edition, 525 sets in morocco leather) £250
East of Suez, Macmillan, 1931 (illustrated by Donald Maxwell) . . . . £25/£10
Selected Poems, Methuen, 1931 . . . . £10/£5
Sixty Poems, Hodder & Stoughton, 1939 . £10/£5
Verse: Definitive Edition, Hodder & Stoughton, 1940 . . . . £15/£5
So Shall Ye Reap: Poems For These Days, Hodder & Stoughton, 1941 . . . . £10/£5
A Choice of Kipling's Verse, Faber & Faber, 1941 (edited by T. S. Eliot) . . . . . . £15/£5

Children's
The Jungle Book, Macmillan, 1894 . . . . £500
The Second Jungle Book, Macmillan, 1895 . £150
'Captains Courageous', a story of the Grand Banks, Macmillan, 1897 . . . . £50
Stalky and Co., Macmillan, 1899 . . . . . £75
Just So Stories for Little Children, Macmillan, 1902 . . . . £250
Puck of Pook's Hill, Macmillan, 1906 . . . £50
ditto, Doubleday Page (U.S.), 1906 (illustrated by Arthur Rackham). £200
Rewards and Fairies, Macmillan, 1910 . . . £50

Novels
The Light That Failed, Lippincott (U.S.), 1890 (12 chapters with happy ending). £150
ditto, Macmillan, 1891 (15 chapters with unhappy ending!) £50
The Naulahka, a story of West and East, Heinemann, 1892 (with W. Balestier) £50
Kim, Doubleday Page (U.S.), 1901 . . . . £100
ditto, Macmillan, 1901 . . . . £50

Short Stories
Plain Tales from the Hills, Thacker Spink (Calcutta), 1888 . . . . £1,500
ditto, Macmillan, 1890 . . . . £125
Soldiers Three, A.H. Wheeler (Allahabad), 1888 £250
ditto, Sampson Low, 1890. . . . . £75
The Story of the Gadsby's, A.H. Wheeler (Allahabad), 1888 . . . . £250
ditto, Sampson Low, 1890, ... £75
In Black and White, A.H. Wheeler (Allahabad), 1888. . . . . £250
ditto, Sampson Low, 1890 . . . . £75
Under the Deodars, A.H. Wheeler (Allahabad), 1888 . . . . £250
ditto, Sampson Low, 1890 . . . . £75
The Phantom Rickshaw and Other Tales, A.H. Wheeler (Allahabad), [1888] £250
ditto, Sampson Low, 1890 . . . . £75
Wee Willie Winkie and Other Child Stories, A.H. Wheeler (Allahabad), 1888 . . . . . . £250
ditto, Sampson Low, 1890 . . . . £75
The Courting of Dinah Shad and Other Stories, Harper (U.S.), 1890 . . . . £250
The City of Dreadful Night and Other Sketches, A.H. Wheeler (Allahabad), 1890 (suppressed edition) £1,000
ditto, as ***The City of Dreadful Night and Other Places***, A.H. Wheeler (Allahabad), 1891 (unsuppressed edition) £250
ditto, Sampson Low, 1891 . . . . £75
Life's Handicap, being stories of mine own people, Macmillan, 1891 . . . . £50
Many Inventions, Macmillan, 1893 . . . . £50
Soldier Tales, Macmillan, 1896 (reprints from ***The Story of the Gadsbys*** and ***In Black and White***) £50
The Day's Work, Doubleday & McClure (U.S.), 1898 . . . . £75
ditto, Macmillan, 1898 . . . . £50
The Kipling Reader, Macmillan, 1900 . . . . £25
Traffics and Discoveries, Macmillan, 1904 . . £50
They, Macmillan, 1905 (from ***Traffics and Discoveries***) £45
The Brushwood Boy, Macmillan, 1907 (from ***The Day's Work***) £25
Actions and Reactions, Macmillan, 1909 . . £50
Abaft the Funnel, Dodge (U.S.), 1909 . . . £125
A Diversity of Creatures, Macmillan, 1917 . . £25
Land and Sea Tales for Scouts and Guides, Macmillan, 1923 . . . . £30/£15
Debits and Credits, Macmillan, 1926 . . £30/£15
Thy Servant A Dog, Told by Boots, Macmillan, 1930 . . . . £30/£15
Humorous Tales, Macmillan, 1931 . . . £30/£15
Animal Stories, Macmillan, 1932 . . . £30/£15
Limits and Renewals, Macmillan, 1932 . . £30/£15
All The Mowgli Stories, Macmillan, 1933 . £50/£25
Collected Dog Stories, Macmillan, 1934 . £30/£15
Ham and the Porcupine, Doubleday Doran (U.S.), 1935 . . . . £30/£15
The Maltese Cat, Macmillan 1936 (from ***The Day's Work***). . . . . £40/£15
More Selected Stories, Macmillan, 1940 . £30/£15
Twenty-One Tales, Reprint Society, 1946 . £10/£5
Ten Stories, Pan, 1947 (wraps) £5
A Choice of Kipling's Prose, Macmillan, 1952 £10/£5
Complete Works: The Sussex Edition, Macmillan, 1937-1939 (35 vols) . . . . £2,000 the set

---

C.H.B. KITCHIN

(b.1895 d.1967)

A novelist, poet and musician, it is as the author of a handful of detective novels that Kitchen is best known.

Detective Novels

Death of My Aunt, Hogarth Press, 1929. . £200/£45
ditto, Harcourt Brace (U.S.), 1930 . . . £45/£10
Crime at Christmas, Hogarth Press, 1934 . £200/£45
Death of his Uncle, Constable, 1939 . . £50/£15
The Cornish Fox, Secker & Warburg, 1949 £35/£10

Other Novels

Streamers Waving, Hogarth Press, 1925 . £150/£45
Mr Balcony, Hogarth Press, 1927 . . . £125/£30
The Sensitive One, Hogarth Press, 1921 . £100/£20
Olive E, Constable, 1937 . . . . . . £20/£10
Birthday Party, Constable, 1938 . . . . £20/£10
The Auction Sale, Secker & Warburg, 1949 £25/£10
The Secret River, Secker & Warburg, 1956 £15/£5
Ten Pollitt Place, Secker & Werburg, 1957 £15/£5
The Book of Life, Davies, 1960 . . . . £10/£5
A Short Walk in Williams Park, Chatto & Windus, 1971 . . . . £10/£5

Short Stories

Jumping Joan and Other Stories, Secker & Warburg, 1954 . . . . £15/£5

Poetry

Curtains, Blackwell, 1919 (wraps) £50
Winged Victory, Blackwell, 1921 (wraps) . . £40

ARTHUR KOESTLER

(b.1905 d.1983)

A novelist and philosopher, all of Koestler's books are more or less an analysis of the turmoil in Europe in the years preceding World War Two.

Autobiography

Spanish Testament, Gollancz, 1937 . . . . £150/£25
ditto, Gollancz, 1937 (Left Book Club, wraps) £35
ditto, as ***Dialogue with Death***, Macmillan (U.S.), 1942 (abridged). . . . . £15/£5
Scum of the Earth, Cape, 1941 . . . . £35/£10
ditto, Macmillan (U.S.), 1941. . . . . . £15/£5
Arrow in the Blue, Collins/Hamilton, 1952 . £20/£5
ditto, Macmillan (U.S.), 1952. . . . . £15/£5
The Invisible Writing, Collins/Hamilton, 1954 £15/£5
ditto, Macmillan (U.S.), 1954. . . . . £10/£5
Stranger on the Square, Hutchinson, 1984 (unfinished, by Arthur and Cynthia Koestler) . . . . £10/£5
ditto, Random House (U.S.), 1984 . . . . £10/£5

Novels

The Gladiators, Cape, 1939 . . . . . . £45/£10
ditto, Macmillan (U.S.), 1939. . . . . . £15/£5
Darkness at Noon, Cape, 1940 . . . . £50/£15
ditto, Macmillan (U.S.), 1941. . . . . . £10/£5
ditto, Franklin Library (U.S.), 1970 (signed, limited edition) £95
Arrival and Departure, Cape, 1943 . . . £25/£10
ditto, Macmillan (U.S.), 1943. . . . . £15/£5
Thieves in the Night, Macmillan, 1946 . . £15/£5
ditto, Macmillan (U.S.), 1946. . . . . £10/£5
The Age of Longing, Collins, 1951 . . . £15/£5
ditto, Macmillan (U.S.), 1951. . . . . £10/£5
The Call-Girls, Hutchinson, 1972 . . . . £10/£5
ditto, Random House (U.S.), 1973 . . . £10/£5

Essays

The Yogi and the Commissar, Cape, 1945 . £15/£5
ditto, Macmillan (U.S.), 1945. . . . . £10/£5
Insight and Outlook, Macmillan, 1949 . . £10/£5
ditto, Macmillan (U.S.), 1949. . . . . £10/£5
The Trail of the Dinosaur, Collins, 1955 . £10/£5
ditto, Macmillan (U.S.), 1955. . . . . £10/£5
Reflections on Hanging, Gollancz, 1957 . £10/£5
ditto, Macmillan (U.S.), 1957. . . . . £10/£5
The Lotus and the Robot, Hutchinson, 1960 £10/£5
ditto, Macmillan (U.S.), 1961. . . . . £10/£5
Hanged by the Neck, Penguin, 1961. . . . £10/£5
Drinkers of Infinity: Essays 1955-1967, Hutchinson, 1968 . . . . £10/£5
ditto, Macmillan (U.S.), 1969. . . . . £10/£5
The Lion and the Ostrich, O.U.P., 1973 . £10/£5
The Heel of Achilles: Essays, Hutchinson, 1974 . . . . £10/£5
ditto, Random House (U.S.), 1975 . . . £10/£5
Janus: A Summing Up, Hutchinson, 1978 . £10/£5
ditto, Random House (U.S.), 1978 . . . £10/£5
Bricks to Babel, Hutchinson, 1980 . . . £10/£5
ditto, Random House (U.S.), 1981 . . . £10/£5

Non Fiction

Promise and Fulfilment, Macmillan, 1949 . £15/£5
ditto, Macmillan (U.S.), 1949. . . . . £10/£5
The Sleepwalkers, Hutchinson, 1959 . . £15/£5
ditto, Macmillan (U.S.), 1959. . . . . £10/£5
The Act of Creation, Hutchinson, 1964 . . £15/£5
ditto, Macmillan (U.S.), 1964. . . . . £10/£5
The Ghost in the Machine, Hutchinson, 1967 £20/£5
ditto, Macmillan (U.S.), 1968. . . . . £10/£5
The Case of the Midwife Toad, Hutchinson, 1971 . . . . £10/£5

ditto, Random House (U.S.), 1972 . . . £10/£5
The Roots of Coincidence, Hutchinson, 1972 £10/£5
ditto, Random House (U.S.), 1972 . . . £10/£5
The Challenge of Chance, Hutchinson, 1973 (with Alister Hardy and Robert Harvie) . . . £10/£5
ditto, Random House (U.S.), 1975 . . . £10/£5
The Thirteenth Tribe, Hutchinson, 1976 . £10/£5
ditto, Random House (U.S.), 1976 . . . £10/£5

DEAN KOONTZ

(b.1945)

Koontz's writing career began in 1956 when, at the age of twenty, he won an *Atlantic Monthly* fiction competition. His world wide sales amount to close on 100 million.

Novels

Star Quest, Ace (U.S.), 1968 (with ***Doom of the Green Planet*** by Emil Petaja, wraps) £10
The Fall of the Dream Machine, Ace (U.S.), 1969 (with ***The Star Venturers***, wraps) £20
Fear That Man, Ace (U.S.), 1969 (with ***Toyman*** by E.C. Tubb, wraps) £10
Anti-Man, Paperback Library (U.S.), 1970 (wraps) £15
Beastchild, Lancer (U.S.), 1970 (wraps) . . £20
Dark of the Woods and ***Soft Come The Dragons***, Ace (U.S.), 1970 (wraps) £10
The Dark Symphony, Lancer (U.S.), 1970 (wraps) £25
Hell's Gate, Lancer (U.S.), 1970 (wraps) . . £20
The Crimson Witch, Curtis (U.S.), 1971 (wraps) £20
A Darkness in My Soul, Daw (U.S.), 1972 (wraps) £10
ditto, Dobson, 1979 . . . . £65/£20
The Flesh in the Furnace, Bantam (U.S.), 1972 (wraps) £25
Starblood, Lancer (U.S.), 1972 (wraps) . . . £15
Time Thieves, Ace (U.S.), 1972 (with ***Against Arcturus*** by Susan K. Putney, wraps) . . . £10
ditto, Dobson, 1977 . . . . £75/£25
Warlock, Lancer (U.S.), 1972 (wraps) . . . £10
Writing Popular Fiction, Writers' Digest Fiction (U.S.), 1973 . . . . £45/£15
A Werewolf Among Us, Ballantine (U.S.), 1973 (wraps) £15
The Haunted Earth, Lancer (U.S.), 1973 (wraps) £15
Hanging On, M. Evans (U.S.), 1973 . . £75/£25
ditto, Barrie & Jenkins, 1974 (wraps) . . . £10
Demon Seed, Bantam (U.S.), 1973 (wraps) . £15
ditto, Corgi, 1977 (wraps). £10
After the Last Race, Athenaeum (U.S.), 1974 £75/£25
Nightmare Journey, Putnam (U.S.), 1975 . £100/£25
Night Chills, Atheneum (U.S.), 1976 . . £100/£30
ditto, W.H. Allen, 1977 . . . . . . £75/£25
The Vision, Putnam (U.S.), 1977. . . . £80/£25
ditto, Corgi, 1980 (wraps). £10
ditto, W.H. Allen, 1988 . . . . . . £45/£15
Whispers, Putnam (U.S.), 1980 . . . . £200/£50
ditto, W.H. Allen, 1981 . . . . . . £75/£25
How To Write Best-Selling Fiction, Writers' Digest Books (U.S.), 1981 . . . . £50/£15
ditto, Popular Press (U.S.), 1981 . . . . £20/£5
Phantoms, Putnam (U.S.), 1983 . . . . £75/£25
ditto, W.H. Allan, 1983 . . . . . . £25/£15
Darkness Comes, W.H. Allen, 1984 . . £125/£35
ditto, as ***Darkfall***, Berkeley (U.S.), 1984 . £15/£5
Twilight Eyes, Land of Enchantment (U.S.), 1985 . . . . £35/£15
ditto, Land of Enchantment (U.S.), 1985 (signed, illustrated collector's edition, 50 copies) . . £350
ditto, Land of Enchantment (U.S.), 1985 (signed edition, 200 copies, d/w and slipcase) . . £200/£125
ditto, W.H. Allen, 1987 . . . . . . £50/£20
Strangers, Putnam (U.S.), 1986 . . . . £25/£5
ditto, W.H. Allen, 1987 . . . . . . £25/£5
Watchers, Putnam (U.S.), 1987 . . . . £20/£5
ditto, Headline, 1987 . . . . £20/£5
Lightning, Putnam (U.S.), 1987 . . . . £20/£5
ditto, Headline, 1988 . . . . £20/£5
Oddkins, Warner (U.S.), 1988 . . . . £25/£10
ditto, Headline, 1988 . . . . £20/£5
Midnight, Putnam (U.S.), 1989 . . . . £15/£5
ditto, Headline, 1989 . . . . £15/£5
Bad Place, Putnam (U.S.), 1990 . . . . £15/£5
ditto, Putnam (U.S.), 1990 (250 signed, numbered copies, d/w and slipcase) . . . . £125/£75
ditto, Headline, 1990 . . . . £15/£5
Cold Fire, Putnam (U.S.), 1991 . . . . £10/£5
ditto, Putnam (U.S.), 1991 (750 signed, numbered copies, d/w and slipcase) . . . . £100/£65
ditto, Headline, 1991 (200 signed, numbered copies) . . . . £125/£100
ditto, Headline, 1991 . . . . £10/£5
Hideaway, Putnam (U.S.), 1992 . . . . £10/£5
ditto, Putnam (U.S.), 1991 (800 signed, numbered copies, d/w and slipcase) . . . . £100/£65
ditto, Headline, 1992 . . . . £10/£5
Dragon Tears, Putnam (U.S.), 1993 . . . £10/£5
ditto, Putnam (U.S.), 1991 (700 signed, numbered copies, d/w and slipcase) . . . . £100/£65
ditto, Headline, 1993 . . . . £10/£5
Mr Murder, Headline, 1993 . . . . . £10/£5
ditto, Putnam (U.S.), 1993 . . . . . . £10/£5
ditto, Putnam (U.S.), 1991 (600 signed, numbered copies, d/w and slipcase) . . . . £100/£65
Winter Moon, Headline, 1994 . . . . £20/£5
ditto, Ballantine (U.S.), 1994 (wraps) £5
Dark Rivers of the Heart, Knopf, 1994 . . £10/£5
ditto, Headline, 1994 . . . . £10/£5

Icebound, Headline, 1995 . . . . . £10/£5
Strange Highways, Warner (U.S.), 1995 . £10/£5
ditto, Headline, 1995 . . . . £10/£5
Intensity, Knopf, 1995 . . . . £10/£5
ditto, Headline, 1995 . . . . £10/£5
Ticktock, Headline, 1996 . . . . £10/£5
ditto, Ballantine (U.S.), 1996 (wraps) £5
Sole Survivor, Knopf, 1997 . . . . . . £10/£5
ditto, Headline, 1997 . . . . £10/£5

Titles written with Gerda Koontz
Bounce Girl, Cosmo (U.S.), 1970 . . . £30/£10
The Underground Lifestyles Handbook, Aware Press (U.S.), 1970 . . . . £25/£10
The Pig Society, Aware Press (U.S.), 1970 . £25/£10

Written as 'David Axton'
Prison of Ice, Lippincott (U.S.), 1976 . . £200/£45
ditto, W.H. Allen, 1977 . . . . £100/£35

Written as 'Brian Coffey'
Blood Risk, Bobbs-Merrill (U.S.), 1973 . . £150/£45
ditto, Arthur Barker, 1974 . . . . . . £75/£25
Surrounded, Bobbs-Merrill (U.S.), 1974 . £150/£50
ditto, Arthur Barker, 1975 . . . . . . £75/£25
The Wall of Masks, Bobbs-Merrill (U.S.), 1975 . . . . £100/£25
The Face of Fear, Bobbs-Merrill (U.S.), 1977 . . . . £150/£50
ditto, Peter Davis, 1978 (pseud. 'K.R. Dwyer') £75/£25
The Voice of the Night, Doubleday (U.S.), 1980 . . . . £200/£65
ditto, Robert Hale, 1981 . . . . £45/£15

Written as 'Deanna Dwyer'
The Demon Child, Lancer (U.S.), 1971 (wraps) £15
Legacy of Terror, Lance (U.S.), 1971 (wraps) £15
Children of the Storm, Lancer (U.S.), 1972 (wraps) £15
The Dark of Summer, Lancer (U.S.), 1972 (wraps) £15
Dance With the Devil, Lancer (U.S.), 1972 (wraps) £15

Written as 'K.R. Dwyer'
Chase, Random House (U.S.), 1972 . . . £125/£40
ditto, Arthur Barker, 1974 . . . . . £75/£25
Shattered, Random House (U.S.), 1972 . . £150/£45
ditto, Arthur Barker, 1974 . . . . . . £75/£25
Dragonfly, Random House (U.S.), 1975. . £100/£30
ditto, Peter Davis, 1977 . . . . £45/£20

Written as 'John Hill'
The Long Sleep, Popular Library (U.S.), 1975 (wraps) £15

Written as 'Leigh Nichols'
The Key to Midnight, Pocket (U.S.), 1979 (wraps) £15
ditto, Magnum, 1980 (wraps) £10
ditto, Dark Harvest (U.S.), 1989 . . . . . £25/£10
The Eyes of Darkness, Pocket (U.S.), 1981 (wraps) £10
ditto, Piatkus, 1981 . . . . £25/£5
ditto, Dark Harvest (U.S.), 1981 (400 signed, numbered copies, d/w and slipcase) . . . . . £50/£35
The House of Thunder, Pocket (U.S.), 1982 (wraps) £10
ditto, Fontana, 1983 (wraps) £10
ditto, Dark Harvest (U.S.), 1988 (550 signed, numbered copies, d/w and slipcase) . . . . . £50/£35
Twilight, Pocket (U.S.), 1984 (wraps) . . . £10
ditto, as ***The Servants of Twilight***, Fontana, 1985 (wraps) £10
ditto, as ***The Servants of Twilight***, Dark Harvest (U.S.), 1988 (450 signed copies, d/w and slipcase) £50/£35
The Door to December, NAL (U.S.), 1985 (wraps, pseud. 'Richard Paige') £10
ditto, Fontana, 1987 (wraps, pseud. 'Leigh Nichols') £10
Shadowfires, Pocket (U.S.), 1987 (wraps) . . £10
ditto, Fontana, 1987 (wraps) £10
ditto, Collins, 1987 . . . . £45/£20
ditto, Dark Harvest (U.S.), 1990 . . . . . £10/£5

Written as 'Anthony North'
Strike Deep, Dial (U.S.), 1974 . . . . £150/£50

Written as 'Owen West'
The Funhouse, Jove (U.S.), 1980 (wraps) . . £10
ditto, Doubleday (U.S.), 1980 . . . . . £15/£5
ditto, Sphere, 1981 (wraps) £10
The Mask, Jove (U.S.), 1980 (wraps) £10
ditto, Coronet/Hodder, 1983 (wraps). . . . £10
ditto, Headline, 1989 . . . . £30/£10

Written as 'Aaron Wolfe'
Invasion, Laser Books (U.S.), 1975 (wraps) . £15

PHILIP LARKIN

(b.1922 d.1985)

A poet and novelist, *XX Poems* was the first of Larkin's collections to realise his own distinctive voice, although *The Less Deceived* was his first popular success.

Verse
The North Ship, The Fortune Press, 1945 £850/£200
ditto, The Fortune Press, 1945 [1965] (unauthorised

second edition, maroon cloth) . . . . . £75/£25
ditto, Faber, 1966 . . . . £45/£15
XX Poems, privately printed, 1951 (100 copies, not for sale, wraps) £1,000
The Fantasy Poets No. 21, Fantasy Press, 1954 (300 copies) £500
The Less Deceived, Marvell Press, 1955 £450/£125
ditto, Marvell Press, 1955 (wraps) £40
ditto, St Martin's Press (U.S.), 1960 . . . £65/£20
The Whitsun Weddings, Faber, 1964 . . £100/£25
ditto, Random House (U.S.), 1964 . . . £65/£20
The Explosion, Poem of the Month Club, 1970 (broadsheet, 1,000 signed copies) £125
High Windows, Faber, 1974 . . . . . £40/£15
ditto, Farrar Straus (U.S.), 1974 . . . . £25/£10
Femmes Damnées, Sycamore Press, 1978 (broadsheet) £30
Aubade, Penstermon Press (U.S.), 1980 (250 numbered, initialed copies, wraps, in envelope) £150
Collected Poems, Faber, 1988 . . . . £25/£10
ditto, Farrar Straus (U.S.), 1988 . . . . £20/£5

Novels

Jill, The Fortune Press, 1946 . . . . . £300/£65
ditto, Faber, 1964 . . . . £75/£25
ditto, St Martin's Press (U.S.), 1964 . . . £50/£20
A Girl in Winter, Faber, 1947 . . . . £500/£100
ditto, St Martin's Press (U.S.), 1957 . . . £75/£20

Recordings

Listen Presents Philip Larkin Reading 'The Less Deceived', Listen/The Marvell Press, 1959 . £25
ditto, Listen/The Marvell Press, 1959 (100 copies signed by the author). £100
Philip Larkin Reads and Comments on 'The Whitsun Weddings', Listen Records [1965] £25
British Poets of Our Time, Philip Larkin 'High Windows': Poems Read by the Author, Argo [1975] £25

Others

All What Jazz: A Record Diary, 1961-68, Faber, 1970 . . . . £45/£15
ditto, St Martin's Press (U.S.), 1970 . . . £25/£10
Philip Larkin Talks to Eboracum, [Eboracum, 1970] (wraps) £50
The Oxford Book of Twentieth Century English Verse, O.U.P., 1973 (edited by Larkin) . £25/£10
Required Writing, Miscellaneous Pieces, 1955-1982, Faber, 1983 (wraps) £20
ditto, Farrar Straus (U.S.), 1983 . . . . £20/£5
ditto, Faber, 1984 (hardback). . . . . £50/£15
Selected Letters of Philip Larkin, 1940-1985, Faber, 1992 . . . . £25/£10
ditto, Farrar Straus (U.S.), 1993 . . . . £15/£5

D.H. LAWRENCE

(b.1885 d.1930)

A versatile and controversial modernist writer whose achievements have often been overshadowed by the various court cases they have provoked, especially the trial of *Lady Chatterly's Lover*.

Novels

The White Peacock, Duffield (U.S.), 1911 . . £3,000
ditto, Heinemann, 1911 . . . . £500
The Trespasser, Duckworth, 1912 . . . . £600
ditto, Kennerley (U.S.), 1912 . . . . . . £250
Sons and Lovers, Duckworth, 1913 . . . . £500
ditto, Kennerley (U.S.), 1913 . . . . . . £250
The Rainbow, Methuen, 1915 . . . . . £500
ditto, Huebsch (U.S.), 1916 . . . . . . £175
The Lost Girl, Secker, 1920 . . . . £600/£100
ditto, Seltzer (U.S.), 1921 . . . . . . £75/£25
Women in Love, privately printed (U.S.), 1921 (1,250 numbered, copies) £350
ditto, Secker, 1921 . . . . £300/£25
ditto, Secker, 1922 (50 signed copies) . . . £1,500
Aaron's Rod, Seltzer (U.S.), 1922 . . . £150/£45
ditto, Secker, 1922 . . . . £150/£45
Kangaroo, Secker, 1923 . . . . . £125/£35
ditto, Seltzer (U.S.), 1923 . . . . . . £100/£25
The Boy in the Bush, Secker, 1924 (with M.L. Skinner) . . . . £150/£25
ditto, Seltzer (U.S.), 1924 . . . . . . £100/£25
The Plumed Serpent, Secker, 1926 . . . £150/£35
ditto, Knopf (U.S.), 1926 . . . . £75/£25
Lady Chatterly's Lover, privately printed (Florence), 1928 (1,000 signed, numbered copies, plain protective jacket). . . . . £2,500/£1,750
ditto, privately printed (Florence), 1928 (second edition, wraps) £200
ditto, privately printed (Paris), 1929 (wraps) . £100
ditto, Secker, 1932 (expurgated edition) . . £100/£25
ditto, Knopf (U.S.), 1932 (expurgated edition) . . . . £375/£45
ditto, Grove Press (U.S.), 1959 (unexpurgated edition). . . . . £50/£15
ditto, Penguin, 1960 (unexpurgated edition, wraps) £10
The Virgin and the Gypsy, Orioli (Florence), 1930 (810 copies) . . . . £300/£125
ditto, Secker, 1930. . . . . £100/£25
ditto, Knopf (U.S.), 1930 . . . . . . £75/£25
Mr Noon, C.U.P., 1984 . . . . . . £15/£5
ditto, Viking (U.S.), 1985 . . . . . . £10/£5

Verse

Love Poems and Others, Duckworth, 1913 . . £200

ditto, Kennerley (U.S.), 1913 . . . . . . £150
Amores, Duckworth, 1916 . . . . . . £75
ditto, Huebsch (U.S.), 1916 . . . . . . £35
Look! We have come through!, Chatto and Windus, 1917 . . . . £75
New Poems, Secker, 1918 (wraps) £100
ditto, Huebsch (U.S.), 1920 . . . . . . £25
Bay, A Book of Poems, Beaumont, 1919 . . £75
ditto, Beaumont, 1919 (30 signed copies) . . £750
Tortoises, Seltzer (U.S.), 1921 . . . . £200/£35
Birds, Beasts and Flowers, Seltzer (U.S.), 1923 . . . . £65/£25
ditto, Secker, 1923 . . . . £45/£20
ditto, Cresset Press, 1923 (500 copies) . . £125
The Collected Poems of D. H. Lawrence, Secker, 1928 (2 vols) . . . . £75/£35
ditto Secker, 1928 (100 signed copies, d/w and slipcase) £750
Pansies, Secker, 1929 . . . . £50/£20
ditto, Secker, 1929 (250 signed copies). £250
ditto, Stephenson, 1929 (500 signed copies, wraps) £250
ditto, privately printed [for Frieda Lawrence] (U.S.), 1954 (750 numbered copies, glassine d/w) £25/£15
ditto, privately printed [for Frieda Lawrence] (U.S.), 1954 (250 numbered copies, signed by Frieda Lawrence, glassine d/w) . . . . . . £40/£30
Nettles, Faber & Faber, 1930 (wraps) . . £35
The Triumph of the Machine, Faber, [1930] (wraps) £30
Last Poems, G. Orioli (Florence), 1932 . . £250/£100
ditto, Secker, 1933. . . . . £45/£20
The Ship of Death, Secker, 1933 . . . . £75
Poems, Heinemann, 1939 (2 vols) . . . . £35/£10
Fire and Other Poems, Book Club of California, 1940 (100 copies) . . . . £300/£100
The Complete Poems, Heinemann, 1957 (3 vols) . . . . £40/£25
ditto, Viking (U.S.), 1964 (2 vols, slipcase) . £30/£20

Short Stories

The Prussian Officer and Other Stories, Duckworth, 1914 . . . . £150/£25
ditto, Huebsch (U.S.), 1916 . . . . . . £100/£20
England, My England, Seltzer (U.S.), 1922 £75/£25
ditto, Secker, 1924. . . . . £75/£25
The Ladybird, The Fox, The Captain's Doll, Secker, 1923 . . . . £60/£20
ditto, as ***The Captain's Doll***, Seltzer (U.S.), 1923 . . . . £40/£15
St Mawr, Secker, 1925 . . . . £150/£30
Glad Ghosts, Ernest Benn, 1926 (500 copies, wraps) £75
Sun, Archer, 1926 (100 copies, expurgated). . £350
ditto, Black Sun Press (Paris), 1928 (wraps) . £650
ditto, Black Sun Press (Paris), 1928 (15 signed copies in glassine d/w and gold folder ,wraps). . . . £2,500
ditto, Black Sun Press (Paris), 1928 (150 copies in gold folder, wraps). £1,000
Rawdon's Roof, Mathews and Marrot, 1928 (530 signed, numbered copies) . . . . . £250/£175
The Woman Who Rode Away, Secker, 1928 £75/£20
ditto, Knopf (U.S.), 1928 . . . . . . £65/£20
The Escaped Cock, Black Sun Press (Paris), 1929 (450 numbered copies, wraps, with tissue d/w and slipcase) . . . . £300/£175
ditto, Black Sun Press (Paris), 1929 (50 signed copies) . . . . £600/£250
ditto, as ***The Man Who Died***, Secker, 1931 (2,000 copies) . . . . £75/£35
Love Among the Haystacks, Nonesuch Press, 1930 (1,600 numbered copies) . . . . . £75/£35
ditto, Secker, 1930. . . . . £25/£10
ditto, Haldeman Julius (U.S.), 1941 (wraps). . £25
The Lovely Lady, Secker, 1932 [1933] . . £75/£25
ditto, Viking (U.S.), 1933 . . . . . . £45/£15
The Tales of D H Lawrence, Secker, 1934 . £25/£10
A Modern Lover, Secker, 1934 . . . . £25/£10
ditto, Viking (U.S.), 1934 . . . . £25/£10

Plays

The Widowing of Mrs Holroyd, Kennerley (U.S.), 1914 . . . . £40
ditto, Duckworth, 1914 . . . . £35
Touch and Go, Daniel, 1920 . . . . . £125/£35
ditto, Seltzer (U.S.), 1920 . . . . . . £100/£35
David, Daniel, 1926 . . . . £75/£25
ditto, Knopf (U.S.), 1926 . . . . . . £75/£25
The Plays, Secker, 1933 . . . . . . £25/£10
A Collier's Friday Night, Secker, 1934 . . £25/£10
The Complete Plays, Heinemann, 1965 . . £25/£10
ditto, Viking (U.S.), 1965 . . . . £25/£10

Miscellaneous

Twilight in Italy, Duckworth, 1916 . . . . £200
ditto, Huebsch (U.S.), 1916 . . . . £100
Movements in European History, O.U.P., 1921 (pseud. Lawrence H. Davison) £75
Sea and Sardinia, Seltzer (U.S.), 1921 . . . . £75
ditto, Secker, 1923. . . . . £25
Psychoanalysis and the Unconscious, Seltzer (U.S.), 1921 . . . . £250/£75
ditto, Secker, 1923 . . . . £200/£50
Fantasia of the Unconscious, Seltzer (U.S.), 1922 . . . . £200/£45
ditto, Secker, 1923. . . . . £200/£50
Studies in Classic American Literature, Seltzer (U.S.), 1923 . . . . £200/£45
ditto, Secker, 1924 . . . . £200/£50
Reflections on the Death of a Porcupine and Further

Essays, Centaur Press (U.S.), 1925 (925 copies) £150
ditto, Simpkin, Marshall, Hamilton, Kent, 1925 (475 numbered copies) £150
Mornings in Mexico, Secker, 1927 . . . £100/£35
ditto, Knopf (U.S.), 1927 . . . . £75/£25
The Paintings of D.H. Lawrence, The Mandrake Press, 1929 (510 copies). £500
Pornography and Obscenity, Faber & Faber, 1929 (wraps) £20
ditto, Faber & Faber, 1929 (cloth) £40
Assorted Articles, Secker, 1930 . . . . £40/£15
ditto, Knopf (U.S.), 1930 . . . . £40/£15
Apropos of Lady Chatterly's Lover, Mandrake Press, 1930 . . . . £35/£15
Apocalypse, Orioli (Florence), 1931 (750 copies) . . . . £150/£75
ditto, Secker, 1932 (750 numbered copies) . £75/£25
ditto, Secker, 1932. . . . . £30/£10
ditto, Viking (U.S.), 1932. . . . . . . £25/£10
The Letters of D. H. Lawrence, Heinemann, 1932. . . . . £100/£40
ditto, Heinemann, 1932 (525 numbered parchment bound copies). £200
ditto, Viking (U.S.), 1932. . . . . . . £25/£10
Etruscan Places, Secker, 1932 . . . . £200/£45
Pornography and So On, Faber, 1936 . . £75/£25
Phoenix: The Posthumous Papers of D. H. Lawrence, Heinemann, 1936 . . . . . . £35/£15
The Manuscripts of D. H. Lawrence, Los Angeles Public Library (U.S.), 1937 (750 copies, wraps) £25
D.H. Lawrence's Letters to Bertrand Russell, Gotham Book Mart (U.S.), 1948 (950 copies) . . £50/£20
Sex, Literature and Censorship, Twayne (U.S.), 1953 . . . . £20/£5
ditto, Heinemann, 1955 . . . . £20/£5
Collected Letters, Heinemann, 1962 . . . £40/£15
ditto, Viking (U.S.), 1962 (2 vols) . . . £30/£10
Letters to Martin Secker, privately printed, 1970 (500 numbered copies) . . . . £45/£15
The Letters, C.U.P., 1979 (vol. I) . . . £25/£10
The Letters, C.U.P., 1981 (vol. II) . . . £25/£10

T.E. LAWRENCE
(b.1888 d.1935)

A soldier and author, Lawrence is popularly known as 'Lawrence of Arabia'. His account of the revolt, *The Seven Pillars of Wisdom*, is seen as a masterpiece by many.

Seven Pillars of Wisdom, Oxford Edition, 1922 (8 copies) £25,000
ditto, London, 1924 (first proof copy) . . . £2,500
ditto, London, 1925, (second proof, 100 copies) £2,000
ditto, Cranwell, Subscribers' Edition, 1926 (169 copies) £20,000
ditto, Cranwell, Subscribers' Edition, 1926 (32 presentation copies) £20,000
ditto, Doubleday Doran (U.S.), 1926 (copyright edition, 22 copies). £12,500
ditto, Jonathan Cape, 1935 (750 copies, d/w and slipcase) . . . . £1,000/£500
ditto, Jonathan Cape, 1935 . . . . . £150/£35
ditto, Jonathan Cape, 1935 (60 copies) . . . £750
ditto, Doubleday Doran (U.S.), 1935. . . £100/£25
ditto, Doubleday Doran (U.S.), 1935 (750 copies, d/w and slipcase) . . . . . . £1,000/£400
Revolt in the Desert, Jonathan Cape, 1927 . £200/£45
ditto, Jonathan Cape, 1927 (315 large paper copies) . . . . £1,000/£500
ditto, Doubleday Doran (U.S.), 1927. . . £100/£35
ditto, Doubleday Doran (U.S.), 1927 (250 large paper copies) £750
The Mint, Doubleday Doran, (U.S.), 1936 (pseud. '352087 A/C Ross', U.S. copyright edition, 50 copies) £20,000
ditto, Jonathan Cape, 1955 (first unexpurgated U.K. edition, 2,000 copies, slipcase) . . . . £125/£100
ditto, Jonathan Cape, 1955 (first U.K. trade edition, expurgated) . . . . £25/£10
ditto, Doubleday Doran, (U.S.), 1955 (1,000 numbered copies, slipcase) . . . . £150/£100
ditto, Doubleday Doran, (U.S.), 1957 . . £15/£5
Crusader Castles, Golden Cockerel Press, 1936 (2 vols, 1000 copies, no d/w or slipcase) . . . £800
*ditto, **The Thesis***, Golden Cockerel Press, 1936 (75 copies) £1,000
*ditto, **The Letters***, Golden Cockerel Press, 1936 (35 copies) £1,500
ditto, Doubleday Doran (U.S.), 1937 (copyright edition) £400
The Diary of T.E. Lawrence MCMXI, Corvinus Press, 1937 (30 copies on 'Canute' paper) £4,000
ditto, Corvinus Press, 1937 (40 copies on 'Medway' paper) £2,500
ditto, Corvinus Press, 1937 (130 copies on parchment-style paper) £1,750
ditto, Doubleday Doran, U.S., 1937 (copyright edition, 50 copies). £3,000
An Essay on Flecker, Corvinus Press, 1937 (26 copies, slipcase) . . . . £2,500/£2,000
ditto, Corvinus Press, 1937 (4 copies, vellum) . £3,500
ditto, Corvinus Press, 1937 (2 copies, leather) . £5,000
ditto, Doubleday Doran (U.S.), 1937 (copyright edition of approx 56 copies, wraps). £1,250
Two Arabic Folk Tales, Corvinus Press, 1937 (31 copies) £1,750

Secret Dispatches from Arabia, Golden Cockerel Press, 1939 (Nos. 1-30, printed on Arnold hand-made paper, bound in white pig-skin, with supplement) £2,000
ditto, Golden Cockerel Press, 1939 (Nos. 31-1,000, printed on Arnold hand-made paper, bound in quarter Niger, without supplement) £400
ditto, Bellew, 1991 (revised edition) £10
Men in Print, Golden Cockerel Press, 1940 (nos. 1-30, bound in full Niger, with supplement, slipcase) . . . . £1,750/£1,250
ditto, Golden Cockerel Press, 1940 (nos. 31-500) £400
The Essential T.E. Lawrence, Jonathan Cape, 1951 . . . . £35/£10
ditto, Dutton (U.S.), 1951 . . . . . £35/£10
Evolution of a Revolt, Early Postwar Writings of T.E. Lawrence, The Pennsylvania State University Press (U.S.), 1968 . . . . £35/£15

Translations by 'J.H. Ross'
The Forest Giant, by Adrien Le Corbeau, Jonathan Cape, 1924 . . . . £75/£25
ditto, Harper & Bros. (U.S.), 1924 (1st issue with translator incorrectly given as L.H. Ross) . £75/£25

Translations by 'T.E. Shaw'
The Odyssey of Homer, Bruce Rogers, 1932, (530 copies, slipcase) . . . . . . £1,500/£1,000
ditto, O.U.P. (U.S.), 1932 . . . . £75
ditto, O.U.P. (U.S.), 1932 (32 copies) . . . £500
ditto, O.U.P., 1935. . . . . £75/£30

Letters
Letters from T.E. Shaw to Bruce Rogers, privately printed by Bruce Rogers, 1933 (300 copies) . £750
More Letters from T.E. Shaw to Bruce Rogers, privately printed by Bruce Rogers, 1936 (300 copies) £500
A Letter from T.E. Lawrence to His Mother, Corvinus Press, 1936 (30 copies) £1,250
Letter from T.E. Shaw to Viscount Carlow, Corvinus Press, 1936, (17 copies) £1,000
The Letters of T.E. Lawrence, Cape, 1938 . £100/£35
ditto, Doubleday Doran (U.S.), 1939. . . £45/£15
ditto, Dent, 1988 (new edition) . . . . £20/£5
T.E. Lawrence To His Biographers, Faber, 1938 (500 copies signed by Graves and Hart, 2 vols with d/ws, in slipcase) . . . . £450/£400
ditto, Doubleday Doran, 1938 (500 copies signed by Graves and Hart, 2 vols with d/ws, in slipcase) . . . . £450/£400
Eight Letters from T.E.L., privately printed [Corvinus Press], 1939 (50 copies) £750
Selected Letters of T.E. Lawrence, World Books, 1941 . . . . £5

Shaw-Ede: T.E. Lawrence's letters to H.S. Ede, 1927-35, Golden Cockerel Press, 1942 (nos. 1-130, bound in full morocco, with facsimile reproductions of 5 of the letters) £1,000
ditto, Golden Cockerel Press, 1942 (nos. 31-500) £300
The Home Letters of T.E. Lawrence and His Brothers, Blackwell, 1954 . . . . . £125/£35
ditto, Macmillan (U.S.), 1954. . . . . . £75/£25
From a Letter of T.E. Lawrence, Officina Bodoni, 1959 (75 copies) £150
T.E.L., Five Hitherto Unpublished Letters, privately printed, 1975 (30 copies, wraps) £150
Fifty Letters, Humanities research centre (U.S.), 1962 (wraps) £30
Letters to E.T. Leeds, Whittington Press, 1988 (650 copies, slipcase) £100

Edited by Lawrence
Minorities, Cape, 1971 . . . . . . £40/£15
ditto, Cape, 1971 (125 copies signed by C. Day-Lewis) £300
ditto, Doubleday (U.S.), 1972 . . . . £35/£15

JOHN LE CARRÉ
(b.1931)

A novelist whose thrillers have examined the grey, dubious world of Cold War spying. As the years have passed his 'fiction' is seen to have been more and more perceptive.

Novels
Call for the Dead, Gollancz, 1961 . . £1,500/£250
ditto, Walker (U.S.), 1962 . . . . . £250/£35
A Murder of Quality, Gollancz, 1962 . £1,450/£250
ditto, Walker (U.S.), 1963 . . . . . £200/£35
The Spy Who Came in from the Cold, Gollancz, 1963 . . . . £250/£35
ditto, Coward McGann (U.S.), 1963 . . . £65/£15
The Looking-Glass War, Heinemann, 1965 £50/£10
ditto, Coward McGann (U.S.), 1965 . . . £25/£5
A Small Town in Germany, Heinemann, 1968 £35/£10
ditto, Coward-McCann (U.S.), 1968 (500 signed copies, tissue d/w) . . . . £200/£175
ditto, Coward McGann (U.S.), 1968 . . . £20£5
The Naive and Sentimental Lover, Hodder & Stoughton, 1971 . . . . £25/£5
ditto, Knopf (U.S.), 1971 . . . . . . £15/£5
Tinker, Tailor, Soldier, Spy, Hodder & Stoughton, 1974 . . . . £25/£5
ditto, Knopf (U.S.), 1974 . . . . £15/£5
The Honourable Schoolboy, Franklin Center: Franklin Library for The First Edition Society (U.S.), 1977 £75

ditto, Knopf (U.S.), 1977 . . . . £15/£5
ditto, Hodder & Stoughton, 1977. . . . . £25/£5
Smiley's People, Franklin Center: Franklin Library for The First Edition Society (U.S.), 1979 . . £100
ditto, Hodder & Stoughton, 1980. . . . . £35/£5
ditto, Knopf (U.S.), 1980 . . . . £15/£5
ditto, Knopf (U.S.), 1980 (signed sheet tipped-in) . . . . £60/£30
The Little Drummer Girl, Knopf (U.S.), 1983 £10/£5
ditto, Knopf (U.S.), 1983 (signed sheet tipped-in) . . . . £75/£40
ditto, Book of the Month Club (U.S.), 1983 (1,048 signed copies, slipcase) . . . . £100/£75
ditto, Hodder & Stoughton, 1983 . . . £15/£5
A Perfect Spy, Hodder & Stoughton, 1986 . £15/£5
ditto, London Limited Editions/Hodder & Stoughton, 1986 (250 signed copies, glassine d/w). . £125/£100
ditto, Knopf (U.S.), 1986 . . . . . . £10/£5
ditto, Knopf (U.S.), 1986 (signed sheet tipped-in) . . . . £60/£30
The Russia House, Knopf (U.S.), 1989 . . £10/£5
ditto, Knopf (U.S.), 1989 (signed sheet tipped-in) . . . . £60/£30
ditto, Hodder & Stoughton, 1989. . . . . £10/£5
ditto, Hodder & Stoughton, 1989 (collector's edition, 500 copies, quarter leather, slipcase) . . £75/£50
ditto, London Limited Editions, 1989 (250 signed copies, glassine d/w) . . . . £125/£75
The Secret Pilgrim, Hodder & Stoughton, 1991 £15/£5
ditto, Knopf (U.S.), 1991 . . . . £10/£5
ditto, Knopf (U.S.), 1991 (signed sheet tipped-in) . . . . £60/£30
The Night Manager, Hodder & Stoughton, 1993 . . . . £10/£5
ditto, Knopf (U.S.), 1993 . . . . £10/£5
ditto, Knopf (U.S.), 1993 (signed sheet tipped-in) . . . . £50/£25
Our Game, Hodder & Stoughton, 1995 (1st issue) . . . . £125/£50
ditto, Hodder & Stoughton, 1995 (2nd issue) £10/£5
ditto, Knopf (U.S.), 1995 . . . . £10/£5
The Tailor of Panama, Hodder & Stoughton, 1996 . . . . £10/£5
ditto, Knopf (U.S.), 1996 . . . . £10/£5

Collections

The Le Carré Omnibus, Gollancz, 1964 . £75/£25
The Quest for Karla, Hodder & Stoughton. 1982 . . . . £25/£5
ditto, Knopf (U.S.), 1982 . . . . £15/£5

Others

The Clandestine Muse, Seluzicki (U.S.), 1986 (250 signed copies) £150
Vanishing England, Salem House (U.S.), 1987 (with Gareth H. Davies) . . . . £35/£15
Nervous Times: An Address Given at the Savoy Hotel..., Anglo-Israel Association, 1998 (250 signed, numbered copies) £100

RICHARD LE GALLIENNE

(b.1866 d.1947)

Generally disregarded simply because he survived the 1890s, Le Gallienne is not overlooked by all collectors of the period.

Fiction

The Student and the Body-Snatcher and Other Tales, Elkin Mathews, 1890 (with R.K. Leather) . . £65
The Book-Bills of Narcissus, Frank Murray, 1891 £45
Prose Fancies, Elkin Mathews & John Lane, 1894 £10
Prose Fancies: Second Series, John Lane, 1896 £10
The Quest of the Golden Girl, John Lane, 1896 £50
The Romance of Zion Chapel, John Lane, 1898 £25
Young Lives, A Tale, Arrowsmith, 1899 . . £25
The Worshipper of the Image, John Lane, 1900 £25
Sleeping Beauty and Other Prose Fancies, John Lane, 1900 . . . . £25
The Life Romantic, Including the Love-Letters of the King, Hurst & Blackett, 1901 . . . . . £25
Painted Shadows, John Lane, 1908 [1907] . . £25
Little Dinners with The Sphinx and Other Prose Fancies, John Lane, 1909 . . . . . . £25
The Maker of Rainbows, with Other Fairy-Tales and Fables, Harper, 1912 . . . . £20
The Highway to Happiness, T. Werner Laurie, [1914] £15
Pieces of Eight, Collins, 1918 . . . . . £15
Old Love Stories Retold, John Lane, 1924 . £35/£10
The Magic Seas, H. Toulmin, 1930 . . . £35/£10

Verse

My Ladies' Sonnets and Other 'Vain and Amatorious' Verses, with Some of Graver Mood, privately printed, 1887 . . . . £150
ditto, privately printed, 1887 (50 signd copies) . £300
Volumes in Folio, Elkin Mathews, 1889 . . £125
ditto, Elkin Mathews, 1889 (250 copies) . . £300
ditto, Elkin Mathews, 1889 (50 large paper copies)£300
English Poems, Elkin Mathews & John Lane, 1892 £50
A Fellowship in Song, Elkin Mathews & John Lane, 1893 (with A. Hayes and N. Gale) £20
Robert Louis Stevenson: An Elegy and Other Poems, John Lane, 1895 . . . . £10
ditto, John Lane, 1895 (500 copies) £100
ditto, John Lane, 1895 (75 large paper copies) . £200
Holly and Mistletoe, Marcus Ward, 1896 (with E.

Nesbit and N. Gale) £45
Rubaiyat of Omar Khayyam: A Paraphrase, Grant Richards, 1897 . . . . £25
Odes from the Divan of Hafiz, Duckworth, 1903 £40
Omar Repentant, Grant Richards, 1908 . . . £20
New Poems, John Lane, 1910 . . . . . . £10
The Lonely Dancer and Other Poems, John Lane, 1914 . . . . £10
The Silk-Hat Soldier and Other Poems, John Lane, 1915 (wraps) £20

Non Fiction
George Meredith: Some Characteristics, Elkin Mathews, 1890 . . . . £10
The Religion of a Literary Man, Elkin Mathews & John Lane, 1893 . . . . £10
Retrospective Reviews: A Literary Log, John Lane, 1896, 2 vols) £15
If I Were God, privately printed, 1897 . . . . £30
Rudyard Kipling: A Criticism, John Lane, 1900 £25
Travels in England, Grant Richards, 1900 . . . £25
The Beautiful Life of Rome, Simpkin, Marshall, Hamilton, Kent & Co, 1900 . . . . . . £10
An Old Country House, Grant Richards, 1902 . £30
October Vagabonds, John Lane, 1910 . . . £10
Attitudes and Avowals, John Lane, 1910 [1911] £10
Vanishing Roads and Other Essays, Putnam, 1915 £10
The Romantic 90s, Putnam, 1926 . . . £50/£15
From a Paris Garret, Richards Press, 1936. £30/£10
The Cry of the Little Peoples, privately printed, 1941 . . . . £25

EDWARD LEAR
(b.1812 d.1888)

Popularly known as a nonsense poet, Lear, an accomplished artist and travel-writer, illustrated his own verse.

Nonsense Books
A Book of Nonsense, Thomas Maclean, 1846 (pseud 'Derry Down Derry', 2 vols, wraps) . . £50,000
ditto, Thomas Maclean, 1855 (no pseud, two volumes, wraps) £5,000
ditto, Routledge, 1861 (enlarged edition) . . £500
ditto, Routledge, 1861 (enlarged edition) . . £500
Nonsense Songs, Stories, Botany and Alphabets, Robert John Bush, 1871 . . . . £500
More Nonsense, Pictures, Rhymes, Botany, Robert John Bush, 1872 [1874] £450
Laughable Lyrics, A Fourth Book of Nonsense Poems, Songs, Botany, Music, etc., Robert John Bush, 1877 . . . . £450
The Jumblies and Other Nonsense Poems, Songs, Botany, Music, Warne, 1877 [1876] £175
Nonsense Drolleries, Warne, 1889 . . . . £125
A Nonsense Birthday Book, Warne, [1894]. . £75
Nonsense Songs and Stories, Warne, 1895 . . £75
Nonsense Songs and Laughable Lyrics, Little, Brown & Co (U.S.), 1899 . . . . £75
ditto, Peter Pauper Press (U.S.), 1935 (650 copies) £50
The Pelican Chorus and Other Nonsense Verses, Warne, 1900 . . . . £125
Queery Leary Nonsense, Mills & Boon, 1911 . £50
Callico Pie, Warne, [1924] . . . . . £75/£25
Facsimile of A Nonsense Alphabet, Warne, 1926 (1,000 numbered copies) £65
The Owl and the Pussy Cat, Warne, [1924] £75/£35
The Pobble, Hugh Sharpe, 1934 (50 copies) . £250
The Quangle Wangle's Hat, Hugh Sharp, 1933 (50 copies) £250
Edward Lear's Nonsense Songs, Chatto & Windus, 1938 . . . . £35/£15
A Book of Lear, Penguin, 1939 (wraps with d/w) . . £10/£5
Edward Lear's Nonsense Omnibus, Odhams, 1943 . . . . £25/£10
The Complete Nonsense of Edward Lear, Faber, 1947 . . . . £25/£10
Edward Lear's Nonsense Alphabet, Collins, [1949] . . . . £25/£15
A Nonsense Alphabet, H.M.S.O., 1952 . . . . £10
Teapots and Quails and Other Nonsense, John Murray, 1953 . . . . £35/£15
ditto, Harvard University (U.S.), 1953 . . £25/£10
ABC, Constable, 1965. . . . . £15/£5
A Book of Nonsense, Peter Owen, 1972 (illustrated by Mervyn Peake) . . . . £25/£10
Bosh and Nonsense, Allen Lane, 1982 . . £15/£5

Natural History
Illustrations of the Family Psittacide, or Parrots, R. Ackerman & E. Lear, 1832 . . . . . £75,000
Gleanings from The Menagerie and Aviary at Knowsley Hall, privately printed, Knowsley, 1846 . . . . £10,000
Tortoises, Terrapins and Turtles Drawn from Life, Henry Sotheran & Joseph Baer, 1872 (with James de Carle Sowerby) £2,000
The Lear Coloured Bird Book for Children, Mills and Boon, [1912] £40
Edward Lear's Parrots, Duckworth, 1949 (12 plates) . . . . £75/£30
The Birds of Edward Lear, A Selection, Ariel Press, 1975 (1000 copies, 12 plates) . . . . £150/£100

Travel
Views in Rome and Its Environs, Thomas Maclean,

1841 (25 plates) £1,500
Illustrated Excursions in Italy, Thomas Maclean, 1846 (first series, 30 plates) . . . . . . £1,500 each
Illustrated Excursions in Italy, Thomas Maclean, 1846 (second series, 25 plates) . . . . . £1,500 each
Journals of a Landscape Painter in Albania, Richard Bentley, 1851 (21 plates) £1,000
Journals of a Landscape Painter in Southern Calabria, Richard Bentley, 1852 (2 maps, 20 plates) £500
Views in the Seven Southern Ionian Islands, E. Lear, 1863 (20 plates) £5,000
ditto, Oldham, 1979 (facsimile reprint of 1,000 numbered copies, 20 plates). . . . . . £100/£65
Journals of a Landscape Painter in Corsica, Robert John Bush, 1870 (41 plates). £500
Lear in Sicily, Duckworth, 1938 . . . . £35/£15
Edward Lear's Journals, A Selection, Arthur Barker, 1952 (4 plates) . . . . £45/£20
Edward Lear's Indian Journal, Jarrolds, 1953 (9 plates). . . . . £45/£20
Edward Lear in Southern Italy, W. Kimber, 1964 (20 plates). . . . . £100/£35
Edward Lear in Greece, W. Kimber, 1965 (20 plates) . . . . £100/£35
Edward Lear in Corsica, W. Kimber, 1966 £100/£35
Lear's Corfu, Corfu Travel, 1965 (8 illustrations) . . . . £25/£10

Letters

The Letters of Edward Lear, T. Fisher Unwin, 1907 (20 plates) £50
Letters ... to Chichester Fortescue Lord Carlingford, and Frances Countess Waldegrave, Duffield (U.S.), [1908]. £45
The Later Letters of Edward Lear, T. Fisher Unwin, 1911 . . . . £25
A Letter from Edward Lear to George William Curtis, Harvard Printing Office (U.S.), 1947 (660 copies, wraps). £5
Selected Letters, Clarendon Press, 1988. . £25/£10

Others

Three Poems by Tennyson Illustrated by Edward Lear, Bousson, Valadon & Co., Scribner & Welford, 1889 (100 copies signed by Tennyson, 24 illustrations by Lear) £2,500
Edward Lear on My Shelves, privately printed by William Osgood Field, 1933 . . . . . . £500

LAURIE LEE
(b.1914 d.1997)

Lee was primarily a poet, best known for his volumes of autobiography. *Cider with Rosie* is a nostalgic memoir of his Gloucestershire childhood.

Autobiography

Cider with Rosie, Hogarth Press, 1959 . . £60/£15
ditto, as ***The Edge of Day***, Morrow (U.S.), 1960 . . . . £40/£10
As I Walked Out One Midsummer Morning, Deutsch, 1969 . . . . £20/£5
ditto, Atheneum (U.S.), 1969 . . . . . . £10/£5
A Moment of War, Viking, 1991. . . . . £10/£5
ditto, New Press (U.S.), 1991 . . . . . £10/£5
Red Sky at Sunrise, Viking, 1992 (collects above autobiographical works) . . . . . . £10/£5

Verse

The Sun My Monument, Hogarth Press, 1944 £65/£25
ditto, Doubleday (U.S.), 1947 . . . . . £40/£15
The Bloom of Candles, Lehmann, 1947. . £40/£15
New Poems, 1954, M. Joseph, 1954 . . . £25/£10
My Many-Coated Man, Deutsch, 1955 . . £25/£10
ditto, Coward McGann (U.S.), 1957 . . . £15/£5
Pocket Poets, Studio Vista, 1960. . . . . . £5
15 poems for William Shakespeare, Trustees and Guardians of Shakespeare's Birthplace, 1964 (wraps). £20
Pergamon Poets 10, Pergamon Press, 1970 (wraps) £5
Selected Poems, Deutsch, 1983 (wraps) £5
Fish and Water, Friends of the Cheltenham Festival, [1991] (broadsheet) £15
Boy in Ice, Turret Bookshop, [1991] (broadsheet) £40

Plays

Peasant's Priest, Friends of Canterbury Cathedral, 1947 . . . . £30/£10
The Voyage of Magellan, Lehmann, 1948 . £60/£15

Others

Land at War, H.M.S.O., 1945 (anonymous, wraps) £25
We Made a Film in Cyprus, Longman, 1947 (with Ralph Keene). . . . . £65/£25
Vassos the Goatherd: A Story of Cyprus, Pilot Press, 1947 . . . . £45/£15
An Obstinate Exile, privately printed (U.S.), 1951 (glassine d/w). . . . . £125/£100
A Rose for Winter: Travels in Andalusia, Hogarth Press, 1955 . . . . £50/£10
ditto, Morrow (U.S.), 1956 . . . . . . £30/£10
Epstein: A Camera Study, Deutsch, 1956 . £35/£10
ditto, Deutsch, 1956 (200 signed copies, slipcase) . . . . £250/£200

Man Must Move, Rathbone, 1960 . . . £25/£10
ditto, as ***The Wonderful World of Transportation***, Doubleday (U.S.), 1961 (with David Lambert) £20/£5
Atlantic Fairway, Cunard Line, [1962] (wraps) £15
The Firstborn, Hogarth Press, 1964 . . . £25/£10
ditto, Morrow (U.S.), 1964 . . . . £15/£5
Paintings and Drawings of the Gypsies of Granada, Athelnay Books (U.S.), 1969 . . . . . £10
I Can't Stay Long, Deutsch, 1975 . . . £10/£5
ditto, Atheneum (U.S.), 1976 . . . . . . £10/£5
Innocence in the Mirror, Morrow (U.S.), 1978 £10/£5
Two Women, Deutsch, 1983 . . . . . £10/£5

J. SHERIDAN LE FANU

(b.1814 d.1873)

Anglo-Irish writer of mystery, supernatural and historical romances.

Novels

The Cock and Anchor, Curry, Longmans, Fraser, 1845, (anonymous, 3 vols, boards) £1,250
ditto, as ***Morley Court***, Chapman & Hall, 1873 (revised edition) £45
The Fortunes of Colonel Torlogh O'Brien, McGlashan, Orr, 1847 (anonymous) . . . £300
The House by the Church-Yard, Tinsley, 1863 (3 vols, royal blue cloth) £3,000
ditto, Tinsley, 1863 (3 vols, green cloth) . . £2,000
Wylder's Hand, Bentley, 1864 (3 vols) . . . £1,250
Uncle Silas, Bentley, 1864 (3 vols) £1,250
Guy Deverell, Bentley, 1865 (3 vols) . . . £1,000
All in the Dark, Bentley, 1866 (2 vols, claret cloth) £750
ditto, Bentley, 1866 (presentation copies, 2 vols, white cloth) £1,500
The Tenants of Malory, Tinsley, 1867, (3 vols) £1,000
A Lost Name, Bentley, 1868 (3 vols) . . . £1,000
Haunted Lives, Tinsley, 1868, (3 vols) . . . £1,000
The Wyvern Mystery, Tinsley, 1869, (3 vols) £1,000
Checkmate, Hurst & Blackett, 1871 (3 vols) £1,000
The Rose and The Key, Chapman & Hall, 1871 (3 vols) £1,000
Willing to Die, Hurst & Blackett, 1873 (3 vols) £800

Short Stories and Collected Editions

Ghost Stories and Tales of Mystery, McGlashan, Orr, 1851 (anonymous, with gold blocking to front board). £3,000
ditto, McGlashan, Orr, 1851 (anonymous, no gold blocking to front board) £600
Chronicles of Golden Friars, Bentley, 1871 (3 vols) £1,500
In A Glass Darkly, Bentley, 1872, (3 vols) . . £2,000
The Purcell Papers, Bentley, 1880, (3 vols) £1,500
The Watcher, Downey, [1894] £350
The Evil Guest, Downey, [1895] £400
A Chronicle of Golden Friars, Downey, 1896 £65
Madam Crowl's Ghost, Bell, 1923 . . . £250/£75
Green Tea and Other Ghost Stories, Arkham House (U.S.), 1945 . . . . £125/£45
A Strange Adventure in the Life of Miss Laura Mildmay, Home & Van Thal, 1947 . . £25/£10
Best Ghost Stories, Dover (U.S.), 1964 (wraps) £5
Ghost Stories and Mysteries, Dover (U.S.), 1975 (wraps) £5
Borrhomeo The Astrologer, Tragara Press (Edinburgh), 1985, (wraps). £25

Verse

The Poems of Joseph Sheridan Le Fanu, Downey, 1896 . . . . £75

URSULA LE GUIN

(b.1929)

An American novelist, poet and critic, Le Guin is admired for her science fiction novels and for the 'Earthsea' fantasy books for children.

Children's Titles

A Wizard of Earthsea, Parnassus Press, (U.S.), 1968 (faint vertical line or smudge on title page, d/w priced $3.95) . . . . £1,000/£300
ditto, Parnassus Press, (U.S.), 1968 (no line or smudge, unpriced d/w) . . . . £125/£25
ditto, Penguin Books: Puffin, 1971 (wraps, illustrated by Ruth Robbins) £10
ditto, Gollancz, 1971 . . . . £150/£35
The Tombs of Atuan, Atheneum (U.S.), 1971 . . . . £125/£25
ditto, Gollancz, 1972 . . . . £100/£20
The Farthest Shore, Atheneum (U.S.), 1972 £100/£20
ditto, Gollancz, 1973 . . . . £65/£15
Very Far Away From Anywhere Else, Atheneum (U.S.), 1976 . . . . £25/£5
ditto, as ***A Very Long Way from Anywhere Else***, Gollancz, 1976 . . . . £20/£5
Leese Webster, Atheneum (U.S.), 1979 . . £20/£5
ditto, Gollancz, 1981 . . . . £15/£5
The Beginning Place, Harper (U.S.), 1980 . £20/£5
ditto, as ***Threshold***, Gollancz, 1980 . . . £20/£5
Visit from Dr Katz, Atheneum (U.S.), 1988 (picture book; boards). £5
ditto, Collins, 1988 . . . . £5
Catwings, Orchard (U.S.), 1988 . . . . £10/£5

Catwings Return, Orchard (U.S.), 1989 . . £10/£5
Fire and Stone, Atheneum (U.S.), 1989 . . £10/£5
Tehanu, Atheneum (U.S.), 1990 . . . . £10/£5
ditto, Gollancz, 1990 . . . . £10/£5

Novels
The Left Hand of Darkness, Ace (U.S.), 1969 (wraps) £15
ditto, Walker (U.S.), 1969 . . . . . £150/£35
ditto, Macdonald, 1969 . . . . £75/£20
City of Illusions, Ace (U.S.), 1971 (wraps) . . £5
ditto, Gollancz, 1971 . . . . £65/£15
ditto, Garland (U.S.), 1975 (no d/w) £35
Rocannon's World, Ace (U.S.), 1966 (wraps) . £5
ditto, Tandem, 1972 (wraps) £5
ditto, Garland (U.S.), 1975 (no d/w) £35
Planet of Exile, Ace (U.S.), 1966 (wraps) . . £5
ditto, Tandem, 1972 (wraps) £5
ditto, Garland (U.S.), 1975 (no d/w) £35
The Lathe of Heaven, Scribner (U.S.), 1971 £125/£25
ditto, Gollancz, 1972 . . . . £65/£20
The Dispossessed, Harper (U.S.), [1974] . £125/£25
ditto, Gollancz, 1974 . . . . £50/£20
The Word for World is Forest, Putnam (U.S.), 1976 . . . . £25/£5
ditto, Gollancz, 1977 . . . . £15/£5
Malafrena, Putnam (U.S.), 1979 . . . . . £15/£5
ditto, Gollancz, 1980 . . . . £10/£5
The Eye of the Heron, Harper (U.S.), 1982. £15/£5
ditto, Gollancz, 1983 . . . . £10/£5
The Visionary, Capra (U.S.) 1985 (with ***Wonders Hidden*** by Scott Saunders, wraps) £5
Always Coming Home, Harper (U.S.), 1985 £10/£5
ditto, Harper (U.S.), 1985 (unspecified number of signed copies with cassette in slipcase) . £100/£35
ditto, Gollancz, 1986 . . . . £10/£5
ditto, Gollancz, 1986 (100 signed copies with cassette in slipcase) . . . . £75/£35
Searoad, Harper (U.S.), 1991 . . . . £10/£5
ditto, Gollancz, 1992 . . . . £10/£5

Short Stories
From Elfland to Ploughkeepsie, Pendragon Press/Oregon Press (U.S.), 1973 (26 signed hardback copies, no d/w) £250
ditto, Pendragon Press/Oregon Press (U.S.), 1973 (100 signed copies, wraps) £50
ditto, Pendragon Press/Oregon Press (U.S.), 1973 (650 trade copies, wraps) £15
Wild Angels, Capra Press (U.S.), 1973 (200 signed, numbered copies) £45
The Wind's Twelve Quarters, Harper (U.S.), 1975 . . . . £25/£5
ditto, Gollancz, 1976 . . . . £20/£5
Orsinian Tales, Harper (U.S.), 1976. . . £20/£5
ditto, Gollancz, 1977 . . . . £10/£5
The Water is Wide, Pendragon Press (U.S.), 1976 (50 signed copies, no d/w) £100
ditto, Pendragon Press (U.S.), 1976 (950 signed copies) . . . . £15/£5
The Compass Rose, Pendragon Press/Underwood-Miller (U.S.), 1982 (550 signed copies) . £45/£25
ditto, Harper (U.S.), 1982. . . . . £30/£10
ditto, Gollancz, 1983 . . . . £25/£5
Gwilan's Harp, Lord John Press (U.S.), 1981 (50 signed, numbered handbound, cloth copies of 350) £100
ditto, Lord John Press (U.S.), 1981 (300 signed copies of 350, wraps in d/w) . . . . £25/£10
Buffalo Gals and Other Animal Presences, Capra Press (U.S.), 1987 . . . . £15/£5
ditto, Gollancz, 1990 . . . . £10/£5

Verse
Hard Words and Other Poems, Harper (U.S.), 1981 . . . . £20/£5
Wild Oats and Fireweed, Harper (U.S.), 1988 £10/£5

Others
Dreams Must Explain Themselves, Algol Press (U.S.), 1973 (1,000 numbered copies, wraps) £15
King Dog, Capra Press (U.S.), 1986 (with Tess Gallagher, bound in with ***Dostoevsky: A Screenplay*** by Raymond Carver, wraps). £25
ditto, Capra (U.S.), 1985 (200 copies signed by all authors, wraps) £100
Language of the Night: Essays on Fantasy and Science Fiction, Putnam (U.S.), 1979 . . £15/£5
ditto, Women's Press, 1989 (revised edition, wraps) £5
Dancing at the Edge of the World: Thoughts on Words, Women and Places, Grove Press (U.S.), 1989 . . . . £10/£5
ditto, Gollancz, 1989 . . . . £10/£5

ROSAMOND LEHMANN

(b.1903 d.1990)

A writer whose novels often deal with the emotional development of womanhood.

Novels
Dusty Answer, Chatto & Windus, 1927 . . £50/£15
ditto, Holt (U.S.), 1927 . . . . £25/£10
A Note in Music, Chatto & Windus, 1930 . £30/£10
ditto, Holt (U.S.), 1930 . . . . £15/£5
ditto, Holt (U.S.), 1930 (300 signed copies) . £60
Invitation to the Waltz, Chatto & Windus, 1932 . . . . £30/£10

ditto, Holt (U.S.), 1932 . . . . . . £15/£5
The Weather in the Streets, Collins, 1936 . £45/£15
ditto, Reynal Hitchcock (U.S.), 1936. . . £15/£5
The Ballad and the Source, Collins, 1944 . £20/£5
ditto, Reynal Hitchcock (U.S.), 1945. . . £10/£5
The Echoing Grove, Collins, 1953 . . . £10/£5
ditto, Harcourt Brace (U.S.), 1953 . . . £10/£5
The Sea-Grape Tree, Collins, 1976 . . . £10/£5
ditto, Harcourt Brace (U.S.), 1977 . . . £10/£5

Short Stories

The Gipsy's Baby and Other Stories, Collins, 1946 . . . . £20/£5
ditto, Reynal Hitchcock (U.S.), 1947. . . £15/£5

Others

Letter to a Sister, Hogarth Press, 1931 (wraps) £15
ditto, Harcourt Brace (U.S.), 1932 . . . . £10
No More Music, Collins, 1939 . . . . £25/£10
ditto, Reynal Hitchcock (U.S.), 1945. . . £10/£5
A Man Seen Afar, Spearman, 1965 (with W. Tudor Pole) . . . . £10/£5
The Swan in the Evening: Fragments of an Inner Life, Collins, 1967 . . . . £10/£5
ditto, Harcourt Brace (U.S.), 1967 . . . £10/£5
Letters from Our Daughters, College of Psychic Studies, 1972 (with Cynthia Hill Sandys, 2 vols) £15

ELMORE LEONARD

Elmore Leonard had his first success in 1951 when *Argosy* magazine published his short story "Trail of the Apache." Despite early recognition as the writer of westerns, his crime novels have become more popular in recent years, in part due to the attentions of Hollywood. Quentin Tarantino ("Pulp Fiction") directed "Jackie Brown," a film based on Leonard's novel *Rum Punch*, in 1997.

The Bounty Hunters, Houghton-Mifflin (U.S.), 1953 . . . . £1,250/£400
ditto, Ballantine (U.S.), 1953 (wraps) . . . £75
The Law at Randado, Houghton-Mifflin (U.S.), 1954 . . . . £1,000/£250
Escape from Five Shadows, Houghton-Mifflin (U.S.), 1956 . . . . £600/£150
Last Stand at Saber River, Dell (U.S.), 1959 (wraps) £25
Hombre, Ballantine (U.S.), 1961 (wraps) . . £50
ditto, Armchair Detective, 1989 . . . . £15/£5
ditto, Armchair Detective, 1989 (26 signed, lettered copies, slipcase) £75
The Big Bounce, Fawcett Gold Medal (U.S.), 1969 (wraps) £25
The Moonshine War, Doubleday (U.S.), 1969 . . . . £300/£65
Valdez is Coming, Fawcett Gold Medal (U.S.), 1970 (wraps) £25
Forty Lashes Less One, Bantam (U.S.), 1972 (wraps) £25
Mr. Majestyk, Dell (U.S.), 1974 (wraps) . . . £25
Fifty-Two Pickup, Delacorte (U.S.), 1974 . £100/£25
ditto, Secker & Warburg, 1974 . . . . £75/£25
The Hunted, Dell (U.S.), 1977 (wraps) . . . £25
Swag, Delacorte (U.S.), 1976. . . . . £100/£25
Unknown Man No. 89, Delacorte (U.S.), 1977 . . . . £250/£45
ditto, Secker & Warburg, 1977 . . . £75/£25
The Switch, Bantam (U.S.), 1978 (wraps) . . £25
Gunsights, Bantam (U.S.), 1979 (wraps) . . £25
Gold Coast, Bantam (U.S.), 1980 (wraps) . . £20
City Primeval, Arbor House (U.S.), 1980 . £35/£10
Split Images, Arbor House (U.S.), 1981. . £35/£10
Cat Chaser, Arbor House (U.S.), 1982 . . £25/£10
Stick, Arbor House (U.S.), 1983 . . . . £25/£10
LaBrava, Arbor House (U.S.), 1983 . . . £25/£10
Glitz, Arbor House (U.S.), 1986 . . . . £25/£10
ditto, (26 signed lettered copies in slipcase) . £200
ditto, (500 signed copies in slipcase) £50
Bandits, Arbor House, 1987 . . . . . £25/£10
Touch, Arbor House (U.S.), 1987 . . . £20/£10
Freaky Deaky, Arbor House/Morrow (U.S.), 1988 . . . . £20/£10
Killshot, Arbor House/Morrow (U.S.), 1989 £15/£5
Get Shorty, Delacorte (U.S.), 1990 . . . £15/£5
Maximum Bob, Delacorte, 1991 . . . . £15/£5
Rum Punch, Delacorte, 1992 . . . . £20/£5
Pronto, Delacorte, 1993 . . . . . . £10/£5
Out of Sight Delacorte (U.S.), 1996 . . . £10/£5
Jackie Brown, Dell, 1997 (wraps) £5
The Tonto Woman and other Western Stories, Delacorte (U.S.), 1998 . . . . . . £10/£5
Cuba Libre, Delacorte (U.S.), 1998 . . . £10/£5
Be Cool, Delacorte (U.S.), 1999 . . . . £10/£5

C.S. LEWIS

(b.1898 d.1963)

Arguably best known for his children's books, Lewis also wrote a handful of science fiction novels, and a great number of theological works.

Children's

The Lion, The Witch and The Wardrobe, Bles, 1950 . . . . £1,750/£300
ditto, Macmillan (U.S.), 1950. . . . . £750/£200

Prince Caspian: The Return to Narnia, Bles, 1951 . . . . £750/£150
ditto, Macmillan (U.S.), 1951. . . . . . £400/£50
The Voyage of the 'Dawn Treader', Bles, 1952 . . . . £750/£150
ditto, Macmillan (U.S.), 1952. . . . . . £400/£50
The Silver Chair, Bles, 1953 . . . . . £750/£150
ditto, Macmillan (U.S.), 1953. . . . . . £250/£50
The Horse and His Boy, Bles, 1954 . . . . £700/£150
ditto, Macmillan (U.S.), 1954. . . . . . £200/£25
The Magician's Nephew, Bles, 1955 . . £750/£150
ditto, Macmillan (U.S.), 1955. . . . . . £250/£25
The Last Battle, Bles, 1956 . . . . . £750/£150
ditto, Macmillan (U.S.), 1956. . . . . . £250/£25

Novels

Out of the Silent Planet, Bodley Head, 1938 . . . . £750/£100
ditto, Macmillan (U.S.), 1943 . . . . £125/£35
Perelandra, Bodley Head, 1943 . . . . . £300/£75
ditto, Macmillan (U.S.), 1944. . . . . . £125/£35
That Hideous Strength: A Modern Fairy-Tale for Grown-Ups, Bodley Head, 1945 . . . . £200/£45
ditto, Macmillan (U.S.), 1946. . . . . . £100/£25
Till We Have Faces: A Myth Retold, Bles, 1956 . . . . £75/£25
ditto, Harcourt Brace & Co (U.S.), 1957 . £35/£10

Short Stories

The Dark Tower and Other Stories, Collins, 1977 . . . . £30/£10
ditto, Harcourt, Brace (U.S.), 1977 . . . £25/£10

Verse

Spirits in Bondage, Heinemann, 1919 (pseud. 'Clive Hamilton') . . . . £200/£40
Dymer, Dent, 1926 (pseud. 'Clive Hamilton') . £175
ditto, Dutton (U.S.), 1926. . . . . £150
Hamlet, the Prince or the Poem, British Academy, 1942 (wraps) £45
Poems, Bles, 1964. . . . . £50/£15
ditto, Harcourt, Brace (U.S.), 1965 . . . £25/£10
Narrative Poems, Bles, 1969. . . . . . £15/£5

Christian Titles

The Pilgrim's Regress: An Allegorical Apology for Christianity, Reason and Romanticism, Dent, 1933 . . . . £75/£25
The Problem of Pain, Centenary Press, 1940 £50/£15
ditto, Bles, 1943 . . . . £30/£10
ditto, Macmillan (U.S.), 1943. . . . . £25/£5
The Screwtape Letters, Bles, 1942 . . . . £250/£35
ditto, Saunders (U.S.), 1942 . . . . . . £125/£15
Broadcast Talks: Right and Wrong: A Clue to the Meaning of the Universe, and What Christians Believe, Bles, 1942 . . . . £50/£15
Christian Behaviour: A Further Series of Broadcast Talks, Bles, 1943 . . . . £30/£10
ditto, Macmillan (U.S.), 1945. . . . . . £20/£5
The Abolition of Man: or Reflections on Education with Special Reference to the Teaching of English in the Upper Forms of Schools, O.U.P., 1943 £25/£10
ditto, Macmillan (U.S.), 1947. . . . . . £25/£10
Beyond Personality: The Christian Idea of God, Bles, 1944 . . . . £35/£10
The Great Divorce: A Dream, Bles, 1945 . £35/£10
Miracles: A Preliminary Study, Bles, 1947. £25/£10
Vivisection, The National Anti-Vivisection Society [1947] (wraps) £95
Mere Christianity, Bles, 1952 . . . . £15/£5
Reflections on the Psalms, Bles, 1958 . . £15/£5
ditto, Harcourt Brace (U.S.), 1958 . . . £15/£5
Shall We Lose God in Outer Space?, SPCK, 1959 (wraps) £65
The Four Loves, Bles, 1960 . . . . . . £15/£5
ditto, Harcourt Brace (U.S.), 1960 . . . £15/£5
The World's Last Night, Harcourt Brace (U.S.), 1960 . . . . £30/£10
Beyond the Bright Blur, Harcourt Brace (U.S.), 1963 . . . . £25/£10
Letters to Malcolm chiefly on Prayer, Bles, [1964] . . . . £15/£5
ditto, Harcourt Brace (U.S.), 1964 . . . £15/£5
Screwtape Proposes a Toast and Other Pieces, Bles, 1965 . . . . £15/£5
Christian Reflections, Bles, 1967 . . . £10/£5
Letters to an American Lady, Eerdmans (U.S.), 1967 . . . . £15/£5
The Joyful Christian, Macmillan (U.S.), 1977 £10/£5

Academic

The Allegory of Love: A Study in Medieval Tradition, O.U.P., 1936 . . . . £45/£15
ditto, O.U.P. (U.S.), 1936 . . . . . . £45/£15
Rehabilitations and Other Essays, O.U.P., 1939 . . . . £40/£15
The Personal Heresy: A Controversy, O.U.P., 1939 (with E.M.W. Tillyard) . . . . . . £35/£10
A Preface to Paradise Lost, O.U.P., 1942 . £35/£15
Arthurian Torso, O.U.P., 1948 (with Charles Williams) . . . . £75/£35
ditto, O.U.P. (U.S.), 1948 . . . . . . £75/£35
English Literature in the Sixteenth Century, Excluding Drama, O.U.P., 1954 . . . £45/£15
ditto, O.U.P. (U.S.), 1954 . . . . . . £45/£15
Studies in Words, C.U.P., 1960 . . . £15/£5
ditto, Macmillan (U.S.), 1960. . . . . £10/£5
An Experiment in Criticism, C.U.P., 1961 £35/£15
ditto, Macmillan (U.S.), 1961. . . . . £30/£10
They Asked for a Paper, Bles, 1962 . . . £15/£5

The Discarded Image, C.U.P., 1964. . . . £10/£5
Of Other Worlds, Bles, 1966. . . . . . £10/£5
Studies in Mediaeval and Renaissance Literature, C.U.P., 1966 . . . . £10/£5
Spenser's Images of Life, C.U.P., 1961 . . £10/£5

Autobiography
Surprised by Joy, Bles, 1955. . . . . . £35/£15
ditto, Harcourt Brace (U.S.), 1956 . . . . £30/£10
A Grief Observed, Faber, 1961 (pseud. 'N.W. Clerk') . . . . £50/£15
ditto, Seabury (U.S.), 1963 . . . . . £25/£10

MATTHEW GREGORY LEWIS

(b.1775 d.1818)

Lewis is best remembered for his Gothic classic, *The Monk*, a scandal when it was published in 1796, and for many years after.

Fiction
The Monk, Bell, [March] 1796 (1st issue with 'In Three Volumes' *above* quotation on title page, 3 vols) £3,000
ditto, Bell, [April] 1796 (2nd issue with 'In Three Volumes' *below* quotation on title page, 3 vols) £1,750
The Bravo of Venice, A Romance, J.F. Hughes, 1804 [1805]. £250
Feudal Tyrants, or, The Counts of Carlsheim and Sargans: a Romance, J.F. Hughes, 1806 (4 vols) £750
Romantic Tales, Longman, Hurst, Rees & Orme, 1808 (4 vols) £750

Verse and Ballads
The Love of Gain, A Poem Imitated from the Thirteenth Satire of Juvenal, J. Bell, 1799 . £250
Tales of Wonder, W. Bulmer/J. Bell, 1801 (2 vols) £150
Poems, Hatchard, 1812 . . . . £250
The Isle of Devils, 'Advertiser', Jamaica, 1627 . £100
ditto, George T. Juckes, 1912 (250 copies) . . £45

Non Fiction
Journal of a West India Proprietor, Kept During a Residence in the Island of Jamaica, John Murray, 1834 . . . . £250
Journal of a West India Proprietor, 1815-17, Routledge, 1929 . . . . £50/£25

NORMAN LEWIS

(b.1908 d.1993)

A travel writer and novelist, Lewis was hailed by Graham Greene as one of the best writers of the twentieth century

Travel
Spanish Adventure, Gollancz, 1935 . . . £100/£35
ditto, Holt (U.S.), 1935 . . . . . . £50/£15
Sand and Sea in Arabia, Routledge, 1938 . £75/£25
A Dragon Apparent, Travels In Indo-China, Cape, 1951 . . . . £50/£20
ditto, Scribner's (U.S.), 1951 . . . . . £25/£10
Golden Earth, Travels In Burma, Cape, 1952 £45/£20
ditto, Scribner's (U.S.), 1952 . . . . . £20/£10
The Changing Sky, The Travels of a Novelist, Cape, 1959 . . . . £40/£15
ditto, Pantheon (U.S.), 1959 . . . . . . £20/£10
The Honoured Society, The Mafia Conspiracy Observed, Collins, 1964 . . . . . . £40/£15
ditto, Putnam's (U.S.), 1964 . . . . . £20/£10
Naples '44, Collins, 1978 . . . . . . £40/£15
ditto, Pantheon (U.S.), 1978 . . . . . £20/£10
Voices of the Old Sea, Hamish Hamilton, 1984 £25/£5
ditto, Viking (U.S.), 1985. . . . . . £15/£5
A Goddess in the Stones, Travels In India, Cape, 1991 . . . . £20/£5
ditto, Holt (U.S.), 1992. . . . . . . £10/£5
An Empire of the East, Travels In Indonesia, Cape, 1993 . . . . £15/£5

Novels
Samara, Cape, 1949 . . . . £35/£10
Within the Labyrinth, Cape, 1950 . . . £20/£5
ditto, Carroll & Graf (U.S.), 1986. . . . £10/£5
A Single Pilgrim, Cape, 1953 . . . . £10/£5
ditto, Rinehart & Co. (U.S.), 1953. . . . £10/£5
The Day of the Fox, Cape, 1955 . . . . £10/£5
ditto, Rinehart & Co. (U.S.), 1955. . . . £10/£5
The Volcanoes Above Us, Cape, 1957 . . £10/£5
Darkness Visible, Cape, 1960 . . . . £10/£5
The Tenth Year of the Ship, Collins, 1962 £10/£5
ditto, Harcourt, Brace (U.S.), 1962. . . . £10/£5
A Small War Made to Order, Collins, 1966 £10/£5
ditto, Harcourt, Brace (U.S.), 1966. . . . £10/£5
Every Man's Brother, Heinemann, 1967 £10/£5
Flight from a Dark Equator, Collins, 1972 £10/£5
The Sicilian Specialist, Random House (U.S.), 1974 . . . . £10/£5
ditto, Collins, 1975 . . . . £10/£5
The German Company, Collins, 1979 . . £10/£5
The Cuban Passage, Collins, 1982 . . . £10/£5
ditto, Pantheon (U.S.), 1982. . . . . . £10/£5
A Suitable Case for Corruption, Hamish Hamilton,

1984 . . . . £10/£5
The Man in the Middle, Pantheon (U.S.), 1984 £10/£5
The March of the Long Shadows, Secker & Warburg, 1987 . . . . £10/£5

Miscellaneous
Jackdaw Cake, Hamish Hamilton, 1985. . £15/£5
ditto, as ***I Came, I Saw***, Picador, 1994 (enlarged edition) . . . . £10/£5
A View of the World, Eland, 1986 . . . £10/£5
The Missionaries, Secker & Warburg, 1988 £10/£5
ditto, McGraw-Hill (U.S.), 1988.. . . . . £10/£5
To Run Across the Sea, Cape, 1989 . . . £10/£5
The World, The World, Cape, 1996 . . . £10/£5
ditto, Holt (U.S.), 1996. . . . . £10/£5

DAVID LINDSAY

(b.1878 d.1945)

British novelist whose curious metaphysical writings are not widely known. Among devotees, however, he is considered highly original and interesting.

Novels
A Voyage to Arcturus, Methuen, 1920 (first binding, 8 page catalogue at rear) . . . . . £1,250/£450
ditto, Methuen, 1920 (second binding without catalogue at rear) . . . . £1,000/£350
ditto, Macmillan (U.S.), 1963. . . . . . £65/£20
The Haunted Woman, Methuen, 1922 . . £250/£75
ditto, Newcastle (U.S.), 1975 (wraps) . . . £10
Sphinx, John Long, 1923 . . . . . . £250/£75
Devil's Tor, Putnam, 1932 . . . . . £250/£75
The Violet Apple and The Witch, Chicago Review Press (U.S.), 1975 . . . . £50/£15

DAVID LODGE

(b.1935)

Also a professor and literary critic, Lodge's novels are the most keenly sought after titles.

Novels
The Picturegoers, MacGibbon & Kee, 1960 £250/£45
Ginger, You're Barmy, MacGibbon & Kee 1962 . . . . £75/£20
ditto, Doubleday (U.S.), 1965 . . . . £45/£15
The British Museum is Falling Down, MacGibbon & Kee, 1965. . . . . £75/£20
ditto, Holt Rinehart (U.S.), 1967 . . . . £45/£15
Out of the Shelter, Macmillan, 1970. . . £75/£20
Changing Places; A Tale of Two Campuses, Secker & Warburg, 1975 . . . . £65/£15
ditto, Viking (U.S.), 1979. . . . . . . £25/£10
How Far Can You Go?, Secker & Warburg, 1980 . . . . £65/£15
ditto, as ***Souls and Bodies***, Morrow (U.S.), 1982 . . . . £15/£5
Small World, Secker & Warburg, 1984 . . £25/£10
ditto, Macmillan (U.S.), 1985. . . . . . £15/£5
Nice Work, Secker & Warburg, 1988 . . £10/£5
ditto, Viking, 1989. . . . . £10/£5
Paradise News, Secker & Warburg, 1991 . £10/£5
ditto, Viking (U.S.), 1992. . . . . . . £10/£5

Play
The Writing Game, Secker & Warburg, 1991 £10/£5

Others
The Language of Fiction, Routledge, 1966 £15/£5
ditto, Columbia University Press (U.S.), 1966 £15/£5
Graham Greene, Columbia University Press (U.S.), 1966 (wraps) £25
The Novelist at the Crossroads and Other Essays on Fiction and Criticism, Roudedge, 1971 £10/£5
ditto, Cornell University Press (U.S.), 1971 £10/£5
Evelyn Waugh, Columbia University Press (U.S.), 1971 (wraps) £10
Twentieth Century Literary Criticism, Longman, 1972 . . . . £10/£5
The Modes of Modern Writing: Metaphor, Metonymy and the Typology of Modern Literature, Arnold, 1977 . . . . £10/£5
ditto, Cornell University Press (U.S.), 1977 £10/£5
Working with Structuralism: Essays and Reviews on Nineteenth and Twentieth Century Literature, Routledge, 1981 . . . . £10/£5
Write On, Secker & Warburg, 1986 . . . £10/£5
After Bakhtin: Essays on Fiction and Criticism, Routledge, 1990 . . . . £10/£5

JACK LONDON

(b.1876 d.1916)

The highly successful writer of many adventure stories, London took part in the Klondike gold rush of 1897 and used this experience as the background for much of his work.

Novels
A Daughter of the Snows, Lippincott (U.S.), 1902 . . . . £250
ditto, Isbister, 1904 . . . . £75
The Kempton-Wace Letters, Macmillan (U.S.), 1903

(with Anna Strunsky. 1st issue without authors names on title page) £300
ditto, Macmillan (U.S.), 1903 (2nd issue with authors names on title page) £250
ditto, Isbister, 1903 . . . . £50
The Call of the Wild, Macmillan (U.S.), 1903 . £350
ditto, Heinemann, 1903 . . . . £125
The Sea-Wolf, Macmillan (U.S.), 1904 . . . £100
ditto, Heinemann, 1904 . . . . £50
The Game, Macmillan (U.S.), 1905 . . . . £75
ditto, Heinemann, 1905 . . . . £50
White Fang, Macmillan (U.S.), 1906 . . . £75
ditto, Methuen, 1907 . . . . £50
Before Adam, Macmillan (U.S.), 1907 . . . £75
ditto, Macmillan Colonial Library Edition, 1907 £45
ditto, Werner Laurie, [1908] £45
The Iron Heel, Macmillan (U.S.), 1908 . . . £50
ditto, Everett, [1908] £45
Martin Eden, Macmillan (U.S.), 1909 . . . £75
ditto, Heinemann, 1910 . . . . £45
Burning Daylight, Macmillan (U.S.), 1910 . . £50
ditto, Heinemann, 1911 . . . . £45
Adventure, Nelson, [1911] £75
ditto, Macmillan (U.S.), 1911. . . . . . £75
The Abysmal Brute, The Century Co. (U.S.), 1913 £50
ditto, Newnes, [1914] £45
John Barleycorn, The Century Co. (U.S.), 1913 £50
ditto, as ***John Barleycorn or Alcoholic Memoirs***, Mills & Boon, 1914 . . . . £45
The Valley of the Moon, Macmillan (U.S.), 1913 £50
ditto, Mills & Boon, 1914. . . . . £45
The Mutiny of the Elsinor, Macmillan (U.S.), 1914 . . . . £75
ditto, Mills & Boon, 1915. . . . . £50
The Scarlet Plague, Macmillan (U.S.), 1915 . £75
ditto, Mills & Boon, 1915. . . . . £50
The Jacket, Mills & Boon, 1915 . . . . . £50
ditto, as ***The Star Rover***, Macmillan (U.S.), 1915 £75
The Little Lady of the Big House, Macmillan (U.S.), 1916 . . . . £50
ditto, Mills & Boon, 1916. . . . . £45
Jerry of the Islands, Macmillan (U.S.), 1917 . £50
ditto, Mills & Boon, 1917. . . . . £45
Michael, Brother of Jerry, Macmillan (U.S.), 1917 . . . . £50
ditto, Mills & Boon, 1918. . . . . £45
Hearts of Three, Mills & Boon, 1918 . . . £45
ditto, Macmillan (U.S.), 1920. . . . . . £200/£45
The Assassination Bureau Ltd, McGraw-Hill (U.S.), 1963 (completed by Robert L. Fish) . . £15/£5
ditto, Deutsch, 1964 . . . . £15/£5

Short Stories

The Son of the Wolf: Tales of the Far North, Houghton, Mifflin (U.S.), 1900 . . . . . £300
ditto, Isbister, 1902 . . . . £150
The God of His Fathers, & Other Stories, McClure, Philips (U.S.), 1901 . . . . £200
ditto, Isbister, 1902 . . . . £150
Children of the Frost, Macmillan (U.S.), 1902 £125
ditto, Macmillan, 1902 . . . . £75
The Faith of Men, and Other Stories, Macmillan (U.S.), 1904 . . . . £125
ditto, Heinemann, 1904 . . . . £75
Tales of the Fish Patrol, Macmillan (U.S.), 1905 £100
ditto, Heinemann, 1906 . . . . £75
Moon-Face, and Other Stories, Macmillan (U.S.), 1906 . . . . £75
ditto, Heinemann, 1906 . . . . £50
Love of Life, and Other Stories, Macmillan (U.S.), 1907 . . . . £75
ditto, Everett, [1908] £50
Lost Face, Macmillan (U.S.), 1910 . . . . £75
ditto, Mills & Boon, [1915] £50
When God Laughs, and Other Stories, Macmillan (U.S.), 1911 . . . . £75
ditto, Mills & Boon, 1912. . . . . £50
South Sea Tales, Macmillan (U.S.), 1911 . . £75
ditto, Mills & Boon, 1912. . . . . £50
The House of Pride and Other Tales of Hawaii, Macmillan (U.S.), 1912 . . . . £75
ditto, Mills & Boon, 1914. . . . . £50
A Son of the Sun, Doubleday, Page & Co. (U.S.), 1912 . . . . £75
ditto, Mills & Boon, 1913. . . . . £50
Smoke Bellew, The Century Co. (U.S.), 1912 . £75
ditto, Mills & Boon, 1913. . . . . £50
The Night-Born, The Century Co. (U.S.), 1913 £75
ditto, Mills & Boon, 1916. . . . . £50
The Strength of the Strong, Macmillan (U.S.), 1914 . . . . £75
ditto, Mills & Boon, 1917. . . . . £50
The Turtles of Tasman, Macmillan (U.S.), 1916 £75
ditto, Mills & Boon, 1917. . . . . £50
The Human Drift, Macmillan (U.S.), 1917 . . £75
ditto, Mills & Boon, 1919. . . . . £50
The Red One, Macmillan (U.S.), 1918 . . . £100
ditto, Mills & Boon, 1919. . . . . £50
On The Makaloa Mat, Macmillan (U.S.), 1919 £75
ditto, as ***Island Tales***, Mills & Boon, 1920 £400/£75
Dutch Courage, and Other Stories, Macmillan (U.S.), 1922 . . . . £1,250/£250
ditto, Mills & Boon, 1923. . . . . . . £250/£50

Others

The Cruise of the Dazzler, The Century Co. (U.S.), 1902 . . . . £1,000
ditto, Hodder & Stoughton, 1906. . . . . £350
The People of the Abyss, Macmillan (U.S.), 1903 £200
ditto, Isbister, 1903 . . . . £75

War of the Classes, Macmillan (U.S.), 1905 . £200
ditto, Heinemann, 1905 . . . . £50
Scorn of Women, Macmillan (U.S.), 1906 . . £350
ditto, Macmillan, 1906 . . . . £125
The Road, Macmillan (U.S.), 1907 . . . . £250
ditto, Mills & Boon, 1914. . . . . £100
Revolution, Kerr (U.S.), 1910 (wraps) . . . £100
Revolution and Other Essays, Macmillan (U.S.), 1910 . . . . £350
ditto, Mills & Boon, 1920. . . . . . . £100/£25
Theft: A Play in Four Acts, Macmillan (U.S.), 1910 . . . . £400
ditto, Macmillan, 1910 . . . . £100
The Cruise of the Snark, Macmillan (U.S.), 1911 £100
ditto, Mills & Boon, 1913. . . . . £35
Jack London By Himself, Macmillan (U.S.), [1913] £125
ditto, Mills & Boon, 1913. . . . . £100
The Acorn-Planter; A California Forest Play, Macmillan (U.S.), 1916 . . . . £500
ditto, Mills & Boon, 1916. . . . . £200
Letters from Jack London, The Odyssey Press (U.S.), 1965 . . . . £40/£20

Collected Editions
The Works of Jack London, Macmillan (U.S.), 1919 (21 vols) £750

ANITA LOOS
(b.1893 d.1981)

In her reminiscences Loos offers a picture of American life and society similar to Fitzgerald's. *Gentlemen Prefer Blondes* is her classic.

Novels
Gentlemen Prefer Blondes, Boni & Liveright, (U.S.), 1925 (1st issue with "Divine" for "Devine" on contents page) . . . . £150/£25
ditto, Brentano's, 1926 . . . . . . £40/£15
ditto, Brentano's, 1926 (1,000 signed copies) . £75
But Gentlemen Marry Brunettes, Boni & Liveright (U.S.), 1927 . . . . £35/£10
ditto, Brentano's, 1928 . . . . £25/£10
A Mouse is Born, Doubleday & Co. (U.S.), 1951 . . . . £15/£5
ditto, Jonathan Cape, 1951 . . . . . . £15/£5
No Mother To Guide Her, Viking Press (U.S.), 1961 . . . . £10/£5
ditto, Arthur Barker, 1961 . . . . . . £10/£5

Others
A Girl Like I, Viking Press (U.S.), 1966 . £15/£5
ditto, Hamish Hamilton, 1967 . . . . . £10/£5
Twice Over Lightly, Harcourt Bruce Jovanovich (U.S.), 1972 (with Helen Hayes) . . . . . £10/£5
Kiss Hollywood Goodbye, Viking Press (U.S.), 1974 . . . . £10/£5
ditto, W.H. Allen, 1974 . . . . £10/£5
A Cast of Thousands, Viking Press (U.S.), 1975 . . . . £10/£5
Fate Keeps on Happening, Dodd, Mead & Co. (U.S.), 1984 . . . . £10/£5
ditto, Harrap, 1985 . . . . £10/£5

H.P. LOVECRAFT
(b.1890 d.1937)

Born in Providence, Rhode Island (U.S.), where he lived for the rest of his life, Lovecraft is famous for his weird fiction. Arkham House have issued revised and corrected editions of all the major Lovecraft stories in recent years.

The Shunned House, The Recluse Press (U.S.), 1928 (original unbound sheets, 300 printed of which c.75 may survive) £6,000
ditto, copies bound by R.H. Barlow (U.S.), 1934/35 (c.8 may exist) £8,000
ditto, Arkham House (U.S.), 1959 (unbound sheets, 50 sets) £2,000
ditto, Arkham House (U.S.), 1961 (bound, 100 copies, no d/w) £2,000
ditto, Arkham House (U.S.), (counterfeit edition, 1965/66) £500
The Cats of Ulthar, Dragon-Fly Press (U.S.), 1935 (42 copies) £1,000
The Shadow Over Innsmouth, Visionary Publishing (U.S.), 1936 (150-200 copies) . . £4,000/£2,000
H.P.L., Corwin Stickney (U.S.), 1937 (poetry, limited to 23 copies) £1,500
History of the Necronomicon, Rebel Press (U.S.), 1938 (wraps) £500
Notes and the Commonplace Book, Futile Press (U.S.), 1938 (no d/w) £1,500
The Outsider and Others, Arkham House (U.S.), 1939 . . . . £1,250/£500
Fungi from Yuggoth, Evans (U.S.), 1943 (wraps) £750
Beyond the Wall of Sleep, Arkham House (U.S.), 1943 . . . . £1,250/£400
The Weird Shadow Over Innsmouth, Bart House (U.S.), 1944 (wraps) £35
Marginalia, Arkham House (U.S.), 1944 . £200/£65
The Dunwich Horror and Other Weird Tales, Armed Services Edition (U.S.), 1945 (wraps) . . . £35
Best Supernatural Stories, Tower Books (U.S.), 1945

. . . . £25/£10

The Dunwich Horror, Bart House (U.S.), 1945 (wraps) £20

Supernatural Horror in Literature, Abramson (U.S.), 1945 (no d/w) £50

The Lurker at the Threshold, Arkham House (U.S.), 1945 (novel by Derleth) . . . . £65/£25

ditto, Museum Press, 1948 . . . . . £200/£40

ditto, Gollancz, 1968 . . . . £40/£15

The Lurking Fear and Other Stories, Avon (U.S.), 1947 (wraps) £15

Something About Cats, Arkham House (U.S.), 1949 . . . . £125/£45

The Haunter of the Dark, Gollancz, (U.K.), 1951 . . . . £50/£15

The Case of Charles Dexter Ward, Gollancz, (U.K.), 1951 . . . . £100/£40

The Lovecraft Collector's Library, S.S.R. Publications (U.S.), 1952-55 (7 vols, 75 copies) £125

The Curse of Yig, Arkham House (U.S.), 1953 (by Zealia B. Bishop) £50

The Challenge from Beyond, Evans (U.S.), 1954 £40

The Dream Quest of Unknown Kadath, Shroud (U.S.), 1955 (50 copies bound in cloth) £250

ditto, Shroud (U.S.), 1955 (1,400+ copies in wrappers) £60

ditto, Shroud (U.S.), 1955 (12 numbered copies clothbound by Gerry de la Ree in 1972) . £100/£50

The Survivor and Others, Arkham House (U.S.), 1957 (completed by Derleth) . . . . £75/£35

The Shuttered Room and Other Pieces, Arkham House (U.S.), 1959 . . . . £125/£45

Dreams and Fancies, Arkham House (U.S.), 1962. . . . . £125/£45

Some Notes on a Nonentity, Arkham House (U.S.), 1963 (wraps) £100

The Dunwich Horror and Others, Arkham House (U.S.), 1963 . . . . £75/£30

Collected Poems, Arkham House (U.S.), 1963 £65/£25

At the Mountains of Madness, Arkham House (U.S.), 1964 . . . . £65/£20

ditto, Gollancz, (U.K.), 1966 . . . . . . £65/£20

Dagon and Other Macabre Tales, Arkham House (U.S.), 1965 . . . . £65/£20

ditto, Gollancz (U.K.), 1967 . . . . £60/£20

Selected Letters, Volume I, Arkham House (U.S.), 1965 . . . . £30/£10

The Dark Brotherhood, Arkham House (U.S.), 1966 . . . . £65/£20

Three Tales of Horror, Arkham House (U.S.), 1967 . . . . £75/£25

Selected Letters, Volume II, Arkham House (U.S.), 1968 . . . . £30/£10

The Shadow out of Time, Gollancz, U.K., 1968 . . . . £45/£15

The Prose Poems: Ex Oblivione, Memory, Nyarlathotep, What the Moon Brings, Squires (U.S.), 1969-1970 (25 lettered copies of 125, 4 booklets in envelopes) £100

ditto, Squires (U.S.), 1969-1970 (99 numbered copies of 125, 4 booklets, in envelopes) £200

The Horror in the Museum and Other Revisions, Arkham House (U.S.), 1970. . . . . . . £45/£15

Selected Letters Volume, III, Arkham House (U.S.), 1971 . . . . £75/£45

Ec'h-Pi-El Speaks, de la Ree (U.S.), 1972 (25 cloth bound copies, no d/w) £125

ditto, de la Ree (U.S.), 1972 (475 copies, wraps) £25

The Watchers Out of Time and Others, Arkham House (U.S.), 1974 (stories completed by Derleth) £45/£15

Lovecraft at Last, Carrollton Clark (U.S.), 1975 ("Collectors edition", 1,000 copies in slipcase) £75

ditto, Carrollton Clark (U.S.), 1975 (2,000 copies) £45

Medusa: A Portrait, Oliphant Press (U.S.), 1975 (500 numbered copies in wrappers) £20

The Occult Lovecraft, de la Ree (U.S.), 1975 (128 numbered cloth bound copies, no d/w) . . . £45

ditto, de la Ree (U.S.), 1975 (990 copies, wraps) £10

Selected Letters, Volume IV, Arkham House (U.S.), 1976 . . . . £25/£10

Selected Letters, Volume V, Arkham House (U.S.), 1976 . . . . £25/£10

To Quebec and the Stars, Grant (U.S.), 1976 £25/£10

Antarktos, Fantome Press (U.S.), 1977 (150 copies, wraps). £15

A Winter Wish and Other Poems, Whispers Press (U.S.), 1977 (26 copies signed and lettered in slipcase) £300

ditto, Whispers Press (U.S.), 1977 (200 signed, numbered copies in slipcase and d/w) . . £50/£25

ditto, Whispers Press (U.S.), 1977 (trade edition, 2,000 copies) . . . . £30/£15

Uncollected Prose and Poetry, Vol I, Necronomicon Press (U.S.), 1978 (wraps) £10

ditto, Vol II, Necronomicon Press (U.S.), 1980 (wraps) £10

ditto, Vol III, Necronomicon Press (U.S.), 1982 (wraps) £10

Ashes and Others, Miskatonic University Press (U.S.), 1983 (wraps) £10

The Best of H.P. Lovecraft, Del Rey/Ballantine (U.S.), 1982 (wraps) £5

The Illustrated Fungi from Yuggoth, Strange Co. (U.S.), 1983 (wraps) £5

Juvenilia:, 1895-1905, Necronomicon Press (U.S.), 1984 (wraps) £5

Saturnalia and Other Poems, Crypt of Cthulhu (U.S.), 1984 (wraps) £5

Uncollected Letters, Necronomicon Press (U.S.), 1986 (wraps) £5

Medusa and Other Poems, Crypt of Cthulhu (U.S.), 1986 (wraps) £5

PETER LOVESEY
(b.1936)

An author of detective fiction whose early works as if they will become very collectable.

Novels

Wobble to Death, Macmillan, 1970 . . . £150/£45
ditto, Dodd Mead (U.S.), 1970 . . . . £50/£15
The Detective Wore Silk Drawers, Macmillan, 1971 . . . . £35/£5
ditto, Dodd Mead (U.S.), 1971 . . . . £20/£5
Abracadaver, Macmillan, 1972 . . . . £25/£5
ditto, Dodd Mead (U.S.), 1972 . . . . £15/£5
Mad Hatter's Holiday, Macmillan, 1973 . £20/£5
ditto, Dodd Mead (U.S.), 1973 . . . . £15/£5
Invitation to a Dynamite Party, Macmillan, 1974 . . . . £15/£5
ditto, as ***The Tick of Death***, Dodd Mead (U.S.), 1974 . . . . £15/£5
A Case of Spirits, Macmillan, 1975 . . . £15/£5
ditto, Dodd Mead (U.S.), 1975 . . . . £15/£5
Swing, Swing Together, Macmillan, 1976 . £15/£5
ditto, Dodd Mead (U.S.), 1976 . . . . £15/£5
Golden Girl, Cassell 1977 (pseud. 'Peter Lear') £10/£5
Waxwork, Macmillan 1978 . . . . . £10/£5
ditto, Pantheon (U.S.), 1978 . . . . . £10/£5
Spider Girl, Cassell 1980 (pseud. 'Peter Lear') £20/£5
ditto, Viking (U.S.), 1980. . . . . . . £20/£5
The False Inspector Dew, Macmillan, 1982 £10/£5
ditto, Pantheon (U.S.), 1982 . . . . . £10/£5
Keystone, Macmillan, 1983 . . . . . £10/£5
ditto, Pantheon (U.S.), 1983 . . . . . £10/£5
The Secret of Spandau, Michael Joseph, 1986 (pseud. 'Peter Lear') . . . . £15/£5
Rough Cider, Bodley Head, 1986 . . . £10/£5
ditto, Mysterious Press (U.S.), 1987 . . . £10/£5
Bertie and the Tinman, Bodley Head, 1987 £10/£5
ditto, Mysterious Press (U.S.), 1988 . . . £10/£5
On the Edge, Mysterious Press, 1989 . . £10/£5
ditto, Mysterious Press, 1989 (250 signed, numbered proof copies, wraps) £25
ditto, Mysterious Press (U.S.), 1989 . . . £10/£5
Bertie and the Seven Bodies, Mysterious Press, 1990 . . . . £10/£5
ditto, Mysterious Press (U.S.), 1990 . . . £10/£5
The Last Detective, Scorpion Press, 1991 (99 signed, numbered copies, acetate d/w) . . . . £75/£65
ditto, Scribners, 1991 . . . . £10/£5
ditto, Doubleday (U.S.), 1991 . . . . £10/£5
Diamond Solitaire, Little Brown, 1992 . . £10/£5
ditto, Mysterious Press (U.S.), 1993 . . . . £10/£5
Bertie and the Crime of Passion, Little Brown, 1993 . . . . £10/£5
ditto, Mysterious Press (U.S.), 1993 . . . £10/£5
The Summons, Little Brown, 1995 . . . £10/£5
ditto, Mysterious Press (U.S.), 1995 . . . £10/£5
Bloodhounds, Little Brown, 1996 . . . £10/£5
ditto, Mysterious Press (U.S.), 1996 . . . £10/£5
Upon a Dark Night, Little Brown, 1997. . £10/£5
ditto, Mysterious Press (U.S.), 1998 . . . £10/£5
Do Not Exceed the Stated Dose, Mysterious Press (U.S.), 1998 . . . . £10/£5
ditto, Crippen & Landru, 1998 (250 signed, numbered copies with booklet) . . . . £35/£25
ditto, Little Brown, 1998 . . . . £10/£5
The Vault, Little Brown, 1999 . . . . £10/£5

Short Stories

Butchers and Other Stories of Crime, Macmillan 1985
ditto, Mysterious Press, 1987 . . . . . £10/£5
The Staring Man and Other Stories, Eurographica (Helsinki), 1988 (350 signed, numbered copies, wraps with d/w) £75

MALCOLM LOWRY
(b.1909 d.1957)

Few of Lowry's books were published in his lifetime. *Under the Volcano* is regarded as his best work.

Ultramarine, Cape, 1933 . . . . . . £3,000/£300
ditto, Lippincott (U.S.), 1962, (revised edition) £50/£20
ditto, Cape, 1963, (revised edition) . . . £45/£15
Under the Volcano, Reynal & Hitchcock, 1947 . . . . £650/£150
ditto, Cape, 1947 . . . . £350/£75
Selected Poems of Malcolm Lowry, City Lights, 1961 (wraps) £25
Hear Us O Lord from Heaven They Dwelling Place, Lippincott (U.S.), 1961 . . . . . . £30/£10
ditto, Cape, 1962 . . . . £25/£10
Selected Letters of Malcolm Lowry, Lippincott (U.S.), 1965 . . . . £25/£10
ditto, Cape, 1967 . . . . £25/£10
Lunar Caustic, Grossman (U.S.), 1968 . . £200/£45
ditto, Cape, 1968 . . . . £45/£15
Dark as the Grave Wherein My Friend is Laid, New American Library (U.S.), 1968 . . . . £25/£10
ditto, Cape, 1969 . . . . £25/£10
October Ferry to Gabriola, World (U.S.), 1970 £15/£5
ditto, Cape, 1971 . . . . £10/£5
Malcolm Lowry, Psalms and Songs, New American

Library, 1975 . . . . £20/£5
Notes on a Screenplay for F. Scott Fitzgerald's Tender is the Night, Bruccoli, 1976 . . £20/£5
The Collected Letters Volume One: 1926-1946, University Of Toronto Press, 1995 . . . £25/£10
The Collected Letters of Malcolm Lowry. Volume Two: 1946-57, University Of Toronto Press, 1995 . . . . £25/£10

ROSE MACAULAY

(b.1881 d.1958)

The author of many clever, 'intelligent' novels, Macaulay was a member of the Bloomsbury Group.

Novels

Abbots Verney, Murray, 1906 . . . . . £30
The Furnace, Murray, 1907 . . . . . . £25
The Secret River, Murray, 1909 . . . . . £25
The Valley Captives, Murray, 1911 . . . . £25
Views and Vagabonds, Murray, 1912 . . . £25
The Lee Shore, Hodder & Stoughton, 1912. . £25
The Making of a Bigot, Hodder & Stoughton, 1914 . . . . £15
Non-Combatants and Others, Hodder & Stoughton, 1916 . . . . £15
What Not: A Prophetic Comedy, Constable, 1918 £15
Potterism: A Tragi-Farcical Tract, Collins, 1920 . . . . £45/£15
Dangerous Ages, Collins, 1921 . . . . £35/£10
Mystery at Geneva, Collins, 1922 . . . £25/£10
Told By an Idiot, Collins, 1923 . . . . £20/£5
ditto, Boni & Liveright, 1923 . . . . £20/£5
Orphan Island, Collins, 1924 . . . . £20/£5
Crewe Train, Collins, 1926 . . . . . £20/£5
ditto, Boni & Liveright, 1926. . . . . £20/£5
Keeping Up Appearances, Collins, 1928 . £20/£5
Staying With Relations, Collins, 1930 . . . £20/£5
They Were Defeated, Collins, 1932 . . . £20/£5
ditto, as ***The Shadow Flies***, Harper & Bros, 1934 . . . . £20/£5
Going Abroad, Collins, 1934. . . . . £20/£5
ditto, Harper & Bros, 1934 . . . . . £20/£5
I Would Be Private, Collins, 1937 . . . £20/£5
ditto, Harper & Bros, 1937 . . . . . £20/£5
And No Man's Wit, Collins, 1940 . . . £15/£5
ditto, Little, Brown (U.S.), 1940 . . . . £15/£5
The World My Wilderness, Collins, 1950 . £15/£5
ditto, Little, Brown (U.S.), 1950 . . . . £15/£5
The Towers of Trebizond, Collins, 1956 . £15/£5
ditto, Farrar, Straus (U.S.), 1957 . . . . £15/£5

Verse

The Two Blind Countries, Sidgwick & Jackson, 1914 . . . . £25
Three Days, Constable, 1919. . . . . . £25
ditto, Dutton (U.S.), 1919. . . . . . . £25

Travel

They Went to Portugal Too, Jonathan Cape, 1946 . . . . £20/£5
Fabled Shore: From the Pyrenees to Portugal, Hamish Hamilton, 1949 . . . . . . £20/£5
ditto, Farrar, Straus (U.S.), 1949 . . . . £15/£5
Pleasure of Ruins, Weidenfeld & Nicolson, 1953 . . . . £20/£10

Others

A Casual Commentary, Methuen, 1925 . . £15/£5
Catchwords and Claptrap, Hogarth Press, 1926 £45
Some Religious Elements in English Literature, Hogarth Press, 1931 . . . . . . £35/£10
Milton, Duckworth, 1934 . . . . £10
ditto, Harper & Row (U.S.), 1935 . . . £20/£10
Personal Pleasures, Gollancz, 1935 . . . £30/£10
ditto, Macmillan (U.S.), 1936. . . . . £20/£10
The Writings of E.M. Forster, Hogarth Press, 1938 . . . . £50/£20
ditto, Harcourt Brace (U.S.), 1938 . . . £20/£5
Life Among the English, Collins, 1942 . . £10/£5
Letters to a Friend: 1950 - 1952, Collins, 1961 £10/£5
ditto, Atheneum (U.S.), 1962. . . . . £10/£5
Last Letters to a Friend, 1952 - 1958, Collins, 1962 . . . . £10/£5
ditto, Atheneum (U.S.), 1963 . . . . . £10/£5
Letters to a Sister, Collins, 1964 . . . . £10/£5
ditto, Atheneum (U.S.), 1964 . . . . . £10/£5

GEORGE MACDONALD

(b. 1824 d.1905)

A Scottish author, Macdonald is perhaps best known for his children's book *At the Back of the North Wind*, and his adult fantasy *Phantastes*

Children's

Dealings with the Fairies, Strahan, 1867 . . £750
At the Back of the North Wind, Strahan, 1871 £2,000
ditto, George Routledge, [no date] . . . £2,000
Ranald Bannerman's Boyhood, Strahan, 1871 £500
The Princess and the Goblin, Strahan, 1872 . £1,000
Gutta Percha Willie, King, 1873. . . . . £300
The Wise Woman, Strahan, 1875 . . . . £150
ditto, as ***The Lost Princess, or The Wise Woman***, Wells, Gardner (U.S.), 1895 . . . . . £50
The Princess and the Curdie, Chatto & Windus, 1883 . . . . £250

Cross Purpose and the Shadows, Blackie, 1886 £15
The Light Princess and Other Fairy Tales, Blackie, 1891 . . . . £65
ditto, Putnam (U.S.), 1893 . . . . £20
The Golden Key, The Bodley Head, 1972 . . £20/£5

Verse
Within and Without: a Dramatic Poem, Longman, 1855 . . . . £1,250
Poems, Longman, 1857 . . . . £300
The Disciple and Other Poems, Strahan, 1867 £250

Translations
Twelve of the Spiritual Songs of Novalis, Strahan, 1851 . . . . £500
Exotics, Strahan, 1851 . . . . £500

Others
Phantastes; a Faerie Romance, Smith, Elder, 1858 . . . . £1,250
ditto, Chatto & Windus, 1894 . . . . . . £750
David Elginbrod, Hurst & Blackett, 1863 (3 vols) £500
ditto, Loring (U.S.), 1863 . . . . £250
Adela Cathcart, Hurst & Blackett, 1864 (3 vols) £250
ditto, Loring (U.S.), [1864] £200
The Portent, Smith, Elder, 1864 . . . . . . £400
ditto, Loring (U.S.), [1864] £200
Alec Forbes of Howglen, Hurst & Blackett, 1865 (3 vols) £750
Annals of a Quiet Neighbourhood, Hurst & Blackett, 1867 (3 vols) £750
Unspoken Sermons, Strahan, 1867 . . . . £450
ditto, Second series, Longmans 1885 . . . . £100
ditto, Third series, Longmans 1889 . . . . £100
Guild Court, Hurst & Blackett, 1868 (3 vols) . £250
Robert Falconer, Hurst & Blackett, 1868 (3 vols) £250
ditto, Loring (U.S.), [1868] £200
The Seaboard Parish, Tinsley, 1868 (3 vols) . £200
England's Antiphon, Macmillan, [1868] . . £100
The Miracles of Our Lord, Strahan, 1870 . . £75
Works of fancy and Imagination, Strahan, 1871 (10 vols) £750
Wilfred Cumbermede, Hurst & Blackett, 1872 (3 vols) £150
The Vicar's Daughter, Tinsley, 1872 (3 vols) . £150
Malcolm, King, 1875 (3 vols) £150
St George and St Michael, King, 1876 (3 vols) £150
Thomas Wingfold, Hurst & Blackett, 1876 (3 vols) £150
The Marquis of Losse, Hurst & Blackett, 1877 (3 vols) £150
Paul Faber, Hurst & Blackett, 1879 (3 vols) . £150
Sir Gibbie, Hurst & Blackett, 1879 (3 vols) . . £150
A Book of Strife, privately printed, 1880 . . £1,000
ditto, privately printed, 1882 . . . . £750
ditto, Longman, 1889 . . . . £450
Mary Marston, Sampson, Low, 1881 (3 vols) . £150
Warlock O'Glen Warlock, Lothrop (U.S.) 1881 £175
ditto, Harper & Brothers (U.S.), 1881 (wraps) . £35
ditto, as ***Castle Warlock***, Sampson, Low, 1882 (3 vols) £175
Orts, Sampson Low, 1882 . . . . £125
Weighed and Wanting, Sampson, Low, 1882 (3 vols) £150
The Gifts of the Child Christ, Sampson Low, 1882 (2 vols) £75
A Threefold Cord: Poem, by Three Friends, edited by MacDonald, privately printed, (1883) . . . £350
Donal Grant, Kegan Paul, 1883 (3 vols) . . £150
What's Mine's Mine, Kegan Paul, 1886 (3 vols) £200
Home Again, Kegan Paul, 1887 . . . . . £150
The Elect Lady, Kegan Paul, 1888 . . . . £150
There and Back, Kegan Paul, 1891 (3 vols) . £175
A Rough Shaking, Blackie, 1891 . . . . . £150
The Flight of the Shadow, Kegan Paul, 1891 . £150
The Hope of the Gospel, Ward, Lock, 1892 . £50
Heather and Snow, Chatto & Windus, 1893 (2 vols) £100
A Dish of Orts, Sampson Low, 1893. . . . £75
Poetical Works, Chatto & Windus, 1893 (2 vols) £100
Lilith, Chatto & Windus, 1895 . . . . . £150
Salted with Fire, Hurst & Blackett, 1897 . . £50
Far Above Rubies, Dodd Mead (U.S.), 1899 . £50
Fairy Tales, Fifield, 1904 (five parts) . . . £125
ditto, Fifield, 1904 (1 vol.) £70

ROSS MACDONALD

(b.1915)

Macdonald is the best known of the many pseudonyms for Kenneth Millar, an American writer of detective novels, who also writes under his own name.

'Ross Macdonald' Novels
The Barbarous Coast, Knopf (U.S.), 1956 . £600/£75
ditto, Cassell, 1957 . . . . £75/£20
The Doomsters, Knopf (U.S.), 1958 . . . £500/£50
ditto, Cassell, 1958 . . . . £25/£10
The Galton Case, Knopf (U.S.), 1959 . . £300/£40
ditto, Cassell, 1960 . . . . £25/£10
The Fergusson Affair, Knopf (U.S.), 1960 . £300/£40
ditto, Collins, 1961 . . . . £25/£10
The Wycherley Woman, Knopf (U.S.), 1961 £300/£40
ditto, Collins, 1961 . . . . £25/£10
The Zebra-Striped Hearse, Knopf (U.S.), 1962 . . . . £125/£30
ditto, Collins, 1963 . . . . £25/£10

The Chill, Knopf (U.S.), 1964 . . . . £125/£30
ditto, Collins, 1964 . . . . £40/£10
The Far Side of the Dollar, Knopf (U.S.), 1965 . . . . £35/£10
ditto, Collins, 1965 . . . . £20/£10
Black Money, Knopf (U.S.), 1966 . . . . £35/£10
ditto, Collins, 1966 . . . . £25/£10
The Instant Enemy, Knopf (U.S.), 1968 . £25/£10
ditto, Collins, 1968 . . . . £25/£10
The Goodbye Look, Knopf (U.S.), 1969 . £20/£10
ditto, Collins, 1969 . . . . £15/£5
The Underground Man, Knopf (U.S.), 1971 £15/£5
ditto, Collins, 1971 . . . . £10/£5
Sleeping Beauty, Knopf (U.S.), 1973 . . £15/£5
ditto, Collins, 1973 . . . . £10/£5
The Blue Hammer, Knopf (U.S.), 1976. . £15/£5
ditto, Collins, 1976 . . . . £10/£5
Lew Archer, Private Investigator, Mysterious Press (U.S.), 1977 (250 numbered, signed copies, acetate d/w and slipcase). . . . . £125/£65

Other Titles as 'Ross Maconald'
On Crime Writing, Capra Press (U.S.), 1973 (250 signed, numbered copies) . . . . . £65/£35
ditto, Capra Press (U.S.), 1973 (wraps) £15
Self Portrait, Ceaselessly Into The Past, Capra Press (U.S.), 1981 (250 signed, numbered copies) £65/£35
ditto, Capra Press (U.S.), 1981 (wraps) . . . £15

'Kenneth Millar' Novels
The Dark Tunnel, Dodd Mead (U.S.), 1944 . . . . £1,500/£150
ditto, as ***I Die Slowly***, Lion, 1955, ... £25/£10
Trouble Follows Me, Dodd Mead (U.S.), 1946. . . . . £1,000/£100
ditto, as ***Night Train***, Lion, 1955. . . . £20/£5
Blue City, Knopf (U.S.), 1947 . . . . . £200/£75
ditto, Cassell, 1949 . . . . £25/£10
The Three Roads, Knopf (U.S.), 1948 . . £75/£15
ditto, Cassell, 1950 . . . . £25/£10

'John Ross Macdonald' Novels
The Drowning Pool, Knopf (U.S.), 1950 £1,000/£75
ditto, Cassell, 1952 . . . . £25/£10
The Way Some People Die, Knopf (U.S.), 1951 . . . . £750/£75
ditto, Cassell, 1953 . . . . £50/£15
The Ivory Grin, Knopf (U.S.), 1951 . . . . £750/£75
ditto, Cassell, 1953 . . . . £50/£15
Meet Me at the Morgue, Knopf (U.S.), 1953 £250/£45
ditto, as ***Experience with Evil***, Cassell, 1954 £25/£10
Find a Victim, Knopf (U.S.), 1954 . . . . £150/£35
ditto, Cassell, 1955 . . . . £25/£10

'John Ross Macdonald' Short Stories
The Name is Archer, Bantam (U.S.), 1955 (wraps) £25

'John Macdonald' Novels
The Moving Target, Knopf (U.S.), 1949 . £450/£45
ditto, Cassell, 1951 . . . . £125/£25

IAN McEWAN
(b.1948)

The writer of obsessive, often explicit novels and short stories, McEwan was the first former student to receive recognition following attendance of Malcolm Bradbury's creative writing course at the University of East Anglia.

Short Stories
First Love, Last Rites, Cape, 1975 . . . £200/£35
ditto, Random House (U.S.), 1975 . . . £30/£10
In Between the Sheets, Cape, 1978 . . . £50/£15
ditto, Simon & Schuster (U.S.), 1979 . . £20/£5
The Short Stories, Cape, 1995 . . . . £15/£5

Novels
The Cement Garden, Cape, 1978 . . . £40/£15
ditto, Simon & Schuster (U.S.), 1978 . . £15/£5
The Comfort of Strangers, Cape, 1981 . . £20/£5
ditto, Simon & Schuster (U.S.), 1981 . . £10/£5
The Child in Time, Cape, 1987 . . . . £15/£5
ditto, London Limited Editions (150 numbered, signed copies in glassine jacket) . . . . . £75/£65
ditto, Houghton Mifflin (U.S.), 1987. . . £10/£5
The Innocent, Cape, 1990 . . . . . £15/£5
ditto, Doubleday (U.S.), 1990 . . . . £10/£5
Black Dogs, Cape, 1992 . . . . . . £15/£5
ditto, London Limited Editions, 1992 (150 numbered, signed copies in glassine jacket) . . . £65/£50
ditto, Doubleday (U.S.), 1992 . . . . £10/£5
Enduring Love, Cape, 1997 . . . . . £10/£5
ditto, Doubleday (U.S.), 1998 . . . . £10/£5
Amsterdam, Cape, 1998 . . . . . . £10/£5
ditto, Doubleday (U.S.), 1999 . . . . £10/£5

Children's
Rose Blanche, Cape, 1983 . . . . . £20/£5
The Daydreamer, Cape, 1994 . . . . £10/£5
ditto, Harper Collins (U.S.), 1994 . . . £10/£5

Miscellaneous
British Films at the London Film Festival, Filmways, 1979 [1980] (wraps) £25
The Imitation Game: Three Plays for Television, Cape, 1981 . . . . £25/£5

ditto, Houghton Mifflin (U.S.), 1982. . . . £10/£5
Or Shall We Die?, Cape, 1983 . . . . . £35/£15
The Ploughman's Lunch, Methuen, 1985 (wraps) £10
Soursweet, Faber, 1988 (wraps) £10
A Move Abroad, Picador, 1989 (wraps) . . £5

JOHN McGAHERN
(b.1934)

A novelist and short story writer whose works, wherever they are set, always refer back to the author's native Ireland.

Novels
The Barracks, Faber, 1963 . . . . . . £350/£75
ditto, Macmillan (U.S.), 1964. . . . . . £30/£10
The Dark, Faber, 1965 . . . . £125/£25
ditto, Knopf (U.S.), 1966 . . . . £25/£10
The Leavetaking, Faber, 1974 . . . . £35/£10
ditto, Little, Brown (U.S.), 1974 . . . . £20/£5
The Pornographer, Faber, 1979 . . . . £35/£10
ditto, Harper & Row (U.S.), 1979 . . . £15/£5
Amongst Women, Faber, 1990 . . . . £10/£5
ditto, Viking (U.S.), 1990 . . . . . . £10/£5

Short Stories
Nightlines, Faber, 1970 . . . . . . £50/£10
ditto, Little, Brown (U.S.), 1971 . . . . £20/£5
Getting Through, Faber, 1978 . . . . £35/£10
ditto, Harper & Row (U.S.), 1980 . . . £15/£5
High Ground, Faber, 1985 . . . . . £20/£5
ditto, Viking (U.S.), 1987. . . . . . . £10/£5
The Collected Stories, Faber, 1992 . . . £25/£10
ditto, Knopf (U.S.), 1993 . . . . . . £20/£5

Plays
The Power of Darkness, Faber, 1991 (wraps) . £15

ARTHUR MACHEN
(b.1863 d.1947)

A novelist, short story writer and essayist, Machen is generally read for his tales of horror and the supernatural although his work is predominantly of a mystical cast. His *Bowmen* was the origin of the 'Angels of Mons' myth in the First World War.

Verse
Eleusinia, privately printed, 1881 (wraps) . £20,000

Novels
The Chronicle of Clemendy, Carbonnek, 1888 (250 numbered copies) £200
ditto, privately printed Carbonnek (U.S.), 1923 (1,050 numbered, signed copies) . . . . . £150/£50
ditto, Martin Secker, 1925 [1926], (100 signed, numbered copies) £125
ditto, Martin Secker, 1925, (trade edition) . £35/£15
The Great God Pan, John Lane, 1894 . . . £150
The Three Impostors, John Lane, 1895 . . . £150
ditto, Roberts Bros (U.S.), 1895 . . . . . £150
ditto, Knopf (U.S.), 1923 . . . . £45/£20
The Hill of Dreams, Grant Richards, 1907 . . £100
ditto, Martin Secker, [1922] (150 signed, numbered copies) £250
The Great Return, The Faith Press, 1915 . £100/£45
The Terror, Duckworth & Co., 1917 . . £150/£30
The Secret Glory, Martin Secker, 1922 . . £75/£25
The Green Round, Ernest Benn, 1933 . . £125/£35
ditto, Arkham House (U.S.), 1968 . . . £50/£20

Short Stories
The House of Souls, Grant Richards, 1906 . . £100
The Bowmen, Simpkin Marshall, 1915 . . . £25
ditto, Simpkin Marshall, 1915 (enlarged edition) £25
The Shining Pyramid, Covici-McGee (U.S.), 1923 (875 numbered copies) £75
Ornaments In Jade, Knopf (U.S.), 1924 (1,000 signed, numbered copies, slipcase) £95
The Shining Pyramid, Martin Secker, 1925 (different from above ***Shining Pyramid***) . . . . £45/£25
ditto, Martin Secker, 1925 (250 signed, numbered copies) . . . . £125/£75
The Cosy Room, Rich & Cowan, 1936 . . £250/£125
The Children of the Pool, Hutchinson & Co., 1936 . . . . £200/£100
Ritual and Other Stories, Tartarus Press, 1992 . . . . £45/£10

Essays
Strange Roads & With the Gods in Spring, The Classic Press, 1923 . . . . £25
ditto, The Classic Press, 1924 (300 signed, numbered copies) £100
The Grande Trouvaille: A Legend of Pentonville, privately printed, 1923 (250 signed, numbered copies, wraps) £50
The Collector's Craft, privately printed, 1923 (250 numbered copies, wraps) £50
ditto, privately printed, 1923 (unknown number also signed, wraps) £150
Dog and Duck, Knopf (U.S.), 1924 . . . £50/£10
ditto, Jonathan Cape, [1924] (900 numbered copies) . . . . £65/£30
ditto, Jonathan Cape, [1924] (150 of above numbered

and signed) . . . . £150/£75
The Glorious Mystery, Covici-McGee (U.S.), 1924 (pictorial boards) . . . . £150/£75
Dreads and Drolls, Martin Secker, 1926 . £45/£20
ditto, Martin Secker, 1926 (100 signed, numbered copies) . . . . £125/£75
Notes and Queries, Spurr & Swift, 1926 (265 signed, numbered copies) £125
Tom O' Bedlam and His Song, The Appellicon Press (U.S.), 1930 (200 signed copies, slipcase) £100/£75
Beneath the Barley, privately printed, 1931 (25 signed, numbered copies, wraps) £75
The Glitter of the Brook, Postprandial Press (U.S.), 1932 (10 copies) £250
Bridles and Spurs, The Rowfant Club (U.S.), 1951 (178 numbered copies, slipcase) £200
ditto, The Rowfant Club (U.S.), 1951 (offprint of the Preface only 25 copies) £75
A Critical Essay, privately printed (U.S.), 1953 (50 copies) £100
A Note on Poetry, Four Ducks Press (U.S.), 1959 (50 numbered copies) £100
From the London Evening News, Four Ducks Press (U.S.), 1959 (50 numbered copies) £100
The Secret of the Sangraal, Tartarus Press, 1996 (250 copies) . . . . £45/£15

Autobiography
Far Off Things, Martin Secker, 1922 (100 signed, numbered copies) £125
ditto, Martin Secker, 1922 (trade edition) . £50/£25
ditto, Knopf (U.S.), 1923 . . . . £45/£15
Things Near and Far, Martin Secker, 1923 (100 signed, numbered copies) £125
ditto, Martin Secker, 1923 . . . . . £75/£25
ditto, Knopf (U.S.), 1923 . . . . £45/£15
The London Adventure, Martin Secker, 1924 £40/£20
ditto, Martin Secker, 1924 (200 signed, numbered copies) £100
ditto, Knopf (U.S.), 1924 . . . . £45/£15
In the Eighties, privately printed, 1931 . . . £75
ditto, Twyn Barlwm Press, 1933 (50 numbered copies) £40

Translations
The Heptameron, by Queen Margaret of Navarre, privately printed [Dryden Press], 1886 . . . £50
The Fortunate Lovers, Redway, 1887 (a selection of the above) £30
Fantastic Tales, or The Way to Attain, privately printed, Carbonnek, 1889 [1890] (500 numbered copies) £40
ditto, privately printed, Carbonnek, 1889 [1890] (large paper issue, 50 signed, numbered copies) . . £150
ditto, privately printed Carbonnek (U.S.), 1923 (1050 numbered, signed copies) . . . . . . £75/£35
The Memoirs of Casanova, privately printed, 1894 (12 vols, 1,000 copies) £300
ditto, privately printed 1894 (large paper issue, 50 numbered sets) £500
ditto, privately printed 1894 (3 numbered sets, Japanese vellum) £750
Casanova's Escape from the Leads, Casanova Society, 1925 . . . . £25/£10
ditto, Knopf (U.S.), Borzoi Pocket Books No. 28 [1925] . . . . £25/£10

Others
The Anatomy of Tobacco, George Redway, 1884 £225
ditto, Knopf (U.S.), 1926 . . . . . . £50/£20
Don Quijote de la Mancha, George Redway, 1887 (wraps) £250
Hieroglyphics, Grant Richards, 1902 . . . £30
ditto, Kennerley (U.S), 1923 . . . . . . £50
ditto, Knopf (U.S), 1923 . . . . . . £50/£20
The House of the Hidden Light, privately printed, 1904 (with A.E. Waite) £5,000
Dr. Stiggins, Francis Griffiths, 1906 . . . . £45
ditto, Knopf (U.S), 1925 . . . . . . £50/£10
War and the Christian Faith, Skeffington & Son, 1918 . . . . £40
Arthur Machen, a novelist of ecstay and sin, Walter M. Hill (U.S.), 1918. (250 copies) £100
Precious Balms, Spurr & Swift, 1924 (265 signed, numbered copies) £100
The Canning Wonder, Chatto & Windus, 1925 . . . . £65/£20
ditto, Chatto & Windus, 1925 (130 signed, numbered copies) £75
ditto, Knopf (U.S.), 1926 . . . . . . £30/£10
A Preface to Casanova's Escape from the Leads, The Casanova Society, 1925 (25 copies, wraps) . £150
A Souvenir of Cadby Hall, J. Lyons and Co. Ltd, 1927 . . . . £75
Parish of Amersham, Mason, 1930 (wraps) . £35
An Introduction to J. Gawsworth: Above the River, privately printed, 1931 (12 signed, numbered copies, wraps) £250
A Few Letters from Arthur Machen, The Rowfant Club (U.S.), 1932 (170 copies) £125
A.L.S., Four Ducks Press (U.S.), 1956 (50 numbered copies) £125
Starrett Vs. Machen, Autolycus Press (U.S.) 1977 £30
Dreams and Visions, by Morchard Bishop, Caermaen Books, 1987 (wraps) £10
Selected Letters, The Aquarian Press, 1988 . . £10/£5

Collected Edition
The Caerleon Edition, Martin Secker, 1923 (9 vols) . . . . £500/£300

COLIN MACINNES

(b.1914 d.1976)

Chiefly read today for his 'London Trilogy' novels, which jauntily catch the changing mood of 1950s and 60s society.

Novels

To The Victors The Spoils, MacGibbon & Kee, 1950 . . . . . £100/£25
June in Her Spring, MacGibbon & Kee, 1952 £50/£15
City of Spades, MacGibbon & Kee, 1957 . £40/£10
ditto, Macmillan (U.S.), 1958. . . . . £20/£5
Absolute Beginners, MacGibbon & Kee, 1959 . . . . £100/£25
ditto, Macmillan (U.S.), 1960. . . . . £25/£10
Mr Love and Justice, MacGibbon & Kee, 1960 . . . . £30/£10
ditto, Dutton (U.S.), 1961. . . . . . £20/£5
All Day Saturday, MacGibbon & Kee, 1966 £30/£10
Sweet Saturday Night, MacGibbon & Kee, 1967 . . . . £20/£5
Westward to Laughter, MacGibbon & Kee, 1969 . . . . £20/£5
ditto, Farrar Straus (U.S.), 1970 . . . . £15/£5
Three Years to Play, MacGibbon & Kee, 1970 £15/£5
ditto, Farrar Straus (U.S.), 1970 . . . . £10/£5
Out of the Garden, Hart-Davis MacGibbon, 1974 . . . . £10/£5

Collected Editions

Visions of London, MacGibbon & Kee, 1969 £15/£5
ditto, as ***The London Novels***, Farrar Straus (U.S.), 1969 . . . . £15/£5

Essays

England, Half English, MacGibbon & Kee, 1961 . . . . £30/£10
ditto, Random House (U.S.), 1962 . . . £20/£5
Posthumous Essays, Brian & O'Keefe, 1977 £15/£5
Out of the Way: Later Essays, Brian & O'Keefe, 1980 . . . . £15/£5

Others

London: City of Any Dream, Thames & Hudson, 1962 . . . . £25/£10
Australia and New Zealand, Time (U.S.), 1966 (with the editors of ***Life***) . . . . £15/£5
Loving Them Both: A Study of Bisexuality and Bisexuals, Brian & O'Keefe, 1973 . . . £25/£10
'No Novel Reader', Brian & O'Keefe, 1975 £15/£5

ALASTAIR MACLEAN

(b.1923 d.1987)

A successful popular novelist, Maclean used wartime experiences with the Royal Navy as the background to his first novel, *HMS Ulysses*. A series of naval and military thrillers followed, characterised by an attention to detail and compelling plots.

Novels

HMS Ulysses, Collins, 1955 . . . . . £40/£10
ditto, Doubleday (U.S.), 1956 . . . . £10/£5
The Guns of Navarone, Collins, 1957 . . £25/£10
ditto, Doubleday (U.S.), 1957 . . . . £10/£5
South By Java Head, Collins, 1958 . . . £15/£5
ditto, Doubleday (U.S.), 1958 . . . . £10/£5
The Last Frontier, Collins, 1959. . . . £10/£5
ditto, as ***The Secret Ways***, Doubleday (U.S.), 1959 . . . . £10/£5
Night Without End, Collins, 1960 . . . £10/£5
ditto, Doubleday (U.S.), 1960 . . . . £10/£5
Fear is the Key, Collins, 1961 . . . . £10/£5
ditto, Doubleday (U.S.), 1961 . . . . £10/£5
The Snow on the Ben, Ward Lock, 1961 (pseud. 'Ian Stuart'), Collins, 1961 . . . . . . £10/£5
The Dark Crusader, Collins, 1961 (pseud. 'Ian Stuart') . . . . £10/£5
ditto, as ***The Blake Shrike***, Scribner (U.S.), 1961 . . . . £10/£5
The Golden Rendezvous, Collins, 1962 . . £10/£5
ditto, Doubleday (U.S.), 1962 . . . . £10/£5
The Satan Bug, Collins, 1962 (pseud. 'Ian Stuart') . . . . £20/£5
ditto, Scribner (U.S.), 1962 . . . . . £10/£5
Ice Station Zebra, Collins, 1963 . . . . £15/£5
ditto, Doubleday (U.S.), 1963 . . . . £10/£5
When Eight Bells Toll, Collins, 1966 . . £10/£5
ditto, Doubleday (U.S.), 1966 . . . . £10/£5
Where Eagles Dare, Collins, 1967 . . . £20/£5
ditto, Doubleday (U.S.), 1967 . . . . £10/£5
Force 10 from Navarone, Collins, 1968 . £20/£5
ditto, Doubleday (U.S.), 1968 . . . . £10/£5
Puppet on a Chain, Collins, 1969 . . . £10/£5
ditto, Doubleday (U.S.), 1969 . . . . £10/£5
Caravan to Vaccares, Collins, 1970 . . . £10/£5
ditto, Doubleday (U.S.), 1970 . . . . £10/£5
Bear Island, Collins, 1971 . . . . . £10/£5
ditto, Doubleday (U.S.), 1971 . . . . £10/£5
The Way to Dusty Death, Collins, 1973 . . £10/£5
ditto, Doubleday (U.S.), 1973 . . . . £10/£5
Breakheart Pass, Collins, 1974 . . . . £10/£5
ditto, Doubleday (U.S.), 1974 . . . . £10/£5
Circus, Collins, 1975 . . . . . . £10/£5
ditto, Doubleday (U.S.), 1975 . . . . £10/£5
The Golden Gate, Collins, 1976 . . . . £10/£5

ditto, Doubleday (U.S.), 1976 . . . . . £10/£5
Death from Disclosure, Hale, 1976 (pseud. 'Ian Stuart') . . . . £10/£5
Flood Tide, Hale, 1977 (pseud. 'Ian Stuart'). £10/£5
Sand Trap, Hale, 1977 (pseud. 'Ian Stuart') . £10/£5
Seawitch, Collins, 1977 . . . . £10/£5
ditto, Doubleday (U.S.), 1977 . . . . £10/£5
Goodbye, California, Collins, 1978 . . . £10/£5
ditto, Doubleday (U.S.), 1978 . . . . £10/£5
Fatal Switch, Hale, 1978 (pseud. 'Ian Stuart') £10/£5
A Weekend to Kill, Hale, 1978 (pseud. 'Ian Stuart') . . . . £10/£5
Athabasca, Collins, 1980 . . . . £10/£5
ditto, Doubleday (U.S.), 1980 . . . . £10/£5
River of Death, Collins, 1981 . . . . £10/£5
ditto, Doubleday (U.S.), 1982 . . . . £10/£5
Partisans, Collins, 1982 . . . . £10/£5
ditto, Doubleday (U.S.), 1983 . . . . £10/£5
Floodgate, Collins, 1983 . . . . . . £10/£5
ditto, Doubleday (U.S.), 1984 . . . . £10/£5
San Andreas, Collins, 1984 . . . . . £10/£5
ditto, Doubleday (U.S.), 1985 . . . . £10/£5
The Lonely Sea, Collins, 1985 . . . . £10/£5
ditto, Doubleday (U.S.), 1985 . . . . £10/£5
Santorini, Collins, 1986 . . . . £10/£5

Others
All About Lawrence of Arabia, Allen, 1962 £15/£5
ditto, as ***Lawrence of Arabia***, Random House (U.S.), 1961 . . . . £10/£5
Captain Cook, Collins, 1971 . . . . . . £10/£5
ditto, Doubleday (U.S.), 1972 . . . . . £10/£5
Alistair MacLean Introduces Scotland, Deutsch, 1972 . . . . £10/£5

LOUIS MACNEICE

(b.1907 d.1963)

A poet often associated with Auden and Spender, MacNeice employs similar devices of irony and satire.

Verse
Blind Fireworks, Gollancz, 1929 . . . . £500/£125
Poems, Faber, 1935 . . . . £200/£45
Poems, Random House (U.S.), 1937. . . . £75/£25
The Earth Compels, Faber, 1938 . . . . £125/£35
Autumn Journal, Faber, 1939 . . . . . £150/£35
ditto, Random House (U.S.), 1939 . . . . £25/£10
The Last Ditch, Cuala Press (Dublin), 1940 (450 copies, tissue d/w) . . . . £150/£100
ditto, Cuala Press (Dublin), 1940 (25 signed copies) £400
Selected Poems, Faber, 1940 . . . . . . £15/£5
Poems, 1925-1940, Random House (U.S.), 1940 . . . . £15/£5
Plant and Phantom, Faber, 1941 . . . . £30/£10
Springboard: Poems, 1941-44, Faber, 1944 £30/£10
ditto, Random House (U.S.), 1945 . . . . £20/£5
Holes in the Sky: Poems, 1944-47, Faber, 1948 . . . . £25/£10
ditto, Random House (U.S.), 1949 . . . £20/£5
Collected Poems, 1925-48, Faber, 1949. . £30/£10
Ten Burnt Offerings, Faber, 1951 . . . £30/£10
ditto, O.U.P. (U.S.), 1953 . . . . . . £20/£5
Autumn Sequel, Faber, 1954. . . . . . £25/£10
The Other Wing, Faber, 1954 (wraps) £15
Visitations, Faber, 1957 . . . . £20/£5
ditto, O.U.P. (U.S.), 1958 . . . . . . £20/£5
Eighty-Five Poems, Faber, 1959. . . . . £20/£5
ditto, O.U.P. (U.S.), 1959 . . . . . . £20/£5
Solstices, Faber, 1961 . . . . £20/£5
ditto, O.U.P. (U.S.), 1961 . . . . . . £20/£5
The Burning Perch, Faber, 1963 . . . £20/£5
ditto, O.U.P. (U.S.), 1963 . . . . . . £20/£5
Selected Poems, Faber, 1964 . . . . . £10/£5
Collected Poems, Faber, 1966 . . . . . £15/£5
ditto, O.U.P. (U.S.), 1967 . . . . . . £10/£5

Novel
Roundabout Way, Putman, 1931 (pseud. 'Louis Malone') . . . . £250/£75

Translations
The Agamemnon of Aeschylus, Faber, 1936 £35/£10
ditto, Harcourt Brace (U.S.), 1937. . . . £25/£10
Goethe's Faust Parts I & II, Faber, 1951 . £30/£10
ditto, O.U.P. (U.S.), 1952 . . . . . . £25/£10

Plays
Out of the Picture, Faber, 1937 . . . . . £50/£15
ditto, Harcourt Brace (U.S.), 1938. . . . £35/£15
Christopher Columbus, Faber, 1944. . . . £30/£10
The Dark Tower, Faber, 1947 . . . . . £30/£10
The Mad Islands and The Administrator, Faber, 1964 . . . . £15/£5
One for the Grave, Faber, 1968 . . . . . £15/£5
ditto, O.U.P. (U.S.), 1968 . . . . . . £10/£5
Persons from Porlock and Other Plays, BBC, 1969 . . . . £15/£5

Essays
Modern Poetry: A Personal Essay, O.U.P. (U.S.), 1938 . . . . £25/£10
The Poetry of W.B. Yeats, O.U.P. (U.S.), 1941. . . . . £45/£15
Meet the U.S. Army, H.M.S.O., 1943 (anonymous, wraps). £300
Varieties of Parable, C.U.P., 1965 . . . . £15/£5

Children's

The Penny That Rolled Away, Putnam (U.S.), 1954 . . . . £75/£25

ditto, as ***The Sixpence That Rolled Away***, Faber, 1956 . . . . £75/£25

Autobiography

The Strings are False, Faber, 1965 . . . £25/£10

ditto, O.U.P. (U.S.), 1966 . . . . . £20/£10

Others

Letters from Iceland, Faber, 1937 (with W.H. Auden). . . . . £75/£25

ditto, Harcourt Brace (U.S.), 1937 . . . £50/£15

Zoo, Joseph, 1938 . . . . £125/£35

I Crossed the Minch, Longman, 1938 . . £150/£35

Astrology, Aldus, 1964 . . . . £15/£5

ditto, Doubleday (U.S.), 1964 . . . . £10/£5

NORMAN MAILER

(b.1923)

An American novelist and journalist, Mailer excels at taking real events and subjecting them to his own fictional representation.

Fiction and Non Fiction

The Naked and the Dead, Rinehart (U.S.), 1948 . . . . £125/£30

ditto, Wingate, 1949 . . . . £75/£25

Barbary Shore, Rinehart (U.S.), 1951 . . £95/£25

ditto, Cape, 1952 . . . . £45/£15

The Deer Park, Putnam (U.S.), 1955 . . £65/£20

ditto, Wingate, 1957 . . . . £35/£10

The White Negro, City Lights Books (U.S.) 1957 (35 cents cover price, wraps) £150

ditto, City Lights Books (U.S.) 1957 (50 cents cover price, wraps) £15

Advertisements for Myself, Putnam (U.S.), 1959 . . . . £35/£10

ditto, Deutsch, 1961 . . . . £25/£10

The Presidential Papers, Putnam (U.S.), 1963 £25/£10

ditto, Deutsch, 1961 . . . . £20/£5

An American Dream, Dial Press (U.S.), 1965 £30/£10

ditto, Deutsch, 1965 . . . . £20/£5

Cannibals and Christians, Dial Press (U.S.), 1966 . . . . £25/£5

ditto, Deutsch, 1967 . . . . £20/£5

Why are We in Vietnam?, Putnam (U.S.), 1967 . . . . £25/£10

ditto, Weidenfeld & Nicholson, 1969 . . £15/£5

The Armies of the Night, NAL (U.S.), 1968 (wraps) £10

ditto, NAL (U.S.), 1968 . . . . £20/£10

ditto, Weidenfeld & Nicholson, 1968 . . £15/£5

Miami and the Siege of Chicago, World (U.S.), 1968 . . . . £15/£5

ditto, Weidenfeld & Nicholson, 1968 . . £15/£5

A Fire on the Moon, Little Brown (U.S.), 1970 £15/£5

ditto, Weidenfeld & Nicholson, 1970 . . £15/£5

The Prisoner of Sex, Little Brown (U.S.), 1971 £15/£5

ditto, Weidenfeld & Nicholson, 1970 . . £15/£5

Maidstone, NAL (U.S.), 1971 (wraps) . . . £10

Existential Errands, Little Brown (U.S.), 1972 £15/£5

St. George and the Godfather, Arbor House (U.S.), 1972 . . . . £15/£5

Marilyn, Grosset & Dunlap (U.S.), 1973 . £15/£5

Faith of Graffiti, Praeger Publishers (U.S.), 1974 (350 signed copies, slipcase) . . . . . . £100/£80

The Fight, Little Brown (U.S.), 1975 . . £10/£5

ditto, Hart-Davis, MacGibbon, 1975 . . . £10/£5

Some Honourable Men, Little Brown (U.S.), 1976 . . . . £10/£5

Genius and Lust, Grove Press (U.S.), 1976 £25/£10

A Transit to Narcissus, Howard Fertig (U.S.), 1978 . . . . £100/£45

The Executioner's Song, Little Brown (U.S.), 1979 . . . . £10/£5

ditto, Hutchinson , 1979 . . . . £10/£5

Of Women and their Elegance, Simon and Schuster (U.S.), 1980 . . . . £25/£10

ditto, Hodder & Stoughton, 1980 . . . . £25/£10

Of a Small and Modest Malignancy, Lord John Press (U.S.), 1980 (300 signed, numbered copies, slipcase). . . . . £50/£35

ditto, Lord John Press (U.S.), 1980 (100 deluxe signed, numbered copies, slipcase) . . . . . £100/£75

Pieces, Little Brown (U.S.), 1982 (wraps) . . £10

Pontifications, Little Brown (U.S.), 1982 (wraps) £10

Ancient Evenings, Little, Brown (U.S.), 1983 £20/£5

ditto, Little, Brown (U.S.), 1983 (350 signed, numbered copies, slipcase) . . . . £45/£35

ditto, Macmillan, 1983 . . . . . . £15/£5

Tough Guys Don't Dance, Random House (U.S.), 1984 . . . . £15/£5

ditto, Franklin Library (U.S.), 1984 (signed limited edition, slipcase) £45

ditto, Joseph, 1984. . . . . £10/£5

The Last Night, Targ Editions (U.S.), 1984 (250 signed copies, tissue d/w) . . . . £65/£50

A Fragment from Vietnam, Eurographica (Helsinki), 1985 (350 signed, numbered copies, wraps) . £75

Conversations with Norman Mailer, University Press of Mississippi (U.S.), 1988 . . . . . £20/£5

Harlot's Ghost, Random House (U.S.), 1991 £15/£5

ditto, Joseph, 1991. . . . . £10/£5

Portrait of Picasso As a Young Man, Atlantic Monthly Press (U.S.) 1995 . . . . £10/£5

Oswald's Tale, Franklin Library, 1995 (signed limited edition) £35
ditto, Random House (U.S.), 1995 . . . . £10/£5
ditto, Little, Brown, 1995 . . . . . . £10/£5
The Gospel According to the Son, Little, Brown (U.S.), 1997 . . . . £10/£5
ditto, Little, Brown, 1997 . . . . £10/£5
Time of Our Time, Random House (U.S.), 1998 . . . . £10/£5

Verse
Deaths for the Ladies and Other Disasters, Putnam (U.S.), 1961 (wraps) £15
ditto, Deutsch, 1962 . . . . £15/£5

Play
The Deer Park, Dell (U.S.), 1967 (wraps) . . £10
ditto, Weidenfeld, 1970 . . . . £10

KATHERINE MANSFIELD
(b.1888 d.1923)

Katherine Mansfield was born in New Zealand, where her work was first published, but she moved to England in 1908 in pursuit of a literary career. Best known for her elegant short stories, Mansfield died of tuberculosis at the age of 35.

Fiction
In a German Pension, Stephen Swift, 1911 £600/£100
ditto, Constable, 1926 (new edition) . . . £25/£10
ditto, Knopf (U.S.), 1926 . . . . £45/£15
Prelude, Hogarth Press, 1918. . . . . . . £1,000
ditto, as ***The Aloe***, Constable, 1930 (750 copies, revised version, edited by J.M. Murry) . . . £250/£75
ditto, Knopf (U.S.), 1930 (975 numbered copies) . . . . £175/£50
Je ne Parle pas Francais, Heron Press, 1919 (100 copies) £500
Bliss and Other Stories, Constable, 1920 . £400/£45
ditto, Knopf (U.S.), 1923 . . . . £250/£35
The Garden Party and Other Stories, Constable, 1922 (1st issue, "sposition" for "position" on p.103, red d/w, blue lettering, 25 copies) . . . £1,000/£300
ditto, Constable, 1922 (2nd issue) . . . £125/£30
ditto, Verona Press, 1947 (alternative selection of stories, lithos by Marie Laurencin, slipcase) . . . . £750/£650
ditto, Knopf (U.S.), 1922 . . . . £75/£20
The Doves' Nest and Other Stories, Constable, 1923 (1st issue, verso of title page blank, 25 copies) . . . . £1000/£800
ditto, Constable, 1923 (2nd issue) . . . £200/£25
ditto, Knopf (U.S.), 1923 . . . . £75/£20
Something Childish and Other Stories, Constable, 1924 (1st issue, verso of title page blank, 34 copies) . . . . £600/£550
ditto, Constable, 1924 (2nd issue) . . . £75/£15
ditto, as ***The Little Girl and Other Stories***, Knopf (U.S.), 1924 . . . . £250/£30
The Collected Stories of Katherine Mansfield, Constable, 1946 . . . . £50/£20
Selected Stories of Katherine Mansfield, O.U.P. Worlds Classics, 1953 (edited and with an introduction by D.M. Davin) . . . . £15/£5
Thirty-Four Short Stories, Collins, 1957 . £10/£5
The Stories of Katherine Mansfield, O.U.P., 1985 (edited by A. Alpers). . . . . . . £15/£5

Other Works
Poems, Constable, 1923 . . . . £65
ditto, Knopf, 1924 . . . . £15/£5
ditto, Constable, 1930 (enlarged edition) . £25/£10
The Journal of Katherine Mansfield, Constable, 1927 . . . . £35/£10
ditto, Knopf (U.S.), 1927 . . . . £35/£10
ditto, Constable, 1954 (revised and enlarged, edited by J.M. Murry) . . . . £25/£10
The Letters of Katherine Mansfield, Constable, 1928 (2 vols, edited by J.M. Murry) . . . . £30/£15
Novels and Novelists, Constable, 1930 (edited by J.M. Murry) . . . . £35/£15
ditto, Knopf (U.S.), 1930 . . . . £35/£15
Reminiscences of Tolstoy, Chekhov and Gorky, Hogarth Press, 1934 (translation with Virginia Woolf and S.S. Koteliansky) £30
To Stanislaw Wyspianski, privately printed, 1938 (poem, limited to 100 copies) £75
The Scrapbook of Katherine Mansfield, Constable, 1939 (edited by J.M. Murry) . . . . . £35/£10
ditto, Knopf (U.S.), 1940 . . . . £30/£15
Katherine Mansfield's Letters to John Middleton Murry, 1913-1922, Constable, 1951 . . £30/£10
ditto, Knopf (U.S.), 1951 . . . . £30/£10
Katherine Mansfield, Letters and Journals, Allen Lane, 1977 (edited and with and introduction by C.K. Stead) . . . . £15/£5
The Urewera Notebook, O.U.P., 1978 (edited by Ian Gordon) . . . . £15/£5
The Collected Letters of Katherine Mansfield Vol 1, 1903-1917, O.U.P., 1984 (edited by Vincent O'Sullivan and Margaret Scott) . . . . £10/£5
ditto ***Vol 2, 1918-1919***, O.U.P., 1987 . . £10/£5
The Critical Writings of Katherine Mansfield, Macmillan, 1986 . . . . £10/£5

NGAIO MARSH

(b.1899 d.1982)

A Kiwi writer of detective fiction whose novels are considered amongst the best of the genre. She was awarded the O.B.E. in 1948 and made a D.B.E. in 1966.

Novels

A Man Lay Dead, Bles, 1934 . . . . £400/£125
ditto, Sheridan (U.S.), 1942 . . . . . £150/£45
Enter a Murderer, Bles, 1935 . . . . £300/£100
ditto, Sheridan (U.S.), 1942 . . . . . £100/£35
Death in Ecstasy, Bles, 1936 . . . . . £200/£75
ditto, Sheridan (U.S.), 1941 . . . . . £90/£30
The Nursing Home Murder, Bles, 1936 (with H. Jellett) . . . . £250/£75
ditto, Sheridan (U.S.), 1941 . . . . . £75/£25
Vintage Murder, Bles, 1937 . . . . . £125/£45
ditto, Sheridan (U.S.), 1940 . . . . . £75/£25
Artists in Crime, Bles, 1938 . . . . . £125/£45
ditto, Ferman (U.S.), 1938 . . . . . £75/£25
Death in a White Tie, Bles, 1938 . . . . £100/£30
ditto, Ferman (U.S.), 1938 . . . . . £50/£20
Overture to Death, Collins, 1939 . . . £175/£50
ditto, Little, Brown (U.S.), 1939 . . . . £50/£20
Death at the Bar, Collins, 1940 . . . . £75/£25
ditto, Little, Brown (U.S.), 1940 . . . . £40/£15
Death of a Peer, Little, Brown (U.S.), 1940 £75/£25
ditto, as ***Surfeit of Lampreys***, Collins, 1941 £175/£50
Death and the Dancing Footman, Collins, 1941 . . . . £75/£25
ditto, Little, Brown (U.S.), 1941 . . . . £35/£15
Colour Scheme, Collins, 1943 . . . . £65/£25
ditto, Little, Brown (U.S.), 1943 . . . . £35/£15
Died in the Wool, Collins, 1945 . . . . £50/£20
ditto, Little, Brown (U.S.), 1945 . . . . £35/£15
Final Curtain, Collins, 1947 . . . . . £50/£20
ditto, Little, Brown (U.S.), 1947 . . . . £35/£15
Swing Brother Swing, Collins, 1949. . . £50/£20
ditto, as ***Wreath for Riviera***, Little, Brown (U.S.), 1949 . . . . £50/£20
Opening Night, Collins, 1951 . . . . £30/£10
ditto, as ***Night at the Vulcan***, Little, Brown (U.S.), 1951 . . . . £30/£10
Spinsters in Jeopardy, Little, Brown (U.S.), 1953 . . . . £30/£10
ditto, Collins, 1954 . . . . £25/£10
Scales of Justice, Collins, 1955 . . . . £25/£10
ditto, Little, Brown (U.S.), 1955 . . . . £25/£10
Death of a Fool, Little, Brown (U.S.), 1956 £25/£10
ditto, as ***Off with His Head***, Collins, 1957 £25/£10
Singing in the Shrouds, Little, Brown (U.S.), 1958 . . . . £25/£10
ditto, Collins, 1959 . . . . £25/£10
False Scent, Little, Brown (U.S.), 1959 . . £25/£10
ditto, Collins, 1960 . . . . £25/£10
Hand in Glove, Little, Brown (U.S.), 1962 £25/£10
ditto, Collins, 1962 . . . . £25/£10
Dead Water, Little, Brown (U.S.), 1963 . . £25/£10
ditto, Collins, 1964 . . . . £25/£10
Killer Dolphin, Little, Brown (U.S.), 1966 . £25/£10
ditto, as ***Death at the Dolphin***, Collins, 1967 £25/£10
Clutch of Constables, Collins, 1968 . . . £25/£10
ditto, Little, Brown (U.S.), 1969 . . . . £15/£5
When in Rome, Collins, 1970 . . . . £25/£10
ditto, Little, Brown (U.S.), 1970 . . . . £15/£5
Tied up in Tinsel, Collins, 1972 . . . . £25/£10
ditto, Little, Brown (U.S.), 1972 . . . . £15/£5
Black as He's Painted, Collins, 1974 . . £25/£10
ditto, Little, Brown (U.S.), 1974 . . . . £15/£5
Last Ditch, Collins, 1977 . . . . . . £25/£10
ditto, Little, Brown (U.S.), 1977 . . . . £15/£5
Grave Mistake, Collins, 1978 . . . . £25/£10
ditto, Little, Brown (U.S.), 1978 . . . . £15/£5
Photo-Finish, Collins, 1980 . . . . . £25/£10
ditto, Little, Brown (U.S.), 1980 . . . . £15/£5
Light Thickens, Collins, 1982 . . . . £25/£10
ditto, Little, Brown (U.S.), 1982 . . . . £15/£5

W. SOMERSET MAUGHAM

(b.1874 d.1965)

For many years Maugham was better known as a playwright than a novelist. He is also an acknowledged master of the short story.

Novels

Liza of Lambeth, T. Fisher Unwin, 1897 . . £350
The Making of a Saint, T. Fisher Unwin, 1898 £100
The Hero, Hutchinson, 1901 . . . . . . £100
Mrs Craddock, Heinemann, 1902 . . . . £125
The Merry-Go-Round, Heinemann, 1904 . . £100
The Bishop's Apron, Chapman & Hall, 1906 . £75
The Explorer, Heinemann, 1908 . . . . . £75
The Magician, Heinemann, 1908 . . . . . £75
Of Human Bondage, Heinemann, 1915 . . . £150
The Moon and Sixpence, Heinemann, 1919 . £50
The Painted Veil, Heinemann, 1925 . . . £225/£50
Cakes and Ale, Heinemann, 1930 . . . £200/£45
ditto, with 'The Skeleton in the Cupboard', Heinemann, [1954] (eightieth birthday edition, 1,000 signed copies) £250
The Narrow Corner, Heinemann, 1932 . . £65/£15
Theatre, Heinemann, 1937 . . . . . £45/£15
Christmas Holiday, Heinemann, 1939 . . £45/£15
Up at the Villa, Heinemann, 1941 . . . £45/£15
The Razor's Edge, Heinemann, 1944 . . £45/£15

Then and Now, Heinemann, 1946 . . . £45/£15
Catalina, Heinemann, 1948 . . . . . . £45/£15

Short Stories
Orientations, T. Fisher Unwin, 1899 . . . . £100
The Trembling of a Leaf, Heinemann, 1921 . £35
The Casuarina Tree, Heinemann, 1926 . . £200/£35
Ashenden, Heinemann, 1928 . . . . . £250/£50
Six Stories Written in the First Person Singular, Heinemann, 1931 . . . . £50/£15
Ah King, Heinemann, 1933 . . . . . . £65/£15
Cosmopolitans, Heinemann, 1936 . . . £50/£15
The Mixture as Before, Heinemann, 1940 . £45/£15
Creatures of Circumstance, Heinemann, 1947 . . . . £45/£15
Quartet, Heinemann, 1948 . . . . . . £45/£15
Trio, Heinemann, 1950 . . . . £40/£10
Encore, Heinemann, 1952 . . . . . . £35/£10

Plays
A Man of Honour, Chapman and Hall, 1903 . £75
Lady Frederick, Heinemann, 1912 . . . . £75
Jack Straw, Heinemann, 1912 . . . . . £75
Mrs Dot, Heinemann, 1912 . . . . . . £75
Penelope, Heinemann, 1912 . . . . . . £75
The Explorer, Heinemann, 1912 . . . . . £75
The Tenth Man, Heinemann, 1913 . . . . £65
Landed Gentry, Heinemann, 1913 . . . . £65
Smith, Heinemann, 1913 . . . . £65
The Land of Promise, 1913 . . . . . . £65
The Unknown, Heinemann, 1920 . . . . £50
The Circle, Heinemann, 1921 . . . . . £50
Caesar's Wife, Heinemann, 1922 . . . . £50
East of Suez, Heinemann, 1922 . . . . . £50
Our Betters, Heinemann, 1923 . . . . . £50
Home and Beauty, Heinemann, 1923 . . . £50
The Unattainable, Heinemann, 1923 . . . £50
Loaves and Fishes, Heinemann, 1924 . . . £45
The Constant Wife, Heinemann, 1927 . . . £45
The Letter, Heinemann, 1927 . . . . . £45
The Sacred Flame, Heinemann, 1928 . . . £45
The Breadwinner, Heinemann, 1930 . . . £35
For Services Rendered, Heinemann, 1932 . . £35
Sheppey, Heinemann, 1933 . . . . . . £35
The Noble Spaniard, Evans Brothers, 1953 . . £25

Travel
The Land of the Blessed Virgin, Heinemann, 1905 £75
On a Chinese Screen, Heinemann, 1922 £125/£45
The Gentleman in the Parlour, Heinemann, 1930 . . . . £100/£30
Don Fernando, Heinemann, 1935 . . . £75/£25

Essays
Books and You, Heinemann, 1940 . . . £40/£15
The Writer's Point of View, C.U.P., 1951 . £20/£5
The Vagrant Mood, Heinemann, 1952 . . £20/£5
ditto, Heinemann, 1952 (500 signed copies). . £75
Ten Novels and Their Authors, Heinemann, 1954 . . . . £20/£5

Others
The Summing-Up, Heinemann, 1938 . . £45/£15
France at War, Heinemann, 1940 . . . £40/£15
Strictly Personal, Heinemann, 1942 . . . £25/£10
A Writer's Notebook, Heinemann, 1949 . . £20/£5
ditto, Heinemann, 1949 (1,000 signed copies) . £125

A.A. MILNE
(b.1882 d.1956)

Milne was a freelance journalist in London, then assistant editor of *Punch*, before becoming a full-time writer from 1918. He is famous for his plays and children's books, although he also wrote novels, short stories, poetry and essays.

Children's Titles
Once on a Time: A Fairy Story, Hodder & Stoughton, 1917 (illustrated by H.M. Brock) £45
ditto, Hodder & Stoughton, [1925] (illustrated by Charles Robinson) . . . . £125/£25
When We Were Very Young, Methuen, 1924 (verse, illustrated by E.H. Shepard) . . . . £2,500/£750
ditto, Methuen, 1924 (verse, illustrated by E.H. Shepard, 100 numbered copies, signed by the author and artist) . . . . £4,500/£3,000
ditto, Methuen, 1974 (300 numbered copies, signed by Christopher Milne) . . . . £300/£150
Vespers: A Poem, Methuen, [1924] (illustrated by E.H. Shepard, music by H. Fraser-Simson) . . £125/£45
Fourteen Songs, Methuen, 1924 (illustrated by E.H. Shepard, music by H. Fraser-Simson) . . £175/£65
Make-Believe: A Children's Play in a Prologue and Three Acts, Methuen, 1925 . . . . £75/£25
A Gallery of Children, Stanley Paul, 1925 (illustrated by H. Willebeek le Mair) . . . . . £200/£65
ditto, Stanley Paul, 1925 (500 numbered copies, signed by the author) . . . . £500/£300
The King's Breakfast, Methuen, 1925 (illustrated by E.H. Shepard, music by H. Fraser-Simson) £175/£50
Winnie-the-Pooh, Methuen, 1926 (stories, illustrated by E.H. Shepard) . . . . £500/£200
ditto, Methuen, 1926 (deluxe edition: red, green or blue leather binding, in slipcase) . . . . . £1,750/£750
ditto, Methuen, 1926 (350 copies, signed by the author and artist, d/w and slipcase) . . . £3,500/£1,750
ditto, Methuen, 1926 (20 special copies, signed by the

author and artist) £6,000
ditto, Methuen, 1973 (illustrated in colour by E.H. Shepard) . . . . £40/£15
ditto, Methuen, 1976 (stories, illustrated by E.H. Shepard, 300 numbered copies, signed by Christopher Milne). . . . . £300/£150
Teddy Bear and Other Songs From 'When We Were Very Young', Methuen, 1926 (illustrated by E.H. Shepard, music by H. Fraser-Simson) . . £175/£50
ditto, Methuen, 1926 (100 numbered copies copies, signed by the author and artist and composer, d/w and slipcase) £500
Now We Are Six, Methuen, 1927 (verse, illustrated by E.H. Shepard) . . . . £250/£75
ditto, Methuen, 1927 (deluxe edition: red, blue or green leather binding, in slipcase) . . . . £500/£200
ditto, Methuen, 1927 (200 numbered copies, signed by the author and artist) £2,000
ditto, Methuen, 1927 (20 special copies, signed by the author and artist) £3,500
ditto, Methuen, 1976 (300 numbered copies, signed by Christopher Milne) . . . . £400/£150
Songs from 'Now We Are Six', Methuen, 1927 (music by H. Fraser-Simson) . . . . . . £175/£45
ditto, Methuen, 1927 (100 signed copies) . . £650
More Very Young Songs, Methuen, 1928 . £175/£60
ditto, Methuen, 1928 (100 numbered copies, signed by the author and artist and composer, d/w and slipcase) £500
The House at Pooh Corner, Methuen, 1928 (stories, illustrated by E.H. Shepard). . . . . £450/£175
ditto, Methuen, 1928 (350 numbered copies, signed by the author and artist). . . . . £3,500/£1,750
ditto, Methuen, 1928 (20 special copies, signed by the author and artist) £6,000
ditto, Methuen, 1928 (deluxe edition: red, green or blue leather binding, in slipcase) £2,000
ditto, Methuen, 1974 (illustrated in colour by E.H. Shepard) . . . . £45/£20
The Christopher Robin Calendar 1929, Methuen 'Ephemerides' series, [1928] (verse, illustrated by E.H. Shepard) £75
The Christopher Robin Story Book, Methuen, 1928 (selections from 'When We Were Very Young', 'Now We Are Six', 'Winnie-the-Pooh' and 'The House at Pooh Corner', new preface by the author) £225/£65
The Hums of Pooh, Methuen, 1929 (illustrated by E.H. Shepard, music by H. Fraser-Simson) . . £175/£45
ditto, Methuen, 1929 (100 numbered copies, signed by the author and artist and composer, d/w and slipcase). £500
Toad of Toad Hall: A Play Taken from Kenneth Grahame's 'The Wind in the Willows', Methuen, 1929 . . . . £100/£25
ditto, Methuen, 1929 (200 numbered copies, signed by Kenneth Grahame and A. A. Milne) . £1,000/£500
Tales of Pooh, Methuen: 'Modern Classics' series, [1930], (selections from 'Winnie-The-Pooh' and 'The House at Pooh Corner', illustrated by E.H. Shepard) . . . . £150/£65
The Christopher Robin Birthday Book, Methuen, 1930 (selections from 'When We Were Very Young', 'Now We Are Six', 'Winnie-the-Pooh' and 'The House at Pooh Corner', illustrated by E.H. Shepard) £125/£50
The Christopher Robin Verses, Methuen, 1932 (contains 'When We Were Very Young' and 'Now We Are Six', illustrated by E.H. Shepard) . . £200/£75
Introducing Winnie-the-Pooh, Methuen, 1947 £75/£35
The World of Pooh, Methuen, 1958 . . £75/£35
The World of Christopher Robin, Methuen, 1959 . . . . £75/£35
Prince Rabbit and The Princess Who Could Not Laugh, Ward Lock, 1966 (illustrated by Mary Shepard) . . . . £35/£15
The Pooh Story Book, Methuen, 1967 . . £50/£20
The Christopher Robin Verse Book, Methuen, 1969 (illustrated by E.H. Shepard) . . . . £50/£20

Adult Titles: Fiction

Mr Pim, Hodder & Stoughton, 1921, (novel) £75/£25
The Red House Mystery, Methuen, 1922 (novel) . . . . £500/£150
The Secret and Other Stories, Methuen/Fountain Press (U.S.), 1929 (742 signed copies) £200
Chloe Marr, Methuen, 1946 . . . . £25/£10
Birthday Party and Other Stories, Dutton (U.S.), 1948. . . . . £25/£10
ditto, Methuen, 1949 . . . . £25/£10
A Table Near the Band, Methuen, 1950 (stories) . . . . £35/£15

Plays

First Plays, Chatto & Windus, 1919 (contains 'Wurzel-Flummery', 'The Lucky One', 'The Boy Comes Home', 'Belinda' and 'The Red Feathers') . . . £25/£10
Second Plays, Chatto & Windus, 1921 (contains 'Make-Believe', 'Mr Pim Passes By, 'The Camberley Triangle', 'The Romantic Age' and 'The Stepmother') . . . . £25/£10
Three Plays, Putnam (U.S.), 1922 (contains 'The Dover Road', 'The Truth about Blayds' and 'The Great Broxopp'). . . . . £25/£10
ditto, Chatto & Windus, 1923 . . . . £25/£10
Success, Chatto & Windus, 1923 . . . £25/£10
The Man in the Bowler Hat, Samuel French (U.K./U.S.), 1923 . . . . £15
Four Plays, Chatto & Windus, 1926 (contains 'To Have the Honour, Meet the Prince', 'Ariadne', 'Portrait of a Gentleman in Slippers' and 'Success') £25/£10
More Plays, Chatto & Windus, 1935 (contains 'The

Ivory Doors', 'The Fourth Wall' and 'Other People's Lives') . . . . £20/£5
Four Plays, Penguin, 1939 (contains 'To Have the Honour', 'Belinda', 'The Dover Road' and 'Mr Pim Passes By', wraps) £5
The Ugly Duckling, Samuel French, 1941 . . £10
Before the Flood, Samuel French (U.K./U.S.), 1951 £5

Verse
For the Luncheon Interval: Cricket and Other Verses, Methuen, 1925 (wraps) £35
Behind the Lines, Methuen, 1940 . . . £25/£10
The Norman Church, Methuen, 1948 . . £25/£10

Others
Lovers in London, Alston Rivers, 1905 . . . £75
The Day's Play, Methuen, 1910 (sketches) . . £15
The Holiday Round, Methuen, 1912 (sketches) £15
Once a Week, Methuen, 1914 . . . . . . £10
Happy Days, George H. Doran (U.S.), 1915 . £10
Not That It Matters, Methuen, 1919 . . . . £10
If I May, Methuen, 1920 . . . . £30/£10
The Sunny Side, Methuen, 1921 . . . . £30/£10
The Ascent of Man, Ernest Benn, 1928 . . £30/£10
By Way of Introduction, Methuen, 1929 . £30/£10
ditto, Dutton (U.S.), 1929 (166 signed, large paper copies) £250
Those Were the Days, Methuen, 1929 . . £30/£10
Two People, Methuen, 1931 . . . . . £30/£10
Four Days Wonder, Methuen, 1933 . . . £30/£10
Peace with Honour, Methuen, 1934 . . £25/£10
Miss Elizabeth Bennett, Chatto & Windus, 1936 . . . . £30/£10
It's Too Late Now, Methuen, 1939 . . . £30/£10
War With Honour, Macmillan, 1940 . . £25/£10
War Aims Unlimited, Methuen, 1941 (wraps) . £15
The Pocket Milne, Dutton (U.S.),1941 . . £25/£10
ditto, Methuen, 1942 . . . . £20/£5
Year In, Year Out, Methuen, 1952 . . . £25/£10

MARGARET MITCHELL

(b.1900 d.1949)

Gone With the Wind was the result of ten years work, a distillation of all of the American Civil War stories Mitchell had heard. Her 1000 page novel won the Pulitzer Prize, has sold over 25 million copies and is translated into 27 different languages.

Gone With the Wind, Macmillan (U.S.), 1936 (d/w with *Gone With the Wind* listed in second column of book list on back panel) . . . . . . £4,000/£200
ditto, Macmillan (U.S.), 1936 (d/w with *Gone With the Wind* listed at top of list in first column on back panel) . . . . £750/£200
ditto, Macmillan, 1936 . . . . . . £300/£75

NAOMI MITCHISON

(b.1897)

A novelist with a long career, her works of the 20s and 30s are held in highest esteem, especially those which evoke classical Greece and Rome. Mitchison also wrote a great deal of fiction for children.

Novels
The Conquered, Cape, 1923 . . . . . . £125/£45
Cloud Cuckoo Land, Cape, 1925 . . . . £40/£15
The Corn King and the Spring Queen, Cape, 1931 . . . . £30/£15
We Have Been Warned, Constable, 1935 . £30/£15
Beyond this Limit, Cape, 1935 . . . . . £40/£15
The Blood of the Martyrs, Constable, 1939 . £20/£5
The Bull Calves, Cape, 1947 . . . . . £25/£5
Lobsters on the Agenda, Gollancz, 1952 . £15/£5
Behold Your King, Muller, 1957 . . . . £15/£5
Memoirs of a Spacewoman, Gollancz, 1962 £15/£5
When We Become Men, Collins, 1965 . . £15/£5
Cleopatra's People, Heinemann, 1972 . . £15/£5
Solution Three, Dobson, 1973 . . . . . £15/£5
Not By Bread Alone, Marion Boyars, 1983 . £15/£5
Early in Orcadia, R. Drew, 1987 . . . £10/£5
The Oath Takers, Bainain Books, 1991 . . £10/£5
Sea-Green Ribbons, Bainain Books, 1991 . £10/£5

Short Stories
When the Bough Breaks and Other Stories, Cape, 1924 . . . . £35/£10
Black Sparta, Greek Stories, Cape, 1928 . £30/£10
Barbarian Stories, Cape, 1929 . . . . £30/£10
The Powers of Light, Pharos, 1932 . . . £30/£10
Images of Africa, Canongate, 1980 . . . £10/£5
What Do You Think of Yourself? Scottish Short Stories, P. Harris, 1982 . . . . £10/£5
Beyond this Limit, Selected Shorter Fiction, Scottish Academic Press, 1986 . . . . £10/£5

Short Stories and Poetry
The Delicate Fire, Cape, 1933 . . . . . £30/£10
The Fourth Pig, Constable, 1936 . . . £15/£5
Five Men and a Swan, Allen & Unwin, 1957 £10/£5
A Girl Must Live, R. Drew, 1990 . . . £10/£5

Poetry
The Laburnum Branch, Cape, 1926 . . £25/£10
The Alban Goes Out, Raven Press, 1939 (wraps) £50

The Cleansing of the Knife and Other Poems, Canongate, 1978 . . . . £10/£5

Plays
The Price of Freedom, Cape, 1931 . . . £25/£5
As It Was in the Beginning, Cape, 1939 . £10/£5
Spindrift, French, 1951 (wraps) £5

MARY RUSSELL MITFORD
(b.1787 d.1855)

Our Village is Mitford's classic, although it is only one book among verse, sketches, novels and short stories. She supported her father through her writing after he had ruined the family through his extravagance.

Verse
Poems, Valpy & Longman, 1810. . . . . £250
ditto, Valpy & Rivington, 1811 . . . . . £75
Christina, Valpy & Rivington, 1811. . . . £75
Narrative Poems on the Female Character in the Various Relations of Life, Volume 1, Valpy & Rivington, 1813 . . . . £75
Dramatic Scenes, Sonnets and Other Poems, Geo. B Whittaker, 1827 . . . . £50

Sketches
Our Village, G & W.B. Whittaker, 1824, Vol. 1 £200
ditto, G & W.B. Whittaker, 1824, Vol. 2 . . £175
ditto, G & W.B. Whittaker, 1824, Vol. 3 . . £150
ditto, G & W.B. Whittaker, 1824, Vol. 4 . . £150
ditto, G & W.B. Whittaker, 1824, Vol. 5 . . £150
Belford Regis, Bentley, 1835 (3 vols) . . . £150

Novels
Atherton and Other Tales, Hurst & Blackett, 1854 (3 vols) £100

Plays
Foscari, Whittaker, 1826, ... £45
Foscari and Julian, Whittaker, 1827. . . . £35
Charles I, John Duncombe, 1834 . . . . £35
Sadak and Kalasrade, Lyceum Opera House, 1835 . . . . £75
Dramatic Works, Hurst & Blackett, 1854 (2 vols) £50

Short Stories
American Stories, First Series, Whittaker, Treacher, 1831 (3 vols) £175
Country Stories, Saunders & Otley, 1837 . . £75

Others
Lights and Shadows of American Life, Colborn & Bentley, Treacher, 1832 (3 vols) £200

NANCY MITFORD
(b. 1904 d.1973)

Although she was also a biographer, Mitford's satirical novels of bohemian life are her most appreciated works.

Novels
Highland Fling, Hamish Hamilton, 1931 . £75/£35
Christmas Pudding, Butterworth, 1932 . . £75/£25
Wigs on the Green, Hamish Hamilton, 1935 £75/£25
Pigeon Pie: A Wartime Receipt, Hamish Hamilton, 1940 . . . . £45/£20
The Pursuit of Love, Hamish Hamilton, 1945 £35/£15
Love in a Cold Climate, Hamish Hamilton, 1949 . . . . £35/£15
The Blessing, Hamish Hamilton, 1951 . . £25/£10
Don't Tell Alfred, Hamish Hamilton, 1960 . £25/£10

Biography
Madame de Pompadour, Hamish Hamilton, 1954 . . . . £25/£10
Voltaire in Love, Hamish Hamilton, 1957 . £25/£10
The Sun King: Louis XIV at Versailles, Hamish Hamilton, 1966 . . . . £20/£5
ditto, Arcadia Press, 1970 (265 signed copies) . £75
Frederick the Great, Hamish Hamilton, 1970 £20/£5

Play
The Little Hut, Hamish Hamilton, 1951 . . £35/£15

Essays
The Water Beetle, Hamish Hamilton, 1962 £30/£10

Translation
The Princess de Cleeves, by Madame de Lafayette, Hamish Hamilton, 1950 . . . . £35

Editor
The Ladies of Alderley, Hamish Hamilton, 1938 . . . . £45/£15
The Stanleys of Alderley, Hamish Hamilton, 1938 . . . . £45/£15
Noblesse Oblige, Hamish Hamilton, 1962 . £40/£15

MICHAEL MOORCOCK
(b.1939)

A wide-ranging author writing predominantly in the fields of science fiction and fantasy.

Elric of Melnibone Titles
The Stealer of Souls, Neville Spearman, 1963 (orange boards) . . . . £125/£100
ditto, Neville Spearman, 1963 (green boards) £35/£10
Stormbringer, Herbert Jenkins, 1965 . . £150/£45
ditto, Daw (U.S.), 1977 (wraps, revised edition) . £5
The Sleeping Sorceress, New English Library, 1971 . . . . £25/£10
ditto, as ***The Vanishing Tower***, Daw (U.S.), 1977 (wraps) £10
ditto, as ***The Vanishing Tower***, Archival Press (U.S.), 1981 (with slipcase) . . . . £65/£40
ditto, as ***The Vanishing Tower***, Archival Press (U.S.), 1981 (150 signed copies, with slipcase) . £150/£125
Elric of Melnibone, Hutchinson, 1972 . . £25/£10
ditto, as ***The Dreaming City***, Lancer (U.S.), 1972 (wraps, with unauthorised cuts) £10
ditto, Blue Star (U.S.), 1977 (in slipcase) . £65/£40
ditto, Blue Star (U.S.), 1977 (150 signed copies, in slipcase) . . . . £150/£125
Elric: The Return to Melnibone, Unicorn, 1973 (soft cover, graphic novella illustrated by Philippe Druillet) £45
The Jade Man's Eyes, Unicorn, 1973 (wraps) . £10
Sailor on the Seas of Fate, Quartet, 1976 . £25/£10
The Weird of the White Wolf, Daw (U.S.), 1977 (wraps) £10
The Bane of the Black Sword, Daw (U.S.), 1977 (wraps) £10
Elric at the End of Time, Paper Tiger, 1987 £20/£5
ditto, Paper Tiger, 1987 . . . . £5
The Fortress of the Pearl, Gollancz, 1989 . £20/£5
The Revenge of the Rose, Grafton, 1991 . £20/£5

A Warrior of Mars Titles
Warriors of Mars, Compact, 1965 (wraps, as 'Edward P. Bradbury') £15
ditto, as ***The City of the Beast***, Lancer, 1970 (wraps, as Michael Moorcock) £10
ditto, as ***City of the Beast, Or Warriors of Mars***, Daw (U.S.), 1979 (wraps, as Michael Moorcock) . £5
Blades of Mars, Compact, 1965 (wraps, as 'Edward P. Bradbury') £15
ditto, as ***The Lord of the Spiders***, Lancer, 1971 (wraps, as Michael Moorcock) £10
Barbarians of Mars, Compact, 1965 (wraps, as 'Edward P. Bradbury') £15
ditto, as ***Masters of the Pit***, New English Library, 1971 (wraps, as Michael Moorcock) £10

Nick Allard/Jerry Cornell Titles
The LSD Dossier, by Roger Harris, Compact, 1966 [rewritten by Moorcock, wraps]. £20
Somewhere in the Night, Compact, 1966 (wraps, pseud. Bill Barclay) £20
ditto, as ***The Chinese Agent***, Macmillan (U.S.), 1970 (revised edition, by Michael Moorcock) . £25/£10
Printer's Devil, Compact, 1966 (wraps, as Bill Barclay) £15
ditto, as ***The Russian Intelligence***, Savoy, 1980 (wraps, revised edition) £10
ditto, as ***The Russian Intelligence***, New English Library, 1983 (revised edition) . . . . £20/£5

Hawkmoon (The History of the Runestaff) Titles
The Jewel in the Skull, Lancer (U.S.), 1967 (wraps) £10
ditto, White Lion, 1973 . . . . £25/£10
ditto, Daw (U.S.), 1977 (wraps, revised edition) . £5
Sorcerers Amulet, Lancer (U.S.), 1968 (wraps) £10
ditto, as ***The Mad God's Amulet***, Mayflower, 1969 (wraps) £5
ditto, as ***The Mad God's Amulet***, White Lion, 1973 . . . . £25/£10
ditto, as ***The Mad God's Amulet***, Daw (U.S.), 1977 (wraps, revised edition) £5
Sword of the Dawn, Lancer (U.S.), 1968 (wraps) £10
ditto, as ***The Sword of the Dawn***, White Lion, 1973 . . . . £25/£10
ditto, as ***The Sword of the Dawn***, Daw (U.S.), 1977 (revised edition, wraps) £5
The Secret of the Runestaff, Lancer (U.S.), 1969 (wraps) £10
ditto, as ***The Runestaff***, Mayflower, 1969 (wraps) £5
ditto, as ***The Runestaff***, White Lion, 1974 . £25/£10
ditto, as ***The Runestaff***, Daw (U.S.), 1977 (wraps, revised edition) £5

Jerry Cornelius Titles
The Final Programme, Avon (U.S.), 1968 (cut version) . . . . £35/£10
ditto, Avon (U.S.), 1968 (cut version, wraps) . £10
ditto, Allison & Busby, 1969 (full text) . . £35/£10
A Cure for Cancer, Allison & Busby, 1971 (plain dustjacket) . . . . £35/£10
ditto, Allison & Busby, 1971 [1976] (pictorial dustjacket) . . . . £25/£10
ditto, Fontana, 1979 (revised edition, wraps) . . £5
The English Assassin, Allison & Busby, 1972 (multiple figure dustjacket) £35/310
ditto, Allison & Busby, 1976 (single-figure dustjacket). . . . . £25/£10
ditto, Fontana, 1979 (revised edition, wraps) . . £5
The Lives and Times of Jerry Cornelius, Allison & Busby, 1976 . . . . £25/£10

ditto, Harrap, 1987 (expanded edition) . . £20/£10
ditto, Grafton, 1987 (expanded edition, wraps) . . £5
The Adventures of Una Persson and Catherine Cornelius in the Twentieth Century, Quartet, 1976 . . . . £25/£10
ditto, Quartet, 1976 (wraps) £5
The Condition of Muzak, Allison & Busby, 1977 . . . . £25/£10
ditto, Allison & Busby, 1977 (wraps) . . . £10
ditto, Fontana, 1978 (revised edition, wraps) . £5
The Great Rock 'N' Roll Swindle, Virgin, 1980 (newspaper) £25
ditto, Virgin, 1981 (wraps) £10
The Entropy Tango, New English Library, 1981 . . . . £15/£5

Karl Glogauer Titles
Behold the Man, Allison & Busby, 1969 . £30/£10
Breakfast in the Ruins, New English Library, 1972 . . . . £25/£10

The Eternal Champion Titles
The Eternal Champion, Dell (U.S.), 1970 (wraps) £10
ditto, Harper & Row (U.S.), 1978 (revised edition) . . . . £30/£10
Phoenix in Obsidian, Mayflower, 1970 (wraps) £10
ditto, as ***The Silver Warriors***, Dell (U.S.), 1973 (wraps) £5
The Swords of Heaven, The Flowers of Hell, Simon & Schuster (U.S.), 1979 (graphic novella, with Howard V. Chaykin, softcover) £30
Das Ewige Schwert, Bastel Lübbe (Germany), 1986 (wraps) £5
ditto, as ***The Dragon in the Sword***, Ace (U.S.), 1986 (cut text) £10
ditto, as ***The Dragon in the Sword***, Grafton, 1987 (full text) . . . . £20/£5

Corum (The Swords Trilogy) Titles
The Knight of Swords, Mayflower, 1971 (wraps) £10
ditto, Allison & Busby, 1977 . . . . . £20/£5
The Queen of the Swords, Berkeley (U.S.), 1971 (wraps) £10
The King of the Swords, Berkeley (U.S.), 1971 (wraps) £10

Oswald Bastaple Titles
The Warlord of the Air, Ace (U.S.), 1971 (wraps) £10
ditto, New English Library, 1971 (censored text) . . . . £20/£5
The Land Leviathan, Quartet, 1974 . . . £20/£5
ditto, Quartet, 1974 (wraps) £5
The Steel Tsar, Granada, 1981 (wraps) £5

The Dancers at the End of Time Titles
An Alien Heat, MacGibbon & Kee, 1972 . £45/£15
The Hollow Lands, Harper & Row (U.S.), 1974 . . . . £30/£10
Legends from the End of Time, Harper & Row (U.S.), 1976 . . . . £30/£10
The End of All Songs, Harper & Row (U.S.), 1976 . . . . £30/£10
The Transformation of Miss Mavis Ming, W.H. Allen, 1977 . . . . £50/£20
ditto, as ***A Messiah at the End of Time***, Daw (U.S.), 1978 (wraps) £10

Corum (The Chronicles of Corum) Titles
The Bull and the Spear, Allison & Busby, 1973 . . . . £30/£10
The Oak and the Ram, Allison & Busby, 1973 . . . . £30/£10
The Sword and the Stallion, Allison & Busby, 1974 . . . . £30/£10

Hawkmoon (The Chronicles of Castle Brass) Titles
Count Brass, Mayflower, 1973 (wraps) . . . £10
The Champion of Garathorm, Mayflower, 1973 (wraps) £10
The Quest for Tanelorn, Mayflower, 1975 (wraps) £10

Hawklords Titles
The Time of the Hawklords, Aidan Ellis, 1976 (with Michael Butterworth) . . . . . . £35/£15
Queens of Deliria, Star, 1977 (by Michael Butterworth, wraps). £10

Colonel Pyat Titles
Byzantium Endures, Secker & Warburg, 1981 £15/£5
The Laughter of Carthage, Secker & Warburg, 1984 . . . . £15/£5
Jerusalem Commands, Cape, 1992 (buff endpapers) . . . . £15/£5
ditto, Cape, 1992 (white endpapers) . . . £10/£5

Von Bek Titles
The War Hound and The World's Pain, Timescape (U.S.), 1981 . . . . £30/£10
The City in the Autumn Stars, Grafton, 1986 £20/£5

Other Novels
Caribbean Crisis, Fleetway Publications, 1962 (pseud. 'Desmond Reid', wraps) £40
The Sundered Worlds, Compact, 1965 (wraps). £10
ditto, as ***The Blood Red Game***, Sphere, 1970 (wraps) £5
ditto, as ***The Sundered Worlds***, Roc, 1992 (revised edition, wraps) £5

The Fireclown, Compact, 1965 (wraps) . . £10
ditto, as ***The Winds of Limbo***, Wraps Library (U.S.), 1969 (wraps) £5
The Twilight Man, Compact, 1966 (wraps) . £10
ditto, as ***The Shores Of Death***, Sphere, 1970 (wraps) £5
The Wrecks of Time, Ace (U.S.), 1967 (cut text, with 'Tramontane' by Emil Petaja, wraps) . . . £10
ditto, as ***The Rituals of Infinity***, Arrow, 1971 (full text, wraps) £5
ditto, as ***The Wrecks Of Time***, Roc, 1994 (full text, wraps) £5
The Ice Schooner, Sphere, 1969 (wraps) . . £10
ditto, Harper & Row, 1977 (revised edition) £35/£10
ditto, Harrap, 1985 (re-revised edition) . . £20/£5
The Black Corridor, Ace (U.S.), 1969 (cut text, wraps) £10
ditto, Mayflower, 1969 (wraps, full text) . . £5
ditto, Ace [book club] (U.S.), 1970 (cut text) £15/£5
The Distant Suns, Unicorn, 1975 (with Philip James, wraps) £10
Gloriana, or The Unfulfill'd Queen, Allison & Busby, 1978 . . . . £25/£10
ditto, as ***Gloriana; Or, The Unfulfill'd Queen***, Orion-Phoenix, 1993 (revised edition, wraps) . . £5
The Real Life of Mr Newman, A.J. Callow, 1979 (500 copies, wraps) £15
The Golden Barge, 1979 (wraps) £10
ditto, New English Library, 1983 (no illustrations) . . . . £20/£5
The Brothel in Rosenstrasse, New English Library, 1982 . . . . £20/£5
Mother London, Secker & Warburg, 1988 . £20/£5

Short Stories
The Deep Fix, Compact, 1966 (pseud. 'James Colvin', wraps) £15
The Time Dweller, Hart Davis, 1969 . . £75/£25
The Singing Citadel, Mayflower, 1970 (wraps) £5
Moorcock's Book of Martyrs, Quartet, 1976 (wraps) £5
ditto, as ***Dying For Tomorrow***, Daw (U.S.), 1978 (wraps) £5
Sojan, Savoy, 1977 . . . . £10
My Experiences in the Third World War, Savoy, 1980 (wraps) £10
Elric at the End of Time, New English Library, 1984 . . . . £20/£5
The Opium General and Other Stories, Harrap, 1984 . . . . £15/£5
Casablanca, Gollancz, 1989 . . . . . £15/£5

Omnibus Editions
The Swords Trilogy, Berkley (U.S.), 1977 (wraps) £10
ditto, Gregg Press (U.S.), 1980 . . . . £30/£10
ditto, as ***The Swords of Corum***, Grafton, 1986 £15/£5
The Cornelius Chronicles, Avon (U.S.) 1977 (wraps) £5
ditto, as ***The Cornelius Quartet***, Orion-Phoenix, 1993 (revised edition) . . . . £20/£5
ditto, as ***The Cornelius Quartet***, Orion-Phoenix, 1993 (revised edition, wraps) £5
The Chronicles of Corum, Berkeley (U.S.), 1978 (wraps) £5
ditto, Grafton, 1986 . . . . £15/£5
The History of The Runestaff, Granada, 1979 £35/£15
The Black Corridor and The Adventures of Una Persson and Catherine Cornelius, Dial Press (U.S.), 1979 [1980] (wraps) £10
Warrior of Mars, New English Library, 1981 £30/£10
The Dancers at the End of Time, Granada, 1981 . . . . £30/£10
The Nomad of Time, Nelson Doubleday [book club] (U.S.), 1982 . . . . £15/£5
The Elric Saga Part One, Nelson Doubleday [book club] (U.S.), 1984 . . . . £15/£5
The Elric Saga Part Two, Nelson Doubleday [book club] (U.S.), 1984 . . . . £15/£5
The Chronicles of Castle Brass, Granada, 1985 £15/£5
The Cornelius Chronicles Vol. II, Avon (U.S.), 1986 (wraps) £5
The Cornelius Chronicles Vol. III, Avon (U.S.), 1987 (wraps) £5
The Cornelius Chronicles Book One, Fontana, 1988 (wraps) £5
The Cornelius Chronicles Book Two, Fontana, 1988 (wraps) £5
Tales from the End of Time, Guild America [book club] (U.S.), 1989 . . . . £15/£5
A Cornelius Calendar, Orion-Phoenix, 1993 £15/£5
ditto, Orion-Phoenix, 1993 (wraps) . . . £5
Behold the Man and Other Stories, Orion-Phoenix, 1994 . . . . £10
ditto, Orion-Phoenix, 1994 (wraps) £5

Omnibus Editions
(The Tale of the Eternal Champion)
Von Bek, Orion-Millennium, 1992 . . . £10/£5
ditto, Orion-Millennium, 1992 (wraps) . . . £5
The Eternal Champion, Orion-Millennium, 1992 . . . . £10/£5
ditto, Orion-Millennium, 1992 (wraps) . . . £5
Hawkmoon, Orion-Millennium, 1992 . . . £10/£5
ditto, Orion-Millennium, 1992 (wraps) . . . £5
Corum, Orion-Millennium, 1992. . . . £10/£5
ditto, Orion-Millennium, 1992 (wraps) . . . £5
Sailing to Utopia, Orion-Millennium, 1993 . £10/£5
ditto, Orion-Millennium, 1993 (wraps) . . . £5
A Nomad of the Time Streams, Orion-Millennium, 1993 . . . . £10/£5

ditto, Orion-Millennium, 1993 (wraps) . . . £5
The Dancers at The End of Time, Orion-Millennium, 1993 . . . . £10/£5
ditto, Orion-Millennium, 1993 (wraps) . . . £5
Elric of Melnibon, Orion-Millennium, 1993 £10/£5
ditto, Orion-Millennium, 1993 (wraps) . . . £5
The New Nature of the Catastrophe, Orion-Millennium, 1993 (with Langdon Jones) . £10/£5
ditto, Orion-Millennium, 1993 (wraps) . . . £5
The Prince with the Silver Hand, Orion-Millennium, 1993 . . . . £10/£5
ditto, Orion-Millennium, 1993 (wraps) . . . £5
Legends from The End of Time, Orion-Millennium, 1993 . . . . £10/£5
ditto, Orion-Millennium, 1993 (wraps) . . . £5
Stormbringer, Orion-Millennium, 1993 . . £10/£5
ditto, Orion-Millennium, 1993 (wraps) . . . £5
Earl Aubec and Other Stories, Orion-Millennium, 1993 . . . . £10/£5
ditto, Orion-Millennium, 1993 (wraps) . . . £5
Count Brass, Orion-Millennium, 1993 . . £10/£5
ditto, Orion-Millennium, 1993 (wraps) . . . £5

Boxed sets
The History of the Runestaff, Mayflower [1973] (wraps, in slipcase) £10
Mighty Moorcock, Quartet [1974] (wraps, in slipcase). £10
Multi-Dimensional Moorcock, Quartet, [1975] (wraps, in slipcase) £10
The Chronicles of Count Brass, Mayflower/Granada, [1977] (wraps, in slipcase) £10
The Dancers at The End of Time, Mayflower, [1978] (wraps, in slipcase) £10
The Jerry Cornelius Quartet, Fontana, [1979] (wraps, in slipcase) £10
The Books of Corum, Granada, [1981] (wraps, in slipcase) £10

Non Fiction
Epic Pooh, British Fantasy Society, 1978 (500 copies, wraps). £15
The Retreat from Liberty, Zomba, 1983 (wraps) £10
Letters from Hollywood, Harrap, 1986 . . £20/£5
Wizardry and Wild Romance, Gollancz, 1987 £20/£5
ditto, Gollancz, 1987 (wraps). £5
Fantasy: The 100 Best Books, Xanadu, 1988 (with James Cawthorn). . . . . £15/£5
ditto, Xanadu, 1988 (50 signed copies) . . . £50
Death Is No Obstacle, Savoy, 1992 (with Colin Greenland) . . . . £15/£5

BRIAN MOORE
(b.1921)

An Irish author of novels which deal powerfully with the torments of guilt and sexual obsession in relation to Catholicism.

Novels
Wreath for a Redhead, Harlequin (Canada), 1951 (pseud. 'Michael Bryan', wraps) £150
ditto, as ***Sailor's Leave***, Pyramid Books (U.S.), 1953 (wraps) £45
The Executioners, Harlequin (Canada), 1951 (pseud. 'Michael Bryan', wraps) £75
French For Murder, Fawcett (U.S.), 1954 (pseud. 'Bernard Mara', wraps) £50
ditto, L. Miller & Sons, 1956 (pseud. 'Bernard Mara', wraps). £50
A Bullet for My Lady, Fawcett (U.S.), 1955 (pseud. 'Bernard Mara', wraps) £50
ditto, L. Miller & Sons, 1956 (pseud. 'Bernard Mara', wraps). £50
Judith Hearne, Deutsch, 1955 . . . . £500/£100
ditto, as ***The Lonely Passion of Judith Hearne***, Little, Brown (U.S.), 1956 . . . . £75/£25
ditto, McClelland & Stewart (Canada), 1964 (wraps) £35
This Gun for Gloria, Dell (U.S.), 1956 (pseud. 'Bernard Mara', wraps) £45
ditto, L. Miller & Sons, 1956 (pseud. 'Bernard Mara', wraps). £35
Intent to Kill, Dell (U.S.), 1956 (pseud. 'Michael Bryan', wraps) £45
ditto, Eyre & Spottiswoode, 1956 (pseud. 'Michael Bryan') . . . . £150/£45
The Feast of Lupercal, Little, Brown (U.S.), 1957 . . . . £75/£25
ditto, Deutsch, 1958 . . . . £50/£20
ditto, as ***A Moment of Love***, Longacre, 1960 £25/£10
Murder in Majorca, Dell (U.S.), 1957 (pseud. 'Michael Bryan', wraps) £45
ditto, Eyre & Spottiswoode, 1958 (pseud. 'Michael Bryan') . . . . £65/£20
The Luck of Ginger Coffey, Little, Brown (U.S.), 1960 . . . . £75/£25
ditto, Deutsch, 1960 . . . . £45/£15
An Answer from Limbo, Little, Brown (U.S.), 1962 . . . . £50/£20
ditto, Deutsch, 1963 . . . . £40/£15
The Emperor of Ice-Cream, Viking Press (U.S.), 1965 . . . . £30/£10
ditto, McClelland & Stewart (Canada), 1965 £30/£10
ditto, Deutsch, 1966 . . . . £25/£10
I Am Mary Dunne, McClelland & Stewart (Canada), 1968 . . . . £25/£10

ditto, Viking Press (U.S.), 1968 . . . . £25/£10
ditto, Cape, 1968 . . . . £25/£10
Fergus, Holt Rinehart (U.S.), 1970 . . . £15/£5
ditto, McClelland & Stewart (Canada), 1970 £15/£5
ditto, Cape, 1971 . . . . £15/£5
Catholics, McClelland & Stewart (Canada), 1972 . . . . £15/£5
ditto, Cape, 1972 . . . . £15/£5
ditto, Holt Rinehart (U.S.), 1973 . . . . . £10/£5
The Great Victorian Collection, Farrar Straus (U.S.), 1975 . . . . £15/£5
ditto, McClelland & Stewart (Canada), 1975 £15/£5
ditto, Cape, 1975 . . . . £15/£5
The Doctor's Wife, Farrar Straus (U.S.), 1976 £15/£5
ditto, McClelland & Stewart (Canada), 1976 £15/£5
ditto, Cape, 1976 . . . . £15/£5
The Mangan Inheritance, Farrar Straus (U.S.), 1979 . . . . £15/£5
ditto, McClelland & Stewart (Canada), 1979 £15/£5
ditto, Cape, 1979 . . . . £15/£5
The Temptation of Eileen Hughes, Farrar Straus (U.S.), 1981 . . . . £15/£5
ditto, McClelland & Stewart (Canada), 1981 £15/£5
ditto, Cape, 1981 . . . . £15/£5
Cold Heaven, Holt Rinehart (U.S.), 1983. . £15/£5
ditto, McClelland & Stewart (Canada), 1983 £15/£5
ditto, Cape, 1983 . . . . £15/£5
Black Robe, Dutton (U.S.), 1985. . . . £15/£5
ditto, McClelland & Stewart (Canada), 1985 £15/£5
ditto, Cape, 1985 . . . . £15/£5
ditto, Cape, 1985 (50 numbered, signed copies, bound by Kenny's of Galway, slipcase) £75
The Color of Blood, Dutton (U.S.), 1987 . £10/£5
ditto, McClelland & Stewart (Canada), 1987 £10/£5
ditto, as ***The Colour of Blood***, Cape, 1987 . £15/£5
Lies of Silence, Bloomsbury, 1990 . . . . £15/£5
ditto, London Limited Editions, 1990 (250 numbered, signed copies, acetate d/w) . . . . . £65/£55
ditto, McClelland & Stewart (Canada), 1990 £15/£5
ditto, Doubleday (U.S.), 1990 . . . . £10/£5
No Other Life, Bloomsbury, 1993 . . . £10/£5
ditto, Knopf (Canada), 1993 . . . . . £15/£5
ditto, Doubleday (U.S.), 1993 . . . . £10/£5
The Statement, Bloomsbury, 1995 . . . £10/£5
ditto, Dutton (U.S.), 1996. . . . . . . £10/£5

Short Stories

Two Stories, California State University (U.S.), 1978 (300 signed, numbered copies) £50
ditto, California State University (U.S.), 1978 (26 lettered copies) £75

Others

Canada, Time Life International (U.S.), 1965 . £15
The Revolution Script, McClelland & Stewart (Canada), 1971 . . . . £20/£5
ditto, Holt Rinehart (U.S.), 1971 . . . . £15/£5
ditto, Cape, 1971 . . . . £15/£5
Autobiography, Partridge Press, 1995 . . . £10/£5

JOHN MORTIMER

(b.1923)

A playwright and barrister, Mortimer was called to the Bar in 1948 and became a QC in 1966. Rumpole, his fictional, incorrigible barrister, has been successfully and popularly televised.

Novels

Charade, Bodley Head, 1947. . . . . . £40/£15
ditto, Viking (U.S.), 1986 . . . . £10/£5
Rumming Park, Lane, 1948 . . . . . £35/£15
Answer Yes or No, Lane, 1950 . . . . £25/£10
ditto, as ***The Silver Hook***, Morrow (U.S.), 1950 £20/£5
Like Men Betrayed, Collins, 1953 . . . . £20/£5
ditto, Lippincott (U.S.), 1954 . . . . . . £15/£5
The Narrowing Stream, Collins, 1954 . . £20/£5
ditto, Viking (U.S.), 1989 . . . . £10/£5
Three Winters, Collins, 1956. . . . . . £20/£5
Will Shakespeare: The Untold Story, Hodder, 1977 . . . . £10/£5
ditto, Delacourt (U.S.), 1978 . . . . . . £10/£5
Paradise Postponed, Viking, 1985 . . . £10/£5
ditto, Viking (U.S.), 1985 . . . . £10/£5
Summer's Lease, Viking, 1988 . . . . £10/£5
ditto, Viking (U.S.), 1988 . . . . £10/£5
ditto, Franklin Library (U.S.), 1988 (signed limited edition) £35
ditto, London Limited Editions, 1990 (250 signed copies) £35
Titmuss Regained, Viking, 1990. . . . £10/£5
ditto, Viking (U.S.), 1990 . . . . £10/£5
Dunster, Viking, 1992 . . . . £10/£5
ditto, Viking (U.S.), 1993 . . . . £10/£5

Stories

Rumpole of the Bailey, Penguin, 1978 (wraps) £20
ditto, Penguin (U.S.), 1980 (wraps) £10
ditto, Armchair Detective Library (U.S.), 1991 (100 signed copies, slipcase) £45
The Trials of Rumpole, Penguin, 1979 (wraps) £10
ditto, Penguin (U.S.), 1981 (wraps) £10
Rumpole's Return, Penguin, 1980 (wraps) . . £10
ditto, Penguin (U.S.), 1982 (wraps) £10
Rumpole for the Defence, Penguin, 1982 (wraps) £5
Rumpole and the Golden Thread, Penguin (U.S.), 1983 (wraps) £10
Rumpole's Last Case, Penguin, 1987 (wraps) . £10

ditto, Penguin (U.S.), 1988 (wraps) £10
Rumpole and the Age of Miracles, Penguin, 1988 (wraps) £10
ditto, Penguin (U.S.), 1989 (wraps) £10
Rumpole à la Carte, Viking, 1990 . . . £15/£5
ditto, Viking (U.S.), 1990 . . . . £10/£5
Rumpole on Trial, Viking, 1992 . . . . £10/£5
ditto, Penguin (U.S.), 1992 . . . . . . £10/£5
Rumpole and the Angel of Death, Viking, 1995 £10/£5
ditto, Penguin (U.S.), 1995 . . . . . . £10/£5

Plays
Three Plays, Elek, 1958 . . . . . . £30/£10
ditto, Grove Press (U.S.), 1962 . . . . £20/£5
The Wrong Side of the Park, Heinemann, 1960 £20/£5
Lunch Hour, French, 1960 (wraps) £10
Lunch Hour and Other Plays, Methuen, 1960 £20/£5
Two Stars For Comfort, Methuen, 1962 . £15/£5
A Flea in Her Ear, French, 1967 (wraps) . . . £5
ditto, French (U.S.), 1967 (wraps) £5
The Judge, Methuen, 1967 . . . . . . £10/£5
Five Plays, Methuen, 1970 . . . . . £10/£5
Come As You Are: Four Short Plays, Methuen, 1971 . . . . £10/£5
A Voyage Round My Father, Methuen, 1971 £20/£5
Knightsbridge, French, 1973 (wraps) £5
Collaborations, Methuen, 1973 . . . . £10/£5
The Fear of Heaven, French, 1978 (wraps) . . £5
Heaven and Hell, French, 1978 (wraps). . . . £5
Edwin and Other Plays, Penguin, 1984 (wraps) . £5
Three Boulevard Farces, Penguin, 1985 (wraps) . £5

Collected Editions
Rumpole, Allen Lane, 1980 . . . . . £10/£5
Regina v. Rumpole, Allen Lane, 1981 . . £10/£5
The First Rumpole Omnibus, Penguin, 1983 £10/£5
The Second Rumpole Omnibus, Viking, 1987 £10/£5
ditto, Penguin (U.S.), 1988 . . . . . £10/£5
The Rapstone Chronicles, Viking, 1991 . £10/£5

Autobiography
Clinging to the Wreckage, Weidenfeld & Nicolson, 1982 . . . . £10/£5
ditto, Ticknor & Fields (U.S.), 1982 . . . £10/£5
Murderers and Other Friends, Viking, 1994 £10/£5
ditto, Viking (U.S.), 1994 . . . . . . £10/£5

Others
With Love and Lizards, Joseph, 1957 (written with Penelope Mortimer) . . . . £25/£10
No Moaning at the Bar, Bles, 1957 (pseud. 'Geoffrey Lincoln') . . . . £30/£10
In Character, Allen Lane, 1983 . . . . £10/£5
Character Parts, Viking, 1986 . . . . £10/£5

IRIS MURDOCH
(b.1919 d.1999)

An artist and philosopher, Murdoch employs a blend of realism and symbolism in her highly regarded novels.

Novels
Under the Net, Chatto & Windus, 1954 . . £350/£100
ditto, Viking (U.S.), 1954 . . . . £75/£25
The Flight from the Enchanter, Chatto & Windus, 1956 . . . . £250/£75
ditto, Viking (U.S.), 1956 . . . . £40/£15
The Sandcastle, Chatto & Windus, 1957 . £150/£65
ditto, Viking (U.S.), 1957 . . . . £40/£15
The Bell, Chatto & Windus, 1958 . . . £75/£25
ditto, Viking (U.S.), 1958 . . . . £15/£5
A Severed Head, Chatto & Windus, 1961 . £75/£25
ditto, Viking (U.S.), 1961 . . . . £15/£5
An Unofficial Rose, Chatto & Windus, 1962 £35/£10
ditto, Viking (U.S.), 1962 . . . . £15/£5
The Unicorn, Chatto & Windus, 1963 . . £25/£10
ditto, Viking (U.S.), 1963 . . . . £10/£5
The Italian Girl, Chatto & Windus, 1964 . £25/£10
ditto, Viking (U.S.), 1964 . . . . £10/£5
The Red and the Green, Chatto & Windus, 1965 . . . . £20/£5
ditto, Viking (U.S.), 1965 . . . . £10/£5
The Time of the Angels, Chatto & Windus, 1966 . . . . £20/£5
ditto, Viking (U.S.), 1966 . . . . £10/£5
The Nice and the Good, Chatto & Windus, 1968 . . . . £20/£5
ditto, Viking (U.S.), 1968 . . . . £10/£5
Bruno's Dream, Chatto & Windus, 1969 . £20/£5
ditto, Viking (U.S.), 1969 . . . . £10/£5
A Fairly Honourable Defeat, Chatto & Windus, 1970 . . . . £20/£5
ditto, Viking (U.S.), 1970 . . . . £10/£5
An Accidental Man, Chatto & Windus, 1971 £10/£5
ditto, Viking (U.S.), 1972 . . . . £10/£5
The Black Prince, Chatto & Windus, 1973 . £10/£5
ditto, Viking (U.S.), 1973 . . . . £10/£5
The Sacred and Profane Love Machine, Chatto & Windus, 1974 . . . . £10/£5
ditto, Viking (U.S.), 1974 . . . . £10/£5
A Word Child, Chatto & Windus, 1975 . . £10/£5
ditto, Viking (U.S.), 1975 . . . . £10/£5
Henry and Cato, Chatto & Windus, 1976 . £10/£5
ditto, Viking (U.S.), 1976 . . . . £10/£5
The Sea, the Sea, Chatto & Windus, 1978 . £10/£5
ditto, Viking (U.S.), 1978 . . . . £10/£5
Nuns and Soldiers, Chatto & Windus, 1980 £10/£5
ditto, Viking (U.S.), 1981 . . . . £10/£5
The Philosopher's Pupil, Chatto & Windus, 1983 . .

. . . . £10/£5
ditto, Viking (U.S.), 1983 . . . . . . £10/£5
The Good Apprentice, Chatto & Windus, 1985 £10/£5
ditto, London Limited Editions, 1985 (250 signed copies, glassine d/w) . . . . £75/£65
ditto, Viking (U.S.), 1985 . . . . . . £10/£5
The Book and the Brotherhood, Chatto & Windus, 1987 . . . . £10/£5
ditto, Viking (U.S.), 1988 . . . . . . £10/£5
ditto, Franklin Library (U.S.), 1988 (signed limited edition) £75
The Message to the Planet, Chatto & Windus, 1989 . . . . £10/£5
ditto, London Limited Editions, 1989 (150 signed copies, glassine d/w) . . . . £75/£65
ditto, Viking (U.S.), 1990 . . . . . . £10/£5
Green Knight, Chatto & Windus, 1993 . . £10/£5
ditto, Viking (U.S.), 1994 . . . . . . £10/£5
Jackson's Dilemma, Chatto & Windus, 1995 £10/£5
ditto, Viking (U.S.), 1995 . . . . . . £10/£5

Plays

A Severed Head, Chatto & Windus, 1964 (with J.. Priestley) . . . . £50/£20
The Italian Girl, French, 1969 (with James Saunders) £40
The Three Arrows and The Servants and the Snow: Two Plays, Chatto & Windus, 1973 . . £25/£10
ditto, Viking (U.S.), 1974 . . . . . . £10/£5
Acastos: Two Platonic Dialogues, Chatto & Windus, 1986 . . . . £10/£5
ditto, Viking (U.S.), 1987 . . . . . . £10/£5
Three Plays, Chatto & Windus, 1989 . . . £10
Joanna Joanna, A Play in Two Acts, Colophon Press, 1994 (12 signed copies, leather, slipcase) . . £200
ditto, Colophon Press, 1994 (143 signed copies) £90
One Alone, Colophon Press, 1995 (26 lettered, signed copies) £125
ditto, Colophon Press, 1995 (200 signed copies, pbk) £30

Verse

A Year of Birds, Compton Press, 1978 (350 signed, numbered copies, no d/w) £95
Something Special, Four Poems and a Story, Eurographica (Helsinki), 1990 (350 signed, numbered copies, wraps in d/w) . . . . . . £100/£75

Others

Sartre: Romantic Rationalist, Bowes & Bowes, 1953 . . . . £100/£30
ditto, Yale University Press (U.S.), 1953 . £50/£20
The Sovereignty of Good, CUP, 1967 (wraps) . £65
ditto, Routledge, 1971 (containing extra essays) . . . . £65/£25
ditto, Schocken Books (U.S.), 1971 . . . £15/£5
The Fire and the Sun: Why Plato Banished the Artists, O.U.P., 1977 . . . . £25/£10
Reynolds Stone, Warren Editions, 1981 (750 signed copies, wraps) £30
The Existential Political Myth, Delos Press, 1989 (45 signed copies of 270, wraps, slipcase) . . . £75
ditto, Delos Press, 1989 (225 numbered copies of 270, wraps, slipcase) £45
Metaphysics as a Guide to Morals, Chatto & Windus, 1992 . . . . £20/£5
ditto, Allen Lane (U.S.), 1993 . . . . £10/£5
Existentials and Mystics, Delos Press, 1993 (100 signed copies of 500, wraps, slipcase) . . . £50
ditto, Delos Press, 1993 (400 numbered copies of 500, wraps) £35
ditto, Allen Lane (U.S.), 1998 . . . . £10/£5

VLADIMIR NABOKOV

(b.1899 d.1977)

A naturalised American novelist, short story writer and poet, Nabokov's first published works were written in his native Russian and were critically acclaimed. During the second half of his career, he achieved a somewhat notorious success with *Lolita*.

Novels

Camera Obscura, Long, 1937 . . . £5,000/£750
ditto, as ***Laughter in the Dark***, Bobbs Merrill (U.S.), 1938 (revised edition) . . . . . . £500/£250
Despair, Long, 1937 . . . . . . £1,000/£250
ditto, Putnam (U.S.), 1966 (revised edition). £100/£35
ditto, Weidenfeld , 1966 (revised edition) . £100/£35
The Real Life of Sebastian Knight, New Directions (U.S.), 1941 (woven red burlap, no d/w) . . £250
ditto, New Directions (U.S.), 1941 (smooth red cloth) . . . . £200/£75
ditto, Editions Poetry, 1945 . . . . £75/£25
Bend Sinister, Holt (U.S.), 1947 . . . . £150/£50
ditto, Weidenfeld, 1960 . . . . . . £100/£35
Lolita, Olympia Press (Paris), 1955 (2 vols, wraps) £2,000
ditto, Putnam (U.S.), 1958 . . . . . £200/£50
ditto, Weidenfeld, 1959 . . . . . . £125/£40
Pnin, Doubleday (U.S.), 1957 . . . . £150/£45
ditto, Heinemann, 1957 . . . . . . £125/£40
Invitation to a Beheading, Putnam (U.S.), 1959 . . . . £50/£15
ditto, Weidenfeld, 1960 . . . . . . £40/£15
Pale Fire, Putnam (U.S.), 1961 . . . . £35/£15
ditto, Weidenfeld, 1962 . . . . . . £35/£15
The Gift, Putnam (U.S.), 1963 . . . . £35/£15

ditto, Weidenfeld, 1963 . . . . £35/£15
The Defence, Weidenfeld, 1964 . . . . £35/£15
ditto, as ***The Defense***, Putnam (U.S.), 1964 . £35/£15
The Eye, Phaedra (U.S.), 1965 . . . . £35/£15
King, Queen, Knave, McGraw-Hill (U.S.), 1968 . . . . £35/£15
ditto, Weidenfeld, 1968 . . . . £35/£15
Ada, McGraw-Hill (U.S.), 1969 . . . . . £25/£10
ditto, Weidenfeld, 1969 . . . . £25/£10
Mary, McGraw-Hill (U.S.), 1970 . . . . £20/£5
ditto, Weidenfeld, 1971 . . . . £20/£5
Glory, McGraw-Hill (U.S.), 1971 . . . . £20/£5
ditto, Weidenfeld, 1972 . . . . £20/£5
Transparent Things, McGraw-Hill (U.S.), 1973 £20/£5
ditto, Weidenfeld, 1973 . . . . £20/£5
Look at the Harlequins!, McGraw-Hill (U.S.), 1974 . . . . £20/£5
ditto, Weidenfeld, 1975 . . . . £20/£5

Short Stories
Nine Stories/Direction Two, New Directions (U.S.), 1947 (wraps) £150
Nabokov's Dozen, Doubleday (U.S.), 1958 . £100/£35
ditto, Heinemann, 1959 . . . . £75/£25
ditto, as ***Spring in Fialta***, Popular Library (U.S.), 1959 (wraps) £20
Nabokov's Quartet, Phaedra (U.S.), 1966 . £25/£10
ditto, Weidenfeld, 1967 . . . . £25/£10
A Russian Beauty and Other Stories, McGraw-Hill (U.S.), 1973 . . . . £25/£10
ditto, Weidenfeld, 1973 . . . . £25/£10
Tyrants Destroyed and Other Stories, McGraw-Hill (U.S.), 1975 . . . . £20/£10
ditto, Weidenfeld, 1975 . . . . £20/£10
Details of a Sunset and Other Stories, McGraw-Hill (U.S.), 1976 . . . . £20/£10
ditto, Weidenfeld, 1976 . . . . £20/£10

Collected Edition
Nabokov's Congeries, Viking Press (U.S.), 1968 . . . . £15/£5

Verse
Poems, Doubleday (U.S.), 1959 . . . . . £175/£45
ditto, Weidenfeld, 1961 . . . . £100/£35
Poems and Problems, McGraw-Hill (U.S.), 1971 . . . . £50/£20
ditto, Weidenfeld, 1972 . . . . £45/£15

Plays
The Waltz Invention, Phaedra (U.S.), 1966 £25/£10
Lolita: A Screenplay, McGraw-Hill (U.S.), 1974 . . . . £25/£10

Others
Nikolai Gogol, New Directions (U.S.), 1944 £150/£45
ditto, Editions Poetry, 1947 . . . . . . £100/£35
Strong Opinions, McGraw-Hill (U.S.), 1973 £25/£10
ditto, Weidenfeld, 1974 . . . . £20/£5
The Nabokov/Wilson Letters:, 1940-1971, Farrar Straus (U.S.), 1978 . . . . £15/£5
ditto, Weidenfeld, 1979 . . . . £15/£5
Lectures on Literature, Harcourt Brace (U.S.), 1980 . . . . £20/£5
ditto, Weidenfeld, 1980 . . . . £15/£5
Lectures on Russian Literature, Harcourt Brace (U.S.), 1981 . . . . £20/£5
ditto, Weidenfeld, 1982 . . . . £15/£5
Lectures on Don Quixote, Harcourt Brace (U.S.), 1983 . . . . £20/£5
ditto, Weidenfeld, 1983 . . . . £15/£5

Autobiography
Conclusive Evidence: A Memoir, Harper (U.S.), 1951 . . . . £175/£50
ditto, as ***Speak, Memory: A Memoir***, Gollancz, 1952 . . . . £50/£20
ditto, as ***Speak, Memory: An Autobiography***, Putnam (U.S.), 1966 (revised edition) . . . . £50/£20
ditto, as ***Speak, Memory: An Autobiography***, Weidenfeld, 1967 (revised edition) . . . £25/£10

SHIVA NAIPAUL
(b.1945 d.1985)

A Trinidadian novelist, Shiva Naipaul's three novels effectively mix satire and compassion.

Novels
Fireflies, Deutsch, 1970 . . . . £65/£20
ditto, Knopf (U.S.), 1971 . . . . £35/£15
The Chip-Chip Gatherers, Deutsch, 1973 . £50/£20
ditto, Knopf (U.S.), 1973 . . . . £20/£5
A Hot Country, Hamilton, 1983 . . . . £10/£5
ditto as ***Love and Death in a Hot Country***, Viking (U.S.), 1984 . . . . £10/£5

Short Stories
The Adventures of Gurudeva, Deutsch, 1976 £25/£10

Travel
North of South: An African Journey, Deutsch, 1978 . . . . £15/£5
ditto, Scribner (U.S.), 1979 . . . . . £15/£5
Black and White, Hamilton, 1980 . . . . £10/£5
ditto, as ***Journey to Nowhere: A New World Tragedy***, Simon & Schuster (U.S.), 1981 . . . . £10/£5

Beyond the Dragon's Mouth, Hamilton, 1984 £10/£5
ditto, Viking (U.S.), 1985 . . . . . . £10/£5
An Unfinished Journey, Hamilton, 1986 . £10/£5
ditto, Viking (U.S.), 1987 . . . . . . £10/£5

V.S. NAIPAUL
(b.1932)

A distinguished Trinidadian novelist, V.S. Naipaul uses such twentieth century uncertainties as imperialism and colonialism as the motivation behind his work.

Novels
The Mystic Masseur, Deutsch, 1957. . . £275/£65
ditto, Vanguard Press (U.S.), 1959 . . . £50/£15
The Suffrage of Elvira, Deutsch, 1958 . . £400/£100
A House for Mr Biswas, Deutsch, 1961 . . £350/£75
ditto, McGraw-Hill (U.S.), 1962 . . . . £50/£15
Mr Stone and the Knights Companion, Deutsch, 1963 . . . . £125/£35
ditto, Macmillan (U.S.), 1964. . . . . £50/£15
The Mimic Men, Deutsch, 1967 . . . . £75/£20
ditto, Macmillan (U.S.), 1967. . . . . £40/£15
In a Free State, Deutsch, 1971 . . . . £65/£20
ditto, Knopf (U.S.), 1971 . . . . . . £25/£10
Guerrillas, Deutsch, 1975 . . . . . £20/£5
ditto, Knopf (U.S.), 1975 . . . . . . £15/£5
A Bend in the River, Deutsch, 1979 . . . £20/£5
ditto, Knopf (U.S.), 1979 . . . . . . £15/£5
The Enigma of Arrival, Viking, 1987 . . £15/£5
ditto, Knopf (U.S.), 1987. . . . . . £10/£5
A Way in the World: A Sequence, Heinemann , 1987 . . . . £15/£5
ditto, Knopf (U.S.), 1994 (advance copy, signed, in slipcase) . . . . £45/£25
ditto, Knopf (U.S.), 1994 . . . . . . £10/£5

Short Stories
Miguel Street, Deutsch, 1959. . . . . £200/£50
ditto, Vanguard Press (U.S.), 1960 . . . £75/£25
A Flag on the Island, Deutsch, 1967 . . £40/£15
ditto, Macmillan (U.S.), 1968. . . . . £35/£10

Others
The Middle Passage, Deutsch, 1962. . . £75/£20
ditto, Macmillan (U.S.), 1963. . . . . £65/£20
An Area of Darkness, Deutsch, 1964 . . £65/£20
ditto, Macmillan (U.S.), 1965. . . . . £50/£15
The Loss of El Dorado, Deutsch, 1969 . . £35/£10
ditto, Knopf (U.S.), 1970 . . . . . . £25/£10
The Overcrowded Barracoon, Deutsch, 1972 £45/£15
ditto, Knopf (U.S.), 1972 . . . . . . £35/£10
India: A Wounded Civilisation, Deutsch, 1977. . . . . £35/£10
ditto, Knopf (U.S.), 1977 . . . . . . £25/£10
The Return of Eva Peron: with The Killings in Trinidad, Deutsch, 1980. . . . . . £20/£5
ditto, Knopf (U.S.), 1980 . . . . . . £15/£5
Congo Diaries, Sylvester and Orphanos, 1980 (300 signed, numbered copies, no d/w) £75
Among the Believers: An Islamic Journey, Deutsch, 1981 . . . . £20/£5
ditto, Franklin Library (U.S.), 1981 (signed limited edition) £45
ditto, Knopf (U.S.), 1981 . . . . . . £15/£5
Finding the Centre: two narratives, Deutsch, 1984 . . . . £15/£5
ditto, Knopf (U.S.), 1984 . . . . . . £15/£5
A Turn in the South, Viking, 1989 . . . £15/£5
ditto, Knopf (U.S.), 1989 . . . . . . £15/£5
ditto, Franklin Library (U.S.), 1989 (signed limited edition) £40
India: A Million Mutinies Now, Heinemann, 1990 . . . . £15/£5
ditto, London Limited Editions (150 signed, numbered copies) £50
ditto, Viking (U.S.), 1991 . . . . . . £10/£5
Conversations with V.S.Naipaul, University Press of Mississippi (U.S.), 1995 . . . . . £20/£5
Beyond Belief : Islam Excursions Among the Converted Peoples, Little, Brown, 1998 . £15/£5
ditto, Random House (U.S.), 1991 . . . £10/£5

VIOLET NEEDHAM
(b.1876 d.1967)

A children's author, Violet Needham was 63 before her first book was published.

The Black Riders, Collins, 1939 . . . . £50/£20
The Emerald Crown, Collins, 1940 . . . £50/£20
The Stormy Petrel, Collins, 1942 . . . £50/£20
The Horn of Merlyns, Collins, 1943. . . £25/£10
The Woods of Windri, Collins, 1944 . . £25/£10
The House of the Paladin, Collins, 1945 . £25/£10
The Changeling of Monte Lucio, Collins, 1946 . . . . £25/£10
The Bell of the Four Evangelists, Collins, 1947 . . . . £25/£10
The Boy in Red, Collins, 1948 . . . . £25/£10
The Betrayer, Collins, 1950 . . . . . £25/£10
Pandora of Parrham Royal, Collins, 1951 . £50/£20
The Avenue, Collins, 1952 . . . . . £25/£10
How Many Miles to Babylon, Collins, 1953 £45/£15
Adventures at Hampton Court, Lutterworth Press,

1954 . . . . £45/£15

Richard and the Golden Horse Shoe, Collins, 1954 . . . . £50/£20

The Great House of Estraville, Collins, 1955 £50/£20

The Secret of the White Peacock, Collins, 1956 . . . . £50/£20

Adventures at Windsor Castle, Lutterworth Press, 1957 . . . . £45/£15

The Red Rose of Ruvina, Collins, 1957 . . £50/£20

KAY NIELSEN

(b.1886 d.1957)

A Danish illustrator, Nielsen moved to London in 1911, and was commissioned to illustrate Quiller-Couch's *In Powder and Crinoline* by Hodder & Stoughton, followed by a series of 'Gift Books'.

In Powder and Crinoline, Old Fairy Tales, retold by Sir Arthur Quiller-Couch, Hodder & Stoughton, [1913]. £650

ditto, Hodder & Stoughton, [1913] (large paper edition) £1,250

ditto, Hodder & Stoughton, [1913] (deluxe edition, 500 signed copies) £2,000

ditto, as ***Twelve Dancing Princesses and Other Fairy Tales***, George H. Doran (U.S.) [1923] . . £450

East of the Sun and West of the Moon, Old Tales from the North, retold by Peter C. Asbjörnsen and Jorgen Moe, Hodder & Stoughton, [1914] . . £1,250

ditto, Hodder & Stoughton, [1914] (deluxe edition, 500 copies) £1,500

ditto, George H. Doran (U.S.) [1914] . . . £200

Hans Andersen's Fairy Tales, Hodder & Stoughton, [1924]. £450

ditto, Hodder & Stoughton, [1924] (deluxe edition, 500 signed copies, issued with d/w) . . £1,500/£1,000

ditto, Hodder & Stoughton, [1924] (deluxe edition, 500 signed copies, white velum binding) . . . £1,500

ditto, Doran (U.S.), 1924 . . . . £200

Hansel and Gretel and Other Stories, Hodder & Stoughton, [1925] £750

ditto, Hodder & Stoughton, [1925] (600 signed copies, cream buckram binding) £1,500

ditto, Doran (U.S.), [1925] £400

Red Magic: A Collection of the World's Best Fairy Tales from all Countries, edited by Romer Wilson, Cape, 1930 . . . . £600/£150

PATRICK O'BRIAN

(b.1914)

Born in Ireland, O'Brian suffered from a severe illness for which 'sea-voyages' were prescribed, resulting in a life-long love of the sea. His 'Jack Aubrey' series of novels deal with the larger-than-life hero's naval career.

Novels

Three Bear Witness, Secker & Warburg, 1952 . . . . £300/£75

ditto, as ***Testimonies***, Harcourt, Brace & Co. (U.S.), [1952]. . . . . £150/£35

ditto, as ***Testimonies***, Harper Collins, 1994 . £20/£5

The Catalans, Harcourt, Brace & Co. (U.S.), [1953] . . . . £350/£75

ditto, as ***The Frozen Flame***, Hart-Davis, 1953 . . . . £350/£75

Richard Temple, Macmillan, 1962 . . . £125/£35

Master and Commander, Lippincott (U.S.), 1969 . . . . £300/£65

ditto, Collins, 1970 . . . . £500/£125

Post Captain, Collins, 1972 . . . . . £250/£45

ditto, Lippincott (U.S.), 1972 . . . . . £225/£35

H.M.S. Surprise, Collins, 1973 . . . . £350/£45

ditto, Lippincott (U.S.), 1973 . . . . . £150/£35

The Mauritius Command, Collins, 1977 . £300/£45

ditto, Stein & Day (U.S.), 1978 . . . . £150/£35

Desolation Island, Collins, 1978 . . . . £275/£40

ditto, Stein & Day (U.S.), 1979 . . . . £125/£25

The Fortune of War, Collins, 1979 . . . £225/£40

ditto, Norton (U.S.), 1991 (wraps) £25

The Surgeon's Mate, Collins, 1980 . . . £500/£65

ditto, Norton (U.S.), 1992 (wraps) £25

The Ionian Mission, Collins, 1981 . . . £400/£50

ditto, Norton (U.S.), 1992 (wraps) £20

Treason's Harbour, Collins, 1983 . . . £250/£45

ditto, Norton (U.S.), 1992 (wraps) £20

The Far Side of the World, Collins, 1984 . £200/£40

ditto, Norton (U.S.), 1992 (wraps) £20

The Reverse of the Medal, Collins, 1986 . £175/£35

ditto, Norton (U.S.), 1992 (wraps) £20

The Letter of Marque, Collins, 1988 . . £150/£35

ditto, Norton (U.S.), 1991. . . . . . £25/£10

The Thirteen-Gun Salute, Collins, 1989 . £145/£35

ditto, Norton (U.S.), 1991. . . . . . £25/£10

The Nutmeg of Consolation, Collins, 1991 [1990]. . . . . £100/£25

ditto, Norton (U.S.), 1991. . . . . . £25/£10

Clarissa Oakes, Harper Collins, 1992 . . £65/£20

ditto, as ***The Truelove***, Norton (U.S.), 1992 £25/£10

The Wine-Dark Sea, Harper Collins, 1993 . £50/£15

ditto, Norton (U.S.), 1993. . . . . . £15/£5

The Commodore, Harper Collins, 1994 . . £50/£15

ditto, Norton (U.S.), 1994 . . . . . . £15/£5
ditto, Norton (U.S.), 1994 (200 signed, numbered copies, slipcase) . . . . £150/£125
The Yellow Admiral, Norton (U.S.), 1996 . £20/£5
ditto, Harper Collins, 1997 . . . . . £25/£5
The Hundred Days, Harper Collins, 1998 . £20/£5
ditto, Norton (U.S.), 1998. . . . . . . £15/£5

Short Stories
The Last Pool and Other Stories, Secker & Warburg, 1950 . . . . £450/£100
The Walker and Other Stories, Harcourt, Brace & Co. (U.S.), [1955]. . . . . £150/£45
ditto, as ***Lying in the Sun and Other Stories***, Hart-Davis, 1956 (slightly different contents) . £175/£50
The Chian Wine and Other Stories, Collins, 1974 . . . . £125/£30
Collected Short Stories, Harper Collins, 1994 £50/£15
ditto, as ***The Rendezvous and Other Stories***, Norton (U.S.), 1994 . . . . £40/£15

Children's
The Road to Samarcand, Hart-Davis, 1954 £20/£35
The Golden Ocean, Hart-Davis, 1956 . . £250/£45
ditto, John Day (U.S.), 1957 . . . . . . £225/£35
The Unknown Shore, Hart-Davis, 1959. . . £175/£40

Non Fiction
Men-Of-War, Collins, 1974 . . . . . £75/£20
ditto, Norton (U.S.), 1995. . . . . . . £25/£10
Pablo Ruiz Picasso: A Biography, Collins, 1976 . . . . £75/£25
ditto, as ***Picasso: Pablo Ruiz Picasso: A Biography***, Putnam (U.S.), [1976] . . . . . . £75/£25
Joseph Banks: A Life, Collins Harvill, 1987 £65/£20
ditto, Godine (U.S.), 1992 . . . . . . £35/£10

Translations
The Quicksand War, by Lucian Bodard, Faber, 1967 . . . . £75/£20
The Italian Campaign, by Michael Mohart, Weidenfeld, 1967 . . . . £75/£20

Editor
A Book of Voyages, Home and Van Thal, 1947 . . . . £350/£75

EDNA O'BRIEN
(b.1932)

An Irish novelist and short story writer, often concentrating on the position of women in society. Her novels are a blend of bleakness and quiet joy.

Novels
The Country Girls, Hutchinson, 1960 . . £60/£15
ditto, Knopf (U.S.), 1960 . . . . £25/£5
The Lonely Girl, Cape, 1962 . . . . . £40/£10
ditto, Random House (U.S.), 1962 . . . £30/£10
Girls in Their Married Bliss, Cape, 1964 . £20/£5
ditto, Houghton Mifflin (U.S.), 1968. . . £15/£5
August is a Wicked Month, Cape, 1965. . £20/£5
ditto, Simon & Schuster (U.S.), 1965 . . £15/£5
Casualties of Peace, Cape, 1966. . . . £25/£5
ditto, Simon & Schuster (U.S.), 1967 . . £15/£5
A Pagan Place, Weidenfeld, 1970 . . . £15/£5
ditto, Knopf (U.S.), 1970 . . . . £15/£5
Night, Weidenfeld, 1972 . . . . . . £15/£5
ditto, Knopf (U.S.), 1973 . . . . . . £15/£5
Johnnie, I Hardly Knew You, Weidenfeld, 1977 . . . . £15/£5
ditto, as ***I Hardly Knew You***, Doubleday (U.S.), 1978 . . . . £10/£5
The High Road, Weidenfeld, 1988 . . . £15/£5
ditto, London Limited Editions, 1988 (150 signed copies, tissue d/w) . . . . . . £50/£40
ditto, Farrar Straus (U.S.), 1988. . . . . £10/£5
Time and Tide, Viking, 1992. . . . . £10/£5
ditto, Farrar Straus (U.S.), 1992. . . . . £10/£5
House of Splendid Isolation, Weidenfeld, 1994 £10/£5
ditto, Farrar Straus (U.S.), 1994. . . . . £10/£5
Down by the River, Weidenfeld, 1995 . . £10/£5
ditto, Farrar Straus (U.S.), 1997. . . . . £10/£5

Short Stories
The Love Object, Cape, 1968. . . . . £20/£5
ditto, Knopf (U.S.), 1969 . . . . . . £10/£5
A Scandalous Woman, Weidenfeld, 1974 . £15/£5
ditto, Harcourt Brace (U.S.), 1974 . . . £10/£5
Mrs Reinhardt and Other Stories, Weidenfeld, 1978 . . . . £15/£5
ditto, as ***A Rose in the Heart***, Doubleday (U.S.), 1979 . . . . £10/£5
Returning, Weidenfeld, 1982 . . . . £15/£5
A Fanatic Heart, Weidenfeld, 1985 . . . £10/£5
ditto, Franklin Library (U.S.), (signed, limited edition). £20
ditto, Farrar Straus (U.S.), 1984. . . . . £10/£5
Lantern Slides, Weidenfeld, 1990 . . . £10/£5
ditto, Farrar Straus (U.S.), 1990 . . . . . £10/£5

Collected Editions
The Collected Edna O'Brien, Collins, 1978 £15/£5
Some Irish Loving, Weidenfeld, 1979 . . £15/£5
ditto, Harper (U.S.), 1979. . . . . . . £10/£5
The Country Girls Trilogy and Epilogue, Farrar Straus (U.S.), 1986 . . . . £10/£5
ditto, Cape, 1987 . . . . £10/£5

Children's

The Dazzle, Hodder & Stoughton, 1981 . . £15/£5
Christmas Treat, Hodder & Stoughton, 1982 £10/£5
Tales for Telling: Irish Folk and Fairy Stories, Pavilion, 1986 . . . . £10/£5

Plays

A Pagan Place, Faber, 1973 . . . . . . £25/£10
Virginia, Hogarth Press, 1981 . . . . . . £10
ditto, Harcourt Brace (U.S.), 1981 . . . . £10

Others

Zee & Co, Weidenfeld, 1971 . . . . . . £25/£10
Mother Ireland, Weidenfeld, 1976 . . . £15/£5
ditto, Harcourt Brace (U.S.), 1976 . . . £15/£5
Arabian Days, Horizon Press (U.S.), 1977 . £10/£5
ditto, Quartet, 1977 . . . . £10/£5
James and Nora, Lord John Press (US), 1981 (26 signed, lettered copies of 276, slipcase) . £75/£65
ditto, Lord John Press (US), 1981 (250 signed, numbered copies of 276) . . . . . . £50/£40

JOE ORTON

(b.1933 d.1967)

Orton's black farces are a skilful blend of the crude and the clever. His irreverence and ear for comic dialogue are unique.

Plays

Entertaining Mr Sloane, Hamish Hamilton, 1964 . . . . £75/£20
ditto, Grove Press (U.S.), 1965 (wraps) . . . £25
Loot, Methuen, 1967 . . . . £30/£10
ditto, Grove Press (U.S.), 1968 . . . . . £10
Crimes of Passion, Methuen, 1967 . . . £25/£10
ditto, Grove Press (U.S.), 1968 . . . . . £10
What the Butler Saw, Methuen, 1969 . . £25/£10
ditto, Grove Press (U.S.), 1969 . . . . . £10
Funeral Games and The Good and Faithful Servant, Methuen, 1970 . . . . £25/£10
Joe Orton: The Complete Plays, Eyre Methuen, 1976 . . . . £15/£5
ditto, Grove Press (U.S.), 1977 . . . . . £10

Screenplay

Up Against It, Eyre Methuen, 1979 . . . £15/£5
ditto, Grove Press (U.S.), 1979 . . . . £10/£5

Novel

Head to Toe, Blond, 1971 . . . . . £20/£5
ditto, St Martins (U.S.), 1971. . . . . £10/£5

Others

The Orton Diaries, Methuen, 1986 . . . £15/£5
ditto, Harper & Row (U.S.), 1986 . . . . £10/£5

GEORGE ORWELL

(b.1903 d.1950)

A left-wing novelist, essayist and journalist, Orwell, a pseudonym for Eric Blair, is famous for his bleak political satires *Animal Farm* and *Nineteen Eighty Four*.

Novels

Burmese Days, Harper (U.S.), 1934 . . . £650/£100
ditto, Gollancz, 1935 . . . . £750/£125
A Clergyman's Daughter, Gollancz, 1935 . £650/£125
ditto, Harper (U.S.), 1936. . . . . . . £500/£100
Keep the Aspidistra Flying, Gollancz, 1936 £650/£100
ditto, Harcourt Brace (U.S.), 1956 . . . £75/£15
Coming Up for Air, Gollancz, 1939 . . £1,500/£150
ditto, Harcourt Brace (U.S.), 1950 . . . £75/£25
Animal Farm, Secker, 1945 . . . . . . £400/£50
ditto, Harcourt Brace (U.S.), 1946 . . . £75/£25
Nineteen Eighty-Four, Secker, 1949 (maroon d/w) . . . . £450/£50
ditto, Secker, 1949 (green d/w) . . . . £300/£50
ditto, Harcourt Brace (U.S.), 1949 . . . £75/£25

Non Fiction

Down and Out in Paris and London, Gollancz, 1933 . . . . £1,250/£250
ditto, Harper (U.S.), 1933. . . . . . £750/£200
The Road to Wigan Pier, Gollancz, 1937 (Left Book Club Edition). £40
ditto, Gollancz, 1937 . . . . £650/£125
ditto, Gollancz, 1937 (200 copies of the Left Book Club Edition bound separately, without the preface) £200
ditto, Supplementary Left Book Club Edition (part one only, plus photographs) £200
ditto, Harcourt Brace (U.S.), 1958 . . . £45/£15
Homage to Catalonia, Secker, 1938. . . £500/£75
ditto, Harcourt Brace (U.S.), 1952 . . . £45/£15
The Lion and the Unicorn, Secker, 1941 (Searchlight Books, No.1) . . . . £75/£20
James Burnham and the Managerial Revolution, Socialist Book Centre, 1946 (wraps) . . . £200

Essays

Inside the Whale, Gollancz, 1940 . . . £600/£75
Critical Essays, Secker, 1946. . . . . £50/£15
ditto, as ***Dickens, Dali and Others***, Reynal (U.S.), 1946 . . . . £50/£15

The English People, Collins, 1947 . . . £30/£10
Shooting an Elephant, Secker, 1950 . . £45/£10
ditto, Harcourt Brace (U.S.), 1950 . . . £40/£10
Such, Such Were the Joys, Harcourt Brace (U.S.), 1953 . . . . £50/£15
ditto, as ***England, Your England***, Secker, 1953 . . . . £45/£15
The Decline of the English Murder and Other Essays, Penguin, 1965 (wraps) £10
The War Broadcasts, BBC/Duckworth, 1985 £15/£5
The War Commentaries, BBC/Duckworth, 1985 . . . . £15/£5

Selected and Collected Editions
The Orwell Reader, Harcourt Brace (U.S.), 1956 . . . . £35/£10
Selected Essays, Penguin, 1957 (wraps) . . . £10
Selected Writings, Heinemann, 1958 . . £15/£5
The Collected Essays, Journalism and Letters, Secker, 1968 (4 vols) . . . . £150/£45
ditto, Harcourt Brace (U.S.), 1968 (4 vols) . £145/£40
The Penguin Complete Longer Non-fiction of George Orwell, Penguin, 1983 (wraps) £5

JOHN OSBORNE

(b.1929 d.1994)

The author of *Look Back in Anger*, which won the 1956 Evening Standard Award for Best Play, is well known for his 'kitchen sink' dramas.

Plays
Look Back in Anger, Faber, 1957 . . . £60/£15
ditto, Criterion (U.S.), 1957 . . . . . £30/£10
The Entertainer, Faber, 1957 . . . . £40/£10
ditto, Criterion (U.S.), 1958 . . . . . £20/£5
Epitaph for George Dillon, Faber, 1958 (with Anthony Creighton) . . . . £25/£10
ditto, Criterion (U.S.), 1958 . . . . . £10/£5
The World of Paul Slickey, Faber, 1959 . £25/£10
ditto, Criterion (U.S.), 1961 . . . . . £10/£5
A Subject of Scandal and Concern, Faber, 1961 . . . . £35/£15
Luther, Faber, 1961 . . . . £25/£10
ditto, Dramatic Publishing Co. (U.S.), 1961 £10/£5
Plays for England, Faber, 1963 . . . . £25/£10
ditto, Criterion (U.S.), 1964 . . . . . £10/£5
Inadmissible Evidence, Faber, 1965 . . . £25/£10
ditto, Grove Press (U.S.), 1965 . . . . £10/£5
A Patriot for Me, Faber, 1966 . . . . £25/£10
ditto, Random House (U.S.), 1970 . . . . £10/£5
Time Present and ***Hotel in Amsterdam***, Faber, 1968 £20/£5
The Right Prospectus, Faber, 1970 . . . . £15/£5
Very Like a Whale, Faber, 1971 . . . . £15/£5
West of Suez, Faber, 1971 . . . . . £15/£5
The Gift of Friendship, Faber, 1972. . . £15/£5
A Sense of Detachment, Faber, 1973 . . £15/£5
The End of Me Old Cigar, Faber, 1975 . . £15/£5
Watch It Come Down, Faber, 1975 . . . £15/£5
You're Not Watching Me, Mummy, and ***try a Little Tenderness***, Faber, 1978 . . . . . £15/£5
A Better Class of Person and ***God Rot Tunbridge Wells***, Faber, 1985 . . . . £15/£5
Dejavu, Faber, 1992 . . . . £10/£5

Autobiography
A Better Class of Person, Faber, 1981. . . £20/£5
ditto, Dutton (U.S.), 1981 . . . . . . £10/£5
Almost a Gentleman: An Autobiography, Vol II, 1955 -1966, Faber, 1991 . . . . . . £15/£5

Translations/Adaptations
A Bond Honoured, Faber 1966 (from Lope de Vega's ***La Fianza Satisfecha***) . . . . . . £15/£5
Hedda Gabler, Faber 1972 (Ibsen) . . . £10/£5
The Picture of Dorian Gray: A Moral Entertainment, Faber, 1973 (Oscar Wilde) . . . . £10/£5
A Place Calling Itself Rome, Faber, 1973 (based on Shakespeare's ***Coriolanus***) . . . . . £10/£5
Strindberg's 'The Father' and Ibsen's 'Hedda Gabler', Faber, 1989 . . . . £10/£5

Others
Look Back in Anger, Four Square Books, 1960 (novelisation by John Burke, wraps) . . . £5
The Entertainer, Four Square Books, 1960 (novelisation by John Burke, wraps) . . . £5
Tom Jones: A Film Script, Faber, 1964. . £20/£5
ditto, Grove Press (U.S.), 1964 . . . . £10/£5
Damn You, England: Collected Prose, Faber, 1994 . . . . £10/£5

WILFRED OWEN

(b.1893 d.1918)

Owen suffered trench fever and concussion in World War One and was diagnosed 'shell-shocked.' While waiting to return to the trenches he drafted and revised his best poems, but was killed in action only a week before the Armistice.

Verse
Poems, Chatto & Windus, 1920 . . . . £1,500,£200
ditto, Huebsch (U.S.), n.d. [1921] . . . . £750/£150
The Poems of Wilfred Owen, Chatto & Windus 1931 . . . . £200/£50

ditto, Viking (U.S.), 1931 . . . . . . £45/£15
Thirteen Poems, Gehenna Press (U.S.), 1956 (illustrated by Shahn and Baskin, 400 signed copies) £250
ditto, Gehenna Press (U.S.), 1956 (35 signed copies with portrait proof) £750
The Collected Poems of Wilfred Owen, Chatto & Windus, 1963. . . . . £30/£10
ditto, New directions (U.S.), 1964 . . . £25/£10
The Complete Poems and Fragments, Chatto & Windus, 1983 (2 vols, d/ws and slipcase) . £75/£45

Others

Collected Letters, O.U.P., 1967 . . . . £75/£25

MERVYN PEAKE

(b.1911 d.1968)

Peake's strength in both his writing and drawing is in the creation of atmosphere through often grotesque detail. His verse is of the nonsense school.

Verse

Shapes and Sounds, Chatto & Windus, 1941 £200/£50
Rhymes Without Reason, Eyre & Spottiswoode, 1944. . . . . £100/£30
The Glassblowers, Eyre & Spottiswoode, 1950 . . . . £75/£25
The Rhyme of the Flying Bomb, Dent, 1962 £40/£10
Poems and Drawings, Keepsake Press, 1965 (150 copies, wraps) £200
A Reverie of Bone, Rota, 1967 (320 copies, wraps with d/w) . . . . £100/£50
A Book of Nonsense, Owen, 1972 . . . . £25/£10
ditto, Dufour (U.S.), 1975. . . . . . £20/£10
Selected Poems, Faber, 1972 . . . . . £25/£10
Twelve Poems, 1939-1960, Bran's Head, 1975 (350 numbered copies, wraps with glassine dw). £40/£30

Novels

Titus Groan, Eyre & Spottiswoode, 1946 . £200/£25
ditto, Reynal and Hitchcock (U.S.), 1946 . £75/£15
Gormenghast, Eyre & Spottiswoode, 1950 . £125/£20
ditto, Weybright & Talley, (U.S.), 1967 . £15/£5
Mr Pye, Heinemann, 1953 . . . . . £50/£15
Titus Alone, Eyre & Spottiswoode, 1959 . £75/£20
ditto, Weybright & Talley, (U.S.), 1967 . £15/£5
ditto, Eyre & Spottiswoode, 1970 (revised edition). . . . . £25/£5

Children's

Captain Slaughterboard Drops Anchor, Country Life, 1939 . . . . £1,000/£250
ditto, Eyre and Spottiswoode, 1945 . . . £300/£75
ditto, Macmillan, (U.S.), 1967 . . . . £30/£10
Letters from a Lost Uncle from Polar Regions, Eyre & Spottiswoode, 1948 . . . . £75

Others

The Craft of the Lead Pencil, Wingate, 1946 . £60
The Drawings of Mervyn Peake, Grey Walls Press, 1949 . . . . £75/£35
Figures of Speech, Gollancz, 1954 . . . £50/£20
The Drawings of Mervyn Peake, Davis-Poynter, 1974 . . . . £30/£10
Mervyn Peake: Writings and Drawings, Academy, 1974 . . . . £20/£10
ditto, St Martin's (U.S.), 1974 . . . . £20/£10
Peake's Progress: Selected Writings and Drawings, John Lane, 1979 . . . . £20/£10
ditto, Overlook Press (U.S.), 1981 . . . £20/£10

CHARLES PERRAULT

(b.1628 d.1703)

A French author and folklorist who popularised and gave lasting form to such fairy tales as *Little Red Riding Hood* and *Cinderella*.

Histoires, Ou Contes du Tempes Passé, Avec des Moralitez, (Paris), 1697 . . . . £7,500
Les Contes de Perrault, (Paris), 1862 (illustrated by Gustav Doré) £250
Perrault's Popular Tales, edited by Andrew Lang, Clarendon Press, 1888 . . . . £75
Tales of Passed Times, Dent, 'Temple Classics for Young People' series, [1899] (illustrated by Charles Robinson). £50
Contes de Perrault, adapted by Kathleen Fitzgerald, Siegle & Hill, 1910 (illustrated by Margaret Tarrant) £75
Perrault's Fairy Tales, translated by S.R. Littlewood, Herbert Daniel, [1911] (illustrated by Honor C. Appleton) £75
The Sleeping Beauty and Other Tales, Blackie, [1912] (illustrated by John Hassall). £50
Fairy Tales, Dent, [1913] (illustrated by Charles Robinson). £65
Cinderella, adapted by E.L. Elias, Harrap, [1915] (illustrated by Willy Pogany) £40
ditto, adapted by Githa Sowerby, Hodder & Stoughton, [1915] (illustrated by Millicent Sowerby) . . £75
ditto, adapted by Charles S. Evans, Heinemann, 1919 (illustrated by Arthur Rackham, pictorial boards) £150
ditto, Heinemann, 1919 (deluxe, 525 signed copies, printed on handmade paper, green boards with tan

cloth spine) £500

ditto, Heinemann, 1919 (deluxe, 325 signed copies, printed on Japanese vellum, vellum-backed cream boards) £750

The Sleeping Beauty, adapted by Charles S. Evans, Heinemann, 1920 (illustrated by Arthur Rackham, pictorial boards with red cloth backstrip) . . £100

ditto, Heinemann, 1920 (deluxe 625 signed copies, vellum-backed cream boards) £500

Old Time Stories, translated by A.E. Johnson, Constable, 1921 (illustrated by W. Heath Robinson; cloth or buckram binding) £250

The Fairy Tales of Charles Perrault, Harrap, [1922] (illustrated by Harry Clarke, cloth or buckram binding) £250

ditto, Harrap, [1922] (deluxe edition, Persian Levant leather binding) £450

Tales of Past Times, Selwyn & Blount, 1922 (illustrated by John Austen) £75

ditto, Selwyn & Blount, 1922 (200 copies, signed by the artist) £150

ELLIS PETERS

(b.1913 d.1995)

Edith Pargeter has written many books under her own name and such pseudonyms as Jolyon Carr and Peter Benedict. However, it is as Ellis Peters that she is best known. As Peters she has given the world a literary sleuth who is also a Benedictine monk, the now televised Brother Cadfael.

Brother Cadfael Novels

A Morbid Taste for Bones: A Mediaeval Whodunnit, Macmillan, 1977 . . . . £600/£75

ditto, Morrow (U.S.), 1978 . . . . . £250/£35

One Corpse Too Many, Macmillan, 1979 . £400/£75

ditto, Morrow (U.S.), 1980 . . . . . £150/£25

Monk's Hood, Macmillan, 1980 . . . . £400/£75

ditto, Morrow (U.S.), 1981 . . . . . £50/£15

Saint Peter's Fair, Macmillan, 1981. . . . £300/£50

ditto, Morrow (U.S.), 1981 . . . . . £40/£15

The Leper of Saint Giles, Macmillan, 1981. £150/£40

ditto, Morrow (U.S.), 1982 . . . . . £30/£15

The Virgin in the Ice, Macmillan, 1982. . £125/£25

ditto, Morrow (U.S.), 1983 . . . . . £35/£15

The Sanctuary Sparrow, Macmillan, 1983 . £100/£20

ditto, Morrow (U.S.), 1983 . . . . . £30/£10

The Devil's Novice, Macmillan, 1983 . . £100/£20

ditto, Morrow (U.S.), 1984 . . . . . £30/£10

Dead Man's Ransom, Macmillan, 1984. . £90/£15

ditto, Morrow (U.S.), 1984 . . . . . £35/£10

The Pilgrim of Hate, Macmillan, 1984 . . £90/£15

ditto, Morrow (U.S.), 1984 . . . . . £25/£10

An Excellent Mystery, Macmillan, 1985 . £85/£15

ditto, Morrow (U.S.), 1986 . . . . . £20/£5

The Raven in the Foregate, Macmillan, 1986 £40/£10

ditto, Morrow (U.S.), 1986 . . . . . £20/£5

The Rose Rent, Macmillan, 1986 . . . £40/£10

ditto, Morrow (U.S.), 1986 . . . . . £20/£5

The Hermit of Eyton Forest, Headline, 1987 £40/£10

ditto, Mysterious Press (U.S.), 1988 . . . £20/£5

The Confession of Brother Haluin, Headline, 1988 . . . . £40/£10

ditto, Mysterious Press (U.S.), 1989 . . . £20/£5

The Heretic's Apprentice, Headline, 1989 . £35/£10

ditto, Mysterious Press (U.S.), 1990 . . . £20/£5

The Potter's Field, Headline, 1989 . . . £25/£10

ditto, Mysterious Press (U.S.), 1990 . . . £20/£5

The Summer of the Danes, Headline, 1991. £25/£10

ditto, Mysterious Press (U.S.), 1990 . . . £20/£5

The Holy Thief, Headline, 1992 . . . . £20/£5

ditto, Mysterious Press (U.S.), 1993 . . . £20/£5

Brother Cadfael's Penance, Headline, 1994 £15/£5

ditto, Headline, 1994 (97 signed, numbered uncorrected proof copy, wraps) £100

Brother Cadfael Short Stories

A Rare Benedict, Headline, 1988 . . . £25/£5

ditto, Mysterious Press (U.S.), 1989 . . . £20/£5

The 'Felse' Series

Death and the Joyful Woman, Collins, 1961 £125/£25

ditto, Doubleday (U.S.), 1961 . . . . £100/£25

Flight of a Witch, Collins, 1964 . . . . £100/£25

ditto, Mysterious Press (U.S.), 1991 . . . £20/£5

A Nice Derangement of Epitaphs, Collins, 1965 . . . . £100/£25

The Piper on the Mountain, Collins, 1966 . £50/£15

ditto, Morrow (U.S.), 1966 . . . . . £45/£10

Black is the Colour of My True-Love's Heart, Collins, 1967 . . . . £50/£15

ditto, Morrow (U.S.), 1967 . . . . . £45/£10

The Grass Widow's Tale, Collins, 1968. . £50/£15

The House of Green Turf, Collins, 1969 . £45/£10

ditto, Morrow (U.S.), 1969 . . . . . £30/£10

Mourning Raga, Macmillan, 1969 . . . £45/£10

ditto, Morrow (U.S.), 1970 . . . . . £20/£5

The Knocker on Death's Door, Macmillan, 1970 . . . . £40/£10

ditto, Morrow (U.S.), 1971 . . . . . £20/£5

Death to the Landlords!, Macmillan, 1972 . £30/£10

ditto, Morrow (U.S.), 1972 . . . . . £20/£5

City of Gold and Shadows, Macmillan, 1973 £30/£10

ditto, Morrow (U.S.), 1974 . . . . . £20/£5

Rainbow's End, Macmillan, 1978 . . . £30/£10

ditto, Morrow (U.S.), 1979 . . . . . £20/£5

Novels by Edith Pargeter
Hortensius, Friend of Nero, Lovat Dickson, 1936 (125 signed copies) . . . . £400/£75
ditto, Greystone Press (U.S.), 1937 . . . £100/£35
Iron-Bound, Lovat Dickson, 1936 . . . £250/£50
The City Lies Foursquare, Heinemann, 1939 £100/£15
Ordinary People, Heinemann, 1941 . . . £75/£15
She Goes to War, Heinemann, 1942 . . . £75/£15
The Eighth Champion of Christendom, Heinemann, 1945 . . . . £50/£15
Reluctant Odyssey, Heinemann, 1946 . . . £50/£15
Warfare Accomplished, Heinemann, 1947 . £50/£15
By Firelight, Heinemann, 1948 . . . . £45/£15
The Fair Young Phoenix, Heinemann, 1948 £45/£15
Lost Children, Heinemann, 1942. . . . £45/£15
Fallen into the Pit, Heinemann, 1951 . . £45/£15
Holiday with Violence, Heinemann, 1952 . £45/£15
This Rough Magic, Heinemann, 1953 . . £45/£15
Most Loving Mere Folly, Heinemann, 1953 £45/£15
The Soldier at the Door, Heinemann, 1954 . £45/£15
A Means of Race, Heinemann, 1956. . . £45/£15
The Heaven Tree, Heinemann, 1960 . . £40/£15
The Green Branch, Heinemann, 1962 . . £35/£10
The Scarlet Seed, Heinemann, 1963 . . £35/£10
A Bloody Field by Shrewsbury, Macmillan, 1972 . . . . £35/£10
Sunrise in the West, Macmillan, 1974 . . £35/£10
The Dragon at Noonday, Macmillan, 1975 . £35/£10
The Hounds of Sunset, Macmillan, 1976 . £35/£10
Afterglow and Nightfall, Macmillan, 1977 . £35/£10
The Marriage of Meggotta, Macmillan, 1979 £35/£10

Short Stories by Edith Pargeter
The Assize of the Dying, Heinemann, 1958 £50/£15
ditto, Doubleday (U.S.), 1958 . . . . £25/£10
The Lily Hand, Heinemann, 1965 . . . £75/£15

Novels by Ellis Peters
Death Mask, Collins, 1959 . . . . . £125/£35
ditto, Doubleday (U.S.), 1960 . . . . £100/£25
The Will and the Deed, Collins, 1960 . . £75/£20
Funeral of Figaro, Collins, 1962 . . . £65/£15
ditto, Morrow (U.S.), 1964 . . . . . £45/£10
The Horn of Roland, Macmillan, 1974 . . £60/£15
ditto, Morrow (U.S.), 1974 . . . . . £40/£10
Never Pick Up Hitchhikers!, Macmillan, 1976 £50/£10
ditto, Morrow (U.S.), 1974 . . . . . £30/£10

Novels by Jolyon Carr
Murder in the Dispensary, Herbert Jenkins, 1938 . . . . £175/£45
ditto, Post Mort (U.S.), 1999 (350 signed, numbered copies, no d/w) £50
Freedom for Two, Herbert Jenkins, 1938 . £150/£40
Death Comes by Post, Herbert Jenkins, 1940 £150/£40
Masters of the Parachute Mail, Herbert Jenkins, 1940 . . . . £150/£40

Novels by John Redfern
The Victim Needs a Nurse, Jarrolds, 1940 . £150/£35

Others
The Coast of Bohemia, Heinemann, 1950 (by Edith Pargeter) . . . . £75/£25
Strongholds and Sanctuaries, Sutton, 1993 £35/£10

GLADYS PETO

(b.1890 d.1977)

A British illustrator who contributed an illustrated diary to the *Sketch* between 1915 and 1926. She published a number of light-hearted travel books, but it is her series of children's annuals from the 1930s that are generally collected.

Gladys Peto's Children Annual 1923, Sampson Low, 1923 . . . . £50
Gladys Peto's Children Annual 1924, Sampson Low, 1924 . . . . £50
Daphne and the Fairy and Other Stories, Sampson Low, 1924 . . . . £75
Joan's Visit to Toyland and Other Tales, Sampson Low, 1924 . . . . £75
Snowman and Other Tales, Sampson Low, 1924 £75
Gladys Peto's Children's Book, Sampson Low, 1925 . . . . £50
Malta and Cyprus, Dent, 1926 . . . . . £75
The China Cow and Other Stories, by Sewell Stokes and others, Sampson Low, [1929] £50
Gladys Peto's Bedtime Stories, Shaw, [1931] . £50
Twilight Stories, Shaw, [1932] £50
Gladys Peto's Girls' Own Stories, Shaw. [1933] £50
Sunshine Tales, Shaw, [1935] £50
The Four-Leaved Clover and Other Stories, Juvenile Productions, [1937] £50

HAROLD PINTER

(b.1930)

A playwright who created, in his best work, a 'comedy of menace'; claustrophobic situations in which there is an indefinable threat hanging over the characters.

Plays
The Birthday Party, Encore Publishing, [1959] (wraps) £75

The Birthday Party and Other Plays, Methuen, 1960 . . . . £50/£15
ditto, Grove (U.S.), 1961 . . . . £25/£10
The Caretaker, Encore Publishing, 1960 (wraps) £65
ditto, Methuen, 1960 . . . . £45/£10
A Night Out, French, 1961 (wraps) £10
A Slight Ache and Other Plays, Methuen, 1961 . . . . £25/£10
The Birthday Party and The Room, Grove Press (U.S.), 1961 . . . . £15/£5
The Collection, French, 1962. . . . . . . £15
Three Plays, Grove Press (U.S.), 1962 . . . £15/£5
The Lover, Dramatists Play Service (U.S.), 1965 £15
The Dwarfs and Eight Review Sketches, Dramatists Play Service (U.S.), 1965 (wraps) £15
The Homecoming, Methuen, 1965 . . . . £15/£5
ditto, Grove Press (U.S.), 1966 . . . . . £10/£5
ditto, Karnac, 1969 (200 signed, numbered copies) £65
The Collection and The Lover, Methuen, 1966 £15/£5
Tea Party, Methuen, 1965 . . . . . . £15/£5
ditto, Vanista (Zagreb), 1965 (280 numbered copies) £50
ditto, Grove Press (U.S.), 1966 . . . . . £10/£5
Tea Party and Other Plays, Methuen, 1967 £10/£5
Early Plays, Grove Press (U.S.), 1968 (wraps) £10
Landscape, Pendragon Press, 1968 (2,000 numbered copies) £45
Landscape and Silence, Methuen, 1969. . £15/£5
ditto, Grove Press (U.S.), 1970 . . . . . £10/£5
Old Times, Eyre Methuen, 1971 . . . . £15/£5
ditto, Karnac, 1971 (150 signed, nubered copies) £75
ditto, Grove Press (U.S.), 1971 . . . . . £10/£5
No Man's Land, Eyre Methuen, 1975 . . . £15/£5
ditto, Karnac, 1975 (150 signed, numbered copies, glassine d/w) £65
ditto, Grove Press (U.S.), 1975 . . . . . £10/£5
Betrayal, Eyre Methuen, 1978 . . . . £15/£5
ditto, Karnac, 1978 (150 signed, numbered copies) £65
ditto, Grove Press (U.S.), 1979 . . . . . £10/£5
The Hothouse, Eyre Methuen, 1980 . . . . £15/£5
ditto, Grove Press (U.S.), 1989 . . . . . £10/£5
Other Places, Methuen, 1982. . . . . . £15/£5
ditto, Grove Press (U.S.), 1983 . . . . . £10/£5
One for the Road, Methuen, 1985 . . . . £15/£5
Mountain Language, Faber, 1988 . . . . £15/£5
ditto, Grove Weidenfeld, (U.S.), 1988 . . . £10/£5
The Heat of the Day, Faber, 1989 . . . . £15/£5
ditto, Grove Weidenfeld, (U.S.), 1990 . . . £10/£5
Party Time, Faber, 1991 . . . . £15/£5
Moonlight, Faber, 1993 . . . . £10/£5

Verse
Poems, Enitharmon Press, 1968 (200 signed copies, no d/w) £100
ditto, Enitharmon Press, 1971 (2nd edition, enlarged, 100 signed copies) £75
Poems and Prose, 1949-1977, Grove Press, 1978 . . . . £10/£5
ditto, Eyre Methuen, 1978 . . . . £10/£5
I Know The Place, Greville Press, 1979 (500 signed copies, no d/w) £50
11 Early Poems, Greville Press, 1992 (wraps) . £10

Novel
The Dwarfs, Faber, 1990 . . . . £15/£5
ditto, London Limited Editions, 1990 (150 signed copies) . . . . £65/£35
ditto, Grove Weidenfeld (U.S.), 1990 . . . £10/£5

Others
The Homecoming: Images, by Harold Cohen, Cohen, 1968 (175 copies) £75
ditto, Cohen, 1968 (25 copies, additional set of plates, slipcase) £150
Mac, Pendragon Press, 1968 (2,000 numbered copies, no d/w) £30
Five Screenplays, Methuen, 1971 . . . . £15/£5
ditto, Methuen, 1971 (wraps) £5
ditto, Karnac, 1971 (150 signed, numbered copies) £75
ditto, Grove (U.S.), 1973 . . . . £10/£5
Monologue, Covent Garden Press, 1973 . £25/£10
ditto, Covent Garden Press, 1973 (100 signed copies in slipcase) . . . . £125/£100
The Proust Screenplay, Grove Press (U.S.), 1977 . . . . £10/£5
ditto, Eyre Methuen, 1978 . . . . £10/£5
The French Lieutenant's Woman, A Screenplay, Cape, 1981 . . . . £15/£5
ditto, Little Brown (U.S.), 1981 . . . . . £15/£5
ditto, Little Brown (U.S.), 1981 (360 signed, numbered copies) . . . . £75/£45
The French Lieutenant's Woman and Other Screenplays, Methuen, 1982 . . . £15/£5
The Comfort of Strangers and Other Screenplays, Faber, 1990 . . . . £15/£5

SYLVIA PLATH
(b.1932 d.1963)

American poet whose poems display an ironic tone and an undercurrent of terror. Married to Ted Hughes, she committed suicide in 1963.

Verse
Sculptor, Grecourt Review, 1959 (wraps) . . £1,000
A Winter Ship, Tragara Press (Edinburgh), 1960 (anonymous leaflet) £700
The Colossus and Other Poems, Heinemann, 1960 .

. . . . £600/£150
ditto, Knopf (U.S.), 1962 . . . . £150/£45
ditto, as ***The Colossus***, Heinemann, 1967 . £15/£5
Ariel, Faber, 1965 . . . . £150/£20
ditto, Harper (U.S.), 1966. . . . . £100/£15
Uncollected Poems, Turret Books, 1965 (150 copies, wraps) £100
Wreath for a Bridal, Sceptre Press, 1970 (150 copies, wraps) £100
Million Dollar Month, Sceptre Press, 1971 (150 copies, wraps) £100
Fiesta Melons: Poems, Rougemont Press, 1971 (75 copies of 150, signed by Ted Hughes) . . £250/£175
ditto, Rougemont Press, 1971 (75 unsigned copies of 150) . . . . £125/£45
Child, Rougemont Press, 1971 (325 copies, wraps with d/w) . . . . £75/£35
Crystal Gazer, Rainbow Press, 1971 (400 copies, slipcase) . . . . £100/£65
ditto, Rainbow Press, 1971 (80 morocco bound copies) £200
Lyonesse, Rainbow Press, 1971 (300 copies bound in quarter leather) £150
ditto, Rainbow Press, 1971 (90 copies bound in full calf) £300
ditto, Rainbow Press, 1971 (10 bound in vellum) £500
Crossing the Water, Faber, 1971. . . . . £50/£15
ditto, Harper (U.S.), 1971. . . . . . . £40/£10
Winter Trees, Faber, 1971 . . . . . . £25/£10
ditto, Harper (U.S.), 1972. . . . . . . £15/£5
Pursuit, Rainbow Press, 1973 (100 copies) . . £100
Two Poems, Sceptre Press, [1980] (225 of 300 copies, wraps) £30
ditto, Sceptre Press, [1980] (75 "especial" of 300 copies, wraps) £60
Two Uncollected Poems, Anvil Press, 1980 (450 copies, wraps) £25
Collected Poems, Faber, 1981 . . . . £20/£5
ditto, Harper (U.S.), 1981. . . . . . . £10/£5
Dialogue Over a Ouija Board, Rainbow Press, 1981 (140 copies) £100

Novel
The Bell Jar, Heinemann, 1963 (pseud. 'Victoria Lucas') . . . . £1,000/£200
ditto, Faber, 1966 (as 'Sylvia Plath') . . . £50/£15
ditto, Harper, (U.S.), 1971 (as 'Sylvia Plath') £40/£10

Plays
Three Women, Turret Books, 1968 (180 copies, glassine d/w) . . . . £150/£125

Children's
The Bed Book, Faber, 1976 . . . . . £35/£10
ditto, Harper (U.S.), 1976. . . . . . . £25/£10

Others
The Art of Sylvia Plath: A Symposium, Faber, 1970 . . . . £50
Letters Home, Harper (U.S.), 1975 . . . . £20/£5
ditto, Faber, 1976 . . . . £20/£5
Johnny Panic and the Bible of Dreams and Other Writings, Faber, 1977 . . . . £20/£5
Johnny Panic and the Bible of Dreams: Short Stories, Prose and Diary Excerpts, Harper (U.S.), 1979 . . . . £20/£5
The Magic Mirror: A Study of the Doublein Two of Dostoevsky's Novels, Embers Handpress, 1989 (50 copies, 'Oxford Hollow' binding, slipcase) £200/£125
ditto, Embers Handpress, 1989 (176 copies, in dustjacket) . . . . £125/£65

EDGAR ALLAN POE
(b.1809 d.1849)

An American poet and short story writer, Poe is best known for often anthologised horror tales such as 'The Fall of the House of Usher'. 'The Murder in the Rue Morgue' signalled the birth of the detective fiction genre.

Verse
Tamerlane and Other Poems, by a Bostonian, Calvin F.S. Thomas (U.S.), 1827 (wraps) . . . £100,000
ditto, Redway, 1884 (100 copies) £1,500
Al AAraaf, Tamerlane and Minor Poems, Hatch & Dunning (U.S.), 1829 . . . . £40,000
Poems, Elam Bliss (U.S.), 1831 . . . . . £15,000
The Raven and Other Poems, Wiley & Putnam (U.S.), 1845 (wraps) £40,000
ditto, Wiley & Putnam, 1845 (cloth) £30,000

Fiction
The Narrative of Arthur Gordon Pym of Nantucket, Harper Bros. (U.S.), 1838 (anonymous) . . £2,500
ditto, Wiley & Putnum, 1838 (cloth) £1,000
Tales of the Grotesque and Arabesque, Lea & Blanchard (U.S.), 1840 (page 213 wrongly numbered, 2 vols). £14,000
ditto, Lea & Blanchard (U.S.), 1840 (page 213 correctly numbered, 2 vols) £9,000
ditto, Lea & Blanchard (U.S.), 1840 (page 213 correctly numbered, 1 vol.) £7,000
The Murders in the Rue Morgue, and the Man that was Used Up, William H. Graham (U.S.), 1843 (wraps) £15,000
Tales, Wiley & Putnum (U.S.), 1845 (wraps) £25,000
ditto, Wiley & Putnam, 1845 . . . . . . £12,500
Eureka, A Prose Poem, Putnam (U.S.), 1848 . £2,500

Others
The Conchologist's First Book, Haswell, Barrington & Baswell (U.S.), 1839 (coloured plates) . . . £1,500
ditto, Haswell, Barrington & Baswell (U.S.), 1839 (uncoloured plates) £1,000
ditto, 1840 (2nd edition) £250
Mesmerism, 'In Articulo Mortis', Short & Co., 1846 (wraps) £1,000

BEATRIX POTTER
(b.1866 d.1943)

British author and illustrator. *The Tale of Peter Rabbit* was first written down in a letter to the son of one of her governesses. It was later privately printed in an edition of 250 copies, the first of a highly successful series of books for the very young.

The Tale of Peter Rabbit, privately printed, [1901] (250 copies, flat spine) £20,000
ditto, privately printed, 1902 (200 copies, round spine) £15,000
ditto, Warne, [1902] (trade edition, cloth) . . £3,000
ditto, Warne, 1902 (trade edition, boards) . . £2,000
ditto, Warne, 1902 (deluxe edition) £4,000
ditto, Warne, 1993 (boxed set containing facsimiles of the 1901 first edition, the first Warne cloth-bound edition of 1902, and the original 'Peter Rabbit' letter from Beatrix Potter, 750 numbered sets) . . £100
The Tailor of Gloucester, privately printed, 1902 (500 copies) £2,500
ditto, Warne, 1903 (trade edition) £500
ditto, Warne, 1903 (deluxe edition) £4,000
ditto, Warne, 1903 (art cloth binding) . . . £2,500
ditto, Warne, 1968 (facsimile of the original manuscript and illustrations, 1,500 numbered copies in box) . . . . £75/£45
ditto, Warne, 1969 (facsimile of the original manuscript) £45
The Tale of Squirrel Nutkin, Warne, 1903 . . £350
ditto, Warne, 1903 (deluxe edition) £4,000
ditto, Warne, 1903 (art cloth binding) £2,500
The Tale of Benjamin Bunny, Warne, 1904 . £350
ditto, Warne, 1904 (deluxe edition) £4,000
The Tale of Two Bad Mice, Warne, 1904 . . £250
ditto, Warne, 1904 (deluxe edition) £4,000
The Tale of Mrs Tiggy-Winkle, Warne, 1905 . £300
ditto, Warne, 1905 (deluxe edition) £4,000
The Pie and the Patty Pan, Warne, 1905 (large format) £150
ditto, Warne, 1905 (deluxe edition) £2,500
The Tale of Mr Jeremy Fisher, Warne, 1906 . £175
ditto, Warne, 1906 (deluxe edition) £2,500
The Story of a Fierce Bad Rabbit, Warne, 1906 (panorama) £350
The Story of Miss Moppet, Warne, 1906, (panorama) £350
The Tale of Tom Kitten, Warne, 1907 . . . £250
ditto, Warne, 1907 (deluxe edition) £2,500
The Tale of Jemima Puddle-Duck, Warne, 1908 . . . . £350
ditto, Warne, 1908 (deluxe edition) £2,500
The Roly-Poly Pudding, Warne, 1908 (large format) £300
ditto, as ***The Tale of Samuel Whiskers***, Warne, [1926] £125
The Tale of the Flopsy Bunnies, Warne, 1909 . £300
ditto, Warne, 1909 (deluxe edition) £2,500
Ginger and Pickles, Warne, 1909 (large format) £200
The Tale of Mrs Tittlemouse, Warne, 1910. . £225
ditto, Warne, 1910 (deluxe edition) £2,500
Peter Rabbit's Painting Book, Warne, [1911] . £300
The Tale of Timmy Tiptoes, Warne, 1911 . . £250
ditto, Warne, 1911 (deluxe edition) £2,250
The Tale of Mr Tod, Warne, 1912 . . . . £250
The Tale of Pigling Bland, Warne, 1913 . . £250
Appley Dapply's Nursery Rhymes, Warne, 1917 . . . . £300
Tom Kitten's Painting Book, Warne, 1917 . . £250
The Tale of Johnny Town-Mouse, Warne, [1918] £200
Cecily Parsley's Nursery Rhymes, Warne, 1922, (small format) £450
Jemima Puddle-Duck's Painting Book, Warne, [1925] £200
Peter Rabbit's Almanac for 1929, Warne, [1928] £350
The Fairy Caravan, McKay (U.S.), 1929 . . £125
ditto, Warne, 1952. . . . . £100/£50
The Tale of Little Pig Robinson, Warne, [1930] (large format) . . . . £350/£200
Sister Anne, McKay (U.S.), 1932 . . . . . £125
Wag-By-Wall, Warne, [1944] (100 copies) . . £300
Jemima Puddle-Duck's Painting Book, From the Original Designs by B. Potter, Warne [1954] £50
Jeremy Fisher's Painting Book, From the Original Designs by B. Potter, Warne, [1954] . . . £50
Peter Rabbit's Painting Book, From the Original Designs by B. Potter, Warne, [1954] . . . £50
Tom Kitten's Painting Book, From the Original Designs by B. Potter, Warne, [1954] . . . £50
The Tale of the Faithful Dove, Warne, [1955] (100 copies, illustrated by Marie Angel) £1,000
The Sly Old Cat, Warne, 1971 (issued with d/w) . . . . £20/£5
The Tale of Tupenny, Warne, 1973 (illustrated by Marie Angel) . . . . £10/£5

EZRA POUND
(b.1885 d.1972)

An American poet, Pound is generally acknowledged as one of the prime movers of modern poetry.

Verse

A Lume Spento, Antonini (Venice), 1908 (100 copies, wraps). £25,000
ditto, New Directions (U.S.), 1965 (acetate d/w) . . . . £45/£15
ditto, Faber, 1965 . . . . £20/£5
A Quinzane for this Yule, privately printed, 1908 (wraps) £20,000
ditto, Elkin Mathews, 1908 (wraps) £7,500
Personae, Elkin Mathews, 1909 (500 copies) . £500
ditto, Boni and Liveright (U.S.), 1926. . . . £450/£75
Exultations, Elkin Mathews, 1909 (500 copies) £350
Provenca, Small Maynard (U.S.), 1910 (200 copies) £350
Canzoni, Elkin Mathews, 1911 (grey cloth, author's name on cover) £300
ditto, Elkin Mathews, 1911 (brown boards, without author's name on cover) £200
Ripostes, Stephen Swift, 1912 . . . . . . £500
ditto, Small Maynard (U.S.), 1913 . . . . . £250
Lustra, Elkin Mathews, [1916] (200 numbered copies, unexpurgated version for private circulation) £1,000
ditto, Elkin Mathews, 1916 (expurgated trade edition) £600
ditto, Knopf (U.S.), 1917 . . . . . . £1,250/£400
Pavannes and Divisions, Knopf (U.S.), 1918 . £150
ditto, Peter Owen, 1960 . . . . £35/£10
Quia Pauper Amavi, The Egoist, [1919] (100 signed copies, handmade paper) £1,500
ditto, The Egoist, [1919] (10 signed copies, roman numerals) £3,500
ditto, The Egoist, [1919] £300
The Fourth Canto, Ovid Press, 1919 (40 copies for private circulation) £5,000
Hugh Selwyn Mauberley, Ovid Press, 1920 (165 unsigned copies) £2,500
ditto, Ovid Press, 1920 (35 signed copies) . . £5,000
Umbra, Elkin Mathews, 1920 . . . . . £400/£150
ditto, Elkin Mathews, 1920 (100 signed copies) £2,000
ditto, Elkin Mathews, 1920 (signed, lettered copies) £4,000
Poems, 1918-21, Boni and Liveright (U.S.), 1921 . . . . £450/£175
Indiscretions; Or, Une Revue de Deux Mondes, Three Mountains Press, 1923 (300 numbered copies) £500
ditto, Three Mountains Press, 1923 (300 numbered copies, unbound sheets) £400
A Draft of XVI Cantos, Three Mountains Press, 1925 (90 copies) £1,500
A Draft of Cantos 12-27, Three Mountain Press, 1928 . . . . £500
Selected Poems, Faber, 1928 (100 signed copies) £2,000
ditto, Faber, 1928 . . . . £250/£100
A Draft of XXX Cantos, Hours Press, 1930 (200 unsigned copies) £1,250
ditto, Hours Press, 1930 (10 signed copies) . . £6,000
ditto, Farrar & Rinehart (U.S.), 1933 ("shit" on page 62). £750
ditto, Farrar & Rinehart (U.S.), 1933 ("sh-t" on page 62). . . . . £200/£45
ditto, Faber, 1933 . . . . £100/£35
Imaginary Letters, Black Sun Press (Paris), 1930 (50 signed copies on Japansese vellum, wraps with glassine d/w and slipcase) £2,000
ditto, Black Sun Press (Paris), 1930 (300 copies, wraps with glassine d/w and slipcase) £350
Eleven New Cantos: XXXI-XLI, Farrar & Rineheart (U.S.), 1934 . . . . £145/£40
ditto, as ***Draft of Cantos XXXI-XLI***, Faber, 1935 . . . . £125/£30
Homage to Sextus Propertius, Faber, 1934 £150/£45
The Fifth Decad of Cantos, Faber, 1937 . £150/£45
ditto, Farrar & Rinehart (U.S.), 1937. . . . £90/£25
ditto, New Directions (U.S.), 1940 . . . . £90/£25
Cantos LII-LXXI, Faber, 1940 . . . . . £150/£45
ditto, New Directions (U.S.), 1940 (500 copies with envelope and pamphlet) . . . . £200/£75
ditto, New Directions (U.S.), 1940 (500 copies without envelope and pamphlet) . . . . £100/£35
The Pisan Cantos, New Directions (U.S.), 1948 . . . . £250/£70
ditto, Faber, 1949 . . . . £250/£50
Section: Rock-Drill, Pesce d'Oro (Milan), 1955 £200
ditto, New Directions (U.S.), 1956 . . . . £45/£15
ditto, Faber, 1957 . . . . £45/£15
Diptych Rome-London, New Directions (U.S.), 1957 (125 signed copies in slipcase) £750
ditto, Faber, 1957 (50 signed copies in slipcase) £1,000
ditto, Vanni Scheiwiller (Italy), 1957 (25 signed copies in slipcase) £1,500
Thrones, Pesce d'Oro (Milan), 1959 (300 copies) £125
ditto, New Directions (U.S.), 1959 . . . . £45/£15
ditto, Faber, 1960 . . . . £45/£15
The Cantos, Faber, 1964 (all 109 cantos) . £35/£10
Cavalcanti Poems, New Directions (U.S.), [1966] (200 signed copies, glassine d/w, slipcase) £1,500/£1,250
ditto, Faber, (1966) (190 signed copies in slipcase). . . . . £1,000/£850
Drafts and Fragments of Cantos CX-CXVII, New Directions (U.S.), 1969 . . . . £40/£15
ditto, New Directions (U.S.), 1969 (200 signed, numbered copies, slipcase) . . . . . . £500/£400
ditto, Stone Wall Press (U.S.), 1969 (10 signed,

numbered copies, slipcase) . . . . £1,000/£850
ditto, Faber, 1970 (200 signed, numbered copies, slipcase) . . . . £300/£250
ditto, Faber, 1970 . . . . £40/£15

Others
The Spirit of Romance, Dent, 1910 . . . . £300
ditto, Dutton (U.S.), 1910. . . . . £200
Cathay, Elkin Mathews, 1915 (wraps) . . . £300
Gaudier-Brzeska, Bodley Head, 1916 (with design on front cover) £500
ditto, Bodley Head, 1916 (without design on front cover) £250
ditto, Lane (U.S.), 1916 . . . . £350
Instigations, Boni & Liveright (U.S.), 1920 £700/£200
Antheil and the Treatise on Harmony, Three Mountains Press (Paris), 1924 (400 copies, wraps) £400
ditto, Three Mountains Press (Paris), 1924 (40 copies, Arches paper, wraps) £700
ditto, Contact Editions/Three Mountains Press (Paris), 1924 (unsold copies of above, wraps) . . . £300
ditto, Pascal Covici (U.S.), 1927 . . £200/£50
How to Read, Harmsworth, 1931 . . . £200
ABC of Economics, Faber, 1933. . . . £125/£35
ditto, New Directions (U.S.), 1940 . . . £75/£25
ABC of Reading, Routledge, 1934 . . . £125/£35
ditto, Yale University Press (U.S.), 1934 . £75/£25
Make it New, Faber, 1934 . . . . . £125/£35
ditto, Yale University Press (U.S.), 1935 . £75/£25
Social Credit, Nott, [1935 or 37?] (wraps) . . £125
Polite Essays, Faber, 1937 . . . . . £125/£35
ditto, New Directions (U.S.), 1940 . . . £75/£25
Guide to Kulchur, Faber, 1938 . . . . £125/£35
ditto, New Directions (U.S.), 1938 . . . £75/£25
Patria Mia, Seymour, 1950 . . . . . £75/£25
ditto, Owen (U.S.), 1962 . . . . . . £35/£15
The Letters of Ezra Pound, Harcourt Brace (U.S.), 1950 . . . . £40/£10
ditto, Faber, 1951 . . . . £35/£10
The Translations of Ezra Pound, Faber, 1953 £50/£15
ditto, New Directions (U.S.), 1953 . . . £50/£15
Literary Essays of Ezra Pound, Faber, 1954 £40/£10
ditto, New Directions (U.S.), 1954 . . . £40/£10
Impact, Essays on Ignorance and the Decline of American Civilisation, Regenery (U.S.), 1960 . . . . £35/£10
Pound/Joyce, New directions (U.S.), 1967 . £25/£10
ditto, Faber, 1968 . . . . £25/£10
Selected Prose, 1909-65, Faber, 1973 . . £25/£10
ditto, New Directions (U.S.), 1975 . . . £25/£10
An Autobiographical Outline, Nadja, 1980 (200 copies, wraps) £45
Pound/Ford, Faber, 1982. . . . . . £25/£10

ANTHONY POWELL
(b.1905)

As a novelist Powell is best known for the series of novels having the general title *Dance to the Music of Time.*

'Dance to the Music of Time' Novels
A Question of Upbringing, Heinemann, 1951 . . . . £750/£125
ditto, Scribner (U.S.), 1951 . . . . . £100/£25
A Buyer's Market, Heinemann, 1952 . . £600/£100
ditto, Scribner (U.S.), 1953 . . . . . £95/£25
The Acceptance World, Heinemann, 1955 . £250/£35
ditto, Farrar Straus (U.S.), 1956 . . . . £45/£15
At Lady Molly's, Heinemann, 1957 . . . £75/£20
ditto, Little, Brown (U.S.), 1958 . . . . £30/£10
Casanova's Chinese Restaurant, Heinemann, 1960 . . . . £75/£15
ditto, Little, Brown (U.S.), 1960 . . . . £30/£10
The Kindly Ones, Heinemann, 1962. . . . £50/£15
ditto, Little, Brown (U.S.), 1962 . . . . £15/£5
The Valley of Bones, Heinemann, 1964. . £50/£15
ditto, Little, Brown (U.S.), 1964 . . . . £15/£5
The Soldier's Art, Heinemann, 1966. . . £35/£10
ditto, Little, Brown (U.S.), 1966 . . . . £15/£5
The Military Philosophers, Heinemann, 1968 £35/£10
ditto, Little, Brown (U.S.), 1969 . . . . £15/£5
Books Do Furnish a Room, Heinemann, 1971 £30/£10
ditto, Little, Brown (U.S.), 1971 . . . . £10/£5
Temporary Kings, Heinemann, 1973 . . £25/£10
ditto, Little, Brown (U.S.), 1963 . . . . £10/£5
Hearing Secret Harmonies, Heinemann, 1975 £25/£10
ditto, Little, Brown (U.S.), 1975 . . . . £10/£5
All twelve *Dance to the Music of Time* novels £2,500

Other Novels
Afternoon Men, Duckworth, 1931 . . £2,000/£400
ditto, Holt (U.S.), 1932 . . . . . . £500/£125
Venusberg, Duckworth, 1932 . . . £1,750/£300
ditto, Holliday (U.S.), 1952 . . . . . £20/£5
From a View to a Death, Duckworth, 1933. . . . . £1,500/£250
ditto, as ***Mr Zouch: Superman***, Vanguard Press, 1934 . . . . £250/£45
ditto, Little, Brown (U.S.), 1964 . . . . £20/£5
Agents and Patients, Duckworth, 1936 . £1,250/£200
ditto, Holliday (U.S.), 1952 . . . . . £20/£5
What's Become of Waring, Cassell, 1939 £750/£175
ditto, Little, Brown (U.S.), 1963 . . . . £20/£5
O, How the Wheel Becomes It, Heinemann, 1983 . . . . £20/£5
ditto, Holt Rinehart (U.S.), 1983 . . . . £10/£5
The Fisher King, Heinemann, 1985 . . . £30/£5
ditto, Norton (U.S.), 1986. . . . . . £10/£5

Autobiography
Infants of the Spring, Heinemann, 1976 . £20/£5
ditto, Holt Rinehart (U.S.), 1976 . . . . . £10/£5
Messengers of the Day, Heinemann, 1978 . £20/£5
ditto, Holt Rinehart (U.S.), 1978 . . . . . £10/£5
Faces in My Time, Heinemann, 1980 . . £20/£5
ditto, Holt Rinehart (U.S.), 1981 . . . . £10/£5
The Strangers all are Gone, Heinemann, 1982 £20/£5
ditto, Holt Rinehart (U.S.), 1983 . . . . . £10/£5

Others
Caledonia: A Fragment, privately printed, 1934 (100 copies) £2,550
John Aubrey and His Friends, Heinemann, 1948 . . . . £45/£10
ditto, Scribner (U.S.), 1949 . . . . . £40/£10
The Garden of God and The Rest I'll Whistle, Heinemann, 1971 . . . . . £25/£5
ditto, Little, Brown (U.S.), 1971 . . . . £10/£5
Journals, 1982-1986, Heinemann, 1995 . £10/£5
Journals, 1987-1989, Heinemann, 1996 . £10/£5
A Reference for Mellors, Moorhouse and Sorensen, 1994 (26 signed copies of 326, quarter goatskin, slipcase) £250
ditto, Moorhouse and Sorensen, 1994 (100 signed copies of 326) £100
ditto, Moorhouse and Sorensen, 1994 (200 copies of 326, wraps) £25

JOHN COWPER POWYS
(b.1872 d.1963)

Novelist, poet and essayist, Powys's historical romances are very highly rated by his readers, although his work has never received much general literary recognition.

Novels
Wood and Stone, A Romance, G.A. Shaw (U.S.), 1915 . . . . £50
ditto, Heinemann, [1917] £25
Rodmoor, A Romance, G.A. Shaw, 1916 . . £45
Ducdame, Doubleday Page (U.S.), 1925 . £125/£30
ditto, Grant Richards, 1925 . . . . . . £125/£30
Wolf Solent, Simon & Schuster (U.S.), 1929 (2 vols, slipcase) . . . . £125/£25
ditto, Jonathan Cape, 1929 (1 vol.) . . . . £125/£25
A Glastonbury Romance, Simon & Schuster (U.S.), 1932 . . . . £75/£25
ditto, Simon & Schuster (U.S.), 1932 (204 signed, numbered copies, no d/w) £150
ditto, John Lane, 1929 (1 vol.) . . . . £75/£25
Weymouth Sands, Simon & Schuster (U.S.), 1934 . . . . £75/£25
ditto, as ***Jobber Skald***, John Lane, 1935 (revised text) . . . . £45/£15
ditto, Jonathan Cape, 1963 (unexpurgated version) . . . . £15/£5
Maiden Castle, Simon & Schuster (U.S.), 1936 . . . . £45/£10
ditto, Cassell, 1937 . . . . £45/£10
Morwyn, or The Vengeance of God, Cassell, 1937 . . . . £75/£25
Owen Glendower, Simon & Schuster (U.S.), 1940 (2 vols) . . . . £75/£25
ditto, John Lane, 1941 (1 vol.) . . . . £75/£25
Porius, Macdonald, 1951 . . . . £25/£10
ditto, Macdonald, 1951 (200 signed copies). . £75
ditto, Philosophical Library (U.S.), 1952 . £25/£10
The Inmates, Macdonald, 1952 . . . . £25/£10
Atlantis, Macdonald, 1954 . . . . . . £25/£10
The Brazen Head, Macdonald, 1956 . . £25/£10
All or Nothing, Macdonald, 1960 . . . . £25/£10

Short Stories
The Owl, the Duck and - Miss Rowe! Miss Rowe!, Black Archer Press (U.S.), 1930 (250 signed copies, slipcase) . . . . £125/£100
Up and Out, Macdonald, 1957 . . . . £25/£10

Verse
Corinth, privately printed, 1891 ("English Verse" on front cover, wraps) £2,000
Odes and Other Poems, Rider & Co., 1896 . . £350
Poems, Rider & Co., 1899 . . . . £250
Wolf's Bane, Rhymes, G.A. Shaw (U.S.), 1916 £35
Mandragora, Poems, G.A. Shaw, 1917 . . . £50
Samphire, Poems, T. Selzer (U.S.), 1922 . £75/£35
Lucifer, A Poem, Macdonald, 1956 (560 signed, numbered copies, acetate d/w) . . . . . £135/£100
John Cowper Powys: A Selection from His Poems, Macdonald, 1964. . . . . £20/£10

Others
The War and Culture, G.A. Shaw (U.S.), 1914 (boards) £50
ditto, G.A. Shaw (U.S.), 1914 (wraps) . . . £45
ditto, as ***The Menace of German Culture***, 1915 £50
Visions and Revisions, G.A. Shaw (U.S.), 1915 . . . . £25/£10
Confessions of Two Brothers, Manas Press (U.S.), 1916 (with Llewelyn Powys) . . . . £75/£25
One Hundred Best Books, G.A. Shaw (U.S.), 1916 . . . . £50/£10
Suspended Judgements, Essays on Books and Sensations, G.A. Shaw (U.S.), 1916 . . £75/£20
The Complex Vision, Dodd Mead (U.S.), 1920 . . . . £25/£10

The Art of Happiness, Haldeman-Julius, 1923 (wraps) £10
Psychoanalysis and Morality, Jessica Colbert (U.S.), 1923 (500 numbered copies) £50
ditto, Random House, 1925 (approximately 50 copies of the above were rebound and signed by J.C. Powys) £150
The Religion of a Sceptic, Dodd Mead (U.S.), 1925 (1,000 copies) . . . . £25/£10
The Secret of Self-Development, Haldeman-Julius, 1926 (wraps) £15
The Art of Forgetting the Unpleasant, Haldeman-Julius, 1928 (wraps) £15
The Meaning of Culture, Norton (U.S.), 1929 £20/£5
ditto, Cape, 1930 . . . . £15/£5
In Defence of Sensuality, Simon & Schuster (U.S.), 1930 . . . . £45/£10
ditto, Gollancz, 1930 . . . . £35/£10
Debate! 15 Modern Marriage a Failure?, Discussion Guild (U.S.), 1930 (with Bertrand Russell) £1,000
Dorothy M. Richardson, Joiner & Steele, 1931 . . . . £40/£10
ditto, Joiner & Steele, 1931 (60 signed, numbered copies) . . . . £125/£75
A Philosophy of Solitude, Simon & Schuster (U.S.), 1933 . . . . £20/£5
Autobiography, Simon & Schuster (U.S.), 1934 £20/£5
ditto, Bodley Head, 1934 . . . . £20/£5
The Art of Happiness, Simon & Schuster (U.S.), 1935 (not the 1923 version) . . . . . . £25/£10
ditto, The Bodley Head, 1935 . . . . . £25/£10
Enjoyment of Literature, Simon & Schuster (U.S.), 1938 . . . . £25/£10
ditto, as ***The Pleasures of Literature***, Cassell, 1938 (contains one extra essay) . . . . . . £25/£10
Mortal Strife, Jonathan Cape, 1941 . . . . £25/£10
The Art of Growing Old, Jonathan Cape, 1944 £25/£10
Dostoievsky, John Lane, 1946 . . . . . £25/£10
Pair Dadeni, or The Cauldron of Rebirth, Druid Press, 1946 . . . . £25/£10
Obstinate Cymric, Essays 1935-47, Druid Press, 1947 . . . . £40/£15
Rabelais, John Lane, 1948 . . . . . . £20/£5
ditto, Philosophical Library (U.S.), 1951 (500 copies) £15
In Spite Of, A Philosophy for Everyman, Macdonald, 1952 . . . . £20/£5
ditto, Philosophical Library (U.S.), 1953 . £15/£5
The Letters of John Cowper Powys to Louis Wilkinson, 1935-1956, Macdonald, 1958 . £20/£5
Homer and the Aether, Macdonald, 1959 . £15/£5
Letters to Nicholas Ross, Bertram Rota, 1971 . £10

LLEWELYN POWYS
(b.1884 d.1939)

Although he wrote three novels, the author's reputation rests upon his collected essays, many detailing his observations of Africa.

Novels

Black Laughter, Harcourt Brace (U.S.), 1924 £35/£10
The Verdict of Bridlegoose, Harcourt Brace (U.S.), 1926 . . . . £35/£10
ditto, Jonathan Cape, 1927 (900 signed, numbered copies) . . . . £35/£20
Apples Be Ripe, Harcourt Brace (U.S.), 1930 £50/£20
ditto, Longman, 1930 . . . . £50/£20

Essays

Ebony and Ivory, American Library Service (U.S.), 1923 . . . . £35/£10
Thirteen Worthies, American Library Service (U.S.), 1923 . . . . £35/£10
ditto, Grant Richards, 1924 . . . . . £35/£10
Honey and Gall, Haldeman-Julius (U.S.), 1924 (wraps) £10
Cup Bearers of Wine and Hellebore, Haldeman-Julius (U.S.), 1924 (wraps) £10
The Cradle of God, Harcourt Brace (U.S.), 1929 . . . . £25/£10
ditto, Cape, 1924 . . . . £25/£10
The Pathetic Fallacy, Longmans Green, 1930 £15/£5
Impassioned Clay, Longmans Green (U.S.), 1931 . . . . £65/£25
ditto, Longmans Green, 1930 . . . . . . £50/£15
Now that the Gods are Dead, Equinox Press (U.S.), 1932 (400 signed copies) £175
Glory of Life, Golden Cockerel Press, 1934 (277 numbered copies) £200
ditto, John Lane, 1938. . . . . £65/£15
Earth Memories, John Lane, 1934 . . . £35/£15
ditto, Simon & Schuster (U.S.), 1938 . . £25/£10
Damnable Opinions, Watts, 1935 . . . £20/£5
Dorset Essays, Bodley Head, 1935 . . . £30/£10
The Twelve Months, Bodley Head, 1936 . £25/£10
ditto, Bodley Head, 1936 (100 signed copies) . £100
Somerset Essays, Bodley Head, 1937 . . £25/£10
A Baker's Dozen, Trovillion Press, 1940 (493 signed, numbered copies, in slipcase) . . . . £60/£45
ditto, Bodley Head, 1941 . . . . £20/£10
Old English Yuletide, Trovillion Press, 1940 (202 numbered copies, signed by the printers, in slipcase) . . . . £75/£65
Swiss Essays, Bodley Head, 1947 . . . £20/£10
Somerset and Dorset Essays, Bodley Head, 1957 . . . . £20/£10

Autobiography

Skin for Skin, Harcourt Brace (U.S.), 1925 . £30/£10
ditto, Jonathan Cape, 1927 (900 signed, numbered copies) . . . . £40/£25
Love and Death, Bodley Head, 1939 . . £25/£10
ditto, Simon & Schuster (U.S.), 1941 . . . £20/£5

Others

Henry Hudson, John Lane, 1927 (1000 copies) . . . . £45/£15
ditto, Harper & Brothers (U.S.), 1928 . . £25/£10
Out of the Past, Grey Bow Press, 1928 (25 copies) £150
A Pagan's Pilgrimage, Harcourt Brace (U.S.), 1931 . . . . £30/£10
The Life and Times of Anthony A. Wood, Wishart & Co., 1932 . . . . £30/£10
Rats in the Sacristy, Watts & Co., 1937. . £25/£10
The Book of Days, Golden Cockerel Press, 1937 (300 copies) £150
ditto, Golden Cockerel Press, 1937 (nos. 1-55 bound in red leather & signed by artist) £250
ditto, Golden Cockerel Press, 1937 (nos. 1-5 on lamb's vellum, bound in red leather & signed by artist) £1000
The Letters of Llewelyn Powys, Bodley Head, 1943 . . . . £25/£10
Advice to a Young Poet, Letters Between Llewelyn Powys and Kenneth Hopkins, Bodley Head, 1949 (issued as a volume in the Uniform Edition of the Works of Llewelyn Powys) . . . . £20/£10
So Wild a Thing, Letters to Gamel Woolsey, Ark Press, 1973 . . . . £15

T.F. POWYS
(b.1875 d.1953)

The author of a number of eccentric novels which offer a highly personal and idiosyncratic view of both God and human nature.

Novels

Black Bryony, Chatto & Windus, 1923 . . £40/£10
ditto, Knopf (U.S.), 1923 . . . . £30/£10
Mark Only, Chatto & Windus, 1924. . . £40/£10
ditto, Knopf (U.S.), 1924 . . . . . . £30/£10
Mr Tasker's Gods, Chatto & Windus, 1925. £40/£10
ditto, Knopf (U.S.), 1925 . . . . £30/£10
Mockery Gap, Chatto & Windus, 1925 . . £35/£10
ditto, Knopf (U.S.), 1925 . . . . . . £25/£10
Innocent Birds, Chatto & Windus, 1926 . £35/£10
ditto, Knopf (U.S.), 1926 . . . . £25/£10
Mr Weston's Good Wine, Chatto & Windus, 1927 (660 copies) . . . . £200/£65
ditto, Viking (U.S.), 1928 . . . . £30/£10
ditto, Chatto & Windus, 1928. . . . . . £30/£10
Kindness in a Corner, Chatto & Windus, 1930 £30/£10
ditto, Chatto & Windus, 1930 (206 signed, numbered copies) £50
ditto, Viking (U.S.), 1930. . . . . . . £25/£5
Unclay, Chatto & Windus, 1931 . . . . £30/£10
ditto, Chatto & Windus, 1931 (large paper edition of 160 copies) £65
ditto, Viking (U.S.), 1932. . . . . . . £25/£5

Short Stories

The Left Leg, Chatto & Windus, 1923 . . £40/£10
ditto, Knopf U.S.), 1923 . . . . £30/£10
A Stubborn Tree, privately printed, 1926 (100 copies). £125
Feed My Swine, E. Archer, 1926 (100 copies) . £75
A Strong Girl, E. Archer, 1926 (100 copies) . £75
What Lack I Yet?, E. Archer, 1926 . . . . . £35
ditto, E. Archer, 1926 (100 signed, numbered copies) £100
ditto, E. Archer, 1926 (25 signed, numbered copies on Japanese vellum) £200
The Rival Pastors, E. Archer, 1927 (100 signed, numbered copies, in envelope) . . . . £75/£50
The House with the Echo, Chatto & Windus, 1928 . . . . £35/£10
ditto, Chatto & Windus, 1928 (206 numbered, signed copies) £145
ditto, Viking (U.S.), 1929. . . . . . . £25/£5
The Dewpond, Elkin Matthews, 1928 (530 signed, numbered copies) . . . . £50/£25
Fables, Viking Press, (U.S.), 1929 . . . . £30/£10
ditto, Chatto & Windus, 1929 (750 signed copies) . . . . £75/£30
Christ in a Cupboard, Blue Moon Booklets no. 5, 1930 (500 numbered, signed copies, wraps) . . . £35
ditto, Blue Moon Booklets no. 5, 1930 (100 small-format copies 'for presentation', wraps). . . £30
The Key of the Field, Furnival Books no.1, 1930 (550 signed copies) £50
The White Paternoster, Chatto & Windus, 1930 . . . . £25/£10
ditto, Chatto & Windus, 1930 (310 copies) . . £145
ditto, Viking, 1931. . . . . £25/£10
Uriah on the Hill, Minority Press, 1930 (wraps, in envelope) . . . . £30/£15
Uncle Dottery, Douglas Cleverdon, 1930 (350 numbered, signed copies) £90
ditto, Douglas Cleverdon, 1930 (nos. 1-50, containing extra set of plates) £175
The Only Penitent, Chatto & Windus, 1931 £20/£5
ditto, Chatto & Windus, 1931 (large paper edition of 160 signed, numbered copies) £65
When Thou Wast Naked, Golden Cockerel Press, 1931

(edition of 500 numbered, signed copies) . . £95
The Tithe Barn, privately printed, 1932 (350 signed, numbered copies) £45
ditto, privately printed, 1932 (50 copies on Japanese vellum, bound in white buckram) £150
The Two Thieves, Chatto & Windus, 1932 . £50/£15
ditto, Chatto & Windus, 1932 (85 signed, numbered copies) £115
ditto, Viking, 1933. . . . . £25/£10
Captain Patch, Chatto & Windus, 1935 . . £35/£10
Make Thyself Many, Grayson & Grayson, 1935 (285 signed, numbered copies) . . . . . £125/£45
Goat Green, Golden Cockerel Press, 1937 (150 signed, numbered copies, slipcase) . . . . . £100/£65
ditto, Golden Cockerel Press, 1937 . . . £25/£10
Bottle's Path, Chatto & Windus, 1946 . . £25/£10
God's Eyes A-Twinkle, Chatto & Windus, 1947 . . . . £25/£10
Rosie Plum, And Other Stories, Chatto & Windus, 1966 . . . . £15/£5
Two Stories, Brimmell, 1967 (525 numbered copies) £45
ditto, Brimmell, 1967 (25 numbered copies on hand-made paper, signed by Reynolds Stone) . . . £95
Three Short Stories, Dud Noman Press, 1971 (150 numbered copies, acetate d/w) . . . £35/£30

Others

An Interpretation of Genesis, privately printed, 1907 (100 copies) £400
ditto, Chatto & Windus, 1929 (490 signed copies, slipcase) . . . . £65/£20
ditto, Viking (U.S.), 1929 (260 signed copies, slipcase) . . . . £100/£75
The Soliloquy of a Hermit, G.A. Shaw (U.S.), 1916 . . . . £75
ditto, as ***The Soliloquies of a Hermit***, Melrose, 1918 . . . . £35

TERRY PRATCHETT
(b.1948)

Author of the hugely successful 'Discworld' novels, which began with *The Colour of Magic.*

Novels

The Dark Side of the Sun, Colin Smythe, 1976 . . . . £400/£150
STRATA, Colin Smythe, 1981 . . . . £275/£100
The Colour of Magic, Colin Smythe, 1983 £750/£250
ditto, Colin Smythe, 1989 (new edition) . . £50/£15
The Light Fantastic, Colin Smythe, 1986 . £275/£75
Equal Rites, Gollancz/Colin Smythe, 1987 . £100/£20
Mort, Gollancz/Colin Smythe, 1987 . . . £100/£20
Sourcery, Gollancz/Colin Smythe, 1988. . £100/£20
Wyrd Sisters, Gollancz, 1988. . . . . £45/£15
Pyramids, Gollancz, 1989 . . . . . £45/£15
Guards! Guards!, Gollancz, 1989 . . . £40/£10
Eric, Gollancz, 1990 (large format) . . . £35/£10
Moving Pictures, Gollancz, 1990 . . . £35/£10
Good Omens, Gollancz, 1990 (with Neil Gaiman) . . . . £30/£10
Reaper Man, Gollancz, 1991. . . . . £30/£10
Witches Abroad, Gollancz, 1991. . . . £30/£10
Small Gods, Gollancz, 1992 . . . . . £25/£5
Lords and Ladies, Gollancz, 1992 . . . £25/£5
Men at Arms, Gollancz, 1993 . . . . £25/£5
Soul Music, Gollancz, 1994 . . . . . £20/£5
Interesting Times, Gollancz, 1994 . . . £15/£5
Maskerade, Gollancz, 1995 . . . . . £15/£5
Feet of Clay, Gollancz, 1996 . . . . . £10/£5
Hogfather, Gollancz, 1996 . . . . . £10/£5
Jingo, Gollancz, 1997. . . . . . . £10/£5
Last Continent, Doubleday, 1998 . . . £10/£5

Children's

The Carpet People, Colin Smythe, 1971 . £300/£75
Truckers, Doubleday, 1989 . . . . . £20/£5
Diggers, Doubleday, 1990 . . . . . £15/£5
Wings, Doubleday, 1990 . . . . . . £15/£5
Only You Can Save Mankind, Doubleday, 1992 . . . . £15/£5
Johnny and the Dead, Doubleday, 1993 . £10/£5
Johnny and the Bomb, Doubleday, 1996 . £10/£5
Carpe Jugulum, Doubleday, 1998 . . . £10/£5

Others

The Unadulterated Cat, Gollancz, 1986 (wraps) £40
Terry Pratchett's Truckers, Picture Corgi, 1992, (wraps) £5
The Streets of Ankh-Morpork, Corgi, 1993 (with Stephen Briggs) £5
The Discworld Companion, Gollancz, 1994 (with Stephen Briggs) . . . . £10/£5

ANTHONY PRICE
(b.1928)

A crime novelist and journalist, Price won the Crime Writers Association's Silver Dagger award with his first book, *The Labyrinth Makers*, and later the Gold Dagger with *Other Paths to Glory*.

Novels

The Labyrinth Makers, Gollancz, 1970 . . £225/£50
ditto, Doubleday (U.S.), 1971 . . . . £35/£10

The Alamut Ambush, Gollancz, 1971 . . . £100/£25
ditto, Doubleday (U.S.), 1972 . . . . . £20/£5
Colonel Butler's Wolf, Gollancz 1972 . . £75/£20
ditto, Doubleday (U.S.), 1973 . . . . £20/£5
October Men, Gollancz, 1973 . . . . £75/£15
ditto, Doubleday (U.S.), 1974 . . . . £20/£5
Other Paths to Glory, Gollancz, 1974 . . £75/£15
ditto, Doubleday (U.S.), 1975 . . . . £20/£5
Our Man in Camelot, Gollancz, 1975 . . £75/£15
ditto, Doubleday (U.S.), 1976 . . . . £20/£5
War Game, Gollancz, 1976 . . . . . £65/£10
ditto, Doubleday (U.S.), 1977 . . . . £20/£5
The '44 Vintage, Gollancz, 1978. . . . . £65/£10
ditto, Doubleday (U.S.), 1979 . . . . £10/£5
Tomorrow's Ghost, Gollancz, 1979 . . . £50/£10
ditto, Doubleday (U.S.), 1979 . . . . £10/£5
The Hour of the Donkey, Gollancz, 1980 . £45/£10
Soldier No More, Gollancz, 1981 . . . £35/£10
ditto, Doubleday (U.S.), 1982 . . . . £10/£5
The Old Vengeful, Gollancz, 1982 . . . £15/£5
ditto, Doubleday (U.S.), 1983 . . . . £10/£5
Gunner Kelly, Gollancz, 1983 . . . . £15/£5
ditto, Doubleday (U.S.), 1984 . . . . £10/£5
Sion Crossing, Gollancz, 1984 . . . . £15/£5
ditto, Mysterious Press (U.S.), 1985 . . . £10/£5
Here Be Monsters, Gollancz, 1985 . . . £15/£5
ditto, Mysterious Press (U.S.), 1985 . . . £10/£5
For the Good of the State, Gollancz, 1986 . £15/£5
ditto, Mysterious Press (U.S.), 1987 . . . £10/£5
A New Kind of War, Gollancz, 1987 . . . £15/£5
ditto, Mysterious Press (U.S.), 1988 . . . £10/£5
A Prospect of Vengeance, Gollancz, 1988 . £10/£5
ditto, The Armchair Detective (U.S.), 1990 . £10/£5
The Memory Trap, Gollancz 1989 . . . £10/£5

Non Fiction
The Eyes of the Fleet, Hutchinson, 1990 . £10/£5

J.B. PRIESTLEY
(b.1894 d.1984)

Priestley was born in Bradford, the son of an elementary schoolmaster, and became a clerk after leaving school. He served with distinction in the West Riding and Devonshire Regiments during the First World War, afterwards studying politics and history at Cambridge. His output was prodigious, including many more non fiction titles.

Novels
Adam in Moonshine, Heinemann, 1927. . £75/£45
Benighted, Heinemann, 1927. . . . . . £25/£60
Farthing Hall (with Hugh Walpole), Macmillan, 1929 . . . . £50/£10
The Good Companions, Heinemann, 1929 . £25/£10
Angel Pavement, Heinemann, 1930 . . . £25/£10
ditto, Heinemann, 1930 (1,025 signed copies) . £50
Faraway, Heinemann, 1932 . . . . . £15/£5
Wonder Hero, Heinemann, 1933. . . . . £15/£5
The Walk in the City: The Lovers in the Stone Forest, Heinemann, 1936 . . . . £15/£5
The Doomsday Men: An Adventure, Heinemann, 1938 . . . . £15/£5
Let the People Sing, Heinemann, 1939 . £15/£5
Black-Out in Gretley: A Story of - and for - Wartime, Heinemann, 1942 . . . . £15/£5
Daylight on Saturday: A Novel about an Aircraft Factory, Heinemann, 1943 £15/£5
Three Men in New Suits, Heinemann, 1945 £15/£5
Bright Day, Heinemann, 1946 . . . . . £15/£5
Jenny Villiers: A Story of the Theatre, Heinemann, 1947 . . . . £15/£5
Festival at Farbridge, Heinemann, 1951 . £15/£5
The Magicians, Heinemann, 1954 . . . £15/£5
Low Notes on a High Level: A Frolic, Heinemann, 1954 . . . . £15/£5
Saturn Over the Water, Heinemann, 1961 . £10/£5
The Shapes of Sleep: A Topical Tale, Heinemann, 1962 . . . . £10/£5
Sir Michael and Sir George, Heinemann, 1964 £10/£5
Lost Empires, Heinemann, 1965 . . . . £15/£5
Salt is Leaving: A Detective Story, Heinemann, 1966 . . . . £10/£5
It's an Old Country, Heinemann, 1967 . . £10/£5
Out of Town (volume one of ***The Image Men***), Heinemann, 1968 . . . . . . £10/£5
London End (volume two of ***The Image Men***), Heinemann, 1969 . . . . £10/£5
Found, Lost, Found or The English Way of Life, Heinemann, 1976. . . . . £10/£5

Short Stories
The Town Major of Miraucourt, Heinemann, 1930 . . . . £20/£5
ditto, Heinemann, 1930 (525 copies signed by the author, in slipcase) . . . . £75/£50
Albert Goes Through, Heinemann, 1933 . £15/£5
Going Up (stories and sketches), Heinemann, 1933 . . . . £15/£5
The Other Place, Heinemann, 1953 . . . £15/£5
The Thirty-First of June: A tale of true love, enterprise and Progress in the Arthurian and ad-atomic ages, Heinemann, 1961 . . . . . £15/£5
Snoggle: A Story for Anybody Between 9 and 90, Heinemann, 1971 . . . . . . £10/£5
The Carfit Crisis and Two Other Stories, Heinemann, 1975 . . . . £10/£5

V. S. PRITCHETT
(b.1900 d.1997)

A writer and critic, Pritchett's books range widely through many genres encompassing travel, essays, short stories, novels and memoirs.

Novels
Clare Drummer, Benn, 1929 . . . . . £175/£45
Shirley Sanz, Gollancz, 1932 . . . . . £150/£35
ditto, as ***Elopement into Exile***, Little, Brown (U.S.), 1932 . . . . £35/£10
Nothing Like Leather, Chatto & Windus, 1935 . . . . £125/£30
ditto, Macmillan (U.S.), 1935 . . . . . £25/£10
Dead Man Leading, Chatto & Windus, 1937 £75/£20
ditto, Macmillan (U.S.), 1937 . . . . . £30/£10
Mr Beluncle, Chatto & Windus, 1951 . . £50/£15
ditto, Harcourt Brace (U.S.), 1951 . . . £15/£5

Short Stories
The Spanish Virgin and Other Stories, Benn, 1930 . . . . £100/£30
You Make Your Own Life, Chatto & Windus, 1938 . . . . £50/£15
It May Never Happen and Other Stories, Chatto & Windus, 1945 . . . . £25/£10
ditto, Reynal (U.S.), 1947 . . . . £15/£5
Collected Stories, Chatto & Windus, 1956 . £15/£5
The Sailor, The Sense of Humour and Other Stories, Knopf (U.S.), 1956 . . . . £20/£5
When My Girl Comes Home, Chatto & Windus, 1961. . . . . £20/£5
ditto, Knopf (U.S.), 1961 . . . . £10/£5
The Key to My Heart, Chatto & Windus, 1963 £25/£10
ditto, Random House (U.S.), 1964 . . . . £10/£5
The Saint and Other Stories, Penguin, 1966 . £5
Blind Love and Other Stories, Chatto & Windus, 1969 . . . . £15/£5
ditto, Random House (U.S.), 1970 . . . . £10/£5
The Camberwell Beauty and Other Stories, Chatto & Windus, 1974 . . . . £15/£5
ditto, Random House (U.S.), 1974 . . . . £10/£5
Selected Stories, Chatto & Windus, 1978 . £10/£5
ditto, Random House (U.S.), 1978 . . . . £10/£5
On the Edge of the Cliff, Random House (U.S.), 1979 . . . . £10/£5
ditto, Chatto & Windus, 1980 . . . . . £10/£5
Collected Stories, Random House (U.S.), 1982 £10/£5
ditto, Chatto & Windus, 1982 . . . . . £10/£5
More Collected Stories, Random House (U.S.), 1983 . . . . £10/£5
ditto, Chatto & Windus, 1983 . . . . . £10/£5
A Careless Widow and Other Stories, Chatto & Windus, 1989 . . . . £10/£5
ditto, Random House (U.S.), 1989 . . . . £10/£5
Complete Short Stories, Chatto & Windus, 1990 . . . . £10/£5
ditto, as ***Complete Collected Stories***, Random House (U.S.), 1991 . . . . £10/£5

Others
Marching Spain, Benn, 1928 . . . . . £100/£45
In My Good Books, Chatto & Windus, 1942 £25/£10
The Spanish Temper, Chatto & Windus, 1954 £20/£5
Foreign Faces, Chatto & Windus, 1964 . £15/£5
The Working Novelist, Chatto & Windus, 1965 £15/£5
A Cab at the Door, Chatto & Windus, 1968 £10/£5
Midnight Oil, Chatto & Windus, 1971 . . £10/£5
The Tale Bearers, Chatto & Windus, 1980 . £10/£5

BARBARA PYM
(b.1913 d.1980)

The author of delicate, sad comedies, often set against a background of middle-class churchgoing characters.

Novels
Some Tame Gazelle, Cape, 1950 . . . £300/£75
ditto, Dutton (U.S.), 1983 . . . . . . £15/£5
Excellent Women, Cape, 1952 . . . . £225/£45
ditto, Dutton (U.S.), 1978 . . . . £20/£5
Jane and Prudence, Cape, 1953 . . . . £225/£45
ditto, Dutton (U.S.), 1981 . . . . £10/£5
Less Than Angels, Cape, 1955 . . . . £200/£45
ditto, Vanguard (U.S.), 1957 . . . . . £35/£10
A Glass of Blessings, Cape, 1959 . . . £175/£40
ditto, Dutton (U.S.), 1980 . . . . . . £10/£5
No Fond Return of Love, Cape, 1961 . . £150/£40
ditto, Dutton (U.S.), 1982 . . . . . . £10/£5
Quartet in Autumn, Macmillan, 1977 . . £35/£10
ditto, Dutton (U.S.), 1978 . . . . £20/£5
The Sweet Dove Died, Macmillan, 1978 . . £30/£5
ditto, Dutton (U.S.), 1979 . . . . £10/£5
A Few Green Leaves, Macmillan, 1980 . . £25/£5
ditto, Dutton (U.S.), 1980 . . . . £10/£5
An Unsuitable Attachment, Macmillan, 1982 £25/£5
ditto, Dutton (U.S.), 1982 . . . . £10/£5
Crampton Hodnet, Macmillan, 1985 . . £15/£5
ditto, Dutton (U.S.), 1985 . . . . £10/£5
An Academic Question, Macmillan, 1986 . £10/£5
ditto, Macmillan (U.S.), 1986 . . . . . £10/£5
Civil to Strangers, Dutton (U.S.), 1988 . . £10/£5

Journals
A Very Private Eye, Macmillan, 1984 . . £15/£5
ditto, Dutton (U.S.), 1984 . . . . . . £10/£5

ELLERY QUEEN

'Ellery Queen' was the pseudonym for Frederic Dannay and Manfred B. Lee, cousins who entered a detective prize story contest with *The Roman Hat Mystery*. This was the beginning of their successful writing career, and the career of their fictional detective, Ellery Queen. They also penned a handful of 'Barnaby Ross' novels. 'Ellery Queen' novels by other writers have also been included.

Novels

The Roman Hat Mystery, Gollancz, 1929 . £300/£45
The French Powder Mystery, Gollancz, 1930 . . . . £200/£45
The Dutch Shoe Mystery, Gollancz, 1931 . £150/£35
The Greek Coffin Mystery, Gollancz, 1932. £150/£35
The Egyptian Cross Mystery, Gollancz, 1933 £150/£35
The American Gun Mystery, Gollancz, 1933 £150/£35
The Ellery Queen Omnibus, Gollancz, 1934 £75/£20
The Siamese Twin Mystery, Gollancz, 1934 £100/£20
The Chinese Orange Mystery, Gollancz, 1934 . . . . £100/£20
The Spanish Cape Mystery, Gollancz, 1935 £75/£20
Halfway House, Gollancz, 1936 . . . . £75/£20
The Door Between, Gollancz, 1937 . . . £75/£20
The Devil To Pay, Gollancz, 1938 . . . £75/£20
The Four of Hearts, Gollancz, 1939. . . £75/£20
The Dragon's Teeth, Gollancz, 1939 . . £75/£20
Ellery Queen, Master Detective, Grosset & Dunlap (U.S.), 1941 (wraps, may not be by Dannay and Lee). £10
The Penthouse Mystery, Grosset & Dunlap (U.S.), 1941 (may not be by Dannay and Lee) . . . £10
The Perfect Crime, Grosset & Dunlap (U.S.), 1942 (may not be by Dannay and Lee) £10
Calamity Town, Gollancz, 1942 . . . . £50/£15
There Was an Old Woman, Gollancz, 1944 £40/£10
ditto, as ***The Quick and the Dead***, Pan, 1961 £20/£5
The Murderer is a Fox, Gollancz, 1945. . £20/£5
Ten Days' Wonder, Gollancz, 1948 . . . £20/£5
Cat of Many Tails, Gollancz, 1949 . . . £20/£5
Double, Double, Gollancz, 1950 . . . . £20/£5
The Origin of Evil, Gollancz, 1951 . . . £20/£5
The King is Dead, Gollancz, 1952 . . . £15/£5
The Scarlet Letters, Gollancz, 1953 . . . £15/£5
The Glass Village, Gollancz, 1954 . . . £15/£5
Inspector Queen's Own Case, Gollancz, 1956 £15/£5
The Hollywood Murders, Lippincott (U.S.), 1956 (may not be by Dannay and Lee) . . . . . £15/£5
The Finishing Stroke, Gollancz, 1958 . . £15/£5
The Scrolls of Lysis, Simon & Schuster (U.S.), 1962 (may not be by Dannay and Lee) . . . £15/£5
The Player on the Other Side, Gollancz, 1963 £15/£5
And on the Eighth Day, Gollancz, 1964 (may not be by Dannay and Lee) . . . . £15/£5
The Fourth Side of the Triangle, Gollancz, 1965 . . . . £15/£5
Sherlock Holmes Versus Jack the Ripper, Gollancz, 1967 . . . . £125/£35
Face to Face, Gollancz, 1967 . . . . £15/£5
The House of Brass, Gollancz, 1968 . . £15/£5
Cop Out, Gollancz, 1969 . . . . . . £15/£5
The Last Woman in His Life, Gollancz, 1970 £15/£5
A Fine and Private Place, Gollancz, 1971 . £15/£5
Four Men Called John, Gollancz, 1976 . £15/£5

'Ellery Queen' Short Stories

The Adventures of Ellery Queen, Gollancz, 1935 . . . . £75/£20
The New Adventures of Ellery Queen, Gollancz, 1940 . . . . £75/£15
The Case Book of Ellery Queen, Gollancz, 1949 . . . . £35/£10
Calendar of Crime, Gollancz, 1952 . . . . £20/£5
QBI: Queen's Bureau of Investigation, Gollancz, 1955 . . . . £20/£5
Queen's Full, Random House (U.S.), 1965 . £15/£5
ditto, Gollancz, 1966 . . . . £15/£5
QED: Queen's Experiments in Detection, Gollancz, 1969 . . . . £15/£5

'Ellery Queen' Non Fiction Titles

Queen's Quorum, Gollancz, 1953 . . . . £25/£5
In the Queen's Parlour, Gollancz, 1957 . £20/£5
Deadlier than the Male, Transworld, 1966 (may not be by Dannay and Lee) . . . . £15/£5

'Barnaby Ross' Titles

The Tragedy of X, Cassell & Co., 1932 . . £150/£35
The Tragedy of Y, Cassell & Co., 1932 . . £150/£35
The Tragedy of Z, Cassell & Co., 1933 . . £150/£35
Drury Lane's Last Case, Cassell & Co., 1933 £150/£35

JONATHAN RABAN

(b.1942)

Raban's early works are academic, but he now has a considerable reputation as a travel writer.

Travel Titles

Soft City, Collins, 1974 . . . . . . £30/£5
ditto, Dutton (U.S.), 1974. . . . . . . £25/£5
Arabia Through the Looking Glass, Collins, 1979 . . . . £25/£5
ditto, as ***Arabia A Journey Through the Labyrinth***, Simon Schuster (U.S.), 1979 . . . . £15/£5
Old Glory, Collins, 1981 . . . . . . £15/£5

ditto, Simon Schuster (U.S.), 1981 . . . . £10/£5
Coasting, Collins, 1986 . . . . £15/£5
ditto, Simon Schuster (U.S.), 1987 . . . . £10/£5
Hunting Mr Heartbreak, Collins, 1990 . . £10/£5
ditto, Harper Collins (U.S.), 1991 . . . . £10/£5

Novels
Foreign Land, Collins, 1985 . . . . . . £15/£5
ditto, Viking (U.S.), 1985 . . . . £10/£5
Bad Land, Picador, 1996 . . . . £10/£5
ditto, Pantheon (U.S.), 1996 . . . . . . £10/£5

Academic Titles
The Technique of Modern Fiction, Arnold, 1968 . . . . £100/£25
Huckleberry Finn, Arnold, 1968 . . . £50/£10
Society of the Poem, Harrap, 1971 . . . . £25/£5

Others
For Love and Money, Collins, 1987 . . . . £10/£5
ditto, Harper & Row (U.S.), 1989 . . . . £10/£5
God, Man and Mrs Thatcher, Chatto & Windus (wraps) £10

ARTHUR RACKHAM
(b.1867 d.1939)

A highly successful illustrator, Rackham's early gift books are his most sought after titles, especially in deluxe editions.

To the Other Side, by Thomas Rhodes, George Philip, 1893 (wraps, also illustrated by Alfred Bryan) £250
The Dolly Dialogues, by Anthony Hope, Westminster Gazette Library: Volume One, [July] 1894 (wraps, first issue with 'Dolly' running head) . . . £150
ditto, Westminster Gazette Library: Volume One, [July] 1894 (wraps, second issue with 'The Dolly Dialogues' running head) £75
ditto, Westminster Gazette Library: Volume One, [August] 1894 (cloth edition) £75
The Illustrated Guide to Wells-next-the-Sea, by Lingwood Lemmon, Jarrolds, [1894] (wraps) . £300
ditto, Jarrolds, [1894] (first cloth issue, date on title page) £150
Sunrise-Land - Rambles in Eastern England, by Mrs Alfred Berlyn, Jarrolds, 1894 (mauve pictorial cloth). £175
ditto, Jarrolds, 1894 (cheaper edition, white boards) £100
The Zankiwank and the Bletherwitch, Dent, 1896. . . . . £500
The Money Spinner and Other Character Notes, by Henry Seaton Merriman and S.G. Tallentyre, Smith Elder, 1896 . . . . £100
In the Evening of His Days - A Study of Mr Gladstone in Retirement, Westminster Gazette, 1896 £125
The Grey Lady, by Henry Seatom Merriman, Smith Elder, 1897 . . . . £50
Two Old Ladies, Two Foolish Fairies and a Tom Cat, The Surprising Adventures of Tuppy and Tue, Cassell, 1897 . . . . £250
Charles O'Malley, The Irish Dragoon, by Charles Lever, Service & Paton, 1897 . . . . . £100
Evelina, by Frances Burney, George Newnes, 1898 . . . . £100
The Ingoldsby Legends, [by R.H. Barham], J.M. Dent, 1898 (gilt lettering on cover and spine) . . £75
ditto, J.M. Dent, 1907 (second edition, revised and enlarged, 560 signed copies) £1,000
ditto, J.M. Dent, 1907 (trade edition of above) . £200
East Coast Scenery, by William J. Tate, Jarrolds, 1899 . . . . £125
Feats on the Fjord, by Harriet Martineau, J.M. Dent, 1898 (blue leather edition) £50
ditto, J.M. Dent, 1898 (blue cloth edition) . . £45
ditto, as ***Feats on the Fjord and Merdhin***, Dent: Everyman Library, [1910] £20
Tales from Shakespeare, by Charles and Mary Lamb, J.M. Dent, 1899 (blue leather edition) . . . £45
ditto, J.M. Dent, 1899 (blue cloth edition) . . £40
ditto, J.M. Dent, 1909 (deluxe edition, 750 signed copies) £750
ditto, J.M. Dent, 1909 (trade edition of above) . £75
Gulliver's Travels, by Jonathan Swift, J.M. Dent, 1900 (blue leather edition). £45
ditto, J.M. Dent, 1900 (blue cloth edition) . . £40
ditto, J.M. Dent, 1909 (deluxe edition, 750 signed copies) £750
ditto, J.M. Dent, 1909 (trade edition of above) . £75
Fairy Tales of the Brothers Grimm, Freemantle, 1900 . . . . £200
The Argonauts of the Amazon, by C.R. Kenyon, W & R Chambers, 1901 (light blue cloth) . . £25
More Tales of the Stumps, Horace Bleackley, Ward Lock, 1902 . . . . £150
Brains and Bravery, Being Stories told by ..., W & R Chambers, [1903] (red or blue cloth) . . . £75
ditto, W & R Chambers, 1903 (later edition, green cloth) £75
The Grey House on the Hill, by Hon. Mrs Greene, Thomas Nelson, [1903] £20
Littledom Castle and Other Tales, by Mrs M.H. Speilmann, George Routledge, 1903 . . . £100
The Greek Heroes, Cassell, 1903 (limp green buckram) £60
Two Years Before the Mast, by Richard Henry Dana, Collins, [1904] £25

Where Flies the Flag, by Henry Harbour, Collins [1904]. £25
Molly Bawn, by Mrs Hungerford, George Newnes: Newnes Sixpenny Novels, [1904] (wraps) . . £100
Red Pottage, by Mary Cholmondeley, George Newnes: Newnes Sixpenny Novels, [1904] (wraps) . . £100
Rip van Winkle, by Washington Irving, Heinemann, 1905 (deluxe edition, 250 signed copies) . £1,750
ditto, Heinemann, 1905 (trade edition) £300
Peter Pan in Kensington Gardens, by J.M. Barrie, Hodder & Stoughton, 1906 (deluxe edition, 500 signed copies) £2,500
ditto, Hodder & Stoughton, 1906 (trade edition) £450
The Peter Pan Portfolio, Hodder & Stoughton, [1912] (500 boxed portfolios, signed by publishers) £1,000
Puck of Pook's Hill, by Rudyard Kipling, Doubleday (U.S.), 1906 . . . . £100
Good Night, by Eleanor Gates, Thomas Y. Crowell (U.S.), [1907]. £100
Alice's Adventures in Wonderland, by Lewis Carroll, William Heinemann, [1907] (deluxe edition of 1,130 copies) £1,000
ditto, William Heinemann, [1907] (trade edition) £125
The Land of Enchantment, by Alfred E. Bonser, Cassell, 1907 (first binding, green cloth). . . £75
ditto, Cassell, 1907 (second binding, cocoa cloth) £35
A Midsummer's Night Dream, by William Shakespeare, William Heinemann, 1908 (deluxe edition, 1,000 signed copies) £1,000
ditto, William Heinemann, 1908 (trade edition) £250
Undine, by De La Motte Fouque, William Heinemann, 1909 (deluxe edition, 1,000 signed copies) £1,000
ditto, William Heinemann, 1909 (trade edition) £150
Grimm's Fairy Tales, Constable, 1909 (title page reads 'The Fairy Fales of the Brothers Grimm', 750 signed copies) £2,500
ditto, Constable, 1909 (trade edition) . . . £500
The Book of Betty Barber, by Maggie Browne, Duckworth, [1910] £125
The Bee Blowaways, by Agnes Grozier Herbertson, Cassell, [1910] £150
Stories of King Arthur, by A.L. Haydon, Cassell, 1910 . . . . £50
The Rhinegold and The Valkyrie, by Richard Wagner, William Heinemann, 1910 (deluxe edition, 1,150 signed copies £750
ditto, William Heinemann, 1910 (trade edition) £150
The Peradventures of Private Pagett, by Major W.P. Drury, Chapman & Hall, 1911 . . . . . £50
Aesop's Fables, William Heinemann, 1912 (deluxe edition, 1,450 signed copies. £1,000
ditto, William Heinemann, 1912 (trade edition) £150
Mother Goose: The Old Nursery Rhymes, William Heinemann, 1913 (deluxe edition, 1,130 signed copies £750
ditto, William Heinemann, 1913 (trade edition) £200
Arthur Rackham's Book of Pictures, William Heinemann, 1913 (deluxe edition, 1,030 signed copies) £750
ditto, William Heinemann, 1913 (trade edition) £150
A Christmas Carol, by Charles Dickens, Heinemann, 1915 (olive green cloth). £125
ditto, Heinemann, 1915 (deluxe edition, 525 signed copies, full vellum) £1,000
ditto, Heinemann, 1915 (publishers special binding, brown leather) £250
The Allies' Fairy Book, by various, Heinemann, 1916 (slate blue cloth) £100
ditto, Heinemann, 1916 (deluxe 525 signed copies, blue cloth) £500
Little Brother and Little Sister, by the Brothers Grimm, Constable, 1917 (light green cloth) . £250
ditto, (deluxe 525 signed copies, including one signed colour plate laid in, light grey cloth) £750
The Romance of King Arthur, And his Knights of the Round Table, by Thomas Malory and Alfred Pollard, Macmillan, 1917 (dark blue cloth) £150
ditto, Macmillan, 1917 (deluxe 500 signed copies, full vellum) £1,000
English Fairy Tales, by Flora Annie Steel, Macmillan, 1918 (red cloth) £125
ditto, Macmillan, 1918 (deluxe edition limited to 500 signed copies, full vellum) £500
The Springtide of Life: Poems of Childhood, by Algernon Charles Swinburne, Heinemann, 1918 (green cloth) £100
ditto, Heinemann, 1918 (deluxe 765 signed copies, vellum-backed cream boards) £500
ditto, Heinemann, 1918 (publishers special binding of dark green mottled leather) £150
ditto, Heinemann, 1918 [1925] (later issue, as trade edition but top edge not gilt) £30
Snickerty Nick and the Giant, by Julia Ellsworth Ford, Moffat, Yard & Co (U.S.), 1919 (3 colour plates and 10 black and white drawings, light blue cloth) £125
ditto, Suttonhouse (U.S.), 1933 (new edition, with music by C.A. Ridgeway) £100
Some British Ballads, by various, Constable [1919] (light blue cloth) £100
ditto, Constable [1919] (575 deluxe signed copies, vellum-backed cream boards) £500
ditto, Constable (with 'Heinemann' at the foot of the spine) [1924] . . . . £100/£35
Cinderella, by Charles Perrault, Heinemann, 1919 (pictorial boards). £125
ditto, Heinemann, 1919 (deluxe 'paper' 525 signed copies, printed on handmade paper, green boards with tan cloth spine) £500
ditto, Heinemann, 1919 (deluxe 'vellum' 325 signed copies, printed on Japanese vellum, vellum-backed

cream boards) £850

The Sleeping Beauty, by Charles Perrault, Heinemann, 1920 (pictorial boards with red cloth backstrip) . . . . £200/£100

ditto, Heinemann, 1920 (deluxe 625 signed copies, vellum-backed cream boards) £650

Irish Fairy Tales, by James Stephens, Macmillan, 1920 (green cloth) . . . . £275/£150

ditto, Macmillan, 1920 (deluxe 520 signed copies, vellum-backed white boards) £1,000

Hansel & Gretel and Other Tales, by the Brothers Grimm, Constable, 1920 (20 colour plates and 28 black and white drawings, trade edition only, dark blue cloth) . . . . £250/£125

ditto, as ***Snowdrop and Other Tales***, by the Brothers Grimm, Constable, 1920 (20 colour plates and 29 black and white drawings, trade edition only, dark blue cloth) . . . . £250/£125

Comus, by John Milton, Heinemann [1921] (green cloth) . . . . £250/£125

ditto, Heinemann [1921] (deluxe 550 signed copies, vellum-backed cream boards) £800

A Dish of Apples, by Eden Phillpotts, Hodder & Stoughton, 1921 (grey cloth) . . . . . £150/£75

ditto, Hodder & Stoughton, 1921 (deluxe 500 copies signed by author and artist, cream buckram) . £400

A Wonder Book, by Nathaniel Hawthorne, Hodder & Stoughton [1922] (red cloth) . . . . . £300/£150

ditto, Hodder & Stoughton [1922] (deluxe 600 signed copies, cream buckram) £800

Where the Blue Begins, by Christopher Morley, Heinemann [1925] (blue cloth) . . . . . £225/£100

ditto, Heinemann [1925] (deluxe 175 signed copies, cream boards with black cloth spine) £500

Poor Cecco, by Margery Williams Bianco, Chatto & Windus, 1925 [May, 1926] (yellow cloth) . £250/£100

ditto, George H. Doran (U.S.), 1925 (deluxe 105 copies signed by the author, vellum-backed blue boards) £3,500

A Road to Fairyland, by Erica Fay, George Putnam's Sons Ltd, 1926 (colour frontispiece only, trade edition only, U.K. issued in grey cloth with blue lettering, U.S. issued in red cloth with gilt lettering) . £250/£100

The Tempest, by William Shakespeare, Heinemann/ Doubleday, 1926 (olive green or grey-black cloth) . . . . £275/£125

ditto, Heinemann/ Doubleday, 1926 (deluxe 520 signed copies, vellum-style boards with vellum spine) £850

The Lonesomest Doll, by Abbie Farwell Brown, Houghton Mifflin (U.S.), 1928 (4 full-page illustrations and 26 black and white drawings, trade edition only, pictorial light-tan cloth) . . £275/£150

The Legend of Sleepy Hollow, by Washington Irving, Harrap, 1928 (green cloth) . . . . . £225/£125

ditto, Harrap, 1928 (deluxe 375 signed copies, full vellum) £750

ditto, Harrap, 1928 (publisher's special binding, grey or brown leather) £250

The Vicar of Wakefield, by Oliver Goldsmith, Harrap, 1929 (dark green cloth) . . . . . . £200/£100

ditto, Harrap, 1929 (deluxe 775 signed copies, full vellum) £500

ditto, Harrap, 1929 (publisher's special binding, olive persian morocco). £250

The Chimes, by Charles Dickens, with an introduction by Edward Wagenknecht, Limited Editions Club (U.K./U.S.), 1931 (6 full-page and 14 smaller black and white drawings, 1,500 copies signed by the artist, tan buckram in pictorial slipcase) . . . £450/£350

The Night Before Christmas, by Clement C. Moore, Harrap, 1931 (wraps with d/w) . . . £100/£65

ditto, Harrap, 1931 (deluxe 550 signed copies, limp vellum in slipcase) . . . . £1,000/£800

The Compleat Angler, by Izaak Walton, Harrap, 1931 (dark blue cloth) . . . . £250/£125

ditto, Harrap, 1931 (deluxe 775 signed copies, full vellum) £500

ditto, Harrap, 1931 (publisher's special binding, dark green or brown leather) £250

Fairy Tales, by Hans Anderson, Harrap, 1932 (rose-red cloth) . . . . £250/£125

ditto, Harrap, 1932 (deluxe 525 signed copies, full vellum) £750

ditto, Harrap, 1932 (publisher's special binding, full morocco) £300

The King of the Golden River, by John Ruskin, Harrap, 1932 (wraps with d/w) . . . . . . £100/£60

ditto, Harrap, 1932 (deluxe 570 signed copies, limp vellum) £500

Goblin Market, by Christina Rossetti, Harrap, 1933 (wraps with d/w) . . . . £100/£60

ditto, Harrap, 1933 (deluxe 410 signed copies, limp vellum) £500

The Arthur Rackham Fairy Book, by various, Harrap, 1933 (red cloth) . . . . £250/£125

ditto, Harrap, 1933 (deluxe 460 signed copies, full vellum) £750

The Pied Piper of Hamelin, by Robert Browning, Harrap, 1934 (wraps with d/w) . . . . . £100/£60

ditto, Harrap, 1934 (deluxe 410 signed copies, limp vellum) £500

Tales of Mystery and Imagination, by Edgar Allan Poe, Harrap, 1935 (grey-black cloth) . . . £275/£150

ditto, Harrap, 1935 (deluxe 460 signed copies, full vellum) £850

ditto, Harrap, 1935 (publisher's special binding, dark blue morocco) £400

Peer Gynt, by Henrik Ibsen, Harrap, 1936 (orange-brown cloth) . . . . £250/£125

ditto, Harrap, 1936 (deluxe 460 signed copies, full

vellum) £650

ditto, Harrap, 1936 (publisher's special binding, green morocco) £250

A Midsummer Night's Dream, by William Shakespeare, Limited Editions Club (U.S.), 1939 (deluxe 1,950 copies) £500

ditto, Weidenfeld & Nicholson, 1977 (12 colour plates, including 6 not previously published) £50

The Wind in the Willows, by Kenneth Grahame, Limited Editions Club (U.S.), 1940 (deluxe 2,020 copies, signed by the designer Bruce Rogers, cloth-backed patterned boards) £1,250

ditto, Heritage Press (U.S.), 1940 (blue-mauve cloth) . . . . £125/£75

ditto, Methuen (U.K.), 1950 (green cloth) . £125/£75

ditto, Methuen, 1951 (deluxe 500 copies, full white calf) £1,000

Haddon Hall Library Titles

Wild Life in Hampshire Highlands, by George A.B. Dewar, Dent, 1899 . . . . £50

ditto, Dent, 1899 (deluxe edition) £100

Our Gardens, by S. Reynolds Hole, Dent, 1899 £40

ditto, Dent, 1899 (deluxe edition, signed by Hole) £100

Fly Fishing, by Sir Edward Grey, Dent, 1899 . £75

ditto, Dent, 1899 (deluxe edition) £150

Our Forests and Woodlands, by John Nisbet, Dent, 1900 . . . . £35

ditto, Dent, 1900 (deluxe edition) £100

Hunting, by J. Otho Paget, Dent, 1900 . . . . £50

ditto, Dent, 1900 (deluxe edition) £150

Outdoor Games, Cricket & Golf, by Hon R.H. Lyttelton Dent, 1901 . . . . £75

ditto, Dent, 1901 (deluxe edition) £150

Bird Watching, by Edmund Selous, Dent, 1901. £50

ditto, Dent, 1901 (deluxe edition) £100

Shooting, by Alexander Innes Shand, Dent, 1902. £50

ditto, Dent, 1902 (deluxe edition) £150

Farming, by W.M. Todd, Dent, 1903 . . . . £35

ditto, Dent, 1903 (deluxe edition) £100

ARTHUR RANSOME

(b.1884 d.1967)

Author of the much loved 'Swallows and Amazons' series of books for children, Arthur Ransome also wrote for adults.

'Swallows and Amazons' Titles

Swallows and Amazons, Cape, 1930 . £1,000/£65

Swallowdale, Cape, 1931 . . . . . . £450/£45

Peter Duck, Cape, 1932 . . . . . . £225/£45

Winter Holiday, Cape, 1933 . . . . . . £225/£45

Coot Club, Cape, 1934 . . . . £225/£45

ditto, Lippincott (U.S.), 1935 . . . . . . £75/£25

Pigeon Post, Cape, 1936 . . . . £225/£45

ditto, Lippincott (U.S.), 1937 . . . . . . £75/£25

We Didn't Mean to Go to Sea, Cape, 1937 . £125/£35

ditto, Macmillan (U.S.), 1938. . . . . . £75/£25

Secret Water, Cape, 1939. . . . . . . £125/£35

ditto, Macmillan (U.S.), 1940. . . . . . £75/£25

The Big Six, Cape, 1940 . . . . £100/£25

Missee Lee, Cape, 1941 . . . . £100/£25

The Picts and the Martyrs, or Not Welcome At All, Cape, 1943 . . . . £90/£25

ditto, Macmillan (U.S.), 1943. . . . . . £45/£10

Great Northern, Cape, 1947 . . . . . . £75/£20

ditto, Macmillan (U.S.), 1948. . . . . . £45/£10

Other Children's Titles

Pond and Stream, Treherne, 1906 . . . . £145

The Child's Book of the Seasons, Treherne, 1906 £145

The Things in Our Garden, Treherne, 1906 . £145

Highways and Byways in Fairyland, Pinafore Library, [1906]. £165

The Imp and the Elf and the Ogre, Nisbet, 1910 £150

The Hoofmarks of the Faun, Martin Secker, 1911 . . . . £150

Old Peter's Russian Tales, T. C. & E. C. Jack, 1916 . . . . £150

Aladdin, Nisbet, [1919] £150

ditto, Nisbet, [1919] (250 signed copies) . . £1,000

Adult Titles

The ABC of Physical Culture, Drane, 1904 . £45

The Souls of the Streets, Brown Langham, 1904 £250

The Stone Lady, Brown Langham, 1905 . . £75

Bohemia in London, Chapman & Hall, 1907 . £75

A History of Storytelling, Jack, 1909 . . . £75

Edgar Allan Poe, Secker, 1910 . . . . . . £100

Oscar Wilde, Secker, 1912 . . . . £75

Portraits and Speculations, Macmillan, 1913 . £45

The Elixir of Life, Methuen, 1915 . . . . £45

Six Weeks in Russia in 1919, Allen & Unwin, 1919 (wraps) £75

The Crisis in Russia, Allen & Unwin, 1921. . £75

The Soldier and Death, J. C. Wilson, 1921 . . £45

Racundra's First Cruise, Allen & Unwin, 1923. . . . . £225/£125

ditto, Huebsch (U.S.), 1923 . . . . . . £100/£30

The Chinese Puzzle, Allen & Unwin, 1927 . £150/£45

Rod and Line, Cape, 1929 . . . . . . £400/£100

Mainly About Fishing, A. & C. Black, 1959 £150/£40

The Autobiography of Arthur Ransome, Cape, 1976 . . . . £20/£5

FORREST REID

(b.1875 d.1947)

An author whose evocations of his native Ulster landscape, and youth, are tinged with the supernatural.

Novels

The Kingdom of Twilight, Fisher Unwin, 1904 £125
The Garden God, David Nutt, 1905 . . . . £125
The Bracknels, Edward Arnold, 1911 . . . . £75
ditto, as ***Denis Bracknel***, Faber, 1947 revised edition) . . . . £15/£5
Following Darkness, Edward Arnold, 1912. . £75
The Gentle Lover, Edward Arnold, 1913 . . £75
At the Door of the Gate, Edward Arnold, 1915. £75
The Spring Song, Edward Arnold, 1916 . . £75
Pirates of the Spring, Fisher Unwin, 1919 [1920] . . . . £60/£20
Pender Among the Residents, Collins, 1922 £50/£10
Demophon, Collins, 1927 . . . . . £50/£10
Uncle Stephen, Faber, 1931 . . . . . £50/£10
Brian Westby, Faber, 1934 . . . . . £50/£10
The Retreat, Faber, 1936 . . . . . . £40/£10
Peter Waring, Faber, 1937 . . . . . £35/£10
Young Tom, Faber, 1944 . . . . . . £15/£5

Short Stories

A Garden by the Sea, Fisher Unwin, 1918 . . £50

Others

W.B. Yeats, A Critical Study, Secker, 1915 . . £40
Apostate, Constable, 1926 (50 signed copies) . £150
ditto, Constable, 1926 . . . . £50/£15
ditto, Faber, 1947 (engravings by Reynolds Stone) . . . . £45/£15
Illustrators of the Sixties, Faber & Gwyer, 1928 £150
Walter de la Mare, A Critical Study, Faber, 1929 £30
Private Road, Faber, 1940 . . . . . £20/£5
Retrospective Adventures, Faber, 1941 . . £35/£10
Notes and Impressions, The Mourne Press, 1942 £50
Poems from the Greek Anthology, Faber, 1943 £10/£5
The Milk of Paradise, Faber, 1946 . . . £10/£5

RUTH RENDELL

(b.1930)

A novelist and short story writer, Rendell is popularly known for the Wexford detective stories and novels. Other fiction written under her own name explores wider issues of criminal maladjustment, while the 'Barbara Vine' books tend to investigate darker psychological motivation.

'Wexford' Novels

From Doon with Death, Long, 1964 . £1,250/£150
ditto, Doubleday (U.S.), 1965 . . . . £200/£25
A New Lease of Death, Long, 1967 . . . £450/£50
ditto, Doubleday (U.S.), 1967 . . . . £150/£15
Wolf to the Slaughter, Long, 1967 . . . £450/£45
ditto, Doubleday (U.S.), 1968 . . . . £150/£15
The Best Man to Die, Long, 1969 . . . £200/£35
ditto, Doubleday (U.S.), 1970 . . . . £75/£15
A Guilty Thing Surprised, Hutchinson, 1970 £150/£25
ditto, Doubleday (U.S.), 1970 . . . . £60/£10
No More Dying, Then, Hutchinson, 1971 . £75/£25
ditto, Doubleday (U.S.), 1972 . . . . £35/£10
Murder Being Done Once, Hutchinson, 1972 £75/£20
ditto, Doubleday (U.S.), 1972 . . . . £35/£10
Some Lie and Some Die, Hutchinson, 1973. £50/£15
ditto, Doubleday (U.S.), 1973 . . . . £30/£10
Shake Hands for Ever, Hutchinson, 1975 . £50/£15
ditto, Doubleday (U.S.), 1975 . . . . £30/£10
A Sleeping Life, Hutchinson, 1978 . . . £25/£5
ditto, Doubleday (U.S.), 1978 . . . £15/£5
Put on by Cunning, Hutchinson, 1981 . . £20/£5
ditto, as ***Death Notes***, Pantheon, 1981 . . £10/£5
The Speaker of Mandarin, Hutchinson, 1983 £20/£5
ditto, Pantheon, 1983 . . . . £10/£5
An Unkindness of Ravens, Hutchinson, 1985 £20/£5
ditto, Pantheon, 1985 . . . . £10/£5
The Veiled One, Hutchinson, 1988 . . . £15/£5
ditto, Pantheon, 1988 . . . . £10/£5
Kissing the Gunner's Daughter, Hutchinson, 1992 . . . . £15/£5
ditto, Warner (U.S.), 1992 . . . . . £10/£5
Simisola, Hutchinson, 1994 . . . . . £15/£5
ditto, Crown (U.S.), 1995 . . . . . . £10/£5
Roadrage, Hutchinson, 1997 . . . . . £15/£5
ditto, Scorpion Press, 1997 (99 signed copies) . £75

Omnibus Editions

A Wexford Omnibus, Hutchinson, 1988. . £15/£5
A Second Wexford Omnibus, Hutchinson, 1989 £10/£5
The Third Wexford Omnibus, Hutchinson, 1989 . . . . £10/£5
The Fourth Wexford Omnibus, Hutchinson, 1990 . . . . £10/£5
Wexford Omnibus 5, Hutchinson, 1991 . . £10/£5

Other Novels

To Fear a Painted Devil, Long, 1965 . . £750/£100
ditto, Doubleday (U.S.), 1965 . . . . £150/£15
Vanity Dies Hard, Long, 1965 . . . . £450/£45
ditto, as ***In Sickness and in Health***, Doubleday (U.S.), 1966 . . . . £100/£15
The Secret House of Death, Long, 1968 . £450/£45
ditto, Doubleday (U.S.), 1969 . . . . £100/£15
One Across, Two Down, Hutchinson, 1971 . £175/£25

ditto, Doubleday (U.S.), 1971 . . . . £50/£10
The Face of Trespass, Hutchinson, 1974 . £75/£15
ditto, Doubleday (U.S.), 1974 . . . . £25/£10
A Demon in My View, Hutchinson, 1976 . £75/£15
ditto, Doubleday (U.S.), 1977 . . . . £25/£10
A Judgement in Stone, Hutchinson, 1977 . £35/£10
ditto, Doubleday (U.S.), 1978 . . . . £10/£5
Make Death Love Me, Hutchinson, 1979 . £30/£10
ditto, Doubleday (U.S.), 1979 . . . . £10/£5
The Lake of Darkness, Hutchinson, 1980 . £25/£10
ditto, Doubleday (U.S.), 1980 . . . . £10/£5
Master of the Moor, Hutchinson, 1981 . . £20/£5
ditto, Pantheon (U.S.), 1982 . . . . . £10/£5
The Killing Doll, Hutchinson, 1984 . . . £20/£5
ditto, Pantheon (U.S.), 1984 . . . . . £10/£5
The Tree of Hands, Hutchinson, 1984 . . £20/£5
ditto, Pantheon (U.S.), 1985 . . . . . £10/£5
Live Flesh, Hutchinson, 1986 . . . . £20/£5
ditto, Pantheon (U.S.), 1986 . . . . . £10/£5
A Dark Adapted Eye, Viking, 1986 (pseud. 'Barbara Vine') . . . . £20/£5
ditto, Bantam (U.S.), 1986 . . . . £5
A Warning to the Curious, Hutchinson, 1987 £20/£5
A Fatal Inversion, Viking, 1987 (pseud. 'Barbara Vine') . . . . £15/£5
ditto, Bantam (U.S.), 1987 . . . . £5
Heartstones, Hutchinson, 1987 . . . . £15/£5
ditto, Harper (U.S.), 1987. . . . . . . £10/£5
Talking to Strange Men, Hutchinson, 1987. £15/£5
ditto, Harper (U.S.), 1987. . . . . . . £10/£5
The House of Stairs, Viking, 1989 (pseud. 'Barbara Vine') . . . . £15/£5
ditto, Crown (U.S.), 1989 . . . . £10/£5
The Bridesmaid, Hutchinson, 1989 . . . £15/£5
ditto, Mysterious Press (U.S.), 1989 . . . £10/£5
Gallowglass, Viking, 1990 (pseud. 'Barbara Vine') . . . . £15/£5
ditto, Crown (U.S.), 1990 . . . . £10/£5
Going Wrong, Hutchinson, 1990. . . . . £15/£5
ditto, Mysterious Press (U.S.), 1990 . . . £10/£5
King Solomon's Carpet, Viking, 1991 (pseud. 'Barbara Vine') . . . . £15/£5
ditto, Crown (U.S.), 1992 . . . . £10/£5
Asta's Book, Viking, 1993 (pseud. 'Barbara Vine') . . . . £15/£5
ditto, Scorpion Press, 1993 (99 signed copies) . £75
The Crocodile Bird, Hutchinson, 1993 . . £10/£5
ditto, London Limited Editions, 1993 (150 signed copies, glassine d/w) . . . . £75/£65
ditto, Crown (U.S.), 1993 . . . . £10/£5
No Night is Too Long, Viking, 1994 . . £10/£5
ditto, Harmony (U.S.), 1994 . . . . . . £10/£5
The Brimstone Wedding, Harmony (U.S.), 1995 . . . . £10/£5
ditto, Viking, 1996. . . . . £10/£5
Keys to the Street, Hutchinson, 1996 . . £10/£5
ditto, Crown (U.S.), 1996 . . . . £10/£5
The Chimney Sweeper's Boy, Viking, 1998 £10/£5
ditto, Harmony (U.S.), 1998 . . . . . . £10/£5
A Sight for Sore Eyes, Hutchinson, 1998 . £10/£5
ditto, Crown (U.S.), 1998 . . . . . . £10/£5
ditto, Scorpion Press, 1998 (99 signed copies) . £75

Short Stories

The Fallen Curtain and Other Stories, Hutchinson, 1976 . . . . £100/£25
ditto, Doubleday (U.S.), 1976 . . . . . £50/£15
Means of Evil and Other Stories, Hutchinson, 1979 . . . . £30/£10
The Fever Tree and Other Stories, Hutchinson, 1982 . . . . £40/£10
ditto, Pantheon (U.S.), 1983 . . . . . £20/£5
The New Girlfriend and Other Stories of Suspense, Hutchinson, 1986 . . . . £20/£5
ditto, Pantheon (U.S.), 1986 . . . . . £10/£5
Three Cases for Inspector Wexford, Eurographica (Helsinki), 1986 (350 signed copies, wraps) . £75
Collected Short Stories, Hutchinson, 1987 . £10/£5
ditto, Pantheon (U.S.), 1988 . . . . . £10/£5
The Copper Peacock and Other Stories, Hutchinson, 1991 . . . . £15/£5
ditto, Mysterious Press (U.S.), 1991 . . . £10/£5
Blood Lines, Hutchinson, 1995 . . . £10/£5
ditto, Crown (U.S.), 1996 . . . . . . £10/£5

Non Fiction

Matters of Suspense, Eurographica (Helsinki), 1986 (350 signed copies, wraps) £75
Ruth Rendell's Suffolk, Muller, 1989 . . £25/£5
Undermining the Central Line, Chatto and Windus, 1989 (with Colin Ward, signed, wraps) . . £25
ditto, Chatto and Windus, 1989 (unsigned copies) £10

JEAN RHYS

(b.1894 d.1979)

Powerfully clear and imaginative writing peoples Rhys's novels with strong female characters, although the protagonists are often lonely and lacking in direction.

Novels

Postures, Chatto & Windus, 1928 . . £1,000/£100
ditto, as ***Quartet***, Simon & Schuster, 1929 . £75/£20
After Leaving Mr Mackenzie, Cape, 1931 . £500/£75
ditto, Knopf (U.S.), 1931 . . . . . . £100/£15
Voyage in the Dark, Constable, 1934 . . £400/£65
ditto, Morrow (U.S.), 1935 . . . . . £250/£45

Good Morning, Midnight, Constable, 1939. £30/£50
ditto, Harper & Row (U.S.), [1970] . . . £15/£5
Wide Sargasso Sea, Deutsch, 1966 . . . £75/£15
ditto, Norton (U.S.), 1966. . . . . . . £15/£5

Short Stories
The Left Bank and Other Stories, Cape, 1927 . . . . £450/£75
ditto, Harper (U.S.), 1927. . . . . . . £225/£50
Tigers Are Better Looking, Deutsch, 1968 . £50/£15
ditto, Harper (U.S.), 1974. . . . . . . £15/£5
Sleep It Off Lady, Deutsch, 1976 . . . £15/£5
ditto, Harper (U.S.), 1976. . . . . . . £15/£5

Translation
Perversity, by Francis Carco (translated by "Ford Maddox Ford" [Jean Rhys], Covici (U.S.), 1928 . . . . £125/£30

Others
My Day, Three Pieces, Frank Hallman (U.S.), 1975 (wraps) £10
ditto, Frank Hallman (U.S.), 1975 (750 copies) £35/£25
ditto, Frank Hallman (U.S.), 1975 (26 signed, lettered copies) £125
Letters, 1931-1966, Deutsch, 1984 . . . £15/£5
ditto, Viking (U.S.), 1984. . . . . . . £15/£5
Smile Please, An Unfinished Biography, Deutsch, 1979 . . . . £15/£5
ditto, Harper (U.S.), 1980. . . . . . . £15/£5

ANNE RICE
(b.1941)

Interview with the Vampire started life as a cult best-seller and found itself two decades later as a Hollywood film. Under her pen-names Rice also publishes erotica.

Novels
Interview with the Vampire, Knopf (U.S.), 1976 . . . . £400/£45
ditto, Macdonald/Raven Books, 1976 . . £150/£35
The Feast of All Saints, Simon & Schuster (U.S.), 1979 . . . . £100/£25
Cry to Heaven, Knopf (U.S.), 1982 . . . £25/£10
ditto, Chatto & Windus, 1990 . . . . £15/£5
Beauty's Punishment, Dutton (U.S.), 1984 (pseud. 'A. N. Roquelaure') . . . . £125/£35
ditto, Futura Books, 1987 (wraps, pseud. 'A. N. Roquelaure') £10
Beauty's Release, Dutton (U.S.), 1985 (pseud. 'A. N. Roquelaure') . . . . £125/£35
ditto, Future Books, 1988 (wraps, pseud. 'A. N. Roquelaure') £10
The Vampire Lestat, Knopf (U.S.), 1985 . £125/£35
ditto, Futura Books, 1986 (wraps) £5
ditto, Macdonald, 1987 (first hardback) . . £25/£10
Exit to Eden, Arbor House (U.S.), 1985 (pseud. 'Anne Rampling') . . . . £60/£15
ditto, Macdonald, 1986 (pseud. 'Anne Rampling') . . . . £10/£5
Belinda, Arbor House (U.S.), 1986 (pseud. 'Anne Rampling') . . . . £20/£5
ditto, Macdonald, 1987 (pseud. 'Anne Rampling') . . . . £15/£5
The Claiming of Sleeping Beauty, Dutton (U.S.), 1983 . . . . £125/£35
ditto, Future Books, 1987 (pseud. 'A. N. Roquelaure', wraps). £5
ditto, Macdonald, 1988 . . . . £15/£5
The Queen of the Damned, Knopf (U.S.), 1988 £20/£5
ditto, Macdonald, 1988 . . . . £15/£5
The Mummy, or Ramses the Damned, Ballantine Books (U.S.), 1989 . . . . £10
ditto, Chatto & Windus, 1989 . . . . . £150/£25
The Witching Hour, Knopf (U.S.), 1990 . £15/£5
ditto, Chatto & Windus, 1991 . . . . £10/£5
The Tale of the Body Thief, Knopf (U.S.), 1992 . . . . £15/£5
ditto, Chatto & Windus, 1992 . . . . £10/£5
Lasher, Knopf (U.S.), 1993 . . . . . . £15/£5
ditto, Chatto & Windus, 1993 . . . . £10/£5
Taltos, Lives of the Mayfair Witches, Knopf (U.S.), 1994 . . . . £10/£5
ditto, Chatto & Windus, 1994 . . . . £10/£5
The Anne Rice Omnibus, Little Brown, 1994 £10/£5
Memnoch the Devil, Knopf (U.S.), 1995 . £10/£5
ditto, Chatto & Windus, 1995 . . . . £10/£5
Servant of the Bones, Knopf (U.S.), 1996 . £10/£5
ditto, Chatto & Windus, 1996 . . . . £10/£5
Violin, Chatto & Windus, 1997 . . . . £10/£5
ditto, Knopf (U.S.), 1997 . . . . £10/£5
Pandora, Knopf (U.S.), 1998. . . . . . £10/£5
ditto, Chatto & Windus, 1998 . . . . £10/£5
The Vampire Armand, Trice (U.S.), 1998 (26 signed, lettered copies, bound in full leather) . . . £400
ditto, Trice (U.S.), 1998 (50 signed, deluxe copies, quarterbound in leather) £200
ditto, Trice (U.S.), 1998 (250 signed, numbered copies) £75
ditto, Knopf (U.S.), 1998 . . . . £10/£5
ditto, Chatto & Windus, 1998 . . . . £10/£5
Vittorio the Vampire, Knopf (U.S.), 1998 . £10/£5

FRANK RICHARDS

(b.1876 d.1961)

Under the pseudonym of 'Frank Richards', Charles Hamilton created the everlasting, rotund schoolboy, Billy Bunter.

Billy Bunter of Greyfriars School, Skilton, 1947 . . . . £75/£15
Billy Bunter's Banknote, Skilton, 1948 . . £60/£10
Billy Bunter's Barring-Out, Skilton, 1948 . £50/£10
Billy Bunter's Christmas Party, Skilton, 1949 £50/£10
Billy Bunter in Brazil, Skilton, 1949 . . £50/£10
Bessie Bunter of Cliff House School, Skilton, 1949 (pseud. 'Hilda Richards'). . . . . . £45/£10
Billy Bunter's Benefit, Skilton, 1950 . . £50/£10
Billy Bunter among the Cannibals, Skilton, 1950 . . . . £45/£10
Billy Bunter's Postal Order, Skilton, 1951 . £45/£10
Billy Bunter Butts In, Skilton, 1951 . . . . £45/£10
Billy Bunter and the Blue Mauritius, Skilton, 1952 . . . . £50/£10
Billy Bunter's Beanfeast, Cassell, 1952 . . £45/£10
Billy Bunter's Brain-Wave, Cassell, 1953 . £45/£10
Billy Bunter's First Case, Cassell, 1953. . £45/£10
Billy Bunter the Bold, Cassell, 1954. . . £30/£5
Bunter Does His Best, Cassell, 1954 . . £30/£5
Billy Bunter's Double, Cassell, 1955 . . £30/£5
Backing Up Billy Bunter, Cassell, 1955 . £30/£5
Lord Billy Bunter, Cassell, 1956 . . . £25/£5
The Banishing of Billy Bunter, Cassell, 1956 £25/£5
Billy Bunter's Bolt, Cassell, 1957 . . . £25/£5
Billy Bunter Afloat, Cassell, 1957 . . . £25/£5
Billy Bunter's Bargain, Cassell, 1958 . . £20/£5
Billy Bunter the Hiker, Cassell, 1958 . . £20/£5
Bunter Out of Bounds, Cassell, 1959 . £20/£5
Bunter Comes for Christmas, Cassell, 1959 £20/£5
Bunter the Bad Lad, Cassell, 1960 . . . £20/£5
Bunter Keeps It Dark, Cassell, 1960 . . £20/£5
Billy Bunter's Treasure-Hunt, Cassell, 1961 £20/£5
Billy Bunter at Butlins, Cassell, 1961 . . £20/£5
ditto, Butlins Beaver Club edition, 1961 . £15/£5
Bunter the Ventriloquist, Cassell, 1961 . £20/£5
Bunter the Caravanner, Cassell, 1962 . . £20/£5
Billy Bunter's Bodyguard, Cassell, 1962 . £20/£5
Big Chief Bunter, Cassell, 1963 . . . . £20/£5
Just Like Bunter, Cassell, 1963 . . . . £20/£5
Bunter the Stowaway, Cassell, 1964 . . £20/£5
Thanks to Bunter, Cassell, 1964 . . . . £20/£5
Bunter the Sportsman, Cassell, 1965 . . £20/£5
Bunter's Last Fling, Cassell, 1965 . . . £20/£5

W. HEATH ROBINSON

(b.1872 d.1944)

A British author and illustrator, Robinson did not find his own distinctive style until *The Adventures of Uncle Lubin*. He is popularly known for his illustrations of preposterous inventions.

Written and Illustrated by Heath Robinson

The Adventures of Uncle Lubin, Grant Richards, 1902 . . . . £350
ditto, Grant Richards, 1925 (new edition) . £100/£35
The Child's Arabian Nights, Grant Richards, 1903 . . . . £300
Bill the Minder, Constable, 1912 . . . . £450
ditto, Constable, 1912 (380 signed copies bound in vellum) £1,250
ditto, Holt (U.S.), 1912 . . . . £400
Peter Quip in Search of a Friend, S.W. Partridge [1922]. £1,000
My Line of Life, Blackie, 1938 . . . . £150/£60
Let's Laugh, A Book of Humorous Inventions, Hutchinson, [1939] . . . . £75/£25

Illustrated by Heath Robinson

Danish Fairy Tales and Legends, by H. C. Andersen, Bliss Sands & Co., 1897. . . . . . . £75
The Life and Exploits of Don Quixote, by Cervantes, Bliss Sands & Co., 1897. . . . . . . £45
The Pilgrim's Progress, by John Bunyan, Bliss Sands & Co., 1897 . . . . £60
The Giant Crab and Other Tales from Old India, by W.H.D. Rouse, Nutt, 1897 . . . . . . £350
The Queen's Story Book, edited by L. Gomme, Constable, 1898 . . . . £60
The Arabian Nights Entertainments, Newnes/ Constable, 1899 . . . . £75
Fairy Tales from Hans Christian Andersen, Dent, 1899 . . . . £100
The Talking Thrush, by W.H.D. Rouse, Dent, 1899 . . . . £275
The Poems of Edgar Allan Poe, Bell, 1900. . £150
ditto, Bell, 1900 (75 copies on Japanese vellum) £750
Tales for Toby, by A.R. Hope, Dent, 1900 . . £45
The Adventures of Don Quixote, by Cervantes, Dent, 1902 . . . . £65
Mediaeval Stories, by H. Schuck, Sands, 1902 . £50
The Surprising Travels and Adventures of Baron Munchausen, by R.E. Raspe, Grant Richards, 1902 . . . . £75
Tales from Shakespeare, by C. and M. Lamb, Sands, [1902]. £65
Rama and the Monkeys, edited by G Hodgson, Dent, 1903 . . . . £65
The Works of Mr Francis Rabelais, Grant Richards,

1904 (2 vols) £250
Stories from Chaucer, edited by J.H. Kelman, Jack [1905] £50
Two Memoirs of Barry Lydon and Men's Wives, by W.M. Thackeray, Caxton, [1906] £50
Stories from the Iliad, edited by Jeanie Lang, Jack [1906] £35
Stories from the Odyssey, edited by Jeanie Lang, Jack [1906] £35
The Monarchs of Merry England, by Roland Carse, Alf Cooke [1907] (4 vols, wraps) £200
More Monarchs of Merry England, by Roland Carse, T. Fisher Unwin [1908] £175
Twelfth Night, by W. Shakespeare, Hodder & Stoughton [1908] £175
ditto, Hodder & Stoughton [1908] (350 signed copies, bound in vellum) £350
A Song of the English, by Rudyard Kipling, Hodder & Stoughton [1909] £45
ditto, Hodder & Stoughton [1909] (500 signed copies, bound in vellum) £200
The Collected Verse of Rudyard Kipling, Doubleday Page (U.S.), 1910 . . . . £100
The Dead King, by Rudyard Kipling, Hodder & Stoughton, 1910 (wraps) £45
Hans Andersen's Fairy Tales, Constable, 1913 £500
ditto, Constable, 1913 (100 signed copies, bound in vellum) £1,750
A Midsummer Night's Dream, by W. Shakespeare, Constable, 1914 . . . . £200
ditto, Constable, 1914 (150 of 250 signed copies bound in green boards) £450
ditto, Constable, 1914 (100 of 250 copies bound in vellum) £600
The Water Babies, by Charles Kingsley, Constable, 1915 . . . . £100
Peacock Pie, by Walter de la Mare, Constable, 1916 . . . . £75
Old Time Stories, by C. Perrault, Constable, 1921 . . . . £200/£75
Topsy Turvey Tales, by E. S. Munro, John Lane, 1923 . . . . £175/£75
The Incredible Adventures of Professor Branestawm, by Norman Hunter, John Lane, 1933 . . £125/£40
Balbus, A Latin Reading Book, by G.M. Lyne, E. Arnold, 1934 . . . . £75/£25
Heath Robinson's Book of Goblins, Hutchinson [1934] . . . . £200/£75
Once Upon A Time, by L. M. C. Clopet, Muller, 1934. . . . . £175/£75
The Adventures of Don Quixote, by Cervantes, Dent, 1953 . . . . £50/£15

SAX ROHMER
(b.1886 d.1959)

Rohmer was the pseudonym for Arthur Ward. Many of his exotic thrillers follow the devilish exploits of the sinister Dr Fu Manchu.

Fu Manchu Novels
The Mystery of Fu Manchu, Methuen, 1913 . £750
The Devil Doctor, Methuen, 1916 . . . . . £500
The Si-Fan Mysteries, Methuen, 1917 . . . . £200
The Daughter of Fu Manchu, Cassell, 1931 . . . . £750/£100
The Mask of Fu Manchu, Cassell, 1933 . £750/£100
The Bride of Fu Manchu, Cassell, 1933 . £450/£65
The Trail of Fu Manchu, Cassell, 1934. . £200/£30
President Fu Manchu, Cassell, 1936 . . £150/£25
The Drums of Fu Manchu, Cassell, 1939 . £200/£30
The Island of Fu Manchu, Cassell, 1941 £200/£30
Re-Enter Dr Fu Manchu, Herbert Jenkins, 1957 . . . . £150/£20
Emperor Fu Manchu, Herbert Jenkins, 1959 £150/£20
The Wrath of Fu Manchu, Tom Stacey, 1973 £65/£15

Omnibus Editions
The Book of Fu Manchu, Hurst & Blackett, 1929 . . . . £350/£30

Other Novels
10.30 Folkestone Express, Lloyds Home Novels No. 41 [no date] £250
The Sins of Severac Bablon, Cassell, 1914 . £250
The Yellow Claw, Methuen, 1915 . . . . . £200
Brood of the Witch Queen, Pearson, 1918 . . £250
The Orchard of Tears, Methuen, 1919 . . . £150
The Quest of the Sacred Slipper, Pearson, 1919 £125
Dope, Cassell, 1919 . . . . £125
The Golden Scorpion, Methuen, 1919 . . . £125
The Green Eyes of Bast, Cassell, 1920 . . £200/£30
Bat-Wing, Cassell, 1921 . . . . £200/£30
Fire-Tongue, Cassell, 1921 . . . . . . £600/£75
Grey Face, Cassell, 1924 . . . . £200/£30
Yellow Shadows, Cassell, 1925 . . . . . £250/£40
Moon of Madness, Cassell, 1927 . . . . £250/£40
She Who Sleeps, Cassell, 1928 . . . . . £250/£40
The Emperor of America, Cassell, 1929 . £300/£50
The Day the World Ended, Cassell, 1930 . £250/£40
Tu'an Hee See Laughs, Cassell, 1932 . . £250/£40
The Bat Flies Low, Cassell, 1935 . . . £300/£50
White Velvet, Cassell, 1936 . . . . . . £250/£40
Seven Sins, Cassell, 1944. . . . . . . £150/£35
Wulfheim, Jarrolds, 1950 (pseud. 'Michael Furey') . . . . £150/£35
Hangover House, Herbert Jenkins, 1950 . £125/£20
Sins of Sumuru, Herbert Jenkins, 1951 . . £125/£20

Slaves of Sumuru, Herbert Jenkins, 1952 . £125/£20
Virgin in Flames, Herbert Jenkins, 1953 . £125/£20
The Moon is Red, Herbert Jenkins, 1954 . £125/£20
Sand and Satin, Herbert Jenkins, 1955 . . £125/£20
Sinister Madonna, Herbert Jenkins, 1956 . £125/£20

Short Stories
The Exploits of Captain O'Hagan, Jarrolds, 1916 . . . . £400
Tales of Secret Egypt, Methuen, 1918 . . . £350
The Dream Detective, Jarrolds, 1920 . . £750/£200
The Haunting of Low Fennel, Pearson, 1920 . . . . £750/£125
Tales of Chinatown, Cassell, 1922 . . . £650/£75
Tales of East and West, Cassell, 1932 . . £250/£35
Salute to Bazarada, Cassell, 1939 . . . £125/£25
Egyptian Nights, Hale, 1944 . . . . . . £125/£25
The Secret of Holm Peel, and Other Strange Stories, Ace (U.S.) 1970 (wraps). £10

Non Fiction Titles
Pause!, Greening, 1910 (anonymous) . . . £500
Little Tich, Greening, 1911 . . . . £500
The Romance of Sorcery, Methuen, 1914 . . £400

FREDERICK ROLFE (BARON CORVO)

(b.1860 d.1913)

The author of a number of almost indigestible semi-autobiographical novels, Rolfe had an unbelievably self-destructive paranoia. He is read for his Toto tales and for the minor classic *Hadrian VII*. Sadly, he only really reached the level of genius in his vituperative letters to self-created enemies.

Tarcissus: The Boy Martyr of Rome, privately printed [1880] (wraps) £600
Stories Toto Told Me, Bodley Head, 1898 . . £200
The Attack on St. Winefride's Well, privately printed [1898] (anonymous, wraps) £500
In His Own Image, Bodley Head, 1901 . . . £100
Chronicles of the House of Borgia, Grant Richards, 1901 . . . . £100
Hadrian the Seventh, Chatto & Windus, 1904 . £250
Don Tarquinio, Chatto & Windus, 1905 . . £75
Don Renato, An Ideal Content, Francis Griffiths, 1909 . . . . £100
ditto, Chatto & Windus, 1963 (200 copies in slipcase) . . . . £100/£75
The Weird of the Wanderer, by Prospero and Caliban, William Rider, 1912 . . . . £250
The Bull Against the Enemy of the Anglican Race, Corvine Society, 1929 (50 copies, wraps) . . £200
Hubert's Arthur, by Prospero and Caliban, Cassell, 1935 . . . . £175/£50
The Desire and Pursuit of the Whole, Cassell [1934] . . . . £75/£25
Three Tales of Venice, The Corvine Press [1950] (150 numbered copies) £200
Amico di Sandro, A Fragment of a Novel, The Peacocks Press, 1951 (150 numbered copies) £350
Letters to Grant Richards, The Peacocks Press, 1951 (200 numbered copies) £300
The Cardinal Prefect of Propaganda, Nicholas Vane, 1957 (262 copies) £125
Nicholas Crabbe, Chatto & Windus, 1958 . £35/£10
ditto, Chatto & Windus, 1958 (215 numbered, large paper copies in slipcase). . . . . . . £125/£100
The Centenary Edition of the Letters of Frederick William Rolfe, Nicholas Vane, 1959 . . . £200
Letters to Pirie Gordon and Leonard Moore, Nicholas Vane, 1959-60 (350 copies, 2 vols). . . . £200
A Letter to Father Beauclerk, Tragara Press (Edinburgh), 1960 (20 copies) £200
Letters to Leonard Moore, Cecil & Amelia Woolf, 1960 (260 numbered copies) £100
Letters of Baron Corvo to Kenneth Grahame, The Peacocks Press, 1962 (40 copies) £200
Without Prejudice - One Hundred Letters from Frederick William Rolfe, Baron Corvo to John Lane, privately printed for Allen Lane, 1963 (600 copies) £150
A Letter to a Small Nephew Named Claude, Iowa City, 1964 (134 copies) £150
Letters to James Walsh, Bertram Rota, 1972 (500 copies) £75
Ballade of Boys Bathing, Tragara Press (Edinburgh), 1972 (200 numbered copies) £75
Collected Poems of Fr Rolfe, Baron Corvo, Cecil & Amelia Woolf, 1974 . . . . £20/£5
ditto, Cecil & Amelia Woolf, 1974 (200 numbered copies) £75
The Reverse Side of the Coin, Tragara Press (Edinburgh), 1974 (95 copies) £75
The Venice Letters, Cecil & Amelia Woolf, 1974 . . . . £100/£25
The Armed Hands, and Other Stories, Cecil & Amelia Woolf, 1974 . . . . £20/£5
ditto, Cecil & Amelia Woolf, 1974 (200 numbered copies) £75
Aberdeen Interval, Tragara Press (Edinburgh), 1975 (140 copies) £65
Different Aspects: Frederick William Rolfe and the Foreign Office, Tragara Press (Edinburgh), 1977 (125 copies) £50
Frederick Rolfe and 'The Times' 4-12 Feb, 1901, Tragara Press (Edinburgh), 1975 (175 copies). £45

Letters to Harry Bainbridge, Enitharmon Press, 1977 (350 of 395 copies) £40
ditto, Enitharmon Press, 1977 (45 numbered copies of 395) £150

Miscellaneous
The Rubaiyat of Umar Khaiyam, John Lane, 1903 (translated by Rolfe) £150
Agricultural and Pastoral Prospects of South Africa, by Col. Owen Thomas, Archibald Constable, 1904 (ghost-written by Rolfe) £100

RUPERT

see Mary Tourtel

SALMAN RUSHDIE

(b.1947)

Salman Rushdie, purveyor of post-modernist pyrotechnics, was born in Bombay but migrated to Britain in 1965. His writing is often described as *magic realism*, and has brought him great literary respect.

Novels
Grimus, Gollancz, 1975 . . . . £250/£35
ditto, Overlook Press (U.S.), 1979 . . . £100/£20
Midnight's Children, Knopf (U.S.), 1981 . £200/£35
ditto, Cape, 1981 . . . . £300/£45
Shame, Cape, 1983 . . . . £25/£10
ditto, Knopf (U.S.), 1983 . . . . £20/£5
The Satanic Verses, Viking, 1988 . . . £75/£20
ditto, Viking, 1988 (100 arabic numbered copies) £500
ditto, Viking (U.S.), 1988 . . . . . £35/£10
ditto, Penguin, 1988 (suppressed edition, wraps) £350
The Moor's Last Sigh, Cape, 1995 . . . £15/£5
ditto, Cape, 1995 (200 signed copies, no d/w) . £100
ditto, Cape, 1995 (2,500 copies in slipcase with facsimilie signature) . . . . £65/£45
ditto, Pantheon (U.S.), 1995 . . . . . £10/£5
ditto, Pantheon (U.S.), 1995 (1,000 signed advance reading copies, wraps, in slipcase) . . . £75/£50
The Ground Beneath Her Feet, Cape, 1999 £15/£5
ditto, Cape, 1999 (150 signed copies, full leather bound, in slipcase) . . . . £200/£150
ditto, Holt (U.S.), 1999 . . . . £10/£5

Children's
Haroun and the Sea of Stories, Granta, 1990 £15/£5
ditto, Granta, 1990 (251 signed copies) . . . £150
ditto, Viking (U.S.), 1991 . . . . . . £10/£5

Short Stories
Two Stories, privately printed, 1989 (60 signed copies of 72) £750
ditto, privately printed, 1989 (12 specially bound, signed copies of 72) £1,750
East, West, Cape, 1994 . . . . . . £15/£5
ditto, Pantheon (U.S.), 1994 . . . . £10/£5

Others
The Jaguar Smile: A Nicaraguan Journey, Picador, 1987 . . . . £10/£5
ditto, Viking (U.S.), 1987 . . . . £10/£5
Is Nothing Sacred?, Granta, 1990 . . . £10/£5
Imaginary Homelands: Essays and Criticism, Granta, 1991 . . . . £10/£5
ditto, Viking (U.S.), 1991 . . . . £10/£5
The Wizard of Oz, B.F.I., 1992 (wraps) . . . £15

VITA SACKVILLE-WEST

(b.1892 d.1962)

The Land brought Vita Sackville-West recognition, winning her the Hawthornden prize. A writer of both poetry and prose, she was also a passionate gardener. It is said the she was the model for Virginia Woolf's *Orlando*.

Novels
Heritage, Collins, 1919 . . . . £75
The Dragon in Shallow Waters, Collins, 1921 . . . . £300/£125
Challenge, Doran (U.S.), 1923 . . . £250/£125
Grey Wethers, Heinemann, 1923. . . . . £225/£65
Seducers in Equador, Hogarth Press, 1924 £200/£45
ditto, Doran (U.S.), 1925 . . . . £100/£25
The Edwardians, Hogarth Press, 1930 . . £200/£45
ditto, Hogarth Press, 1930 (125 copies) . . . £450
ditto, Doran (U.S.), 1930 . . . . £75/£20
All Passion Spent, Hogarth Press, 1931 . . £250/£50
ditto, Doran (U.S.), 1931 . . . . £75/£20
Family History, Hogarth Press, 1932 . . £150/£45
The Death of Noble Godavary and Gottfried Kunstler, Benn, 1932 (wraps) £25
The Dark Island, Hogarth Press, 1934 . . £125/£45
ditto, Doran (U.S.), 1934 . . . . £75/£20
Grand Canyon, Michael Joseph, 1942 . . £65/£20
ditto, Doran (U.S.), 1942 . . . . £45/£15
Devil at Westease, Doubleday Doran (U.S.), 1947 . . . . £175/£45
The Easter Party, Michael Joseph, 1953 . £35/£15
ditto, Doubleday (U.S.), 1953 . . . . . £25/£10
No Signposts in the Sea, Michael Joseph, 1961 . . . . £25/£10

ditto, Doubleday (U.S.), 1961 . . . . £15/£5

Short Stories
The Heir, privately printed, [1922] (100 signed copies) £350
ditto, Heinemann, 1922 . . . . . . £200/£50
Thirty Clocks Strike the Hour and Other Stories, Doubleday Doran (U.S.), 1934 . . . . £125/£45

Verse
Chatterton, privately printed, 1909 (wraps) . £2,000
Constantinople, Eight Poems, privately printed, Complete Press, 1915 (wraps) £250
Poems of West and East, John Lane, 1917 . . £65
Orchard and Vineyard, John Lane, 1921 . £125/£25
The Land, Heinemann, 1926 . . . . . £125/£25
ditto, Heinemann, 1926 (125 copies, slipcase) . . . . £250/£175
King's Daughter, Hogarth Press, 1929 . . £100/£30
ditto, Doubleday (U.S.), 1930 . . . . £75/£25
Sissinghurst, Hogarth Press, 1931 (500 signed, numbered copies, hand-printed by the Woolfs) £300
Invitation to Cast Out Care, Faber, 1931 . £50/£20
ditto, Faber, 1931 (200 copies) £125
V. Sackville-West, Benn, 1931 . . . . . £10
Collected Poems, Volume One, Hogarth Press, 1933 . . . . £100/£35
ditto, Hogarth Press, 1933 (150 copies) . . . £200
Solitude, Hogarth Press, 1938 . . . . £75/£25
Selected Poems, Hogarth Press, 1941 . . £45/£15
The Garden, Michael Joseph, 1946 . . . £60/£20
ditto, Michael Joseph, 1946 (500 signed copies, plain d/w) . . . . £250/£100

Travel
Passenger to Tehran, Hogarth Press, 1926 £250/£75
Twelve Days, Hogarth Press, 1928 . . . £250/£50

Gardening
Some Flowers, Cobden-Sanderson, 1937 . £75/£30
Country Notes, Michael Joseph, 1939 . . £75/£30
ditto, Harper (U.S.), 1940. . . . . . . £40/£10
Country Notes in Wartime, Hogarth Press, 1940 . . . . £65/£15
In Your Garden, Michael Joseph, 1951 . . £45/£15
Hidcote Manor Garden, Country Life, 1952 £25/£10
In Your Garden Again, Michael Joseph, 1953 £45/£15
More For Your Garden, Michael Joseph, 1955. . . . . £35/£10
Even More For Your Garden, Michael Joseph, 1958 . . . . £35/£10
A Joy of Gardening, Harper & Row (U.S.), 1958 . . . . £25/£10
V. Sackville-West's Garden Book, Michael Joseph, 1968 . . . . £20/£5
ditto, Atheneum (U.S.), 1968 . . . . . . £15/£5
The Illustrated Garden Book, Michael Joseph, 1986 . . . . £15/£5

Historical and Biographical
Knole and the Sackvilles, Heinemann, 1922 £125/£35
ditto, Doran (U.S.), 1922 . . . . £100/£25
Aphra Benn, The Incomparable Astrea, Gerald Howe, 1927 . . . . £100/£35
ditto, Viking (U.S.), 1928 . . . . £75/£30
Andrew Marvell, Faber, 1929 . . . . £65/£20
ditto, Faber, 1929 (75 signed copies) £200
Saint Joan of Arc, Cobden-Sanderson, 1936 £45/£15
ditto, Cobden-Sanderson, 1936 (120 copies) . £150
ditto, Doubleday (U.S.), 1936 . . . . £30/£10
Joan of Arc, Hogarth Press, 1937 . . . £65/£15
Pepita, Hogarth Press, 1937 . . . . . £65/£10
ditto, Doubleday (U.S.), 1937 . . . . £30/£10
English Country Houses, Collins, 1941 . . £25/£5
ditto, Collins, 1941 (bound in green cloth) . £35/£20
The Eagle and the Dove, Michael Joseph, 1943 . . . . £30/£10
Daughter of France, Michael Joseph, 1959 £30/£10
ditto, Doubleday (U.S.), 1959 . . . . . £30/£10

Others
The Diary of the Lady Anne Clifford, Heinemann, 1923 (edited by V. Sackville-West) . . £150/£40
Rilke, Hogarth Press, 1931 (translation) . . £75/£20
The Women's Land Army, Michael Joseph, 1944 . . . . £40/£15
Nursery Rhymes, Dropmore Press, 1947 (550 copies) . . . . £150/£45
ditto, Dropmore Press, 1947 (25 signed copies of the above). . . . . £750/£500
Faces: Profiles of Dogs, Harvill Press, 1961 £20/£5
Dearest Andrew, Letters to Andrew Reiber, 1951-62, Michael Joseph, 1979 . . . . . . £20/£10
Letters from V. Sackville-West to Virginia Woolf, Michael Joseph, 1984 . . . . . . £20/£5

SAKI

(b.1870 d.1916)

Saki was a pseudonym adopted by H. H. Munro for his predominantly humorous novels and short stories. Although his writing is whimsical and satirical, some critics have noted the darker undercurrent of the alienated outsider.

Novels
The Unbearable Bassington, John Lane, 1912 . £50
When William Came, John Lane, 1913 . . . £40

The Collected Novels and Plays, John Lane, The Bodley Head, 1933. . . . . £35/£15

Short Stories

Reginald, Methuen, 1904 . . . . £100

Reginald in Russia and Other Sketches, Methuen, 1910 . . . . £45

The Chronicles of Clovis, John Lane, 1911 . . . £45

Beasts and Superbeasts, John Lane, 1914 . . £25

The Toys of Peace, John Lane, The Bodley Head, 1919 . . . . £25

The Square Egg and Other Sketches, John Lane, The Bodley Head, 1924 . . . . £35/£10

The Collected Short Stories, John Lane, The Bodley Head, 1930 . . . . £20/£5

Others

The Rise of the Russian Empire, Grant Richards, 1900 . . . . £45

The Westminster Alice, Westminster Gazette, 1902 (wraps) £225

ditto, Westminster Gazette, 1902 (boards) . . £125

J.D. SALINGER

(b.1919)

Essentially a one-novel novelist, the author of *The Catcher in the Rye* was born in New York. He now lives in Cornish, New Hampshire.

Novels

The Catcher in the Rye, Little Brown (U.S.), 1951 . . . . £2,000/£150

ditto, Hamish Hamilton, 1951 . . . . £300/£65

Short Stories

Nine Stories, Little Brown (U.S.), 1953 . . £750/£150

ditto, as ***For Esme - With Love and Squalor and Other Stories***, Hamish Hamilton, 1953 . . . . £150/£35

Franny and Zooey, Little Brown (U.S.), 1961 £75/£20

ditto, Heinemann, 1963 . . . . £35/£10

Raise High the Roof Beam, Carpenters and Seymour: An Introduction, Little Brown (U.S.), 1963 £45/£10

ditto, Heinemann, 1963 . . . . £25/£10

The Complete and Uncollected Short Stories of J. D. Salinger, no publisher named, 1974 (2 vols, wraps, first vol. saddle-stitched and the second vol. perfect bound., pirated edition) £450

SARBAN

(b.1910 d.1989)

Pseudonym used by John W. Wall, a diplomat for many years stationed in the Middle-East.

Ringstones and other stories, Davies, 1951 £125/£30

The Sound of His Horn, Davies, 1952 . . £150/£35

The Doll Maker, Davies, 1953 . . . . £250/£50

SIEGFRIED SASSOON

(b.1886 d.1967)

A poet and author of autobiography and semi-autobiographical novels, his *Memoirs of a Fox-Hunting Man* won both the Hawthenden and Tait Black Memorial Prizes.

Novels

Memoirs of a Fox-Hunting Man, Faber, 1928 (anonymous) . . . . £150/£50

ditto, Faber, 1928 (limited edition) £250

ditto, Faber, 1929 (illustrated edition) . . £100/£50

ditto, Coward McGann (U.S.), 1929 . . . £75/£10

Memoirs of an Infantry Officer, Faber, 1930 £100/£25

ditto, Faber, 1930 (750 signed copies) . . . £200

ditto, Coward McGann (U.S.), 1930 . . . £45/£15

ditto, Faber, 1931 (illustrated edition, 320 signed copies) £500

ditto, Faber, 1931 (illustrated edition, 12 signed copies) £1,000

Sherston's Progress, Faber, 1936 . . . £75/£20

ditto, Faber, 1936 (300 signed copies) . . . £150

ditto, Doubleday (U.S.), 1936 . . . £25/£10

The Complete Memoirs of George Sherston, Faber, 1937 . . . . £25/£10

ditto, Doubleday (U.S.), 1937 . . . . £15/£5

Verse

An Ode for Music, privately printed, 1912 (50 copies). £500

The Daffodil Murderer, Richmond, 1913 (wraps) £125

The Old Huntsman, Heinemann, 1917 (with errata slip and d/w) . . . . £300/£75

ditto, Dutton (U.S.), 1917. . . . . . £275/£65

Counter-Attack, Heinemann, 1918 . . . . £350

ditto, Heinemann, 1918 (wraps) £200

ditto, Dutton (U.S.), 1918. . . . . . . £50

The War Poems of Siegfried Sassoon, Heinemann, 1919 . . . . £175/£45

Recreations, privately printed, 1923 (75 copies of 81) £250

ditto, privately printed, 1923 (6 copies of 81) . £500
Selected Poems, Heinemann, 1925 . . . £50/£20
Satirical Poems, Heinemann, 1926 . . . £100/£35
ditto, Viking (U.S.), 1926 . . . . £100/£35
Nativity, Faber, 1927 (350 numbered copies, wraps) £35
ditto, Faber, 1927 (wraps) £15
ditto, William Edwin Rudge (U.S.), 1927 (27 copies to secure copyright) £125
The Heart's Journey, Heinemann and Crosby Gaige (U.S.), 1928 (590 signed copies) . . . . £200/£125
ditto, Heinemann and Crosby Gaige (U.S.), 1928 (9 copies on green paper) £500
ditto, Heinemann, 1928 . . . . £75/£20
ditto, Harper (U.S.), 1929 . . . . . . £45/£15
To My Mother, Faber, 1928 . . . . . £40/£15
ditto, Faber, 1928 (500 signed large paper copies) £100
In Sicily, Faber, 1930 . . . . £40/£15
ditto, Faber, 1928 (400 signed large paper copies) £100
Poems by Pinchbeck Lyre, Duckworth, 1931 (glassine d/w) . . . . £55/£50
To the Red Rose, Faber, 1931 . . . . £60/£15
Prehistoric Burials, Knopf (U.S.), 1932 (Borzoi Chap Book) £35
The Road to Ruin, Faber, 1933 . . . . . £60/£15
Vigils, [Douglas Cleverdon], 1934 (272 signed copies, Niger morocco) £125
ditto, Heinemann, 1935 . . . . £60/£15
ditto, Viking (U.S.), 1936 . . . . £40/£10
Rhymed Ruminations, Faber, 1940 . . . . £35/£10
ditto, Viking (U.S.), 1941 . . . . £25/£10
Poems Newly Selected, Faber, 1940 . . . £25/£10
Collected Poems, Faber, 1947 . . . . £40/£15
ditto, Viking (U.S.), 1949 . . . . £30/£10
Sequences, Faber, 1956 . . . . £30/£10
ditto, Viking (U.S.), 1957 . . . . £25/£10
Collected Poems, 1908-1956, Faber, 1961 . £20/£10
An Octave, privately printed, 1966 (350 copies, wraps, slipcase) . . . . £75/£50

Others
The Old Century and Seven More Years, Faber, 1938. . . . . £45/£15
ditto, Viking (U.S.), 1939 . . . . £30/£10
The Weald of Youth, Faber, 1941 . . . £40/£10
ditto, Viking (U.S.), 1942 . . . . £25/£10
Siegfried's Journey, Faber, 1945 . . . £35/£10
ditto, Viking (U.S.), 1946 . . . . £15/£5
Meredith, Constable, 1948 . . . . . . £20/£10
ditto, Viking (U.S.), 1948 . . . . £20/£10
The Path to Peace, Stanbrook Abbey Press, 1960 (500 copies, quarter vellum) £150
Something About Myself by Siegfried Sassoon, aged 11, Stanbrook Abbey Press, 1966 (350 copies, wraps) £50

Diaries, 1920-1922, Faber, 1981 . . . . £20/£10
Diaries, 1915-1918, Faber, 1983 . . . . £20/£10
Diaries, 1923-1925, Faber, 1984 . . . . £20/£10
Siegfried Sassoon: Letters to Max Beerbohm with a Few Answers, Faber, 1986 . . . . . . £20/£5

THE SAVOY

After leaving "The Yellow Book", Aubrey Beardsley joined with Arthur Symons to produce, "The Savoy", published by Leonard Smithers. Smithers later bound and published sets of all 8 issues in pictorial cloth in 3 volumes.

No.1, January 1896 (including Christmas card) . £65
No.2, April, 1896 . . . . £50
No.3, July, 1896 . . . . £50
No.4, August, 1896 . . . . £50
No.5, September, 1896 . . . . £50
No.6, October, 1896 . . . . £50
No.7, November 1896 . . . . £50
No.8, December 1896 . . . . £50

All 8 issues, 3 vols £1,500

DOROTHY L. SAYERS
(b.1893 d.1957)

Principally a writer of detective fiction, Sayers' novels follow the exploits of Lord Peter Wimsey.

Novels
Whose Body?, Boni & Liveright (U.S.), 1923 . . . . £1,500/£350
ditto, Unwin, 1923 . . . . £1,500/£350
Clouds of Witness, Unwin, 1926 . . . £1,000/£200
ditto, Dial Press (U.S.), 1927. . . . . £750/£150
Unnatural Death, Benn, 1927 . . . £1,000/£200
ditto, as ***The Dawson Pedigree***, Dial Press (U.S.), 1928 . . . . £1,000/£200
The Unpleasantness at the Bellona Club, Benn, 1928 . . . . £1,000/£200
ditto, Brewer (U.S.), 1928 . . . . . £750/£150
Strong Poison, Gollancz, 1930 . . . . . £600/£75
ditto, Harcourt (U.S.), 1930 . . . . . . £500/£45
The Documents in the Case, Benn, 1930 (with Robert Eustace) . . . . £500/£45
ditto, Brewer (U.S.), 1930 . . . . . . £400/£35
The Five Red Herrings, Gollancz, 1931 . £600/£75
ditto, as ***Suspicious Characters***, Harcourt (U.S.), 1931 . . . . £500/£45

Have His Carcase, Gollancz, 1932 . . . £500/£45
ditto, Harcourt (U.S.), 1932 . . . . . £400/£35
Murder Must Advertise, Gollancz, 1933 . £500/£45
ditto, Harcourt (U.S.), 1933 . . . . . £450/£35
The Nine Tailors, Gollancz, 1934 . . . £450/£35
ditto, Harcourt (U.S.), 1934 . . . . . £450/£35
Gaudy Night, Gollancz, 1935 . . . . £450/£35
ditto, Harcourt (U.S.), 1936 . . . . . £450/£35
Busman's Honeymoon, Harcourt (U.S.), 1937 . . . . £450/£35
ditto, Gollancz, 1937 . . . . £450/£35

Short Stories
Lord Peter Views the Body, Gollancz, 1928 £750/£75
ditto, Brewer (U.S.), 1929 . . . . . £500/£50
Hangman's Holiday, Gollancz, 1933 . . £450/£35
In the Teeth of the Evidence, Gollancz, 1940 £400/£35
ditto, Harcourt (U.S.), 1940 . . . . . £350/£30
Talboys, Harper & Row (U.S.), 1972 . . . £20/£5

Collected Editions
Lord Peter, A Collection of All the Lord Peter Wimsey Stories, Harper & Row (U.S.), 1972 . . £25/£10
Striding Folly, New English Library, 1973 . £25/£10

'Chain' Novels with other authors
The Floating Admiral, Hodder and Stoughton, [1931] . . . . £600/£125
Ask a Policeman, Arthur Barker, [1933] £500/£100
Six Against the Yard, Selwyn & Blount, 1936 . . . . £500/£100
Double Death, Gollancz, 1939 . . . £500/£100

Verse
OP. I, Blackwell, 1916 (wraps) £200
Catholic Tales and Christian Songs, Blackwell, 1918 (wraps) £125

Plays
Busman's Honeymoon, Gollancz, 1937 . £250/£40
ditto, Gollancz, 1937 (wraps) £100
ditto, Harcourt Brace (U.S.), 1937 . . £125/£25
The Zeal of Thy House, Gollancz, 1937 . £25/£10
ditto, Harcourt Brace (U.S.), 1937 . . £25/£10
The Devil to Pay, Gollancz, 1937 . . . £35/£15
ditto, Harcourt Brace (U.S.), 1941 . . £25/£10
He that Should Come, Gollancz, 1939 (wraps in d/w) . . . . £20/£10
The Man Born to be King, Gollancz, 1943 . £60/£15
The Just Vengeance, Gollancz, 1946 (wraps) . £10
Four Sacred Plays, Gollancz, 1948 . . . . £5
The Emperor Constantine, Gollancz, 1951 . £20/£5

Essays
Begin Here, Gollancz, 1940 . . . . . £75/£25
The Mind of the Maker, Methuen, 1941 . £25/£10
ditto, Harcourt (U.S.), 1941 . . . . . £15/£5
Unpopular Opinions, Gollancz, 1946 . . £25/£10
ditto, Harcourt (U.S.), 1947 . . . . . £15/£5
Creed or Chaos and Other Essays, Methuen, 1947 . . . . £15/£5
ditto, Harcourt (U.S.), 1949 . . . . . £15/£5
Introductory Papers on Dante, Methuen, 1954. . . . . £25/£10
Further Papers on Dante, Methuen, 1957 . £20/£10
The Poetry of Search and the Poetry of Statement, Gollancz, 1963 . . . . £15/£5
Christian Letters to a Post-Christian World, William Eerdmans (U.S.), 1969 . . . . . . £10/£5
A Matter of Eternity, William Eerdmans (U.S.), 1973 . . . . £10/£5
Wilkie Collins: A Critical and Bibliographical Study, University of Toledo, 1977 . . . . . £10/£5

Children's
Even the Parrot, Methuen, 1944 . . . . £65/£20

Others
Papers Relating to the Family of Wimsey, privately printed, Humphrey Milford, [1936] (approximately 500 copies) £100
Account of Lord Mortimer Wimsey, Hermit of the Wash, 'Printed by M. Bryan, 1816' [O.U.P., 1937] £100
The Wimsey Family, A Fragmentary History, Gollancz, 1977 . . . . £35/£10

ANNA SEWELL
(b.1820 d.1878)

Black Beauty was Anna Sewell's only novel, written in an attempt to encourage the better treatment of horses.

Black Beauty: His Grooms and Companions. The Autobiography of a Horse, Jarrold, 1877 . £3,500

TOM SHARPE
(b.1928)

Tom Sharpe became a full-time novelist in 1971 with the publication of *Riotous Assembly*. His books have been filmed, with varying degrees of success.

Novels
Riotous Assembly, Secker & Warburg, 1971 £200/£25
ditto, Viking (U.S.), 1971 . . . . . . £65/£15

Indecent Exposure, Secker & Warburg, 1973 £150/£20
Porterhouse Blue, Secker & Warburg, 1974 £150/£20
ditto, Prentice-Hall(U.S.), 1974 . . . . . £65/£15
Blott on the Landscape, Secker & Warburg, 1975 . . . . £45/£10
ditto, Random House (U.S.), 1985 . . . £10/£5
Wilt, Secker & Warburg, 1976 . . . . £35/£10
ditto, Random House (U.S.), 1984 . . . £10/£5
The Great Pursuit, Secker & Warburg, 1977 £20/£5
ditto, Harper (U.S.), 1978. . . . . . . £15/£5
The Throwback, Secker & Warburg, 1978 . £20/£5
ditto, Random House (U.S.), 1985 . . . . £10/£5
The Wilt Alternative, Secker & Warburg, 1979 £20/£5
ditto, Random House (U.S.), 1984 . . . £10/£5
Ancestral Vices, Secker & Warburg, 1980 . £20/£5
ditto, St Martin's (U.S.), 1980 . . . . . £15/£5
Vintage Stuff, Secker & Warburg, 1982. . £20/£5
ditto, Random House (U.S.), 1985 . . . . £10/£5
Wilt on High, Secker & Warburg, 1984 . . £15/£5
ditto, Random House (U.S.), 1985 . . . . £10/£5
Granchester Grind, A Porterhouse Chronicle, Secker & Warburg, 1995 . . . . £10/£5
The Midden, Deutsch/Secker & Warburg, 1996 £10/£5
ditto, Overlook (U.S.), 1997 . . . . . £10/£5

GEORGE BERNARD SHAW

(b.1856 d.1950)

Primarily a playwright, Shaw's dramatic works are often satirical attacks on convention and cant. His many other writings are also highly political. In 1925 he was awarded the Nobel Prize for Literature, but he later declined offers of a peerage and the Order of Merit.

Novels

Cashel Byron's Profession, Walter Scott, 1886, (wraps) £750
An Unsocial Socialist, Swan, Sonnenschein, Lowrey & Co., 1887 . . . . £500
Love Among the Artists, Herbert S. Stone (U.S.), 1905 . . . . £250
The Irrational Knot, Archibald Constable, 1905 £50
Immaturity, Constable, 1930 . . . . £25

Political Works

A Manifesto, Fabian Society Tract No. 2, 1884 £100
To Provident Landlords and Capitalists, Fabian Society Tract No. 3, 1885 (anonymous) . . £75
The True Radical Programme, Fabian Society Tract No. 6, 1887 (anonymous) £75
Fabian Essays in Socialism, Fabian Society, 1889 £75
Anarchism Versus State Socialism, Henry Seymour, 1889 . . . . £75
What Socialism Is, Fabian Society Tract No. 13, 1890 (anonymous) £75
The Legal Eight Hours Question, R. Forder, 1891 £75
Quintessence of Ibsenism, Walter Scott, 1891 . £75
ditto, Constable, 1913 (extended edition) . . £25
Fabian Election Manifesto, Fabian Society Tract No. 40, 1892 (anonymous) £100
The Fabian Society: What it has Done, etc, Fabian Society Tract No. 41, 1892 . . . . £75
Vote! Vote! Vote!, Fabian Society Tract No. 43, 1892 (anonymous) £75
The Impossibilities of Anarchism, Fabian Society Tract No. 45, 1893 . . . . £75
A Plan of Campaign for Labour, Fabian Society Tract No. 49, 1894 . . . . £75
Report on Fabian Policy, Fabian Society Tract No. 70, 1896 (anonymous) £50
On Going to Church, Roycraft Printing Shop (U.S.), 1896 . . . . £500
Women as Councillors, Fabian Society Tract No. 93, 1900 . . . . £75
Fabianism and the Empire: A Manifesto, Grant Richards, 1900 . . . . £50
Socialism for Millionaires, Fabian Society Tract No. 107, 1901 . . . . £50
Common Sense of Municipal Trading, Constable, 1904 . . . . £50
Election Address, Fabian Society, 1904 . . . £50
Fabianism and the Fiscal Question, Fabian Society Tract No. 116, 1904 . . . . £35
Is Free Trade Alive or Dead?, George Standring, 1906 . . . . £75
Statement of the Evidence in Chief of G. B. S. Before the Joint Select Committee on Stage Plays, privately printed, 1909 . . . . £200
Rent and Value, Fabian Society Tract No. 142, 1909 . . . . £35
Socialism and Superior Brains, Fabian Society Tract No. 146, 1910 . . . . £35
The Case for Equality, Address to the Political & Economic Circle National Liberal Club, 1913 £35
Commonsense about The War, 'New Statesman' supplement, 1914 . . . . £35
How to Settle the Irish Question, Talbot and Constable, 1917 . . . . £35
Peace Conference Hints, Constable, 1919 . . £25
Socialism and Ireland, 'New Commonwealth' supplement, 1919 . . . . £25
Ruskin's Politics, Ruskin Centenary Council, 1921 £50
A Discarded Defence of Roger Casement, privately printed by Clement Shorter, 1922 (25 copies) £200
The Unprotected Child & The Law, The Six Point Group, [1923] £25
Bernard Shaw and Fascism, Favil Press, 1927 £15

The Intelligent Woman's Guide to Socialism, Constable, 1928 . . . . £20
The League of Nations, Fabian Society Tract No. 226, 1929 . . . . £25
A Little Talk on America, Friends of the Soviet Union, 1931, (50 copies). £75
A Political Madhouse in America and Nearer Home, Constable, 1933 . . . . £20
The Future of Political Science in America, Dodd Mead (U.S.), 1933 . . . . £20
Are We Heading for War?, Labour Party, 1934 £20
Everybody's Political What's What?, Constable, 1944 . . . . £10
Fabian Essays, C. Allen & Unwin, 1948 . . £10
Shaw on Censorship, Shavian Tract No. 3, 1955 £10

MARY SHELLEY
(1797-1815)

Famous for *Frankenstein* of course, but her few other works are also keenly sought by collectors. There is apparently some doubt about her authorship of the first title

Verse
Mounseer Nongtonpaw, Baldwin, Juvenile Series, 1808 . . . . £500

Novels
Frankenstein, or, the Modern Prometheus, Lackington, Hughes, Harding, Mayor & Jones, 1818, (3 vols) £50,000
ditto, Whitaker, 1823 (second edition, 2 vols) . £2,000
ditto, Lea and Blanchard (U.S.), 1833 . . . £,2000
Valperga, or the Life and Adventures of Castruccio, Prince of Lucca, Whittaker, 1823 (3 vols). . £600
The Last Man, Colburn, 1826 (3 vols) . . . £1,000
The Fortunes of Perkin Warbeck, Colburn and Bentley, 1830 (3 vols) £1,500
Lodore, Bentley, 1835 (3 vols) £500
Falkner, Sanders and Ottley, 1837 (3 vols) . . £600
Mathilde, 1959 (unfinished) £25

Others
Rambles in Germany and Italy, 1840, 1842 and 1843, Moxon, 1844 (2 vols) £100

M.P. SHIEL
(b.1865 d.1947)

The author of fantasy and science fiction, Matthew Phipps Shiel's short stories are rather luxuriant. His 'Prince Zaleski' tales, for example, offer a detective far more decadent than that other drug-taking dilettante, Sherlock Holmes.

Short Stories
Prince Zaleski, John Lane, 1895 . . . . . £150
ditto, Roberts Brothers (U.S.), 1895 . . . . £150
Shapes in the Fire, John Lane, 1896. . . . . £125
ditto, Roberts Brothers (U.S.), 1896 . . . . £125
The Pale Ape, T. Werner Laurie, [1911] . . £150
Here Comes the Lady, The Richards Press, [1928] . . . . £150/£45
The Invisible Voices, The Richards Press, 1935 (with John Gawsworth). . . . . £150/£45
ditto, Vanguard Press (U.S.), 1936 . . . £100/£35
The Best Short Stories of M.P. Shiel, Gollancz 1948 . . . . £35/£10
Xélucha and Others, Arkham House (U.S.), 1975 . . . . £20/£5
Prince Zaleski and Cummings King Monk, Mycroft & Moran (U.S.), 1977 . . . . £20/£5

Novels
The Rajah's Sapphire, Ward, Lock & Bowden, 1896 . . . . £250
The Yellow Danger, Grant Richards, 1898 . £125
ditto, R.F. Fenno & Co. (U.S.), 1899. . . . . £100
Contraband of War, Grant Richards, 1899 . . £100
ditto, The Gregg Press (U.S.), 1968 (no d/w) . £20
Cold Steel, Grant Richards, 1899. . . . . . £100
ditto, Brentano's (U.S.), 1900. . . . . . . £100
ditto, Gollancz, 1929 (revised edition, 105 signed copies, half vellum) £250
The Man Stealers, Hutchinson & Co., 1900 . £100
ditto, Lippincott (U.S.), 1900 . . . . . . £75
The Lord of the Sea, Grant Richards, 1901 . . £100
ditto, Frederick A. Stokes Co. (U.S.), 1901 . . £75
ditto, Gollancz, 1929 (revised edition, 105 signed copies, half vellum) £250
The Purple Cloud, Chatto & Windus, 1901. £250
ditto, Gollancz, 1929 (revised edition, 105 signed copies, half vellum) £300
ditto, Vanguard Press (U.S.), 1930 (revised) £45/£10
The Weird o' It, Grant Richards, 1902 . . . £100
Unto the Third Generation, Chatto & Windus, 1903 . . . . £75
The Evil That Men Do, Ward, Lock & Co. Ltd, 1904 . . . . £75
The Lost Viol, Edward J. Clode (U.S.), 1905 . £100
ditto, Ward, Lock & Co. Ltd, 1905 (copyright edition).

. . . . £250
ditto, Ward, Lock & Co. Ltd, 1908 . . . . £50
The Yellow Wave, Ward, Lock & Co. Ltd, 1905 (authors name spelt 'Sheil' on title page) . . £75
ditto, Ward, Lock & Co. Ltd., 1905 (authors name spelt correctly on title page) £45
ditto, Thomas Langton (Canada), 1905 (authors name spelt 'Sheil' on title page) £45
The Last Miracle, T. Werner Laurie, 1906 [1907] £50
The White Wedding, T. Werner Laurie, [1908]. £45
The Isle of Lies, T. Werner Laurie, [1909] . . £45
This Knot of Life, Everett & Co., [1909] . . £45
The Dragon, Grant Richards, 1913 (advance copy, green cloth) £100
ditto, Grant Richards, 1913 . . . . . . £40
ditto, Edward J. Clode (U.S.), 1914 . . . . £40
ditto, as ***The Yellow Peril***, Gollancz, 1929 (revised edition, 105 signed copies, half vellum) . . £200
Children of the Wind, Grant Richards, 1923 £200/£40
ditto, Knopf (U.S.), 1923 . . . . £175/£40
How The Old Woman Got Home, The Richards Press, 1927 . . . . £150/£40
ditto, Vanguard Press (U.S.), 1928 . . . £100/£20
Dr Kranski's Secret, The Vanguard Press (U.S.), 1929 . . . . £150/£25
ditto, Jarrolds, 1930 . . . . £100/£25
The Black Box, The Vanguard Press (U.S.), 1930 . . . . £150/£25
ditto, The Richards Press, 1931 . . . . £100/£25
Say Au R'Voir But Not Goodbye, Ernest Benn Ltd, 1933 (wraps) £40
This Above All, The Vanguard Press (U.S.), 1933 . . . . £75/£20
ditto, as ***Above All Else***, Lloyd Cole, 1943 . £65/£15
The Young Men Are Coming, Allen & Unwin, 1937 . . . . £65/£20
ditto, Vanguard Press (U.S.), 1937 . . . . £65/£20

Others
Richards Shilling Selection from Edwardian Poets - M. P. Shiel, The Richards Press, 1936 (wraps) £30
Science, Life and Literature, Williams & Norgate Ltd, 1950 . . . . £25/£10

NEVIL SHUTE
(b.1899 d.1961)

A popular novelist, Shute's *On the Beach*, about the survivors of a nuclear holocaust, is arguably his most important work.

Novels
Marazan, Cassell, 1926 . . . . £150/£35
So Disdained, Cassell, 1926 . . . . . £125/£25
Lonely Road, Heinemann, 1932 . . . . . £100/£25
Ruined City, Heinemann, 1938 . . . . . £100/£25
What Happened to the Corbetts, Heinemann, 1939 . . . . £75/£25
An Old Captivity, Heinemann, 1940 . . . £75/£25
Landfall, Heinemenn, 1940 . . . . . . £75/£25
Pied Piper, Heinemann, 1942 . . . . . £50/£15
Pastoral, Heinemann, 1944 . . . . . . £50/£15
Most Secret, Heinemann, 1945 . . . . . £50/£15
The Chequer Board, Heinemann, 1947 . . £40/£10
No Highway, Heinemenn, 1948 . . . . . £40/£10
A Town Like Alice, Heinemann, 1950 . . £50/£15
Round the Bend, Heinemann, 1951 . . . £25/£10
The Far Country, Heinemann, 1952. . . £25/£10
In the Wet, Heinemann, 1953 . . . . . £25/£10
Requiem for a Wren, Heinemann, 1955. . £20/£5
Beyond the Black Stump, Heinemann, 1956 £20/£5
On the Beach, Heinemann, 1957. . . . £20/£5
The Rainbow and the Rose, Heinemann, 1958 £20/£5
Trustee from the Toolroom, Heinemann, 1960 £20/£5
Stephen Morris, Heinemann, 1961 . . . . £20/£5

Autobiography
Slide Rule, Heinemann, 1954. . . . . . £20/£5

Drama
Viland the Good, Heinemann, 1946 . . . . £40/£15

ALAN SILLITOE
(b.1928)

A novelist and poet, Sillitoe's reputation rests principally on *Saturday Night and Sunday Morning*.

Novels
Saturday Night and Sunday Morning, Allen, 1958 . . . . £125/£25
ditto, Knopf (U.S.), 1958 . . . . . . £45/£15
The General, Allen, 1960. . . . . . . £25/£5
ditto, Knopf (U.S.), 1960 . . . . £10/£5
Key to the Door, Macmillan, 1961 . . . £15/£5
ditto, Knopf (U.S.), 1961 . . . . £10/£5
The Death of William Posters, Macmillan, 1965 . . . . £15/£5
ditto, Knopf (U.S.), 1965 . . . . £10/£5
A Tree on Fire, Macmillan, 1967 . . . £15/£5
ditto, Knopf (U.S.), 1967 . . . . £10/£5
A Start in Life, Allen, 1970 . . . . . £15/£5
ditto, Scribner (U.S.), 1971 . . . . . . £10/£5
Travels in Nihilon, Allen, 1971 . . . . £15/£5
ditto, Scribner (U.S.), 1972 . . . . . . £10/£5
Raw Material, Allen, 1972 . . . . . . £15/£5

ditto, Scribner (U.S.), 1973 . . . . . . £10/£5
Flame of Life, Allen, 1974 . . . . £10/£5
The Widower's Son, Allen, 1976. . . . . £10/£5
ditto, Harper (U.S.), 1977 . . . . . . £10/£5
The Storyteller, Allen, 1979 . . . . . £10/£5
ditto, Simon & Schuster (U.S.), 1980 . . £10/£5
Her Victory, Granada, 1982 . . . . . £10/£5
ditto, Watts (U.S.), 1982 . . . . £10/£5
The Lost Flying Boat, Granada, 1983 . . £10/£5
ditto, Little, Brown (U.S.), 1983 . . . . £10/£5
Down from the Hill, Granada, 1984 . . . £10/£5
Life Goes On, Granada, 1985 . . . . £10/£5
Out of the Whirlpool, Hutchinson, 1987 . £10/£5
ditto, Harper (U.S.), 1988. . . . . . £10/£5
The Open Door, Grafton, 1989 . . . . £10/£5
Lost Loves, Grafton, 1990 . . . . . £10/£5
Snowstop, Harper Collins, 1992 . . . . £10/£5

Verse
Without Beer or Bread, Outpost Publications, 1957 (wraps) £200
The Rats and Other Poems, Allen, 1960 . £25/£10
A Falling out of Love and Other Poems, Allen, 1964 . . . . £15/£5
Love in the Environs of Voronezh, Macmillan, 1968 . . . . £10/£5
ditto, Doubleday (U.S.), 1968 . . . . . £10/£5
Shaman and Other Poems, Turret Books, 1973 (500 signed copies) . . . . £35/£20
Barbarians and Other Poems, Turret Books, 1973 (500 signed copies) . . . . £35/£20
From Canto Two of 'The Rats', published by the author, 1973 (wraps). £15
Storm: New Poems, Allen, 1974. . . . £15/£5
Snow on the North Side of Lucifer, Allen, 1979 . . . . £15/£5
Sun Before Departure: Poems, 1974-1984, Granada, 1984 . . . . £10/£5
Tides and Stone Walls, Grafton, 1986 . . £10/£5
Three Poems, Worlds Press, 1988 . . . . £20

Stories
The Loneliness of the Long Distance Runner, Allen, 1959 . . . . £75/£20
ditto, Knopf (U.S.), 1959 . . . . £35/£10
The Ragman's Daughter, Allen, 1963 . . £15/£5
ditto, Knopf (U.S.), 1963 . . . . . . £10/£5
Guzman Go Home, Macmillan, 1968 . . £15/£5
ditto, Doubleday (U.S.), 1968 . . . . £10/£5
Men, Women, and Children, Allen, 1973 . £10/£5
ditto, Doubleday (U.S.), 1974 . . . . . £10/£5
The Second Chance and Other Stories, Cape, 1981 . . . . £10/£5
ditto, Simon & Schuster (U.S.), 1981 . . £10/£5
The Far Side of the Street, W.H. Allen, 1988 £15/£5

Plays
All Citizens are Soldiers, Macmillan, 1969 (adaptation with Ruth Fainlight) £10
ditto, Dufour (U.S.), 1969. . . . . . . £10
Three Plays, Allen, 1978 . . . . £10/£5

Children's
The City Adventures of Marmalade Jim, Macmillan, 1967 . . . . £15
Big John and the Stars, Robson, 1977 . . . £10
The Incredible Fencing Fleas, Robson, 1978 . £10
Marmalade Jim at the Farm, Robson, 1982 . £10
Marmalade Jim and the Fox, Robson, 1984 . £10

Others
The Road to Volgograd, Allen, 1964 . . £15/£5
ditto, Knopf (U.S.), 1964 . . . . . . £10/£5
Mountains and Caverns, Allen, 1975 . . £10/£5
The Saxon Shore Way, Hutchinson, 1983 . £10/£5
Alan Sillitoe's Nottinghamshire, Grafton, 1987 £10/£5
Every Day of the Week: An Alan Sillitoe Reader, W. H. Allen, 1987 . . . . £10/£5
Life Without Armour, HarperCollins, 1995. £10/£5
Leading the Blind, Picador, 1995 . . . . £10/£5

GEORGES SIMENON

(b.1903 d.1989)

Born in Belgium, Simenon's literary output was prodigious, and much of it has not been translated into English. He is known especially for his Inspector Maigret novels.

Maigret Novels
The Crime of Inspector Maigret, Covici (U.S.), 1932 . . . . £1,000/£150
ditto, as ***Introducing Inspector Maigret***, Hurst and Blackett, 1933 . . . . £750/£75
Inspector Maigret Investigates, Hurst and Blackett, 1933 . . . . £450/£45
The Triumph of Inspector Maigret, Hurst and Blackett, 1934 . . . . £450/£45
The Patience of Maigret, George Routledge & Sons, 1939 . . . . £100/£20
Maigret Travels South, George Routledge & Sons, 1940 . . . . £75/£15
Maigret Abroad, George Routledge & Sons, 1940 . . . . £75/£15
Maigret to the Rescue, George Routledge & Sons, 1940 . . . . £75/£15
Maigret Keeps a Rendez-Vous, George Routledge & Sons, 1940 . . . . £50/£10
Maigret Sits It Out, George Routledge & Sons, 1941

. . . . £50/£10
Maigret and M. L'Abbé, George Routledge & Sons, 1941 . . . . £40/£10
Maigret on Holiday, Routledge and Kegan Paul, 1950 . . . . £25/£5
Maigret Right and Wrong, Hamish Hamilton, 1954 . £25/£5
Maigret and the Young Girl, Hamish Hamilton, 1955 . . . . £25/£5
Maigret and the Burglar's Wife, Hamish Hamilton, 1955 . . . . £25/£5
Maigret's Revolver, Hamish Hamilton, 1956 £25/£5
My Friend Maigret, Hamish Hamilton, 1956 £25/£5
Maigret Goes to School, Hamish Hamilton, 1957 . . . . £25/£5
Maigret's Little Joke, Hamish Hamilton, 1957 £25/£5
Maigret and the Old Lady, Hamish Hamilton, 1958 . . . . £25/£5
Maigret's First Case, Hamish Hamilton, 1958 £25/£5
Maigret has Scruples, Hamish Hamilton, 1959 £25/£5
Maigret and the Reluctant Witnesses, Hamish Hamilton, 1959 . . . . £25/£5
Madame Maigret's Friend, Hamish Hamilton, 1960 . . . . £25/£5
Maigret Takes a Room, Hamish Hamilton, 1960 . . . . £25/£5
Maigret in Court, Hamish Hamilton, 1961 . £25/£5
Maigret Afraid, Hamish Hamilton, 1961 . £25/£5
Maigret in Society, Hamish Hamilton, 1962 £25/£5
Maigret's Failure, Hamish Hamilton, 1962 £25/£5
Maigret's Memoirs, Hamish Hamilton, 1963 £25/£5
Maigret and the Lazy Burglar, Hamish Hamilton, 1963 . . . . £25/£5
Maigret's Special Murder, Hamish Hamilton, 1964 . . . . £25/£5
Maigret and the Saturday Caller, Hamish Hamilton, 1964 . . . . £25/£5
Maigret Loses His Temper, Hamish Hamilton, 1965 . . . . £25/£5
Maigret Sets a Trap, Hamish Hamilton, 1965 £25/£5
Maigret on the Defensive, Hamish Hamilton, 1966 . . . . £25/£5
The Patience of Maigret, Hamish Hamilton, 1966 . . . . £25/£5
Maigret and the Headless Corpse, Hamish Hamilton, 1967 . . . . £25/£5
Maigret and the Nahour Case, Hamish Hamilton, 1967 . . . . £25/£5
Maigret's Pickpocket, Hamish Hamilton, 1968 £25/£5
Maigret Has Doubts, Hamish Hamilton, 1968 £25/£5
Maigret Takes the Waters, Hamish Hamilton, 1969 . . . . £25/£5
Maigret and the Minister, Hamish Hamilton, 1969 . . . . £20/£5
Maigret Hesitates, Hamish Hamilton, 1970 £20/£5
Maigret's Boyhood Friend, Hamish Hamilton, 1970 . . . . £20/£5
Maigret and the Wine Merchant, Hamish Hamilton, 1971 . . . . £20/£5
Maigret and the Killer, Hamish Hamilton, 1971 £20/£5
Maigret and the Madwoman, Hamish Hamilton, 1972 £20/£5
Maigret and the Flea, Hamish Hamilton, 1972 £20/£5
Maigret and Monsieur Charles, Hamish Hamilton, 1973 . . . . £20/£5
Maigret and the Dosser, Hamish Hamilton, 1973 . . . . £20/£5
Maigret and the Millionaires, Hamish Hamilton, 1974 . . . . £20/£5
Maigret and the Gangsters, Hamish Hamilton, 1974 . . . . £20/£5
Maigret and the Loner, Hamish Hamilton, 1975 20/£5
Maigret and the Man on the Boulevard, Hamish Hamilton, 1975 . . . . £20/£5
Maigret and the Black Sheep, Hamish Hamilton, 1976 . . . . £20/£5
Maigret and the Ghost, Hamish Hamilton, 1976 . . . . £20/£5
Maigret and the Spinster, Hamish Hamilton, 1977 . . . . £20/£5
Maigret and the Hotel Majestic, Hamish Hamilton, 1977 . . . . £20/£5
Maigret in Exile, Hamish Hamilton, 1978 . £15/£5
Maigret and the Toy Village, Hamish Hamilton, 1978 . . . . £15/£5
Maigret's Rival, Hamish Hamilton, 1979 . £15/£5
Maigret in New York, Hamish Hamilton, 1979 £15/£5
Maigret and the Coroner, Hamish Hamilton, 1980 . . . . £15/£5

Maigret Short Stories
Maigret's Christmas, Hamish Hamilton, 1976 . £10
Maigret's Pipe, Hamish Hamilton, 1977. . £20/£5

Other Novels
The Disintegration of J.P.G. George, Routledge & Sons, 1937 . . . . £300/£45
In Two Latitudes, George Routledge & Sons, 1942 . . . . £125/£25
Affairs of Destiny, George Routledge & Sons, 1942 . . . . £75/£20
The Man who Watched the Trains Go By, George Routledge & Sons, 1942. . . . . . . £70/£15
Havoc by Accident, George Routledge & Sons, 1943 . . . . £70/£15
Escape in Vain, George Routledge & Sons, 1943 . . . . £65/£15
On the Danger Line, George Routledge & Sons, 1944 . . . . £65/£15
The Shadow Falls, George Routledge & Sons, 1945 .

. . . . £65/£15
The Lost Moorings, George Routledge & Sons, 1946 . . . . £45/£10
Magnet of Doom, George Routledge & Sons, 1948 . . . . £45/£10
Black Rain, Routledge and Kegan Paul, 1949 £45/£10
Chit of a Girl, Routledge and Kegan Paul, 1949 . . . . £45/£10
A Wife at Sea, Routledge and Kegan Paul, 1949 . . . . £45/£10
Strange Inheritance, Routledge and Kegan Paul, 1950 . . . . £35/£10
Poisoned Relations, Routledge and Kegan Paul, 1950 . . . . £35/£10
The Strangers in the House, Routledge and Kegan Paul, 1951 . . . . £35/£10
The Window over the Way, Routledge and Kegan Paul, 1951 . . . . £35/£10
The House by the Canal, Routledge and Kegan Paul, 1952 . . . . £35/£10
The Burgomaster of Furnes, Routledge and Kegan Paul, 1952 . . . . £35/£10
The Trial of Bébé Donge, Routledge and Kegan Paul, 1952 . . . . £35/£10
The Stain on the Snow, Routledge and Kegan Paul, 1953 . . . . £35/£10
Aunt Jeanne, Routledge and Kegan Paul, 1953 . . . . £35/£10
Act of Passion, Routledge and Kegan Paul, 1953 . . . . £35/£10
Across the Street, Routledge and Kegan Paul, 1954 . . . . £35/£10
Ticket of Leave, Routledge and Kegan Paul, 1954 . . . . £35/£10
Violent Ends, Hamish Hamilton, 1954 . . £30/£10
Danger Ahead, Hamish Hamilton, 1955. . £30/£10
A Sense of Guilt, Hamish Hamilton, 1955 . £30/£10
The Judge and the Hatter, Hamish Hamilton, 1956 . . . . £25/£5
The Sacrifice, Hamish Hamilton, 1956 . . . £25/£5
The Little Man from Archangel, Hamish Hamilton, 1957 . . . . £25/£5
The Stowaway, Hamish Hamilton. 1957. . . £25/£5
The Son, Hamish Hamilton, 1958 . . . . £20/£5
Inquest on Bouvet, Hamish Hamilton, 1958 £20/£5
The Negro, Hamish Hamilton, 1959 . . . . £20/£5
Striptease, Hamish Hamilton, 1959 . . . . £20/£5
In Case of Emergency, Hamish Hamilton, 1960 . . . . £15/£5
Sunday, Hamish Hamilton, 1960. . . . £15/£5
The Premier, Hamish Hamilton, 1961 . . . £15/£5
The Widower, Hamish Hamilton, 1961 . . £15/£5
The Fate of the Malous, Hamish Hamilton, 1962 . . . . £15/£5
Pedigree, Hamish Hamilton, 1962 . . . . £15/£5
Account Unsettled, Hamish Hamilton, 1962 £15/£5
A New Lease of Life, Hamish Hamilton, 1963 £15/£5
The Iron Staircase, Hamish Hamilton, 1963 £15/£5
The Patient, Hamish Hamilton, 1963 . . . £15/£5
The Train, Hamish Hamilton, 1964 . . . £15/£5
The Door, Hamish Hamilton, 1964 . . . . £15/£5
The Blue Room, Hamish Hamilton, 1965 . £15/£5
The Man with the Little Dog, Hamish Hamilton, 1965 . . . . £15/£5
The Accomplices, Hamish Hamilton, 1966 . £15/£5
The Little Saint, Hamish Hamilton, 1966 . £15/£5
The Confessional, Hamish Hamilton, 1967 . £15/£5
Monsieur Monde Vanishes, Hamish Hamilton, 1967 . . . . £15/£5
The Old Man Dies, Hamish Hamilton, 1968 £15/£5
The Neighbours, Hamish Hamilton, 1968 . £15/£5
The Prison, Hamish Hamilton, 1969. . . £15/£5
Big Bob, Hamish Hamilton, 1969 . . . £15/£5
The Man on the Bench in the Barn, Hamish Hamilton, 1970 . . . . £10/£5
November, Hamish Hamilton, 1970 . . . £10/£5
The Rich Man, Hamish Hamilton, 1971. . £10/£5
Teddy Bear, Hamish Hamilton, 1971 . . £10/£5
When I was Old, Hamish Hamilton, 1972 . £10/£5
The Disappearance of Odile, Hamish Hamilton, 1972 . . . . £10/£5
The Cat, Hamish Hamilton, 1972 . . . . £10/£5
The Glass Cage, Hamish Hamilton, 1973 . £10/£5
The Innocents, Hamish Hamilton, 1973. . £10/£5
The Venice Train, Hamish Hamilton, 1974. £10/£5
The Magician, Hamish Hamilton, 1974 . . £10/£5
Betty, Hamish Hamilton, 1975 . . . . £10/£5
The Others, Hamish Hamilton, 1975 . . £10/£5
Three Beds in Manhattan, Hamish Hamilton, 1976 . . . . £10/£5
The Girl in his Past, Hamish Hamilton, 1976 £10/£5
Four Days in a Lifetime, Hamish Hamilton, 1977 . . . . £10/£5
The Bottom of the Bottle, Hamish Hamilton, 1977. . . . . £10/£5
The Girl with a Squint, Hamish Hamilton, 1978 £10/£5
The Family Lie, Hamish Hamilton, 1978 . £10/£5
The Night Club, Hamish Hamilton, 1979 . £10/£5
The Long Exile, Hamish Hamilton, 1983 . £10/£5
The Reckoning, Hamish Hamilton, 1984 . £10/£5
The Couple from Poitiers, Hamish Hamilton, 1985 . . . . £10/£5
The Outlaw, Hamish Hamilton, 1986 . . £10/£5
Uncle Charles, Hamish Hamilton, 1988 . . £10/£5
The Rules of the Game, Hamish Hamilton, 1989 . . . . £10/£5

Collected Editions

African Trio, Hamish Hamilton, 1979 . . £15/£5
The White Horse Inn, Hamish Hamilton, 1980 £15/£5

Other Short Stories
The Little Doctor, Hamish Hamilton, 1978 . £10/£5

Autobiography
Letter to my Mother, Hamish Hamilton, 1976 £20/£5
Intimate Memoirs, Hamish Hamilton, 1984 £20/£5

EDITH SITWELL
(b.1887 d.1964)

A poet and critic, Edith Sitwell co-founded the anthology *Wheels* with her brothers Osbert and Sacheverell in 1916, as a revolt against contemporary poetry. A penchant for experimentation and an eccentric and outrageous dress-sense made her a well-known literary figure.

Verse
The Mother and Other Poems, Blackwell, 1915 (500 copies) £200
Twentieth Century Harlequinade and Other Poems, Blackwell, 1916 (with Osbert Sitwell, 500 copies, wraps) £200
Clown's House, Blackwell, 1918 (750 copies, wraps) £150
The Wooden Pegasus, Blackwell, 1920 (750 copies) . . . . £125/£30
Facade, Favil Press, 1922 (150 signed copies, wraps) £225
Bucolic Comedies, Duckworth, 1923 . . £50/£15
The Sleeping Beauty, Duckworth, 1924 . . £65/£20
Troy Park, Duckworth, 1925 . . . . . £65/£20
Poor Young People, The Fleuron, 1925 (with Osbert & Sacheverell Sitwell, 375 numbered copies) £125/£50
The Augustan Books of Modern Poetry: Edith Sitwell, Benn, 1926 . . . . £10
Elegy on Dead Fashion, Duckworth, 1926 (225 signed copies) £150
Rustic Elegies, Duckworth, 1927 . . . . £65/£15
Popular Song, Faber & Gwyer, 1928 (wraps) . £10
ditto, Faber & Gwyer, 1928 (500 signed, numbered copies) £40
Five Poems, Duckworth, 1928 (275 copies). £100/£45
Gold Coast Customs and Other Poems, Duckworth, 1929 . . . . £40/£10
In Spring, privately printed, 1931 (290 copies). £45
ditto, privately printed, 1931 (edition of 15 signed copies) £200
Jane Barston, 1719-1746, Faber, 1931 (wraps) £15
ditto, Faber, 1931 (274 signed copies, wraps) £45
Epithalamium, Duckworth, 1931 (900 copies) £35/£15
ditto, Duckworth, 1931 (100 signed copies). . £50
Five Variations on a Theme, Duckworth, 1933 . . . . £40/£10
Street Songs, Macmillan, 1942 . . . . £25/£10
Green Song and Other Poems, Macmillan, 1944 . . . . £25/£10
The Shadow of Cain, John Lehmann, 1947 . £20/£5
Poor Men's Music, Fore Publications, 1950 (wraps) £10
Gardeners and Astronomers, Macmillan, 1953 £20/£5
The Outcasts, Macmillan, 1962 . . . . £15/£5

Collected Verse
Collected Poems, Duckworth, 1930 . . . . £45/£15
ditto, Duckworth, 1930 (320 signed copies). £225/£75
Selected Poems, Duckworth, 1936 . . . £45/£15
Poems Old and New, Faber, 1940 . . . £25/£10
The Song of the Cold, Macmillan, 1945. . £15/£5
The Canticle of the Rose, Macmillan, 1949. £15/£5
Facade and Other Poems, 1920-1935, Duckworth, 1950 . . . . £15/£5
Selected Poems, Penguin, 1952 (wraps). . . £5
Collected Poems, Duckworth, 1957 . . . £20/£5
The Pocket Poets, Vista, 1960 (wraps) . . . £5

Autobiography
Taken Care Of, Hutchinson, 1965 . . . £15/£5

Others
Poetry and Criticism, Hogarth Press, 1925 (wraps) £45
Alexander Pope, Faber, 1930 . . . . £30/£10
ditto, Faber, 1930 (220 signed copies) £125
Bath, Faber, 1932 . . . . £35/£10
The English Eccentrics, Faber, 1933 . . £140/£35
Aspects of Modern Poetry, Duckworth, 1934 £20/£5
Victoria of England, Faber, 1938 . . . £65/£15
I Live Under a Black Sun, Gollancz, 1937 . £75/£20
Trio: Dissertations on Some Aspects of National Genius, Macmillan, 1938 (with Osbert and Sacheverell Sitwell) . . . . . . £25/£10
English Women, Collins, 1942 . . . . £20/£5
A Poet's Notebook, Macmillan, 1943 . . £15/£5
Fanfare for Elizabeth, Macmillan, 1946 . £15/£5
A Notebook on William Shakespeare, Macmillan, 1948 . . . . £15/£5
The Queens and the Hive, Macmillan, 1962 £15/£5
Selected Letters, Macmillan, 1970 . . . £10/£5

OSBERT SITWELL

(b.1892 d.1969)

A poet and novelist, Osbert also wrote a number of volumes of family memoirs.

Verse

Twentieth Century Harlequinade and Other Poems, Blackwell, 1916 (with Edith Sitwell, 500 copies, wraps) £200
The Winstonburg Line, Hendersons, 1919 (wraps) £125
Argonaut and Juggernaut, Chatto & Windus, 1919 . . . . £25
At the House of Mrs Kinfoot, Favil Press, 1921 (wraps) £125
Out of the Flame, Grant Richards, 1923 . £45/£10
Poor Young People, The Fleuron, 1925 (with Edith & Sacheverell Sitwell, 375 numbered copies) £125/£50
Winter the Huntsman, The Poetry Bookshop, 1927 . . . . £10
England Reclaimed, Duckworth, 1927 . . £45/£10
ditto, Duckworth, 1927 (165 signed copies). £75/£45
Miss Mew, Mill House Press, 1929 (101 signed copies) £85
Collected Satires and Poems, Duckworth, 1931 . . . . £30/£10
ditto, Duckworth, 1931 (110 signed copies). . £65
Three-Quarter Length Portrait of Michael Arlen, Heinemann, 1931 (520 signed copies) . £65/£45
Three-Quarter Length Portrait of the Viscountess Wimborne, Cambridge, 1931 (57 signed copies) £125
Mrs Kimber, Macmillan, 1937 (500 copies). . £25
Selected Poems, Old and New, Duckworth, 1943 . . . . £20/£5
Four Songs of the Italian Earth, Banyan Press, 1945 (260 copies, wraps) £75
Demos the Emperor, Macmillan, 1949 (wraps). £10
ditto, Macmillan, 1949 (500 signed copies, wraps) £35
Wrack at Tidesend, Macmillan, 1952 . . £10/£5
On the Continent, Macmillan, 1958 . . . £10/£5
Poems About People, Duckworth, 1965. . £10/£5

Autobiography

Left Hand, Right Hand!, Macmillan, 1945 . £15/£5
The Scarlet Tree, Macmillan, 1946 . . . £15/£5
Great Morning, Macmillan, 1948 . . . £15/£5
Laughter in the Next Room, Macmillan, 1949 £15/£5
Noble Essences, Macmillan, 1950 . . . £15/£5

Others

Who Killed Cock Robin?, C. W. Daniel, 1921 (wraps) £50
Triple Fugue, Grant Richards, 1924 . . . £50/£20
Discursions on Travel, Art and Life, Grant Richards, 1925 . . . . £45/£10
Before the Bombardment, Duckworth, 1926 £25/£10
All At Sea, Duckworth, 1927 (with Sacheverell Sitwell) . . . . £25/£10
The People's Album of London Statues, Duckworth, 1928 . . . . £35/£10
ditto, Duckworth, 1928 (116 signed copies). . £60
The Man Who Lost Himself, Duckworth, 1929 . . . . £25/£10
Dumb Animal and Other Stories, Duckworth, 1930 . . . . £15/£5
ditto, Duckworth, 1930 (110 signed copies) £75/£40
Dickens, Chatto & Windus, 1932 . . . £25/£10
ditto, Chatto & Windus, 1932 (110 signed copies) £75
Winters of Content, Duckworth, 1932 . . £15/£5
Miracle on Mount Sinai, Duckworth, 1933 £50/£10
Brighton, Faber, 1935 (with Margaret Barton) £25/£10
Penny Foolish, A Book of Tirades and Panegyrics, Macmillan, 1935 . . . . £20/£5
Those Were the Days: Panorama with Figures, Macmillan, 1938 . . . . £15/£5
Trio: Dissertations on Some Aspects of National Genius, Macmillan, 1938 (with Edith and Sacheverell Sitwell) . . . . £25/£10
Escape with Me: An Oriental Sketch Book, Macmillan, 1939 . . . . £35/£10
Open the Door!, Macmillan, 1941 . . . £25/£10
A Place of One's Own, Macmillan, 1941 . £25/£10
Gentle Caesar, Macmillan, 1942 (with R. J. Minney) . . . . £10/£5
Sing High! Sing Low!, Macmillan, 1944 . £10/£5
A Letter to My Son, Home & Van Thal, 1944 (wraps with d/w) . . . . £10/£5
The True Story of Dick Whittington: A Christmas Story for Cat Lovers, Home & Van Thal, 1945 . . . . £20/£5
Alive - Alive-Oh! and Other Stories, Pan, 1947 (wraps) £5
The Novels of George Meredith and Some Notes on the English Novel, O.U.P., 1947 (wraps) . . £5
Death of a God and Other Stories, Macmillan, 1949 . . . . £20/£5
Collected Stories, Duckworth/Macmillan, 1952 £15/£5
The Four Continents, Macmillan, 1954 . . £15/£5
Fee Fi Fo Fum! A Book of Fairy Stories, Macmillan, 1959 . . . . £15/£5
A Place of One's Own and Other Stories, Icon, 1961 (wraps) £5
Tales My Father Taught Me, Macmillan, 1962 £15/£5
Pound Wise, Hutchinson, 1963 . . . . £10/£5

SACHEVERELL SITWELL
(b.1897 d.1988)

A more 'traditional' poet than his brother and sister, Sacheverell's most important writings were on art and music criticism.

Verse

The People's Palace, Blackwell, 1918 (400 copies, wraps) £125
Doctor Donne and Gargantua, First Canto, Favil Press, 1921 (101 signed, numbered copies, wraps) £125
The Hundred and One Harlequins, Grant Richards, 1922 . . . . £35/£10
The Parrot, The Poetry Bookshop, 1923 . . £35
The Thirteenth Caesar and Other Poems, Grant Richards, 1924 . . . . £65/£25
Exalt the Eglantine and Other Poems, The Fleuron, 1924 (370 copies) £50
Poor Young People, The Fleuron, 1925 (with Osbert & Edith Sitwell, 375 numbered copies) . . . £125/£50
The Cyder Feast and Other Poems, Duckworth, 1927 (1000 unsigned copies) . . . . £25/£10
ditto, Duckworth, 1927 (165 signed copies). £50/£35
The Augustan Books of Modern Poetry: Sacheverell Sitwell, Benn, 1928 . . . . £10
Two Poems, Ten Songs, Duckworth, 1929 (275 signed copies) £125
Dr Donne & Gargantua: The First Six Cantos, Duckworth, 1930. . . . . £25/£10
ditto, Duckworth, 1930 (215 signed copies). . £125
Canons of Giant Art: Twenty Torsos in Heroic Landscapes, Faber, 1933 . . . . . . £25/£10
Collected Poems, Duckworth, 1936 . . . £20/£5
Selected Poems, Duckworth, 1948 . . . £10/£5

Autobiography

Journey to the Ends of Time, Cassell, 1959 £15/£5

Others

Southern Baroque Art, Grant Richards, 1924 £45/£15
All Summer in a Day, Duckworth, 1926 . £35/£10
All At Sea, Duckworth, 1927 (with Osbert Sitwell). . . . . £25/£10
German Baroque Art, Duckworth, 1927 . £40/£15
A Book of Towers and Other buildings of Southern Europe, Etchells & Macdonald, 1928 (350 copies) £150
The Gothick North, Duckworth, 1929/30, (3 vols) . . . . £125/£50
ditto, Duckworth, 1938, (1 vol.) . . . . £45/£15
Beckford and Beckfordism, An Essay, Duckworth, 1930 (265 signed copies) £40
Far from My Home: Stories Long and Short, Duckworth, 1931. . . . . £45/£15
ditto, Duckworth, 1931 (110 signed copies). £75/£50
Spanish Baroque Art, Duckworth, 1931 . £30/£10
Mozart, Peter Davies, 1932 . . . . . £25/£10
Liszt, Faber, 1934 . . . . £20/£10
Touching the Orient: Six Sketches, Duckworth, 1934 . . . . £25/£10
A Background for Domenico Scarlatti, 1685-1757, Faber, 1935 . . . . £25/£10
Dance of the Quick and the Dead, Faber, 1936 . . . . £45/£10
Conversation Pieces, Batsford, 1936 . . £50/£20
Narrative Pictures, Batsford, 1937 . . . £50/£20
La Vie Parisienne: A Tribute to Offenbach, Faber, 1937 . . . . £25/£10
Trio: Dissertations on Some Aspects of National Genius, Macmillan, 1938 (with Osbert and Edith Sitwell) . . . . £25/£10
Roumanian Journey, Batsford, 1938 . . £15/£5
Edinburgh, Faber, 1938 . . . . £20/£5
German Baroque Sculpture, Duckworth, 1938 . . . . £30/£10
The Romantic Ballet in Lithographs of the Time, Faber, 1938 . . . . £45/£20
Old Fashioned Flowers, Country Life, 1939 £65/£25
Mauretania: Warrior, Man and Woman, Duckworth, 1940 . . . . £20/£10
Poltergeists, Faber, 1940 . . . . . . £25/£10
Sacred and Profane Love, Faber, 1940 . £25/£10
Valse des Fleurs, Faber, 1941 . . . . £15/£5
Primitive Scenes and Festivals, Faber, 1942 £35/£10
The Homing of the Winds and Other Passages in Prose, Faber, 1942 . . . . £15/£5
Splendours and Miseries, Faber, 1943 . . £15/£5
British Architects and Craftsmen, Batsford, 1945 . . . . £25/£10
The Hunters and the Hunted, Macmillan, 1947 £20/£5
The Netherlands, Batsford, 1948 . . . £15/£5
Morning, Noon & Night in London, Macmillan, 1948 . . . . £15/£5
Theatrical Figures in Porcelain, Curtain Press, 1949 . . . . £25/£10
Spain, Batsford, 1950 . . . . £15/£5
Cupid and the Jacaranda, Macmillan, 1952 £20/£5
Truffle Hunt, Robert Hale, 1953. . . . £20/£5
Fine Bird Books, Collins, 1953 (295 signed copies, slipcase) . . . . £750/£600
Portugal and Madeira, Batsford, 1954 . . £15/£5
Selected Works, Robert Hale, 1955 . . . £15/£5
Great Flower Books, Collins, 1956 (295 signed copies, slipcase) . . . . £750/£600
Denmark, Batsford, 1956. . . . . . . £15/£5
Arabesque and Honeycomb, Robert Hale, 1957 . . . . £25/£10
Malta, Batsford, 1958. . . . . £20/£5

Bridge of the Brocade Sash, Weidenfeld & Nicolson, 1959 . . . . £15/£5
Golden Wall and Mirador: From England to Peru, Weidenfeld & Nicolson, 1961 . . . . . £15/£5
The Red Chapels of Banteai Srei, Weidenfeld & Nicolson, 1962 . . . . £30/£10
Monks, Nuns and Monasteries, Weidenfeld & Nicolson, 1965 . . . . £25/£10
Southern Baroque Revisited, Weidenfeld & Nicolson, 1967 . . . . £35/£10
Gothic Europe, Weidenfeld & Nicolson, 1969 £15/£5
For Want of the Golden City, Thames and Hudson, 1973 . . . . £20/£5

CLARK ASHTON SMITH

(b.1893 d.1961)

An American poet and author of fantasy fiction, Clark Ashton Smith was a member of the circle of writers surrounding H.P. Lovecraft. His work is recognisable by its rich vocabulary.

The Star-Treader and Other Poems, A. M. Robertson (U.S.), 1912 . . . . £200
Odes and Sonnets, The Book Club of California (U.S.), 1918 (wraps) £250
Ebony and Crystal, Auburn Journal Press (U.S.), 1922 (250 signed, numbered copies) £250
Sandalwood, privately printed (U.S.), 1925 (250 signed, numbered copies, wraps) £250
The Immortals of Memory, Stellar Publishing Corporation (U.S.), 1932 (wraps) £100
The Double Shadow and Other Fantasies, Auburn Journal Press (U.S.), 1933 . . . . . . £200
The White Sybil, Fantasy Publications (U.S.), 1935 (wraps) £125
Nero and Other Poems, Futile Press (U.S.), 1937 £150
Out of Space and Time, Arkham House, 1942 . . . . £450/£125
Lost Worlds, Arkham House, 1944 . . . £175/£60
Genius Loci and Other Tales, Arkham House, 1948 . . . . £95/£35
The Ghoul and the Seraph, Gargoyle Press, 1950 (wraps) £200
The Dark Chateau, Arkham House, 1958 . £300/£125
Spells and Philtres, Arkham House, 1958 . £300/£125
Abominations of Yondo, Arkham House, 1960 . . . . £95/£35
Hesperian Fall, Clyde Beck, 1961 (wraps) . . £150
Poems in Prose, Arkham House, 1964 . £80/£30
Tales of Science and Sorcery, Arkham House, 1964 . . . . £80/£30
Other Dimensions, Arkham House, 1970 . £65/£25
Selected Poems, Arkham House, 1971 . . £75/£25
Planets and Dimensions, Mirage (U.S.), 1973 (wraps) £30
Grotesques and Fantastiques, De la Ree (U.S.), 1973 (500 numbered copies, wraps) £25
ditto, De la Ree (U.S.), 1973 (50 hardback copies) £75
Klarkash-Ton and Monstro Ligriv, De la Ree (U.S.), 1974 (500 numbered copies, wraps) £25
The Black Book, Arkham House, 1979 . . . . £40
A Rendezvous in Averoigne, Arkham House, 1988 . . . . £25/£10

STEVIE SMITH

(b.1902 d.1971)

A poet and novelist, Smith often illustrated her work with naive line drawings somewhat in the style of Edward Lear.

Novel

Novel on Yellow Paper, Cape, 1936 . . . . £350/£40
ditto, Morrow (U.S.), 1937 . . . . . . £150/£30
Over the Frontier, Cape, 1939 . . . . . £75/£25
The Holiday, Chapman & Hall, 1949 . . £75/£25
ditto, Smithers (U.S.), 1950 . . . . . . £65/£15

Verse

A Good Time was Had by All, Cape, 1937 £200/£40
Tender Only to One, Cape, 1938. . . . . £100/£25
Mother, What is Man?, Cape, 1942 . . . . £100/£25
Harold's Leap, Chapman & Hall, 1950 . . £50/£15
Not Waving but Drowning, Deutsch, 1957 . £100/£25
Selected Poems, Longman, 1962. . . . . £35/£10
ditto, New directions (U.S.), 1964 (wraps) . . £10
The Frog Prince and Other Poems, Longman, 1966 . . . . £35/£10
The Best Beast, Knopf, 1969 . . . . . . £35/£10
Francesca in Winter, Poem of the Month Club, 1970 (signed broadsheet) £40
Two in One, Longman, 1971 . . . . . . £15/£5
Scorpion and Other Poems, Longman, 1971 £20/£5
Collected Poems, Lane, 1975. . . . . . £75/£10
ditto, O.U.P. (U.S.), 1976. . . . . . . £40/£10

Others

Cats in Colour, Batsford, 1959 . . . . . £15/£5
ditto, Viking (U.S.), 1959. . . . . . . £15/£5
Me Again: Uncollected Writings, Virago, 1981 £15/£5
ditto, Farrar Straus (U.S.), 1982 . . . . £15/£5
Stevie Smith: A Selection, Faber, 1983 . . £10/£5
ditto, Faber (U.S.), 1982 . . . . £10/£5

C.P. SNOW

(b.1905 d.1980)

Possessing a Ph.D in Chemistry, C.P. Snow wrote a number of technical papers before becoming well known for his detective novels, the first of which was published in 1932. He was awarded a CBE in 1943 and a knighthood in 1957. He accepted a Life Peerage in 1964.

'Strangers and Brothers' Titles

Strangers and Brothers, Faber, 1940 (later re-titled ***George Passant***) . . . . £300/£65
ditto, Scribner (U.S.), 1960 . . . . . . £25/£5
The Light and the Dark, Faber, 1947 . . £40/£10
ditto, Macmillan (U.S.), 1948. . . . . £15/£5
Time of Hope, Faber, 1949 . . . . . £40/£10
ditto, Macmillan (U.S.), 1950. . . . . £15/£5
The Masters, Macmillan, 1951 . . . . £25/£10
ditto, Macmillan (U.S.), 1951. . . . . £15/£5
The New Men, Macmillan, 1954 . . . . £15/£5
ditto, Scribner (U.S.), 1954 . . . . . £10/£5
Homecomings, Macmillan, 1956 . . . £25/£10
ditto, as ***Homecoming***, Scribner (U.S.), 1956 £15/£5
The Conscience of the Rich, Macmillan, 1958 £15/£5
ditto, Scribner (U.S.), 1958 . . . . . £15/£5
The Affair, Macmillan, 1960 . . . . . £15/£5
ditto, Scribner (U.S.), 1960 . . . . . £10/£5
Corridors of Power, Macmillan, 1964 . . £15/£5
ditto, Scribner (U.S.), 1964 . . . . . £10/£5
The Sleep of Reason, Macmillan, 1968 . £15/£5
ditto, Scribner (U.S.), 1969 . . . . . £10/£5
Last Things, Macmillan, 1970 . . . . £10/£5
ditto, Scribner (U.S.), 1970 . . . . . £10/£5
Strangers and Brothers, Macmillan, 1972 (omnibus edition) . . . . £15/£5

Other Novels

Death Under Sail, Heinemann, 1932 . . £150/£40
ditto, Scribner (U.S.), 1959 . . . . . £15/£5
New Lives for Old, Gollancz, 1933 (published anonymously). £50
The Search, Gollancz, 1934 . . . . £125/£30
ditto, Bobbs-Merrill (U.S.), 1935. . . . £65/£15
ditto, Scribner (U.S.), 1958 . . . . . £25/£10
The Malcontents, Macmillan, 1972 . . . £10/£5
ditto, Scribner (U.S.), 1972 . . . . . £10/£5
In Their Wisdom, Macmillan, 1974 . . . £10/£5
ditto, Scribner (U.S.), 1974 . . . . . £10/£5
A Coat of Varnish, Macmillan, 1979 . . £10/£5
ditto, Scribner (U.S.), 1979 . . . . . £10/£5
ditto, Franlklin Library (U.S.), 1979 . . . . £25

Others

Richard Aldington, Heinemann, [1938] (wraps) £35
Two Cultures and the Scientific Revolution, C.U.P. (U.S.), 1959 . . . . £15/£5
Science and Government, O.U.P., 1961. . £10/£5
ditto, Harvard U.P. (U.S.), 1961 . . . . £10/£5
Variety of Men, Macmillan, 1968 . . . £15/£5
ditto, Scribner (U.S.), 1968 . . . . . £10/£5
The State of Siege, Scribner (U.S.), 1969 . £10/£5
Public Affairs, Scribner (U.S.), 1971 . . £10/£5
Trollope, Macmillan, 1975 . . . . . £15/£5
ditto, Scribner (U.S.), 1975 . . . . . £10/£5
The Realists, Macmillan, 1978 . . . . £10/£5
ditto, Scribner (U.S.), 1978 . . . . . £10/£5
The Physicists, Macmillan, 1981. . . . £10/£5
ditto, Little Brown (U.S.), 1981 . . . . £10/£5

ALEXANDER SOLZHENITSYN

(b.1918)

Since being deported from Russia Solzhenitsyn has lost some of his mystique, although none of his reputation as a fine writer.

Novels

One Day in the Life of Ivan Denisovich, Praeger (U.S.), 1963 . . . . £75/£20
ditto, Dutton (U.S.), 1963 . . . . . . £25/£10
ditto, Gollancz, 1963 . . . . £25/£10
We Never Make Mistakes: Two Short Novels, University of South Carolina (U.S.), 1963 . £20/£5
The First Circle, Harper & Row, 1968 . . £25/£10
ditto, Collins, 1968 . . . . £25/£15
Cancer Ward, Bodley Head, 1968-1969 (2 vols) . . . . £40/£15
ditto, Farrar Straus (U.S.), 1959 (1 vol.) . . £20/£10
August, 1914, Bodley Head, 1972 . . . £20/£5
ditto, Farrar Straus (U.S.), 1972 . . . . £20/£5
The Gulag Archipelago, Harper (U.S.), 1974 £15/£5
ditto, Collins, 1974 . . . . £15/£5
The Gulag Archipelago, 2, Harper (U.S.), 1975 . . . . £10/£5
ditto, Collins, 1975 . . . . £10/£5
The Gulag Archipelago, 3, Harper (U.S.), 1976 £10/£5
ditto, Collins, 1978 . . . . £10/£5

Plays

The Love-Girl and the Innocent, Bodley Head, 1969 . . . . £20/£5
ditto, Farrar Straus (U.S.), 1970 . . . . £15/£5
Candle in the Wind, University of Minnesota (U.S.), 1973 . . . . £15/£5
ditto, Bodley Head/O.U.P., 1973 . . . . £15/£5
Victory Celebrations, Bodley Head, 1983 . £10/£5
Prisoners, Bodley Head, 1983 . . . . . £10/£5

Others

Stories and Prose Poems, Bodley Head, 1971 £15/£5

ditto, Farrar Straus (U.S.), 1971 . . . . . £15/£5

"One Word of Truth ...", Bodley Head, 1972 (wraps) £15

ditto, as ***A World Split Apart***, Harper (U.S.), 1980 . . . . £10

Letter to Soviet Leaders, Index on Censorship, 1974 (wraps) £5

ditto, Harper (U.S.), 1974 . . . . £10/£5

From under the Rubble, Little Brown (U.S.), 1975 . . . . £10/£5

ditto, Collins, 1975 . . . . £10/£5

Lenin in Zurich, Farrar Straus (U.S.), 1976. £10/£5

ditto, Bodley Head, 1976 . . . . . . £10/£5

Warning to the Western World, Bodley Head/BBC, 1976 (wraps) £10

ditto, as ***Speeches to the Americans***, Farrar Straus, 1976 . . . . £10/£5

Alexander Solzhenitsyn Speaks to the West, Bodley Head, 1979 . . . . £10/£5

The Mortal Danger, Bodley Head, 1980 . £10/£5

ditto, Harper (U.S.), 1980 . . . . £10/£5

The Oak and the Calf, Harper (U.S.), 1980. £10/£5

ditto, Bodley Head, 1980 . . . . . . £10/£5

Verse

Prussian Nights, Collins/Harvill, 1977 . . £10/£5

ditto, Farrar Straus (U.S.), 1977 . . . . . £10/£5

MURIEL SPARK

(b.1918)

A novelist, poet and short story writer, Spark's first novel, *The Comforters* was very well received. All of her novels are written with elegance and detachment, and are full of black humour and irony.

Novels

The Comforters, Macmillan, 1957 . . . £200/£35

ditto, Lippincott (U.S.), 1957 . . . . . £100/£25

Robinson, Macmillan, 1958 . . . . . £150/£30

ditto, Lippincott (U.S.), 1958 . . . . . £75/£20

Memento Mori, Macmillan, 1959 . . . £125/£30

ditto, Lippincott (U.S.), 1959 . . . . . £75/£20

The Ballad of Peckham Rye, Macmillan, 1960 . . . . £75/£20

ditto, Lippincott (U.S.), 1960 . . . . . £30/£10

The Bachelors, Macmillan, 1960 . . . . £45/£15

ditto, Lippincott (U.S.), 1961 . . . . . £15/£5

The Prime of Miss Jean Brodie, Macmillan, 1961 . . . . £65/£20

ditto, Lippincott (U.S.), 1962 . . . . . £45/£15

The Girls of Slender Means, Macmillan, 1963 £45/£10

ditto, Knopf (U.S.), 1963 . . . . £15/£5

The Mandelbaum Gate, Macmillan, 1965 . £20/£5

ditto, Knopf (U.S.), 1965 . . . . £15/£5

The Public Image, Macmillan, 1968 . . £20/£5

ditto, Knopf (U.S.), 1968 . . . . £15/£5

The Driver's Seat, Macmillan, 1970 . . . £20/£5

ditto, Knopf (U.S.), 1970 . . . . £15/£5

Not to Disturb, Macmillan, 1971 . . . . £20/£5

ditto, Observer Books, 1971 (500 signed copies, glassine d/w) . . . . £75/£50

ditto, Viking (U.S.), 1972 . . . . £15/£5

The Hothouse by the East River, Macmillan, 1973 . . . . £15/£5

ditto, Viking (U.S.), 1973 . . . . £15/£5

The Abbess of Crewe: A Modern Morality Tale, Macmillan, 1974 . . . . £15/£5

ditto, Viking (U.S.), 1974 . . . . £15/£5

The Takeover, Macmillan, 1976 . . . . £15/£5

ditto, Viking (U.S.), 1976 . . . . £10/£5

Territorial Rights, Macmillan, 1979 . . . £10/£5

ditto, Coward McGann (U.S.), 1979 . . . . £10/£5

Loitering With Intent, Bodley Head, 1981 . £10/£5

ditto, Coward McGann (U.S.), 1981 . . . . £10/£5

The Only Problem, Bodley Head, 1984 . . £10/£5

ditto, Franklin Library (U.S.), 1984 (signed edition) £35

ditto, Coward McGann (U.S.), 1984 . . . £10/£5

A Far Cry from Kensington, Constable, 1988 £10/£5

ditto, London Limited Editions, 1988 (150 signed, numbered copies, glassine d/w) . . . . £65/£50

ditto, Houghton Mifflin (U.S.), 1988 . . . £10/£5

Symposium, Constable, 1990 . . . . . . £10/£5

ditto, Houghton Mifflin (U.S.), 1990 . . . £10/£5

Reality and Dreams, Constable, 1996 . . £10/£5

Omnibus Editions

The Muriel Spark Omnibus, Constable, 1993 (vol. 1) . . . . £10/£5

The Muriel Spark Omnibus, Constable, 1994 (vol. 2) . . . . £10/£5

The Muriel Spark Omnibus, Constable, 1996 (vol. 3) . . . . £10/£5

Verse

Out of a Book, Millar & Burden, [1933] (broadside, written as 'Muriel Camberg') £750

The Fanfarlo, Hand & Flower Press, 1952 (wraps) £75

Collected Poems I, Macmillan, 1967 . . £20/£5

ditto, Knopf (U.S.), 1968 . . . . £20/£5

Going Up to Sotheby's and Other Poems, Granada, 1982 (wraps) £10

Short Stories
The Go-Away Bird and Other Stories, Macmillan, 1958 . . . . £175/£35
ditto, Lippincott (U.S.), 1960 . . . . . £45/£15
The Seraph and the Zambesi, Lippincott (U.S.), 1960 (privately printed, wraps) £45
Collected Stories, Macmillan, 1967 . . . £20/£5
ditto, Knopf (U.S.), 1968 . . . . £15/£5
Bang-Bang You're Dead and Other Stories, Granada, 1982, (wraps). £10
The Stories of Muriel Spark, Dutton (U.S.), 1985 . . . . £10/£5
ditto, Bodley Head, 1987 . . . . £10/£5
The Portobello Road and Other Stories, Eurographica (Helsinki), 1990 (350 signed copies, wraps) . £75
Harper and Wilton, Colophon Press, 1996 (100 signed copies) £75

Children's
The Very Fine Clock, Knopf (U.S.), 1968 . £45/£20
ditto, Macmillan, 1968 . . . . £25
French Window, Colophon Press, 1993 (105 signed copies) £60
ditto, Colophon Press, 1994 (12 signed copies, leather) £150

Plays
Voices at Play, Macmillan, 1961 . . . . £25/£5
ditto, Lippincott (U.S.), 1962 . . . . . £10/£5
Doctors of Philosophy, Macmillan, 1963 . £25/£5
ditto, Knopf (U.S.), 1966 . . . . £10/£5

Others
Reassessment, Reassessment Pamphlet No.1, [1948], (single sheet, folded). £50
Child of Light: A Reassessment of Mary Wollstonecraft Shelley, Tower Bridge, 1951 £75/£25
ditto, Folcroft Library Editions (U.S.), 1976 £20/£5
Emily Bronte: Her Life and Work, Owen, 1953 (with Derek Stanford) . . . . £40/£10
ditto, Coward McGann (U.S.), 1966 . . . £25/£5
John Masefield, Nevill, 1953 . . . . £35/£10
ditto, Folcroft Library Editions (U.S.), 1977 £15/£5
The Essence of the Brontes, P Owen, 1993 £15/£5

Autobiography
Curriculum Vitae: A Volume of Autobiography, Constable, 1992 . . . . £10/£5
ditto, Houghton Mifflin (U.S.), 1993. . . £10/£5

STEPHEN SPENDER
(b.1909 d.1995)

Early in his poetic career Spender displays a lyricism which he did not continue. In later years he put more of his energies into critical works.

Verse
Nine Experiments by S. H. S.: Being Poems Written at the Age of Eighteen, hand-printed by Spender, 1928 (wraps) £7,500
Twenty Poems, Blackwell, 1930 (75 signed copies of 135, wraps) £500
ditto, Blackwell, 1930 (55 unsigned copies of 135, wraps). £250
Poems, Faber, 1933 . . . . £100/£25
ditto, Random House (U.S.), 1934 . . . £65/£20
Vienna, Faber, 1934 . . . . £45/£15
ditto, Random House (U.S.), 1935 . . . £25/£10
The Still Centre, Faber, 1939. . . . . £45/£15
Selected Poems, Faber, 1940 . . . . . . £25/£5
Ruins and Visions, Faber, 1942 . . . . £35/£10
ditto, Random House (U.S.), 1942 . . . £25/£10
Spiritual Exercises, Curwen Press, 1943 (125 copies) £250
Poems of Dedication, Faber, 1947 . . . £30/£10
ditto, Random House (U.S.), 1947 . . . £25/£10
The Edge of Being, Faber, 1949 . . . . £30/£10
ditto, Random House (U.S.), 1949 . . . £25/£10
Sirmione Peninsula, Faber, 1954 . . . £20/£10
Collected Poems, 1928-1953, Faber, 1955 . £25/£10
ditto, Random House (U.S.), 1955 . . . £25/£10
Inscriptions, Poetry Book Society, 1958 . . £20
Selected Poems, Random House (U.S.), 1964 £15/£5
ditto, Faber, 1965 . . . . £15/£5
The Generous Days, Faber, 1971 . . . £15/£5
ditto, Random House (U.S.), 1971 . . . £15/£5
Recent Poems, Anvil Press Poetry, 1978 (400 signed copies, wraps) £40
Dolphins, Faber, 1994 . . . . . . £10/£5
ditto, Faber, 1994 (limited, signed edition) . . £35
ditto, St. Martin's Press (U.S.), 1994 . . . £10/£5

Novels
The Backward Son, Hogarth Press, 1940 . £150/£40
The Temple, Faber, 1988 . . . . . . £10/£5
ditto, Grove Press (U.S.), 1988 . . . . £10/£5

Short Stories
The Burning Cactus, Faber, 1936 . . . £50/£15
ditto, Random House (U.S.), 1936 . . . £25/£10
Engaged in Writing and The Fool and The Princess, Hamish Hamilton, 1958 . . . . . . £10/£5
ditto, Farrar Straus (U.S.), 1958 . . . . £10/£5

Plays

Trial of a Judge, Faber, 1938 . . . . £25/£5
ditto, Random House (U.S.), 1938 . . . £20/£5
Danton's Death, Faber, 1939 (adaptation with Goronwy Rees) . . . . £20/£5
Oedipus Trilogy, Faber, 1985 . . . . £10/£5
ditto, Random House (U.S.), 1985 . . . £10/£5

Prose

The Destructive Element, Cape, 1935 . . £25/£10
ditto, Houghton Mifflin (U.S.), 1935. . . £25/£10
Forward from Liberalism, Gollancz, 1937 £45/£15
ditto, Left Book Club, 1937 . . . . . £20/£5
ditto, Random House (U.S.), 1937 . . . £10/£5
The New Realism: A Discussion, Hogarth Press, 1939 (wraps) £30
Life and the Poet, Secker & Warburg, 1942 £10/£5
Citizens in War - And After, Harrap, 1945 . £20/£5
European Witness: Impressions of Germany in, 1945, Hamish Hamilton, 1946 . . . . . . £20/£5
Poetry Since 1939, Longmans, Green, 1946 (wraps) £15
World Within World, Hamish Hamilton, 1951 £15/£5
ditto, Harcourt Brace (U.S.), 1951 . . . £10/£5
Learning Laughter, A Study of Children in Israel, Weidenfeld & Nicolson, 1952 . . . . £15/£5
The Creative Element, Hamish Hamilton, 1953 £10/£5
ditto, British Book Center (U.S.), 1954 . . £10/£5
The Making of a Poem, Hamish Hamilton, 1955 . . . . £10/£5
The Struggle of the Modern, Hamish Hamilton, 1963 . . . . £10/£5
ditto, Univ of California Press (U.S.), 1954 . £10/£5
The Year of the Young Rebel, Weidenfeld & Nicholson, 1969 . . . . £10/£5
ditto, Random House (U.S.), 1969 . . . . £10/£5
Love-Hate Relations: A Study of Anglo-American Sensibilities, Hamish Hamilton, 1974 . . . £10/£5
ditto, Random House (U.S.), 1974 . . . . £10/£5
T. S. Eliot, Fontana, 1975. . . . . £10
The Thirties and After: Poetry, Politics and People, 1933-75, Fontana, 1975 . . . . . . £10/£5
ditto, Random House (U.S.), 1978 . . . . £10/£5
Letters to Christopher, Black Sparrow Press, 1980 £25
China Diary, Thames and Hudson, 1982 . £30/£10
ditto, Abrams (U.S.), 1982 . . . . . . £15/£5
Journals, 1939-83, Faber, 1985 . . . . £10/£5
ditto, Random House (U.S.), 1986 . . . £10/£5

Others

W.H. Auden, A Memorial Address Delivered at Christ Church Cathedral, Oxford on 27 October, 1973, Faber, 1975 (wraps) £75
W.H. Auden, A Tribute, Weidenfeld & Nicholson, 1975 . . . . £15/£5
ditto, Macmillan (U.S.), 1975 . . . . . £10/£5

JOHN STEINBECK

(b.1902 d.1968)

An American novelist, *The Grapes of Wrath* is perhaps his best known work, and was later made into a classic film. He was awarded the Nobel Prize for Literature in 1962.

Novels

Cup of Gold, McBride (U.S.), 1929 . . £4,500/£750
ditto, Heinemann, 1937 . . . . . £750/£150
The Pastures of Heaven, Brewer (U.S.), 1932 . . . . £2,750/£500
ditto, Allan, 1933 . . . . £750/£150
To a God Unknown, Ballou (U.S.), 1933 £4,500/£750
ditto, Heinemann, 1935 . . . . £750/£150
Tortilla Flat, Covici Friede (U.S.), 1935 £1,000/£150
ditto, Covici Friede (U.S.), 1935 (500 advance review copies in wraps) £750
ditto, Heinemann, 1935 . . . . £500/£125
In Dubious Battle, Covici Friede (U.S.), 1936 . . . . £750/£150
ditto, Covici Friede (U.S.), 1936 (99 signed, numbered copies, tissue d/w and black slipcase) £3,000/£2,500
ditto, Heinemann, 1936 . . . . . £400/£65
Of Mice and Men, Covici Friede (U.S.), 1937 . . . . £750/£150
ditto, Heinemann, 1937 . . . . . . £250/£45
The Grapes of Wrath, Viking (U.S.), 1939 . . . . £1,250/£150
ditto, Heinemann, 1939 . . . . . . £200/£35
The Moon is Down, Viking (U.S.), 1941 . £35/£10
ditto, Heinemann, 1942 . . . . £30/£10
Cannery Row, Viking (U.S.), 1945 (first issue, buff cloth) . . . . £650/£75
ditto, Viking (U.S.), 1945 (second issue, yellow cloth). . . . . £200/£25
ditto, Heinemann, 1945 . . . . £25/£5
The Wayward Bus, Viking (U.S.), 1947. . £100/£20
ditto, Heinemann, 1947 . . . . £75/£15
The Pearl, Viking (U.S.), 1947 . . . . £100/£20
ditto, Heinemann, 1948 . . . . . . £35/£10
Burning Bright, Viking (U.S.), 1950 . . £100/£15
ditto, Heinemann, 1951 . . . . £25/£5
East of Eden, Viking (U.S.), 1952 . . . £400/£75
ditto, Viking (U.S.), 1952 (1,500 signed, numbered copies) . . . . £1,250/£850
ditto, Heinemann, 1952 . . . . . . £100/£25
Sweet Thursday, Viking (U.S.), 1954 . . £65/£15
ditto, Heinemann, 1954 . . . . £45/£10
The Short Reign of Pippin IV: A Fabrication, Viking

(U.S.), 1957 . . . . £40/£10
ditto, Heinemann, 1957 . . . . £30/£5
The Winter of Our Discontent, Viking (U.S.), 1961 . . . . £20/£10
ditto, Heinemann, 1961 . . . . £30/£5

Short Stories
The Red Pony, Covici Friede (U.S.), 1937 (690 signed copies, slipcase) . . . . £1,000/£750
ditto, Covici Friede (U.S.), 1937 (signed, lettered copies, slipcase) . . . . . . £1,750/£1,500
ditto, Viking (U.S.), 1945 (enlarged edition, slipcase no d/w) . . . . £25/£15
The Long Valley, Viking (U.S.), 1938 . . £250/£35
ditto, Heinemann, 1939 . . . . £150/£25

Plays
Of Mice and Men, Covici Friede (U.S.), 1937 . . . . £750/£150

Screenplay
The Forgotten Village, Viking (U.S.), 1941 £25/£10
Viva Zapata!, Edizioni Filmcritica (Italy), 1952 £25
ditto, Viking (U.S.), 1975 . . . . £25
ditto, Yolla Bolly Press (U.S.), 1991 (190 numbered copies signed by the artist, slipcase) . . . £600
ditto, Yolla Bolly Press (U.S.), 1991 (40 signed deluxe copies signed by the artist, with *Zapata The Man, The Myth, And The Mexican Revolution*, also signed) £1,250
ditto, Heinemann , 1991 . . . . . . £75/£25

Others
Sea of Cortez: A Leisurely Journal of Travel and Research, Viking, 1941 (with Edward F. Ricketts) . . . . £500/£50
ditto, Viking, 1941 (with Edward F. Ricketts, advance proof copy, wraps) £1,000
ditto, as ***The Log from the Sea of Cortez***, Viking, 1951 . . . . £200/£20
ditto, as ***The Log from the Sea of Cortez***, Heinemann, 1958 . . . . £75/£15
Bombs Away: The Story of a Bomber Team, Viking, 1942 . . . . £125/£20
A Russian Journal, Viking, 1948 . . . £75/£20
ditto, Heinemann, 1949 . . . . £50/£15
Once There Was a War, Viking (U.S.), 1958 £75/£20
ditto, Heinemann, 1959 . . . . £50/£15
Travels With Charley in Search of America, Viking (U.S.), 1962 . . . . £40£10
ditto, Heinemann, 1962 . . . . £35/£10
Speech Accepting the Nobel Prize for Literature, Viking (U.S.), 1962 . . . . £75
America and Americans, Viking, 1966 . . £35/£10
ditto, Heinemann, 1966 . . . . £35/£10
The Acts of King Arthur and His Noble Knights, Farrar Straus (U.S.), 1976 . . . . . . £10/£5
ditto, Heinemann, 1977 . . . . £10/£5

COUNT ERIC STENBOCK
(b.1860 d.1895)

The most self-conscious of all 1890's decadents, Stenbock impressed his contemporaries by his personality and wealth rather than by his morbidly sensitive and self-financed poetry and prose.

Verse
Love, Sleep and Dreams, Shrimpton & Son/Simpkin Marshall & Co., 1881 [?] £1,000
Myrtle, Rue and Cypress, privately printed by Hatchards, 1883 . . . . £850
ditto, Hermitage Books, 1992 (60 numbered copies) £45
The Shadow of Death, The Leadenhall Press, 1893 . . . . £850
On the Freezing of the Baltic Sea, privately printed for Timothy d'Arch Smith, 1961 . . . . . . £50

Short Stories
Studies of Death: Romantic Tales, David Nutt, 1894 . . . . £1,000
ditto, Durtro Press, 1996 [1997] £60
The True Story of a Vampire, Tragara Press (Edinburgh), 1989 (reprinted from Studies of death, 110 numbered copies) £45

ROBERT LOUIS STEVENSON
(b.1850 d.1894)

A novelist, essayist and poet, many of Stevenson's romances have become classics of English literature, although such novels as *Treasure Island* and *Kidnapped* are often relegated to the category of children's fiction.

Fiction
New Arabian Nights, Chatto & Windus, 1882 (2 vols) £400
Treasure Island, Cassell, 1883 . . . . . £5,000
Prince Otto, Chatto & Windus, 1885 . . . £250
The Dynamiter, More New Arabian Nights, Longmans Green & Co., 1885 (with Fanny van de Grift Stevenson, boards) £250
ditto, Longmans Green & Co., 1885 (with Fanny van de

Grift Stevenson, wraps) £275
The Strange Case of Dr Jekyll and Mr Hyde, Scribner (U.S.), 1886 (wraps) £1,250
ditto, Scribner (U.S.), 1886 (boards) £1,250
ditto, Longmans Green & Co., 1886 (wraps) £1,000
ditto, Longmans Green & Co., 1886 (boards) £1,000
Kidnapped, Cassell, 1886 . . . . £500
The Merry Men and Other Tales, Chatto & Windus, 1887 . . . . £150
The Black Arrow, Cassell, 1888 (wraps) . . £250
ditto, Cassell, 1888 (boards) £150
The Master of Ballantrae, Cassell, 1889 . . £225
The Wrong Box, Longmans Green & Co., 1889 (with L. Osbourne) £125
The Wrecker, Cassell, 1892 (with L. Osbourne) £100
Three Plays, D. Nutt, 1892 (with W. Henley) . £300
ditto, D. Nutt, 1892 (with W. Henley, 30 copies on Japanese vellum) £1,500
ditto, D. Nutt, 1892 (with W. Henley, 100 on Dutch handmade paper) £1,000
Catriona, Cassell, 1893 . . . . £150
Island Nights' Entertainments, Cassell, 1893 . £150
The Ebb-Tide, Heinemann, 1894 (with L. Osbourne) £30
Valima Letters, Methuen, 1895 . . . . . £50
Weir of Hermiston, Chatto & Windus, 1896 . £50
St. Ives, Scribners (U.S.), 1897 (with Quiller Couch) £75
ditto, Heinemann, 1898 (with Quiller Couch) . £50

Verse

A Child's Garden of Verses, Longmans Green & Co., 1885 . . . . £1,250
Underwoods, Chatto & Windus, 1887 . . . £45
Ballads, Scribners (U.S.), 1890 . . . . . £45
ditto, Chatto & Windus, 1890 . . . . . £45
Songs of Travel and Other Verses, Chatto & Windus, 1896 . . . . £40
Verses by R.L.S., privately printed, The De Vinne Press (U.S.), 1912 (100 presentation copies) . . . £300

Non Fiction

The Pentland Rising, Elliot, 1866 (annonymous, wraps) £2,000
The Charity Bazaar, privately printed, 1868 (signed, wraps) £300
ditto, privately printed, 1868 (unsigned, wraps) . £150
An Inland Voyage, Kegan Paul, 1878 . . . £300
Edinburgh: Picturesque Notes, Seeley & Co., 1879 . . . . £200
Travels With a Donkey in the Cevennes, Kegan Paul, 1879 . . . . £300
Virginibus Puerisque, Kegan Paul, 1881 . . £150
Familiar Studies of Men and Books, Chatto & Windus, 1882. . . . . £125
The Silverado Squatters, Chatto & Windus, 1883 £125
Memories and Portraits, Chatto & Windus, 1887 £50
Memoir of Fleeming Jenkin, Scribners (U.S.), 1887 . . . . £35
Father Damien, An Open Letter, privately printed, (Australia,) 1890 (wraps, 25 copies) . . . £1,250
ditto, privately printed (Edinburgh), 1890 (unbound sheets in portfolio) £450
ditto, Chatto & Windus, 1890 (wraps) £250
In the South Seas, Cassell (copyright edition), 1890 . . . . £1,000
ditto, Edinburgh edition, 1896 (with 15 of 35 letters) £75
ditto, Chatto & Windus, 1900 . . . . . £35
Across the Plains, Chatto & Windus, 1892 . . . £25
A Footnote to History, Cassell, 1892 . . . £40
The Amateur Emigrant, Stone & Kimball (U.S.), 1895 . . . . £25
Essays of Travel, Chatto & Windus, 1905 . . £20
Essays in the Art of Writing, Chatto & Windus, 1905 . . . . £20
Lay Morals and Other Papers, Chatto & Windus, 1911 . . . . £15
Records of a Family of Engineers, Chatto & Windus, 1912 . . . . £15

BRAM STOKER

(b.1847 d.1905)

Born and educated in Dublin, Stoker was the author of a number of novels of mystery and romance, the most famous of which was *Dracula*.

Novels

The Snake's Pass, Sampson Low, 1891 [1890] £400
The Watter's Mou', Constable, 1895 . . . £250
The Shoulder of Shasta, Constable, 1895 . . £350
Dracula, Constable, 1897. . . . . . . £3,000
Miss Betty, Pearson, 1898 . . . . . . £300
The Mystery of the Sea, Heinemann, 1902 . . £200
The Jewel of the Seven Stars, Heinemann, 1903 £300
The Man, Heinemann, 1905 . . . . . . £250
Lady Athyne, Heinemann, 1908 . . . . . . £200
The Lady of the Shroud, Heinemann, 1909 . . £175
The Lair of the White Worm, Rider, 1911 . . £175

Short Stories

Under the Sunset, Sampson Low, 1882 [1881] . £250
Snowbound, Collier, 1908 (wraps) £75
Dracula's Guest and Other Weird Stories, Routledge, 1914 . . . . £100
The Dualists, Tragara Press (Edinburgh), 1986, (wrappers) £25

Non Fiction
The Duties of the Clerks of Petty Sessions in Ireland, John Falconer, 1879 . . . . £200
A Glimpse of America, Sampson Low, 1886, (wraps) £65
Personal Reminiscences of Henry Irving, Heinemann, 1906, (two vols) £75
Famous Impostors, Sidgwick and Jackson, 1910 £100

TOM STOPPARD
(b.1937)

A prolific playwright, Stoppard was born in Czechoslovakia, taken to Singapore as an infant, and finished his education in England.

Plays
Rosencrantz and Guildenstern are Dead, Faber, 1967 . . . . £250/£50
ditto, Faber, 1967 (wraps). £40
ditto, Grove Press (U.S.), 1967 . . . . £150/£25
The Real Inspector Hound, Faber, 1968 . £200/£45
ditto, Faber, 1968 (wraps). £25
ditto, Grove Press (U.S.), 1969 (wraps) . . . £20
Enter a Free Man, Faber, 1968 . . . . £150/£35
ditto, Faber, 1968 (wraps). £25
ditto, Grove Press (U.S.), 1972 (wraps) £20
Albert's Bridge and If You're Glad I'll be Frank: Two Plays for Radio, Faber, 1969 (wraps) £35
After Magritte, Faber, 1971 (wraps) £50
ditto, Grove Press (U.S.), 1972 (wraps) £15
Jumpers, Faber, 1971 . . . . £75/£20
ditto, Faber, 1971 (wraps). £30
ditto, Grove Press (U.S.), 1972 . . . . . £35/£10
Artist Descending a Staircase and Where Are They Now?: Two Plays for Radio, Faber, 1973 . £45/£15
Travesties, Faber, 1975 . . . . . . £60/£15
ditto, Faber, 1975 (wraps). £20
ditto, Grove Press (U.S.), 1975 . . . . . . £15
Dirty Linen and New-Found-Land, Ambiance/Almost Free Playscript, 1976 . . . . £25
ditto, Inter Action, 1976 (1,000 signed, numbered copies, wraps) £40
ditto, Grove Press (U.S.), 1976 . . . . £35/£10
ditto, Faber, 1976 . . . . £10
The Fifteen Minute Hamlet, French, 1976 (wraps) £25
Albert's Bridge & Other Plays, Grove Press (U.S.), 1977 . . . . £20/£5
Every Good Boy Deserves Favour and Professional Foul, Faber, 1978 . . . . £50/£15
ditto, Faber, 1978 (wraps). £15
ditto, Grove Press (U.S.), 1978 . . . . £25/£10
Night and Day, Faber, 1978 . . . . . £40/£10
ditto, Grove Press (U.S.), 1979 . . . . £25/£10
Undiscovered Country, Faber, 1980 (wraps) . £45
Dogg's Hamlet, Cahoot's Macbeth, Inter-Action, 1979 (2,000 numbered copies, wraps) £35
ditto, Faber, 1980 . . . . £20
On the Razzle, Faber, 1981 (wraps) £20
The Real Thing, Faber, 1982. . . . . £15
ditto, Faber, 1982 (500 signed copies, broadside) £125
ditto, Faber (U.S.), 1984 (revised edition) . £20/£5
The Dog It was That Died and Other Plays, Faber, 1983 . . . . £15
Four Plays for Radio, Faber, 1984 . . . . £10
Squaring the Circle, Faber, 1984 . . . . . £10
Rough Crossing, Faber, 1985 . . . . . . £10
Hapgood, Faber, 1988 . . . . £10
Radio Plays 1964-1983, Faber, 1990 . . . £10
In the Nation State, Faber, 1991 . . . . . £10
Television Plays, 1965-84, Faber, 1993 . . £35/£10
Indian Ink, Faber, 1995 . . . . £30/£10
ditto, Faber, 1995 (wraps). £10

Novels
Lord Malquist and Mr Moon, Blond, 1966 £65/£15
ditto, Knopf (U.S.), 1968 . . . . £25/£10

Others
Rosencrantz and Guildenstern Are Dead: The Film, Faber, 1991 . . . . £15

DAVID STOREY
(b.1933)

A novelist and playwright, much of Storey's writing considers the problems of working class characters as they move into middle class surroundings and/or a mid-life crisis.

Novels
This Sporting Life, Longmans, 1960 . . £150/£30
ditto, Macmillan (U.S.), 1960. . . . . . £25/£10
Flight into Camden, Longmans, 1961 . . £75/£20
ditto, Macmillan (U.S.), 1961. . . . . . £25/£10
Radcliffe, Longmans, 1963 . . . . . . £30/£10
ditto, Coward McGann (U.S.), 1964 . . . £20/£5
Pasmore, Longman, 1972. . . . . . . £15/£5
ditto, Dutton (U.S.), 1974 . . . . £10/£5
A Temporary Life, Lane, 1973 . . . . . £15/£5
ditto, Dutton (U.S.), 1974. . . . . . . £10/£5
Saville, Cape, 1976 . . . . £20/£5
ditto, Harper (U.S.), 1977. . . . . . . £10/£5
A Prodigal Child, Cape, 1981 . . . . . £15/£5
ditto, Dutton (U.S.), 1982. . . . . . . £10/£5
Present Times, Cape, 1984 . . . . . . £15/£5

Plays
The Restoration of Arnold Middleton, Cape, 1967 . . . . £20/£5
In Celebration, Cape, 1969 . . . . . . £20/£5
ditto, Grove Press (U.S.), 1975 . . . . . £10/£5
The Contractor, Cape, 1970 . . . . . . £15/£5
ditto, Random House (U.S.), 1971 . . . . £10/£5
Home, Cape, 1970. . . . . £15/£5
ditto, Random House (U.S.), 1971 . . . . £10/£5
The Changing Room, Cape, 1972 . . . . £10/£5
ditto, Random House (U.S.), 1972 . . . . £10/£5
The Farm, Cape, 1973 . . . . £10/£5
Cromwell, Cape, 1973 . . . . £10/£5
Life Class, Cape, 1975 . . . . £10/£5
Mother's Day, Cape, 1977 . . . . . . £10/£5
Early Days, Penguin, 1980 . . . . £10
Sisters, Penguin, 1980. . . . . £10
The March on Russia, French, 1989 . . . . £10

Humour
Edward, Lane, 1973 . . . . £10/£5

Verse
Storey's Lives: Poems, 1951-1991, Cape, 1992 £15/£5

GILES LYTTON STRACHEY

(b.1880 d.1932)

Lytton Strachey was educated at Liverpool and Cambridge Universities and became a prominent member of the Bloomsbury Group. Best known for biographies, he also wrote poetry, reviews and essays.

Landmarks in French Literature, Williams and Norgate, 1912 (first issue) £95
ditto, Holt (U.S.), 1912 . . . . £10
Eminent Victorians, Chatto & Windus, 1918 . £45
ditto, Putnam (U.S.), 1918 . . . . £15
Queen Victoria, Chatto & Windus, 1921 . £75/£25
ditto, Harcourt (U.S.), 1921 . . . . . . £45/£15
Books and Characters, Chatto & Windus, 1922 . . . . £45/£15
ditto, Harcourt (U.S.), 1922 . . . . . . £25/£10
Pope: The Leslie Stephen Lecture, CUP, 1925. . . . . £30/£10
ditto, Harcourt (U.S.), 1926 . . . . . . £25/£10
Elizabeth and Essex, Chatto & Windus, 1928 £35/£10
ditto, Harcourt Brace/Crosby Gaige (U.S.), 1928 . . . . £20/£5
ditto, Harcourt Brace/Crosby Gaige (U.S.), 1928 (1,060 signed copies) £50
Portraits in Miniature, Chatto & Windus, 1931 . . . . £30/£10
ditto, Chatto & Windus, 1931 (260 signed copies) £125
ditto, Harcourt (U.S.), 1931 . . . . . . £15/£5
Characters and Commentaries, Chatto & Windus, 1933 . . . . £45/£15
ditto, Harcourt (U.S.), 1933 . . . . . . £30/£10
Virginia Woolf and Lytton Strachey: Letters, Hogarth Press, 1956 . . . . £65/£20
ditto, Harcourt (U.S.), 1956 . . . . £25/£10
Spectatorial Essays, Chatto & Windus, 1964 £15/£5
ditto, Harcourt (U.S.), 1965 . . . . £10/£5
Ermyntrude and Esmeralda, Blond, 1969 (17 illustrations by Erte) . . . . £45/£15
ditto, Stein & Day (U.S.), 1969 . . . . £25/£10
Lytton Strachey by Himself, Heinemann, 1971 (edited Michael Holroyd) . . . . £10/£5
ditto, Holt, Rhinehart & Winston (U.S.), 1971 £10/£5
Lytton Strachey: The Really Interesting Question, Weidenfeld & Nicholson, 1972 (edited Paul Levy) . . . . £15/£5
ditto, Coward, McCann (U.S.), 1973. . . . £15/£5
The Shorter Strachey, O.U.P., 1980 (edited Michael Holroyd) . . . . £10/£5

MONTAGUE SUMMERS

(b.1880 d.1948)

A strange but scholarly character, Summers published many books on the supernatural as well as 17th century theatre and the Gothic novel.

Major Works
The Marquis de Sade, The British Society for the Study of Sex Psychology, 1920 (wraps) . . £40
The History of Witchcraft and Demonology, Kegan Paul, 1926 . . . . £100/£50
ditto, Knopf (U.S.), 1926 . . . . £65/£35
The Geography of Witchcraft, Kegan Paul, 1927 . . . . £65/£35
ditto, Knopf (U.S.), 1927 . . . . £45/£25
Essays in Petto, Fortune Press, [1928] . . £125/£65
ditto, Fortune Press, [1928] (70 numbered copies) £200
The Discovery of Witches, Cayme Press, 1928 (wraps) £45
The Vampire: His Kith and Kin, Kegan Paul, 1928 . . . . £65/£30
ditto, University Books (U.S.), 1966 . . . . £15/£5
The Vampire in Europe, Kegan Paul, 1929. £85/£25
ditto, Dutton (U.S.), 1929 . . . . £75/£25
The Werewolf, Kegan Paul, 1933 . . . £125/£45
ditto, Dutton (U.S.), 1934 . . . . £75/£25
The Restoration Theatre, Kegan Paul, 1934 £45/£20
ditto, Macmillan (U.S.), 1934. . . . . . £35/£20
A Bibliography of the Restoration Drama, Fortune

Press [1935] . . . . £25/£10
ditto, Fortune Press [1935] (250 copies) . . £45/£35
ditto, Fortune Press [1943] (revised and enlarged edition) . . . . £25/£10
The Playhouse of Pepys, Kegan Paul, 1935 £40/£15
ditto, Macmillan (U.S.), 1935. . . . . £35/£15
A Popular History of Witchcraft, Kegan Paul, 1937 . . . . £35/£10
The Gothic Quest, Fortune Press, [1938] (950 copies) . . . . £125/£50
A Gothic Bibliography, Fortune Press [1940] (750 copies) . . . . £125/£50
Witchcraft and Black Magic, Rider, [1946] £25/£10
The Physical Phenomena of Mysticism, Rider, [1950] £25
The Galanty Show: An Autobiography, Cecil Woolf, 1980 . . . . £20/£5
Letters to an Editor, Tragara Press (Edinburgh), 1986 (145 numbered copies, wraps) £35

Others
Antinous and Other Poems, Sisley's [1907] . £200
The Source of Southerne's The Fatal Marriage, C.U.P., 1916 (wraps) £45
The Double Dealer, [Incorporated Stage Society], [1916] (wraps) £35
Orrey's The Tragedy of Zoroastres, C.U.P., 1917 (wraps) £45
Love for Love, [Incorporated Stage Society], [1917] (wraps) £35
A Great Mistress of Romance, Royal Society of Literature, [1917] (wraps) £45
The Way of the World, [Incorporated Stage Society], [1918] (wraps) £35
Jane Austen: An Appreciation, Royal Society of Literature, [1918] (wraps) £45
The Provok'd Wife, Incorporated Stage Society, [1919] (wraps) £35

GRAHAM SWIFT

(b.1949)

A novelist whose acclaim was based largely on *Waterland* until *Last Orders* won the 1996 Booker Prize.

Novels
The Sweet-Shop Owner, Allen Lane, 1980 . £150/£35
ditto, Washington Square(U.S.), 1985 (wraps) . £10
Shuttlecock, Allen Lane, 1981 . . . . £100/£25
ditto, Washington Square(U.S.), 1985 (wraps) . £10
Waterland, Heinemann, 1983 . . . . £50/£10
ditto, Poseidon (U.S.), 1984 . . . . . £20/£5
Out of This World, Viking, 1988 . . . £15/£5
ditto, Poseidon (U.S.), 1988 . . . . . £10/£5
Ever After, Picador, 1992 . . . . . £15/£5
ditto, Knopf (U.S.), 1992 . . . . . £10/£5
Last Orders, Picador, 1996 . . . . . £15/£5
ditto, Knopf (U.S.), 1996 . . . . . £10/£5

Short Stories
Learning to Swim and Other Stories, London Magazine Editions, 1982 . . . . . £75/£20
ditto, Knopf (U.S.), 1992 . . . . . £10/£5

A.J.A. SYMONS

(b.1900 d.1941)

A biographer, bibliographer and book collector, Symons' masterpiece is *The Quest for Corvo.*

A Bibliography of the First Editions of Books by William Butler Yeats, First Edition Club, 1924 (500 copies) £75
Frederick Baron Corvo, Sette of Odd Volumes, 1927 (199 copies, wraps) £100
Emin: The Governor of Equatoria, The Fleuron, 1928 (300 copies, wraps) £100
ditto, Falcon Press, 1950 . . . . . . £20/£5
An Episode in the Life of the Queen of Sheba Redicovered by A.J.A. Symons, privately printed, 1929 (150 copies, wraps) £100
H.M. Stanley, Duckworth, 1933 . . . . £15/£5
ditto, Falcon Press, 1950 . . . . . . £15/£5
The Quest for Corvo, Cassell, 1934 . . . £65/£15
Essays and Biographies, Cassell, 1969 (edited by Julian Symons) . . . . £10/£5
A.J.A. Symons to Wyndham Lewis: Twenty-Four Letters, Tragara Press, 1982 (120 copies, wraps) £45
Two Brothers: Fragments of a Correspondence, Tragara Press, 1985 (105 copies, wraps) . . £35
ditto, Tragara Press, 1985 (25 copies, signed by Julian Symons, wraps) £75

JULIAN SYMONS

(b.1912 d.1994)

A novelist and critic, Symons' speciality is detective fiction. He co-founded the Crime Writers Association in 1953.

Novels
The Immaterial Murder Case, Gollancz, 1945 . . . . £100/£25

ditto, Macmillan (U.S.), 1957. . . . . £40/£15
A Man Called Jones, Gollancz, 1947 . . £35/£10
Bland Beginning, Gollancz, 1949 . . . £35/£20
ditto, Harper (U.S.), 1949. . . . . . . £25/£10
The 31st of February, Gollancz, 1950 . . £35/£20
ditto, Harper (U.S.), 1950. . . . . . . £15/£5
The Broken Penny, Gollancz, 1952 . . . £35/£10
ditto, Harper (U.S.), 1953. . . . . . . £15/£5
The Narrowing Circle, Gollancz, 1954 . . £35/£10
ditto, Harper (U.S.), 1954. . . . . . . £15/£5
The Paper Chase, Collins, 1956 . . . . £25/£5
ditto, as ***Bogue's Fortune***, Harper (U.S.), 1957 £20/£5
The Colour of Murder, Collins, 1957 . . £25/£5
ditto, Harper (U.S.), 1957. . . . . . . £15/£5
The Gigantic Shadow, Collins, 1958 . . £25/£5
ditto, as ***Pipe Dream***, Harper, 1958 . . . £15/£5
The Progress of a Crime, Collins, 1960. . £25/£5
ditto, Harper (U.S.), 1960. . . . . . . £15/£5
The Killing of Francie Lake, Collins, 1962. £25/£5
ditto, as ***The Plain Man***, Harper, 1962 . . £10/£5
The End of Solomon Grundy, Collins, 1964 £20/£5
ditto, Harper (U.S.), 1964. . . . . . . £10/£5
The Belting Inheritance, Collins, 1965 . . £15/£5
ditto, Harper (U.S.), 1965. . . . . . . £10/£5
The Man Who Killed Himself, Collins, 1967 £15/£5
ditto, Harper (U.S.), 1967. . . . . . . £10/£5
The Man Whose Dreams Came True, Collins, 1969 . . . . £15/£5
ditto, Harper (U.S.), 1969. . . . . . . £10/£5
The Man Who Lost His Wife, Collins, 1971 £15/£5
ditto, Harper (U.S.), 1971. . . . . . . £10/£5
The Players and the Game, Collins, 1971 . £15/£5
ditto, Harper (U.S.), 1972. . . . . . . £10/£5
The Plot Against Roger Rider, Collins, 1973 £15/£5
ditto, Harper (U.S.), 1973. . . . . . . £10/£5
A Three Pipe Problem, Collins, 1975 . . £15/£5
ditto, Harper (U.S.), 19725. . . . . . . £10/£5
The Blackheath Poisonings, Collins, 1978 . £15/£5
ditto, Harper (U.S.), 1979. . . . . . . £10/£5
Sweet Adelaide, Collins, 1980 . . . . £15/£5
ditto, Harper (U.S.), 1980. . . . . . . £10/£5
The Detling Murders, Macmillan, 1982. . £15/£5
ditto, as ***The Detling Secret***, Viking, 1983 . £10/£5
The Name of Annabel Lee, Macmillan, 1983 £15/£5
ditto, Viking (U.S.), 1983. . . . . . . £10/£5
The Criminal Comedy of the Contented Couple, Macmillan, 1985 . . . . £15/£5
ditto, as ***A Criminal Comedy***, Viking (U.S.), 1986 . . . . £10/£5
The Kentish Manor Murders, Macmillan, 1988 £15/£5
ditto, Viking (U.S.), 1988. . . . . . . £10/£5
Death's Darkest Face, Macmillan, 1990 . £15/£5
ditto, Viking (U.S.), 1990. . . . . . . £10/£5
Something Like a Love Affair, Macmillan, 1992 . . . . £15/£5
ditto, Mysterious Press (U.S.), 1992 . . . £10/£5
Playing Happy Families, Macmillan, 1994 . £15/£5
ditto, Mysterious Press (U.S.), 1995 . . . £10/£5
A Sort of Virtue, Macmillan, 1996 . . . £10/£5

Omnibus
The Julian Symons Omnibus, Collins, 1966 £10/£5

Stories
Murder, Murder, Fontana, 1961 . . . . . £10
Francis Quarles Investigates, Panther, 1965 . £10
The Tigers of Subtopia and Other Stories, Macmillan, 1981 . . . . £15/£5
ditto, Viking (U.S.), 1983. . . . . . . £10/£5
Somebody Else and Other Stories, Eurographica (Helsinki), 1990 (wraps). £35
Portraits of the Missing, Deutsch, 1991. . £15/£5
The Man Who Hated Television and Other Stories, Macmillan, 1995 . . . . £10/£5
Murder Under the Mistletoe, Severn House, 1993 . . . . £10/£5

Others
Confusions About X, Fortune Press, [1939] £100/£25
The Second Man, Routledge, 1943 . . . . £45/£10
The Modern Crime Story, Tragara Press (Edinburgh), 1980 (125 signed copies) £45
ditto, Eurographica (Helsinki), 1988 (350 signed copies) £35
Makers of the New, Deutsch, 1987 . . . £10/£5
ditto, Random House (U.S.), 1987 . . . . £10/£5
The Thirties and the Nineties, Carcanet, 1990 . £5

W.M. THACKERAY
(b.1811 d.1863)

Charlotte Brontë's favourite author, Thackeray's most famous work is *Vanity Fair*.

Novels
Vanity Fair: A Novel Without a Hero, Bradbury & Evans, 1848 (20 parts in 19; yellow wraps) £1,000
ditto, Bradbury & Evans, 1848 (first book edition, made up of the original parts; with the woodcut [later suppressed] of Lord Steyne on page 336) . . £2,000
The History of Pendennis, His Fortunes and Misfortunes, His Friends and His Greatest Enemy, Bradbury & Evans, 1850 (24 parts in 23; yellow wraps). £750
ditto, Bradbury & Evans, 1849[-50] (2 vols) . £1,000
The History of Henry Esmond, Esq. A Colonel In the Service of Her Majesty Q. Anne. Written by Himself, Smith Elder, 1852 (3 vols) £500

The Newcomes: Memoirs of a Most Respectable Family, Bradbury & Evans, 1855 (24 parts in 23, yellow wraps). £500
ditto, Bradbury & Evans, 1854[-55] (2 vols) . £750
The Memoirs of Barry Lyndon, Esq., of The Kingdom of Ireland, Bradbury & Evans, 1856 (wraps) . £500
The Virginians: A Tale of the Last Century, Bradbury & Evans, 1859 (24 parts, yellow wraps) . . £400
ditto, Bradbury & Evans, 1858[-59] (2 vols) . £500
Lovel the Widower, Smith Elder, 1861 . . . £250
The Adventures of Philip on His Way Through the World; Shewing Who Robbed Him, Who Helped Him, and Who Passed Him By, Smith Elder, 1862 (3 vols) £400
Denis Duval, Smith Elder, 1867 . . . . . £250

Christmas Books
Mrs Perkins's Ball, Chapman & Hall, [1847] ('By Mr M.A. Titmarsh') £400
"Our Street", Chapman & Hall, 1848 ('By Mr M.A. Titmarsh'). £400
Doctor Birch and His Young Friends, Chapman & Hall, 1849 ('By Mr M.A. Titmarsh') . . . £400
The Kicklebury's on the Rhine, Chapman & Hall, 1850 ('By Mr M.A. Titmarsh'). £400
The Rose and the Ring, or, The History of Prince Gigilo and Prince Bulbo: A Fireside Pantomime for Great and Small Children, Chapman & Hall, 1855 ('By Mr M.A. Titmarsh'). £500
Christmas Books, Chapman & Hall, 1857 . . £250

Tales and Sketches
Comic Tales and Sketches, Hugh Cunningham, 1841 ('Edited and Illustrated by Mr Michael Angelo Titmarsh'; no reference to 'Vanity Fair') . . £750
The Book of Snobs, Punch Office, 1848 (wraps) £350
The History of Samuel Titmarsh and the Great Hoggarty Diamond, Bradbury & Evans, 1849 £350
Rebecca and Rowena: A Romance Upon Romance, Chapman & Hall, 1850 ('By Mr Michael Angelo Titmarsh'). £350
The Fatal Boots and **Cox's Diary**, Bradbury & Evans, 1855 (wraps) £350
The Little Dinner at Timmins's and ***The Bedford-Row Conspiracy***, Bradbury & Evans, 1856 (wraps) £350
The Memoirs of Mr Charles J. Yellowplush and ***The Diary of C. Jeames de la Pluche, Esq.***, Bradbury & Evans, 1856 (wraps) £350
The Fitz-Boodle Papers and ***Men's Wives***, Bradbury & Evans, 1857 (wraps) £350
A Shabby Genteel Story, Bradbury & Evans, 1857 (wraps) £350

Non Fiction
The Paris Sketch Book, John Macrone, 1840 ('by Mr Titmarsh', 2 vols). £750
The Irish Sketch Book, John Macrone, 1843 ('by Mr Titmarsh', 2 vols). £750
Notes of a Journey from Cornhill to Grand Cairo, By Way of Lisbon, Athens, Constantinople, and Jerusalem, Chapman & Hall, 1846 ('by Mr M.A. Titmarsh) £500
The English Humorists of the Eighteenth Century: A Series of Lectures Delivered in England, Scotland and the United States of America, Smith Taylor, 1853 . . . . £250
The Four Georges: Sketches of Manners, Morals, Court and Town Life, Smith Elder, 1861 . . £250
The Roundabout Papers, Smith Elder, 1863 . £250

Collected Editions
The Works of William Makepeace Thackeray, Smith Elder 'Library Edition', Smith Elder, 1869-86 (24 vols) £500
The Works of William Makepeace Thackeray, Smith Elder/Ritchie Edition, Smith Elder, 1898-99 (24 vols). £400
The Oxford Thackeray, O.U.P./Saintsbury Edition, O.U.P, [1908] (17 vols) £250
The Works of William Makepeace Thackeray, Smith Elder 'Centenary Biographical Edition', Smith Elder, 1910-11 (26 vols). £750

PAUL THEROUX
(b.1941)

An American novelist and travel writer, Theroux first came to the attention of the critics with the publication of *The Great Railway Bazaar* and *The Old Patagonian Express*

Novels
Waldo, Houghton Mifflin (U.S.), 1967 . . £150/£35
ditto, Bodley Head, 1968 . . . . . . £75/£20
Fong and the Indians, Houghton Mifflin (U.S.), 1968. . . . . £125/£35
ditto, Hamilton, 1976 . . . . £65/£20
Girls at Play, Houghton Mifflin (U.S.), 1969 £65/£20
ditto, Bodley Head, 1969 . . . . . . £35/£15
Murder in Mount Holly, Ross, 1969 . . £650/£125
Jungle Lovers, Houghton Mifflin (U.S.), 1971 £75/£20
ditto, Bodley Head, 1971 . . . . . . £75/£20
Saint Jack, Bodley Head, 1973 . . . . £35/£10
ditto, Houghton Mifflin (U.S.), 1973. . . £35/£10
The Black House, Hamilton, 1974 . . . £25/£5
ditto, Houghton Mifflin (U.S.), 1974. . . £20/£5
The Family Arsenal, Hamilton, 1976 . . £25/£5
ditto, Houghton Mifflin (U.S.), 1976. . . £25/£5

Picture Palace, Hamilton, 1978 . . . . £20/£5
ditto, Houghton Mifflin (U.S.), 1978. . . £20/£5
The Mosquito Coast, Hamilton, 1981 . . £20/£5
ditto, Houghton Mifflin (U.S.), 1982. . . £15/£5
ditto, Houghton Mifflin (U.S.), 1982 (350 signed copies, slipcase) . . . . £100/£65
Doctor Slaughter, Hamilton, 1984 . . . £15/£5
ditto, as ***Half Moon Street***, Houghton Mifflin (U.S.), 1984 . . . . £15/£5
O-Zone, Hamilton, 1986 . . . . £15/£5
ditto, Putnam (U.S.), 1986 . . . . . £10/£5
My Secret History, Hamish Hamilton, 1989. £10/£5
ditto, London Limited Editions, 1989 (150 signed, numbered copies) £75
ditto, Putnam (U.S.), 1989 . . . . . £10/£5
Doctor Demarr, Hutchinson, 1990 . . . £10/£5
Chicago Loop, Hamish Hamilton, 1990 . . £10/£5
ditto, Random House (U.S.), 1991 . . . . £10/£5
Millroy the Magician, Hamish Hamilton, 1993 £10/£5
ditto, Random House (U.S.), 1994 . . . . £10/£5
My Other Life, Houghton Mifflin (U.S.), 1996 £10/£5
Kowloon Tong, Houghton Mifflin (U.S.), 1997 £10/£5
ditto, Franklin Library (U.S.), 1998 (1,350 signed copies) £40

Short Stories

Sinning with Annie and Other Stories, Houghton Mifflin (U.S.), 1972 . . . . £75/£20
ditto, Hamilton, 1975 . . . . £25/£10
The Consul's File, Hamilton, 1977 . . . £20/£5
ditto, Houghton Mifflin (U.S.), 1977. . . £15/£5
World's End, Hamilton, 1980 . . . . £10/£5
ditto, Houghton Mifflin (U.S.), 1980. . . £10/£5
The London Embassy, Hamilton, 1982 . . £10/£5
ditto, Houghton Mifflin (U.S.), 1983. . . £10/£5

Travel

The Great Railway Bazaar: By Train Through Asia, Hamilton, 1975 . . . . £100/£25
ditto, Houghton Mifflin (U.S.), 1975. . . £65/£20
The Old Patagonian Express: By Train Through the Americas, Hamilton, 1979 . . . . . £20/£5
ditto, Houghton Mifflin (U.S.), 1979. . . £20/£5
The Kingdom by the Sea, Hamilton, 1983 . £10/£5
ditto, Houghton Mifflin (U.S.), 1983. . . £10/£5
ditto, Houghton Mifflin (U.S.), 1983 (250 signed, numbered copies, slipcase) . . . . . £50/£35
Sailing through China, Russell, 1984 (150 [400] signed copies, glassine d/w) . . . . . £75/£65
ditto, Houghton Mifflin (U.S.), 1984. . . £10/£5
Patagonia Revisited, Russell, 1985 (with Bruce Chatwin) . . . . £20/£10
ditto, Russell, 1985 (250 copies, cellophane d/w) . . . . £175/£150
ditto, Houghton Mifflin (U.S.), 1986. . . £20/£10
ditto, as ***Nowhere Is a Place***, Sierra Club (U.S.), 1991 . . . . £20/£10
Sunrise with Seamonsters, Hamilton, 1985 . £10/£5
ditto, Houghton Mifflin (U.S.), 1985. . . £10/£5
The Imperial Way, Hamilton, 1985 (with Steve McCurry) . . . . £10/£5
ditto, Houghton Mifflin (U.S.), 1985. . . £10/£5
Riding the Iron Rooster: By Train Through China, Hamish Hamilton, 1988 . . . . £10/£5
ditto, Putnam (U.S.), 1988 . . . . . . £10/£5
Pillars of Hercules, Putnam (U.S.), 1995 . £10/£5

Others

V.S. Naipaul: An Introduction to his Work, Deutsch, 1972 . . . . £600/£125
ditto, Africana (U.S.), 1972 . . . . . £125/£35
A Christmas Card, Hamilton, 1978 . . . . £10/£5
ditto, Houghton Mifflin (U.S.), 1978. . . £10/£5
London Snow, Russell, 1979 (450 signed copies, glassine d/w) . . . . £100/£85
ditto, Hamilton, 1980 . . . . £15/£5
ditto, Houghton Mifflin (U.S.), 1980. . . £15/£5
The Turn of the Years, Russell, 1982 (150 signed copies) £100
The Shortest Day of the Year: A Christmas Fantasy, Sixth Chamber Press, 1986 (175 signed copies) £60
ditto, Sixth Chamber Press, 1986 (26 signed copies on handmade paper) £100
Sir Vidia's Shadow, Houghton Mifflin (U.S.), 1998 . . . . £10/£5

DYLAN THOMAS

(b.1914 d.1953)

Notorious fitzrovian poet and playwright, Thomas died after taking morphine and drinking around a dozen whiskies in the White Horse Tavern in Greenwich Village, New York.

18 Poems, The Sunday Referee/The Parton Bookshop, 1934 (first issue, c.250 copies, flat spine) £,1750/£400
ditto, The Sunday Referee/The Parton Bookshop, 1934 (second issue, c.250 copies, round-backed spine) . . . . £350/£100
Twenty-Five Poems, Dent, 1936 . . . . £600/£150
The Map of Love: Verse and Prose, Dent, 1939 . . . . £250/£45
The World I Breathe, New Directions (U.S.), 1939 . . . . £400/£40
Portrait of the Artist as a Young Dog, Dent, 1940 . . . . £300/£60
ditto, New Directions (U.S.), 1940 . . . £200/£35
From In Memory of Ann Jones, Caseg Press, [1942],

(500 copies, broadside) £250
New Poems, New Directions (U.S.), 1943 (paper boards) . . . . £200/£75
ditto, New Directions (U.S.), 1943 (wraps) . £75
Deaths and Entrances, Dent, 1946 . . . . £250/£75
ditto, Gregynog Press, 1984 (250 copies, John Piper illustrated edition, in slipcase). . . . . £250/£100
ditto, Gregynog Press, 1984 (28 roman numbered copies, in slipcase). . . . . £750/£650
Selected Writings of Dylan Thomas, New Directions (U.S.), 1946 . . . . £125/£25
Twenty-Six Poems, Dent/New Directions, [1950] (Nos I-X signed, numbered copies of 150, printed on Japanese vellum, in slipcase) £6,000
ditto, Dent/New Directions, [1950] (Nos 11-60 signed, numbered copies of 150, slipcase) £2,000
ditto, Dent/New Directions, [1950] (Nos 61-147 signed, numbered copies of 150, slipcase) £2,000
In Country Sleep and Other Poems, New Directions (U.S.), 1952 . . . . £200/£65
ditto, New Directions (U.S.), 1952 (100 signed, numbered copies, in slipcase) . . £2,000/£1,750
Collected Poems, 1934-1952, Dent, 1952 . £75/£15
ditto, Dent, 1952 (65 signed, numbered copies) £2,000
ditto, New Directions (U.S.), 1953 . . . £65/£10
The Doctors and the Devils, Dent, 1953 . £25/£5
ditto, New Directions (U.S.), 1953 . . . . £20/£5
Two Epigrams Of Fealty, privately printed for members of the Court of Redonda, 1947, (30 numbered copies, folded leaflet) £200
Galsworthy and Gawsworth, privately printed for members of the Court of Redonda (1953), (30 numbered copies, folded leaflet) £200
Under Milk Wood: A Play for Voices, Dent, 1954 . . . . £100/£15
ditto, New Directions (U.S.), 1954 . . . . £45/£10
Quite Early One Morning, Dent, 1954 . . £75/£15
ditto, New Directions (U.S.), 1954 . . . . £35/£10
Conversation About Christmas, New Directions (U.S.), 1954 (wraps, in envelope) . . . £125/£95
Adventures in the Skin Trade and Other Stories, New Directions (U.S.), 1955 . . . . . . £100/£20
ditto, Putnam , 1955 . . . . £100/£20
A Prospect of the Sea, Dent, 1955 . . . £35/£10
A Child's Christmas in Wales, New Directions (U.S.), 1954 [1955]. . . . . £65/£15
ditto, New Directions (U.S.), [1969] (100 copies, illustrated by Fritz Eichenberg, with signed portfolio) . . . . £350/£200
ditto, New Directions (U.S.), [1969] (trade edition illustrated by Fritz Eichenberg) . . . . £35/£10
ditto, Dent, 1978 (illustrated by Edward Ardizzone) . . . . £25/£10
Letters to Vernon Watkins, Dent/Faber, 1957 £25/£5
ditto, New Directions (U.S.), 1957 . . . £20/£5
The Beach of Falesa, Stein & Day (U.S.), 1963 (film script) . . . . £25/£5
ditto, Cape, 1964 . . . . £20/£5
Twenty Years A-Growing, Dent, 1964 (film script) . . . . £20/£5
Rebecca's Daughters, Triton, 1965 (film script with a foreword by Sidney Box) . . . . . . £20/£5
ditto, Little, Brown (U.S.), 1965 . . . . £15/£5
Me and My Bike, McGraw Hill (U.S.), 1965 £45/£15
ditto, Triton, 1965 (film script) . . . . £35/£10
ditto, Triton, 1965 (500 copies, in slipcase) . £75/£50
The Doctor and the Devils and Other Scripts, New Directions (U.S.), 1966 . . . . . . £15/£5
Selected Letters of Dylan Thomas, Dent, 1966 £20/£5
ditto, New Directions (U.S.), 1967 . . . £20/£5
The Notebooks of Dylan Thomas, New Directions (U.S.), 1967 . . . . £20/£5
ditto, as ***Poet in the Making: The Notebooks of Dylan Thomas***, Dent, 1968 . . . . £20/£5
Twelve More Letters, Turret Books, 1969 (175 copies, acetate d/w) . . . . £65/£55
ditto, Turret Books, 1969 (26 lettered copies, acetate d/w) . . . . £125/£100
Dylan Thomas: Early Prose Writings, Dent, 1971 . . . . £15/£5
ditto, New Directions (U.S.), 1972 . . . . £15/£5
The Death of the King's Canary, Hutchinson, 1976 (with John Davenport) . . . . £10/£5
ditto, Viking (U.S.), 1976. . . . . £10/£5
Drawings to Poems by Dylan Thomas by Ceri Richards, Enitharmon Press, 1980 (180 copies) £75
Collected Letters, Dent, 1985. . . . . . £20/£5
ditto, Macmillan (U.S.), 1976. . . . . . £20/£5
Dylan Thomas: The Notebook Poems, 1930-1934, Dent, 1989 . . . . £15/£5
Dylan Thomas: The Broadcasts, Dent, 1991 £10/£5

EDWARD THOMAS

(b.1878 d.1917)

Not a "war poet", although he did die in the First World War, Edward's love of nature comes through in his best work.

Verse

Six Poems, Pear Tree Press, [1916] (pseud. Edward Eastway, copies in boards of total edition of 100) £250
ditto, Pear Tree Press, [1916] (pseud. Edward Eastway, copies in wraps of total edition of 100). . . £250
ditto, Pear Tree Press, 1927 . . . . £125
Poems, Selwyn & Blount, 1917 (525 copies, pseud. Edward Eastway). £125
ditto, Holt (U.S.), 1917 (525 copies). £125

Last Poems, Selwyn and Blount, 1918 . . . £90
Collected Poems, Selwyn and Blount, 1920 . . £95
ditto, Selwyn and Blount, 1920 (deluxe edition, 100 copies) £200
Augustan Books of Modern Poetry - Edward Thomas, Benn, [1926] (wraps) £5
Selected Poems, Gregynog Press, 1926 (275 copies) £200
ditto, Gregynog Press, 1926 (25 specially bound copies) £750
Two Poems, Ingpen & Grant, 1927 (85 copies) £75
Collected Poems, Ingpen & Grant, 1928 . . . £30
The Last Sheaf, Cape, [1928] . . . . £45/£20

Others

The Woodland Life, Blackwood, 1897 . . . . £300
Horae Solitaire, Duckworth, 1902 (300 copies) £150
ditto, Dutton (U.S.), [1902] £100
Oxford, A & C Black, [1903]. £40
ditto, A & C Black, [1903] (deluxe edition, 300 copies) £175
Rose Acre Papers, Langham, 1904 . . . . £100
Beautiful Wales, A & C Black, 1905 . . . £75
The Heart of England, Dent, 1906 . . . . £50
ditto, Dutton (U.S.), [1906] £40
Richard Jefferies, Hutchinson, 1909 . . . £50
ditto, Little Brown (U.S.), 1909 . . . . . £40
The South Country, Dent, 1909 . . . . . £50
Rest and Unrest, Duckworth, 1910 . . . . £45
ditto, Dutton (U.S.), 1910. . . . . £45
Rose Acre Papers, Duckworth, 1910 . . . . £35
Feminine Influence on the Poets, Secker, 1910 £45
ditto, John Lane (U.S.), 1911 . . . . . . £35
Windsor Castle, Blackie & Son, 1910 . . . £45
The Isle of Wight, Blackie & Son, 1911. . . £45
Light and Twilight, Duckworth, 1911 . . . . £30
Maurice Maeterlink, Methuen, [1911] . . . £30
Celtic Stories, Clarendon Press, 1911 . . . £75
The Tenth Muse, Secker, [1911]. £35
Algernon Charles Swinburne, Secker, 1912 . £35
George Borrow, Chapman and Hall, 1912 . . £25
Lafcadio Hearn, Houghton Mifflin (U.S.), 1912 £20
ditto, Constable, 1912 . . . . £20
Norse Tales, Clarendon Press, 1912 . . . . £45
The Icknield Way, Constable, 1913 . . . . £75
The Country, Batsford, [1913] £50
The Happy-Go-Lucky Morgans, Duckworth, [1913] £200
Walter Pater, Secker, 1913 . . . . £25
In Pursuit of Spring, Nelson, [1914] £75
Four and Twenty Blackbirds, Duckworth, [1915] £40
The Life of the Duke of Marlborough, Chapman and Hall, 1915 . . . . £20
Keats, Jack, 1916 . . . . £15
ditto, Dodge (U.S.), [1916] £15

A Literary Pilgrim in England, Dodd, Mead (U.S.), 1917 . . . . £25
ditto, Methuen, [1917] £20
Cloud Castle, Duckworth, [1922] . . . . £100/£25
ditto, Dutton (U.S.), [1923] . . . . . £65/£15
Essays of Today and Yesterday, Harrap, [1926] (wraps) £20
Chosen Essays, Gregynog Press, 1926 (350 copies) £75
The Childhood of Edward Thomas, Faber, 1938 £25
The Friend of the Blackbird, Pear Tree Press, 1938 . . . . £50
The Prose of Edward Thomas, Falcon Press, 1948 . . . . £30/£10
Letters from Edward Thomas to Gordon Bottomley, O.U.P., 1968 . . . . £20/£5
Autumn Thoughts, Tragara Press, 1975 (190 numbered copies, wraps) £45
The Diary of Edward Thomas, Whittington Press, 1977 (575 copies, slipcase) . . . . . £100/£75
Edward Thomas on the Countryside: A Selection, Faber, 1977 . . . . £10/£5
Edward Thomas: A Centenary Celebration, Eric and Joan Stevens, 1978 (75 copies signed by the artist) £75
Four Letters to Frederick Evans, Tragara Press, 1978 (150 numbered copies, wraps) £40
Reading out of Doors, Tragara Press, 1978 (110 numbered copies, wraps) £35
The Chessplayers, and other essays, Whittington Press, 1981 (375 copies). £75
A Selection of Letters to Edward Garnett, Tragara Press, 1981 (175 numbered copies, wraps). . £40
The Letters of Edward Thomas to Jesse Berridge, Enitharman, 1981 . . . . £25
The Fear of Death, Tragara Press, 1982 (95 numbered copies, wraps) £45
A Sportsman's Tale, Tragara Press, 1983 (125 numbered copies, wraps) £40
A Handful of Letters: Edward and Helen Thomas, Tragara Press, 1985 (wraps). £20

FLORA THOMPSON

(b.1877 d.1947)

Flora Thompson's autobiographical writings are popularly collected together as *Lark Rise to Candleford*. Her descriptions of countryside life are precise and unsentimental.

Verse

Bog Myrtle and Peat, Allan, 1921 (wraps) . . £65

Prose

Guide to Liphook, Bramshott and Neighbourhood, Williams, 1925 (wraps) £20
Lark Rise, O.U.P., 1939 . . . . £65/£20
Over to Candleford, O.U.P., 1941 . . . £50/£15
Candleford Green, O.U.P., 1943 . . . £50/£15
Lark Rise to Candleford, O.U.P., 1945 . . £50/£20
ditto, Crown (U.S.), 1983 . . . . . . £10/£5
Still Glides the Stream, O.U.P., 1948 . . £25/£5
ditto, Crown (U.S.), 1984 . . . . . . £10/£5
A Country Calendar, O.U.P., 1979 . . . £10/£5
The Peverel Papers, Century, 1986 . . . £10/£5

COLIN THUBRON

(b.1939)

Popularly considered a travel writer, Thubron's novels are also critical and commercial successes.

Travel

Mirror to Damascus, Heinemann, 1967 . . £50/£15
ditto, Little, Brown (U.S.), 1968 . . . . £25/£10
The Hills of Adonis: A Quest In Lebanon, Heinemann, 1968 . . . . £25/£5
ditto, Little, Brown (U.S.), 1969 . . . . £20/£5
Jerusalem, Heinemann, 1969. . . . . £25/£5
ditto, Little, Brown (U.S.), 1969 . . . . £20/£5
Journey into Cyprus, Heinemann, 1975. . £40/£10
Istanbul, Time Life, 1978 (with others) . . . £25
The Venetians, Time Life, 1980 (with others) . £10
The Ancient Mariners, Time Life, 1981 (with others) £10
Among the Russians, Heinemann, 1983. . £30/£10
ditto, as ***Where the Nights are Longest: Travels by Car Through Western Russia***, Random House (U.S.), 1984 . . . . £20/£5
Behind the Wall: A Journey Through China, Heinemann, 1987 . . . . £25/£10
ditto, Atlantic Monthly Press (U.S.), 1988 . £15/£5
The Silk Road - China: Beyond the Celestial Kingdom, Pyramid, 1990 . . . . . £45/£20
ditto, Simon and Schuster (U.S.), 1990 . . £45/£20
The Lost Heart of Asia, Heinemann, 1994 . £15/£5
ditto, Harper Collins (U.S.), 1994 . . . £10/£5

Novels

The God in the Mountain, Heinemann, 1977 £30/£10
ditto, Norton (U.S.), 1977. . . . . . £10/£5
Emperor, Heinemann, 1978 . . . . . £25/£10
A Cruel Madness, Heinemann, 1984 . . £15/£5
ditto, Atlantic Monthly Press (U.S.), 1985 . £10/£5
Falling, Heinemann, 1989 . . . . . £10/£5
ditto, Atlantic Monthly Press (U.S.), 1990 . £10/£5
Turning Back the Sun, Heinemann, 1991 . £10/£5
ditto, Harper Collins (U.S.), 1992 . . . £10/£5
Distance, Heinemann, 1996 . . . . . £10/£5

Others

The Royal Opera House, Covent Garden, Hamish Hamilton, 1982 . . . . £10/£5

J. R. R. TOLKIEN

(b.1892 d.1973)

John Ronald Reuel Tolkien was born in South Africa but educated in Britain. He was appointed Professor of Anglo-Saxon at Oxford in 1925 and published a number of related academic works. He is best known for his novels dealing with the mythical land of 'Middle-Earth'.

Middle-Earth Novels

The Hobbit, Allen & Unwin, 1937 . . £6,000/£400
ditto, Houghton Mifflin (U.S.), 1938. . £4,000/£250
The Fellowship of the Ring, being the First Part of 'The Lord of the Rings', Allen & Unwin, 1954 . . . . £2,000/£125
ditto, Houghton Mifflin (U.S.), 1954. . . £450/£45
The Two Towers, being the Second Part of 'The Lord of the Rings', Allen & Unwin, 1954 . £1,000/£75
ditto, Houghton Mifflin (U.S.), 1955. . . £200/£35
The Return of the King, being the Third Part of 'The Lord of the Rings', Allen & Unwin, 1955 . £750/£65
ditto, Houghton Mifflin (U.S.), 1956. . . £200/£35
The Lord of the Rings, Allen & Unwin, 1962 (first combined edition, three books in grey box) £75/£50
ditto, Allen & Unwin, 1964 (deluxe combined edition, three books bound in buckram, decorated box) . . . . £125/£75
The Silmarillion, Allen & Unwin, 1977 (printed by either Billing & Sons or William Clowes) . £20/£5
ditto, Houghton Mifflin (U.S.), 1977. . . £15/£5

History of Middle-Earth Titles

The Book of Lost Tales, Part 1, Allen & Unwin, 1983 . . . . £10/£5
ditto, Houghton Mifflin (U.S.), 1984. . . £10/£5
The Book of Lost Tales, Part 2, Allen & Unwin, 1984 . . . . £10/£5
ditto, Houghton Mifflin (U.S.), 1984. . . £10/£5
The Book of Lost Tales, Part 3: The Lays of Beleriand, Allen & Unwin, 1985 . . . £10/£5
ditto, Houghton Mifflin (U.S.), 1985. . . £10/£5
The Book of Lost Tales, Part 4: The Shaping of Middle-Earth, Allen & Unwin, 1986 . . £10/£5
ditto, Houghton Mifflin (U.S.), 1986. . . £10/£5

The Lost Road and Other Writings, Unwin Hyman, 1987 . . . . £10/£5
ditto, Houghton Mifflin (U.S.), 1987. . . . £10/£5
The Return of the Shadow: The History of the Lord of the Rings, Part 1, Unwin Hyman, 1988 . £10/£5
ditto, Houghton Mifflin (U.S.), 1988. . . . £10/£5
Treason in Isengard: The History of the Lord of the Rings, Part 2, Unwin Hyman, 1989 . . £10/£5
ditto, Houghton Mifflin (U.S.), 1989. . . £10/£5
The War of the Ring: The History of the Lord of the Rings, Part 3, Unwin Hyman, 1990 . . £10/£5
ditto, Houghton Mifflin (U.S.), 1990. . . £10/£5
Sauron Defeated: The History of the Lord of the Rings, Part 4, Unwin Hyman, 1992 . . £10/£5
ditto, Houghton Mifflin (U.S.), 1992. . . £10/£5

Other Middle-Earth Titles
The Adventures of Tom Bombadil and Other Verses from 'The Red Book', Allen & Unwin, 1962 £75/£20
ditto, Houghton Mifflin (U.S.), 1963. . . £50/£15
The Road Goes Ever On: A Song Cycle, Houghton Mifflin (U.S.), 1967 . . . . £35/£10
ditto, Allen & Unwin, 1968 . . . . . . £35/£10
Bilbo's Last Song, Houghton Mifflin (U.S.), 1974 . . . . £25/£5
ditto, Allen & Unwin, 1974 (poster) £10
Unfinished Tales, Allen & Unwin, 1980 . £15/£5
ditto, Houghton Mifflin (U.S.), 1980. . . £15/£5

Other Prose
Farmer Giles of Ham, Allen & Unwin, 1949 £200/£45
ditto, Houghton Mifflin (U.S.), 1950. . . £75/£15
Tree and Leaf, Allen & Unwin, 1964 . . £100/£20
ditto, Houghton Mifflin (U.S.), 1965. . . £35/£10
The Tolkien Reader, Ballantine (U.S.), 1966 £25/£10
Smith of Wootton Major, Allen & Unwin, 1967 £35
ditto, Houghton Mifflin (U.S.), 1967. . . £30/£10
The Father Christmas Letters, Allen & Unwin, 1976 . . . . £15/£5
ditto, Houghton Mifflin (U.S.), 1976. . . £15/£5
Pictures by J.R.R. Tolkien, Allen & Unwin, 1979 . . . . £25/£10
ditto, as ***The Pictures of J.R.R. Tolkien***, Houghton Mifflin (U.S.), 1979 . . . . £25/£10
Poems and Stories, Allen & Unwin, 1980 . £25/£5
ditto, Houghton Mifflin (U.S.), 1980. . . £15/£5
Letters, Allen & Unwin, 1981 . . . . £10/£5
ditto, Houghton Mifflin (U.S.), 1981. . . £10/£5
Mr Bliss, Allen & Unwin, 1982 . . . . . £10/£5
ditto, Houghton Mifflin (U.S.), 1983. . . £10/£5
Finn and Hengest: The Fragment and the Episode, Allen & Unwin, 1983 . . . . . . £10/£5
ditto, Houghton Mifflin (U.S.), 1983. . . . £10/£5

Other Verse
Songs for the Philologists, privately printed, 1936 . . . . £1,250
The Homecoming of Beorhtnoth, Allen & Unwin, 1975 . . . . £15/£5

Academic
A Middle English Vocabulary, O.U.P., 1922 (wraps) £450
ditto, O.U.P. (U.S.), 1922. . . . . £75
Sir Gawain and the Green Knight, O.U.P., 1925 (with errata slip) . . . . £200/£75
ditto, O.U.P. (U.S.), 1925. . . . . £75
Beowulf: The Monsters and the Critics, British Academy, [1936] (wraps) £100
ditto, Folcroft Editions (U.S.), 1972 . . . . £10
Sir Gawain and the Green Knight, Pearl, and Sir Orfeo, Allen & Unwin, 1975 . . . . £10/£5
ditto, Houghton Mifflin (U.S.), 1975. . . £10/£5

MARY TOURTEL
(b.1873 d.1948)

Rupert Bear was the best known creation of this British author and illustrator. Rupert first appeared in the Daily Express during 1920. Tourtel stopped working on the cartoon strip in 1935 due to failing eyesight. The very collectable series of Rupert Annuals began in the following year after the strip was taken over by Alfred Bestall. It is now drawn by John Harrold.

Rupert Annuals
1936, Daily Express, 1936 (with dustjacket) £1,500
ditto, Daily Express, 1936 (without dustjacket) . £350
1937, Daily Express, 1937 . . . . £250
1938, Daily Express, 1938 . . . . £250
1939, Daily Express, 1939 . . . . £250
1940, Daily Express, 1940 . . . . £350
1941, Daily Express, 1941 . . . . £350
1942, Daily Express, 1942 (wraps) £500
1943, Daily Express, 1943 (wraps) £300
1944, Daily Express, 1944 (wraps) £200
1945, Daily Express, 1945 (wraps) £200
1946, Daily Express, 1946 (wraps) £75
1947, Daily Express, 1947 (wraps) £65
1948, Daily Express, 1948 (wraps) £65
1949, Daily Express, 1949 (wraps) £65
1950-59, Daily Express, 1950-59 (boards) . £50 each
1960-68, Daily Express, 1960-68 ('magic painting' pages not coloured in) . . . . . . £150 each
1960-68, Daily Express, 1960-68 ('magic painting' pages coloured in) . . . . £25 each

1969, Daily Express, 1969 . . . . £10
1970-89, Daily Express, 1970-89 . . . . £5
1990, Daily Express, 1990 (anniversary issue) . £10
1991-97, Daily Express, 1991-97 . . . £5 each

Rupert Annuals - Facsimiles
1936, Daily Express, 1985 . . . . £40
1937, Daily Express, 1986 . . . . £30
1938, Daily Express, 1989 . . . . £35
1939, Daily Express, 1991 . . . . £15
1940, Daily Express, 1992 . . . . £15
1941, Daily Express, 1993 . . . . £10
1942, Daily Express, 1994 . . . . £10

Monster Rupert Annuals
Monster Rupert, Sampson Low, [1931] (Rupert with wolf) £200
Monster Rupert, Sampson Low, [1932] (Rupert on log) £200
Monster Rupert, Sampson Low, [1933] (Rupert with bird) £200
Monster Rupert, Sampson Low, [1934] (Rupert with small boy in storeroom) £200
Monster Rupert, Sampson Low, [1948] (Rupert on log, with d/w) £35
Monster Rupert, Sampson Low, [1949] (Rupert with fox, with d/w). £35
Monster Rupert, Sampson Low, [1950] (Rupert helping boy out of hole, with d/w, with all cut-outs intact) £50
Monster Rupert, Sampson Low, [1953] (with all cut-outs intact) £40

'Rupert' Books
The Adventures of Rupert the Little Lost Bear, Nelson, [1921] £500
The Little Bear and the Fairy Child, Nelson, [1922] £350
Margot the Midget and Little Bear's Christmas, Nelson, [1922] £350
The Little Bear and the Ogres, Nelson, 1922 . £350
'Rupert Little Bear's Adventures', Sampson Low, 1924-25 (3 books) . . . . £350 each
'Rupert - Little Bear Series', Sampson Low, 1925-27 (6 books) . . . . £350 each
'Little Bear Library' titles, Sampson Low, [1928-1936] (numbered 1-46) . . . . £25 each
The Rupert Story Book, Sampson Low, [1938] £150
Rupert Little Bear: More Stories, Sampson Low, [1939]. £150
Rupert Again, Sampson Low, [1940] . . . £150

'Adventure' Titles *(all in card covers)*
No. 1, Daily Express £30
Nos. 2-9, Daily Express . . . . £20 each
No. 10, Daily Express . . . . £25 each
Nos. 11-20, Daily Express . . . . . . £20 each
Nos. 21-30, Daily Express . . . . . . £25 each
Nos. 31-35, Daily Express . . . . . . £25 each
Nos. 36-40, Daily Express . . . . . . £25 each
Nos. 41-45, Daily Express . . . . . . £25 each
Nos. 46-48, Daily Express . . . . . . £60 each
No. 49, Daily Express £75
No. 50, Daily Express £100

Daily Express Children's Annuals
Daily Express Children's Annual, 1930, Lane, 1930 . . . . £100
Daily Express Children's Annual, 1931, Lane, 1931 . . . . £100
Daily Express Children's Annual, 1932, Lane, 1932 . . . . £75
Daily Express Children's Annual, 1933, Lane, 1933 . . . . £75
Daily Express Children's Annual, 1934, Lane, 1934 . . . . £75

Other Collectable Titles by Mary Tourtel
A Horse Book, Grant Richards 'Dumpy Books for Children' series No. 10, 1901, ... £75
The Humpty Dumpty Book, Nursery Rhymes Told in Pictures, Treherne, [1902] £75
The Three Little Foxes, Grant Richards 'Dumpy Books for Children's series No. 21, 1903 . . . . . £75

WILLIAM TREVOR
(b.1928)

A novelist and short story writer, Trevor's work often deals with the corruption of innocence.

Novels
A Standard of Behaviour, Hutchinson, 1958 . . . . £500/£200
ditto, Sphere, 1967 (revised edition, wraps) . . £10
The Old Boys, Bodley Head, 1964 . . . £125/£35
ditto, Viking (U.S.), 1964 . . . . £65/£15
The Boarding House, Bodley Head, 1965 . £125/£35
ditto, Viking (U.S.), 1965 . . . . £65/£15
The Love Department, Bodley Head, 1966 £125/£35
ditto, Viking (U.S.), 1967 . . . . £65/£15
Mrs Eckdorf in O'Neill's Hotel, Bodley Head, 1969 . . . . £65/£15
ditto, Viking (U.S.), 1970 . . . . £45/£10
Miss Gomez and the Brethren, Bodley Head, 1971 . . . . £65/£15
Elizabeth Alone, Bodley Head, 1973 . . £50/£15
ditto, as ***Dreaming***, Stellar Press, 1973 (extract from

Elizabeth Alone, 225 copies, wraps) £100
ditto, Viking (U.S.), 1974 . . . . . . £35/£10
The Children of Dynmouth, Bodley Head, 1976 . . . . £35/£10
ditto, Viking (U.S.), 1977 . . . . £15/£5
Other People's Worlds, Bodley Head, 1980. £20/£5
ditto, Viking (U.S.), 1981 . . . . £10/£5
Fools of Fortune, Bodley Head , 1983 . . £20/£5
ditto, Bodley Head, 1983 (50 numbered, signed copies, bound by Kenny's of Galway, slipcase). . . £75
ditto, Viking (U.S.), 1983 . . . . £10/£5
The Silence in the Garden, Bodley Head, 1988 £15/£5
ditto, London Limited Editions, 1988 (150 numbered, signed copies, glassine d/w) . . . . . £75/£50
ditto, Viking (U.S.), 1988 . . . . £10/£5
Two Lives, Viking (U.K.), 1991 . . . . £10/£5
ditto, Viking (U.S.), 1991 . . . . £10/£5
Felicia's Journey, Viking (U.K.), 1994 . . £10/£5
ditto, Viking (U.S.), 1995 . . . . £10/£5

Short Stories
The Day We Got Drunk on Cake, Bodley Head, 1967 . . . . £400/£40
ditto, Viking (U.S.), 1968 . . . . £65/£15
The Ballroom of Romance, Bodley Head, 1972 . . . . £125/£35
ditto, Viking (U.S.), 1972 . . . . £45/£10
The Last Lunch of the Season, Covent Garden Press, 1973 (100 numbered, signed copies of 600, wraps) £45
ditto, Covent Garden Press, 1973 (500 copies of 600, wraps) £25
Angels at the Ritz and Other Stories, Bodley Head, 1975 . . . . £45/£15
ditto, Viking (U.S.), 1976 . . . . £25/£10
Old School Ties, Lemon Tree Press, 1976 . £75/£20
Lovers of Their Time and Other Stories, Bodley Head, 1978 . . . . £30/£10
ditto, Stellar Press, 1973 (extract, 225 copies, wraps) £125
ditto, Viking (U.S.), 1978 . . . . £20/£5
The Distant Past, Poolbeg Press (Dublin), 1979 £20
Beyond the Pale, Bodley Head, 1981 . . £20/£5
ditto, Viking (U.S.), 1982 . . . . £10/£5
The News From Ireland and Other Stories, Bodley Head, 1986 . . . . £25/£5
ditto, Bodley Head, 1986 (50 numbered, signed copies, bound by Kenny's of Galway, slipcase). . . £125
ditto, Viking (U.S.), 1986 . . . . £15/£5
Nights at the Alexandria, Hutchinson, 1987 £15/£5
ditto, Harper (U.S.), 1987 . . . . £10/£5
Family Sins and Other Stories, Bodley Head, 1990 . . . . £10/£5
ditto, Viking (U.S.), 1990 . . . . £10/£5
The Collected Stories, Viking (U.K.), 1990 . £15/£5
ditto, Viking (U.K.), 1990, (100 signed copies) . . . . £150/£75
Marrying Damian, Colophon Press, 1995 (175 numbered signed copies, wraps) £50
ditto, Colophon Press, 1994 (26 signed copies, slipcase) . . . . £125/£100
After Rain, Viking, 1996 . . . . . . £15/£5
ditto, Viking (U.S.), 1996 . . . . £10/£5
Death of a Professor, Colophon Press, 1997 (200 numbered signed copies, wraps) £50
ditto, Colophon Press, 1997 (26 signed copies, slipcase) . . . . £125/£100

Plays
The Girl, French, 1968 (wraps) £25
The Old Boys, Poynter, 1971 (wraps) £25
Going Home, French, 1972 (wraps) £10
A Night With Mrs Da Tonka, French, 1972 (wraps) £10
Marriages, French, 1973 (wraps) £10
Scenes from an Album, Co-op Books (Dublin), 1981 (wraps) £15

Children's
Juliet's Story, O'Brien Press (Dublin), 1991 £25/£10
ditto, Bodley Head, 1992 . . . . £15/£5
ditto, Simon & Schuster (U.S.), 1992 . . £10/£5

Others
A Writer's Ireland, Viking (U.S.), 1984 . . £15/£5
ditto, Thames & Hudson, 1984 . . . . . £15/£5
Excursions in the Real World, Hutchinson/Random House, 1993 . . . . £15/£5
ditto, Knopf (U.S.), 1994 . . . . £10/£5

ANTHONY TROLLOPE
(b.1815 d.1882)

Trollope's two most important series of novels are based around the fictitious cathedral town of Barchester. Arguably his greatest contribution to society, however, was the introduction of the pillar-box.

The Macdermots of Ballycoran, Newby, 1847 (3 vols) £6,000
The Kellys and the O'Kelleys, Colburn, 1848 (3 vols) £1,500
La Vendee, Colburn, 1850 (3 vols) £2,000
The Warden, Longman, 1855 . . . . £1,500
Barchester Towers, Longman, 1857 (3 vols) £6,500
The Three Clerks, Bentley, 1858 (3 vols) . £2,000
Doctor Thorne, Chapman & Hall, 1858 (3 vols) £5,000

The Bertrams, Chapman & Hall, 1859 (3 vols) £2,000
Castle Richmond, Chapman & Hall, 1860 (3 vols) . . . £,2000
Framley Parsonage, Smith Elder, 1861 (3 vols) £3,000
Tales of All Countries, Chapman & Hall, 1861 £500
Orley Farm, Chapman & Hall, 1862 (2 vols) £3,000
Tales of All Countries: Second Series, Chapman & Hall, 1863 . . . £500
Rachel Ray, Chapman & Hall, 1863 (2 vols) £1,250
The Small House at Allington, Smith Elder, 1864 (2 vols) . . . £2,000
Can You Forgive Her, Chapman & Hall, 1864 (2 vols) . . . £2,000
Miss Mackenzie, Chapman & Hall, 1865 (2 vols) . . . £2,000
The Belton Estate, Chapman & Hall, 1866 (3 vols) . . . £2,500
Nina Balakta, Blackwood, 1867 (2 vols) . £1,750
The Last Chronicles of Barset, Smith Elder, 1867 (2 vols) . . . £1,500
The Claverings, Smith Elder, 1867 (2 vols) . . £750
Lotta Schmidt and Other Stories, Strahan, 1867 £350
Linda Tressel, Blackwood, 1868 (2 vols) . . . £750
Phineas Finn, The Irish Member, Virtue, 1869 (2 vols) . . . £500
He Knew He Was Right, Strahan, 1869 (2 vols) £1,500
The Vicar of Bullhampton, Bradbury, Evans, 1870 . . . £500
The Struggles of Brown, Jones and Robinson, Smith Elder, 1870 . . . £500
Sir Harry Hotspur of Humblethwaite, Hurst and Blackett, 1871 . . . £1,000
Ralph the Heir, Hurst and Blackett, 1871 (3 vols) . . . £2,000
The Golden Lion of Granpere, Tinsley, 1872 . £450
The Eustace Diamonds, Chapman & Hall, 1873 (3 vols) . . . £750
Phineas Redux, Chapman & Hall, 1874 (2 vols) £450
Lady Anna, Chapman & Hall, 1874 (2 vols) £2,000
Harry Heathcote of Gangoil, Sampson Low, 1874 . . . £450
The Way We Live Now, Chapman & Hall, 1875 (2 vols) . . . £1,000
The Prime Minister, Chapman & Hall, 1877 (4 vols) . . . £1,000
The American Senator, Chapman & Hall, 1877 (3 vols) . . . £1,500
Is He Popenjoy?, Chapman & Hall, 1878 (3 vols) £500
An Eye for an Eye, Chapman & Hall, 1879 (2 vols) . . . £400
John Caldigate, Chapman & Hall, 1879 (3 vols) . . . £1,250
Cousin Henry, Chapman & Hall, 1879 (2 vols) £450
The Duke's Children, Chapman & Hall, 1880 (3 vols). . . . £750
Dr Wortle's School, Chapman & Hall, 1881 (2 vols) . . . £1,000
Ayala's Angel, Chapman & Hall, 1881 (3 vols) £2,000
Why Frau Frohmann Raised Her Prices and Other Stories, Ibister, 1882. . . . £750
Kept in the Dark, Chatto & Windus, 1882 (2 vols). . . . £1,000
Marion Fay, Chapman & Hall, 1882 (3 vols) . £1,500
The Fixed Period, Blackwood, 1882 (2 vols) . £1,000
Mr Scarborough's Family, Chatto & Windus, 1883 (3 vols) . . . £1,250
The Landleaguers, Chatto & Windus, 1883 (3 vols) . . . £1,450
An Old Man's Love, Blackwood, 1884 (2 vols volumes) . . . £450
The Noble Jilt, Constable, 1923 . . . £250

Others
The West Indies and the Spanish Main, Chapman & Hall, 1859 . . . £500
North America, Chapman & Hall, 1862 (2 vols) £1,000
Hunting Sketches, Chapman & Hall, 1863 . . £500
Travelling Sketches, Chapman & Hall, 1866 . £500
Clergymen of the Church of England, Chapman & Hall, 1866 . . . £650
An Editor's Tales, Strahan, 1870. . . . £450
The Commentaries of Caesar, Blackwood, 1870 £250
Australia and New Zealand, Chapman & Hall, 1873 (2 vols) . . . £750
South Africa, Chapman & Hall, 1878 (2 vols) . £150
How the 'Mastiffs' Went to Iceland, Virtue, 1878 £650
Thackeray, Macmillan, 1879. . . . £500
The Life of Cicero, Chapman & Hall, 1880 (2 vols) . . . £250
Lord Palmerston, Ibister, 1882 . . . £250
An Autobiography, Blackwood, 1883 (2 vols) . £500
London Tradesmen, Mathews & Marrot, 1927 £50

BARRY UNSWORTH
(b.1930)

Unsworth is not as widely known as he might be, despite *Sacred Hunger* being jointly awarded the 1992 Booker Prize.

Novels
The Partnership, Hutchinson New Authors, 1966 . . . £125/£25
The Greeks Have a Word For It, Hutchinson, 1967 . . . £65/£20
The Hide, Gollancz, 1970 . . . £65/£20
ditto, Norton (U.S.), 1996. . . . £10/£5
Mooncranker's Gift, Lane, 1973 . . . £35/£10

ditto, Houghton Mifflin (U.S.), 1974 . . . £20/£5
The Big Day, Joseph, 1976 . . . . . £25/£5
ditto, Mason/Charter (U.S.), 1976 . . . £15/£5
Pascali's Island, Joseph, 1980 . . . . £20/£5
ditto, as ***The Idol Hunter***, Simon & Schuster (U.S.), 1980 . . . . £15/£5
The Rage of the Vulture, Granada, 1982 . £20/£5
ditto, Houghton Mifflin (U.S.), 1982 . . . £15/£5
Stone Virgin, Hamish Hamilton, 1985 . . £20/£5
ditto, Houghton Mifflin (U.S.), 1986 . . . £15/£5
Sugar and Rum, Hamish Hamilton, 1988 . £10/£5
Sacred Hunger, Hamish Hamilton, 1992 . £10/£5
ditto, Doubleday (U.S.), 1992 . . . . £10/£5
Morality Play, Hamish Hamilton, 1995 . . £10/£5
ditto, Doubleday (U.S.), 1995 . . . . £10/£5
After Hannibal, Hamish Hamilton, 1996 . £10/£5
ditto, Doubleday (U.S.), 1997 . . . . £10/£5

JOHN UPDIKE

(b.1932)

American novelist, short story writer and critic, Updike has the reputation of a keen observer of American life.

Verse

The Carpentered Hen and Other Tame Creatures, Harper (U.S.), 1938 . . . . £250/£45
ditto, as ***Hoping for a Hoopoe***, Gollancz, 1959 . . . . £150/£25
Telephone Poles, Knopf (U.S.), 1963 . . £65/£20
ditto, Deutsch, 1963 . . . . £40/£10
Dog's Death, Scott (U.S.), 1965 (100 signed copies, broadside) £75
Bath After Sailing, Pendulum Press, 1968 (125 signed copies, wraps) £225
Midpoint and Other Poems, Knopf (U.S.),1964 . . . . £35/£10
ditto, Knopf (U.S.),1964 (350 signed copies in d/w) . . . . £125/£45
ditto, Deutsch, 1969 . . . . £20/£5
The Angels, King and Queen Press (U.S.), 1968 (150 copies, wraps in envelope) . . . . . £400/£350
On Meeting Authors, Wickford Press (U.S.), 1968 (250 copies, wraps) £400
Dance of the Solids, Scientific American (U.S.), [1970] (wraps) £400
Seventy Poems, Penguin, 1971 . . . . . £15
Six Poems, Aloe Editions (U.S.), 1973 (100 signed, numbered copies, wraps) £200
Cunts, Hallman (U.S.), 1974 (250 signed copies) £125
Sunday in Boston, Rook Press (U.S.), 1975 (100 copies signed by author and illustrator, broadside) £75
ditto, Rook Press (U.S.), 1975 (100 copies signed by author only, broadside) £75
ditto, Rook Press (U.S.), 1975 (100 unsigned copies, broadside) £25
Tossing and Turning, Knopf (U.S.), 1977 . £20/£5
ditto, Deutsch, 1977 . . . . £15/£5
From the Journal of a Leper, Lord John Press (U.S.), 1983 (300 signed, numbered copies) . . . £60
Sixteen Sonnets, Ferguson (U.S.), 1979 (250 signed, numbered copies, wraps) £100
The Beloved, Lord John Press (U.S.), 1978 (100 signed, numbered deluxe copies) £75
ditto, Lord John Press (U.S.), 1978 (300 signed, numbered copies) £45
Facing Nature, Knopf (U.S.), 1985 . . . £15/£5
ditto, Deutsch, 1986 . . . . £10/£5
A Pear Like a Potato, Santa Susanna Press (U.S.), 1986 . . . . £40
Two Sonnets, Northouse & Northouse (U.S.), 1987 (40 signed, roman numbered copies) £200
ditto, Northouse & Northouse (U.S.), 1987 . . £40
Recent Poems, Eurographica (Helsinki), 1992 (350 signed, numbered copies, wraps) . . . £100
Collected Poems 1953-1993, Knopf (U.S.), 1993 . . . . £20/£10
Down Time, Firefly Press (U.S.), 1997 (90 signed copies, broadside) £100

Novels

The Poorhouse Fair, Knopf (U.S.), 1959 . £125/£35
ditto, Gollancz, 1959 . . . . £75/£15
Rabbit, Run, Knopf (U.S.), 1960 . . . . £300/£35
ditto, Deutsch, 1961 . . . . £50/£10
The Centaur, Knopf (U.S.), 1963 . . . £50/£15
ditto, Deutsch, 1963 . . . . £25/£10
Of the Farm, Knopf (U.S.), 1965 . . . £30/£10
ditto, Deutsch, 1973 . . . . £15/£5
Couples, Knopf (U.S.), 1968 . . . . £25/£5
ditto, Deutsch, 1968 . . . . £15/£5
Rabbit Redux, Knopf (U.S.), 1971 . . . £25/£5
ditto, Knopf (U.S.), 1971 (350 signed copies, slipcase, clear d/w) . . . . £125/£100
ditto, Deutsch, 1972 . . . . £15/£5
A Month of Sundays, Knopf (U.S.), 1975 . £25/£5
ditto, Deutsch, 1975 . . . . £15/£5
Marry Me, Knopf (U.S.), 1976 . . . . £20/£5
ditto, Deutsch, 1977 . . . . £15/£5
The Coup, Knopf (U.S.), 1978 . . . . £15/£5
ditto, Deutsch, 1979 . . . . £10/£5
Rabbit is Rich, Knopf (U.S.), 1981 . . . £15/£5
ditto, Knopf (U.S.), 1981 (350 signed copies) £100/£75
ditto, Deutsch, 1982 . . . . £10/£5
Bech is Back, Knopf (U.S.), 1982 . . . £15/£5
ditto, Knopf (U.S.), 1982 (500 signed, numbered copies) . . . . £100/£75

ditto, Deutsch, 1983 . . . . £10/£5
The Witches of Eastwick, Knopf (U.S.), 1984 £15/£5
ditto, Franklin Library (U.S.), 1984 (signed copies) £35
ditto, Deutsch, 1984 . . . . £15/£5
Roger's Version, Knopf (U.S.), 1986 . . . £10/£5
ditto, Franklin Library (U.S.), 1986 (signed copies) £35
ditto, Deutsch, 1986 . . . . £10/£5
S, Knopf (U.S.), 1988 . . . . £10/£5
ditto, Deutsch, 1988 . . . . £10/£5
Rabbit at Rest, Knopf (U.S.), 1990 . . . £10/£5
ditto, Deutsch, 1991 . . . . £10/£5
Brazil, Knopf (U.S.), 1994 . . . . . £10/£5
In the Beauty of the Lilies, Knopf (U.S.), 1996 £10/£5
Toward the End of Time, Knopf (U.S.), 1997 £10/£5

Short Stories
The Same Door, Knopf (U.S.), 1959 . . £200/£30
ditto, Deutsch, 1962 . . . . £75/£20
Pigeon Feathers, Knopf (U.S.), 1962 . . . £100/£20
ditto, Deutsch, 1962 . . . . £45/£15
The Music School, Knopf (U.S.), 1966 . . £150/£53
ditto, Deutsch, 1973 . . . . £45/£15
Bech: A Book, Knopf (U.S.), 1970 . . . £20/£5
ditto, Knopf (U.S.), 1970 (500 signed copies, slipcase) . . . . £75/£50
ditto, Deutsch, 1970 . . . . £15/£5
Museums and Women and Other Stories, Knopf (U.S.), 1972 . . . . £15/£5
ditto, Knopf (U.S.), 1972 (350 signed copies, slipcase) . . . . £75/£50
ditto, Deutsch, 1973 . . . . £15/£5
Warm Wine: An Idyll, Albodocani Press (U.S.), 1973 (250 signed copies) £100
Problems and Other Stories, Knopf (U.S.), 1979 . . . . £10/£5
ditto, Deutsch, 1980 . . . . £10/£5
Too Far to Go: The Maples Stories, Fawcett (U.S.), 1979 . . . . £10/£5
Trust Me, Knopf (U.S.), 1987 . . . . £10/£5
ditto, Deutsch, 1987 . . . . £10/£5
The Afterlife, Sixth Chamber Press, 1987 (175 signed copies, no d/w) £100
ditto, Knopf (U.S.), 1994 . . . . £10/£5

Children's
The Magic Flute, Knopf (U.S.), 1962 (cloth, in d/w) . . . . £350/£65
ditto, Knopf (U.S.), 1962 (pictorial boards, no d/w) £300
A Child's Calendar, Knopf (U.S.), 1965 . £65/£20

Others
The Ring, Knopf (U.S.), 1964 . . . . . £10
Assorted Prose, Knopf (U.S.), 1965 . . . . £25/£10
ditto, Knopf (U.S.), 1965 (signed copies, unspecified number) £100
ditto, Deutsch, 1965 . . . . £20/£5
Bottom's Dream: Adapted from William Shakespeare's 'A Midsummer Night's Dream', Knopf (U.S.), 1969 . . . . £65/£15
A Good Place, Aloe Editions (U.S.), 1973 (100 signed, numbered copies, wraps) £200
Picked-Up Pieces, Knopf (U.S.), 1976 . . £20/£5
ditto, Knopf (U.S.), 1976 (250 signed, numbered copies, slipcase) . . . . £100/£75
ditto, Deutsch, 1976 . . . . £15/£5
Three Illuminations in the Life of an American Author, Targ Editions (U.S.), 1979 (350 signed, numbered copies) . . . . £85/£65
Hugging the Shore, Knopf (U.S.), 1983 . £15/£5
ditto, Deutsch, 1984 . . . . £15/£5
Self-Consciousness: Memoirs, Knopf (U.S.), 1989 . . . . £15/£5
ditto, Deutsch, 1989 . . . . £10/£5
Just Looking: Essays on Art, Knopf (U.S.), 1989 . . . . £20/£5
ditto, Deutsch, 1989 . . . . £20/£5
Odd Jobs: Essays and Criticism, Knopf (U.S.), 1991 . . . . £10/£5
ditto, Deutsch, 1991 . . . . £10/£5
Memories of the Ford Administration, Knopf (U.S.), 1992 . . . . £10/£5
Golf Dreams, Knopf (U.S.), 1996 . . . £10/£5

Plays
Buchanan Dying, Knopf (U.S.), 1974 . . £25/£10
ditto, Deutsch, 1974 . . . . £20/£5

FLORENCE UPTON
(b.1873 d.1922)

Born in New York, Florence Upton moved to England in her twenties. She illustrated the 'Golliwogg' stories (in verse and prose) written by her mother, Bertha Upton. Thus started a whole 'Golliwogg' craze.

The Adventures of Two Dutch Dolls and a Golliwogg, Longmans [1895] £250
The Golliwogg's Bicycle Club, Longmans, [1896] £200
Little Hearts, Routledge, 1897 . . . . . £200
The Vege-Men's Revenge, Longmans, [1897] . £200
The Golliwogg at the Seaside, Longmans, 1898 £200
The Golliwogg in War!, Longmans, 1899 . . £200
The Golliwogg's Polar Adventures, Longmans, [1900] £250
The Golliwogg's 'Auto-Go-Cart', Longmans, [1901] .

. . . . £200
The Golliwogg's Air-Ship, Longmans, [1902] . £200
The Golliwogg's Circus, Longmans, [1903] . £200
The Golliwogg in Holland, Longmans, [1904] . £200
The Golliwogg's Fox-Hunt, Longmans, [1905] £200
The Golliwogg's Desert Island, Longmans. [1906] £200
The Golliwogg's Christmas, Longmans, 1907 £200
The Adventures of Borbee and the Wisp: The Story of a Sophisticated Little Girl and an Unsophisticated Little Boy, Longmans, 1908. . . . . . . £150
Golliwogg in the African Jungle, Longmans, 1909 . . . . £250

JULES VERNE

(b.1828 d.1905)

Born in Nantes, France, Verne studied law in Paris and began his literary career while working at the Stock Exchange. Famous for his escapist adventure novels and short stories, Verne also wrote opera libretti and plays.

Fiction

Five Weeks in a Balloon, Chapman & Hall, 1870 £250
A Journey to the Centre of the Earth, Griffith & Farran, 1872 [1871] £750
Twenty Thousand Leagues Under the Seas, Sampson Low, 1873 [1872] £600
From the Earth to the Moon Direct in 97 Hours, 20 Minutes, and a Trip Round it, Sampson Low, 1873 . . . . £500
Meridiana: The Adventures of Three Englishmen and Three Russians in South Africa, Sampson Low, 1873 . . . . £150
The Fur Country, Sampson Low, 1874 [1873] £125
Around the World in Eighty Days, Sampson Low, 1874 [1873] £300
A Floating City, and The Blockade Runners, Sampson Low, 1874 . . . . £125
Dr Ox's Experiment and Other Stories, Sampson Low, 1875 . . . . £100
The Mysterious Island, Sampson Low, 1875 (3 vols: *Dropped from the Clouds*, *Abandoned* and *The Secret of the Island*) £400
The Adventures of Captain Hatteras: The English at the North Pole, Routledge, 1875 [1874] . . £100
The Field of Ice, Routledge, 1876 . . . . £100
The Chancellor: The Survivors of the Chancellor, Sampson Low, 1875 . . . . £125
Martin Paz, Sampson Low, 1876 . . . . £100
A Winter Amid the Ice and Other Stories, Sampson Low, 1876 . . . . £75
A Voyage Round the World, Routledge, 1876-1877 (3 vols: *South America*, *Australia* and *New Zealand*) £250
Michael Strogoff, Sampson Low, 1877 [1876] £125
The Child of the Cavern, Sampson Low, 1877 . £125
Hector Servadac, Sampson Low, 1878 . . . £125
Dick Sands, The Boy Captain, Sampson Low, 1879 [1878]. £125
The Begum's Fortune, Sampson Low, 1880 [1879] £100
The Tribulations of a Chinaman, Sampson Low, 1880 . . . . £100
The Steam House, Sampson Low, 1881 (2 vols: *Demon of Cawnpore* and *Tigers and Traitors*) £250
The Giant Raft, Sampson Low, 1881 (2 vols: *Down the Amazon* and *The Cryptogram*) £250
Godfrey Morgan, A Californian Mystery, Sampson Low, 1883 . . . . £100
The Green Ray, Sampson Low, 1883 . . . £125
Keraban the Inflexible, Sampson Low, 1884-5 (2 vols: *The Captain of the Guidara* and *Scarpante the Spy*) £125
The Vanished Diamond, Sampson Low, 1885 . £75
The Archipelago on Fire, Sampson Low, 1886 £125
Mathias Sandorf, Sampson Low, 1886 . . . £125
The Clipper of the Clouds, Sampson Low, 1887 £100
The Lottery Ticket, Sampson Low, 1887 . . £100
The Flight to France, Sampson Low, 1888. . £100
North Against South, Sampson Low, 1888 . . £100
Adrift in the Pacific, Sampson Low, 1889 . . £100
A Family Without a Name, Sampson Low, 1891 [1890] £100
The Purchase of the North Pole, Sampson Low, 1891 [1890] £100
Caesar Cascabel, Sampson Low, 1891 . . . . £100
Mistress Branican, Sampson Low, 1892 . . £100
The Castle of the Carpathians, Sampson Low, 1893 . . . . £100
Claudius Bombarnac, Sampson Low, 1894. . £100
Foundling Mick, Sampson Low, 1895 . . . £100
Captain Antifer, Sampson Low, 1895 . . . £100
The Floating Island, Sampson Low, 1896 . . £100
Clovis Dardentor, Sampson Low, 1897 . . . £100
For the Flag, Sampson Low, 1897 . . . . £100
An Antarctic Mystery, Sampson Low, 1898. . £125
The Will of an Eccentric, Sampson Low, 1900. £65
The Chase of the Golden Meteor, Grant Richards, 1909 . . . . £45
Master of the World, Sampson Low, [1914] . £45
The Lighthouse at the End of the World, Sampson Hall, [1923] . . . . £100/£35
Second Patrie: Their Island Home, Sampson Low, [1923] . . . . £75/£20
The Castaways of the Flag, Sampson Low, [1923] . . . . £75/£20

The Barsac Mission: Into the Niger Bend, Arco, 1960 . . . . £25/£10
The City in the Sahara, Arco, 1960 . . . . £25/£10
The Survivors of the Jonathan: The Masterless Man, Arco, 1962 . . . . £25/£10
The Unwilling Dictator, Arco, 1962. . . . £25/£10
The Golden Volcano: The Claim on Forty Mile Creek, Arco, 1962 . . . . £25/£10
Flood and Fame, Arco, 1962 . . . . £25/£10
The Secret of the Wilhelm Storitz, Arco, 1964 £25/£10
The Village in the Treetops, Arco, 1964 . £25/£10
Salvage from the 'Cynthia', Arco, 1964 . £25/£10
Yesterday and Tomorrow, Arco, 1965 . . £25/£10
The Thompson Travel Agency: Package Holiday, Arco, 1965 . . . . £25/£10
End of the Journey, Arco, 1965 . . . . £25/£10
Drama in Livonia, Arco, 1967 . . . . £25/£10
The Danube Pilot, Arco, 1967 . . . . £25/£10
The Sea Serpent, Arco, 1967. . . . . £25/£10

Non Fiction
The Exploration of the World (B.C. 505 - A.D. 1700), Sampson Low, 1879 . . . . £75
The Great Navigators of the Eighteenth Century, Sampson Low, 1880 . . . . £75
The Great Explorers of the Nineteenth Century, Sampson Low, 1881 . . . . £75

GORE VIDAL

(b.1925)

An American novelist and essayist, Vidal offers a sharp insight into contemporary American life.

Novels
Williwaw, Dutton (U.S.), 1946 . . . . £250/£35
ditto, Heinemann, 1970 . . . . £25/£10
In a Yellow Wood, Dutton (U.S.), 1947 . . £150/£15
The City and The Pillar, Dutton (U.S.), 1948 £125/£15
ditto, Lehmann, 1949 . . . . £25/£10
ditto, Dutton (U.S.), 1965 (revised edition) . £15/£5
ditto, Heinemann, 1966 (revised edition) . £15/£5
The Season of Comfort, Dutton (U.S.), 1949 £100/£10
A Search for The King, Dutton (U.S.), 1950 £100/£15
Dark Green, Bright Red, Dutton (U.S.), 1950 £75/£10
ditto, Lehmann, 1950 . . . . £25/£5
The Judgement of Paris, Dutton (U.S.), 1952 £75/£10
ditto, Heinemann, 1953 . . . . £20/£5
Death in The Fifth Position, Dutton (U.S.), 1952 (pseud. 'Edgar Box') . . . . £150/£20
ditto, Heinemann, 1954 . . . . £75/£15
Death Before Bedtime, Dutton (U.S.), 1953 (pseud. 'Edgar Box') . . . . £150/£20
ditto, Heinemann, 1954 . . . . £65/£15
Death Likes It Hot, Dutton (U.S.), 1954 (pseud. 'Edgar Box') . . . . £150/£20
ditto, Heinemann, 1955 . . . . £65/£15
Messiah, Dutton (U.S.), 1954 . . . . £50/£10
ditto, Heinemann, 1955 . . . . £25/£10
Julian, Little, Brown (U.S.), 1964 . . . £35/£10
ditto, Heinemann, 1964 . . . . £20/£5
Washington DC, Little, Brown (U.S.), 1967 £25/£5
ditto, Heinemann, 1967 . . . . £15/£5
Myra Breckinridge, Little, Brown (U.S.), 1968 £15/£5
ditto, Blond, 1968 . . . . £15/£5
Two Sisters, Little, Brown (U.S.), 1970 . . £15/£5
ditto, Heinemann, 1970 . . . . £10/£5
Burr, Random House (U.S.), 1973 . . . £10/£5
ditto, Heinemann, 1974 . . . . £10/£5
Myron, , Random House (U.S.), 1974 . . £10/£5
ditto, Heinemann, 1975 . . . . £10/£5
1876, Random House (U.S.), 1976 . . . £10/£5
ditto, Random House (U.S.), 1976 (300 signed copies, slipcase) . . . . £60/£45
ditto, Heinemann, 1976 . . . . £10/£5
Kalki, Random House (U.S.), 1978 . . . £10/£5
ditto, Heinemann, 1978 . . . . £10/£5
Creation, Random House (U.S.), 1981 . . £10/£5
ditto, Random House (U.S.), 1981 (500 signed copies, slipcase) . . . . £65/£50
ditto, Heinemann, 1981 . . . . £10/£5
Duluth, Random House (U.S.), 1983 . . £10/£5
ditto, Heinemann, 1983 . . . . £10/£5
Lincoln, Random House (U.S.), 1984 . . £10/£5
ditto, Franklin Library (U.S.), 1984 (350 signed copies) £40
ditto, Heinemann, 1984 . . . . £10/£5
Empire, Random House (U.S.), 1987 . . £10/£5
ditto, Franklin Library (U.S.), 1987 (350 signed copies) £40
ditto, Deutsch, 1987 . . . . £10/£5
Hollywood, Random House (U.S.), 1990 . £10/£5
ditto, Deutsch, 1990 . . . . £10/£5
View from The Diner's Club, Random House (U.S.), 1991 . . . . £10/£5
ditto, Deutsch, 1991 . . . . £10/£5
Live from Golgotha, Random House (U.S.), 1992 . . . . £10/£5
ditto, Deutsch, 1992 . . . . £10/£5

Short Stories
A Thirsty Evil: 7 Short Stories, Zero Press (U.S.), 1956 . . . . £100/£20
ditto, Heinemann, 1958 . . . . £30/£10
The Ladies in The Library and Other Stories, Eurographica (Helsinki), 1985 (350 signed copies) . . . . £75/£35

Plays

Visit to a Small Planet and Other Television Plays, Little, Brown (U.S.), 1957 . . . . . £50/£10
The Best Man, Little, Brown (U.S.), 1960 . £25/£10
Three Plays, Heinemann, 1962 . . . . . £25/£10
Romulus: A New Comedy, Dramatists Play Service (U.S.), 1962 (wraps) £15
Weekend, Dramatists Play Service (U.S.), 1968 (wraps) £10
An Evening with Richard Nixon, Random House (U.S.), 1972 . . . . £15/£5

Essays

Rocking The Boat, Little, Brown (U.S.), 1962 £30/£10
ditto, Heinemann, 1963 . . . . £25/£10
Reflections Upon a Sinking Ship, Little, Brown (U.S.), 1969 . . . . £15/£5
ditto, Heinemann, 1969 . . . . £15/£5
Homage to Daniel Shays: Collected Essays 1952-1972, Random House (U.S.), 1972 . . . . £15/£5
ditto, as ***Collected Essays 1951-1972***, Heinemann, 1974 . . . . £15/£5
Matters of Fact and Fiction: Essays, 1973-1976, Random House (U.S.), 1977 . . . £10/£5
ditto, Heinemann, 1977 . . . . £10/£5
Armageddon? Essays 1985-1987, Deutsch, 1987 . . . . £10/£5
ditto, as ***At Home***, Random House (U.S.), 1988 £10/£5
United States: Essays, 1951-92, Deutsch, 1993 £10/£5

Others

Great American Families, Norton (U.S.), 1977 (with others). . . . . £15/£5
ditto, Times, 1977 . . . . £10/£5
Vidal in Venice, Weidenfeld, 1984 . . . £10/£5
ditto, Summit (U.S.), 1985 . . . . . . £10/£5
Screening History, Harvard University Press (U.S.), 1992 . . . . £10/£5
ditto, Deutsch, 1992 . . . . £10/£5
Palimpsest, Random House (U.S.), 1995 £10/£5
ditto, Deutsch, 1995 . . . . £10/£5

KURT VONNEGUT
(b.1911)

An American novelist, Vonnegut's experiences as a prisoner of war in Dresden during World War Two have influenced much of his writing.

Novels

Player Piano, Scribner (U.S.), 1952 . . . £450/£35
ditto, Macmillan, 1953 . . . . £150/£25
The Sirens of Titan, Fawcett (U.S.), 1959 (wraps) £75
ditto, Houghton Mifflin (U.S.), 1961. . . . £450/£45
ditto, Gollancz, 1962 . . . . £250/£25
Mother Night, Fawcett (U.S.), 1962 (wraps) . £50
ditto, Harper &Row (U.S.), [1966] . . . £200/£30
ditto, Cape, 1968 . . . . £50/£15
Cat's Cradle, Holt Rinehart (U.S.), 1963 . £300/£25
ditto, Gollancz, 1963 . . . . £125/£20
God Bless You, Mr Rosewater, Holt Rinehart (U.S.), 1965 . . . . £200/£20
ditto, Cape, 1965 . . . . £100/£20
Slaughterhouse-Five, Delacorte (U.S.), 1969 £300/£25
ditto, Cape, 1970 . . . . £125/£20
ditto, Franklin Library (U.S.), 1978 (signed copies) £45
Breakfast of Champions, Delacorte (U.S.), 1973 . . . . £20/£5
ditto, Cape, 1973 . . . . £20/£5
Slapstick, Delacorte (U.S.), 1976 . . . . £20/£5
ditto, Delacorte (U.S.), 1976 (250 signed, numbered copies, slipcase) . . . . £125/£100
ditto, Cape, 1976 . . . . £20/£5
ditto, Franklin Library (U.S.), 1976 (signed copies) £45
Jailbird, Delacorte (U.S.), 1979 . . . . £15/£5
ditto, Delacorte (U.S.), 1979 (500 signed copies, slipcase) . . . . £100/£75
ditto, Cape, 1979 . . . . £15/£5
ditto, Franklin Library (U.S.), 1979 (signed copies) £45
Deadeye Dick, Delacorte (U.S.), 1981 . . £15/£5
ditto, Delacorte (U.S.), 1981 (300 signed copies, slipcase) . . . . £125/£100
ditto, Cape, 1983 . . . . £10/£5
Galapagos, Delacorte (U.S.), 1985 . . . £15/£5
ditto, Delacorte (U.S.), 1985 (500 signed copies, slipcase) . . . . £100/£75
ditto, Cape, 1985 . . . . £15/£5
ditto, Franklin Library (U.S.), 1985 (signed copies) £45
Bluebeard, Delacorte (U.S.), 1987 . . . £10/£5
ditto, Delacorte (U.S.), 1987 (500 signed copies, slipcase) . . . . £100/£75
ditto, Cape, 1988 . . . . £10/£5
Hocus Pocus; Or, What's The Hurry Son?, Putnam (U.S.), 1990 . . . . £10/£5
ditto, Cape, 1990 . . . . £10/£5

Short Stories

Canary in a Cathouse, Fawcett (U.S.), 1961 (wraps) £125
Welcome to The Monkey House, Delacorte (U.S.), 1968 . . . . £250/£35

Plays

Happy Birthday, Wanda June, Delacorte (U.S.), 1971 . . . . £225/£30
ditto, Cape, 1973 . . . . £125/£20
Between Time and Timbuctoo, Delacorte (U.S.), 1971 . . . . £250/£35

Others

Wampeters, Foma, and Granfalloons: Opinions, Delacorte (U.S.), 1974 . . . . . . £40/£10

ditto, Cape, 1975 . . . . £25/£10

Palm Sunday, Delacorte (U.S.), 1981 . . £15/£5

ditto, Delacorte (U.S.), 1981 (500 signed copies, slipcase) . . . . £100/£75

ditto, Cape, 1981 . . . . £15/£5

Fates Worse Than Death: An Autobiographical Collage of The 1980's, Putnam (U.S.), 1991 £10/£5

ditto, Putnam (U.S.), 1991 (200 signed, numbered copies) £125

ditto, Cape, 1991 . . . . £10/£5

LOUIS WAIN

(b.1860 d.1939)

Highly successful British illustrator, well known for his drawings of cats.

Books Written and Illustrated by Louis Wain

Dreams by French Firesides, A & C Black, 1890 (pseud. 'Richard Leander') £75

Miss Lovemouse's Letters, Nelson, 1896 . . . £75

Puppy Dogs' Tales, Nelson, 1896 . . . . £75

The Children's Tableaux: The Three Little Kittens, Nister, 1896 . . . . £75

The Dandy Lion, by Louis Wain and Clifton Bingham, Nister, [1900]. £200

Fun All The Way, Nister, 1900 . . . . . £45

Cats, Sands, [1901] (pseud. 'Grimalkin'). . . £200

Fun For Everyone, Nister, 1902. . . . . £45

Fun and Frolic, by Louis Wain and Clifton Bingham, Nister, [1902]. £375

Pa Cats, Ma Cats, and Their Kittens, Raphael Tuck, [1902] (pseud. 'Father Tuck') £400

The Louis Wain Nursery Book, Clarke, [1902] £75

Louis Wain's Cats and Dogs, Raphael Tuck, 1902 . . . . £200

Big Dogs, Little Dogs, Cats and Kittens, Raphael Tuck, [1903] £350

Comic Annuals ABC, by Louis Wain, Collins, [1903] £200

Louis Wain's Baby's Picture Book, Clarke, 1903 £100

Louis Wain's Dog Painting Book, Raphael Tuck, 1903 . . . . £100

Louis Wain's Cat Painting Book, Raphael Tuck, 1903 . . . . £100

Louis Wain's Summer Book, Hutchinson, 1903 £100

The Louis Wain Kitten Book, Treherne, [1903] (printed on one side of the page) £350

Funny Animals and Stories About Them, Clarke, 1904 . . . . £200

In Animal Land with Louis Wain, Partridge, [1904] £300

Kits and Cats, Raphael Tuck, 1904 . . . . . £200

Louis Wain's Animal Show: With Stories in Prose and Verse, Clarke, 1905. . . . . £200

Louis Wain's Summer Book for 1906, King, 1906 . . . . £100

Animal Playtime, Clarke, 1908 . . . . . £150

In Story Land with Louis Wain, Raphael Tuck, 1912 . . . . £350

Louis Wain's Painting Book, Shaw, 1912 . . £100

Louis Wain's Father Christmas, Shaw, 1912 . £100

Animal Happyland, Clarke, 1913 . . . . . £100

Happy Hours with Louis Wain, Shaw, 1913 . £200

A Cat Alphabet and Picture Book for Little Folk, Blackie, [1914] £200

Animal Picture-Land, Clarke, 1914 . . . . £250

Daddy Cat, Blackie & Sons, [1915] £350

Little Red Riding Hood and Other Tales, Gale & Poleden, [1917] £100

Cinderella and Other Fairy Tales, Gale & Poleden, 1917 . . . . £100

Cats at Play, Blackie, 1917 . . . . . . £200

Rosy Cheeks Funny Book, Nister, [c.1917]. . £50

The Story of Tabbykin Town in School and at Play, Faulkner, [1920] (pseud. 'Kittycat'). £200

Pussy Land, Geographia, [1920]. £200

The Kitten's House, Valentine, 1922 . . . £200

Charlie's Adventures, Valentine, 1922 . . . . £200

Comical Kittens, Valentine, [1922] (painting book with paints and brush) £75

Louis Wain's Children's Book, Hutchinson, [1923] £150

Souvenir of Louis Wain's Work, Louis Wain Fund, 1925 . . . . £100

ditto, as ***Animals 'Xtra' and Louis Wain's Annual 1925***, Louis Wain Fund, [1925]. £100

Louis Wain's Animal Book, Collins, 'Bumper Book', [1928]. £75

Louis Wain's Great Big Midget Book, Dean, 1934 £75

Annuals

Louis Wain's Annual, Treherne, 1901 . . . £250

Louis Wain's Annual for 1902, Treherne, 1902 £200

Louis Wain's Annual 1903, Hutchinson, 1903 . £200

Louis Wain's Annual 1905, King, 1905. . . £200

Louis Wain's Annual for 1906, Shaw, 1906 . £200

Louis Wain's Annual 1907, Bemrose, 1907 . £150

Louis Wain's Annual 1908, Bemrose, 1908 . £150

Louis Wain's Annual 1909-10, Allen, 1909 . £150

Louis Wain's Annual 1910-11, Allen, 1910 . £150

Louis Wain's Annual 1911, Shaw, 1911 . . £150

Louis Wain's Annual 1911-12, Shaw, 1911 . £150

Louis Wain's Annual 1912, Shaw, 1912 . . £150

Louis Wain's Annual 1913, Shaw, 1913 . . £150

Louis Wain's Annual 1914, Shaw, 1914 . . £150
Louis Wain's Annual 1915, Shaw, 1915 . . £175
Louis Wain's Annual 1921, Hutchinson, 1921 . £150

Books Illustrated by Louis Wain
Madame Tabby's Establishment, by Kari, Macmillan, 1886 . . . . £300
Our Farm: The Trouble and Successes Thereof, by F. W. Pattenden, Clarke, 1888 . . . . £75
Peter, A Cat O' One Tail: His Life and Adventures, by Charles Morley, Pall Mall Gazette Extras, 1892 £100
Old Rabbit, The Voodoo and Other Sorcerers, by M.A. Owen, Unwin, 1893 . . . . £75
More Jingles, Jokes and Funny Folks, by Clifton Bingham, Nister, 1898 . . . . £100
The Monkey That Would Not Kill, by Henry Drummond, Hodder & Stoughton, 1898 . . £50
Pussies and Puppies: With Verses and Tales by Various Writers, Partridge, [1899] £100
The Living Animals of The World, by C.J. Cornish, [1901] £75
All Sorts of Comical Cats, by Clifton Bingham, Nister, 1902 . . . . £375
Ping-Pong Calendar for 1903, by Clifton Bingham, Raphael Tuck, [1903] £175
Kittenland, by Clifton Bingham, Collins, [1903] £350
With Louis Wain to Fairyland, by Nora Chesson, Raphael Tuck, [1904] £350
Funny Favourites, by Clifton Bingham, Nister, 1904 . . . . £200
Claws and Paws: Stories and Pictures from Kittenland and Puppyland, by C. Bingham, Nister, [1904] £350
Cat Tales, by W.L. Alden, Digby Long, 1905 . £250
The Adventures of Friskers and His Friends, by Marian Hurrell, Culley, 1907 . . . . . £150
Mephistopheles: The Autobiography and Adventures of a Tabby Cat, by C.Y. Stephens, Jarrold, 1907 £150
The Kings and The Cats: Munster Fairy Tales for Young and Old, by John Hannon, Burns & Oates, [1908] £150
Cat's Cradle: A Picture Book for Little Folk, by May Clariss Byron, Blackie, [1908] £150
Full of Fun, by Clifton Bingham, Nister, [1908] £150
Holidays in Animal Land, by A.W. Ridler, Clarke, [1909] £150
Two Cats at Large: A Book of Surprises, by S.C. Woodhouse, Routledge, [1910] £200
The Merry Animal Picture Book, by A.W. Ridler, Clarke, [1910] £150
The Happy Family, by Edric Vredenburg, Raphael Tuck, 1910 . . . . £400
Such Fun with Louis Wain, by Norman Gale, Raphael Tuck, 1910 . . . . £200
Cats at School, by S.C. Woodhouse, Routledge, [1911] £150
Animals in Fun-Land, by A.W. Rider, Clarke, 1911 . . . . £200
Merry Times in Animal-Land, by A.W. Rider, Clarke, 1912 . . . . £200
The Cats Scouts: A Picture Book for Little Folk, by Jessie Pope, Blackie, [1912] £350
Louis Wain's Happy Land, by A.W. Ridler, Shaw, 1912 . . . . £100
Tinker, Tailor, by Eric Vredenburg, Raphael Tuck, 1914 . . . . £350
Animal Fancy-Land, by A.W. Rider, Clarke, 1915 . . . . £200
Little Soldiers, by May Crommelin, Hutchinson, [1915] £100
Merry Times with Louis Wain, by Dorothy Black, Raphael Tuck, 1916 . . . . £200
The Tales of Little Priscilla Purr, by Cecily M. Rutley, Valentine, 1920 . . . . £100
The Tale of Naughty Kitty Cat, by Cecily M. Rutley, Valentine, 1920 . . . . £100
The Tale of Peter Pusskin, by Cecily M. Rutley, Valentine, 1920 . . . . £100
The Tale of The Tabby Twins, by Cecily M. Rutley, Valentine, 1920 . . . . £100
The Teddy Rocker: Naughty Teddy Bear, by Cecily M. Rutley, Valentine, 1921 (shape book) . . £150
The Pussy Rocker: Polly Puss, by Cecily M. Rutley, Valentine, 1921 (shape book) £150

ALFRED WAINWRIGHT

(d.1907 d.1991)

Wainwright was the author and illustrator of numerous guides to the fells of England and Scotland.

A Pictorial Guide to the Lakeland Fells Titles
The Eastern Fells, Henry Marshall, 1955 (in 'second impression' dustjacket) . . . . . . £175/£150
The Far Eastern Fells, Henry Marshall, 1957 . . . . £165/£65
The Central Fells, Henry Marshall, 1958 . £150/£65
The Southern Fells, Henry Marshall, 1960 . £150/£65
The Southern Fells, Henry Marshall, 1962 . £150/£65
The North-Western Fells, Westmorland Gazette, 1964 . . . . £150/£65
The Western Fells, Westmorland Gazette, 1966 . . . . £150/£65

Lakeland Sketchbooks
A Lakeland Sketchbook, Westmorland Gazette, 1969 . . . . £75/£25
A Second Lakeland Sketchbook, Westmorland Gazette, 1970 . . . . £50/£20

A Third Lakeland Sketchbook, Westmorland Gazette, 1971 . . . . £30/£10
A Fourth Lakeland Sketchbook, Westmorland Gazette, 1972. . . . . £30/£10
A Fifth Lakeland Sketchbook, Westmorland Gazette, 1973 . . . . £30/£10

Scottish Mountain Drawings
The Northern Highlands, Westmorland Gazette, 1974 . . . . £20/£20
The North-West Highlands, Westmorland Gazette, 1976 . . . . £40/£15
The Western Highlands, Westmorland Gazette, 1976 . . . . £40/£15
The Central Highlands, Westmorland Gazette, 1977 . . . . £40/£15
The Eastern Highlands, Westmorland Gazette, 1978 . . . . £40/£15
The Islands, Westmorland Gazette, 1979 . £40/£15

Others
Fellwanderer, The Story Behind the Guidebooks, Westmorland Gazette, 1966. . . . . . £25/£10
Pennine Way Companion, Westmorland Gazette, 1968 . . . . £75/£25
Walks in Limestone Country, Westmorland Gazette, 1970 . . . . £50/£20
Walks on the Howgill Fells, Westmorland Gazette, 1972 . . . . £40/£15
A Coast to Coast Walk, St Bees Head to Robin Hood's Bay, Westmorland Gazette, 1973 . . . . £40/£15
The Outlying Fells of Lakeland, Westmorland Gazette, 1974. . . . . £40/£15
Westmorland Heritage, Westmorland Gazette, 1974 (1,000 signed copies) . . . . . . £500/£200
ditto, Westmorland Gazette, 1988 . . . . £15/£5
A Dales Sketchbook, Westmorland Gazette, 1976 . . . . £35/£15
Kendal in the Nineteenth Century, Westmorland Gazette, 1977. . . . . £75/£15
A Second Dales Sketchbook, Westmorland Gazette, 1978 . . . . £35/£15
A Furness Sketchbook, Westmorland Gazette, 1978 . . . . £35/£15
Walks from Ratty, Ravenglass and Eskdale Railway Co, 1978 . . . . £35/£15
A Second Furness Sketchbook, Westmorland Gazette, 1979 . . . . £35/£15
Three Westmorland Rivers, Westmorland Gazette, 1979 . . . . £35/£15
A Lune Sketchbook, Westmorland Gazette, 1980 . . . . £35/£15
A Ribble Sketchbook, Westmorland Gazette, 1980. . . . . £35/£15
An Eden Sketchbook, Westmorland Gazette, 1980 . . . . £35/£15
Lakeland Mountain Drawings, Westmorland Gazette, 1980 (5 vols) . . . . £35/£15 each
Welsh Mountain Drawings, Westmorland Gazette, 1981 . . . . £35/£15
A Bowland Sketchbook, Westmorland Gazette, 1981 . . . . £35/£15
A North Wales Sketchbook, Westmorland Gazette, 1982 . . . . £35/£15
A Wyre Sketchbook, Westmorland Gazette, 1982 . . . . £35/£15
A South Wales Sketchbook, Westmorland Gazette, 1983 . . . . £35/£15
Wainwright in Lakeland, Abbott Hall Art Gallery, 1983 (1,000 signed copies) . . . . . £450/£175
A Peak District Sketchbook, Westmorland Gazette, 1984 . . . . £35/£15
Fellwalking with Wainwright, Michael Joseph, 1984 (photographs by Derry Brabbs) . . . . £15/£5
Old Roads of Eastern Lakeland, Westmorland Gazette, 1985. . . . . £10/£5
Wainwright on the Pennine Way, Michael Joseph, 1985 (photographs by Derry Brabbs) . . £10/£5
A Pennine Journey, Michael Joseph, 1986 . £10/£5
Wainwright's Coast to Coast Walk, Michael Joseph, 1987 (photographs by Derry Brabbs) . . £10/£5
Ex-Fellwanderer, Westmorland Gazette, 1987 £10/£5
Wainwright in Scotland, Michael Joseph, 1988 (photographs by Derry Brabbs). . . . £10/£5
Fellwalking with a Camera, Westmorland Gazette, 1988 . . . . £10/£5
Wainwright on the Lakeland Mountain Passes, Michael Joseph, 1989 (photographs by Derry Brabbs) £10/£5
Wainwright in the Limestone Dales, Michael Joseph, 1991 (photographs by Ed Geldard). . . . £10/£5
Wainwright's Favourite Lakeland Mountains, Michael Joseph, 1991 (photographs by Derry Brabbs) . . . . £10/£5
Wainwright in the Valleys of Lakeland, Michael Joseph, 1992 (photographs by Derry Brabbs) £10/£5
Memoirs of a Fellwanderer, Michael Joseph, 1993 . . . . £10/£5
Wainwright: His Tour of the Lake District, Whitsuntide, 1931, Michael Joseph, 1993 (photographs by Ed Geldard) . . . . £10/£5
The Walker's Log Book, Michael Joseph, 1993 £10/£5

Other Titles Illustrated by Wainwright
Inside the Real Lakeland, by A.H. Griffin, Guardian Press, 1961 . . . . £40/£15
Scratch and Co., by Molly Lefebure, Gollancz, 1968 . . . . £15/£5
The Hunting of Wilberforce Pike, by Molly Lefebure, Gollancz, 1970 . . . . £10/£5

The Plague Dogs, by Richard Adams, Allen Lane, 1977 . . . . £10/£5
Guide to the View from Scafel Pike, Chris Jesty Panoramas, 1978 . . . . £10/£5

A.E. WAITE

(b.1857 d.1942)

An occultist, poet, bohemian and mystic, Waite's contribution to the literature of the occult is highly regarded by devotees.

Principal Works

The Real History of The Rosicrucians, George Redway, 1887 . . . . £75
A Handbook of Cartomancy, George Redway, 1889 (pseud. 'Grand Orient') £60
The Interior Life from The Standpoint of The Mystics, 'Light', [1891] £125
The Occult Sciences, Kegan Paul, Trench, Trübner and Co., 1891 . . . . £75
Azoth: or The Star in The East, Theosophical Publishing Society, 1893 . . . . . . £100
Devil-Worship in France, George Redway, 1896 £65
The Book of Black Magic and Pacts, Redway, 1898 (500 copies) £120
The Life of Louis Claude de Saint-Martin, Philip Wellby, 1901 . . . . £100
The Doctrine and Literature of The Kabalah, Theosophical Publishing Society, 1902 . . £75
Studies in Mysticism, Hodder & Stoughton, 1906 £65
The Hidden Church of The Holy Graal, Rebman Ltd, 1909 . . . . £75
The Key to The Tarot, William Rider and Son Ltd, 1910 . . . . £50
ditto, 1920 (new edition) £45
The Pictorial Key to The Tarot, William Rider and Son Ltd, 1911 . . . . £50
The Book of Ceremonial Magic, William Rider and Son Ltd, 1911 . . . . £50
The Secret Tradition in Freemasonry, Rebman Ltd, 1911 . . . . £45
The Secret Doctrine in Israel, William Rider and Son Ltd, 1913 . . . . £65
The Way of Divine Union, William Rider and Son Ltd, 1915 . . . . £200
Deeper Aspects of Masonic Symbolism, privately printed, 1915 . . . . £45
New Encyclopaedia of Freemasonry, William Rider and Son Ltd, 1921 . . . . £75/£45
Robert Fludd and Freemasonry, offprint, (1922) £45
Raymond Lully, William Rider and Son Ltd, 1922 . . . . £75/£45
Saint-Martin, William Rider and Son Ltd, 1922 . . . . £65/£35
Lamps of Western Mysticism, Kegan Paul, Trench, Trübner and Co., 1923 . . . . . . £60/£35
The Brotherhood of The Rosy Cross, William Rider and Son Ltd, 1924 . . . . £75/£25
Emblematic Freemasonry, William Rider and Son Ltd, 1925 . . . . £65/£35
The Secret Tradition in Alchemy, Kegan Paul, Trench, Trübner and Co., 1926 . . . . . . £75/£35
The Holy Kabbalah, William and Norgate Ltd, 1929 . . . . £50/£30
The Holy Grail, William Rider and Son Ltd, 1933 . . . . £65/£35
The Secret Tradition in Freemasonry, Rider and Co., 1937 . . . . £65/£35
Shadows of Life and Thought, Selwyn and Blount, 1938 . . . . £65/£30

Verse

An Ode to Astronomy and Other Poems, 1877?, (100 copies) £3,000
A Lyric of The Fairyland, Catty, 1879 . . . £2,000
A Soul's Comedy, George Redway, 1887 . . £65
Lucastra, James Burns, [1890] £65
A Book of Mystery and Vision, Philip Wellby, 1902 . . . . £45
ditto, Philip Wellby, 1902 (10 signed copies on Japanese vellum) £200
Strange Houses of Sleep, Philip Wellby, 1906 (250 signed, numbered copies, with Arthur Machen) £100
The Collected Poems of Arthur Edward Waite, Rider, 1914 (2 vols) £50
The Book of The Holy Graal, J.M. Watkins, 1921 (500 copies) . . . . £65/£35
The Open Vision, Shakespeare Head Press, 1959 (500 copies) . . . . £20/£10

Fiction

Prince Starbeam, James Burns, 1889 . . . £75
The Golden Stairs, Theosophical Publishing Society, 1893 . . . . £75
Belle and The Dragon, James Elliot, 1894 . . £75
Steps to The Crown, Philip Wellby, 1906 . . £45
The Quest of The Golden Stairs, Theosophical Publishing House Ltd, [1927] £35

Others

Israfel, Letters, Visions and Poems, E.W. Allen, 1886 . . . . £65
ditto, James Elliot and Co., 1894 (enlarged edition) £65
The House of The Hidden Light, privately printed, 1904 (with Arthur Machen) £1,000
The Hermetic Text Society, Philip Wellby, 1907 £50

EDGAR WALLACE

1875 1932

Wallace's output of books was vast, and he made no attempt to disguise the fact that it was popular rather than critical success that he craved. In this ambition he was incredibly successful.

Novels

The Four Just Men, Tallis Press, 1905 (numbered competition slip) £100
ditto, Tallis Press, 1906 (includes chapter 12, a letter from Manfred as solution) £30
ditto, Tallis Press, 1911 (includes full chapter 12) £20
ditto, Small Maynard (U.S.), 1920 . . . £75/£20
Angel Esquire, Arrowsmith, 1908 . . . . £40
ditto, Holt (U.S.), 1908 . . . . £40
The Council of Justice, Ward Lock, 1908 . . £75
Captain Tatham of Tatham Island, Gale and Polden, 1909 . . . . £75
ditto, as ***The Island of Galloping Gold***, Newnes, 1916 . . . . £15
ditto, as ***Eve's Island***, Newnes, 1926 [wraps] . £30
The Duke in the Suburbs, Ward Lock, 1909 . £50
The Nine Bears, Ward Lock, 1910 . . . . £75
ditto, as ***The Other Man***, Dodd, Mead (U.S.), 1911 £50
ditto, as ***Silinski, Master Criminal***, World Syndicate, 1930 . . . . £20/£5
Private Selby, Ward Lock, 1912 . . . . . £65
The People of the River, Ward Lock, 1912 . . £30
Grey Timothy, Ward Lock, 1913. . . . . £30
ditto, as ***Pallard the Punter***, Ward Lock, 1914 (wraps) £25
The River of Stars, Ward Lock, 1913 . . . £30
The Fourth Plague, Ward Lock, 1913 . . . £45
ditto, Doubleday Doran (U.S.), 1930. . . £30/£10
The Admirable Carfew, Ward Lock, 1914 . . £20
The Melody of Death, Arrowsmith, 1915 . . £45
ditto, Dial (U.S.), 1927 . . . . . . £25/£10
1925: The Story of a Fatal Peace, Newnes, 1915 (wraps) £75
The Man Who Bought London, Ward Lock, 1915 £45
The Clue of the Twisted Candle, Small Maynard (U.S.), 1916 . . . . £30
ditto, Newnes, 1917 . . . . £25
A Debt Discharged, Ward Lock, 1916 . . . £55
The Tomb of Ts'in, Ward Lock, 1916 . . . £225
The Just Men of Cordova, Ward Lock, 1917 . £30
ditto, Doubleday Doran (U.S.), 1929. . . . £15
The Secret House, Ward Lock, 1917 . . . £30
ditto, Small Maynard (U.S.), 1919 . . . . £15
Kate Plus Ten, Small Maynard (U.S.), 1917 . £50
ditto, Ward Lock, 1919 . . . . £45
The Keepers of the King's Peace, Ward Lock, 1917 . . . . £30
Down Under Donovan, Ward Lock, 1918 . . £30
Those Folk of Bulboro, Ward Lock, 1918 . . £50
Lieutenant Bones, Ward Lock, 1918 . . . £30
Tam of the Scouts, Newnes, 1918 . . . . £35
ditto, as ***Tam O' the Scoots***, Small Maynard (U.S.), 1919 . . . . £30
The Man Who Knew, Small Maynard (U.S.), 1918 £30
ditto, Newnes, 1919 . . . . £30
The Real Shell-Man, John Waddington, 1919 (wraps). £45
The Fighting Scouts, Pearson, 1919. . . . £25
The Green Rust, Ward Lock, 1919 . . . . £30
ditto, Small Maynard (U.S.), 1920 . . . £30/£10
Jack O' Judgement, Ward Lock, 1920 . . £65/£15
ditto, Small Maynard (U.S.), 1921 . . . £30/£10
The Daffodil Mystery, Ward Lock, 1920 . £75/£15
ditto, as ***The Daffodil Murder***, Small Maynard (U.S.), 1921. . . . . £65/£15
The Book of All Power, Ward Lock, 1921 . £25/£10
The Angel of Terror, Hodder & Stoughton, 1922 . . . . £30/£10
ditto, Small Maynard (U.S.), 1922 . . . £30/£10
Sandi, The King-Maker, Ward Lock, 1922 £30/£10
Captains of Souls, Small Maynard (U.S.), 1922 . . . . £50/£15
ditto, John Long, 1923 . . . . . . £50/£15
The Flying Fifty-Five, Hutchinson, 1922 . £75/£15
The Crimson Circle, Hodder & Stoughton, 1922 . . . . £50/£15
ditto, Doubleday Doran (U.S.), 1929. . . £25/£10
Mr. Justice Maxell, Ward Lock, 1922 . . £75/£15
The Valley of Ghosts, Odhams, 1922 . . £75/£15
ditto, Small Maynard (U.S.), 1923 . . . £35/£10
The Clue of the New Pin, Hodder & Stoughton, 1923 . . . . £25/£10
ditto, Small Maynard (U.S.), 1923 . . . £25/£10
The Books of Bart, Ward Lock, 1923 . . £25/£10
The Green Archer, Hodder & Stoughton, 1923 £20/£5
ditto, Small Maynard (U.S.), 1924 . . . £20/£5
Blue Hand, Small Maynard (U.S.), 1923 . £30/£10
ditto, Ward Lock, 1925 . . . . . . £30/£10
The Fellowship of the Frog, Small Maynard (U.S.), 1923 . . . . £65/£15
ditto, Ward Lock, 1925 . . . . . . £65/£15
The Missing Million, John Long, 1923 . . £75/£15
ditto, as ***The Missing Millions***, Small Maynard (U.S.), 1925 . . . . £35/£10
The Dark Eyes of London, Ward Lock, 1924 £30/£10
ditto, Doubleday Doran (U.S.), 1929. . . £25/£5
The Sinister Man, Hodder & Stoughton, 1924 £20/£5
ditto, Small Maynard (U.S.), 1925. . . . £15/£5
Room 13, John Long, 1924 . . . . . £50/£15
The Three Oak Mystery, Ward Lock, 1924 £65/£15
Double Dan, Hodder & Stoughton, 1924 . £20/£5
ditto, as ***Diana of Kara-Kara***, Doubleday Doran (U.S.),

1924 . . . . £20/£5
The Face in the Night, John Long, 1924 . £50/£15
ditto, Doubleday Doran (U.S.), 1929. . . £30/£10
Flat 2, Garden City (U.S.), 1924 (wraps) . . £25
ditto, John Long, 1927 . . . . £15/£5
The Black Avons, George Gill, 1925, (four paperbacks) £75
The Strange Countess, Hodder & Stoughton, 1925 . . . . £25/£10
ditto, Small Maynard (U.S.), 1926 . . £15/£5
A King by Night, John Long, 1925 . . . £50/£15
ditto, Doubleday Page (U.S.), 1926 . . . £40/£10
The Gaunt Stranger, Hodder & Stoughton, 1925 . . . . £15/£5
ditto, as ***The Ringer***, Doubleday Page (U.S.), 1926 . . . . £15/£5
The Three Just Men, Hodder & Stoughton, 1925 . . . . £20/£5
ditto, Doubleday Doran (U.S.), 1929 . . £15/£5
The Man from Morocco, John Long, 1925 . £20/£5
ditto, as ***The Black***, Doubleday Doran (U.S.), 1930 . . . . £15/£5
The Daughters of the Night, Newnes, 1925 £35/£10
The Hairy Arm, Small Maynard (U.S.), 1925 £25/£10
ditto, as ***The Avenger***, John Long, 1926 . . £25/£10
The Door with Seven Locks, Hodder & Stoughton, 1926 . . . . £15/£5
ditto, Doubleday Doran (U.S.), 1926. . . £15/£5
Sanders, Hodder and Stoughton, 1926 . . £20/£5
ditto, as ***Mr. Commissioner Sanders***, Doubleday Doran (U.S.), 1930 . . . . £20/£5
We Shall See, Hodder & Stoughton, 1926 . £20/£5
ditto, as ***The Gaol-Breakers***, Doubleday Doran (U.S.), 1931 . . . . £20/£5
The Black Abbot, Hodder & Stoughton, 1926 £30/£10
ditto, Doubleday Page (U.S.), 1927 . . . £30/£10
The Terrible People, Hodder & Stoughton, 1926 . . . . £15/£5
ditto, Doubleday Page (U.S.), 1926 . . £15/£5
The Day of Uniting, Hodder & Stoughton, 1926 . . . . £20/£5
ditto, Mystery league (U.S.), 1930 . . . £20/£5
Penelope of the Polyantha, Hodder & Stoughton, 1926 . . . . £20/£5
The Joker, Hodder & Stoughton, 1926 . . £15/£5
ditto, as ***The Colossus***, Doubleday Doran (U.S.), 1932. . . . . £15/£5
The Square Emerald, Hodder & Stoughton, 1926 . . . . £15/£5
ditto, as ***The Girl from Scotland Yard***, Doubleday Doran (U.S.), 1927 . . . . £15/£5
The Yellow Snake, Hodder & Stoughton, 1926 £10/£5
Barbara on Her Own, Newnes, [1926] . . £20/£5
The Million Dollar Story, Newnes, 1926 (wraps) £35
The Northing Tramp, Hodder & Stoughton, 1926 . . . . £20/£5
ditto, Doubleday Doran (U.S.), 1929. . . £15/£5
The Hand of Power, John Long, 1926 . . £25/£5
ditto, Mystery League (U.S.), 1930 . . . £20/£5
The Traitor's Gate, Hodder & Stoughton, 1927 £20/£5
ditto, Doubleday Page (U.S.), 1927 . . . £15/£5
The Man Who Was Nobody, Ward Lock, 1927 . . . . £30/£10
The Feathered Serpent, Hodder & Stoughton, 1927 . . . . £10/£5
ditto, Doubleday Doran (U.S.), 1928. . . £15/£5
Terror Keep, Hodder & Stoughton, 1927 . £20/£5
ditto, Doubleday Page (U.S.), 1927 . . . £20/£5
Big Foot, John Long, 1927 . . . . . £20/£5
Number Six, Newnes, 1927 (wraps) £30
The Squeaker, Hodder & Stoughton, 1927 . £10/£5
ditto, as ***The Squealer***, Doubleday Doran (U.S.), 1928. . . . . £15/£5
The Forger, Hodder & Stoughton, 1927 . £20/£5
ditto, as ***The Clever One***, Doubleday Doran (U.S.), 1928 . . . . £20/£5
The Double, Hodder & Stoughton, 1928 . £20/£5
ditto, Doubleday Doran (U.S.), 1928. . . £20/£5
The Twister, John Long, 1928 . . . . £15/£5
ditto, Doubleday Page, 1929 . . . . . . £15/£5
The Flying Squad, Hodder & Stoughton, 1928 £15/£5
ditto, Doubleday Doran (U.S.), 1928. . . £15/£5
The Gunner, Long, 1928 . . . . . . £15/£5
ditto, as ***Gunman's Bluff***, Doubleday Doran (U.S.), 1929 . . . . £15/£5
Four Square Jane, Readers Library, 1929 . £20/£5
The India-Rubber Men, Hodder & Stoughton, 1929 . . . . £15/£5
ditto, Doubleday Doran, 1930 . . . . £15/£5
The Terror, Collins, 1929 (wraps) . . . £15/£5
The Golden Hades, Collins, 1929 . . . £20/£5
The Green Ribbon, Hutchinson, 1929 . . £15/£5
ditto, Doubleday Doran, 1930 . . . . £15/£5
White Face, Hodder & Stoughton, 1930 . £15/£5
ditto, Doubleday Doran (U.S.), 1931. . . £15/£5
The Calendar, Collins, 1930 . . . . . £20/£5
ditto, Doubleday Doran, 1931 . . . . . £20/£5
The Clue of the Silver Key, Hodder & Stoughton, 1930 . . . . £15/£5
ditto, as ***The Silver Key***, Doubleday Doran (U.S.), 1930 . . . . £15/£5
The Lady of Ascot, Hutchinson, 1930 . . £15/£5
The Devil Man, Collins, 1931 . . . . £30/£10
ditto, Doubleday Doran (U.S.), 1931. . . £30/£10
On the Spot, John Long, 1931 . . . . £20/£5
ditto, Doubleday Doran (U.S.), 1931. . . £20/£5
The Man at the Carlton, Hodder & Stoughton, 1931 . . . . £15/£5
ditto, Doubleday Doran (U.S.), 1932. . . £15/£5
The Coat of Arms, Hutchinson, 1931 . . £20/£5

ditto, as ***The Arranways Mystery***, Doubleday Doran (U.S.), 1932 . . . . £20/£5
When the Gangs Came to London, John Long, 1932 . . . . £75/£10
ditto, Doubleday Doran (U.S.), 1932. . . £65/£10
King Kong, Grosset & Dunlap (U.S.), 1932 (with Merian C. Cooper) . . . . . . £1,250/£200
ditto, Corgi, 1966 (wraps). £5
The Frightened Lady, Hodder & Stoughton, 1933 . . . . £15/£5
ditto, as ***The Mystery of the Frightened Lady***, Doubleday Doran (U.S.), 1933 . . . . £15/£5

Stories

Smithy, Tallis Press, 1905 (card covers). . . £100
Smithy Abroad, Hulton, 1909 (card covers). . £250
Sanders of the River, Ward Lock, 1911 . . £70
ditto, Doubleday Doran (U.S.), 1930. . . £20/£5
Bosambo of the River, Ward Lock, 1914 . . £35
Smithy's Friend Nobby, Town Topics, 1914 . £250
ditto, as ***Nobby***, Newnes, [1916] £20
Bones, Ward Lock, 1915 . . . . £30
Smithy and the Hun, Pearson, 1915 (card covers) £300
Smithy, Not to Mention Nobby Clark and Spud Murphy, Newnes, 1915 (card covers) . . . £100
The Adventures of Heine, Ward Lock, 1919 . £25
Bones in London, Ward Lock, 1921. . . £35/£10
Law of the Four Just Men, Hodder and Stoughton, 1921 . . . . £125/£50
ditto, as ***Again the Three Just Men***, Doubleday Doran (U.S.), 1933 . . . . £30/£10
Chick, Ward Lock, 1923 . . . . £100/£35
Bones of the River, Newnes, [1923] . . . £20/£5
Educated Evans, Webster, [1924] . . . . £25/£10
The Mind of Mr. J.G. Reeder, Hodder & Stoughton, 1925 . . . . £20/£5
ditto, as ***The Murder Book of Mr. J.G. Reeder***, Doubleday Doran (U.S.), 1929 . . . . £15/£5
More Educated Evans, Webster, [1926] . £20/£5
The Brigand, Hodder & Stoughton, 1927 . £15/£5
This England, Hodder & Stoughton, [1927] £20/£5
The Mixer, John Long, 1927 . . . . . £15/£5
Good Evans, Webster, [1927] . . . . £20/£5
Again the Three Just Men, Hodder & Stoughton, 1928 . . . . £15/£5
ditto, as ***The Law of the 3 Just Men***, Doubleday Doran (U.S.), 1931 . . . . £15/£5
Again Sanders, Hodder & Stoughton, [1928] £20/£5
ditto, Doubleday Doran (U.S.), 1929. . . £20/£5
The Orator, Hutchinson, 1928 . . . . £20/£5
Elegant Edward, Readers Library, [1928] . £15/£5
The Thief in the Night, Readers Library, 1928 £20/£5
Forty Eight Short Stories, Newnes, 1929 . £20/£5
Planetoid 127 and The Sweizer Pump, Readers Library, 1929. . . . . £20/£5
Again the Ringer, Hodder & Stoughton, 1929 £15/£5
ditto, as ***The Ringer Returns***, Doubleday Doran, 1931. . . . . £15/£5
The Cat Burglar, Newnes, 1929 (wraps) . . £20
Circumstantial Evidence, Newnes, 1929 (wraps) £25
ditto, as ***Circumstantial Evidence and Other Stories***, World Syndicate, 1934 . . . . £20/£5
Fighting Snub Reilly, Newnes, 1929 (wraps) . £20
ditto, as ***Fighting Snub Reilly and Other Stories***, World Syndicate (U.S.), 1934 . . . . . £20/£5
The Ghost of Down Hill, and The Queen of Sheba's Belt, Readers Library, 1929. . . . . £20/£5
The Little Green Man, Newnes, 1929 (wraps) . £20
The Prison-Breakers, Newnes, 1929 (wraps) . £20
Red Aces, Being Three Cases of Mr. Reeder, Hodder & Stoughton, 1929 . . . . £20/£5
ditto, Doubleday Doran (U.S.), 1930. . . £20/£5
The Lone House Mystery, Collins, 1929 . £20/£5
The Black, Readers Library, 1929 . . . £20/£5
ditto, Digit Books, 1962 (wraps) £10
For Information Received, Newnes, 1929 . £100/£25
The Governor of Chi-Foo, Newnes, 1929 (wraps) £20
ditto, as ***The Governor of Chi-Foo and Other Stories***, World Syndicate (U.S.), 1933 . . . . £20/£5
The Lady of Little Hell, Newnes, 1929 (wraps) £75
The Reporter, Readers Library, 1929 . . £20/£5
The Big Four, Readers Library, 1929 . . £20/£5
The Iron Grip, Readers Library, 1929 . . £20/£5
Killer Kay, Newnes, 1930 (wraps) £100
The Lady Called Nita, Newnes, 1930 (wraps) £150
Mrs William Jones and Bill, Newnes, 1930 (wraps) £75
The Guv'nor and Other Stories, Collins, 1932 £20/£5
ditto, as ***Mr. Reeder Returns***, Doubleday Doran (U.S.), 1932 . . . . £20/£5
Sergeant Sir Peter, Chapman and Hall, 1932 £30/£10
ditto, Doubleday Doran, 1933 . . . . . £25/£10
The Steward, Collins, 1932 . . . . . . £20/£5
Mr. J.G. Reeder Returns, Collins, 1934. . . £15/£5
The Last Adventure, Hutchinson, 1934 . . £35/£10
The Woman from the East and Other Stories, Hutchinson, 1934 . . . . £35/£10
The Undisclosed Client, Digit, 1963 (wraps) . £10

Verse

The Mission that Failed, T. Maskew Miller, 1898 (wraps) £350
War and Other Poems, Eastern Press, 1900 . £200
Writ in the Barracks, Methuen, 1900 . . . £250

Others

Unofficial Dispatches, Hutchinson, [1901] . . £40
Famous Scottish Regiments, Newnes, 1914 (wraps) £75
Field Marshal Sir John French and His Campaigns,

Newnes, 1914 (wraps) £75

Heroes All, Gallant Deeds of the War, Newnes, 1914 . . . . £30

The Standard History of the War, Newnes, [1914-15] (4 vols) £45

Kitchener's Army and the Territorial Forces: The Full Story of a Great Achievement, Newnes, 1915 (6 vols, wraps) £75

War of the Nations, Newnes, 1915-17 (12 vols, wraps) £75

People: A Short Autobiography, Hodder & Stoughton, 1926 . . . . £25/£10

ditto, Doubleday Doran (U.S.), 1929. . . . £25/£10

My Hollywood Diary, Hutchinson, [1932] . £20/£5

MINETTE WALTERS

A contemporary crime writer, Minette Walters owes much of her popularity to highly successful television adaptations of her books.

Novels

The Ice House, Macmillan, 1992 . . . . £600/£45

ditto, Macmillan, 1992 (variant jacket, two heads under the ice) . . . . £1,250/£45

ditto, St Martin's Press (U.S.), 1992 . . . £150/£20

The Sculptress, Macmillan, 1993 . . . £45/£10

ditto, St Martin's Press (U.S.), 1992 . . . £20/£5

The Scold's Bridle, Macmillan, 1994 . . £25/£5

ditto, Scorpion Press, 1994 (75 signed copies) . £100

ditto, Scorpion Press, 1994 (15 lettered copies). £250

ditto, St Martin's Press (U.S.), 1994 . . . £20/£5

The Dark Room, Macmillan, 1995 . . . £15/£5

ditto, Putnam's (U.S.), 1996 . . . . . . £15/£5

The Echo, Macmillan, 1997 . . . . . . £15/£5

ditto, Putnam's (U.S.), 1997 . . . . . . £10/£5

The Breaker, Macmillan, 1998 . . . . £15/£5

ditto, Putnam's (U.S.), 1999 . . . . . £10/£5

SYLVIA TOWNSEND WARNER
(b.1893 d.1978)

A talented novelist, poet and short story writer, Warner's concerns are often with the ordinary and overlooked members of society. By examining the detail of their lives she shows what extraordinary people they often are.

Verse

The Espalier, Chatto and Windus, 1925 . £100/£25

ditto, Dial Press (U.S.), 1925 . . . . . £100/£25

Time Importuned, Chatto and Windus, 1928 £100/£25

ditto, Viking Press (U.S.), 1928 . . . . £100/£25

Opus 7, Chatto and Windus, 1931 . . . £20/£10

ditto, Chatto and Windus, 1931 (110 signed, numbered copies) £85

ditto, Viking Press (U.S.), 1931 . . . . £25/£10

Rainbow, Borzoi (U.S.), 1932 (wraps, in envelope) . . . . £75/£65

Whether a Dove or Seagull, Viking Press (U.S.), 1933 . . . . £75/£20

ditto, Chatto and Windus, 1934, (with Valentine Ackland) . . . . £65/£20

Boxwood, Monotype Corporation, 1957 (500 copies, withdrawn) £100

ditto, Monotype Corporation, 1958 (500 copies). £75

ditto, Chatto and Windus, 1960 (enlarged edition) . . . . £35/£10

King Duffus, privately printed, 1968 (wraps) . £75

Twelve Poems, privately circulated booklet, 1977 (duplicated sheets, stapled) £80

ditto, Chatto and Windus, 1980 (reissue) . £10/£5

ditto, as ***Azrael***, Libanus Press, 1978, (200 copies, wraps) £65

Collected Poems, Carcanet Press/Viking Press (U.S.), 1982 . . . . £25/£10

Selected Poems, Carcanet Press, 1985 (wraps) £10

Novels

Lolly Willowes, Chatto and Windus, 1926 . £65/£15

ditto, Viking Press (U.S.), 1926 . . . . £65/£15

Mr Fortune's Maggot, Chatto and Windus, 1927 . . . . £50/£15

ditto, Viking Press (U.S.), 1927 . . . . £50/£15

The True Heart, Chatto and Windus, 1929 . £50/£15

ditto, Viking Press (U.S.), 1929 . . . . £50/£15

Summer Will Show, Chatto and Windus, 1936 £40/£10

ditto, Viking Press (U.S.), 1936 . . . . . £25/£10

After The Death of Don Juan, Chatto and Windus, 1938 . . . . £30/£10

ditto, Viking Press (U.S.), 1938 . . . . £25/£10

The Corner that Held Them, Chatto and Windus, 1948 . . . . £20/£10

ditto, Viking Press (U.S.), 1948 . . . . £20/£10

The Flint Anchor, Chatto and Windus, 1954 £30/£10

ditto, Viking Press (U.S.), 1954 . . . . £25/£10

Short Stories

The Maze, Fleuron, 1928 (signed, wraps) . . £75

Some World Far From Ours and 'Stay Corydon, Thou Swain', Mathews and Marrot, 1929 (531 numbered, signed copies) . . . . . £35/£20

Elinor Barley, Cresset Press, 1930 (350 numbered, signed copies on mould made paper, slipcase). . . . . £100/£125

ditto, Cresset Press, 1930 (30 numbered and signed

copies on hand made paper, extra set of engravings, slipcase) . . . . £400/£275
A Moral Ending, W Jackson, 1930 (550 numbered, signed copies) £45
The Salutation, Chatto and Windus, 1932 . £75/£35
ditto, Viking Press (U.S.), 1932 . . . . . £75/£35
More Joy in Heaven, Cresset Press, 1935 . £35/£10
The Cat's Cradle Book, Viking Press (U.S.), 1940 . . . . £40/£15
ditto, Chatto and Windus, 1960 . . . . . £25/£10
A Garland of Straw, Chatto and Windus, 1943 £30/£10
ditto, Viking Press, 1943 . . . . £25/£10
The Museum of Cheats, Chatto and Windus, 1947 . . . . £30/£10
ditto, Viking Press (U.S.), 1947 . . . . . £25/£10
Winter in The Air Chatto and Windus, 1955 £25/£10
ditto, Viking Press (U.S.), 1956 . . . . . £20/£5
A Spirit Rises, Chatto and Windus, 1962 . £25/£10
ditto, Viking Press (U.S.), 1962 . . . . . £20/£5
Sketches from Nature, privately printed, 1963 (wraps) £75
A Stranger with a Bag, Chatto and Windus, 1966 . . . . £25/£10
ditto, as ***Swans on an Autumn River***, Viking Press (U.S.), 1966 . . . . £20/£5
Two Conversation Pieces, privately printed, 1967 (wraps) £65
The Innocent and The Guilty, Chatto and Windus, 1971 . . . . £15/£5
ditto, Viking Press (U.S.), 1971 . . . . . £15/£5
Kingdoms of Elfin, Chatto and Windus, 1977 £15/£5
ditto, Viking Press (U.S.), 1977 . . . . . £15/£5
Scenes of Childhood, Chatto and Windus, 1981 £10/£5
ditto, Viking Press (U.S.), 1981 . . . . . £10/£5
One Thing Leading to Another, Chatto and Windus, 1984 . . . . £10/£5
ditto, Viking Press (U.S.), 1984 . . . . . £10/£5
Selected Stories, Chatto and Windus, 1989 . £15/£5
ditto, Viking Press (U.S.), 1989 . . . . . £15/£5

Translations
By Way of Saint-Beuve, by Marcel Proust, Chatto and Windus, 1958. . . . . £25/£10
A Place of Shipwreck, by Jean Rene Huquenin, Chatto and Windus, 1963 . . . . £25/£10

Other Works
Somerset, Paul Elek, 1949, (withdrawn). . £40/£20
Jane Austen, Longmans Green, 1941 (wraps) . £10
T.H. White, A Biography, Jonathan Cape, 1967 £15/£5
ditto, Viking Press (U.S.), 1968 . . . . . £10/£5
Letters, Chatto and Windus, 1982 . . . . £20/£10
The Diaries of Sylvia Townsend Warner, Chatto and Windus, 1994. . . . . £15/£5

EVELYN WAUGH

(b.1903 d.1966)

Waugh is best known for his humorous, satirical novels. He also wrote a number of travel books.

Verse
The World to Come: A Poem in Three Cantos, privately printed, 1916 . . . . £6,000

Novels
Decline and Fall, Chapman & Hall, 1928 £2,500/£250
ditto, Doubleday (U.S.), 1929 . . . . . £750/£75
ditto, Farrar (U.S.), 1929 . . . . £500/£50
ditto, Chapman & Hall, 1937 (12 copies) . . £2,000
Vile Bodies, Chapman & Hall, 1930 . . £,1,750/£200
ditto, Farrar (U.S.), 1930 . . . . £500/£50
ditto, Chapman & Hall, 1937 (12 copies) . . £2,000
Black Mischief, Chapman & Hall, 1932. . £500/£150
ditto, Chapman & Hall, 1932 (250 signed copies) . . . . £1,000/£650
ditto, Farrar (U.S.), 1932 . . . . £250/£50
ditto, Chapman & Hall, 1937 (12 copies) . . £2,000
A Handful of Dust, Chapman & Hall, 1934 . . . . £1,500/£150
ditto, Farrar (U.S.), 1934 . . . . £400/£75
ditto, Chapman & Hall, 1937 (12 copies) . . £2,000
Scoop, Chapman & Hall, 1938 . . . . £650/£75
ditto, Little, Brown (U.S.), 1938 . . . . £225/£45
Put Out More Flags, Chapman & Hall, 1942 £350/£45
ditto, Little, Brown (U.S.), 1942 . . . . £125/£30
Work Suspended, Chapman & Hall, 1942 (unfinished novel, 500 copies) . . . . £200/£65
Brideshead Revisited, privately printed for the author, 1945 [1944] (50 copies). £3,000
ditto, Chapman & Hall, 1945 . . . . . . £450/£45
ditto, Little, Brown (U.S.), 1945 . . . . £125/£25
ditto, Little, Brown (U.S.), 1945 (600 copies) . . . . £500/£150
Scott-King's Modern Europe, Chapman & Hall, 1947 . . . . £45/£15
ditto, Little, Brown (U.S.), 1949 . . . . £35/£10
The Loved One, Chapman & Hall, 1948 . £75/£25
ditto, Chapman & Hall, 1948 (250 signed, numbered copies, glassine d/w). . . . . . . £750/£650
ditto, Little, Brown (U.S.), 1948 . . . . £35/£10
Helena, Chapman & Hall, 1950 . . . . £35/£10
ditto, Chapman & Hall, 1950 (50 deluxe copies for presentation) £1,750
ditto, Little, Brown (U.S.), 1950 . . . . £25/£10
Men at Arms, Chapman & Hall, 1952 . . £50/£15
ditto, Little, Brown (U.S.), 1952 . . . . £35/£10
Love Among The Ruins, Chapman & Hall, 1953 . . . . £35/£10
ditto, Chapman & Hall, 1953 (350 signed copies,

glassine d/w) . . . . £350/£275
Officers and Gentlemen, Chapman & Hall, 1955 . . . . £50/£15
ditto, Little, Brown (U.S.), 1955 . . . . . £35/£10
The Ordeal of Gilbert Pinfold, Chapman & Hall, 1957 . . . . £35/£10
ditto, Chapman & Hall, 1957 (50 large copies for presentation) £1,500
ditto, Little, Brown (U.S.), 1957 . . . . . . £25/£10
Unconditional Surrender, Chapman & Hall, 1961 . . . . £35/£10
ditto, as ***The End of The Battle***, Little, Brown (U.S.), 1961 . . . . £15/£5
Basil Seal Rides Again, Chapman & Hall, 1963 (750 signed copies, glassine d/w) . . . . £400/£100
ditto, Chapman & Hall, 1963 . . . . . . £45/£15
ditto, Little, Brown (U.S.), 1963 . . . . . £45/£15
ditto, Little, Brown (U.S.), 1963 (1000 signed copies, glassine d/w) . . . . £250/£225

Short Stories
Mr Loveday's Little Outing, Chapman & Hall, 1936 . . . . £1,000/£100
ditto, Little, Brown (U.S.), 1936 . . . . . £450/£45
Charles Ryder's Schooldays and Other Stories, Little, Brown (U.S.), 1982 . . . . £15/£5

Essays
PRB: An Essay on The Pre-Raphaelite Brotherhood, privately printed, 1926 . . . . £3,000
The Holy Places, Queen Anne Press, 1952 (50 signed copies) . . . . £750/£650
ditto, Queen Anne Press, 1952 (900 copies) £750/£100

Travel
Labels, Duckworth, 1930 . . . . £250/£50
ditto, Duckworth, 1930 (110 signed copies, page of manuscript laid in) £1,250
ditto, as ***A Bachelor Abroad***, Farrar (U.S.), 1932 . . . . £125/£25
Remote People, Duckworth, 1931 . . . £250/£50
ditto, as ***They Were Still Dancing***, Farrar (U.S.), 1932 . . . . £125/£25
Ninety-Two Days, Duckworth, 1934. . . . £250/£50
ditto, Farrar (U.S.), 1934 . . . . £125/£25
Waugh in Abyssinia, Longman, 1936 . . . £250/£50
ditto, Farrar (U.S.), 1936 . . . . £125/£25
Robbery Under Law, Chapman & Hall, 1939 £250/£50
ditto, as ***Mexico: An Object Lesson***, Little, Brown (U.S.), 1939 . . . . £150/£35
When The Going Was Good, Duckworth, 1946 . . . . £150/£35
ditto, Little, Brown (U.S.), 1947 . . . . . £75/£20
A Tourist in Africa, Chapman & Hall, 1960 £45/£15
ditto, Little, Brown (U.S.), 1960 . . . . . £45/£15

Biography
Rosetti, Duckworth, 1928 . . . . . . £500/£100
ditto, Dodd (U.S.), 1928 . . . . £250/£65
Edmund Campion, Longman, 1935 . . . £250/£50
ditto, Longman, 1935 (50 signed copies) . . £750
ditto, Sheed (U.S.), 1935 . . . . £125/£35
Ronald Knox, Chapman & Hall, 1959 . . £25/£5
ditto, Little, Brown (U.S.), 1960 . . . . . £25/£5

Others
An Open Letter to his Eminence the Cardinal Archbishop of Westminster, privately printed, 1933 . . . . £2,000
Wine in Peace and War, Saccone & Speed, [1947] . . . . £100/£35
A Little Learning, Chapman & Hall, 1964 . £25/£5
ditto, Little, Brown (U.S.), 1964 . . . . . £15/£5
Diaries, Weidenfeld, 1976 . . . . £25/£5
ditto, Little, Brown (U.S.), 1976 . . . . . £15/£5
A Little Order, Methuen, 1977 . . . . . £20/£5
ditto, Little, Brown (U.S.), 1981 . . . . . £10/£5
The Letters of Evelyn Waugh, Weidenfeld, 1980 . . . . £10/£5
ditto, Ticknor & Fields (U.S.), 1980 . . . . £10/£5
The Essays, Articles and Reviews of Evelyn Waugh, Methuen, 1983 . . . . £10/£5
ditto, Little, Brown (U.S.), 1984 . . . . . £10/£5

MARY WEBB
(b.1881 d.1927)

Webb only found success as a novelist after being championed by Stanley Baldwin, then Prime Minister. Her books are Hardyesque, with nature powerfully and beautifully described, and peopled by characters who battle grimly against fate.

Novels
The Golden Arrow, Constable, 1916 . . . £125
ditto, Dutton (U.S.), 1918. . . . . £30
Gone to Earth, Constable, 1917 (dark red cloth) £100
ditto, Dutton (U.S.), 1917. . . . . £30
The House in Dormer Forest, Hutchinson, [1920] . . . . £125/£35
Seven For A Secret, Hutchinson, 1922 . . £125/£30
ditto, Doran (U.S.), 1923 . . . . £125/£30
Precious Bane, Cape, 1924 . . . . . . £200/£75
ditto, Modern Library (U.S.), 1926 . . . . £25/£10
Armour Wherein He Trusted, Cape, 1929 . £30/£15
ditto, Dutton (U.S.), 1929. . . . . £25/£10

Short Stories
The Chinese Lion, Rota, 1937 (350 copies, glassine

d/w and slipcase) . . . . £100/£75

Verse
Poems and The Spring of Joy, Cape, 1928 £35/£15
ditto, Dutton (U.S.), 1929 . . . . . . £25/£10
Fifty-One Poems, Cape, 1946 . . . . £20/£5
ditto, Dutton (U.S.), 1946 . . . . . . £20/£5

Others
Spring of Joy: A Little Book of Healing, J.M. Dent & Sons, 1917 . . . . £45
A Mary Webb Anthology, Cape, 1935 (illustrated by Rowland Hilder and Norman Hepple) . . £15/£5
The Essential Mary Webb, Cape, 1949 . . £15/£5

DENTON WELCH

(b.1915 d.1948)

Welch studied painting at Goldsmiths' School of Art, London, until a bicycle accident in 1935 severed his spine and left him temporarily paralysed and permanently ill. He took up writing as a career, producing three highly autobiographical books and numerous fragments.

Novels
Maiden Voyage, Routledge, 1943 . . . . £125/£30
ditto, Fischer (U.S.), 1944 . . . . . . £65/£20
In Youth is Pleasure, Routledge, 1944 [1945] £75/£25
ditto, Fischer (U.S.), 1946 . . . . . . £65/£20
A Voice Through a Cloud, John Lehmann, 1950 . . . . £50/£15

Short Stories/Miscellaneous
Brave and Cruel and Other Stories, Hamish Hamilton, 1948 [1949] . . . . £65/£15
A Last Sheaf, John Lehmann, 1951 . . . £45/£15
I Left My Grandfather's House, James Campbell, 1958 (150 copies) £75
ditto, The Lion and Unicorn Press, 1958 (200 copies) £75
Dumb Instrument, Enitharmon Press, 1976 (a selection of poems and fragments, 600 copies) £45
The Denton Welch Journals, Hamish Hamilton, 1952 (edited by Jocelyn Brooke) . . . . . £20/£5
The Journals of Denton Welch, Allison & Busby, 1984 (edited by Michael De-la-Noy) . . £15/£5
ditto, Dutton (U.S.), 1984 . . . . . . £15/£5
A Lunch Appointment, Elysium Press (U.S.), 1993 (150 copies, bound in black silk) £75
ditto, Elysium Press (U.S.), 1993 (20 copies, bound in black silk), signed by Edmund White, with an extra signed etching by Le-Tan) £250

FAY WELDON

(b.1931)

A novelist and writer for television drama, Weldon's popular success was *The Life and Loves of a She Devil*.

Novels
The Fat Woman's Joke, MacGibbon & Kee, 1967 . . . . £75/£25
ditto, as ***... and the Wife Ran Away***, McKay (U.S.), 1968 . . . . £50/£15
Down Among the Women, Heinemann, 1971 £25/£5
ditto, St. Martins Press (U.S.), 1972 . . . £15/£5
Female Friends, Heinemann, 1971 . . . £25/£5
ditto, St. Martins Press (U.S.), 1974 . . . £15/£5
Remember Me, Hodder & Stoughton, 1976 . £15/£5
ditto, Random House (U.S.), 1976 . . . £15/£5
Little Sisters, Hodder & Stoughton, 1977 . £15/£5
ditto, as ***Words of Advice***, Random House (U.S.), 1977 . . . . £15/£5
Praxis, Hodder & Stoughton, 1978 . . . £15/£5
ditto, Summit (U.S.), 1978 . . . . . £15/£5
Puffball, Hodder & Stoughton, 1980 . . £15/£5
ditto, Summit (U.S.), 1980 . . . . . £15/£5
The President's Child, Hodder & Stoughton, 1983 . . . . £15/£5
ditto, Doubleday (U.S.), 1983 . . . . £15/£5
The Life and Loves of a She Devil, Hodder & Stoughton, 1984 . . . . £15/£5
ditto, Pantheon (U.S.), 1984 . . . . . £10/£5
The Shrapnel Academy, Hodder & Stoughton, 1986 . . . . £10/£5
ditto, Viking (U.S.), 1987 . . . . . . £10/£5
The Heart of the Country, Century Hutchinson, 1987 . . . . £10/£5
ditto, Viking (U.S.), 1988 . . . . . . £10/£5
The Hearts and Lives of Men, Heinemann, 1987 . . . . £10/£5
ditto, Viking (U.S.), 1988 . . . . . . £10/£5
The Rules of Life, Century Hutchinson, 1987 £10/£5
ditto, Harper & Row (U.S.), 1987 . . . £10/£5
Leader of the Band, Hodder & Stoughton, 1988 £10/£5
ditto, Viking (U.S.), 1989 . . . . . . £10/£5
The Cloning of Joanna May, Collins, 1989 £10/£5
ditto, Viking (U.S.), 1989 . . . . . . £10/£5
Darcy's Utopia, Collins, 1990 . . . . £10/£5
ditto, Viking (U.S.), 1991 . . . . . . £10/£5
Life Force, Harper Collins, 1992 . . . . £10/£5
ditto, Viking (U.S.), 1992 . . . . . . £10/£5
Growing Rich, Harper Collins, 1992 . . £10/£5
Affliction, Harper Collins, 1993 . . . . £10/£5
ditto, as ***Trouble***, Viking (U.S.), 1993 . . £10/£5

Splitting, Harper Collins, 1995 . . . . £10/£5
ditto, Atlantic Monthly Press (U.S.), 1995 . £10/£5
Worst Fears, Harper Collins, 1996 . . . £10/£5
ditto, Atlantic Monthly Press (U.S.), 1996 . £10/£5
Big Girls Don't Cry, Harper Collins, 1997 . £10/£5
ditto, as ***Big Women***, Atlantic Monthly Press (U.S.), 1997 . . . . £10/£5

Short Stories
Watching Me Watching You, Hodder & Stoughton, 1981 . . . . £15/£5
ditto, Summit (U.S.), 1981 . . . . . £10/£5
Polaris, Hodder & Stoughton, 1985 . . . £10/£5
ditto, Penguin (U.S.), 1989 (wraps) . . . £10/£5
Moon Over Minneapolis, Collins, 1991 . . £10/£5
A Question of Timing, Colophon Press, 1992 (100 signed, numbered copies of 225, wraps) . . £20
Angel, All Innocence and Other Stories, Bloomsbury, 1995 . . . . £5
Wicked Women, Harper Collins, 1997 . . . £10/£5
ditto, Atlantic Monthly Press (U.S.), 1997 . £10/£5
A Hard Time To Be A Father, Harper Collins, 1998 . . . . £10/£5

Children's Books
Wolf The Mechanical Dog, Collins, 1988 . £15/£5
Party Puddle, Collins, 1989 . . . . . £15/£5
Nobody Likes Me, Bodley Head, 1997 . . £10/£5

Others
Letters to Alice, Michael Joseph/Rainbird Books, 1984 . . . . £15/£5
ditto, Taplinger (U.S.), 1985 . . . . . £15/£5
Rebecca West, Penguin, 1985 . . . . £10/£5
Sacred Cows, Chatto & Windus, 1989 (wraps) . £5

H.G. WELLS
(b.1886 d.1946)

A versatile novelist whose work ranges from innovative science fiction through to social realism, Wells was also the author of works on politics, society and history.

Novels
The Time Machine, Heinemann, 1895 (grey cloth) £500
ditto, Heinemann, 1895 (red cloth) £200
ditto, Heinemann, 1895 (wrappers) £1,000
ditto, Henry Holt (U.S.), 1895 ('H.S. Wells' on title page) £500
The Wonderful Visit, Dent, 1895 . . . . . £250
The Island of Doctor Moreau, Heinemann, 1896 (monogram blind-stamped on back board) . . £400
ditto, Heinemann, 1896 (no monogram) . . . £250
The Wheels of Chance, Dent, 1896 . . . . £150
The Red Room, Stone and Kimball (U.S.), 1896 (12 copies only) £10,000
The Invisible Man, Pearson, 1897 . . . . £450
The War of The Worlds, Heinemann, 1898 . . £500
When The Sleeper Wakes, Harpers, 1899 . . £150
ditto, Thomas Nelson, 1910 (revised edition) . £25
Love and Mr Lewisham, Harpers, 1900 . . . £100
The First Men in The Moon, Newnes, 1901 . £350
The Sea Lady: A Tissue of Moonshine, Methuen, 1902 . . . . £300
The Food of The Gods, Macmillan, 1904 . . £75
A Modern Utopia, Chapman & Hall, 1905 . . £75
Kipps, Macmillan, 1905 . . . . £75
In The Days of The Comet, Macmillan, 1906 . £75
The War in The Air, George Bell, 1908 . . . £150
Tono Bungay, Macmillan, 1909 . . . . . £75
Ann Veronica, T. Fisher Unwin, 1909 . . . £75
The History of Mr Polly, Thomas Nelson, 1910 £75
The New Machiavelli, John Lane the Bodley Head, 1911 . . . . £30
Marriage, Macmillan, 1912 . . . . £30
The Passionate Friends, Macmillan, 1913 . . £30
The World Set Free, Macmillan, 1914 . . . £30
The Wife of Sir Isaac Harman, Macmillan, 1914 £30
Boon, T. Fisher Unwin, 1915 . . . . . . £25
Bealby, Methuen, 1915 . . . . £20
The Research Magnificent, Macmillan, 1915 . £20
Mr Britling Sees It Through, Cassell, 1916 . . £20
The Soul of a Bishop, Cassell, 1917 . . . . £15
Joan and Peter, Cassell, 1918 . . . . . . £15
The Undying Fire, Cassell, 1919 . . . . £15
The Secret Places of The Heart, Cassell, 1922 £45/£15
Men Like Gods, Cassell, 1923 . . . . . £50/£20
The Dream, Jonathan Cape, 1924 . . . . £50/£20
Christina Alberta's Father, Jonathan Cape, 1925 . . . . £35/£15
The World of William Clissold, Ernest Benn, 1926 (3 vols) . . . . £95/£35
ditto, Ernest Benn, 1926 (218 deluxe signed copies, 3 vols) £250
The Short Stories of H.G. Wells, Ernest Benn, 1927 . . . . £45/£20
Meanwhile, Ernest Benn, 1927 . . . . £45/£15
Mr Blettsworthy on Rampole Island, Ernest Benn, 1928 . . . . £50/£20
The King Who Was a King, The book of a film, Ernest Benn, 1929 . . . . £45/£15
The Autocracy of Mr Parham, Heinemann, 1930 . . . . £50/£20
The Bulpington of Blup, Hutchinson, 1932 £40/£15
The Shape of Things to Come, The Ultimate Revolution, Hutchinson, 1933 . . . . . £75/£35

ditto, as ***Things to Come: A Film Story***, Cresset Press, 1935 . . . . £45/£15
The Croquet Player, Chatto & Windus, 1936 £50/£20
Man Who Could Work Miracles: A Film Story, Cresset Press, 1936 . . . . £45/£15
Star Begotten, Chatto & Windus, 1937 . . £50/£20
Brynhild, Methuen, 1937 . . . . . . £45/£15
The Camford Visitation, Methuen, 1937 . £45/£15
The Brothers, Chatto & Windus, 1938 . . £45/£15
Apropos of Dolores, Jonathan Cape, 1938 . £45/£15
The Holy Terror, Michael Joseph, 1939. . £45/£15
The Final Men, Phantagraph Press, 1940 (wraps) £50
Babes in The Darkling Wood, Secker & Warburg, 1940 . . . . £45/£15
All Aboard for Ararat, Secker & Warburg, 1940 . . . . £45/£13
You Can't Be Too Careful, Secker & Warburg, 1941 . . . . £40/£15

Omnibus Editions
Three Prophetic Novels of H.G. Wells, Dover, 1960 (wraps) £10

Short Stories
Select Conversations with an Uncle, Lane, 1895 £250
The Stolen Bacillus and Other Incidents, Methuen, 1895 . . . . £250
The Plattner Story and Others, Methuen, 1897 £175
Thirty Strange Stories, Edward Arnold (U.S.), 1897 . . . . £150
Tales of Space and Time, Harpers, 1899 . . £250
Twelve Stories and a Dream, Macmillan, 1903 £125
The Country of The Blind, and Other Stories, Nelson, 1911 . . . . £50
ditto, Golden Cockerel Press, 1939, (signed, limited edition) £450
The Door in The Wall and Other Stories, Mitchell Kennerley, 1911 (limited edition, handmade paper) £200
ditto, Mitchell Kennerley, 1915 (60 signed copies) £350

Children's
Floor Games, Palmer, 1911 . . . . £75
Little Wars, Palmer, 1913. . . . . £45
The Adventures of Tommy, Harrap, 1929 . £65/£25

Others
Text-Book of Biology, W.B. Clive, 1893 (2 vols, with 47 two-page plates) £350
ditto, W.B. Clive, 1894 (revised edition of Part 1) £25
ditto, as ***Text-Book of Zoology***, W.B. Clive, 1898 (revised edition) £25

MARY WESLEY
(b.1912)

Mary Wesley had her first novel published at the age of 70, and continues to write, living rather a hermit-like existence in Devon.

Novels
The Sixth Seal, Macdonald, 1969 . . . . £45/£10
ditto, Stein & Day (U.S.), 1971 . . . . . £15/£5
Jumping The Queue, Macmillan, 1983 . . £35/£10
ditto, Penguin (U.S.), 1988 . . . . . . £10/£5
Haphazard House, Dent, 1983 . . . . . £15/£5
The Camomile Lawn, Macmillan, 1984. . £30/£10
ditto, Summit (U.S.), 1985 . . . . . . £10/£5
Harnessing Peacocks, Macmillan, 1985 . £15/£5
ditto, Scribner (U.S.), 1986 . . . . . . £10/£5
The Vacillations of Poppy Carew, Macmillan, 1986 . . . . £15/£5
ditto, Penguin (U.S.), 1988 . . . . . . £10/£5
Not That Sort of Girl, Macmillan, 1987. . £15/£5
ditto, Viking (U.S.), 1988. . . . . . . £10/£5
Second Fiddle, Macmillan, 1988. . . . £15/£5
ditto, Viking (U.S.), 1989. . . . . . . £10/£5
A Sensible Life, Bantam, 1990 . . . . . £10/£5
ditto, Viking (U.S.), 1990. . . . . . . £10/£5
A Dubious Legacy, Bantam, 1992 . . . . £10/£5
ditto, Viking (U.S.), 1992. . . . . . . £10/£5
An Imaginative Experience, Bantam, 1994 £10/£5
ditto, Viking (U.S.), 1995. . . . . . . £10/£5
Part of the Furniture, Bantam, 1997 . . £10/£5
ditto, Viking (U.S.), 1997. . . . . . . £10/£5

Collected Edition
The Mary Wesley Omnibus, Macmillan, 1992 £10/£5

REBECCA WEST
(b.1892 d.1983)

Throughout her many and diverse writings, West was preoccupied with the idea of original sin. She was made a Dame in 1959.

Novels
The Return of the Soldier, Century Publishing (U.S.), 1918 . . . . £50
ditto, Nisbet, 1918. . . . . £45
The Judge, Hutchinson, 1922 . . . . £100/£25
ditto, Doran (U.S.), 1922 . . . . £50/£10
Harriet Hume, A London Fantasy, Hutchinson, 1929. . . . . £100/£20
ditto, Doran (U.S.), 1929 . . . . . . £50/£10
War Nurse, Cosmopolitan Book Co (U.S.), 1930

(anonymous) . . . . £45/£10
The Harsh Voice, Cape, 1935 . . . . £20/£5
ditto, Doubleday (U.S.), 1935 . . . . £15/£5
The Thinking Reed, Viking Press (U.S.), 1936 £25/£5
ditto, Hutchinson, [1936] . . . . . . £25/£5
The Fountain Overflows, Viking (U.S.), 1956 £15/£5
ditto, Macmillan, 1957 . . . . £15/£5
The Birds Fall Down, Macmillan, 1966. . £10/£5
ditto, Viking (U.S.), 1966 . . . . £15/£5
This Real Night, Macmillan, 1984 . . . £15/£5
ditto, Viking (U.S.), 1985. . . . . . . £10/£5
Cousin Rosamund, Macmillan, 1985 . . £10/£5
ditto, Viking (U.S.), 1986 . . . . £10/£5
Sunflower, Virago, 1986 . . . . . . £10/£5
ditto, Viking (U.S.), 1987. . . . . . . £10/£5

Others
Henry James, Nisbet, 1916 . . . . £45
ditto, Holt (U.S.), 1916 . . . . £25
The Strange Necessity, Cape, 1928 . . . . £35/£10
ditto, Doran (U.S.), 1928 . . . . £25/£10
Lions and Lambs, Cape, 1928 . . . . £40/£15
D.H. Lawrence, Secker, 1930 . . . . £35/£15

ditto as ***Elegy***, Phoenix (U.S.), 1930 (250 signed copies, glassine d/w) . . . . £65/£50
Ending in Earnest: A Literary Log, Doubleday Doran (U.S.), 1931 . . . . £20
Arnold Bennett Himself, John Day (U.S.), 1931 (wraps) £15
St Augustine, Appleton (U.S.), 1933 . . . £35/£10
ditto, Davies, 1933. . . . . £35/£10
A Letter to Grandfather, Hogarth Press, 1933 (wraps). £25
The Modern "Rake's Progress", Hutchinson, 1934 . . . . £20
ditto, Hutchinson, 1934 (250 signed copies). . £45
Black Lamb and Grey Falcon, Viking Press (U.S.), 1941 (2 vols) . . . . £75/£35
ditto, Macmillan, 1942 (2 vols) . . . . £75/£5
The Meaning of Treason, Viking Press (U.S.), 1947 . . . . £15/£5
ditto, Macmillan, 1949 . . . . £15/£5
A Train of Powder, Macmillan, 1955 . . . £15/£5
ditto, Viking (U.S.), 1955. . . . . . . £15/£5
The Court and the Castle, Yale University Press (U.S.), 1957 . . . . £15/£5
ditto, Macmillan, 1958 . . . . £15/£5
The Vassal Affair, Sunday Telegraph, 1963 (wraps) £10
McLuhan and the Future of Literature, The English Association, 1969 (wraps) £25
Rebecca West, A Celebration, Macmillan, 1977 £10/£5
ditto, Viking (U.S.), 1977. . . . . . . £10/£5
1900, Weidenfeld & Nicolson, 1982. . . . £10/£5

ditto, Viking (U.S.), 1982. . . . . . £10/£5
The Young Rebecca, Virago, 1982 . . . £10/£5
ditto, Viking (U.S.), 1982. . . . . . . £10/£5
Family Memories, Virago, 1987. . . . £10/£5
ditto, Viking (U.S.), 1988. . . . . . . £10/£5
The Only Poet and Short Stories, Virago, 1992 £10/£5

EDITH WHARTON
(b.1862 d.1937)

An American novelist and short story writer, with *The Age of Innocence* she became the first woman to be awarded the Pulitzer Prize.

Novels and Novellas
The Touchstone, Scribner's (U.S.), 1900 . . £150
ditto, as ***A Gift from The Grave***, John Murray, 1900 . . . . £150
The Valley of Decision, Scribner's (U.S.), 1902 (2 vols) £150
ditto, John Murray, 1902 . . . . £75
Sanctuary, Scribner's (U.S.), 1903 . . . . £125
ditto, Macmillan, 1903 . . . . £75
The House of Mirth, Scribner's (U.S.), 1905 . £75
ditto, Macmillan, 1905 . . . . £65
Madam de Treymes, Scribner's (U.S.), 1907 . £45
ditto, Macmillan, 1907 . . . . £45
The Fruit of The Tree, Scribner's (U.S.), 1907. £45
ditto, Macmillan, 1907 . . . . £45
Ethan Frome, Scribner's (U.S.), 1911 (first issue: top edge gilt) £250
ditto, Macmillan, 1911 . . . . £100
ditto, Scribner's (U.S.), 1922 (2,000 copies, new introduction, slipcase) . . . . £65/£50
ditto, Limited Editions Club (U.S.), 1939 (1,500 signed copies, slipcase) . . . . £45/£40
The Reef, D. Appleton & Co. (U.S.), 1912 . . £40
ditto, Macmillan, 1912 . . . . £35
The Custom of The Country, Scribner's (U.S.), 1913 . . . . £40
ditto, Macmillan, 1913 . . . . £35
Summer, Appleton & Co. (U.S.), 1917 . . . £45
ditto, Macmillan, 1917 . . . . £35
The Marine: A Tale of The War, Appleton & Co. (U.S.), 1918 . . . . £35
ditto, Macmillan, 1918 . . . . £25
The Age of Innocence, Appleton & Co., 1920 (first issue: 'burial', p.186, no mention of Pulitzer Prize on d/w) . . . . £3,000/£250
The Glimpses of The Moon, Appleton & Co., 1922 . . . . £175/£35
ditto, Chapman and Hall, 1922 . . . . . £75/£15
A Son at The Front, Scribners (U.S.), 1923. £175/£35

ditto, Macmillan, 1923 . . . . £150/£25
Old New York, Appleton & Co., 1924 (4 vols) . . . . £450/£100
The Mother's Recompense, Appleton & Co., 1925 . . . . £150/£20
Twilight Sleep, Appleton & Co., 1927 . . . £125/£15
The Children, Appleton & Co., 1928 . . . £125/£15
Hudson River Bracketed, Appleton & Co., 1929 . . . . £125/£15
The Gods Arrive, Appleton & Co., 1932 . £125/£15
The Buccaneers, Appleton & Co., 1938. . £125/£15

Short Stories
The Greater Inclination, Scribners (U.S.), 1899 (first issue: 'Wharton' only on spine) £250
ditto, John Lane, 1899. . . . . £125
Crucial Instances, Scribner's (U.S.), 1901 . . £125
ditto, John Murray, 1901 . . . . £75
The Descent of Man and Other Stories, Scribner's (U.S.), 1904 . . . . £100
ditto, Macmillan, 1904 . . . . £75
The Hermit and The Wild Woman, and Other Stories, Scribners (U.S.), 1908 . . . . £100
ditto, Macmillan, 1908 . . . . £75
Les Metteurs en Scene, (Paris), 1909 (in French) £50
Tales of Men and Ghosts, Scribners (U.S.), 1910 £100
ditto, Macmillan, 1910 . . . . £75
Xingu and Other Stories, Scribner's (U.S.), 1916 £35
ditto, Macmillan, 1916 . . . . £35
Here and Beyond, Appleton & Co., 1926 . £125/£25
Certain People, Appleton & Co., 1930 . . £125/£25
Human Nature, Appleton & Co., 1933 . . £125/£25
The World Over, Appleton & Co., 1936. . £125/£25
Ghosts, Appleton & Co., 1937 . . . . . £125/£25
The Collected Short Stories of Edith Wharton, Scribner's (U.S.), 1968 . . . . £45/£15
Quartet: Four Stories, Allen Press (U.S.), 1975 (140 copies) £300
The Ghost Stories of Edith Wharton, Constable, 1975 . . . . £25/£10
The Stories of Edith Wharton, Simon & Schuster, 1988 & 1989 (2 vols) . . . . £30/£10

Verse
Verses, privately printed (U.S.), 1908 (wraps; pseud. 'Edith Newbold Jones') £20,000
Artemis to Actaeon and Other Verses, Scribner's (U.S.), 1909 . . . . £125
ditto, Macmillan, 1909 . . . . £75
Twelve Poems, The Medici Society, 1926 (130 signed copies) . . . . £2,000/£1,000

Others
The Decoration of Houses, Scribner's (U.S.), 1897 (with Ogden Codman Jr.) £700
Italian Villas and Their Gardens, Century (U.S.), 1904 . . . . £500
ditto, John Lane, 1904. . . . . £400
Italian Backgrounds, Scribner's (U.S.), 1905 . £100
ditto, Macmillan, 1905 . . . . £75
A Motor-Flight through France, Scribner's (U.S.), 1908 . . . . £75
ditto, Macmillan, 1908 . . . . £65
Fighting France: From Dunkerque to Belfort, Scribner's (U.S.), 1915 . . . . £65
ditto, Macmillan, 1915 . . . . £45
French Ways and Their Meaning, Appleton & Co. (U.S.), 1919 . . . . £65
ditto, Macmillan, 1919 . . . . £45
In Morocco, Scribner's (U.S.), 1920 . . . £125/£35
ditto, Macmillan, 1920 . . . . £125/£30
The Writing of Fiction, Scribner's, 1925 . £125/£20
A Backward Glance, Appleton-Century, 1934 . . . . £125/£20
An Edith Wharton Treasury, Appleton-Century-Crofts (U.S.), [1950]. . . . . £25/£10
The Letters of Edith Wharton, Simon & Schuster, 1988 . . . . £20/£5

DENNIS WHEATLEY
(b.1897 d.1977)

Wheatley's headstone describes him as the 'Prince of Thriller Writers', and with worldwide sales of more than 45 million copies few would argue with the claim. Best known for his black magic books, he also wrote historical and adventure novels.

Duke de Richleau Titles
The Forbidden Territory, Hutchinson, [1933] £30/310
The Devil Rides Out, Hutchinson, [1935] £30/£10
The Golden Spaniard, Hutchinson, [1938] £20/£5
Three Inquisitive People, Hutchinson, [1940] £20/£5
Strange Conflict, Hutchinson, [1941] . . . £20/£5
Codeword - Golden Fleece, Hutchinson, [1946] £15/£5
The Second Seal, Hutchinson, 1950 . . . . £10/£5
The Prisoner in The Mask, Hutchinson, 1957 £10/£5
Vendetta in Spain, Hutchinson, 1961 . . . £10/£5
Dangerous Inheritance, Hutchinson, 1965 £10/£5
Gateway to Hell, Hutchinson, 1970 . . . £10/£5

Gregory Sallust Titles
Black August, Hutchinson, [1934] . . . . £15/£5
Contraband, Hutchinson, [1936]. . . . . £15/£5
The Scarlet Impostor, Hutchinson, [1940] £10/£5
The Black Baroness, Hutchinson, [1940] £10/£5
'V' for Vengeance, Hutchinson, [1942] . . £10/£5
Come into my Parlour, Hutchinson, [1946] £10/£5

Faked Passport, Hutchinson, [1949]. . . £10/£5
The Island Where Time Stands Still, Hutchinson, 1954 . . . . £10/£5
Traitor's Gate, Hutchinson, 1958 . . £10/£5
The Used Dark Forces, Hutchinson, 1964 £10/£5
The White Witch of The South Seas, Hutchinson, 1968 . . . . £10/£5

Julian Day Titles
The Quest of Julian Day, Hutchinson, [1939] £15/£5
The Sword of Fate, Hutchinson, [1941] . . £10/£5
The Bill for The Use of a Body, Hutchinson, 1964 . . . . £10/£5

Roger Brook Titles
The Launching of Roger Brook, Hutchinson, [1947] . . . . £15/£5
The Shadow of Tyburn Tree, Hutchinson, [1948] . . . . £15/£5
The Rising Storm, Hutchinson, [1949] . . £15/£5
The Man Who Killed The King, Hutchinson, 1951 . . . . £10/£5
The Dark Secret of Josephine, Hutchinson, 1955 . . . . £10/£5
The Rape of Venice, Hutchinson, 1959 . . £10/£5
The Sultan's Daughter, Hutchinson, 1963 . £10/£5
The Wanton Princess, Hutchinson, 1966 . £10/£5
Evil in a Mask, Hutchinson, 1969 . . . £10/£5
The Ravishing of Lady Mary Ware, Hutchinson, 1971 . . . . £10/£5
Desperate Measures, Hutchinson, 1974 . . £10/£5

Other Titles
Such Power is Dangerous, Hutchinson, [1933] £15/£5
The Fabulous Valley, Hutchinson, [1934] . £15/£5
The Eunuch of Stamboul, Hutchinson, [1935] £15/£5
They Found Atlantis, Hutchinson, [1936] . £15/£5
The Secret War, Hutchinson, [1937] . . £15/£5
Uncharted Seas, Hutchinson, [1938] . . £15/£5
Sixty Days to Live, Hutchinson, [1939] . . £15/£5
The Man Who Missed The War, Hutchinson, [1945] . . . . £15/£5
The Haunting of Toby Jug, Hutchinson, [1948] £15/£5
Star of Ill-Omen, Hutchinson, 1952 . . . £10/£5
To The Devil - A Daughter, Hutchinson, 1953 £10/£5
Curtain of Fear, Hutchinson, 1953 . . . £10/£5
The Ka of Gifford Hillary, Hutchinson, 1956 £10/£5
The Satanist, Hutchinson, 1960 . . . . £10/£5
Mayhem in Greece, Hutchinson, 1962 . . £10/£5
Unholy Crusade, Hutchinson, 1967 . . . £10/£5
The Strange Story of Linda Lee, Hutchinson, 1972 . . . . £10/£5
The Irish Witch, Hutchinson, 1973 . . . £10/£5
The Deception Planners: My Secret War, Hutchinson, 1980 . . . . £10/£5

Short Stories
Mediterranean Nights, Hutchinson, [1942] £10/£5
Gunmen, Gallants and Ghosts, Hutchinson, [1943] . . . . £15/£5

Non Fiction
Old Rowley: A Private Life of Charles II, Hutchinson, 1933 . . . . £20/£5
Red Eagle: A Life of Marshal Voroshilov, Hutchinson, 1937 . . . . £15/£5
Total War, Hutchinson, [1941] . . . . . £20/£5
The Seven Ages of Justerini's, Riddle Books, 1949 . . . . £10/£5
ditto, as ***1749-1965: The Eight Ages of Justerini's'***, Dolphin, 1965 . . . . £10/£5
Of Vice and Virtue, privately printed, 1950 . . £75
Stranger than Fiction, Hutchinson, 1959 . £10/£5
Saturdays with Bricks and Other Days Under Shell-Fire, Hutchinson, 1961 . . . . . £10/£5
The Devil and All His Works, Hutchinson, 1971 . . . . £15/£5

Autobiography
The Young Man Said: 1897-1914, Hutchinson, 1977 . . . . £20/£5
Officer and Temporary Gentleman: 1914-1919, Hutchinson, 1978 . . . . £20/£5
Drink and Ink: 1919-1977, Hutchinson, 1979 £20/£5
The Time Has Come, Arrow, 1981 (wraps). . . £5

Crime Dossiers
Murder Off Miami, Hutchinson, [1936] (with J. G. Links). £35
ditto, as ***File on Bolitho Lane***, Morrow (U.S.), 1936 . . . . £35
Who Killed Robert Prentice?, Hutchinson, [1937] (with J. G. Links). £35
ditto, as ***File on Robert Prentice***, Greenburg (U.S.), 1937 . . . . £35
The Malinsay Massacre, Hutchinson, [1938] (with J. G. Links) £35
Herewith The Clues!, Hutchinson, [1939] (with J. G. Links) £35

PATRICK WHITE
(b.1912 d.1990)

An Australian novelist, short story writer and dramatist, White won the Nobel Prize for Literature in 1973.

Novels
Happy Valley, Harrap, 1939 . . . . £2,000/£200

ditto, Viking (U.S.), 1940 . . . . . £1,750/£200
The Living and the Dead, Viking (U.S.), 1941 . . . . £600/£100
ditto, Routledge, 1941 . . . . £600/£100
The Aunt's Story, Routledge, 1948 . . . £500/£75
ditto, Viking (U.S.), 1948 . . . . . . £250/£45
The Tree of Man, Viking (U.S.), 1955 . . £75/£20
ditto, Eyre & Spottiswoode, 1956 . . . £25/£5
Voss, Viking (U.S.), 1957 . . . . . . £40/£10
ditto, Eyre & Spottiswoode, 1957 . . . £40/£10
Riders in the Chariot, Viking (U.S.), 1961 . £35/£10
ditto, Eyre & Spottiswoode, 1961 . . . £35/£10
The Solid Mandala, Eyre & Spottiswoode, 1966 . . . . £25/£10
ditto, Viking (U.S.), 1966 . . . . . . £25/£10
The Vivesector, Cape, 1970 . . . . . £20/£5
ditto, Viking (U.S.), 1970 . . . . . . £20/£5
The Eye of the Storm, Cape, 1973 . . . . £20/£5
ditto, Viking (U.S.), 1974 . . . . . . £20/£5
A Fringe of Leaves, Cape, 1976 . . . . £20/£5
ditto, Viking (U.S.), 1976 . . . . . . £20/£5
The Twyborn Affair, Cape, 1979 . . . £20/£5
ditto, Viking (U.S.), 1980 . . . . . . £20/£5
Memoirs of Many in One, Cape, 1986 . . £15/£5
ditto, Viking (U.S.), 1986 . . . . . . £15/£5

Short Stories
The Burnt Ones, Eyre & Spottiswoode, 1964 £35/£10
ditto, Viking (U.S.), 1964 . . . . . . £20/£5
The Cockatoos, Cape, 1974 . . . . . £20/£5
ditto, Viking (U.S.), 1975 . . . . . . £20/£5
Three Uneasy Pieces, Pascoe (Australia), 1987 (wraps) £10
ditto, Penguin (U.S.), 1988 . . . . . £15/£5
ditto, Viking (U.S.), 1988 . . . . . . £15/£5

Verse
Thirteen Poems, privately printed, 1930 . . £2,000
The Ploughman and Other Poems, Beacon Press (Australia), 1935 (200 copies) . . . £2,500/£500

Plays
Four Plays, Eyre & Spottiswoode, 1965 . £75/£15
ditto, Viking (U.S.), 1966 . . . . . . £65/£15
The Night of the Prowler, Penguin/Cape, 1978 (wraps) £10
Big Toys, Currency Press (Australia), 1978 (wraps) £10
Netherwood, Currency Press (Australia), 1983 (wraps) £10
Signal Driver, Currency Press (Australia), 1983 (wraps) £10

Others
Flaws in the Glass, Cape, 1981 . . . . £15/£5
ditto, Viking (U.S.), 1982 . . . . . . £10/£5

Patrick White Speaks, Primavera Press (Australia), 1989 . . . . £15/£5
ditto, Cape, 1990 . . . . £15/£5

T.H. WHITE
(b.1906 d.1964)

A novelist and children's writer, White's major success was the re-telling of the Arthurian legends in a series of novels which began with *The Sword in the Stone.*

Novels
Dead Mr Nixon, Cassell, 1931 (with R. McNair Scott) . . . . £300/£65
Darkness at Pemberley, Gollancz, 1932 . £250/£65
ditto, Century (U.S.), 1933 . . . . . . £125/£25
They Winter Abroad, Gollancz, 1932 (pseud. 'James Aston') . . . . £225/£45
ditto, Viking (U.S.), 1932 . . . . . . £200/£35
First Lesson, Gollancz, 1932 (pseud. 'James Aston') . . . . £225/£45
ditto, Knopf (U.S.), 1933 . . . . . . £200/£35
Farewell Victoria, Collins, 1933 . . . . £200/£35
ditto, Smith & Haas (U.S.), 1934 . . . . £100/£20
Earth Stopped, Or Mr Marx's Sporting Tour, Collins, 1934 . . . . £150/£25
ditto, Putnam (U.S.), 1935 . . . . . £75/£20
Gone to Ground, Collins, 1935 . . . . £150/£25
ditto, Putnam (U.S.), 1935 . . . . . £125/£20

Children's
The Sword in The Stone, Collins, 1938 . . £400/£50
ditto, Putnam (U.S.), 1939 . . . . . £125/£25
The Witch in The Wood, Putnam (U.S.), 1939 . . . . £125/£25
ditto, Collins, 1940 . . . . £400/£50
The Ill-Made Knight, Putnam (U.S.), 1940 . £125/£25
ditto, Collins, 1941 . . . . £400/£50
Mistress Masham's Repose, Putnam (U.S.), 1946 . . . . £30/£10
ditto, Cape, 1947 . . . . £25/£10
The Elephant and The Kangaroo, Putnam (U.S.), 1947 . . . . £25/£10
ditto, Cape, 1948 . . . . £20/£5
The Master, An Adventure Story, Cape, 1957 £25/£10
ditto, Putnam (U.S.), 1957 . . . . . £20/£5
The Once and Future King, Collins, 1958 £150/£35
ditto, Putnam (U.S.), 1958 . . . . . £100/£20
The Book of Merlyn, University of Texas Press (U.S.), 1977 . . . . £15/£5
The Maharajah and Other Stories, Putnam (U.S.), 1981 . . . . £15/£5
ditto, MacDonald, 1981 . . . . £15/£5

Verse

Cambridge Poetry, No. 8, Hogarth Living Poets, Hogarth Press, 1929 . . . . £250

Loved Helen and Other Poems, Chatto & Windus, 1929 . . . . £250/£75

ditto, Viking (U.S.), 1929 . . . . £200/£50

The Green Bay Tree, or The Wicked Man Touches Wood, Songs for Sixpence, No. 3, Heffer, 1929 (wraps) £250

Verses, Shenval Press, 1962 (100 numbered copies) £750

A Joy Proposed, Bertram Rota, 1980 (500 numbered copies) . . . . £25/£10

ditto, University of Georgia Press (U.S.), 1983 £15/£5

Non Fiction

England Have My Bones, Collins, 1936 . £125/£25

ditto, Macmillan (U.S.), 1936. . . . . £45/£15

Burke's Steerage, Or The Amateur Gentleman's Introduction to Noble Sports and Pastimes, Collins, 1938 . . . . £100/£20

ditto, Putnam (U.S.), 1939 . . . . . £75/£15

The Age of Scandal, Cape, 1950. . . . £25/£10

ditto, Putnam (U.S.), 1950 . . . . . £25/£10

The Goshawk, Cape, 1951 . . . . . . £65/£15

ditto, Putnam (U.S.), 1952 . . . . . . £45/£10

The Scandalmonger, Cape, 1952 . . . . £25/£10

ditto, Putnam (U.S.), 1952 . . . . . £15/£5

The Godstone and The Blackymor, Cape, 1959 . . . . £25/£10

ditto, Putnam (U.S.), 1959 . . . . . . £15/£5

America At Last, The American Journal of T.H. White, Putnam (U.S.), 1965. . . . . £10/£5

The White/Garnett Letters, Cape, 1968 . . £15/£5

ditto, Viking (U.S.), 1968. . . . . . . £10/£5

Letters to a Friend, The Correspondence Between T.H. White and L.J. Potts, Putnam (U.S.), 1982 . . . . £10/£5

ditto, Alan Sutton, 1984 (enlarged edition) . £10/£5

OSCAR WILDE

(b.1854 d.1900)

Known principally a playwright, Wilde was also a fine essayist, poet and novelist. Even today his public persona often overshadows his considerable literary achievements.

Verse

Ravenna, Thomas Shrimpton, 1878 (wraps) £1,000

Poems, David Bogue, 1881 (750 copies printed and issued as 3 editions) £750

ditto, Mathews and Lane, 1892 (220 signed copies) £2,750

The Sphinx, Mathews & Lane, 1894 (200 copies) £4,000

ditto, Mathews & Lane, 1894 (25 large paper copies) £5,000

ditto, John Lane, The Bodley Head, 1910 (cheap edition) £25

The Ballad of Reading Gaol, Leonard Smithers, 1898. . . . . £250

ditto, Leonard Smithers, 1898 (30 numbered copies) £1,750

ditto, Leonard Smithers, 1898 (third edition, 99 signed copies) £2,000

Short Stories

The Happy Prince and Other Tales, David Nutt, 1888 . . . . £750

ditto, David Nutt, 1888 (75 signed copies, large hand made paper edition) £3,000

ditto, Duckworth, 1913 (illustrated by Charles Robinson). £75

ditto, Duckworth, 1913 (250 copies signed by artist, in slipcase) . . . . £500/£400

Lord Arthur Saville's Crime and Other Stories, Osgood, McIlvaine & Co., 1891 . . . . £200

A House of Pomegranates, Osgood, McIlvaine & Co., 1891 . . . . £750

Plays

Vera, or The Nihilists Ranken & Co., 1880 (grey wraps). £12,500

ditto, privately printed (U.S.), 1882 (wraps). £10,000

The Duchess of Padua, privately printed (U.S.), 1883 (20 copies printed as manuscript) . . . £10,000

ditto, Methuen, 1907 . . . . £500

Salome, Drama en un Acte, Librairie de L'art Independant/ Elkin Mathews et John Lane, 1893 £450

ditto, Librairie de L'art Independant/ Elkin Mathews et John Lane, 1893 (50 tall copies on hand made paper). £1,500

Lady Windermere's Fan, Elkin Mathews and John Lane, 1893 . . . . £750

ditto, Elkin Mathews and John Lane, 1893 (50 deluxe copies on hand made paper) £1,500

Salome, Elkin Mathews and John Lane, 1894 (875 copies, illustrated by Beardsley) £750

ditto, Elkin Mathews and John Lane, 1893 (100 large paper copies) £2,500

A Woman of No Importance, John Lane, 1894 £750

ditto, John Lane, 1894 (50 deluxe copies on hand made paper) £1,500

The Importance of Being Earnest, Smithers, 1899 . . . . £750

ditto, Smithers, 1899 (12 copies on Japanese vellum) £5,000

ditto, Smithers, 1899 (100 signed, deluxe copies) £2,500
ditto, [Methuen], 1910 (1200 copies) . . . £75
An Ideal Husband, Smithers, 1899 . . . . £250
ditto, Smithers, 1899 (12 copies on Japanese vellum) £5,000
ditto, Smithers, 1899 (100 signed, deluxe copies) £2,500

Novel
The Picture of Dorian Gray, Ward, Lock, 1891 . . . . £1,000
ditto, Ward, Lock, 1891 (250 signed, numbered, large paper copies) £2,500

Essays
Intentions, Osgood, McIlvaine & Co., 1891 . £200
The Soul of Man Under Socialism, Humphreys, 1895 (50 copies, brown paper wraps) £450
ditto, Humphreys, 1907 (with bookmark) . . . £35
The Portrait of Mr W.H., Smithers, 1904 (200 copies) £250
Essays, Criticisms and Reviews, Wright & Jones, 1901 . . . . £75
De Profundis, Methuen, [1905] £50
ditto, Methuen, [1905] (200 copies on hand-made paper) £250
ditto, Methuen, [1905] (50 copies on Japanese vellum) £1,500
The Suppressed Portions of De Profundis, Paul Reynolds (U.S.), 1913 (15 copies) . . . £1,500

Others
Phrases and Philosophies for The Use of The Young, privately printed, A. Cooper, 1894 (wraps) . £250
Children in Prison and Other Cruelties of Prison Life, Murdoch & Co., [1898] (wraps) £750
Poems in Prose, Carrington, 1905 (50 copies on Imperial Japanese vellum) £250
ditto, Carrington, 1905 (50 copies on Japanese vellum) £250
Wilde and Whistler: An Acrimonious Correspondence in Art, Smithers, 1906 (400 copies, wraps) . £200
After Berneval, Letters of Oscar Wilde to Robert Ross, Beaumont Press, 1922 (limited edition) . . £200
Some Letters from Oscar Wilde to Alfred Douglas, 1892-1897, privately printed (U.S.), 1924 (225 copies, slipcase) . . . . £250/£200
The Letters of Oscar Wilde, Hart-Davis, 1962 £75/£30

Selected Work
Oscariana, privately printed by Humphreys, 1895 (50 copies in buff paper wraps) £200
ditto, Humphreys, 1910 (200 copies in Japanese vellum wrappers) £250
ditto, Humphreys, 1910 (50 copies on Japanese vellum) £300
Sebastian Melmoth, Humphries, 1904 . . . £50

CHARLES WILLIAMS

(b.1886 d.1945)

The author of many books on theological subjects, Williams also wrote a number of supernatural thrillers dealing with the conflict between good and evil.

Verse
The Silver Stair, Herbert & Daniel, [1912] . . £250
Poems of Conformity, Humphrey Milford, 1917 £100
Divorce, Humphrey Milford, 1920 . . . £200/£50
Windows of Night, Humphrey Milford, 1925 £175/£45
Heroes and Kings, Sylvan Press, 1930 (300 copies) £200
Taliessin Through Logres, O.U.P., 1938 . £30/£10
The Region of The Summer Stars, Editions Poetry, 1944 . . . . £40/£15

Novels
War in Heaven, Gollancz, 1930 . . . . £125/£35
ditto, Pellegrini & Cudahy (U.S.), 1949 . . £60/£15
Many Dimensions, Gollancz, 1931 . . . £125/£35
ditto, Pellegrini & Cudahy (U.S.), 1949 . . £60/£15
The Place of The Lion, Gollancz, 1931 . . £150/£40
ditto, Gollancz, 1931 (wraps) £25
ditto, Norton (U.S.), 1932 . . . . . . £125/£30
The Greater Trumps, Gollancz, 1932 . . £125/£30
ditto, Pellegrini & Cudahy (U.S.), 1950 . . £60/£15
Shadows of Ecstasy, Gollancz, 1933 . . £125/£25
ditto, Pellegrini & Cudahy (U.S.), 1950 . . £60/£15
Descent into Hell, Faber, 1937 . . . . £75/£20
ditto, Pellegrini & Cudahy (U.S.), 1949 . . £60/£15
All Hallows Eve, Faber, 1945 . . . . £75/£20
ditto, Pellegrini & Cudahy (U.S.), 1948 . . £60/£15

Drama
The Masque of The Manuscript, privately printed, 1927 (100 copies, wraps) £200
A Myth of Shakespeare, O.U.P., 1928 . . £200/£75
The Masque of Perusal, privately printed, 1929 (100 copies, wraps) £200
Three Plays, O.U.P., 1931 . . . . . £65/£20
Thomas Cranmer of Canterbury, H. J. Goulden, 1936 (wraps) £45
ditto, O.U.P., 1936. . . . . £45/£15
Judgement at Chelmsford, O.U.P., 1939 (wraps) £50
The House of The Octopus, Edinburgh House, 1945 . . . . £45/£10
Flecker of Dean Close, Canterbury Press, 1946 . .

. . . . £50/£10
Seed of Adam and Other Plays, O.U.P., 1948 £25/£10
Collected Plays, O.U.P., 1963 . . . . £20/£10

Biography
Bacon, Arthur Barker, 1933 . . . . . £125/£25
James I, Arthur Barker, 1934 . . . . . £125/£25
Rochester, Arthur Barker, 1935 . . . . £125/£25
Queen Elizabeth, Duckworth, 1936 . . . £100/£20
Henry VII, Arthur Barker, 1937 . . . . . £100/£20

Theology
He Came Down from Heaven, Heinemann, 1938 . . . . £45/£10
The Descent of The Dove, Longmans, Green, 1939 . . . . £40/£10
Witchcraft, Faber, 1941 . . . . £75/£20
The Forgiveness of Sins, Bles, 1942 . . . £35/£10

Criticism
Poetry at Present, Clarendon Press, 1930 . £45/£15
The English Poetic Mind, Clarendon Press, 1932 . . . . £40/£10
Reason and Beauty in The Poetic Mind, Clarendon Press, 1933 . . . . £40/£10
Religion and Love in Dante, Dacre Press, [1941] (wraps) £25
The Figure of Beatrice, Faber, 1943 . . . £75/£20
Arthurian Torso, O.U.P., 1948 (with C. S. Lewis) . . . . £75/£35
The Image of The City, O.U.P., 1958 . . . £25/£10

TENNESSEE WILLIAMS

(b.1911 d.1983)

An American playwright, many of whose works have been filmed. Most of Williams' plays show a sympathy with lost, lonely and self-punishing characters.

Plays
Battle of Angels, New Directions (U.S.), 1945 £50/£15
The Glass Menagerie, Random House (U.S.), 1945 . . . . £100/£20
ditto, Lehmann, 1948 . . . . £65/£15
You Touched Me, French (U.S.), 1947 (with Donald Windham, wraps) £20
A Streetcar Named Desire, New Directions (U.S.), 1947 . . . . £75/£15
ditto, Lehmann, 1949 . . . . £65/£15
Summer and Smoke, New Directions (U.S.), 1948 . . . . £60/£15
ditto, Lehmann, 1952 . . . . £50/£15

The Rose Tattoo, New Directions (U.S.), 1951 £35/£10
ditto, Secker & Warburg, 1954 [1955] . . £35/£10
I Rise in Flame, Cried the Phoenix, A Play about D.H. Lawrence, New Directions (U.S.), 1951 £30/£10
Camino Real, New Directions (U.S.), 1953 . £50/£15
ditto, Secker & Warburg, 1958 . . . . . £35/£10
Cat on a Hot Tin Roof, New Directions (U.S.), 1955 . . . . £60/£15
ditto, Secker & Warburg, 1956 . . . . £35/£10
Suddenly Last Summer, New Directions (U.S.), 1958 . . . . £35/£10
A Perfect Analysis Given by a Parrot, Dramatic Play Services (U.S.), [1958] (wraps) £20
Orpheus Descending/Battle of Angels, New Directions, (U.S.), 1958 . . . . . . £45/£10
Orpheus Descending, New Directions, (U.S.), 1959 . . . . £45/£10
ditto, Secker & Warburg, 1958 . . . . . £25/£10
Garden District, Secker & Warburg, 1959 . £25/£10
Sweet Bird of Youth, New Directions (U.S.), 1959 . . . . £45/£10
ditto, Secker, 1961. . . . . £25/£10
Three Players of a Summer Game, Secker & Warburg, 1960 . . . . £25/£10
Period of Adjustment/High Point over a Cavern/A Serious Comedy, New Directions (U.S.), 1960 . . . . £35/£10
ditto, Secker, 1961. . . . . £25/£10
The Night of the Iguana, New Directions (U.S.), 1961 . . . . £45/£10
ditto, Secker, 1963. . . . . £20/£5
The Milk Train Doesn't Stop Here Anymore, New Directions (U.S.), 1964 . . . . . . £25/£10
ditto, Secker, 1964. . . . . £15/£5
The Mutilated, Dramatists Play Service (U.S.), 1967 (wraps) £15
The Gnaediges Fraulein, Dramatists Play Service (U.S.), 1967 (wraps) £15
Kingdom of Earth: The Seven Descents of Myrtle, New Directions (U.S.), 1968 . . . . £25/£10
ditto, as ***The Kingdom of Earth: The Seven Descents of Myrtle***, Dramatists Play Service (U.S.), 1969 (wraps) £10
The Two-Character Play, New Directions (U.S.), 1969 . . . . £10/£5
In The Bar of a Tokyo Hotel, Dramatists Play Service (U.S.), 1969 (wraps) £10
Small Craft Warnings, New Directions (U.S.), 1972 . . . . £15/£5
Vieux Carre, New Directions (U.S.), 1979 . £10/£5
A Lovely Sunday for Creve Coeur, New Directions (U.S.), 1980 . . . . £10/£5
Steps Must Be Gentle, Targ (U.S.), 1980 . £10/£5
Clothes for a Summer Hotel, A Ghost Play, Dramatists Play Service (U.S.), 1981 (wraps) £5

It Happened the Day the Sun Rose, Sylvester & Orphanos (U.S.), 1981 . . . . . . £10/£5
The Remarkable Rooming House of Mme Le Monde, Albondocani Press (U.S.), 1984 . . . £15/£5
The Red Devil Battery Sign, New Directions (U.S.), 1988 . . . . £15/£5
Not About Nightingales, Methuen, 1998 (wraps) £5

Novels
The Roman Spring of Mrs Stone, New Directions (U.S.), 1950 . . . . £45/£15
ditto, New Directions (U.S.), 1950 (500 signed copies in slipcase) . . . . £175/£150
ditto, Lehmann, 1950 . . . . £25/£10
Moise and the World of Reason, Simon & Schuster (U.S.), 1975 . . . . £15/£5
ditto, Simon & Schuster (U.S.), 1975 (350 signed copies) £150

Short Stories
One Arm and Other Stories, New Directions (U.S.), 1948 . . . . £50/£15
ditto, New Directions (U.S.), 1948 (1,500 copies on laid paper, slipcase) . . . . £150/£125
Hard Candy, A Book of Stories, New Directions (U.S.), 1954 . . . . £40/£15
ditto, New Directions (U.S.), 1954 (1,500 copies on laid paper, slipcase) . . . . £150/£125
Man Brings This Up Road, Street & Smith (U.S.), 1959 . . . . £20/£10
Three Players of a Summer Game and Other Stories, Secker & Warburg, 1960 . . . . . £20/£10
Grand, House of Books (U.S.), 1964 . . £20/£10
ditto, House of Books (U.S.), 1964 (300 signed copies, tissue d/w) £200
The Knightly Quest, A Novella and Four Short Stories, New Directions (U.S.), 1967 . . £15/£5
Eight Mortal Ladies Possessed, A Book of Stories, New Directions (U.S.), 1974 . . . . £15/£5
ditto, Secker & Warburg, 1975 . . . . £10/£5
Collected Stories, New Directions (U.S.), 1985 £15/£5

Screenplays
Baby Doll, The Script for a Film, New American Library (U.S.), 1956 (wraps) £10
ditto, Secker & Warburg, 1957 . . . . £20/£5
The Fugitive Kind, Signet (U.S.), 1960 (wraps) £10
Stopped Rocking and Other Screenplays, New Directions (U.S.), 1984 . . . . £15/£5

Poetry
In The Winter of Cities, New Directions (U.S.), 1956 . . . . £45/£15
ditto, New Directions (U.S.), 1956 (500 signed copies, slipcase) £200
Androgyne, Mon Amour, New Directions (U.S.), 1977 . . . . £15/£5
ditto, New Directions (U.S.), 1956 (200 signed copies, slipcase) £200

Other Titles
Lord Byron's Love Letter, An Opera in One Act, Ricordi (U.S.), [1955] . . . . . . £30/£10
Memoirs, Doubleday (U.S.), 1975 . . . £35/£15
ditto, Doubleday (U.S.), 1975 (400 signed copies in slipcase) £200
ditto, W.H. Allen, 1976 . . . . £15/£5
Tennessee Williams' Letters to Donald Windham, 1940-1965, Verona, 1976 . . . . . £15/£5
ditto, Holt (U.S.), 1977 . . . . . . £15/£5
Where I Live, Selected Essays, New Directions (U.S.), 1976 . . . . £15/£5
Conversations with Tennessee Williams, University Press of Mississippi (U.S.), 1986 . . . £15/£5

HENRY WILLIAMSON
(b.1895 d.1977)

Williamson's most successful writings are considered to be his nature novels, such as *Tarka the Otter* and *Salar the Salmon.* It is generally acknowledged that these owe a debt to the 19th century naturalist Richard Jefferies. Williamson's right-wing political sympathies during the 1930s did much to damage his reputation.

A Chronicle of Ancient Sunlight Titles
The Dark Lantern, Macdonald, 1951 . . £50/£10
Donkey Boy, Macdonald, 1952 . . . . £50/£10
Young Phillip Maddison, Macdonald, 1953 £50/£10
How Dear is Life, Macdonald, 1954 . . . £50/£10
A Fox Under My Cloak, Macdonald, 1955 . £65/£15
The Golden Virgin, Macdonald, 1957 . . £50/£10
Love and The Loveless: A Soldiers Tale, Macdonald, 1958 . . . . £50/£10
A Test To Destruction, Macdonald, 1960 . £45/£10
The Innocent Moon, Macdonald, 1961 . . £45/£10
It Was The Nightingale, Macdonald, 1962 £45/£10
The Power of The Dead, Macdonald, 1963 £45/£10
The Phoenix Generation, Macdonald, 1965 £40/£10
A Solitary War, Macdonald, 1966 . . . £40/£10
Lucifer Before Sunrise, Macdonald, 1967 . £40/£10
The Gale of The World, Macdonald, 1969 . £60/£15

Other Fiction
The Beautiful Years, Collins, 1921 . . . £400/£50
ditto, Faber, 1929 (revised edition) . . . £45/£15
ditto, Faber, 1929 (200 signed copies, revised edition). £125

Dandelion Days, Collins, 1922 . . . . £100/£20
ditto, Faber, 1930 (revised edition) . . . £25/£10
ditto, Faber, 1930 (200 signed copies, revised edition). £125
The Dream of Fair Women, Collins, 1924 . £75/£15
ditto, Faber, 1931 (revised edition) . . . £20/£5
ditto, Faber, 1931 (200 signed copies, revised edition). £100
The Peregrin's Saga, Collins, 1923 (600 copies) £100
ditto, as ***Sun Brothers***, Dutton (U.S.), 1925 . . £75
The Old Stag, Putnam, 1926 . . . . . £100/£25
Tarka The Otter, Putnams, 1927 (100 signed copies, privately printed for subscribers) £700
ditto, Putnam, 1927 (1000 copies) £125
The Pathway, Cape, 1928 . . . . . £65/£10
ditto, Faber, 1931 (200 signed copies) . . . £150
The Linhay on The Downs and The Firing Gatherer, Woburn Press, 1929 (530 copies) . . . . £55/£35
ditto, Cape, 1934 (revised and enlarged edition) . . . . £45/£15
The Patriot's Progress, Bles, 1930 . . . . £40/£10
ditto, Bles, [1930] (350 signed copies) . . £200/£150
The Star Born, Faber, 1933 . . . . . £40/£10
ditto, Faber, 1933 (70 signed copies) . . . £300
ditto, Faber, 1948 (revised edition) . . . £20/£5
The Gold Falcon or The Haggard of Love, Faber, 1933 (anonymous) . . . . £65/£25
ditto, Faber, 1947 (revised edition) . . . £20/£5
Salar The Salmon, Faber, 1935 . . . . . £100/£20
ditto, Faber, 1935 (13 numbered copies signed and corrected by the author) £1,500
The Sun in The Sands, Faber, 1945 . . . £25/£10
The Phasian Bird, Faber, 1948 . . . . £25/£10
Tales of Moorland and Estuary, Macdonald, 1953 . . . . £25/£10
Collected Nature Stories, Macdonald, 1970 £10/£5
The Scandaroon, Macdonald, 1972 . . . . £20/£5
ditto, Macdonald, 1972 (250 signed copies, slipcase) . . . . £75/£50

Omnibus Editions
The Flax of Dream, Faber, 1936 . . . . £25/£10
ditto, Faber, 1936 (200 copies) £150

Children's
Scribbing Lark, Faber, 1948 . . . . . £25/£10

Non Fiction
The Lone Swallows, Collins, 1922 (500 copies) £250
ditto, Collins, 1928 (revised edition) . . . £35/£10
The Wet Flanders Plain, Beaumont Press, 1929 (80 of 320 copies, signed copies on handmade parchment vellum) £400
ditto, Beaumont Press, 1929 (240 of 320 copies, numbered, on handmadė paper) £225
ditto, Faber, 1929 (revised edition) . . . £65/£15
The Ackymals, Windsor Press (U.S.), 1929 (225 signed copies, slipcase) . . . . £150/£125
The Village Book, Cape, 1930 . . . . £35/£10
ditto, Cape, 1930 (504 signed copies) . . . £100
The Wild Red Deer of Exmoor, Faber, 1931 (75 copies) £125
ditto, Faber, 1931 . . . . £45/£15
The Labouring Life, Cape, 1932. . . . £50/£15
ditto, Cape, 1932 (122 signed copies, acetate d/w) . . . . £150/£125
ditto, as ***As The Sun Shines***, Dutton, 1933 . £20/£5
On Foot in Devon, Maclehose, 1933 . . £50/£15
Devon Holiday, Cape, 1935 . . . . . £40/£15
Goodbye West Country, Putnam, 1937 . . £40/£15
The Children of Shallowford, Faber, 1939 . £35/£10
ditto, Faber, 1959 (revised edition) . . . £15/£5
The Story of a Norfolk Farm, Faber, 1941 . £30/£10
Genius of Friendship - T.E. Lawrence, Faber, 1941 . . . . £50/£20
Norfolk Life, Faber, 1943 (with Lilias Rider Haggard). . . . . £25/£10
Life in a Devon Village, Faber, 1945 . . £20/£5
Tales of a Devon Village, Faber, 1945 . . £20/£5
A Clear Water Stream, Faber, 1958 . . . £20/£5
In The Woods, St Albert's Press, 1960 (50 numbered and signed copies, wraps) £75
ditto, St Albert's Press, 1960 (950 numbered copies, wraps). £35

A.N. WILSON
(b.1950)

A prolific writer, Wilson is at his best in his tragicomic novels.

Novels
The Sweets of Pimlico, Secker & Warburg, 1977 . . . . £200/£45
Unguarded Hours, Secker & Warburg, 1978 £50/£10
Kindly Light, Secker & Warburg, 1979 . . £25/£5
The Healing Art, Secker & Warburg, 1980 £25/£5
Who Was Oswald Fish?, Secker & Warburg, 1981 . . . . £10/£5
Wise Virgin, Secker & Warburg, 1982 . . £10/£5
ditto, Viking (U.S.), 1983 . . . . . . £10/£5
Scandal, Hamish Hamilton, 1983 . . . . £10/£5
ditto, Viking (U.S.), 1984 . . . . . . £10/£5
Gentlemen in England, Hamish Hamilton, 1985 . . . . £10/£5
ditto, Viking (U.S.), 1986 . . . . . . £10/£5
Love Unknown, Hamish Hamilton, 1986 . £10/£5
ditto, Viking (U.S.), 1987 . . . . . . £10/£5

Incline Our Hearts, Hamish Hamilton, 1988 £10/£5
ditto, Viking (U.S.), 1989 . . . . £10/£5
A Bottle in The Smoke, Sinclair-Stevenson, 1989 . . . . £10/£5
ditto, Viking (U.S.), 1990 . . . . £10/£5
Daughters of Albion, Sinclair-Stevenson, 1991 £10/£5
ditto, Viking (U.S.), 1991 . . . . . . £10/£5
Vicar of Sorrows, Sinclair-Stevenson, 1993. £10/£5
ditto, Norton (U.S.), 1994. . . . . . . £10/£5
Hearing Voices, Sinclair-Stevenson, 1995 . £10/£5
ditto, Norton (U.S.), 1996. . . . . . . £10/£5
A Watch in the Night, Sinclair-Stevenson, 1996 £10/£5
ditto, Norton (U.S.), 1996. . . . . . £10/£5
A Watch in the Night, Murray , 1998 . . £10/£5
ditto, Norton (U.S.), 1998. . . . . . £10/£5

Biography
The Laird of Abbottsford: A View of Walter Scott, O.U.P., 1980 . . . . £25/£5
The Life of John Milton, O.U.P., 1983 . . £15/£5
Hilaire Belloc, Hamish Hamilton, 1984 . . £10/£5
ditto, Atheneum (U.S.), 1984 . . . . . £10/£5
Tolstoy: A Biography, Hamish Hamilton, 1988 £10/£5
ditto, Norton (U.S.), 1988. . . . . . £10/£5
Eminent Victorians, BBC, 1989 . . . . £10/£5
ditto, Norton (U.S.), 1990. . . . . £10/£5
C. S. Lewis; A Biography, Collins, 1990 . £10/£5
ditto, Norton (U.S.), 1990. . . . . . £10/£5
Jesus, Sinclair-Stevenson, 1992 . . . . £10/£5
ditto, Norton (U.S.), 1992. . . . . . £10/£5
The Rise and Fall of the House of Windsor, Sinclair-Stevenson, 1993 . . . . £10/£5
ditto, Norton (U.S.), 1993. . . . . . £10/£5
Paul: The Mind of the Apostle, Norton (U.S.), 1997 . . . . £10/£5

Verse
Lilibet: An Account in Verse of The Early Years of The Queen Until The Time of Her Accession, Blond & Briggs, 1984 . . . . £10

Essays
How Can We Know? An Essay on The Christian Religion, Hamish Hamilton, 1985 . . . . £10
ditto, Atheneum (U.S.), 1985 . . . . . . £10
The Church in Crisis, Hodder & Stoughton, 1986 (with Charles Moore and Gavin Stamp) . . £10
Penfriends from Porlock: Essay and Reviews, 1977-1986, Hamish Hamilton, 1988 . . . . £10/£5
ditto, Norton (U.S.), 1989. . . . . . £10/£5

Children's
Stray, Walker Books, 1987 . . . . . . £15/£5
ditto, Orchard (U.S.), 1989 . . . . . . £10/£5
The Tabitha Stories, Walker Books, 1988 . £15/£5
ditto, as ***Tabitha***, Orchard (U.S.), 1989 . . £10/£5
Hazel The Guinea-pig, Walker Books, 1989 £10/£5

Others
Landscape in France, Elm Tree, 1987 . . £10/£5
ditto, St Martin's Press (U.S.), 1988 . . . £10/£5

ANGUS WILSON
(b.1913 d.1991)

A novelist and short story writer, Wilson's critical writings are highly regarded, particularly his studies of Zola and Dickens.

Novels
Hemlock and After, Secker & Warburg, 1952 £30/£10
ditto, Viking (U.S.), 1952. . . . . . £20/£5
Anglo-Saxon Attitudes, Secker & Warburg, 1956 . . . . £25/£10
ditto, Viking (U.S.), 1956. . . . . . £15/£5
The Middle Age of Mrs Eliot, Secker & Warburg, 1958 . . . . £20/£5
ditto, Viking (U.S.), 1959. . . . . . £10/£5
The Old Men at The Zoo, Secker & Warburg, 1961 . . . . £20/£5
ditto, Viking (U.S.), 1961. . . . . . £10/£5
Late Call, Secker & Warburg, 1964 . . . £20/£5
ditto, Viking (U.S.), 1965. . . . . . £10/£5
No Laughing Matter, Secker & Warburg, 1967 £10/£5
ditto, Viking (U.S.), 1967. . . . . . £10/£5
As if by Magic, Secker & Warburg, 1973 . £10/£5
ditto, Viking (U.S.), 1973. . . . . . £10/£5
Setting The World on Fire, Secker & Warburg, 1980 . . . . £10/£5
ditto, Viking (U.S.), 1980. . . . . . £10/£5

Stories
The Wrong Set and Other Stories, Secker & Warburg, 1949 . . . . £85/£20
ditto, Morrow (U.S.), 1950 . . . . . . £35/£10
Such Darling Dodos and Other Stories, Secker & Warburg, 1950 . . . . £65/£20
ditto, Morrow (U.S.), 1951 . . . . . . £25/£10
A Bit Off The Map and Other Stories, Secker & Warburg, 1957 . . . . £15/£5
ditto, Viking (U.S.), 1957. . . . . . £10/£5
Death Dance: 25 Stories, Viking (U.S.), 1969 £10/£5
Collected Stories, Secker & Warburg, 1987 £10/£5
ditto, Viking (U.S.), 1987. . . . . . £10/£5

Plays
The Mulberry Bush, Secker & Warburg, 1956 £30/£10

Others

Emile Zola, Secker & Warburg, 1952 . . . £45/£15
ditto, Morrow (U.S.), 1952 . . . . . . £25/£10
For Whom The Cloche Tolls, Methuen, 1953 (with Philippe Jullian) . . . . £25/£10
ditto, Curtis Books (U.S.), 1953 (wraps). . . £5
The Wild Garden: or, Speaking of Writing, University of California Press (U.S.), 1963. . . . £10/£5
ditto, Secker & Warburg, 1963 . . . . £10/£5
Tempo: The Impact of Television on The Arts, Studio Vista, 1964 . . . . £10/£5
ditto, Dufour (U.S.), 1966. . . . . . £10/£5
The World of Charles Dickens, Secker & Warburg, 1970 . . . . £10/£5
ditto, Viking (U.S.), 1970. . . . . . . £10/£5
The Strange Ride of Rudyard Kipling, Secker & Warburg, 1977 . . . . £15/£5
ditto, Viking (U.S.), 1978. . . . . . . £10/£5
Diversity and Depth in Fiction: Selected Critical Writings, Secker & Warburg, 1983. . . . £10/£5
ditto, Viking (U.S.), 1983. . . . . . £10/£5
Reflections in a Writer's Eye, Secker & Warburg, 1986 . . . . £10/£5
ditto, Viking (U.S.), 1986. . . . . . £10/£5

JEANETTE WINTERSON

(b.1959)

A winner of numerous awards, Winterson's first book, *Oranges Are Not The Only Fruit* remains the classic.

Novels

Oranges Are Not The Only Fruit, Pandora Press, 1985 (wraps) £150
ditto, Atlantic Monthly Press (U.S.), 1987 (wraps) . £10
ditto, Guild, 1990 . . . . £40/£10
Boating for Beginners, Methuen, 1985 . . £150/£25
The Passion, Bloomsbury, 1987. . . . £25/£5
ditto, Atlantic Monthly Press (U.S.), 1988 . £25/£5
Sexing The Cherry, Bloomsbury, 1989 . . £25/£5
ditto, Atlantic Monthly Press (U.S.), 1990 . £15/£5
Written on The Body, Cape, 1992 . . . £15/£5
ditto, Knopf (U.S.), 1993 . . . . . . £15/£5
Art and Lies, Cape, 1994 . . . . . £10/£5
ditto, Knopf (U.S.), 1993 . . . . . . £10/£5
Gut Symmetries, Granta, 1997 . . . . £10/£5
ditto, Knopf (U.S.), 1997 . . . . . . £10/£5

Short Stories

The World and Other Places, Cape, 1998 . £10/£5
The Dreaming Place, Ulysses, 1998 (150 signed copies) £50

Others

Art Objects: Ecstasy and Effrontery, Cape, 1995 . . . . £20/£5
ditto, Knopf (U.S.), 1996 . . . . . . £15/£5
Fit for the Future, Pandora Press, 1986. . £150/£30
ditto, Pandora Press, 1986 (wraps) £30

WISDEN CRICKETERS' ALMANACKS

The cricketers' bible.

	Hard cover	Soft cover
1864		£5,000
1865		£3,500
1866		£3,500
1867		£2,500
1868		£1,500
1869		£1,500
1870		£1,500
1871		£500
1872		£500
1873		£400
1874		£450
1875		£2,000
1876		£600
1877		£700
1878		£400
1879		£500
1880		£400
1881-1888		£300
1889		£400
1890-1895		£200
1896-1899	£400	£200
1900-1915	£300	£150
1916	£750	£600
1917	£350	£150
1918	£350	£150
1919	£350	£150
1920-1930	£150	£100
1930-1940	£200	£125
1941	£400	£200
1942	£300	£150
1943	£300	£160
1944	£250	£120
1945	£120	£80
1946-1950	£80	£60
1950-1959	£25	£20
1960-1969	£25	£20
1970	£30	£20
1971	£35	£25
1972-present	£15	£10

P.G. WODEHOUSE

(b.1881 d.1975)

A prolific comic author, Wodehouse's world is light, smart, superficial, and if you enjoy his humour, highly addictive.

Jeeves and Wooster Novels

Thank You, Jeeves, Jenkins, 1934 . . . £750/£150
ditto, Little Brown (U.S.), 1934 . . . . £300/£75
Right Ho, Jeeves, Jenkins, 1934 . . . . £750/£100
ditto, as ***Brinkley Manor***, Little Brown (U.S.), 1934 . . . . £250/£75
The Code of The Woosters, Jenkins, 1938 . £600/£100
ditto, Doubleday (U.S.), 1938 . . . . £250/£75
Joy in The Morning, Doubleday (U.S.), 1946 . . . . £125/£30
ditto, Jenkins, 1947 . . . . £100/£25
The Mating Season, Jenkins, 1949 . . . £75/£20
ditto, Didier (U.S.), 1949 . . . . . . £75/£20
Ring for Jeeves, Jenkins, 1953 . . . . £75/£20
ditto, as ***The Return of Jeeves***, Doubleday (U.S.), 1953 . . . . £75/£20
Jeeves and The Feudal Spirit, Jenkins, 1954 £100/£25
ditto, as ***Bertie Wooster Sees It Through***, Simon and Schuster (U.S.), 1955 . . . . . . £75/£20
Jeeves in The Offing, Jenkins, 1960 . . . £60/£15
ditto, as ***How Right You Are, Jeeves***, Simon and Schuster (U.S.), 1960 . . . . . . £60/£15
Stiff Upper Lip, Jeeves, Jenkins, 1963 . . £50/£15
ditto, Simon and Schuster (U.S.), 1963 . . £50/£15
Much Obliged, Jeeves, Barrie & Jenkins, 1971 £25/£10
ditto, as ***Jeeves and The Tie that Binds***, Simon and Schuster (U.S.), 1971. . . . . . . £25/£10
Aunts Aren't Gentlemen, Barrie & Jenkins, 1974 . . . . £25/£10
ditto, as ***The Cat-Nappers***, Simon and Schuster (U.S.), 1974 . . . . £25/£10

Jeeves and Wooster Short Stories

The Man With Two Left Feet, Methuen, 1917 . £250
ditto, Burt (U.S.), 1933 . . . . . . £125/£25
My Man Jeeves, Newnes, 1919 . . . . . £250
The Inimitable Jeeves, Jenkins, 1923 . . £600/£175
ditto, as ***Jeeves***, Doran (U.S.), 1923 . . . £500/£150
Carry On Jeeves, Jenkins, 1925 . . . . £600/£175
ditto, Doran (U.S.), 1927 . . . . . . £500/£150
Very Good, Jeeves, Jenkins, 1930 . . . £600/£175
ditto, Doubleday (U.S.), 1930 . . . . £500/£150
A Few Quick Ones, Jenkins, 1959 . . . £75/£20
ditto, Simon and Schuster (U.S.), 1959 . . £60/£20
Plum Pie, Jenkins, 1966 . . . . . . £60/£20
ditto, Simon and Schuster (U.S.), 1967 . . £50/£15

Jeeves and Wooster Omnibus Editions

Jeeves Omnibus, Jenkins, 1931 . . . . £100/£30
The World of Jeeves, Jenkins, 1967 . . . . £35/£10

Other Novels

The Pothunters, Black, 1902 (plain binding) . £2,000
ditto, Macmillan (U.S.), 1924 . . . . £500/£150
A Prefect's Uncle, Black, 1903 . . . . . . £700
ditto, Macmillan (U.S.), 1924 . . . . £500/£150
The Gold Bat, Black, 1904 . . . . £700
ditto, Macmillan (U.S.), 1923 . . . . £400/£75
William Tell Told Again, A. & C. Black, 1904 £750
The Head of Kay's, A. & C. Black, 1905 . . £600
ditto, Macmillan (U.S.), 1922 . . . . £500/£125
Love Among The Chickens, Newnes, 1906 . . £2,500
ditto, Circle Publishing Co. (U.S.), 1909 . . £500
The White Feather, A. & C. Black, 1907 . . £1,000
ditto, Macmillan (U.S.), 1922 . . . . £500/£125
Not George Washington, Cassell, 1907 (written with H. Westbrook) £2,000
The Swoop, Alston Rivers, 1909 (wraps) . . £2,000
Mike, A. & C. Black, 1909 . . . . . . £750
ditto, Macmillan (U.S.), 1924 . . . . £400/£75
ditto, as ***Enter PSmith***, Black, 1935 (re-issue of second part of ***Mike***) . . . . £300/£65
ditto, as ***Mike at Wrykn***, Jenkins, 1953, and ***Mike and PSmith***, Jenkins, 1953 (2 vol. re-issue, novel revised) . . . . £125/£25 each
A Gentleman of Leisure, Alston Rivers, 1910 . £600
ditto, as ***The Intrusion of Jimmy***, Watt (U.S.) 1910 . . . . £500
PSmith in The City, A. & C. Black, 1910 . £450
The Prince and Betty, Mills and Boon, 1912 . £750
The Prince and Betty, Watt (U.S.), 1912 (different from above) £600
ditto, as ***PSmith Journalist***, A. & C. Black, 1915 . . . . £450
The Little Nugget, Methuen, 1913 . . . . £500
ditto, Watt (U.S.), 1914 . . . . £300
Something Fresh, Methuen, 1915 . . . . £1,250
ditto, as ***Something New***, Appleton (U.S.), 1915 £750
Uneasy Money, Appleton (U.S.), 1916 . . . £250
ditto, Methuen, 1917 . . . . £1,000
Piccadilly Jim, Dodd Mead (U.S.), 1917 . . £250
ditto, Jenkins, 1918 . . . . £500
A Damsel in Distress, Doran (U.S.), 1919 . . £200
ditto, Jenkins, 1919 . . . . £450
Their Mutual Child, Boni & Liveright (U.S.), 1919 . . . . £200
ditto, as ***The Coming of Bill***, Jenkins, 1920 . . . . £1,000/£150
The Little Warrior, Doran (U.S.), 1920 . . £800/£200
ditto, as ***Jill The Reckless***, Jenkins, 1921 £1,500/£350
The Girl on The Boat, Jenkins, 1922 . £1,500/£300
ditto, as ***Three Men and a Maid***, Doran, 1922 (revised

version) . . . . £600/£125
The Adventures of Sally, Jenkins, 1922 . £1,200/£250
ditto, as ***Mostly Sally***, Doran (U.S.), 1923 £600/£125
Leave it to PSmith, Jenkins, 1923 . . £1,000/£200
ditto, Doran (U.S.), 1923 . . . . . . £1,000/£200
Bill The Conqueror, Jenkins, 1924 . . £1,000/£200
ditto, Doran (U.S.), 1925 . . . . £350/£100
Sam The Sudden, Methuen, 1925 . . . . £750/£125
ditto, as ***Sam in The Suburbs***, Doran (U.S.), 1925 . . . . £250/£50
The Small Bachelor, Methuen, 1927 . . . £750/£125
ditto, Doran (U.S.), 1927 . . . . £250/£50
Money for Nothing, Jenkins, 1928 . . . £750/£125
ditto, Doran (U.S.), 1928 . . . . £250/£50
Summer Lightning, Jenkins, 1929 . . . . £750/£125
ditto, as ***Fish Preferred***, Doubleday, 1929 £500/£100
Big Money, Doubleday (U.S.), 1931 . . . £250/£50
ditto, Jenkins, 1931 . . . . £750/£100
If I Were You, Doubleday (U.S.), 1931 . . £250/£50
ditto, Jenkins, 1931 . . . . £500/£100
Doctor Sally, Methuen, 1932 . . . . . £450/£100
Hot Water, Jenkins, 1932 . . . . . . £450/£100
ditto, Doubleday (U.S.), 1932 . . . . £250/£50
Heavy Weather, Jenkins, 1933 . . . . £500/£125
ditto, Little Brown (U.S.), 1933 . . . . £500/£125
The Luck of The Bodkins, Jenkins, 1935 . £300/£45
ditto, Little Brown (U.S.), 1935 . . . . £250/£50
Laughing Gas, Jenkins, 1936 . . . . £400/£100
ditto, Doubleday (U.S.), 1936 . . . . £250/£50
Summer Moonshine, Doubleday (U.S.), 1937 . . . . £150/£45
ditto, Jenkins, 1938 . . . . £400/£100
Uncle Fred in The Springtime, Jenkins, 1939 . . . . £300/£65
ditto, Doubleday (U.S.), 1939 . . . . £150/£45
Quick Service, Jenkins, 1940 . . . . . £150/£25
ditto, Doubleday (U.S.), 1940 . . . . £100/£20
Money in The Bank, Doubleday (U.S.), 1942 £200/£25
ditto, Jenkins, 1946 . . . . £100/£20
Full Moon, Jenkins, 1947 . . . . £100/£25
ditto, Doubleday (U.S.), 1947 . . . . £100/£25
Spring Fever, Doubleday (U.S.), 1948 . . £100/£25
ditto, Jenkins, 1948 . . . . £100/£25
Uncle Dynamite, Jenkins, 1948 . . . . . £100/£25
ditto, Didier (U.S.), 1948 . . . . . . £100/£25
The Old Reliable, Jenkins, 1951 . . . . £75/£15
ditto, Doubleday (U.S.), 1951 . . . . £75/£15
Barmy in Wonderland, Jenkins, 1952 . . £75/£15
ditto, as ***Angel Cake***, Doubleday (U.S.), 1952 £75/£15
Pigs Have Wings, Jenkins, 1952 . . . . £75/£15
ditto, Doubleday (U.S.), 1952 . . . . £75/£15
French Leave, Jenkins, 1956 . . . . . £50/£15
ditto, Simon and Schuster, 1959 . . . . £50/£15
Something Fishy, Jenkins, 1957 . . . . £50/£15
ditto, as ***The Butler Did It***, Simon and Schuster (U.S.), 1957 . . . . £50/£15
Cocktail Time, Jenkins, 1958 . . . . . £50/£15
ditto, Simon and Schuster (U.S.), 1958 . . £50/£15
The Ice in The Bedroom, Simon and Schuster (U.S.), 1961 . . . . £50/£15
ditto, as ***Ice in The Bedroom***, Jenkins, 1961 £50/£15
Service with a Smile, Simon and Schuster (U.S.), 1961 . . . . £45/£10
ditto, Jenkins, 1962 . . . . £45/£10
Biffen's Millions, Simon and Schuster (U.S.), 1964 . . . . £45/£10
ditto, as ***Frozen Assets***, Jenkins, 1964 . . £45/£10
Galahad at Blandings, Jenkins, 1965 . . . £40/£10
ditto, as ***The Brinkmanship of Galahad Threepwood***, Simon and Schuster (U.S.), 1967 . . . £30/£10
The Purloined Paperweight, Simon and Schuster (U.S.), 1967 . . . . £50/£15
ditto, as ***Company for Henry***, Jenkins, 1967 £65/£20
Do Butlers Burgle Banks?, Simon and Schuster (U.S.), 1968 . . . . £65/£20
ditto, Jenkins, 1968 . . . . £75/£20
A Pelican at Blandings, Jenkins, 1969 . . £45/£10
ditto, as ***No Nudes is Good Nudes***, Simon and Schuster (U.S.), 1970 . . . . £30/£10
The Girl in Blue, Barrie & Jenkins, 1970 . £25/£10
ditto, Simon and Schuster (U.S.), 1971 . . £25/£10
Pearls, Girls and Monty Bodkin, Barrie & Jenkins, 1972 . . . . £25/£10
ditto, as ***The Plot That Thickened***, Simon and Schuster (U.S.), 1973 . . . . £25/£10
Bachelors Anonymous, Barrie & Jenkins, 1973 . . . . £25/£10
ditto, Simon and Schuster (U.S.) ,1974 . . £25/£10
Sunset at Blandings, Chatto & Windus, 1977 (unfinished novel, finished by Richard Usborne) . . . . £25/£10
ditto, Simon and Schuster (U.S.), 1977 . . £25/£10
Sir Agravaine, Blandford, 1984 . . . . £25/£10

Other Short Stories

Tales of St Austin's, Black, 1903 . . . . £450
ditto, Macmillan (U.S.), 1923 . . . . £400/£125
The Man Upstairs, Methuen, 1914 . . . . . £400
Indiscretions of Archie, Jenkins, 1921 . £,1250/£250
ditto, Doran (U.S.), 1921 . . . . . . £500/£150
The Clicking of Cuthbert, Jenkins, 1922 £1,000/£200
ditto, as ***Golf Without Tears***, Doran (U.S.), 1924 . . . . £500/£150
Ukridge, Jenkins, 1924 . . . . . . £1,000/£200
ditto, as ***He Rather Enjoyed It***, Doran (U.S.), 1926 . . . . £650/£150
The Heart of a Goof, Jenkins, 1926 . . . £125/£30
ditto, as ***Divots***, Doran (U.S.), 1927 . . . £100/£25
Meet Mr Mulliner, Jenkins, 1927 . . . £200/£30
ditto, Doran (U.S.), 1928 . . . . . . £100/£25

Mr Mulliner Speaking, Jenkins, 1929 . . £200/£30
ditto, Doubleday (U.S.), 1930 . . . . £100/£25
Mulliner Nights, Jenkins, 1933 . . . . £150/£25
ditto, Doubleday (U.S.), 1933 . . . . £100/£25
Blandings Castle, Jenkins, 1935 . . . . £300/£75
ditto, Doubleday (U.S.), 1935 . . . . £250/£65
Young Men in Spats, Jenkins, 1936 . . . £225/£50
ditto, Doubleday (U.S.), 1936 . . . . £175/£45
Lord Emsworth and Others, Jenkins, 1937 . £250/£65
ditto, as ***Crime Wave at Blandings***, Doubleday (U.S.), 1937 . . . . £200/£50
Eggs, Beans and Crumpets, Jenkins, 1940 . £250/£65
ditto, Doubleday (U.S.), 1940 . . . . £100/£25
Nothing Serious, Jenkins, 1950 . . . . £100/£25
ditto, Doubleday (U.S.), 1951 . . . . . £50/£15

Other Omnibus Editions
Nothing but Wodehouse, Doubleday (U.S.), 1932 . . . . £200/£40
Mulliner Omnibus, Jenkins, 1935 . . . £100/£25
Weekend Wodehouse, Jenkins, 1939 . . £100/£25
ditto, Doubleday (U.S.), 1939 . . . . £100/£25
Wodehouse on Golf, Doubleday (U.S.), 1940 £200/£40
The World of Mr Mulliner, Barrie & Jenkins, 1972 . . . . £15/£5
ditto, Taplinger (U.S.), 1974 . . . . . £10/£5
The Golf Omnibus, Barrie & Jenkins, 1973 £15/£5
ditto, Simon and Schuster (U.S.), 1974 . . £10/£5
The World of PSmith, Barrie & Jenkins, 1974 £15/£5
The World of Ukridge, Barrie & Jenkins, 1975 £15/£5
The World of Blandings, Barrie & Jenkins, 1975 . . . . £15/£5
The Uncollected Wodehouse, Seabury Press (U.S.), 1976 . . . . £25/£5
Vintage Wodehouse, Barrie & Jenkins, 1977 £15/£5
Tales from The Drones Club, Hutchinson, 1982 . . . . £15/£5
Wodehouse Nuggets, Hutchinson, 1983 £15/£5
The World of Uncle Fred, Hutchinson, 1983 £10/£5
The World of Wodehouse Clergy, Hutchinson, 1984 . . . . £10/£5
The Hollywood Omnibus, Hutchinson, 1985 £10/£5
Wodehouse on Cricket, Hutchinson, 1987 . £10/£5
The Aunts Omnibus, Hutchinson, 1989 . . £10/£5

Autobiography
Performing Flea, Jenkins, 1953 . . . . £75/£20
ditto, as ***Author! Author!***, Simon and Schuster (U.S.), 1962 . . . . £45/£15
Bring on The Girls, Simon and Schuster (U.S.), 1953 (with Guy Bolton) . . . . £50/£15
ditto, Jenkins, 1954 (differences from above) £50/£15
America I Like You, Simon and Schuster (U.S.), 1956 . . . . £50/£15
ditto, as ***Over Seventy***, Jenkins, 1957 (revised) £50/£15

Others
The Globe By The Way Book, Globe, 1907 (written with H. Westbrook, wraps) £5,000
Louder and Funnier, Faber, 1932 . . . £350/£100
The Parrot and Other Poems, Hutchinson, 1988 . . . . £10/£5
Yours, Plum, Hutchinson, 1990 . . . . £10/£5

TOM WOLFE
(b.1930)

An American novelist and journalist, Wolfe developed a 'new journalism', reporting hard facts with a spectacular and emotional graphic style.

Essays
The Kandy-Kolored Tangerine Flake, Farrar Straus (U.S.), 1965 . . . . £75/£15
ditto, as ***Streamline Baby***, Cape, 1966 . . £45/£10
The Pump House Gang, Farrar Straus (U.S.), 1968 . . . . £20/£5
ditto, as ***The Mid-Atlantic Man and Other New Breeds in England***, Weidenfeld & Nicolson, 1969 £20/£5
The Electric Kool-Aid Acid Test, Farrar Straus (U.S.), 1968 . . . . £75/£15
ditto, Weidenfeld & Nicolson, 1968 . . . £45/£10
Mauve Gloves and Madmen, Clutter and Vine and Other Stories, Farrar Straus (U.S.), 1976 . £20/£5
In Our Time, Farrar Straus (U.S.), 1980 . £10/£5
ditto, Picador, 1980 (wraps) £5

Journalism and Others
Radical Chic and Mau-Mauing The Flak Catchers, Farrar Straus (U.S.), 1970 . . . . . £20/£5
ditto, Joseph, 1971. . . . . £20/£5
The Painted Word, Farrar Straus (U.S.), 1975 £15/£5
The Right Stuff, Farrar Straus (U.S.), 1979 £15/£5
ditto, Cape, 1979 . . . . £15/£5
From Bauhaus to Our House, Farrar Straus (U.S.), 1981 . . . . £20/£5
ditto, Cape, 1982 . . . . £15/£5
A Man in Full, Farrar Straus (U.S.), 1998 . £10/£5

Fiction
The Purple Decades, Farrar Straus (U.S.), 1982 . . . . £20/£10
ditto, Farrar Straus (U.S.), 1982 (450 signed copies, slipcase) . . . . £75/£50
The Bonfire of The Vanities, Farrar Straus (U.S.), 1987 . . . . £30/£10
ditto, Franklin Library (U.S.), 1987 (250 signed copies, slipcase) . . . . £175/£150
ditto, Cape, 1988 . . . . £25/£5

VIRGINIA WOOLF
(b.1882 d.1941)

Woolfe's London home became the centre of the Bloomsbury Group. *To the Lighthouse* and *The Waves*, with their innovative stream-of-consciousness style, brought her to the forefront of Modernism.

Novels

The Voyage Out, Duckworth, 1915 . . . . £750
ditto, Doran (U.S.), 1920 (revised text) . £1,250/£150
ditto, Duckworth, 1920 (revised text) . £1,250/£150
Night and Day, Duckworth, 1919 . . . . £200
ditto, Doran (U.S.), 1920 . . . . . £1,250/£150
Jacob's Room, Hogarth Press, 1922 . . £2,500/£500
ditto, Hogarth Press, 1922 (40 signed copies) . £5,000
ditto, Harcourt Brace (U.S.), 1923 . . £1,000/£250
Mrs Dalloway, Hogarth Press, 1925 . . £7,500/£750
ditto, Harcourt Brace (U.S.), 1925 . . . . £750/£100
To The Lighthouse, Hogarth Press, 1927 £7,500/£750
ditto, Harcourt Brace (U.S.), 1927 . . . £750/£100
Orlando: A Biography, Crosby Gaige (U.S.), 1928 (861 numbered, signed copies) £1,000
ditto, Hogarth Press, 1928 . . . . . £750/£100
The Waves, Hogarth Press, 1931 . . . . £500/£65
ditto, Harcourt Brace (U.S.), 1931 . . . £150/£25
Flush: A Biography, Hogarth Press, 1933 . £200/£35
ditto, Harcourt Brace (U.S.), 1933 . . . . £75/£15
The Years, Hogarth Press, 1937 . . . . £250/£45
ditto, Harcourt Brace (U.S.), 1937 . . . . £75/£15
Between The Acts, Hogarth Press, 1941 . . £200/£25
ditto, Harcourt Brace (U.S.), 1941 . . . . £75/£15

Short Stories

Two Stories, Hogarth Press, 1917 (150 copies, wraps) £4,000
Kew Gardens, Hogarth Press, 1919 (150 copies, in wraps.) £3,500
Monday or Tuesday, Hogarth Press, 1921 (1,000 copies) £750
ditto, Harcourt Brace (U.S.), 1921 . . . . £750
A Haunted House, Hogarth Press, 1943 £150/£20
ditto, Harcourt Brace (U.S.), 1944 . . . . £65/£15
Nurse Lugton's Golden Thimble, Hogarth Press, 1966 (glassine d/w). . . . . £75/£65
Mrs Dalloway's Party, Hogarth Press, 1973 £30/£10
The Pargiters, Hogarth Press, 1977 . . . £20/£5
ditto, Harcourt Brace (U.S.), 1977 . . . . £15/£5

Essays

Mr Bennett and Mrs Brown, Hogarth Press, 1924 (wraps) £200
The Common Reader, Hogarth Press, 1925. . . . . £1,000/£200
ditto, Harcourt Brace (U.S.), 1925 . . . . £350/£75
A Room of One's Own, Fountain Press (U.S.) /Hogarth Press, 1929 (492 signed copies). . £2,500/£1,750
ditto, Hogarth Press, 1929 . . . . . . £500/£75
ditto, Harcourt Brace (U.S.), 1929 . . . £400/£35
Street Haunting, Westgate Press (U.S.), 1930 (500 signed copies, slipcase) . . . . £650/£500
On Being Ill, Hogarth Press, 1930 (250 signed copies) . . . . £1,500/£750
Beau Brummell, Rimington & Hooper (U.S.), (550 signed copies, glassine d/w, slipcase) . . £750/£650
A Letter to A Young Poet, Hogarth Press, 1932 (wraps) £35
The Common Reader: Second Series, Hogarth Press, 1932 . . . . £400/£50
ditto, Harcourt Brace (U.S.), 1932 . . . . £125/£35
Walter Sickert: A Conversation, Hogarth Press, 1934 (wraps) £50
The Roger Fry Memorial Exhibition, Bristol, 1935 (125 copies) £450
Three Guineas, Hogarth Press, 1938 . . £300/£65
ditto, Harcourt Brace (U.S.), 1938 . . . . £200/£40
Reviewing, Hogarth Press, 1939 (wraps) . . £25
The Death of The Moth, Hogarth Press, 1942 £75/£20
ditto, Harcourt Brace (U.S.), 1942 . . . . £60/£15
The Moment and Other Essays, Hogarth Press, 1947 . . . . £50/£15
ditto, Harcourt Brace (U.S.), 1948 . . . . £45/£15
The Captain's Death Bed, Harcourt Brace (U.S.), 1950 . . . . £65/£20
ditto, Hogarth Press, 1950 . . . . . £45/£15
Granite and Rainbow, Hogarth Press, 1958. £65/£20
ditto, Harcourt Brace (U.S.), 1958 . . . £45/£15
Contemporary Writers, Hogarth Press, 1965 £25/£5
ditto, Harcourt Brace (U.S.), 1966 . . . . £20/£5
Books and Portraits, Hogarth Press, 1977 . £15/£5
ditto, Harcourt Brace (U.S.), 1977 . . . . £10/£5
The London Scene, Hogarth Press, 1982 . £15/£5
ditto, Random House (U.S.), 1982 . . . . £10/£5
The Essays of Virginia Woolf, Volume I, Chatto & Windus, 1986. . . . . £30/£10
ditto, ***Volume II***, Chatto & Windus, 1987 . £30/£10
ditto, ***Volume III***, Chatto & Windus, 1988 . £30/£10
ditto, ***Volume IV***, Chatto & Windus, 1994 . £30/£10

Biography

Roger Fry: A Biography, Hogarth Press, 1940 . . . . £250/£35
ditto, Harcourt Brace (U.S.), 1940 . . . . £200/£30

Autobiography

Moments of Being, Sussex University Press, 1976 . . . . £10/£5
ditto, Harcourt Brace (U.S.), 1976 . . . . £25/£5

Comedy

Freshwater, Hogarth Press, 1976 . . . £25/£5
ditto, Harcourt Brace (U.S.), 1976 . . . £25/£5

Others

A Writer's Diary, Hogarth Press, 1953 . . £75/£20
ditto, Harcourt Brace (U.S.), 1954 . . . £35/£20
Virginia Woolf and Lytton Strachey: Letters, Hogarth Press, 1956 . . . . £40/£10
ditto, Harcourt Brace (U.S.), 1956 . . . £30/£10
The Flight of The Mind: The Letters of Virginia Woolf, 1888-1912, Hogarth Press, 1975 . £25/£5
The Question of Things Happening: The Letters of Virginia Woolf, 1912-1922, Hogarth Press, 1976 . . . . £20/£5
ditto, Harcourt Brace (U.S.), 1976 . . . £20/£5
The Diary of Virginia Woolf, Volume 1, 1915-1919, Hogarth Press, 1977 . . . . £15/£5
ditto, Harcourt Brace (U.S.), 1977 . . . £15/£5
A Change of Perspective: The Letters of Virginia Woolf, 1923-1928, Hogarth Press, 1977 . £15/£5
ditto, Harcourt Brace (U.S.), 1977 . . . £15/£5
The Diary of Virginia Woolf, Volume II, 1920-1924, Hogarth Press, 1978 . . . . £15/£5
ditto, Harcourt Brace (U.S.), 1978 . . . £15/£5
A Reflection of The Other Person: The Letters of Virginia Woolf, 1929-1931, Hogarth Press, 1978 . . . . £15/£5
ditto, Harcourt Brace (U.S.), 1978 . . . £15/£5
The Sickle Side of The Moon: The Letters of Virginia Woolf, 1931-1935, Hogarth Press, 1979 . £15/£5
ditto, Harcourt Brace (U.S.), 1979 . . . £15/£5
The Diary of Virginia Woolf, Volume III:, 1925-1930, Hogarth Press, 1980 . . . . £15/£5
ditto, Harcourt Brace (U.S.), 1980 . . . £15/£5
Leave The Letters Till We're Dead: The Letters of Virginia Woolf, 1936-1941, Hogarth Press, 1980 . . . . £15/£5
ditto, Harcourt Brace (U.S.), 1980 . . . £15/£5
The Diary of Virginia Woolf Volume IV, 1931-1935, Hogarth Press, 1982 . . . . £15/£5
ditto, Harcourt Brace (U.S.), 1982 . . . £15/£5
The Diary of Virginia Woolf, Volume V, 1936-1941, Chatto & Windus, 1984 . . . . . . £15/£5
ditto, Harcourt Brace (U.S.), 1984 . . . £15/£5
Paper Darts: The Illustrated Letters, Collins & Brown, 1992 . . . . £15/£5

JOHN WYNDHAM

(b.1903 d.1969)

Wyndham is the pen name used by John Wyndham Parkes Lucas Beynon Harris, and he has written under several other variations of his name. He is best known for his peculiarly British science fiction novels.

Novels

The Secret People, Newnes [1935] (pseud. 'John Beynon') . . . . £300/£75
Foul Play Suspected, Newnes [1935] (pseud. 'John Beynon') . . . . £300/£75
Planet Plane, Newnes [1936] (pseud 'John Beynon') . . . . £250/£45
ditto, as ***Stowaway to Mars***, Coronet, 1972 (wraps) £5
Love in Time, Utopian Publications, 1945 (pseud. 'Johnson Harris') . . . . £250/£45
The Day of The Triffids, Michael Joseph, 1951 . . . . £300/£45
ditto, Doubleday (U.S.), 1951 . . . . £250/£35
The Kraken Wakes, Michael Joseph, 1953 . £125/£25
ditto, Ballantine (U.S.), 1953 . . . . . £100/£20
Re-Birth, Ballantine (U.S.), 1955 . . . £100/£20
ditto, as ***The Chrysalids***, Michael Joseph, 1955. . . . . £100/£20
The Midwich Cuckoos, Michael Joseph, 1957 . . . . £100/£20
ditto, Ballantine (U.S.), 1957 . . . . . £75/£15
Trouble with Lichen, Michael Joseph, 1960 £45/£10
ditto, Ballantine (U.S.), 1960 (wraps) £10
Chocky, Michael Joseph, 1968 . . . . £35/£10
ditto, Ballantine (U.S.), 1968 (wraps) £10
Web, Michael Joseph, 1979 . . . . . £20/£5

Short Stories

Jizzle, Dennis Dobson, 1954 . . . . . £125/£30
Seeds of Time, Michael Joseph, 1956 . . £75/£15
Tales of Gooseflesh and Laughter, Ballantine (U.S.), 1956 (wraps) £10
The Outward Urge, Michael Joseph, 1959 (with 'Lucas Parkes') . . . . £65/£15
ditto, Ballantine (U.S.), 1959 (wraps) £10
Consider Her Ways, Michael Joseph, 1961 . £30/£10
The Infinite Moment, Ballantine (U.S.), 1961 (wraps) £10
A John Wyndham Omnibus, Michael Joseph, 1964 . £35/£10
The Best of John Wyndham, Sphere, 1973 (wraps) £5
ditto, as ***The Man from Beyond***, Michael Joseph, 1975 . . . . £10/£5
Wanderers of Time, Coronet, 1973 (wraps) . . £5
Sleepers of Mars, Coronet, 1973 (wraps) . . . £5
Exiles on Asperus, Coronet, 1979 (wraps) . . . £5

THE YELLOW BOOK

A literary and art periodical considered to be outrageous and decadent in its day. Many contributors went on to become major literary figures. It was Aubrey Beardsley's distinctive artwork that upset most commentators.

Volume 1, Matthews and Lane, April, 1894 . . £35
Volume 2, Matthews and Lane, July, 1894 . . £35
Volume 3, Lane/Bodley Head, October, 1894 . £35
Volume 4, Lane/Bodley Head, January, 1895 . £35
Volume 5, Lane/Bodley Head, April, 1895 . . £25
Volume 6, Lane/Bodley Head, July, 1895 . . £25
Volume 7, Lane/Bodley Head, October, 1895 . £25
Volume 8, Lane/Bodley Head, January, 1896 . £25
Volume 9, Lane/Bodley Head, April, 1896 . . £25
Volume 10, Lane/Bodley Head, July, 1896 . . £25
Volume 11, Lane/Bodley Head, October, 1896 . £25
Volume 12, Lane/Bodley Head, January, 1897 . £25
Volume 13, Lane/Bodley Head, April, 1897 . £25
Complete set, (evenly coloured spines) . . . £600

APPENDIX

W. HARRISON AINSWORTH (b.1805 d.1882)
The Tower of London, Bentley, 1840 (13 parts in 12, wraps). £500
ditto, Bentley, 1840 . . . . £250

LOUISA MAY ALCOTT (b.1832 d.1888)
Little Women, Roberts Bros (U.S.), 1868-69 (2 vols) £5,000

RICHARD HARRIS BARHAM (b.1788 d.1845)
The Ingoldsby Legends, (first series) Bentley, 1840 . . . . £125
ditto, (second series) Bentley, 1842 . . . . £100
ditto, (third series) Bentley, 1847. . . . . £100

WILLIAM BECKFORD (b.1759 d.1844)
An Arabian Tale, Johnson, 1786 (a.k.a. ***Vathek***, anonymous) £650

THOMAS BEWICK (b.1753 d.1828)
A General History of Quadrupeds, Bewick, Beilby & Hodgson, 1790 . . . . £600

WILLIAM BLAKE (b.1757 d.1827)
Songs of Innocence and Experience, 1789 £200,000

ROLF BOLDREWOOD (b.1826 d.1915)
Robbery Under Arms, Remington, 1888 (3 vols) £1,000

GEORGE BORROW (b.1803 d.1881)
Wild Wales, Murray, 1862 (3 vols) £250

JAMES BOSWELL (b.1740 d.1795)
The Life of Samuel Johnson, Baldwin, Dilly, 1791 (2 vols) £4,000

JOHN BUNYAN (b.1628 d.1688)
The Pilgrim's Progress, Nath. Ponder, Peacock, 1678 . . . . £7,500

ROBERT BURNS (b.1759 d.1796)
Poems, Chiefly in the Scottish Dialect, Wilson, 1786 . . . . £10,000

ROBERT BURTON (b.1577 d.1640)
The Anatomy of Melancholy, Lichfield and Short for Henry Cripps, 1621 . . . . £20,000

SAMUEL BUTLER (b.1835 d.1902)
Erewhon or Over the Range, Trubner & Co, 1831 (anonymous) £125
The Way of All Flesh, Grant Richards, 1903 . £200

SAMUEL TAYLOR COLERIDGE (b.1772 d.1834)
Lyrical Ballads, Longman, 1798 . . . . . £6,000

WILLIAM CONGREVE (b.1670 d.1729)
The Way of the World, Tonson, 1700 . . . £2,000

STEPHEN CRANE (b.1871 d.1900)
The Red Badge of Courage, Appleton (U.S.), 1895 . . . . £2,000

HARRY CROSBY (b.1922 d.1898)
The Collected Poems, Black Sun Press, 1931 (500 copies, 4 vols in box) £1,000

ALEISTER CROWLEY (b.1875 d.1947)
The Diary of a Drug Fiend, Collins, 1922 £900/£125
Moonchild, Mandrake Press, 1929 . . . £150/£35

W. H. DAVIES (b.1871 d.1940)
The Autobiography of a Super-Tramp, Fifield, 1908 . . . . £75

THOMAS DE QUINCEY (b.1785 d.1859)
Confessions of an English Opium Eater, Taylor & Hessey, 1822 . . . . £750

HENRY FIELDING (b.1707 d.1754)
The History of Tom Jones, Millar, 1749 (6 vols) £2,500

EDWARD FITZGERALD (b.1809 d.1883)
Rubáiyát of Omar Khayyám, Quaritch, 1859 £10,000

JOHN GAY (b.1685 d.1732)
The Beggar's Opera, Watts, 1728 . . . . £500

OLIVER GOLDSMITH (b.1730 d.1774)
The Vicar of Wakefield, Newbery, 1766 (2 vols, anonymous) £1,500

NADINE GORDIMER (b.1923)
Face to Face, Silver Leaf Books (Johannesburg), 1949 . . . . £450/£65

KENNETH GRAHAME (b.1859 d.1932)
Wind in the Willows, Methuen, 1908 . . . £1,250

JOHN GRAY (b.1866 d.1934)
Silverpoints, Elkin Mathews and John Lane, 1893 (250 numbered copies) £800

GEORGE and WEEDON GROSMITH (b.1847 d.1912, and b.1854 d.1919,)
The Diary of a Nobody, Arrowsmith, 1892 . . £250

NATHANIEL HAWTHORNE
(b.1804 d.1864)
Fanshawe, Marsh & Capen, 1828 . . . . £7,500
The Scarlet Letter, Ticknor, Reed & Fields (U.S.), 1850 . . . . £3,000
The House of the Seven Gables, Ticknor, Reed & Fields (U.S.), 1851 . . . . £1,000

A.E. HOUSMAN (b.1859 d.1936)
A Shropshire Lad, Kegan Paul, Trench, Trubner & Co., 1896 . . . . £1,500

W.H. HUDSON (b.1841 d.1922)
The Purple Land, Sampson Low, 1885 . . . £750

THOMAS HUGHES (b.1822 d.1896)
Tom Brown's Schooldays, Macmillan, 1857 . £500

LIONEL JOHNSON (b.1867 d.1902)
Poems, Elkin Mathews/Copeland & Day, 1895 (25 signed copies) £4,000
ditto, Elkin Mathews/Copeland & Day, 1895 (750 copies) £500

SAMUEL JOHNSON (b.1709 d.1784)
A Dictionary of the English Language, various publishers, 1775 (2 vols) £5,000

BEN JONSON (b.1572 d.1637)
The Workes of Benjamin Jonson, [first volume], Will Stansby, 1616 . . . . £2,000
ditto, [second volume], Richard Meighen, 1640 £1,500

NIKOS KAZANTZAKIS (b.1885 d.1957)
Zorba the Greek, Lehman, 1952 . . . . . £45/£15
ditto, Simon & Schuster (U.S.), 1953 . . £30/£10

CHARLES KINGSLEY (b.1819 d.1875)
The Water Babies, Macmillan, 1863 (first issue, containing 'L'Envoi') £400
ditto, Macmillan, 1863 (later issues) £100

CHARLES LAMB (b.1775 d.1834)
Tales From Shakespeare, Hodgkins, 1807 (2 vols) £1,500

WYNDHAM LEWIS (b.1882 d.1957)
The Apes of God, The Arthur Press, 1930 (750 signed copies) . . . . £200/£100
ditto, Nash & Grayson, 1931 . . . . . £100/£25

EDWARD BULWER LYTTON (b.1803 d.1873)
The Last Days of Pompeii the Wanderer, Bentley, 1834 (anonymous, 3 vols) £500

RICHARD MARSH (b.1857 d.1915)
The Beetle, Skeffington, 1897 . . . . . . £300

Rev. C.R. MATURIN (b.1782 d.1824)
Melmoth the Wanderer, Constable, 1820 (4 vols) £1,750

HERMAN MELVILLE (b.1819 d.1891)
The Whale, Bentley, 1851 (3 vols) . . . £45,000
ditto, as ***Moby Dick***, Harper (U.S.), 1851 . £10,000

ARTHUR MILLER (b.1915)
All My Sons, Reynal & Hitchcock (U.S.), 1947. £200/£40
Death of a Salesman, Viking (U.S.), 1949 £300/£35
ditto, Cresset, 1949 . . . . £75/£20

HENRY MILLER (b.1891 d.1980)
The Tropic of Cancer, Obelisk Press (Paris), 1934 (wraps) £2,500
ditto, Grove Press (U.S.), 1961 (100 signed copies) £1,000
ditto, Grove Press (U.S.), 1961 . . . . . £75/£20

ditto, Calder, 1963 . . . . £45/£15
The Tropic of Capricorn, Obelisk Press (Paris), 1939 (wraps) £1,500
ditto, Grove Press (U.S.), 1961 . . . . £75/£20
ditto, Calder, 1964 . . . . £45/£15

JOHN MILTON (b.1608 d.1674)
Paradise Lost, Parker, 1667 . . . . . £30,000
Paradise Regain'd, Starkey, 1671 . . . £1,500

BILL NAUGHTON (b.1910 d.1992)
Alfie, MacGibbon & Kee, 1966 . . . . . £50/£10

BARONESS ORCZY (b.1865 d.1947)
The Scarlet Pimpernel, Greening, 1905 . . £65

JOHN POLIDORI (b.1795 d.1821)
The Vampyre, Sherwood, Neely and Jones, 1819 . . . . £1,750

ALEXANDER POPE (b.1688 d.1744)
The Rape of the Lock, Lintott, 1714 (wraps) £3,500

MARIO PUZO (b.1920)
The Godfather, Putnam (U.S.), 1969 . . £150/£25
ditto, Heinemann, 1969 . . . . . . £45/£15

THOMAS PYNCHON (b.1937)
V, Lippincott (U.S.), 1963 . . . . . £600/£65
ditto, Cape, 1963 . . . . £200/£30

CHARLES READE (b.1814 d.1884)
The Cloister and the Hearth, Trubner, 1861 (4 vols) £600

SAMUEL RICHARDSON (b.1689 d. 1761)
Pamela, Rivington, 1741-1742 (4 vols) . . £5,000

CHRISTINA ROSSETTI (b.1830 d. 1894)
Goblin Market, Macmillan, 1862 . . . . £1,000

DANTE GABRIEL ROSSETTI (b.1828 d. 1882)
Poems, privately printed, 1869 (wraps) . . £1,000
ditto, Ellis, 1870 . . . . £250

PHILIP ROTH (b.1933)
Goodbye Columbus and ***Five Short Stories***, Houghton Mifflin (U.S.), 1959 . . . . £400/£45
ditto, Deutsch, 1959 . . . . £100/£20

SIR WALTER SCOTT (b.1771 d.1832)
Ivanhoe, Constable, 1820 (3 vols) £500

RONALD SEARLE (b.1920)
Hurrah for St Trinian's, Macdonald, 1948 . £35/£10
ditto, Macdonald (U.S.), 1948 . . . . £25/£10

PETER SHAFFER (b.1926)
Equus, Deutsch, 1973 . . . . £50/£15
ditto, Atheneum (U.S.), 1974 . . . . . £25/£10

PERCY BYSSHE SHELLEY (b.1792 d.1822)
Queen Mab, privately printed, 1812 (with title page) £7,000
ditto, privately printed, 1812 (without title page) £500
Poetical Works, Kelmscott Press (1894-1895) (250 copies, 3 vols) £1,500

EDMUND SPENSER (b.1552 d.1599)
The Faerie Queen, Ponsonbie, 1590-1596 (2 vols) £15,000

WALLACE STEVENS (b.1879 d.1955)
Harmonium, Knopf (U.S.), 1923 . . . £2,500/£450
Idea of Order, Alcestis (U.S.), 1935 (135 signed copies, glassine d/w, slipcase) . . . £1,250/£850
ditto, Knopf (U.S.), 1936 . . . . . . £450/£75

LAURENCE STERNE (b.1713 d.1768)
The Life and Opinions of Tristram Shandy, Gentleman, Ravanat and Dodsley, 1760-67 (9 vols) £2,500

HARRIET BEECHER STOWE (b.1811 d.1896)
Uncle Tom's Cabin, Jewett (U.S.), 1852 (2 vols, wraps) £5,000
ditto, Jewett (U.S.), 1852 (2 vols, wraps) . £3,500
ditto, Cassell, 1852 . . . . £450

WILLIAM STYRON (b.1925)
Lie Down in Darkness, Bobbs-Merrill (U.S.), 1951 . . . . £175/£30

ELIZABETH TAYLOR (b.1912 d.1976)
At Mrs Lippincote's, Davies, 1945 . . . £75/£20
ditto, Knopf (U.S.), 1946 . . . . . . £45/£15

COLIN WILSON (b.1931)
The Outsider, Gollancz, 1956 . . . . £65/£15
ditto, Houghton Mifflin (U.S.), 1956 . . . £45/£15

LEONARD WOOLF (b.1880 d.1969)
The Village in the Jungle, Arnold, 1913 (U.S.), 1852 . . . . £150/£25
ditto, Harcourt Brace (U.S.), 1926 . . . £35/£10